CRITICAL SURVEY

OF

POETRY

Second Revised Edition

Volume 4

Horace - Osip Mandelstam

Editor, Second Revised Edition
Philip K. Jason
United States Naval Academy

Editor, First Edition, English and Foreign Language Series
Frank N. Magill

SALEM PRESS, INC.
Pasadena, California   Hackensack, New Jersey

Editor in Chief: Dawn P. Dawson
Managing Editor: Christina J. Moose
Developmental Editor: Tracy Irons-Georges
Research Supervisor: Jeffry Jensen
Acquisitions Editor: Mark Rehn
Photograph Editor: Philip Bader
Manuscript Editors: Sarah Hilbert, Leslie Ellen Jones,
Melanie Watkins, Rowena Wildin
Assistant Editor: Andrea E. Miller
Research Assistant: Jeff Stephens
Production Editor: Cynthia Beres
Layout: Eddie Murillo

Library of Congress Cataloging-in-Publication Data

Critical survey of poetry / Philip K. Jason, editor.—2nd rev. ed.
    p. cm.
Combined ed. of: Critical survey of poetry: foreign language series, originally published 1984, Critical survey of poetry: supplement, originally published 1987, and Critical survey of poetry: English language series, rev. ed. published 1992. With new material. Includes bibliographical references and index.
    ISBN 1-58765-071-1 (set : alk. paper) — ISBN 1-58765-075-4 (v. 4 : alk. paper) —
1. Poetry—History and criticism—Dictionaries. 2. Poetry—Bio-bibliography. 3. Poets—Biography—Dictionaries. I. Jason, Philip K., 1941 -   .

PN1021 .C7 2002
809.1′003—dc21
2002008536

Third Printing

PRINTED IN THE UNITED STATES OF AMERICA

CONTENTS

COMPLETE LIST OF CONTENTS

VOLUME 1

VOLUME 2

VOLUME 3

VOLUME 4

VOLUME 5

VOLUME 6

VOLUME 7

VOLUME 8

CRITICAL SURVEY
OF
POETRY

HORACE

Quintus Horatius Flaccus

Born: Venusia, Italy; December 8, 65 B.C.E.
Died: Rome, Italy; November 27, 8 B.C.E.

PRINCIPAL POETRY

Satires, 35 B.C.E., 30 B.C.E. (English translation, 1567)

Epodes, c. 30 B.C.E. (English translation, 1638)

Odes, 23 B.C.E., 13 B.C.E. (English translation, 1621)

Epistles, c. 20-15 B.C.E. (English translation, 1567; includes *Ars poetica*, c. 17 B.C.E.; *The Art of Poetry*)

Carmen Saeculare, 17 B.C.E. (*The Secular Hymn*, 1726)

OTHER LITERARY FORMS

Horace is noted for his poetry and the literary theory in *Ars poetica*.

ACHIEVEMENTS

Horace is the premier Roman lyric poet. He invented what was to become a particularly influential verse genre, the poetic autobiography. A transmitter and re-shaper of early Greek poetry, he turned an essentially minor form (compared with epic and tragedy) into a vehicle for incisive and important political and philosophical statements, while retaining the melodic qualities of his Greek predecessors Sappho, Alcaeus, Anacreon, and Callimachus, among others. Horace's poetry stands at the midpoint between two conceptions of lyricism: the early Greek mode of socially oriented "occasional" verse, on one hand, and modern meditative poetic statement, on the other. Indeed, he did much to bring the latter into being.

Aside from the Horatian lyric stance, the poet bequeathed to Western literature a model technique, one often imitated though rarely equaled. The technique is painstaking; mosaic art is perhaps the best metaphor for it. Friedrich Nietzsche described its effects with wonder: "Every word, by sound, by position, and by meaning, diffuses its influence to right, to left, and over the whole." Again, Horace had illustrious Greek predecessors in us-ing such verbal artistry, notably the Hellenistic poet Callimachus, whose insistence on brevity, exactness, and the "thin" Muse (as opposed to the inflated pseudo-epic style) is repeatedly alluded to by his Roman imitator two centuries later. Horace used the Callimachean aesthetic rule to measure and castigate earlier Roman poets, especially Lucilius, whom he made his model in the *Satires*. It is clear, moreover, that Horace made the artistic rule into a moral precept as well, a rule for pragmatic, practical behavior (as opposed to self-deceiving, "inflated" self-importance and its attendant vices). In this admirable synthesis, he again blended a typically Roman concern for morality with a Greek love of formal beauty.

In addition to these innovations by mediation of Greek and Roman elements, Horace appears to have been the first Roman poet—and perhaps the only one, next to Vergil—to have meditated on the role of rhetoric in verse. There is a constant tension in Horatian verse between communication, using all the devices of the long classical tradition of rhetoric, and contemplation, dwelling on image, sound, and ambiguity within the space of an individual poem, with little apparent concern to "persuade" a reader. The main lines of this opposition will be seen in Horace's poetic career: from writing *Epodes*, almost all of which address an audience explicitly, urging action or hurling insult, the poet proceeded to the composition of *Satires* or, as he called them, *sermones*, "conversations." Then, having experimented with public and semiprivate modes of discourse, his poetry turns inward to private concerns in the *Odes*; if Horace "reveals" himself at all in the four books of *Odes*, it is only behind a series of masks. Next, he turns to a communicative genre again in the *Epistles*, but here the ostensible "letter" form is still less revealing than one might expect: The poems pretend to be real missives when they are in fact artfully contrived peeks at a persona. Consequently, the "real" Horace is never seen; his image is fractured by a hall-of-mirrors display of poetic skill. It is significant, in fact, that the ancient "Life" of Horace tells how the poet arranged a gallery of mirrors around the sides of his bedroom; the same urge powers the life and the work of this enigmatic man.

Such a personality exerted a powerful attraction on succeeding generations of poets. Horace, unlike most ancient pagan authors, was read and studied during the Middle Ages (if only for his easily excerpted moral maxims), so that many manuscripts of his poems survived to the Renaissance, at which time his poetry could be appreciated in its fullness by such men as Pierre de Ronsard, Petrarch, Michel de Montaigne, and, later, Ben Jonson, Andrew Marvell, Robert Herrick, and John Milton. Horace's *Odes* in particular became popular, sometimes to the disadvantage of the poetry, which was misunderstood as the offhand versifying of a jolly, rotund Epicurean, or distorted to read like the precepts of a Christian moralist. By early in the twentieth century, the *Odes* had been translated more than one hundred times in England and France and nearly as often in Germany and Italy. In short, Horace's own predictions of poetic immortality were fulfilled, for he had written at the conclusion of the first three books of the *Odes*: ". . . I have completed a memorial more lasting than bronze . . . not all of me will die; I shall avoid the goddess of death (most of me). . . ."

BIOGRAPHY

Horace gives more details about his own life, in writing intended for the public, than any other Roman author. His poetry, however, is not undiluted autobiography; even when he purports to tell the truth about his younger days, it can be shown that he is distorting facts slightly for effect. Thus, while it is probably true that Horace's father was a freed slave, as the poet reports in a touching tribute, it is probably not the case that he was "poor in a thin little piece of land," as Horace would have his reader believe. Horace's father must have had a greater income than that if he could afford to send his son to Rome for schooling alongside the offspring of Roman knights and senators, bypassing the local academy at which the sons of settlers and centurions were taught. It appears that life as an auctioneer's agent (*coactor*) was sufficiently rewarding for the poet's father.

Horace's early education, then, resembled that of any upper-class Roman of the day: study of the Greek classics, primarily Homer, first in the antique translation of Livius Andronicus, later in the original. Unlike most freedmen's sons, Horace continued his education on the "university" level at Athens, where he studied moral philosophy; no doubt he also continued to read Greek poetry, since his earliest productions show wide ac-

Horace (Kim Kurnizki)

quaintance with the body of lyric verse from the seventh century B.C.E. on. Finally, it was in Athens that Horace began his education in a harder school. There Brutus, the slayer of Julius Caesar, came, eager for new recruits, a few months after the murder in 44 B.C.E.; Horace, along with other young Romans, such as Cicero's son Marcus, joined the campaign against the followers of Caesar in the civil war. As military tribune, Horace took part in the Battle of Philippi of 42 B.C.E., in which his leader, Brutus, met defeat.

On his return home, Horace evidently found that his father's land had been confiscated, to be given to veterans of the victorious army. In an autobiographical section of one epistle, Horace claims that the resulting poverty drove him to write poetry. One must see through Horace's artful irony once again: He cites this bit of personal history in the context of explaining why, at his advanced age, he has been slow to write; there is no pressing need, the poet says, since he is well-off now. Yet Horace could not have been poverty-stricken in his early years, since he was able to purchase the rather high post of scribe to the magistrates, an office which had responsibilities for keeping official records. This employment probably gave him time to write the *Epodes* and the early poems of the *Satires*, and this poetry, in turn, led to his greater fortune.

Horace had the good luck to become a friend of the poet Vergil, who was five years his senior and already a rising talent; Vergil introduced Horace to his own patron, Maecenas, and, nine months after the meeting, Maecenas invited the young Horace to join his circle of writers. Ironically, Maecenas, as well as being an amateur poet and patron of the arts, was a sort of minister of culture to Horace's former military enemy, Octavian, soon to become the Emperor Augustus and now nominal "first citizen" of the Roman state. Horace was eventually recognized by the Emperor and was even offered a position as private secretary, which he refused; it seems the poet preferred the delights of the Sabine farm, a gift to him from Maecenas about 31 B.C.E., to the bustle of Rome and official business.

Horace remained obedient to the commands of Augustus in the literary sphere, however, composing the fourth book of *Odes* specifically at his request. Augustus as a greatly admired figure, savior of the Roman state, also plays a role in Horace's more political poems, in particular the so-called Roman odes. Horace was so successful in treading the line between personal and public commitments with regard to Augustus that he remained in the good graces of the emperor to his death; he named Augustus his heir, but the latter's true fortune was to inherit mention in Horace's poems.

Other details of Horace's life are often deduced from his poetry, but it has been sufficiently shown that this is a risky undertaking. Often, the "incidents" alleged to have taken place reflect Horace's reading of earlier poetry: He loses his shield in battle, for example, only because the Greek poets Archilochus and Alcaeus (and probably Anacreon) did the same, according to their poems; such was literary convention.

The most that one can say about Horace's later life is that it was comfortable; it included the refreshments of country living as well as the latest in Roman gossip and enabled the poet to nurture his muse while avoiding the frequent pressures to write anything other than what he wished—military epic, for instance.

Horace was buried on the Esquiline hill, near the grave of his friend and patron Maecenas, whose death preceded his by a few months.

ANALYSIS

Certain recurring themes and continuing preoccupations can be traced throughout Horace's work: the tendency, from the start of his writing career, to combine Greek and Roman motifs and techniques; his insistence, again from the very start, on a certain "Alexandrian" (or Callimachean) style; his increasing awareness of poetry as personal communication as well as public statement; and his concern with Roman politics of the day.

The seventeen poems which later grammarians and scribes called "epodes" (from the Greek word denoting the shorter line of a couplet) Horace called *iambi* (iambics), a title which would have carried several significant messages to an attentive literate audience. In a collection of iambic poetry, the contemporary reader of Horace's poems would expect savage invective verses. This had been the traditional content of *iambi* since the seventh century B.C.E., when the Greek poet Archilochus of Paros used the form to compose abusive satires of his contemporaries. Archilochus's verse was so effective that its victims, a prospective father-in-law among them, reportedly committed suicide. Horace's *iambi* do reflect this tradition—but only to a small degree. Epodes 4, 6, 8, 10, and 12 are surely Archilochean in inspiration: They exhibit the typical direct address to the victim (a degenerate rich man, an unnamed enemy, or lust-crazed hags, in Horace's poems); obscenity and colloquial speech (only here in Horatian verse); and the "animal persona" device often adopted by the Greek poet (such as the implicit equation of the poet with a wolf, and the ironic reversal in another epode, in which a formidable hag becomes wolf to Horace's lamb). Furthermore, Horace hints that he is adopting the Archilochean mode; he refers in epode 6 to the "spurned son-in-law" who had his revenge on "faithless Lycambes" (the name of Archilochus's victim), and in epode 10 he uses the very same motif that the Greek poet had employed, wishing horrible shipwreck on an enemy.

The reader who had expected to find pure invective in Horace's *iambi*, however, would be disappointed. In what was to become his typical fashion, Horace inserted elements of the traditional genre only to play with them in a sophisticated remodeling of tradition. So it is that the remaining epodes hint at invective poetry but then veer off into other generic types—praise poetry, love poetry, *recusatio* (refusal), pastoral, and variations of these. In this refashioning, Horace again had some precedent in Callimachus, the third century Greek poet, who had also written *iambi* but had used them for yet another prodigious display of esoteric mythical and historical allusion.

EPODES

What is most fresh in Horace's *Epodes* is the use of the form for direct address on current topics. Epodes 1, 7, 9, and 16 all touch on the civil war between Brutus and the followers of Caesar (and later, Antony and Octavian). The introductory poem, as is customary, is addressed to Horace's patron, Maecenas, and so was probably the last poem to be written. As in epode 9, here the topic of war is only background to the main theme of the poem: Maecenas is sailing off to Actium with Octavian; Horace, cleverly using military and political language, pledges his loyalty to the patron and adopts the stance of an *imbellis*, or "noncombatant," poet. Although it might appear to be a minor point, such a stance is crucial to Horace as poet of the *Epodes*. From the start, he is hinting that it will not be his chosen task to praise Maecenas or Octavian for military victories. Horace is, instead, to live a modest existence at home, viewing war only from a distance and being free to write humorously about anything he might like—as he proceeds to do in the remaining epodes. The poem is, then, introduction, apology, refusal, and praise of the patron. Even at this early point of his career, Horace is a master of *multum in parvo*, "saying much in a short space."

The prevalence of humorous poems in the *Epodes*, such as epode 2 (a mock pastoral put in the mouth of a Roman moneylender), epode 3 (a mock threat to Maecenas for a gift of garlic), and epode 5 (the baroque lament of a witch's victim), further emphasizes the serious intent of civil war poems such as epode 7, in which Horace berates the fratricidal citizens of the city of Romulus and Remus (a fratricidal pair). At the same time, even in the "serious" poems, Horace does not forget his role—he is a poet, not a social reformer. Thus, the final civil war poem, epode 16, resembles epode 7

in its refusal to offer solutions to the conflict. It might appear that the poet does come up with an answer in this address to an imaginary Roman assembly: He proposes an expedition to the Isles of the Blest and the abandonment of all of Rome's problems. The reader must see through Horace's dramatic setting, however: The assembly cannot have been Roman (and therefore the possibility of the proposal being accepted is rejected); the details of the Isles of the Blest are too obviously the stock motifs of impossible pastoral scenes, common from Hesiod on. Ending as it does with the word *fuga* (flight), the poem is better interpreted as Horace's ironic reply to the escapist element at Rome: Civil war is in the blood, and there is no flight. This is invective in sheep's clothing.

A final indication of Horatian artistry in the *Epodes* arises from the deployment of the poems within the book. Scholars have noticed symmetry in theme between epodes 5 and 17 (both about Canidia the witch), epodes 6 and 15 (revenge warnings), epodes 8 and 12 (abuse of hags), epodes 9 and 13 (symposium settings), and epodes 11 and 14 (love elegies).

SATIRES

By 30 B.C.E., Horace had published another carefully arranged collection of poems, the *Satires*, consisting of two books, each containing about one thousand dactylic hexameter verses and dealing with an astonishing array of topics, from the history of the genre (which Horace traced to Greek Old Comedy) to travel narrative to imaginary conversations in the Underworld. The title *Satires*, in fact, is misleading: There is little abuse here, no invective directed against historical personages (the names all being stock characters), and little, if any, serious intent to correct morals. The poet seems to have referred to his work as *sermones* (conversations); this title far better describes the content and style of the poems.

While the *Epodes* follows a principle of opposite arrangement, those near the beginning of the book being echoed symmetrically by poems near the end, the *Satires* can be read in sections which form a clear progression, from moralizing harangue through autobiographical essays to anecdotes of Roman life; then, after an "apology" poem, the second book presents a new strategy of poetic setting: All eight poems are somehow dialogues, with named or imaginary interlocutors. The now-familiar Horatian device of variety in content subjected to strict formal control appears not only on the level of arrangement. Within individual poems, Horace strives for the effect of random conversation, yet this "talk" is not merely transcribed street speech. It is artistically abbreviated and modified to fit smoothly into the difficult hexameter meter. The ability to overcome such technical difficulties marks Horace as a master. A few examples might illustrate this achievement.

First, Horace does not claim for himself the honor of having invented the "conversation" genre, although this is surely his innovation in the history of *satura* (satire). Instead, he names the earlier Roman poet Lucilius as his model. Satire I.4, in which he discusses his debt, however, also contains the specific objections which Horace makes to Lucilian style, and these form a sort of poetic creed for the later poet. Lucilius (whose huge output survives only in fragments) "used to recite two hundred verses an hour, standing on one foot, as a grand performance," says Horace; there would be much to excise from such versifying. For Horace, brevity is art. Again, Horace sees poetry as hard work; Lucilius, he alleges, was "lazy at bearing the labor of writing correctly."

In true ironic fashion, Horace proceeds to undercut his assertions by claiming that he is not a "real" poet himself, but only someone who enjoys enclosing talk in meter. He makes the statement in order to avoid being called a savage satirist by the industrious, greedy Romans: *His* "work" is only play, Horace says, and not the dangerous occupation which many consider it.

To diminish further the threat of his satire, Horace makes the famous claim that, whereas epic, high-poetic diction is instantly recognizable, if one were to subtract meter from his own poems, there would not be even "the limbs of a sundered poet" left over. At times, as in the nine-line parenthetical remark embedded in the *Satires*, Horace goes to extremes to prove that his poetry is more like conversation. The conceit adds all the more irony to these compositions, as it is clear from such poems as the programmatic satire I.10 on which side of the stylistic question Horace really stands. Here, in the final poem of the first book (as traditional as opening poems for the placing of poetic credos), he provides the most concise rationale for his own style:

And so it's not enough to make the hearer laugh;
(Yet this is also a virtue of some sort)
One needs conciseness, so that the thought runs on,
Doesn't tangle itself up with words that burden tired ears.
And talk should have now a sad, often a happy cast,
Doing the part now of an orator, now again a poet.

This creed, at least, is one Horace follows. Poet and rhetorician, in the *Satires* he merges low style (stemming from the commonplace style of third century Greek popular moral sermons) with high (that of earlier Greek and Roman epic, tragic, and lyric verse). Carefully chosen diction jostles home truths in the poems, making the *Satires* an authentic image of Rome itself, where all types of humanity could be seen. As the English Augustan poets knew, satire is the urban genre *par excellence*; Horatian satire, in its gently teasing pretense of "talking" to the city, is central to later examples of this poetic mode.

ODES

If the *Satires* is still fresh after two thousand years, that fact is partly the result of Horace's completely original choice of tone, a strength which sustains the *Odes* as well. In this collection of eighty-eight poems in various meters, supplemented by a later fifteen poems, the poet most often speaks in the first person to another. Maecenas, Vergil, Augustus, and other actual contemporaries are among the addressees; so are various divinities and inanimate objects (a boat, a wine jar, a spring). Yet these are far from being simple poetic letters—Horace would experiment with the epistle form a few years later. Rather, they use the convention of an addressee to proceed in one of two directions: Either the topic changes abruptly from the person addressed to what is really the subject of the poem, or the addressee *becomes* the topic. An example of the first type is *Odes*, book 1, in which Maecenas, addressed in the first two lines as "defense" and "pleasing source of pride" (*dulce decus*) for the poet, drops out of sight for the next thirty lines while Horace develops his contrast between the poet and other occupations; the poet is humble by comparison but also free and secluded:

As for me, ivy on literary brows
Transports me to gods' company; the cool wood grove,
Light choruses of Nymphs with Satyrs
Keep me from the crowd. . . .

Only in line thirty-five does Maecenas reappear: "If *you* count me with lyric's inspired bards, head held high I'll hit the stars," the poet concludes. Thus, the poem defines the poet (or at least that "I" which is Horace's poetic personality) instead of focusing on communication with the addressee.

In the second type of ode, the poems in which the addressee becomes the topic, Horace pays most attention to creating dramatic and often humorous situations by means of unexpected words, mere hints about time, place, and background, and artfully withheld information about the character of the speaker. Even though he appears to offer us slices of his own life, Horace is at the farthest possible remove from confessional poetry in the *Odes*. The second type integrates the addressee into the poem more completely; it contains examples of Horace's better poems. One such, *Odes*, book 1, deals with love (as about one-third of the odes do), but in a typically oblique way, as part of a short moralizing discourse in the words of an unnamed narrator. The first word of the poem puts the reader into the scene. "*You* see how Mt. Soracte stands, white in deep snow. . . ." Outside, all is ice-jammed; trees and rivers freeze over; inside, by contrast, warmth rules, as the speaker orders "Thaliarche" (a slave?—the Greek name, "festival ruler," has significance) to pile more logs on the fire and pour more wine. Once allowed to eavesdrop on the domestic conversation, the reader is lured into imagining details which Horace slyly keeps concealed: The speaker must be an older man, since he takes the role of adviser ("Leave the rest to the gods; don't seek to know tomorrow's fate"). Ending his bland dismissals in a tightly worded vignette, he specifies what activities the young man beside him should be pursuing: "Now, go after the whispers in the evening, the welcome laugh that gives away the girl hiding in an intimate nook, the pledge-ring snatched from a wrist, or a finger barely resisting." The shift in what occupies the speaker's mind is enough to characterize him for any reader, and one rereads the poem with a fresh eye. Is it the snow ("white," line one, like his description of "white-haired old age," line seventeen) which reminds the poem's persona of death? Is the frozen world somehow to be reconciled with the melting girl? Thirty nouns, eighteen adjectives, and almost no exposition, in Horace's hands, can prompt

such larger questions. If the *Odes* approaches philosophic concerns, it is solely through such intense viewing of the physical world in all of its contrasts, not through the obvious (and often ironically placed) moral platitudes which one also finds in Horace.

The two forms of address, then—self-reflective poems to real persons and dramatic, self-concealing poems to imaginary ones—between them utilize all the old lyric themes, of love, death, wine, and mythology. As in the poetry of one of his Greek models, the sixth century Alcaeus, the seemingly unpoetic theme of politics also finds a place in Horace's poetry. Horace lacks Alcaeus's direct involvement in local affairs, yet his lyrics allow the public voice of the *Epodes* and *Satires* to emerge, as it does most clearly in book 3 of the *Odes*. Ironically, this public poetry cycle begins with a reassertion of the poet as master of esoteric art: "I hate and shun the uninitiated crowd." He calls himself "priest of the Muses." Like the distancing achieved by masks in drama, or by animal personas in fables, this withdrawal enables Horace to speak his mind more plainly. In theme, these "Roman Odes" cover the Roman ethical vocabulary: *paupertas* (a noble small means); *virtus* (courage and incorruptibility); *justitia* (the rule of law); *imperium* (the rule of appointed power).

Horace inevitably associates the last mentioned with Augustus, whom he praises as equal to the divinized heroes of Greek myth, but in the same poem he also advises against too ambitious a campaign in the East. It is worth noting how Horace can give advice without becoming dangerously offensive. First, he places the warning in the veiled words of the goddess Juno, who speaks within the poem in a mythological excursus. Second, he employs the technique of *recusatio* in order to avoid getting deeply into the subject. The poem ends: "Muse, where are you heading? Don't go telling the talks of gods; attenuate in small music the great affairs." More than in the *Epodes*, where the technique first appears, the poet of the *Odes* restricts his topics by this Callimachean device; his subject is love affairs, not statecraft.

Horace innovates further, using this lyric device, by turning the stylistic call for "small" (*tenuis*, or "thin") themes into a moral imperative, most clearly in *Odes*, book 2, to Grosphus. Because neither riches nor political power give personal peace or stop anxiety, the solution, says Horace, is good-humored resignation in rustic seclusion. "*Small* fields" and the "*thin* breath of a Greek rustic Muse" (Greek because Horace in the *Odes* imitates the meter and often the content of Sappho and Alçaeus)—these are the poet's fated gifts. The implied "seclusion" is only part of Horace's poetic strategy, and it need not have been actual: A true recluse does not write verse like this or attempt to justify his personal integration of life and style.

EPISTLES

In the *Epistles*, both the ironic tension and the philosophical tone of the Grosphus ode find expression as Horace returns to humorous hexameter verse. The twenty poems of the first book show the poet applying the combined lessons of his earlier work. As in the *Odes*, each poem is addressed to someone, ensuring tonal control; as in the *Satires*, each pretends to instruct the reader on some moral point. The persona adopted now is that of an eclectic philosopher, "sworn to no one school." The letter form allows a joking, rapid, conversational style, and the style, in turn, disguises Horace's serious pronouncements on subjects ranging from the psychology of the Roman practical mind, to Stoicism, to the client-patron relationship. Some of the scattered short poems resemble actual letters; the longer poems, meanwhile, read like an epistolary novel in their gradual creation of character: that of a gentleman-farmer-poet of small means but rich in insight (especially into his fickle nature: "At Rome I want Tibur, at Tibur, Rome. . . .").

Although Horace, in the introductory poem of the first book, claims to have abandoned lyric verse, this does not mean that he has forgotten his high standards of craftsmanship. In a gibe at his imitators, he shows that he prides himself on the pioneering achievement of the *Epodes* and *Odes*, particularly the latter, in which he still has confidence despite the poor public reception. A final example of his craftsmanship appears as the last epistle in the book, where Horace addresses the collection as he would caution a recently freed slave eager to participate in the life of the city. It is an extended metaphor; the poet warns that "you will be loved while you are still young—then you'll end up teaching small boys in a small town somewhere" (a common occupation for old slaves as well as old books). What the book will teach is Horace himself, "who stretched his wings out bigger

than his nest . . . a slight man, tanned and graying, quick to anger but easy to calm down."

Only with this exhibition of the unique Horatian combination of humor with precise literary estimation in mind should one read the most famous and most imitated epistle, the *Ars poetica* (c. 17 B.C.E.), which forms the finale to the second book. That work, also, is a letter; it purports to instruct the sons of Piso about poetry. Many attempts have been made to detect various technical theories behind the work, but it is, rather, an amusing and eclectic virtuoso piece. After four hundred lines of animated, veering argumentation, its primary message comes to this: Write verse the way I have done, with clarity, wit, and flair, learnedly, laboriously, and playfully. So one returns, again, to the Horatian corpus, not to any one statement *about* poetry, but in order to learn how to write verse. It is a good principle in reading Horace and, indeed, all literature.

BIBLIOGRAPHY

Fraenkel, Edouard. *Horace.* Oxford: Clarendon Press, 1957. Extensive twentieth century commentary on the poet's works. Although not intended as a biography, a chapter on Horace's life is thorough and illuminating. Concentrates on close readings of selected poems which illustrate the range of Horace's tastes, interests, and abilities. Carefully researched and documented; most useful for those with some knowledge of Latin literature and culture.

Levi, Peter. *Horace: A Life.* New York: Routledge, 1998. Biography of the poet intended for general readers with little understanding of classical life or literature. Emphasizes the personal relationships that inspired his poetry; provides insight into the historical events that shaped Horace's thought. Offers close textual analysis of key works, including an extensive discussion of *Ars Poetica*.

Oliensis, Ellen. *Horace and the Rhetoric of Authority.* New York: Cambridge University Press, 1998. An advanced introduction to Horace dealing with his poetic career and all of the genres in which he worked, with an emphasis on the social dimensions of Horace's poetry.

Reckford, Kenneth J. *Horace.* New York: Twayne, 1969. Excellent general survey of the poet's life and literary career. Attempts to trace the development of Horace's imagination through the poetry. Provides readings of several important poems, including the odes and satires. Includes a brief bibliography of secondary sources about the poet and his age.

West, David. *Reading Horace*. Edinburgh: Edinburgh University Press, 1967. Reviews the canon, concentrating on the odes; assists readers interested in classical poetry in understanding the complexity of Horace's major works through close readings of selected poems. Attempts to correct misrepresentations of the poet that crept into critical studies during previous decades. Argues that Horace's use of metaphor has not been fully appreciated.

Williams, Gordon. *Horace*. Oxford: Clarendon Press, 1972. Brief, personal reading of the major works by a distinguished Horatian scholar. While acknowledging the importance of previous criticism, attempts to interpret Horace directly from his poetry. Devotes individual chapters to each of the genres in which Horace worked.

Richard Peter Martin;
bibliography updated by Laurence W. Mazzeno

A. E. HOUSMAN

Born: Fockbury, Worcestershire, England; March 26, 1859
Died: Cambridge, England; April 30, 1936

PRINCIPAL POETRY

A Shropshire Lad, 1896
Last Poems, 1922
More Poems, 1936
Collected Poems, 1939

OTHER LITERARY FORMS

A. E. Housman's only work of prose fiction is *A Morning with the Royal Family*, a youthful fantasy printed without his permission in 1882 in the *Bromsgrovian* and unpublished elsewhere. His translations total 102 lines from Aeschylus's *Hepta epi Thēbas* (467 B.C.E.; *Seven Against Thebes*), Sophocles' *Oidipous epi Kolōnōi* (401 B.C.E.; *Oedipus at Colonus*), and Euripides' *Alkēstis* (438 B.C.E.; *Alcestis*) and first appeared in A. W. Pollard's *Odes from the Greek Dramatists* in 1890. They have since been included in the *Collected Poems*. Henry Maas has collected more than eight hundred of Housman's letters, which, though not in the great tradition of English letter-writing, shed considerable light on the poet's enigmatic personality.

ACHIEVEMENTS

Although A. E. Housman's fame today rests on a handful of poems, it was to classical scholarship that he devoted most of his life. For nearly fifty years he was a professor of Latin, first at University College, London, and later at Cambridge University. A profound and prolific scholar fluent in five languages, he published in that time approximately two hundred critical papers and reviews spanning the entire spectrum of classical literature from Aeschylus to Vergil. This work consists mainly of textual emendations of corrupt manuscripts and is highly technical, providing a stark contrast to the lucid simplicity of his poetry. Titles such as "Emendationes Propertianae," "The Codex Lipsiensis of Manilius," and "Adversaria Orthographica" abound in *The Classical Papers of A. E. Housman* (1972), collected and edited by J. Diggle and F. R. D. Goodyear in three volumes. In addition, Housman has left behind editions of Ovid, Juvenal, Lucan, and Manilius and several major lectures, including *The Confines of Criticism* (1969) and *The Name and Nature of Poetry* (1933).

Housman held no illusions either about the power of classical knowledge to influence human character or the extent of its appeal, but he nevertheless placed the highest premium on learning for its own sake and was a relentless seeker after truth using the method of textual criticism, which he defined in *The Application of Thought to Textual Criticism* (1922) as "the science of discovering error in texts and the art of removing it." This was for him "an aristocratic affair, not communicable to all men, nor to most men." The one thing most necessary to be a textual critic "is to have a head, not a pumpkin, on your shoulders, and brains, not pudding, in your head." He applied to others the same rigorous standards of scholarship that he set for himself, and he had no sympathy for incompetence in any form. He was particularly annoyed by the practice of modern criticism of following one manuscript whenever possible instead of weighing the relative merits of alternative manuscripts, a practice, he writes in his preface to Juvenal (1905), designed "to rescue incompetent editors alike from the toil of editing and from the shame of acknowledging that they cannot edit." His harshest words are reserved for self-complacent and insolent individuals masquerading as sane critics. His vituperative attacks on Elias Stoeber and Friedrick Jacob in his 1903 preface to Manilius may be taken as typical: "Stoeber's mind, though that is no name to call it by, was one which turned as unswervingly to the false, the meaningless, the unmetrical, and the ungrammatical, as the needle to the pole," and "Not only had Jacob no sense for grammar, no sense for coherency, no sense for sense, but being himself possessed by a passion for the clumsy and the hispid he imputed this disgusting taste to all the authors whom he edited." The

A. E. Housman (Library of Congress)

extent of Housman's learning and the unbridled candor of his judgments made him a respected and feared polemicist and perhaps the most formidable classicist of his age. W. H. Auden called him "The Latin Scholar of his generation."

Throughout his career Housman repeatedly denied having any talent for literary criticism, and he turned down the Clark Lectureship in English Literature at Trinity College, Cambridge, on the ground that he did not qualify as a literary critic, who, he wrote in *The Confines of Criticism*, is rarer than "the appearance of Halley's comet." When he was at University College, London, he delivered papers on various English poets including Matthew Arnold, Algernon Charles Swinburne, and Alfred, Lord Tennyson, but he refused to allow them to be published and apparently resented the demands the Literary Society made on him, writing in his preface to Arthur Platt's *Nine Essays* (1927) that "Studious men who might be settling *Hoti's* business and properly basing *Oun* are expected to provide amusing discourses on subjects of which they have no official knowledge and upon which they may not be titled even to open their mouths." Nevertheless, Housman's several excursions into literary criticism reflect a great sensitivity to such central concerns as the integrity of literary texts and the debasement of language. In its emphasis on the numinous intractability of great poetry, *The Name and Nature of Poetry* is an oblique repudiation of the intellectualism of T. S. Eliot and I. A. Richards. Housman's criticism shows the influence of Matthew Arnold, but the importance he attached to the undergirding of impressionistic judgments with sound scholarship goes beyond that Victorian sage.

As a poet, Housman was successful to the point of celebrity. *A Shropshire Lad* was initially slow to catch on with the reading public, but after Grant Richards took over as Housman's publisher, it became a great success on both sides of the Atlantic. Its moody *Weltschmerz* caught the *fin de siècle* state of mind, just as *Last Poems* captured the ennui of a war-weary generation. Today the inevitable reaction has set in and Housman's poetry is not as highly regarded as it once was. The melancholy of his poems too often seems uninformed by spiritual struggle, but the plaintive lyricism of his best work has a universal and enduring appeal.

BIOGRAPHY

Alfred Edward Housman was born on March 26, 1859, in Fockbury, Worcestershire, into an ancient family of preachers and farmers whose English roots extended back to the fourteenth century. His great-grandfather on his father's side, an evangelical preacher who lived out his life with a wife and eight children in genteel poverty, was shy and unassertive in manner but inwardly tough, capable of bearing up under the hardships of life with manly fortitude. Housman was able to observe at first hand that stoicism, which informs so much of his mature poetry, in his own mother, Sarah, whose prolonged suffering and death after bearing seven children was a model of quiet courage. In the words of George L. Watson, "With his grimly stoical demeanor, Housman often recalled some ancestral farmer, glowering at the inclement weather" (*A. E. Housman: A Divided Life*, 1957). No such family precedent exists for Housman's career as a scholar unless it be a distant cousin on his father's side who was a lecturer in Greek and Divinity at Chichester College, and still less exists for the poet's rejection of the Church within a year of his mother's death.

The death of Housman's mother on his twelfth birthday brought a traumatic end to his childhood and left him with a profound sense of loss from which he never fully recovered. He had adored the witty, intelligent woman who took pride in her descent from Sir Francis Drake, and her death created a vacuum which could not be filled by his father, Edward, a lackluster solicitor who took increasingly to drink during Sarah's illness and who, two years after her death, married his cousin Lucy and began a long slide into poverty, dying after many years of broken health in 1894. Alfred was never close to his father. He regarded his drunkenness and general improvidence as intolerable weaknesses and held him in barely concealed contempt. He was, however, close to his six brothers and sisters during his early life and, as the oldest, conducted literary parlor games for them, taking the lead in writing nonsense verse, a practice that continued during summer vacations through his college years.

Sarah's death was not permitted to interrupt for long Housman's studies at nearby Bromsgrove School, where he had enrolled on a scholarship in the fall of 1870. Bromsgrove was an old and reputable public school and provided an excellent foundation in the classics, English, and French. As a student, Housman was introspective and shy and was known as "Mouse" by his classmates. Throughout his childhood, he was afflicted with a nervous disorder and while a student at Bromsgrove he had violent seizures which the headmaster attributed to St. Vitus's dance (chorea). Later in life this nervous condition took the form of occasional facial contortions which might "incongruously reappear in the course of the most impersonal lectures, as he read aloud one of the odes of Horace, leaving his astonished students 'afraid the old fellow was going to cry,'" in the words of George L. Watson. His nervous affliction notwithstanding, Housman seemed to thrive on the rigorous eleven-hour-a-day regimen at Bromsgrove School. In 1874, he appeared for the first time in print with a poem in rhymed couplets about the death of Socrates for which he won the prize for composition in English verse and which he delivered on Commencement Speech Day. It was published in the *Bromsgrove Messenger* on August 8, 1874, much to his later chagrin. In adult life, Housman was always jealous of his reputation and forbade the publication of his juvenilia and occasional addresses, which he felt did not meet the high standards he set for himself.

Housman's career at Bromsgrove School ended in triumph as he won the Lord Lyttelton prize for Latin verse, the honorarium for Greek verse, and the Senior Wattell prize, along with a generous scholarship to St. John's College, Oxford. At least some of Housman's success at this time can be attributed to Herbert Millington, who became headmaster at Bromsgrove School in 1873. A man of keen intellect, Millington presented a formidable figure to the students, and Housman felt some hero-worship for him, referring to him much later as a good teacher for a clever boy. Millington was the most important role model of Housman's youth.

In the fall of 1877, Housman entered Oxford and within a few days was writing irreverently to his stepmother about the solemn Latin ceremony of matriculation. He joined the Oxford Union, and although he was inactive he was "an avowed member and staunch champion of the Conservative faction" (Watson). Generally, however, Housman remained uninvolved in the life of the university. He was unimpressed by its professors and attended only one lecture by the illustrious Benjamin Jowett. Housman came away disgusted by Jowett's disregard for the "niceties" of scholarship. A lecture by John Ruskin also left Housman unimpressed. Housman later wrote that "Oxford had not much effect on me." This was not entirely the case, for it was at Oxford that he began to develop in earnest his capacity for classical scholarship. Passively resisting the conventional curriculum, Housman early in his Oxford career decided to devote his energies to the text of the Latin poet Propertius, whose garbled works required extensive editorial attention. He continued to work on Propertius for the remainder of his time at Oxford. George Watson writes that Housman was already "embarking on those problems of conjectural emendation which are the acme of classical learning." It was also at this time that Housman began keeping a commonplace book of his favorite quotations, which tended toward the sepulchral, as one might expect of a young man whose only adornments for his college rooms were Albrecht Dürer's "Melancholia" and "The Knight, Death and the Devil." Housman's favorite poem during his early Oxford years was Arnold's *Empedocles on Etna* (1852), which he said contained "all the law and the prophets." He was attracted to Thomas Hardy's early novels for their gloomy stoicism. For a time Housman flirted with the poetry of Swinburne and wrote an antiecclesiastical poem, "New-Year's Eve," modeled on Swinburne's style.

Clearly the most important thing that happened to Housman during these years was his friendship with Moses Jackson, which had a deep and lasting effect on him. Among the first people he met at Oxford were A. W. Pollard and Jackson. He liked them both, but he was especially attracted to the latter. Jackson was everything that Housman was not: sociable, handsome, athletic, charismatic. A brilliant student of engineering, he excelled with ease at everything he did. The three became fast friends, and in 1879, Housman won a first class in Moderations but his failure to win either the Hertford Classical Scholarship or the Newdigate Prize for English verse was an omen of worse to come. In his last year at Oxford, Housman shared rooms with Pollard and Jackson and according to Watson this "was to be the most perturbed and momentous period of his life."

There is convincing evidence that at this time Housman developed a passionate attachment for Jackson, which he kept hidden from everyone at great psychic cost to himself. He became irritable and moody, but his friends apparently suspected nothing. He failed his examination in Greats, and in the summer of 1881, he returned to his family in disgrace. Andrew S. Gow in his *A. E. Housman: A Sketch* (1936) attributes Housman's failure to the nature of the curriculum, which emphasized history and philosophy at the expense of literature, but the weight of more recent opinion, including that of Watson and Maude M. Hawkins (*A. E. Housman: Man Behind a Mask*, 1958) places the blame on Housman's changed feelings for Jackson.

Housman returned to Oxford in the fall of 1881 to qualify for the lowly pass degree. He worked occasionally as a tutor in Greek and Latin at his old school and studied intensively for the Civil Service Examination. In December, 1882, he moved to London to share lodgings with Jackson and Jackson's younger brother, Adalbert, and went to work in the Patent Office, where he spent the next ten years registering trademarks. From this point until 1885, not one letter emerged from Housman and not even a brother and sister could gain access to him when they came to live in London. In 1886, Housman, seeking the peace of solitude, took private rooms in Highgate, and from this time on, his "invariable mode of life," according to Watson, would be "monastic seclusion." Only the Jackson brothers were encouraged to intrude upon his privacy.

In 1888 Housman broke upon the scholarly world with an avalanche of brilliant critical articles that won for him an international reputation (and would secure for him the chair in Latin at University College, London, in 1892). When one remembers that these early scholarly publications were researched in the evenings at the British Museum after a full day at the Patent Office, his accomplishment must be seen as nothing short of heroic. His *Introductory Lecture* (1937) was given on October 3, 1892, at University College and earned for him the lasting respect of his colleagues. Housman's scholarly writing continued unabated during his years there. He continued to work on the manuscripts of Propertius, edited works by Ovid and Juvenal, and in 1897 came out with a brilliant series of papers on the

Heroides. In the meantime, Moses Jackson had gone to live in India and Adalbert had died, plunging Housman into near suicidal gloom which was to persist at intervals for the rest of his life and which could be relieved only by creative activity. In 1896, *A Shropshire Lad* appeared, published at his own expense, and 1899 saw the first paper on Manilius, the poet who was to become the object of Housman's most important work of scholarship. His edition of Manilius appeared in five books over a twenty-seven-year period, "a monument of incomparable skill and thankless labour."

The eventual success of *A Shropshire Lad* and Housman's recognized position as a scholar of the first rank made him something of a celebrity, and during his last ten years at University College, he would dine at the Café Royal with a select circle of friends that included his brother Laurence, his publisher Grant Richards, his faculty colleague Arthur Platt, and a few others. By now Housman was a connoisseur of fine food and wine and an accomplished dinner conversationalist. He remained aloof from the London literary scene, however, and had little appreciation for the serious writers of his day, including the poet William Butler Yeats. On a lesser level, he intensely disliked the novels of John Galsworthy, and when James Joyce's *Ulysses* (1922) was published, Housman sniffed, "I have scrambled and waded through and found one or two half-pages amusing." Nor did he display any interest in music or painting. About such composers as Ralph Vaughan Williams and Charles Butterworth, who set some of his poems to music, Housman remarked, "I never hear the music, so I do not suffer."

In October, 1911, Housman was elected Kennedy Professor of Latin at Cambridge University and a fellow of Trinity College. His brilliant inaugural lecture on *The Confines of Criticism* remained unpublished during his lifetime because he was unable to verify a reference in it to Percy Bysshe Shelley. At the university, Housman became a member of a select group of the faculty known as "The Family," which met twice a month for dinner. At these ritual banquets, Housman proved a good raconteur and was a well-accepted member of the group, but according to Gow, he held himself back from intimate friendships with his colleagues for fear of rejection or disappointment. He was equally distant toward his students; and his lectures, which he gave twice weekly in all three academic terms, were sparsely attended both because of the highly technical nature of his subject matter and the coldness of his demeanor on the platform. Throughout his twenty-five years at Cambridge, Housman continued to publish widely, directing his major efforts to the edition of Manilius. He was both respected as a great scholar and feared as a devastating polemicist. *Last Poems*, which appeared in 1922, was a great success. In the spring of 1933, Housman was prevailed upon to give the Leslie Stephen Lecture. He delivered *The Name and Nature of Poetry* on the twenty-second anniversary of his inaugural lecture as Kennedy Professor of Latin. In the summer of 1935, an ill Housman rallied enough strength for one last trip to France, where he had vacationed regularly since 1897. Weakened by heart disease, he died in Cambridge on April 30, 1936. In the words of Watson, he "wore in absolute repose a look of 'proud challenge.'"

ANALYSIS

A. E. Housman once remarked, with that scathing condescension of which he was a master, that Swinburne "has now said not only all he has to say about everything, but all he has to say about nothing." Actually, when Housman was at Oxford he fell under Swinburne's powerful spell. His "New Year's Eve" (*Additional Poems*, XXI), written about 1879, celebrates the death of the gods in a labored imitation of the "Hymn to Proserpine": "Divinities disanointed/ And kings whose kingdom is done." The poem is interesting but uninspired, and it is good that Housman early rejected Swinburne as a model. Still, one wishes that Housman had possessed more of the older poet's exuberance of imagination and richness of rhetoric, for it is in these qualities that his poetry is most deficient.

Practically all of his poems are variations on the related themes of mortality and the miseries of the human condition; while a close reading reveals considerably more variety than at first appears, it is nevertheless true that the body of Housman's poetry is slighter than that of any other English poet of comparable reputation. The authorized canon consists of only three small volumes, which were published separately: *A Shropshire Lad*, *Last Poems*, and the posthumous *More Poems*. The twenty-three *Additional Poems* and three verse translations have been added to the *Collected Poems* for a total of 175 original poems. All are short, some no more than a stanza in length. The predominant form is the lyric. The tone is characteristically mournful and the mood elegiac. It is useless to look for any kind of development, either of substance or technique, in these poems, for most of them were written in the 1890's when Housman was under great psychological stress. They are intensely autobiographical inasmuch as they spring from the deep well of Housman's psyche, but few refer to specific events in his life. Housman's passion for privacy was as great as Robert Browning's, and he was attracted to the lyric as a verse form largely because of its essential impersonality. The emotion of his poems is usually general, an undifferentiated *Weltschmerz*, and such dramatic elements as may occur as persona and setting are characteristically undefined. The extremely personal and revealing "The world goes none the lamer" (*More Poems*, XXI) and "Because I liked you better" (*More Poems*, XXXI) are exceptional.

DOOMED LOVE

In the world of Housman's poetry, which is more obviously consistent than that of more complex poets, youth fades into dust, lovers are unfaithful, nature is lovely but indifferent, and death is the serene end of everything. These great archetypal themes have given rise to some of the world's finest poetry, from Sir Walter Raleigh's "The Nymph's Reply to the Shepherd" to William Butler Yeats's "Sailing to Byzantium." What makes them interesting in Housman's poetry are the particular forms in which they are cast. "With rue my heart is laden" (*A Shropshire Lad*, LIV), a poem sometimes set to music, may be taken as exemplary of his lyricism:

> With rue my heart is laden
>   For golden friends I had,
> For many a rose-lipt maiden
>   And many a lightfoot lad.
> By brooks too broad for leaping
>   The lightfoot boys are laid;
> The rose-lipt girls are sleeping
>   In fields where roses fade.

In this lyric of studied simplicity there is a classical blending of form and substance. The simple and inven-

tive diction; the Latinate syntax, parallelism, and balance; the alternating seven- and six-syllable lines restrain still further the already generalized emotion; and while the poem is cold and artificial, it has a kind of classical grace. A comparison with William Wordsworth's "A Slumber Did My Spirit Seal" will reveal the power of a great sensibility working through the constraints of classical form to convey a sense of profound personal feeling.

In too many of Housman's lyrical poems, including the well-known "When I was one-and-twenty" (*A Shropshire Lad*, XIII) and "When first my way to fair I took" (*Last Poems*, XXXV), the feeling is severely attenuated by a mannered flatness, and the passion that the poet undoubtedly experienced is swallowed up by the generalization of the emotion. At worst, the feeling degenerates into the bathos of "Could man be drunk for ever" (*Last Poems*, X) or the histrionic posturing of "Twice a week the winter thorough" (*A Shropshire Lad*, XVII), but at their best there is a genuine communication of feeling, as in "Yonder see the morning blink" (*Last Poems*, XI) and "From far, from eve and morning" (*A Shropshire Lad*, XXXII). There is a thin line between the expression of the poignancy of existence and sentimentality, and it is a tribute to Housman's tact that he so seldom crosses it.

Housman's poems work best when the emotion is crystallized by a dramatic context, as in some of the love pieces and the poems about soldiers in which the oracular pronouncements about the miseries of living which so easily lapse into an unacceptable didacticism are subordinated to more concrete situations. "Oh see how thick the goldcup flowers" (*A Shropshire Lad*, V) is a clever and humorous dialogue between a young blade and a girl who spurns his advances, but beneath the surface gaiety there is the slightest suggestion of the mortality and faithlessness of lovers. In "Delight it is" (*More Poems*, XVIII) the youthful speaker addresses the maiden in words of reckless honesty—"Oh maiden, let your distaff be/ And pace the flowery meads with me/ And I will tell you lies"—and one is to assume that he is a prototype of all young lovers.

In "Spring Morning" (*Last Poems*, XVI), the idyllic beauty of an April morning and the universal renewal of life in the spring place in ironic relief the "scorned unlucky lad" who "Mans his heart and deep and glad/ Drinks the valiant air of dawn" even though "the girl he loves the best/ Rouses from another's side." The speaker of "This time of year" (*A Shropshire Lad*, XXV) is more fortunate, but only because the former lover of his sweetheart has died. "Is my team ploughing" (*A Shropshire Lad*, XXVII) dramatizes a similar situation in which the surviving youth has taken his dead friend's girl. In a dialogue that extends beyond the grave, the living lover tells his dead friend: "I cheer a dead man's sweetheart/ Never ask me whose." One of the most effective of Housman's love poems is "Bredon Hill" (*A Shropshire Lad*, XXI), in which the sound of the church bells reminds the speaker of the untimely death of his sweetheart. The poem ends ambiguously with the distraught lover saying to the humming steeples: "Oh, noisy bells, be dumb/ I hear you, I will come." Also with death in mind is the speaker of "Along the field" (*A Shropshire Lad*, XXVI), who a year before had heard the aspen predict the death of his sweetheart. The prediction fulfilled, he now walks beside another girl, and under the aspen leaves he wonders if they "talk about a time at hand/ When I shall sleep with clover clad/ And she beside another lad."

In all of these poems love is doomed to transience by infidelity or death. This, they say, is the human condition. In virtually all of them, death has supplanted sex as the major ingredient, making them unique in English love poetry.

DEATH

Death is also, less surprisingly, the main element in most of Housman's military poems. The poems about soldiers, with the exception of the frequently anthologized "Epitaph on an Army of Mercenaries" (*Last Poems*, XXXVII), are not as well known as some of Housman's other poetry. At first sight they may seem somewhat out of place, but it is not surprising that an introverted classical scholar of conservative convictions should glamorize the guardians of the empire. The attitude toward the soldier is consistently one of compassion and respect and the poems convey a depth of sincerity not always felt elsewhere. The prospect of young men going to die in foreign lands in the service of the queen takes on an added poignancy from the death of Housman's younger brother, Herbert, who was killed in

the Boer War. On another level, a soldier's death is an honorable form of suicide and a way to attain lasting fame. "The Deserter" (*Last Poems*, XIII) and "The Recruit" (*A Shropshire Lad*, III) may be taken as typical. In the first, the lass, rejected by her lover so that he may rejoin his comrades, upbraids him and others like him for scouring "about the world a-wooing/ The bullet to their breast"; in the second, the lad is promised eternal fame either as a returning hero or as a slain comrade. In "Lancer" (*Last Poems*, VI), the speaker affirms his coming death with the ringing refrain of "*Oh who would not sleep with the brave?*" In these poems Housman succeeds in investing Thanatos, characteristically an enervated and sterile attitude, with a singular vitality. The placid stoicism of the soldiers makes these ultimately the least melancholy of all of Housman's poems.

The melancholy that permeates virtually every line of Housman's poetry is a matter of temperament more than of a well-wrought metaphysics. He affirms the existence of the soul in such poems as "The Immortal Part" (*A Shropshire Lad*, XLIII) and "Be still, my soul" (*A Shropshire Lad*, XLVIII) even as he denies its immortality, the agnostic "Easter Hymn" (*More Poems*, I) notwithstanding. Such monologues to the dead as "To an Athlete Dying Young" (*A Shropshire Lad*, XIX) and "Shot? so quick, so clean an ending?" (*A Shropshire Lad*, XLIV) are intended as no more than poetic license. Death is seen as the final, desirable release from the Sisyphean exhaustion of living. Thanatos ultimately leads to suicide, which in several of the poems is prescribed as the best antidote for the illness of life. Other strategies for coping with the suffocating consciousness of "our long fool's-errand to the grave" are hedonism and, more logically, stoicism.

HEDONISM AND STOICISM

In Housman's hedonistic poems, the traditional sexuality of the *carpe diem* theme has been eliminated. In his most rousing invitation to pleasure, "Think no more lad" (*A Shropshire Lad*, XLIX), the lad is told to "be jolly/ Why should men make haste to die?" Such pleasures as "jesting, dancing, drinking" stave off the darkness, since "'tis only thinking/ Lays lads underground." The other exercises in hedonism are more subdued. The speaker of "Loveliest of trees" (*A Shropshire Lad*, II), aware of his limited time, will go about the woodlands

"To see the cherry hung with snow," and "The Lent Lily" (*A Shropshire Lad*, LXXIX) invites anyone who will listen to enjoy the spring and gather all the flowers that die on Easter Day. In "Reveille" (*A Shropshire Lad*, IV), the lad is enjoined to rise and enjoy the morning, for "Breath's a ware that will not keep/ Up, lad: when the journey's over/ There'll be time enough to sleep." "Ho, everyone that thirsteth" (*More Poems*, XXII) makes an effective use of the living waters of Scripture as a metaphor of fulfillment. The poem concludes that "he that drinks in season/ Shall live before he dies," but the "lad that hopes for heaven/ Shall fill his mouth with mold."

Stoicism is a more satisfying way of coming to grips with the human condition, and it provides the basis for several of Housman's most rewarding poems, including "The Oracles" (*Last Poems*, XXV), "The Sage to the Young Man" (*More Poems*, IV), and "The chestnut casts his flambeaux" (*Last Poems*, IX). In this last poem, an embittered young man drinking in a tavern deplores the passing of another spring and curses "Whatever brute and blackguard made the world" for cheating his "sentenced" soul of all that it has ever craved. Then with dramatic suddenness, he sees that "the troubles of our proud and angry dust/ Are from eternity," and this leads to his stoic affirmation that "Bear them we can, and if we can we must." The idea here that human misery is both certain and universal is the central focus of such powerful poems as "The First of May" (*Last Poems*, XXXIV), "Westward on the high-hilled plains" (*A Shropshire Lad*, LV), and "Young is the blood" (*More Poems*, XXXIV). In "Young is the blood," the speaker identifies his own pain in a youth he espies whistling along the hillside highway and proclaims in the succession of the generations "that the sons of Adam/ Are not so evil-starred/ As they are hard." This is the heart of Housman's stoicism, and this is one of his more honest and successful poems.

In a number of Housman's poems, the universalization of the existential predicament embodies a vision of the remote past that suggests the ultimate insignificance of everything. The speaker of "When I watch the living meet" (*A Shropshire Lad*, XII) is reminded by the moving pageant filing through the street of the dead nations of the past where "revenges are forgot/ And the hater hates no more," just as the speaker of "On Wenlock

Edge" (*A Shropshire Lad*, XXXI) is put in mind by a storm of "the old wind in the old anger" threshing the ancient Roman city of Uricon. He knows the storm will pass even as "the Roman and his trouble," both now "ashes under Uricon." The perspective shifts to the future in "I wake from dreams" (*More Poems*, XLIII) and "Smooth between sea and land" (*More Poems*, XLV), which present visions of apocalyptic dissolution.

The poetry of Housman is the poetry of negation. Most of it is shot through with a nameless melancholy and much of it is pessimistic. His lyrics invite comparison with Hardy's, with which they are often included in anthologies, but they reflect none of Hardy's moral depth. They are closer in spirit to those of Heinrich Heine, whom Housman mentioned as one of the three major influences on his work, along with the English ballads and the songs of William Shakespeare. Housman's *Weltschmerz* struck a deep chord in two generations of English readers, making *A Shropshire Lad* and *Last Poems* two of the most popular volumes of poetry of their period. Today, Housman's reputation is tempered by the knowledge that his poetry, though capable of creating haunting moods, neither expands nor deepens one's self-awareness nor one's awareness of life, despite his claim in "Terence, this is stupid stuff" (*A Shropshire Lad*, LXII) that it prepares one for life's rigors. For this reason Housman must be considered a minor poet.

OTHER MAJOR WORKS

LONG FICTION: *A Morning with the Royal Family*, 1882.

NONFICTION: *The Application of Thought to Textual Criticism*, 1922; *The Name and Nature of Poetry*, 1933; *Introductory Lecture*, 1937; *Selected Prose*, 1961 (John Carter, editor); *The Confines of Criticism*, 1969; *The Letters of A. E. Housman*, 1971 (Henry Maas, editor); *The Classical Papers of A. E. Housman*, 1972 (J. Diggle and F. R. D. Goodyear, editors).

EDITED TEXTS: *M. Manilii Astronomicon Liber Primus*, 1903; *Ivnii Ivvenalis Satvrae*, 1905; *M. Manilii Astronomicon Liber Secundus*, 1912; *M. Manilii Astronomicon Liber Tertius*, 1916; *M. Manilii Astronomicon Liber Quartus*, 1920; *M. Annaei Lvcani Belli Civilis Libri Decem*, 1926; *M. Manilii Astronomicon Liber Quintus*, 1930.

BIBLIOGRAPHY

Graves, Richard Perceval. *A. E. Housman: The Scholar-Poet*. London: Routledge & Kegan Paul, 1979. A fine, balanced biography, drawing on material previously unpublished from public and private sources. Especially significant is Graves's reconciliation of Housman's romantic poetry and classical scholarship. Extensive notes and a bibliographical essay make this volume an especially useful study.

Haber, Tom Burns. *A. E. Housman*. Boston: Twayne, 1967. A biographical study of the poet with separate chapters on his major collections of poetry, two chapters on "literary tastes and influences," and a "retrospect and summing-up." Extensive notes, references, and an annotated bibliography make this book a valuable introductory work, although superseded, in some respects, by later biographies.

Holden, Alan W., and J. Roy Birch. *A. E. Housman: A Reassessment*. New York: St. Martin's Press, 2000. A collection of both biographical and critical essays which uncover the deceptive simplicity of Housman's poetry and life. Includes bibliographical references and index.

Leggett, B. J. *Housman's Land of Lost Content: A Critical Study of "A Shropshire Lad."* Knoxville: University of Tennessee Press, 1970. Contending that *A Shropshire Lad* contains most of Housman's enduring poems, Leggett provides a painstaking analysis of its structure and its theme ("the problem of change"). Leggett aims to shift discussion away from Housman's personality. The bibliography is especially helpful in bringing together the fragmentary and scattered commentary on Housman.

_____. *The Poetic Art of A. E. Housman*. Lincoln: University of Nebraska Press, 1978. A useful study divided by topics: the use of metaphor, nature poetry, structural patterns, Housman, T. S. Eliot, and "critical fashion in the thirties." Leggett devotes two chapters to Housman's theory and practice of poetry, since this has been a contested point in literary criticism. Supplemented by extensive notes but no bibliography.

Naiditch, P. G. *Problems in the Life and Writings of A. E. Housman*. Beverly Hills, Calif.: Krown & Spellmam, 1995. A lucid and readable biographical account with lasting contributions to knowledge of a great and controversial scholar. Includes a bibliography and index.

Page, Norman. *A. E. Housman: A Critical Biography*. New York: Schocken Books, 1983. A succinct account drawing on published and unpublished sources, with separate chapters on Housman's classical scholarship and the development of his poetry. The introduction is especially helpful on the biographer's method, on his evaluation of previous biographies, and on his decision to separate discussions of the life and the work.

Ricks, Christopher, ed. *A. E. Housman: A Collection of Critical Essays*. Englewood Cliffs, N.J.: Prentice-Hall, 1968. The learned introduction concentrates on the quality and critical reception of the poet's work. The collection includes several fine essays by distinguished poets and critics. The list of important dates in Housman's life is sketchy, and the brief bibliography is out of date.

Robert G. Blake;
bibliography updated by the editors

RICHARD HOWARD

Born: Cleveland, Ohio; October 13, 1929

PRINCIPAL POETRY

Quantities, 1962
The Damages, 1967
Untitled Subjects, 1969
Findings: A Book of Poems, 1971
Two-Part Inventions, 1974
Fellow Feelings, 1976
Misgivings, 1979
Lining Up, 1984
Quantities/Damages: Early Poems, 1984
No Traveller, 1989
Selected Poems, 1991 (Hugh Haughton and Adam Phillips, editors)
Like Most Revelations: New Poems, 1994
Trappings: New Poems, 1999

OTHER LITERARY FORMS

Richard Howard wrote extensively about the work of other authors in a collection of criticism titled *Alone with America: Essays on the Art of Poetry in the United States Since 1950* (1969). The book has been praised for its objectivity in discussing his subjects' entire literary career. Whenever he has known the writer personally, he uses his experience to enhance his understanding of the poet's work, always focusing on the work, which he quotes extensively and comments on elaborately. He has also gained a considerable reputation as a translator of French literature, having produced works of such writers as André Gide, Albert Camus, Roland Barthes, Simone de Beauvoir, Stendhal, and many others.

ACHIEVEMENTS

More than any other modern poet, Richard Howard has developed the dramatic monologue into an expressive literary form. Without restricting himself formally, he has used the dramatic monologue in book after book to portray actual and imaginary figures, to create the mood and manners (at least in voice) of earlier epochs, and to link in one literary creation multiple perspectives on the artistic experience, especially that of the homosexual artist. At the same time, Howard has acquired considerable respect as a translator of important French writers, establishing himself as one of the best authorities of these writers. His scores of translations include works of philosophy, literary criticism, and fiction.

In 1966, he was awarded a Guggenheim Fellowship in poetry and, in 1970, a grant from the National Institute of Arts and Letters. His volume of poetry *Untitled Subjects* (1969) received a Pulitzer Prize in 1970, and his work has earned him many other awards, including the American Book Award for his 1983 translation of *Les Fleurs du mal* by Charles Baudelaire. In 1984 he was made a Chevalier de l'Ordre National du Mérite by the French government and in 1989 he received the Academy of American Poets Fellowship. In 1996, he received a MacArthur Fellowship. He is a member of the American Academy and Institute of Arts and Letters and serves as a chancellor of the Academy of American Poets.

Richard Howard (© Rollie McKenna)

BIOGRAPHY

Richard Howard was born an only child in Cleveland, Ohio, on October 13, 1929. His childhood home, which was well stocked with books, provided the youth with a strong literary foundation. His mother had attended Vassar and developed friends whose literary tastes influenced Howard. One of his mother's friends, Ida Treat, a novelist who helped some French writers with their autobiographies, further interested the youth in the literary life. On a trip to Florida, an aunt from Vienna who lived with the Howard family taught the five-year-old Richard to speak French. In his teens he continued to read avidly, and his literary interests included Greek mythology. At Columbia, he met a group of young poets, among whom was John Hollander, who furthered Howard's interest in reading literature, especially poetry, and he developed a particular liking for the poetry of Ezra Pound, Marcel Proust, and W. H. Auden, who later became his mentor.

Howard earned a B.A. at Columbia University in 1951 and an M.A. the following year. A fellowship allowed him to continue his study at the Sorbonne from

1952 to 1953. Returning to the United States, he worked as a lexicographer until 1957 and began translating, soon becoming a prolific and highly respected translator of French literature, focusing on the most important French authors.

Howard has served as poetry editor of several prestigious journals, including *Poetry Review*, *New American Review*, and *New Republic*, and he was president of the PEN American Center from 1979 to 1980. He served as the poet laureate of New York State from 1994 to 1996. He has also taught at a number of prestigious universities. In 1983, he was the Luce Visiting Scholar at the Whitney Humanities Center at Yale; he taught writing at the University of Houston in Houston, Texas, from 1987 to 1997. From Houston he moved to New York City to teach in the writing division of the School of the Arts at Columbia University. He also became editor of *The Paris Review* and *Western Humanities Review*.

ANALYSIS

Richard Howard has developed a wide acquaintance with the leading American poets of his day and won great respect for his critical objectivity and insight. His steady stream of translations has established him as a major authority of French literature. However, his reputation as a poet overshadows his other contributions, significant as they are. Early in his career he established the dramatic monologue as his most characteristic form, seeing it as a way of bringing the past and present together and as a way of layering meanings in a poem through the voices of multiple personas. Speaking through other voices, he once said, has enabled him to represent his own experience better than he otherwise could present it. In this form, he could portray characters and circumstances in a way that made his poetry both intensely expressive yet emphatically impersonal. At the same time, he uses his gallery of portraits and chorus of voices to explore the relation of the past and present, death and loss, and creative success and failure, as well as the passage of time and issues relating to the homosexual artist. In the exploration, he also creates a vivid presence of his characters and their circumstances.

QUANTITIES AND THE DAMAGES

Howard's first two collections of poems were praised for their polished language, flawless rhythms, and lin-

guistic effects. His themes include personal loss, the passage of time, survival, and acceptance. Critics noted Howard's "formal virtuosity and a knack for aphorism." In *Quantities*, Howard experiments in form with an almost restless energy, scarcely rhyming yet retaining regularity in line and stanza length, unifying his poem with a fluid rhythm, image, and sound. He sees the world with a fresh eye and conveys what he sees freshly:

> The sea's green fur begins at length
> To grow against you, and your own
> Accustomed skin gives way to end
>
> In a flourish of salt, swart hair.

In such lines, Howard sees landscape as a sensual presence, and he expresses it in a controlled, sinuous line. Throughout both collections, he seems to be sailing in a literary sea, searching, like Odysseus, for his home. The poems are shorter than his later poems, and the persona often appears to be speaking for Howard himself. Rhyme surfaces here and there in the poems, French and Latin commingle with the English text, and other poets are named, as if beckoned to join the poet in his search for expression and identification. His interest in other times and places is reflected in many titles, such as "To Aegidius Cantor" and "Eusebius to Florestan: On Aproxexia." A sense of loss informs many of the poems, as in the following lines: "Find/ my love: no islands/ for me. Lost/ my love last/ night on the islands." The lines themselves are islands of meaning, separate yet linked to others, incomplete yet part of a whole. Howard's form expresses both ambivalence and conviction.

UNTITLED SUBJECTS

The island metaphor is central to Howard's poetic journey: People, places, and poems are discrete entities that are temporary stops in his journey. The verse epistle, which closely resembles the dramatic monologue, takes central position in *Untitled Subjects*, which won for Howard a Pulitzer Prize. In these poems, whose titles are simply dates, from 1801 to 1915, Howard creates a variety of personas, male and female alike, and reveals subject and circumstance through the voice of the poem's fictive writer. Howard said that translating the work of others is for him an erotic experience, for he enters the mind of the other author in the most intimate ways. The same experience probably led him to embrace the forms of these poems, for he and his character become one voice, intimately bound to one personality.

Howard's many obscure references throughout the volume challenge the reader to stay fixed on what they do to portray the personality of the poem's persona, as in "1897," when Gladstone says, "'Ah, my boy . . .'/ 'we are well away from Balmorality here,/ the terrible Tartanitis which overtook/ the Throne in my time, hard upon/ the Morte d'Albert.'" Howard trusts that the reader will understand references to the death of Queen Victoria's consort, Prince Albert in 1861, the play on the name of the royal castle at Balmoral, and the allusion to Sir Thomas Malory's *Le Morte d'Arthur* in 1485.

FINDINGS AND TWO-PART INVENTIONS

In his following collections, Howard continued to employ the dramatic monologue, varying its subjects and voices to explore and reveal character. In *Findings* he offers elaborate descriptions of snakes, dragons, works of art, and places: "But at night these ashes glow, this dust kindles; like/ the Sultan's topaz, sallow/ then suddenly red, the moon turns Greek/ fire, catches" (in "From Beyoglu"). The poems in *Two-Part Inventions* represent historical figures in dialogue. In a long exchange between Oscar Wilde and Walt Whitman, Howard explores the relation of traditional form and formal freedom. In another poem, the sculptor Auguste Rodin discusses the sexual implications of his creations with a homosexual, who sees the artistic and the homosexual as sharing "the miseries/ of continued possession" and "the struggles of continued exorcism."

MISGIVINGS AND LINING UP

In the middle part of *Misgivings*, Howard takes another creative turn by addressing thirteen photographs of nineteenth century poets and musicians, including the photographer himself, Nadar (Gaspard-Félix Tournachon). Howard's descriptions of the portraits give them a life and character that contrasts poignantly with the stillness of the subjects. Howard returns to this form in *Lining Up*, making it seem as though he is engaged in familiar conversation with his subject. Though he varies the look of poems, their stanza patterns, and their line lengths, his style remains consistent, marked by precise descriptions, historical references, and conversational tone. The remarkable result is that the reader feels in-

cluded in this conversation even though the subjects, references, and language are often beyond reach.

NO TRAVELLER AND LIKE MOST REVELATIONS

Howard favors the long poem, which allows him to develop his subjects like a novelist, filling it with scenes and conversations that give historical context to his ideas and enable him to present his thoughts from different perspectives and in different voices. *No Traveller* opens with one of Howard's most celebrated poems, "Even in Paris," a thirty-page narrative that follows the poet Wallace Stevens on a visit to Paris in 1952. Told in a sequence of letters between three characters, the poem contrasts the distinctive tones and points of view that identify each character. Ivo's letter is lively: "Now Roderick, according/ to Richard, our *anonimo* was none/ other than the Fourteenth Way of Looking at/ a Bleak Bard." By contrast, Richard is somber, sardonic: "Christmas is a deadly season here,/ illustrating the old Parisian rule:/ every silver lining is tarnished by clouds." Both styles are characteristic of Howard's poetry, especially the later poems. His animated style shows elaborately on play, sound, rhythm, and shorter lines; his more somber, serious, or reflective style relies on similar features, but the mood is darkened by the subject, the sounds, and the lines' tendency to lengthen: "Another *fine*, another *fin-de-siecle/* feast of fast with dying dowagers."

Like Most Revelations contains features that are characteristic of Howard, but the subjects are more serious and concerned with current issues and urban scenes. Howard speaks of friends who have died of AIDS; homosexuality is a subject in many of the poems, and the book's final poem is contemporary about a news story of a man with AIDS who beat up homosexuals.

TRAPPINGS

Trappings offers readers the same virtuosity that has become Howard's trademark. The central poem is a typical example of his inventiveness. The poem is a sequence on the subject of John Milton dictating *Paradise Lost* (1667, 1674) to his two daughters, the whole combining different points of view, styles, and forms and addressing various paintings that depict Milton dictating. Each voice is distinct and reveals a thought or perspective that brings life and meaning to a moment in time. The book's characteristic wit and exuberance; the inventive spirit and ornate, convoluted manner of mingling diverse personalities and complex forms; and Howard's preoccupation with gay issues, the classical past, literature, painting, and music, with artists, poets, musicians, seeking and having, losing and finding—all of these features give his poetry a uniqueness, texture, and flexibility that continue to surprise and delight.

OTHER MAJOR WORKS

NONFICTION: *Alone with America: Essays on the Art of Poetry in the United States Since 1950*, 1969.

TRANSLATIONS: *The Immoralist*, 1970 (of André Gide); *Les Fleurs du mal*, 1983 (of Charles Baudelaire); *The Charterhouse of Parma*, 1999 (of Stendhal); *The Little Prince*, 2000 (of Antoine Saint-Exupéry).

EDITED TEXTS: *Preferences*, 1974; *The Best American Poetry*, 1995.

BIBLIOGRAPHY

Bergman, David. *Gaiety Transfigured: Gay Self-Representation in American Literature*. Madison: University of Wisconsin Press, 1991. Bergman devotes a chapter to the poetry of Walt Whitman, John Ashbery, and Richard Howard, tracing their ideas of selfhood in their poetry and connecting these ideas to their homosexuality. The remaining nine chapters of this book establish the context in which gay writers express their sexuality.

Howard, Richard, and Marilyn Hacker. "The Education of a Poet: A Colloquy with Richard Howard and Marilyn Hacker." *The Antioch Review* 58 (Summer, 2000): 261. In this interview, Howard and Hacker stress the need for beginning poets to read literature, especially that of other poets. Howard's comments include some useful autobiographical information not found elsewhere.

Longenbach, James. "Richard Howard's Modern World." *Salmagundi*, no. 108 (Fall, 1995): 141-163. Longenbach's lengthy examination focuses on the themes of loss and recovery in Howard's poetry and on the distinction between the intimate self and the poet's private life. Longenbach argues that Howard has sought to blur the line between the personal and the impersonal in his poetry.

_____. "Sex and Style in Contemporary American Poetry." *Raritan* 19, no. 4 (Spring, 2000): 7-22. Long-enbach argues that poetic style does not necessarily reflect the poet's sexuality and defends Howard's poetry against the charge that it is too prettified. Longenbach asserts that cultural expectations see the plain style as manly and the decorative style "ladylike," but the work of several modern poets shows that the poet's sexuality need not determine the poet's style.

Martin, Robert K. *The Homosexual Tradition in American Poetry: An Expanded Edition*. Iowa City: University of Iowa Press, 1998. Martin's survey of homosexual poetry from Walt Whitman to the late 1990's provides an excellent context in which to read Howard's work. Martin's study is complimentary and focuses on Howard's skill in using the literary monologue to portray various character types. Martin sees Howard's homosexuality as a central issue in the poet's work and shows how the past plays a major role in Howard's thinking. An excellent bibliography concludes the book.

Bernard E. Morris

SUSAN HOWE

Born: Boston, Massachusetts; June 10, 1937

PRINCIPAL POETRY

Hinge Picture, 1974
The Western Borders, 1976
Secret History of the Dividing Line, 1978
Cabbage Gardens, 1979
The Liberties, 1980
Pythagorean Silence, 1982
Defenestration of Prague, 1983
Articulation of Sound Forms in Time, 1987
A Bibliography of the King's Book: Or, Eikon Basilike, 1989
The Europe of Trusts, 1990
Singularities, 1990
The Nonconformist's Memorial: Poem, 1993
Frame Structures: Early Poems, 1974-1979, 1996
Pierce-Arrow, 1999
Bed Hangings, 2001

OTHER LITERARY FORMS

Because her poetry is engendered both by a close attention to the minims of language and by a constant examination of the ground from which the language stems, Howe has come into association with the group known as the Language Realists, or the school known as Language Poetry, publishing in the magazines of that movement as well as in several anthologies predominantly or wholly of Language Realism: *The L = A = N = G = U = A = G = E Book* (1984), *21 + 1 American Poets Today* (a bilingual edition, 1986), *In the American Tree* (1986), and *Language Poetry* (1987).

Susan Howe has also published several reviews and *My Emily Dickinson* (1985). This last, a book-length consideration of Dickinson's work, elucidates the poetry not only of its subject but also of its author, and it is central to an understanding of her oeuvre.

ACHIEVEMENTS

In the years since she began to publish her poetry, Susan Howe has established herself as a poet of profound engagement with the problematic of Being in the era she confronts. Her work also addresses the meaning of being American and being a woman, in order to strip away obsolete ideas concerning both America and Woman and to discover the realities of these conditions in the present.

Howe has twice received the American Book Award of the Before Columbus Foundation, in 1982 for *Pythagorean Silence* and again in 1985 for *My Emily Dickinson*. In 1980, she received a Pushcart Prize for "The Art of Literary Publishing," an interview she conducted with James Laughlin; in 1986, she was awarded a writer's fellowship by the New York State Arts Council; in 1989, she received a second Pushcart Prize. In 1985, she participated in the Colloquium on New Writing held by the Kootenay School for Writers in Vancouver, Canada, and in that same year was writer in residence at New College in San Francisco. In 1986, she spoke on Emily Dickinson to a conference on H. D. and Emily Dickinson held at San Jose State University. In 1989, a complete issue of a journal called *The Difficulties* was devoted to discussion of her work. *The Birth-Mark: Unsettling the Wilderness in American Literary History* was named one of the "International Books of the Year"

by the *Times Literary Supplement* in 1993. She was a John Simon Guggenheim Memorial fellow and won the Ray Harvey Pearce Award, both in 1996, and was a recipient of the New York State Council Writers in Residency grant for a poetry workshop at Lake George, New York. In 2000, she was elected Chancellor of the Academy of American Poets.

BIOGRAPHY

Susan Howe was born in Boston, Massachusetts, on June 10, 1937. With the exception of a relatively brief period in Buffalo, New York, her childhood and adolescence were spent in Boston and Cambridge, where she attended the Beaver Country Day School, from which she was graduated in 1955. Also in 1955, she began a year's study at the Gate Theater, Dublin, Ireland, acting and designing sets. From 1957 to 1961, she attended the Museum School of Fine Arts in Boston. She next took up residence in New York City, working as a painter and exhibiting her paintings at a number of galleries, including the Kornblee. In 1961 she married Harvey Quaytman, and their daughter Rebecca was born that same year. When her marriage ended in 1966, Howe began living with the sculptor David von Schlegell, and in 1967, their son Mark was born. The couple was married in 1976.

In 1971, Howe moved to Guilford, Connecticut, which has been her residence for more than thirty years. From 1975 to 1980, she produced the program Poetry for WBAI, New York City's Pacifica Radio station. In 1988-1989, she was Butler Fellow at the State University of New York, Buffalo, where she continued to teach into the 1990's. In 1990-1991, she was a visiting professor of writing at Temple University in Philadelphia. She maintains a lecture and reading schedule, is active in the American Academy of Poets, and is also a painter who has exhibited her work at galleries in New York City.

ANALYSIS

Susan Howe's poetry challenges habitual assumptions on many levels, but the level the reader is most likely to notice first is the syntactic; what Howe says of Emily Dickinson can with equal force be applied to herself: "In prose and poetry she explored the implications of breaking the law just short of breaking off communication with a reader." Generally, Howe's poems make much use of the page, where the white space is allowed to interrupt the sequence of print, so that a variety of statements may be derived from relatively few phrases, and the overall thrust of the syntax is continually thwarted. Denied easy access to an overarching meaning, the reader must work with smaller units (phrase, line, couplet) and can only gradually constitute the meaning of the whole. This process parallels the approach to Being advocated both explicitly and implicitly in Howe's work. The presumptions of categorical value which modern Western culture persists in advocating are resisted at every turn, for Howe sees (and reveals) just how damaging such presumptions and categories can be. Often, she labors to construct a fresh view of her subject, be it Esther Johnson (known to Jonathan Swift's readers as Stella), Emily Dickinson, or American theologian Jonathan Edwards. To this end, Howe employs the various devices of deconstruction, notably the fracturing of sentence, phrase, or even word.

Such a project inevitably must challenge received notions of the poetic. It is for this reason that traditional forms are absent from Howe's poetry. Such forms by their very ease of recognition would defeat her purpose. To arouse the critical faculties in her reader, Howe must abjure whatever constructions might encourage a reader to glide effortlessly onward: The work must be difficult, not only to reflect accurately the difficulty of living but also to remind the reader at each turn of his or her preconceptions concerning the nature of reality, art, and the very act of reading. For Howe, as for other poets wedded to this task, the question then becomes, What portion of the inherited conceptions of beauty, truth, and the good ought to be retained (as inherent to the art of poetry), and what portion uprooted and discarded (as inimical to a faithful representation of the present)? Language, derived from Being, comes then to govern Being; the reader projects back onto the world expectations previously drawn therefrom: Yet the world is always in process, always changing, always endangering our assumptions and rendering them obsolete. It is therefore to language itself, argue poets who share Howe's address, that the poet ought to draw attention; the reader must be kept aware of the ways in which language governs not only one's concepts but also one's perceptions, and it is

for this reason that Howe through "parataxis and rupture" never lets her readers forget the effect of words and phrases on content. Content, in fact, always includes the agony of choice, whether it be the deliberations as to formal procedure or their counterparts in other modes of action.

Inescapably, Howe is, by birth and gender, both American and a woman, subject to the assumptions of those categories, and at once in revolt against such predications and eager to discover their underlying realities. In *My Emily Dickinson*, she would rescue the Dickinson of her particular vision from the several inadequate characterizations which prevent, to Howe's view, a full experience of the poetry. To this end, Howe, in a work that is cousin to both William Carlos Williams's *In the American Grain* (1925) and Charles Olson's *Call Me Ishmael* (1947), rereads the contribution of figures vital to Dickinson's production: Elizabeth Barrett Browning and Robert Browning, James Fenimore Cooper, Emily Brontë, Charles Dickens, Jonathan Edwards, Ralph Waldo Emerson, Cotton Mather, Mary Rowlandson, William Shakespeare, Henry David Thoreau, and Thomas Wentworth Higginson. Howe finds that, approached from this rich assortment of angles, Dickinson's poetry yields a wealth of information about Being in general, but also about being American and being a woman, and about how a poetry grows consanguineously. Howe is severe with certain feminist critics who, while lauding Dickinson, laud a Dickinson who is essentially the creation of patriarchal vision, swallowing whole this distortion. Toward the end of *My Emily Dickinson*, Howe observes: "Victorian scientists, philosophers, historians, intellectuals, poets, like most contemporary feminist literary critics—eager to discuss the shattering of all hierarchies of Being—didn't want the form they discussed this in to be shattering." Howe's poetic practice is the negation of this widespread and persistent error.

"The lyric poet," Howe writes in *My Emily Dickinson*, "reads a past that is a huge imagination of one form," and while the labor of precursors in one sense is enormously beneficial, providing as it does countless elucidations of Being, in another sense it becomes a mighty burden, because of the irresistible nature of pre-existing formulations, whether to the poet or to her audience, formulations which nevertheless demand to be resisted if one is to come to a personal definition of one's epoch. Howe, then, in her determination to "make it new," aligns herself with such high modernists as Ezra Pound, Gertrude Stein, and William Carlos Williams, although she must also—for the reasons given above—keep her project distinct from theirs. The world in the 1970's and 1980's is far from the world of the 1910's and 1920's; Howe is among those who see the poet's calling as a demand to make forms consonant with her own day.

THE LIBERTIES

The analysis provided during the 1960's and 1970's of dominant patriarchal elements in Western society is one example of this altered ideology to which Howe would be responsible. Therefore *The Liberties*, a book of poetry whose sufficient cause is the largely masculine-engendered version of Esther Johnson, known—and it is the commonality of this means of recognition Howe intends to attack—as Dean Swift's Stella. Howe would liberate from this patriarchal version another picture of this historical personage. As she writes in another context (in her analysis of the received idea we termed "Emily Dickinson"): "How do I, choosing messages from the code of others in order to participate in the universal theme of Language, pull SHE from all the myriad symbols and sightings of HE?" In *The Liberties*, Howe begins by providing a prose sketch, "Fragments of a Liquidation," whose import can best be summarized by repeating the last two sentences of its first paragraph: "Jonathan Swift, who gave allegorical nicknames to the women he was romantically involved with, called her 'Stella.' By that name she was known to their close friends, and by that name she is known to history." The poems that follow spring from Howe's desire to liberate Esther from Stella and, by extension, Howe's own self from equally pernicious assumptions. In practice, it is not always possible to distinguish from each other these twin liberations, and so a composite woman, struggling to be freed from the roles provided for her by men and a male-dominated history, becomes the shadow heroine of Howe's pages.

If the method is to question in this manner, and to reconstitute a truer history, the technique that Howe develops and that is consonant with her method is to call meaning into question not only at the level of the sentence (these poems are so severely underpunctuated that the reader usually must decide the limits of the sentence) but also at the level of the phrase or even the word. One poem, for example, begins "and/ she/ had a man's dress mad/ e/ though her feet ble/ d/ skimming the surf/ ace," a series of ruptures which militates against any "skimming of the surface" on the reader's part.

In a subsequent section of *The Liberties*, Howe extends her attention to William Shakespeare's Cordelia, surely attractive to Howe for her refusal to accede to the patriarchal demand to accord with the picture of herself her father wished to perpetuate. This section, titled "White Foolscap," puns on "fool's cap" and thus reminds the reader that Cordelia is a dramatic character whose only "real" context is the play *King Lear*, complete with Fool. Yet the title also refers to the blank page that the writer addresses: metaphorically, the nothingness into which she throws herself, composing. In the next section, "God's Spies," a playlet, Stella and Cordelia meet, together with the ghost of Jonathan Swift; the women are dressed as boys in their early teens. The action is fragmented, the dialogue sparse, truncated, enigmatic. The longest speech is Stella's, a poem the historical Stella wrote, very much in the manner of Swift: When it is done, Stella shoots herself. To so sink herself in the style of another, Howe is saying, is tantamount to suicide.

The third and final section of *The Liberties*, "Formation of a Separatist, I," is prospective, as the previous sections were retrospective. Howe has composed these poems of isolated words—single words with white space between each, arranged in blocks—and celebrates their individual tones, rather than their syntactic possibilities. There are, however, other poems in this section which depend upon phrases and sentences; in fact, the book ends with these lines: "Tear pages from a calendar/ scatter them into sunshine and snow." The nightmare of history disperses into a present which is subject to elements in their own nature.

PYTHAGOREAN SILENCE

Pythagorean Silence is also divided into three sections: The first, "Pearl Harbor," opens with a poem titled "Buffalo, 12.7.41" and the announcement of the cataclysm that has unleashed such terrible forces upon the second half of the century, the cataclysm that has so thoroughly trammeled survivors and inheritors in an ethical dilemma that becomes, for the artist, an aesthetic dilemma as well. Theodor Adorno, the German theoretician of art and society, averred that it has become impossible, since Auschwitz, to write poetry; the tens of millions murdered since 1941 cry out whenever Being is addressed. A character in Howe's poem, who is called TALKATIVE, "says we are all in Hell": Howe suggests that a truer use of language, one less suspect (in Howe's world and work, all talking *about* things is seen as vitiated by its own remove), can be found in biblical Rachel's inconsolable cry: "her cry/ silences/ whole/ vocabularies/ of *names*/ for *things*." The problem with the declaration that we are all in Hell arises from the clichéd nature of the phrase, which works against an experience of its meaning. Howe's "negative poetry" would undo prior namings where these have become impenetrably familiar. This is why she nudges her poems along through puns: In the pun, other meanings break through the intended singularity of usage, the law of logical syntax is transgressed by the play of several possibilities. "Connections between unconnected things are the unreal reality of Poetry," she asserts in *My Emily Dickinson*.

In section 2, the title section of *Pythagorean Silence*, the initial poem opens with a pun arising from the fracturing of a single word: "He plodded away through drifts of i/ ce." "Drifts of i" suggests the accumulation of personal, even egocentric, experience, with "drifts" implying the contingent nature of such accumulations, accrued as "the wind listeth." The line's extension equates "i" with "ice"—a frozen lump of such subjectivity. Yet Pythagoras broke through the amassed subjectivity of his experience to accomplish, with his theorem, the objective; to the extent that he is the hero of this sequence and this book, Howe implicitly urges emulation of his persistence. The "silence" of her title—which Howe discovered in a footnote in E. R. Dodd's *The Greeks and the Irrational*—refers to the silence maintained by initiates of the Pythagorean rites prior to their more active worship, a form of meditation. Indeed, the impression of her poetry is of (to echo William Butler Yeats) "speech after long silence," a use of language directly opposed to unthinking, unfeeling chatter.

Notice should be taken, however, of Howe's statement in *My Emily Dickinson:*

> at the center of Indifference I feel my own freedom . . . the Liberty in wavering. Compression of possibilities tensing to spring. Might and might . . . mystic illumination of analogies . . . instinctive human supposition that any word may mean its opposite. Occult tendency of opposites to attract and merge.

Taking this as a rule of thumb and applying it to the claim that Pythagoras is the hero in her book, the reader will consider the possibility that he is also the villain, capable of leading the unsuspecting into frozen wastes of abstruse speculation. Nor will this afterthought annul the previous reading, but rather coexist with it. Howe's greatest clarity lies in her ability to imply and exemplify the insupportable partiality of any single answer.

Single answers, after all, like universal concepts, are acts of enclosure, a delimiting of the possible; historically, they have been imposed by men upon women and children, by imperialists upon territories hitherto regarded as "unknown," terra incognita, full of hidden terrors—even as women and children for the dominant male. Howe herself, in an article published in *Politics and Poetic Form* (edited by Charles Bernstein; New York: Segue, 1989), addresses these issues, remarking that that sum of single answers, knowledge, "no matter how I get it, involves exclusion and repression." She continues

> National histories hold ruptures and hierarchies. On the scales of global power what gets crossed over? Foreign accents mark dialogues that delete them. . . . When we move through the positivism of literary canons and master narratives, we consign our lives to the legitimation of power, chains of inertia, an apparatus of capture.

It has become part of the burden of Howe's poetry to make plain enough these concerns, to confront, although at oblique angles, readers with modes of capture and unfreedom of which they may have been unaware. Her method is to locate the mortmain of the past in documents—demotic narratives of escape and capture, for example—of the past, and in instanced persistence of past patterns into the conduct of the present. In this second endeavor, she may take herself as instance, although the work never resembles autobiography in any of its conventional senses. When all is said and done, however, a poem itself is a form of enclosure, even as the choice of a place of one's own, an affirmation of belonging (as in Howe's case, being a New Englander). Clearly, then, such acceptance of limitation can be a source of strength, succor, and enabling. Even though Howe admits that all power is unstable, she does not deny its existence. There is a push-pull in her poetry, then, between the need for limits and a suspicion of them: Are they freely elected? Or are they imposed from without?

THE NONCONFORMIST'S MEMORIAL

The Nonconformist's Memorial challenges traditional beliefs and conceptions of history from both a nonconforming feminist and a deconstructionist point of view. The book has four long sequences that are divided into two sections, "Turning" and "Conversion." The book's structure, as well as Howe's thematic approach and her use of expressionism, echoes T. S. Eliot's *Four Quartets*. She imitates his style, however, in an ironic way, acting as a counterpoint in many instances to his religious themes and suggestions for bringing the soul closer to God. For example, the two poems in "Turning" describe female speakers' struggle with their religious faith. In "The Nonconformist's Memorial," the speaker raises questions about the practice of "true submission and subjection," because "self-concealment" (Eliot's proposal) has failed to lead the speaker to the anticipated union with God; it has, instead, thrown her into bewilderment and physical darkness. The sense of estrangement is created by the harsh tone in lines such as "Stop clinging to me" and "Don't touch me" and by Howe's use of large gaps between stanzas, ruptures that visually display the poet's thematic concerns.

In another of the collection's notable poems, "Melville's Marginalia," Howe explores the contributions of an Irish poet—that history has deemed "minor"—to Herman Melville's research. In her teaching of *Billy Bud* in the early 1990's, Howe discovered a book titled *Melville's Marginalia*, a collection of marginal notations and annotations that Melville marked in books from his library. She learns that in fact, James Clarence Mangan was "a rebel politically, and a rebel intellectually and spiritually–a rebel with his whole heart and

soul singing against the spirit of the age." Her poem of this subject follows the structural pattern that Howe has established in other poems in the book. They objectify the speaker's struggle to decipher the meaning of the words in Melville's comments on Magnan, as well as the meaning of Magnan's own writings. The chaotic movements of lines in the beginning of the poem again make certain parts hardly readable. The first half of the poem is also frequently disrupted by prose sections that include works from Magnan's writings and the speaker's meditation. Literally and figuratively then, Howe's deconstructionist exploration of Magnan brings his work and persona out of the margins and into a concrete place in history.

FRAME STRUCTURES AND PIERCE-ARROW

After *The Nonconformist's Memorial*, Howe's *Frame Structures* reissued early poems in new versions, along with an introduction, "Frame Structures," in which Howe looked back on the themes and motifs of her early poetry and her movement from the visual arts to poetry. It was six years after *The Noncormist's Memorial*, however, before Howe produced a collection of new poems, *Pierce-Arrow*. The book brings historiography and poetry together, focusing on nineteenth century pragmatist philosopher Charles Sanders Peirce and Juliette, his wife. Howe addresses her first section, "Arisbe," to a biographical essay on Peirce and poems about his work. The middle section, "The Leisure of the Theory Class," is full of allusions to philosophers and literary figures whose relations are both blurred and solidified in Howe's poems. The final section, "Ruckenfigur," takes as its theme the legend of Tristan and Isolde, the tragic lovers. A mixture of prose and poetry, full of dense and at times pedantic references, *Pierce-Arrow* is a tour de force of history, biography, poetry, and scholarship.

OTHER MAJOR WORKS

NONFICTION: *Religious Literature of the West*, 1971 (with John Raymond Whitney); *My Emily Dickinson*, 1985; *Incloser*, 1992; *The Birth-Mark: Unsettling the Wilderness in American Literary History*, 1993; *"Sorting Facts: Or, Nineteen Ways of Looking at Marker" in Beyond Document: Essays on Nonfiction Film*, 1996.

BIBLIOGRAPHY

Campbell, Bruce. "Ring of Bodies/Sphere of Sound." *The Difficulties* 3, no. 2 (1989). According to Campbell, Howe "is a kind of post-structuralist visionary." He explains that this "means that, while attuned to a transcendental possibility, she is fully aware of how mediated both language and consciousness are." While she must therefore explore history, she mistrusts it, and cannot "accept it as truth."

Chamberlain, Lori. Review of *Defenestration of Prague*, by Susan Howe. *Sulfur* 9 (1984). A useful look at this book—a sound, informal approach, which is the one that yields the best results for this poet. Chamberlain sees heterogeneity as always threatening to undermine unity in this work. Howe, Chamberlain notes, overlays self-remembering via various allegories with her remembering of Ireland. Chamberlain finds the final section "the most uneven," containing "lists of words that do not invite the reader's participation in this archeology of memory."

Daly, Lew. *Swallowing the Scroll: Late in a Prophetic Tradition with Poetry of Susan Howe and John Taggart*. Buffalo, N.Y.: M Press, 1994. A critial essay comparing the work of Susan Howe and John Taggart.

DuPlessis, Rachel Blau. "'Whowe' On Susan Howe." In *The Pink Guitar*. New York: Routledge, Chapman & Hall, 1990. A comprehensive review of Howe's work from a feminist viewpoint: "Howe appears to be on the cusp between two feminisms: the one analyzing female difference, the other 'feminine' difference. For the latter, she is close to Julia Kristeva, who evokes marginality, subversion, dissidence as antipatriarchal motives beyond all limits." DuPlessis is a thoroughly informed adjudicator of postmodern poetry; this is an excellent essay.

Naylor, Paul. *Poetic Investigations: Singing the Holes in History*. Evanston, Ill.: Northwestern University Press, 1999. A critical survey of English Commonwealth and American experimental and avant-garde literature of the twentieth century. Covering the work of Susan Howe, Kamau Brathwaite, Nathaniel Macky, and Lyn Hejinian. Includes bibliographical references and index.

O'Brien, Geoffrey. "The Way We Word." *The Village Voice Literary Supplement*, December, 1990. Deeper than most journalistic notices, this article provides some firm handles for raising Howe's work to consideration. "The complex structures, images and narratives Howe evokes [are] not written down; they exist in the margins of what *is* written down." O'Brien notes Howe's use of "runes, scratches, accretions of speech" and a vocabulary that "restores an awareness of the immensity of a single word."

Quartermain, Peter. "And The Without." *The Difficulties* 3, no. 2 (1989). Finds Howe more subject to language than master thereof—approvingly, for this brings her poetry nearer to experience, creating a reality that culture seldom acknowledges. Quartermain reads text meticulously and succeeds in giving the impression that this is an excellent way to read Howe's poems.

David Bromige,
updated by Sarah Hilbert

LANGSTON HUGHES

Born: Joplin, Missouri; February 1, 1902
Died: New York, New York; May 22, 1967

PRINCIPAL POETRY

The Weary Blues, 1926
Fine Clothes to the Jew, 1927
Dear Lovely Death, 1931
The Negro Mother, 1931
The Dream Keeper and Other Poems, 1932
Scottsboro Limited: Four Poems and a Play in Verse, 1932
A New Song, 1938
Shakespeare in Harlem, 1942
Jim Crow's Last Stand, 1943
Lament for Dark Peoples, 1944
Fields of Wonder, 1947
One Way Ticket, 1949
Montage of a Dream Deferred, 1951
Selected Poems of Langston Hughes, 1959
Ask Your Mama: Or, Twelve Moods for Jazz, 1961

The Panther and the Lash: Or, Poems of Our Times,
  1967
The Poems: 1921-1940, 2001 (Dolan Hubbard, editor)
The Poems: 1941-1950, 2001 (Hubbard, editor)

OTHER LITERARY FORMS

In addition to his prolific production of poetry, Langston Hughes wrote, translated, edited and/or collaborated on works in a number of other genres. He wrote two novels, *Not Without Laughter* (1930) and *Tambourines to Glory* (1958), and produced several volumes of short stories, including *The Ways of White Folks* (1934), *Laughing to Keep from Crying* (1952), and *Something in Common and Other Stories* (1963). Hughes's short fiction also includes several collections of stories about his urban folk philosopher, Jesse B. Semple (Simple): *Simple Speaks His Mind* (1950), *Simple Takes a Wife* (1953), *Simple Stakes a Claim* (1957), *The Best of Simple* (1961), and *Simple's Uncle Sam* (1965).

Hughes published several works for young people, including the story *Popo and Fifina: Children of Haiti* (1932), with Arna Bontemps; biographies of black Americans in *Famous American Negroes* (1954), *Famous Negro Music Makers* (1955), and *Famous Negro Heroes of America* (1958); and a series of "first book" histories for young people, such as *The First Book of Negroes* (1952), *The First Book of Jazz* (1955), and *The First Book of Africa* (1960).

Hughes's histories for adult readers include *Fight for Freedom: The Story of the NAACP* (1962) and two pictorial histories in collaboration with Milton Meltzer, *A Pictorial History of the Negro in America* (1956) and *Black Magic: A Pictorial History of the Negro in American Entertainment* (1967). Other experimental volumes of photo essays are *The Sweet Flypaper of Life* (1955), with photographs by Roy DeCarava, and *Black Misery* (1969), with illustrations by Arouni.

Major translations by Hughes include *Cuba Libre* by Nicolás Guillén (1948), with Ben Carruthers; *Gypsy Ballads*, by Federico García Lorca (1951); and *Selected Poems of Gabriela Mistral* (1957).

Hughes was also productive as a playwright, although his plays did not enjoy much critical or financial success. They include *Mulatto* (1935); *Little Ham* (1935); *Simply Heavenly* (1957), based on the characters in his Simple stories; and *Tambourines to Glory* (1963), adapted from his novel. The last play was billed as a "gospel song-play," and Hughes created four other plays in that category: *Black Nativity* (1961), *Gospel Glory* (1962), *Jerico-Jim Crow* (1964), and *The Prodigal Son* (1965). These productions are of interest mainly because they underscore Hughes's heartfelt sympathy with the black folk life of America, a love affair he carried on throughout his works.

Hughes wrote the libretti for several operas, a screenplay–*Way Down South* (1939), with Clarence Muse—radio scripts, and song lyrics. His most famous contribution to musical theater, however, was the lyrics he wrote for Kurt Weill and Elmer Rice's musical adaptation of Rice's *Street Scene* (1947).

Over the years, Hughes also wrote several nonfiction articles, mainly focused on his role as a poet and his love of black American music—jazz, gospel, and the blues. Perhaps his most important article was his first: "The Negro Artist and the Racial Mountain," published in *The*

Langston Hughes (Library of Congress)

Nation on June 23, 1926, in defense of the idea of a black American literary style, voice, and subject matter.

Anthologies of Hughes's work include *The Langston Hughes Reader* (1958), and *Five Plays* (1963), edited by Walter Smalley. Hughes himself edited many volumes of work by black American writers, including *The Poetry of the Negro, 1746-1949* (1949), with Arna Bontemps; *The Book of Negro Folklore* (1959), also with Bontemps; *New Negro Poets: U.S.A.* (1964); *The Book of Negro Humor* (1966); and *The Best Short Stories by Negro Writers: An Anthology from 1899 to the Present* (1967).

Finally, there are the two volumes of autobiography, *The Big Sea: An Autobiography* (1940) and *I Wonder as I Wander: An Autobiographical Journey* (1956). A planned third volume was not completed.

ACHIEVEMENTS

All of his works illustrate the depth of Langston Hughes's commitment to a celebration of black American life in all its forms and make immediately evident the reason why he has been proclaimed "The Poet Laureate of Black America." As a young poet he won prizes in contests sponsored by *The Crisis* and *Opportunity*, and his first two volumes of poetry, *The Weary Blues* and *Fine Clothes to the Jew*, won critical acclaim. Hughes also won a Harmon Gold Award for his novel *Not Without Laughter*, as well as a Rosenwald Fund Fellowship in the early 1930's, which enabled him to make his first cross-country reading tour.

His stature as a humorist grew from his creation of Jesse B. Semple, also known as Simple, a Harlem barstool philosopher in the tradition of American folk humor ranging from Davy Crockett to Mr. Dooley. Hughes wrote about Simple in columns published in the *Chicago Defender*, begun in the 1940's and continuing into the 1960's. His Simple columns also appeared in the *New York Post* between 1962 and 1965. Publication of his five books of Simple sketches increased the readership of that sage of Harlem with his views on life in white America.

Although Hughes never had any one big seller, his efforts in so many fields of literary endeavor earned for him the admiration and respect of readers in all walks of life. Certainly, too, Hughes is a major poetic figure of his time and perhaps the best black American poet.

BIOGRAPHY

James Mercer Langston Hughes (the first two names were soon dropped) was born in Joplin, Missouri, on February 1, 1902. His parents, James Nathaniel and Carrie Mercer Langston Hughes, separated when Hughes was young; by the time he was twelve, he had lived in several cities: Buffalo, Cleveland, Lawrence and Topeka, Kansas, Colorado Springs, and Mexico City (where his father lived). Until 1914, however, Hughes lived mainly with his maternal grandmother in Lawrence.

Hughes began writing poetry during his grammar school days in Lincoln, Illinois. While attending Cleveland's Central High School (1916-1920), Hughes wrote his first short story, "Mary Winosky," and published poems in the school's literary publications. The first national publication of his work came in 1921, when *The Crisis* published "The Negro Speaks of Rivers." The poem had been written while Hughes was taking a train on his way to see his father in Mexico City, a visit that the young man dreaded making. His hatred for his father, fueled by his father's contempt for poor people who could not make anything of themselves, actually led to Hughes's being hospitalized briefly in 1919.

Hughes's father did, however, send his son to Columbia University in 1921. Although Hughes did not stay at Columbia, his experiences in Harlem laid the groundwork for his later love affair with the city within a city. Equally important to Hughes's later work was the time he spent at sea and abroad during this period of his life. His exposure to American blues and jazz players in Paris nightclubs and his experiences in Europe, and especially in Africa, although brief, provided a rich source of material that he used over the next decades in his writing.

The years between 1919 and 1929 have been variously referred to as the Harlem Renaissance, the New Negro Renaissance, and the Harlem Awakening. Whatever they are called, they were years of rich productivity within the black artistic community, and Hughes was an important element in that Renaissance. While working as a busboy in the Wardman Park Hotel in Washington, D.C., in 1925, Hughes showed some of his poems—"Jazzonia," "Negro Dancers," and "The Weary Blues"—to Vachel Lindsay, who read them during one of his performances that same evening. The next day,

Hughes was presented to the local press as "the busboy poet." With that introduction, and with the aid of people such as writer Carl Van Vechten and Walter White (of the NAACP), Hughes's popularity began to grow. He published *The Weary Blues* in 1926 and entered Lincoln University in Pennsylvania, where he completed his college education. The 1920's also saw the publication of his second volume of poems, *Fine Clothes to the Jew*, and the completion of his first novel, *Not Without Laughter.*

During much of the early 1930's, Hughes traveled abroad. He went to Cuba and Haiti during 1931-1932 and joined a group of young writers and students from Harlem on a film-making trip to Russia in 1932-1933. Publishing articles in Russian journals enabled him to extend his own travels in the Far East; he also began to write short stories during that time. By 1934, he had written the fourteen stories that he included in *The Ways of White Folks.*

During the mid-1930's, several of Hughes's plays were produced: *Mulatto* (1935), and *Little Ham* were among them. In the course of having these plays performed, Hughes started the Harlem Suitcase Theatre in 1938, the New Negro Theatre in Los Angeles (1939), and the Skyloft Players of Chicago (1941).

After the publication of his first autobiographical volume, *The Big Sea*, Hughes spent time in Chicago with the group he had founded there. When America entered World War II, Hughes produced material for the war effort, ranging from "Defense Bond Blues" to articles on black American participation in the war. In addition, during the 1940's, he began work on his translations of the poetry of Nicolás Guillén, wrote essays for such diverse magazines as the *Saturday Review of Literature* and *Negro Digest*, wrote the lyrics for *Street Scene*, and published three volumes of poetry: *Shakespeare in Harlem, Fields of Wonder*, and *One Way Ticket.*

Also in the 1940's, Hughes "discovered" Jesse B. Semple. Drawing inspiration from a conversation he had in a bar with a worker from a New Jersey war plant—during which the man complained to his nagging girl friend, "You know white folks don't tell colored folks what cranks crank"—Hughes developed the framework for his Simple stories. He combined his own authorial voice, the voice of Simple's learned interrogator (even-

tually named Boyd), and the voice of Simple himself to weave a mixture of folk humor that has direct ties back to the "old southwest" humor of Mark Twain and his contemporaries.

The next decades saw continued production of poetry and other writing by Hughes. He wrote his pictorial histories and his "first books" for children. He continued his public readings, often accompanied by piano and/or jazz orchestra—a prototype of the Beat poets. His second volume of autobiography, *I Wonder as I Wander*, was published in 1956, and *The Langston Hughes Reader*, an extensive collection of his work in several genres, appeared two years later. The last two volumes of his new poetry, *Ask Your Mama* and *The Panther and the Lash*, continued his experimentation with incorporating jazz and folk elements in his poetry.

Hughes spent the last years of his life living and working in Harlem. He encouraged younger black writers, publishing several stories by newcomers in his *The Best Short Stories by Negro Writers*, as well as including works by established older writers such as Ralph Ellison and Richard Wright. Hughes died on May 22, 1967, in Harlem, the city that so inspired and informed his best work. No one caught the magic that Harlem represented during his lifetime in quite the way that Hughes did.

ANALYSIS

Langston Hughes often referred to three poets as his major influences: Paul Laurence Dunbar, Carl Sandburg, and Walt Whitman. If one were to assay which qualities of Hughes's poetry show the influence of which poet, one might say that Hughes got his love of the folk and his lyric simplicity from Dunbar, his attraction to the power of the people—especially urban dwellers—and his straightforward descriptive power from Sandburg, and his fascination with sensual people—people of the body rather than the mind—and his clear sense of rhythm from Whitman. No one would draw such a clear delineation, but the elements described are essential elements of Hughes's poetry. His work explores the humor and the pathos, the exhilaration and the despair, of black American life in ways that are sometimes conventional and sometimes unique. He explored the blues as a poetic form, and he peopled his poems with Harlem dancers, as well as with a black mother trying to explain her life to her son. He worked with images of dreams and of "dreams deferred"; he looked at life in the middle of America's busiest black city and at the life of the sea and of exploration and discovery. Always, too, Hughes examined the paradox of being black in mostly white America, of being not quite free in the land of freedom.

The poetry of Langston Hughes is charged with life and love, even when it cries out against the injustice of the world. He was a poet who loved life and loved his heritage. More than any other black American writer, he captured the essence of the complexity of a life that mixes laughter and tears, joy and frustration, and still manages to sing and dance with the spirit of humanity.

THE WEARY BLUES

Hughes's first collection of poetry, *The Weary Blues*, contains samples of many of the poetic styles and themes of his poetry in general. The collection begins with a celebration of blackness ("Proem") and ends with an affirmation of the black American's growing sense of purpose and equality "Epilogue" ("I, Too, Sing America"). In between, there are poems that sing of Harlem cabaret life and poems that sing the blues. Some of the nonblues poems also sing of a troubled life, as well as an occasional burst of joy. Here, too, are the sea poems drawn from Hughes's traveling experiences. All in all, the sparkle of a love of life in these poems was that which caught the attention of many early reviewers.

The titles of some of the poems about cabaret life suggest their subject: "Jazzonia," "Negro Dancers," "The Cat and the Saxaphone (2 A.M.)," and "Harlem Night Club." "The Cat and the Saxaphone (2 A.M.)" is especially intriguing because it intersperses a conversation between two "jive" lovers with the first chorus of "Everybody Loves My Baby," producing the effect of a jazz chorus within the song's rhythmic framework.

Part of the controversy which flared in the black community during the Harlem Renaissance involved whether an artist should present the "low-life" elements or the more conventional middle-class elements in black American life. Hughes definitely leaned toward the former as the richer, more exciting to portray in his poetry.

Because the blues tradition is more tied to the common folk than to the middle-class, Hughes's interest in the possibilities of using the blues style in his poetry is

not surprising. He took the standard three-line blues stanza and made it a six-line stanza to develop a more familiar poetic form; the repetition common in the first and second lines in the blues becomes a repetition of the first/second and third/fourth lines in Hughes's poems. As in the traditional blues, Hughes varies the wording in the repeated lines—adding, deleting, or changing words. For example, here is a stanza from "Blues Fantasy":

> My man's done left me,
> Chile, he's gone away.
> My good man's left me,
> Babe, he's gone away.
> Now the cryin' blues
> Haunts me night and day.

Often exclamation points are added to suggest more nearly the effect of the sung blues.

There are not as many blues poems in this first collection as there are in later ones such as *Fine Clothes to the Jew* and *Shakespeare in Harlem*. (The latter contains a marvelous seven-poem effort titled "Seven Moments of Love," which Hughes subtitled "An Un-Sonnet Sequence in Blues.") The title poem of his first collection, "The Weary Blues," is an interesting variation because it has a frame for the blues which sets up the song sung by a blues artist. The poet recalls the performance of a blues singer/pianist "on Lenox Avenue the other night" and describes the man's playing and singing. Later, the singer goes home to bed, "while the Weary Blues echoed through his head." Over the years, Hughes wrote a substantial number of blues poems and poems dealing with jazz, reflecting clearly his love for the music that is at the heart of the black American experience.

Some of the poems in *The Weary Blues* are simple lyrics. They are tinged with sadness ("A Black Pierrot") and with traditional poetic declarations of the beauty of a loved one ("Ardella"). The sea poems are also, by and large, more traditional than experimental. Again, their titles reflect their subject matter: "Water-Front Streets," "Port Town," "Sea Calm," "Caribbean Sunset," and "Seascape."

A few of these early poems reflect the gentle but insistent protest that runs through Hughes's poems; they question the treatment of black Americans and search for a connection with the motherland, Africa. The last section of the book is titled "Our Land," and the first poem in the section, "Our Land: Poem for a Decorative Panel," explores the idea that the black American should live in a land of warmth and joy instead of in a land where "life is cold" and "birds are grey." Other poems in the section include "Lament for Dark Peoples," "Disillusion," and "Danse Africaine." Perhaps the most poignant poem in the book is also in this last section: "Mother to Son." The poem is a monologue in dialect in which a mother encourages her son to continue the struggle she has carried on, which she likens to climbing a rough, twisting staircase: "Life for me ain't been no crystal stair./ It's had tacks in it . . . And places with no carpet on the floor—/ Bare." The collection's final poem, "Epilogue" ("I, Too, Sing America"), raises the hope that some day equality will truly be reached in America for the "darker brother" who is forced "to eat in the kitchen/ When company comes." Taken together, the poems of *The Weary Blues* make an extraordinary first volume of poetry and reveal the range of Hughes's style and subject matter.

The next two principal volumes of poetry, *Fine Clothes to the Jew* and *The Dream Keeper and Other Poems*, present more of Hughes's blues poems (the latter volume is primarily in that genre) and more poems centering on Harlem's night life. The final two volumes, *Ask your Mama* and *The Panther and the Lash*, continue the experiment of combining musical elements with poetry and offer some of Hughes's strongest protest poetry.

ASK YOUR MAMA

Ask Your Mama is dedicated to "Louis Armstrong— the greatest horn blower of them all." In an introductory note, Hughes explains that "the traditional folk melody of the 'Hesitation Blues' is the leitmotif for this poem." The collection was designed to be read or sung with jazz accompaniment, "with room for spontaneous jazz improvisation, particularly between verses, when the voice pauses." Hughes includes suggestions for music to accompany the poetry. Sometimes the instructions are open ("delicate lieder on piano"), and sometimes they are more direct ("suddenly the drums roll like thunder as the music ends sonorously"). There are also suggestions for specific songs to be used, including "Dixie" ("impishly"), "When the Saints Go Marchin' In" and "The Battle Hymn of the Republic." As a final aid, Hughes includes at the end of his collection "Liner Notes" for, as he says, "the Poetically Unhep."

Throughout, the poems in *Ask Your Mama* run the current of protest against "the shadow" of racism that falls over the lives of the earth's darker peoples. Shadows frequently occur as images and symbols, suggesting the fear and the sense of vague existence created by living in oppression. "Show Fare, Please" summarizes the essence of the poet's feeling of being left out because he does not have "show fare," but is also suggests that "the show" may be all illusion anyway. Not all the poems are so stark; the humor of Hughes's earlier work is still very much in evidence. In "Is It True," for example, Hughes notes that "everybody thinks that Negroes have the *most* fun, but, of course, secretly hopes they do not—although curious to find out if they do."

THE PANTHER AND THE LASH

The Panther and the Lash, the final collection of Hughes's new poetry, published the year he died, also contains some of his most direct protest poetry, although he never gives vent to the anger which permeated the work of his younger contemporaries. The collection is dedicated "To Rosa Parks of Montgomery who started it all . . ." in 1955 by refusing to move to the back of a bus. The panther of the title refers to a "Black Panther" who "in his boldness/ Wears no disguise,/ Motivated by the truest/ Of the oldest/ Lies"; the lash refers to the white backlash of the times (in "The Backlash Blues").

The book has seven sections, each dealing with a particular part of the subject. "Words on Fire" has poems on the coming of the Third World revolution, while "American Heartbreak" deals with the consequences of "the great mistake/ That Jamestown made/ Long ago"; that is, slavery. The final section, "Daybreak in Alabama," does, however, offer hope. In spite of past and existing conditions, the poet hopes for a time when he can compose a song about "daybreak in Alabama" that will touch everybody "with kind fingers."

OTHER MAJOR WORKS

LONG FICTION: *Not Without Laughter*, 1930; *Tambourines to Glory*, 1958.

SHORT FICTION: *The Ways of White Folks*, 1934; *Simple Speaks His Mind*, 1950; *Laughing to Keep from Crying*, 1952; *Simple Takes a Wife*, 1953; *Sim-*

ple Stakes a Claim, 1957; *The Best of Simple*, 1961; *Something in Common and Other Stories*, 1963; *Simple's Uncle Sam*, 1965.

PLAYS: *Troubled Island*, pr. 1935 (opera libretto); *Mulatto*, pb. 1935; *Little Ham*, pr. 1935; *Don't You Want to Be Free?*, pb. 1938; *Freedom's Plow*, pb. 1943; *Street Scene*, pr., pb. 1947 (lyrics; music by Kurt Weill and Elmer Rice); *Simply Heavenly*, pr. 1957 (opera libretto); *Black Nativity*, pr. 1961; *Tambourines to Glory*, pr., pb. 1963; *Five Plays*, pb. 1963 (Walter Smalley, editor); *Jerico-Jim Crow*, pr. 1964; *The Prodigal Son*, pr. 1965.

NONFICTION: *The Big Sea: An Autobiography*, 1940; *Famous American Negroes*, 1954; *Famous Negro Music Makers*, 1955; *The Sweet Flypaper of Life*, 1955 (with Roy DeCarava); *A Pictorial History of the Negro in America*, 1956; *I Wonder as I Wander: An Autobiographical Journey*, 1956; *Famous Negro Heroes of America*, 1958; *Fight for Freedom: The Story of the NAACP*, 1962; *Black Magic: A Pictorial History of the Negro in American Entertainment*, 1967 (with Meltzer); *Black Misery*, 1969 (illustrations by Arouni); *Arna Bontemps—Langston Hughes Letters*, 1980.

CHILDREN'S LITERATURE: *Popo and Fijina: Children of Haiti*, 1943 (story; with Arna Bontemps); *The First Book of Negroes*, 1952; *The First Book of Rhythms*, 1954; *The First Book of Jazz*, 1955; *The First Book of the West Indies*, 1955; *The First Book of Africa*, 1960.

TRANSLATIONS: *Masters of the Dew*, 1947 (of Jacques Roumain; with Mercer Cook); *Cuba Libre*, 1948 (of Nicolás Guillén; with Ben Carruthers); *Gypsy Ballads*, 1951 (of Federico García Lorca); *Selected Poems of Gabriela Mistral*, 1957.

EDITED TEXTS: *The Poetry of the Negro, 1746-1949*, 1949 (with Arna Bontemps); *The Book of Negro Folklore*, 1959 (with Bontemps); *New Negro Poets: U.S.A.*, 1964; *The Book of Negro Humor*, 1966; *The Best Short Stories by Negro Writers: An Anthology from 1899 to the Present*, 1967.

SCREENPLAY: *Way Down South*, 1939 (with Clarence Muse).

MISCELLANEOUS: *The Langston Hughes Reader*, 1958.

BIBLIOGRAPHY

Berry, Faith. *Langston Hughes: Before and Beyond Harlem*. New York: Wings Books, 1995. The first biography based on primary sources and interviews, which sets out to re-create the historical context in which Hughes lived and worked. Berry quotes an unusual number of poems in their entirety and includes extensive discussions of his poetry throughout the biography.

Bloom, Harold, ed. *Langston Hughes*. New York: Chelsea House, 1989. An up-to-date collection of some of the best literary criticism of Hughes's works, with several articles on his poetry. Unfortunately, these reprinted essays do not have notes. Bloom's introduction is perfunctory. Supplemented by a useful bibliography and an index.

Emanuel, James A. *Langston Hughes*. Boston: Twayne, 1967. A concise overview of Hughes's extraordinary career as a poet, playwright, literary critic, dramatist, and man of letters. Emanuel takes a thematic approach, showing how Hughes's concerns with his race, prejudice, Harlem, and his own past figure in his individual works. Contains a chronology, an annotated bibliography, and notes.

Harper, Donna Sullivan. *Not So Simple: The "Simple" Stories by Langston Hughes*. Columbia: University of Missouri Press, 1995. Harper analyzes Hughes's development of the satirical stories with the character Jesse B. Simple. Covering the changes in the character from 1943 to 1965 starting in Hughes's column in the *Chicago Defender* and ending in the *New York Post*, Harper searches for the deeper meanings behind the stories. With a bibliography of the columns from 1942 to 1949, and the contents of the first collection of stories.

Miller, R. Baxter. *The Art and Imagination of Langston Hughes*. Lexington: University Press of Kentucky, 1989. Divides Hughes's imagination into the "autobiographical," the "apocalyptic," the "lyrical," the "political," and the "tragicomic." Baxter carefully examines Hughes's technique and style, and each chapter focuses on a poem or other work central to an appreciation and understanding of Hughes's imagination.

Mullen, Edward J., ed. *Critical Essays on Langston Hughes*. Boston: G. K. Hall, 1986. Very useful for its generous selection of contemporary reviews of the poet's work. Separate sections are devoted to articles and essays on Hughes's poetry, prose, and drama. An extensive and well-documented introduction surveys and analyzes the critical reception of the poet's work. The index is especially useful in sorting through this heterogenous material.

Onwuchekwa, Jemie. *Langston Hughes: An Introduction to the Poetry.* New York: Columbia University Press, 1976. Treats Hughes's poetry in thematic terms, with separate chapters on his "black esthetic," the blues, jazz and other musical forms, his social protest verse, his evocation of the ideal ("the dream"), and the poet's place in the "evolution of consciousness in black poetry." Includes an extensive bibliography and an index.

Rampersad, Arnold. *The Life of Langston Hughes, 1902-1941: I, Too, Sing America.* Vol. 1. New York: Oxford University Press, 1986. Situating the poetry and other works in the context of the times and tracing the development of the writer, Rampersad provides acute interpretations of both Hughes's character and career. Distinguished by its fine style and balance, this volume is the definitive biography of the poet.

Edward E. Waldron;
bibliography updated by the editors

TED HUGHES

Born: Mytholmroyd, Yorkshire, England; August 17, 1930

Died: North Tawton, Devon, England; October 28, 1998

PRINCIPAL POETRY

The Hawk in the Rain, 1957
Lupercal, 1960
Wodwo, 1967
Crow: From the Life and Songs of the Crow, 1970, revised 1972
Selected Poems, 1957-1967, 1972

Cave Birds, 1975 (revised as *Cave Birds: An Alchemical Cave Drama,* 1978)
Gaudete, 1977
Remains of Elmet, 1979
Moortown, 1979
Selected Poems, 1957-1981, 1982
River, 1983
Flowers and Insects: Some Birds and a Pair of Spiders, 1986
The Cat and the Cuckoo, 1987
Wolfwatching, 1989
Rain-Charm for the Duchy and Other Laureate Poems, 1992
Three Books, 1993 (includes *Remains of Elmet, Cave Birds,* and *River*)
Elmet, 1994
Collected Animal Poems, 1995
New Selected Poems, 1957-1994, 1995
Birthday Letters, 1998

OTHER LITERARY FORMS

Ted Hughes wrote many poems and tales for children, several stage and radio plays, nonfiction works on William Shakespeare and other writers, and translations of poetry from many languages. Hughes was also a prolific editor and anthologist, having edited several volumes by his wife Sylvia Plath and other poets.

ACHIEVEMENTS

Ted Hughes was undoubtedly one of the major British poets of the twentieth century, and probably the most influential English poet of the post-World War II era. His writing began as a reaction to "The Movement" poetry of the 1950's—a poetry marked by understatement, classical restraint, and a refusal to go beyond everyday reality. By contrast, Hughes signed himself as a poet who distrusted the intellect and the narrow conformity of ordinary activity. His poetry embraces the violent life of nature, particularly as exemplified by animals and birds, but also by persons who allow instincts and drives to reveal a language of the heart. He thus returned English poetry to a romantic tradition, critical of the materialism and soullessness of contemporary society.

He produced poetry regularly, besides editing and dramatizing, particularly for radio. He also wrote exten-

Ted Hughes (© 1991, Jane Bown)

sively for children, in various genres. He became Britain's poet laureate on December 19, 1984—a largely honorary role, but one that carried considerable prestige, bespeaking his acceptance by the British literary establishment. He was awarded the Order of Merit by Queen Elizabeth II for his service to poetry. The Whitbread Award for Book of the Year was awarded posthumously in 1998 for *Birthday Letters*.

BIOGRAPHY

Edward James Hughes was born in a small Yorkshire town on the edge of the moors, only a few miles from where the famous Brontë sisters (Charlotte, Emily, and Anne) had lived. His father, William, a carpenter, had been badly wounded in World War I during the Gallipoli landings. Hughes was the youngest of three children. His brother briefly became a gamekeeper; his sister, Olwyn, became an executor and literary agent for the estate of Sylvia Plath. When Hughes was seven, the family moved to a mining town in south Yorkshire called Mexborough. From the grammar school there, he won an scholarship to attend Cambridge University, and he went to Cambridge in 1951 after two years of national service in the Royal Air Force. Having changed his major from English to archaeology and anthropology, he was graduated in 1954.

Hughes then worked at a number of jobs, including teaching. Although he had been writing poetry from the age of fifteen, he wrote little at Cambridge and attempted to publish only locally at first. In 1956 he met Sylvia Plath, who was two years younger than he and was in Cambridge on a Fulbright Fellowship. At the time of their meeting, she was already a published poet. She began to send his poems to magazines and also entered him for a competition in New York for a first volume of poetry. He won with *The Hawk in the Rain*, and through publication his name quickly became known.

Plath and Hughes were married within four months of meeting. He returned with her to the United States in 1957, where they earned their living by teaching and writing prolifically together. In 1959 they returned to London, Hughes having completed *Lupercal*, helped by a Guggenheim Fellowship. The next year their daughter, Frieda, was born, and the year after that they moved to Devon, in the southwest part of England. Soon after the birth of their second child, Nicholas, in 1962, the marriage collapsed. Plath returned to London and filed for divorce, but during a bitterly cold winter she fell into a deep depression and committed suicide on February 11, 1963.

For some time after Plath's suicide, Hughes wrote only for children. In March, 1969, his new partner, Assia Wevill, and her child Shura both died tragically. Hughes dedicated *Crow*, a volume that marked a new direction in his poetry, to them. The volume also solidified his reputation as a writer and poet.

In 1970 he married Carol Orchard, the daughter of a Devon farmer whose farm he was leasing. *Moortown* includes many details about his experiences there and shows Hughes returning somewhat to the subject matter of his earlier poetry. Controversy over his relationship with Plath continued to dog him, especially in the United States, where his reputation was badly affected. He remained silent about the affair until the publication of *Birthday Letters* in 1997. Only after his death was the publication of Plath's journals allowed by their daughter Frieda.

Apart from periods in London and Yorkshire, where he helped establish the Avron Foundation, which encourages creative writing, he continued to live in Devon until his death in 1998 from cancer. He was sixty-eight. At his memorial service at Westminster Abbey, Hughes's close friend and fellow poet Seamus Heaney stated that Hughes was "a great poet through his wholeness, simplicity and unfaltering truth to his whole sense of the world."

ANALYSIS

Ted Hughes's poetic career was somewhat cyclical. His first volumes of verse contain individual poetic statements on the nature of the created world, focusing on particular animals, plants, people, and seasons. These poems are intended as explorations of identity, of the "thing in itself"—following closely the late Victorian poet Gerard Manley Hopkins, whose emphasis in much of his nature poetry was on the "this-ness" or "selfhood" of each created being.

While Hopkins saw such creation as manifestations of the variety and infiniteness of the Creator, Hughes denied the existence of divinity. In the earlier poetry his metaphysical claims are very limited; at most he acknowledges some sort of unconscious inspiration, in the manner of Robert Graves, whose concept of the "White Goddess" as poetic inspiration and creative spirit influenced him heavily, and also of Dylan Thomas, though at first Hughes lacked the exuberance of these poets.

Yet Hughes increasingly felt the need for some sort of philosophical expression for his romanticism. That expression, when it came, was as surprising as it was forceful. The themes of violence that characterize the early poetry are transformed in the cycle of mythological poems *Crow* and *Gaudete* to an anarchic energy that subverts the organizing institutional principles of humankind, as expressed in religion, culture, and rationality. Hughes's need for a mythology to advance his personal poetic development was akin to that of William Butler Yeats, a poet he much admired (he claimed that at Cambridge he knew all of Yeats by heart).

Again like Yeats, having established a mythology in the middle part of his career and having made some very powerful poetry out of it, Hughes felt free to leave it to one side. Thus, from *Moortown* onward, his poetry tended to return to a more specific focus, based on the natural life surrounding him. He also returned to poems of personal reminiscence and the ritualized violence of war, and as a last gesture, to the publication of poems over his failed marriage to Plath.

THE HAWK IN THE RAIN AND LUPERCAL

Most of Hughes's poetry was first published in various poetry magazines and in literary and other journals, although some was commissioned for specific projects. Critical work on Hughes has grown steadily since the publication of *The Hawk in the Rain*, which was widely recognized from the first as showing great promise. The poems in this volume can be taken alongside those of *Lupercal*, since their composition must be seen as overlapping. One volume contains forty poems, the other forty-one. Rather more from *Lupercal* find their way into Hughes's 1982 *Selected Poems, 1957-1981*.

ANIMAL POEMS

Many of Hughes's most anthologized poems are to be found here—for example, "The Thought Fox," "Hawk Roosting," "Esther's Tomcat," "Six Young Men," "View of a Pig," "An Otter," and "Pike."

Most of these are animal poems that in their specificity, brilliance of imagery, and originality of viewpoint are immediately striking and reasonably accessible. It has been pointed out, as a caution, that only a limited number of poems in *The Hawk in the Rain* are real animal poems. In fact, to believe that the animals presented are real is to misunderstand the poetry, epitomized in "The Thought Fox," which explicitly states that the place of such animals' existence is in Hughes's imagination, for which memory and observation have only provided the raw materials. The majority of his poems are in fact infused with animal imagery. For example, the protagonist of "Famous Poet" is a monster, the subject of "Secretary" is "like a starling under the bellies of bulls," and "A Modest Proposal" is built around the extended simile of two wolves.

Lupercal is perhaps more obviously about animals, and here the nearest influence is D. H. Lawrence. Lawrence, however, develops more moral sympathy for his creatures than does Hughes, whose attitude is far more ambivalent. Hughes frankly admits to terror at times— for example, in "Pike," whose pond he "fished/ With the hair frozen on my head/ For what might move." The pike, like the hawk and the thrushes, is a perfect killing instrument; this reality both fascinates and horrifies Hughes. He recognizes in these creatures depths of darkness that exist within himself. The Jungian idea of a personal shadow is never far distant. In a number of his poems, including "Pike," "An Otter," and "To Paint a Water Lily," the dualism of natural life is vividly portrayed in terms of the surface and depths of water.

In a more ambitious poem, "Mayday on Holderness," this idea is combined with a geographical image of concentric circles. Starting with "the furnace door whirling with larvae" on a pond, through the generating life of the country in springtime, he sees all such draining into the North Sea, beneath which the dead soldiers of Gallipoli lie still, crying, "Mother, Mother!" The "Mother" is profoundly ambiguous, since it is "motherly summer" that moves on the pond in the apparently endless cycle of regeneration ending in (violent) death.

Few of the other poems in these first two volumes—apart from "Pennines in April" and "Wind," in both of which the landscape is seen in terms of the sea—are what might be called regional. Nevertheless, the sense of a northern English countryside is very strong, especially in its bleakness, its mud, and the sheer struggle required to survive there. A number of poems deal with humans who can survive such conditions—"Roarers in a Ring," "Dick Straightup," and "Crag Jack's Apostasy." More significantly, other survivors are praised, though somewhat enigmatically, in "The Retired Colonel" and the powerful "The Martyrdom of Bishop Farrar." What the characters of these poems possess is a physical courage drawn from the deep wellsprings of natural life. Farrar's courage, therefore, is not so much religious or moral as spiritual, in the Lawrentian sense Hughes later developed.

The title poems of both volumes were omitted from *Selected Poems, 1957-1981*. "The Hawk in the Rain," perhaps too reminiscent of Hopkins's "The Windhover," contrasts the earthbound poet, drowning in "the drumming ploughland," to the hawk that "effortlessly at height hangs his still eye." The poet is aware of "the master-/ Fulcrum of violence where the hawk stands still," but the violence emanates not only from the hawk but also toward the hawk, which ultimately crashes to the ground. This awareness of the continuity of forces running through nature, destructive yet energy-giving, is one of the central features of these two volumes. The other title poem, "Lupercalia," celebrates a Roman festival of fertility, Lupercus being a god of prophecy also. The poet perhaps sees himself as a priest celebrating both prophetically and ritualistically the mystery of the fertility of nature, giving birth by sacrificing.

WAR POEMS

Another group of poems is the war poems: not of World War II, as might be expected from a poet whose boyhood was spent in that period, but of World War I, in which his father fought (William Hughes was one of the few survivors of a regiment otherwise wiped out). Later poems, such as "Out" (from *Wodwo*) and "Dust As We Are" (from *Wolfwatching*), explain how the young boy heard his father reenacting these traumatic experiences. Clearly, he entered deeply into his father's sufferings, and the impact of the violence of humankind in war must have shaped his perceptions of universal violence.

WODWO

Between 1960 and 1967 Hughes concentrated on children's poetry and poetic drama. The births of his own two children during these years seem to have moved him to channel his creative effort into working his animal poetry into comic and fable-related material. Hughes did a number of school broadcasts, including a reworking of the Orpheus and Euridice myth. This echoes poignantly Hughes's own personal tragedy at this time, the breaking up of his marriage and his wife's subsequent suicide. Undoubtedly, these sad events affected his poetic output immediately, and in the longer term acted as catalysts for radical changes in style and manner.

The volume that collects Hughes's adult poetry of the period, *Wodwo*, reflects this upheaval. Some critics see it as a pivotal volume in Hughes's development; certainly it must be seen as transitional. In this, and in its overall layout, it is very similar to Robert Lowell's *Life Studies* (1959), published not long before. Like Lowell's volume, *Wodwo* contains two sections of poetry sandwiching several prose pieces, some of which are autobiographical. Although Hughes's stay in the United States had brought him into touch with such American poets as Wallace Stevens, Hart Crane, and Lowell, the differences remain striking. The open confessional style that Lowell (and John Berryman) developed is the very opposite of Hughes's private manner of creating poems from which autobiographical details must be excavated skillfully, fragment by fragment.

Wodwo contains some forty poems, to which a few others were added later. Although the poetry is transitional, Hughes selected a greater proportion of it for his 1982 selection than of any other volume. It moves toward a fabular, allegorical, or mythic approach to animals and plants, as in "The Bear," "The Green Wolf," and "The Howling of Wolves." Each creature in these poems manifests some aspect of a life force, certainly, but in a more ritualistic and metaphysical way than in earlier poems. The title poem tells of some legendary animal seeking its identity, full of questions, exploring the dualism of intention and instinct, of self and not-self. Though still in the romantic tradition, many of the poems seem explicitly antiromantic in sentiment; in "Skylarks," for example, Hughes denies the truth-beauty equation. Despite critical claims to unity, the volume is more a collection of parts: Hughes is still searching for a belief system for his poetic. The arrangement of poems within the volume seems somewhat random, and their internal logic appears arbitrary. The title of one poem, "You Drive in a Circle," is rather apt for the whole collection.

CROW

Nevertheless, a number of poems in *Wodwo* do point forward to Hughes's next volume, *Crow*. "Logos," "Reveille," and "Theology" reorder the Adam and Eve story in the simplistic, demotic comic style that typifies *Crow*. The powerful "Pibroch" suggests the medieval sense of the chain of being, while it denies medieval teleology—leaving a bleakness and pessimism caught also in "Wings" and "Gnat Psalm." Hughes's verse, too, is far more experimental in *Wodwo*, ranging from the tight balladlike form of "The Bear" to the loose "Wodwo," in which punctuation and line structures have almost collapsed. Particularly, Hughes is moving away from poetic rhetoric toward the direct speaking voice (as did Lowell), and the isolation of the single line or phrase is exploited as an alternative to stanza form. Thus, even if *Crow* did come as a shock, there had been hints of it previously.

The cycle of *Crow* actually began as a response to an invitation from the American artist Leonard Baskin to write poems to accompany his drawings of mythic animals, particularly a crow that was half bird, half human. Hughes was already aware of the crow in various Native American legends as a trickster figure, and he saw in this image an "object correlative" on which to construct the mythology he needed for his poetic. The volume is subtitled *From the Life and Songs of the Crow*, suggesting

that the original intention was, as it had been for Yeats, to construct a full mythology. The complete mythology failed to materialize, however—possibly because of certain irresolvable contradictions in the enterprise—and thus there is very much of a provisional feel to the volume. Later editions added several more poems, and there seems to be no internal reason that other poems should not be added, deleted, or rearranged. Nevertheless, *Crow* came as a new, powerful, and quite shocking voice in British poetry in the early 1970's, a voice that most reviewers did recognize as once and for all establishing Hughes as a major poet, if not the major poet of his generation.

Hughes's need for myth springs from two explicit causes, with probably two unstated factors also involved. First is his stated rejection of Christianity, its account of creation and of the Creator, and the nature of its spirituality—a rejection arising from his encounter with narrow fundamentalism in the village chapel of his boyhood. His rejection is in some sense reactionary: He still needs Christian myth, especially the account of the Fall. Many of his poems in *Crow* and elsewhere rework the figures of Adam, Eve, and the serpent, introducing Crow as a "wild card" element to suggest a creative principle separate from the God of the Genesis account (see, for example, "Crow's Theology," "Crow Communes," and "Crow's First Lesson").

Second is his rejection of demythologizing rational humanism and the preeminence of the word as logical utterance and rational discourse. In this he follows William Blake and Robert Graves, as he does stylistically. He sees modern Western civilization as having lost its primitive energies through its superficial materialism and its denial of the spirit. For him, though, the spirit is out of nature, not out of Christianity—there is nothing holy about it, nor any moral necessity to it ("A Disaster" and "Crow's Account of St. George" are illuminating in this regard).

These rejections are explicit. Not openly explored yet clearly influential in Hughes's life are the nuclear threat that hung heavily over the world in the 1960's and 1970's and the tragic deaths of two women close to him. There also seems to have been a difficult, unresolved relationship with his mother. At a psychological level, *Crow* could be interpreted as an attempt to exorcise these tragedies and to resolve his feelings toward the women involved (as in "Criminal Ballad," "Song for a Phallus," "Crow and Mama," and "Lovesong"). On a political level, the nuclear threat could be seen as a subtext, underlining for him the urgency for Western civilization to find new roots to draw upon, however primitive or pagan.

A new influence on Hughes's style in this period was contemporary East European poetry, especially that of Vasko Popa, whose work he helped to make known in the West. Like Popa, Hughes was interested in colloquial, folktale-like myths as images of survival, and he used poem cycles to build up such mythology. The trickster figure is basically a survivor, although the central contradiction is that usually he stays unchanged, whereas Hughes wants Crow to develop and to take on different roles and guises—as victim, helper, rebel, humankind, even Hughes himself as poet.

Crow is anarchic; so is the verse form. Words mean what Hughes wants them to mean. His rejection of rational discourse is exhilarating, creative, and unpredictable; it is also arbitrary, exasperating, and sometimes sheer nonsense, a total poetic joke. Hughes at times seems bardic, the shaman, willing to be possessed by spiritual forces in order to speak wisdom or healing; at other times he seems a naughty boy writing rude words. Yet "the song was worth it," as he writes in the final enigmatic "Two Eskimo Songs." Here also water finishes up "utterly worn out utterly clear." The cycle is meant ultimately as a purification of the will to live: What it does not give is a purpose for living.

GAUDETE

Gaudete (meaning "rejoice") seeks to resolve some of the contradictions of *Crow* by positing a hero and his shadow (to use a Jungian term), or double. This double is, in fact, the protagonist—the Reverend Nicholas Lumb, acting as substitute vicar for a village (Lumb Bank is actually the name of Hughes's house in Yorkshire). In fact, he sets himself up as high priest of a pagan fertility cult and spends his time bringing to life the latent sexuality of the village women by making love to them. In a climactic scene, a young woman is ritually initiated into the pagan cult but is killed by its priestess (or witch), who is jealous of Lumb, since she suspects that he is human enough to want to elope with the girl.

Meanwhile, the village men, out of jealousy and anger, pursue Lumb in a semiritual stag hunt and shoot him. The bodies of the girl, Lumb, and the priestess, who has stabbed herself, are then burned by the men to hide the evidence.

All this main part of the narrative is told in some fifty-five sections of a new, flexible, and pulsating narrative verse, interspersed with passages of poetic prose. The narrative is enfolded by a prologue and an epilogue, which deal with the real vicar, abducted by dark forces out of a dead world in order to heal a woman. For his inability to do this, he is violently beaten in a purgatorial ritual and then resurrected. The fruits of his resurrection, which takes place on the west coast of Ireland, are some forty short, gem-like poems, centering on the theme of suffering and emptying self.

The whole volume is quite extraordinary. Unlike previous volumes, it must be read as a unity—it is impossible to extract, reorder, or add. It is clearly an achieved work: Response is one of purgation or catharsis. The mythic basis is Dionysus and his female followers, the Bacchantae, though ritualistic patterns from other fertility cults are also used. In an interview given in 1971, Hughes called his poetry "a war between vitality and death . . . [which] celebrates the exploits of the warriors on either side." In a reworking of Graves's White Goddess, he links Venus with Sycorax, a female figure turned by the Middle Ages into the figure of Mary, and now lost. Western humanism has served Adonis, the god of rationality. *Gaudete* then becomes the reinstatement of Dionysus—and Venus—as the new spiritual force, Adonis having brought a general death.

In this release, however, men and women become totally separated—the men into their violence, their killer instincts, and the women into their unconscious fertility. Normal men-women relationships necessarily break down. The end is destruction and harm, as damaging as anything Adonis brings. Yet by creating Lumb as a duality, Hughes is able to avoid the dichotomy that he elsewhere describes as possible responses to the energy "of the elemental power circuit of the Universe": Refusal brings death, but acceptance brings destruction. To escape the dichotomy, one needs the purgatorial experience—not the naked instinctual one, though it is necessary to recognize and embrace the shadow within oneself—and through it to come to some sort of resurrection of spirit. Both Lumbs undergo a death. Out of this comes, at the end, a Dickinsonian distillation of regenerative and intuitive wisdom, cryptically and allusively personal. It rounds off a poem that seeks a way forward (not merely a subversion), as an alternative to both Christianity and modern secularism.

CAVE BIRDS

Between *Crow* and *Gaudete*, Hughes produced a number of other volumes, two of which were done in close conjunction with Leonard Baskin. *Cave Birds* was based, like *Crow*, on a series of Baskin drawings of various fabular birds. Hughes then wrote further poems, for most of which Baskin did drawings—some thirty in all. The volume represents a reworking of *Crow* in a much more positive and orderly fashion. A bird—a cockerel to start with—is drawn into the underworld into a Kafka-esque trial scene. As it realizes the guilt of its rationalism, it takes on a series of shifting guises to reach its own hidden psyche. It refuses easy answers, going through execution, a dying to self, until finally it meets (in Jungian fashion) an anima, a female counterpart. Their marriage in "Bride and Groom Lie Hidden for Three Days" suggests renewal through love, reversing poems such as "Lovesong" and "The Lovepet," in which sexual love is shown as purely destructive and possessive. Finally comes resurrection—as a falcon, the Egyptian Horus, a sky god. Thus the book contains a complete cycle of dying and rising, showing the need to die in order to live spiritually. Hughes's final question is "But when will be land on a man's wrist?" At their best, the poems have a beautifully cadenced sensitivity; at worst, they are perhaps too tied to Baskin: Hughes's rhetoric begins to establish itself too easily.

SEASON SONGS

Season Songs was also done with Baskin, but this time Baskin was merely Hughes's illustrator. The pieces in this book were intended for children primarily, but they manifest a delightful marriage of traditional seasonal poetry and the vivid children's poetry of a few years earlier. A number of the poems seem assured of a place in the many anthologies produced for schools. Nature is not romanticized here, but neither is it full of the instinctual violence and bleakness of *Lupercal* or the chaos of *Crow*. "Swifts" and "The Harvest Moon" are good examples of the suppleness of style of which Hughes was now master, and also of his mixing of modern and traditional imagery.

REMAINS OF ELMET

Another volume, *Remains of Elmet*, was produced at this time, in conjunction with the photographer Fay Godwin. A later volume, *River*, was done in the same way. *Remains of Elmet* is a portrait of the region of Hughes's youth, whereas *Season Songs*, anticipating *Moortown*, reflects the Devon countryside and farm where he had settled.

MOORTOWN

Moortown is a mixed volume, almost an anthology in itself. It incorporates a large section of poems centering on the Devon farm, but written over a period of time as a "verse farming diary," and then several separate sequences or minicycles. One of these, "Prometheus on His Crag," had been published separately in 1973, the result of an invitation to take part in a drama festival in Persepolis, Iran. For this occasion Hughes had written a drama, *Orghast*, centered partly on the Prometheus myth. The cycle of poems emerged indirectly from this play as a sort of meditation.

For inclusion in *Moortown*, several more were added, making a total of twenty-one. They trace the sufferings of Prometheus from his first awakening to his agony, chained to a rock, as part of his punishment for stealing fire from the gods (though he does not remember doing so), to his trying to identify the full suffering (the vulture pecking at his liver, the heat and the cold, the permanence of the enchainment), to his coming to terms with it. The vulture is even admired for its being a perfect instrument of punishment. The sequence ends with a poem as full of questions as "Wodwo," but also with a sense of acceptance that the poet's humanity is made up of pain and endurance. The poems themselves are in tightly controlled yet very flexible stanzas, with a typical disintegration at the end into isolated lines and phrases. The imagery, again typically, is startling, violent yet lyrical in its dramaticity.

The second sequence is "Adam and the Sacred Nine." Here again, an originally mythic figure holds this shorter cycle together. Each poem describes a different bird that comes to present itself to Adam—not for him to name, as in the Genesis account, but for him to learn from. One or two poems, such as "The Dove Came," are in the *Crow* style; each bird is symbolic or allegorical and all are far removed from the *Lupercal* treatment. Further sequences are titled "Earth-Numb" and "Seven Dungeon Songs."

The farming poems are more relaxed and personal, focusing largely on the sufferings and joys of the farm animals in creating new life; births and miscarriages are detailed, almost gratuitously at times, along with deaths and partings of mothers and infants. Certainly the treatment suggests that creation, even with human intervention, works poorly. Nevertheless, the quality of felt experience is powerfully portrayed. In this antipastoral, the reader comes to see Hughes as a compassionate, sensitive farmer.

FLOWERS AND INSECTS AND WOLFWATCHING

The farming poems, like *Season Songs*, show Hughes moving away from mythic statements toward more lyrical and personal ones. This tendency continues in *Flowers and Insects* and *Wolfwatching*. In the latter, myth remains in "Two Astrological Conundrums" and "Take What You Want But Pay for It," but "Wolfwatching" is a more orthodox zoo poem, and "The Black Rhino" has an ecological message. Perhaps the most attractive poems here are those of reminiscence, especially concerning his father. The violence of the war poems of *The Hawk in the Rain* is now counterbalanced by a small boy's watching of a shell-shocked father.

BIRTHDAY LETTERS

Fortunately, becoming British poet laureate did not have a negative impact on Hughes's creativity, as can sometimes happen. Although his laureate poems, collected in *Rain-Charm for the Duchy*, were not particularly striking, the publication of the deeply personal *Birthday Letters* was. For the first time, Hughes allowed his account of the Plath marriage to be told, in eighty-eight poems written over a twenty-five-year period. The poems show Hughes as somewhat passive, even as a victim of Plath's instability and hysterical despair. The poems won for Hughes a posthumous Whitbread Award for Book of the Year in 1998.

OTHER MAJOR WORKS

SHORT FICTION: *The Threshold*, 1979; *Difficulties of a Bridegroom*, 1995.

PLAYS: *The Calm*, pr. 1961; *Epithalamium*, pr. 1963; *Seneca's Oedipus*, pr. 1968; *Orghast*, pr. 1971; *Eat Crow*, pr. 1971; *The Story of Vasco*, pr. 1974 (music by Gordon Crosse; adaptation of a play by Georges Schehadé).

RADIO PLAYS: *The House of Aries*, 1960; *A Houseful of Women*, 1961; *The Wound*, 1962; *Difficulties of a Bridegroom*, 1963; *Dogs*, 1964; *The House of Donkeys*, 1965; *The Head of Gold*, 1967.

NONFICTION: *Poetry Is*, 1970; *Shakespeare's Poem*, 1971; *Henry Williamson: A Tribute*, 1979; *Shakespeare and the Goddess of Complete Being*, 1992, rev. 1993; *Winter Pollen: Occasional Prose*, 1994 (W. Scammel, editor).

CHILDREN'S LITERATURE: *Meet My Folks!*, 1961; *The Earth-Owl and Other Moon-People*, 1963; *How the Whale Became*, 1963; *Nessie and the Mannerless Monster*, 1964; *Poetry in the Making: an Anthology of Poems and Programmes*, 1967 (revised as *Poetry Is*, 1970); *The Iron Man: A Story in Five Nights*, 1968 (also as *The Iron Giant*); *Five Autumn Songs for Children's Voices*, 1969; *The Coming of the King and Other Plays*, 1970 (augmented as *The Tiger's Bones and Other Plays for Children*, 1974); *Orpheus*, 1971; *Spring, Summer, Autumn, Winter*, 1974 (revised as *Season Songs*, 1975); *Earth-Moon*, 1976; *Moon-Whales and Other Moon Poems*, 1976; *Moon-Bells and Other Poems*, 1978; *The Pig Organ: Or, Pork with Perfect Pitch*, 1980 (music by Richard Blackfort); *Under the North Star*, 1981; *What Is Truth? A Farmyard Fable for the Young*, 1984; *Collected Poems for Children 1961-1983*, 1985; *Ffangs the Vampire Bat and the Kiss of Truth*, 1986; *Tales of the Early World*, 1988; *The Iron Woman: A Sequel to "The Iron Man,"* 1993; *The Dreamfighter and Other Creation Tales*, 1995; *The Iron Wolf*, 1995; *Shaggy and Spotty*, 1997.

TRANSLATIONS: *Selected Poems*, 1968 (of Yehuda Amichai; with Amichai); *Selected Poems*, 1976 (of János Pilinszky; with János Csokits); *Amen*, 1977 (of Amichai; with Amichai); *Time*, 1979 (of Amichai; with Amichai); *Blood Wedding*, 1996 (of Federico García Lorca); *The Oresteia*, 1999 (of Aeschylus); *Phèdre*, 1998 (of Jean Racine).

EDITED TEXTS: *New Poems*, 1962, 1962 (with Patricia Beer and Vernon Scannell); *Here Today*, 1963;

Selected Poems, 1964 (by Keith Douglas); *Ariel*, 1965 (by Sylvia Plath); *A Choice of Emily Dickinson's Verse*, 1968; *With Fairest Flowers While Summer Lasts: Poems from Shakespeare*, 1971 (also as *A Choice of Shakespeare's Verse*); *Crossing the Water*, 1971 (by Plath); *Winter Trees*, 1971 (by Plath); *Johnny Panic and the Bible of Dreams, and Other Prose Writings*, 1977, augmented 1979 (by Plath); *New Poetry Six*, 1980; *The Collected Poems of Sylvia Plath*, 1982; *1980 Anthology: Arvon Foundation Poetry Competition*, 1982 (with Seamus Heaney); *The Rattle Bag: An Anthology*, 1982 (with Heaney); *Selected Poems*, 1985 (by Plath); *A Choice of Coleridge's Verse*, 1996; *The School Bag*, 1997 (with Heaney); *By Heart: 101 Poems to Remember*, 1997.

BIBLIOGRAPHY

Robinson, Craig. *Ted Hughes as Shepherd of Being.* Basingstoke, England: Macmillan, 1989. Robinson examines Hughes in the light of Martin Heidegger's philosophy, seeking his "redefinition of human maturity in our time." He places Hughes firmly in the Romantic tradition, especially that of William Blake, in his desire for freedom from Enlightenment rationalism. The study covers Hughes's writing through *Flowers and Insects.* Includes a bibliography and an index.

Sagar, Keith. *The Challenge of Ted Hughes.* London: Macmillan, 1994. Sagar is a leading British writer on Hughes, having edited and written several other critical books on him. Includes a bibliography.

Sagar, Keith, and Stephen Tabor. *Ted Hughes: A Bibliography, 1946-1995.* London: Mansell, 1998. A complete bibliography.

Scigaj, Leonard M. *The Poetry of Ted Hughes: Form and Imagination.* Iowa City: Iowa University Press, 1986. This study explores Hughes's Asian influences, and how he has sought to augment the modern Western consciousness. Includes a bibliography and an index.

_____. *Ted Hughes.* Boston: Twayne, 1992. Scigaj is one of the United States' leading exponents of Hughes and rightfully chosen to write this introductory volume in the well-known Twayne series of introductions to major authors.

_____, ed. *Critical Essays on Ted Hughes.* New York: G. K. Hall, 1992. One of the best collections of essays on Hughes. Some other collections are fragmentary or celebratory.

Walder, Dennis. *Ted Hughes.* Philadelphia: Open University Press, 1987. This book is written specifically to accompany *Selected Poems, 1957-1981.* It is basically thematic, focusing on Hughes's myths of violence and masculinity, but seeing these tempered by more recent "feminine" poems. Offers suggestions for further reading and includes an index.

David Barratt, updated by Barratt

RICHARD HUGO

Richard Franklin Hogan
Born: Seattle, Washington; December 21, 1923
Died: Seattle, Washington; October 22, 1982

PRINCIPAL POETRY

A Run of Jacks, 1961
Death of the Kapowsin Tavern, 1965
Good Luck in Cracked Italian, 1969
The Lady in Kicking Horse Reservoir, 1973
What Thou Lovest Well, Remains American, 1975
Thirty-one Letters and Thirteen Dreams, 1977
Selected Poems, 1979
White Center, 1980
The Right Madness on Skye, 1980
Making Certain It Goes On: The Collected Poems of Richard Hugo, 1984

OTHER LITERARY FORMS

Richard Hugo confirmed his reputation as a beloved professor with the 1979 publication of his book on craft, *The Triggering Town: Lectures and Essays on Poetry and Writing.* In the title essay he distinguishes between the initiating or triggering subject of a poem (for him, a small town that has seen better days) and its real subject. A posthumous collection of essays, *The Real West Marginal Way: A Poet's Autobiography*, appeared in 1986, edited by his wife, Ripley S. Hugo, and colleagues Lois M. and James Welch.

Featuring a retired Seattle detective who becomes a deputy sheriff in a small Montana town, Hugo's mystery novel *Death and the Good Life* (1981) was a runner-up for the Pulitzer Prize. A second novel with the same character was planned but never completed. Hugo also published reviews and articles in literary journals; his papers can be found in the University of Washington Archives.

ACHIEVEMENTS

Hugo's poetry earned numerous honors, including the Theodore Roethke Memorial Poetry Prize for *What Thou Lovest Well, Remains American* (1975). In addition, three collections were nominated for the National Book Award. A 1967 Rockefeller Fellowship for creative writing allowed him to travel extensively in Italy and Europe, and in 1977 a Guggenheim Fellowship enabled him to write for a year on Scotland's Isle of Skye.

In the summer of 1971, Hugo held the Roethke Chair at the University of Washington. Six years later he was appointed editor of the Yale Younger Poets Series. President and Mrs. Jimmy Carter honored him at a 1980 White House celebration, and the following year he received the Academy of American Poets Fellowship for distinguished achievement. In 1982, only a few months before his death, Montana State University conferred on him an honorary Doctor of Letters, while the University of Montana presented him with its Distinguished Scholar Award.

BIOGRAPHY

Richard Hugo was born Richard Franklin Hogan, to Franklin James Hogan and the teenage Esther Clara Monk Hogan in White Center, a rough, shabby neighborhood of Seattle. At twenty months he was left with his maternal grandparents, Fred and Ora Monk, when his parents separated, although his mother tried unsuccessfully to reclaim him after she married Herbert Hugo, a Navy man. The boy, who admired his stepfather, legally changed his name to Hugo at nineteen.

A bleak and impoverished childhood with his elderly, inarticulate grandparents left him with a burning sense of inadequacy. His grandfather, a failed tenant farmer from Michigan, was employed by the Seattle Gas Plant. Hugo believed that his strict grandmother, who had barely completed the fourth grade, was a bit crazy. He discovered that fishing gave him a sense of fulfillment (a love that stayed with him), just as playing softball and baseball earned him approval and attention.

He volunteered for the Army Air Corps in December, 1942, to avoid being drafted into World War II. Based in Italy, he completed thirty-five missions as a none-too-accurate bombardier (he may have bombed Switzerland). After the war he returned to his grandparents' home for three years, leaving only after his grandmother's death in 1949. At the University of Washington he earned bachelor's and master's degrees in creative writing, inspired by the legendary poet Theodore Roethke.

In 1951 Hugo married Barbara Williams and worked as a technical writer for the Boeing Company until 1963, when both quit their jobs to spend a year in Italy. He needed to face the demons of war, fear, and memory, and he began to drink heavily. When he returned to the United States as a visiting lecturer at the University of

Richard Hugo

Montana in Missoula, Barbara went on alone to the West Coast; they ultimately divorced in 1966. Thereafter, he remained at the University of Montana except for brief stints at other universities, eventually rising to the rank of professor and director of the creative writing program. His benevolent influence on young writers was extraordinary.

Hugo's life changed dramatically in 1971 when he suffered a nervous breakdown two weeks before the end of his term as visiting poet at the University of Iowa. He returned briefly to the Seattle psychiatrist he had consulted in the 1950's; in addition, a bleeding ulcer forced him to give up alcohol permanently. Nevertheless, these unfortunate events heralded the most productive, satisfying period in his writing life, intensified by his 1974 marriage to Ripley Schemm Hansen, with whom he was happier than he had ever been. In January, 1981, he underwent surgery for lung cancer and seemed to recover, but twenty-one months later he was dead of leukemia, just short of his fifty-ninth birthday. The epitaph on his grave in Missoula is taken from his poem "Glen Uig": "Believe you and I sing tiny/ and wise and could if we had to eat stone and go on."

ANALYSIS

Richard Hugo is identified primarily as a Pacific Northwest poet, but his reputation transcends that of most regional poets, and his fascination with place extends well into Europe. Even though his largely autobiographical poems were written during a period in which confessional poets such as Anne Sexton and Robert Lowell flourished, Hugo speaks through a persona not entirely himself, especially in the early poems. His characteristic stance is that of a failed, lonely alcoholic, even when that description no longer fit him. In later years he was able to discard that hard-voiced persona and write more openly as himself.

A RUN OF JACKS AND DEATH OF THE KAPOWSIN TAVERN

Although Hugo published his first two collections four years apart, many of the poems were written at the same time. These early poems frequently employ more formal structure, soon to be discarded (except for villanelles and syllabic poems) in favor of strong accents and repetition. While both books mirror the landscape of the poet's native Pacific Northwest, the external scene reflects metaphorically the interior world of the persona.

Hugo establishes his poetic territory in 1961 with *A Run of Jacks*. "Ocean on Monday" offers bleak coastal images:

> Here at last is ending.
> Where gray coordinates with nothing
> the horizon wrinkles in the wind.

Seattle's flawed "Duwamish" River, where "Boys [snap] tom cod spines," lies "Midwestern in the heat," and its "curves are slow and sick." The forgotten, desolate places that the poet prefers are embodied by "1614 Boren," an abandoned house in Seattle: "These dirty rooms were dirty even then/ . . ./ and light was always weak and flat." A less gloomy view emerges briefly, for "The world has poison and the world has sperm"; death is accompanied by life. The persona's dual perception is confirmed as he watches a "Neighbor" carried out, "bleeding from the corners of his grin."

Hugo's personal ghosts first appear here, shadows of his unhappy early life. In "Digging Is an Art," he recalls his harsh grandmother: "Now they bury her and the clouds run scared." Many of these images return in *Death of the Kapowsin Tavern*. The title poem, one that introduced many readers to Hugo's work, laments the burned-out ruin of an isolated tavern: "I can't ridge it back again from char." Even the river reappears in the long poem "Duwamish Head": "This river helped me play an easy role—/ to be alone, to drink, to fail."

THE LADY IN KICKING HORSE RESERVOIR

Hugo's fourth collection, *The Lady in Kicking Horse Reservoir* (1973), focuses mostly on Montana. A different sensibility is present here; in an interview Hugo explained that "In Seattle everything is clogged, hidden," but Montana is "open, panoramic." Critic Jonathan Holden calls this the last of Hugo's books "to systematically tout the myth of personal failure." Indeed, the persona embraces his own degradation in "The Only Bar in Dixon" ("Home. Home. I knew it entering") and "The Milltown Union Bar" ("You need never leave. Money or a story/ brings you booze"). Yet in "Degrees of Gray in Philipsburg," a failed mining town, the persona realizes that there is still hope:

The car that brought you here still runs.
The money you buy lunch with,
no matter where it's mined, is silver
and the girl who serves your food
is slender and her red hair lights the wall.

The title poem begins as a revenge fantasy. The dead woman in Kicking Horse Reservoir is a lover who rejected the persona (in reality, one of Hugo's graduate students who married somebody else), but the persona's bitter voice quickly softens to "Sorry. Sorry. Sorry." The woman also undergoes a metamorphosis from death to affirming life, "spill[ing] out/ into weather," irrigating the dry land. The poet begins to make peace with his personal past in "Montgomery Hollow":

> . . . You conquer loss
> by going to the place it happened
> and replaying it, saying the name
> of the face in the open casket right.

That "open casket" holds his grandparents and his early life, and he must look directly at it, without the filtering persona.

WHAT THOU LOVEST WELL, REMAINS AMERICAN

Holden suggests that this award-winning book reveals Hugo's struggle to abandon his alcoholic persona for his own voice and to face his real fear of success. "Goodbye, Iowa" ("Once more you've degraded yourself on the road") recalls his hasty 1971 departure from that state, awash in self-pity. That bathetic voice is countered by another from "Places and Ways to Live," which admits, "That is the crude self I've come to. The man who says/ suffer, stay poor and I can create," but only as a victim. This second voice does not belong to the persona, the protective mask; it is honest, open, even kind.

A more balanced reality emerges, especially in Hugo's poems about the past. The speaker in "Saying Goodbye to Mrs. Noraine," a former neighbor, confesses, "I remembered most things wrong." In "A Snapshot of 15th S.W.," Hugo's childhood home, the poet struggles with his double view of the past: "Burn this shot. That gray is what it is" becomes, finally, "Don't burn it. That gray is what it was." Ultimately, the speaker in "The Art of Poetry" advises "sad Raymond," his former self, "Better to

search your sadness for the man"; better to reject the persona for the real voice.

THE RIGHT MADNESS ON SKYE

With the aid of a new landscape from the Inner Hebrides, Hugo attains his fully mature voice, displaying a relaxed and easy humor and philosophical acceptance. "Letter to Garber from Skye" reveals his affinity for the island: "The sky, water, vegetation and wind are Seattle./ The panoramic bare landscape's Montana. For me, two/ homes in one." The "me" is himself; the past he explores, whether historical or mythic, belongs to the island and its people: displaced crofters, monstrous shape-shifters. His personal poems dwell on more immediate experience.

Hugo always exhibited a fondness for cemeteries. When he envisions his own death here, it is no longer pathetic or mournful. His long poem "The Right Madness on Skye" is written with tongue-in-cheek instructions for his funeral, reminiscent of William Carlos Williams's "Tract." In it, a stolid Harry of Nothingham drives the wagon bearing the speaker, who is only pretending to be dead—a rather morbid joke with the refrain "Have the oxen move on. Tell Harry of Nothingham, slow."

Hugo writes,

> Don't back up for cars. Clear the road for the dead.
> Cry "Fat bag of bones coming through." I heard that note.
> I told you, no trumpets. I told you, five minutes, no more
> for piper and drum. Who's mouthing that organ for nothing?

MAKING CERTAIN IT GOES ON

This posthumous collection contains all but two of the poems published in book form during Hugo's lifetime, as well as twenty-two new ones he wished to include. Of the six Stone Poems, perhaps "Green Stone" is the most poignant, describing the lucky stone he carried during his cancer surgery. "Where the House Was," that boyhood home again, has become a church parking lot, and his memories are no longer nightmares. Hugo also added several elegies, including one for poet James Wright, but the finest of these is "Here, but Unable to Answer," a powerful tribute to his seafaring stepfather: "night sky wide open and you naming/ wisely every star again, your voice enormous/ with the power of moon, of tide."

In his title poem, "Making Certain It Goes On," the drunken fisherman (another version of his former persona) finally dies, becoming part of the tapestry of nature. One finds reconciliation in these last poems, thoughtful maturity, and acceptance of the whole of life.

OTHER MAJOR WORKS

LONG FICTION: *Death and the Good Life*, 1981.

NONFICTION: *The Triggering Town: Lectures and Essays on Poetry and Writing*, 1979; *The Real West Marginal Way: A Poet's Autobiography*, 1986.

BIBLIOGRAPHY

Allen, Michael S. *We Are Called Human: The Poetry of Richard Hugo*. Fayetteville: University of Arkansas Press, 1982. A biocritical study of Hugo's work through *The Right Madness on Skye*. Allen integrates details of the poet's personal life—poverty, early trauma, and the Depression—with the "presence of hurt" found particularly in his earlier work. In an extended discussion of "the Hugo town," he places the poet within the small-town tradition of earlier American writers, including Edgar Lee Masters, Edwin Arlington Robinson, Sherwood Anderson, William Faulkner, and Sinclair Lewis.

Garber, Frederick. "Fat Man at the Margin: The Poetry of Richard Hugo." *Iowa Review* 3, no. 4 (1972): 58-69. A discussion of the inner and outer landscapes of Hugo's first three collections. This stylistic analysis underscores the significance of the word "marginal" in his work.

Gerstenberger, Donna. *Richard Hugo*. Western Writers Series 59. Boise, Idaho: Boise State University, 1983. A study of Hugo's work in the context of Western writing, as he made use of contemporary Western experience and his "complete possession of and by the local region." His awareness of physical space, distance, and direction reflects a Western consciousness as he expresses an inner journey by means of outward scene. Gerstenberger also urges a more precise definition of "regional."

Holden, Jonathan. *Landscapes of the Self: The Development of Richard Hugo's Poetry*. Millwood, N.Y.: Associated Faculty Press, 1986. An insightful psychological reading of all but the final collection, including a worthwhile chapter on *Thirty-one Letters and Thirteen Dreams*. In the early books Hugo "project[s] his inner life onto one derelict landscape after another." Holden argues that Hugo is in fact a confessional poet by his attempt "to transcend personal suffering by converting painful autobiography into a myth." Wishing to supply an adequate context for the poems, Holden includes a detailed biographical chapter based on correspondence with the poet.

Myers, Jack, ed. *A Trout in the Milk: A Composite Portrait of Richard Hugo*. Lewiston, Idaho: Confluence Press, 1982. Includes reprints of interviews with Hugo and some fine critical essays on his work, as well as poems and reminiscences by an impressive group of people who fell under his influence.

Pinsker, Sanford. *Three Pacific Northwest Poets: William Stafford, Richard Hugo, and David Wagoner*. Boston: Twayne, 1987. Contains a lengthy chapter on Hugo's themes and techniques. Pinsker notes that autobiographical poetry presents conflicting demands, combining the tactics of prose fiction (facts and details) and the lyric poem (persona and myth). He compares Hugo's poems with those of Sylvia Plath and Robert Lowell. Although his biographical details are unreliable, he presents an interesting examination of Hugo's language.

Smith, Dave. "Lyrics for Life's Harsh Music." *The New York Times Book Review*, February 26, 1984: 12-13. This review of *Making Certain It Goes On* offers a brief but excellent overview of Hugo's life and poetry from a critic and fellow poet, revealing "a man bearing himself with relentless introspection, intelligence, courage, and withering good humor."

Joanne McCarthy

VICTOR HUGO

Born: Besançon, France; February 26, 1802
Died: Paris, France; May 22, 1885

PRINCIPAL POETRY
Odes et poésies diverses, 1822, 1823
Nouvelles Odes, 1824

Odes et ballades, 1826

Les Orientales, 1829 (*Les Orientales: Or, Eastern Lyrics*, 1879)

Les Feuilles d'automne, 1831

Les Chants du crépuscule, 1835 (*Songs of Twilight*, 1836)

Les Voix intérieures, 1837

Les Rayons et les ombres, 1840

Les Châtiments, 1853

Les Contemplations, 1856

La Légende des siècles, 1859-1883 (5 volumes; *The Legend of the Centuries*, 1894)

Les Chansons des rues et des bois, 1865

L'Année terrible, 1872

L'Art d'être grand-père, 1877

Le Pape, 1878

La Pitié suprême, 1879

L'Âne, 1880

Les Quatre Vents de l'esprit, 1881

The Literary Life and Poetical Works of Victor Hugo, 1883

La Fin de Satan, 1886

Toute la lyre, 1888

Dieu, 1891

Les Années funestes, 1896

Poems from Victor Hugo, 1901

Dernière Gerbe, 1902

Poems, 1902

The Poems of Victor Hugo, 1906

Océan, 1942

OTHER LITERARY FORMS

Besides his rather prolific output in the field of poetry, Victor Hugo achieved prominence in two other genres as well. His novels, for which he is best known in the United States, span most of his literary career and include such recognizable titles as *Le Dernier Jour d'un condamné* (1829; *The Last Day of a Condemned*, 1840), *Notre-Dame de Paris* (1831; *The Hunchback of Notre Dame*, 1833), and *Les Misérables* (1862; English translation, 1862). Hugo was a successful playwright in his time, but only *Hernani* (pr., pb. 1830; English translation, 1830) has received sustained attention. The preface to his play *Cromwell* (pb. 1827; English translation, 1896), however, is frequently studied by scholars be-

cause of its attack on the three unities, so long observed by French classical writers, and because of Hugo's elaboration on his theory of the union of the grotesque and the sublime. His other plays are a *mise en oeuvre* of the dramatic principles found in the *Cromwell* preface.

Although less well known as an essayist, Hugo did write in the genre. His better-known essay collections include *Le Rhin* (1842; *The Rhine*, 1843), *William Shakespeare* (1864; English translation, 1864), *Choses vues* (1887; *Things Seen*, 1887), and *En voyage: Alpes et Pyrénées* (1890; *The Alps and Pyrenees*, 1898). Hugo also wrote and delivered a number of political speeches in the Chambre des Pairs. Among these are the "Consolidation et défense du littoral," which was delivered in the summer of 1846, "La Famille Bonaparte," which was delivered the following spring, and "Le Pape Pie IX," which was presented in January, 1848.

ACHIEVEMENTS

"Ego Hugo": This was the inscription emblazoned on the Gothic armchair that stood in the dining room in the Hugos' Guernsey home. Dubbed an ancestral chair by the poet, it remained conspicuously empty at mealtime. For Victor Hugo's critics, this motto became a symbol of an oversized ego. For his admirers, the empty chair symbolized the greatness of Hugo the poet, if not Hugo the man. Indeed, his place in literature is unquestioned, and no other French poet since has been able to match his production and influence.

Hugo excelled in a wide variety of verse forms: ode, lyric, epic, satire, and heroic narrative. His versatility in mode was matched by variations in tone, from the eloquence and rhetorical precision found in *Les Châtiments* (the chastisements), for example, to the simplicity and grace of *Les Contemplations*. Conventions that were in vogue at the time, such as the marvelous and the fantastic, the medieval and the Oriental, were translated by Hugo into verse. The poet also found inspiration in the imagery of dreams, spiritualism, and metempsychosis. His poetry set the tone and the style for Romantic verse; his choice of subjects and his novel uses of stylistic devices influenced the Parnassians and the Symbolists.

The sheer volume of Hugo's production would have assured him a place in literary history even if the strength and character of the man had not assured his ce-

Victor Hugo (Hulton Archive)

lebrity. Hugo's resiliency allowed him to overcome personal tragedy and to express his grief in verse. He championed causes such as free, compulsory education, universal suffrage, the right to work, and the abolition of the death penalty, before such political postures were popular. In all, Hugo was a man of deep convictions, of great sensibility, and of tremendous ego whose poetic creation reflected all these aspects of his complex personality.

BIOGRAPHY

Victor-Marie Hugo was born at Besançon, the third son of Joseph Léopold Sigisbert Hugo and Sophie Trébuchet. His father, a career military man, served with distinction in the postrevolutionary army. He later became a general and viscount, as well as a close associate of Joseph Bonaparte, Napoleon's brother. Though gifted with military tenacity, the elder Hugo unfortunately was not capable of such steadfastness on the home front. Madame Hugo soon tired of his lusty nature and infidelities, finding relief in the arms of General Victor Fanneau

LaHorie, an opponent of Napoleon, who was Victor Hugo's godfather. Shortly after Hugo's birth, Madame Hugo moved her children to Paris to be near LaHorie. After LaHorie became an enemy of Napoleon's regime, she hid him in her quiet house with a large garden in the rue des Feuillantines. During those eighteen months, the gentle "M. le Courlandais" taught the eight-year-old Hugo to read and translate Tacitus, and he impressed the young boy with the ideal of liberty; indeed, Hugo was to have a lifelong sympathy for the oppressed. In later years, he would fondly remember those days spent playing in the garden with his brother and with a girl named Adèle Foucher. Madame Hugo somehow provided a tranquil environment for her children, unembittered by constant marital strife.

Though LaHorie had provided some formal training, the education of the Hugo brothers remained spotty because of the family's frequent moves. The family took two trips to visit the boys' father: to Italy in 1809 and to Spain in 1811-1812. During that last trip, the boys were enrolled at the Collège des Nobles in Madrid. The year in Spain was to provide Hugo with much material for his later works. The Spanish hero Ernani would become the hero of his play, with the Masserano palace as one of its settings; the hunchback Corcova at the seminary would become the inspiration for Quasimodo; the street Ortoleza reappears in the play *Ruy Blas* (pr., pb. 1838; English translation, 1890).

In 1814, General Hugo insisted that his sons be enrolled at the Pension Cordier, where they spent four years studying the sciences. In order to relieve the drudgery, the brothers wrote poems and plays during their leisure hours. Soon, this pastime became a successful enterprise. At the age of fifteen, Hugo entered the Académie Française's poetry contest, receiving an honorable mention. In 1819, he won two prizes from the Académie des Jeux Floraux of Toulouse. Hugo and his brother Eugène entered law school to please their father but spent most of their efforts in the founding of a magazine called *Le Conservateur littéraire*. Among the early contributors to the venture was Alfred de Vigny, who was to become one of Hugo's closest friends. In this magazine, Hugo published his "Ode sur la mort du duc de Berry" and the first version of what was to become his second novel, *Bug-Jargal* (1826; *The Noble Rival*,

1845). The ode placed Hugo in the favor of the Royalists, among them his idol François-René de Chateaubriand, in whose presence the poet was received shortly after the publication of his ode. Soon, the Hugo brothers were admitted into the Société des Bonnes Lettres, an ultra-Royalist group; by this time, Hugo had adopted his mother's Royalist views.

With the death of his mother in 1821, Hugo entered a period of extreme poverty. He abandoned *Le Conservateur littéraire* and strove to make a living. In 1822, Hugo published the *Odes et poésies diverses*. Conservative and Royalist in content, these odes earned for Hugo a royal pension. He was able to marry his childhood sweetheart, Adèle Foucher, and continue with his literary career.

The years between 1822 and 1828 were filled with creative and literary activities. In 1823, Hugo published the second edition of *Odes et poésies diverses* as well as his first novel, *Han d'Islande* (1823; *Hans of Iceland*, 1845). The following year, Hugo's *Nouvelles Odes* were published. In 1825, Hugo was named, along with Alphonse de Lamartine, to the Legion of Honor "for his noble efforts . . . to sustain the sacred cause of the altar and the throne." The year 1826 saw the publication of Hugo's *Odes et ballads*, as well as his second novel, *The Noble Rival*. The publication the following year of the bold preface to *Cromwell* established Hugo as the spokesman for the new Romantic school. Hugo's father, Léopold, died in 1828, an event which greatly grieved the poet. Since the death of his mother, Hugo and his father had achieved a rapprochement. This friendship rendered the poet more sympathetic to the Bonapartist cause and served to counterbalance the Royalist fervor that he had received from his mother. In that same year, Hugo's play *Amy Robsart* (pr. 1828; English translation, 1895) was presented.

During these years, the Hugo home had become the focal point for the gathering of literary young men caught up in the Romantic revolution against the formalism of the seventeenth and eighteenth centuries, men such as Charles Augustin Sainte-Beuve, Alfred de Vigny, Alfred de Musset, Théophile Gautier, Gérard de Nerval, and Émile and Antoine Deschamps. This group, which became known as the *cénacle*, sought to break the bonds of the dramatic unities, of poetic versification, and of the choice of subject matter, and rallied to expand the imaginative and aesthetic field. Hugo was the unquestioned head of the group. From his ideas and from the discussions that took place in his home during those years sprang new branches of Romanticism, including the Parnassian school.

The next few years were emotionally difficult ones for Hugo. Though he continued to receive acclaim for his new collection of poems *Les Orientales*, striking because of their exoticism; for his play *Hernani*, which heralded a decisive victory for Romantic drama; and for *The Hunchback of Notre Dame*, which established Hugo as a great writer of the historical novel, the security of his home life had begun to crumble. In 1829, Hugo's best friend, Sainte-Beuve, had revealed to the poet his love for Hugo's wife, Adèle. In spite of this revelation, Hugo tried to maintain the friendship, made more difficult by Sainte-Beuve's assertion that his love was reciprocated. In his distress, Hugo found comfort in a relationship with an actress, Juliette Drouet. It was an affair that would last fifty years and that was eventually accepted by Adèle Hugo. Drouet was transformed through her love for the poet into a devoted companion who remained virtually cloistered in her quarters, content to read and to copy his books.

These personal afflictions and affections found expression in the poetic works that followed: *Les Feuilles d'automne* (the leaves of autumn), *Songs of Twilight*, *Les Voix intérieures* (the interior voices), and *Les Rayons et les ombres* (the rays and shadows). These collections contrasted markedly with Hugo's previous poetic works in both tone and style. Unlike the exotic and colorful *Les Orientales*, for example, these poems sought to express the more intimate relationships found in love, childhood, and friendship, as well as in man's association with nature. In 1843, two other disasters, the death of his daughter Léopoldine and the failure of his play *Les Burgraves* (pr., pb. 1843; *The Burgraves*, 1896) caused Hugo to put down his pen for some time. As always, tragedy accompanied success in the poet's life.

Meanwhile, Hugo's political involvement intensified. In 1841, he was elected to the Académie Française. As his prominence grew, it followed that he should be raised to peerage, and this indeed occurred in 1845. From this position, Hugo addressed the parliament on such matters as capital punishment and the plight of the poor, subjects on which he had already written in *The Last Day of a Condemned* and *Claude Gueux* (1834), and which would be fully exploited in a work already in progress at this time, *Les Misérables*. Because of his concern for the ordinary man and the unfortunates, he was elected a "representative of the people" in 1848 and a year later became a Parisian delegate to the Assemblée Nationale. During the 1848 Revolution, Hugo published his opinions in his journal *L'Événement*, and though he was aligned with no particular political party, the periodical was suppressed. He grew increasingly suspicious of Louis Napoleon's ambitions, and though Hugo had originally supported him for the presidency, he delivered a scathing address before the Assemblée in July of 1851 in which he called the president "Napoleon the Little." As a consequence of this attack, Hugo fled France shortly after the *coup d'état* of December, 1851. This event marked another change in the poet's political stance: Having been a Royalist and then a Bonapartist, Hugo next became a Republican.

Hugo went first to Belgium, where he stayed only for a short time, then moved to the Channel Islands of Jersey and then Guernsey, where he finally settled with his family and with Juliette Drouet from 1855 to 1870. These were to be very productive years for Hugo. After a long silence, the poet's voice was again heard in 1853 with the publication of *Les Châtiments*, in which he vehemently denounced Louis Napoleon and his empire. In 1856, Hugo published *Les Contemplations*, in which he integrated lyrics, meditative poems on his daughter's death, and more visionary and mystical verses. In large measure, these poems would influence the Symbolists. With the publication of the first *The Legend of the Centuries* in 1859, an extensive epic that detailed humankind's progress from slavery to freedom, Hugo achieved the unquestioned reputation of "poet-seer."

It was as if Hugo's long silence had caused him to relish his renewed literary voice, for his productivity during the 1860's remained substantial. In 1862, his great novel *Les Misérables* appeared, succeeded by *Les Chansons des rues et des bois* (the songs of the streets and the woods) in 1865. These were followed in 1866 by another novel, *Les Travailleurs de la mer* (1866; *The Toilers of the Sea*, 1866). As always, his literary acclaim

was accompanied by personal sorrow. Adèle Hugo died in 1868 in Brussels of apoplexy. Her wish had been to be buried beside her daughter Léopoldine. Hugo accompanied her body as far as the French frontier. The following year, Hugo's next novel, *L'Homme qui rit* (1869; *The Man Who Laughs*, 1869), was published. It received little acclaim at the time, and it has been only rarely studied since.

The fall of the Second Empire on September 3, 1870, ended Hugo's long exile from France. He returned during turbulent times: The war with Prussia and the civil war which ensued left Hugo disillusioned. During this time, his son Charles died, his daughter Adèle was confined to an asylum, and his son François became gravely ill. Once more, the poet returned to Guernsey, this time not so much to escape political forces as to seek solace. He recorded his feelings in *L'Année terrible* (terrible year).

Hugo returned to Paris in 1873 after finishing his novel *Quatre-vingt-treize* (1874; *Ninety-three*, 1874), which was published the following year. Then seventy-one years old, he found great consolation in his grandchildren, spending long hours with them and sharing childhood delights. For his age, his productivity was amazingly constant. In 1877, there appeared the second volume of *The Legend of the Centuries*, as well as *L'Art d'être grand-père* (the art of being a grandfather). These were followed by *Le Pape* (the pope), *La Pitié suprême* (the supreme pity), *Religions et religion* (1880), *L'Âne* (the ass) and a play, *Torquemada* (wr. 1869, pb. 1882; English translation, 1896). On May 11, 1883, Juliette Drouet died of stomach cancer; her death was a terrible blow to Hugo. He published nothing else during his lifetime except the final volume of *The Legend of the Centuries* in 1883. His health steadily declined, and he died of pneumonia on May 22, 1885. He was buried in the Panthéon beside Voltaire and Rousseau.

In 1875, Hugo had written his literary will, which specified that after his death all of his manuscripts without exception should be published. This testament was faithfully executed, allowing for the appearance of the following posthumous publications: *Théâtre en liberté* (pb. 1886), *La Fin de Satan* (1886; the end of satan), *Toute la lyre* (1888; all of the lyre), *Dieu* (1891; God), *Les Années funestes* (1896; the fatal years), and *Dernière Gerbe* (1902; last sheaf). A portion of his letters, *Correspondence* (1896-1898), and his travel books *En voyage: Alpes et Pyrénées* (1890; *The Alps and Pyrenees*, 1898) and *Choses vues* (1887; *Things Seen*, 1887), were also published.

ANALYSIS

Victor Hugo's poetry took many forms, from the lyric to the epic to the elegiac. Along with this variety of form, the range of the poet's ideas expanded during his long career. From poems with political overtones, Hugo's poetry grew to exhibit the tenets of Romanticism. He wrote of more personal and intimate subjects, such as family and love. He also wrote about humankind's relationship with nature and with the Creator. As Hugo matured, his themes became more philosophical and humanitarian, and his self-appointed role became that of a poet-seer attempting to understand the mysteries of life and creation.

Hugo's shift toward Romanticism and away from political themes first became apparent in *Odes et ballades*. In this collection, the poet makes copious use of the fantastic, the uncanny, and the horrifying, a popular style of the time, exemplified by the German ballads of Gottfried Burger, Christoph Wieland, and Johann Wolfgang von Goethe. Hugo's inspiration was drawn also from contemporary translations of Spanish, English, and French ballads, a diversity of sources that infused his own ballads with eclecticism.

ODES ET BALLADES

In the preface to *Odes et ballades*, Hugo compares the sculptured gardens of Versailles with the primitive forests of the New World. The artificiality of the former, Hugo claims, stands in opposition to the laws of nature, whereas in the untouched forests, "everything obeys an invariable law." The true poet, then, must look to nature as his model, forsaking the contrived in favor of the natural. This was the new precept which Hugo sought to follow in this work.

Hugo received praise from his contemporaries for his imaginative use of his subject matter and for his great technical versatility. He used not only the classical Alexandrine but also other forms of versification, such as the octosyllabic line in the poem "La Fiancée du timbalier" ("The Cymbaleer's Bride") and the little-used Renaissance seven-syllable line in "À Trilby." Though original

and clever, these poems are devoid of the philosophical intent which characterizes the poet's later work. They were pronounced excellent, however, by a young critic for *Le Globe* by the name of Charles-Augustin Sainte-Beuve.

LES ORIENTALES

Les Orientales marks Hugo's departure from neoclassical rhetorical forms and inaugurates his bolder, more colorful style. Hugo's use of metaphor gains precision and originality; he employs verse forms drawn from the Renaissance Pléiade, to which he had been led by Sainte-Beuve.

The most famous poem of *Les Orientales* is "Les Djinns" ("The Djinns"), which exhibits Hugo's technical virtuosity. There is exoticism in the choice of both subject and form; in this, the poem is representative of the entire collection. The djinns are identified as evil spirits who sweep into a town and leave just as quickly. Their anticipated arrival is marked by a mounting from a two-syllable line to a decasyllabic line, while their departure is signaled by a parallel decrescendo. In this manner, Hugo is able to create an atmosphere of mystery and terror, with a contrasting feeling of relief. The poem won the plaudits not only of Hugo's contemporaries, but also of later poets and critics; Algernon Charles Swinburne was to comment that no other poet had "left a more exquisite piece or one more filled with delicate lyricism."

LES FEUILLES D'AUTOMNE

In *Les Feuilles d'automne*, Hugo's lyrical voice achieves maturity. The central themes are those of childhood, nature, and love. Although the style is less spectacular than that of *Les Orientales*, Hugo achieves a profound poetic effect through greater simplicity. His treatment of domestic themes is reminiscent of William Wordsworth, whose works Hugo may have known through the influence of Sainte-Beuve.

The opening poem is a tribute to the poet's mother's love and devotion. This is followed by a warm acknowledgment of his father, in which Hugo recalls the General's house at Blois and mourns his father's death. These panegyrics to his parents set the tone for the entire collection.

Less than a handful of poems deal with the topic of childhood, yet Hugo was the first to introduce this subject into French verse. The masterpiece of the collection is one such poem, "Lorsque l'enfant paraît" ("Infantile Influence"), touching in its description of the young child whose presence signifies a blessed household. Hugo concludes with a prayer imploring God to preserve family and friends from a home without a child. Such a sentimental ending would not have been found in *Les Orientales*, and it manifests a further development in the poet's style.

Another development, but on a different plane, establishes the poet's concern for the correspondences between people and nature, as in the poem "Ce qu'on entend sur la montagne" ("What Is Heard on the Mountain"). The role of the poet becomes significant in such an interchange; he becomes an interpreter in this dialogue, as Hugo announces in "Pan." These assertions were manifest again in later poetic works.

LES RAYONS ET LES OMBRES

In *Les Rayons et les ombres*, Hugo conceives of a social mission for the poet. The poet becomes a sacred dreamer, an impartial observer of his time, seeking inspiration from humankind, nature, and God. This collection is, therefore, rather diverse in its subject matter. There are love poems, poems devoted to nature, verses inspired by a search for religious significance, childhood memories, and poems with greater social content.

Two celebrated poems are to be found in *Les Rayons et les ombres*. The first is "Tristesse d'Olympio," in which the poet is presented as a keeper of the secrets of the universe. The tone of sadness which pervades the piece is in large measure a reflection of the unhappy events of 1837, the year it was written. Sainte-Beuve had published a story titled "Mme de Pontivy," in which he described a love affair similar to his alleged affair with Adèle Hugo. Hugo's daughter Léopoldine had been seriously ill that year. At the same time, the poet himself had been afflicted with an eye disorder. In that same year also, Hugo's brother Eugène died after spending many years in an asylum, his illness caused in large part by Hugo's marriage with Adèle, whom he had also loved. The inspiration for the poem is, therefore, overwhelmingly personal. The mood of the poem reflects Hugo's disillusionment with the mutability of nature. In striking contrast with poems of this same genre, such as Alphonse de Lamartine's "Le Lac" ("The Lake"),

Hugo asserts that, though nature may forget, humankind will not.

The second important poem in this collection is "Oceano Nox." Though it is much shorter and less complicated than "Tristesse d'Olympio," it nevertheless successfully introduces the sea into Hugo's poetic corpus. The poet chose the elegiac form to describe the force of the ocean and the tragedy of men who are engulfed in the sea, remembered only for a short time by their loved ones. The final stanza is powerful in its description of the desperate voices contained in the roar of the sea at night.

"L'EXPIATION"

It was during his stay in Jersey in 1853 that Hugo published *Les Châtiments*, a volume of satiric poetry. The work is a ceaseless diatribe against the Second Empire and Louis Napoleon. Hugo's indignation against the Emperor was inexhaustible. He believed Napoleon to be a tyrant, a ruler who had compromised the liberty of the French people. Hugo evokes every imaginable vituperative image in his denunciation of "Napoleon the Dwarf." Though these pages are replete with a succession of ingenious epithets and metaphors, one poem in this collection is particularly noteworthy, "L'Expiation."

The poem combines both epic and satiric styles; its structure is particularly ingenious. Opening with an account of the glorious reign of Napoleon I, it develops the concept of the crime which the poet must expiate: the *coup d'état* on the *Dix-huit Brumaire* of the revolutionary calendar. Hugo then details the Emperor's retreat from Moscow, his army's struggle in the blinding snow, the loss of countless men to the elements. Napoleon wonders at this point whether this is his punishment. A voice replies: *No*.

The second part of the poem recounts the battle at Waterloo. Hugo describes the conflict at its height. Napoleon witnesses the fall of the French army, and this time he knows that his defeat will be total. Once more the question is asked: Is this the punishment? Once more, the voice answers: *No*.

The third segment of the poem concerns Napoleon's exile on Saint Helena. Hugo ably contrasts the prisoner Napoleon with the formerly glorious emperor. The latter is now preoccupied with the memories of Moscow, with his wife's infidelity, and with the constant surveillance of his jailer, Sir Hudson Lowe. As the fallen emperor lies dying, he once more raises the question: Is this the punishment? This time, the voice replies: *Not yet.*

Thirty years later, Napoleon I is awakened in his tomb by a familiar voice. It is the voice of his nephew, who has debased the name of Napoleon. Now the punishment is clear: The name of Napoleon is to be remembered not in glory but in ignominy.

Though it is known that Hugo researched his subject carefully, the tension and the concentration of events which make this poem so remarkable are his own distinctive contributions. The ingenuity of the threefold intervention of the voice sustains the dramatic movement, while the portrait of Napoleon is a powerful study in contrast.

LES CONTEMPLATIONS

Published in two volumes, titled *Autrefois* (former times) and *Aujourd'hui* (today), *Les Contemplations* has been called by the critic Ferdinand Brunetière "the most lyrical collection in the French language." The dividing line between the two volumes was the death of Hugo's daughter Léopoldine, in 1843. Consequently, the poems in this collection are very personal, yet the poet generalizes his experiences to include the experiences of all people. Central to the work is the relationship of God and humankind, of humankind and external nature, and of life and death.

In this collection, there are two groups of poems that are particularly significant. The first is "Pauca meae," comprising seventeen poems composed between 1841 and 1855. They were inspired by Hugo's daughter, Léopoldine. The best-known poem in this series is "A Villequier," which expresses the poet's deep despair at the loss of his beloved daughter. It treats the poet's attempt to submit to the will of God and to resign himself to a life without his child. Though he is able to achieve the former, complete resignation is something which eludes him. Unable to restrain his emotion, he claims the right to weep. The grief of a father dominates the rest of the poem, which concludes on a note of extreme sadness.

The second important series in *Les Contemplations*, "Au bord de l'infini," comprises twenty-six poems containing a statement of Hugo's philosophical ideas. The poet aspires to penetrate the unknown, perhaps through prayer. His search for truth will be as a winged dreamer

or as a startled wise man. The crowning piece of this series, "Ce que dit la bouche d'ombre" ("What the Mouth of the Shadow Says"), deals with such concepts as Pythagoreanism (in particular, the metempsychosis of souls), Platonism, and pantheism.

"What the Mouth of the Shadow Says" is set at the dolmen of Rozel. There the poet meets a specter with whom he discusses the unity of the universe and the essential vitality of all that is in it. Everything in creation has a soul and a consciousness, but how is this universe to be explained? If God is in everything and everything is in God, then how can one reconcile the imperfections of the world with the perfection that is God? It is here that Hugo introduces the notion of evil. If evil is caused by the absence of light, then the resulting darkness and heaviness can only be associated with matter. Because man is conscious of the difference between darkness and light, he chooses to do evil by his own free will. Moreover, man chooses his own punishment. An evildoer's soul will be metamorphosed into something degrading; the soul of Judas, for example, is to be found in the spit of men. Ultimately, however, there is hope for humankind, a hope that the dualism between light and darkness, between goodness and evil, will be reconciled. It is on this thought that the poem ends.

THE LEGEND OF THE CENTURIES

Considered by many to be the greatest epic poem since the Middle Ages, *The Legend of the Centuries* differs from other epics in its humanitarian concerns. Hugo states in the preface that he is interested in showing the human profile "from Eve, the mother of men, to the Revolution, the mother of peoples." This is to be accomplished with the notion of progress foremost in his mind. This is not a historical collection, but rather, as Charles Baudelaire put it, a collection of those things which are poetic, that is, legend, myth, and fable, those things which tap the deep reservoirs of humanity.

Among the many subjects presented are the following: "Le Sacre de la femme" ("The Crowning of Women"), which opens the volume and which treats the story of Eve, not from the perspective of original sin, but from the perception of idyllic beauty; "La Conscience" ("Conscience"), which is the story of Cain's attempt to flee from the Eye that follows him everywhere, even to his grave; "Booz endormi" ("Boaz Asleep"), which was inspired by the Book of Ruth and in which Hugo attributes to the patriarch Boaz a dream in which he sees a great oak leading from himself to David and finally to Christ; "Le Mariage de Roland," which is considered by critics to be the prototype of the little epic and which presents the four-day struggle between Roland and Olivier, ending with the proposal that Roland marry Olivier's sister; "La Rose de l'infante" ("The Infanta's Rose"), which deals with the destruction in 1588 of the Spanish Armada and describes a great gust of wind which scatters the fleet and simultaneously arrives in the royal garden of Aranjuez, stripping the petals of the rose held by the infanta and scattering them in the nearby fountain; "Le Satyr" ("The Satyr"), which is considered to be the most important philosophical poem of the collection and treats the double nature of man, a being at once allied with the gods because of his spirit, but who now has his feet in the mud; and two poems, "Pleine mer" ("Out at Sea") and "Plein ciel" ("Up in the Sky"), which together constitute "Vingtième siècle," contrasting the evils of old-world war symbolized by the steamship Leviathan with the vision of goodness symbolized by the airship.

LA FIN DE SATAN

Although *La Fin de Satan* was not published until after Hugo's death, it was conceived of during his stay in Guernsey. Hugo's treatment of the fallen angel differs greatly from the Miltonic version. Whereas the fall of Satan in Milton's work is precipitous, in Hugo's version Satan's fall takes thousands of years, while the feathers from his wings fall even more slowly. Furthermore, while Milton's Satan reigns over a host of other devils, Hugo's Satan is alone until he is able to engender a daughter, the veiled Isis-Lilith. It is she who brings evil into the world. After the great Flood, she returns to Earth the three weapons with which Cain had slain Abel: a bronze nail, a wooden club, and a stone. For Hugo, these instruments symbolically represent war, capital punishment, and imprisonment. These three representations determine the structure of the work.

In the first section, "Le Glaive," Hugo illustrates the evils of war through the symbolic character of Nimrod. Hugo's Nimrod is arrogant and bellicose, and his attack on the kingdom of God is doomed to failure. The most remarkable section of this first part concerns another

Hugoesque creation. One of the feathers from Lucifer's wings had not fallen into the abyss, landing instead on the edge of a precipice. The angel, Liberty, engendered from this feather is a creation of God rather than of Satan, and together with Lilith, she represents the dual nature of Lucifer-Satan.

The second section, centering on an earthly drama, is titled "Le Gibet" ("The Cross"). It is divided into three parts: "La Judée," "Jésus-Christ," and "Le Crucifix." Hugo's attack on capital punishment takes the form of a contrast between the innocent Christ, who is crucified, and the guilty Barabbas, who is set free. Hugo adds an effective scene not found in the biblical narration, wherein Barabbas comes to the foot of the Cross after the Crucifixion.

In the meantime, Liberty beseeches God to allow Lucifer to return to the light. Before putting Lucifer into a peaceful sleep, she receives his blessing to undo the work of Lilith on Earth. The final section of the poem, dealing with imprisonment, was not complete at Hugo's death. Hugo, however, did write a conclusion to the work, titled "Satan pardonnée" ("Satan Pardoned"). Liberty is able to gain the salvation of both humankind and Lucifer.

DIEU

Composed in large part during Hugo's stay in Guernsey in 1855, *Dieu* was left unfinished for many years. Hugo returned to it in 1875, and it was published posthumously in 1891. The poem concerns Hugo's search for God. Twenty-one voices warn the poet of the futility of his search for a complete understanding of God; nevertheless, the poet continues on his journey. He meets a series of symbolic birds, for he himself is winged. These birds are emblems of various understandings of the godhead: atheism, skepticism, Manichaeanism, paganism, Judaism, and Christianity. Finally, the poet achieves the light in "La Lumière" ("The Light"), although he is denied complete understanding, for a veil falls before him. Man is to know the secrets of the infinite only in death.

Together with *La Fin de Satan*, *Dieu* represents a synthesis of Hugo's religious and philosophical ideas, revealing the poet as a privileged seeker of truth. Hugo shows himself to be not only a master of versification but also a man consumed by the desire to comprehend the deeper mysteries of existence and of the universe.

OTHER MAJOR WORKS

LONG FICTION: *Han d'Islande*, 1823 (*Hans of Iceland*, 1845); *Bug-Jargal*, 1826 (*The Noble Rival*, 1845); *Le Dernier Jour d'un condamné*, 1829 (*The Last Day of a Condemned*, 1840); *Notre-Dame de Paris*, 1831 (*The Hunchback of Notre Dame*, 1833); *Claude Gueux*, 1834; *Les Misérables*, 1862 (English translation, 1862); *Les Travailleurs de la mer*, 1866 (*The Toilers of the Sea*, 1866); *L'Homme qui rit*, 1869 (*The Man Who Laughs*, 1869); *Quatre-vingt-treize*, 1874 (*Ninety-Three*, 1874);

PLAYS: *Irtamène*, wr. 1816, pb. 1934 (verse drama); *Inez de Castro*, wr. c. 1818, pb. 1863 (verse drama); *Cromwell*, pb. 1827 (verse drama; English translation, 1896); *Amy Robsart*, pr. 1828 (English translation, 1895); *Hernani*, pr., pb. 1830 (verse drama; English translation, 1830); *Marion de Lorme*, pr., pb. 1831 (verse drama; English translation, 1895); *Le Roi s'amuse*, pr., pb. 1832 (verse drama; *The King's Fool*, 1842, also known as The *King Amuses Himself*, 1964); *Lucrèce Borgia*, pr., pb. 1833 (*Lucretia Borgia*, 1842); *Marie Tudor*, pr., pb. 1833 (English translation, 1895); *Angelo, tyran de Padoue*, pr., pb. 1835 (*Angelo, Tyrant of Padua*, 1880); *Ruy Blas*, pr., pb. 1838 (verse drama; English translation, 1890); *Les Burgraves*, pr., pb. 1843 (*The Burgraves*, 1896); *La Grand-mère*, pb. 1865; *Mille Francs de Recompense*, pb. 1866; *Torquemada*, wr. 1869, pb. 1882 (English translation, 1896); *Les Deux Trouvailles de Gallus*, pb. 1881; *Théâtre en liberté*, pb. 1886 (includes *Mangeront-ils?*); *The Dramatic Works*, pb. 1887; *The Dramatic Works of Victor Hugo*, pb. 1895-1896 (4 volumes);

NONFICTION: *La Préface de Cromwell*, 1827 (English translation, 1896); *Littérature et philosophie mêlées*, 1834; *Le Rhin*, 1842 (*The Rhine*, 1843); *Napoléon le petit*, 1852 (*Napoleon the Little*, 1852); *William Shakespeare*, 1864 (English translation, 1864); *Actes et paroles*, 1875-1876; *Histoire d'un crime*, 1877 (*The History of a Crime*, 1877-1878); *Religions et religion*, 1880; *Le Théâtre en liberté*, 1886; *Choses vues*, 1887 (*Things Seen*, 1887); *En voyage: Alpes et Pyrénées*, 1890 (*The Alps and Pyrenees*, 1898); *France et Belgique*, 1892; *Correspondance*, 1896-1898.

MISCELLANEOUS: *Oeuvres complètes*, 1880-1892 (57 volumes); *Victor Hugo's Works*, 1892 (30 volumes); *Works*, 1907 (10 volumes).

BIBLIOGRAPHY

Crockett, Clarence V. *Three Loves Claim Victor Hugo*. New York: Liveright, 1964. Crockett engages in a comprehensive analysis of Hugo as a novelist, a playwright, and a poet.

Frey, John Andrew. *A Victor Hugo Encyclopedia*. Westport, Conn.: Greenwood Press, 1999. A comprehensive guide in English to Victor Hugo. Includes a foreword, a biography, and a bibliography. Frey addresses Hugo as a leading poet, novelist, artist, and religious and revolutionary thinker of France. The balance of the volume contains alphabetically arranged entries discussing his works, characters, and themes, as well as historical persons and places. Includes a general bibliography.

Grant, Elliott M. *The Career of Victor Hugo*. New York: Kraus Reprint, 1969. A thorough biography of Hugo with bibliographic references.

Hudson, William Henry. *Victor Hugo and His Poetry*. New York: AMS Press, 1972. An introductory biography and critical interpretation of some of Hugo's work.

Ireson, J.C. *Victor Hugo: A Companion Guide to His Poetry*. New York: Clarendon Press, 1997. A detailed critical study dealing with Victor Hugo's verse in its totality, showing how each work was composed, how the themes evolved, and the considerations that dictated the sequence of his publications. Includes bibliographic references.

Matthew, Josephson. *Victor Hugo: A Realistic Biography of the Great Romantic*. Garden City, N.Y.: Doubleday, Doran, 1942. This source is useful for biographical details and information about Hugo's influence on literature as a Romantic author.

Peyre, Henri. *Victor Hugo: Philosophy and Poetry*. Tuscaloosa: University of Alabama Press, 1980. A study of Hugo's philosophy as evidenced by his poetry. Contains translations of selected poems with an index and bibliography.

Robb, Graham. *Victor Hugo*. New York: W. W. Norton, 1997. Winner of the 1997 Whitbread Biography

Award, Robb analyzes Victor Hugo's life and work with intelligence and wit. Hugo created much of the legend that grew around him, from his pastoral conception on a mountainside to his heroic republican opposition to Napoleon. Robb unties these myths in a search for the reasons underlying Hugo's re-creation of his own history.

Ward, Patricia. *The Medievalism of Victor Hugo.* University Park: Pennsylvania State University Press, 1975. A study of Hugo's knowledge and use of medieval history and themes. Includes bibliographic references.

Sylvie L. F. Richards;
bibliography updated by Mabel Khawaja

LEIGH HUNT

Born: Southgate, England; October 19, 1784
Died: Putney, England; August 28, 1859

PRINCIPAL POETRY
Juvenilia, 1801
The Feast of the Poets, 1814
The Story of Rimini, 1816
Foliage, 1818
Hero and Leander, and Bacchus and Ariadne, 1819
The Poetical Works of Leigh Hunt, 1923 (H. S. Milford, editor)

OTHER LITERARY FORMS
Leigh Hunt was a poet, familiar essayist, critic, political commentator, playwright, and translator. While he wrote well in all of these genres and with occasional brilliance in some, his reputation as an essayist has best endured. The critical essays reveal a keen sense for what is good in literature; they quote extensively from the works being considered. The familiar essays are famous for their quiet good humor. They are seldom as polished as the essays of Charles Lamb or as perceptive as those of William Hazlitt; still, a few—such as "Getting Up on Cold Mornings" and "Deaths of Little Children"—continue to be anthologized as classics.

ACHIEVEMENTS
In his own time, the general reading public respected Leigh Hunt as an important literary figure, one whose opinions on literature and the political scene were both valid and influential. His role as editor of several periodicals afforded him an effective means of voicing those opinions to a great many readers, far more than expensive books could reach. Thus Hunt was the great popularizer of the Romantic movement in England. Later critics, however, concluded that several of his contemporaries, though then of less influence and popularity, were actually better artists and more profound thinkers. The common twentieth century attitude has tended to ignore Hunt's individual achievements, rather viewing him as the comparatively less important hub of an illustrious literary circle: John Keats, Percy Bysshe Shelley, Lord Byron, Charles Lamb, and William Hazlitt, in particular. More recently, critics have again begun to assess Hunt's own achievements, and while few would allow that he was as fine a poet as Keats, as graceful an essayist as Lamb, or as profound a critic as Hazlitt, still his work does not merit oblivion. His translations are among the finest in English, and he must be credited with increasing the English-speaking world's awareness of Italian literature. His countless journalistic pieces reflect wide reading and high standards of scholarship, and he deserves recognition for his contribution to the quality of popular journalism. A fair assessment of Hunt's literary achievement would have to include his positive influence on the several young poets who went on to surpass their mentor, but that assessment should also not overlook the quality of his own work as a journalist and translator.

BIOGRAPHY
Leigh Hunt was the son of a Philadelphia lawyer who had returned to England at the time of the American Revolution. The father was a highly principled if rather impractical man who changed his profession from lawyer to Unitarian minister and occasional tutor. At seven years of age, young Hunt was sent to school at Christ's Hospital, where Charles Lamb and Samuel Taylor Coleridge had also been students. Hunt's *The Autobiography of Leigh Hunt* (1850) reveals that from his earliest years he was instilled with a hatred of all that is evil.

He detested violence, was shocked by profane language, and opposed tyranny by defending his weaker schoolmates with passive resistance of schoolyard bullies. Hunt stayed at Christ's Hospital until he was fifteen. At seventeen he published a volume of juvenile verse.

In 1808, Hunt became the editor of a journal, *The Examiner*, owned by his brother John. *The Examiner* championed a number of liberal causes: abolition of slavery, freedom of the press, an end to imprisonment for debt. In their catalog of social evils, the Hunts did not hesitate to include even the Prince Regent of England. Their description of the prince as "a violator of his word, a libertine over head and ears in debt and disgrace, a despiser of domestic ties, the companion of gamblers" resulted in a libel case and two years' imprisonment for both brothers. Prison was not very hard on Leigh Hunt. He had a decent room, which he decorated with flowered wallpaper, and in which he received such notable visitors as Byron, Shelley, and Hazlitt. After his release, Hunt published his major poem, *The Story of Rimini*, and became the literary mentor to young Keats. The Tory critics, however, could not forgive the slandering of the prince and viciously attacked Hunt. In 1817, *Blackwood's Magazine* coined the term "cockney school" to describe Hunt's frequently colloquial style, and the appellation was to plague him for many years.

In 1822 Hunt and his family arrived in Italy. Shelley invited him to assume editorship of *The Liberal*, a periodical conceived by Byron and Shelley as a vehicle for their own writings. Shelley drowned soon thereafter, and when Byron, upon whom the Hunts had depended for financial support, left Italy, the family was stranded until 1825, when Hunt borrowed enough money to return to England. He naturally felt that Byron had done him an injustice and in 1828 he published *Lord Byron and Some of His Contemporaries*, presenting a most unfavorable picture of Byron's personal fears and dishonesties. Hunt maintained in the face of widespread adverse criticism that he had included nothing which he did not believe to be entirely true. True or not, few considered it proper to write so about a man who had recently gone to a heroic death.

With the exception of the embarrassment resulting from his identification with the character Harold Skimpole in Charles Dickens's *Bleak House* (1852) (Dickens insisted that any similarity was unintentional), the remainder of Hunt's life was rather uneventful. He wrote voluminously in all literary forms and on countless topics. The concise *Cambridge Bibliography of English Literature* (1965) estimates that a complete edition of his prose works alone would fill forty volumes. He lived to see his liberal ideas become the popular thought of the day and himself a respected figure in the literary community. Hunt's productive life ended peacefully in 1859 while he was visiting one of his oldest friends, the printer Charles Reynell, in Putney.

ANALYSIS

Leigh Hunt's three-volume *The Autobiography of Leigh Hunt* has remained the single most important source of information on both the facts of his life and those personal attributes which influenced his writings. There is, in fact, comparatively little in *The Autobiography of Leigh Hunt* dealing exclusively with Hunt; it is more a series of recollections and examinations of his many literary friends. This fact is of some importance in understanding Hunt the man, for it reflects a total lack of selfishness and a genuine sympathetic concern for the many fortunate people who won his friendship. These friendships were treasured by Hunt, and in the accounts of his youthful infatuations is reflected the simple kindheartedness and romantic idealism which were noted by his contemporaries and by later critics. *The Autobiography of Leigh Hunt* does not follow a strict chronology but is rather a series of units. For example, he describes his parents' lives until their deaths before he discusses his own early years. In fact, Hunt's father lived to see his son a successful editor. This organizational method may well be a result of Hunt's reliance on personal taste. His taste of course was selective; he extracted from his experience what he considered excellent and showed little regard for the organizational coherence of the whole. His literary criticism, indeed even his poetry, displays the same fondness for selection found in his autobiography.

Most critics agree that Hunt's greatest contribution to poetry was not the poetry he himself wrote but his fine criticism of the poetry of others. Again, Hunt's criticism is based on his own excellent taste, but his taste was far more useful in recognizing good literature than in distinguishing what was specifically bad and forming a thoughtful critical opinion as to the nature of the faults. In practice, Hunt the critic was a selector; he chose those passages from a work which especially appealed to his taste and quoted them at length. Thus he assumed that the works would speak for themselves. He did not conceive of a critic as one who thinks for the reader and locks literature into a single interpretation. If Hunt has survived as a critic, it is because his personal taste was so good. At the same time, his natural sensitivity to what is fine in literature may be said to have worked against his ever achieving a place among the very greatest critics. He had no need for detailed analysis to tell him what was fine in art, and he created no aesthetic concepts approaching the sophistication of some of his contemporaries, notably Coleridge. Thus, Hunt cannot be numbered among the important literary theoreticians. His reputation as a quite respectable critic is dependent on the fact that he was perhaps the greatest appreciator of literature in the history of English letters.

The same quality of taste that enabled Hunt to select what was best in the writings of others also influenced his own poetic compositions. That selective talent, however, did not serve Hunt the poet quite so well. In the composition of his own verse, he was inclined to combine lines and passages reflective of specific poetic principles without a view to the appropriateness of the principle in relation to the poem as a whole. For example, Hunt as the great popularizer of Romantic literary ideas did more than William Wordsworth to bring home to the nineteenth century reader the notion that poetry should reflect the language really used by people. Another aim of the Romantics was to make a place in literature for the experiences of the lower classes, comprising that whole stratum of society that neoclassical writers generally ignored. Hunt's conviction that it was the business of poetry to do these things led him, much more than Wordsworth, Coleridge, and his other illustrious contemporaries who shared these ideas, to overlook yet another major principle of composition that had so concerned the neoclassicist: decorum.

Decorum demanded that all of the various elements of a work of art contribute to the unified effect of the work as a whole. Thus, diction must be appropriate to character and action; a king suffering tragedy should not speak like the common man in the street. Decorum

made the poet responsible to the propriety of the particular work. Hunt too often forced the work to comply with principle, and while the principle of natural poetic language suited certain poems, lines such as "The two divinest things this world has got,/ A lovely woman in a rural spot" are jarring. The many critics who have viewed Hunt's poetry with disfavor have really played variations on a single theme: the unevenness of the work. The tone is inappropriate for the subject; good writing is not maintained throughout; the central idea is lost for the digressions. These are all pitfalls into which a reliance on personal taste might lead one, and though Hunt is guilty of all this, it must also finally be acknowledged that this same disregard for uniformity resulted in an important contribution to English poetry of the nineteenth century.

THE STORY OF RIMINI

The unfortunate couplet just quoted is from *The Story of Rimini*, a retelling of Dante's tragic story of Paolo and Francesca and Hunt's most ambitious poetic effort. At the time of its composition, Hunt found John Dryden "The most delightful name to me in English literature." In *The Autobiography of Leigh Hunt* he confesses that while *The Story of Rimini* was intended to reflect the vigor and music of Dryden's natural style, his personal taste produced some variations, such as a more simple diction and less vigorous versification. Obviously the results of these liberties were not always happy. The effect of *The Story of Rimini* on English poetry, however, was certainly positive. The poem contributed greatly to the breakup of the highly polished closed couplet perfected by Alexander Pope; Hunt called for a less rigid couplet structure making use of run-on lines and feminine endings. The poem had a marked influence on the styles of several of his contemporaries. Some of Keats's most important early pieces, such as "I Stood Tip-toe Upon a Little Hill" and "Sleep and Poetry," show the influence of Hunt's couplet. Indeed, the motto for "I Stood Tip-toe" was borrowed from *The Story of Rimini*.

Still, the vicious political critics from *Blackwood's Magazine* and the *Quarterly* who dubbed Hunt the leader of the so-called Cockney School of poetry were not completely wrong in their identification of the poem's faults. The freer couplet form resulted in an easy, almost conversational tone which was only aggravated by colloquial diction. Hunt simply did not recognize that some of the ingredients he selected to mix in this noble experiment were not appropriate to the dignity of the subject. Regardless of particular theories of poetic composition or the unique tastes of any age, a character such as Francesca deserves better than "She had strict notions on the marrying score."

Despite its several flaws, *The Story of Rimini* does contain passages of natural grace and elegance. Clearly Dryden's lesson was not completely lost on Hunt. Moreover, the canon of Hunt's poetry includes some astonishingly pure gems that prove the truth of the judgment of *The Cambridge History of English Literature* (1916) that Hunt's best poetry is better than his best prose. These best efforts are short—sonnets and brief narratives. The rigid structure of the sonnet seems to have provided the direction that Hunt was likely to lose sight of in his longer experiments, and brief narratives prevented those digressions which he was likely to engage in for their own sake and at the expense of the clarity of his theme. The sonnet on "The Nile" is an example of Hunt at his best. Critics have generally praised it over the sonnets on the same topic by Keats and Shelley. Here, Hunt achieves smooth versification with natural rhymes and diction reflective of the tranquil progress of the river through an ancient and glorious landscape. Very unobtrusively, in only the last one and a half lines, meditation on the river is allowed to slide gracefully into a metaphor for meditation on human experience. Had Hunt more often shown the sense of dignity and decorum obvious in "The Nile," his place as an important English poet would be secure.

"ABOU BEN ADHEM"

The best of the brief narratives is also Hunt's most famous poem. "Abou Ben Adhem" first appeared in Samuel Carter Hall's *The Amulet* (1835) and is certainly one of the most frequently anthologized poems in the English language. The poet relates a simple tale, and while an incident of angelic visitation might seem to demand the most heroic language, Hunt wisely understood that the point of the tale is not so much the magnificence of the angel as it is the intimacy that exists between a good person and the divine. The character of Abou Ben Adhem, then, is most important; that character had to be

made to appeal to human readers. Thus, Abou Ben Adhem, secure in his knowledge of what he is, is not intimidated by the angel. His address is respectful but relaxed and touched by humor. He does not disagree with the angel's omission of his name from the list of those who love God but politely suggests an alternative: "I pray thee then/ Write me as one that loves his fellow-men." In this poem of only eighteen lines, Hunt successfully drew a quite sophisticated character and suggested a relationship between God and human beings more subtle than the implied message that God loves people who love their neighbors. In the hands of a lesser poet, "Abou Ben Adhem" might have been an undistinguished exercise in lofty language and baroque figures; the theme would allow such an approach. Indeed, in the hands of Hunt it might have been a hodgepodge of styles and words at war with themes, but in this poem and several others, he managed to keep his eye on the poem itself rather than on assorted notions about poetry.

In his *An Essay on Criticism* (1711), Alexander Pope describes two kinds of literary genius: the genius to create the material of poetry, the rhetorical figures, the variety of styles, and the genius to know how to arrange the material into a unified whole. In this latter respect Hunt too often showed himself deficient. When he managed to overcome that deficiency, as he often did, he showed himself the worthy companion of Keats, Shelley, and the many immortal Romantics who loved him so well.

OTHER MAJOR WORKS

PLAY: *A Legend of Florence*, pr. 1840.

NONFICTION: *Lord Byron and Some of His Contemporaries*, 1828; *Imagination and Fancy*, 1844; *Wit and Humour*, 1846; *Men, Women and Books*, 1847; *The Autobiography of Leigh Hunt*, 1850; *Leigh Hunt's Dramatic Criticism, 1808-1831*, 1949 (Carolyn W. Houtchens and Lawrence H. Houtchens, editors); *Leigh Hunt's Literary Criticism*, 1956 (Houtchens and Houtchens, editors).

BIBLIOGRAPHY

Blainey, Ann. *Immortal Boy: A Portrait of Leigh Hunt.* New York: St. Martin's Press, 1985. This biography adds further dimension to the usual perception of Hunt as a cheerful character by emphasizing the infuriating and melancholic sides of the man. Blainey's brief, well-written portrait focuses on Hunt's vulnerable, human qualities. Includes several illustrations, an extensive bibliography, and an index.

Edgecombe, Rodney Stenning. *Leigh Hunt and the Poetry of Fancy.* Cranbury, N.J.: Associated University Presses, 1994. Critical analysis of selected poetry by Hunt. Includes bibliographical references and index.

Hunt, Leigh. *Leigh Hunt: A Life in Letters, Together with Some Correspondence of William Hazlitt.* Edited and introduced by Eleanor M. Gates. Essex, Conn.: Falls River Publications, 1998. A collection of correspondence that offers invaluable insight into Hunt's life and work.

Johnson, Brimley. *Leigh Hunt.* 1896. New York: Haskell, 1970. This 152-page work examines Hunt's major works in great detail, assessing the writer's ability separately as a journalist, poet, and critic. Johnson suggests that "gratitude" to Hunt for his service to liberalism and his "popularization" of taste should persuade critics to overlook his "shallow" intellect and weak style. Supplemented by an index.

Kendall, Kenneth E. *Leigh Hunt's "Reflector."* Paris: Mouton, 1971. Examines Hunt's first literary periodical as a reflection of contemporary thought and times. Although the short 183-page book looks at other contributors from the Hunt circle, Hunt receives most of the attention. Kendall suggests that *The Reflector* was very important to the literary development of Hunt. Complemented by a bibliography, an index, and appendices.

McCown, Robert A., ed. *The Life and Times of Leigh Hunt: Papers Delivered at a Symposium.* Iowa City: Friends of the University of Iowa Libraries, 1985. A collection of critical essays covering various aspects of Hunt's writings. Titles included are "Leigh Hunt in Literary History: A Response," "Inter Pares: Leigh Hunt as Personal Essayist," and "Leigh Hunt's Dramatic Success: A Legend in Florence." These essays marked the bicentennial of Hunt's birth.

Marshall, William H. *Byron, Shelley, Hunt, and "The Liberal."* Philadelphia: University of Pennsylvania Press, 1960. This 269-page work examines the literary partnership and friendship between George Gordon, Lord Byron, Percy Bysshe Shelley, and Hunt. The work analyzes each number of *The Liberal* in separate chapters and offers a critical study of Hunt as both a writer and an editor. Appendices include a parody of *The Liberal* called *The Illiberal.* Supplemented by a bibliography and an index.

William J. Heim;
bibliography updated by the editors

I

DAVID IGNATOW

Born: Brooklyn, New York; February 7, 1914
Died: East Hampton, New York; November 17, 1997

PRINCIPAL POETRY

Poems, 1948
The Gentle Weight Lifter, 1955
Say Pardon, 1961
Figures of the Human, 1964
Rescue the Dead, 1968
Earth Hard: Selected Poems, 1968
Poems, 1934-1969, 1970
Selected Poems, 1975 (Robert Bly, editor)
Facing the Tree: New Poems, 1975
Tread the Dark, 1978
Sunlight: A Sequence for My Daughter, 1979
Whisper to the Earth, 1981
Leaving the Door Open, 1984
New and Collected Poems, 1970-1985, 1986
Shadowing the Ground, 1991
Against the Evidence: Selected Poems, 1934-1994, 1993
I Have a Name, 1996
At My Ease: Uncollected Poems of the Fifties and Sixties, 1998
Living Is What I Wanted: Last Poems, 1999

OTHER LITERARY FORMS

David Ignatow published several volumes of prose, including *The Notebooks of David Ignatow* (1973), *Open Between Us* (1980), a collection of lectures, interviews, essays, and reviews, and *The One in the Many: A Poet's Memoirs* (1988). In addition, Ignatow published a substantial number of short stories in various small magazines in the 1940's and 1950's. Many of these are collected in *The End Game and Other Stories* (1996). His letters, a treasure trove of personal, aesthetic, and philo-

sophical insight, are collected in *Talking Together: Letters of David Ignatow, 1946-1990* (1992).

ACHIEVEMENTS

Because of his deliberate eschewal of traditional poetic techniques, including rhyme and meter, and his firm insistence upon the "plain style" in contradiction to prevailing modes of the day, David Ignatow endured a long period of public and academic neglect, not unlike that endured by his idol and warm supporter, William Carlos Williams. Also like Williams, he was an early victim of T. S. Eliot's extraordinary success, which has tended to cast much modern American poetry in a convoluted Donne-shadowed mold, despite Eliot's own sympathetic openness to free verse.

Ignatow's first two collections, *Poems* and *The Gentle Weight Lifter*, were decidedly the work of a poet at odds with the dominant mandarin sensibility of the period. The first collection occasioned an enthusiastic review by Williams in *The New York Times* (November 21, 1948), a review that led to a friendship between the two men. Although conversational in style, the poems' simplicity of diction and syntax, their almost clumsy rejection of conventional lyricism, and their steadfast metaphoric sparseness placed them outside the mainstream of contemporary aesthetics, causing more than one critic to label their author a "naif" or "primitive." Randall Jarrell's more accurate review of *The Gentle Weight Lifter* in the *Yale Review* (Autumn, 1955) characterized Ignatow's poetry as "humane, unaffected, and unexciting," noting that he lacked Williams's "heights and depths."

From the beginning, Ignatow proclaimed himself "a man with a small song," identifying most strongly with Walt Whitman and Williams in terms of wanting to articulate the travails and tragedies of the ordinary citizen in his own language. A strong chord of social and political protest inevitably accompanied such a program, and not a little of Ignatow's value resided in his willingness to confront the inequities he saw all around him.

Yet, it must have become increasingly evident to Ignatow that very few of the poems in his first two books were clear successes, for all their integrity of purpose and manner, and that something more was needed if he hoped to achieve the same sort of understated suggestiveness that Ernest Hemingway, an admired fellow writer, had achieved in his best short stories. He had to find a method that could weld Hemingway's lean but loaded sentences to the plain style learned from Williams and the kind of parabolic structures encountered in the Bible (an important source); that is, he needed to use narrative as metaphor but he needed to free it from the innate limitations of a prose mode by more direct confrontations with unconscious forces. Allegory was an obvious answer, as in Stephen Crane's neglected verse, but the specific modernist approach was found in the nightmare revelations of the Surrealists, which seemed to complement perfectly readings in Charles Baudelaire and Arthur Rimbaud.

Consequently, beginning with *Say Pardon*, Ignatow's deceptively modest story-poems started to illuminate deeper, darker undercurrents, started to probe Freudian streams with relentless innocence. In "The Dream" a stranger approaches "to fall down at your feet/ and pound his head upon the sidewalk" until "your life takes on his desperation," even after waking. Like Baudelaire, Ignatow remained a poet of urban landscapes, committed to a moral exploration of man's most ambitious and ambiguous invention, yet he never lost his spiritual roots

David Ignatow

in a Jewish past in his search for godhead and ideal certitudes. In the book's title poem, for example, he advises, "Say pardon/ and follow your own will," but two poems later, "The Complex" addresses the dilemma of a father whose "madness is to own himself/ for what he gives is taken," while another poem, "And I Said," envisions "God" behind "my enemy."

The tension energizing his strongest poems, an ethical and psychological matrix of contending defiance and guilt, often entails a transformation of public material into family dramas, spotlighting an ambivalent father figure, a wronged wife, a victimized son. A prolific writer intent upon processing every vagrant bit of daily experience, however trivial, Ignatow published more poems than he should, far too frequently lapsing into sententious whimsy or belaboring the obvious. This contributed, no doubt, to his dismissal by many academics. It was not until the 1970's and the publication of *Poems 1934-1969* and the *Selected Poems* that the true extent of his contribution to American literature was appreciated, climaxing in the award of the prestigious Bollingen Prize in 1977 and reconfirming the truism that risk-taking and pratfalls are ever the hallmarks of the serious artist.

Fellow poets were more ready to concede and celebrate the sly art beneath Ignatow's rough surfaces—at least poets who shared his concern for establishing an alternative aesthetic closer to the Whitman-Williams line of descent, ranging from Charles Reznikoff to the "deep image" school of Robert Bly, James Wright, and Diane Wakoski. They helped bring Ignatow's verses to the forefront of contemporary American poetry—Bly in particular, through his choices for the *Selected Poems*.

In later years, belying his age, Ignatow continued to evolve, another sign of genuine talent, and relaxed enough, at last, to appreciate poetic stances at the opposite end of the scale, including a growing comprehension of Eliot's technical radicalism and intelligence. If *Tread the Dark* exhibited symptoms of possible fatigue, compulsive reiteration of death threats and near self-parodies, these have since been denied in the moving *Sunlight: A Sequence for My Daughter* and *Whisper to the Earth*, in which the concluding "With Horace" epitomizes Ignatow's determination to dig for rocks, to strike off "his fire upon stone."

Ignatow received the National Institute of Arts and Letters Award (1964), two Guggenheim Fellowships (1965 and 1973), the Shelley Memorial Award (1965), and the Bollingen Prize (1977). In 1992, Ignatow received the Frost Medal along with American poet Adrienne Rich.

BIOGRAPHY

Born February 7, 1914, in Brooklyn, New York, the son of Russian immigrant parents, Max and Yetta (née Reinbach) Ignatow, David Ignatow had the misfortune to graduate from New Utrecht High School in 1932: "I stepped out of high school into the worst economic, social, and political disaster of our times, the Great Depression." He did enroll at Brooklyn College but lasted only half a semester, subsequently schooling himself in literary matters by reading Hemingway, Whitman, Friedrich Nietzsche, Arthur Schopenhauer, Søren Kierkegaard, the Russian novelists, the French poets of the previous century, and the Bible. He worked in his father's commercial pamphlet bindery, running a machine or delivering the finished pamphlets by hand-truck, and wrote stories and poems in his spare hours. Oppressed by the tedious labor, and by an ambivalent, often heated relationship with a hard-driving father, Ignatow envisioned literature as an escape. With his mother's aid, he managed to secure an appointment as a reporter for the WPA (Works Project Administration) Newspaper Project. The year before, his short story "I Can't Stop It" had appeared in *The New Talent* magazine, earning a place on Edward J. O'Brien's Honor List in his *The Best American Short Stories* annual in 1933.

Ignatow was finally able to leave the family business and home in 1935, when he found a cheap apartment in Manhattan's East Village, where he became a part of the literary scene and met artist Rose Graubart, whom he married two years later. Their son David was born in 1937. Financial difficulties harassed the young couple, and in the period from 1939 to 1948 Ignatow was forced to work at a series of low-paying jobs, as night clerk at the sanitation department, as a health department clerk, as an apprentice handyman in the lathe workshop at the Kearny Shipyards in New Jersey, and, for five years, as night admitting clerk at Beth Israel Hospital in New York. It was during his last year at Beth Israel that his

first collection, *Poems*, appeared and garnered an enthusiastic review from William Carlos Williams. Williams, in fact, emerged as a friend, as did Charles Reznikoff, and these two poets probably exerted the most enduring influence upon Ignatow's career.

The year 1955 proved to be crucial in Ignatow's life. *The Gentle Weight Lifter* was published; he was asked to edit the Whitman Centennial issue of the *Beloit Poetry Journal*; and his son began to exhibit the signs of mental illness that would eventually result in his being institutionalized. A daughter, Yaedi, was born the next year, and Ignatow became closely associated with *Chelsea* magazine. In 1961, his third volume of poetry, *Say Pardon*, was published by Wesleyan University Press—destined to remain his publisher for almost two decades—but money was still a pressing problem, and Ignatow worked as a paper salesman in the years between 1962 and 1964, also serving as an auto messenger for Western Union on the weekends. During the same interval, he spent a year as poetry editor of *The Nation* and gave a poetry workshop at the New School for Social Research.

The publication of *Figures of the Human* helped to earn him an award from the National Institute of Arts and Letters in 1964, his first significant token of recognition. This was followed by a Guggenheim Fellowship a year later. In 1965 he also won the Shelley Memorial Award and was a visiting lecturer at the University of Kentucky. Other academic posts came his way: at the University of Kansas in 1966 and at Vassar College from 1967 to 1969. He then accepted positions as poet in residence at York College (CUNY) and as adjunct professor at Columbia University. Editorial assignments included extended stints with *Beloit Poetry Journal* and *Chelsea*, and in 1972 he was among the first associate editors connected with the founding of *The American Poetry Review*, a connection that was dissolved near the decade's end when he and a group of fellow editors resigned in protest over what they perceived as implicit unfairness in the magazine's attitude toward women and minority groups.

In 1973 Ignatow was granted a second Guggenheim Fellowship, but the award that had the most to do with bringing his name before a broader audience was the Bollingen Prize of 1977. The publication of *The Note-*

books of David Ignatow—selections from his journals which the poet hoped, in vain, would result in a wider readership for his poetry—had made clear the terrible cost of being a writer, particularly an antiestablishment writer, in America. It also demonstrated with high principle, brutal candor, and almost claustrophobic narcissism the ultimate advantages and limitations of constantly translating self into truth. Ignatow's career achieved ironic completeness with his election to the presidency of the Poetry Society of America in 1980. He died on November 17, 1997.

ANALYSIS

In his poetry written in the 1930's and 1940's, later gathered in the first section of *Poems 1934-1969*, David Ignatow projected an abiding concern for both the well-made poem, however occasionally denuded of conventional lyric devices, and a reformer's vision of realistic life—in the city, in the streets, in the homes of the poor and outcast, who are romantically linked with the artist's difficult lot. The subjects were traditional—marriage, murder, sex, love's complexities, adolescence, the death of Franklin D. Roosevelt—but their treatment exhibited a diverting ability to make sudden leaps from the banal to the profound, always in language direct enough to disarm. "Autumn Leaves," for example, moves skillfully from an ordinary image of the leaves as Depression victims to a vivid figure of God sprawling beneath a tree, gaunt in giving, "like a shriveled nut where plumpness/ and the fruit have fed the worm." This kind of dramatic shift epitomizes Ignatow's focus on social injustice and his often bitter struggle with a religious heritage and the questionable place of deity in a scheme of things so geared to grind down human hopes.

Surprisingly, many of the early poems betray a professional smoothness and a reliance on metaphor and balanced lines that one might not expect from a disciple of Williams; there is scant sense in these poems of a language straining for experimental intensities. "The Murderer," an undeniable failure, marked by simplistic psychology but true to its author's identification with the underclass, can only express love for "those who cart me off to jail" in easy prose: "I love them too/ for the grief and anger/ I have given." More relevant, the murderer had killed with a knife, that most intimate of weapons,

which reappears again and again in the Ignatow canon, a reflection of the menace and death lurking behind every scene of ordinary existence, as well as symbolic reminder of murderous impulses and contrary fears of castration by the father and his capitalistic society.

POEMS

In *Poems*, which is a bundle of furies, Ignatow's rage against America's hunger for money, "our masterpiece" (according to a poem of that title), rarely escapes self-imposed boundaries. Occasionally, as in "At the Zoo," a quiet pathos gives modest dimensions their proper subject: an elephant trapped and separated from his real self, like the poet of course, in "stingy space and concrete setting." Repeatedly, however, as in "Come!" and "The Poet Is a Hospital Clerk," Ignatow underestimates his audience, wherein lies the innate danger of such songs, and settles for either blatant self-abasement—"I have said it before, I am no good"—or political invective: "Come, let us blow up the whole business;/ the city is insane." At his best, he can produce "Europe and America," merging anger against world ills with ambivalence toward his father, the knife resurfacing in a climax of fused violences:

My father comes of a small hell
where bread and man have been kneaded and baked
    together.
You have heard the scream as the knife fell;
while I have slept
as guns pounded offshore.

THE GENTLE WEIGHT LIFTER

Working with a larger canvas and a surer touch, *The Gentle Weight Lifter* evinces a growing dependence on narrative means and on verbal portraits and mirrors of the people who define Ignatow's imagination. The collection is not unlike Edgar Lee Masters's urbanized *Spoon River Anthology* (1915), although it is brightened by exotic historic additions and splashes of darker Kafkaesque tones. In its quest for parallel lives and allegorical configurations, the collection ranges back in time to ancient Greece, to Oedipus at Colonnus in "Lives II"—tellingly centered on the father, not Antigone, his head in her lap as "he thought surely some cover/ could be found for him"—to Nicias in "The Men Sang," a parable about the poet's generic function, and to the Old Testament in "The Pardon of Cain," which captures Cain in the "joy" of having freed himself from death's insidious allure.

Though not yet prevalent, surrealistic perspectives, when they do appear, tend to be founded upon absurd juxtapositions of mythic and modernist elements, as in "News Report," where "a thing" arises from a sewer to run amok among urban females—primeval sexuality rampant in a city field. Each victim describes her special view, "one giving the shaggy fur, the next the shank bone/ of a beast." In the end, the creature is an obvious refugee from Greek mythology, "the red teeth marks sunk into the thigh/ and the smell of a goat clinging tenaciously." Throughout the book, there is a stubborn quest for philosophic truths at variance with contemporary culture, and the governing voice, confounding Ignatow's own aesthetic, often resounds with a pedant's dense lexicon, as in "The Painter," a sensitive inquiry into a particular artist's world, which has a fourth stanza beginning: "These are not dreams, and the brush stroke is the agent./ At the hour of appropriate exhaustion, leaving the field/ of canvas, she ravens on the transient bread and cheese."

This is far from streamlined narrative terseness, far from the language of the man in the street, and it points up *The Gentle Weight Lifter*'s uneasy transitional quality, despite several remarkable poems, and its abrupt swings between simple allegorical spareness and thicker meditative measures.

SAY PARDON

In *Say Pardon*, much of the uncertainty has disappeared, carrying Ignatow's main voice and means closer to the spare slyness that distinguishes his final style. In *Babel to Byzantium* (1968), James Dickey salutes the collection's "strange, myth-dreaming vision of city life" and isolates, with acute accuracy, its basic modus operandi as "an inspired and brilliantly successful metaphysical reportage." Since it announces a greater willingness to accept a surrealistic path to unconscious resources, without jettisoning conversational immediacy and treasured social and moral concerns, one of the key poems is "How Come?" A naked, unpretentious self funnels the experience into Everyman's tale: "I'm in New York covered by a layer of soap foam." The conceit, whimsy in service of darker designs, is logically de-

veloped, radio newscasts informing him of the foam's spread to San Francisco, Canada, and the Mexican border, climaxing with "God help the many/ who will die of soap foam." Light fantasy has suggested the paradox of drowning in cleanliness, next to American godliness, the pollution of scientific and commercial advances against nature.

The relaxed speech is matter-of-fact, contrasting scaffolding for a surreal flight, not quite as jagged as it will later become in Ignatow's continued effort to simulate urban realities, and the situation adeptly yokes "what-if" fantasy to persistent reformist despair. More touching, though no less characteristic, are two poems about the author's institutionalized son, "In Limbo" and "Sunday at the State Hospital," the former a brief statement of grief, insisting that "there is no wisdom/ without a child in the house," and the latter recounting a visit in which the son cannot eat the sandwich his father has brought him:

> My past is sitting in front of me
> filled with itself
> and trying with almost no success
> to bring the present to its mouth.

A poem called simply "Guilt" lays bare the emotional core of these and other family verses: "Guilt is my one attachment to reality."

Jewish guilt, the anxiety bred of childhood training in a context that conditions love to obedience, outsider status, and unresolved Oedipus complexes, must forever seek release not only in the past, but in a specific religious ethos as well. Thus, the last section of *Say Pardon* is a procession of spiritual selves that assumes a living godhead, who proffers salvation (from guilt, rage, hatred) through the act of loving fatherhood, the "Lord" claiming "you will win your life/ out of my hands/ by taking up your child." These lines are from "I Felt," second in the series of twelve poems, after "The Mountain Is Stripped," where the poet had conceded, "I have been made frail with righteousness:/ with two voices. I am but one person." Because of its inveterate opposition to his rational espousal of liberal dogma and experimental openness, this conservative streak in Ignatow's consciousness, which helps to fuel his moral indignation, generates the lion's share of the tension in some of his strongest poetry. It also explains how such a cosmopolitan individual could, as revealed in *The Notebooks of David Ignatow*, react with abhorrence to homosexuality, viewing it as a degeneration into self-love.

"And I Stand," third in the series, ostensibly a declaration, has the impact of a prayer in its speaker's avowal not to kill his enemy, standing and gazing, instead, past "my enemy at Him." Noah, Samson, and Job, three personifications of a volatile man-god fulcrum, are considered for antithetical urges, their stories rephrased, until the final poem, "The Rightful One," confronts a divine visitation, a New Testament Christ to replace the Old Testament's paternal fierceness, full of forgiveness, "his hair long, face exhausted, eyes sad," with pardon again based on selfless parenthood: "Bless your son . . . / . . . And the Rightful One/ was gone and left a power to feel free." Redemption is not the reader's, however, ideal or otherwise, since boredom is the normal response when any dramatic conflict flattens out into a species of George Santayana's "animal faith," intimating that belief, in this case, is either forced or without sufficient doubt.

FIGURES OF THE HUMAN

Figures of the Human is free of such overt metaphysical gestures toward mental entropy, and more potent as a result. Its first section concentrates on those human figures whose crimes and tragedies populate the daily tabloids; it is tuned to the violence, urban and sudden, that Ignatow deems typical of modern life. A victim, for example, of a random, fatal assault in his own home is elegized in "And That Night." The poem's attitude is one of primitive awe: "You bring up a family in three small rooms,/ this crazy man comes along/ to finish it off." Note how the language refuses mandarin remoteness, and savors instead the vernacular tongue of victim and reporter. Another victim, a nine-year-old girl raped and thrown off a tenement roof, is the voice in "Play Again," which enables Ignatow to grant her (at the brink of poor taste) a sacrificial mission:

> The living
> share me among them. They taste
> me on the ground, they taste me
> in the air descending.

Salvation comes, saving the poem, with a beautiful death plea, as the child and author ask readers to play again

"and love me/ until I really die, when you are old/ on a flight of stairs." A poem called "Two Voices," echoing Alfred, Lord Tennyson, underscores the almost schizophrenic division in self of which the poet is always aware; the retreat into "Baudelaire, Whitman, Eliot" versus the need for active involvement in a present tense is translated into a suicidal leap into a winter lake, which is daring, if deadly, because it challenges "the weather," nature itself.

The rest of *Figures of the Human*, three further sections, varies its approach with frequent recourse to personal days and ways—"My mind is green with anxiety/ about money"—and surreal fantasies, one of which, the brief "Earth Hard," has a delicious Blakean air:

> Earth hard to my heels
> bear me up like a child
> standing on its mother's belly
> I am a surprised guest to the air.

Childhood is an issue in the title poem also, questing after "the childhood spirit" of a maddened beloved for the impulse that impels art as well: "Then are we loved, hand drawing swiftly/ figures of the human struggling awake." This is mission and theme combined, dream explicating experience, and a reply to the savage urge that brings back the "knife" in other poems.

RESCUE THE DEAD

Whatever else it accomplishes, *Figures of the Human* demonstrates the firm command Ignatow had obtained over his unique aesthetic, culminating, four years later, in *Rescue the Dead*, his finest, most consistently effective volume of verse, which is, at times, his most autobiographical. As the title avers, the major goal of the book is to revive the past, the personal dead and strangers and the dead in spirit. A handful of its poems have already been recognized for the virtuoso performances they are, among them "The Boss" and "The Bagel," first and last in the initial section, which is introduced by a "Prologue" that offers up parents "who had small/ comfort from one another." The larger arrangement of the section, which evolves from a bitter portrait of a sinning father into the playful absurdity of a man turning into a rolling bagel, has the additional weight of a small sequence about the father: five poems, beginning with the "Prologue" and concluding with his "Epi-

Critical Survey of Poetry

taph," which prays: "Forgive me, father,/ as I have forgiven you/ my sins."

The Freudian chain has thus been broken, at least for the moment, at least within the limits of the poem, and "Nourish the Crops," the next poem, can proceed to the other father, God, realizing self as the "product of you to whom all life/ is equal." The proposition here is the same frightening one, minus deity, facing Albert Camus and Jean-Paul Sartre in the 1950's, modern man's existential dilemma vis-à-vis an indifferent cosmos. In spite of conflicting religious restraints, for Ignatow the pivotal answer must be imagination, ceaseless reworkings of the Romantic heritage he had forsworn, and an alter ego in pursuit of a bagel, sounding like Williams and Wright, tumbling head over heels, "one complete somersault/ after another like a bagel/ and strangely happy with myself." In the title poem, the climb to redemption is pitted against paradox—"Not to love is to live"—and has the poet conceding his incapacity to choose love over life (survival, materialist wants) and asking that you "who are free/ rescue the dead." A powerful poem at the end of the second section, "The Room," reconfirms the crucial role of imagination in the battle against loneliness, emotional and physical, again seeking, with fluid lyricism, escape from loss of self and others—his bed constructed from "the fallen hairs/ of my love, naked, her head dry"—through a magical transformation, the persona flying around his dark room like a bat or angel.

The fourth section of *Rescue the Dead* is the weakest by far, its lapses made glaring by the general excellence of section three, which focuses on rituals of survival in breathless contrast to the violence of the real world (inner and outer), circling from the murder of innocence in England to a derelict, who returns, like "a grey-haired foetus," to his mother while asleep, and two ignored children in the "East Bronx," sharpening their "knives against the curb." The failure of the section stems from a stubborn determination to fashion vehicles of protest, blunt weapons to combat what is perceived as massive public wrongs, such as the Vietnam War and the Medgar Evers incident, and even contains a poem about "Christ" and dares add the coda of "In My Childhood," a facile memory of a yellow canary and a boy with an air gun. Returning to more complex private visions to tap a wellspring, the fifth section recoups some of the lost poetic

energy, humming appreciations, never without saving shadows, of a put-upon wife, a foraging bum, an old love, and so on. It peaks with "Omen," a sentimental grab for love from sylvan nature that beats false, but provides a smooth thematic entry to the sixth and final section of eleven poems about poetry, three of which are dedicated to admired fellow craftsmen, Denise Levertov, Marianne Moore, and Williams.

Like Stanley Kunitz, whom he closely resembles in his search for paternal, mystical salvation amid alien corn, Ignatow summons up Dante for validation in "Anew," commencing, "Dante forgot to say,/ Thank you, Lord, for sending me/ to hell." The apex of the sequence is "Walk There," an allegorical walk in a dark wood, full of fear, before a heaven is glimpsed: "Ahead, is that too the sky/ or a clearing?/ Walk there." The desire is credible and is honestly earned by prior struggles with private and public demons, but the poetry that inevitably concludes an Ignatow collection, mirroring Dante's *Paradiso*, never equals in intensity and metaphoric convolutions the engrossing journey through infernal regions that got him there.

In the year before his death, Ignatow looked back over this amazingly prolific period and decided that many poems not collected in his several volumes of those decades were worthy enough to be given a new life. Thus, in *At My Ease: Uncollected Poems of the Fifties and Sixties*, Ignatow gathered a rich second harvest.

FACING THE TREE

Facing the Tree is more of a mixed bag than its predecessors, sure of its technique and confident in voice, and including a growing fondness for prose poems, that most dangerous invitation to self-indulgence. The voice of "Reading the Headlines" mates, typically, personal and social anguish: "I have a burial ground in me where I place the bodies/ without fuss or emotion." Whimsy alternates with stark tragedy as the naïve but shrewd narrator reacts to an evil world by laboring to extract some psychological and spiritual truths from its surface madness, filtered, always, through the mesh of a receptive self. The poems that work efficiently, such as "Letter to a Friend," "My Own Line," "The Refuse Man," "Autumn," "In Season," and several untitled prose poems, are those which remember to keep near the taut edge of the parabolic methodology that Ignatow has perfected, avoiding the glibness and rhetorical excess that ruin so many others in the book, notably where they are attached to political frames, such as "My President Weeps" and "Now Celebrate Life and Death."

TREAD THE DARK

Tread the Dark is similarly confident in style and speech, but its obsession with death and the absence of adequate counter-moods numb the reader to its occasional brilliance and successes, such as "The Abandoned Animal," "Death of a Lawn Mower," "The Dead Sea," "The Forest Warden," "An Account in the Present Tense . . . ," "Midnight," and two untitled pieces, numbered 46 and 80. All the poems are numbered, stressing their author's conception of them as a series structured upon the leitmotif of death. In treading the dark, fighting off oblivion with imagination, the poet too often treads familiar waters, flounders into pretentiousness and embarrassing archness, appropriately reaching a nadir in "Epilogue," a short coda that has the persona, aware of being watched by trees ("tall gods") in his study, bow over his typewriter and start "the ceremony/ of a prayer." A year later, the publication of the highly charged *Sunlight* sequence demonstrated that the decline signaled by *Tread the Dark* was temporary.

WHISPER TO THE EARTH

Although not equal to Ignatow's strongest volumes, *Whisper to the Earth* is ripe with readiness, open to new modes, and at peace with the softer hues of twilight and autumn and the death they prefigure. Divided into five sections, the collection's first group of poems, with a single exception, approach nature directly, forsaking urbanscapes in favor of garden meditations upon apples and trees and stones, a strategy for resolving death fears, so that entering the grave will "be like entering my own house." In a poem for his daughter, "For Yaedi," Ignatow claims that when he dies he wants it said, "that I wasted/ hours in feeling absolutely useless/ and enjoyed it, sensing my life/ more strongly than when I worked at it." Elegies fittingly dominate the next two sections, but the ones for his father and mother—"Kaddish," "The Bread Itself," "A Requiem," and "1905"—can be counted among the most evocative poems he has ever written, regardless of their mellow reordering of the past to concentrate upon his parents' genuine gifts to him. The

father is forgiven by way of a comprehension of his own harsh youth in Russia, and the mother is celebrated as the "bread" that sustained him. Tension here is less important than the positive electricity of love heightening the language out of itself and its narrative solidity.

The fourth section, "Four Conversations," is the weakest series in the book, a sequence of dialogues that seems to lead toward Wallace Stevens, but its experimental boldness reflects credit upon Ignatow's resolve not to surrender to old age's penchant for self-parody and safe repetitions. In the final section, the prose poem holds sway, at its tightest in "I Love to Fly," which uses a dream to good effect. The climax is in "With Horace," an identification with the Roman poet that accepts the Sabine Farm wisdom of his retreat from the city to use the experience of his late years as a new tool for penetrating nature's rock hardness.

LATER POEMS

Death is once again center stage in *Shadowing the Ground*, which can be read either as a book-length poem or an ordered sequence of (untitled) poems built around a unifying theme. These sixty-five terse pieces, most only ten lines or fewer, reexamine past deaths of wife and parents and meditate on the poet's death to come. Ignatow's lonely, sagacious voice seems highly restrained, emotion checked by a lifetime of brooding wisdom. *I Have a Name* is a late return to a more characteristic manner, showing the aged poet still exercising a full range of powers. Finally, and posthumously, Ignatow left readers with *Living Is What I Wanted*. Written in the year preceding his death, these poems close a brilliant career in which a poet's courage to acknowledge and grapple with death through all life's turnings has taken him to the inevitable shore. As ever, Ignatow's writings hover between a stoic, intellectual detachment and an honest display of deep emotion.

OTHER MAJOR WORKS

SHORT FICTION: *The End Game and Other Stories*, 1996.

NONFICTION: *The Notebooks of David Ignatow*, 1973; *Open Between Us*, 1980; *The One in the Many: A Poet's Memoirs*, 1988; *Talking Together: Letters of David Ignatow, 1946 to 1990*, 1992.

BIBLIOGRAPHY

Emanuel, Lynn, and Anthony Petrosky. "It's Like Having Something in the Bank: An Interview with David Ignatow." *American Poetry* 3 (Winter, 1986): 64-85. This interview offers valuable insight into Ignatow's poetic philosophy. Ordinary life is his subject, and he tries to show it in a new way. Essential to understanding Ignatow.

Ignatow, David. *The Notebooks of David Ignatow.* Chicago: Swallow Press, 1973. Ignatow allows the reader into his creative process by means of these journals. He offers biographical details as well as insight into his philosophy of writing poetry.

_____. *The One in the Many: A Poet's Memoirs.* Middletown, Conn.: Wesleyan University Press, 1988. Ignatow presents his essays on poetry written over a period of four decades. In them, he reveals that he was obsessed with a single artistic quest: to uncover the human dimension beneath the technical structure of poetic theory. Valuable for any student of Ignatow.

Mazzaro, Jerome. *Postmodern American Poetry.* Urbana: University of Illinois Press, 1980. Mazzaro outlines Ignatow's work, as well as that of six other modern American poets. He includes biographical references and an index. A good, quick overview useful to any student.

Ray, David. "The Survivor's Art: The Notebook of David Ignatow." *Kansas Quarterly* 24/25 (1992/1993): 219-233. A detailed analysis of the demons that tormented Ignatow and fed his art. Ray's retrospective look at this volume is a springboard to a fine discussion of Ignatow's themes and of the creative process.

Sjoberg, Lief. "An Interview with David Ignatow." *Contemporary Literature* 28 (Summer, 1987): 143-162. Ignatow explains to Sjoberg the influence of Walt Whitman and William Carlos Williams on his poetry. Whitman, he says, wrote about everyday life, and Williams wrote in everyday speech. These two influences were Ignatow's salvation in the 1930's and through the 1950's, when the fashion in poetry was lofty abstraction.

Terris, Virginia R., ed. *Meaningful Differences: The Poetry and Prose of David Ignatow.* Tuscaloosa: University of Alabama Press, 1994. Though Terris is clearly an Ignatow partisan, she has gathered more than forty critical voices in a balanced, wide-ranging survey of critical opinion on Ignatow's work.

Wakoski, Diane, Linda M. Wagner, and Milton Hindus. "David Ignatow: Three Appreciations." *American Poetry* 3 (Winter, 1986): 35-51. Wakoski praises Ignatow's use of simple American language, as opposed to a more stylized British idiom. Wagner points out that Ignatow achieves the rhythms of spoken speech through idiomatic phrasing rather than colloquial word choice. Hindus explains the reason that Ignatow and his literary predecessors, William Carlos Williams and Walt Whitman, have been so rarely anthologized.

Edward Butscher,
updated by Philip K. Jason

GYULA ILLYÉS

Born: Rácegrespuszta, Hungary; November 2, 1902
Died: Budapest, Hungary; April 15, 1983

PRINCIPAL POETRY

Nehéz föld, 1928
Sarjúrendek, 1931
Hősökről beszélek, 1933
Szálló egek alatt, 1935
Rend a romokban, 1937
Külön világban, 1939
Összegyüjtött versei, 1940
Egy év, 1945
Osszes versei, 1947
Szembenézve, 1947
Válogatott versei, 1952
Egy mondat a zsarnokságról, 1956 (*One Sentence on Tyranny*, 1957)
Kézfogások, 1956
Új versek, 1961
Nem volt elég, 1962
Nyitott ajtó, 1963 (translation)
Dőlt vitorla, 1965
A költo felel: Válogatott versek, 1966

Poharaim: Összegyujtött versek, 1967

Fekete-fehér, 1968

Abbahagyott versek, 1971

Haza a magasban: Összegyüjtött versek, 1920-1945, 1972

Minden lehet, 1973

Teremteni: Összegyüjtött versek, 1946-1968, 1973

Különös testamentum, 1977

Összegyüjtött versei, 1977 (2 volumes)

Nyitott ajtók: Összegyüjtött versforditások, 1978 (2 volumes)

Közügy, 1981

What You Have Almost Forgotten: Selected Poems, 1999

Charon's Ferry: Fifty Poems, 2000

OTHER LITERARY FORMS

Although principally a poet, Gyula Illyés was also the author of significant prose and drama. Two of his most important prose works appeared in the 1930's: *Puszták népe* (1936; *People of the Puszta*, 1967), widely translated, is partly an autobiographical documentary and partly a sociography of Hungary's poverty-stricken peasantry; *Petőfi* (1936; English translation, 1973) is both a personal confession and a scholarly analysis of the great nineteenth century poet, Sándor Petőfi. Published late in Illyés's life, the essays collected in *Szellem és erőszak* (1978; spirit and violence), officially banned but published in the West in a facsimile edition, reflects his concern about the mistreatment of four million Hungarians living as minorities in countries neighboring Hungary. His principal plays deal with a search for lessons in Hungary's history.

Illyés also excelled as a translator of Louis Aragon, Ben Jonson, Robert Burns, Paul Éluard, Victor Hugo, Jean Racine, François Villon, and others; a collection of his translations was published in 1963 under the title of *Nyitott ajtó* (open door).

ACHIEVEMENTS

Gyula Illyés is internationally recognized as one of the leading poets of the century. French poet and critic Alain Bosquet wrote about him: "Only three or four living poets have been able to identify themselves with the soul of the century. Their genius burns in the Hungarian poet Gyula Illyés." The International Biennale of Poets in Knokke-le-Zoute, Belgium, awarded to him its Grand Prix in 1965, and the University of Vienna awarded to him the Herder Prize in 1970. He received two literary prizes in France: the Ordre des Art et Lettres in 1974 and the Grand Prize in 1978 from the Société des Poètes Français. In 1981, he was awarded the Mondello literary prize in Italy. In 1969, he was elected vice president of the International PEN Club. In Hungary, among many other awards, he was three times the recipient of the Kossuth Prize.

Apart from the highest critical acclaim, Illyés achieved the status of a national poet and an intellectual leader in Hungary and in Europe. His unbending loyalty to the downtrodden and his contributions in clarifying the most important issues of his times earned him an extraordinary moral authority.

BIOGRAPHY

Gyula Illyés was born into a family of poor farm workers on one of the large estates of a wealthy aristocrat. His grandfather was a shepherd and his father a mechanic; the joint efforts of his relatives were needed to

Gyula Illyés (© Hunyady József)

pay for his schooling in Budapest. At the end of World War I, the Austro-Hungarian monarchy collapsed, giving way to a liberal republic, which was taken over by a short-lived Communist regime. Illyés joined the Hungarian Red Army in 1919. After the old regime defeated the revolution, he fled to Vienna in 1920, then went to Berlin, and a year later to Paris. He attended the Sorbonne, studying literature and psychology, and he supported himself by tutoring and by working in a book bindery. His earliest poetry appeared in Hungarian émigré periodicals. During those years, he made the acquaintance of many young French poets, some of whom later became famous as Surrealists: Aragon, Éluard, and Tristan Tzara. In 1926, the political climate became more tolerant in Hungary, and Illyés returned. He worked as an office clerk and joined the circle connected with the avant-garde periodical *Dokumentum*, edited by Lajos Kassák. Some of his early poems caught the eye of Mihály Babits, a leading poet and senior editor of the literary periodical *Nyugat*, and in a short time, Illyés became a regular contributor to that outstanding modern literary forum.

Illyés's first collection of poems was published in 1928, followed by twelve other books of poetry and prose, resulting in literary prizes as well as critical and popular recognition during the next ten years.

Another decisive event in Illyés's life is best described by him:

I have arrived from Paris, being twenty-three-and-a-half years old. My new eyes saw a multitude of horrors when I looked around my birthplace. I had a deep and agonizing experience, I was outraged, shocked and moved immediately to action upon seeing the fate of my own people.

The result of this experience was *People of the Puszta*, a realistic personal account of the hardships and injustices that the poorest estate-servant peasants suffered. With this book, Illyés had joined the literary/political populist movement, which fought between the two world wars for the economic, social, educational, cultural, and political interests of the peasantry and, later, the working class as well.

In 1937, Illyés became one of the editors of *Nyugat*, and, after its cessation, he founded and edited its successor, *Magyar Csillag*.

After World War II, Illyés was offered leading literary and political positions and edited the literary periodical *Válasz* from 1946 to 1949, but as the Stalinist Communist Party, with the help of the occupying Soviet Army, enforced totalitarian control over the country, Illyés withdrew from public life. He continued to write, however, and his poems and plays created during these years of dictatorship address the issues of freedom, power, morality, and hope. His monumental poem *One Sentence on Tyranny*, written in the early 1950's but not published until 1956, was officially banned in Hungary; it became the emblem of the 1956 revolution. After the revolution was crushed by the Soviet Army, Illyés went into passive resistance, not publishing anything until the government's release, in 1960, of most jailed writers.

In the 1960's and 1970's, Illyés published some thirty books, including poems, plays, reports, essays, and translations. In his old age, his themes became increasingly universal, and he died at the height of his creative powers, addressing issues of vital concern not only to his nation but also to humanity at large.

ANALYSIS

Gyula Illyés's immense prestige and world renown were largely the result of his ability to integrate the philosophies and traditions of Eastern and Western Europe, the views and approaches of the rational intellectual and of the lyric dreamer, and the actions of *homo politicus* and *homo aestheticus*. In a 1968 interview, Illyés confided:

With all the literary genres with which I experimented I wanted to serve one single cause: that of a unified people and the eradication of exploitation and misery. I always held literature to be only a tool.

Five sentences later, however, he exclaimed:

I would forgo every single other work of mine for one poem! Poetry is my first, my primary experience and it has always remained that.

André Frenaud has remarked of Illyés that he is a poet ofdiverse and even contradictory impulses: a poet who can be

violent and sardonic, who lacks neither visions coming from deep within, nor the moods of sensuality. He knows the cowardice of man and the courage needed for survival. He knows the past and interrogates the future.

Illyés began his literary career in the 1920's under the influence of Surrealism and Activism. He found his original style and tone at the end of the 1920's and the beginning of the 1930's. Lyric and epic qualities combined with precise, dry, objective descriptions (whose unimpassioned tone is occasionally heated by lyric fervor) determine the singular flavor of his poetry.

NEHÉZ FÖLD AND SARJÚRENDEK

Illyés's first book of poems, *Nehéz föld* (heavy earth), strongly reflects his intoxication with Surrealism and other Western trends. His next collection, *Sarjúrendek*, represents a turning point in his art; in this volume, Illyés turned toward populism and *engagé* realism, although he still retained many stylistic features of the avant-garde.

Illyés's tone became increasingly deep and bitter, his themes historical, and his style more and more intellectual during the 1930's and 1940's. In this period, he wrote many prose works, most of which reflected on historical, social, and political themes. He did not publish any significant collection of new poetry between 1947 and 1956. During this time of harsh political repression, he wrote historical dramas in which he sought to strengthen his people's national consciousness by the examples of great patriots of the past.

Illyés's poetic silence ended in 1956 when he published a volume of poems titled *Kézfogások* (handshakes). This volume initiated another new phase for the poet: His style thereafter was more intellectual, contemplative, dramatic, and analytical. He never lost the lyric quality of his poetry, however, and the passionate lyricism of his tone makes the moral, ethical, and historical analysis of his poems of the next twenty-five years glow with relevance, immediacy, and urgency.

DŐLT VITORLA

A good example of this style is found in his collection *Dőlt vitorla* (tilted sail), published in 1965. This book contains a number of long poems—written in free verse—about his fellow writers and artists, amplifying their messages, identifying with their visions, and offering Illyés's conclusions. The volume also contains a number of prose poems. In his preface, Illyés gives his reasons for using this genre: He states that he wants "to find the most common everyday words to express the most complicated things. . . . To concentrate into a piece of creation all that is beautiful, good and true without glitter and pretention but with innovation and endurance."

Written in the middle 1960's to another writer, "Óda a törvényhozóhoz" ("Ode to the Lawmaker") analyzes the role of poets. The poet is "the chief researcher" who uncovers the future, "the progressive, the fighter, the ground breaker," a destroyer of surface appearances "who separates the bad from the good," who shows when the ugly is beautiful and when the virgin is a harlot. Such experimenters, such researchers, are the writers he celebrates: "They are the ones I profess as examples! They are the ones who signal the direction towards a tomorrow!" The tomorrow that these exemplary researcher-poets promote is one of pluralism and tolerance. In this poem, a passionate lyricist evokes a future which the rational intellectual already knows—a future that requires freedom combined with order. "Make laws, but living laws so that we [can] stay human." The poet demands recognition of shadings and nuances, of the "exception, which may be the rule tomorrow."

How can the individual relate to the modern powers of his world as well as realize his individual goals of freedom and humanity? The title poem of *Dőlt vitorla* offers a clue. "Look—when do mast and sail fly forward most triumphantly? When tilted lowest." The ancient Aesopian parable, about the reed that bows to the wind and survives while the proud oak tree breaks and dies, is given a new dimension in this poem: The boat flies forward while it heels low. The issue of relating to the ruling power structure—of surviving sometimes unbearable dictatorial pressures and of being able to realize oneself in spite of authoritarian inhumanities—has been a perennial problem in Hungary. Illyés's sailboat offers a possible solution to the dilemma of whether one should compromise or perish: It sways, bows, and bends, but using, instead of opposing, the forces of the wind, it dashes ahead.

ONE SENTENCE ON TYRANNY

Sometimes such a solution is not possible: The wind may be a killer hurricane. In totalitarian dictatorships, there is no escape. This is the conclusion of Illyés's devastating diagnosis in *One Sentence on Tyranny*. This 183-line dramatic sentence is a thorough and horrifying analysis of the nature of such total oppression. Tyranny permeates every minute of every hour. It is present in a lover's embrace and a wife's goodbye kisses; it is present not only in the torture chambers but also in the nursery schools, the churches, the parliament, and the bridal bed; it is in everything, so that, finally, man becomes tyranny himself. He creates it, and it stinks and pours out of him; it looks at him from his mirror. Where there is tyranny, all is in vain. In Illyés's poem, the metaphors of Franz Kafka have become dehumanizing and annihilating realities.

The opportunity of people to be happy and free, to be able to fulfill themselves, should not depend on power or brute force. What chance do the weak have? Illyés the lyric poet and the concerned humanist is at his best when he redefines strength and weakness in three long poems written in the 1960's.

In "Ditirambus a nőkhöz" ("Dithyramb to Women"), he contrasts the hard, sharp, strong and proud forms of being with the fragile, yielding, and soft forms, and he finds the latter ones stronger: "Not the stones and not the metals, but grass, loess, sedge became the protest." Not the fortresses but the twig, wax, and pen have carried humans so far. Not the weapons and the kings but the clay, the fur, the hide have become the leaders. Not the armored soldiers storming to victory but the loins and breasts, the singing and the spinning, the everyday-working and humanity-protecting women have become the strongest. "Good" strength is defined here not as the strength of force, weight, uncompromising boldness, and pride, but as the strength of flexibility, endurance, resilience, beauty, and love. The contrast is masterfully woven not only between the forceful and softly enduring but also between the boastfully heroic and the gray, everyday, silent endeavor. As Illyés emphasizes in the concluding lines of another poem, "Hunyadi keze" ("The Hand of Hunyadi"): "Cowardly are the people who are protected by martyrs alone. Not heroic deeds but daily daring, everyday, minute-by-minute courage saves men and countries."

This motif of quiet everyday work and courage gives new dimensions to Illyés's theme of strength in weakness; it provides depth to the idea, further developed in "Az éden elvesztése" ("The Loss of Paradise"), a mod-ern oratorio, a moral-political passion play about the chances of the average weak and powerless human individual to avoid the impending atomic cataclysm. After repudiating those who, because of naïveté, blind faith, fatalism, or determinism, accept the inevitability of an atomic war, Illyés argues with those who would capitulate to the threatening powers because of their feelings of weakness and powerlessness.

In his "Hymn of the Root," Illyés emphasizes that "Leaf and tree live according to what the root sends up to them to eat" and that "from the deepest depths comes everything that is good on this Earth." In a "Parable of the Stairs," he offers a concrete program of "everyday, minute-by-minute courage," by which the seemingly weak and powerless can win over the powerful, over dehumanization, over evil.

> Whenever we correct a mistake, that is a step. Whenever we dress a wound: one step. Whenever we reprimand a bossy person: one step. Whenever we do our job right without needing a reprimand: ten steps. To take a baby in one's arm, to say something nice to its mother. . . .

In the final lines of this oratorio, the prophet urges his people:

> When the day of fury comes,
> when the atom explodes,
> on that final day,
> before that terrible tomorrow,
> people let us dare to do
> the greatest deed:
> .   .   .   .   .   .
> let us begin here, from the depths
> by the strength of our faith,
> .   .   .   .
> let us begin life anew.

OTHER MAJOR WORKS

LONG FICTION: *Hunok Párizsban*, 1946.

PLAYS: *Ozorai példa*, 1952; *Fáklyaláng*, 1953; *Dózsa György*, 1956; *Malom a Séden*, 1960; *Kegyenc*, 1963; *Különc*, 1963; *Tiszták*, 1969; *Testvérek*, 1972; *Sorsválasztók*, 1982.

NONFICTION: *Petőfi*, 1936 (English translation, 1973); *Puszták népe*, 1936 (*People of the Puszta*,

1967); *Magyarok*, 1938; *Ebéd a kastélyban*, 1962; *Kháron ladikján*, 1969; *Hajszálgyökerek*, 1971; *Szellem és erőszak*, 1978; *Naplójegyzetek: 1977-1978*, 1991.

BIBLIOGRAPHY

Kolumbán, Nicholas, ed. *Turmoil in Hungary: An Anthology of Twentieth Century Hungarian Poetry*. St. Paul, Minn.: New Rivers Press, 1982. A collection of Hungarian poetry translated into English with commentary.

Smith, William Jan. Introduction to *What You Have Almost Forgotten*, by Gyula Illyés. Willimantic, Conn.: Curbstone Press, 1999. The well-known poet provides a substantial introduction to Illyés and his poetry.

Tezla, Albert. *An Introductory Bibliography to the Study of Hungarian Literature*. Cambridge, Mass.: Harvard University Press, 1964. Contains publication information and some commentary on Illyés's work.

_____. *Hungarian Authors: A Bibliographical Handbook*. Cambridge, Mass.: Harvard University Press, 1970. Extension of *An Introductory Bibliography to the Study of Hungarian Literature*, and is to be used in conjunction with that work.

Károly Nagy;
bibliography updated by the editors

ISSA

Kobayashi Yatarō
Born: Kashiwabara, Japan; June 15, 1763
Died: Kashiwabara, Japan; January 5, 1827

PRINCIPAL POETRY
Kansei kuchō, 1794
Kansei kikō, 1795
Kyōwa kuchō, 1803
Bunka kuchō, 1804-1808
Shichiban nikki, 1810-1818
Hachiban nikki, 1819-1821
Kuban nikki, 1822-1824
The Autumn Wind, 1957
A Few Flies and I, 1969
The Spring of My Life, and Selected Haiku, 1997

OTHER LITERARY FORMS
Although Issa is known primarily as one of the three great haiku poets, he also wrote prose—in *Chichi no shūen nikki* (1801; *Diary of My Father's Death*, 1992), a response to his father's death—and mixed prose and verse, or *haibun*, in *Oragu haru* (1819; *The Year of My Life*, 1960), an autobiographical account of his most memorable year.

ACHIEVEMENTS
Ezra Pound's recognition of the power of a single image which concentrates poetic attention with enormous force and his examination of the complexity of the Japanese written character led to an increasing awareness of the possibilities of haiku poetry for Western readers in the early part of the twentieth century. Combined with a growing interest in Oriental studies and philosophy, haiku offered an entrance into Japanese concepts of existence concerning the relationship of man and the natural world. Because the brevity of haiku is in such contrast to conventional ideas of a complete poem in the Western tradition, however, only the most accomplished haiku poets have been able to reach beyond the boundaries of their culture.

The most prominent among these are Bashō (1644-1694), Buson (1715-1783), and Issa. As William Cohen describes him, "in humor and sympathy for all that lives, Issa is unsurpassed in the history of Japanese literature and perhaps even in world literature." A perpetual underdog who employed humor as an instrument of endurance, who was exceptionally sensitive to the infinite subtlety of the natural world, and who was incapable of acting with anything but extraordinary decency, Issa wrote poetry that moves across the barriers of language and time to capture the "wordless moment" when revelation is imminent. More accessible than the magisterial Buson, less confident than the brilliant Bashō, Issa expresses in his work the genius that is often hidden in the commonplace. The definition of haiku as "simply what is happening in this place at this moment" is an apt emblem for a poet who saw humans forever poised between the timely and the timeless.

BIOGRAPHY

The poet known as Issa was born Kobayashi Yatarō in 1763 in the village of Kashiwabara, a settlement of approximately one hundred houses in the highlands of the province of Shinano. The rugged beauty of the region, especially the gemlike Lake Nojiri two miles east of the town, led to the development of a tourist community in the twentieth century, but the harsh winter climate, with snowdrifts of more than ten feet not uncommon, restricted growth in Issa's time. The area was still moderately prosperous, however, because there was a central post office on the main highway from the northwestern provinces to the capital city of Edo (now Tokyo). The lord of the powerful Kaga clan maintained an official residence which he used on his semiannual visits to the shogun in Edo, and a cultural center developed around a theater which featured dramatic performances, wrestling exhibitions, and poetry readings.

Issa was the son of a fairly prosperous farmer who supplemented his income by providing horse-pack transportation for passengers and freight. His composition of a "death-verse" suggests a high degree of literary awareness. In the first of a series of domestic tragedies, Issa's mother died when he was three, but his grandmother reared him with deep affection until Issa's father remarried. Although his stepmother treated him well for two years, upon the birth of her first child, she relegated Issa to a role as a subordinate. When she suggested that a farmer's son did not need formal schooling, Issa was forced to discontinue his study of reading and writing under a local master. When her baby cried, she accused Issa of causing its pain and beat him so that he was frequently marked with bruises.

According to legend, these unhappy circumstances inspired Issa's first poem. At the age of nine or so, Issa was unable to join the local children at a village festival because he did not have the new clothes the occasion required. Playing by himself, he noticed a fledgling sparrow fallen from its nest. Observing it with what would become a characteristic sympathy for nature's outcasts, he declared:

Come and play,
little orphan sparrow—
play with me!

The poem was probably written years later in reflection on the incident, but Issa displayed enough literary ability in his youth to attract the attention of the proprietor of the lord's residence, a man skilled in calligraphy and haiku poetry, who believed that Issa would be a good companion for his own son. He invited Issa to attend a school he operated in partnership with a scholar in Chinese studies who was also a haiku poet. Issa could attend the school only at night and on holidays—sometimes carrying his stepbrother on his back—when he was not compelled to assist with farm chores, but this did not prevent him from cultivating his literary inclinations. On one of the occasions when he was assisting his father by leading a passenger on a packhorse, the traveler ruminated on the name of a mountain that they were passing. "Black Princess! O Black Princess!" he repeated, looking at the snow-topped peak of Mount Kurohime. When Issa asked the man what he was doing, he replied that he was trying to compose an appropriate haiku for the setting. To the astonishment of the traveler, Issa proclaimed: "Black Princess is a bride—/ see her veiled in white."

Issa's studies were completely terminated when his grandmother died in 1776. At his stepmother's urgings, Issa was sent to Edo, thrown into a kind of exile in which he was expected to survive on his own. His life in the capital in his teenage years is a mystery, but in 1790 he was elected to a position at an academy of poetics, the Katsushika school. The school had been founded by a friend and admirer of Bashō who named it for Bashō's home, and although Issa undoubtedly had the ability to fulfill the expectations of his appointment, his innovative instincts clashed with the more traditional curriculum already in place at the school. In 1792, Issa voluntarily withdrew from the school, proclaiming himself Haikaiji Issa in a declaration of poetic independence. His literary signature literally translates as "Haikai Temple One-Tea." The title "Haikai Temple" signifies that he was a priest of haiku poetry (anticipating Allen Ginsberg's assertion "Poet is Priest!"), and as he wrote, "In as much as life is empty as a bubble which vanishes instantly, I will henceforth call myself *Issa*, or One Tea." In this way, he was likening his existence to the bubbles rising in a cup of tea—an appropriate image, considering the importance of the tea ceremony in Japanese cultural life.

During the next ten years, Issa traveled extensively, making pilgrimages to famous religious sites and prominent artistic seminars, staying with friends who shared his interest in poetry. His primary residence was in Fukagawa, where he earned a modest living by giving lessons in haikai, possibly assisted by enlightened patrons who appreciated his abilities. By the turn of the century, he had begun to establish a wider reputation and his prospects for artistic recognition were improving, but his father's final illness drew him home to offer comfort and support. His father died in 1801 and divided his estate equally between Issa and his half brother. When his stepmother contested the will, Issa was obliged to leave once again, and he spent the next thirteen years living in Edo while he attempted to convince the local authorities to carry out the provisions of his father's legacy. His frustrations are reflected in a poem he wrote during this time: "My old village calls—/ each time I come near,/ thorns in the blossom."

Finally, in 1813, Issa was able to take possession of his half of the property, and in April, 1814, he married a twenty-eight-year-old woman named Kiku, the daughter of a farmer in a neighboring village. Completely white-haired and nearly toothless, he still proclaimed that he "became a new man" in his fifties, and during the next few years, his wife gave birth to five children. Unfortunately, all of them died while still quite young. Using a familiar line of scripture that compares the evanescence of life to the morning dew as a point of origin, Issa expressed his sense of loss in one of his most famous and least translatable poems:

> This dewdrop world—
> yet for dew drops
> still, a dewdrop world

In May, 1823, Issa's wife died, but he remarried almost immediately. This marriage was not harmonious, and when the woman returned to her parent's home, Issa sent her a humorous verse as a declaration of divorce and as a statement of forgiveness. Perhaps for purposes of continuing his family, Issa married one more time in 1825, his bride this time a forty-six-year-old farmer's daughter. His wife was pregnant when Issa died in the autumn of 1828, and his only surviving child, Yata, was born after his death. Her survival enabled Issa's descendants to retain the property in his home village for which he had struggled during many of the years of his life.

In his last years, while he was settled in his old home, he achieved national fame as a haikai poet. His thoughts as a master were valued, and he held readings and seminars with pupils and colleagues. After recovering from a fairly serious illness in 1820, he adopted the additional title Soseibo, or "Revived Priest," indicating not only his position of respect as an artist and seer but also his resiliency and somewhat sardonic optimism. As a kind of summary of his career, he wrote a poem which legend attributes to his deathbed but which was probably given to a student to be published after his death. It describes the journey of a man from the washing bowl in which a new baby is cleansed to the ritual bath in which the body is prepared for burial: "Slippery words/ from bathtub to bathtub—/ just slippery words." The last poem Issa actually wrote was found under the pillow on the bed where he died. After his house had burned down in 1827, he and his wife lived in an adjoining storehouse with no windows and a leaky roof: "Gratitude for the snow/ on the bed quilt—/ it too is from Heaven." Issa used the word *Jodo* (Pure Land) for Heaven, a term which describes the Heaven of the Buddha Amida. Issa was a member of the largest Pure Land sect, the Shin, and he shared the sect's faith in the boundless love of the Buddha to redeem a world in which suffering and pain are frequent. His final poem is an assertion of that faith in typically bleak circumstances, and a final declaration of his capacity for finding beauty in the most unlikely situations.

ANALYSIS

The haiku is a part of Japanese cultural life, aesthetic experience and philosophical expression. As Lafcadio Hearn noted, "Poetry in Japan is universal as air. It is felt by everybody." The haiku poem traditionally consists of three lines, arranged so that there are five, seven, and five syllables in the triplet. Although the "rules" governing its construction are not absolute, it has many conventions that contribute to its effectiveness. Generally, it has a central image, often from the natural world, frequently expressed as a part of a seasonal reference, and a "cutting word," or exclamation that states or implies the poet's reaction to what he sees. It is the ultimate compression of poetic energy and often draws its strength from the unusual juxtaposition of image and idea.

It is very difficult to translate haiku into English without losing or distorting some of the qualities which make it so uniquely interesting. English syllables are longer than Japanese *jion* (symbol sounds); some Japanese characters have no English equivalent, particularly since each separate "syllable" of a Japanese "word" may have additional levels of meaning; a literal rendering may miss the point while a more creative one may remake the poem so that the translator is a traitor to the original. As an example of the problems involved, one might consider the haiku Issa wrote about the temptations and disappointments of his visits to his hometown. The Japanese characters can be literally transcribed as follows:

Furosato ya *yoru mo sawaru mo bara-no-hana*

(Old village : come-near also touch also thorn's-flowers)

The poem has been translated in at least four versions:

> At my home everything
> I touch is a bramble. (*Asataro Miyamori*)

> Everything I touch
> with tenderness alas
> pricks like a bramble. (*Peter Beilenson*)

> The place where I was born:
> all I come to—all I touch—
> blossoms of the thorn. (*Harold Henderson*)

> My old village calls—
> each time I come near,
> thorns in the blossom. (*Leon Lewis*)

Bashō's almost prophetic power and Buson's exceptional craftsmanship and control may be captured fairly effectively in English, but it is Issa's attitude toward his own life and the world that makes him perhaps the most completely understandable of the great Japanese poets.

His rueful, gentle irony, turning on his own experiences, is his vehicle for conveying a warmly human outlook which is no less profound for its inclusive humor. Like his fellow masters of the haiku form, Issa was very closely attuned to the natural world, but for him, it had an immediacy and familiarity that balanced the cosmic dimensions of the universal phenomena which he observed. Recognizing human fragility, he developed a strong sense of identification with the smaller, weaker creatures of the world. His sympathetic response is combined with a sharp eye for their individual attributes and for subtle demonstrations of virtue and strength amid trying circumstances. Although Issa was interested in most of the standard measures of social success (family, property, recognition), his inability to accept dogma (religious or philosophical) or to overlook economic inequity led him to a position as a semipermanent outsider no matter how successful he might be.

OBSERVER OF NATURAL PHENOMENA

Typically, Issa depicts himself as an observer in the midst of an extraordinary field of natural phenomena. Like the Western Romantic poets of the nineteenth century, he uses his own reactions as a measuring device and records the instinctive responses of his poetic sensibility. There is a fusion of stance and subject, and the man-made world of business and commerce occurs only as an intrusion, spoiling the landscape. What matters is an eternal realm of continuing artistic revelation, the permanent focus of humankind's contemplation: "From my tiny roof/ smooth . . . soft . . ./ still-white snow/ melts in melody." The poet is involved in the natural world through the action of a poetic intelligence which re-creates the world in words and images, and, more concretely, through the direct action of his participation in its substance and shape: "Sun-melted snow . . ./ with my stick I guide/ this great dangerous river." Here, the perspective ranges from the local and the minimal to the massively consequential, but in his usual fashion, Issa's wry overestimation of his actions serves to illustrate his realization of their limits. Similarly, he notes the magnified ambition of another tiny figure: "An April shower . . ./ see that thirsty mouse/ lapping river Sumida." Amid the vast universe, man is much like a slight animal. This perception is no cause for despair, though. An acceptance of limitations with characteristic humor enables him to enjoy his minuscule place among the infinities: "Now take this flea:/ He simply cannot jump . . ./ and I love him for it."

Because he is aware of how insignificant and vulnerable all living creatures are, Issa is able to invest their apparently comic antics with dignity: "The night was hot . . ./ stripped to the waist/ the snail enjoyed the moonlight." The strength of Issa's identification of the correspondence between the actions of human beings and animals enables him to use familiar images of animal behavior to comment on the pomposity and vanity of much human behavior. In this fashion, his poems have some of the satirical edge of eighteenth century wit, but Issa is much more amused than angry: "Elegant singer/ would you further favor us/ with a dance, O Frog?" Or if anger is suggested, it is a sham to feign control over something, because the underlying idea is essentially one of delighted acceptance of common concerns: "Listen, all you fleas . . ./ you can come on pilgrimage, o.k. . . ./ but then, off you git!" Beyond mock anger and low comedy, Issa's poems about his participation in the way of the world often express a spirit of contemplation leading to a feeling of awe. Even if the workings of the natural world remain elusive, defying all real comprehension, there is still a fascination in considering its mysterious complexity: "Rainy afternoon . . ./ little daughter you will/ never teach that cat to dance."

FORBIDDING NATURE

At other times, however, the landscape is more forbidding, devoid of the comfort provided by other creatures. Issa knew so many moments of disappointment that he could not restrain a projection of his sadness into the world: "Poor thin crescent/ shivering and twisted high/ in the bitter dark." For a man so closely attuned to nature's nuances, it is not surprising that nature would appear to echo his own concerns. When Issa felt the harsh facts of existence bearing heavily on him, he might have found some solace in seeing a reflection of his pain in the sky: "A three-day-old moon/ already warped and twisted/ by the bitter cold." Images of winter are frequent in Issa's poetry, an outgrowth of the geographical reality of his homeland but also an indication of his continuing consciousness of loss and discouragement. Without the abundant growth of the summer to provide pleasant if temporary distraction, the poet can-

not escape from his condition: "In winter moonlight/ a clear look/ at my old hut . . . dilapidated." The view may be depressing but the "clear look" afforded by the light is valuable, and in some ways, reassuringly familiar, reminding the poet of his real legacy: "My old father too/ looked long on these white mountains/ through lonely winters."

HOME AND FAMILY

Issa spent much time trying to establish a true home in the land in which he was born because he had a strong sense of the importance of family continuity. He regarded the family as a source of strength in a contentious and competitive environment and wrote many poems about the misfortune of his own family situation. Some of his poems on this subject tend to be extremely sentimental, lacking his characteristic comic stance. The depth of his emotional involvement is emphasized by the stark pronouncement of his query: "Wild geese O wild geese/ were you little fellows too . . ./ when you flew from home?" These poems, however, are balanced by Issa's capacity for finding some unexpected reassurance that the struggle to be "home" is worthwhile: "Home again! What's this?/ My hesitant cherry tree/ deciding to bloom?" Although nothing spectacular happens, on his home ground, even the apparently mundane is dressed in glory: "In my native place/ there's this plant:/ As plain as grass but blooms like heaven." In an understated plea for placing something where it belongs, recalling his ten-year struggle to win a share of his father's property, he declares how he would dispense justice: "Hereby I assign in perpetuity to wit:/ To this wren/ this fence." For Issa, the natural order of things is superior to that of society.

The uncertainty of his position with respect to his family (and his ancestors) made the concept of home ground especially important for Issa as a fixed coordinate in a chaotic universe. His early rejection by his stepmother was an important event in the development of an outlook that counted uncertainty as a given, but his sense of the transitory nature of existence is a part of a very basic strain of Japanese philosophy. The tangible intermixed with the intangible is the subject of many of his poems: "The first firefly . . ./ but he got away and I—/ air in my fingers." A small airborne creature, a figure for both light and flight, is glimpsed but not caught and held. What is seen, discernible, is rarely seen for long and never permanently fixed. The man who reaches for the elusive particle of energy is like the artist who reaches for the stuff of inspiration, like any person trying to grasp the animating fire of the cosmos. The discrepancy between the immutable facts of existence and the momentary, incredible beauty of life at its most moving is a familiar feature of Issa's work: "Autumn breezes shake/ the scarlet flowers my poor child/ could not wait to pick." Issa's famous "Dewdrop" haiku was also the result of the loss of one of his children, but in this poem too, it is the moment of special feeling that is as celebrated—a mixture of sadness and extraordinary perception.

SPIRITUALISM AND FAITH

The consolation of poetry could not be entirely sufficient to compensate for the terrible sense of loss in Issa's life, but he could not accept standard religious precepts easily either. He was drawn to the fundamental philosophical positions of Buddhist thought, but his natural skepticism and clear eye for sham prevented him from entering into any dogma without reservation. Typically, he tried to undermine the pomposity of religious institutions while combining the simplicity of understated spiritualism with his usual humor to express reverence for what he found genuinely sacred: "Chanting at the altar/ of the inner sanctuary . . ./ a cricket priest." Insisting on a personal relationship with everything, Issa venerated what he saw as the true manifestation of the great spirits of the universe: "Ah sacred swallow . . ./ twittering out from your nest in/ Great Buddha's nostril." The humanity of his position, paradoxically, is much more like real religious consciousness than the chanting of orthodox believers who mouth mindless slogans although unable to understand anything of Amida Buddha's message to humankind: "For each single fly/ that's swatted, *'Namu Amida/ Butsu'* is the cry." Above all, Issa was able to keep his priorities clear. One is reminded of the famous Zen description of the universe, "No holiness, vast emptiness," by Issa's determination to keep Buddha from freezing into an icon: "Polishing the Buddha . . ./ and why not my pipe as well/ for the holidays?" As Harold Henderson points out, "the boundless love attributed to Amida Buddha coalesced with his own tenderness toward all weak things—children and animals and insects." Even in those poems of a religious nature which

do not have a humorous slant there is a feeling of humility that is piety's best side: "Before the sacred/ mountain shrine of Kamiji . . ./ my head bent itself." In this poem, too, there is an instinctive response that does not depend on a considered position or careful analysis, thus paralleling Issa's reaction to the phenomena of the natural world, the true focus of his worship.

While most of Issa's haiku are like the *satori* of Zen awareness, a moment of sudden enlightenment expressed in a "charged image," Issa's "voice" also has a reflective quality that develops from a rueful realization of the profound sadness of existence. What makes Issa's voice so appealing in his more thoughtful poems is his expression of a kind of faith in the value of enduring. He can begin the new year by saying: "Felicitations!/ Still . . . I guess this year too/ will prove only so-so." Or he can draw satisfaction from triumphs of a very small scale: "Congratulations Issa!/ You have survived to feed/ this year's mosquitos." The loss of five children and his wife's early death somehow did not lead to paralysis by depression: "If my grumbling wife/ were still alive I just/ might enjoy tonight's moon." When his life seemed to be reduced almost to a kind of existential nothingness, he could see its apparent futility and still find a way to feel some amusement: "One man and one fly/ buzzing together in one/ big bare empty room." Or he could calculate the rewards of trying to act charitably, his humor mocking his efforts but not obscuring the fact that the real reward he obtained was in his singular way of seeing: "Yes . . . the young sparrows/ if you treat them tenderly—/ thank you with droppings."

SOMBER POEMS

There were moments when the sadness became more than his humor could bear. How close to tragic pessimism is this poem, for example: "The people we know . . ./ but these days even scarecrows/ do not stand upright." And how close to despair is this heartfelt lament: "Mother lost, long gone . . ./ at the deep dark sea I stare—/ at the deep dark sea." Issa is one of those artists whose work must be viewed as a connected body of creation with reciprocal elements. Poems such as these somber ones must be seen as dark seasoning, for the defining credo at the crux of his work is that his effort has been worthwhile. In another attempt at a death song, Issa declared: "Full-moon and flowers/ solacing my forty-nine/ foolish years of song." Since death was regarded as another transitory stage in a larger vision of existence, Issa could dream of a less troubled life in which his true nature emerged: "Gay . . . affectionate . . ./ when I'm reborn I pray to be/ a white-wing butterfly." He, knew, however, that this was wishful thinking. In his poetry, he was already a "white-wing butterfly," and the tension between the man and the poem, between the tenuousness of life and the eternity of art, energized his soul. As he put it himself, summarizing his life and art: "Floating butterfly/ when you dance before my eyes . . ./ Issa, man of mud."

OTHER MAJOR WORKS

NONFICTION: *Chichi no shūen nikki*, 1801 (*Diary of My Father's Death*, 1992).

MISCELLANEOUS: *Oragu haru*, 1819 (*The Year of My Life*, 1960); *Issa zenshū*, 1929; *Issa zenshū*, 1979 (9 volumes).

BIBLIOGRAPHY

Blyth, R. H. *Eastern Culture*. Vol. 1 in *Haiku*. Tokyo: Hokusheido Press, 1981. Discusses Issa in the context of the spiritual origins of haiku in Zen Buddhism and other Eastern spiritual traditions. Sees Issa as the poet of destiny, who saw his own tragic experiences as part of the larger motions of fate. Also interprets him both as a poet within Japanese culture and as a poet of universal appeal.

_____. *From the Beginnings Up to Issa*. Vol. 1 in *A History of Haiku*. Tokyo: Hokusheido Press, 1963. Devotes four chapters to Issa, presenting Issa's work in chronological order, ending in the haiku of Issa's old age. Includes interpretations of Issa's work plus examples of his portrayals of plants and the small creatures of the earth and of meaningful personal incidents, such as the deaths of his wife and children. Compares and contrasts him with the great haiku poet Bashō.

Kato, Shulchi. *A History of Japanese Literature*. Vol. 3. Translated by Don Sanderson. New York: Kodansha International, 1990. Includes a short chapter on Issa as a realistic, down-to-earth poet of everyday life and in the context of the Japanese society of the time.

MacKenzie, Lewis, trans. *The Autumn Wind: Selection of the Poems of Issa Kobayashui*. London: John Murray, 1957. Lengthy and informative introduction by the translator to a selection of Issa's haiku. MacKenzie assesses Issa's contributions to the haiku form, includes a detailed narrative of Issa's often troubled life, and comments on individual haiku. Includes both English translations of the poems and phonetic Japanese versions.

Yasuda, Kenneth. *Japanese Haiku: Its Essential Nature, History, and Possibilities in English, with Selected Examples*. Rutland, Vt.: Charles E. Tuttle, 1994. References to Issa and samples of his work in the context of a thorough analysis of the theory and practice of haiku.

Leon Lewis;
bibliography updated by Margaret Boe Birns

J

Women Poets was published in 1972 with a piece by William Stafford. Interviews with her can be found in periodicals such as *Thalia* and *New Letters*, and in the book *Our Other Voices: Nine Poets Speaking* (1991).

ACHIEVEMENTS

Marilyn Hacker once noted, "The work of Josephine Jacobsen is one of the best kept secrets of contemporary American literature. She is a coeval of Auden and Roethke, Bishop, Miles, and Rukeyser." Josephine Jacobsen has won numerous awards. She has received fellowships from Yaddo, the Millay Colony for the Arts, and the MacDowell Colony. Her prizes include an Academy of American Poets Fellowship, the Lenore Marshall Poetry Prize, and numerous O. Henry prizes for her short stories. *In the Crevice of Time: New and Collected Poems* (1995) won the Shelley Memorial Award and the William Carlos Williams Award. It was also a finalist for a National Book Award.

In 1971, Jacobsen was named a consultant in poetry to the Library of Congress, a position she kept until 1973, when she became a honorary consultant in American letters until 1979. She has also served on the literature panel for the National Endowment for the Arts and has belonged to such literary organizations as the Poetry Society of America and PEN Club. She has served on the poetry committee of the Folger Library in Washington, D.C. In 1988, she received the Shelley Memorial Award for lifetime service to literature. In 1994, Jacobsen was inducted into the American Academy of Arts and Sciences.

BIOGRAPHY

Canadian-born American poet Josephine Jacobsen was born in Cobourg, Ontario, Canada, in 1908. Her parents, Joseph Edward and Octavia Boylan, had two children, a daughter and a son. Jacobsen's father died when she was five; she lived with her mother and brother. The family moved around a lot, to such places as New York City, North Carolina, Atlantic City, and Connecticut. When she was fourteen, the family settled down near Baltimore, Maryland. Jacobsen was tutored for awhile, and then entered the Roland Park Country School. Even in these early years, writing poetry was important to her. She was enthralled with

JOSEPHINE JACOBSEN

Josephine Boylan
Born: Cobourg, Ontario, Canada; August 19, 1908

PRINCIPAL POETRY
Let Each Man Remember, 1940
For the Unlost, 1946
The Human Climate: New Poems, 1953
The Animal Inside, 1966
The Shade-Seller: New and Selected Poems, 1974
The Chinese Insomniacs: New Poems, 1981
The Sisters: New and Selected Poems, 1987
Distances, 1991
In the Crevice of Time: New and Collected Poems, 1995

OTHER LITERARY FORMS
Although most noted for her poetry, Josephine Jacobsen has also written short stories. Her collections include *A Walk with Raschid and Other Stories* (1978), *Adios, Mr. Moxley: Thirteen Stories* (1986), and *On the Island: New and Selected Stories* (1989). *What Goes Without Saying: Collected Stories of Josephine Jacobsen* was published by the Johns Hopkins University in 1996. Jacobsen has also produced works of dramatic criticism: *The Testament of Samuel Beckett* (1964; with William R. Mueller) and *Ionesco and Genet: Playwrights of Silence* (1968; also with Mueller). Her lecture before the Library of Congress on May 7, 1973, was printed up as *The Instant of Knowing*. This title later served for a compilation of her prose pieces, *The Instant of Knowing: Lectures, Criticism, and Occasional Prose* (1997), edited by Elizabeth Spires and published by the University of Michigan Press.

Jacobsen's poetry has been recorded by the Library of Congress. Her work has also been adapted to music and performed at the Baltimore Museum of Art. Her lecture *From Anne to Marianne: Some American* education and learning. Her one regret is that she never went to college: "At times, it just lacerates me to think of, oh, if I'd had that experience." After graduating from high school in 1926, Jacobsen joined a semiprofessional theater group. In 1932, she married Eric Jacobsen. They had one son and one grandson, who later died in a tragic accident.

As Elizabeth Spires has pointed out, "Unlike many of her contemporaries, Jacobsen has not pursued a particularly 'literary' life." Though she was publishing in periodicals such as *Poetry* and having small presses steadily publish volumes of her poetry, such as *Let Each Man Remember* in 1940*, For the Unlost* in 1946*, The Human Climate: New Poems* in 1953, and *The Animal Inside* in 1966, it was not until she got a job working with the Library of Congress in 1971, a job which lasted until 1973, that Jacobsen began to get the critical attention she deserved. In 1973, she was named an honorary consultant in poetry to the Library of Congress. In 1974, she published *The Shade-Seller: New and Selected Poems*, her first collection of new and selected poems. During this period, she and her family began to travel widely around the world, to such countries as Spain, Italy, Greece, Kenya, Haiti, and Grenada, where they made a second home. In 1975, Jacobsen received the first of many fellowships to Yaddo. She claimed it is at Yaddo and other writing colonies that she got most of her writing done. In 1978, Jacobsen published her first volume of short stories, *A Walk with Raschid and Other Stories.*

In 1981, she published *The Chinese Insomniacs: New Poems.* This was followed in 1987 with *The Sisters: New and Selected Poems*, which was nominated for a National Book Award and won the Lenore Marshall Poetry Prize.

The 1990's brought her even more critical attention. In 1994, she was inducted into the American Academy of Arts and Letters. In 1995, she published *In the Crevice of Time: New and Collected Poems.* This volume won several awards, including the Shelley Memorial Award and the William Carlos Williams Award.

Even with this attention, she and her work are not as well known as many of her contemporaries—those who sought literary careers and led literary lives. Jacobsen never taught and kept to her own standard of measure-

Josephine Jacobsen (© William L. Klender)

ment: "I have not tried to establish a reputation on any grounds but those of my poetry." She continued to write and publish into the twenty-first century; in April, 2001, *The New Yorker* published one of her poems.

ANALYSIS

Josephine Jacobsen is a writer who wants to be instructed by everything that is in the world. She wants to learn the lessons of time in order to see what, if anything, can survive time's natural ally, death. She is an observer of nature, of culture, and perhaps most of all, of human behavior. Joyce Carol Oates writes that Jacobsen's work "attempts to calibrate, in exquisite, polished and unfailingly intelligent language, the wonders and horrors of the interior landscape." Even the puzzlement of sleep, or lack of sleep, can induce a crisp response, a reason for writing. In her poetry, there is seldom the flash of the screaming image or the pouring forth of raw feeling. She is not a confessional poet, and yet she is smartly modern and curiously enduring, even if not widely known. She is protean; she is a traveler in her thirst for knowledge. Laurence Lieberman states that she is "gifted with the power to get outside her own personality and assume the identity of the subject that absorbs her." Her use of irony and sharp wit can lead to a certain detachment. Yet her goal is to invite the reader into the world, to see it clearly for the first time—as if for all time.

In *In the Crevice of Time* she has sifted through her own work, hewing to a rigorous standard by which she means to preserve a record of what poems she thinks should last. The poems are sorted around years and decades, not titles of former collections, as if part of one large book—a continuous dialogue with the reader.

"LINES TO A POET," "GENTLE READER," AND "THE MONOSYLLABLE"

Throughout her career, Jacobsen has struck a cautionary tone concerning the poet's responsibility toward his or her craft, readers, and other poets. Poems such as "Lines to a Poet," "Gentle Reader," and "The Monosyllable" seem to explore and state Jacobsen's ethics about the craft, purpose, and result of making a poem.

In "Lines to a Poet," the opening line, "Be careful what you say to us now" has the beguiling reversal of the audience instructing the poet. The authority and puck are Frost-like in tone. Yet the world revealed is urban, not rural. Street lamps, jagged windows, and a fountain litter the landscape, not to mention a dead body.

A poem such as "Gentle Reader," wherein the poet is both audience and writer, looks into night thoughts "Late in the night when I should be asleep/ under the city stars" and finds comfort and ecstasy in literature's embrace. Jacobsen's refined yet complex tastes lead her to poets who are "dangerous and steep." Her fellow companions seem to be Emily Dickinson—"O God, it peels me, juices me like a press"—and James Joyce: "saying like Molly, yes, yes, yes O yes." Reading is a sexual orgy that can stamp out dust, death, and time, if only for a spell—if only until sleep or morning comes.

"The Monosyllable" shows the poet isolated yet resplendent in a world of language: "One day/ she fell/in love with its/ heft and speed." Each syllable of sound can be slow or fast, tenor or bass. Yet the outside world, coupled with the necessities of craft, intrudes upon her solipsistic, light-as-a-cloud state: "With it, she said,/ I may,// if I can,/ sleep; since I must,/ die." The one-note "rise" at the end (or bottom) is affirming yet lonely.

"LET EACH MAN REMEMBER"

This early poem, an example of Jacobsen's formal style, also serves as the title to her first collection of poetry. Though it lacks the spare elegance of her more mature work, the poem shows many of Jacobsen's major themes. The scene is "a terrible hour in early morning." This light eventually wakes each man. It can be the light of knowing; ironically, it is also the light each man will again see "when he is at peace in the night." Each man must face his own death. Jacobsen offers little comfort, yet her point is not to despair. Whatever equipment is brought to the battle, whatever character is possessed, people can face what they must with courage because of this lesson learned: "Let each man remember, who opens his eyes to that morning,/ How many men have braced them to meet the light."

"THE SHADE-SELLER"

This poem served as the title poem for her 1974 collection of poetry. Its locale is something out of a Paul Bowles short story, with visitors or tourists stopped by a native who asks a question that is potentially rescuing but has sinister undertones: "'Sombra?' (shadow)" Foregoing a rhyme scheme, Jacobsen instead uses a consistent three-line stanza with a one- or two-word first line. The poem's energy pivots upon the word "Sometimes." In a swift reversal, a day scene is transformed into a night dream—where the dream seems also about the tourist or visitor. However it is she, not the native, who uses the word "sombra." A primeval violence seems to lurk close to the surface, all out of an innocent question. Above all, the poem insists upon its own exact articulations and phrasings.

"IN THE CREVICE OF TIME," "SOFTLY," AND "READING ON THE BEACH"

"In the Crevice of Time," the title poem to Jacobsen's 1995 collection, artistic desire is given early form by the crude representations of the "cave man." His methods and compositions may be different, yet his shaman-like efforts are motivated by the same forces that guide humans' postmodern efforts and trouble their minds: "the knowledge of death, and time the wicked thief,/ and the prompt monster of foreseeable grief." The steady hand paints the pictures of violence and sorrow. It is an act of faith and celebration. The true poet is an archaeologist and preserver of cultural memory.

In "Softly," everywhere people step, they make contact with the dead, even if they do not know it. The poem instructs the reader to know humans' place in this world: "in respect of that fraternity." Without this, one is lost, more lost than the unknown dead. To understand this is to know that people walk with the dead, not just over them. The billions of people who are alive now are miniscule in number compared to the countless dead, who almost seem to make the ground move and breathe.

In "Reading on the Beach" contact with the past is turned into a living act. Through the cold interstices of the universe, through the foam of time itself, people can travel—through the habitual act of reading—and be touched and renewed by the glow of past creations: "On Vasari's foxed page my hand is warmed."

OTHER MAJOR WORKS

SHORT FICTION: *A Walk with Raschid and Other Stories*, 1978; *Adios, Mr. Moxley: Thirteen Stories*, 1986; *On the Island: New and Selected Stories*, 1989; *What Goes Without Saying: Collected Stories of Josephine Jacobsen*, 1996.

NONFICTION: *The Testament of Samuel Beckett*, 1964 (with William R. Mueller); *Ionesco and Genet: Playwrights of Silence*, 1968 (with Mueller).

EDITED TEXT: *From Anne to Marianne: Some American Women Poets*, 1972.

MISCELLANEOUS: *The Instant of Knowing: Lectures, Criticism, and Occasional Prose*, 1997 (Elizabeth Spires, editor).

BIBLIOGRAPHY

Jacobsen, Josephine. "The Mystery of Faith: An Interview with Josephine Jacobsen." Interview by Evelyn Prettyman. *New Letters* 53, no. 4 (Summer, 1987). In this engaging interview, Jacobsen talks about her personal life, her religious faith, and certain themes found within her poems.

Mason, David. *Hudson Review* 49, no. 1 (Spring, 1996). This review of *In the Crevice* praises Jacobsen for the high quality of her writing throughout her long career.

Osterhaus, Joe. Review of *In the Crevice of Time*, by Josephine Jacobsen. *Boston Review* 20, no. 6 (December/January, 1995). This favorable review discusses Jacobsen's 1995 collection of poems. Osterhaus notes the lack of critical attention given her work and suggests reasons why this is so. He argues that Jacobsen's work deserves to be much better known.

Reeve, F. D. Review of *In the Crevice of Time*, by Josephine Jacobsen. *Poetry* 170, no. 1 (April, 1997). This review praises *In the Crevice of Time* and notes that Jacobsen has continued to write quality poetry.

Shaw, Robert B. Review of *The Sisters: New and Selected Poems*, by Josephine Jacobsen. *Poetry* LL11, no. 1 (April 4, 1988). This short but positive review is by a noted critic of contemporary American poetry.

Spires, Elizabeth. "Joy and Terror: The Poems of Josephine Jacobsen." *New Criterion* 14, no. 3 (November, 1995). This article uses *In the Crevice of Time* to look at Jacobsen's entire career. Spires argues for, and discusses the meanings of, several of Jacobsen's major poems.

Robert W. Scott

RANDALL JARRELL

Born: Nashville, Tennessee; May 6, 1914
Died: Chapel Hill, North Carolina; October 14, 1965

PRINCIPAL POETRY

"The Rage for the Lost Penny," in *Five Young American Poets*, 1940
Blood for a Stranger, 1942
Little Friend, Little Friend, 1945
Losses, 1948
The Seven-League Crutches, 1951
Selected Poems, 1955
The Woman at the Washington Zoo, 1960
The Lost World, 1965
The Complete Poems, 1969

OTHER LITERARY FORMS

An important critic and teacher of literature as well as a poet, Randall Jarrell published critical essays, translations, children's books, and a novel. His first book of criticism, *Poetry and the Age* (1953), examines the function of the poet in modern society, the nature of criticism, and the work of John Crowe Ransom, Wallace Stevens, Marianne Moore, and William Carlos Williams. Direct, witty, and sometimes harsh commentary in these essays aims at expanding the appreciative faculty in its broadest sense. The next collection, *A Sad Heart at the Supermarket* (1962), examines values and literature, including the American obsession with consumption. *The Third Book of Criticism* (1969), collected posthumously, includes discussions of Wallace Stevens, Robert Graves, W. H. Auden, Robert Frost, Russian novels, and American poetry since 1900. Close reading, Freudian analysis, myth interpretation, and religious considerations are features of Jarrell's method. His translations include *The Golden Bird and Other Fairy Tales of the Brothers Grimm* (1962) and *Faust, Part I* (1976), as well as other works for children and adults. Jarrell's novel, *Pictures from an Institution* (1954), presents life in an academic community from a satirical point of view. His children's books are *The Gingerbread Rabbit* (1964). *The Bat-Poet* (1964), and *The Animal Family* (1965).

Randall Jarrell (© Philippe Halsman)

ACHIEVEMENTS

Randall Jarrell's reputation as an artist and critic spans a writing career of thirty-three years. Initially recognized as a poet of World War II, Jarrell received a Guggenheim Post-Service Award in 1946. He also served as literary editor of *The Nation*, visiting lecturer at the Salzburg Seminar, and visiting fellow in creative writing at Princeton. Awarded a second Guggenheim Fellowship in 1963, he served as a chancellor of the Academy of American Poets and a member of the National Institute of Art and Letters. One of his collections of poetry and translations, *The Woman at the Washington Zoo*, won the National Book Award for Poetry in 1961. He served as U.S. poet laureate from 1956 to 1958.

Jarrell's chief contribution to the poetry of the twentieth century is his insistence that the experience of ordinary people is worth exploring to discover truth. His work reflects a determination to communicate everyday experience in a language and a form that speaks to the general reader as well as to the literary scholar.

BIOGRAPHY

Randall Jarrell spent his youth in Tennessee and California, living with his grandparents in Hollywood for a time when his parents separated. Although his family expected him to go into his uncle's candy business, Jarrell enrolled in psychology at Vanderbilt University, where he met the poet and critic John Crowe Ransom and, through him, other members of the waning Fugitive movement, including Robert Penn Warren, Allen Tate, and Donald Davidson. In 1937, Jarrell and his associate Peter Taylor followed Ransom to Kenyon College, where Jarrell began a lifelong association with Robert Lowell. During this period, Jarrell also completed work for his M.A. degree in literature, including a critical thesis on A. E. Housman under the direction of Donald Davidson.

Jarrell began his career as a professor at the University of Texas in Austin, where he met Mackie Langham, who became his wife in 1940. He enlisted in a ferry-pilot training program soon after Pearl Harbor, but actually began his military career as a private in the Army Air Corps. He served as a celestial navigation tower operator at Chanute Field in Illinois and Davis-Monthan Field in Arizona. After the war he taught at Sarah Lawrence College and then at the Women's College of the University of North Carolina in Greensboro. In the summer of 1948, Jarrell traveled to Europe, teaching American civilization at the Salzburg Summer Seminar. In 1951 Randall and Mackie Jarrell separated, and in 1952 they were divorced. Jarrell married Mary von Schrader late in 1952.

Jarrell was hospitalized briefly for a nervous disorder in 1965. He continued to teach at the University of North Carolina in Greensboro until October of that year, when he was struck and killed by an automobile in Chapel Hill, North Carolina.

ANALYSIS

Randall Jarrell's poetry speaks with intelligence and humanity about the problem of change as it affects men and women in the twentieth century. Often using the motif of a dreamer awakening in an unfamiliar world, Jarrell probes the experience of each speaker to discover enduring truths, however bleak they may be. Although the speakers in his poems learn that the difference between innocence and experience is often bewilderment and pain, they also express a sense of dignity and affirmation. Whether the focus is on a soldier facing death, a mother relinquishing her son, or a lonely woman wandering in a zoo, Jarrell's poems achieve a balance between the common experience of humanity and the suffering of the individual.

From the beginning of his career, Jarrell confronted the necessity that opposes human desires. In early works such as "For an Emigrant" and "The Refugees," he acknowledges the enormous isolation that engulfs hopeful arrivals gaining their freedom only to endure without identity in their new homeland. On a larger scale, Jarrell also anticipates the self-destructive force of humankind in poems such as "The Automaton" and "The See-er of Cities," in which archetypal death figures hover on the horizons of civilization. Jarrell's lasting concern, however, is the individual's search for meaning in a world of change and death. In "90 North," a poem following the pattern of the dreamer awakening to the world of experience, a child secure in bed at night dreams of discovering the North Pole. Envisioning himself as an adult explorer, the lone survivor of his party, the child reaches his goal only to find darkness and cold. This experience of emptiness and death becomes for him the truth he sought: "Nothing comes from nothing . . ./ Pain comes from the darkness/ And we call it wisdom. It is pain." Next, the child's dream is juxtaposed with an adult's dream in which North has no meaning, for the adult realizes that the dark world of dream is the final reality of humankind's experience, the meaninglessness acceptable only to the unconscious and terrifying to the conscious explorer of existence. A deep-sea diver makes a similar journey in "The Iceberg," finding ultimate annihilation in the "sick ambiguous wisdom of the sea" and surfacing to observe the many faces of the great berg melting as he loses consciousness.

LITTLE FRIEND, LITTLE FRIEND

In his second collection, *Little Friend, Little Friend*, Jarrell's presentation of those affected by World War II reflects the same concern with the extremes of psychological experience, whether at first hand or vicariously. In the war poems, specific characters and settings provide a structural basis and blank verse provides the medium for the voices. In "2nd Air Force," a mother visiting her son at an air base senses the necessary detachment of the young soldiers preparing their bombers, "hopeful cells/ heavy with someone else's death." She knows that her son, like the others, may as easily be a victim, and she ponders whether all her years of hope and care "meant this?" In the course of her meditation, she sees in her imagination the crash of her son in a burning plane; the distress call "little friend," Jarrell's title for the book, is repeated without hope of the young pilot's survival. "Losses," one of the most famous poems in the collection, voices the confusion of young soldiers for whom death has yet no personal meaning. They are amazed when members of their group disappear during training, since ordinary accidents lack the heroism expected in wartime. In their view, "it was not dying: everybody died," and surely they expected more of the experience than to die "like aunts or pets or foreigners."

Even in battle over the unfamiliar cities of the enemy, the youths still fail to comprehend the meaning of their end. The problem, as Jarrell's simple, colloquial speaker addresses it, is that "When we left high school nothing else had died/ For us to figure we had died like." Their dream of life failed to allow for personal experience of death; the cities they bomb are no more to them than names studied in geography class at school.

Jarrell's awareness of the child within each fighting man appears also in "The State" and "The Death of the Ball Turret Gunner," often anthologized for their dramatic appeal. The speaker of the first understands the power of government through the loss of his family. He begins, "When they killed my mother it made me nervous," continuing to lament the loss of his sister, and finally his cat; their disappearance causes the death of his consciousness, underscored by the simple frantic expression of a child. The speaker of "The Death of the Ball Turret Gunner" endures a cycle of birth to death in the course of his service to the "State." Awakening to discover himself in the rotating turret of a fighting plane "six miles from earth, loosed from its dream of life," his nightmare of reality ends violently as it began, but his voice persists: "When I died they washed me out of the turret with a hose." A poem recording a similar awakening with greater detail and tension, "A Pilot from the Carrier," describes a flier's escape from his burning plane and his lengthy parachute descent. Imagery of fire and ice effectively captures the intensity of his struggle to free himself from the "blazing wheel" of the cockpit. As the ball turret gunner falls into the belly of the State, so the pilot descends toward the warmth of earth, its sunlight and stillness contrasting with his frenzied escape. As he hangs suspended over the sea, his new perceptions, "the great flowering of his life," create a sense of detachment and calm. The brilliant gleam of his burning plane as it reaches the water reveals his location to an enemy plane so that he recognizes the approach of death as clearly as if he were "reading a child's first scrawl." In his last moments he learns the lesson of his own vulnerability in the unreasoning natural world. As a bombardier realizes in "Siegfried," death simply comes: "It happens as it does because it does."

The difficulty of reconciling a moral perspective with the life of war is the subject of "Eighth Air Force,"

one of Jarrell's best-known poems. Civilian life and battle merge for the men of this force that bombed continental targets from bases in Britain. Having the opportunity for some domestic comforts, the men groom themselves, keep pets, and even cut flowers. As they lounge, playing cards and counting up their missions, are they murderers because they have fulfilled their duty the day before? The persona delivers no harsh judgment on these whom he observes, for he has been one of them and has survived. As Pilate offered Christ, so he offers these figures for whom he has suffered and lied in his dreams. As he sees it, the guilt must be widely shared: "Men wash their hands, in blood, as best they can." Actor and victim become arbitrary designations once the process of war begins. In this view, to "behold the man" carries complex contradictory associations. The men are saviors of Europe, sinners against their own consciences, and scapegoats for others' blame. As the speaker shares their role, the reader must evaluate the speaker's final judgment that he "finds no fault in this just man," a composite symbol for the Eighth Air Force and humanity itself.

Jarrell also deals with the problems of accepting violence and death as a part of life in "Burning the Letters," portraying the wife of a pilot killed in the Pacific. Her husband died a fiery death, and now, several years later, she burns his letters as a sign of relinquishment. Jarrell notes that she was once a Christian, and, in her meditation, imagery of her husband's death mingles continually with imagery of Christ as she struggles to reconcile the paradox of life exchanged for death. In the context of her loss, Christ appears as a flame and a bird of prey seeking the hidden lives of those who dwell in darkness; then they turn on him, drawing from his life both bread and blood. Entering her dream, the woman sees herself as an aging child, clutching at the Christ figure who devours his own body before flickering away in the darkness. In addition to identifying the death of her husband with the death of Christ, she also recalls the sea burial of her husband in terms of the secretive burial of Christ's body. Like those who buried Christ, and those who bury the dead at sea, she attempts to bury her dead in flames. Although she chooses life for herself, her final prayer is addressed to the grave. Her acceptance of the death of her husband points toward a final emptiness and negation; in this nightmare of experience she acknowledges the same end discovered by the dreaming child in "90 North."

If human experience converges ultimately in isolation, emptiness, and darkness, where is the life men expect to have lived? Dreams also carry out this function in Jarrell's poems. "Absent with Official Leave" records the dream life of a soldier who finds his only protection from painful experience in sleep. There he achieves identity beyond his number and enjoys relationships not controlled by authority. After the lights dim, he enters the larger world "where civilians die/ Inefficiently, in their spare time, for nothing." Curved roads, contrasting sharply with the grids of army life, lead into a pastoral atmosphere where hunters seek birds in sporting fashion. In a cottage, the soldier visualizes the careful work of loving women "tending slow small fires." Their presence signals a transition to the "charmed" world of a fairy tale, where the soldier becomes a bear sheltered by Snow White and Rose Red as snow falls in the form of gentle blossoms. Negative forces appear, also, in the shape of accusing eyes and "grave mysterious beings" from his past, who represent the causes that justify war. Although they mourn his fate hypocritically at best, in his dream they grant him justification, signifying the love that he longs to experience. The poem reflects Jarrell's interest in the fairy tale and myth as a means of wish-fulfillment connected with the unconscious. The dreamer awakes, however, to the darkness of his fellow soldiers. A fuller development of the conflict between the fairy-tale world of dream and the painful nature of reality is "The Marchen," dramatizing men's desires to live and rule over an obstacle-filled environment.

THE SEVEN-LEAGUE CRUTCHES

While many critics believe that Jarrell found his most effective subject in the turmoil of war, his interest in the folktale stimulated a series of meditative poems in the collection *The Seven-League Crutches*. In the well-known poem "A Girl in a Library," Jarrell considers the outlook of a modern young coed napping in the library. Although she is no intellectual (her subjects are home economics and physical education), she too is a dreamer, with the simplicity of a kitten. Unaware of the power that the library offers in terms of art or science,

she rests secure in the method of her modern studies of function and technique. The speaker who observes her, however, recognizes her potential as a woman of virtue and intelligence such as Alexander Pushkin's Tatyana Larina, if she should ever awake from her "sleep of life." Her courses in food preparation and exercise will surely not arouse the soul within her, which "has no assignments/ neither cooks/ Nor referees." The mythic self locked within her, however, balances the speaker's judgment of her superficial dreams and pursuits. Two earlier poems that reflect similar needs among young students are "Children Selecting Books in a Library" and "The Carnegie Library, Juvenile Division." In these poems, children seek intellectual transformation, unknowingly, in the imaginative world of myth and fairy tale, in contrast with the older girl, who will never be significantly changed by anything in the library. She will, however, carry out the rituals of love and suffering that the speaker anticipates in his allusions to the Corn King and Spring Queen of the ancient myths.

Jarrell's interest in the psychology of the fairy tale also appears in several reworkings of well-known works. "A Quilt Pattern" incorporates the plot of "Hansel and Gretel" in a child's dream that forms the narrative line of the poem, enriched with allusions to the Fall of Genesis. Hansel and Gretel are renamed "Good Me and Bad Me" to underscore the psychological aspects of the story. Similarly, Jarrell's version of "Cinderella" portrays her as an ash girl rejecting the world in favor of an "imaginary playmate," the godmother. This Cinderella indulges herself in fantasies that are destructive in the end. She moves from the fireside of her childhood to the furniture of marriage and family life, then finally into the fires of Hell, where she is again happy in isolation from reality. In like manner, Jarrell deals with the other side of fairy tales in "The Sleeping Beauty: Variation of the Prince" and "La Belle au Bois Dormant." In the first reworking of the tale, Jarrell proposes a new ending in which the prince does not awaken the princess with his kiss, but determines to sleep on eternally with her, thus achieving a truly permanent union. The story also embodies a death wish—the desire for an unbroken peace—and a rejection of sexual fulfillment. In "La Belle au Bois Dormant," Jarrell uses the sleeping beauty story in a perverse way to present a woman who has been murdered and dismembered by her lover. The poems are characteristic of Jarrell in the theme of a lonely death without transcendence or hope, but the characters lack the grounding in a human context that enhances Jarrell's best work.

"The Woman at the Washington Zoo"

"The Woman at the Washington Zoo," one of Jarrell's most powerful treatments of human loneliness, reflects the intensity of experience typical of his poetry. An aging woman finds herself envying the caged specimens she observes for the attention they receive, while she remains invisible among the sightseers. Women pass her in brightly colored saris corresponding to the dramatic clothing of the leopard in his cage. The navy print she wears, however, receives no attention, no complaints, and entraps her as surely as iron bars imprison an animal body. The tall columns of Washington serve the same function, in fact, separating the lonely woman from the other workers whom she passes. Her inner cries burst out in frustration at the world's indifference to her suffering. In desperation she covets the experience of violence she sees as the animals devour their meat. Identifying with the offal rejected by all but the vulture, the old woman imagines the hope of a magical transformation and release. Calling out to this ugliest of birds, she visualizes herself among the animal kingdom with man as the ruler: "You know what I was,/ You see what I am: change me, change me!" In the impossibility of her outward renewal is the necessity that frustrates hope; in the expression of her need is release and affirmation of self. Jarrell's poem gives utterance to the suffering of the woman as a type and as an individual, providing a wider recognition of her existence and of the human need for inner change and transformation through love.

The Lost World

Jarrell's last volume of poetry, *The Lost World*, emphasizes the themes of his maturity: aging, loneliness, loss, and the dreamworld where every man is a child. "Next Day," for example, is narrated by a lonely middle-class woman who has suddenly recognized her passage into old age. Her material and social success far surpass that of the woman at the zoo, but she is equally unhappy. The title of the poem refers to the woman's vision of herself in the mirror the day after attending the funeral of a friend her age. In plain language and a contemporary American setting, Jarrell presents ordinary experience with great psychological intensity.

The poems of the final collection also treat the experiences of pain and loss with an affirmative note, for especially in these poems Jarrell develops the power of the dreamworld as real, if only in a metaphorical sense. In "The Lost Children," "The Lost World," and "Thinking of the Lost World," the experience of reality attains for some a magical, mythical quality in its own right. "The Lost Children" originated as a dream recorded by Jarrell's wife and develops a wish-fulfillment sequence found in "They" by Rudyard Kipling. While Kipling's story involves the recovery of a man's beloved child among several who have returned to earth after death, Jarrell's poem uses this dream as a background for a mother's contemplation of the possession and loss of a child as it matures. Each stanza then presents a stage in the process of separation and maturity. Eventually the parent exchanges the parental bond for friendship with the child as an adult, but the initial relationship lives on in the mother's consciousness. The mother compares the persistence of memory to a hide-and-seek game that the little girls still require her to play. The thought of them brings sadness at their separation, but the richness of the association remains.

"The Lost World" recovers portions of Jarrell's own past, using sensory impressions as French novelist Marcel Proust uses them in *Le temps retrouvé* (1927, *The Past Recaptured*). The poem is Jarrell's own, however, although it may have been stimulated by his interest in Proust's *À la recherche du temps perdu* (1913-1927, *Remembrance of Things Past*). Jarrell employs the effective strategies of his thirty years' writing experience to create impressions of his life in Hollywood in the 1920's, combining the world of his neighborhood with the world of art and filmmaking. Although the poem is narrated in the present tense, a sense of the struggle of re-creating time appears periodically as a conflict. Images of Hollywood, boyhood fantasies, and intense moments of pleasure or fear interweave in a journey undertaken to establish relationships between the past and the meaning of the present. "Thinking of the Lost World" considers the importance of the quest for the lost world of childhood. In keeping with the meditative intent of the poem, Jarrell returns from the formalistic use of terza rima that structures "The Lost World" to the conversational free verse characteristic of his later work. The flavor of chocolate tapioca evokes memories for the speaker of the poem as did the taste of the madeleine in Proust's great work of memory, but Jarrell's narrator finds the way into the past more difficult. "The sunshine of the Land/ Of Sunshine is a gray mist now," he admits, and the atmosphere is as polluted as that of an area given up to industry. In the realm of memory he constructs a compensating fantasy, an "undiscovered/ Country between California and Arizona," where his past resides. He longs, too, for the objects of the past: his "Mama's dark blue Buick" or "Lucky's electric" surely could transport him back. His late aunt reappears to him often in the guise of other women, and in this regard his past sustains itself in awakening memory.

The changes in his own body also testify to some remarkable ongoing process that persists despite the attempts of his memory to conserve the lost world of childhood and maturity. For the speaker as for the mother in "The Lost Children," the paradox is that while nothing remains, all of the past belongs to the rememberer. As he says, "My soul has memorized world after world," and in this memory he finds not merely an acceptable end, but happiness. For him, an awareness of the loss is assurance of some existence in the past that transcends time and death. The awareness itself is a "reward," a way of coming to terms with change in human experience, perhaps the central concern of Jarrell's poetry.

Tremendous sensitivity, critical insight, and human concern characterized the work of Jarrell throughout his career. The vigor of his last poems suggests that his work had not reached its end, although much of his talent had fulfilled itself in his last books. Jarrell wrote poetry with a human focus, poetry that is lasting and influential in its attempt to communicate the nature of experience in the modern world.

OTHER MAJOR WORKS

LONG FICTION: *Pictures from an Institution*, 1954.
NONFICTION: *Poetry and the Age*, 1953; *A Sad Heart at the Supermarket*, 1962; *The Third Book of Criticism*, 1969; *Kipling, Auden, and Co.: Essays and Reviews, 1935-1964*, 1981; *Randall Jarrell's Letters: An Autobiographical and Literary Selection*, 1985.

TRANSLATIONS: *The Golden Bird and Other Fairy Tales of the Brothers Grimm*, 1962; *Faust, Part I*, pb. 1976 (of Johann Wolfgang von Goethe's play).
CHILDREN'S LITERATURE: *The Gingerbread Rabbit*, 1964; *The Bat-Poet*, 1964; *The Animal Family*, 1965.

BIBLIOGRAPHY
Bryant, J. A. *Understanding Randall Jarrell*. Columbia: University of South Carolina Press, 1986. An easy book to read. Contains biographical information and an overview of Jarrell's writings, including a breakdown of his earlier poems, his criticism and essays, his children's poems, and his later poetry. Supplemented with a bibliography and an index.
Ferguson, Suzanne. *The Poetry of Randall Jarrell*. Baton Rouge: Louisiana State University Press, 1971. This excellent book stresses Jarrell as first a teacher and second a poet. Ferguson gives a solid, in-depth analysis of his major works, taking selections from all of his different areas of interest. Complemented by a select bibliography and an exhaustive index.
Flynn, Richard. *Randall Jarrell and the Lost World of Childhood*. Athens: University of Georgia Press, 1990. Flynn addresses the importance of Jarrell redetermining the "child's set face" in the tumultuous lifestyle of modern-day society. The critical analysis that he offers is very insightful in this neglected genre of children's poetry, as he sets Jarrell up as one of its masters. Contains a good bibliography and an index.
Hoffman, Frederick. *The Achievement of Randall Jarrell*. Glenview, Ill.: Scott, Foresman, 1970. This short book concentrates on an analysis of Jarrell's poetry, centering on one of his characteristic themes, that of a dreamer being awakened into a reality which is somehow parallel or connected to the dream. Although not comprehensive in the scope of all Jarrell's poetry, it provides excellent coverage within that parameter.
Jarrell, Mary. *Remembering Randall: A Memoir of Poet, Critic, and Teacher Randall Jarrell*. New York: HarperCollins, 1999. Mary Jarrell delivers a focused portrait of her late husband that is in keeping with her sense of propriety. She avoids details of bed-

room behavior and handles Randall's nervous collapse with sympathetic tact. The result is a portrait of a poet, his personality, and his career.

Lowell, Robert, et al., eds. *Randall Jarrell: 1914-1965.* New York: Farrar, Straus & Giroux, 1967. In this book of assorted essays, Jarrell's life is reflected on by many of his friends and scholars. Offers excellent coverage of his dreams, aspirations, and writings as seen from diverse individuals, but gives little critical analysis of his works.

Meyers, Jeffrey. *Manic Power: Robert Lowell and His Circle.* New York: Arbor House, 1987. Investigates the relationships between Robert Lowell, John Berryman, Theodore Roethke, and Jarrell. Meyers gives an in-depth study of the influences these men had on Jarrell and sheds light on the foundations from which his poetry emerged. Supplemented by a select bibliography and an index.

Travisano, Thomas J. *Midcentury Quartet: Bishop, Lowell, Jarrell, Berryman, and the Making of a Postmodern Aesthetic.* Charlottesville: University Press of Virginia, 1999. A survey of the work of four American poets, focusing on their contributions to postmodernism. Intended for a scholarly audience versed in the literary theory of modernism and postmodernism. Includes an excellent supporting bibliography.

Chapel Louise Petty;
bibliography updated by the editors

ROBINSON JEFFERS

Born: Allegheny (now in Pittsburgh), Pennsylvania;
January 10, 1887
Died: Carmel, California; January 20, 1962

PRINCIPAL POETRY

Flagons and Apples, 1912
Californians, 1916
Tamar and Other Poems, 1924
Roan Stallion, Tamar, and Other Poems, 1925

The Women at Point Sur, 1927
Cawdor and Other Poems, 1928
Dear Judas and Other Poems, 1929
Descent to the Dead: Poems Written in Ireland and Great Britain, 1931
Thurso's Landing and Other Poems, 1932
Give Your Heart to the Hawks and Other Poems, 1933
Solstice and Other Poems, 1935
Such Counsels You Gave to Me and Other Poems, 1937
Poems Known and Unknown, 1938
The Selected Poetry of Robinson Jeffers, 1938
Be Angry at the Sun and Other Poems, 1941
Medea, 1946 (verse drama, translation of Euripides)
The Double Axe and Other Poems, 1948
Hungerfield and Other Poems, 1954
The Beginning and the End, 1963
Selected Poems, 1965
The Alpine Christ and Other Poems, 1973
Brides of the South Wind, 1974
What Odd Expedients and Other Poems, 1980
Rock and Hawk: A Selection of Shorter Poems by Robinson Jeffers, 1987
The Collected Poetry of Robinson Jeffers: Volume I, 1920-1928, 1988
The Collected Poetry of Robinson Jeffers: Volume II, 1928-1938, 1989
The Collected Poetry of Robinson Jeffers: Volume III, 1939-1962, 1991

OTHER LITERARY FORMS

Robinson Jeffers explained his own work and expressed his ideas on society and art in some detail in the forewords to the Modern Library edition (1935) of his *Roan Stallion, Tamar, and Other Poems* and his *Selected Poetry of Robinson Jeffers* (1938). Other important prose statements are "Poetry, Gongorism and a Thousand Years," *The New York Times Book Review,* Jan. 18, 1948, pp. 16, 26; *Themes in My Poems* (1956); and *The Selected Letters of Robinson Jeffers, 1897-1962* (1968, Ann N. Ridgeway, editor).

In addition, the poet William Everson has collected, from various forgotten pages, two volumes of poetry that Jeffers had discarded. These volumes reconstitute the work of the transitional period from 1916 to 1922. They are *The Alpine Christ and Other Poems* (1973) and *Brides of the South Wind* (1974).

ACHIEVEMENTS

Many years after his death, Robinson Jeffers remains probably the most controversial American poet, with the exception of Edgar Allan Poe, who has never been termed "major." A number of important writers and critics have ranked him with Walt Whitman and invoked the Greek tragedians in trying to suggest his somber power. In the early years of his fame his books typically went into several editions, and he was the subject of a *Time* magazine cover story. In 1947 his free translation of *Medea* for the New York stage brought him new acclaim as a dramatic poet. Since the early years of his fame, however, some critics, few but influential, were hostile, and others found Jeffers merely uninteresting as the subject of critical examination. The deep division over Jeffers's importance as a poet is seen today in college anthologies: He is given generous space in some and omitted entirely from others. The weight of criticism, however, has been consistently on the positive side. Serious studies have been published about his work which, while strongly favorable, avoid the extravagant praise of some of Jeffers's early admirers. All but the most hostile critics are agreed that he had an unmistakably original voice, strong dramatic talents, and great descriptive ability. He is the only American poet of note since Edwin Arlington Robinson—who praised him highly—to write a large quantity of narrative poetry. Some of Jeffers's short lyrics, moreover, notably "Hurt Hawks," "The Eye," "The Purse-Seine," and "Shine, Perishing Republic," seem destined to become classics. In addition to his poetic gifts, and indeed inseparable from them, is the force of a worldview that is unusual, coherent, and challenging, a set of reasoned attitudes that justifies classifying him as a philosophical poet of unusual interest. Jeffers's radical skepticism about the human race, embodied in his doctrine that man should "uncenter himself" from the universe, is expressed in poetry that draws on considerable scientific and historical study, on thorough knowledge of religious and classical literature, and on deep resources of myth and ritual. It is the combination of poetic power and philosophical stance that argues

strongly for Jeffers's place in a twentieth century pantheon of American poets. Jeffers won a number of important awards, including the Academy of American Poets prize in 1958 and the Shelley Memorial Award in 1960. He was never given the Pulitzer Prize, even though Edna St. Vincent Millay and Louis Untermeyer, among others, repeatedly pressed his case.

BIOGRAPHY

John Robinson Jeffers's life, milieu, and work are of one piece. From his early adulthood, one can see him choosing a place of living and a way of life that are strongly reflected in his poetry and in his occasional prose statements about his work.

When Jeffers was born in Pittsburgh in 1887, his father was forty-nine, his mother twenty-seven. His father's occupation as well as his age set the boy apart; the senior Jeffers had been a Presbyterian minister and was professor of Old Testament literature and exegesis at Western Theological Seminary. Young Robin was an only child for seven years, and he spent much of his time

Robinson Jeffers (Library of Congress)

in solitary wandering or reading on the relatively iso-lated family property. He was later educated in Switzer-land for nearly four years, in schools in which the lan-guage of instruction was either French or German. His father had introduced him to Greek at the age of five, and he also acquired Latin and some Italian. After his parents moved to Los Angeles, he entered Occidental College, where he continued his classical and literary education and supplemented his childhood religious training with courses in biblical literature and theology.

Although popular with his fellow students, Jeffers al-ready was establishing the pattern of his life through his interest in camping and mountain climbing on one hand, and in reading and writing on the other. Graduating at eighteen, he then pursued medical studies at the Univer-sity of Southern California, and later studied forestry, hoping to find a way to support himself amid nature that would permit him time for poetry. A small legacy, how-ever, enabled him to settle, with his bride Una Call Custer, in Carmel, California, in 1914. The whole area, then uncrowded, had a dramatic beauty, and Jeffers called it his "inevitable place." He was profoundly af-fected by its massive simplicity of elements: huge, tree-less mountains plunging directly into the Pacific, broken by occasional narrow canyons in which grew at that time little groves of redwoods; the constant pound and swirl of the sea against bare granite shore-rocks; hawks soar-ing above the cattle-pasturing headlands. In this setting, Jeffers helped masons to construct a simple stone house on Carmel Point, looking directly seaward; and, later, he built with his own hands, using boulders that he labori-ously rolled up from the shore, his famous "Hawk Tower." Evoking with its name the fierce independence of the birds that were one of his favorite subjects, the tower became symbolically for him a place beyond time, a psychological vantage point for his often apoca-lyptic and prophetic stance in the world.

With his wife, to whom he was devoted, Jeffers reared twin sons (a daughter, born previously, lived only a day), and lived quietly in Carmel, departing only for vacations in Taos, New Mexico, and for rare trips to the East Coast or the British Isles. With a very few excep-tions, he did not participate in the round of readings, book reviews, or campus appearances that characterizes the life of so many American poets.

When Jeffers died in 1962, it was in the seaward bed-room of his own house. There, in the poem "The Bed by the Window," he had many years earlier envisioned the day when a ghostly figure would appear, rap with his staff, and say, "Come, Jeffers."

ANALYSIS

Robinson Jeffers's central concept of the universe and of humankind's place in it, all-important in under-standing his poetry, is grounded in his respect for scien-tific thought and in his own historical observations, but strongly colored in its expression by emotion. From sci-ence, he took a cool, analytical view of the human race as one species that evolved in one stage of an ever-evolving, dynamic universe—a mere "fly-speck" in the scheme of things. Perhaps because of his interest in as-tronomy (his younger brother, Hamilton, was for many years a scientist at the Lick Observatory in California), he took an extraterrestrial view even of the earth. The first photograph taken by the astronauts of the earth from the vicinity of the moon represented a view that Jeffers had achieved in his imagination long before: "It is only a little planet/ But how beautiful it is. . . ." In "The Double Axe," Jeffers paid tribute to one of the sci-entists who helped him to achieve this view, Copernicus, hailing him as the first who "pushed man/ Out of his in-sane self-importance. . . ."

A second factor which influenced Jeffers's outlook was his study of history. From the British archaeologist Flinders Petrie and the Italian philosopher Giovanni Battista Vico, Jeffers drew the concept of cultural cycles and the conviction that cultural or national groupings are inherently unstable and social progress temporary. This view, again, was bolstered by his observations of the in-evitable cycles of growth, flowering, and decay in na-ture. It was given special force by Jeffers's belief, influ-enced by Oswald Spengler, that Western civilization was already on the downgrade.

Many scientists share Jeffers's objective view of the world but not the intensity of his feeling for the insig-nificance of humanity or the "beauty of things," his often-used phrase for natural loveliness. The roots of Jeffers's feeling seem to be in the Calvinistic teachings of his father's religion, which proclaimed the glory of God and the nothingness of man. Rejecting his father's

Christian God, Jeffers transferred his religious feeling to a new object, a universe whose parts are all "expressions of the same energy," a dynamic universe, ever in strain and struggle, and ever in that process discovering its own nature. In a letter outlining his views, Jeffers wrote, "This whole is in all its parts so beautiful, and is felt by me to be so intensely in earnest, that I am compelled to love it, and to think of it as divine." He went on to say that he felt there was "peace, freedom, I might say a kind of salvation, in turning one's affections toward this one God, rather than inward on one's self, or on humanity, or on human imagination and abstractions. . . ." Jeffers's sole admission of the possibility that humans could have a positive effect was to say that one may "contribute (ever so slightly) to the beauty of things by making one's own life and environment beautiful. . . ." While he granted that such action could include moral beauty, which he called one of the qualities of humanity, for the most part the weight of his emotions was on the side of sad resignation where the human race was concerned, or actual disgust with its frequent moral ugliness.

Jeffers's intensity of feeling for natural beauty and especially for the dynamism of nature was profoundly affected by his lifelong residence on the spectacular Carmel coast. The area is not only ruggedly beautiful, but is also wracked by periodic events reminding one of the awesome power of nature and of man's uncertain tenure on earth: brush fires that sweep the dry hills in late summer and sometimes destroy farms and homes; earthquakes that shudder along the San Andreas fault; fierce winds that torture the picturesque Monterey cypresses; drenching rains that bring floods and dangerous mudslides. These natural events, recalling the fire, earthquake, wind, and deluge of the biblical apocalypse, appear as major instruments of destruction in many of the narratives, and are centrally important, too, in some of the lyrics. Most important, probably, was the sheer beauty of the surroundings, beauty which Jeffers identified as one of the six major themes in his poems in a talk given in 1941 at the Library of Congress. It is possible to imagine Jeffers living on the coast of Ireland, or in the Scottish Hebrides, or on a mountainside, but not in a quiet New England meadow or an industrial city. He chose his landscape, his "inevitable place," and it in turn formed him and became a major actor in his dramas. Today the Carmel/Big Sur area is known as "Jeffers country."

The expression of his basic attitudes, to which Jeffers eventually gave the name "Inhumanism," took three major forms in poetry: dramatic, narrative, and, loosely considered, lyric. The dramatic poetry includes not only a play primarily intended for stage production, Euripides' *Medea*, but also dramas primarily intended to be read, a Japanese Noh play, and a masque. The narratives and dramas range in length to well above one hundred pages. The lyrics include some poems that are of substantial length—several pages or more. Some poems are mixtures of elements and defy classification.

The narratives and dramas reveal metaphorically—and occasionally through interposed comments—the poet's preoccupation with the self-concern and solipsism of the human race. At the same time, they express Jeffers's sense of the historical cycles of human behavior and of the larger cycle of death and rebirth that Jeffers called, in "Cawdor," the "great Life." To embody these attitudes, Jeffers chose a number of often shocking subjects: incest, murder, rape, self-mutilation because of guilt, suicide, and the sexual feelings of a woman for a horse.

TAMAR

One of the best of the long narratives, the one which caused the greatest initial sensation when it was published with other poems in 1924, is *Tamar*. The setting is an isolated part of the California coast, where the Cauldwell family lives. Circumstances lead the daughter, Tamar, and her brother, Lee, into incest. Later, Tamar learns that her father had committed the same sin with his sister, now long dead. In one strange scene on the beach at night Tamar is possessed sexually by the ghosts of the Indians who once occupied the area; the scene is a kind of descent into death, and after it Tamar is a "flame," self-destructive and demoniac, feeling herself doomed because of her breaking of natural laws. She then tempts her father sexually, as if to prove her depravity, although she commits no sexual act with him. Finally, the entire family is consumed in a fire from which they could have saved themselves had not Tamar, her brother, and her suitor, Will Andrews, been acting out the climax of fierce sexual jealousy.

This seemingly fantastic and occasionally lurid drama was based on one or both of the two biblical Tamar stories, and on Percy Bysshe Shelley's *The Cenci* (1820), all of which include incest. These tales in turn, however, are overshadowed by the Greek myth of the creation of the human race: the incest of Heaven and Earth to produce Titan, and Titan's ensuing incest with his mother, Earth, to produce a child. Thus Jeffers has created a modern story based on layers of myth, reminding readers of the powerful libidinal forces that have been repressed by millennia of taboos but never, as Sophocles and Sigmund Freud noted, eliminated from human nightmares. Further, the isolated home of the Cauldwells on Point Lobos allegorically suggests the entire world, and the initial incest has strong overtones of Adam's fall. Thus man's failure to relate himself humbly to his environment, obeying natural laws such as the ban on incest, is comparable to Adam and Eve ignoring God's command to know their place in the scheme of things. The expulsion of Adam and Eve from paradise is comparable to the troubles visited on the little world of the House of Cauldwell. The story, moreover, is a chapter of apocalypse, with fire—persistently invoked throughout as an agent of cleansing destruction—accomplishing the destruction of Judgment Day. It is prophecy inasmuch as it warns against man's self-concern. It is also persistently evocative, as Robert J. Brophy has pointed out (*Robinson Jeffers: Myth, Ritual, and Symbol in His Narrative Poems*, 1973), of the monomyth of the seasonal cycle of death and rebirth. Yet only in relatively recent years have critics paid systematic attention to the complexity of *Tamar* and Jeffers's other narratives.

NARRATIVES

Jeffers's other narratives similarly explore recurrent patterns of human conduct as expressed in folklore, myth, or religion. "Roan Stallion," the poet's most powerful short narrative, is a modern version of the myth of God uniting with a human. This pattern is seen not only in the Christian story of the fatherhood of Jesus, but also in myths from various cultures, especially the Greek tales of Zeus and his sexual encounters—with Leda, when he took the form of a swan; with Antiope, as a satyr; with Europa, as a bull; and others. "The Tower Beyond Tragedy," one of Jeffers's most successful long poems, is a free adaptation of the first two plays of Aeschylus's *The Oresteia* (458 B.C.E.). In "Cawdor," the poet reworks the Hippolytus story of Euripides, adding an element—self-mutilation—from Sophocles' *Oedipus the King* (429-401 B.C.E.). "The Loving Shepherdess," another relatively early narrative that was well received, is imaginatively based on the Scottish legend of "Feckless Fannie." "Such Counsels You Gave to Me" is built on suggestions from the Scottish ballad "Edward, Edward," which in turn, like all true ballads, invokes deep folk memories. Other narratives explore age-old problems. "Give Your Heart to the Hawks" explores the question of who should administer justice; "Thurso's Landing" considers when, if ever, it is right to take another's life out of pity.

THE WOMEN AT POINT SUR

In one of his early long poems—the longest, in fact, at 175 pages—Jeffers did not base his story on myth or folklore, but created a poem that has become itself a kind of literary legend of magnificent failure: *The Women at Point Sur*. It is a violent, brilliant, chaotic, and difficult-to-comprehend story of a mad minister who collects disciples by telling them that there are no more moral rules and that they can do as their hearts, or bodies, desire. The poem did not generally achieve one of its main purposes, which, as Jeffers put it, was to show "the danger of that 'Roan Stallion' idea of 'breaking out of humanity,' misinterpreted in the mind of a fool or a lunatic." The prologue and other parts are impressive, nevertheless, and the poem has a curiously prescient character. Barclay, who commits an incestuous rape to prove that he is beyond good and evil himself, leads his followers into sex orgies. Not very many years later, the Big Sur area of the poem was the scene of sometimes tragic experimentation in sexual behavior amid some of the more extreme communes and "sensitivity institutes." Further, Barclay's corrupting influence on those around him prefigured the monstrous sway that Charles Manson held over the young women who went out from his remote California hideaway to do murder at his bidding.

SECOND PERIOD

The nature of the narratives and dramas changed somewhat through the years. In Jeffers's first mature period (his youthful work, when he produced two volumes of conventional verse, is of interest only to specialists), the concentration was on writing modern versions of myths, such as *Tamar*. In the second period, ranging from the late 1920's to about 1935, the narratives were realistic, though still based on older stories. Such scenes as the violation of Tamar by ghostly Indians were no longer written. "Cawdor," "Thurso's Landing," and "Give Your Heart to the Hawks" were in this vein, while "Dear Judas," chronologically a part of the period, a play in the Japanese Nō form, was based on myth and religion. In the late 1930's, Jeffers again concentrated on myth. In two of his least successful narratives, "Solstice" and "Such Counsels You Gave to Me," he focused on what Frederick I. Carpenter (*Robinson Jeffers*, 1962) has called "case histories in abnormal psychology." In the same period Jeffers wrote "At the Birth of an Age," a philosophical poem, partly in dramatic form, which has as a central figure a self-torturing Hanged God of the universe. One of the most interesting of Jeffers's poems, it is also one of the most complex and difficult, often appealing primarily to the mind, and having some of the same virtues and faults as Shelley's *Prometheus Unbound* (1820).

"THE DOUBLE AXE"

Jeffers again ventured into the mythic and the supernatural in "The Double Axe," a two-part poem published in 1948. In the first part, "The Love and the Hate," he took an idea from his earlier "Resurrection," a short narrative (1932) about a World War I soldier returned miraculously from the grave. In "The Love and the Hate," Hoult Gore has similarly returned from death in World War II. His denunciation of war and his presentation of the facts about who actually suffers for the pride of patriots and politicians are sometimes eloquent, but the ghoulishness of the central figure, the walking corpse, is so naturally repellent that it is difficult for the reader to sympathize with the hero emotionally, much less to identify with him. Additionally, there are moments when the writing comes close to unintentional humor, as when Gore's widow, first seeing him, says he looks "dreadful." The violence of the action, even though it is meant to be cleansing, is not properly prepared for by the buildup of emotions, so that it seems exaggerated and gratuitous. The second half of the poem, "The Inhumanist," is much more successful. In this poem Jeffers creates a new mythical hero, an old man armed with Zeus's double-bitted axe, which is a symbol both of

divine destruction and procreation. This Inhumanist has various adventures in the course of a complex and sometimes supernatural story. Despite its flaws, which include prosy passages of bitter political ranting, it is one of the essential poems for anyone wishing to achieve a full knowledge of Jeffers's thought.

"HUNGERFIELD"

"The Double Axe," which dealt a heavy blow to Jeffers's reputation, was succeeded by one other major narrative, another excursion into the supernatural, but this time a generally successful one—"Hungerfield." Written after the crushing blow of Una Jeffers's death, "Hungerfield" tells the story of a man who wrestled with death to save his mother from cancer. This violation of natural laws causes all kinds of other natural disasters to occur, recalling the way that the "miracle drugs" and chemical sprays with which people and farmlands are treated cause unforeseen and often disastrous side effects. The Hungerfield story, which also has mythic references (Hungerfield is a Hercules figure), is framed by Jeffers's personal meditation on the death of his wife, and ends with his reconciliation with it. These framing passages lack the compactness and intense poetic power of Jeffers's best lyrics, but their directness, tenderness, and simplicity carry them past the danger of sentimentality and make them moving and effective.

"THE PLACE FOR NO STORY"

The lyric poems, which are here taken to include all the shorter poems that are not basically narratives or dramas, celebrate the same things and denounce the same things as the narratives. Being primarily meditations on one subject, they are more intense and unified, and are free of the problems of multilayered poems such as *The Women at Point Sur*. Typically, a Jeffers lyric describes an experience and comments upon it; and it does this in the simple, declarative voice that stamped every poem with his unique signature.

"The Place for No Story," although exceptionally short, is an excellent example. Jeffers opens with a simple description: "The coast hills at Sovranes Creek:/ No trees, but dark scant pasture drawn thin/ Over rock shaped like flame." Then he describes the "old ocean at the land's foot, the vast/ Gray extension beyond the long white violence." Jeffers describes a herd of cattle on the slope above the sea, and above that "the gray air haunted with hawks. . . ." Ending this section with a colon, he draws, figuratively and spiritually, a deep breath and simply states:

> This place is the noblest thing I have ever seen
> No imaginable
> Human presence here could do anything
> But dilute the lonely self-watchful passion.

There are many qualities to notice in this simple poem, qualities that will stand for those of scores of other lyrics, meditations, mixed-mode poems, and sections of the narratives and dramas. First, there is the voice. It is simple and colloquial, as characteristically attuned to the rhythms of everyday American speech as anything by Robert Frost. The word order is natural. The diction is simple and dignified, but not formal. It reflects Jeffers's conscious decision to focus on things that will endure. It would have been easily comprehensible in sixteenth century England, and will almost certainly be so for centuries to come. The poem is written in the typical style of the mature Jeffers: no rhyme, no regular metrical pattern.

As Jeffers explained, however, he had a sense of pattern that made him disagree with those who called his lines free verse. His feeling, he once wrote, was for the number of beats to the line and also for the quantitative element of long and short syllables. Most of his poems break up into recurring patterns of beats per line—ten and five, six and four, five and three alternations being common. In this poem, less regular than many, there is still a recurrence of four-beat lines, culminating in a pair at the end to make a couplet effect. The longer lines run mostly to six stresses, depending on how the poem is read. Binding the whole together is a subtle pattern of alliteration, a device that Jeffers used with full consciousness of his debt to the strong-stress lines of Anglo-Saxon verse.

In the first few lines, for example, the hard "c" of "coast" is repeated in "Creek" (and picked up much later in another stressed word, "cows"); the "s" in "Sovranes" reappears in "scant" and "shaped"; the "d" in "dark" reappears in "drawn"; the "f" of "flame," in "foot"; the "v" of "vast" in "violence"; the "h" in "hills" appears five lines later in "herd," six lines later in "hardly," seven lines later in "haunted" and "hawks." A notable assonance is "old ocean," which works to slow down its line with its long syllables.

In this short lyric, too, are embodied some of Jeffers's key ideas. The ocean's "violence" reminds the reader of the struggle ever-present in the natural world. The contrast between rock, a symbol of endurance, and flame, a symbol of violent change, suggests that even rocks undergo change from the same process of oxidation that produces flame. Above, the hawks are Jeffers's preferred symbol of independence and of the inexorable violence of nature. The poem simply and unaffectedly celebrates beauty, and at the end reminds the reader of the insignificance of human beings in a universe still discovering itself in the "passion" of its dynamic life.

The qualities found in this short lyric are found in abundance in many other poems of varying length. Among the most notable of the short poems not already cited are "To the Stone-Cutters," "Night," "Boats in a Fog," "Noon," "Rock and Hawk," "Love the Wild Swan," "Return," "All the Little Hoofprints," "Original Sin," "The Deer Lay Down Their Bones," and "For Una."

LONGER LYRICS

Among the longer lyrics, several are important for a full understanding of the poet. Chief among these is *Apology for Bad Dreams*, Jeffers's *ars poetica*. "Meditation on Saviors" and "De Rerum Virtute" are also important philosophical poems, as is "Margrave," a short narrative framed by an approximately equal amount of meditative lyric. Two large sections of "Cawdor" contain particularly powerful lyric sections. These, "The Caged Eagle's Death-Dream" and "The Old Man's Dream After He Died," have been reprinted in *The Selected Poetry of Robinson Jeffers* (1938).

THE BEGINNING AND THE END

After passing through a period (1938-1948) during which many of his poems were bitter political harangues, Jeffers achieved a quieter tone in the poems that were posthumously printed in *The Beginning and the End*. They lack the close texture and the intensity, however, of his better poems from earlier years, and tend to become prosy. At the same time, in their increasing concern with astrophysics, the origins of human life, and the terrible prospect that all may end in a nuclear catastrophe, they explore new territory and provide a fitting, relatively serene end to an enormously productive career.

LEGACY

In seeking to place Jeffers in the continuum of American poets, one is drawn to generalizations that often apply surprisingly well to Walt Whitman, who was temperamentally and sometimes philosophically Jeffers's polar opposite. Like Whitman, Jeffers was a technical innovator, developing a typically long, colloquial line and a voice that can be mistaken for no other. Like Whitman, he was often charged, with some justification, with using inflated rhetoric and exaggeration to achieve his effects, and with repetitiveness. Like Whitman, he was a poet of extremes, and for that reason perhaps he will be best appreciated when some of the political and social passions which he stirred have been forgotten. Like Whitman, too, Jeffers had a well-developed set of attitudes toward society and the world. These views put both men in the prophetic stance at times. Like Whitman, Jeffers was deeply religious in a pantheistic way, and so profoundly conscious of the cycle of birth and regeneration that he thought of death as a redeemer.

Many of these characteristics are those of a public poet, a person in a dialogue with his nation and the world about its life and the right way of living. Beyond these qualities, Jeffers had other attributes of the public poet. He was not only prophetic, admonishing and seeking reform in attitudes and behavior, but also apocalyptic, standing apart and reminding his readers of the immanence and possible imminence of worldly destruction. He was historical, reminding them that cultures and nations had risen and fallen before them. He was an early environmentalist, reminding Americans that they were part of a complex cycle of life, and castigating them for their sins against the earth. He was an explorer of the depths probed by Freud and Carl G. Jung—and thus a psychological poet. He was also a mystical poet—the "Caged Eagle's Death-Dream" constituting a supreme illustration.

The process of sifting out and properly appraising the poems in which Jeffers succeeded in his various roles has begun. No single long narrative has been acclaimed by all favorable critics as entirely successful, but it is certain that at least half a dozen, probably led by "Roan Stallion," will survive. Many lyrics and shorter mixed-mode poems, however, are generally esteemed, and it is these poems that already have assured Jeffers a place among the honored writers of the century. Finally, the quality that seems most likely to ensure Jeffers's future stature is his very lack of timeliness. His references are not to ephemera but to rock, hawk, sea, and mountain—things that will be with the world as long as humans are there to perceive their beauty and their significance.

OTHER MAJOR WORKS

PLAY: *The Cretan Woman*, pr. 1954.

NONFICTION: *Themes in My Poems*, 1956; *The Selected Letters of Robinson Jeffers, 1897-1962*, 1968 (Ann N. Ridgeway, editor).

BIBLIOGRAPHY

Bennett, Melba Berry. *The Stone Mason of Tor House: The Life and Work of Robinson Jeffers*. Los Angeles: Ward Ritchie Press, 1966. Written by a personal friend of the poet, this biography is rather uncritical of his views. Supplemented with an index, illustrations, and bibliographies of works by and about Jeffers.

Brophy, Robert J. *Robinson Jeffers: Myth, Ritual, and Symbol in His Narrative Poems*. Reprint. Hamden, Conn.: Archon Books, 1976. This basic study, often referred to by critics, thoroughly establishes the grounding of Jeffers's narrative works in—among others—Judeo-Christian, Greek, Norse, and Hindu mythologies. Contains illustrations, an index, notes, and a bibliography.

_____, ed. *The Robinson Jeffers Newsletter: A Jubilee Gathering, 1962-1988*. Los Angeles: Occidental College, 1988. A collection of the best articles from the first twenty-five years of the journal devoted to the poet and his works. Includes illustrations.

Everson, William. *The Excesses of God: Robinson Jeffers as a Religious Figure*. Stanford, Calif.: Stanford University Press, 1988. The author, himself a poet, sees Jeffers as a bardic and prophetic man and relates him to the thought of such modern theologians as Mircea Eliade. Contains notes and an index. Everson is also the author, under his previous pen name of Brother Antoninus, of an earlier study on the same subject, *Robinson Jeffers: Fragments of an Older Fury* (1968).

Karman, James. *Robinson Jeffers: Poet of California.* Brownsville, Oreg.: Story Line Press, 1995. A revised and expanded edition of Karman's critical biography which gives insight into the life of Jeffers, his family, and the honor he gave to hard work, self-reliance, and conservation of the environment.

Nolte, William H. *Rock and Hawk: Robinson Jeffers and the Romantic Agony.* Athens: University of Georgia Press, 1978. Relates Jeffers to the traditions of European, English, and American Romantic philosophy and poetry. Supplemented with notes and an index.

Thesing, William B. *Robinson Jeffers and a Galaxy of Writers.* Columbia: University of South Carolina Press, 1995. A collection of critical essays by various authors dealing with Jeffers's life and work. Includes bibliographical references and index.

Vardamis, Alex A. *The Critical Reputation of Robinson Jeffers: A Bibliographical Study.* Hamden, Conn.: Archon Books, 1972. A chronological annotated bibliography of all the books, articles, and reviews about Jeffers from the beginning of his career to 1971. Contains a critical introduction.

Zaller, Robert. *The Cliffs of Solitude: A Reading of Robinson Jeffers.* New York: Cambridge University Press, 1983. An interpretation of Jeffers's entire career, with particular emphasis on the long narratives. Combines the psychoanalytic and mythic viewpoints. Complemented with a chronology, an index, notes, and a bibliography.

Edward A. Nickerson;
bibliography updated by the editors

Juan Ramón Jiménez

Born: Moguer, Spain; December 23, 1881
Died: San Juan, Puerto Rico; May 29, 1958

PRINCIPAL POETRY
Almas de violeta, 1900
Ninfeas, 1900
Rimas, 1902
Arias tristes, 1903
Jardines lejanos, 1904
Pastorales, 1905
Elegías puras, 1908
La soledad sonora, 1908
Elegías intermedias, 1909
Elegías lamentables, 1910
Baladas de primavera, 1911
Pastorales, 1911
Laberinto, 1913
Estío, 1916
Diario de un poeta recién casado, 1917
Poesías escojidas, 1917
Sonetos espirituales, 1917
Eternidades, 1918
Piedra y cielo, 1919
Segunda antolojía poética, 1922
Belleza, 1923
Poesía, 1923
Canción, 1936
La estación total, 1946
Romances de Coral Gables, 1948
Animal de fondo, 1949
Libros de Poesía, 1957
Three Hundred Poems, 1905-1953, 1962
Tercera antolojía poética, 1957
Dios deseado y deseante, 1964

OTHER LITERARY FORMS

Somewhat ironically perhaps, Juan Ramón Jiménez is probably best known for his *Platero y yo* (1914, enlarged 1917; *Platero and I*, 1956), a collection of sketches in prose largely about his native Moguer. As always in Jiménez' noncritical work, however, his poetic vision and lyric expression are most apparent.

ACHIEVEMENTS

In 1903, Juan Ramón Jiménez revealed himself as a prolific poet, and by 1916 no one could surpass Jiménez' position and influence as a poet in the Hispanic world. His twenty-two years spent in the United States, Puerto Rico, Cuba, and South America from 1936 to his death, indicated no overall diminution of his creativity as a writer or of his authority as a critic. Appropriately, both for the excellence of his work and the half century de-

Juan Ramón Jiménez, Nobel laureate in literature for 1956.
(© The Nobel Foundation)

voted to it, he received the Nobel Prize in Literature in 1956, the first Spaniard to win it since 1920.

BIOGRAPHY

Juan Ramón Jiménez was born in Moguer, a typical town in Andalusia, steeped in tradition, colorful but slow-moving. His father, Victor, had come from north-central Spain to make his fortune in viniculture, acquiring extensive vineyards and numerous wineries in Moguer. Purificación, Jiménez' mother, was a native Andalusian and a very good mother, although perhaps too indulgent toward her youngest child, Juan Ramón. The future poet had a comfortable and happy early childhood in the family's new home on the Calle Nueva. Later, he learned to ride and, on horse or donkey, developed his love of nature in the beautiful countryside, which offered some compensation for the scant cultural stimulation of the town. After four or five years of elementary education in Moguer, Jiménez, then eleven years old, was sent with his brother to a Jesuit school near Cádiz, where he completed his secondary studies at age fifteen.

The *colegio* offered the best education available in the region, and Jiménez was a good, well-behaved student. Although somewhat homesick and averse to the school's regimentation, he was alert, imaginative, and intellectually curious, enjoying a variety of subjects, especially drawing and literature. His meditative mind and love of nature inclined him to religion and, despite later aversion to the Church, among the six schoolbooks that he kept permanently were the Bible and Thomas à Kempis's *Imitatio Christi* (c. 1427; *The Imitation of Christ*, c. 1460-1530). Upon graduation, Jiménez went to Seville to study painting and to develop his passion for poetry. His father had wanted him to study law at the university, but he had no interest in prelaw studies and neglected them for the arts. The family's prosperity made it possible for Jiménez to indulge himself and choose between two financially unpromising careers. Some early paintings show that he might have become a fine painter, but the publication of his first poems, evoking favorable criticism, turned him to poetry.

Fatigue and emotional strain in Seville put Jiménez under the care of doctors in Moguer, yet he continued to write feverishly, sending poems to magazines in Madrid and establishing contacts with poets there. Somewhat capricious and unreasonable, he shunned social events in Moguer and, despite two or more youthful love affairs, preferred to be alone. The poems sent by Jiménez to *Vida nueva* met with such favor that the magazine's editor, Francisco Villaespesa, and Rubén Darío, the Nicaraguan poet and leader of *Modernismo* who had been in Spain since 1899, invited the young poet to visit Madrid to help them reform Spanish poetry. Life in Madrid was exciting. Jiménez became close friends with Darío and other contemporary poets, and despite some excesses criticized by the academicians, his first collections were hailed as the work of a promising newcomer. His father's sudden fatal heart attack in 1900 caused Jiménez' nervous illness, which had recurred during the stimulating sojourn in Madrid, to worsen to the point that he required care in a sanatorium in Bordeaux.

In France, Jiménez read Charles Baudelaire and the Symbolist poets and continued to write, expressing his grief, sometimes in the excessively sentimental manner of the nineteenth century, sometimes in a more dignified, authentic style. Returning to Madrid rather than Moguer in 1901, the young poet continued his sheltered, privileged life in the Sanatorio del Rosario. Surrounded by tranquillity and beauty, Jiménez often entertained friends and relatives, more than ever before, and his retreat became a literary salon and social center. His work soon became known in the New World, and his popularity and influence grew with each volume. In 1903, Jiménez and a number of other young poets began to publish the literary journal *Helios*, the eleven issues of which exercised great influence—so much so that Miguel de Unamuno y Jugo, certainly not identified with *Modernismo*, was willing to be a contributor. While Darío gave Spanish poetry new subtlety, beauty, and music, Unamuno's influence deepened and intensified it. Later in 1903, Jiménez went to live with his physician and friend, Dr. Luís Simarra, with whom he remained for two years. With Simarra's encouragement and that of other scholars, Jiménez expanded his knowledge in several fields by reading and attending lectures at the Institución Libre de Enseñanza. The liberal views at this institution further eroded Jiménez' already weakened traditional religious convictions.

Unlike most of his colleagues, Jiménez felt less comfortable in Madrid than in a more rural setting. In 1905, ill again and homesick, he returned to Moguer, where he remained for six years, not with his family but in a house at Fuentepiña owned by them. There he rested and wrote, avoiding society for the most part. In 1910, at the age of twenty-eight, Jiménez was elected to the Royal Spanish Academy, but he declined membership, not only then but also on two subsequent occasions under different political regimes. With his sisters' marriages and other changes, including financial ones, the family's situation declined. Although Jiménez preferred solitude and nature, there were periods of tedium and depression for him, especially as he continued to suffer sporadically from ill health. Occasional amorous interludes were followed by disenchantment, bitterness, and remorse. In 1912, it seemed time to return to Madrid, where, except for brief visits to Moguer, the poet remained until 1936.

In four years at the Residencia de Estudiantes, the heart of intellectual and literary activity in Madrid, in the company of celebrated thinkers and writers, Jiménez completed two volumes of poetry and his prose masterpiece, *Platero and I*. His experimentation in content and form continued, and he gave evidence of increasing maturity in every way. In 1912, too, Jiménez had met Zenobia Camprubí Aymar; they soon became engaged and were married in 1916. Zenobia, who was part American, was lovely—as had been other women in the poet's life—and intelligent, interested in the same things that interested Jiménez. Above all, Zenobia was lively, a quality that proved very helpful for the sober, moody Jiménez. After a trip to New York and his wedding, Jiménez published his *Diario de un poeta recién casado* (diary of a newly married poet), a work marking his entrance to full maturity and long considered his best by the critics and author alike. He continued to grow in all respects, producing more significant poetry in the years from 1916 to 1923 than during any other period in his life, and might have become the "grand old man" of poetry had his temperament permitted.

Like so many other Spanish refugees from the Civil War, Jiménez headed for the United States in 1936, first visiting Washington, D.C., briefly as a cultural emissary of the Spanish Republic, then visiting Puerto Rico and Cuba for three years, finally settling for six years in Coral Gables, Florida, and later in Washington, D.C. His fame as a poet and critic was great, especially in Hispanic circles, and he lectured, read his poetry, and wrote numerous critical essays but produced no new poetic works for a time. Between 1942 and 1951, however, he published four major works and began a fifth that he was not to complete. Despite numerous invitations, Jiménez and his wife rarely left the United States. In 1956, Jiménez won the Nobel Prize for Literature, two days before Zenobia's death from cancer. He died in 1958 and is buried in Moguer with his wife.

ANALYSIS

The Spanish intellectuals and writers of the *generación del 98*, or Generation of '98, saw the need to arouse the national conscience and envisioned a vigorous, creative Spain in every aspect of life. The presence of Rubén Darío in Madrid had drawn many to the city and to *Modernismo*, the literary movement of which he was the chief exponent. Both the French Symbolists, who had largely inspired *Modernismo*, and Darío himself strongly influenced Juan Ramón Jiménez' poetry for more than a decade. In 1903, he published a collection of lyric poems, *Arias tristes* (sad airs), which revealed that he had abandoned the excessive sentimentality and random experimentation and imitation of his earlier collections for a more mature position based on firmer understanding of his talents.

ARIAS TRISTES

Arias tristes is divided into three "movements," each prefaced by the score of a *Lied* by Franz Schubert and dedicated to a friend. In addition, the second part has an epigraph taken from Paul Verlaine, and the third, one from Alfred de Musset. The second part is further prefaced by Jiménez' commentary on his own work, which is "monotonous, full of moonlight and sadness," and concludes with an evocation of Heinrich Heine and Gustavo Adolfo Bécquer as well as of Verlaine and Musset and an entreaty to all kindred spirits to weep for those who never weep. A vague, subdued sadness prevails here as in much Symbolist poetry. Avoiding novelty for the sake of novelty, Jiménez employs the verse of the romance exclusively and with a versatility that remains unmatched. Seemingly artless in its simplicity, the verse reveals great mastery in the use of enjambment, to give it fluency and grace, and in its diction, chosen for maximum musicality as well as meaning. Among the best poems in the collection are those that capture Jiménez' love of his native Andalusian landscape in delicate and original imagery.

JARDINES LEJANOS AND PASTORALES

In part under the influence of Unamuno, who wrote for Jiménez' journal, *Helios*, but favored exploiting traditional Spanish inspiration, but more so under that of his doctor and close friend, Luís Simarro, who introduced him to the principles of liberal education of the Institución Libre de Enseñanza, the poet began to explore sources other than Symbolism and *Modernismo*, and in 1904 and 1905, respectively, produced two collections of verse, in *Jardines lejanos* (distant gardens) and *Pastorales*. The former is full of musical allusions that convey Jiménez' emotional, often sad responses to music, and it has a new, conventional, and superficial

eroticism that separates it from his earlier work. The second volume, like *Arias tristes* and *Jardines lejanos*, is prefaced with musical notations (from Christoph Gluck, Felix Mendelssohn-Bartholdy, and Robert Schumann), and its verse is chiefly that of the romance (usually four-line stanzas, odd lines unrhymed, even lines assonanced), but it is less introverted, less morbid, and less sorrowful than its predecessor. Jiménez' prolonged stay in the Guadarrama Mountains had completed his cure and brought him back to an appreciation of nature, albeit in solitude and mystery.

BALADAS DE PRIMAVERA

For Jiménez, the years from 1906 to 1912, spent in his native Moguer, represented both a physical and a spiritual renewal, as well as a return to *Modernismo*. In no less than nine books of poetry, he again emulated Darío in his experimentation with forms, fascination with the music of words, and joyous eroticism in nature. *Baladas de primavera* (ballads of spring) exemplifies this phase of Jiménez' development. In *Baladas de primavera*, he eschews exotic figures and decor so typical of the Parnassians, Symbolists, and modernists; here, his sensuality is simpler, more tender, and closer to that of Musset, Verlaine, and Francis Jammes, experienced more personally than vicariously. Again, there is the inspiration from the heritage of popular Spanish poetry, evident both in form—as in the use of a rhythmic line as a musical refrain, conveying no particular meaning but with an appealing lilt—and in content, where ingenuous and simple expression belies profound thought or poignant emotion.

LA SOLEDAD SONORA

The trilogy of elegies marked a return to the Baudelairean decadence of some earlier volumes. These poems have little of the spontaneity and musicality of the pastorals and ballads, largely because of the poet's efforts to adapt his material to the fourteen-syllable Alexandrine, usually in four-line stanzas with assonance in the even lines, not Jiménez' best poetic medium. Jiménez continued to modify and perfect the Alexandrine as well as other forms in four more volumes, *La soledad sonora* (the sonorous solitude) being the most representative. This collection articulates with particular clarity the poet's personal view of the world.

The epigraph of *La soledad sonora* is taken from Saint John of the Cross, reinforcing the link with the sixteenth century mystical poet suggested by the title of the collection. The apparent paradox in the antithetical "sonorous solitude" disappears when the reader becomes aware that solitude here does not mean withdrawal from the world but rather intimate communion with it. Moreover, there is much more auditory imagery in this work than before, along with the characteristic range of visual and other sensuous images, made possible for Jiménez by his solitude. The poet's normal tendency to Impressionism extends here to synesthesia, a common feature of *Modernismo* and one to which Jiménez' keen sensory perception easily adapted. The poet's skill in prolonging the perfect instant to render it infinite, occasionally disturbed by thoughts of the passage of time and death, is epitomized in his contemplation of the pine tree by his house at Fuentepiña. Jiménez' perceptions of the odor and sounds of the tree that best characterizes the Andalusian scene are transformed from sensations of the moment into a mystical experience in which he finds himself attuned to the eternal.

SONETOS ESPIRITUALES

Back in Madrid until his exile from Spain, Jiménez associated with many prominent artists and intellectuals, but by this time in his career he was less open to stylistic influences. His *Sonetos espirituales* (spiritual sonnets) are unique in his oeuvre in that they are composed almost exclusively of classic eleven-syllable sonnets with the traditional *abba* rhyme scheme. The discipline of these poems, which are characterized by a high degree of technical perfection, is matched by great emotional restraint. Here, Jiménez achieves a balance between thought and feeling. Despite the great mastery of form, the structural and verbal precision of these poems, genuine emotion prevents exclusive concern with intellectual subtlety, formal perfection, and verbal agility for its own sake. The introductory "Al soneto con mi alma" ("To the Sonnet with My Soul"), with its physical images translated in each case into ideal images and arranged in pairs, contains the essence of the volume. *Estío* (summer) marks further Jiménez' maturation in terms of emotional and poetic authenticity; most notable in *Estío* are the variety, flexibility, and verbal economy of the verse. Jiménez' treatment of love in this volume, inspired by his love for his fiancé, is in marked contrast to the immature eroticism of earlier works.

DIARIO DE UN POETA RECIÉN CASADO

Less than a year after his wedding, Jiménez published *Diario de un poeta recién casado*, a combination of free verse and brief prose pieces generally recognized as a key work, his best, in the poet's own opinion. This collection is composed of six groups of poems, each with a title that identifies its theme. The principal themes of the volume are married love and the poet's metaphysical reflections on his ocean voyage to the United States and return voyage to Spain. This was not only his first contact with America but also his first experience of the sea. The expanse, monotony, and solitude of the gray ocean and gray sky immediately gripped him; he was most impressed by the endless, restless motion of the sea, like the beating of a huge, cosmic heart, giving the ocean a kind of immortality that he had never perceived before. Jiménez' awareness of the sea as an image of the entire physical world, changing constantly yet remaining fundamentally the same, gave *Diario de un poeta recién casado* a metaphysical dimension previously lacking in his verse. The collection marked the mature poet's search for more universal values in poetry and life at a time when the vogue of *Modernismo* had passed. *Diario de un poeta recién casado*, followed by *Eternidades* (eternities), *Piedra y cielo* (rock and sky), *Poesía*, and *Belleza* (beauty), set a new direction for Spanish poetry and established decisively Jiménez' position and influence.

EXPLOITING SPANISH HERITAGE

Like Unamuno and Antonio Machado, Jiménez continued to keep abreast of the latest movements in literature and the arts yet sought inspiration primarily in Spanish traditions. Although it cannot be said that, either by age or temperament, Jiménez had become the "grand old man" of Spanish poetry, he did not recommend novelty for novelty's sake to his fellows, and he began to find fault not only with imitations of foreign works but also with the innovations of the Spanish vanguard poets. (Indeed, he had grown somewhat crotchety and, except for his wife, more solitary than ever.) His own originality was no longer achieved in defiance of tradition, but rather in a harmonious blend of change with the traditional. The *romancero*, Saint John of the Cross, Luis de Góngora y Argote, and Bécquer exemplify the vital heritage that Jiménez and the greatest of his contemporaries would continue to exploit. In fact, the *generación del 27* (Generation of 1927) indirectly took its name from Góngora, whose tricentenary was celebrated in that year and to the admiration of whose virtuosity Jiménez had contributed. The Mexican essayist Alfonso Reyes, Jiménez' longtime friend, compared him physically and spiritually to Góngora as well as to the tortured figures in many of El Greco's paintings.

POETRY FROM THE NEW WORLD

During the first part of Jiménez' new life in the New World, spent in Puerto Rico and Cuba, the poet wrote many articles for newspapers and magazines published in every country of Latin America. For several years, however, he wrote no new poetry, publishing several volumes that were no more than anthologies or rearrangements of old materials, perhaps because he thought that his American readers would find them new. Finally, in Florida, his inspiration returned and, before a trip to Argentina and Uruguay in 1948, he produced *La estación total* (total season) and *Romances de Coral Gables*. Although the former also contains some of his earlier work, Jiménez added much that was a distillation of all of his poetic experience and a reaffirmation of the values of *Diario de un poeta recién casado*. *La estación total* not only is a summation, however, but also points the way to the joyous sense of fulfillment of *Animal de fondo* (animal of depth).

In the collections immediately preceding *La estación total*, Jiménez had expressed the fundamental tension in his being—both a source of inspiration and a soul-wearying affliction. Torn between light and shadow, truth and falsehood, hope and doubt, he would be whole only when these opposites were united, perhaps only in death. Such was Jiménez' recurring theme in the volumes preceding *La estación total*. In contrast, "Desde dentro" ("From Inside"), the first poem of *La estación total*, is positive and confident; in this collection, Jiménez finally attains the transcendent reality that he had grasped imperfectly and fleetingly in earlier work. "Plenitude" might well be the title of the volume, which reveals the poet's awareness of plenitude in three dimensions: the "eternal," seen in nature; the "external," experienced through the senses; and the "inner reality," discovered intuitively. Communicating a sincere, intensely personal religious experience through language alone, these poems are in-evitably marked by a certain obscurity and ambiguity, desirable if readers are to be permitted their own interpretations.

ANIMAL DE FONDO

Animal de fondo was to be the first part of *Dios deseado y deseante* (God desired and desiring), a much larger work that Jiménez never completed. The twenty-nine poems of the collection were not intended to be read as individual pieces but rather as links in a continuous chain. A dynamic rhythm, strongly suggestive of the motion of the ship on which Jiménez sailed to South America, prevails throughout the sequence. Soothed by the gentle movement of the sea, the poet is as satisfied as a child rocked and comforted in his mother's arms, attaining at last the complete sense of fulfillment that he has sought since childhood and to which he has aspired throughout his long, arduous efforts as a poet. Contrary to the tradition of Spanish mysticism, which expresses the divine through the language of human love, Jiménez uses religious metaphors to deify his sensitivity to the beautiful, for poetic creation is also a religious experience, an intimate union, although not, as in the customary mystical sense, a union with God. The theme of "La transparencia Dios, la transparencia" ("Transparency, God, Transparency") is that of the whole collection, expressing the struggle between the poet and his personal god to achieve successful union in art and love, "as a fire with its air" in its ardor. There is some ambiguity in the poems that follow, as Jiménez attempts to distinguish his god from God, often in paradoxical and contradictory terms. Among the several attributes of his god, Jiménez discovers love, found in all the elements but not solely spiritual or divine. "En mi tercero mar" ("On My Third Sea") reveals his god to be one of human love also, that of the poet for his wife, as much physical as spiritual. The poet's "great knowledge" is his awareness of being complete when, as perceiver, he merges with that which is perceived. On the sea, his god is the "mirror" of himself, then, but in "La fruta de mi flor" ("The Fruit of My Flower"), the imagery becomes more abstract, and Jiménez' vision turns inward. The sensibility that has been like a halo about him through life now enters his being, and the flower of promise bears the fruit of fulfillment. Whether Jiménez' mysticism is orthodox or not, the joyous yet humble religious attitude, the flexible meter and other aspects of prosody, and the novel imagery of *Animal de fondo* often remind one of the *canciones del alma* (songs of the soul) of Saint John of the Cross.

It is neither as theologian nor as philosopher but as a great lyric poet that the author of *Animal de fondo* is remembered. Unfortunately, recurring depression prevented Jiménez from maintaining in his last poems the optimism of *Animal de fondo*. In more than fifty years of poetic production, however, Jiménez' aesthetic and spiritual vision remained clear and his creative ability vigorous. Constant renewal kept his work from becoming dated, although his roots were always deep in the Spanish traditions that sustained his entire poetic creation.

OTHER MAJOR WORKS

NONFICTION: *Platero y yo*, 1914, enlarged 1917 (*Platero and I*, 1956); *Españoles de tres mundos*, 1944; *Monumento de amor*, 1959; *La corriente infinita*, 1961; *El trabajo gustoso*, 1961.

BIBLIOGRAPHY

Cole, Leo R. *The Religious Instinct in the Poetry of Juan Ramón Jiménez*. Oxford, England: Dolphin, 1967. A critical analysis of Jiménez's poetry with an emphasis on its religious aspects. Includes a bibliography.

Fogelquist, Donald F. *Juan Ramón Jiménez*. Boston: Twayne Publishers, 1976. An introductory biography and critical analysis of Jiménez's major works. Includes a bibliography of the poet's works.

Jiménez, Juan Ramón. *The Complete Perfectionist: A Poetics of Work*. Edited and translated by Christopher Maurer. New York: Doubleday, 1997. Christopher Maurer, who has written widely on Spanish literature, has collected and categorized the thoughts and aphorisms recorded by Jiménez in his quest for perfection in life and his work. Maurer provides context for the maxims set down by Jiménez, allowing the reader to begin to know Jiménez as a person and a poet as well as a philosopher.

Nicolás, Antonio T. de, ed. and trans. *Time and Space: A Poetic Autobiography—Juan Ramón Jiménez*. New York: Paragon House, 1988. Nicolás provides some excellent translations and a detailed introduction to the prose work *Tiempo* and the prose and poetry of *Espacio*. His well-documented presentation is supported by analysis in a historical context.

Olson, Paul R. *Circle of Paradox: Time and Essence in the Poetry of Juan Ramón Jiménez*. Baltimore: Johns Hopkins University Press, 1967. A critical study of selected poems. Includes bibliographic references.

Urbina, Pedro Antonio. *Actitud modernista de Juan Ramón Jiménez*. Pamplona: Ediciones Universidad de Navarra, 1994. This brilliant analysis resulted from Urbina's Berley lectures. He demonstrates the extent of influence that Jiménez had on the Generation of '27 as well as his ideological and literary influences on European and Latin American writers. In Spanish.

Wilcox, John C. *Self and Image in Juan Ramón Jiménez*. Chicago: University of Illinois Press, 1987. Wilcox examines the evolution of the poetry from pre-Modern origins, through Modernism, and its endurance through the post-Modern era. He focuses on the work as process and reader interpretations from various perspectives, including formalist, structuralist, and poststructuralist readings, as well as other critical readings of the enigmatic poet's prolific corpus.

_____. "T. S. Eliot and Juan Ramón Jiménez: Some Ideological Affinities." In *T. S. Eliot and Hispanic Modernity, 1924-1993*, edited by K. M. Sibbald and Howard Young. Boulder, Colo.: Society of Spanish and Spanish-American Studies, 1994. A discussion of Jiménez's connections with literary movements in England and the United States.

Young, Howard T. *The Line in the Margin: Juan Ramón Jiménez and his Reading in Blake, Shelly, and Yeats*. Madison: University of Wisconsin Press, 1980. This analysis demonstrates the influences upon the poet's work by English poets William Blake, Percy Bysshe Shelly, and William Butler Yeats. Jiménez had translated their poetry, and the Spanish poet's admiration is evident in his own poetry as he departed from his Spanish and French models. This investigation yields interesting biographical data as well as critical readings and literary analyses. The poet's affinity for British literature was evident in his life and work.

Richard A. Mazzara;
bibliography updated by Carole A. Champagne

SAINT JOHN OF THE CROSS

Juan de Yepes y Álvarez

Born: Fontiveros, Spain; June 24, 1542
Died: Úbeda, Spain; December 14, 1591

PRINCIPAL POETRY

"Vivo sin vivir en mí," wr. 1573 ("I Live Yet Do Not Live In Me")

"En una noche oscura," wr. 1577 ("The Dark Night")

"Adónde te escondiste," wr. 1577 ("The Spiritual Canticle")

"Llama de amor viva," wr. 1577 ("The Living Flame of Love")

"En el principio moraba," wr. 1577 ("Ballad on the Gospel 'In the Beginning Was the Word'")

"Que bien sé yo la fonte," wr. 1577 ("Although by Night")

"Encima de las corrientes," wr. 1578 ("Ballad on the Psalm 'By the Waters of Babylon'")

"Entréme donde no supe," wr. c. 1584 ("Verses Written on an Ecstasy")

"Tras de un amoroso lance," wr. c. 1584 ("A Quarry of Love")

The Complete Works of St. John of the Cross, 1864, 1934, 1953

Poems, 1951

OTHER LITERARY FORMS

The following prose works by Saint John of the Cross explicate themes in his poetry, using methodologies of Scholastic criticism: *La subida del Monte Carmelo* (1578-1579; *The Ascent of Mount Carmel*, 1864, 1922), *Cántico espiritual* (c. 1577-1586; *A Spiritual Canticle of the Soul*, 1864, 1909), and *Llama de amor viva* (c. 1582; *Living Flame of Love*, 1864, 1912). Discussion of them in the text is parallel with that of the poems.

ACHIEVEMENTS

With Saint Teresa de Jesús of Ávila, Saint John of the Cross carried out the reform of the Carmelite Order and defended the Descalced Carmelites' rights to self-determination within obedience. In addition to becoming rector of the Carmelite College at Alcaláde Henares

and founder of the Descalced Carmelite College in Baeza, John of the Cross was vicar of the El Calvario Convent in Andalusia and prior of Los Mártires in Granada and of the Descalced Carmelite Monastery in Segovia. Moreover, he participated in the foundation of at least eight Descalced Carmelite houses throughout Spain. John of the Cross was beatified in 1675 by Pope Clement X, canonized in 1726 by Pope Benedict XIII, and declared Doctor of the Church in 1926 by Pope Pius XI.

In Spain, John is considered to be the most successful lyric poet of the sixteenth century because of his harmonious resolution of popular and medieval traditions with the new learning and literary forms of the Renaissance. Beyond Spain, perhaps because of his singular dedication to one ideal and the strength of his vision, his poetry continues to rank among the finest love poetry written in any language.

BIOGRAPHY

From his twenty-first year, Saint John of the Cross dedicated his life and writing to the singular goal of making the adventure of the contemplative life of the anchorite an actuality in sixteenth century Spain. His accomplishment, particularly in literature, far surpassed his expectations.

Saint John of the Cross was born Juan de Yepes y Álvarez in 1542 in the town of Fontiveros in the kingdom of Old Castile. His father, Gonzalo de Yepes, and his mother, Catalina Álvarez, had worked in that small village for thirteen years as silk weavers and merchants, aided by John's older brother, Francisco. Gonzalo de Yepes' great-grandfather had been a favorite of King Juan II; one uncle was an Inquisitor in Toledo; three others were canons; and one was the chaplain of the Mozarabic Chapel in Toledo.

Because of her lower social status, Catalina Álvarez was hated by her husband's family, so much so that upon Gonzalo's death they refused to help her support his three children, forcing them to live in poverty. In 1548, they moved to Arévalo, where Francisco was apprenticed as a weaver and Juan, without success, attempted a variety of trades.

From Arévalo, the Yepes family moved to the town of Medina del Campo, famous since the Middle Ages for its annual three-month-long international trade fair. There, John learned his letters and learned to beg for his Jesuit school. His brother married, and his mother, Catalina, in spite of their difficulties, took in a foundling. In 1556, when Emperor Charles V stopped at Medina on his way to his retirement at the monastery at Yuste, John saw the hero of European spiritual unity. The great moment did not, however, contribute to John's learning a trade. In 1563, he was taken to the Hospital de la Concepción by Don Alonso Álvarez de Toledo, where he became a nurse, working in that profession until he was twenty-one years old.

In 1563, having rejected the offer to become the hospital's chief warder, John left it to profess in the Order of Mount Carmel. The young Spaniard followed the rule of the Order in perfect obedience, according to contemporary accounts, but he spent hours searching for the spirit of the primitive rule in *A Book of the Institutions of the First Monks* (reprinted in 1507). In this fourteenth century work, Juan de Yepes discovered the tradition of the eremitical way, which leads through austerity and isola-

Saint John of the Cross (Library of Congress)

tion to the experience of the Divine Presence. John of the Cross received permission to follow the old rule when he made his final profession before Ángel de Salazar, who had recently allowed Teresa de Jesús to found the Order of Descalced Carmelites in Ávila.

After professing in 1564, the young friar traveled to the University of Salamanca, to which the Spanish then referred as *Roma la chica* because of its large international student body and its superb reputation in theology. The first three years he spent at Salamanca as an *artista*, and the fourth as a theologian studying, not with the famous Francisco Vitoria, father of international law, nor with Luis de León, who taught there between 1565 and 1573, but with the more traditional Father Guevara and Father Gallo, who taught Saint Thomas Aquinas's *Summa theologica* (c. 1265-1274) and Aristotle's *Ethica nicomachea* (c. fourth century B.C.E.). The effect of this study appears in Saint John's later writing. Rather than posing a threat to his mystic contemplation, Scholasticism served to keep his mystic effusions within the confines of reality, fostering a clarity of language and logical development, a lyricism of thought, and a psychology of common sense that made his work accessible to all readers.

The faculty during those years at Salamanca longed for intellectual emancipation, and many, such as Luis de León, were cautioned and often jailed for years by the Inquisition. The debate was between the Scholastics, who authorized only the Latin Vulgate, and the Renaissance-inspired Scripturalists, who wished to translate the Hebrew and Koine Greek into modern languages. Typically, John of the Cross did not involve himself in this intellectual turmoil but continued to seek the solitary spirit of Mount Carmel. His zeal was so great that in 1566, those Carmelite students who were entrusted to his tutelage by the vicar general of the Order, Juan Bautista Rubeo, complained of John's rigor, self-discipline, and near-constant state of contemplation. John's course was not the outward one. Instead of finishing his university career, he left Salamanca in 1567 for Medina del Campo, where he said his first Mass at the Church of Saint Anne in the presence of his brother, the latter's family, and his mother, Catalina Álvarez.

Because it was permissible to do so among the Carmelites, John immediately decided to enter the Carthusian Order for a life of total silence, solitude, and contemplation. His decision was delayed, however, by his meeting Teresa de Jesús, who had come to Medina del Campo, with Juan Bautista Rubeo's blessing, to establish a convent for Descalced Carmelite nuns. Teresa convinced John to follow the contemplative way within his own Order so that her nuns would have a confessor. Moreover, at the time of Teresa's visit, King Philip II wrote to Father Antonio Heredia, the prior of Saint Anne's, giving him permission to reform the Carmelite Order of Monks as well, telling him that a wealthy gentleman had donated a house in the hamlet of Duruelo for that very purpose.

In August, 1568, Teresa, three nuns, one Julián de Ávila, and John of the Cross left Medina del Campo for the city of Valladolid and for Duruelo. Teresa taught John the old rule through example as she commanded his aid in establishing the Convent of El Río de los Olmos outside Valladolid. She then changed his name from Juan de San Matías to John of the Cross. She also persuaded him that recreation in the form of music, song, and dance were necessary (as well as taking long walks, which prevented the Carmelites from becoming surly) and sent him with one workman to prepare the house at Duruelo for the eventual arrival of Father Heredia from Saint Anne's.

During their five weeks of rigorous labor, John revived the mode of desert life of the original Carmelites, going barefoot, wearing serge vestments, fasting, praying, and doing penance. When Father Heredia arrived to take charge, John was careful to observe Vicar General Rubeo's dictates not to depart in principle from the Unmitigated Carmelite Order as already defined, so as to avoid antagonizing them. While Teresa's letters to Heredia reveal her concern regarding the severity of the brothers' penances and flagellations, John's mother Catalina Álvarez came to be their cook, his brother Francisco came to sweep their cells, and Ana Isquierda came to wash and mend their clothes.

From Duruelo, John went to establish religious houses in the towns of Mancera and Pastrana, and in 1570 he went to the University of Alcaláde Henares to found a college for the Order. At Alcalá John tutored his charges in Thomist philosophy, heard their confessions and those of the nuns at the Imagen Convent, and directed the friars in their contemplative life.

In 1571, Teresa de Jesús called John of the Cross to be the confessor at the Convent of the Incarnation in Ávila. She relates that, during the months of December and January, she began to have access to the ineffable experience of *matrimonio* and that John was of immense help to her: "One cannot speak of God to Father John of the Cross because he at once goes into ecstasy and causes others to do the same," she writes. The practical-minded Teresa complained that John's desire to bring everyone to spiritual perfection was a source of constant annoyance. Moreover, testimony from his living companions, Father Germaine and Brother Franciso, claimed that John was tormented with frightful night apparitions and on one occasion was severely beaten by an enraged countryman—all of which he welcomed.

Suddenly, the reformed Order began to encounter difficulty on every level. In 1570, Philip II appointed visitors to examine the houses, an action which angered the Vicar General. Father Rubeo retaliated by appointing various defenders, who were sent to each of the provinces. Teresa left the Convent of the Incarnation and met Father Gracián, who persuaded her to disregard Father Rubeo's orders not to establish houses in Andalusia simply because the Vicar General felt that the vitality of southern Spain was incongruent with the contemplative way. With Gracián's assurance that Philip II would support her, Teresa, then sixty-three years old, went ahead and established houses in Seville, Peñuela, and Granada. Rubeo accordingly declared the Descalced Order disobedient and ordered the immediate evacuation of the Andalusian convents in 1575. Gracián and Teresa refused; he was excommunicated, and she was ordered by the Council of Trent to pick a convent where she would spend the remainder of her days. She refused and decided to spend another year in Seville.

Meanwhile, John of the Cross was still serving as confessor at La Incarnación in Ávila, until Gracián called him and other Descalced Carmelites to Almodóvar in 1576. Father Gracián proposed that the reformed Order name its own definitors and provincials, in effect making themselves independent of the Unmitigated Carmelites under Father Rubeo. At this meeting, John of the Cross wished, as usual, to avoid conflict. In fact, he opposed the election of officers from among the reformed Order, since the Calced brothers already fulfilled these duties, leaving the followers of the reformed Order to their meditations. John's voice went unheard, and Gracián succeeded.

Rubeo reacted by sending Father Jerónimo Tostado to visit the Spanish Descalced houses in order to discourage their expansion. Supposedly, had Teresa and Gracián taken their case to Rome, the Pope could have settled their differences with Rubeo. Philip II, however, was anxious to maintain the traditional Spanish monarchical sovereignty over the Church Militant and impeded Gracián and Teresa's move in that direction.

In 1577, Teresa attempted to return to La Incarnación in Ávila, but Tostado excommunicated all the nuns who voted for her reinstatement as prioress. He evicted them from the convent and denied them access to their confessors. He then tried to persuade John to abandon Teresa and reenter the unreformed Order, promising him a priorship. John refused.

While visiting Teresa, who was living in secrecy in Toledo, John was arrested by the secular arm of the Church, beaten, and locked in isolation. When he was led out for interrogation, he succeeded in escaping back to his cell to destroy letters, only to be recaptured and imprisoned within the Carmelite monastery in a closet at water level on the River Tajo. There he remained from December, 1576, until his escape in August, 1577. Teresa repeatedly wrote Philip II regarding the situation, but her letters went unanswered. Rubeo and Tostado considered Teresa's work finished and John of the Cross to be a rebel who had disobeyed by serving as confessor to the Convent of the Incarnation in Ávila without Rubeo's express permission.

While he was imprisoned, John composed, among others, his poems "The Spiritual Canticle" and "The Living Flame of Love," which, according to nineteenth century Spanish critic Menéndez y Pelayo in his *Historia de los heterodoxos españoles* (1887), "surpass all that has ever been written in Spanish." John was fed bread and water only three times a week on the floor of the refectory, after which he was beaten by each of the friars, who verbally insulted his kneeling form. Occasionally, so that he would not collapse from hunger, he was given rancid sardines.

After loosening the bolts of his cell door during his jailer's absences, John of the Cross lowered himself down a rope made of bedclothes to the monastery garden. There, a stray dog showed him a route of escape. Believing that the Virgin Mary was lifting him, he succeeded in scaling two walls to reach the street. By hiding in doorways of various houses, he made his way in full daylight to the Carmelite Convent of San José, where he found refuge for several days until the nobleman Don Pedro González de Mendoza arranged for his recuperation at the Hospital of Santa Cruz. During John's stay with the nuns of San José, he spoke of his captors in glowing terms as his benefactors who had brought him to an understanding of grace, to which he referred as "the dark light." He recited to the nuns the poems he had composed while in captivity, and one of the nuns wrote them down.

Because Tostado's persecution of the Order had abated, John was soon appointed vicar of the El Calvario monastery in Andalusia. John customarily led the thirty monks into the mountains for evening meditations. According to tradition, they ate only salads made from wild herbs that were carefully chosen by an expert, the cook's mule. On feast days, they dined upon *migajas*, bread fried in oil. At El Calvario, John of the Cross wrote *The Ascent of Mount Carmel*.

One year later, in 1579, John was ordered by Father Ángel de Salazar to take three friars to the university town of Baeza and set up a monastery in an old house; this was to become the College of Our Lady of Mount Carmel. The college quickly became an object of intense curiosity among the faculty at the university, who, believing that John of the Cross enjoyed infused wisdom, respected his insight into the mysteries of the faith and attended his lectures on morals and religious questions. John, however, prudently sent his charges to the university to study theology.

In 1581, John and his companion, Brother Jerome, established a convent of four nuns in Granada. The following year, John was elected prior of the Carmelite monastery there, Los Mártires. The revolt of the Alpujarras, in which Moorish converts to Christianity had elected a king and rejected their new religion, had been suppressed by Philip II ten years prior to John's arrival. Consequently, many of the children born to apostate families now served as slaves or protected servants in the homes of wealthy Old Christian families. Moreover, during those years there lived in Granada a ninety-year-old woman remembered as La Mora de Ubeda, who had gained a reputation among contemporary Muslim theologians for mystic wisdom acquired through the *faqir* tradition. The young *moriscos* drawn to their fathers' faith were threatened with years of rowing in the king's galleys should they wear Moorish clothes, carry Moorish weapons, speak, read, or write Arabic, bathe too frequently, dance the zambra, or play Moorish instruments. John served as confessor to *moriscos* and Old Christians alike, and to those seduced by the splendors of the city crowned by the Alhambra and the Generalife, he taught that "we travel not in order to see but in order not to see."

In Granada, John wrote the books *A Spiritual Canticle of the Soul* and *Living Flame of Love* to distinguish the contemplative way to unity according to the Divine Will from both natural and Muslim mysticism, which often took the form of possession and madness. According to John of the Cross, these states were outwardly nearly indistinguishable from the transports of the dark light of grace; they occurred, he said, not only among Christians drawn to the Illuminist movement but also among the young *moriscos*, upon whom he was often called to perform exorcisms.

While John of the Cross was still at Baeza, a wealthy young Genoese, Jesús María Doria, professed within the Descalced Order and quickly found favor with Teresa de Jesús through Philip II's recommendation. Doria was to be John of the Cross's nemesis. Teresa, well aware of the Italian's keen mind, sent him to her friend Gracián, who in turn sent him as their representative to Rome. In 1582, Doria returned to Spain with special papal privileges, determined to reorganize the Order of Descalced Carmelites according to the *machina* of the Italian houses. In order to do so, he succeeded in having himself elected vicar general of the Order and unsuccessfully tried to send his former superior and continual rival, Gracián, to Mexico. In 1588, through a general conference, he revamped the Order's governing structure. Meanwhile, John of the Cross, while founding monasteries and convents in Córdoba, Segovia, and Málaga, sought to mediate between Doria's missionary zeal to send Carmelites throughout all Christendom and beyond, and Gracián's equal determination to keep the Order small and confined to Spanish soil. At a general

meeting in Almodóvar, John actually spoke out against the hunger for power he saw invading the Order in the guise of worthy projects—but to no avail.

In 1588, John was appointed prior to the convent in Segovia, which became the seat of government of the Order during Doria's frequent trips abroad. Philip II learned of John's able administration and commended him for it. John's companions, however, attested that he scourged himself regularly, was sickly, wore sparto-grass undergarments and chains which drew blood, fasted almost continuously, and refused to wear anything but the heaviest clothing the year round. He slept only three hours each night and still heard confessions and ministered to the sick while trying to reconcile Gracián and Doria. His inner life was such that on occasion he was incapable of carrying out the simplest task, so frequent and overwhelming were his raptures. The last time he saw his brother Francisco, whom he claimed to have loved more than anyone else, John told him of a vision in which Christ asked him his desire. To Christ, John replied, "Suffering to be borne for Your sake and to be despised and regarded as worthless." His prayer was to be answered.

In 1589, the nuns of the Order, convinced that Doria was determined to abolish the reforms initiated by Teresa, petitioned Gracián and John to be separated from the Brothers over whom Doria ruled. Doria learned of the conspiracy from Luis de León and, suspecting that both Gracián and John were supporting the feminine rebellion against him, denounced the two to Philip II, who intervened directly with an order that the nuns remain.

At the next chapter meeting, John was denied any post whatsoever. First the council accepted and then rejected his offer to lead twelve Carmelites to Mexico. He and Gracián were to learn the extent of Doria's anger. In Seville during the chapter meetings, there was such fear of Doria that no one dared to oppose him. John bravely spoke out, accusing Doria of destroying charity, free discussion, and the right to self-determination within the rule. Doria reacted by sending John of the Cross into exile, to the solitude of the desert monastery of Peñuela in Extremadura. Gracián suffered a worse fate, being stripped of his habit, expelled from the Order, and sent begging justice to Rome. The accusation against him was disobedience.

In Peñuela, John of the Cross became seriously ill with an infection and went to Úbeda seeking aid. There, the prior treated him badly because, years earlier, John had scolded him for his manner of preaching. John's ecstatic prayer in Segovia, as reported by his brother Francisco, was answered in Úbeda: "not to die a superior, to die where he was unknown and to die after great suffering."

ANALYSIS

The work of Saint John of the Cross, although not copious, presents a synthesis of medieval learning and Renaissance form, couched in the tradition of Spanish realism. He sought through his poems and books to explain to his Order the nature of the three steps through contemplation to union with the Divine Presence: the *via purgativa*, the *via iluminativa*, and the *via unitativa*. The poem "The Dark Night" and the poet's book-length explication *The Ascent of Mount Carmel* address the beginner or novice, revealing the two spiritual revolutions he will experience; the poem "The Spiritual Canticle" and its book-length explication *A Spiritual Canticle of the Soul* address the *aprovechantes*, who intermittently see their aspirations fulfilled; the poem "The Living Flame of Love" and its explication *Living Flame of Love* address those perfect religious aspirants who seldom cease to experience the dark light of grace. The three poems were written during the imprisonment of John of the Cross in Toledo in 1577, the first book during his priorship at El Calvario in 1578 and the remaining two while he was prior of Los Mártires in Granada in 1581. Although the works become clearer when read in the context of sixteenth century Spain, John of the Cross's method of combining medieval, Renaissance, and popular traditions to explain the mysteries of the faith in terms of universal human experience frees his writing from its historical limitations.

Saint John of the Cross's prose explicates his poetry: *The Ascent of Mount Carmel, A Spiritual Canticle of the Soul*, and *Living Flame of Love* use the methodology of Scholastic criticism to explain the doctrine contained in his three major poems. The author readily admits that the intellect hinders rather than aids one's progress toward meditation, but he maintains that reason, in theology as well as in physics and psychology, is the only re-

liable guide. Reason and the concomitant qualities of simplicity and clarity are extolled as those values most to be esteemed in the religious life of prayer and discipline, so that the contemplative may avoid the danger of becoming attached to the intricate beauty of the ritual rather than to its spirit. The contemplative must present a tabula rasa—freeing his will from the self so that he may be charitable, his understanding from knowledge so that he may have faith, and his memory from continuity so that he may have hope—before he may receive grace.

Reason enables Saint John of the Cross to distinguish the contemplative's two passages through the "dark night," first from initiate to *aprovechante*, then to perfect, from the states of melancholy, *aboulia*, and possession which they closely resemble. The initiate's enthusiasm soon becomes anger in the form of the frustration experienced by a child denied the rewards he seeks, and he is then subject to pride, restlessness, boredom, envy, impatience, fetishism, and dishonesty until, when he least expects it, he "stand[s] alone in the bitter and terrible dark night of the senses" in which the world appears inverted. The initiate entering the first dark night manifests total distraction and fear that he is lost. All of his attempts to regain the source of his former well-being are foiled. Some initiates attempt to begin their discipline again, to no avail. Most, on entering the first dark night, manifest madness in the form of extreme sexual desire, blasphemy, and vertigo.

Once they have overcome these trials, however, the *aprovechantes* may lose their humility and attack with too much confidence, to the point that their experience of grace is self-deceiving and they become blinded by hallucinations, voices, and transports. Since the *aprovechantes* have not completely overcome their former affections, they are in danger of becoming physically and psychologically ill.

According to John of the Cross, the second passage through the dark night to perfection is even more difficult and may last many years. For the physically weak, it is unbearable. The *aprovechantes* experience spiritual poverty, helplessness, detachment, incomprehension, an absence of will, and anguish over losing mind and memory. They may by chance finally acquire wisdom in the form of the dark light of the fire described in *Living Flame of Love*. The perfect is then enjoined to make of his soul a hiding place where the beloved may live with gracious company in pleasure and ease.

Although Saint John of the Cross's psychology is limited to three faculties (the will, reason, and memory) and four interrelated emotions (pleasure, pain, fear, and hope), he provides a clear view of the spiritual adventure of a sixteenth century Spaniard who is not called to the territorial adventure of imperial expansion. In an interesting image, John compares the reluctant adventurer to a canvas that refuses to be still for the artist's brush.

"THE DARK NIGHT"

In "The Dark Night," John of the Cross presents the momentary union of the novice's soul with God in terms of the fulfillment of the desires of two lovers who have been separated. Most directly, the poem re-creates the escape of the beloved at night from her house to a meeting with her lover outside the walls of the city, where they surrender themselves to the rapture of their passion. The beloved recalls her fear, her desire, the necessary deceptions and precaution, the shock of being found by her lover, and the joy of the encounter, with its consequential loss of self in a union with all and nothingness.

The simplicity of the poem gives it its strength and almost hypnotic power. The Spanish is rustic, although not uncultured, and it characterizes the beloved with a pastoral simplicity and innocence as she ventures forth to meet her lover. Morphologically and syntactically, the poet gives the beloved's words some features of that dialect between Gallego-Portuguese and Castilian which characterizes the standard literary form of rustic speech known as *sayagués*. Moreover, the poet employs a stanza which discourages elaboration in favor of simplicity, clarity, and precision. From the soldier-courtier Garcilaso de la Vega (1501-1536), who two decades earlier had revolutionized Spanish poetry by successfully adapting the softer Italian hendecasyllable to the more regularly accented and rigid medieval Spanish verse, John of the Cross borrowed the *lira*. By alternating three heptasyllables and two hendecasyllables within a rhyme scheme which seals the lines by pairing them without regard to length, the poet using the *lira* directs his thought inward and inhibits elaboration. The inward direction of the poem, reflecting the recollection necessary for the beloved's escape, is reinforced by the poet's skillful use of repetition within and between the strophes. Through

onomatopoeia, he re-creates with sibilants and voiceless fricatives the darkness, silence, secrecy, and softness of the adventure.

To overcome the temporal limitation of the language of the poem, the poet uses a series of apostrophes to the night. The poem is a re-creation of the encounter in which the beloved attributes to the night the same immediacy ascribed to the lover. Again, in response to the inward direction of the poem, the apostrophe culminates in the center of the poem, in which the metamorphosis of lover-beloved occurs on the morphological level: "amado con amada/ amada en el amado transformada." The fusion of the lovers becomes confusion, and the sounds of the poem overwhelm the sense, so that the original gender distinction between the allomorphs "amado" and "amada" disappears into "transformada."

"THE SPIRITUAL CANTICLE"

"The Spiritual Canticle" enlarges the theme of "The Dark Night" to include mortification and illumination. The poem, comprising forty *liras*, is an eclogue, modeled on those of Garcilaso de la Vega, in which John of the Cross presents the lovers in a dialogue as shepherds who are now espoused. (In "The Dark Night," they had to escape in order to be united.)

The first stanzas present the beloved initiate moving through the *via purgativa* as a young shepherdess seeking her lover, who has abandoned her soon after revealing his love. Her sense of loss turns her life into an attenuated death and a desperate search for reunion. First, she tries to reach him through other shepherds. Then she abandons both her fears and her pleasures to look for him on her own. As she wanders, the beauty she discovers reminds her of his grace, until she is overwhelmed by longing. The shepherds who speak to her of him merely increase her pain, because she cannot understand the meaning of their words. As she has already surrendered her will to him, she believes her punishment is unjustified, yet she hopes that by his possession of her, she will regain the self she has lost and the reason for being which she lacks. When she least expects it, her lover's eyes appear to her, reflected in a fountain where she quenches her thirst. The *via purgativa* ends with the medieval motif of the maid at the fountain overtaken by a stag.

The next step toward union, the *via iluminativa*, begins with fear. The beloved flees in panic until the lover's words assure her that her flight merely attracts him more, and therefore her attempt to escape is futile. Since the beloved has not acquired perfection, the *via iluminativa* of the *aprovechante* and the *via unitativa* of the perfect become confused. The beloved may ascend to union and also descend to mortification on the secret ladder introduced by the poet in "The Dark Night." In the fourteenth and fifteenth stanzas, the beloved finds union with her lover, expressed as an ecstatic vision of mountains, valleys, strange islands, sweet melodies unheard, and sonorous silence. The vision is enriched by imagery reminiscent of the Old Testament Song of Songs and, because of the absence of verbs, is made to appear simultaneous.

The beloved must descend from union, presented as a garden in Zion, first to mortification in which she defends their vines from foxes; then to illumination in which she weaves their roses into garlands; then back to mortification in order to defend their solitude, to conjure the rain-laden western wind, to restrain the envious, and to hide her lover away in silence while distracting him with the delights of her raptures. To aid his beloved, the lover proudly commands his creation, through song, to abandon them to their rapture. He then proceeds to raise her again to union, regaling her with the fulfillment of her desire, healing her sorrow, defending her tranquillity with the controlled power of lions, the wealth of gold shields or coins, the luxury of purple hangings, and the peace derived from a social structure based upon others' admiration and awe before the brilliance of their passion and the fragrance of their wine that, because of its age, gives delight without sorrow.

In stanzas twenty-six through twenty-nine, the beloved addresses those same admirers of her rapture in order to explain her distraction. She reveals that it derives from the wine that she shares with her lover and that consequently her only concern has become to learn to love well. She explains to them that she will no longer be among them on the commons, because she has become entranced with loving, losing herself only to be found by her lover. In the last ten stanzas, unconcerned that their admirers overhear, she addresses her lover and reveals to them the source of their love. His passion derives from one insignificant grace, presented as a single hair blown across her throat. Because of her humility

and unworthiness, the continuation of that passion arises from the beauty which flows from his eyes, and is reflected in her, as her passion arises from discovering her reflection in him. The verbal tenses of these last eight stanzas refer not to chronology but to the fulfillment of the lover and beloved's purpose. The distinctions among past, present, and future disappear as the lovers explore profound and lofty mysteries. Accordingly, the eclogue ends not in the classical manner of the shepherd's departure with the setting sun, but with the image of horses descending a hill to drink water once the siege they had resisted is lifted.

"THE LIVING FLAME OF LOVE"

The third of the poems written by Saint John of the Cross while in the monastery prison of Toledo, "The Living Flame of Love," continues the allegory of "The Dark Night" and "The Spiritual Canticle." This work presents in four *liras* the song of the beloved to her lover's passion during their ecstatic union. The beloved is now perfect inasmuch as her grace is actual rather than potential. These *liras*, having six rather than five lines and deriving from Garcilaso de la Vega's friend and immediate literary predecessor, Juan Boscán (1500?-1542), are freer, less vacillating and inwardly directed than the first two poems.

The poem is one of the most intense moments in a powerful literary tradition. In it, the beloved sings of the lover's passion as a life-giving and living fire that consumes with fulfillment rather than destruction. The beloved rejoices in her total surrender and pleads to have the rapture made complete by his destruction of the barriers which still divide them. His passion captures, wounds, and subdues her with a gentleness that reveals to her the nature of eternity. The taste of this knowledge turns her heart from the sorrow of living an attenuated death apart from her lover to the joy which his presence infuses as she comes into being through his love. The dark light emanating from her lover's fire illuminates the entirety of her beauty when the poem ends abruptly with her lover's breath rousing her passion again as he awakens on her breast.

Three other poems written in Toledo at the same time do not achieve as perfect a synthesis of the eclogue, Song of Songs, and folk motifs derived from the tradition of the romances and courtly lyrics of the *villancicos* as do the three poems presented here. The *coplas de pie quebrado*, known as "Although by Night," present the medieval motif of the *fonte frida* in such a way that the night acquires at least thirteen different meanings through an equal number of contexts. In the nine *romances* which constitute the "Ballad on the Gospel 'In the Beginning Was the Word,'" the poet employs the same method as in his major poems, explaining the mysteries of the faith in terms of the varieties of human love. In "Ballad on the Psalm 'By the Waters of Babylon,'" the ascetic's sense of alienation and his consequent rejection of the world are presented in terms of the Babylonian captivity of Israel's people, who refuse to sing the jubilant songs of Zion.

OTHER MAJOR WORKS

NONFICTION: *La subida del Monte Carmelo*, 1578-1579 (*The Ascent of Mount Carmel*, 1864, 1922); *Cántico espiritual*, c. 1577-1586 (*A Spiritual Canticle of the Soul*, 1864, 1909); *Llama de amor viva*, c. 1582 (*Living Flame of Love*, 1864, 1912).

MISCELLANEOUS: *The Complete Works of St. John of the Cross*, 1864, 1934, 1953.

BIBLIOGRAPHY

Brenan, Gerald. *St. John of the Cross: His Life and Poetry.* Cambridge, England: Cambridge University Press, 1973. Includes a translation of his poetry by Lynda Nicholson. Bibliography.

John of the Cross, St. *The Poems.* Translated by Roy Campbell, with an introduction by P. J. Kavanagh. London: Harvill Press, 2000. A bilingual edition of the poems that includes useful commentary by Kavanagh.

_____. *The Poems of St. John of the Cross.* Edited by John Frederick Nims. Chicago: University of Chicago Press, 1995. According to the publisher, "this dual-language edition makes available the original Spanish from the Codex of Sanlúcon de Barrameda with facing English translations. The work concludes with two essays—a critique of the poetry and a short piece on the Spanish text that appears alongside the translation—as well as brief notes on the individual poems."

_____. *The Poems of St. John of the Cross.* Trans-

lated by Kenneth Krabbenhoft, illustrated by Ferris Cook. New York: Harcourt, 1999. This beautifully illustrated bilingual edition of the poems that includes a bibliography.

Kavanaugh, Kieran. *John of the Cross: Doctor of Light and Love.* New York: Crossroad, 1999. A study of St. John of the Cross that reprints the poems and includes useful features such as a select bibliography. Illustrated.

Kenneth A. Stackhouse; bibliography updated by the editors

RONALD JOHNSON

Born: Ashland, Kansas; November 25, 1935
Died: Topeka, Kansas; March 4, 1998

PRINCIPAL POETRY
A Line of Poetry, a Row of Tress, 1964
Assorted Jungles: Rousseau, 1966
Gorse/Goose/Rose and Other Poems, 1966
Sunflowers, 1966
Io and the Oxeye Daisy, 1966
The Book of the Green Man, 1967
The Round Earth on Flat Paper, 1968
Reading One and Two, 1968 (2 volumes)
Valley of the Many-Colored Grasses, 1969
Balloons for Moonless Nights, 1969
The Spirit Walks, the Rocks Will Talk, 1969
Songs of the Earth, 1970
Maze/Mane/Wane, 1973
Eyes and Objects, 1976
RADI OS I-IV, 1977
Ark: The Foundations 1-33, 1980
Ark 50: Spires 34-50, 1984
Ark, 1996
To Do as Adam Did: Selected Poems of Ronald Johnson, 2000

OTHER LITERARY FORMS
In addition to his poetry, Ronald Johnson published several cookbooks, including *The Aficionado's South-*

western Cooking (1968), *The American Table* (1984), *Southwestern Cooking, New and Old* (1985), *Simple Fare* (1989), and *Company Fare* (1991).

ACHIEVEMENTS

Prizes awarded to Johnson for his poetry include the Boar's Head Prize for Poetry, in 1960; *Poetry*'s Inez Boulton Award, in 1964; National Endowment for the Arts grants, in 1969 and 1974; and the National Poetry Series Award 1984. His magnum opus, *Ark*, was awarded the *Boston Book Review*'s Bingham Poetry Prize in 1997, shortly before his death. After his death, in 2000, a conference on Johnson's poetry, called "Eye, Ear, and Mind," was held at the State University of New York, Buffalo.

BIOGRAPHY

Ronald Johnson was born and grew up in Ashland, Kansas. He briefly attended the University of Kansas before spending two years in the United States Army, earning as a result the post-Korea veterans' benefits that allowed him to attend and be graduated from Columbia University, New York, in 1960. During the years in New York, he became acquainted with many other artists, poets, and scholars, including poets, such as Charles Olson, associated with Black Mountain College in North Carolina.

In the early 1960's, Johnson traveled in England with poet and publisher Jonathan Williams, and he received inspiration from the country for many of his most memorable poems. During this time he participated in the concrete poetry movement and became a close friend of Ian Hamilton Finlay, one of the best-known poets in the movement.

In 1968, Johnson moved to San Francisco, where, with the exception of two teaching jobs, he was to make his permanent home. He taught creative writing at the University of Kentucky (1971-1972), held the Roethke Chair for Poetry at the University of Washington, Seattle (1973), taught at the Wallace Stegner Writing Workshop at Stanford University (1991), and was Roberta Holloway Poet at the University of California, Berkeley (1994). In 1996, Living Press, in Albuquerque, New Mexico, issued a special broadside edition of *Ark*, "a pyramid of eleven levels and sixty-six quatrains fram[ing]

Johnson's darkest work of verse," as Paul Naylor put it. Johnson died of brain cancer on March 4, 1998.

ANALYSIS

A disciple of Charles Olson, Ronald Johnson followed Olson's intuition that a poem must find the form necessary to its fullest expression. For Johnson, this meant the writing of poems that, by conventional measures of poetry, do not seem to be poems at all. Under the pull of energies initially mobilized during the concrete poetry movement of the early 1960's, Johnson explored the poetic possibilities of typography and the visual presence of a poem as a kind of sign. At the root of his attention is the natural world, its sounds and sights. Out of his deference to this phenomenal world, Johnson devised techniques to register it in a new way. In some of his poems, where his manipulation of typography and instinct for the suggestibility of individual letters is working, the poem becomes a wholly novel visual experience.

From his early concrete poems to his *Ark* series, Johnson sought to bind the world of poetry to the world of made things, and he regarded this as the poet's realm—objects as words and words (as attested by the carefully crafted typography of his pages) as objects. Thus, his work is a rare and refreshing turn-away from the hypersubjectivity and confessionalism of much postmodern poetry. Against the ramblings of selfhood he erects a bright vision, directing one toward the complex and beautiful universe.

VALLEY OF THE MANY-COLORED GRASSES

In his book *Valley of the Many-Colored Grasses*, Ronald Johnson quotes Ralph Waldo Emerson in an epigraph to one of his poems. The quotation attributes to nature the power to use creation as a means of expressing itself: "The air is full of sounds; the sky, of tokens; the ground is all memoranda & signatures." These signs speak to "the intelligent," or human beings with eyes and ears. If "the intelligent" are not suitably articulate to pass on the language Nature speaks, it "waits & works, until, at last, it moulds them to its perfect will & is articulated." Reading the poem following the epigraph, one discovers that it is simply the words of the epigraph "aired out" in free-verse lines, Johnson's spacial arrangement of the words serving to arrest the flow of Emerson's prose and emphasize key perceptions. A poem has been found in Emerson's text.

This poem, titled "Emerson, on Goethe," exemplifies two characteristics of Johnson's thought and writing. The first is his preoccupation with nature, or everything that makes up the cosmos, from ants to stars and not exclusive of what an architect designs or a composer composes. A man is subservient to nature, inhabiting nature, dependent upon nature. Nature produces patterns of order and sentient secretaries, artists of various kinds, who are not justified in feeling alienated from a world so animated and willful. Pervading Johnson's poetry is the idea that a poet is someone who brings nature to the ears and eyes of nonpoets under the command of nature itself. This mission puts Johnson as a poet outside the trend of contemporary poetry, where the poet seems more often the secretary of himself, that subjective complex which utters forth from deep within its private and often obscure consciousness. Johnson's heritage as a writer is much more old-fashioned. His poems frequently refer to writers and painters, for whom the real show is the world outside the self. The Johnson heritage includes, along with the transcendentalist Emerson, the poet William Blake, who saw everything in a grain of sand. It embraces the records Henry Thoreau left of his daily eyework along Walden Pond and the paintings of Joseph Turner, who had himself roped to a ship's mast during a storm, the better to know what he was painting. It welcomes the visionary eye of the painter Samuel Palmer, as in Johnson's poem on Palmer, in which the eye is "covered with fire after every immersion/ in the air" and is taken by nature's leading beyond the horizon, where "it gathers to itself all light/ in visionary harvest." It is the same heritage which guided the poet Ezra Pound, in his World War II prison cage, to find in the wasps and midges in the grass a vision of the highest order, an order uncreated by humans but requiring gifts of sensitivity and vision to recognize.

The second characteristic that Johnson's Emerson "poem" demonstrates is Johnson's unconcern about what is actually a poem. None of its words is Johnson's, but the perception of the words is Johnson's. Perception, attention, and observation are of more value to the poet than so-called originality, not that Johnson as a writer is simply copying down what others have written. His attention is arrested by nature and by other writers who testify to similar devotion, so, if in the course of writing

a poem Johnson remembers that "to Coleridge, the Marigold,/ Monk's-hood, Orange-lily & Indian pink/ flash with light—" the poem is not spoiled by borrowing. On this poet's mind, Johnson's, happened to be the working of another poet's mind, Samuel Taylor Coleridge's. Appropriately, then, the line that follows the one just quoted tells about Charles Darwin's ability to see phosphorus in a horse's eyes. Perhaps the poetic spell is ruined by telling about what a scientist can do, but Johnson is not particularly concerned about "the poem"; he seeks to evoke dazzling examples of human eyesight working in the real world.

THE BOOK OF THE GREEN MAN

Yet Johnson is also concerned about "the poem." He wants his poems to be new, bright, as dazzling as the source of inspiration. To readers familiar with what T. S. Eliot and Ezra Pound did to the form of a poem, Johnson's poetry does not seem unpoetic at all. What does seem uncommon is Johnson's persistent belief in a nature which speaks to human beings. Johnson is not interested merely in objectivity, but in seeing through the objectivity. He pursues the calling of seer, or hearer: A tree and its leaves are never ordinary; commonplace objects speak and establish intimacy, an intimacy which is the vision. Thus, a suite of Johnson's poems in another early book, *The Book of the Green Man*, have sweetly innocent titles: "What the Earth Told Me," "What the Air Told Me," and "What the Leaf Told Me." In this book, Johnson mentions the "skiey influences" that entered into Romantic poet William Wordsworth's pores, sustaining his poetic vision of countryside and lakes. Johnson desires such a relationship. He longs to hear the earth speak, to issue some dark, meditated/ syllable perhaps—/ something more/ than this inarticulate warble and seething." The earth writes to the poet instead:

> Today I saw the word written on the poplar leaves.
> It was "dazzle."
> As a leaf startles out
> from an undifferentiated mass of foliage,
> so the word did from a leaf—.

The poet is Adam in a garden that has not yet been seen with language. Nature continues to educate Adam in this garden, beyond declaring the adjectives through which it is known, with basic scientific facts: "For the tree forms sun into leaves, & its branches & saps/ are solid & liquid states of sun." Johnson would have his reader respond to photosynthesis as a visionary entity, while still bringing along a knowledge of electrochemical force and the laws of physics. When the earth tells the poet that "nothing is allowed to stand still," the commonplace law becomes marvelous in its numberless examples, poplar leaves in the wind being only one in the countless manifold. "In the homage of attentions 'all things/ are in flux,'" Johnson writes, and, throwing a stone into a pond, observes "its circles interlacing/ & radiating out to the most ephemeral edge." Again, the high school physics experiment becomes an occasion for religious meditation.

Writing of Johnson's poetry, Guy Davenport notes that "his every poem has been to trace the intricate and subtle lines of force wherein man can discern the order of his relation to the natural world." Thus, Johnson's desire to make nature have a voice is to regather the modern ear to a hearing of what it has been taught is dead. In his poems, the goal of registering the voice of phenomena is reached by pruning away conventional poetic rhetoric and extruding lines of gnomic brevity. In *The Book of the Green Man*, the theme is that a man desires to enter the green world and be taught by it. The man of the title is that mythical figure from England who, in one of his guises, has leaves growing on his face like a beard and foliage for hair. This man bespeaks that intimacy of botany and humanity which for Johnson is the substratum of his art of writing a poem:

Poems beginning germinal in the instant
—reeling out, unravelling, tendril & silken, into the air—
ethereal growths,
sudden, & peculiar as mushrooms?
Uncrumpling
as moths from cocoons—.

The poet marvels at the relationship between the world and the mind and understands the relationship as something ethereally botanical, biological. In this light, Johnson assembles a corps of writers, from Alexander Pope to Wordsworth to William Klivert, who sensed the heavenly abode which nature suggested. Pope dreamed of planting a cathedral from poplar trees; Johnson dreams in a poem of entering "the architecture of bees" and the mole's passages and the lizard route through "scrolls of leaves." Dominant in all Johnson's work is this urging to go *into* nature, and to recall those writers who attempted the same kind of entry and union.

SONGS OF THE EARTH

In a slender volume published in 1970 titled *Songs of the Earth*, Johnson continued his efforts to listen to the world. He said of the poems: "These songs are listenings, as poems must listen and sing simultaneously." One of the poems is simply the word "earth" repeated without spacing three times in one line, this one line repeated seven times: "eartheartbearth." The eye picks out significant terms hiding in the bushes: art, ear, hear, heart, hearth.

Another poem spaces out the first and last *s* in the word "stones" to reveal "tone." Yet another places the word "wane" in a square grid, the word printed with spaces between the letters and the lines. Within the square thus formed of capital letters the word "anew" appears in lowercase letters. As in nature, there is no waning that leads to nothing; all waning is, rather, a kind of reprocessing, so in the poem the recycling of letters displays new meaning. Such a poem cannot be spoken, and such poetry to Johnson is "a magical world where all is possible and an 'o' can rise, like the real moon, over the word *moon*."

Such writing is sign-making and emphasizes the dominance of the eye as the ruling mode of perception for Johnson. His *Songs of the Earth* was written in response to Gustav Mahler's symphony of the same name. The concrete poems which resulted may have been the product of the poet's listening, but they exist for the reader solely as mute visual patterns, for the eye alone. Johnson considers this not a drawback but a revolution: "We can now make a line of poetry as visible as a row of trees." In a later volume of poetry, titled *Eyes and Objects*, Johnson defines a self as the things it sees: "You are what you look for/ zeroing out on the light-and-dark,/ the X of eyes." His need and intuition as a poet have been to make visible objects for pairs of eyes to converge upon and see.

RADI OS I-IV

Johnson has continued to marvel at the products of the universe and to erect structures to hold his marvelings. A book titled *RADI OS I-IV* is a rewriting by excision of John Milton's *Paradise Lost* (1667, 1674). Milton's text, like his title, undergoes a rereading by Johnson, and what is left after the "erasures"—which explains the spacing in the title (paRADIse lOSt)—is a modern poem, both in appearance and in ideas. One theme is energy, a familiar twentieth century concern. The radii of the sun energize men and also enable them to see. A fragment of the poem reads:

> Too well I see:
> for the mind
> swallowed up
> entire, in the heart
> to work in fire,
> words The Arch.

ARK

The poet takes his vocation, a commitment not without risk, from the energy mysteriously generated by his capacity to be impassioned by the world. *RADI OS I-IV* is one part of Johnson's magnum opus *Ark*, in which the analogy between writing poetry and creating physical structures is declared in the subsection's titles: "The Foundations," "The Spires," and "The Outworks" (also as "The Ramparts"). In a note on *Ark*, Johnson says that he wrote the poem "with stones of words and mortar of song." Individual poems in the work are "Spires," and the reader is impressed by Johnson's unique ability to *arrest* language, whether single words or phrases:

> to say then head wedded nail and hammer to the
> work of vision
> of the word
> at hand
> that is paradise

Ark is that structure so literally prescribed for Noah by God in which he would leave behind the old world and find a new, a terrestrial paradise. It, the ark, is also the arc, the curve of the globe, one segment of which is America, the last promised land humanity was vouchsafed and from which humanity managed to fall, ignoring and persecuting the original inhabitants. Artificers, builders, and poets remain, however—Johnson a member of the host—and they project their various visions. As a builder of his vision, Johnson is in many respects an *arc*hitect, and indeed the poem is a complex struc-

ture, in part built of sections called "Beams," carefully laid out on the page, sometimes in blocks of prose, sometimes in structures that, like George Herbert's "The Altar," represent a physical object—an I-beam in the case of "Beam I."

The vision is work, Johnson reminds the reader: "for if hell indeed rein time stood still/ and paradise thus daily fall/ unlikely wings/ on usual shoulders." Johnson clearly views writing poetry as a religious quest, as the establishment of a testimonial edifice that will inspire belief in the hearts of nonartificers. Behind this poem stand Johnson's predecessors, for whom nature was the first place to look for inspiration—William Blake, Walt Whitman, Henry David Thoreau, and Samuel Palmer. It is a vision that sees swarms of mayflies as bands of angels and an ear for which "even the humble fly/ buzz anthem/ Christ."

TO DO AS ADAM DID

Johnson's last collection of poems, published posthumously in an edition preapred by Peter O'Leary, reissues poems from Johnson's entire career as well as previously unpublished poems that Johnson wrote at the end of his career. Included are selections from seven collections published between 1964 and the 1996 edition of *Ark*, as well as "The Shrubberies" and *Songs of the Earth*, the latter difficult to find after its 1970 edition. Taken in the aggregate, these poems display the full range of Johnson's impressive erudition—his allusions to astronomy, biology, music, ornithology, mythology, botany—in a "cross-cultivation" of idioms that "announce the natural world as our temple," as reviewer Christian Sheppard put it. Rich in quotations and borrowings from the Bible, European literary traditions, and naturalists including Thoreau and Palmer, Johnson's oeuvre transforms these into his own, revivified, vision.

This career-wide collection reminds readers that the poetry of Johnson is inimical to despair and gloom. It derives from a mandate, clearly religious, to make the world seen and heard. In vain a reader will search for confirmations or investigations of the popular twentieth century focus: the self. In abundance, however, the reader will find things for that self to study and see, and constant reminders of what powers of perception a human possesses, and what he or she is supposed to do with them:

Let us grasp at
the gate, unhinge the dark

clear lake

(moon to sky's edge)

awake! awake!

OTHER MAJOR WORKS

NONFICTION: *The Aficionado's Southwestern Cooking*, 1968; *The American Table*, 1984; *Southwestern Cooking, New and Old*, 1985; *Simple Fare*, 1989; *Company Fare*, 1991.

TRANSLATION: *Sports and Divertissments*, 1965 (of notes by Erik Satie for his piano pieces under the same title).

BIBLIOGRAPHY

Chicago Review 42, no. 1 (Winter, 1996). A special section of this issue is devoted to Johnson's poetic monument *Ark*, his lifework, with such contributors as Thom Gunn, Robert Creeley, and Paul Naylor.

Harmon, William. "The Poetry of a Journal at the End of an Arbor in a Watch." *Parnassus: Poetry in Review* 9 (Spring/Summer, 1981): 217-232. For the Johnson scholar, this work represents an apex in the canon of critical evaluations of the poet's works from *A Line of Poetry, a Row of Trees* to *Ark*. Harmon's ambitions often make his writings as complex and dense as the work he is examining. This is a rewarding essay that requires perseverance and determination.

Jaffe, Dan. "Voice of the Poet." *Saturday Review* 52 (September 6, 1969): 29. This review of *Valley of the Many-Colored Grasses* illustrates Johnson's devotion to nature, the inspiration provided by Walt Whitman and the Black Mountain poets, and his decidedly unfashionable language. Jaffe observes that "Grasses" blends the intentions of the Symbolist poets with the imagery of the naturalists to create an energetic expression of the universe.

Johnson, Ronald. *The American Table*. New York: William Morrow, 1984. Although an unconventional source of information, this book provides a fascinating perspective on Johnson's travels throughout America and his ruminations on the country and its diverse communities and lifestyles. Offers glimpses of the significant impact Johnson's travels and exposure to different cultures—from the Shakers to the Southwest and Wyoming to the east coast—have had on his poetry.

Library Journal. "California and the West." 102 (December 15, 1977): 2469. This article evokes the spirit of Guy Davenport, who wrote about Johnson in his collection of essays *The Geography of the Imagination*, in asserting the importance of Johnson's poem *RADI OS I-IV*. It also reiterates the ultimate payoff to the reader who perseveres through this difficult and fragmented poem which is based on John Milton's work.

O'Leary, Peter. Introduction to *To Do as Adam Did*, by Ronald Johnson. Jersey City, N.J.: Talisman, 2000. O'Leary considers Johnson an American counterpart of the great visionary poets, such as Dante, George Herbert, and William Blake.

Stratton, Dirk. *Ronald Johnson*. Boise, Idaho: Boise State University, 1996. A brief but valuable and complete overview of Johnson, part of the Boise State Western Writers series. Includes a four-page bibliography.

Bruce Wiebe,
updated by Christina J. Moose

SAMUEL JOHNSON

Born: Lichfield, Staffordshire, England; September 18, 1709
Died: London, England; December 13, 1784

PRINCIPAL POETRY

London: A Poem in Imitation of the Third Satire of Juvenal, 1738

The Vanity of Human Wishes: The Tenth Satire of Juvenal Imitated, 1749

Poems: The Yale Edition of the Works of Samuel Johnson, 1965 (volume 6; E. L. McAdam, Jr., and George Milne, editors).

OTHER LITERARY FORMS

Samuel Johnson was a journalist, essayist, critic, scholar, lexicographer, biographer, and satirist. Early in his career, he wrote reports on the debates in Parliament for *The Gentleman's Mazagine*. Until 1762, when he received a pension from the British government, Johnson was a professional writer and wrote what publishers would buy. The most important results of his efforts, in addition to his poetry, were his *A Dictionary of the English Language: To Which Are Prefixed, a History of the Language, and an English Grammar* (1755), his essays in *The Rambler* (1750-1752) and *The Idler* (1758-1760), and *Rasselas, Prince of Abyssinia* (1759). *A Dictionary of the English Language* remains one of the outstanding achievements in the study of language. Johnson contracted in 1746 with a group of publishers to write the first comprehensive dictionary of the English language. Nine years later, with the help of only six assistants, he produced a work that is notable for its scholarship and wit. Although scholars fault its etymological notes, its definitions are generally apt and often colored by Johnson's

Samuel Johnson (Library of Congress)

wit, biases, and sound understanding of English usage. *The Rambler* and *The Idler* are composed of periodical essays, which, when combined with those that Johnson wrote for *The Adventurer* (1753-1754), number more than three hundred. The essays discuss literature, religion, politics, and society. They were much admired in Johnson's day, but are less so in the modern era. They are often grave, but rarely dull, and represent some of the finest prose in English. Another important prose work, *Rasselas, Prince of Abyssinia* is Johnson's major contribution to fiction. Like Voltaire's *Candide: Or Optimism* (1759), *Rasselas, Prince of Abyssinia* features a naïve young protagonist whose adventures gradually strip away his illusions. Johnson's work is the less harsh of the two, but is similar in tone.

Johnson's work as a biographer and scholar began early. In 1740, he wrote biographies of Admiral Robert Blake, Sir Francis Drake, and Jean-Philippe Barretier. These works are unoriginal in content. In 1744, he pub-

lished *An Account of the Life of Mr. Richard Savage, Son of the Earl Rivers*, which was later included in *The Lives of the Poets* (1779-1781), although it was often published separately. Savage was a bitter and angry man; Johnson emphasized with dramatic narrative the wrongs society had visited on him. Many years after *An Account of the Life of Mr. Richard Savage, Son of the Earl Rivers*, Johnson agreed to write a series of prefaces to the works of English poets for a group of booksellers. The result was *The Lives of the Poets* (four volumes in 1779 and an additional six volumes in 1781). These essays are marked by Johnson's critical insight and immense knowledge of literature; many are still standard references. Johnson was also an editor, and produced an important edition of Shakespeare with commentary. Some critics have denigrated Johnson's lack of appreciation of Shakespeare's poetry, but his appraisal of the plays is well considered, and his defense of the plays against dogmatic neoclassical criticism is notable for its good sense.

Among Johnson's other significant writings are the political essays *Thoughts on the Late Transactions Respecting Falkland's Islands* (1771) and *Taxation No Tyranny* (1775), and the account of his travels in Scotland with his young Scottish friend, James Boswell, titled *A Journey to the Western Islands of Scotland* (1775). In these works Johnson displays his hatred of war and political profiteering and his acuteness of observation.

ACHIEVEMENTS

The diversity of Samuel Johnson's writings can be daunting; he was a novelist, playwright, essayist, journalist, editor, critic, scholar, biographer, lexicographer, etymologist, moralist, social and political commentator, philosopher, and poet. His poem *London* (1738) was published at least twenty-three times during his lifetime, and the popularity of his poetry contributed much to his reputation as the quintessential *man of letters*. In his era, no one had read more of the world's literature than he, and few equaled his literary achievements. Johnson seems to have so dominated the literary life of England that the period from 1750 to 1784 is often called the Age of Johnson.

"Poet" was a term of honor in eighteenth century England. The poet was at the apex of literature, and Johnson took pleasure in being referred to as one. After his death, his reputation as a poet fell from the high esteem of his contemporaries to a level of near disregard. His best-known poetry is the product of intellectual work, not inspiration. The Romantics and their nineteenth century descendants valued emotional and inspirational verse. Johnson's verse is well organized, often satirical, filled with social commentary and moralizing, and more realistically observational than metaphorical; his poetry is well within the Augustan style. He was among the best poets of his day, his verse being dynamic and rich in thought. He believed that poetry should emphasize the contemporary language of the poet; it should be accessible to the poet's contemporary readers. In this belief he is in the same tradition as John Donne, John Dryden, Alexander Pope, and even poets as Karl Shapiro. The language of Johnson's verse is still accessible to readers; it is distinctive in its combination of precision, nearly explosive anger and contempt, and acute observation of the human condition.

BIOGRAPHY

Many writers have suffered, and many more have pretended to suffer, for their art. Samuel Johnson's own suffering in fact made his art necessary. He was born on September 18, 1709 to Michael Johnson, a bookseller, and Sarah (née Ford), who was then forty years old. The labor had been difficult, and Samuel Johnson was, by his own account, born nearly dead. While he was a child he contracted scrofula and smallpox; he was horribly scarred by the diseases and became deaf in one ear and partially blind in one eye. Although his father was a respectable citizen and even gained a small degree of prominence in 1709 as Sheriff of Lichfield, Johnson's ancestors were of humble background. His parents were unhappy with each other, and their mild mutual hostility contributed to the miseries of their son's life.

In spite of his ugliness, poor background, and unhappy family life, Johnson became a leader among his schoolmates. He was not an ideal student; he would neglect his studies, then in great bursts of energy apply himself to learning. He wrote much as he had studied; for example, *An Account of the Life of Mr. Richard Savage, Son of the Earl Rivers* was written in as little as thirty-six hours, and it has been claimed that *Rasselas, Prince of Abyssinia* was completed in a week. He aspired to be almost anything but a writer. With a small savings he paid for more than a year at Oxford, from October, 1728 to December, 1729, but lack of money forced him to leave. After his father's death in 1731, he tried teaching. He was temperamentally unsuited for teaching; he gesticulated wildly when lecturing, and his bizarre antics confused his students. David Garrick, the actor, was among his pupils, and later helped Johnson have the verse play *Irene: A Tragedy* (1749) produced. Johnson's next ambition was to become a lawyer, but his poverty and physical infirmities inhibited his studies and his ability to pursue strenuous professions. He turned to writing in order to support himself and his wife.

He married Elizabeth Jervis, the widow of Harry Porter, in 1735. She was nineteen years his senior, but provided him with love, a home, and companionship that helped to stabilize his passionate and explosive personality. Acutely aware of his responsibilities as a husband, Johnson took work where he could find it. He moved to London and persuaded the publisher of *The*

Gentleman's Magazine, Edward Cave, to allow him to write for the periodical. During this period of his life he wrote and sold the poem *London*, and tried to interest theater owners in a rough version of *Irene*. As a professional writer who sought to meet the needs of publishers, Johnson wrote essays, reports, poetry, and biographies—whatever would earn him money. *London* was a success and greatly advanced his reputation, but he sold the copyright and profited little from it. His literary labors earned enough for food and a place to live, but he endured bitter poverty.

A group of London publishers contracted with him in 1746 for *A Dictionary of the English Language*, which he completed its compilation seven years later and which was published in 1755. The loyal support of the syndicate of publishers provided him with some small financial security, although his life remained hard. While writing the dictionary with the help of six secretaries, Johnson wrote *The Rambler*, which was published twice weekly from 1750 to 1752. The periodical's reputation was great, but its sales were small. Such was the reputation of the dictionary and *The Rambler* that Johnson became known as "Dictionary Johnson" and "Author of *The Rambler*." In 1749, the poem *The Vanity of Human Wishes* was published. Today it is probably the best known of Johnson's poetic works. Also in that year, David Garrick, Johnson's onetime pupil, by then a famous actor, produced *Irene* at the Drury Lane Theatre. The play lasted for nine nights, a respectable run, and Johnson earned almost two hundred pounds from the production. Subject to depressions in the best of times, Johnson was greatly saddened by the death of his wife in 1752.

From 1755 to 1762, Johnson's most important literary efforts were *The Idler*, which was published from 1758 to 1760 in the *Universal Chronicle*, and *Rasselas, Prince of Abyssinia*. In 1759, Johnson's mother died. Perhaps her illness and death inspired Johnson to contemplate his youth and its disillusionments. The evident result was *Rasselas, Prince of Abyssinia*. Some biographers assert that *Rasselas* was written to pay for his mother's funeral, but most scholars disagree. In 1762, Johnson was awarded an annual pension of three hundred pounds, enough to free him from the necessity of labor.

In 1763, Johnson met James Boswell, a young Scot who would become a favorite companion. It is because of Boswell's *The Life of Samuel Johnson, LL.D.* (1791) that scholars know more about the last twenty years of Johnson's life than they know of the previous fifty-five. Free from financial cares, and afflicted by a variety of physical complaints, Johnson did not write at the prodigious rate that he had when he was younger. His principal literary efforts were *The Lives of the Poets*, a series of prefaces to English poets written for a consortium of booksellers, and *A Journey to the Western Islands of Scotland*, an account of a tour in 1773 with Boswell. Johnson's poetry during his last years consisted primarily of parodies and burlesques written for friends, and Latin verse, composed mostly for his own contemplation. Always a moody and introspective man, his poetry became private and contemplative in his last years. In public, of course, he sought companionship and good conversation, relishing his status as England's leading man of letters. In private, he had an almost morbid dread of death. He believed that people should, at the peril of their souls, fulfill all of their talents; he was acutely aware of his own superior intellectual powers, and believed that he had not properly made use of them. Once in February, 1784, the dropsy that afflicted him disappeared while he prayed, and he took the relief to be a sign from God and spent the last months of his life in spiritual peace. He died on December 13, 1784, and was buried on December 20 in Westminster Abbey, as befitted a poet.

ANALYSIS

Samuel Johnson wrote two major poetic works: *London* and *The Vanity of Human Wishes*. The remaining verse divides into the play *Irene*, poems in Latin, miscellaneous verse in English, and translations from Greek and Latin. *London* was the most popular of Johnson's poems during his life, and it remains the most accessible to modern audiences. Its language is clear and its images straightforward. Like *London*, *The Vanity of Human Wishes* is an imitation of the satires of Juvenal, a Latin poet of the first and second centuries. It is widely regarded as Johnson's poetic masterpiece and is Johnson's effort to convey the essence of the Christian ethos through verse and imagery. The density of its images and ideas makes *The Vanity of Human Wishes* difficult to interpret even for experienced critics. *Irene*, on the other hand, yields readily to interpretation through its strong plot, although its verse, while competent, is unremarkable.

LONDON

Johnson customarily composed his poems mentally before committing them to paper. *London* was composed in this manner; it was written on large sheets of paper in two columns—the left being for the first draft and the right for revisions. Johnson's poetry is firmly in the Augustan tradition, typified in the eighteenth century by the works of Alexander Pope, Jonathan Swift, and Joseph Addison; *London* is characteristically Augustan in its dependence on a Latin model, in this case Juvenal's third satire. When the poem was published, the passages that were derived from Juvenal were accompanied by Juvenal's original lines, which were included at Johnson's request—a common practice at the time. A good edition of *London* will include the relevant Juvenalian passages.

Juvenal's third satire, Johnson's model for *London*, focuses on Rome. In general, Juvenal's satires attack what he perceived to be the immorality of Roman society. In his third satire he cites particulars in the city of Rome itself. Johnson focuses his poem on the city of London and, like Juvenal, cites particulars. He also includes translations from Juvenal's poem and updated versions of some of Juvenal's sentiments. As the accompanying Latin verse shows, Johnson's borrowings are only part of the whole and tend to illustrate the universality of some of the poem's ideas. Too much of *London* is original for it to be simply a translation. For example, Juvenal writes from the point of view of a conservative Roman who believed that his countrymen had grown soft from lack of war and sacrifice, while Johnson writes from the point of view of an eighteenth century Christian who believed that the vices of his age stemmed from his countrymen's failure to recognize the importance of the soul. Johnson was a man of ideas, and his ideas make *London* his own work—a statement of his views of the city when he was a young man of twenty-eight.

London is written in rhyming iambic pentameter couplets. Johnson believed that blank verse could be sustained only by strong images; otherwise, verse needed clear structure and rhyme. His best poetry exemplifies his ideas about prosody; *London*'s heroic couplets follow the model established by Pope. The poem's language is lively and its ideas flow rapidly. Johnson's condemnations are sharply expressed:

> By numbers here from shame or censure free,
> All crimes are safe, but hated poverty.
> This, only this, the rigid law pursues,
> This, only this, provokes the snarling muse.

The city is portrayed as rife with crime, folly, and injustice. King George II is said to be more interested in Hanover than England and London; learning is said to be unrewarded (a favorite theme of Juvenal); government is said to be grasping while the nation sinks; and the city is characterized as architecturally in bad taste. The satire makes London seem bleak and ugly, but the language is exuberant and makes London's faults seem exciting.

The poem's persona (the speaker) is named Thales, who intends to leave London for Cambria (Wales); he craves solitude and peace. Some scholars have identified Thales as the personification of Richard Savage, who had suffered poverty and indignities in London; he left London in 1739 for Wales. Other scholars maintain that Johnson had not yet met Savage, and that *London* was, after all, published in 1738, a year before Savage's migration. This dispute over seeming minutiae represents a major problem that infects much criticism of Johnson's works. Those who support the notion that Savage is the original for Thales sometimes cite Johnson's assertion that anyone who is tired of London is tired of life. They maintain that the poem's point of view is not representative of Johnson but of Savage. Even some critics who do not assert that Savage was the model for Thales dismiss *London* as insincere—as an exercise that does not reflect Johnson's true love for the city.

Students new to the study of Johnson should be wary of reasoning based on Johnson's views in Boswell's *The Life of Samuel Johnson, LL.D.* Boswell's work is monumental; it has helped to shape the modern view of eighteenth century England. Johnson's opinions as reported by Boswell are forcefully expressed and seemingly permanently set, and even knowledgeable scholars have sometimes read into Johnson's early works the views he held when he was a conservative old man. In fact, like most writers who have been fortunate enough to have long careers, Johnson changed his views as he matured, as he read new works, and as he gained new experiences. As a young man, Johnson was rebellious and angry. He was learned and poor; he disliked the Hanoverian monarchy; and the architecture of London in 1738 could be not only ugly but downright dangerous—poorly built walls sometimes collapsed into the streets. The crowding, poverty, and crime of London would probably have shocked any young person from the country who was experiencing it for the first time; Johnson arrived in London in 1737, and the poem appeared in 1738.

THE VANITY OF HUMAN WISHES

The Vanity of Human Wishes, on the other hand, was written when Johnson was in his middle years. Juvenal's satires still interested him, as they did, according to Boswell, in his late years; and *The Vanity of Human Wishes* is an imitation of Juvenal's tenth satire. In this satire, Juvenal shows that people are unable to perceive their own best interests. Some people wish to be eloquent, even though Cicero was doomed by his own eloquence; others seek power, even though Alexander the Great was undone by power. Wise people, Juvenal says, would let the gods choose what is best for them. Typical of the Latin poet, the tenth satire expresses a conservative Roman's disgust with the foolishness of society in the Empire. The dominant themes in the satire would have appealed to Johnson: anger at a people who neglect the ideals that made them great, dismay at the successes of fools at the expense of supposedly intelligent people, and the notion that society's values were distorted, with learning and wisdom ranking below ignorance and vice.

The ethos of *The Vanity of Human Wishes* is Christian. Johnson replaces Juvenal's notion that people do not choose to do what will do them good with the idea that people choose vainly when they choose material and worldly success. Johnson also replaces Juvenal's notion that wise people let the gods choose for them with the idea that wise people put their lives in God's hands. The tenth satire of Juvenal was popular during the Middle Ages because preachers could convert its criticisms of vice into homilies on the dangers of materialism, and it provides ready material for Johnson's portrait of human life gone astray. Nearly 350 lines of his poem are devoted to discussing how people who seek wealth, power, or other earthly pleasures and rewards, fail to find happiness. The poem is thick with images and requires close reading; it is in large part depressingly negative. Much of human life seems hopeless. Even so, Johnson's scope is remarkable; he reaches beyond the range of *London* and beyond the range of Juvenal's satire; he discusses all human beings, everywhere. He cites Thomas Wolsey's power and wealth, Charles XII of Sweden's ambition, the miserable fates of John Churchill Marlborough, who was debilitated by strokes, and Jonathan Swift, who suffered from a disease similar to senile dementia. Neither power, wealth, ambition, honor, nor intellect mean much in the great scheme of life, and none are proof against misery and humiliation.

Johnson leaps back and forth through time, and from one part of the world to another, in his effort to convey the vastness of his topic and universality of his theme. He asserts:

> Unnumber'd suppliants crowd Preferment's gate,
> Athirst for wealth, and burning to be great,
> Delusive Fortune hears th' incessant call,
> They mount, they shine, evaporate, and fall.

A host of examples are mustered to support Johnson's contention that all earthly human wishes are vain; a reader can feel overwhelmed by the images and arguments that Johnson presents. If one does not read the poem carefully, one might interpret it as a despairing depiction of human endeavors and of lives without hope. Some critics call the poem "stoic," as if the only response to the hopelessness of life as depicted by Johnson were withdrawal and endurance. Such a reading misses the poem's fundamental point and fails to recognize Johnson's rejection of stoicism: "Must helpless man, in ignorance sedate,/ Roll darkling down the torrent of his fate?" No, Johnson answers, because "petitions yet remain,/ Which heav'n may hear, nor deem religion vain." God is the solution to the vanities of humanity. Stoicism demands a retreat into one's self; Johnson advocates that one reach outside himself. An important teaching of Christianity in Johnson's day was that one needed to seek beyond the material world for happiness—that unselfishness would bring enduring rewards. Johnson notes the "goods for man the laws of heav'n ordain," "love," "patience," and "faith." He says, "With these celestial wisdom calms the mind." Just as folly is universal, so too is the answer to folly. God responds to anyone who is devoted to Him.

The Vanity of Human Wishes is grim; the poem reflects Johnson's personality and his concerns, and his unhappy view of the disorder of an unfair world is expressed in relentless images. He was also a Christian, holding out hope for himself and the rest of humanity. His poetic skill is revealed in his shift from a lengthy account of the failures of even the best of people to the simple assertion of God's ability to ease the misery of anyone. He uses the heroic couplet, as in *London*, to give his poem a clear structure. Within that structure he maneuvers ideas with seeming ease and resolves the complex problem of the vanity of human wishes with the poetically elegant answer of the Christian ethos.

IRENE

Johnson's play *Irene* was begun while he was still a teacher, before he moved to London in 1737, and he continued to work on it sporadically until 1749, when David Garrick produced it under the title *Mahomet and Irene*. The primary source for the play was the *Generall Historie of the Turkes* (1603), by Richard Knolles. The story is filled with intrigue: Mahomet, the Turkish Sultan, falls in love with a Greek Christian, Irene. He offers her wealth, power, and marriage, if she will renounce Christianity and convert to Islam. His followers are unhappy that their leader, who has conquered Constantinople, would fall for a conquered infidel, and they plot his overthrow. Greeks join in the plotting as well. After some soul-searching and passionate scenes, Irene yields to Mahomet and becomes a victim of the play's intrigues. The plot of *Irene* is surprisingly good, given its neglect by modern readers. Its weakness is in its blank verse, which, as Donald Greene notes in *Samuel Johnson* (1970), has a "sledgehammer monotony." Although the play made money during its run as Garrick's production and was reprinted three times while Johnson lived, it was not a critical success. Its verse is unimaginative and dull, unequal to the strengths of both plot and characters. Johnson reveals insight into his characters, particularly the spiritually struggling Irene, and an ability to present an interesting story.

PROLOGUES, EPITAPHS, ELEGIES

Although *London* and *The Vanity of Human Wishes* are justifiably rated by critics as his best poems, much of Johnson's lesser verse is rewarding. His *Prologue Spoken at the Opening of the Theatre in Drury-Lane* (1747), for example, discusses the merits of drama. In addition to writing prologues that are superior to most others, Johnson was a master of the epitaph and elegy. His "Epitaph on Hogarth" is representative of his ability to evoke pathos in a short poem with such lines as: "Here death has clos'd the curious eyes/ That saw the manners in the face." The poem on William Hogarth, the painter, was something of an exercise for Johnson, written as it was in response to Garrick's request for advice on an epitaph requested by Mrs. Hogarth.

His "On the Death of Dr. Robert Levet" comes more from his heart. The elegy was written in 1782 after the death of the friend and surgeon who had been living in Johnson's home. The poem presents a picture of a man who was "Officious, innocent, sincere,/ Of ev'ry friendless name the friend." Johnson makes the poem a comment on life in general, both its sorrows and glories, and makes the seemingly humble Levet a representative of the best virtues: sacrifice for others, modesty in material desires, and selfless working to improve the lot of humanity. The poem is united by metaphor ("mine" and "caverns") and theme.

WIT AND HUMOR

The somber themes of the elegy and epitaph and the weighty themes of the prologues and major poems might suggest that Johnson's verse is devoted exclusively to the unhappy aspects of life. Such a view, however, would be unbalanced. Even in the bitterness of *London* there is witty wordplay; and Johnson had a remarkable taste for stinging humor. He sent to Mrs. Thrale in 1780 a poem about her scapegrace nephew, John Lade, titled "A Short Song of Congratulation." Lade had recently come into his inheritance, and Johnson lists the various ways that the young man could waste his money. The wit is pointed and accurate; Lade wasted his fortune. Most of Johnson's light verse is extemporaneous, being meant for his friends, rather than for the public, lacking the careful structure of Johnson's other poetry. His Latin poetry, on the other hand, is usually very well constructed.

CRITICAL RESPONSES

Johnson's stature as a poet has varied according to critical fashion. The critics of the Romantic and Victorian periods often dismissed his work as heavy-handed; they favored spontaneity and image over calculation and idea. Johnson was a man of ideas; he thrived on them and loved to toy with them, but his work was also emotional. The critics of the nineteenth century favored lyric poetry over satire and often missed the merits of the poetic tradition in which Johnson's best verse belongs. Twentieth century critics have, in general, rediscovered the virtues of Johnson's prosody. At his best, he fashions his verse with persuasive naturalness. His poetry conveys a powerful vision of the universality of the human condition. *The Vanity of Human Wishes* rightly ranks as one of the best and most important poems of world literature; with *London* and some of the minor poems, taken as a group, it argues powerfully for Johnson's status as a significant poet.

OTHER MAJOR WORKS

LONG FICTION: *Rasselas, Prince of Abyssinia: A Tale by S. Johnson*, 1759 (originally published as *The Prince of Abissinia: A Tale*).

PLAY: *Irene: A Tragedy*, pr. 1749.

NONFICTION: *Marmer Norfolciense*, 1739; *A Compleat Vindication of the Licensers of the Stage*, 1739; *The Life of Admiral Blake*, 1740; *An Account of the Life of John Philip Barretier*, 1744; *An Account of the Life of Mr. Richard Savage, Son of the Earl Rivers*, 1744; *Miscellaneous Observations on the Tragedy of Macbeth*, 1745; *The Plan of a Dictionary of the English Language*, 1747; *Prologue Spoken at the Opening of the Theatre in Drury-Lane*, 1747; essays in *The Rambler*, 1750-1752; essays in *The Adventurer*, 1753-1754; *A Dictionary of the English Language: To Which Are Prefixed, a History of the Language, and an English Grammar*, 1755 (2 volumes); essays in *The Idler*, 1758-1760; preface and notes to *The Plays of William Shakespeare*, 1765 (8 volumes); *The False Alarm*, 1770; *Thoughts on the Late Transactions Respecting Falkland's Islands*, 1771; *The Patriot: Addressed to the Electors of Great Britain*, 1774; *Taxation No Tyranny: An Answer to the Resolutions and Address of the American Congress*, 1775; *A Journey to the Western Islands of Scotland*, 1775; *Prefaces, Biographical and Critical, to the Works of the English Poets*, 1779-1781 (10 volumes; also known as *The Lives of the Poets*); *The Critical Opinions of Samuel Johnson*, 1923, 1961 (Joseph Epes Brown, editor).

TRANSLATIONS: *A Voyage to Abyssinia*, 1735 (of Jerome Lobo's novel); *Commentary on Mr. Pope's Principles of Morality*, 1739 (of Jean-Pierre de Crousaz).

MISCELLANEOUS: *The Works of Samuel Johnson*, 1787-1789.

BIBLIOGRAPHY

Bate, Walter Jackson. *Samuel Johnson*. New York: Harcourt Brace Jovanovich, 1979. This Pulitzer prize-winning biography has shrewd psychological assessments of Johnson's early and major poems.

Boswell, James. *Life of Johnson*. Edited by R. W. Chapman. New York: Oxford University Press, 1998. A massive and exhaustive biography. Boswell has littered the book with countless quotes including Johnson's definitions of oats and lexicographer, his love for his cat Hodge, as well as thousands of bon, and mal, mots.

Eliot, T. S. Introduction to *London and The Vanity of Human Wishes*, by Samuel Johnson. London: Etchells and Macdonald, 1930. Reprinted in *English Critical Essays: Twentieth Century*, edited by Phyllis M. Jones. London: Oxford University Press, 1933. One of Eliot's most brilliant critical pieces, this groundbreaking essay is an indispensable introduction to Johnson's poetry. More than fifty years ago, Eliot proclaimed Johnson's excellence as a poet and declared that *London* and *The Vanity of Human Wishes* were among the finest verse satires in any language.

Greene, Donald. *Samuel Johnson*. 2d ed. Boston: Twayne, 1989. This updated biography offers a vigorous summing-up of Johnson's poetic genius.

Hart, Kevin. *Samuel Johnson and the Culture of Property*. New York: Cambridge University Press, 1999. Hart traces the vast literary legacy and reputation of Johnson. Through detailed analyses of the biographers and critics who carefully crafted and preserved Johnson's life for posterity, Hart explores the emergence of "The Age of Johnson."

Hinnant, Charles H. "The Decline of the Heroic: From *London* to *The Vanity of Human Wishes.*" In *Samuel Johnson: An Analysis*. New York: St. Martin's Press, 1988. This chapter discusses the different approaches of Johnson's two major poems and the changes in artistic vision behind the differences. This essay is a detailed, usually reliable interpretation of both works in relationship to his literary canon.

Johnson, Samuel. *The Poems of Samuel Johnson*. Edited by David Nichol Smith and Edward L. McAdam, Jr. 2d ed. Oxford, England: Clarendon Press, 1974. This pioneering collection arranges all Johnson's poems in chronological order. The editorial and explanatory scholarship is of the highest order. Supervised by J. D. Fleeman in the second edition of 1974, the text is one of the major printings of Johnson's poetry. Prefaces for individual poems provide useful explanations of meaning and any editorial problems.

_____. *Samuel Johnson: Poems*. Edited by Edward L. McAdam, Jr. Vol. 6 in *The Works of Samuel Johnson*. New Haven, Conn.: Yale University Press, 1958. This standard edition offers a chronological arrangement of Johnson's English and Latin poetry, with English translations and solid critical and editorial commentary in footnotes. Based on newly discovered manuscripts and current literary research, this collection is a reliable addition to the modern publication of all Johnson's literary canon. Unlike the above two editions of Johnson's poetry, the Yale collection indulges in some standardization of the original manuscript texts and reduces capitalized common nouns to lower case, in accordance with the guidelines of the Yale Editorial Committee for this project. Prefaces for individual poems provide useful explanations of meaning and any editorial problems.

_____. *Samuel Johnson: The Complete English Poems*. Edited by J. D. Fleeman. New York: Penguin Books, 1971. Another fine chronologically arranged collection of Johnson's poetry. This convenient edition includes Johnson's Latin poems, with English prose translations. Contains excellent editorial scholarship, with incisive endnotes.

Lascelles, Mary M. "Johnson and Juvenal." In *New Light on Dr. Johnson: Essays on the Occasion of His 250th Birthday*, edited by Frederick W. Hilles. New Haven, Conn.: Yale University Press, 1959. This essay is an important study of the poetic transformation of Juvenal's *Satires III* and *X* in, respectively, Johnson's *London* and *The Vanity of Human Wishes*. A comparison of the Latin and English poems demonstrates Johnson's genuine originality, unique Christian vision, and distinctive moral and political concerns.

Naugle, Helen Harrold, and Peter B. Sherry. *A Concordance to the Poems of Samuel Johnson*, Ithaca, N.Y.: Cornell University Press, 1973. This is an alphabetical index of the principal words in Johnson's poetry, citing the passages where they appear. Helpful for identifying both his works and his opinions on issues.

Kirk H. Beetz;
bibliography updated by the editors

_____

Ben Jonson

Born: London, England; June 11, 1573
Died: London, England; August 6, 1637

PRINCIPAL POETRY
Poems, 1601
Epigrams, 1616
The Forest, 1616
Underwoods, 1640
Ben Jonson, 1925-1952 (C. H. Hereford, Percy Simpson, and Evelyn Simpson, editors; includes *Ungathered Verse*)

OTHER LITERARY FORMS

Ben Jonson's fame has rested mainly on his comic drama, especially on the masterpieces of his maturity, *Volpone: Or, The Fox* (1605), *Epicœne: Or, The Silent Woman* (1609), *The Alchemist* (1610), and *Bartholomew*

Fair (1614). Surviving earlier comedies are *The Case Is Altered* (1597), *Every Man in His Humour* (1598, 1605), *Every Man Out of His Humour* (1599), *Cynthia's Revels: Or, The Fountainf Self-Love* (1600-1601), *Poetaster: Or, His Arraignment* (1601), and *Eastward Ho!* (1605, with George Chapman and John Marston). Later comedies are *The Devil Is an Ass* (1616), *The Staple of News* (1626), *The New Inn:Or, The Light Heart* (1629), *The Magnetic Lady: Or, Humours Reconciled* (1632), and *A Tale of a Tub* (1633). Jonson wrote two tragedies, *Sejanus* (1603) and *Catiline* (1611). Two uncompleted works date apparently from the end of his life: the pastoral *The Sad Shepherd* and the tragedy *Mortimer His Fall* (only a few pages).

Jonson's court masques and entertainments may conservatively be said to number about thirty, differing tallies being possible depending on whether minor entertainments of various kinds are counted. Important titles include *The Masque of Blackness* (1605), *The Golden Age Restored* (1616), and *The Gypsies Metamorphosed* (1621). Besides plays, masques, and original nondramatic verse, Jonson wrote and translated a few other works which help to place him in the Renaissance humanistic tradition; all were first published in the 1640-1641 *The Works of Benjamin Jonson*. As a vernacular humanist, Jonson wrote *The English Grammar* (1640); he translated Horace's *Ars poetica* (as *Horace His Art of Poetry*) in 1640; finally, he compiled and translated extracts from classical and modern authors, mostly having to do with ethics, education, and rhetoric; the collection is titled *Timber: Or, Discoveries Made upon Men and Matter* (1641).

ACHIEVEMENTS

Ben Jonson's achievements as a writer of verse can best be summarized by saying that he founded English neoclassicism. Jonson, of course, wrote several decades before what is usually thought of as the neoclassic age, but his work clearly foreshadows that of John Dryden and Alexander Pope. His, like theirs, was a mode of poetry generally imitative of ancient Roman forms, concerned, as important Roman writers had been, with behavior on a specifically human stage of action, and sometimes heroic, often satirical, in tone and stance.

BIOGRAPHY

Benjamin Jonson's father, a minister, died a month before his son's birth. Ben's mother remarried, apparently fairly soon thereafter, the stepfather being a master bricklayer of Westminster. "A friend" enrolled Jonson at Westminster School, but (as he told William Drummond) he was "taken from" school at about the age of sixteen and "put to" a "Craft," presumably bricklaying. Unable to "endure" this occupation, Jonson escaped briefly into the wars with the Netherlands. The next few years (roughly, his early twenties) are the most obscure of Jonson's life. At some point during this time he married and began having children, although practically nothing is known about his wife or family.

Jonson reappears in the late 1590's in theatrical records as an actor and part-time playwright. In these years Jonson was repeatedly at odds with the law, usually because of his involvement with satirical or political drama. He also attracted the authorities' hostility through his conversion to Roman Catholicism. (Eventually he returned to the Church of England, and later in life expressed, above all, distaste for those who claimed

Ben Jonson (Library of Congress)

complete theological certainty.) In the series of comedies of "humours" beginning with *Every Man in His Humour*, Jonson coined an original form of satirical comedy based on the caricature of psychological types. In 1600 to 1601 he temporarily abandoned the open-air "public" playhouses to present his "comical satires" at the more fashionable indoor "private" theater at Blackfriars. The move was part of the provocation of the "stage quarrel" or "war of the theaters," in which Jonson, Thomas Dekker, and John Marston traded plays lampooning one another. Jonson's earliest datable non-dramatic poetry also belongs to these years. From the first, Jonson wrote occasional and panegyric verse addressed to the aristocracy, invoking their patronage.

The first decade and a half of the seventeenth century were the years of Jonson's superb creativity and greatest popularity as a playwright. During those years he was in social contact with fellow playwrights such as William Shakespeare, and also with scholars such as William Camden and John Selden. Jonson's associations, however, were not limited to the theatrical and the learned; he was steadily employed as the writer of court masques throughout the reign of James I. Both the King and the aristocrats at the court responded to Jonson's work for many years with notable offers of support. The years from 1616 through 1624 probably marked the height of his prestige. In 1616 he published *The Workes of Benjamin Jonson* in folio. A royal pension came in the same year and, in 1619, an honorary degree from Oxford. Also gratifying was the gathering around Jonson of the "Tribe of Ben," a circle of poetic "sons," including Thomas Carew and Robert Herrick, who adopted him as their mentor.

The accession of Charles I to the throne in 1625 ended Johnson's tenure as regular writer of masques for the court, and in other respects also the last dozen years of Jonson's life contrast with the preceding successful decades. At some points during these last years, he was clearly in financial need, and in 1628 he suffered a stroke. He was writing comedies again for the popular stage, but none of them won much acclaim. Against such bleak circumstances, however, stands a persistence of poetic energy, embodied in much outstanding verse attributable to these years. Jonson held the regard of his "Sons" until his death in 1637, and beyond: One of them, Sir Kenelm Digby, finally assembled and published Jonson's later, along with his earlier *Works* in 1640-1641.

ANALYSIS

Until the last few decades, attention to Ben Jonson's poetry focused largely on the famous songs and the moving epitaphs on children. Such choices were not ill-advised, but they are unrepresentative. The works in these modes certainly rank among Jonson's most successful, but they differ in tone from Jonson's norm.

Songs such as "Kiss me, sweet: the wary lover" and "Drink to me only with thine eyes" evoke emotions beyond the world of reason or fact, partly through reference to extravagant gestures and implausible experiences: hundreds and thousands of kisses, a wreath that will not die after the beloved has breathed on it. Through rhythms that are stronger and less interrupted than Jonson usually created, the songs activate the capacity to respond sensually and irrationally to language. Some of them create magical secret worlds where sense and emotion are to be experienced in disregard of troubling or qualifying context (the "silent summer nights/ When youths ply their stol'n delights" in "Kiss me, sweet: the wary lover"). Exactly such worlds are created, but also subjected to critique, in *Volpone* and *The Alchemist*.

The epitaphs, particularly those on Jonson's own children ("On my First Son," "On my First Daughter") are so effective because in them subjective emotions strain against rational conviction. Jonson's statement in each of these poems is doctrinal and exemplary, involving resignation to the will of God, but part of the power of the affirmation of belief arises from Jonson's undertone of grief over which faith has won out. Regret and despair have not been reasoned away but are being rationally controlled; consolation is not easy.

Such richly concentrated poems obviously deserve attention; that they should have received exposure to the virtual exclusion of Jonson's less lyrical or emotive verse, however, perhaps represents a holdover from Romantic or Victorian taste for rhapsodic expressions of feeling and imaginative vision in poetry. In fact, the renewal of contact with the Metaphysical sensibility achieved by T. S. Eliot and other critics in the 1920's and 1930's, which brought about the displacement of Victorian approaches to a number of seventeenth century writers, did not do so, immediately or directly, in the case of Jonson as a nondramatic poet. Some of Jonson's works are recognizably close to the secular reaches of John Donne's writing, but the speaker's psychological self-discovery through metaphor, so often the business of a Donne poem, is only occasionally Jonson's way. The contrast is especially clear between Jonson's poetic range and the realm of the meditative, intense, often all-but-private Metaphysical religious lyric. Jonson wrote very few strictly devotional poems; the ode "To Heaven" is probably the only strikingly successful work that could bear that label. In poems such as the ode to Sir Lucius Cary and Sir Henry Morison and the funeral elegies, where the afterlife is mentioned, the relation of humanity as such to divinity is not the real focus of attention. The poems involve tensions mainly between diverse human levels, between more ordinary experience on the one hand and, on the other, an excellence or superiority of nature which Cary, Morison, Lady Jane Pawlet, and the other exemplary figures achieve.

At most, only on the peripheries of Jonson's non-dramatic verse can it be seen to approximate pure emotive lyricism, or can it be cast in Metaphysical terms. Only in the late twentieth century did criticism achieve a modern reunderstanding of Jonson's achievement, involving a strongly positive evaluation of his central, typical poetic work. Jonson emerges in this criticism as decisively a neoclassic artist, the intellectual background of whose poetry is Renaissance humanism.

TIMBER

Jonson appears as a humanistic thinker in his *Timber*, and his career reflected humanistic motivations and aspirations. Fundamentally, Jonson conceived of learning, thought, and language as phases of the active life of man. Humanists conceived of education as the initiation of patterns of wise and effective behavior in the student's life. Humanistic education was largely linguistic, because of the traditional importance of the persuasive linguistic act, the centrality of oratory (or, for the Renaissance, the counseling of the prince and nobles) in the repertory of practical, political skills. Patterns both of moral behavior in general and of speech specifically were normally learned through imitation of the deeds and words of figures from the past; for most humanists,

and very definitely for Jonson, this did not mean that modern men were supposed to become mere apes of their predecessors, but rather that, through first following models, men should exercise and organize their own capacities to a point where they could emulate and rival the ancients, becoming effective on their own terms as the ancients were on theirs.

As a nonaristocratic humanist in a stratified society, Jonson essentially followed a pattern marked out since the time of Thomas More and Thomas Elyot early in the preceding century when he attached himself to noble households and the court. Debarred by birth from directly wielding the largest measure of power in his society, he engaged in action obliquely by speaking to the powerful, counseling and offering praise to encourage the elite in the wise conduct of life and authority. This was the light in which Jonson saw his masques, not only as celebrations, but also as reminders of ideals, such as justice, which should inform the court's activity. A great many of Jonson's moralizing poems addressed to noblemen and others also clearly exhibited actual hortatory intent.

Jonson's thought includes, as one might expect, special factors that set it off somewhat from humanism as it appears in other contexts. For one thing, while Jonson was not an unbeliever, it is certainly true that his humanism does not merge clearly and continuously into moralistic, pastoral Christianity, as had that of Desiderius Erasmus a hundred years before. The ethical universe of *Timber* is one of Roman, not obtrusively Christian, virtues; if anything, Jonson looks forward to later secular rationalism. Another characteristic of Jonson's humanism is the trace of influence from Seneca and Roman Stoicism, apparent in his writing, as elsewhere in early seventeenth century English expression. A main effect of Senecan influence on Jonson seems to have been to encourage a concern with and regard for what can best be called integrity; that is, the correlation of an individual's behavior with his inner nature rather than with outward circumstance. Such concern naturally belonged with the Senecan concept of specifically linguistic behavior which *Timber* expresses—a heightened awareness of style as emerging from and conveying an image of the "inmost" self.

Jonson's neoclassic verse is the poetic cognate of his quite secular, somewhat Senecan version of humanism.

Splitting the relation into separate aspects only for the sake of analysis, one can say that in form Jonson's poems are above all linguistic acts, the talk of a persona to an implied (often, a designated) human audience. In content, the poems are orderings of levels or modes of human behavior.

EPISTLES

Jonson's "An Epistle answering to One that asked to be Sealed of the Tribe of Ben" is identified by its title in terms of the act of communication that it imitates, the letter. Relatively few of Jonson's titles actually include the word "epistle," but many of them involve, or even simply consist of, the designation of an addressee—"To Katherine Lady Aubigny," "To Sir Robert Wroth," and so on. Thus the reader is asked to be aware of many of Jonson's poems not primarily in terms of any myths they may relate or images they may invoke, but as linguistic action, the linguistic behavior of a human speaker toward a human audience.

The fiction of speaker and audience is not an inert element but has an impact on the poem's other aspects. Many qualities of style are conditioned by the character of the addressee and his relation to the speaker. In the "Epistle to Master John Selden," the speaker states that he feels free to use a curt, "obscure," at times almost telegraphic style because "I know to whom I write": He knows that Selden is not only intelligent but also at home with the speaker's ways of thinking. Generally, the grandiloquence, expansiveness, and elaborate structure of public oratory will rarely be appropriate for an epistle or other poem addressed by one person to another.

Jonson's style in "An Epistle answering to One that asked to be Sealed of the Tribe of Ben" is fairly typical of that in a number of his poems. His diction is generally colloquial; Edmund Bolton's characterization of Jonson's "vital, judicious and practicable language" (in Edmund Bolton's *Hypercritica*, c. 1618) is an excellent general description of the style. Syntactic units in Jonson's poems are by and large brief and stopped abruptly so that one jumps (or stumbles) from clause to clause rather than making easy transitions. Units are typically not paired or otherwise arranged symmetrically in relation to one another. The effect in "An Epistle answering to One that asked to be Sealed of the Tribe of Ben" is

one of rather blurting, unpremeditated speech, propelled by some emotional pressure. Structurally, too, the poem seems unpremeditated, beginning with appropriate introductory comments to the would-be discile to whom Ben is writing, then falling away into contemptuous griping about phony elements in Jonson's society, circling down into what reads like underlying anxiety about Jonson's personal situation—and coming through this human situation to a now almost heroic assertion of what it means to be Ben or one sealed of his tribe.

In other poems, the style varies, within a generally informal range. Jonson's meaning can in fact be obscure when the syntax is very broken or a great deal of meaning is concentrated in one phrase; the effect is often that of a rather impatient intelligence, not using more words than it needs to communicate meaning to its immediate addressee. In extreme cases, the reader may feel like an outsider reading a communication not meant for him (see, for example, the "Epistle to Sir Edward Sackville"). Such privacy, immured by style, sets Jonson off somewhat from Augustan neoclassic writers such as Alexander Pope, who usually engage in smoother and more public address.

Titling the poem an "Epistle," besides drawing attention to its character as a linguistic act, also of course associates it with a generic tradition. Seneca was the most influential classical practitioner of the moral epistle as a prose form, Horace of the form in verse. Jonson's epistles and many of his other poems evoke these authors' works in content and style, sometimes through specific allusion. Clearly related to classical tradition, yet utterly topical and personal (with its references to the politics of "Spain or France" and to Jonson's employment as a writer of masques), "An Epistle answering to One that asked to be Sealed of the Tribe of Ben" is a successful act of humanistic imitation. Overt reference to tradition reveals the moral statement of Jonson's poetry in relation to the whole body of classical moral wisdom—and implies that Jonson is not afraid of the juxtaposition.

The particular wisdom of this poem is conveyed most clearly in the description of the course of conduct Jonson has "decreed" for himself, which comes after the middle of the poem's descriptions of a social environment of indulgence of appetite, empty talk, and illusory "Motions." Jonson's resolve is to "Live to that point . . .

for which I am man/ And dwell as in my Center as I can." The image is one of withdrawal from concern for meaningless external situations; it is also a picture of a life standing in relation to some firm, definite principle, as opposed to the poem's earlier images of unfounded judgments and groundless chatter.

The ideas of withdrawal and of a "Center" within the personality are clearly reminiscent of Seneca and Horace. The most characteristic aspect of the poem's meaning is that it consists of definitions not so much of the ideal principle itself as of the behavior which is or is not oriented to it. Jonson is not much concerned with describing the Center except as such, as a point from which surrounding space takes orientation. He is concerned with describing centeredness, and distinguishing it from shapeless and unfocused conditions; or, to return from geometry to humanity, with describing what it is like to operate on a firm moral basis, and distinguishing this from the "wild Anarchy" in which those outside the Tribe of Ben live.

The focus on behavior which is or is not guided, rather than on the available guiding transcendent principle, corresponds to the specifically secular emphasis of Jonson's humanism. There is an almost (though certainly not quite) agnostic quality in Jonson's almost interchangeable references to the "point," the "Center," "heaven," and "reason" as the source of his wisdom and strength. Clearly it is the exemplification of those qualities in life that interests him. Such an interest makes Jonson stand out as strikingly modern against the backdrop, for example, of the highly articulated ideal world of Edmund Spenser; it links Jonson forward to the essence of English neoclassicism, such as in Pope's ethically oriented satires and moral essays.

It should be noted that the movement toward the Center involves choice and effort: Jonson must decree it to himself, and even those who have been once sealed to the tribe of Ben have still to fear the shame of possibly stumbling in reason's sight. For good or evil, no destiny holds Jonson's human beings in place. The ideal principle is only vaguely defined; it is merely an available, not a controlling, factor.

EPIGRAMS

Like the epistles and other more or less epistolary longer poems, Jonson's epigrams are, in form, primarily linguistic acts. They are comments "on" or "to" someone. They are self-consciously brief remarks, aiming to capture the essence of a character—sometimes, implicitly, to reduce an object to its true dimensions (many of Jonson's epigrams are satirical).

The epigrammatic mode is closely related to the epistolary in Jonson's practice and in the tradition out of which he writes. Martial, the Roman epigrammatist whom Jonson regularly imitated, conceived of his works as epistles in brief. Jonson's style has the same constituents. The broken syntax sometimes seems part of epigrammatic compression; sometimes it promotes a casualness which is part of Jonson's reduction and dismissal of a satirized personality, as in epigram 21 ("On Reformed Gamester").

The pentameter couplets in which Jonson writes not only the epigrams but the great bulk of his neoclassic verse are derived partly from normal English practice for nonlyric poetry going back through Geoffrey Chaucer. They are also, however, influenced by a classical form, the elegiac distich—a prosodic vehicle used by, among others, Martial. Readily recognizable and essentially symmetrical, the form tends to stand as a strong balancing, controlling, ordering presence in the poetry in which it appears. Part of its potential is as a structure for concentrated, gnomic, almost proverbial utterance, easy for the reader to carry away in his mind; this potential is best realized when the couplet is a tightly closed unit, as is normally the case in Pope.

Jonson uses the form in the several ways just mentioned. Couplet order underscores orderly, almost (for Jonson) patterned, praise of a firmly centered man in epigram 128 ("To William Roe"). Some epigrams consist of single gnomic couplets (epigram 34, "Of Death"), and others are memorable for neat, closed-couplet wit (epigram 31, "On Banck the Usurer"). Both Jonson's prestige and his virtuoso skill in testing the couplet's range of uses were important in establishing it as the standard neoclassic prosodic structure. Jonson's most characteristic way of exploiting the couplet, however, was not simply to employ, but simultaneously to violate, its order, to write across the prosodic structure as if in disregard of it. Actually, more often than not, in Jonson's verse, syntactic and phrasal breaks do not come at such points within a line as to facilitate the prosodic caesura, nor are they matched with line endings or even the ends of the couplets themselves (see for example epigram 46, "To Sir Luckless Woo-all"). The couplet may be opposed by meaning, along with grammar: Antitheses and other logical and rhetorical structures work at cross purposes with the prosody (epigram 11, "On Some-Thing, that Walks Some-Where").

In such circumstances, the couplet does not cease to be an obtrusive form. Jonson maintains the reader's awareness of it, precisely as a structure that is not managing to control or limit the autonomy of his grammar, rhetoric, and logic. The latter, of course, are the elements of the oratorical presence in the poetry—of Jonson's voice or speech. The net effect is to enhance the sense of the independent liveliness of the speaking persona, his freedom to move about, to understand and to explain in his own way, on his own terms. Jonson's handling of the couplet implies through form a quite radical version of secular humanism, a sense of the detachment of linguistic action (and of man the linguistic actor) from any containing structure.

Many of the same kinds of content are present in the epigrams as in the epistolary writings. The epigrammatic image of William Roe's stable personality, mentioned earlier, is obviously cognate with Ben's self-image in "An Epistle answering to One that asked to be Sealed of the Tribe of Ben," as are such portrayals as those of Sir Henry Nevil (epigram 109), William, Earl of Pembroke (102), and Sir Thomas Roe (98). (The latter contains one of Jonson's more gnomic statements of the concept of the inner-directed and self-sufficient man: "Be always to thy gathered self the same/ And study conscience, more than thou would'st fame.") Satire, often a phase in the epistles, can fill entire epigrams. Something, that Walks Somewhere, Sir Voluptuous Beast (epigrams 35 and 36) and Don Surly (epigram 38) are incisively but fully realized satiric characters, clearly inhabitants of the same world as the "humour" characters Corbaccio and Epicure Mammon in Jonson's plays. Something, that Walks Somewhere, the lord who walks in "clothes brave enough," "buried in flesh, and blood," unwilling to do and afraid to dare, is one of Jonson's most powerful pictures of pointless, disorganized life— almost of disorganized protoplasm. Jonson suggested in many indirect ways that he regarded Horace as his mentor, and his work certainly has many Horatian traits, but his satire sometimes seems to belong less in the Horatian than in the harsher Juvenalian category.

"To Penshurst"

"To Penshurst," one of Jonson's most famous poems, celebrates a different kind of relatedness from the internal centering discussed so far. Here human life is benign because it stands within what men have recently learned to call an ecosystem: a web of connections between elements that feed and feed off one another and through interaction perpetuate one another's well-being. At Penshurst, the Sidney family's country estate, nature freely delivers its supply into the Sidneys' hands; fish and birds "officiously" serve themselves up; but here and even more in the very similar poem "To Sir Robert Wroth," one feels that the humans could have a harvesting function, culling what sometimes seems almost like a glut of natural abundance. In any case, the human lords of Penshurst themselves stand as the basis of further relations, providing a social center to which neighbors from a whole community and guests from farther away "come in." The neighbors bring even more food, and the "provisions" of Penshurst's "liberal board" flow back to them. The system yields more than it can use, and the superflux passes to the unenvied guest and is there, ready to be offered to the king, the regulator of a larger system and community, when he happens into this particular sphere. The system, though nature flows through it, is not mindless. From Penshurst's lady's "huswifery" up through "The mysteries of manners, arms and arts" which the house's children are learning, specifically human roles and human activities have their place in this strong and ample natural and human network; in fact, the sophisticated culture of an ancestral figure of the house, Sir Philip Sidney, can be alluded to without seeming out of place here.

A close modern analog to "To Penshurst" is W. H. Auden's "In Praise of Limestone," where man also meshes with landscape in a perfect way; Auden's description of the limestone system, however, is interrupted by accounts of less pleasing, more technological adjustments of the relation. In "To Penshurst," on the other hand, contrasting satiric pictures or references have less share than in almost any of Jonson's works. Only a few lines, mainly at the poem's beginning and end, succinctly insert Jonson's usual distinctions. Penshurst is Edenic. One is left with the uneasy feeling that the poem's being so much anthologized may be bound up with its being, for Jonson, atypically untroubled.

ODES

Jonson's ode "To the Immortal Memory and Friendship of that Noble Pair, Sir Lucius Cary and Sir H. Morison" stands near the beginning of the history of English efforts to imitate Pindar's odes. It has a complex and stately stanzaic structure. Nevertheless, many traits are carried over from Jonson's epigrammatic and epistolary style, in particular the tendency toward syntax that is at odds with prosodic divisions, of which the poem contains egregious examples: For instance, a stanza break comes in the middle of the name "Ben/ Jonson." An epic, "Heroologia," which Jonson planned, would probably have represented another extension to a new genre of his characteristic manner and ethical matter. The epic was to be in couplets and was to deal with "the Worthies of his country, roused by fame" (reports William Drummond). Like Pope, Jonson actually wrote a mock-epic rather than the serious one; Jonson's work is the "merdurinous" "On the Famous Voyage" (epigram 133).

The ode to Cary and Morison is extreme in imagery as well as in syntacticprosodic tension. It opens with a notorious image, that of the "infant of Saguntum" who retreated back to the womb before it was "half got out," appalled by the horror and devastation of wartime scenes into which it was being born. Jonson goes on to surprise conventional taste even further by suggesting that this vaginal peripety represents a "summ'd" "circle . . . of deepest lore, could we the Center find." References to circle and center of course bring along a whole train of important imagery and structure in Jonson, as well as alluding to the structure of the whole poem, with its repeated peripeteia of "Turn," "Counter-Turn," and "Stand."

The will to shock, or at least to write in uncompromisingly extraordinary ways, may indirectly express the speaker's grief and sense of loss (the poem's occasion is Morison's death). It is certainly connected with a larger demand to see life in an unconventional way, which is the poem's essential consoling strategy. (Jonson speaks of the "holy rage" with which Morison "leap'd the pres-

ent age"; readers are asked to do the same thing, in the same mood.) The distinction that Jonson insists on is between visions of life as "space" and as "act." In terms of the former—sheer duration—Morison's life was indeed lamentably cut off: He lived barely into his twenties. In terms of "act," Morison's life was perfect:

> A Soldier to the last right end
> A perfect Patriot, and a noble friend,
> But most a virtuous Son.
> All Offices were done
> By him, so ample, full and round,
> In weight, in measure, number, sound
> As, though his age imperfect might appear,
> His life was of Humanity the Sphere.

This is, notably, purely secular consolation. There are later references to a "bright eternal day," but it has less to do with Christian Paradise than with a pagan heaven of commemoration, in which Morison (and Cary) may persist as an "Asterism," a constellation. The poem's contrast with "Lycidas" marks the distance between John Milton's more old-fashioned Christian humanism and Jonson's secular mind.

Jubilation, rather than lamentation, over Morison's perfection of "act" is, like most of Jonson's higher choices, not easy to maintain. The speaker's own "tongue" "falls" into mourning at one point. Cary, Morison's great friend who survives him and to whom the poem is at least in part addressed, is exhorted to "call . . . for wine/ And let thy looks with gladness shine"—and to maintain connection. Like the centered men of the epigrams and epistles, and like the Sidneys of Penshurst, Cary is to act in relation, to "shine" on earth in conjunction with Morison's now heavenly light. The function of the poem vis-à-vis Cary is to establish this relation for him, and the broken but single name of Ben Jonson bridges over precisely the two stanzas where the relation of the two friends is most fully discussed.

The poem includes a satirical picture. Contrasting with the vital life of act, the vacuous life of space is personified as a futile careerist, "buoy'd . . . up" in the end only by the "Cork of Title." More than by alternation of satiric and positive images, however, the poem works by a tension constant throughout: the tension between the naturalistic sense of death as an end, which is never really lost, and the other vision which Jonson is insisting upon. The poem is a celebration of secular heroism. It depicts that quality in its subjects ("Nothing perfect done/ But as a Cary, or a Morison"), enacts it in its language, and demands it of its readers. The tension and energy which the poem displays are the reasons for reading Jonson's verse.

OTHER MAJOR WORKS

PLAYS: *The Case Is Altered*, pr. 1597; *The Isle of Dogs*, pr. 1597 (with Thomas Nashe); *Hot Anger Soon Cold*, pr. 1598 (with Henry Chettle and Henry Porter); *Every Man in His Humour*, pr. 1598, revised 1605; *Every Man Out of His Humour*, pr. 1599; *The Page of Plymouth*, pr. 1599 (with Thomas Dekker; no longer extant); *Robert the Second, King of Scots*, pr. 1599 (with Chettle and Dekker; no longer extant); *Cynthia's Revels: Or, The Fountain of Self-Love*, pr. c. 1600-1601; *Poetaster: Or, His Arraignment*, pr. 1601; *Sejanus His Fall*, pr. 1603 (commonly known as *Sejanus*); *Eastward Ho!*, pr., pb. 1605 (with George Chapman and John Marston); *Volpone: Or, The Fox*, pr. 1605; *Epicæne: Or, The Silent Woman*, pr. 1609; *The Alchemist*, pr. 1610; *Catiline His Conspiracy*, pr., pb. 1611 (commonly known as *Catiline*); *Bartholomew Fair*, pr. 1614; *The Devil Is an Ass*, pr. 1616; *The Staple of News*, pr. 1626; *The New Inn: Or, The Light Heart*, pr. 1629; *The Magnetic Lady: Or, Humours Reconciled*, pr. 1632; *A Tale of a Tub*, pr. 1633; *The Sad Shepherd: Or, A Tale of Robin Hood*, pb. 1640 (fragment).

NONFICTION: *The English Grammar*, 1640; *Timber: Or, Discoveries Made upon Men and Matter*, 1641.

TRANSLATION: *Horace His Art of Poetry*, 1640 (of Horace's *Ars poetica*).

MISCELLANEOUS: *The Workes of Benjamin Jonson*, 1616; *The Works of Benjamin Jonson*, 1640-1641 (2 volumes).

BIBLIOGRAPHY

Bamborough, J. B. *Ben Jonson*. London: Hutchinson University Library, 1970. A good standard scholarly biography and literary analysis, fact-filled but not overwhelming. Particularly revealing in placing Jonson in his historical context. Complete with basic index and bibliography.

Barton, Anne. *Ben Jonson, Dramatist*. Cambridge, England: Cambridge University Press, 1984. Barton's approach is comprehensive and magisterial. She covers all aspects of Jonson's life and writing with grace, style, insight, and perception. For a scholarly study, this is hard to put down. Includes a chronology, notes, and an index.

Booth, Stephen. *Precious Nonsense: The Gettysburg Address, Ben Jonson's "Epitaphs on His Children," and "Twelfth Night."* Berkeley: University of California Press, 1998. Using three disparate texts, Booth demonstrates how poetics can triumph over logic and enrich the reading experience. Booth's presentation is playful yet analytical and his unique reading of *Epitaphs on His Children* is a valuable addition to critical thought on Jonson's work.

Brock, D. Heyward. *A Ben Jonson Companion*. Indianapolis: Indiana University Press, 1983. This long-awaited volume provides everything that was promised: a thorough and multifold first reference work with substance and range. Contains illuminating introductions to all the standard topics related to Jonson. The chronologies, indexes, and bibliography are easy to follow.

Chute, Marchette. *Ben Jonson of Westminster*. New York: E. P. Dutton, 1953. An old standard that has not been surpassed, Chute's biography for the general reader is genial, enthusiastic, and bewitching. A good index makes it easier to cross-relate various topics, although the bibliography is badly dated.

Miles, Rosalind. *Ben Jonson: His Life and Work*. London: Routledge & Kegan Paul, 1986. Miles's volume is a fine standard biography-study, especially for the literary background and Jonson's position in Jacobean courtly society. The scholarly apparatus is thorough: a chronology, an index, a select but extensive bibliography, notes, and an appendix.

Riggs, David. *Ben Jonson: A Life*. Cambridge, Mass.: Harvard University Press, 1989. This is a full-scale biography rather than a literary biography such as Miles's; here the works illuminate the life rather than vice versa. The illumination is brilliant. Riggs reviews all the facts and assembles them in memorable order. He includes all the standard scholarly attachments; but the book deserves to be read simply for the revelations it contains for Jonson and his age, most of which are illustrated.

Summers, Claude J., and Ted-Larry Pebworth. *Ben Jonson*. Rev. ed. New York: Twayne, 1999. An introductory overview of Jonson's life and work. Includes bibliographical references and index.

Watson, Robert N. Editor. *Critical Essays on Ben Jonson*. New York: G. K. Hall, 1997. A collection of previously published and new essays edited by an established authority on the life and work of Ben Jonson. Includes an introduction that provides an overview of criticism of Jonson's work over his career. In addition, some previously unpublished interviews, letters, and manuscript fragments are included.

John F. McDiarmid;
bibliography updated by the editors

JUNE JORDAN

Born: Harlem, New York; July 9, 1936
Died: Berkeley, California; June 14, 2002

PRINCIPAL POETRY

Who Look at Me, 1969
Some Changes, 1971
New Days: Poems of Exile and Return, 1974
Things That I Do in the Dark: Selected Poetry, 1977
Passion: New Poems, 1977-1980, 1980
Living Room: New Poems, 1985
Lyrical Campaigns: Selected Poems, 1989
Naming Our Destiny: New and Selected Poems, 1989
Haruko/Love Poems: New and Selected Love Poems, 1993 (pb. in the United States as *Haruko: Love Poems*, 1994)
Kissing God Goodbye: Poems, 1991-1997, 1997

OTHER LITERARY FORMS

June Jordan's literary reputation is based almost equally on her poetry and her political and autobio-

graphical essays, which she considered inextricably connected. Thus her poetry addresses many of the topics she discusses in her major essay collections. In addition she published a novel, books for children and young adults, an illustrated history of the Reconstruction and Civil Rights eras, dramatic pieces, and the prose memoir *Soldier: A Poet's Childhood* (2000).

ACHIEVEMENTS

June Jordan won the Lila Wallace-Reader's Digest Writer's Award (1995), the National Association of Black Journalists Award (1984), and the PEN Center USA West Freedom to Write Award (1991). She was the recipient of grants and fellowships from the Rockefeller Foundation, the National Endowment for the Arts, the New York Foundation for the Arts, and the Massachusetts Council on the Arts. She also won the Prix de Rome in Environmental Design (1970-1971). In 1971, her book *His Own Where* (1971) was nominated for a National Book Award. Her poetry is represented in many major anthologies of contemporary American poetry.

BIOGRAPHY

The essence of June Jordan's life reveals itself in her poetry and in her autobiographical writings, in particular in *Civil Wars* (1981) and her memoir *Soldier: A Poet's Childhood* (2000). She was born in Harlem, the daughter of her father Granville, a Panamanian immigrant, and Mildred, her Jamaican mother. When she was five years old, her parents moved to Brooklyn, and Jordan began her education by commuting to an all-white school. She later attended Northfield School for Girls, a preparatory school in Massachusetts.

Her introduction to poetry came through her father, who forced her to read, memorize, or recite the plays and sonnets of William Shakespeare, the Bible, the poetry of Paul Laurence Dunbar, and the poetry of Edgar Allan Poe, as well as the novels of Sinclair Lewis and Zane Grey. At the age of seven, she began to write poetry herself. Unfortunately her father's pedagogical methods also included beatings for unsatisfactory performance, but Jordan never questioned his love for her, affirming that he had the greatest influence on her poetic and personal development, having given her the idea that "to protect yourself, you try to hurt whatever is out there." Jordan's mother, who committed suicide in 1966, did not oppose her father's harsh treatment of her, and Jordan found this passivity harder to forgive than her father's brutality.

Her interest in poetry was developed at Northfield but was limited mainly to white male poets "whose remoteness from my world . . . crippled my trust in my own sensibilities . . . and generally delayed my creative embracing of my own . . . life as the stuff of my art."

In 1953, at Barnard College, Jordan met Michael Meyer, a white student at Columbia University. They were married in 1955 and Jordan followed her husband to the University of Chicago. The strain of their interracial marriage, at a time when such marriages were frowned upon by the dominant society, began to take its toll, and after a prolonged separation the couple eventually divorced in 1965, leaving Jordan to raise her son Christopher, born in 1958, by herself. Supporting herself at first as a technical writer, journalist, and assistant to Frederick Wiseman (producer of *The Cool World*, a film about Harlem), she began her academic career at the City College of New York in 1967. In 1969, she published her first book, *Who Look at Me*, a series of poetic fragments dealing with the problem of black identity in America, in which she tries to imagine what a white person might see when looking at an African American and what effect such a look can have on the person observed.

In 1970 Jordan traveled to Italy with funding from the Prix de Rome in Environmental Design, which she had won with the support of R. Buckminster Fuller. Her reflections on this journey are contained in her collection *New Days: Poems of Exile and Return*. A breakthrough in her career as a poet came with the publication in 1977 of her best-known collection, *Things That I Do in the Dark*, edited by Toni Morrison.

After the publication of *Who Look at Me*, Jordan published more than twenty books in a variety of genres, including books for children and young adults, political essays, long fiction, plays, and even an opera libretto. She taught at Connecticut College, Sarah Lawrence College, Yale University, and the State University of New York at Stony Brook, eventually taking up a professorship in African studies at the University of California, Berkeley. There she became the head of the popular outreach program Poetry for the People. She was a regular contributor to the liberal periodical *The Progressive*, an

June Jordan

outspoken critic of American foreign aid policy, and an aggressive proponent of affirmative action. Jordan died in June, 2002, after losing her decade-long fight against breast cancer.

ANALYSIS

June Jordan was not an academic, ivory-tower poet given to abstract speculations about the nature of truth and beauty. She was a self-avowed anarchist activist who considered all poems to be political. Indeed, she stated that to her, William Shakespeare's sonnets were examples of status quo politics, mirroring the ideology of an idle leisure class. Her poetic ambition was to be a "people's poet" in the fashion of Pablo Neruda, particularly a black people's poet.

Jordan's early poems are autobiographical and self-reflective, attempting to come to terms with her relationships with her parents and with her son Christopher. Yet even these early poems transcend the purely personal and illustrate her attempt to cope with being both black and a woman in a society that looks upon women of color with indifference, if not with outright hostility. In

Who Look at Me she withstands the gaze of the white observer and finally even returns the look defiantly. Over the years this defiance became increasingly characteristic of her poetry, even as the causes in which she engaged herself proliferated.

Her poetic output was to a large degree a running commentary on the social and political life in the United States, with allusions to sociopolitical events such as the 1991 Clarence Thomas/Anita Hill hearings, Jesse Jackson's 1984 presidential campaign, the 1991 police beating of Rodney King and subsequent trial, and even the controversial events surrounding boxer Mike Tyson. Poems that deal with personal topics, such as being raped and coping with illness, reach outward and become expressions of anger and sympathy for other sufferers of injustice and violence: homosexuals, victims of police brutality, or the people of sub-Saharan Africa, Nicaragua, Bosnia, Kosovo, and Palestine.

Although Jordan's tone is frequently sarcastic, angry, and strident, in some sense all her poems are love poems. Her militancy and unwillingness to be conciliatory appear to be guided by her love for the oppressed and marginalized; her denunciation of the oppressors is accompanied by the call to the victims not to capitulate, to gain and to preserve a sense of self-love and self-worth and then put it into action. This political engagement and her stridency in advocating her causes gained for Jordan many admirers in the women's and civil rights movements. Yet her militancy, particularly her refusal to embrace violence in the fight against oppression and injustice, also caused her to be met with coldness and even hostility in some circles. This may also explain why she was consistently overlooked in the selection for the Pulitzer Prize and the National Book Award, although her work was nominated for the latter in 1971.

SOME CHANGES

Jordan's first substantial collection of poems is divided into four parts, each dedicated to a particular facet of her life that she felt needed revision and change. These poems were written in the years after the suicide of her mother and the dissolution of her own marriage; as such they are an assertion of her new independence as a woman, mother, poet, sexual person, and politically autonomous citizen; therefore she dedicates the volume to "new peoplelife."

This "new peoplelife" involves making peace with her mother and father in the opening poem. For the former, she has a list of promises; her father she would "regenerate." In "Poem for My Family: Hazel Griffin and Victor Hernando Cruz," Jordan expands the meaning of "family" beyond the traditional nuclear family to include all suffering people of her race.

In several other poems in the first half of the collection, Jordan's role as a single, working mother translates into concern for children in general and for her own son in particular. The tone of many of these early poems is dark. In "Not a Suicide Poem," she asserts that

> no one should feel peculiar living
> as they do
> . . . [in] terrific reeking epidermal
> damage
> marrow rot . . .

Other poems, such as "The Wedding" and "The Reception," assert a married woman's personal autonomy. Most notable of these is "Let Me Live with Marriage," a clever deconstruction of Shakespeare's sonnet beginning "Let me not to the Marriage of True Minds." Jordan's wish is to be allowed "to live with marriage/ as unruly as alive/ or else alone and longing/ not too long alone."

After declaring her independence from family and marriage in the first half and coming to terms with her losses ("I Live in Subtraction"), she indicates her growing sense of racial pride and political empowerment in the later poems of *Some Changes*. "What would I do white?" she asks in the opening poem of the third section, in which she declares herself in solidarity with all black people, whom she has incorporated into her extended family. In the final section she expands this family yet more to include all people living in poverty and oppression ("47,000 Windows") before returning to memories of her father and her family's former home on Hancock Street in Brooklyn, emphasizing the emptiness of the house and the forlorn wandering of her father after her mother's suicide ("Clock on Hancock Street").

In the final poem of the collection, pessimistically titled "Last Poem for a Little While," the speaker is saying grace at a Thanksgiving dinner of 1969, in which she thanks God "for the problems that are mine/ and evidently mine alone" and asks her fellow diners to "Pass the Ham./ And wipe your fingers on the flag."

In *Some Changes* Jordan found her independent poetic identity, acknowledging the influence of Shakespeare, T. S. Eliot, Emily Dickinson, and Walt Whitman but striking out confidently on her own path.

NAMING OUR DESTINY

Naming Our Destiny: New and Selected Poems updates *Things That I Do in the Dark* to include her poetry up to 1989. It therefore gives the reader a good sense of which poems from her previous collections Jordan considered most worthy of attention. The volume's first section presents selections from *Things That I Do in the Dark* (1958-1977); the second contains poems from *Passion* (1977-1980); the third is a selection from *Living Room* (1980-1984); the fourth is composed of new poems written between 1984 and 1989.

Part 2 includes her most anthologized piece, "A Poem About My Rights." Jordan claimed that this poem was written in response to having been raped a few months before and that she intended to express her psychological reaction to this event. She emphatically states that victims of violence must resist the temptation to internalize the blame for the violent act and put it squarely on the shoulders of the perpetrators. She then characteristically extrapolates from her personal tragedy to the situation of violated people everywhere: "I am the history of rape/ I am the history of the rejection of who I am." As the poem indicates and as Jordan stated in interviews, the difference between her rape and the situation in apartheid South Africa was, for her, minimal. Her anger at this violation finds expression in the menacing final lines of the poem: "but I can tell you that from now on my resistance/ my simple and daily and nightly self-determination/ may very well cost you your life."

The new poems in *Naming Our Destiny* are collected in the fourth section under the title "North Star," a reference to the Abolitionist newspaper founded by Frederick Douglass in 1847 and to the constellation that served as the navigational guide to Africans making their escape from slavery. Consequently, most of these poems are unabashedly political, taking to task most of Jordan's adversaries: the Israeli occupiers of Palestine; Bernard Goetz, the New York subway vigilante; the white supremacist rulers of South Africa; Ronald Reagan and the Nicaraguan Contras; the Marcos regime in the Philippines; and even Benjamin Franklin for declaring that there could be no lasting peace with Native Americans, "till we have well-drubbed them" ("Poem for Benjamin Franklin"). Other poems pay homage to friends and fellow activists, such as Angela Y. Davis ("Solidarity").

KISSING GOD GOODBYE

This slender collection of poems written between 1991 and 1997 restates many of the themes of Jordan's previous collections, but despite Jordan's battle with breast cancer, the tone of these poems is more optimistic and conciliatory, compared to the anger and stridency of her earlier work. The volume is dedicated to an anonymous lover and to the "Student Poet Revolutionaries" in her Poetry for the People project at Berkeley. Except for a harsh critique of the American air campaign against Iraq ("The Bombing of Baghdad") and the Israeli devastation of Lebanon, the poems are more personal, introspective, and accepting, particularly "First Poem after Serious Surgery" and "merry-go-round poetry."

The majority are intimate haikus and other poems to b.b.L., clearly a treasured lover, but even the lyricism of "Poem #7 for b.b.L.,"

> Baby
> when you reach out
> for me
> I forget everything
> except
> I do remember to breathe. . . .

is tempered in the last lines by a claim to breathing room.

In the title poem, "Kissing God Goodbye," which brings the collection to an end, the kinder and gentler June Jordan gives way once more to the strident activist, pouring sarcasm on what she considers the bigoted rhetoric of the antiabortion movement Operation Rescue:

> You mean to tell me on the 12th day or the 13th
> that the Lord . . .
> decided who could live and who would die? . . .
> You mean to tell me that the planet
> is the brainchild
> of a single
> male
> head
> of household?

In *Kissing God Goodbye*, then, Jordan reasserts her position as a fearless critic of American society and public policy, reconfirming her reputation as one of today's most gifted American poets. The Kosovo poem, "April 10, 1999," will surely strike a responsive chord in many readers:

> Nothing is more cruel
> than the soldiers who command
> the widow
> to be grateful
> that she's still alive.

OTHER MAJOR WORKS

LONG FICTION: *His Own Where*, 1971.

PLAYS: *In the Spirit of Sojourner Truth*, pr. 1979; *For the Arrow That Flies by Day*, pr. 1981; *I Was Looking at the Ceiling and Then I Saw the Sky*, pr., pb. 1995 (libretto and lyrics; music by John Adams).

NONFICTION: *Civil Wars*, 1981; *On Call: Political Essays*, 1985; *Moving Towards Home: Political Essays*, 1989; *Technical Difficulties: African-American Notes on the State of the Union*, 1992; *Affirmative Acts: Political Essays*, 1998; *Soldier: A Poet's Childhood*, 2000.

CHILDREN'S LITERATURE: *Dry Victories*, 1972; *New Life: New Room*, 1975; *Fannie Lou Hamer*, 1972; *Kimako's Story*, 1981.

BIBLIOGRAPHY

Brogan, Jacqueline V. "From Warrior to Womanist: The Development of June Jordan's Poetry." In *Speaking the Other Self: American Women Writers*, edited by Jeanne Campbell Reesman. Athens: University of Georgia Press, 1997. Traces Jordan's growth as a poet, concentrating on her life as a political and social activist.

Brown, Kimberly N. "June Jordan." In *Contemporary African American Novelists: A Bio-bibliographical Critical Sourcebook*, edited by Emmanuel S. Nelson. Westport, Conn.: Greenwood Press, 1999. A useful reference entry in a book devoted to African American writers.

Erickson, Peter. "The Love Poetry of June Jordan." *Callaloo* 9, no. 1 (Winter, 1986): 221-234. Dis-cusses the poems in *Passion*, in particular those selected later for *Things I Do in the Dark*. Claims that attention to Jordan's activist, political poetry has unjustly overshadowed her powerful love poetry.

Franz G. Blaha

JAMES JOYCE

Born: Dublin, Ireland; February 2, 1882
Died: Zurich, Switzerland; January 13, 1941

PRINCIPAL POETRY

Chamber Music, 1907
Pomes Penyeach, 1927
"Ecce Puer," 1932
Collected Poems, 1936

OTHER LITERARY FORMS

Although James Joyce published poetry throughout his career (*Chamber Music*, a group of thirty-six related poems, was in fact his first published book), it is for his novels and short stories that he is primarily known. These works include *Dubliners* (1914), a volume of short stories describing what Joyce saw as the moral paralysis of his countrymen: *A Portrait of the Artist as a Young Man* (1916), a heavily autobiographical account of the growing up of a writer in Ireland at the end of the nineteenth century and the beginning of the twentieth; *Ulysses* (1922), a novel set in Dublin in 1904, recounting the day-long adventures of Leopold Bloom, a modern-day Odysseus who is both advertising man and cuckold, Stephen Dedalus, the young artist of *A Portrait of the Artist as a Young Man* now grown somewhat older, and Molly Bloom, Leopold's earthy wife; and *Finnegans Wake* (1939), Joyce's last published work, not a novel at all in the conventional sense, but a world in itself, built of many languages and inhabited by the paradigmatic Earwicker family.

ACHIEVEMENTS

James Joyce's prose works established his reputation as the most influential writer of fiction of his generation and led English prose fiction from Victorianism into modernism and beyond. To this body of work, Joyce's poetry is an addendum of less interest in itself than it is in relationship to the other, more important, work. At the same time, in the analysis of Joyce's achievement, it is impossible to ignore anything that he wrote, and the poetry, for which Joyce reserved some of his most personal utterances, has its place along with the play *Exiles* (1918)—now seen as more important than it once was—and the essays, letters, and notebooks.

BIOGRAPHY

The life of James Joyce is interwoven so inextricably with his work that to consider one requires considering the other. The definitive biography of Joyce, by Richard Ellmann, is as strong in its interpretation of Joyce's work as it is of his life. If Joyce, as Ellmann suggests in that biography, tended to see things through words, readers must try to see him through *his* words—the words of his work—as well as through the facts of his life.

James Joyce (Library of Congress)

Joyce was born into a family whose fortunes were in decline, the first child to live in the match of a man who drank too much and accumulated too many debts and a woman whose family the Joyces considered beneath them. John Joyce, James's father, became the model for Stephen's father both in *A Portrait of the Artist as a Young Man* and in *Ulysses*, where he is one of the most memorable characters, and also a model for H. C. Earwicker in *Finnegans Wake*. If Joyce's father seemed not to understand his son's work or even to show much interest in it during his lifetime, that work has become a surer form of immortality for him than anything he ever did himself.

Joyce was educated at Clongowes Wood College, a Jesuit school not far from Dublin which he memorialized in *A Portrait of the Artist as a Young Man*, and then later at Belvedere College, also Jesuit, in Dublin. In 1898, upon his graduation from Belvedere, he entered University College, Dublin. At this point in his life, increasingly rebellious against the values of his home and society, Joyce did his first writing for publication. He was graduated from the university with a degree in modern languages in 1902 and then left Dublin for Paris to study medicine. That, however, quickly gave way to Joyce's real desire to write, and he entered a difficult period in which he turned to teaching to earn a living. The problems of the father had become the problems of the son, but during this period Joyce wrote some of his best earlier poems, including what is now the final piece in the *Chamber Music* sequence. With the death of his mother imminent in April, 1903, Joyce returned to Dublin, where, the following winter, he began to write the first draft of *A Portrait of the Artist as a Young Man* (known as *Stephen Hero*).

By far the most important event after Joyce's return to Ireland, however, was his meeting in June, 1904, with the woman who was to become his mate for the rest of his life, Nora Barnacle, whose roots (like those of the family Joyce) were in Galway, the westernmost county in Ireland. If Joyce's mother's family had seemed too low for the Joyces, Nora's family was even lower on the social scale, but Joyce, like Stephen Dedalus, was to escape the net of convention and take the woman he loved away from Ireland to live in a succession of temporary residences on the Continent while he established himself as a major writer. The model, at least in part, for Molly Bloom and also for Anna Livia Plurabelle, Nora, not Joyce's legal wife until 1931, was the mother of their two children—Giorgio, born in 1905, and Lucia, born in 1907—and Joyce's main emotional support for almost four decades.

From the time Joyce and Nora moved to the Continent until the outbreak of World War I, they lived chiefly in Trieste, a port city in northeastern Italy which in appearance seemed more Austrian than Italian; there Joyce taught English in a Berlitz School, and wrote; he returned to Ireland only twice, in 1909 and again in 1912, for what turned out to be his last visit. With the outbreak of the war, Joyce and his family moved to Zurich, which was neutral ground, and in 1920—after a brief sojourn once again in Trieste—moved to Paris, where they were to remain until the fall of France twenty years later.

Paris in the 1920's, Ernest Hemingway was to write years later, was a "moveable feast," but Joyce, as always, was a selective diner, an integral part of the literary life of Paris at that time, yet aloof from it, imaginatively dwelling in the Dublin of 1904, the year he had met Nora. Having published *Chamber Music*, *Dubliners*, *A Portrait of the Artist as a Young Man*, and *Exiles*, Joyce had embarked on his most ambitious project to date—a treatment in detail of one day in Dublin—June 16, 1904—and the adventures of a modern-day Odysseus, Leopold Bloom, ultimately to be his greatest single achievement in characterization. The serialization of *Ulysses* had begun in 1918; its publication in book form waited until Joyce's fortieth birthday, on February 2, 1922. Because of publication difficulties resulting from censorship, Joyce did not realize much financially from the book until later in his life, and remained dependent upon a succession of patrons and subscribers not only for its initial publication but also for his livelihood. With its publication, however—difficult though it was to achieve—came the recognition of Joyce as the greatest living novelist in English, a master stylist who had managed (as such major figures as T. S. Eliot and Ezra Pound were quick to see) to give the modern experience a historical dimension which so many realistic novels had lacked.

As recognition of *Ulysses* came, Joyce characteristically moved on to something different (in a sense, in his published work he almost never repeated himself, in style or in form, though he dealt continuously with certain themes), publishing in 1924 the first portion of what for years was termed "Work in Progress" and then ultimately became *Finnegans Wake*. This novel broke new ground in the same way *Ulysses* did, in its rendering of unconscious universal experiences and in its use of language; but it took much longer for it to achieve general recognition as a masterpiece. Plagued throughout his lifetime by financial problems, health problems (especially with his eyes), and family problems (his daughter's mental health was always fragile, and she has lived most of her life in a sanatorium), Joyce remains the prime example of the artist as exile.

ANALYSIS

Chamber Music appeared in 1907, but James Joyce had been working on the poems which comprise the volume for some time before that date. As early as 1905 he had worked out a plan for the poems, different from the one finally devised for the 1907 version but perhaps more revealing of the thematic content of the poetry. With the addition of several poems not in the 1905 scheme, *Chamber Music* came to thirty-six poems of varying lengths and forms, the work of a young man who had already largely abandoned poetry in favor of prose fiction.

CHAMBER MUSIC

In many ways the poems of *Chamber Music* are typical of the period in which they were written. The poetry of the late nineteenth century in English has a hothouse quality; like the French Symbolist, who—next to the English Romantics—provided the chief inspiration throughout this period, the poets of the *fin de siècle* eschewed ordinary life in favor of an aesthetic ideal. This was in fact the final flowering of the ideal of art for art's sake so important to nineteenth century literature and art, an attitude which the young Joyce flirted with and ultimately abandoned, satirizing it in the pages of *A Portrait of the Artist as a Young Man*. In the poems of *Chamber Music*, however, the satire is less easy to detect, and *fin de siècle* themes provide the basis of many of the poems in the sequence. The dominant note of the poetry of the *fin de siècle* is one of weariness or sadness, the favorite time dusk or night, the favorite stance one of retreat; in Joyce's *Chamber Music* poems, as later in *A Portrait of the Artist as a Young Man*, such favorite attitudes are questioned but not totally rejected. If the final note is one of anger or bitterness rather than simply of sadness or despair, there is still a strong enough taste of the latter to mark the poems—even the celebrated number XXXVI—as the work of a young man who has grown up in the last important moment of aestheticism. Even so, the experience of the young man who is the principal speaker of the sequence of poems seems ultimately to toughen him in a way more typical of Joyce than of the poetry of the *fin de siècle*.

In Joyce's 1905 sequence, the personas of the poems are more easily perceived, the themes developed in them clearer, as William York Tindall was first to point out at length in his 1954 edition of *Chamber Music*. In that sequence there are thirty-four poems, designated first in the following list, with the numbers from the 1907 edition in Roman numerals in parentheses immediately after: 1 (XXI), 2 (I), 3 (III), 4 (II), 5 (IV), 6 (V), 7 (VIII), 8 (VII), 9 (IX), 10 (XVII), 11 (XVIII), 12 (VI), 13 (X), 14 (XX), 15 (XIII), 16 (XI), 17 (XIV), 18 (XIX), 19 (XV), 20 (XXIII), 21 (XXIV), 22 (XVI), 23 (XXXI), 24 (XXII), 25 (XXVI), 26 (XII), 27 (XXVII), 28 (XXVIII), 29 (XXV), 30 (XXIX), 31 (XXXII), 32 (XXX), 33 (XXXIII), and 34 (XXXIV).

This sequence has certain important features. Poem 1 (XXI) introduces the young man of the sequence, a sort of romantic rebel in the tradition of the Shelleyan hero, a "high unconsortable one" more in love with himself than with anyone else. This theme of aloofness and narcissism is struck in several poems following this one—in 2 (I), 3 (III), and 4 (II)—but by 5 (IV) the young man has not only become the speaker of the poem, but he has also found someone to love. Poem 6 (V) gives her a name—"Goldenhair"—and establishes the theme of the next group of poems: the young man in pursuit of Goldenhair, in the traditional rites of courtship. In 7 (VIII) he pursues her through the "green wood" and in 8 (VII) he sees her among the apple trees, vernal settings for these ancient rites. In 9 (IX), however, he cannot find her, and 10 (XVII) explains why: Here the third persona of the sequence is introduced—the rival who is a friend of the young man and who, at the same time, is threatening his relationship with Goldenhair: "He is a stranger to me

now/ Who was my friend." Poem 11 (XVIII), addressed both to Goldenhair and to the rival, complains of the failure of friends and suggests that another woman may well give the young man succor. As the poems proceed, this other woman takes on a variety of connotations, until finally, in 17 (XIV) the young man imagines his union with her in terms suggesting that she has combined characteristics, in Tindall's words, "of church, mother, muse, nation, and soul." After 17, the poems do variations on the themes of separation and lost love, ending in 33 (XXXIII) and 34 (XXXIV) on a decidedly wintry note: "The voice of the winter/ Is heard at the door./ O sleep, for the winter/ Is crying, 'Sleep no more.'"

This pattern of love challenged by a rival and ending in bitter or mixed feelings occurs elsewhere in Joyce's work, most notably in *A Portrait of the Artist as a Young Man* and in the play *Exiles*, where, as a test of a relationship, it provides the major theme. *Chamber Music* thus becomes an early working out of this theme, though Joyce ultimately agreed to an ordering of the poems (devised by his brother Stanislaus) different from the one of 1905—allowing for an ending on a much stronger note with poem XXXVI, beginning "I hear an army charging upon the land," which was not part of the 1905 sequence at all and which suggests an attitude that is more than simply passive or accepting on the part of the young man. These little poems, while carrying the weight of themes developed more completely in Joyce's later work, are also lyrics light and fresh enough to serve as the basis of songs. Joyce himself set a number of them to music, and over the years they have been set by many other composers as well.

Poem 16 (XI) illustrates the technique of the lyrics of *Chamber Music*. The diction is simple but frequently archaic—note the use of "thee" and "thy," "hast" and "doth," in keeping with much of the lyric poetry of the 1890's—and the tone light and songlike, with touches of irony apparent only in the last few lines of the second stanza. This irony is heralded in line 9 by the verb "unzone," which stands out in a poem of otherwise simple diction. Like many such words in these poems, "unzone" is unusual for the accuracy with which it is used (compare, for example, "innumerous" in poem 19 [XV]), Joyce returning to its original meaning of "encircle" or "surround," derived by way of the Latin *zone* from Greek *zona*, or "girdle." What is frequently most distinctive about Joyce's choice of words, in prose as well as in poetry, is their accuracy. In this context, the contrast between the formality of "unzone" and the "girlish bosom" of the next line, reinforced by the irony in other poems of the series dealing with the wooing of Goldenhair, makes the reader question her innocence if not the young man's intentions.

The repetition of the opening lines of 16 is another notable feature of the series. In 12 (VI) one can see the same quality on a somewhat larger scale, the final line pointing back to the beginning of the poem. If the poems of *Chamber Music* are relatively simply lyrics, they have their own complexities and ambiguities, as this poem shows. The "bosom" of the first stanza is conceivably Goldenhair's, but may also be interpreted as that of mother or church. "Austerities," like "bosom" used twice in the poem, in particular leads the reader to think so, the bosom or heart leading to an ascetic, not hedonistic, form of satisfaction for the young man. In this poem the young man flees from the relationship with Goldenhair and seeks other means of satisfaction. The language of the poem creates irony through repetition, forcing the reader to reexamine the premises of the relationship described. If this technique is much simpler than the one Joyce employed in his prose master-pieces, it is certainly a technique of the same order.

POMES PENYEACH

In 1927, Joyce published a second volume of poetry with the unassuming title *Pomes Penyeach*. The occasion for the volume was largely negative; stung by criticism of "Work in Progress" from people such as Ezra Pound, who had been so supportive of *Ulysses*, Joyce wished to show that he could also produce a relatively simple volume of lyrics. Unfortunately, for the taste of the time the lyrics were too simple and the volume went largely ignored; Pound himself suggested that Joyce should have reserved the poems for the Bible or the family album. This criticism now seems unfair, or at least out of proportion. The thirteen poems of *Pomes Penyeach* do not in any sense break new ground in English poetry, but they provide a kind of personal comment on Joyce's private life which is not easy to find in the prose works, and some of them are also simply good lyrics in the manner of *Chamber Music*.

The poems represent work of a period of approximately twenty years, beginning with "Tilly," composed in 1903 just after Joyce's mother's death, and ending with "A Prayer" of 1923, though stylistically they are of a piece. In this poetry Joyce favored a diction and tone which seemed archaic by the late 1920's, and did so without any of the irony apparent or at least incipient in certain poems of *Chamber Music*. If the mood of these poems did not suit the times in which they appeared, neither did it seem to suit the style of the supreme punster of "Work in Progress." They provide the single instance in Joyce's published work of an anachronism—a work which looks back in style and tone, in this case to the poetry of Joyce's youth and young manhood, rather than forward in time—and this accounts in part for their unenthusiastic reception.

In *Pomes Penyeach* the poems occur in roughly chronological order, in the order of their composition, and may be grouped according to subject matter. Some celebrate Joyce's feelings toward his children, as in "A Flower Given to My Daughter" or "On the Beach at Fontana," while others refer to feelings provoked in him by women he fancied himself to be in love with, either in the Trieste period or in Zurich during World War I. Some poems suggest certain of the prose works, such as "She Weeps over Rahoon" with its echoes of the long story "The Dead," written some five years before the poem. The final poem of the group, "A Prayer," returns to the mood of the darker poems in *Chamber Music* and to the image of woman as vampire which occurs so frequently in the poetry and art of the *fin de siècle*. It also suggests the strain of masochism which shows itself so often in Joyce's work in connection with sensuous pleasure. All in all, these lyrics provide an engaging record of various moods of Joyce as he passed into middle age, tempered by the public reputation he had acquired by that time.

"A Flower Given to My Daughter" and "A Prayer" illustrate the extremity of mood and variety of technique of these poems. In the first, the inverted word order and quaint diction of the poem—"sere" is the best example of the latter—do not keep the last line from being extremely touching, in part because it is so realistic a description. Joyce manages in the best of *Pomes Penyeach* to find just such a strong line with which to end, establishing a kind of contrast between the somewhat antique technique of the poem and conclusions remarkable for their simplicity and strength. "A Prayer" is far more dramatic in tone, but here the long lines and the rolling words ("remembering" followed by "pitying") also carry the reader into the joy become anguish of the final lines. In these poems as in others of the group, Joyce seems to be using the style and tone of another time with sometimes deadly effect—a conscious archaism rather than the more distanced irony of some of the poems of *Chamber Music*.

"ECCE PUER"

In 1932, Joyce published his last poem, "Ecce Puer," a touching commemoration of two occasions—the death of his father and the birth of his grandson and namesake Stephen James Joyce, the son of Giorgio and his wife Helen. "Tilly," the first item of *Pomes Penyeach*, was written on the occasion of the death of his mother and is in many ways the strongest of the group; "Ecce Puer"—written just after the death of John Joyce— is even stronger. For felt emotion conveyed, it has no equal among Joyce's works in this form, and its concluding stanza is all the more touching for its echoes of the theme of paternity so important to *Ulysses*—"A child is sleeping:/ An old man gone./ O, father forsaken,/ Forgive your son!" In fact, the poem was completed not many days after the tenth anniversary of the publication of *Ulysses*, which provides yet a third occasion for its composition.

SATIRIC POEMS

In addition to *Chamber Music*, *Pomes Penyeach*, and "Ecce Puer," Joyce published occasional broadsides— satiric poems to express his unhappiness over various literary matters. These include "The Holy Office" (1904) (now the rarest of all the published works of Joyce), an attack on the Irish literary movement by a young writer who already knew that his work was to be essentially different from theirs, and "Gas from a Burner" (1912), an attack on the Dublin publisher who ultimately burned the proofs of *Dubliners* rather than print what he considered an indecent book.

Finally, in *A Portrait of the Artist as a Young Man*, one of the crucial moments occurs (in the final part of the book) when Stephen Dedalus composes a poem in the form of a villanelle. This poem, while technically

not Joyce's, represents as sure a comment as Joyce ever made on the aestheticism of the 1890's, and thus stands in contrast with *Pomes Penyeach*, which echoes the themes and tones of that time.

Joyce's poetry was ultimately expressed most fully in his prose works, where the traditional distinctions between poetry and prose are effectively blurred. Perhaps in the end, his lyric poetry is best viewed as a minor expression—almost a form of relaxation—of a master stylist in prose.

OTHER MAJOR WORKS

LONG FICTION: *A Portrait of the Artist as a Young Man*, 1914-1915 (serial), 1916 (book); *Ulysses*, 1922; *Finnegans Wake*, 1939; *Stephen Hero*, 1944.

SHORT FICTION: *Dubliners*, 1914.

PLAY: *Exiles*, pb. 1918.

NONFICTION: *Letters of James Joyce*, 1957-1966 (3 volumes; Stuart Gilbert, editor); *The Critical Writings of James Joyce*, 1959; *Selected Letters of James Joyce*, 1975 (Richard Ellmann, editor); *The James Joyce Archives*, 1977-1979 (64 volumes); *On Ibsen*, 1999; *Occasional, Critical, and Political Writing*, 2000.

BIBLIOGRAPHY

Boyle, Robert, S. J. "The Woman Hidden in James Joyce's *Chamber Music*." In *Women in Joyce*, edited by Suzette Henke and Elaine Unkeless. Urbana: University of Illinois Press, 1982. Boyle describes the woman in the early poems to be an "ideal woman" created out of Joyce's imagination. She is, however, narcissistic and capable of malice. One of the best essays on the poems.

Ellmann, Richard. *James Joyce*. Ithaca, N.Y.: Cornell University Press, 1989. Ellman discusses the background, contexts, publication, and reception of all Joyce's poems and includes critical discussions of each book. Indispensable for the study of Joyce.

Fargnoli, A. Nicholas, and Michael Patrick Gillespie. *James Joyce A to Z: The Essential Reference to the Life and Work*. New York: Oxford University Press, 1996. Alphabetically arranged entries of varying lengths treat the major themes, places, people, characters, and other elements of Joyce's life and work.

Howarth, Herbert. "*Chamber Music* and Its Place in the Joyce Canon." In *James Joyce Today: Essays on the Major Works*, edited by Thomas F. Staley. Bloomington: Indiana University Press, 1966. An excellent discussion of the technique of the poems and the technique's purpose. Howarth feels that Joyce's purpose was music and that he partially achieved that. He also finds similar structures in the poems that are found in the major works.

McCourt, John. *James Joyce: A Passionate Exile.* New York: St. Martin's Press, 2001. Photos and sketches embellish this account of the life, times, relationships, and works of Joyce. Excellent introductory text, particularly for its illustrations.

O'Brien, Edna. *James Joyce.* New York: Viking Penguin, 1999. In this short biography, relative to some of the exhaustive works on Joyce that are available, O'Brien has produced spirited narrative with insight on Joyce's art and life.

Power, Arthur. *Conversations with James Joyce.* 1974. Reprint. Foreword by David Norris. Dublin: Lilliput Press, 1999. Power, a young Irish art critic working in Paris, sustained a friendship with Joyce during the 1920's that resulted in many fascinating discussions on literature, politics, and life, which he re-creates here. Powell honestly admits that his renditions are from memory, but they are nevertheless authentic and true to Joyce's private character.

Schwaber, Paul. *The Cast of Characters: A Reading of Ulysses.* New Haven, Conn.: Yale University, 1999. A literature professor and a psychoanalyst, Schwaber uses knowledge from both fields in an analysis of characterization in *Ulysses*. Schwaber illuminates the psychological depths of Joyce's characters.

Theall, Donald F. *James Joyce's Techno-Poetics.* Toronto: University of Toronto Press, 1997. Representative of a new wing of Joyce studies, Theall's work examines Joyce as a progenitor of today's cyberculture. Bibligraphy, index.

Tindall, William York. Introduction to *Chamber Music*, by James Joyce. New York: Columbia University Press, 1954. The best introduction to the poems available. Tindall explains the background and publishing history of the poems and makes some cogent critical comments on their nature and value. Joyce disdained his earliest work, but Tindall quotes friends who knew how "precious" the poems were to him.

Wilson, Edmund. Review of *Pomes Penyeach*. In *James Joyce: The Critical Heritage*, edited by Robert H. Deming. 2 vols. New York: Barnes & Noble Books, 1970. Praises Joyce's advance in skill and power from *Chamber Music*. The creation of such lyrics is, he suggests, "difficult and rare." *Pomes Penyeach* is a slim volume, but Wilson finds it to be "real poetry" and among the "purest of our time."

Archie K. Loss;
bibliography updated by the editors

JUDAH HA-LEVI

Born: Tudela, Kingdom of Pamplona (now in Spain); c. 1075
Died: Egypt; July, 1141

PRINCIPAL POETRY

Dīwān, twelfth century
Selected Poems of Jehudah Halevi, 1924, 1925, 1928, 1942, 1973
Die schönen Vermasse, 1930
Kol Shirei Rabbi Yehudah Halevi, 1955
Shirei ha-qodesh, 1978
Ninety-two Poems and Hymns of Yehuda Halevi, 2000

OTHER LITERARY FORMS

Primarily famous as a poet, Judah ha-Levi also wrote an apologetic religious treatise, the *Kuzari* (twelfth century; English translation, 1947), and several letters, in the rhymed prose characteristic of formal Hebrew and Arabic letters of the Middle Ages, which have been preserved and are of interest for their literary style. One of these is translated in Benzion Halper's *Post-Biblical Hebrew Literature* (1921) and reprinted in Franz Kobler's *Letters of Jews Through the Ages*. Some important Judeo-Arabic letters were translated into English by S. D. Goitein, "Judeo-Arabic Letters from Spain," in J. M. Barral, editor, *Orientalia Hispanica*, 1974.

ACHIEVEMENTS

In order to understand Judah ha-Levi's position as one of the foremost Hebrew poets not only of the medieval period but also of all time, it is necessary to survey briefly the "firmament" in which he is said to be one of the shining stars—that is, medieval Hebrew poetry. Hebrew poetry began with the Bible, and it would even be possible to argue that secular poetry began there as well, if such books as the Song of Songs may be understood to be secular rather than allegorical. In the Hellenistic period, Jewish poets wrote some Greek verse, and apparently some verse in Persian during the period of the post-Talmudic era in Babylonia. It was the influence of Arabic poetry, however, throughout the Muslim world—where the majority of Jews in the medieval period lived—that aroused Jewish intellectuals to attempt a renaissance of the Hebrew language. Hebrew had long been relegated to religious poetry (*piyyut*) for recitation in the synagogue and some few compositions on purely religious subjects. Simply by composing Hebrew poetry on secular themes, and using adaptations of Arabic meter, Judah ha-Levi's predecessors were effecting a linguistic revolution. These first efforts began in Muslim Spain in the tenth century, and quickly reached a level of excellence in the eleventh century with the generation preceding ha-Levi.

Samuel ibn Nagrillah, born in Córdoba at the height of the cultural flourishing of Muslim civilization in Spain, rose to a position of power almost unheard of for a Jew at that time and in that area; he became prime minister and commander in chief of the armies of the Muslim kingdom of Granada (there were other Jewish ministers and even prime ministers in Muslim Spain and elsewhere, but he was the first known Jewish general since the one who served Cleopatra). As an active soldier, fighting battles against the enemies of his kingdom every year for eighteen years, he wrote virtually the only Hebrew war poetry extant. In addition, he found time to compose no less than three volumes of Hebrew poetry on a variety of themes, as well as a work on grammar and a book on Jewish law.

Solomon ibn Gabirol was the other outstanding Hebrew poet of that period. Although his life was marked by frustration and suffering, his poetry can only be described as brilliant, often rising above whatever his misfortunes may have been to sing the lyric themes of love, nature, wine, and other topics. He began writing while still a teenager and expressed the audacity and hubris of youth in some of his early poems, praising his own poetry and fame. He was a philosopher and a mystic—more famous in the Christian world for his *Fons vitae* (the Latin translation of his original work) than among his fellow Jews. Both of these elements are present in many of his poems, some of which reveal profound philosophical insights or are tinged with mystical longings. Most famous of these is the lengthy religious-mystical-philosophical poem *Keter malkhut*, translated frequently into numerous languages (perhaps the best version in English is *The Kingly Crown*, translated by Bernard Lewis).

Contemporary with Judah ha-Levi, although his senior and for many years his mentor and friend, was the great Moses ibn Ezra of Granada. Perhaps the finest of the Hebrew poets of medieval Spain and certainly the most complex, he has been the least understood and appreciated. His poetry is far from simple; it consists of an intricate filigree of biblical language, with allusions to the Talmud, the Midrash, and Arabic poetry and letters. This texture is characteristic of the other medieval Hebrew poets as well, but Ibn Ezra's style is particularly complex. A philosopher as well as a poet (his work in this field still has not been completely edited), he also wrote the only important medieval work on Hebrew poetics. This work details the history of Hebrew poetry and poets to his time, analyzing at length the various rhetorical devices and poetic embellishments employed over the years.

Judah ha-Levi thus came at the end of what could be termed the "classical period" of medieval Hebrew poetry, and the period in which he lived and wrote was by no means as conducive to creative production as that of the previous generations of poets. Following a civil war which led to the destruction in 1013 of the central caliphate of Córdoba, the Muslim part of Spain was divided into a series of *taifa* (city-state) kingdoms, such as that of Granada, of which the poet Ibn Nagrillah was prime minister. These were generally weak and divided among themselves, with constant fighting and quarreling, thus providing the opportunity for which the Christians had long been waiting. Ferdinand I was able to unite Leon and Castile and begin the "reconquest" of Muslim Spain. Alfonso VI succeeded in conquering Toledo in 1085; in response to this loss of territory the Muslims invited the fanatic Almoravids of North Africa to invade Spain and help rid them of the Christian threat. In 1090, the Almoravid troops entered Granada, an event which came just after the massacre of many Jews there. The Christian reconquest itself had serious repercussions for the entire Jewish community, both in Christian and in Muslim Spain. Caught between invading Christian troops and Almoravid Muslim forces, Jews fought and suffered on both sides. The poet Moses ibn Ezra was forced to flee from Granada, as were most of the Jews there, and he spent many years wandering in exile in Christian Spain, primarily in Navarre. During the same period, Judah ha-Levi wandered from city to city in Muslim Spain, and it appears almost fruitless to try to trace these wanderings. In spite of this less-than-ideal situation, he managed to produce a very respectable body of poetry, both secular and religious in theme.

Even in his own time, or soon thereafter, Judah ha-Levi was recognized as one of the greatest of the Spanish Hebrew poets. His contemporary and friend Moses ibn Ezra may not have shared this opinion, since in his work on poetics he mentions Judah only as a composer of some riddles, but this judgment may have been written before the poet had done most of his best work. Judah al-Harizi (who lived in the early thirteenth century) said of Judah ha-Levi's poems that they are "sweeter than honey" adding that "he took all the treasures from the treasury of poetry and locked its gate after him." Abraham Bedersi of Provence (who also lived in the thirteenth century) said of Judah ha-Levi, "He prevailed over his fellow-poets; to ha-Levy say: My perfection and my light." Nearly all of the nineteenth century scholars who pioneered in the study of Hebrew poetry concurred. Heinrich Heine, who acquired his limited knowledge of Hebrew poetry from reading the German works of some of these scholars, joined in praise of Judah ha-Levi. Heine, in his "Princezzin Sabbath" ("Princess Sabbath"), erroneously attributes to ha-Levi the famous *piyyut* "Lekha dodi" (actually written by Solomon Alkabes) recited at Friday evening services.

Heine dedicated four lengthy poems to Judah ha-Levi. The first of these is a highly romantic and inaccu-

rate picture of the poet's youth. The second, "Beiden Wassern Babels," one of Heine's finest poems, has a reference to "Ghaselen" as one of the various kinds of poems which Judah ha-Levi wrote. This may puzzle some readers: The term is a transliteration of Arabic *ghazel* (erotic poetry), a form in which ha-Levi excelled. In the final poem, "Meine Frau ist nicht zufrieden," Heine explains to his wife that the three stars of Hebrew poetry were ha-Levi, Ibn Gabirol, and Ibn Ezra; he advises her to abandon her theaters and concerts long enough to devote some years to studying Hebrew, so that she can read their poems in their original language.

BIOGRAPHY

Yehuda ben Shemuel ha-Levi, in Arabic surnamed Ab al-Ḥasan, was born in Tudela, Spain. His father is referred to in a letter as a rabbi and great scholar, but this may have been merely a courtesy. Otherwise, nothing is known of him. There is absolutely no evidence to support the oft-repeated claim that Judah studied either with the great Isaac Alfasi in Lucena or with his successor Joseph ibn Megash. It is true that ha-Levi composed a eulogy on the death of the former, but this was not unusual considering that Alfasi was the greatest rabbi in Spain, and many poets composed eulogies in his honor. At some time during his youth, certainly not later than 1089, ha-Levi left Christian Spain for Andalusia in Muslim Spain and sent a letter to Moses ibn Ezra in Granada, together with an imitation of one of Ibn Ezra's poems. Thus began a long friendship with Ibn Ezra and his brothers that lasted until their death.

Like many Jews in medieval Spain, Judah ha-Levi was trained in medicine, and he practiced as a doctor at a later period in his life. Although he was probably wealthy in his later years, and even engaged in commerce, in his younger life he received financial support by writing poetry in praise of patrons.

Judah ha-Levi had one daughter, who is supposed to have written at least two poems and who was married to Isaac ibn Ezra (the son of the great biblical commentator, Abraham ibn Ezra, himself a poet but not related to Moses ibn Ezra). Isaac, also a poet of note in later years, accompanied his father-in-law on his famous journey, when, at about the age of fifty, ha-Levi decided to leave his beloved Spain and go to the Holy Land. He and his companions arrived in Egypt in 1140. He remained in Egypt for a year, and died there in July, 1141.

ANALYSIS

Judah ha-Levi may not entirely deserve his reputation as the greatest of medieval Hebrew poets, a reputation which is based largely on nineteenth century scholarship, when little was known of the work of other Hebrew poets of the period; certainly, however, he is one of the four greatest. He mastered most of the themes typical of Hebrew poetry: wine, love (both of women and of boys), nature, friendship, panegyric, complaint, humor. Ha-Levi wrote a number of religious or "liturgical" poems as well. Like most of the religious poems that come from the Spanish school, they are far simpler in style and vocabulary than the secular verse. His secular poetry, which constitutes the largest part of his work, is often difficult and at times stiff, but he can move the modern reader with his emotions; he can arouse a smile and even a laugh. Some of his love poetry, dealing with both sexes, ranks among the finest in Hebrew verse. There is no doubt, however, that the poetry for which he is most famous and was best remembered is his "Zion" poetry. The poet came to the conclusion that, like the rabbi in his religious treatise, the *Kuzari*, he had to abandon his "temporary home" in the Exile and go to the land scared to his people: "My heart is in the East [Zion] and I am in the ends of the West [Spain]; How can I taste what I eat, and how can it be sweet?"

Leaving his home was not easy, however, and one of ha-Levi's most poignant poems describes his emotions about leaving his daughter and his grandson and namesake, Judah:

> I do not worry about property or possessions
> nor wealth nor all my losses—
> Except that I foresake my offspring,
> sister of my soul, my only daughter.
> I shall forget her son, a segment of my heart,
> and I have, except for him, nothing to discuss—
> Fruit of my womb and child of my delights;
> how can Judah forget Judah?

"ODE TO ZION"

Of all the poems which ha-Levi wrote while contemplating his trip, and during the perilous sea voyage which he so well describes (the meter of one poem makes the reader "feel" the motion of the sea during a storm), none is more famous than the "Zionide" ("Ode to Zion"), which has been translated into numerous languages in many versions. Of all the poems ever written by Jew or Gentile in praise of Zion, this is surely the best known and the most stirring.

The poem opens with the poet's plaintive query to Zion concerning the scattered Jewish people who daily seek the welfare of Zion: "Do you inquire of the welfare of your captives?" There follows the famous line in which the poet says that in his dreams of the return of the people to Zion, he is "a lute for [their] songs." He mentions his desire to wander in the now-desolate land, and all the places which he names are places where God appeared to Jacob; thus, they are symbolic of the holiness of the land and also reflect Judah ha-Levi's interest in revelation, an interest which is central also in the *Kuzari*. "There," in Jerusalem, "your Creator opened facing the gates of heaven your [Zion's] gates," he says, reflecting the rabbinic allegory, borrowed in turn by Christian writers, indicating that there is a heavenly city of Jerusalem corresponding to the earthly one, the gates of which are the gates of Heaven. In Jerusalem, the poet says, he shall prostrate himself "and delight in [the city's] stones exceedingly and favor [its] dust," a reference to Psalm 102:15.

From his ecstatic vision of himself walking barefoot in the land, verging on allegory ("the life of souls is the air of your land, and of flowing myrrh the dust of your earth, and flowing honey your rivers"), the poet turns to polemics against the Muslims, who had conquered and inhabited the land, profaning, in his eyes, the sacredness of the place. The reader must remember that this poem was written while the poet was still in Muslim Spain, and—almost as if he were afraid to express anti-Muslim sentiment openly, even in Hebrew—he hides behind allusions; for example, "How can the light of day be sweet to my eyes while I see in the mouths of crows the corpses of your eagles?" becomes fully intelligible only when the reader realizes that the Hebrew word for ravens (or crows), *orvim*, is almost identical in sound to the Hebrew word for "Arabs," *Aravim*.

From the pit of captivity, he says, the exiled people are longing for return: "the flocks of your multitude which have been exiled and scattered/ from mountain to hill and have not forgotten your folds." These lines echo Jeremiah 50:6: "My people hath been lost sheep, their shepherds have caused them to go astray . . . they have gone from mountain to hill, they have forgotten their resting place." Because the Jews of medieval Spain knew the Old Testament books almost by heart, such allusions would not have been lost on them.

Another significant allusion is found in the line: "Shinar and Pathros—can they compare to you in greatness, or their vanity be likened to your perfection and enlightenment?" Shinar and Pathros are biblical terms for Babylonia and Egypt, but the reader cannot help feeling that there is yet another meaning: the medieval Muslim lands that represented the culture with which the Jews of Spain, at least, were trying to compete.

From praise of Jerusalem, the poet turns, prophet-like, to consolation, declaring that God longs once again to make the city a habitation for His glory. The poem concludes in a mood that is both a challenge and a litany of praise: "Happy he who waits, and arrives, and sees the ascendancy of your light, and upon whom breaks your dawns—/ To see the goodness of your chosen and to rejoice in your happiness in your return to your former youth!"

LEGACY

"Ode to Zion" became almost an anthem of the Jewish people in the Middle Ages and for centuries afterward, although astonishingly few know it today. It entered into the liturgy and was recited in synagogue services throughout the world. No other Hebrew poem was so frequently imitated by so many poets in different lands.

In recent years, the revival of Hebrew as a living language has prompted renewed interest in the entire corpus of Hebrew poetry, and several excellent anthologies have been published, ranging from biblical verse to modern Hebrew poetry written in Israel. In this renaissance of Hebrew poetry, the works of Judah ha-Levi have been discovered by a new generation of readers.

MAJOR PUBLICATION OTHER THAN POETRY

NONFICTION: *Kuzari*, twelfth century (English translation, 1947).

BIBLIOGRAPHY

Druck, David. *Yehuda Halevy: His Life and Works.* New York: Bloch, 1941. A biographical and critical survey of Judah ha-Levi's life and work.

Goitein, Shelomo Dov. "The Last Phase of Rabbi Judah ha-Levy's Life in Light of the Genizah Papers." *Tarbiz* 24 (1954): 21-47. Biographical and historical details of Judah ha-Levi's life.

Schirmann, Jefim. "The Journey of Judah Halevi." *Judaism* 2 (1953): 353-362. A biography of the poet and philosopher.

Silman, Yochanan. *Philosopher and Prophet: Judah Halevi, the Kuzari, and the Evolution of His Thought.* Translated by Lenn J. Schramm. Albany: State University of New York Press, 1995. A biographical and historical study of Judah ha-Levi's life and philosophical thought. Includes bibliographical references and index.

Norman Roth (including translations);
bibliography updated by the editors

DONALD JUSTICE

Born: Miami, Florida; August 12, 1925

PRINCIPAL POETRY

The Summer Anniversaries, 1960, rev. ed. 1981
A Local Storm, 1963
Night Light, 1967, rev. ed. 1981
Sixteen Poems, 1970
From a Notebook, 1972
Departures, 1973
Selected Poems, 1979
The Sunset Maker: Poems, Stories, a Memoir, 1987
New and Selected Poems, 1995
Orpheus Hesitated Beside the Black River: Poems, 1952-1997, 1998

OTHER LITERARY FORMS

Best known for his poetry, Donald Justice has also written plays, short stories, critical essays, reviews, and the libretto for Edward J. Miller's opera *The Young God*.

His stories "The Lady" and "Vineland's Burning," first published in *The Western Review*, were included in the O. Henry Awards *Prize Stories* of 1950 and 1954. Both portray characters who are locked inside themselves; like a number of Justice's poems, these stories discover the humanity of people who might be overlooked as uninteresting or dismissed as insane. The nonfiction *Platonic Scripts* (1984) is a collection of essays and interviews; Justice's criticism and reviews demonstrate the same concern for craftsmanship that characterizes his own poetry and fiction.

ACHIEVEMENTS

Donald Justice started collecting literary awards after the publication of his first book, *The Summer Anniversaries*, which won the Lamont Poetry Selection in 1959. He went on to win the Inez Boulton Prize from *Poetry* magazine in 1960, the Pulitzer Prize in poetry in 1980 for *Selected Poems*, the Harriet Monroe Award from the University of Chicago in 1984, a Bollingen Prize for poetry in 1991, and the Lannan Literary Award for poetry in 1996. He received a National Book Award nomination in 1973 for *Departures* and a National Book Critics Circle Award nomination in 1988 for *The Sunset Maker: Poems, Stories, a Memoir*. He became an American Academy of Poets fellow in 1988. Among his other honors are grants in poetry from the Rockefeller and Guggenheim Foundations, and a grant in theater from the Ford Foundation.

BIOGRAPHY

Born and reared in Miami, Donald Justice was graduated from the University of Miami in 1945. He received an M.A. degree from the University of North Carolina in 1947 and a Ph.D. from the University of Iowa in 1954. From 1948 to 1949, he attended Stanford University to study with Yvor Winters. Among his other teachers were Karl Shapiro, Robert Lowell, and John Berryman. He married Jean Ross in 1947 and had one son.

Justice has taught at various universities, including Syracuse, the University of California at Irvine, Princeton, and the Universities of Iowa and Virginia. He joined the faculty of the University of Florida at Gainesville in 1982, where he taught until 1992, when he retired from teaching.

ANALYSIS

Donald Justice is a consummate craftsman. His carefully polished work demonstrates the power and beauty of the appropriate form. He deals with his major themes, change and loss, by fashioning poems which allow him and the reader to contemplate things that cannot stay. He is a literary, some would say academic, poet. If his range is limited, he does not overextend or repeat himself. His voice is quiet, nostalgic but not sentimental, and sometimes ironic. Whether he is writing about artistic activity or more ordinary experiences and people, his personas and other characters are "real," humanly significant. Instead of saying, "This is the way I feel," he says that "This is how things go."

The character of Donald Justice's work is most clearly seen against the background of major developments in contemporary poetry. Like most American poets of the 1950's, he worked within the formalist tradition. In the next decade he became involved in the translation of contemporary French and Mexican poets. Following this immersion in the "new surrealism," he began to use suggestive images and freer forms. He has not, however, reacted against T. S. Eliot's ideal of the impersonal poet, nor has he repudiated meter, rhyme, and other traditional artifices; he values them because they provide aesthetic distance during the composing process and an intelligible, satisfying shape for the completed poem.

Justice has observed that "one of the motives for writing is surely to recover and hold what would otherwise be lost totally—memory or experience." He regards the poem not as an expression of the writer's personality but as an artifact which registers a significant perception ("The Effacement of Self: An Interview with Donald Justice," in *Ohio Review* 16, no. 3, 1975). In "Meters and Memory" he argues that it is technical skill that makes a subject "accessible to memory, repeatedly accessible, because it exists finally in a form that can be perused at leisure, like a snapshot in an album" (*The Structure of Verse*, 1979, Harvey Gross, editor). Artifice, then, is not incompatible with genuine expression; it is one of the "fixatives" that constitute art—indeed, that make it possible.

THE SUMMER ANNIVERSARIES

Justice's mastery of literary forms and commitment to pattern are evident in *The Summer Anniversaries*, which

Donald Justice

includes syllabic and accentual poems, sestinas, and sonnets. More than a third of the poems in this collection are rhymed, and most of the others use repetition, assonance, or consonance in place of end-rhyme. No slave to convention, Justice varies traditional forms as he explores his major themes: childhood, loss, and memory. "Sonnet to My Father" pays respects to the Italian sonnet, but Justice substitutes repetition for rhyme. It is fitting that the second, third, sixth, and seventh lines end with "mine," for the poem is about the speaker's participation in his father's dying. The end-words of lines nine through eleven—"die," "place," and "there,"—are mirrored at the ends of the poem's final lines—"there," "place," "die." This repetition represents the son's identification with the father, made explicit in the last line: "while I live, you cannot wholly die." As in most of Justice's early work, the diction, while not elevated, is elegant. The poem is a carefully controlled expression of emotion.

Justice uses archaic diction in the remarkable "Tales from a Family Album," a syllabic poem of five nine-line stanzas. The speaker feels constrained to speak of his family's "doom," the effect, or cause, of their "acquain-

tance/ Not casual and not recent with a monster." Although their ancestral tree might be represented by an ordinary Georgia chinaberry, they have known uncommon tragedy. Even now there lives a cousin with a paw print on his forehead, and the speaker vividly recalls the fate of another "kinsman" who attempted to write the family history: He "perished,/ Calling for water and the holy wafer,/ Who had, ere that, resisted much persuasion." With characteristic gentle irony, Justice uses old-fashioned vocabulary and syntax to portray an imaginative Southerner who longs to be respected as a gentleman.

"In Bertram's Garden," a poem concerned with a young woman's loss of innocence, best illustrates Justice's use of convention and allusion. As Michael Rewa has shown in "'Rich Echoes Reverberating': The Power of Poetic Convention" (*Modern Language Studies* 9, no. 1, 1978-1979), the poet examines Jane's fall ironically but not unsympathetically by alluding to Ben Jonson's celebration of chastity in "Queen and Huntress, chaste and fair." (Justice's poem uses the same rhyme scheme as Jonson's and, in the third stanza, the same meter.) Jane's seducer, Bertram, reminiscent of the cynical lover in William Shakespeare's *All's Well That Ends Well* (c. 1602-1604), is also associated with corruption and Cupid, the antitheses of chastity. By placing his poem within a tradition, Justice provides a moral basis for assessing the seduction. As is true of many of his works, "In Bertram's Garden" will be most appreciated by a highly literate audience, but even the reader unaware of its references to Jonson, Shakespeare, Alfred, Lord Tennyson, and perhaps Andrew Marvell will understand why Jane is to "lie down with others soon/ Naked to the naked moon." Toyed with and cast aside, she can no more recover her belief in love than she can retrieve her virginity.

During the 1960's, a number of American poets were making statements on public issues and writing about personal tragedies. *Night Light* includes a few poems critical of the pragmatism, conformity, and latent authoritarianism he saw in mid-twentieth century America. "Memo from the Desk of X" and "For a Freshman Reader" anticipate a not-too-distant time when poetry will become extinct, to be replaced by a "more precise" statement. The undergraduate is advised not to "bother with odes," not to risk "singing": "The day will come when once more/ Lists will be nailed to the door/ And numbers stamped on the chest/ Of anyone who says No" ("For a Freshman Reader"). "To the Hawks," dated February, 1965, sees the escalation of American involvement in Southeast Asia as the beginning of the end of the world. The poet's vision of dawning horror is held in place by sixteen pairs of five-syllable lines. Only the title and dedication (*"McNamara, Rusk, Bundy"*) mark the poem as an occasional piece: It might have been written yesterday.

While Robert Lowell, John Berryman (both had been Justice's teachers), and other "confessional poets" probed their traumas and anxieties, Justice wrote guardedly and ironically about the self. "A Local Storm" mocks the ego that takes a storm as a personal threat. In "Heart," Reason speaks to Passion: After urging that "we" should behave maturely, "more becomingly," the speaker finally admits that self-indulgence is irresistible. "We will take thought for our good name"—after one more revel. "Early Poems" comments on Justice's work: "How fashionably sad my early poems are!" he exclaims. "The rhymes, the meters, how they paralyze." Such manicured structures attract "no one" now; it is time for renewal. After a "long silence" comes "the beginning again." Written at (and about) a time when many poets were avoiding rhyme, meter, and logical structure, "Early Poems" is neatly rhymed and carefully ordered. Although responsive to contemporary developments, Justice is not a trendsetter or camp follower. "Early Poems" is followed by two blank pages and then "The Thin Man," thirty syllables spoken by a persona who relishes "rich refusals"; Justice, beginning again, departed from the beautiful intricacies of formalism and developed a plainer style.

There are no sonnets or sestinas in *Night Light*; there are two prose poems. Rhyming infrequently, Justice experiments with varying line lengths and minimal punctuation. "Dreams of Water" consists of three short lyrics linked by subject and mood; reluctant to relinquish the unifying power of symmetry, Justice gives each poem the same shape: three three-line stanzas followed by a single line.

NIGHT LIGHT

Most of *Night Light* is concerned with neither the self nor poetry but with obscure people—an anonymous servant and artist who lived centuries ago; the man at the corner who might be a salesman, a tourist, or an assassin; people in bus stops; the stranger whose lights are burning at 3:00 A.M.; men turning forty; a woman whose letters are sold at auction. Imagining what their lives might be like, Justice conveys a sense of their humanity and, in some cases, their otherness. "The Man Closing Up," free verse "improvisations on themes from Guillevic," is unified by images of decay and enclosure. Cutting off all outside influences, the title character climbs up into himself like someone ascending the stairs of a lighthouse. Still more unreachable and mysterious are the suicides, once regarded as friends, who refused to show themselves in life and now must always be strangers ("For the Suicides of 1962").

Night Light, written in the early and middle 1960's, is a transitional book. Still committed to the polish and detachment favored by T. S. Eliot and the New Critics, Justice did not reject, as some contemporaries did, the patterned regularity of meter and rhyme, but he more frequently allowed his forms to "make themselves up as the poems get written."

DEPARTURES

The aptly named *Departures* deals with endings, partings, and other moments when one realizes the futility of trying to deflect time. Several of Justice's speakers and characters are weary or broken. "A Letter" sketches the desperation of a woman in an asylum. Depressed, disoriented, and troubled by painful memories, she thinks of exposing her "wounds" and her bosom to "the young doctor/ Who has the power to sign prescriptions, passes." Reading her letter, the speaker in the poem understands that she cannot escape her sadness. If she is released, she will return to the city (itself a sanatorium, Justice suggests) to resume her former habits—and find herself "suddenly/ Ten years older, tamed now, less mad, less beautiful." In "A Dancer's Life," neither neurosis nor sex obscures a celebrated dancer's vision of the emptiness of her life. Although she is still famous and beautiful enough to attract young men, she realizes that she has already passed her peak and thinks, "How disgusting it always must be to grow old."

The title *Departures* also reflects a change in Justice's style. There are few signs of formalism. Some pieces are fragments, bits from a notebook. Two consist entirely of questions, two of riddles. Justice uses occasional rhyme, assonance, consonance, and other means of structuring his poems. "Absences," an evocation of subtle, evanescent things and experiences, is composed of related images. The dreamlike companion poem "Presences" uses repetition and association to convey the paradoxical constancy of loss and change. Most of the key words and end words in "Presences" are repeated; departures, disappearances, and transitions are dreams and drifting clouds, "going away in the night again and again," yet they persist in the mind as they do in the poem. Justice's statement that he likes a poem "to be organized," "to have an apprehensible structure," is not surprising. His typical poem is not contained by, but *is*, its structure. Often it further defines itself in relation to other works of art.

By identifying various sources (including Rafael Alberti, Eugene Guillevic, César Vallejo, and Ingmar Bergman) and noting that some of his poems "come, in part, from chance methods," he asks the reader to consider the way in which the individual poem develops and its relation to other compositions. For this unromantic writer, poetry is a tradition and a craft, not just the pronouncement of a personal vision. Justice presents even first-person narratives as things composed, not manifestations of his unique sensibility. A poem based on the premise that "Donald Justice is dead" and buried under "the black marl of Miami" is titled "Variations on a Text by Vallejo." Poets, human beings—not just "I"—find ways to deal with mortality. Justice has explained his use of chance methods as "a further means of keeping [himself] distant" from his materials. By shuffling cards on which he had written sentences and words that interested him, then exercising "aesthetic choice," he formed some lines and images that he was able to develop into poems (*Ohio Review* 16).

A third of the poems in *Departures* are concerned with artists and art, especially with poetry. "Self-Portrait as Still Life" distinguishes two kinds of artists: those who wish to come, singing and playing guitars, "into the picture," and those who say, "Myself, I'm not about to/ Disturb the composition." Two other poems assess contemporary poetry and Justice's relation to it. The "I" of "The Telephone Number of the Muse" dryly but with some regret chronicles the end of his affair with the mistress who now wishes to be "only friends." He still calls her sometimes, long distance, "And she still knows my voice, but I can hear,/ Always beyond the music of her phonograph,/ The laughter of the young men with their keys." Youths who barge unprepared and uninvited into the muse's presence are satirized in "Sonatina in Green" ("for my students"). The young anticipate ecstasy; they do not think of work. The ironic poet, an experienced teacher of writing and literature, also looks askance at "[The] few with the old instruments,/ Obstinate, sounding the one string"—limiting themselves to the music of another time instead of responding to the requirements of the present. The poem argues that there is too much performance, too much publication, too little craftsmanship: "There has been traffic enough/ In the boudoir of the muse." Justice himself is a relatively reticent poet, publishing only ninety-eight titles (some poems have two or more parts) in his first three books.

SELECTED POEMS

Selected Poems includes seventy-six poems from the previous collections, arranged, as he puts it, "in fair chronological order." He revised many poems as he prepared this book. A group of sixteen previously uncollected titles, also arranged chronologically, once again demonstrates his stylistic virtuosity. As Dana Gioia has observed, *Selected Poems* "reads almost like an anthology of the possibilities of contemporary poetry" (*Southern Review* 17, Summer, 1981). The earliest poem is a Shakespearean sonnet; there are several free-verse poems, while other compositions, including some of the most recent ones in the collection, are rhymed.

In the middle and late 1970's Justice continued to observe ordinary people and seemingly insignificant incidents and places, sometimes drawing upon memory, as he had done at the beginning of his career. "Childhood," set in Miami in the 1930's, is narrated in the present tense. Justice represents the texture of the child's "long days": the Sunday boredom, his delight in the starry ceiling of the Olympia Theater, the exhilarating crime of using a drinking fountain for "colored" people. This personal poem is placed, as Justice tends to do, in relation to tradition: There is an epigraph from Arthur Rimbaud, and the work is dedicated to William Wordsworth, Rimbaud, Hart Crane, and Rafael Alberti, "the poets of a mythical childhood."

"First Death," a narrative in tetrameter couplets, uses concrete details to re-create the child's loneliness, restlessness, and fear in the three days following his grandmother's death. Justice comments on the poem's subject and form in *Fifty Contemporary Poets: The Creative Process* (1977). This essay elucidates what might be called his philosophy of composition. As he recalls, "First Death" began with his writing couplets about "nothing" until an image activated boyhood memories. Writing in a tight form about the child he was in 1933 provided "the illusion of distance" that makes him a craftsman. Although the poem is easily paraphrased, Justice remarks that its form—the shaping and cadences and rhymes that "*fix* the poem, as the right solution fixes the snapshot"—gave its maker the pleasure of finding an appropriate form and enables the reader to experience the child's misery. Justice concludes that he likes the poem "because it records something otherwise lost."

All of Justice's poems are attempts "to keep memorable what deserves to be remembered." He captures the essence of a fantasy, experience, or memory in a vivid detail or image—funeral flowers "sweating in their vases," the "clean blue willowware" prayed over in Depression Miami, the pianist rapt in his finger exercises, Death's extended hand "a little cage of bone"—and "fixes" it with a form appropriate to it, using free verse, metrics, syllabics, rhyme, or any device or convention that helps to make it durable. Much of his work develops by alluding to or departing from other poems or art forms, European and Latin American as well as Anglo-American. For Justice, the choice to make craft, not the self, his chief concern has meant freedom to develop his individual talent.

NEW AND SELECTED POEMS

New and Selected Poems opens with fifteen new poems from Justice. Readers can discern the subtle changes that have occurred in Justice's style and themes over his three and a half decades of writing, seeing, for example, a gradual enlargement and exactitude of tone and scope, and an increasing use of dissonance. His growth is witnessed in "In Memory of the Unknown Poet, Robert Boardman Vaughn," a villanelle written in the early 1990's and distinguished by some critics as one of this century's best. In it, Justice erodes the elegant repetitions with urban images of "toppled ashcans" and drunken ambulations "between St. Mark's Place and the Bowery." His minimalism here is evident not only in length but, as critics have noted, with "a capacity for selflessness" and a "humility before his subjects."

The works in this collection are accessible to a broad range of readers, showing an extraordinary range of modes and forms—from the sonnet to the sestina—and displaying the "personal" without being self-indulgent. It is a controlled poetry, cast in subtleties and nuances rather than bright and primary colors, and both the new and old poems are evocative recollections, improvisations, and meditations. Justice's preoccupation with the figure of Orpheus is again present here. Orpheus's glance back at Eurydice on their way back to the world of light marks the moment and condition of loss as well as the threshold where narratives begin. Similarly, Justice often employs the moment of looking back, casting his words into a particular Orphic tradition that elegizes even while it creates new forms. "The Artist Orpheus," one of the most striking of his new poems, presents a portrait of the poet: "It was a tropical landscape, much like Florida's, which he knew./ (Childhood came blazing back at him)." A companion poem to "The Artist Orpheus" is the elegy for the poet Henri Coulette, "Invitation to a Ghost." The speaker invokes the dead poet as a muse, "I ask you to come back," and as an allusion to Jean Cocteau's figure of Orpheus, "Let it be as though a man could go backwards through death." Not only is the living poet attempting to invoke the presence of the dead poet, but also to reinstate the fullness of memory, that is, to "correct me if I remember it badly."

OTHER MAJOR WORKS

NONFICTION: *Platonic Scripts*, 1984; *Oblivion: On Writers and Writing*, 1998.

EDITED TEXTS: *The Collected Poems of Welden Kees*, 1960, revised 1975; *The Collected Poems of Henri Coulette*, 1990.

TRANSLATION: *Contemporary French Poetry*, 1965 (with Alexander Aspel).

BIBLIOGRAPHY

De Jong, Mary Gosselink. "Musical Possibilities: Music, Memory, and Composition in the Poetry of Donald Justice." *Concerning Poetry* 18 (1985): 57-66. De Jong explores the influences of music upon the structures, techniques, and metaphors in Justice's work. The work is both specific (citing the poet's references to Mozart and Thomas Higgins) and general (indicating the poet's use of musical qualities such as rhyme, assonance, and repetition). The extensive footnotes also contribute to this essay's value.

Ehrenpreis, Irvin. "Boysenberry Sherbet." *The New York Review of Books* 22 (October 16, 1975): 3-4. Ehrenpreis explores Justice's stylistic relationships and similarities with such poets as John Ashbery and Wallace Stevens. He also examines the poet's themes including lovers, children, the aged, and the weak. Other subjects covered are the creative process, his distinct refinement of syntax, and his new technique that abandons regular meters for free verse.

Gioia, Dana, and William Logan. *Certain Solitudes: On the Poetry of Donald Justice.* Fayetteville: University of Arkansas Press, 1997. A collection of essays covering Justice's career to 1996, including some biographical material with critical analysis of his works. Includes bibliographic references.

Hamilton, David, and Lowell Edwin Folsom. "An Interview with Donald Justice." *The Iowa Review* 10 (Spring/Summer, 1980): 1-21. This extensive interview features Justice discussing a wide range of subjects, from the qualifications for selecting poems to explorations of specific imagery in a particular poem, such as "The Bridge." So extensive and thorough is this interview that it is difficult to imagine a topic not covered. An accessible and valuable source for all students of Justice's work.

Howard, Richard. *Alone with America: Essays on the Art of Poetry in the United States.* New York: Atheneum, 1950. The extensive chapter on Justice reviews the poet's focused interests, his singular artistic identity, the distinct elegance of his voice, and the "major resolution of the minor" in Justice's poetry. Howard justifies his assertions and assists the reader's comprehension by extensively quoting the poetry he discusses.

St. John, David. "Scripts and Water, Rules and Riches." *The Antioch Review* 43, no. 3 (1985): 309-319. An excellent, in-depth review of Justice's *Platonic Scripts* combined with quotations from an interview with Justice and a lucid interpretation of his work and evaluation of his importance in the world of poetry. This essay is extremely accessible, well written, and essential to anyone with an interest in Justice and his work.

Spiegelman, Willard. "The Nineties Revisited." *Contemporary Literature* 42, no. 2 (Summer, 2001): 206-237. Spiegelman discusses ten poets from the twentieth century, including A. R. Ammons, Robert Creeley, and Donald Justice, and reflects on whether these poets are representative of poetry during the 1990's.

Mary De Jong,
updated by Sarah Hilbert

K

PATRICK KAVANAGH

Born: Inniskeen, Ireland; October 21, 1904
Died: Dublin, Ireland; November 30, 1967

OTHER LITERARY FORMS

Three fictional autobiographies–*The Green Fool* (1938), *Tarry Flynn* (1948), and *By Night Unstarred* (1977)—are based on Patrick Kavanagh's early years in County Monaghan. The latter part of *By Night Unstarred* pursues his life into Dublin. Various prose essays and occasional pieces can be found in *Collected Pruse* (1967) and *November Haggard: Uncollected Prose and Verse of Patrick Kavanagh* (1971). *Kavanagh's Weekly*, a magazine which published thirteen issues between April 12 and July 15, 1952, contains a variety of fiction, commentary, and verse which was written under various pseudonyms but is almost all Kavanagh's own work (reprinted, 1981). *Lapped Furrows: Correspondence, 1933-1967* (1969) and *Love's Tortured Headland* (1978) reprint correspondence and other documents between 1933 and 1967. Since the poet's death, his brother Peter has been editing and publishing his work, and Peter's biography, *Sacred Keeper* (1980), contains a number of previously unpublished or unreprinted documents. Despite the claims of various titles, Kavanagh's work remains uncollected. A poem ("The Gambler") was adapted for ballet in 1961, and *Tarry Flynn* was dra-

matized in 1966; each was performed at the Abbey Theatre.

ACHIEVEMENTS

Despite handicaps of poverty, physical drudgery, and isolation, Patrick Kavanagh became the leading figure in the "second generation" of the Irish Literary Revival. He practically reinvented the literary language in which rural Ireland was to be portrayed. Bypassing William Butler Yeats, J. M. Synge, and Lady Gregory, he returned for a literary model to a fellow Ulsterman, William Carleton, and to his own experience of country life as a subject. He invested his fiction and poetry with fresh regional humor which did not sentimentalize or condescend to its characters. His vision is fundamentally religious, imbued with a Catholic sacramental view of nature. His various criticisms of Irish life and institutions arise from an unrefined but genuine spirituality. The quality of Kavanagh's work is uneven, and his public attitudes are inconsistent. Even so, the sincerity of his best work, its confidence in its own natural springs, its apparent artlessness, its celebration of local character, place, and mode of expression, make him the most widely felt literary influence on the poets of contemporary Ireland, most significantly on those with similar backgrounds, such as John Montague and Seamus Heaney.

BIOGRAPHY

Patrick Kavanagh was the fourth of ten children of James Kavanagh, a shoemaker, and his wife Bridget. The Kavanagh home is in Mucker, a townland of Inniskeen, County Monaghan, near the Armagh (and now Northern Ireland) border. The boy attended Kednaminsha National School until he was thirteen, when he was apprenticed to his father's trade. Later, he worked a small farm purchased in the nearby townland of Shancoduff. His first literary influences were the school anthologies which featured Henry Wadsworth Longfellow, Charles Kingsley, William Allingham, Alfred, Lord Tennyson, Robert Louis Stevenson, and Thomas Moore, and his earliest poems were written in school notebooks. As he worked on his small farm, he nurtured his taste on magazines picked up at fairs in the town of Dundalk. His keen observations of country life, its customs, characters, and speech patterns, together with his growing awareness of his sensitivity which set him apart from his peers, are well set forth in his account of his early life, *The Green Fool*. Many of his early poems appeared in the 1930's in *The Irish Statesman*, whose editor, Æ (George William Russell), was the first to recognize and cultivate the peasant poet. Æ Russell introduced him to modern world literature, providing him with books, advice, payment, and introductions to the Irish literary establishment. Of the books given him by Russell, *Gil Blas of Santillane* (1715, 1724, 1735), *Ulysses* (1922), and *Moby Dick* (1851) remained the classics most revered by Kavanagh.

After he moved to Dublin in 1939, he supported himself as a journalist. Throughout the 1940's he wrote book and film reviews, a range of critical and human interest pieces, city diaries, and various pieces for *The Irish Press* (as "Piers Plowman"), *The Standard, The Irish Times*, and *Envoy*. During that time, the long poem *The Great Hunger*, his second poetry collection, *A Soul for Sale*, and the novel *Tarry Flynn* appeared, so that following the deaths of Yeats (1939) and James Joyce

Patrick Kavanagh

(1941), he emerged as the central figure in Irish literary life. His most ambitious journalistic venture was in 1952 when, with his brother's financial and managerial assistance, he produced *Kavanagh's Weekly*, which ran for thirteen issues (April 12-July 5). This production comprises the fullest expression of Kavanagh's "savage indignation" at the mediocrity of Irish life and letters. It is useful as a document of the Dublin ethos in the early 1950's and in reading Kavanagh's poetry of the same period. In October, 1952, *The Leader* responded—in a spirit typical of the infamous factionalism of Dublin's literary politics—with a malicious "Profile," which prompted Kavanagh to file suit for libel. Following a celebrated trial, which Kavanagh lost, he fell dangerously ill with lung cancer.

He made a dramatic physical recovery, however, which in turn revivified his creative powers. This second birth resulted in a group of poems—mainly sonnets—written in 1955 and 1956—set in and around the Rialto Hospital and by the Grand Canal, Dublin, and published in *Recent Poems* and *Come Dance with Kitty Stobling and Other Poems*. Thereafter he went into a slow decline, physically and creatively. In April, 1967, he married Katherine Moloney, but he died the following November. He is buried in Inniskeen.

His brother Peter (twelve years his junior) was Kavanagh's constant correspondent, financier, confidant, critic, and promoter. He edited and published many works arising from this fraternal collaboration, including *Lapped Furrows: Correspondence, 1933-1967*; *November Haggard: Uncollected Prose and Verse of Patrick Kavanagh*; *The Complete Poems of Patrick Kavanagh*, which supersedes and corrects *Collected Poems*; a bibliography, *Garden of the Golden Apples* (1972); and a documentary biography, *Sacred Keeper*. Despite its title, *Collected Pruse* contains only a sampling of Kavanagh's prose works.

ANALYSIS

Although he frequently and vehemently denied it, Patrick Kavanagh was a distinctively Irish poet. He had already formed his own voice by the time he discovered—or was discovered by—the Revival and became a leading figure in the "second generation." Kavanagh was not a Celtic mythologizer such as W. B. Yeats, a conscious dialectician such as J. M. Synge, a folklorist such as Lady Gregory, an etymologist such as James Joyce, or a Gaelic revivalist such as Douglas Hyde. He felt and wrote with less historical or political consciousness than his progenitors. His gifts and temperament made him an outsider in Inniskeen, his lack of formal education and social grooming excluded him from Dublin's middle-class literary coteries, and his moral sensibility excluded him from Bohemia.

Yet in retrospect, Kavanagh emerges as the dominant Irish literary personality between 1940 and 1960. Although he admired each of the Revival's pioneers for particular qualities, he regarded the Irish Literary Revival in the main as an English-inspired hoax. The romanticized peasant, for example, he considered the product of Protestant condescension, and he felt that too many writers of little talent had misunderstood the nature of Yeats's and Joyce's genius and achievements, so that the quality of "Irishness" replaced sincerity.

Against a pastiche of literary fashions which misrepresented the peasant, attempted the revival of the Irish language, promoted nationalism in letters and in politics, Kavanagh posited his own belief in himself, in his powers of observation, and his intimate knowledge of the actual lives of country people. Kavanagh's subsequent popular success in Ireland and his influence on the "third generation" are attributable to several distinct characteristics: his parochialism, which he defined as "confidence in the social and artistic validity of his own parish"; his directness, the apparent offhandedness of his work, and his freedom from literary posing; his deep Catholicism, which went beyond sentimentality and dogma; his imaginative sympathy for the ordinary experiences of country people; his comedy; his repose; his contemplative appreciation of the world as revelation; and his sincerity, his approval of feelings arising only from a depth of spirit. Although he has often been admired for one or more of these virtues, and although his manner often masked these qualities, they must be taken as a whole in accounting for his character as a poet. He disdained the epithet "Irish poet," yet shares with each of the pioneers of the Revival one or more signally "Irish" characteristics.

Kavanagh's creative development followed three stages: first, the works of intimacy with and disengagement from the "stony grey soil" of parochial Monaghan; second, the works which show his involvements with Dublin or national cultural issues; and third, his "rebirth" in the post-1955 reconciliation of public and private selves, when rural parish and national capital find mutual repose.

His two most successful fictional works, *The Green Fool* and *Tarry Flynn*, provide a rich lode of documentation of their author's country background and the growth of his sensibility. Some of his finest lyrics come from this period, along with his magnum opus, *The Great Hunger*. All of these works are set in the same few townlands, and the theme is the revelation of grace in ordinary things and tasks. Through these poems, and from *The Green Fool* to *Tarry Flynn*, the poet's confidence in his own visionary gifts progressively deepens, even though the expression is often uncertain. In a handful of lyrics, however, such as "Ploughman," "Inniskeen Road: July Evening," "A Christmas Childhood," "Spraying the Potatoes," "Shancoduff," and "Epic," Kavanagh's technique realizes his intentions. In each of these, the chance appearances belie the deft design, and the natural voice of the countryman is heard for the first time since Carleton in Irish literature.

"SHANCODUFF"

"Shancoduff" (*The Complete Poems of Patrick Kavanagh*) is one of Kavanagh's most successful expressions of his parochial voice and is a representative early poem. The small farmer's pride in his bare holding is seemingly disquieted by a casual comment from passing strangers: "By heavens he must be poor." Until this uninvited, materialistic contrast with other places intrudes, this little world, although uncomfortable, has been endurable. Now it may not be so.

Before the cattle drovers assess the farm, the readers have seen it through the eyes of its owner, and they do not need to be told that he is a poet. With him they have first observed these hills' exemplary, incomparable introspection (lines 1-7). Even as his readers are being invited to contemplate the hills' ontological self-sufficiency, however, the poet, by necessity a maker of comparisons, introduces mythological and geographical allusions from the larger world. Even though these references—to Lot's wife, the Alps, and the Matterhorn—ostensibly imply his sympathy with his property's self-justification, their very statement admits some kind of comparison and betrays the principle it proposes. This and the irony in "fondle" arrange the scene for the dour pragmatism of the jobbers. Shancoduff is very poor land, poets do make poor farmers, or farmers make poor poets, and the eavesdropping owner-farmer-poet seems disconcerted. The question in line 16 is slyly rhetorical, however; the poet's evident disdain for the jobbers implies that his heart may not be quite so "badly shaken."

The poem operates by a set of contrasts which set the cold, wet, dark, ungainly native places against apparently more positive reflections from the outside. Earth and water oppose air and fire; St. Patrick's see of Armagh (and/or ancient Ulster's adjacent capital of Emhain Macha) is a counterattraction to the foreign cities of dubious renown—Sodom, Rome, London, even perhaps Tokyo. The gauche place-names of Kavanagh's parish do not seem to invite tourists, yet they combine in shaping the poet's attitude to these humble townlands and the design of the poem (see also "Old Black Pocket"; "Glassdrummond," "Streamy/Green Little Hill"; "Featherna," "Streamy"; with the "Big Forth" they compose an ancient, native estate).

"Shancoduff" uses seasonal, biblical, and religious images to suggest his parochial independence from urban cultures, while foreshadowing several motifs which run through Kavanagh's later works: his distrust of cities and critics, his investment of local dialect or commonplace phrases with larger, often mystical, reference, his disdain for positivist assessments, and his cutting irony. Yet, despite the representative nature of its content, it must be admitted that by its total coherence and clarity this poem stands out from most of his work.

THE GREAT HUNGER

The Great Hunger is Kavanagh's most ambitious poem and is one of signal importance in the literature of modern Ireland. First published in 1942, it is 756 lines long, in fourteen sections. It narrates the life of Patrick Maguire, a peasant farmer whose life is thwarted by physical poverty, Jansenism, and the lack of imagination. The poem is Kavanagh's most extensive rebuke to the idealization of the peasant: A report "from the other side of the ditch," it has great reportorial force. For just as it describes the degradation of the rural poor, it also

projects Maguire sympathetically as a figure of keen self-awareness and spiritual potential. Maguire's anguish is muffled and extended by his procrastination, the dull round of gossip, gambling, and masturbation. The Church distorts his natural religious sensibilities into patterns of guilt, which, together with his mother's hold on the farm, conspire to justify his pusillanimity. Woman is the embodiment of life's potentialities, and Maguire's failure to marry is thus the social expression of his spiritual retardation.

The title recalls the potato famine of 1845 to 1847, when starvation and disease ravaged the population and caused long-term psychological and social harm. The mood of the people turned pessimistic as they accepted the disaster as a judgment from an angry deity, and they turned penurious. This historical catastrophe had a deeply depressing effect on rural life, enlarged the power of the Church, reduced national self-confidence, and led to the disuse of the native language and the loss of the gaiety and spontaneity for which the Irish had been renowned. Kavanagh's poem reflects several of these effects with unflinching honesty.

The poem is a tour de force of descriptive writing, technical variation, and complex tonal control. In the modernist mode, it utilizes the rhythms and idioms of jazz, nursery rhymes, ballads, the Hiberno-English dialect, the Bible, the pastoral, and the theater, with only occasional lapses in momentum. The poet stands at very little distance from his subject; the tone is somber to bitter. Kavanagh shows compassion rather than condescension toward his protagonist; the humor is grim and restrained. *The Great Hunger* suffers by its occasional stridency, but its urgency and commitment do not diminish it as much as its author would have readers think when he later disowned it as "lacking the nobility and repose of poetry" (*Self-Portrait*).

By the time Kavanagh had made that statement, he had gone through some important changes in spirit. Even though *The Great Hunger* established his reputation in Dublin's literary life, he suffered from lack of patronage and managed to survive only by journalism. That activity he undertook with zest and courage—witness *Kavanagh's Weekly*—but it brought to the fore some of his insecurities which found expression in flailing abuse of his rivals and in sententious dogma on a range of public issues. As the objects of his satirical verses changed, the central vision began to disintegrate. The bitter libel suit against *The Leader* was a personal disaster. His bout with lung cancer took him close to death, and his creative energies had reached their nadir. His remarkable physical recovery, however, led to a spiritual revivification on the banks of the Grand Canal, Dublin, in the year following the summer of 1955.

RECENT POEMS AND COME DANCE WITH KITTY STOBLING

This reinvigoration of spirit is reflected in a group of sonnets published in *Recent Poems* and *Come Dance with Kitty Stobling*, notably the title poem of the latter, along with "Canal Bank Walk," "The Hospital," and "Lines Written on a Seat on the Grand Canal." As his various accounts (notably in *Self-Portrait*) of this experience testify, Kavanagh rediscovered his original capacities to see, accept, and celebrate the ordinary. In these poems, the original innocence of the Monaghan fields graces his experience of Dublin, mediated by his hospitalization and the repose offered by the environment of the Grand Canal. Kavanagh purged these poems of many defects which had marred his previous work—contentiousness, self-pity, shrill engagement in passing events, messianic compulsions—all of which arose from relative shallows.

In "Lines Written on a Seat on the Grand Canal," for example, there is a nicely balanced irony in the mock-heroic view of self, which is deftly subsumed by the natural grace observed in the setting. The artificial roar is drowned by the seasonal silence. The well-tempered voice of the poet commands original simplicities with easeful assurance. The poet's memorial, "just a canal-bank seat for the passer-by," summarizes Kavanagh's testament: his acknowledgment of Yeats, his self-definition as observer, namer, and diviner, and his humility as no more than a "part of nature." The countryman, the poet, the visionary, the Irishman, and the citizen are finally reconciled to one another. Although the poem appears to mirror the persona's affection of indifference, its taut conclusion indicates that casualness has not been easily won.

The accomplishment of these late poems notwithstanding, Kavanagh retained a sense of defeat to the end of his career. He never overcame a defensiveness arising from his deprived youth. He rarely reconciled his feelings for his Monaghan sources and his need for a Dublin audience. His *The Complete Poems of Patrick Kavanagh* shows how small a proportion of his total production is truly successful. Nevertheless, his impact on Irish cultural life is large, and this is attributable to the color of his personality, the humor of his prose, and his unsentimental social criticism, as much as to his poetic oeuvre.

OTHER MAJOR WORKS

LONG FICTION: *The Green Fool*, 1938; *Tarry Flynn*, 1948; *By Night Unstarred*, 1977.

PLAY: *Tarry Flynn*, pr. 1966.

NONFICTION: *Lapped Furrows: Correspondence, 1933-1967*, 1969 (with Peter Kavanagh); *Love's Tortured Headland*, 1978 (with Peter Kavanagh and others).

MISCELLANEOUS: *Kavanagh's Weekly*, 1952 (serial), 1981 (facsimile); *Self-Portrait*, 1964; *Collected Pruse*, 1967; *November Haggard: Uncollected Prose and Verse of Patrick Kavanagh*, 1971 (Peter Kavanagh, editor).

BIBLIOGRAPHY

Agnew, Una. *The Mystical Imagination of Patrick Kavanagh*. Blackrock, County Dublin, Ireland: Columba Press, 1998. A critical study of selected works by Kavanaugh. Includes bibliographical references and indexes.

Garratt, Robert F. *Modern Irish Poetry: Tradition and Continuity from Yeats to Heaney*. Berkeley: University of California Press, 1986. The chapter devoted to Kavanagh is divided into four parts: his criticism of the Irish Literary Revival and revisionist reading of William Butler Yeats, his early poetic realism, his poetic rebirth in the "Canal Bank" poems, and the development of his influential poetics of the local and familiar, which influenced the next generation.

Heaney, Seamus. *The Government of the Tongue*. New York: Farrar, Straus & Giroux, 1988. This collection of prose by Kavanagh's most famous successor contains a lecture in which Kavanagh's poetry is seen in two stages: the "real topographical presence" of the early poems, followed by the "luminous spaces" of the late poems. The essay shows the importance of Kavanagh for younger Irish poets in the words of one of the best.

Kavanagh, Peter. *Sacred Keeper: A Biography of Patrick Kavanagh*. The Curragh, Ireland: Goldsmith Press, 1980. This partisan biography by the poet's devoted brother claims to avoid the lies and legends of "the eccentric, the drunkard, the *enfant terrible* of Dublin" in favor of the facts, lovingly recorded in a pastiche of letters, poems, photographs, articles, and reminiscences.

Nemo, John. *Patrick Kavanagh*. Boston: Twayne, 1979. Like other volumes in the Twayne series, this study provides a useful overview of Kavanagh's life and work, along with a chronology and a bibliography. The examination of the poetry is thorough and authoritative.

O'Brien, Darcy. *Patrick Kavanagh*. Lewisburg, Pa.: Bucknell University Press, 1975. This brief book in the Irish Writers series sketches the poet's career, dwells somewhat on the libel action, examines the poetry, and speculates on his stature and influence. Contains a chronology and a select bibliography.

Quinn, Antoinette. *Patrick Kavanagh*. Syracuse, N.Y.: Syracuse University Press, 1991. A critical assessment of Kavanaugh's oeuvre. Includes bibliographical references and indexes.

Ryan, John. *Remembering How We Stood: Bohemian Dublin at Mid-Century*. New York: Taplinger, 1975. A chapter of this colorful, if respectful, memoir captures "Paddy Kavanagh," the picturesque eccentric and pub crawler, in the local atmosphere of literary Dublin from 1945 to 1955. Entertaining, anecdotal, but not thoroughly reliable.

Warner, Alan. *Clay Is the Word: Patrick Kavanagh, 1904-1967*. Dublin: Dolmen Press, 1973. The first full-length study and the best introduction to Kavanagh, Warner's book is engaging in tone, discursive in method, and speculative in its conclusions. Makes use of reminiscences of those who knew the poet, as well as literary analyses of the poems. Includes a checklist of publications by and about Kavanagh.

Cóilín Owens;
bibliography updated by the editors

NIKOS KAZANTZAKIS

Born: Heraklion, Crete; February 18, 1883
Died: Freiburg, Germany; October 26, 1957

PRINCIPAL POETRY

Odysseia, 1938 (*The Odyssey: A Modern Sequel*, 1958)
Iliad, 1955 (modern version, with Ioannis Kakridis)
Odysseia, 1965 (modern version, with Kakridis)

OTHER LITERARY FORMS

Although Nikos Kazantzakis himself always regarded *The Odyssey: A Modern Sequel* as his crowning achievement, he has received international acclaim primarily as a novelist; in addition, he is recognized in his own country and to a lesser extent throughout Europe as a playwright, essayist, translator, and writer of travel books. His travelogues of Russia, Spain, and Great Britain combine vivid description with political and cultural commentary. A prolific translator, he has provided his countrymen with modern Greek renditions of many Western writers, including Friedrich Nietzsche, Jules Verne, Charles Darwin, Henri Bergson, and Dante. Kazantzakis collaborated on a modern Greek translation of Homer's *Odyssey* (c. 800 B.C.E.; English translation, 1614) and *Iliad* (c. 800 B.C.E.; English translation, 1611). Kazantzakis's published novels include *Toda-Raba* (1929; English translation, 1964); *De tuin der Rotsen* (1939, better known as *Le Jardin des rochers*; *The Rock Garden*, 1963); *Vios kai politeia tou Alexe Zormpa* (1946; *Zorba the Greek*, 1952); *Ho Christos xanastauronetai* (1954; *The Greek Passion*, 1953, also known as *Christ Recrucified*); *Ho Kapetan Michales* (1953; *Freedom or Death*, 1956; also known as *Freedom and Death: A Novel*); *Ho teleutaios peirasmos* (1955; *The Last Temptation of Christ*, 1960; also known as *The Last Temptation*); *Ho phtochoules tou Theou* (1956; *Saint Francis*, 1962).

ACHIEVEMENTS

Though for English-speaking readers, Nikos Kazantzakis's achievements as a novelist may continue to overshadow his performance as a poet, anyone wishing to understand the success of the novels both as literary masterpieces and as philosophical documents must turn to *The Odyssey: A Modern Sequel* to discover the roots of Kazantzakis's genius.

Readers who become acquainted with Kazantzakis in translation cannot fully appreciate one of the most significant aspects of his work. Modern Greek is actually two languages: demotic, or spoken Greek, which is highly colloquial, and *Katharevousa*, or purist Greek, which is much more formal, containing many words not used in everyday speech. Among partisans of demotic, Kazantzakis was a member of the most radical group. He campaigned to have it adopted as the official language of the nation—the language used in schools. He wrote educational materials in demotic, as well as essays and popular articles advocating its use; he intransigently employed words and constructions rejected by all but the most extreme demoticists.

Nowhere is Kazantzakis's passion for demotic demonstrated more clearly than in *The Odyssey*. He composed this masterwork over a period of fourteen years, during which he spent much time traveling the back roads of his own country, gathering words in the way a more traditional scholar might gather old letters or documents. Indeed, *The Odyssey* has been described by author Peter Bien as a repository of demotic words and phrases, an encyclopedic compendium of the spoken language gathering the pungent idioms of Greek fishermen and shepherds, country people and common folk.

Hence, at its best, *The Odyssey* has an immediacy and a freshness in its imagery that truly makes it a rival of its classical forebear. At its worst, however, as many critics have been quick to point out, the language of the poem violates the very principles that it is supposed to embody, for Kazantzakis's extreme demoticism led him to employ many rare words—words which the Greek reader is unlikely to have encountered anywhere else, either in speech or in writing. Nevertheless, the popularity of *The Odyssey* with the general public in Greece attests the overall success of Kazantzakis's project. The English-speaking reader is fortunate to have Kimon Friar's gifted translation, which preserves the simple, colloquial nature of Kazantzakis's original Greek. Friar also mirrors Kazantzakis's meter in English by using iambic hexameter in his translation.

The ability to synthesize the apparently conflicting philosophical views of Nietzsche and Bergson and to transform this new view of man into art is Kazantzakis's unique achievement as a writer. Nowhere does that synthesis become more apparent than in *The Odyssey*, where these two opposing philosophies appear almost at war in a plethora of images that vivify abstract philosophical principles. In the poem, one can see the idea of man's existential struggle to assert his individuality and importance in a world without meaning portrayed with insight and technical skill. Kazantzakis's Odysseus, like the heroes of his later novels, appears larger than life, for Kazantzakis believed that the truly great man always rises above the limitations of the flesh and works toward a state of complete spirituality, setting himself apart from the masses, who are content to live without questioning the meaning of their existence. Like other great writers of the twentieth century, Kazantzakis has been able to mine the events of his own life, the history of his nation, and the myths of Western culture with equal success to produce poetry that strikes the reader with its penetrating insight into universal human problems.

BIOGRAPHY

Nikos Kazantzakis was born in 1883, in a land that had for centuries been the site of bitter struggles for independence from the Turks. One of his first memories was of a night when, at the age of six, while with his family hiding from the Turks, his father made him swear to help kill the women of their family rather than let the marauders have their way with them. Fortunately, Kazantzakis did not have to carry out the promise.

In 1902, Kazantzakis left Crete to study at the University of Athens. Upon graduation in 1906, he departed for Paris, where he was introduced to the works of Nietzsche and Bergson. Kazantzakis returned to Athens, where he presented his dissertation on Nietzsche to the faculty of the university to gain a teaching position there. A proponent of "positive nihilism," Kazantzakis saw himself as a prophet who would use his art to "save" the world. Until 1921, he remained in Greece, writing (primarily plays) and taking an active part in business and government. For a brief period, he was a member of the Greek government under prime minister Eleftherios Venizelos, but when Venizelos fell from power, Kazantzakis, disillusioned, left for Paris.

Kazantzakis spent much of the remainder of his life in restless travel. Even during the periods when he was relatively settled on the island of Aegina, he was often away, either to the mainland of Greece or to other parts of Europe. His 1907 marriage to Galatea Alexiou lasted only briefly, and he enjoyed a succession of female companions in the various places he visited. His relationship with Helen Samiou, which began in 1924, finally culminated in marriage in 1945.

In the mid-1920's, Kazantzakis traveled in France, Germany, Austria, and Italy, and later to the Middle East and Egypt, living on the scant revenues from works submitted to Greek magazines. His professed Communism caused him some trouble at home but secured for him an invitaton to the tenth anniversary of the Russian Revolution in Moscow in 1927. His experiences there provided the material for a book in which he explained his theory of "metacommunism."

During the 1920's, Kazantzakis decided to embody his own beliefs about the role and destiny of modern man in a long sequel to Homer's *Odyssey.* In 1924, Kazantzakis began the first draft of the poem. For the next fourteen years, he worked on this project diligently, carefully revising and shaping the work he was to consider his masterpiece. The poem went through numerous revisions—including seven major drafts—but always Kazantzakis had in mind his goal of re-creating in the Homeric character a concrete representation of modern man's struggle to give meaning to his life. During these years, Kazantzakis's own life was something of a struggle. He spent part of the time in Gottesgab, Czechoslovakia, part in other areas of Europe, especially Spain, constantly engaged in other works to support himself and Helen Samiou so that he could continue with his poem.

The experiences garnered during these years of travel found their way into *The Odyssey,* too, as Kazantzakis himself pointed out in letters to numerous friends. In 1938, an American patroness was so moved by the beauty of the poem that she offered to fund the publication of a limited edition. Kazantzakis accepted, and in that year a press run of three hundred copies was issued under the supervision of Helen Samiou. Though the poem was slow to gain critical acceptance, the young people of Greece and Crete found much to like in Kazantzakis's epic.

Kazantzakis's personal odyssey took him to Great Britain in 1939, then back to Aegina, where he spent the war years writing and translating and quietly supporting the resistance movement against the German occupation force. Although in 1941 he had said that he was not comfortable working as a novelist, in 1943, Kazantzakis turned to that form to portray a part of his personal history; the result was his most famous work, known to English-speaking readers as *Zorba the Greek.*

In 1946, the Greek Society of Men of Letters proposed Kazantzakis for the Nobel Prize in Literature. That nomination was repeated several times in succeeding years, and men such as Thomas Mann and Albert Schweitzer supported Kazantzakis's candidacy. Though he never received the Nobel Prize, Kazantzakis seemed unaffected. The postwar years saw him resume his travels on the Continent and in Great Britain, and in 1947, he was appointed director of UNESCO's Department of Translation of the Classics. During the final years of his life, he resurrected old manuscripts and returned to subjects that had haunted him for years, producing a series of novels. He continued to write plays as well and planned several major dramas that never materialized. During the 1950's, sponsorship by literary figures such as Max Tau in Germany, Borje Knos in Sweden, and Max Schuster in America provided opportunities for Kazantzakis's works to reach audiences throughout Europe and the English-speaking world.

By 1952, Kazantzakis's health had begun to fail, and in 1954 he enrolled in a clinic in Freiburg, where he was diagnosed as suffering from a form of leukemia. Undaunted, he continued to write and travel, returning to Freiburg for treatment when necessary. On a tour of Japan and China in 1957, he received a bad vaccination; though he returned immediately to Freiburg for medical attention, he died in the clinic there on October 26.

ANALYSIS

It has been said that Nikos Kazantzakis tells one story and that his novels, plays, and poems merely provide different historical backdrops to a single universal theme: the struggle of man to learn the truth about himself and about God. There is little doubt that man's search for God is at the center of all of Kazantzakis's writings, and his early philosophical tract, *Salvatores Dei: Asketike* (1927; *The Saviors of God: Spiritual Exercises*, 1960), provides a gloss for his entire life's work. Initially a follower of Nietzsche, who had proclaimed the death of God, Kazantzakis adopted the belief that the God of the Christian and Jewish traditions was indeed dead, that the hard facts of evolution had proven conclusively that traditional beliefs were inadequate to explain or justify the human condition. Nevertheless, Kazantzakis did not abandon the notion of God altogether; rather, for him the term "God" represented a kind of omega point, a teleological focus for all of man's endeavors toward self-fulfillment. In a curious twist of logic, Kazantzakis saw God as needing man as much as man needs Him, for God is created by man as the embodiment of all that man hopes to be. Ultimately, though, man must come to the realization that life is essentially meaningless, and that whatever meaning man gives to his existence is purely self-imposed. It is the fate of the truly heroic individual to pursue the quest for meaning in spite of his knowledge that the quest is futile, to raise a cry against this horrible fact that the only end for man is the abyss of nothingness that awaits him at death. It should not be surprising, then, to find that the poem Kazantzakis considered his greatest literary achievement deals with religious and philosophical questions, and that his hero wrestles with metaphysical issues.

THE ODYSSEY

The reader first confronting Kazantzakis's *The Odyssey* is most often struck by its length; twice as long as its Homeric namesake, the poem is consciously epic both in scope and in structure. Kazantzakis employed traditional conventions, but he did so in a way that was distinctly modern. The hero's voyage and quest provide the structural framework in which dozens of seemingly disparate adventures reveal character and illuminate themes. The diversity of action and the cast of characters are exceptionally great, as is the geographical sweep of the poem: Odysseus begins his second great voyage in Greece, travels across the Mediterranean Sea and the African continent, and ends his wanderings in the Antarctic.

The Odyssey: A Modern Sequel can best be classified as part of a tradition started soon after Homer composed his *Odyssey*, that of the "continuation" epic. The poem relates the further adventures of Odysseus, who as early as the fifth century B.C.E. was considered by readers of Homer's epic to be ill suited to a life of leisure on Ithaca after twenty years of wandering about the Mediterranean basin. From his classical source, Kazantzakis has taken not only his main character, but also others whose stories he chooses to complete (Telemachus, Laertes). Kazantzakis has also gone to the *Iliad* for a handful of other Homeric figures (Helen of Troy, Menelaus, Idomeneus). Figures from Greek mythology such as Heracles, Tantalus, and Prometheus figure prominently in the work as well.

Following the long-standing tradition of Homeric continuations, Kazantzakis begins *The Odyssey* with his hero already returned to power in Ithaca, having killed Penelope's suitors. Odysseus's wanderlust leads him to reject quickly the domestic life on his island (his people, including Telemachus, find him unbearable as well). Odysseus assembles about him a band of adventurers with whom he departs on a journey he knows will end in death. In succession, he travels to Sparta, where he abducts a willing Helen, languishing at home with Menelaus; to Knossos, where he helps topple a society that, though once the cradle of Western civilization, is now hopelessly corrupt; to Africa, where he fights to overthrow the ineffectual and decadent Pharaoh and his court; and through the African desert and up the Nile to its source, where he constructs a city for his followers, a band that now numbers in the hundreds. His utopian city is destroyed by an earthquake, however, and at that point Odysseus abandons all of his followers and becomes a great ascetic, wandering alone about Africa until he reaches the ocean. There, he embarks on a ship built in the shape of a coffin, sailing south to the Antarctic; in that southern clime, he has one last brush with civilization, in an Eskimo-like village whose inhabitants are all killed by a natural disaster just as Odysseus leaves them. The hero then sails alone until he meets his death on an iceberg.

This short summary hardly does justice to the wide variety of incidents that make up the poem. Throughout, however, Kazantzakis gives his work unity through a series of images that constantly remind the reader that the poem is more than mere adventure. As Kimon Friar points out in the introduction to his translation, "sun, flame, fire, and light compose the chief imagery" in the poem; these symbolize for Kazantzakis pure spirit—the real goal of Odysseus's search. Perhaps almost as important is Kazantzakis's use of birds to suggest both the various qualities of human characters and the constant struggle of man to emerge from the physical world and enter the realm of the purely spiritual. Most important among these references are those which associate human characteristics with specific species. Odysseus's mind is described on more than one occasion as a "hovering hawk" or a "hunting hawk"; the hero calls himself a "black crow" patiently waiting to wreak destruction; on another occasion, he speaks of his mind as "an eagle, grasping Africa in its claws." Helen is a "decoy-bird"; Odysseus's heart is like a "caged bird"; he is told by a wise craftsman in Knossos that freedom makes one's soul soar like "a giddy bird." On numerous occasions, bird imagery is used to explain the nature of God himself. One example is particularly illustrative. Speaking with a fellow prisoner in Egypt, Odysseus says that God "spreads the enormous wing of good from his right side,/ the wing of evil from his left, then springs and soars./ If only we could be like God, to fly with wayward wings!"

THE NATURE OF ODYSSEUS AS HERO

Perhaps the best way to appreciate both the poetry and the philosophy of Kazantzakis's epic is to examine the nature of his hero. Though modeled closely on Homer's Odysseus, Kazantzakis's Odysseus carries a greater symbolic load than his classical predecessor. First, he is a representative of the author himself. During the years when Kazantzakis was first composing the poem, he once referred to himself as "Don Odysseus," and indeed the experiences Kazantzakis gleaned from a lifetime of travel are embodied in his hero. Furthermore, Odysseus is presented as a type of Everyman—or better, of existential man. His external travels are paralleled by the internal struggle he constantly faces within himself as he tries to free himself from the entanglements of the flesh and "ascend to God." Odysseus is constantly reminding himself and others that nothing in life has any real meaning, but the struggle to establish meaning (even while knowing that the attempt will end in failure) motivates him and gives him real stature among men.

Always fond of adjectives, Kazantzakis uses them lavishly to describe Odysseus. The epithets that characterize Kazantzakis's hero reveal similarities with his Homeric predecessor and establish his position as a Kazantzakian seeker for God and truth. At times, he is the crafty, ruthless warrior of Homer's *Odyssey*, called by various sobriquets: "archer," "fox-minded man," "much-traveled man," "worldwide roamer," "double faced," "resourceful," "sly," "swifthanded." He is, unlike the classical Odysseus, also a "soul seizer," "soul leader," "deep-sighted man," the "man of seven souls," often a "heaven baiter" and a "mind battler." He takes on the characteristics of other famous characters, or meets with them in various guises in the course of his wanderings. In the crucial books of the poem immediately preceding the construction of his ideal city (books 12 through 15), he shares many characteristics with the biblical Moses, leading his people out of Egypt, communing with his "God" atop the mountain, entering into a promised land and establishing a utopian community. Later, he meets with Captain Sole (Don Quixote) and the black fisher boy (Christ), with whom he debates about the right way to face the trials of life.

Face them he does, directly and uncompromisingly, in a fashion distinctly Kazantzakian. Odysseus at times indulges almost to excess in the pleasures of the flesh; at other times, he eschews such activity with intensity and sincerity. In him, perhaps more than in any other character in the canon of Kazantzakis's works, one can see the twin tendencies toward asceticism and sensuality that Kazantzakis perceived to be the essence of the human condition.

Odysseus's clear vision of the human condition causes him to act ruthlessly at times, even with his God. For him, man's greatest task is to defy his fate and assert his independence: "I drink not to the gods," he tells his people upon returning to Ithaca, "but to man's dauntless mind!" "The awesome ancient gods are now but poor bugbears," he says on another occasion. When Menelaus tells him that man becomes a kind of god by following his fate, Odysseus replies: "I think man's greatest duty on earth is to fight his fate,/ to give no quarter and blot out his written doom./ This is how mortal man may even surpass his god!" Clearly, Odysseus's "God" is not the traditional Christian deity; rather he is the God

Kazantzakis conceived of early in his own life, described in *The Saviors of God* as a deity dependent on man for his existence as much as man is traditionally thought to depend on God.

Thus, Odysseus proclaims a new set of commandments for the existential world. The "ten commandments" he chisels in stone in his new city in Africa provide a capsule of Kazantzakis's own philosophy: "God groans, he writhes within my heart for help"; God "chokes" in the ground, and "leaps from every grave"; God "stifles" all living things, and all living things "are his cofighters." Man himself must "love wretched man at length, for he is you, my son." Additionally, he must "love plants and beasts . . . the entire earth." Man must each day "deny [his] joys, [his] wealth, [his] victories, all" because "the greatest virtue on earth is not to become free/ but to seek freedom in a ruthless, sleepless strife."

Beside his commandments, Odysseus carves an arrow shooting toward the sun, symbolizing man's ascent toward the special God that Kazantzakis conceives of as one with man in the struggle to make meaning of his existence. By these rules, Kazantzakis's hero lives his own life; by them, Kazantzakis suggests that modern man may come to give meaning to his life, not because life has meaning, but because the struggle to achieve human perfectibility will itself provide joy (the Bergsonian élan vital) in the midst of the tragedy that Kazantzakis, following Nietzsche, sees at the root of the human condition.

OTHER MAJOR WORKS

LONG FICTION: *Toda Raba*, 1929 (English translation, 1964); *De tuin der Rosten*, 1939 (better known as *Le Jardin des rochers*; *The Rock Garden*, 1963); *Vios kai politeia tou Alexe Zormpa*, 1946 (*Zorba the Greek*, 1952); *Ho Kapetan Michales*, 1953 (*Freedom or Death*, 1956; also known as *Freedom and Death: A Novel*); *Ho Christos xanastauronetai*, 1954 (*The Greek Passion*, 1953; also known as *Christ Recrucified*); *Ho teleutaios peirasmos*, 1955 (*The Last Temptation of Christ*, 1960; also known as *The Last Temptation*); *Ho phtochoules tou Theou*, 1956 (*Saint Francis*, 1962; also known as *God's Pauper: Saint Francis of Assisi*); *Aderphophades*, 1963 (*The Fratricides*, 1964).

PLAYS: *Melissa*, pr. 1939; *Kouros*, pr. 1955; *Christophoros Kolomvos*, pr. 1956; *Three Plays: Melissa, Kouros, Christopher Columbus*, pb. 1969.

NONFICTION: *Salvatores Dei: Asketike*, 1927; (*The Saviors of God: Spiritual Exercises*, 1960); *Ho Morias*, 1937 (serial), 1961 (book; *Journey to the Morea*, 1965); *Ispania*, 1937 (*Spain*, 1963); *Iaponia-Kina*, 1938 (*Japan/China*, 1963); *Anghlia*, 1941 (*England*, 1965); *Anaphora ston Greko: Mythistorema*, 1961 (autobiography; *Report to Greco*, 1965).

BIBLIOGRAPHY

Bien, Peter. *Kazantzakis: Politics of Spirit.* Princeton, N.J.: Princeton University Press, 1989. This study focuses on the evolution of Kazantzakis's personal philosophy up to the point of his publication in 1938 of *The Odyssey: A Modern Sequel.* Properly documented with a rich international bibliography, a detailed chronology, and an index of names and titles.

Dombrowski, Daniel A. *Kazantzakis and God.* Albany, N.Y.: State University of New York Press, 1997. An established authority on the life and literature of the Cretan writer, Dombrowski here focuses on significant aspects of Kazantzakis's theological thought.

Middleton, Darren J. N., and Peter Bien. *God's Struggler: Religion in the Writings of Nikos Kazantzakis.* Macon, Ga.: Mercer University Press, 1996. Two authorities on Kazantzakis's life and literature explore the author's intellectual growth as a theological thinker.

Newton, Rick M. "Homer and the Death of Kazantzakis' Odysseus." *Classical and Modern Literature: A Quarterly* 9, no. 4 (Summer, 1989): 327-338. This study contrasts Homer's Odysseus with Kazantzakis's more extensive treatment of the hero's death voyage. Provides insights into Kazantzakis's poetics.

Reece, Andrew. "Kazantzakis' St. Francis and the Cynics." *Classical and Modern Literature Quarterly* 18, no. 1 (Fall, 1997): 71-77. A study of Kazantzakis's debt to ancient writings on Cynicism for his concept of perfect asceticism, personified by Saint Francis of Assisi in his novel *Poor Man.*

Laurence W. Mazzeno;
bibliography updated by Elaine Laura Kleiner

JOHN KEATS

Born: Moorfields, London, England; October 31, 1795

Died: Rome, Italy; February 23, 1821

PRINCIPAL POETRY

Poems, 1817

Endymion: A Poetic Romance, 1818

"Lamia," "Isabella," "The Eve of St. Agnes," and Other Poems, 1820

Life, Letters, and Literary Remains of John Keats, 1848

The Fall of Hyperion: A Dream, 1856

OTHER LITERARY FORMS

In *The Use of Poetry* (1933), T. S. Eliot referred to the letters of John Keats as "the most notable and the most important ever written by any English poet," primarily because "there is hardly one statement of Keats about poetry, which . . . will not be found to be true." The letters also offer an important gloss on specific poems and have thus become important for understanding Keats. Besides many passing comments of brilliance, the central concept of the letters is "negative capability." As defined by Keats, it is the capability to remain "in uncertainties, Mysteries, doubts, without any irritable reaching after fact & reason" (I, 193), which implies a disinterestedness that permits even competing ideas full play to reach their potential. In his letters, Keats often carried an idea to its extreme with extraordinary intellectual flexibility; another day, its opposite will surface to be worked out, as all things "end in speculation" (I, 387). The concept is also taken to include Keats's understanding of the poetical character, or the ability to surrender one's personal self to create characters and objects with independent life. Keats believed that the artist's first responsibility was to create beauty, which implies that the artist's personally held ideas and beliefs should be temporarily suspended or treated only partially so as to realize fully the work's aesthetic potential. Through the use of sympathetic imagination, Keats attempted to become the thing he was creating, to intensely identify with its life, not to find his personal life reflected in it. The standard edition of Keats's letters is *The Letters of John Keats, 1814-1821* (2 volumes; 1958, Hyder Edward Rollins, editor). Text citations are to that edition.

ACHIEVEMENTS

Without being facetious, one could identify John Keats's greatest achievement as becoming one of the greatest poets of the English language in twenty-five years, three months, and twenty-three days of life, for Keats died before the age of twenty-six. Douglas Bush has said that no other English poet would rank as high as Keats if he had died as young—not William Shakespeare, John Milton, or Keats's greatest contemporary, William Wordsworth. Whereas other poets, especially his Romantic contemporaries, have gone in and out of critical fashion, Keats's reputation has endured since shortly after his death.

John Keats (Library of Congress)

Keats followed the Shakespearean model of impersonality in art; that is, the surrendering of self to the fullest development of character and object, and it is this impersonality, coupled with intensity, that makes his poetry readily accessible to a wide range of modern readers. The reader does not have to re-create Keats's time, empathize with Romantic norms and beliefs, or identify with the poet's unique biographical experiences, to appreciate his poetry fully. Keats is sane, honest, and open; his art is varied, intense, and rich in texture and experience. As he said of his poetic model, Shakespeare, Keats was as little of an egotist as it was possible to be, in the Romantic period, at least, in the creation of art.

BIOGRAPHY

Though the events of John Keats's life are meager, his biography has fascinated many. Keats did not have a single physical, social, familial, or educational advantage in life, nothing to prepare for or enhance the development of his genius. Internally, however, he was afire with ambition and the love of beauty. Even at that, he did not discover his poetic vocation until late, given the fact that he died at the age of twenty-five and spent the last eighteen months of his life in a tubercular decline. His career lasted from 1816, when Keats renounced the practice of medicine, to the fall of 1819, when he stopped working on his last great, though incomplete, poem, *The Fall of Hyperion: A Dream* (1856). One almost has to count the months, they are so few and precious. In fact, in a single month, May, 1819, he wrote four of his great odes—"Ode to a Nightingale," "Ode on a Grecian Urn," "Ode on Melancholy," and ironically, "Ode on Indolence."

This remarkable and courageous poet, the oldest of four children, was born to keepers of a London livery stable. His father was killed in a fall from a horse when John was eight; his mother died from tuberculosis when he was fourteen. His relatives arranged for schooling and apothecary training so that he might make a living, but the year he received his certificate, 1816, he began to devote himself to poetry. He wrote some good, but mostly bad, poetry, or at least poetry that does not add much to his reputation, until the summer of 1818. His reward was a brutal review of his major early work, *Endymion*, in a leading magazine of the day. Keats was

criticized so severely that Percy Bysshe Shelley speculated that the review began Keats's physical decline.

Actually, the truth was much worse. Keats was nursing his brother Tom, who was dying from tuberculosis, when the reviews came out. Though he was too strong in character to be deeply affected by criticism, especially when he was a more astute critic of his poetry than his readers, a contagious illness could hardly be thwarted with character. In the fall of 1818, Keats also fell deeply in love with Fanny Brawne. They intended to marry, but his illness soon made their future together impossible. Sadly, the futility of their love and passion offered important inspiration to Keats's poetry. By late fall, 1819, in the same year that he had written "The Eve of St. Agnes," the odes, *Lamia*, and *The Fall of Hyperion*, his illness was severe enough to arouse his deep concern. In July, 1820, his influential volume *"Lamia," "Isabella," "The Eve of St. Agnes," and Other Poems* was published. Keats, however, now separated from Fanny, ill, in desperate need of money, and unable to achieve his major ambition of writing a "few fine Plays" in the manner of Shakespeare, was utterly despondent. He later spent a few months under the care of the Brawnes, but left England for Italy in September, 1820, in an attempt to save his life in the milder Italian weather. Joseph Severn, a dear friend, nursed him until his death in Rome in February, 1821.

Forever thinking aloud in his letters about the central concerns of existence, Keats once found purpose in this earthly life as "a vale of soul-making"; that is, while every human being perhaps contains a spark of divinity called soul, one does not attain an identity until that soul, through the medium of intelligence and emotions, experiences the circumstances of a lifetime. Thus the world has its use not as a vale of tears, but, more positively, as a vale of becoming through those tears. Keats's soul flourished as rapidly as his genius, and the poetry is evidence of both.

ANALYSIS

Lieben und arbeiten—to love and to work—are, psychologists say, the principal concerns of early adulthood. In John Keats's case, they became, as well, the dominant themes of his most important poetry. The work theme includes both the effort and the love of creating beauty and the immortality Keats longed for as recompense. Once, perhaps exaggerating, Keats wrote that "the mere yearning and fondness" he had "for the Beautiful" would keep him writing "even if [his] night's labours should be burnt every morning and no eye ever shine upon them." Not passing, however, was the tenacity of his ambition: "I would sooner fail than not to be among the greatest." Keats's quest for immortality takes several forms: It appears openly, especially in the sonnets and in "Ode on Indolence" and "Ode to Psyche" as the anxieties of ambition—being afforded the time, maintaining the will and energy, and, not least, determining the topic, or territory, for achievement. It includes a metamorphosis fantasy, whereby the young poet, whether immortal as in *Hyperion: A Fragment* (1820) or mortal as in the revised *The Fall of Hyperion*, becomes deified or capable of immortal poetry through absorption of divinely granted knowledge. The ambition/work theme also takes a self-conscious turn in *The Fall of Hyperion*, questioning the value to a suffering humankind of the dreamer-poet's life and work.

The love theme explores dreams of heterosexual bliss, but it also moves into the appropriate relationships to be had with art and nature. The imagination is the ally of love's desires; reality and reason are their nemeses. In "The Eve of St. Agnes," a better lover, in *Lamia*, a better place, are dreams which dissipate in the light of reality and reason. "Ode to a Nightingale" attempts a flight from reality through identification with beautiful song rather than through dream, but the result is an intensification of distress. "Ode on Melancholy," "To Autumn," and "Ode on a Grecian Urn," however, suggest perspectives on the human condition, nature, and art that can be maintained with honesty and deeply valued without recourse to dream. One could say that Keats's love theme moves toward the understanding and acceptance of what is.

Concomitant with the maturation of theme and perspective is Keats's stylistic development. Like most poets, Keats went through phases of imitation during which he adapted the styles and themes he loved to his own work and ambitions. Leigh Hunt, Edmund Spenser, John Milton, and always Shakespeare, provided inspiration, stylistic direction, and a community of tradition. Regardless of origin, the principal traits of Keats's style

are these: a line very rich with sound pattern, as in "with brede/ of marble men and maidens overwrought," which also includes puns on "brede" ("breed") and "overwrought" (as "delicately formed on" and as "overly excited"); synaesthetic imagery, or imagery that mingles the sense ("soft incense," "smoothest silence"); deeply empathic imagery ("warmed jewels," "all their limbs/ Locked up like veins of metal, crampt and screwed"); stationing or positioning of characters to represent their dramatic condition (so Saturn after losing his realm, "Upon the sodden ground/ His old right hand lay nerveless, listless, dead,/ Unsceptered; and his realmless eyes were closed"); the use of the past participle in epithets ("purple-stained mouth," "green-recessed woods"); and, of course, as with every great writer, that quality which one can only describe as *Je ne sais quoi*—I know not what—as in the lines from the sonnet "Bright Star": "The moving waters at their priest-like task/ Of pure ablution round earth's human shores."

Themes of ambition and accomplishment inform many of Keats's sonnets. The claiming of territory for achievement is the focus of "How Many Bards Gild the Lapses of Time," "On First Looking into Chapman's Homer," "Great Spirits Now on Earth Are Sojourning," and the great "Ode to Psyche." In "On First Looking into Chapman's Homer," for example, Keats recounts the discovery of Homer's "demesne." The extended metaphor of the sonnet is narrator-reader as traveler, poet as ruler, poem as place. The narrator, much-traveled "in the realms of gold," has heard that Homer rules over "one wide expanse," yet he has never "breath[ed] its pure serene." During the oration of Chapman's translation, however, he is as taken as an astronomer "When a new planet swims into his ken" or as an explorer, such as "stout Cortez," when "He stared at the Pacific—and all his men/ Looked at each other with a wild surmise—/ Silent, upon a peak in Darien." The complementary images of the distant planet and the immense ocean suggest both the distance the narrator is from Homeric achievement and its epic proportions. His reaction, though, represented through the response of Cortez, is heartening: while lesser beings look to each other for cues on what to think, how to react, the greater explorer stares at the challenge, with "eagle eyes," to measure the farthest reaches of this new standard for achievement.

Following the lead of his contemporary William Wordsworth, though with a completely original emphasis, Keats's territory for development and conquest became the interior world of mental landscape and its imaginings. Wordsworth had defined his territory in his "Prospectus" to *The Recluse* (1798) as "the Mind of Man—/ My haunt, and the main region of my song." Whereas Wordsworth believed that mind, "When wedded to this goodly universe/ In love and holy passion," could create a vision of a new heaven and a new earth, Keats initially sought to transcend reality, rather than to transform it, with the power of the imagination to dream. "Ode to Psyche" explores Keats's region and its goddess, who was conceived too late in antiquity for fervid belief. While Wordsworth asserts in "Lines Composed a Few Miles Above Tintern Abbey" (1798) that "something far more deeply interfused" could sanctify our experience with nature, Keats locates days of "holy . . . haunted forest boughs" back in a past that precedes even his goddess of mind. The only region left for her worship must be imagined, interior. As priest, not to nature, but to mind, the poet says he will be Psyche's "choir" to "make delicious moan/ Upon the midnight hours," her voice, lute, pipe, incense, shrine, grove, oracle, her "heat/ Of pale-mouthed prophet" dreaming in "some untrodden region of [his] mind." In the "wide quietness" of this sacred microcosm, "branchèd, thoughts, . . ./ Instead of pines shall murmur in the wind"; a "wreathed trellis of working brain" will dress "its rosy sanctuary"; the goddess's "soft delight" will be all that "shadowy thought can win." In keeping with the legend of Cupid as lover of Psyche, a casement will remain open at night "To let the warm Love in!" Keats's topic becomes, then, how the mind is stimulated by desire to create imagined worlds, or dreams, rather than, as in Wordsworth's case, how the mind is moved by love to re-create its perception of the real world.

HYPERION

Besides finding his territory for achievement, Keats struggled as well with the existential issues of the artist's life—developing the talent and maintaining the heart to live up to immense ambitions. It is to be doubted whether poets will ever be able to look to Shakespeare or to Milton as models without living in distress that deepens with every passing work. The "writing of a few fine Plays," meaning Shakespearean drama, remained Keats's greatest ambition to the end. Yet the achievement of *Paradise Lost* (1667) haunted him as well, and the first *Hyperion* was an attempt in its mold. Keats became more critical of Milton's achievement during the course of composing *Hyperion*, however, for it was, "though so fine in itself," a "curruption [sic] of our Language," too much in "the vein of art," rather than the "true voice of feeling." In fact, Keats gave up *Hyperion* because Milton's influence weighed so heavily that he could not distinguish the poem's excessively self-conscious artistry from its true beauty derived from accurate feeling.

Aesthetic considerations aside, a recurring theme in Keats's works of epic scope was the fantasy of poetic metamorphosis. The sonnet "On Sitting Down to Read King Lear Once Again" introduces the wish for transformation that will enable the poet to reach Shakespearean achievement. The metaphor is consumption and rebirth through fire, as adapted from the Egyptian legend of the phoenix bird, which was said to immolate itself on a burning pile of aromatic wood every five hundred years to engender a new phoenix from its ashes. The narrator-poet lays down his pen for a day so that he might "burn through" Shakespeare's "fierce dispute/ Betwixt damnation and impassion'd clay." To "burn through" must be read two ways in the light of the phoenix metaphor—as reading passionately through the work and as being burned through that reading. He prays to Shakespeare and the "clouds of Albion" not to let him "wander in a barren dream" when his long romance, *Endymion*, is concluded, but that "when . . . consumed in the fire" of reading *King Lear*, he may be given "new phoenix wings to fly at [his] desire." Out of the self-immolating achievement of reading will arise a poet better empowered to reach his quest.

The transformation theme of *Hyperion* exceeds the passionate wishfulness of "On Sitting Down to Read King Lear Once Again" by stressing the need for "knowledge enormous," as befits the poem's epic ambitions. *Hyperion* is a tale of succession in which the Titans are supplanted by the Olympians as the reigning monarchs of the universe, with focus upon Hyperion the sun god being replaced by Apollo, the new god of poetry and light. It has been suggested that *Hyperion* becomes Keats's allegory for his own relationship with his poetic contemporaries, especially Wordsworth. Keats had said that Wordsworth was Milton's superior in understanding, but this was not owing to "individual greatness of Mind" as much as to "the general and gregarious advance of intellect." *Hyperion* embodies this hypothesis of progress in its succession and transformation themes.

The poem opens with Saturn, who was the supreme god of the Titans, in a position of perfect stasis—the stationing referred to above—stupefied by his loss of power—"His old right hand lay nerveless, listless, dead,/ Unsceptered." Thea, the bewildered wife of the as-yet-undeposed Hyperion, visits to commiserate. She informs Saturn that the new gods are wholly incompetent; Saturn's "sharp lightning in unpracticed hands/ Scorches and burns our once serene domain." The question is: Why, with the world running perfectly, was there a need for change? Saturn, an image of pomposity and egotism, perhaps inspired by Wordsworth's character, knows only of his personal loss:

> I have left
> My strong identity, my real self,
> Somewhere between the throne, and where I sit
> Here on this spot of earth.

"Thea, Thea! Thea!" he moans, "where is Saturn?" Meanwhile, Hyperion is pacing his domain in the region of the sun, wondering: "Saturn is fallen, am I too to fall?" In his anxiety he overreacts, attempting to wield more power than he ever possessed by making the sun rise early. "He might not," which dismays him tremendously. The first book of this unfinished three-book epic ends with Hyperion sailing to earth to be with his fallen peers.

At the same time, Saturn and Thea also reach those "regions of laborious breath" where the gods sit

> Dungeoned in opaque element, . . .
> Without a motion, save of their big hearts
> Heaving in pain, and horribly convulsed
> With . . . boiling gurge of pulse.

The Titans receive their deposed king with mixed response—some groan, some jump to their feet out of old respect, some wail, some weep. Saturn, being unable to

satisfy their need to know why and how they have fallen, calls upon Oceanus, the former god of the sea, for not only does he "Ponderest high and deep," he also looks content! Oceanus then reveals a law of succession particularly appropriate for the early nineteenth century: "We fall," he says, "by course of Nature's law, not force/ Of thunder, or of Jove." Blinded by sheer supremacy, Saturn has not realized that, as he was not the first ruler, so he will not be the last. Nature's law is the law of beauty. Just as heaven and earth are more beautiful than chaos and darkness, and the Titans superior in shape and will to heaven and earth, so the new gods signal another significant advance in being; "a fresh perfection treads,/ A power more strong in beauty, born of us/ And fated to excel us," Oceanus explains, "as we pass/ In glory that old Darkness." In short, the eternal law is that "first in beauty should be first in might."

On Apollo's isle the important transformation is about to begin. Apollo, as a good Keatsean poet, can make stars throb brighter when he empathizes with their glory in his poetry; yet he is inexplicably sad. Mnemosyne the muse seeks to assist her favorite child, who aches with ignorance. She emits what he needs to know and he flushes with

> Names, deeds, gray legends, dire events, rebellions,
> Majesties, sovran voices, agonies
> Creations and destroyings, all at once
> Pour[ing] into the wide hollows of [his] brain.

Apollo shouts, "knowledge enormous makes a God of me" and "wild commotions shook him, and made flush/ All the immortal fairness of his limbs." It is like a death pang, but it is the reverse, a dying into life and immortal power. The poem ends incomplete with Apollo shrieking, Mnemosyne arms in air, and the truncated line—"and lo! from all his limbs/ Celestial * * *." No one has been able to conjecture to the satisfaction of anyone else where the poem might have gone from there, although the result of Apollo's transformation seems inevitable. He would replace Hyperion, effortlessly, in this pre-Darwinian, pre-Freudian, universe where sons, like evolving species, acquire power over the earth without conscious competition with their fathers. As Oceanus indicates, the Titans are like the

forest-trees, and our fair boughs
Have bred forth . . .
. . . eagles golden-feathered, who do tower
Above us in their beauty, and must reign
In right thereof.

However timorously, it would follow that Keats, bred on Spenser, Shakespeare, Milton, and Wordsworth, would have to live up to, if not exceed, their accomplishments.

This myth of progress would necessarily still require the superior poem to be written to support its prophetic validity. Keats knew that he needed deeper knowledge to surpass Wordsworth, but there was not much he could do about it. Though it was an attractive imagining, no god was likely to pour knowledge into the wide hollows of his brain. "I am . . . young writing at random—straining at particles of light in the midst of a great darkness," he wrote with characteristic honesty, "without knowing the bearing of any one assertion of any one opinion." Ironically, his dilemma brought out the strength his modern readers prize most highly, his courageous battling with, to use his favorite phrase of Wordsworth's, "the Burthen of the mystery." Caught in this impasse between noble ambition and youthful limitation, Keats's spirit understandably failed in weaker moments. His self-questioning was exacerbated when he reflected upon the frailty of earthly achievement. Such is the torment in "On Seeing the Elgin Marbles," the Grecian ruins brought to England by Lord Elgin.

The narrator opens feeling "Like a sick eagle looking at the sky" in the face of the magnificent architectural ruins. Ironically, they are only the "shadow of a magnitude" that once was, an insubstantial image emphasizing how much has been lost rather than how much was once achieved. Human achievement wasted by time brings the narrator a "most dizzy pain" born of tension between body and soul over committing one's life to mortal achievement. In "Ode on Indolence," Keats enjoys a temporary respite from his demons—love, ambition, and poetry—in a state of torpor in which the body temporarily overpowers spirit. One morning the shadows come to him: love the "fair Maid"; "Ambition, pale of cheek,/ And ever watchful with fatiguèd eye"; and, "the demon Poesy." At first he burns to follow and aches

for wings, but body prevails: even poetry "has not a joy—/ . . . so sweet as drowsy noons,/ And evenings steeped in honeyed indolence." The victory is transitory outside the poem; within it, a respite from ambition, love, and work is accepted.

THE FALL OF HYPERION

All of these issues—the quest for immortality; the region of quest as dream; the transformation essential to achieve the quest; the spiritual weakness inevitably felt in the face of the challenge to be immortal; and, beyond all these, an altruism that seeks to distinguish between the relative value of humanitarian works and poetry in behalf of suffering humanity—are melded in Keats's second quest for epic achievement, *The Fall of Hyperion*. Following a brief introduction, the poem moves to a dream arbor reserved for the dreamer, who "venoms all his days,/ Bearing more woe than all his sins deserve." Remnants of a feast strew the ground; the narrator eats, partakes of a draft of cool juice and is transported through sleep and reawakening to a second dream kingdom. He finds himself this time amid remnants of an ancient religious festival. These dream regions represent Keats's aspirations to romance and epic respectively. Off in the west, he sees a huge image being ministered to by a woman. The image is Saturn; the minister is Moneta, Mnemosyne's surrogate. Moneta's face is curtained to conceal the immense knowledge her eyes can reveal to those worthy of receiving her immortal knowledge. She challenges the narrator to prove himself so worthy by climbing the altar stairs to immortality, or dying on the spot. Cold death begins to mount through his body; in numbness he strives to reach the lowest step—"Slow, heavy, deadly was my pace: the cold/ Grew stifling, suffocating, at the heart;/ And when I clasped my hands I felt them not." At the last moment, he is saved; his "iced feet" touch the lowest step and "life seemed/ To pour in at the toes." He learns that he has been saved because he has felt for the suffering of the world, though he is only a dreamer, without hope for himself or of value to others. True poets, Moneta tells him, pour balm upon the world; dreamers increase the vexation of humankind.

Although in his letters Keats gave precedence to "fine doing" over "fine writing" as "the top thing in the world," the poem does not clarify whether humanitarians are above the poets of humankind, though both are unquestionably above the dreamers. The poem then moves to the metamorphosis that will make the dreamer a poet through the acquisition of knowledge. Moneta's bright-blanched face reveals the immortal sorrow she has endured for eons; her eyes hold the narrator enthralled with the promise of the "high tragedy" they contain, for their light and the sorrowful touch of her voice reveal deep knowledge. He begs to know and she relates the fall of the Titans. The revelation begins the narrator's transformation: "Whereon there grew/ A power within me of enormous ken./ To see as a God sees." His vision opens with the "long awful time" Saturn sat motionless with Thea at his feet. In anguish the narrator sits on a tree awaiting action, but the pain must be endured, for knowledge does not come easily or quickly, not even in a dream. The narrator curses his prolonged existence, praying that death release him from the vale, until Saturn moves to speak and the narrator witnesses scenes of the beginning of things from *Hyperion*. The poem continues but this version also ends incomplete, with Hyperion flaring to earth.

It is a poignant fact that Keats never believed that his poetry, his work, had come to anything, his epic endeavors left incomplete, no "few fine Plays" written. Writing to Fanny Brawne in February, 1820, he said that he had frequently regretted not producing one immortal work to make friends proud of his memory. Now frighteningly ill, the thought of this failure and his love for Fanny were the sole two thoughts of his long, anxious nights. Quoting Milton's lines on fame from "Lycidas," Keats wrote to her: "Now you divide with this (may *I* say it) 'last infirmity of noble minds' all my reflection."

Their love had earlier spawned his most important love poems, though he refused his created lovers the bliss of unreflecting love. It would seem unfortunate that dreams do not outlast the act of dreaming, but Keats's romances, "The Eve of St. Agnes" and *Lamia*, approach wish-fulfillment more critically. "The Eve of St. Agnes" permits a love dream to become flesh to provoke a dreamer's response to the contrast between dream and reality, though they are, in person, the same; *Lamia* permits a too-ordinary mortal to enter the love dream of a lovely immortal to elicit the likely response of the

nondreamer to the experience of continuous, in this case, carnal, perfection. Together the poems serve to show that lovers cannot have it either way: Either reality will not be good enough for the dreamer, or the dream will not satisfy the extra-romantic desires of the nondreamer.

"THE EVE OF ST. AGNES"

"The Eve of St. Agnes" presents an array of wish-fulfilling mechanisms that seek to alter, control, or purify reality—praying, suffering, drinking, music, ritual, dance, and, at the center, dreaming. This poem with a medieval setting opens with a holy beadsman, "meagre, barefoot, wan," praying to the Virgin in the castle's icy chapel. Though he is fleetingly tempted to walk toward the music dancing down the hall from a party within, he turns to sit among "rough ashes" in recompense for his and others' sins. Among others praying this frigid night is Madeline, who follows the ritual of St. Agnes: If a maiden refrains from eating, drinking, speaking, listening, looking anywhere, except up to heaven, and lies supine when she retires, she will be rewarded with the vision of her future husband. The irony of the patron saint of virgins inspiring a heterosexual vision is lost on the young girl, panting as she prays for all "the bliss to be before to-morrow morn." Meanwhile, Porphyro, her love, is in reality racing across the moors to worship his Madeline. As Madeline works on her dream, Porphyro will act on his desired reality—getting into Madeline's bedroom closet where "he might see her beauty unespied,/ And win perhaps that night a peerless bride."

The lovers' stratagems provide a weird culmination, though they move in complementary pattern. While Madeline is undergoing her ritualistic deprivations, Porphyro is gathering, through the assistance of her wily old nurse, Angela, a banquet of delights to fulfill deliciously her sensual needs; while she undresses, he gazes, of course, unseen; while she silently sleeps, he pipes in her ear "La belle dame sans merci." When she awakens to find the man of her dream at her side, however, the seemingly perfect solution is shattered. Madeline's dream of Porphyro was better than Porphyro and she tells him so: "How changed thou art! how pallid, chill, and drear!" She implores that he return to her as the dream. Porphyro arises, "Beyond a mortal man impassioned far/ At these voluptuous accents" and like a throbbing star

. . . . . .

Into her dream he melted, as the rose
Blendeth its odor with the violet—
Solution sweet.

The moon of St. Agnes, which has been languishing throughout the poem, sets as Madeline loses her virginity. Madeline, however, comes out of the experience confused; she wanted a dream, not reality, and apparently she could not distinguish between them at their climax. Now bewildered, and feeling betrayed and vulnerable to abandonment, she chides Porphyro for taking advantage. He assures her of his undying devotion and the two flee the sleeping castle into the storm, for he has prepared a home for her in the southern moors. The drunken revelers from the party lie benightmared; Angela soon dies "palsy-twitched"; and the loveless beadsman, after thousands of Aves, sleeps forever among his ashes.

A skeptical reading of the poem has found Porphyro a voyeur and (perhaps) a rapist, Madeline a silly conjurer whose machinations have backfired; an optimistic reading has Madeline and Porphyro ascending to heaven's bourn. The language, imagery, and structure allow both interpretations, which is the way of complex ironic honesty. The dream experience, for example, has two parts: the first when Madeline awakens to find Porphyro disappointingly imperfect; the second when the two blend into "solution sweet." It would seem that dream and reality have unified in the second part, but the first part is not thereby negated. Rather, the lovers are lost in sensory intensity, which, according to Keats, makes "all disagreeables evaporate." Whether the moment of intensity is worth the necessary conjuration before or the inevitable disillusionment afterward is a judgment on the nature of romance itself, down to this very day.

Lamia

Lamia provides the nondreamer, Lycius, with much more than the two ordinary lovers of "The Eve of St. Agnes" are permitted; but the question is whether more is better. T. S. Eliot wrote that humankind cannot stand very much reality; Keats suggests in *Lamia* that neither can we bear very much dreaming. Lamia, as imagination incarnate, provides her lover Lycius with a realized dream of carnal perfection that extends continuously until he tires of her adoration. When Lamia, once bound in serpent form, was capable of sending her imagination abroad to mingle among the mortals of Corinth, she saw Lycius in a chariot race and fell in love. After being released from her serpent prison house by another immortal, Hermes, in an exchange of wish fulfillments, she assumes a glorious woman's body to attract Lycius. She is successful, but a series of compromises must be made to win him and satisfy his desires. Those compromises are the record of imagination's degeneration. Because Lycius is so overwhelmed by her beauty, he believes she must be immortal and loses his confidence. She "throws the goddess off" to encourage his masculinity. When he tires of the carnal pleasure she provides in the "purple-lined palace of sweet sin," she begs on her knees that he might preserve the privacy of their dream, for she knows of her vulnerability to reason. The sight of her begging brings out the sadist in Lycius, who "takes delight in her sorrows, soft and new." His passion grown cruel, Lamia plays the complementary masochist, burning, loving the tyranny. She grants his wish that they should be married before all of Corinth, and creates a feast and a vision of palatial splendor for the "gossip rout." The philosopher Apollonius, tutor to Lycius, crashes the party to destroy the dream with his "keen, cruel, perceant, stinging" eye. Apollonius is reason to Lamia's imagination, and in the confrontation between them, Lamia dissipates; Lycius the scholar-lover dies because he is incapable of balancing reason and imagination; and Apollonius is left with a Pyrrhic victory, for he has lost his pupil whom he intended to save.

Ironically, the loss of the dream, the dreamers, and the battle is not even tragic because not one was worthy of salvation. Lycius risks his dream so that his friends will look with admiration, but his friends choke over his good fortune; Lamia concedes to this foolish vanity; and Apollonius, the brilliant sophist, mistakes the whole situation, feeling that Lycius has become the prey of Lamia. More than saying that dreams cannot mix with reality, *Lamia* warns that imagination cannot be prostituted to the pleasure principle. Dreams are pure and sensitive constructs inspired by love, created for the psyche by the imagination. The eye of self-consciousness; participation with others, including loved ones; the dictates of forces less pure than love—all cause dissolution of the ephemeral dream.

"ODE TO A NIGHTINGALE"

"Ode to a Nightingale" leaves the medium of the dream for empathic identification with a natural being that seems to promise transcendence of the human condition. Again, a transcendence of self is fleetingly achieved, leaving the poet, *in propria persona*, more isolated and bewildered thereafter. He opens the poem having returned from identification with the bird's "happiness" that causes and permits it to sing "of summer in full-throated ease." The poet, however, is now drowsy and numb, so far has he sunk from that high experience of unself-conscious joy. He wishes for any wine, human or divine, that might effect a dissolution of consciousness and a return to the bird; for among men, "but to think is to be full of sorrow/ And leaden-eyed despairs." The transience of the physical splendor of beauty, of the psychological heights of love; the tragedy of early death, the indignity of aging to death; participation in human misery—all have thwarted any love or hope he might feel for the human condition.

In the fourth stanza the poet seems to join the bird, but ambiguously. After exhorting his imagination and/or the bird to fly "Away! away!" where he will reach it on "the viewless wings of Poesy," he seems to achieve the connection: "Already with thee! tender is the night." The eighth and final stanza supports the interpretation of his extended identification, for it has the poet being tolled back from the bird "to my sole self." Before the identification in stanza four, however, he has qualified the power of those viewless wings to keep him in stable flight, for "the dull brain perplexes and retards." Consequently, throughout the poem, he is neither entirely with the bird, nor entirely in his metaphysical agony, but rather in a state of mixed or split consciousness that leads to the poem's concluding questions: "Was it vision, or a waking dream?/Fled is that music:—Do I wake or sleep?" In the sixth stanza, for example, as he sits in his "embalmèd darkness" in the arbor, he says, "Darkling I listen; and, for many a time/ I have been half in love with easeful Death." Shortly, he seems to be lost in the ecstasy of the bird's song. Yet immediately he retracts, for common sense tells him that, if he were dead,

his ears would be in vain, and "To thy high requiem" of the bird, he would "become a sod."

The seventh stanza distinguishes the immortality of the bird's song from the mortality of the poet, and for another passing moment he seems to experience identification as he slips into empathy with those through time who have also heard the immortal song, especially Ruth of the Old Testament: "Perhaps the self-same song that found a path/ Through the sad heart of Ruth, when, sick for home,/ She stood in tears amid the alien corn." This song that flows through time sparks both the poet's identification with it and his empathy for fellow beings. He is not as explicit as Walt Whitman would be in defining immortality as empathy for all beings and experiences of all times, but his revealed feeling for others is the eternal human counterpart to the song that eternally elicits the feeling. Still, the great divider between the bird and poet is the poet's self-consciousness. The bird, unaware of its individuality and coming death, is more a medium of the song of its species than a being in its own right. The poet withdraws completely in the final stanza to his "sole self." The imagination cannot support the identification with a dissimilar being for very long. The bird's song fades until it is metaphorically dead to the poet, "buried deep/ In the next valley glades." The stimulus for experience now fled, the poet recognizes the division he has undergone between empathy and identity, being in out of self, with neither strain coming to resolution. The bewilderment of the conclusion reflects perfectly the imperfect resolution of his experience.

"ODE ON MELANCHOLY" AND "TO AUTUMN"

The "Ode on Melancholy" offers perhaps the most positive perspective possible to one who appreciates this tragedy of the human condition. Its psychology is a variant of Satan's from *Paradise Lost:* "Evil, be thou my good." The poet advises that when the "melancholy fit shall fall," as fall it must, one should not seek to escape with "poisonous wine," "nightshade," or other agents that would "drown the wakeful anguish of the soul," for that very anguish is the catalyst for more intensely valuing transient beauty, joy, and love. Even the anger of a loved one will reach a value transcending relationship, if we "Emprison her soft hand, and let her rave,/ And feed deep, deep upon her peerless eyes." The glow fired by her passion, the beauty, joy, and pleasure that accompany love, all must dwindle, die, depart, sour; but if one holds an awareness of their end while indulging in their prime, the triumph of deep inclusive response will reward the sensitive soul with ultimate mortal value. It will be among Melancholy's "cloudy trophies hung," which is to say, the "sadness of her might" will hold him forever sensitive to the richness of transience.

In like manner, "To Autumn" offers a pespective on nature in the ultimate richness of its condition. It has always been difficult for poets to look upon nature without moralizing its landscape for human edification. The Romantic period especially sought its morality from nature and its processes. Keats, however, describes nature without pressing metaphor out of it; his goal is to offer it as worthy in itself so that we might love it for itself. If there are analogues between human nature and nature, they are not the subject, concern, or purpose of the poem. As several critics have noted, the stanzas move from the late growth of summer to the fulfillment of autumn to the harvested landscape; correspondingly, the imagery moves from tactile to visual to auditory in an ascension from the most grossly physical to the most nonphysical. The sun and the season are in league to load and bless the vines with fruit, and in a string of energetic infinitives, the push of life's fulfillment is represented: "To bend with apples the mossed cottage trees," to "fill all fruit with ripeness to the core," "To swell the gourd, and plump the hazel shells," "to set budding more,/ And still more, later flowers for the bees." An image of surfeited bees, who think summer will never end, their "clammy cells" are so "o'er-brimmed," concludes the first stanza.

Stanza two presents the personification of autumn "sitting careless on a granary floor"; sound asleep "Drowsed with the fume of poppies" in the fields; "by a cyder press, with patient look," watching the "last oozings hours by hours." The harvested stubble plains of stanza three provoke the poet's question, "Where are the songs of spring?" Even so, the question is raised more to dismiss it as irrelevant than to honor its inevitability. Autumn has its own music and the poem softly presents it: as the stubble plains are covered with the rosy hue of the dying day, the "small gnats mourn," "full-grown lambs loud bleat," "Hedge crickets sing," "with treble soft/ The red-breast whistles from a garden-croft," and "gathering swallows twitter in the skies." The suggestion of ani-

mate life singing unconsciously in its joy, while just as unconsciously readying for winter, signals the end of the natural year. Unlike Shelley, however, who in "Ode to the West Wind" looks through the fall and coming winter to spring as an analogue of rebirth for humankind, Keats allows not more than a suggestion of what is to follow, and that only because it belongs to the sound and action of the season. Autumn is accepted for itself, not as an image, sign, or omen of spiritual value. Ripeness is all.

"ODE ON A GRECIAN URN"

As "Ode on Melancholy" and "To Autumn" established perspectives on the human condition and nature, so "Ode on a Grecian Urn" establishes a relationship with art. This ode begins and ends by addressing the urn as object, but the subject-object duality is dissolved in the third of the five stanzas. The experiential movement of the poem is from ignorance through identification to understanding. The poet addresses the urn as a "bride of quietness," "still unravished" by passing generations. It is a "foster child of silence and slow time." Once the child of the artist and his time, the urn belongs not to eternity, for it is vulnerable to destruction, but to the timeless existence of what endures. It is a sylvan historian, containing a narrative relief of the beings and scenes of its surface. The poet asks questions of it as historian; what gods, music, bacchanalian frenzy it images. All is silent; but that is best, we learn, for "Heard melodies are sweet, but those unheard/ Are sweeter," free to become as flawless as imagination can wish. The second stanza finds the poet moving close, addressing the urn's individuals. The "Fair youth" who pipes the song so softly that only the spirit hears, the "Bold lover" who has neared the lips of his maiden, both arouse the poet-lover's empathy.

In the third stanza, the poet participates fully in the urn's existence as he inspires scenery and youths with imaginative fervor. The "happy, happy boughs! that cannot shed/ [their] leaves, nor ever bid the spring adieu"; the "happy melodist, unwearied,/ Forever piping songs forever new"; and, above all, "more happy love! more happy, happy love!/ Forever warm and still to be enjoyed,/ Forever panting, and forever young"—none of it can pass. Nature, art, and love remain in the glow of their promise. The love on the urn arouses a special contrast with "breathing human passion . . ./ That leaves a heart high-sorrowful and cloyed,/ A burning forehead, and a parching tongue." The fourth stanza begins to pull out of intense identification, with questions on the urn's religious scene: "Who are these coming to the sacrifice?" To what "green altar" does the priest lead his sacrificial heifer? What town do they come from that will be emptied of its inhabitants forever? Stanza five again addresses the urn as object, but with increased understanding over stanza one. She is now "Attic shape! Fair Attitude! with brede/ Of marble men and maidens overwrought." The bride, though unravished and wed to quietness, has her breed of beings, themselves passionately in pursuit of experience. She is a "silent form" that "dost tease us out of thought/ As doth eternity: Cold Pastoral!" If her silence provokes participation so that viewers lose self-consciousness in her form, then truly they are teased out of thought, as the poet was in stanza three. Why, though, is she a "Cold Pastoral!"

Critics have taken this to be the poet's criticism of the urn in her relationship with those who contemplate her; perhaps it is best, however, that the urn remain cold, if she is to encourage and reward the viewers' empathy. Stanza three criticized human passion for its torrid intensity in contrast with the urn's image of love "Forever *warm* and [thus] still to be enjoyed." The urn remains a cold object until it is kindled by the viewers' passion. When the mortals of the present generation have been wasted by time, the urn will continue to exist for others, "a friend to man," to whom it (or the poet) has this to say: "Beauty is truth, truth beauty—that is all/ Ye know on earth, and all ye need to know."

Much ink has been spilled over these final lines of the "Ode on a Grecian Urn" and the technicalities of this famous problem for criticism must be at least briefly addressed. The difficulty is in determining who is saying what to whom; the issue has a mundane origin in punctuation. According to the text of the *Lamia* volume, the lines should be punctuated with the quotation marks enclosing only the beauty-truth statement: "'Beauty is truth, truth beauty'—that is all. . . .'" If the lines are punctuated thus, the urn makes the beauty-truth statement, and the poet himself offers the evaluation of it, either to the urn, to the figures on the urn, or to the reader. Many scholars, however, see the matter differently; they would place the entire aphorism within quotations, based upon

manuscript authority: "'Beauty is truth . . . need to know." With this punctuation, the urn is talking to man. Both choices lead to problematic interpretations. In the former case, it does not make much sense for the poet to speak to the urn or to its images about "all ye know on earth," as if there were someplace else for the urn to know something. There might be an afterlife where things can be known, but not for the urn. It would be odd for the poet to speak to the reader in that way, too. The inconsistency in tone would be especially awkward. Several lines earlier, he had joined his reader in saying to the urn: "Thou . . . dost tease us out of thought." To refer now to "us" as *ye*, as in "that is all/ Ye know on earth," is out of tone. On the other hand, the argument against the urn speaking the entire aphorism is directed against its sufficiency. It has been argued that human beings need to know a great deal more than "Beauty is truth, truth beauty," no matter how one tries to stretch the meanings of the terms to make them appear all-inclusive. There is no way to resolve this critical problem with confidence, though trying to think through it will provide an exercise in Keatsean speculation at its best.

To agree that the experience the poet undergoes is entirely satisfactory might be enough, though there is not critical unanimity about this, either. Lovers about to kiss, rather than kissing; trees in their springtime promise, rather than in fruition; a song that has to be imagined; a sacrifice still to be made, rather than offered—all can suggest experience short of perfection. Yet, like Keats's dreams which surpass reality, these figures are safely in their imaginative prime. The kiss, after all, may not be as sweet as anticipated; the fruit may be blighted; the song may be tiresome or soon grow so; the sacrifice may be unacceptable.

In fact, a reader comes to Keats's poetry as the poet himself came to the urn. Like all great art, Keats's poetry is evocative; it leads its readers' emotions and thoughts into and then out of its formal beauty to teach and delight. One can stand back and examine its formal perfection; one can ask questions of it about human nature and its desires for being and loving. Yet only through the experience of it can one learn what it has to teach; only after one goes through the empathy of Keats's narrator in stanza three can one speak with confidence of its meaning.

OTHER MAJOR WORKS

NONFICTION: *The Letters of John Keats, 1814-1821*, 1958 (2 volumes; Hyder Edward Rollins, editor).

MISCELLANEOUS: *Complete Works*, 1900-1901 (5 volumes; H. B. Forman, editor).

BIBLIOGRAPHY

Bate, Walter Jackson. *John Keats*. Cambridge, Mass.: Harvard University Press, 1963. If there is one single book that students of Keats's life and poetry should have at their side, it is this superb critical biography. Bate is accurate with biographical details, subtle in his analyses of Keats's psychology and how it influenced his poetry, and always reliable when discussing the style and themes of the poems.

Bloom, Harold, ed. *John Keats: Modern Critical Views*. New York: Chelsea House, 1985. Eleven essays, most of them reprinted from longer works, which make up a representative collection of modern approaches to Keats. Some of the essays are difficult, and familiarity with the poems and earlier critical approaches to them is recommended. Individual poems discussed are *Endymion* (Stuart Sperry), "To Autumn" (Geoffrey Hartman), *Hyperion* (Paul Sherwin), *Lamia* (Leslie Brisman), "Ode on Indolence" (Helen Vendler), and the two *Hyperions*. Contains several general essays, including Paul de Man's frequently cited overview of Keats's poetry.

Christensen, Allan C. *The Challenge of Keats: Bicentenary Essays, 1795-1995*. Atlanta, Ga.: Rodopi, 2000. Contributors to this volume reexamine some of the criticisms and exaltations of Keats in order to find a new analysis of his achievement. Delivers an appraisal of the historical and cultural contexts of Keats's work and an in-depth discussion of the influences and relationships among Keats and other poets.

Cox, Jeffrey N. *Poetry and Politics in the Cockney School: Keats, Shelley, Hunt, and Their Circle*. New York: Cambridge University Press, 1998. This monograph in the Cambridge Studies in Romanticism series examines the "second generation" of Romantics (those associated with Leigh Hunt) and challenges the common idea that the original Romantics, including Keats, were solitary figures, instead postu-lating the social nature of their work. An entire chapter, "John Keats, Coterie Poet," is devoted to Keats.

Dickstein, Morris. *Keats and His Poetry: A Study in Development*. Chicago: University of Chicago Press, 1971. Studies the development of Keats's attitude to consciousness, defined as "self-awareness and awareness of the world that surrounds, nurtures, and conditions the self." Dickstein argues that Keats's poetry developed from early escapism to self-awareness and awareness of the tragic dimension to existence. Provides detailed analysis of *Endymion*, the odes, and some of the minor poems that have received less critical attention.

Evert, Walter H. *Aesthetic and Myth in the Poetry of Keats*. Princeton, N.J.: Princeton University Press, 1965. An important and frequently cited study of Keats's aesthetic ideas and his use of a mythic structure to express them. Argues persuasively that the Greek myth of Apollo gave Keats a vision of human life operating in harmony with the cycle of life and growth in nature. The longest discussion is of *Endymion*, but Evert also provides illuminating readings of most of the other major poems.

McFarland, Thomas. *The Masks of Keats: The Endeavour of a Poet*. New York: Oxford University Press, 2000. The well-known scholar of Romantic literature surveys the essence of Keats.

Motion, Andrew. *Keats*. New York: Farrar, Straus and Giroux, 1998. A biography that emphasizes Keats's politics as well as his poetry and personality. Motion won a Whitbread Prize for his biography of Philip Larkin, but *Keats* is his first dealing with the Romantic period. Highlighting the tough side of Keats's character, Motion puts to rest the image of Keats as little more than a sickly dreamer.

O'Flinn, Paul. *How to Study Romantic Poetry*. New York: St. Martin's Press, 2001. A useful study guide for introductory students, including overviews and outlines for Coleridge, Wordsworth, Blake, and Keats.

Robinson, Jeffrey C. *Reception and Poetics in Keats: My Ended Poet*. New York: St. Martin's Press, 1998. Readings of other poets' poems addressed to or about Keats, followed by an examination of Keats as a precursor to the visionary open-form poetry of some of the modern age's experimental poets.

Sitterson, Joseph C., Jr. *Romantic Poems, Poets, and Narrators*. Kent, Ohio: Kent State University Press, 2000. An examination of narrative and point of view in the poetry of the Romantic poets William Wordsworth, Samuel Taylor Coleridge, William Blake, and Keats. Close readings of the major poems, including *Lamia*, from various critical perspectives. Bibliographical references, index.

Sperry, Stuart M. *Keats the Poet*. Princeton, N.J.: Princeton University Press, 1973. One of the most respected studies. In the first chapter, Sperry discusses the importance of "sensation" to Keats and the philosophic and aesthetic theories underlying it. The second chapter discusses analogies between chemical processes as known in Keats's day and Keats's descriptions of the poetic process. Readings of all the major poems follow in chronological order, as Sperry traces Keats's intellectual and poetic development, with emphasis on Keats's view of the poetic process.

Van Ghent, Dorothy. *Keats: The Myth of the Hero*. Princeton, N.J.: Princeton University Press, 1983. This unusual book, which was completed in the 1960's and published posthumously, applies mythic and archetypal criticism to Keats. Although this approach is not currently fashionable, Van Ghent's readings of all the major poems in terms of the quest myth of the hero, as described by mythologist Joseph Campbell, are fresh and insightful.

Waldoff, Leon. *Keats and the Silent Work of Imagination*. Urbana: University of Illinois Press, 1985. A psychoanalytic study of the role of imagination in Keats's poetry and development. Waldoff extends earlier studies by taking into account the "unconscious dimension" of imagination, how it functions to give expression to the deepest images, feelings, and thoughts in Keats's psyche and art. The psychoanalysis is Freudian, but it is not applied dogmatically, and the result is some thought-provoking close readings of the major poems that reveal the recurring conflicts in Keats's mind.

Richard E. Matlak;
bibliography updated by the editors

WELDON KEES

Born: Beatrice, Nebraska; February 24, 1914
Died: San Francisco, California; July 18, 1955

PRINCIPAL POETRY
The Last Man, 1943
The Fall of the Magicians, 1947
Poems, 1947-1954, 1954
The Collected Poems of Weldon Kees, 1960, revised 1975

OTHER LITERARY FORMS

While the poetry of Weldon Kees eventually dominated his literary career, he began by publishing more than three dozen short stories in little magazines, such as *The Prairie Schooner*, that were scattered throughout the Midwest. From his first published story in 1934 (while still an undergraduate) to his last one in 1940 ("The Life of the Mind"), Kees's reputation grew steadily and impressively. He was frequently cited in annual anthologies such as those published by New Directions. Edward J. O'Brien designated twenty of his stories as "distinctive" in his *Best Short Stories*, an annual distillation from thousands of stories published in English; indeed, O'Brien's 1941 volume was dedicated to Kees. Kees's commitment to short fiction, however, had already waned by then.

In addition to short stories, Kees published a number of reviews in prestigious periodicals such as *Poetry, The Nation*, and *The New York Times Book Review*. His interests were astonishingly diverse, and he reviewed books of poetry, fiction, music, art, criticism, and psychology. In 1950, Kees served as art critic for *The Nation*, publishing an important series of articles on the "abstract expressionists." He also wrote the essay "Muskrat Ramble: Popular and Unpopular Music," based on his study of jazz, which was anthologized for its insights into popular culture. Kees also tried his hand at writing plays, and he left behind an experimental, off-Broadway sort of play, *The Waiting Room* (1986).

Besides writing, Kees managed to make, or help to make, several short "art films" that are representative of American expressionist cinematography of the period.

Weldon Kees

important in unacknowledged quarters of contemporary poetry. The inclusion of Kees in *The Norton Anthology of Modern Poetry* (1973) would expand his audience. His editor, Donald Justice, saw fit to revise *The Collected Poems* fifteen years after initial publication. Larry Levis, whose first three books have each won a major national award, includes the eulogy "My Only Photograph of Weldon Kees" in his book *The Dollmaker's Ghost* (1981).

If, as Rexroth has suggested, Kees was "launched" into poetry by Conrad Aiken, T. S. Eliot, and W. H. Auden, he also assimilated the objectivist viewpoint of William Carlos Williams, the incremental method of Ezra Pound, the prose rhythms of Kenneth Fearing, and the proletarian realism of James T. Farrell, in moving far beyond those early influences. Kees may, indeed, yet be seen as an important figure in the transition from modernist poetics to the postmodern sensibility, with its preoccupation with loss, fictions of the self, and parody of older forms.

More than as an unknown link in the history of poetics or as an artist of amazing versatility, Kees's achievement is a poetry that is singularly voiced in its blunt honesty and articulate despair over the loss of Walt Whitman's American idealism. There is no poet in all of American literature more bitter than Kees; yet that "permanent and hopeless apocalypse" (Rexroth) in which he lived does not hinder his eloquence, nor does it erode an eerie serenity that constantly seems to accept certain doom. Kees even seems to anticipate the now-familiar despair of the nuclear age in his poem "Travels in North America," in which he declares that "the sky is soiled" by the "University of California's atom bomb." Had he been publishing in the 1960's or the 1970's, Kees might be read widely. As Rexroth has concluded, the poems of Kees may simply have been "just a few years too early."

Notable are *The Adventures of Jimmy*, for which he wrote a jazz score, and *Hotel Apex*, his own psychological study of urban disintegration. His filmmaking extended to studies in child and group psychology that led to an association with the psychiatrists Gregory Bateson and Jurgen Ruesch; with the latter, Kees coauthored *Nonverbal Communication: Notes on the Visual Perception of Human Relations* (1956), which contains a stunning series of still photographs taken by Kees himself. Published after his disappearance in 1955, this volume and *The Collected Poems* are essential for an understanding of Kees's poetry.

ACHIEVEMENTS

While Weldon Kees was fairly well known and critically acclaimed by reviewers such as Rexroth in his own time, his work is now all but forgotten. A thorough assessment of his place in American poetry remains to be done, yet one senses that Kees has been influential and

BIOGRAPHY

Weldon Kees remained in his birthplace, the small town of Beatrice in rural Nebraska, until he attended the University of Nebraska. His childhood and adolescence appear typical of the era and place. By the time Kees had been graduated from a liberal arts curriculum in 1935, he had made a sufficient impression on Professor L. C. Wimberly to become a regular contributor and reviewer for *The Prairie Schooner.* After serving as an editor for the Federal Writers' Project in Lincoln, Kees moved to Denver in 1937 to work as a librarian, eventually becoming director of the Bibliographical Center of Research for the Rocky Mountain Region. His first published poem, "Subtitle," appeared that year in an obscure little magazine called *Signatures*; from then on, Kees turned increasingly toward poetry for the expression of his artistic vision.

By 1943, Kees had moved to New York, where he worked as a journalist for *Time* and became involved in documentary filmmaking. That year also saw the publication of his first book of poems, *The Last Man*, by the Colt Press in San Francisco. Midway through the 1940's, Kees took up painting, choosing to identify himself with what was to be known as the abstract expressionist movement. He exhibited his work in one-man shows at the Peridot Gallery; at least once, his paintings were shown with those of Hans Hofmann, William de Kooning, Jackson Pollock, and Robert Motherwell—the major artists of the movement. Kees also found time to continue writing poems, and they appeared in *Poetry, The New Yorker*, and *Harper's*, among other leading journals. His second collection of poems, *The Fall of the Magicians*, was published in 1947.

Kees abandoned New York for San Francisco sometime in 1951. There he began serious study of jazz piano and jazz composition. He continued his work in cinematography and made several movies himself. Kees also began exploring nonverbal signs with Jurgen Ruesch and interpersonal cues with Gregory Bateson in an attempt to grasp the commonplace, to exploit it, and to express it immediately and directly by a method that was "spare, rigorous, and clinical." Meanwhile, he continued to paint and write; in 1954, his last book, *Poems, 1947-1954*, was published in San Francisco.

Aside from Kees's far-ranging activities and multitalented pursuits, his life to this point, in the words of Justice, seems to have been "a fairly typical career for any writer reaching manhood in the depression and passing through a time of political crisis and war." On July 18, 1955, however, Kees's car was found abandoned on the approach to the Golden Gate Bridge. In a review that appeared that same day in *The New Republic*, Kees had written of "our present atmosphere of dis-

trust, violence, and irrationality" that led to "so many human beings murdering themselves—either literally or symbolically. . . ." Justice reports that in the weeks before his car was found, Kees had spoken to friends both of suicide and of going away to Mexico to begin a new life. His disappearance, it seems, was not an act of sudden or impulsive desperation, but rather the culmination of nearly two decades in which his poetry shows an increasing despair that grew deeper with his avid scrutiny of humanity in contemporary society and his insistent denial of those superficial values by which human beings sought to order their lives. Whether Kees did commit suicide or whether he simply fled from any previous social context in his life, his disappearance was the ultimate symbolic act against what he perceived to be an indifferent society seized by the doldrums of pervasive mediocrity.

ANALYSIS

Perhaps the neglect that Weldon Kees's poetry has suffered results from the lack of a single, brilliant "masterpiece." There is no long poem, no ambitious project or sequence like those on which many modern and contemporary poets have founded their reputations. There is no pretentious, gaudy innovation of form that would assure him a place in debates on "technical craft." Many of Kees's poems suffer from flaws such as awkward allusions or tedious repetitions, but despite all such deficiencies his work is original for its soft voice that expresses a tone of hard bitterness. That voice is not especially pleasing in its barrage of satiric details, yet it retains a unique capacity to haunt the memory of anyone who has read his poems. Donald Justice is surely correct in asserting that Kees's poetry "makes its deepest impression when read as a body of work rather than a collection of isolated moments of brilliance," for "there is a cumulative power to the work as a whole to which even the weaker poems contribute."

In Kees's early poems such as "The Speakers," one detects the unmistakable echoes of T. S. Eliot, while a poem such as "Variations on a Theme by Joyce" employs a Joycean "war in the words." Even in those first poems, however, Kees comes quickly to his own sense of rhythm and tone. While he played with formalism by using the villanelle and the sestina, and while he experimented with form in such poems as "Fuge" and "Round," Kees settled in to a rhythmic prose line that was more flexible than traditional meter and more restrictive than free verse. Possessing a naturally good ear, Kees successfully wed form and content by starting with facts and things and then consummated them by placing the right words in the right order—in short, a wholly natural proselike but lyrical style. The consequent unobtrusive tone of the poems is the very heart of Kees's poetic vision.

Kees chose as an epigraph to his final book a passage from Nathaniel Hawthorne's *The Marble Faun* (1860) that reveals much about Kees's own perspective in his poetry. His quest was to enter "those dark caverns into which all men must descend, if they would know anything beneath the surface and illusive pleasures of existence." Hawthorne's novel itself is a study of ambivalent meaning in a world scattered among the fragments of tradition and the incomprehensible debris that is left to the artist. Seeing himself in a similar world, but facing an even more painful disintegration than Hawthorne had perceived, Kees sought to enter his own "dark caverns" by explicating and disclosing the ironies of the "surface" and satirizing the "pleasures of existence." Whatever hope marks that quest—and it does not appear with any frequency—can be found in the intense scrutiny of both personal and public experience, capable not only of recognizing and accepting continuous despair, but also of remaining detached from its implications. Kees proposes a self-protective hope, simple, isolated, solitary, and stationary, out of which, with absolute denial, the self can create a system of values by which it can survive—honestly and naturally—with perhaps its greatest pleasure being in art itself.

"FOR MY DAUGHTER"

The pervasive anguish and bitterness that runs through Kees's poetry like grain through wood appeared in his earliest work. In the early poem "For My Daughter," as the speaker gazes into his "daughter's eyes," he perceives "hintings of death" which he knows "she does not heed." Continuing his contemplation of the destruction of her youth, he fears that she will be subjected to the "Parched years that I have seen" and intensifies his dread by assuming that she will be ravished by "lingering/ Death in certain war." Worse yet, the speaker bemoans the possibility—even probability—that his daughter will be "fed on hate" and learn to relish "the sting/ Of other's agony" in which the masochism of self-destruction overwhelms the tenderness of love. In the midst of such bleak projection, Kees undermines the speaker's fearful uncertainties. "These speculations," says the speaker, "sour in the sun." Just as the reader begins to applaud the father for coming to his senses and rejecting his indulgent morbidity, Kees delivers an excruciating shock in the last line: "I have no daughter. I desire none." The reader now realizes that the despair is even greater than he had supposed; the speaker has already chosen not to have children, because he sees nothing but betrayal and suffering in his vision of the future. He chooses to withhold his own "procreative urge," viewing it as his own inevitable complicity in the suffocation of the unborn generations.

"THE CONVERSATION IN THE DRAWING ROOM"

That rather private sense of futility gives way in other poems to a dramatic rendering of an equally futile sense in interpersonal relationships. In "The Conversation in the Drawing Room," Kees creates a dialogue between Hobart, a young man aghast at a "spot of blood" that is "spreading" on the room's wall, and Cousin Agatha, who refuses to acknowledge his hysteria as anything but the result of reading *The Turn of the Screw* (Henry James, 1898) before bedtime. Agatha sees herself as compassionate and progressive; she remarks that the "weather is ideal" and ruminates on joining "a new theosophist group" as Hobart announces that the spot is "growing brighter." When he urges her to examine it, she dismisses it as an "aberration of the wallpaper" and suggests that he suffers from indigestion. When Hobart points out that the spot has become "a moving thing/ That spreads and reaches from the wall," Agatha's response denies even his presence: "I cannot listen to you any more just now." After treating her lily with "another aspirin" and finding her own "barbital," Agatha leaves Hobart twitching, "rather feebly," in the aftermath of a convulsion "on the floor," while speculating that his "youthful animal spirits" and "a decided taste for the macabre" have been responsible for his disconcerting "gasping and screaming." Declaring that it is "a beautiful afternoon," Agatha anticipates her evening dinner party and rejoices smugly that "everything is blissfully quiet now" so that she can depart for her routine afternoon nap. Quite apart from her perception of herself, Kees portrays a drastic indifference on Agatha's part that is the result of her mundane, trivial allegiance to and affirmation of the social and spiritual contexts that she unquestionably accepts as her own. Her unexamined, callous optimism has, in fact, destroyed not only her cousin Hobart, but also her own ability to see beyond the surface of a superficial value system. Agatha has not the slightest notion of the presence of evil in the world. Her refusal to acknowledge it is her constant contribution to its growth.

THE ROBINSON POEMS

Kees was later to extend his satirical attack on the shallow values of society in a more mature series of poems that center on Robinson, an archetypal ordinary man who has little idea who he is, what he is doing, or where he has been. In the Robinson poems, however, Kees offers sympathy with ridicule, compassion with condemnation, and self-irony with parody. These poems, "Robinson," "Aspects of Robinson," "Robinson at Home" and "Relating to Robinson," show a curious use of the persona in that Robinson is usually absent or nearly absent from the poems. Kees writes primarily of the things or places that once affirmed his existence: The remnants of his life and actions are all that remain of him. When Robinson is present, he is isolated by a room, a hallway or a stairway, or he is insulated from the world to which he attempts to relate by a deep and troubled sleep. When Robinson looks into a "mirror from Mexico," he finds that it "reflects nothing at all." The pages in his books are blank. He attempts to telephone himself at his own empty house. His existence consists solely of traces of himself that he can no longer discern. Throughout the poems, Robinson speaks only once—and then out of a nightmare: "There is something in this madhouse that I symbolize—/ This city—nightmare—black. . . ." Hardly capable of such a statement in his waking state, Robinson speaks here as much for Kees as for himself. What Kees has sought to use as a device, the persona of absence, has resulted, because of his empathy with that persona, in the presence of his own voice. Kees's satire has become self-irony. The shallow life that he had wished to parody has become all too much a part of his own life.

By the final poem in the series, "Relating to Robinson," Kees's pretense of the persona itself has dissolved: "We were alone there, he and I,/ Inhabiting the empty street." The speaker confesses freely that Robinson is a fiction of himself: "His voice/ Came at me like an echo in the dark." As the creator of the persona, the poet must now accept those aspects of himself that he has sought to keep at a distance by his use of the device. Consequently, he must now accept the paradox that he himself is as much the creation of Robinson as Robinson is the product of his art, for he has now "no certainty,/ There in the dark, that it was Robinson/ Or someone else." In his exploration of "surfaces" and his analysis of "illusive pleasures," Kees has successfully overcome the phenomenological alienation between subject and object, but the intensity of his involvement in doing so has left him hopelessly entangled in the very shallowness he had hoped to overturn. His success is his failure.

"A SALVO FOR HANS HOFMANN"

In the wake of this tendency to undermine his own quest (his villanelles and sestinas fail precisely because they cannot contain his blunt confrontation with experience without seeming stillborn themselves), Kees developed a poetic technique that embodies his denial of false values, perhaps best illustrated in "A Salvo for Hans Hofmann," which reveals a good deal more about Kees than it does about the painter. Kees's antagonistic method intends to enter "the slashed world traced and traced again" so that by his entry it is "enriched, enlarged, caught in a burning scrutiny" which will illuminate "like fog-lamps on a rotten night" the decay and debris of contemporary civilization. He sifts through the surfaces, "the scraps of living," that continuously "shift and change," with the hope that by that very act, those fragments can be "shaped to a new identity" for both the self and the world. He seeks a path through the rubble where "the dark hall/ Finds a door" and, purging the pain, "the wind comes in." The search itself, however, remains suspect; the last line of the poem comments on the momentary fragility of any new identity: "A rainbow sleeps and wakes against the wall." If a splendid, euphoric new identity has been rekindled from the debris, then in all probability it too will be contained by experience and thus contaminated just as it has been before. The greater terror, however, is that the "rainbow" itself, while apparently new in its radiant beauty, may not be even a new identity of elusive quality but merely one more delusion grounded in the shallow pleasure of a two-dimensional painting. Once again, Kees finds himself turned back upon himself, just as he did in the Robinson poems.

"THE TURTLE"

It is this insistent turning back upon itself of the poem (and the poet) that crushes the faint hope of the self-protecting solipsism such as that found in "The Turtle." In this poem, probably written in the late 1940's, Kees seems to cling to a hope that serene detachment can shelter him from his excavations of despair. As he watches a turtle "beside the road," he is also aware of the "smells/ Of autumn closing in." His sense of dormancy, decay, and death, however, are not merely those associated with seasonal change, for there is little that would foreshadow rebirth in spring. The ominous smells are qualified by the din of "night traffic roaring by" on the superhighway that marks a civilization moving too fast to keep up with itself. His inner response is to feel "a husk . . . inside me, torpid, dry," like stale air "from a long-closed room" that "drifts through an opening door" into a tentative, fragile freedom from the indifferent rush of the world. His hope, at best, is to move "as a turtle moves/ Into the covering grass"; that is, Kees seeks a Whitmanesque union with the earth that offers little distinction between life and death. The tenuous, plodding movement away from both the psychological turmoil and the speeding reality of "night traffic" is a denial both of the artifacts of civilization and of the human beings who have allowed such disintegration to occur. That denial undermines even an illusion of hope, for it implies the further denial of one's own life and art.

The slow retreat of the hard-shelled self seen in "The Turtle" into a place "far in the woods, at night" could not be sustained when the creature and its creations began to consume themselves. Kees fell prey to his own methods and convictions, for they carried him to a point of moral dilemma beyond which he could not return. His only choice, then, would seem to have been either the ultimate denial of suicide, or a purgative flight from the self-entangled surfaces to a possibility of a new identity. Many suicides by American poets seem ironically to have confirmed their stature in a world that they re-

jected. The very ambiguity of Kees's disappearance withholds the rather twisted fascination of the "poet and his suicide" from the shallowness of a society that he denied. Kees's art contains the prophecy that art must move beyond itself to some form of pure action. That was to mean for Kees that he would leave his readers with a mystery that would "cleanse/ What ever it is that a wound remembers/ After the healing ends."

OTHER MAJOR WORKS

SHORT FICTION: *The Ceremony and Other Stories*, 1983.

PLAY: *The Waiting Room*, pb. 1986.

NONFICTION: *Nonverbal Communication: Notes on the Visual Perception of Human Relations*, 1956 (with Jurgen Ruesch; includes photographs by Kees); *Reviews and Essays, 1936-55*, 1988.

BIBLIOGRAPHY

Cotter, Holland. "The Absent Irascible: Weldon Kees in Postwar New York." *The New York Times*, April 30, 1999, p. 38. A description of Kees's paintings and a brief profile of his work in visual art and poetry.

Elledge, Jim. *Weldon Kees: A Critical Introduction.* Metuchen, N.J.: Scarecrow Press, 1985. The first book-length study of Kees's work, this volume collects nearly fifty essays and reviews—all of the important criticism published before 1985. Eleven previously "lost" poems, a bibliographic checklist, and an index to Kees's works are also included.

Knoll, Robert E., ed. "The New York Intellectuals, 1941-1950: Some Letters by Weldon Kees." *Hudson Review* 38 (Spring, 1985): 15-55. After a brief biography, Knoll quotes and comments on some of Kees's correspondence from the 1940's. This focused collection of letters provides a fascinating glimpse of intellectual society at the time.

_____. *Weldon Kees and the Midcentury Generation: Letters, 1935-1955.* Lincoln: University of Nebraska Press, 1986. Consists mostly of extracts from letters written by Kees and contains lengthy and useful commentaries by the editor. Begins with a chapter on Kees's early life and goes on to assemble a satisfying biography of the poet/musician/filmmaker from his letters. Includes more than thirty illustrations.

Nelson, Raymond. "The Fitful Life of Weldon Kees." *American Literary History* 1 (Winter, 1989): 816-852. This brief but informative biographical essay shows the similarities between Kees's life and death and those of his unhappy contemporaries John Berryman, Randall Jarrell, Robert Lowell, and Delmore Schwartz. The essay is sensitive to Kees's dreams and failures, and appreciative of his successes.

Nemerov, Howard. "On Weldon Kees: An Introduction to His Critical Writings." *The Prairie Schooner* 61 (Winter, 1987): 33-36. This is a personal reminiscence and evaluation by a man who was a close friend and correspondent of Kees during the 1940's. Nemerov is pleased that Kees's poetry has received such high acclaim and makes a case for further study and appreciation of his critical essays and reviews.

Smith, William Jay. "A Rendezvous with Robinson." *Sequoia*, Spring, 1979, 9-11. This brief reminiscence describes Kees's generosity and encouragement toward Smith when both were young writers in the 1940's. Smith's article is one of several in this special issue of *Sequoia*, which addressed the question "Is Weldon Kees America's Greatest Forgotten Poet?"

Michael Loudon;
bibliography updated by the editors

ROBERT KELLY

Born: Brooklyn, New York; September 24, 1935

PRINCIPAL POETRY

Armed Descent, 1961
Her Body Against Time, 1963
A Joining: A Sequence for H. D., 1967
Twenty Poems, 1967
Axon Dendron Tree, 1967
Finding the Measure, 1968
Songs I-XXX, 1968
Sonnets, 1968
The Common Shore, Books I-V: A Long Poem About America in Time, 1969

Kali Yuga, 1970
Flesh, Dream, Book, 1971
Ralegh, 1972
The Pastorals, 1972
The Mill of Particulars, 1973
The Loom, 1975
The Lady Of, 1977
The Convections, 1978
The Book of Persephone, 1978
The Cruise of the Pnyx, 1979
Kill the Messenger Who Brings Bad News, 1979
Spiritual Exercises, 1981
The Alchemist to Mercury, 1981
Under Words, 1983
Not This Island Music, 1987
The Flowers of Unceasing Coincidence, 1988
Oahu, 1988
A Strange Market, 1992
Mont Blanc, 1994
Red Actions: Selected Poems, 1960-1993, 1995
The Time of Voice, 1998

OTHER LITERARY FORMS

Although Robert Kelly is known primarily for his poetry, it is his fiction that has generated the most enthusiastic reviews. The fiction consists of one novel, *The Scorpions* (1967), a fanciful travelogue, *Cities* (1971), and two collections of stories, *A Transparent Tree* (1985) and *Doctor of Silence* (1988). Kelly has consented to more than half a dozen published interviews, has written prefaces for eight books by other authors, and has contributed occasional statements on film, poetry, and related topics to numerous periodicals since the early 1960's. One collection of such writings was published in 1971, *In Time*, and this book has taken its place as the most significant summation of Kelly's poetics.

ACHIEVEMENTS

Robert Kelly has written and published abundantly since his first book appeared in 1961. Recognized at once as one of the most gifted poets of his generation, he has subsequently lived up to his potential by deviating from his original promise over and over again. The first twenty-five years of Kelly's career saw the publication of more than three thousand pages of poetry and nearly one thousand pages of prose. What is remarkable is the consistency of the work and the variety of its forms. It seems certain that Kelly's contribution to the long poem will itself command respect for some time to come. At the same time, he is an adroit miniaturist, a most elegant prose stylist, and a discerning commentator on the work of other poets.

Kelly's prolific body of work is predicated on the fundamental commitment to poetry as a grand project, shared among all of its practitioners. His work is keenly motivated by a sense of poetry as a monumental structure, like a cathedral, arising through centuries of sustained craftsmanship—involving generations and entire communities. The sense of the poem as an addressing of communal concerns is evident throughout Kelly's collections.

On a more private level, Kelly's work is of considerable interest both as the daily registration of poetry and as process. Because there has been no slackening of energy as the decades have gone by, Kelly's poetry is an invaluable testimony to a demystification of the Romantic legacy of inspiration and divine election. The Kelly poem is a distinct engagement with vision and plenitude as daily obligations. Failure is as inextricably written into the work as success, given the improvisatory legacy of sheer dailiness as a modus operandi.

As several critics noted in a special issue of *Vort* devoted to Kelly in 1974, he is possessed by a rare gift of prosody. This has helped make even his minor efforts seem virtuous in comparison with the preponderance of bad habits prevalent in contemporary free-verse practice. This is all the more astonishing considering Kelly's staggering productivity. The size of his oeuvre has, almost from the beginning, kept his work from being as widely read as that of some of his parsimonious contemporaries. Read even in patches, however, it leaves a lasting impression of energy and eloquence, colloquial ease, and formal grace—a combination rare in the poetry of any period.

BIOGRAPHY

Robert Kelly was born and reared in Brooklyn, in a stimulating urban environment that nourished much of his early poetry. Quite precocious, Kelly entered the City College of New York at age fifteen and entered Columbia at nineteen as a graduate student of medieval studies. The stability of his life as a professor at Bard College since 1962 has afforded Kelly a reliability of circumstance to devote himself to poetry on a prodigious scale. Furthermore, the professorial role at a small college has meant that his daunting intellectual fortitude has been at the service of his poetry rather than diverted into formal scholarship as such.

At the beginning of his career, in the late 1950's and early 1960's, Kelly was associated with a circle of poets that included Paul Blackburn, David Antin, Jerome Rothenberg, Armand Schwerner, George Economou, Diane Wakoski, and Clayton Eshleman. Kelly and Rothenberg in particular rose to some prominence as exponents of "deep image," a short-lived but effective stance for young unknown poets to take, insofar as their manifestos commanded respect and their poetry was taken to be a rich demonstration of the theory. Kelly edited two ephemeral magazines in the early 1960's—*Trobar* and *Matter*—which helped establish him as a proponent of the free-verse line of poetry indebted to Charles Olson, Robert Duncan, and Louis Zukofsky among then-living masters.

Robert Kelly (© Mary Moore Goodlett)

From 1967 to 1973, Kelly served as associate editor for Clayton Eshleman's widely influential magazine *Caterpillar*. Kelly's involvement ensured that such contemporaries as Kenneth Irby and Gerrit Lansing were regularly featured in the magazine, as well as students and young protégés such as Thomas Meyer, Charles Stein, Richard Grossinger, Harvey Bialy, and Bruce McClelland. This was a period of extraordinary productivity for Kelly himself, making *Caterpillar* a showcase for his many forays into the long poem, culminating in the magazine's final issues with glimpses of the masterwork *The Loom*.

The demise of *Caterpillar* marked the end of a certain burgeoning of public poetry in the United States, not only for Kelly but also for his generation. Kelly subsequently became more involved at Bard College on administrative levels, continuing to teach but also becoming director of the writing program of the Avery Graduate School of the Arts. Kelly has been a recipient of a fellowship from the National Endowment of the Arts. His collection *Kill the Messenger Who Brings Bad News* was awarded the first annual prize in poetry at the Los Angeles Times Book Awards in 1980. In 1981, his archives were acquired by the Poetry/Rare Books Collection of the University Libraries, State University of New York at Buffalo. He received the American Book Award, Before Columbus Foundation, in 1991, for *In Time*.

ANALYSIS

Robert Kelly's first book, *Armed Descent*, showed some indebtedness to Ezra Pound's balance of line, presentation of a numinous world through direct images, and rhythmically modulated musicality. Most striking, however, was not the debt but the originality and the confidence. It was a sensuous poetry, a demonstration of Kelly's proclamation that the fundamental rhythm of a poem was the rhythm of images. Each poem contended in its own way for the proposition that visible realities be read as spiritual clarities. The spirit made flesh was the manifest mystery, but there was a practical injunction as well: "The gateway is the visible; but we must go in."

Kelly's imaginistic skills might have easily been directed toward the production of autonomous free association. It was within his means to become a giant among American Surrealist poets. He was engaged in a quest which could not rest comfortably on surfaces, however, nor reside in a simple succession of images. In his 1968 retrospective pamphlet *Statement*, Kelly stressed that the significant term in "deep image" had been the word *deep:* It was depth that was striven for in poems. Images were simply material agencies and were to be regarded as cues, clues, tangible signs of spiritual intensity.

The sense of depth, in conjunction with the concept of the image, led Kelly to postulate a location "behind the brain" where human lives as experienced through sense and image are "slain/ minute by minute." The Catholicism of Kelly's childhood has persisted in his poetry in the form of guiding images. This epiphany of "the place of the death of Images" is, suitably, from the poem "In Commentary on the Gospel According to Thomas" (in *The Alchemist to Mercury*), and it should be noted that the epigraphs to *Armed Descent* are also drawn from that apocryphal gospel. Kelly was fascinated with the image as something that is born or appears (is a *phenomenon*, from the Greek word for "to appear," *phaino*), dies or lapses, and then reappears or is resurrected. Kelly's Christian roots go deep in this image cycle, of which Christ and the grail chalice that holds his life's blood are the sustaining images. Kelly's is a patently antiauthoritarian Christian vision, however, informed by pagan rites, gnostic and neoplatonist philosophy, heretical sects, and alchemy.

SUMMONING THE DREAM WORLD

The sense of depth for which Kelly was striving in his early poetry soon became associated with what he called "The Dream Work" (in *In Time*). By linking the production of images in a poem with that productive energy of the dream world, Kelly was able to ground his poetics in a mode of psychic creation going on all the time. This certainly facilitated his orientation to poetry as daily practice. Unlike such previous poetics as that of the French Surrealists, who were fascinated with dream imagery, Kelly's was concerned with drawing psychic energy from the depths from which dreams speak, *not* using the poem as a means of reporting on or approximating dream states. Kelly's success is most evident in the narrative passages of *The Loom*, where such dreamlike images as the detached skull or a notch of coffin-shaped sunlight seen through a keyhole become the stimulus for meditations which are somnambulistic yet acutely conscious at the same time.

THE ALCHEMICAL QUEST FOR UNIVERSAL INTIMACY

Given Kelly's training as a medieval scholar, it is no surprise that his poems evoke the world of the books of hours, the body as a zone of astrological inscriptions and humors, and the spirit as a vehicle for ascent through the plectrum of the harmoniously organized stars and planets. "Finding the measure" (the title of his most acclaimed book), in its literal sense, refers to the process of modulating the rhythms of attention to the shape of the language in its shapely apparition as a poem. Finding the measure for Kelly has all the force of a cosmological prescription as well: "Finding the measure is finding the/ specific music of the hour,/ the synchronous/ consequence of the motion of the whole world." At this level, finding the measure is a mode of tuning or attunement, a means of "keeping in touch" with a cosmos that is intimate (a microcosm) despite its infinitude (a macrocosm). "In the burgeoning optimism of unlimited desire, I reach out for universal intimacy" wrote Kelly in "An Alchemical Journal" (in *The Alchemist to Mercury*). In various ways, the poetry has clearly manifested such unlimited desire in the forms of both sacred and profane yearning. Much of the best work of the late 1960's and early 1970's chronicles this reaching out for universal intimacy in the images provided by alchemy.

Because alchemy is a lapsed language of science, there have been complaints of esotericism directed at Kelly. It is true that much of the work of *Songs I-XXX* and *Flesh, Dream, Book* is densely allusive. Some simple reminders, however, are in order. Kelly's skills as an image maker have always been prodigious. Even the poems most saturated with arcane lore are guided by the familiar Christian cycle of personal redemption. For Kelly, alchemy was of use in clarifying the concept of the grail. Alchemy was an allegorical presentation of quest motifs intrinsic to the grail legend; in fact, the fundamental concept in alchemy is that of the *vessel*.

In Kelly's work, the experience of being *embodied*—being subjected to growth and decay—is the essence of the alchemical work. The body is the vessel, and the experience is oracular: "Every orifice is a sybil's cave." Every vessel is a chalice or grail, a body that fills, overflows, spills, and is emptied out. This is the cycle of redemption written into Kelly's work from his earliest long poem "The Exchanges" (in *The Alchemist to Mercury*) to "The Emptying" (in *Spiritual Exercises*), passing through such large mediating epiphanies as "Arnolfini's Wedding" and "The World" in *The Mill of Particulars* and *The Loom*.

There are not so much difficulties in Kelly's work as there are mysteries, because mystery is at the heart of it. Kelly's is the *mysterium tremendum* of sanctity and grace; his single most abiding theme (and the most exacting single pronouncement of his poetics) is the "nonstop imagery of making love salvation." It is Christian in its overall motivation, while allowing for the nonstop profanity of image-making and of "making love." In one of his poems, in fact, Kelly toys with the notion that images are to the eyes what sex is to the body. Both are engaged in a quest for depth, an inkling of that place where images and bodily energies are quelled.

THE LOOM

It seems plausible that, in the long run, Kelly's most acclaimed book will be the four-hundred-page poem *The Loom*. This poem oscillates between meditations and narrative, coiling images and insights around the slender axis of the very short line, often consisting of only three or four words. In *The Loom*, Kelly has not so much found his measure as returned to it, in that one of his most compelling early poems was the short-lined, book-length *Axon Dendron Tree*. *The Loom* is a book in which all Kelly's obsessions (sex, death, pain, revelation, transfiguration) are ceaselessly recycled toward a resolution of metabolism, a quieting in which a "sacred language" can be "known best/ when you're hardly listening." Readers of *The Loom*, in fact, can come to know the specific cycle of the alchemical great work through the poem, for it duplicates the prescribed stages of alchemical transmutation of base metal into gold without drawing any attention to this as such. The reader not privy to alchemical lore can be satisfied by *The Loom* without even knowing that an immense catalog of occult data is circulating through the text, in the form of narratives and precise images, all of which seem "natural" and not imposed. This is a singular achievement, to transmit secret information in the form of a transparent, lucid text which can be comprehended on an initial (aesthetic, psychological, and philosophic) level without reference to the underlying allegory.

THE FLOWERS OF UNCEASING COINCIDENCE

Kelly's long 1988 poem, *The Flowers of Unceasing Coincidence*, is composed of 672 short meditations, some as short as a single word (#15: "dreads") but most five to six lines long. The overall effect is of a series of epiphanies, such as #83:

> pervading everything the scent of bliss benefits all
>   beings who have heard the Whisper

The image of an island recurs throughout the poems, but the whole work can itself be seen as a poetic archipelago, chunks of words poking up through an ocean of inchoate existence. Although not narrative by any stretch of the imagination, the poem seems to be structured around a voyage from the Middle East and India through Persian Gulf and the Greek islands—or is it a mythological voyage through the sources of Western paganism? As critic Paul Christensen noted, "The poem luxuriates in pagan vision; gods proliferate, the female is deified, her flesh exalted. The sea is full of islands where the gods wait patiently for mortal believers. The same imagery and allusions to pagan forms were always there in Kelly's poetry and prose, but in *The Flowers of Unceasing Coincidence* one cannot distinguish Pan from Kelly any longer."

Kelly's work enacts a quest for attaining spiritual intensities in the world of physical forms and forces. It is continually resourceful at generating images that aid the contemplation of this enduring contradiction. The reader's gratitude and perplexity are registered in the image of the poet going into a hardware store to buy a pair of needle-nosed pliers and spark plugs, "as if I were a man on earth": One is moved or unsettled or both, according to one's lights, by the stubborn grace of Kelly's *as if.*

OTHER MAJOR WORKS

LONG FICTION: *The Scorpions*, 1967; *Cities*, 1971.

SHORT FICTION: *A Transparent Tree*, 1985; *Doctor of Silence*, 1988.

NONFICTION: *In Time*, 1971.

MISCELLANEOUS: *The Garden of Distances: Drawings and Poems*, 1999.

BIBLIOGRAPHY

Barne, Dennis. "Nothing but Doors: An Interview with Robert Kelly." *Credences*, n.s. 3 (Fall, 1985): 100-122. This interview focuses on Kelly's involvement with the periodicals *Chelsea*, *Trobar*, and *Maller*. Kelly comments on many of his contemporaries, their work, and the influences that shaped his own verse and thought. Gives a good portrait of the poet's career and personality.

Christensen, Paul. "The Resurrection of Pan." *Southwest Review* 78, no. 4 (1993): 506-528. A close reading of *The Flowers of Unceasing Coincidence* in the context of the fascination with paganism in modern poetry. Illustrates the influences of Pound and Olson on Kelly's poetry.

Kelly, Robert. "Robert Kelly." *Vort* 2, no. 2 (1974). A long and detailed interview with Kelly conducted by Barry Alpert.

Ossman, David. *The Sullen Art*. New York: Corinth Books, 1963. This collection contains a conversation with Robert Kelly covering his notions on what poetry is and how it works. Kelly is approached from his position as editor of the poetry magazine *Trobar* discussing other poets, but for the most part, the interview focuses on his thoughts regarding his own work in relation to his contemporaries. A very interesting interview.

Rasula, Jed. "Robert Kelly: A Checklist." *Credences*, n.s. 3 (Spring, 1984): 91-124. Books, pamphlets, broadsides, separate publications, and contributions to books and periodicals make up this list. An excellent source showing the considerable extent of Kelly's output.

_____. "Ten Different Fruits on One Different Tree: Reading Robert Kelly." *Credences*, n.s. 3 (Spring, 1984): 127-175. A review of Kelly's career and a publishing history that sorts through and presents the scope of the poet's works. Helpful parts of this guide are a list of select poems to introduce the novice to Kelly's verse, a discussion and chronology of the longer poems, analyses of several books (*Finding the Measure*, *The Loom*), and a look at Kelly's craft as a formalist.

Vort 5 (1974). This special issue periodical dedicated to Kelly predates the publication of *The Loom*. Contains critical appraisals and personal tributes to Kelly.

Jed Rasula,
updated by Leslie Ellen Jones

X. J. KENNEDY

Born: Dover, New Jersey; August 21, 1929

PRINCIPAL POETRY

Nude Descending a Staircase: Poems, Song, a Ballad, 1961
Growing into Love, 1969
Bulsh, 1970
Breaking and Entering, 1971
Emily Dickinson in Southern California, 1974
Celebrations After the Death of John Brennan, 1974
Three Tenors, One Vehicle, 1975 (song lyrics in sections by Kennedy, James Camp, and Keith Waldrop)
French Leave: Translations, 1983
Hangover Mass, 1984
Cross Ties: Selected Poems, 1985
Dark Horses: New Poems, 1992

OTHER LITERARY FORMS

Although X. J. Kennedy is best known for his poetry, he has also written reviews, several highly successful textbooks, and two novels for children, *The Owlstone Crown* (1983) and its sequel, *The Eagle as Wide as the World* (1997). Kennedy established himself as a witty and discriminating judge of contemporary poetry through a series of book reviews published in *Poetry* magazine from 1961 through 1966. The lively and lucid style developed in these essays played an important part in the success of his various textbooks and anthologies, which include *Mark Twain's Frontier* (1963, edited with James Camp), *An Introduction to Poetry* (1966, 1982, 1990), *Pegasus Descending: A Book of the Best Bad Verse* (1971, edited with James Camp and Keith Waldrop), *Messages: A Thematic Anthology of Poetry* (1973), *An Introduction to Fiction* (1976, revised 1979, 1987, 1991, 1999, edited with Dana Gioia), *Literature: An Introduction to Fiction, Poetry, and Drama* (1976, revised 1979, 1987, 1991, 1995, 1999, 2002, edited with Dana Gioia), *Tygers of Wrath: Poems of hate, anger, and invective* (1981), and *The Bedford Reader* (1982, edited with Dorothy Kennedy). Much of his output in the 1990's was children's poetry: *Fresh Brats* (1990), *The Kite That*

Braved Old Orchard Beach: Year-round Poems for Young People (1991), *The Beasts of Bethlehem* (1992), *Drat Those Brats: Children's Poems* (1993), *Uncle Switch: Looney Limericks* (1997), and *Elympics* (1999).

ACHIEVEMENTS

X. J. Kennedy's literary reputation rests almost exclusively on five volumes of poetry: *Nude Descending a Staircase*, *Growing into Love*, *Emily Dickinson in Southern California*, *Cross Ties*, and *Dark Horses*. Of his other published volumes, *Bulsh* has been unpopular and difficult to find in libraries; the title poem (reprinted in *Breaking and Entering*) is an entertaining but unimportant satire skewering a modern pretender to sainthood. Most of the poems in *Breaking and Entering* are reprinted from Kennedy's other volumes. *Celebrations After the Death of John Brennan* is a series of memorial verses inspired by the death of one of Kennedy's former students; it was published in a very limited edition. *Three Tenors, One Vehicle* includes only a few song lyrics by Kennedy, most of which are available in his major collections.

The remaining volumes are intended for children. Over the years, Kennedy has always remained interested in the challenge of composition for an audience that demands nothing more than clarity, wit, and fun. Indeed, he once described children's verse as a form of escape for poets "suffering psychic hangovers from excess doses of Kierkegaard and Freud" and longing to return to "a cosmos where what matters is whether a rabbit can find its red balloon again." Although Kennedy has written a juvenile novel (*The Owlstone Crown*) and several volumes of children's verse, his literary achievement is measured largely in terms of his serious poetry. The poems in *Nude Descending a Staircase* won for him the Lamont Award from the Academy of American Poets, and the Bess Hokin Prize from *Poetry* magazine. The publication of *Growing into Love* brought him the Shelley Memorial Award for 1969; and *Emily Dickinson in Southern California* and *Celebrations After the Death of John Brennan* in 1974 brought the Golden Rose from the New England Poetry Club. He won the *Los Angeles Times* Award in 1985 and the American Academy Braude Award in 1989. He has been a Bread Loaf Fellow in poetry (1960), a winner of a National Council on the Arts grant (1967-1968), and a Guggenheim Fellow (1973-1974). In 2000, the National Council of Teachers of English awarded Kennedy their Award for Excellence in Poetry for Children.

Although Kennedy is often dismissed as a witty minor poet—a self-described "whittler of little boats in bottles"—he may in time be awarded higher stature. He has published sparingly and slowly. More prolific contemporary poets naturally tend to attract more frequent attention and thus are more likely to attain a loftier status in the hierarchy of living poets. Kennedy's verse, however, is of astonishing technical proficiency. Most likely, a large percentage of the poems in his volumes will withstand the test of time. Indeed, they have had to wear well before Kennedy himself would consent to their publication in book form; their appeal to other readers is demonstrated by their frequent inclusion in anthologies.

Kennedy has lived by his "Prayer to an Angry God" that in rereading his own words he should "Not spare,/ But smite." If there is justice in heaven or value in such textbook advice, he should eventually reap his reward.

X. J. Kennedy (© Christopher Longyear)

BIOGRAPHY

The only child of a Roman Catholic father and a Methodist mother, Joseph Charles Kennedy (who later assumed the nom de plume X. J. Kennedy) must have sensed early in childhood the atmosphere of spiritual tension and uncertainty that is the most distinguishing and thought-provoking aspect of his poetry. A probable self-portrait of the youthful Kennedy occurs in "Poets," a brilliant and ironic sketch of the sensitive, dithering, bespectacled youths who, like stupid swans trapped in ice, can sometimes be freed to soar in dazzling glory. When only twelve, Kennedy published mimeographed science-fiction fan magazines titled *Vampire* and *Terrifying Test-Tube Tales*.

He was graduated from Seton Hall University (1950) and took a master's degree from Columbia University (1951) before enlisting in the Navy. After his tour of duty, he spent a year studying in Paris, where he received a *certificat* in 1956. From 1956 to 1962 he pursued doctoral studies at the University of Michigan and came into contact with an elite coterie of young poets from the Detroit-Ann Arbor area. Among his friends of the period were Keith Waldrop, James Camp, Donald Hall, John Frederick Nims, and W. D. Snodgrass. He left Ann Arbor without completing work for his degree, spent one year teaching at the Woman's College of the University of North Carolina, and then joined the faculty of Tufts University, where he eventually rose to be a full professor. In 1979 he left Tufts and became a freelance writer, a career he has followed for the rest of his life. In this he is perhaps remarkable as one of the few modern poets to support himself wholly by his craft.

From 1961 to 1964 Kennedy was the poetry editor of the *Paris Review*. In 1971 he and his wife founded *Counter/Measures, a Magazine of Rime, Meter, and Song*, to counter the trend toward poetry in "open forms"—the kind of free verse that Kennedy has satirically described as "Disposable stuff, word-Kleenex." The last issue of the magazine appeared in 1974, and Kennedy's later verse has itself occasionally been written in open forms.

ANALYSIS

During a memorable exchange of opinions in the *Saturday Review*, John Ciardi insisted to X. J. Kennedy that poets writing in traditional forms strive to create artifacts for posterity and must therefore believe that there *will be* some posterity. In contrast, those writing casual, formless free verse "reject the idea of the artifact" as the result of a belief "that there is no world to follow, or none worth addressing." Kennedy disagreed. Not only did he contend that a poet such as Gary Snyder, who writes in open forms, manifestly believes in an Asian concept of human continuity, but he also argued that the effort to create a permanent artifact in traditional poetic form does not necessarily imply a belief in any posterity to enjoy that artifact. Instead, he insisted that, "Even if it all goes blooey tomorrow, the act of trying to write a poem as well as possible is a good way of living until then."

The exchange illuminates the ethical as well as the artistic views of X. J. Kennedy. Recognizing the unsettling changes in art and life, and looking ruefully upon the weakening social and literary conventions, Kennedy continually seeks to resolve the tension between the traditional and the trendy, reactionary and radical. Through the course of his three major books of poetry, his world view shifts from a militant traditionalism (implying belief in God, in ever-renewing life, and in conventional verse forms) into a tolerant uncertainty. His recent poems display a lack of faith in traditional values, combined with a lack of trust in the new. Thus, he seems to stand on shifting ground, offering brilliant satirical insights into the modern world, but little advice about how best to live in that world. Indeed, he no longer seems as certain as he once was that traditional values offer "a good way of living until then."

Nude Descending a Staircase

A number of poems in Kennedy's first book, *Nude Descending a Staircase*, express his belief that the time is out of joint. In its very title, for example, "B Negative" suggests the dehumanizing effect of modern urban life. The poem's protagonist is given no name. Instead, he is identified only by his blood type and by an abbreviated description of his characteristics: "M/ 60/ 5 FT. 4/ W PROT." His monologue depicts the sterile environment of the city, where he discovers that it is spring by the increased litter of coughdrop boxes and "underthings cast off," rather than by daisies in the grass. Spring makes little mark on the city, "No bud from branches of con-

crete." The city is an unnatural, artificial place where pigeons too fat to stand peck shoelaces and eat sacks of corn as if they "grew on a stalk." It is a place so costly that grown men sleep on subways "tucked in funny sheets" taken from the daily newspaper. It is so dense that the sun cannot penetrate to the street level, and so frigid that spring has no "abiding heat." Here a man's virility can wither to impotence after years pronging litter, or shabbily sustained through steamy musings over the gaudy pages of a movie magazine. In the city the seasons have scant significance, and human life, stripped of its own seasonal qualities, becomes scanty too. The city blocks and cubic rooms create human integers that "wake one day to find [themselves] abstract." In cementing over human roots and rhythms, modern urban life generates abnormal beings who become either suicidal or sadistic.

The poem's diction and imagery are especially effective in suggesting the violence inherent in city surroundings. The daisies, for example, are described as "white eyeballs in the grass." The pick with which the speaker prongs litter is called a "stabpole." The subway riders are observed by "guards." The radio is turned off with a "squawk as if your hand/ Had shut some human windpipe with a twist." In this menacing environment the "routed spirit flees" or looks around "for a foothold—in despair." What comfort life is capable of offering lingers only as a memory of the past. In lines futilely addressed to a lost lover, the speaker laments that he can no longer remember "the twist that brought me to your street," nor can he summon up her face or recall her "outline on the sheet." At least for this speaker, the warmth of the past is irretrievable and the future offers only an increasingly frigid isolation.

Elsewhere in this first book of verse, however, Kennedy is confident that survival and sanity can be maintained in the changing modern world. Procreation can assure survival and continuity between past and future, while religion can provide the same sort of guidelines for a sane life that the rules of rhyme and meter provide for a sane poetry. Thus, after surveying various signs of foreboding (slips in the hangman's knot and the price of stocks, movement of mountains, proliferating madness), the poem "All-Knowing Rabbit" concludes with consolation. The rabbit, who eats voraciously to feed the offspring growing in her womb, smugly ponders "All secrets of tomorrow, of the Nile . . . And munches on, with giaconda smile." The rabbit, the Nile, and the giaconda smile are symbols of fecundity. At this stage in his career, it does not occur to Kennedy that exceptional fertility is itself one of the dangers of the mad world he inhabits. Furthermore, in this book Kennedy perceives only dimly the chinks in the armor of conventional religious faith. His poem "In Faith of Rising" sounds more like Gerard Manley Hopkins or George Herbert than the work of a man reared in an era when one catchphrase was, "God is dead." Kennedy's poem is a pious statement of trust that after death God will "cast down again/ Or recollect my dust."

The confident reverence of "In Faith of Rising" is, however, atypical even in Kennedy's early poetry. "First Confession" is much more representative of his general approach, in both content and style. The first confession inspires awe in the child who perceives the priest as a "robed repositor of truth," burns in his guilt while awaiting penance, and later kneels to take communion in "seraphic light." From the more experienced retrospective of the adult, however, the events take on comic overtones. He sees ludicrous elements coexisting with sanctity. The child "scuffed,/ Steps stubborn" to the confessional. His list of sins included the "sip snitched" from his father's beer and a bribe paid his girlfriend to pull down her pants. He zealously said his penance twice to "double-scrub" his soul.

Kennedy emphasizes the disjunction between the holy and the humorous by deliberate incongruity in his choice of words. Formal language exuding a dusty odor of sanctity mingles with the stale stench of street speech. The "curtained portal," the "robed repositor of truth," and the dignified priest's "cratered dome" are somewhat sullied by contact with a diminutive sinner who snitches from his "old man's beer" and who bribes his girl "to pee." The priest himself becomes the object of mirth when he doles out penance "as one feeds birds." Even the sacrament of communion is trivialized at the end when the child sticks out his tongue at the priest: "A fresh roost for the Holy Ghost."

The mood that unfolds through "First Confession" is less skeptical than satirical. Modern humans—both priest and penitent—seem out of place within the ancient traditions of the Roman Catholic Church, just as the poem's use of contemporary slang seems to desecrate its setting. This sense of disjunction, of times out of joint, is characteristic of Kennedy's subsequent poetry.

GROWING INTO LOVE

By the time *Growing into Love* appeared in 1969, Kennedy's faith in the traditions of Roman Catholicism had weakened to the point where he could write in "West Somerville, Mass.": "My faith copped out. Who was it pulled that heist?" Here again one sees the bizarre verbal incongruity that had characterized "First Confession," but Kennedy has moved from satire of tottering traditions to outright skepticism and agnosticism. Nevertheless, he clearly feels a loss in abandoning his faith. A number of poems in the volume show his longing for the solidity of the past and his loathing of the impermanence of the present.

In "Cross Ties," for example, the speaker, walking along a railroad track "where nothing travels now but rust and grass," says, "I could take stock in something. . . . Bearing down Hell-bent from behind my back." Figuratively, the speaker's situation is also Kennedy's. Uncomfortable in the present, Kennedy walks a track deserted by others. His poems rhyme and scan and he is predisposed toward tradition. In one sense, then, the speaker, like Kennedy, longs for a return to the past when trains served functions now taken over by semitrucks, superhighways, and motels. Both Kennedy and the speaker also long to believe in their lost religious faith with its freight of forces for good and evil. The speaker hears this phantom train's whistle in the "curfew's wail," sees its headbeam in the full moon, and hears the screech of "steel wrenched taut till severed" (the train's brakes?) in the hawk's cry. He explains the fact that no Hell-bent force strikes him down by hypothesizing that he is "Out of reach/ Or else beneath desiring," and he concludes by observing that when he spills the salt he throws some to the devil and he still allows the priest to bless his child.

The superficial appearance of faith in God and Satan is undercut, however, by closer analysis. The speaker begins by saying that he "could take stock in" this malign force. A statement beginning "I could take stock in . . ." normally continues with a conditional clause: for example, "I could take stock in purple people-eaters if someone could show me their lairs." The absence of the expected conditional clause implies that the speaker cannot state the conditions that must be met before he really *believes*. Moreover, it is clear that the speaker willfully imagines the malign force behind his back. He knows that the tracks are deserted, and he knows too that the curfew's wail, the moon's head beam, and the hawk's cry are wholly natural phenomena. He uses these aspects of everyday reality in an attempt to scare himself into a faith in Satanic evil, for if there is a devil to fear there must also be a deity to love. He is, however, unsuccessful. As he walks along, "tensed for a leap" and trying to imagine some evil behind him, he declares himself "unreconciled/ To a dark void all kindness." This neatly ambiguous phrase could mean that he is unreconciled to an indifferent universe, a malign universe, or a Godless universe, but, whatever it means, it falls far short of positive faith in God. It is a phrase, then, that hedges its bets just as the speaker does with a pinch of salt and a mist of holy water.

The poem's title, "Cross Ties," has a similar multiplicity of meanings. In a naturalistic sense, the poem is about walking on railroad ties, and the title reflects that subject. Yet the poet's central interest is in the ties of emotion between the longing for the past years when engines rode the tracks and the longing for the faith in God that typified those years. Indeed, the poem's title, by suggesting the form of the crucifix, itself links the literal, historical, and religious implications of the poem.

Kennedy's consciousness of the disjunction caused by changes in the modern world finds expression in several poems in *Growing into Love* that deal with the American landscape. In "Main Road West," the television set in a motel room suddenly goes dead, and the speaker, left with "No magazines, no book but the Good Book," is forced to observe and reflect. He finds himself in a denatured environment. Although trees with leaves are few and "The wind's turned off," a sign for used cars burns brightly, keeping out the starlight, "As though stars will be foresworn, or stared down." Thus, the traveler sees that natural resources are being displaced by mechanical artifice.

"Driving Cross-country" makes the parallel point that imaginative resources are also being destroyed through mass-produced mediocrity. The poem begins with a series of baffling and discontinuous allusions to

twentieth century counterparts of fairy-tale figures (Jack the Giant-killer, Cinderella, Sleeping Beauty). Collectively, these allusions illustrate how meager is the spirit of the present in comparison with the traditional legends of the past. The Jack the Giant-killers of today sing to cornstalks in Keokuk, and contemporary Cinderellas (with names like Ella Ashhauler) try to scrounge free meals in the Stoplight Lounge. The only magic of the age is that which has filled the nation with identical motel rooms—each deloused and designed by computer to offend no one. Victims of "Some hag's black broth," Americans hurtle down endless highways knowing that "We had a home. It was somewhere./ We were there once upon a time."

In these poems, as in "Cross Ties," there is a longing for a return to a better past—where nature reigned unchained and where natural man indulged in fantasy and belief. Similar points are made in "Peace and Plenty." Pineclad hills lie stunned and bound by chains of motels; the river is so choked with debris that it cannot choose its course; the new-fallen snow must "Lay bare her body to the Presto-Blo"; and the blown rose finds her "quietus . . . inside the in-sink waste-disposer." By personifying and feminizing the hills, river, snow, and rose, Kennedy creates an image of nature ravished by the vile artificial constructions of man—the motels, engines, chemical wastes, snowblowers, and disposals.

Kennedy's rejection of mechanized and plasticized society is, however, refreshingly apolitical and unpredictable. In 1961, in apparent reaction to the space flights of Yuri Gagarin and Alan Shepard, Kennedy published "The Man in the Manmade Moon," a scathing satire on space flight and those who seek to promote it. Yet by 1969 his views had begun to change. In "Space," he reflects on man's increasing power over nature, a power bemoaned in "Main Road West," "Driving Cross-country," and "Peace and Plenty." He finds that the ability to escape from earth and let the unweighted heart beat freely has appeal, and the whole process of sending massive projectiles careening through the heavens at the flick of a switch makes Kennedy wonder what life will be like after this power spreads and increases: "Who will need long to savor his desire . . . when acts, once dreamt, transpire?" Will man return to the womb? Indeed, is the fetal crouch of the astronauts on takeoff and the fixation with landing on the moon (a traditional symbol of femininity) a disguised attempt to return to the womb? Kennedy explores these questions with sensitivity. Ultimately, he finds that he shares the same desires for escape that have moved men with slide rules to "Render our lusts and madnesses concrete." In a bar or at the wheel of a car, he too attempts to "shrug the world's dull weight" and is surprised to find himself, "Out after what I had long thought I'd hate."

Similarly, in "The Medium Is the Message" Kennedy contemplates the music-oriented youth of America, "transistors at their brains,/ Steps locked to rock." He concludes that "The rude beast slouches"—that Yeats's second coming is at hand and that "words in lines" will soon be obsolete. The modern age rejects the traditional iambic rhythms of the heart and insists instead on a rock music that beats to the "rush-hour traffic's fits and starts." So much is vintage Kennedy— rejecting contemporary changes in favor of the traditional past—but he surprises the reader when he admits that he would drop out only if he could pack along his own high-technology conveniences: "my hi-fi set,/ Electric light, a crate of books, canned beer. . . ."

EMILY DICKINSON IN SOUTHERN CALIFORNIA

Kennedy continues to explore his sense of disjunction between past values and present vicissitudes in *Emily Dickinson in Southern California* (1974), but the acute sense of impending disaster that had prompted earlier allusions to Yeats's "The Second Coming" is here replaced by his bemused transplantation of Emily Dickinson into Southern California. Although the title series of poems, like so much of Kennedy's verse, develops in part through incongruity, here the incongruities are more amusing than upsetting. The whole idea of observing the laid-back, let-it-all-hang-out California scene from the perspective of a wry and reclusive nineteenth century spinster is itself incongruous and delightful. Unfortunately, Kennedy does relatively little with this idea. Seven of the nine poems in the series are simple imitations of Dickinson's style and make no effort to force her approach into a confrontation with the modern world.

Kennedy's "Two Views of Rime and Meter" are written in free verse, a form that Kennedy rarely used in his earlier volumes. The first poem compares meter with the repetitious thud of a carpet beater, and rhyme with the glittering dust. The second compares meter with the rhythm of copulation, and rhyme with the pleasure of simultaneous orgasm. The implications of the first metaphor are that meter and rhyme are monotonous, routine, and stale, while the implications of the second are that both devices are human, primal, delightful, and creative. The two views are incompatible and incongruous; as elsewhere, Kennedy's own position remains unresolved.

To the extent, however, that the debate about meter and rhyme is part of the larger debate about tradition and change, other aspects of the volume suggest Kennedy's increasing sympathy with the twentieth century. There is, for example, the fact that eight of the seventeen pieces in the volume can be classified as free verse. Furthermore, "Categories," a poem that specifically examines modern changes, concludes that one must come to understand transformations and adapt to circumstances. Although species collide, styles expire, and the century clots or collapses, man can begin to understand if "through the tip of his tongue he hear bright red." If this incongruous and paradoxical advice means anything at all, it certainly demands breaking free of perceptual limitations in the effort to grasp a new reality. Similarly, the poem's very last lines show that one must break free of the limitations of tradition. A novice Buddhist monk, "a scrubber of pots," is capable of teaching his master that, having "hatched from names" and lacking clean plates, one can "Serve cake on a shut fan." Thus, the old must learn from the young and the tradition-bound mind must hatch into a new freedom in order to adapt to difficulties.

Appropriately, the poem starts out with six lines of fairly standard iambic pentameter but becomes increasingly free from formal metrical constraints as it proceeds. If anything, this poem is even more sensitive to the rhythms and sounds of poetic language than many of Kennedy's rigorously metrical compositions. Fifteen of the poem's twenty lines can be classified as loose iambic pentameter, but Kennedy repeatedly alters the iambic rhythm to correspond with his rhetorical emphases. Thus, three of the poem's first four syllables are stressed in making the point that "Nothing stays put." An extra accented syllable is packed into the third line, making the description of the "too-close-following cars" onomatopoeic. The century's collapse through the "mind's pained hour-glass" throbs more forcefully because of the series of strong stresses, as does the need to "hear bright red." Perhaps, however, the last line of the poem is the finest example of Kennedy's liberation. Not only is the assertion that one can "Serve cake on a shut fan" an apt imagistic summary of the change in Kennedy's views and the point of the whole poem, but it is also impossible to scan. It has two stresses, two rests, and two more stresses. What could be more rhythmical and yet further from traditional meter?

This change in Kennedy's attitudes toward traditional thinking and traditional poetics was also reflected in a changed view of the American landscape. Perhaps man's creations do litter the land, but Kennedy has moved far from the depressed mood of the collector of debris in "B Negative" and the discouraged travelers of "Main Road West" and "Driving Cross-country." Now he is capable of writing a poem titled "Salute Sweet Deceptions," in which he observes that in certain lights bare bricks turn amber, beer cans resemble stars, and raindrops clinging to telephone wires look like a "seedpearl necklace."

CROSS TIES

In 1985 Kennedy published *Cross Ties: Selected Poems*, an ample and accurate sampler from his poetic oeuvre—though the back cover of the book is inaccurate in claiming that it includes "every poem that the poet cares to save." Kennedy explains, "That blurb was read to me over the phone for approval, one sleepy morning, and that devastating claim buzzed right on by. There are many poems I couldn't put in *Cross Ties* that I wouldn't destroy just yet, including nearly everything in the books of verse for children." Indeed, the bulk of Kennedy's verse in the 1980's was addressed to children. *Hangover Mass* 1984 was a notable exception.

Kennedy's poetic output in the 1980's demonstrated his continuing interest in standard verse forms, and a number of the poems reflect nostalgia for the past. In "Hangover Mass," for example, he reminisces about his youthful attendance at late-morning Mass with his father; in "One-Night Homecoming" he writes about a brief visit to his aging parents and his emotions as he once again lies in "childhood's bed"; and in "The Death

of Professor Backwards" he writes an amusingly sentimental epitaph for a murdered vaudeville performer whose chief claim to fame was an ability to speak backward: "Transposed perfectly them at back hurl he'd/ Out called crowd the hecklers any whatever." Could it be that this praise of the curmudgeonly Professor Backwards, written in cross-rhymed iambic pentameter, is partially motivated by Kennedy's own desire to go backward and to cling to the old forms still? If so, this is an instance in which form is closely matched to substance and yet another indication of Kennedy's remarkable skillfulness.

DARK HORSES

Kennedy's collection *Dark Horses*, published in 1992, directly addressed the apparent contradictions between "serious" and "light" poetry in "On Being Accused of Wit." He claims himself to be actually "witless," but his list of fellow witless ones suggests that his witlessness is that of a holy fool:

> Witless, that juggler rich in discipline
> Who brought the Christchild all he had for gift,
> Flat on his back with beatific grin
> Keeping six slow-revolving balls aloft.

Formalism taken to its extreme may become lifeless when form is all it has to offer. Kennedy illustrates the virtues of form as an underlying scaffolding that supports the brilliance of wit. Kennedy's verbal sleights-of-hand, evident throughout the poems in this collection, not only exhibit his technical virtuosity but also playfully link his individual works to the larger web of Western poetry. Wit is only witty in the context of shared tradition that provides a context for the reference.

Kennedy's poetry, as it always has been, is dominated by incongruity, but the intense longing for tradition has been modified by a mellow toleration of the times, and the intense commitment to meter and rhyme has been balanced by an interest in exploring the many forms of modern poetry. Kennedy once said, "Writing in rhythm and rhyme, a poet is involved in an enormous, meaningful game not under his ego's control. He is a mere mouse in the lion's den of the language—but with any luck, at times he can get the lion to come out."

OTHER MAJOR WORKS

CHILDREN'S LITERATURE: *One Winter Night in August and Other Nonsense Jingles*, 1975 (poetry); *The Phantom Ice Cream Man: More Nonsense Verse*, 1979; *Did Adam Name the Vinegarroon?*, 1982 (poetry); *The Owlstone Crown*, 1983; *The Forgetful Wishing Well: Poems for Young People*, 1985; *Brats*, 1986 (poetry); *Ghastlies, Goops, and Pincushions: Nonsense Verse*, 1989; *Fresh Brats*, 1990 (poetry); *The Kite That Braved Old Orchard Beach: Year-round Poems for Young People*, 1991; *The Beasts of Bethlehem*, 1992 (poetry); *Drat Those Brats: Children's Poems*, 1993; *The Eagle as Wide as the World*, 1997; *Uncle Switch: Looney Limericks*, 1997 (poetry); *Elympics*, 1999 (poetry).

EDITED TEXTS: *Mark Twain's Frontier*, 1963 (with James Camp); *Pegasus Descending: A Book of the Best Bad Verse*, 1971 (with James Camp and Keith Waldrop); *Messages: A Thematic Anthology of Poetry*, 1973; *An Introduction to Fiction*, 1976, revised 1979, 1987, 1991, 1999 (with Dana Gioia); *Literature: An Introduction to Fiction, Poetry, and Drama*, 1976, revised 1979, 1987, 1991, 1995, 1999, 2002 (with Dana Gioia); *Tygers of Wrath: Poems of Hate, Anger, and Invective*, 1981; *The Bedford Reader*, 1982 (with Dorothy Kennedy); *Knock at a Star: A Child's Introduction to Poetry*, 1982 (with Dorothy M. Kennedy).

BIBLIOGRAPHY

Bjork, Robert E. "Kennedy's 'Nothing in Heaven Functions as It Ought.'" *Explicator* 40 (Winter, 1982): 6-7. This explication develops the premise that the poem "exploits the concept of norm and deviation . . . to deal with the nature of heaven and hell, questioning our conventional notions about each." Bjork argues that Kennedy cleverly deviates from the reader's expectations of a Petrarchan sonnet in order to demonstrate that "Nothing in heaven, or in this sonnet, functions as it ought."

Ciardi, John. "Counter/Measures: X. J. Kennedy on Form, Meter, and Rime." *Saturday Review* 4 (May 20, 1972): 14-15. Ostensibly, John Ciardi (who was a major poet in his own right) was interviewing X. J. Kennedy about the purpose of Kennedy's literary magazine, *Counter/Measures*. In fact, however, the interview presents both poets with opportunities to formulate their ideas about the merits of form in poetry and the possibility that poems can be enduring "artifacts."

Collins, Michael. "The Poetry of X. J. Kennedy." *World Literature Today* 61, no. 1 (1987): 55-58. This essay provides an overview of Kennedy's poetic achievement. Its main thesis is that Kennedy writes in a way that characteristically fuses "the serious and playful" and that "Kennedy is a poet of contemporary middle-class America."

Kennedy, X. J. "The Poet in the Playpen." *Poetry* 105 (December, 1964): 190-193. In this review of children's books by Marianne Moore, Rumer Godden, and J. R. R. Tolkien, Kennedy formulates a defense of juvenile literature. He observes that "Randall Jarrell and John Ciardi of late seem to write more books for children than for the rest of us" and comments, "It is almost as if we were back in the days when a Blake or a Smart could expect nobody but children to listen to him."

Prunty, Wyatt. *"Fallen from the Symboled World": Precedents for the New Formalism*. New York: Oxford University Press, 1990. In arguing for the existence of a new formalism that takes "doubt as its starting point" and "builds relation from the ground up," Prunty briefly cites Kennedy as a poet of particular power. Kennedy's "On a Child Who Lived One Minute" is called a "little masterpiece" because the contrasts between gentleness and harshness in rhythm, rhyme, and diction "match Kennedy's attitude toward the infant girl's death," creating "the fusion of an abiding absurdity with which we all live."

Sharp, Ronald A. "Kennedy's 'Nude Descending a Staircase.'" *Explicator* 37 (Spring, 1979): 2-3. Sharp largely ignores the similarities between Kennedy's poem and Marcel Duchamps's painting titled *Nu descendant un escalier*, but he does demonstrate that "the poem turns on an implicit analogy between beautiful women and beautiful poems: Both are composed of individually beautiful parts but their unity is dynamic."

Jeffrey D. Hoeper,
updated by Leslie Ellen Jones

JANE KENYON

Born: Ann Arbor, Michigan; May 23, 1947
Died: Wilmot, New Hampshire; April 22, 1995

PRINCIPAL POETRY
From Room to Room, 1978
The Boat of Quiet Hours, 1986
Let Evening Come, 1990
Constance, 1993
Otherwise: New and Selected Poems, 1996

OTHER LITERARY FORMS

Although Jane Kenyon mainly wrote poetry, she also wrote an occasional essay. Many of these were first written for the *Concord (N.H.) Monitor.* Selected essays and interviews are collected in *A Hundred White Daffodils: Essays, Interviews, the Akhmatova Translations, Newspaper Columns, and One Poem* (1999). Her translations of Anna Akhmatova are collected in *Twenty Poems of Anna Akhmatova* (1985).

ACHIEVEMENTS

Jane Kenyon's poetic achievement gained recognition while she was still a student at the University of Michigan, where in 1969 she received the Avery and Jules Hopwood Award. Later she also received a Guggenheim Prize and a Fellowship Grant from the National Endowment for the Arts.

Along with Joyce Peseroff, Kenyon cofounded and coedited *Green House*, a journal dedicated to publishing the best in contemporary poetry and, in particular, representing contemporary female poets. She was also involved in readings and support activities for Alice James Books, a cooperative publishing venture that encouraged female authors. In 1986 Kenyon, with her husband Donald Hall, visited China and Japan as visiting writers sponsored by the State Department Cultural Exchange. They visited India under similar auspices in 1991 and 1993.

BIOGRAPHY

Jane Kenyon grew up on the outskirts of Ann Arbor, Michigan, on a rural road across from a working farm. Besides instilling her with a love for rustic countryside

and gardening, the household itself was alive with music, also nurturing Kenyon's lifelong love for all musical forms. Kenyon's father, Reuel, was a jazz musician who had toured Europe before returning to the United States during the Depression era to play nightclubs. At one such club, he met Pauline, an eighteen-year-old nightclub singer. After marrying they settled down near Ann Arbor, taking their love and talent for music with them. In addition to playing clubs, Reuel started teaching piano lessons. When Jane and her older brother, Reuel, Jr., were born, Pauline, a skilled seamstress, began taking in commissioned work and providing sewing lessons. Music still dominated the house. Two upright pianos stood in the living room; a large phonograph stood in the hallway. Jane fell asleep at night listening to the strains of classical music drifting up to her second-story bedroom.

Through fourth grade Kenyon attended a rural, one-room schoolhouse. There were four children in her kindergarten class. Then she took the bus to a large Ann Arbor school. Nearly nine hundred students were in her graduating high school class. Several important happenings marked her school years. The first was her relationship with her grandmother, Dora Kenyon, the subject of several poems and essays. Grandmother viewed the world through narrow religious eyes. She saw the Apocalypse coming at any moment and expected, for herself and her granddaughter, a rigorous body of rules to make sure they arrived at the proper spot when the Apocalypse came. Kenyon did not take kindly to her grandmother's theology of fear and rules. By the time she was in junior high, Kenyon had renounced all religious practices. Simultaneously, her strong individual character emerged. Something of a rebel at heart, Kenyon developed a disdain of rules simply for the sake of rules. The final significant item during her school years may be most important, for, while in eighth grade, Kenyon received a book of poetry—translations of Chinese poems into English—and began writing her own poems.

Kenyon's first serious encounter with depression occurred when she started at the University of Michigan. Although she was later to say that her illness (later professionally diagnosed as bipolar disorder) had been lodged in her genetic code since birth, this is the first time it significantly interfered with her life. She dropped

Jane Kenyon (© William Abranowicz)

out of the university during her freshman year and worked at a gift shop. She returned the following year as a French major, also exercising her love of music by singing in and traveling with the Michigan Chorale.

In the spring semester of 1969, Kenyon enrolled in Donald Hall's popular course Introduction to Poetry for Non-English Majors. The following semester Kenyon took Hall's creative-writing course. The friendship between the two deepened, and they married in April, 1972. That same year Kenyon received her M.A. in English and began working on the Modern English Dictionary project at the university.

The two moved to Hall's ancestral farmhouse near Wilmot, New Hampshire, in 1975, permitting both to devote themselves to full-time writing careers. The twenty years at Eagle Pond Farm were a boon to Kenyon's writing. Her art depended upon the clear, elemental image— what she called the "luminous particular"—and the New England landscape supplied a rich backdrop for her range of imagery. At Eagle Pond Farm Kenyon found close friends, with whom she started a writer's workshop. Most significantly, perhaps, she rediscovered and

renewed her spiritual faith while attending, along with Hall, South Danbury Christian Church.

During those years at Eagle Pond Farm, however, personal tragedies also intervened. Kenyon's father died of cancer. Her mother also died. Kenyon herself underwent surgery for a cancerous salivary gland. Donald Hall underwent two major surgeries for cancer, first for colon cancer then for a metastasis of the cancer to the liver. At the same time Kenyon's depressive episodes grew more frequent and more intense. The forceful way she confronted these episodes in her poetry spoke to many readers who also suffered from the disorder. The intrusion of suffering on life became one of the major themes of her later poetry.

Jane Kenyon was diagnosed with leukemia on January 31, 1994. For a year she endured a battery of treatments, including a bone marrow infusion in Seattle on November 18, 1994. Upon her return to New Hampshire on February 24, 1995, there was reason for optimism. Blood counts improved. Then, on April 11, tests showed the return of leukemia. Kenyon died at home on April 22, 1995.

ANALYSIS

Jane Kenyon's readership and consequent critical attention increased steadily throughout her career. When she died she was fully confident of her own techniques and at the height of her poetic voice. In her works her life and art intertwine like a fine cross-stitch. She was an artist of exquisitely intense lyrics that, like faceted diamonds casting prismatic light, threw off soundings of the human soul.

Several premises in particular guided her artistry. She always sought, as she said, the intense, passionate lyric. Indeed, the heightened musical qualities of her verse have been well recognized. In 1997 composer William Bolcom produced a score titled *Briefly It Enters: A Cycle of Songs from Poems of Jane Kenyon*. Also in 1997 J. Mark Scearce composed *American Triptych*, based on Kenyon's three poems of that same title.

Furthermore, Kenyon sought the "right" word, a process that appeared in the extensive drafting of her poems. The right word for her was a "naming" word, one that immediately evoked the essence of the object. She preferred Old English stock words and used relatively few Latinate/

Romance derivations. Kenyon's use of imagery and figurative language formed the lifeblood of the poem, permitting the reader to see things in new and surprising ways. Her aim throughout her career was to allow the reader to enter the poem and share the experience.

FROM ROOM TO ROOM

Although Kenyon had published many of the poems from this 1978 volume individually in leading periodicals, she still faced the usual difficulties of locating a publisher for the collection. Eventually she published it with Alice James Press. Several of the poems were composed during her days at the University of Michigan, but the volume is woven tightly thematically: the convergence of past memories upon the present moment at Eagle Pond Farm. She has now moved into the farmhouse, and even while recording childhood memories she senses the whispers of Hall's ancestors all around her. In "Finding a Long Gray Hair" she describes herself as washing the floors, "repeating/ the motions of other women/ who have lived in this house." Then, when she finds a long gray hair floating in the pail, she feels "my life added to theirs." It is at once a volume of dislocation and of finding one's place as she moves from room to room in the new house.

THE BOAT OF QUIET HOURS

Most of the poems for this 1986 volume were written during the five-year period of Kenyon's work translating Akhmatova. The individual poems bear far more vitality, precision of imagery and language, and confidence than those in *From Room to Room*. Moreover, many poems are more overtly personal. For the first time the reader sees Kenyon openly encountering her struggle with depression. Similarly, there are many poems directly encountering her spiritual questions and beliefs. Yet alongside such poems appear many others of the pastoral sort she had written earlier. The poems are infused with concrete images from Eagle Pond Farm. In "The Pond at Dusk" she writes, "A fly wounds the water but the wound/ soon heals." Often, as with Robert Frost, nature is a springboard into metaphorical speculation. Often Kenyon leaves those speculations open-ended, for the reader to resolve.

LET EVENING COME

The themes of Kenyon's previous volume—her search for the divine, understanding her illness, her playfulness and joy in nature—continue in *Let Evening Come* (1990). Yet, those themes turn more intensely personal and introspective. This volume has been a favorite of readers and reviewers alike, heralded for the skillful mastery of craft and the honest engagement with the thematic issues. The volume includes the much-admired "Three Songs at the End of Summer" and what may well be Kenyon's masterpiece, "Let Evening Come." The haunting lyrics of the poem trace the shifting evening light: "Let the light of late afternoon/ shine through chinks in the barn, moving/ up the bales as the sun moves down." The imprecatory word "let" appears twelve times in the poem, signaling at once ease in the passage of light but also the fact that one cannot really do anything about it anyway. Thus, the last stanza arrives as a benediction of peace: "Let it come, as it will, and don't/ be afraid. God does not leave us/ comfortless, so let evening come."

CONSTANCE

Although it is her briefest volume, *Constance* (1993) displays Kenyon at the peak of her power. Unlike the peaceful acceptance of *Let Evening Come*, however, the energy here is raw, centered particularly in one of her most powerful poems, "Having It out with Melancholy." This was a difficult poem for Kenyon to write, each of the nine parts put through dozens of drafts. It is ruthless in its honesty: "A piece of burned meat/ wears my clothes, speaks/ in my voice." Unfortunately, many people read the poem with focus on the first eight parts—the battle with depression. However, Kenyon did not leave it there. Part 9, "Wood Thrush," responds to the entire preceding poem. The poet awakens not in pain but to early June light, where she is "overcome// by ordinary contentment." Kenyon refuses here, as she did in life, to give in to any bleak nihilism. Her vital spirit always sought the joy of "ordinary contentment."

Other poems in this important volume also examine her depression, but the struggle is often modulated by quiet language and natural imagery. In "August Rain, After Haying," for example, the concluding stanza makes a suggestive connection between natural rhythms and the disorder of her own spirit: "The grass resolves to grow again,/ receiving the rain to that end,/ but my disordered soul thirsts/ after something it cannot name." The pattern of using the natural image to speculate upon the human condition, a trait Kenyon used since her early career, is mastered fully in this volume.

OTHERWISE

Before Kenyon had her bone marrow infusion, plans were under way for a volume of collected works. Donald Hall had made photocopies of her poems from which to work. When they returned to New Hampshire, Kenyon expected to engage the work as her strength increased. Her energy was set back, however, by sudden gallbladder surgery. Then came the news that the leukemia had returned. Kenyon had strength to work on the volume with her husband for only about three days, during which they read and included or rejected poems. On several poems Kenyon had made minor revisions, which Hall later discussed with Kenyon's closest writing friends.

The volume includes twenty new poems. Several of these reflect on the deaths of Kenyon's parents and on Hall's mother's death. The volume also includes "Woman, Why Are You Weeping?," a poem that Kenyon had previously withheld from publication. During their trips to India, Kenyon had fallen in love with the country but was also disconcerted by the harsh juxtaposition of lush natural beauty and an impoverished people. "Woman, Why Are You Weeping?" places the narrator-poet in her own church back in the United States, but she is remembering her encounter with the corpse of an infant floating in the river while she was on a sightseeing tour. That vision haunted her, and she tried to come to grips with it in the poem by combining the biblical story of the angel appearing to Mary Magdalene at the empty tomb, her own place in the church, and the forsakenness of the infant in the river.

OTHER MAJOR WORKS

TRANSLATION: *Twenty Poems of Anna Akhmatova*, 1985.

MISCELLANEOUS: *A Hundred White Daffodils: Essays, Interviews, the Akhmatova Translations, Newspaper Columns, and One Poem*, 1999.

BIBLIOGRAPHY

Hall, Donald. "With Jane and Without: An Interview with Donald Hall." Interview by Jeffrey S. Cramer. *Massachusetts Review* (Winter, 1998): 493. Hall discusses his marriage to Kenyon and how his poetry improved after they became close.

Hornback, Bert, ed. *Bright, Unequivocal Eye: Poems, Papers, and Remembrances from the First Jane Kenyon Conference*. New York: Peter Lang, 2000. This conference, held in 1998, was the occasion for friends and scholars of Jane Kenyon to commemorate her life and death. Notable are remembrances from Gregory Orr, Alice Mattison, and Wendell Berry.

Mattison, Alice. "'Let It Grow in the Dark Like a Mushroom': Writing with Jane Kenyon." *Michigan Quarterly Review* 39, no. 1 (Winter, 2000): 120. Mattison recounts her years in a workshop with Kenyon. Correspondence between the two is included.

Timmerman, John H. *Jane Kenyon: A Literary Life*. Grand Rapids, Mich.: Wm. B. Eerdmans, 2002. This work is the first full study of Kenyon's life and art. Making use of drafts of poems in the Jane Kenyon Archives at the University of New Hampshire, the author demonstrates the development of Kenyon's artistic craft. Previously unpublished materials and interviews with Donald Hall provide a detailed biography of the poet's life.

John H. Timmerman

VLADISLAV KHODASEVICH

Born: Moscow, Russia; May 28, 1886
Died: Paris, France; June 14, 1939

PRINCIPAL POETRY
Molodost', 1908
Shchastlivy domik, 1914
Putem zerna, 1920
Tyazhelaya lira, 1922
Evropeiskaya noch', 1927

OTHER LITERARY FORMS

In addition to his poetry, Vladislav Khodasevich published many critical essays and memoirs. The most important of these are collected in *Nekropol'* (1939), *Literaturnye stat'i i vospominaniia* (1954), and *Belyi koridor: Isbrannaia proza v dvukh tomakh* (1982). His biography of the eighteenth century poet Gavrila Derzhavin (*Derzhavin*, 1931) is also notable. As is the case with Khodasevich's poetry, very little of his prose is available in English translation.

ACHIEVEMENTS

Vladislav Khodasevich was one of the most highly regarded Russian poets of his own time and is one of the least known of ours. Twelve years of poetic silence before his death contributed to that obscurity, and a virtual ban on publishing his work in the then Soviet Union as well as difficult relations within the Russian émigré community in Western Europe negatively affected his reputation for years. Interest in him revived in the 1980's, when a growing interest in him emerged in both the Soviet Union and the West.

BIOGRAPHY

Vladislav Felitsianovich Khodasevich was born in Moscow on May 28 (May 16, Old Style), 1886. Neither his father nor his mother was a native Russian (Felitsian Khodasevich was Polish, Sophie Brafman a Jewish convert to Catholicism and a fervent Polish nationalist), but perhaps as much because of his background as despite it, young Khodasevich considered himself thoroughly Russian in both allegiance and sensibility. The youngest of six children, he was educated at Moscow's Third Classical Gimnazium. Even before he left school, his ambitions turned to writing, and it was through a schoolmate that he made his first shy forays into the febrile world of *fin de siècle* Moscow literary life—the world of Valery Bryusov, Andrey Bely, and Aleksandr Blok. After graduation, Khodasevich began writing and publishing, and except for an almost comic bureaucratic interlude immediately after the revolution, he practiced no other profession.

Chronic ill health aggravated by hardship and privation kept Khodasevich out of military service during World War I and the Russian Revolution. In April of 1921, Khodasevich moved with his second wife, Anna Chulkova, and her son Garik to St. Petersburg, the abandoned capital, to work and live in the subsidized House

Vladislav Khodasevich (Russian Literature Triquarterly)

of the Arts. It was there that Khodasevich, in a concentrated burst of energy, wrote many of his finest poems. Roughly one year later, however, spurred by private difficulties and by doubts about the future for writers in the new Soviet state, he and young poet Nina Berberova left for Western Europe. Khodasevich, like many other artists and intellectuals who left at the same time, did not expect his sojourn there to be a permanent one, and he maintained literary and personal ties with his homeland. Yet Khodasevich soon found himself on the list of those who were to be barred from returning, and his skepticism about the Soviet Union began to harden into conviction.

Khodasevich was not of like mind with much of the émigré community, and although he settled permanently in Paris in 1927, he—like Marina Tsvetayeva—found that their aesthetic isolation in Russian letters and their lack of a convenient niche was to become an oppressive physical and spiritual isolation as well. Khodasevich, unlike Tsvetayeva, was never ostracized by fellow émigrés and was able to earn a meager living writing criticism for Russian periodicals, but there were few kindred spirits to be found among his own countrymen, let alone among the left-leaning French intellectual community of 1930's Paris. Khodasevich believed that he was witnessing the final eclipse of Russian letters and, ironically, continued to insist on the primacy of tradition even as his own poetics were discarding their much-vaunted classical proportions.

Khodasevich's last years were difficult ones: He wrote practically no poetry after 1927, and a final break with Berberova in 1932, financial straits, and failing health all contributed to depression. He did remarry and continue to write remarkable prose, and he was at work on an Alexander Pushkin study when he was fatally stricken with cancer in 1939. He died in the spring of that year.

ANALYSIS

A pupil of the Symbolists who soon freed himself from their poetics if not their perceptions, a contemporary of Boris Pasternak, Anna Akhmatova, Marina Tsvetayeva, and Osip Mandelstam but resembling none of them, Vladislav Khodasevich is a poet not easily classified. He is often described as a classicist because of his loyalty to Alexander Pushkin and Russian verse tradition, yet his always ironic and sometimes bleak vision of the world is no less a product of the twentieth century. His poetic output was small and his demands on himself severe, but his mature verse, with its paradoxical combination of domesticity and exile, banality and beauty, harmony and grotesquerie, places him among the finest Russian poets of the twentieth century.

Khodasevich made his poetic debut in the heyday of Russian Symbolism. For the Symbolists, passion was the quickest way to reach the limits of experience necessary for artistic creation, and so all the motifs which accompany the Symbolist/Decadent notion of love—pain, intoxication, hopelessness—are explored by Khodasevich, diligent student of decadence, in his first collection.

MOLODOST'

In *Molodost'* (youth), Khodasevich treats the transcendent themes of death, love, art, and eternity (so dear to the Symbolist canon) to both facile versifying and facile dramatization. His lyric voice is that of the seer, the magus, the seeker—a pale youth with burning eyes,

a self-conscious poet risking all for revelation and encounters with mystic dread. *Molodost'* is the work of a talented beginner, but no more.

The poems are infused with vague mystery and vague premonitions, full of hints of midnight trysts at crypts, of confounding of realities, of fashionable madness and jaded melancholy. Khodasevich's problem is the problem of Symbolism in general: Its claim to universality of experience was undercut by the lack of any universal, or even coherent, symbolic system. In seeking to create a language of those "Chosen by Art" they plumbed for the emblematic, "creative" meaning of words, but the choosing and the chosen—hence the meaning—might vary from salon to salon. No word or deed was safe from symbolic interpretation, but the poet's own self-absorbed consciousness was the sole arbiter of meaning. Indeed, at times it seemed that literature itself was secondary to the attempt to divine hidden meaning in everyday events, thereby creating a life which itself was art enough.

Khodasevich's poetics would begin to change with the advent of his next book, but his apprenticeship among the Symbolists would affect him for the rest of his life. From them, he learned to perceive human existence as the tragic incompatibility of two separate realities, and all of his poetic life would be an attempt to reconcile them.

SHCHASTLIVY DOMIK

His second volume of verse, *Shchastlivy domik* (the happy little house), shows Khodasevich replacing his early mentors—Bely, Blok, Bryusov, Innokenty Annensky—with eighteenth and nineteenth century classics such as Pushkin, Evgeny Baratynsky, and Derzhavin. His new persona is both more accessible and more distant than the pale pre-Raphaelite youth of the first book: He is more personal and biographical, surrounded by more concrete visual imagery and fewer abstractions, although the stylization, the deliberate archaisms, and the traditional meter in which those details are given serve to keep the poet's mask a generalized one—one poet among many, the latest heir to an elegiac tradition. *Shchastlivy domik* is still a diary of the emotions, kept by a self-absorbed "I," but here the spheres of emotion and art begin to separate. This poet belongs to a guild of craftsmen, not a hieratic brotherhood intent on perceiving life as a work in progress. A sense of history and linear time replaces the boundless "I" of the Symbolist/Decadent, defining both past and present and imposing different sorts of limits on the power of language to conjure, transform, or even affect reality. In this context, death becomes an even rather than a sensuous state of mind, and art becomes a means of overcoming death by very virtue of its formality and conventionality. These characteristics, not sibylline utterances, will carry the work beyond its creator's physical end.

Gone, then, are sadness and frustration at the utter futility of words, replaced by a less literal quietism— elegiac contemplation, meditation, and pride not in one's own oracular powers but in a tradition. Dignified humility replaces bombast, domesticity replaces exotica, and Pushkin is the chief guide. Although Khodasevich never lost his sense of the split between the world of appearance and the higher reality, in this collection he discovered inspiration in everydayness, in ordinary, prosaic, humble moments. In his next collection, his first book of truly mature work, he worked out the poetics appropriate to that discovery.

PUTEM ZERNA

Most of the major poems in *Putem zerna* (the way of grain) were finished by 1918, but the book itself did not see print until 1920. In lexicon, choice of themes, and lyric voice, it is a testament to a sober but still joyful everyday life; the poet is an ordinary human, subject to the laws of time and space, vulnerable to cold, hunger, illness, and death, no more and no less significant than any other man on the street. Like his fellow Muscovites in times of war and revolution, he observes history, participates in it "like a salamander in flame," but possesses no Symbolist second sight and no power to guess, let alone prophesy, the future. Although the poet, unlike his fellows, does have occasion to transcend his human limits, his small epiphanies, too, depend on the physical world. Their source is earthly. They derive from moments in which the poet experiences an acute awareness of things heard, felt, seen, smelled, and tasted.

Straightforward syntax, simplicity of lexicon, an intimate, slightly ironic, conversational tone, and the unrhymed iambic pentameter of the longer poems all make *Putem zerna* a deliberately prosaic book of poetry.

Its persona is both public and private—public in his identification with the lives and deaths of his fellow creatures, private in facing his own mortality. The two are linked by the central metaphors of the book; the biblical seed which dies to be born again and the life-giving bread baked from buried grain—the eternal cycle of being.

Many of the book's poems have an identifiable setting in both space and time, coordinates usually lacking in Khodasevich's earlier works. The homely images of Moscow neighborhoods lead to meditations on the passing of time, nations, generations, and the poet himself as he feels the onset of physical weakness, illness, and old age. The poems chronicle what Khodasevich called "holy banality": common, collective experiences such as hauling wood, selling herring rations to buy lamp oil, and watching the local coffin maker finish his latest order. Moments of transcendence come unrequested and unexpected, with the thump of a seamstress's treadle or the sight of an all-too-ordinary suicide in a local park. The thump of the poet's own rocking chair, for example, marking time, sparks this moment in "Epizod" ("Episode"). In this poem, the observer of others leaves his own body and instead observes himself—thin, pale, dying, cigarette in hand. He also observes all the objects surrounding him—a bookcase, the ubiquitous yellow wallpaper of modest, older apartments, Pushkin's death mask, the children, and their sleds. As the soul returns to its body, it journeys over water—a crossing of Lethe described in painstakingly physical terms.

The balance achieved in *Putem zerna* is both an acrobatic and a poetic feat, as Khodasevich points out in one of his short poems. It requires both muscle and brain. In his incarnation as ordinary man, Khodasevich has to balance life against death; in his role as poet, he has to balance creativity and the everyday world. For the moment, poetry makes that reconciliation possible by imposing order on the chaos and disarray of everyday life. Yet just as the poet cannot exist without the man, the poetry cannot exist without the chaos.

TYAZHELAYA LIRA

If earthly and divine principles complement each other in *Putem zerna*, they come into conflict in Khodasevich's 1922 collection, *Tyazhelaya lira* (the heavy lyre). Here the divine side of the poet's nature turns dominant, becomes a condition for the existence of all else. Poetic order is no longer simply one possible means of reconciliation but the only order possible if the "I" is to survive in any way. Equilibrium shifted, the prosy external world lends itself less and less to ordering. Unlike the poet in the previous collection (an ordinary man save for his flashes of kinship with "child, flower, beast"), the poet of *Tyazhelaya lira* is unmistakably a creature different from his fellows, one for whom the creative moment has expanded to fill his entire consciousness. His state is one of constant awareness of human limitations and his own duality, of constant service to his craft. This awareness reveals not affinities but differences, not community but isolation.

Exalted, yes, but smug—never. Khodasevich's version of the conventional antagonism between the two worlds of the poet is not at all simple and clear-cut. The two realities are mutually exclusive yet do, paradoxically, overlap. Each seeks to free itself of the other, but only in their uncomfortable union does the lyric "I" of this collection exist. This voice may be much more ironic and self-deprecating than that of the high priests of Symbolism, but the poet's gifts—vision and "secret hearing"—allow him to see and hear, not over, but through physical existence. They allow him to escape, however briefly, from his captivity in an aging, unattractive, bodily prison. Indeed, the collection is dominated by a set of images which provide that escape to the soul's true homeland: Eyes, windows, mirrors, and reflections all open onto another reality, an escape route for the spirit. Wings, wounds (sometimes mortal, death being the ultimate flight), verbs with transitional prefixes, and negative definitions also belong to a poetics whereby the word, the soul, and the spirit break out of the enclosed cell of body or world. Angels, Psyche, Lucifer, an automobile winged by headlights, and acid consuming a photographic negative move across and through the tissue of existence.

One of the most striking poems of the collection, "Ballada" ("Ballad"), describes another journey out of the body. Here, as in "Episode," the poet is transformed into a creature with knowledge of the realms of both life and death. In both cases, the journey to the underworld begins with the speaker of the poem alone in his room, surrounded by familiar objects; the room has a window,

and time passes strangely. Yet while "Episode" ends with a return to the mortal body and an understanding of life and death as kindred states, "Ballad" ends with the man transfigured, changed into Orpheus, and that transformation takes place because of poetry. Cut by the sharp blade of music, the man grows up and out of himself, setting dead matter into motion with him, recreating both himself and the world around him. His instrument, his blade, is the heavy lyre handed him through the wind.

EVROPEISKAYA NOCH'

Khodasevich's last book, *Evropeiskaya noch'* (European night), did not appear separately but came out as part of his *Sobranie stikhov* (collected verse) of 1927. Like his two earlier books, *Evropeiskaya noch'* treats of both spiritual and material worlds. The epiphanies of *Putem zerna*, however, are long gone, as are the neat oxymorons and epigrammatic resolutions of *Tyazhelaya lira*. There are no escape routes here. Instead, there is the Gnostic's anti-Paradise, a grotesque Gogolian world of inferior time and space, demoniac in its unrelenting banality and tawdry stupidity. The poet is doubly exiled, for even language seems to have lost its ability to transform either the self or what surrounds it. Now the physical world shapes both the language and the voice, distorting them and depriving them of their fragile unity and identity. The possibility—or rather impossibility—of creativity involves three things: the victory of matter over spirit and the distortion of both; the confusion of masks, or the poet's inability to recognize even himself; and the dismemberment of the once coherent lyric "I," as in a poem which ends with the poet exploding, flying apart "Like mud, sprayed out by a tire/ To alien spheres of being."

Savagely funny, *Evropeiskaya noch'* covers a world densely populated by humans, animals, and objects as well as the trappings, gadgetry, and attitudes of the modern century. Animate and inanimate objects obey the same laws, are objects of the same verbs, undergo the same processes. The natural world is at best askew, at worst hostile. The luminous, sanctified domesticity of *Putem zerna* has turned paltry and pitiful, the entire universe reduced to a collection of "poor utensils." The lyric hero, a petty Cain, is exiled from his age and from himself: "Like a fly on sticky paper/ He trembles in our time." Too inarticulate to give voice, he merely groans in mute despair.

The breakup of coherent vision and the loss of sense of self and genuine creativity take poetic form in the breakup of a once smooth line, disjointed stanzaic structure, abrupt changes of rhythm, and incongruous rhyme. Imagery, too, disintegrates: The poet looks in mirrors and cannot recognize his past selves in the aging face confronting him, gazes at a shiny tabletop and sees his own severed head reflected in the window of a passing streetcar, looks at the "asphalt mirror" of a Berlin street at night and sees himself and his friends as monsters, mutants, and human bodies topped by dogs' heads. The creation of art, so closely tied to the re-creation of self, seems impossible in a world of dusty galleries and cheap cinemas. Appropriately enough, *Evropeiskaya noch'* ends with a counterfeit act of creation, a parody of Jehovah's Fourth Day and of the poet's ability to bring dead matter to life. In this last poem, called "Zvezdi" ("Stars"), the cosmos emerges at the wave of a seedy conductor's baton. The show begins, and light comes forth from darkness in the form of prostitutes: the chorus line as the Big Dipper and the soloists as the North Star and "l'Étoile d'Amour." In Khodasevich's earlier works, the poet had been able to create or re-create an earlier, truer existence, a cosmos of his own. He came to doubt his ability to perform such a task. In Khodasevich's later poems, it appears that corrupt and perverted forms—vaudeville comedians and down-and-out dancing girls—may be the only artistic order left to the modern world.

OTHER MAJOR WORKS

NONFICTION: *Derzhavin*, 1931; *Nekropol'*, 1939; *Literaturnye stat'i i vospominaniia*, 1954; *Belyi koridor: Isbrannaia proza v dvukh tomakh*, 1982.

MISCELLANEOUS: *Sobranie stikhov*, 1927.

BIBLIOGRAPHY

Bethea, David M. *Khodasevich: His Life and Art*. Princeton, N.J.: Princeton University Press, 1983. A thorough study by a leading Western expert on Khodasevich. The monograph examines Khodasevich's life and works, underscoring his main achievements in poetic artistry and his contribution to the Russian literature at home and in exile.

Hughes, Robert P. "Khodasevich: Irony and Dislocation: A Poet in Exile." In *The Bitter Air of Exile: Russian Writers in the West, 1922-1972*, edited by Simon Karlinsky and A. Appel, Jr. Berkeley: University of California Press, 1977. Main stations in Khodasevich's life are marked, followed by brief but pertinent comments on his poetry and his place in Russian literature.

Khodasevich, Valentina, and Olga Margolina-Khodasevich. *Unpublished Letters to Nina Berberova*. Edited by R. D. Sylvester. Berkeley, Calif.: Berkeley Slavic Specialties, 1979. Previously unpublished letters casting light on Khodasevich. Bibliographical references, illustrated.

Miller, Jane A. "Xodasevi's Gnostic Exile." *South and East European Journal* 28, no. 2 (1984): 223-233. Miller concentrates on Khodasevich's exile poetry, notably on *Tyazhelaya lira* and *Evropeiskaya noch'*. She points out the success of the former and the relative failures of the latter. She also broaches the question of creativity and the artist, especially his mirror of himself and his relation to the material world around him.

Nabokov, Vladimir. "On Khodasevich." In *The Bitter Air of Exile: Russian Writers in the West, 1922-1972*, edited by Simon Karlinsky and Alfred Appel, Jr. Rev. ed. Berkeley: University of California Press, 1977. A terse but significant article on Khodasevich, written in 1939 in Russian on his death. The article has added weight because it was written by another famous writer in exile.

Poggioli, Renato. "Vladislav Khodasevich." *Poets of Russia, 1880-1930*. Cambridge: Harvard University Press, 1960. A brief evaluation by one of the best American scholars of Russian literature. Poggioli succeeds in pointing out in a few strokes the main features of Khodasevich's poetry.

Smith, G. S. "Stanza Rhythm and Stress Load in the Iambic Tetrameter of V. F. Xodasevi." *South and East European Journal* 24, no. 1 (1980): 25-35. A meticulous, expert analysis of this particular aspect of Khodasevich's poetry, bolstered by pertinent examples and charts.

Jane Ann Miller;
bibliography updated by Vasa D. Mihailovich

HENRY KING

Born: Worminghall, Buckinghamshire, England; baptized January 16, 1592
Died: Chichester, Sussex, England; September 30, 1669

PRINCIPAL POETRY

Poems, Elegies, Paradoxes, and Sonnets, 1657
Poems and Psalms, 1843
Poems, 1965 (Margaret Crum, editor)

OTHER LITERARY FORMS

Henry King's significant literary remains other than poetry are his Latin verses and his surviving sermons, which span almost a half-century and provide an excellent record of his ministerial concerns. They have not, however, been collected.

ACHIEVEMENTS

A full assessment of Henry King's poetic stature has been slow to evolve. It appears that among his contemporaries, King was renowned less as a poet than as a churchman, as an eminent preacher and respected bishop of Chichester, and there is no evidence to suggest that King would have preferred to be viewed in any other way. It was only in the period during which for political reasons he was forcibly denied his bishopric that King, at a rather advanced age, published his poetry, and his output is relatively modest—by the reckoning of his most modern editor, Margaret Crum (*Poems*, 1965), only eighty-six poems, exclusive of his little-read and little-esteemed metrical transcriptions of the Psalms. Though the widespread appearance of a number of King's poems in various manuscripts both during his life and for several decades after his death would attest to some popularity, King's poetic achievement as a whole was left to rest in oblivion throughout the eighteenth and much of the nineteenth centuries.

Newly edited and republished in 1843, King's poems attracted some of the attention paid in the late nineteenth and early twentieth centuries to England's poetic antiquities and seventeenth century divines, and when King's good friend and religious associate John Donne came to be "rediscovered" and reacclaimed as one of England's great poets, King's poetic canon began to receive its first sustained critical study. Comparisons with Donne's verse have been inevitable and not wholly to King's advantage. King's personal association with Donne and a general resemblance between the cerebral and sometimes recondite imagery that King employs and the ingeniously involved "conceits" made famous by Donne have led to King's being labeled one of the lesser disciples of Donne's "school," or what Samuel Johnson dubbed the "metaphysical" mode of poetry. That King's imagery is less "knotty" and philosophically adventurous than Donne's and that King's verse lacks the dramatic impact so conspicuous in Donne's have made it easy to confuse difference with inferiority and to view King, not as a poet with his own concerns and idiom, but simply as Donne's unsuccessful imitator. Moreover, the high percentage of his verse which is "occasional," that is, which was prompted by and composed for a particular event, may suggest that his poetry lacks the spontaneity and originality the modern reader demands of poetry.

With closer scrutiny, however, has come the recognition not only that King may owe as much to Ben Jonson as he does to Donne, but also, and more important, that, far from being anyone's servile imitator, King studied and emulated the example of older contemporaries such as Donne and Jonson, while fashioning a poetic style through which he spoke with his own distinctive, ever thoughtful, frequently meditative, voice. In the evolution of poetic techniques and tastes in the seventeenth century, King's volume of published verse is a valuable document, encompassing as it does a period of forty-five years (1612-1657), and at once reflecting the poetic practices of the Elizabethan period and presaging those of the Restoration and neoclassicism. To the epigrammatic plainness and conciseness of Jonson's iambic pentameter and tetrameter rhymed couplets, King brings a refinement of expression that heralds the lapidary smoothness cultivated by practitioners of the rhymed couplet form in the middle and later decades of the century, and if some of King's images recall the kind of imagery brought into vogue by Donne near the beginning of the century, the polished trenchancy of some of King's more satiric and polemical pieces foreshadows the great heroic verse satires of John Dryden near the end of the century.

Above all, King's poetry is of immense interest as a lucid record of a poet's response to a most turbulent and critical period in English history, a period which brought fundamental changes to England's political, social, and religious institutions, and which challenged the perceptive poet to examine the purposes and value of his art. Like the actors Hamlet so esteemed, King's poems are "the abstract and brief chronicles of the time," and King himself a diligent poetic chronicler of the significant literary-historical events of his lifetime: the deaths of great poets, the births and deaths of princes and heirs to the throne, the travails and deaths of monarchs. To these subjects King brought the unifying perspective of a poet nurtured in the Renaissance view of the cosmos and disposed to see in the events of the world—no matter how great or small—the workings of a divinely ordered universe. Thus, side by side in King's poetic "Kalendar" stand poems on affairs of state and affairs of the heart; and in the upheavals of the politic body and the death of a king, as in personal disruptions and the death of a wife, King is prepared to read the hints of a greater disorder and the portents of a world with, in Donne's words, "all cohaerance gone." It is in its power to illuminate these correspondences between the "greater" and "lesser" worlds, and between the poet's private self and his public role, that the signal achievement of King's poetry lies.

BIOGRAPHY

Even a cursory examination of the poet's background will suffice to show that Henry King's art is very much a reflection of the life that produced it. Born in 1592, King was the eldest of five sons of John King, scion of an aristocratic family and renowned Anglican divine and eventual bishop of London. Since John King intended each of his sons to enter the ministry, Henry received an education befitting a man of learning. As a youngster, he attended the Westminster School, where Ben Jonson, among many other notables, had studied, and where, as part of his classical training, he became practiced in the techniques of versification. After he left Westminster he proceeded to Oxford, where he took his B.A. degree in 1611, his M.A. in 1614, and his B.D. and D.D. in 1625.

The oldest son of an influential clergyman, King came into contact as a child and young man with some of the most distinguished churchmen and courtiers of the time, among whom was John Donne. Donne was a good friend of John King and, according to Donne's early biographer, Izaak Walton, grew to be no less fond of Henry. In 1616, as a young student of divinity, King was named to the clerical office of Prebendary of St. Paul's Church, where several years later Donne would become Dean. Their relationship remained close, and shortly before his death in 1631, Donne made King his legal executor. King's final service for Donne came in the form of the funeral elegy he composed, "Upon the Death of my ever Desired friend Dr. Donne Deane of Pauls."

From the example of his father, from his formal education, and, not improbably, from his acquaintance with Donne would emerge the intellectual cast of mind and the religious and political propensities that would permanently shape King's life, his career, and, no less so, his poetry. From all that is known of it, King's life appears to have been a genuinely religious one, predicated on a belief that God's ordinances were embodied in two temporal institutions: the Church and the Crown. Thus, religious orthodoxy and political conservatism were the mainstays of his thought and colored almost everything he wrote. No personal loss—not even the death of his young wife in 1624—could overturn his religious convictions, and, while in his verse he acknowledges the pain of loss most frankly, as he does in the celebrated elegy he wrote for his wife, "The Exequy," his affirmation of the triumph of the immortal soul over death is nonetheless assured.

Nor did the tribulations of the civil tumult weaken his adherence to either Church or monarch, despite the considerable privations his loyalty cost him. In 1643, a victory of the forces representing the Parliamentary and Puritan factions over the Royalist army led to the ejection of King from the bishopric of Chichester to which he had been elevated only a year before. Stripped of almost all of his property and personal papers, King existed on rather modest means—apparently not without some harassment—for the next seventeen years, until, with the Restoration of the monarchy in the person of Charles II, King returned to his church in Chichester.

In the years immediately following his ejection, King wrote his most staunchly partisan and pro-Royalist verse, culminating in by far his longest and most passionate pieces, the elegies written just after the execution of Charles I in 1648, "A Deepe Groane, fetch'd at the Funerall of that incomparable and Glorious Monarch," and "An elegy upon the most Incomparable King Charls the First."

Yet, as strong as King's personal convictions were, his best verse is curiously undogmatic. The depth of King's learning and belief manifests itself not in a welter of information to be presented as absolute truth, but in a self-assured spirit of inquiry. If King shares anything with Donne, it is the pleasure he takes in exploring an idea through the play of language and metaphor. Like Donne, King seems often to be probing, discovering the essential likenesses in things that have ostensibly little in common, between an emotional state or religious point, for example, and the physical properties of the universe. Thus, when King takes a position on an issue, he does not presume its correctness but demonstrates it carefully and seriously, yet imaginatively. It is the depth of both his convictions and intelligence that leaves the reader with the sense of having shared or worked through with the poet the experience he presents in his verse. King's poetic corpus may be relatively small, but a survey of his poems gives one the impression of having learned a good deal about their author precisely because King shows so much, not only of what he thinks, but how he thinks as well.

ANALYSIS

Like most of the technically accomplished poets of his era, Henry King was proficient in a wide range of forms and styles. Yet the form which seems to have been most congenial to his poetic temper, and in which he wrote his most memorable pieces, was the elegy. Constituting a significant part of his rather compact volume, elegies punctuate King's entire poetic career, accounting for his first datable poem, "An Elegy Upon Prince Henryes Death" (1612), and his last, "An Elegy Upon my Best Friend L. K. C." (Lady Katherine Cholmondeley, 1657). Indeed—though it is unlikely that King himself would have coveted this distinction—the list of notable personages memorialized so eloquently in his

funeral poems might well give King claim to the title of elegiac poet laureate of the seventeenth century.

ELEGIES

That what King calls the "Elegiack Knell" peals so resonantly in his verse is in part a measure of the "occasional" and "public" character much of his poetry assumed. For King, as for many of his contemporaries, private experience and public events were not inimical as poetic subjects, but complementary; in both lay hints of universal significance for the discerning poet to interpret and elucidate. Thus, a poem called forth by a particular "occasion"—the birth of a child or the death of a celebrated war hero—could serve as a vehicle for recording, for solemnizing, the significance of an event for both the poet and the world at large. No "occasion," though, fulfills this purpose more ably than that of death, for no event is at once so private and so public, and when, in turn, death deprives the world of an individual of special importance, a "Matchlesse" wife, or a "most Incomparable" monarch, for example, the scope of the loss is all the more conspicuous, its implications all the more universal. The "weeping verse" and funeral rites invoked in King's elegies are in part, then, a literary convention by means of which King affirms and reaffirms the common basis of experience that he as a poet shares with the public about whom and for whom he writes.

Still, to suggest that the elegiac strain in King's verse is in some sense "conventional" is not to impugn or belittle what it may reveal about the innermost concerns of King's poetic psyche. In her seminal discussion of "The Laureate Hearse" in *Studies in Seventeenth Century Poetic* (1950), Ruth Coons Wallerstein persuasively argued that the response to death in the elegiac poems of the seventeenth century crystallized the deepest spiritual and poetic preoccupations of the era, a thesis to which King's elegies prove no exception. For King the "occasion" of death subjected the aspirations of life and art to their most intense scrutiny. In metaphoric terms, King conceived of death as a literary text, the "Killing rhetorick" and "Grammer" of which contained lessons about human experience that King seems never to have tired of reading.

Just how tireless this reading was is suggested not only by the sheer frequency with which elegiac themes appear in King's verse but also by their appearance in poems that are not explicitly funereal pieces and have little ostensibly to do with the issues of death and mourning. A conspicuous example is the poem King wrote in honor of the newly born Prince Charles, titled "By Occasion of the young Prince his happy birth. May 29-1630." No subject, one would think, has less to do with death than does birth, and, in an ethos in which the divine right of kings was a respected principle, no birth would be a source of as much public rejoicing as would that of a prince and heir apparent. Yet, at the outset of the poem, the reader finds King laboring, not to express his joy but to explain why he has hesitated to write, why at first, in fact, he "held it some Allegiance not to write." What has tempered King's celebrative mood is the recognition that everything that makes the arrival of Prince Charles a welcome event entails a sobering reflection about his father, King Charles. In the advent of a child abides the hope of immortality, along, unfortunately, with the acknowledgment of mortality. Hence, even a newly born child is a *memento mori*, and in that book of harsh lessons by which King metaphorically conceived of death, children form "The Smiling Preface to our Funerall." The arrival of a prince, connoting as it does the hope of a smooth succession and continuity in the royal line, underscores the inevitability of the death of the monarch; to acclaim the birth of Charles the Prince is, King fears, to anticipate and make seem all the more imminent the passing away of Charles the King.

Such insights bring King to something of a dilemma. As a loyal Englishman he would like to use his poetic gifts to frame a compliment to the Crown. Yet his poetic vision enables, obliges, him to see the infant prince both for what he is and for what he represents. The apprehension of mortality and the rhetoric of death force King to see and say things inappropriate to the ostensibly complimentary occasion; but to excise his elegiac concerns, King implies, is to render his compliment hollow and poetically false.

King's solution, both in this poem and in many others, is to reconcile his elegiac presentiments with his religious convictions and to turn the occasion of paying a compliment into an opportunity for teaching a salutary lesson. True, the birth of an heir is a tacit intimation of mortality, but mortality itself is but a milestone on the soul's journey to immortality, and but the last instance of

finitude before all time is transformed into the infinitude of life everlasting. To pretend to ignore death, to be obsessed with prolonging life on earth, is to repudiate a fundamental article of faith: "And wee in vaine were Christians, should wee/ In this world dreame of Perpetuitye." Rather deftly, King pays the royal father the ultimate compliment of eschewing flattery and appealing, instead, to wisdom and Christian humility to accept a wholesome truth: "Decay is Nature's Kalendar; nor can/ It hurt the King to think He is a Man." With these reflections articulated, and with the fullest implications of the Prince's birth understood, King can with more genuine enthusiasm acclaim the happy event and even look forward to that time when young Charles will "lead Succession's goulden Teame" and ascend to his father's throne.

"THE EXEQUY"

The poem on "the young Prince" exemplifies the pattern of argumentation that King pursues in much of his verse, wherein, with varying degrees of success and conviction, he strives to achieve a synthesis in which elegiac sadness and pessimism over the transience of this world is answered by religious belief in the permanence of the next. Nowhere, perhaps, is this religious elegiac vision more moving and more triumphant than in King's most frequently anthologized piece, the poem he wrote upon the death of his young wife Anne, "The Exequy."

What at first seems peculiar about this poem, which deals with so emotionally charged an experience, and which ultimately manages to be so moving, is that it at first appears so distanced, so oddly impersonal. Little is learned about Anne herself, and one wonders at first whether King is merely making use of the death of his wife as a pretext for a philosophical discourse. One has only to read a little way into the poem to discover that it is delivered as a meditation in which Anne is a rather abstracted presence. The title of the poem may promise that it is addressed "*To* his Matchlesse never to be forgotten Freind" [italics added], but the poem opens with the poet apostrophizing a burial monument, "Thou Shrine of my Dead Saint." To the extent that Anne herself is addressed at all within the first ten lines of the piece, it is not as a person but as "Deare Losse." It is this "Losse" that consumes all the poet's emotional energy, but that energy has been subsumed in study, in a commitment to do nothing but "meditate" on the loss itself. It is the "Deare Losse" which forms "the Book,/ The Library whereon I took."

Although the poet at first seems to be distanced from Anne, it is precisely this distancing that establishes the emotional tension and intensity within the poem. The poet must turn to the study of his loss because that is all that is left him; all that remains of Anne, after all, is the "Lov'd Clay" lying in the tomb. In the discipline of meditation, then, the poet finds a method of coping with death and a means by which he may explore the psychology of grief and "compute the weary howres/ With Sighes dissolved into Showres."

Initially, at least, meditation enables the poet, not so much to allay his grief, as to define its scope. The emotional void left by the death of Anne makes existence as a whole a desolation because it was Anne who gave existence its meaning. Here the influence of Donne upon King becomes readily apparent, for in attempting to define the impact of his wife's loss, King employs the kind of imagery used by Donne to illustrate the experiences of separation and loss in poems such as "A Valediction: Forbidding Mourning" and "A Nocturnal upon Saint Lucy's Day." The extinction of Anne's life is like the extinction of the sun, since it was she who brought "Light and Motion" to the poet's now darkened "Hemispheare." Yet this is a "straunge Ecclipse," one "As ne're was read in Almanake," because it was not caused by the obstruction of the moon but by the earth itself, which in reclaiming Anne's "Lov'd Clay" has "interposed" itself between the poet and his sun.

What makes this "Ecclipse" especially "straunge" is not merely its provenance but its duration. Unlike a "normal" solar eclipse, this one is not transitory, but will endure as long as the earth endures. The eclipse of the poet's world is not an extraordinary phenomenon but a systemic and all too ordinary condition. With the recognition of this fact comes the realization of the immensity of the poet's loss. In depriving the poet of his wife, mortality has made earthly existence at once a void and a barrier to their reunion that can only be surmounted by the extinction of existence itself.

Still, implanted in the depths of King's sorrow are the very seeds of his remission, although King's recognition and articulation of this truth proceed as much from the promptings of his faith as from the workings of his intellect. If by dying, Anne has succumbed to the mortality inherent in her earthly nature, it follows that all things earthly, including the earth itself, must inevitably succumb as well. Thus, the onerous sentence of King's grief bears with it the promise of a terminus, and King can look forward to that apocalyptic "Day" when a "fierce Feaver must calcine/ The Body of this World," even as a more localized fever has already consumed the body of Anne, "My Little World."

The expectation of the world's dissolution would not be much of a source of comfort to the poet were it not coupled with his unqualified belief in a universal Resurrection. On this premise turns the argument—and the mood—of the latter parts of the poem. Death becomes, then, less a boundless condition than a transitional event: The death of the body brings about the liberation of the soul, while the death of earthly existence is the purificatory and regenerative mechanism by which "our Bodyes shall aspire/ To our Soules blisse." So it is that no hint of equivocation mars the confidence with which the poet envisions that endless day on which "wee shall rise,/ And view our selves with cleerer eyes/ In that calme Region, where no Night/ Can hide us from each other's sight." Moreover, that the poet begins to use pronouns such as "wee" and "us" suggests that the reunion with Anne to be attained in the general Resurrection is already under way, and that the gulf created by death which had so tormented the poet at the outset of the piece has already been bridged by the poetic process of meditation. Death becomes less an insuperable foe than a functionary accountable to a higher power. Anne's tomb is less a devourer of her flesh than a temporary custodian whose duty will be to return on the day of the Resurrection an accurate "reck'ning" of "Each Grane and Atome of this Dust." Nothing has been, or will be, lost.

At the same time, it is a measure of the complexity and artistry of King's vision that no matter how assured his faith leads him to be about the ultimate implications of death, its immediate reality remains no less horrid. Although King's quickened religious insight may enable him to think of Anne now, not as someone gone forever, but as his temporarily sleeping bride, there is something chillingly reminiscent of Juliet's entombment in the Capulets' charnel house in the picture of King's young wife, enfolded with "Black Curtaines," lying on "Thy cold bed/ Never to be disquieted." Death seems no less importunate, no less an interloper, and when the poet poignantly takes "My last Goodnight" he forcibly acknowledges that he is still very much wedded to the things of this world, "to that Dust/ It so much loves." Indeed, the poet's resounding triumph in the conclusion of the poem takes the form of a paradox: The more fully he affirms his mortality the more clearly he beholds the date of his transcendence, the very rapidity with which mortality encroaches setting the pace by which immortality approaches. It is this image of mortality fused with immortality in one relentless motion that resonates in the cadences of King's parting assurance to his wife that "My pulse, like a soft Drum/ Beates my Approach, Tells Thee I come," while the resolute stroke of eight monosyllabic words underscores the poet's final promise that "I shall at last sitt downe by Thee."

"SIC VITA"

Elegiac sadness for the human condition merges with religious conviction in King's poem to his wife to produce an illusion of poise and inner assurance which make the poem one of the great elegies of the language and, not surprisingly, his most highly esteemed work. In other poems, King's vision is more darkly elegiac, his remorse over the fragility of human existence less evenly tempered by the consolation of faith. One striking instance is the twelve-line epigram titled, "Sic Vita," a poem very much in the *memento mori* tradition, the very compression and conciseness of which give dramatic immediacy to its familiarly elegiac theme that existence is transitory and all too peremptorily brief. In the first six lines of the poem, King presents a series of six exquisite and ephemeral natural phenomena whose exquisiteness, in fact, arises from their ephemeral character and from the teasing hope they engender that somehow they can be preserved, frozen in time. The space is very small, but King manages to select examples that are representative of the diverse operations of the natural world, both great and small: a falling star, a soaring eagle, the fecundity of spring, a gust of wind on the sea, some dew drops, some bubbles on the surface of water. All of these are introduced as terms of one extended simile, and in the seventh and eighth lines one discovers that what draws them together, besides their ephemeral attractiveness, is that they are emblems of man. Man is but one more image of transience, and, like the other entities of nature, he too has a life and "Light" that are "borrow'd" and will be "streight Call'd in, and Pay'd to Night."

If it took only one eight-line sentence to establish the common bond between man and the other elements of his universe, it takes only one four-line sentence to make the implications of this bond briskly and brusquely clear. Swept up in the annihilative rush of time, mortality, and King's swiftly paced iambic tetrameter verse are all the things of nature, including man and, worse, all traces of man's life: "The Dew dryes up: The Starr is shott:/ The Flight is past: And Man Forgott."

For King, the brevity of existence is, however, often only a catalyst for other, even more somber, ruminations about the human condition. Indeed, the importunity of death would hold little but terror for King did he not see it as the culmination of the sorrows that afflict and waste a man's life. "What is th' Existence of Man's Life?" King asks rhetorically at the outset of "The Dirge," only to answer the question immediately: "open Warr, or Slumber'd Strife," from which "Death's cold hand" alone provides a reprieve. What makes this "strife" most pernicious is that it arises from the disorders that original sin has wrought upon the human soul and psyche, effectively making man his own implacable foe, in whom "each loud Passion of the Mind/ Is like a furious gust of Wind."

"THE DIRGE"

It is this perception that makes King, at his most pessimistic, a satirist in the vein of the writer of Ecclesiastes, a scourge of vanity, of the delusions and emptiness that are the inveterate accessories of one's existence. Such is certainly the stance King assumes in "The Dirge," in which he concludes by employing one of William Shakespeare's recurrent metaphors, likening man's existence to a play, "a weary Enterlude," the acts of which are consumed by man's "vaine Hope and vary'd Feares," and the only fitting "Epilogue" to which is "Death." Even more stridently contemptuous is the assessment of man and his aspirations that King offers in "An Elegy Occasioned by Sicknesse." Here illness becomes a meditative device to turn one's attention inward and "Make Man into his proper Opticks look,/ And so become the Student and the Book." What this self-inventory reveals is rather deflating. From conception and birth man is ordained to emerge as little else but "complicated Sin." At the height of his pretensions he is merely "Poore walking Clay," fated to be "a short-liv'd Vapour upward wrought,/ And by Corruption unto nothing brought."

In the face of these dour appraisals of man's worth, the value and role that King allots in his poetry to meditation and the self-scrutiny entailed in meditation become clear. Central to King's excoriation of human vanity is the premise that man's intellect is a casualty of his spiritual defects, that vanity prevents man, for all his apparent intellectual attainments, from knowing himself and what conduces to his own good. Thus, the meditative strain so recurrent in King's poems has, in part, a hortatory function and invites man to lay aside the studies of the external world with which he is so preoccupied in order to study himself, his "proper Opticks," the better to confront and dispel, if possible, the mists impairing his vision.

"THE LABYRINTH"

Such is the challenge posed in "The Labyrinth," which opens with the proposition that "Life is a crooked Labyrinth" in which man is "dayly lost" and then proceeds to draw the reader into a scrutiny of the conundrums that lie at the heart of human conduct. How can it be that man can know what is good, resolve to do the good, and then lapse and relapse into wrong, ever erring, never extricating himself from the labyrinth his will has created? "Why is the clearest and best judging Mind/ In her own Ill's prevention dark and blind?" What contrition can possibly be effective when the mind has become so practiced at begging forgiveness while rationalizing the commission of sin, when, like the usurper King Claudius in *Hamlet, Prince of Denmark* (pr. c. 1600-1601), the sinner cannot in good conscience seek to undo what he has done since he knows that he would do it again? The more thoughtfully the reader ponders these questions, the more surely he is drawn into the labyrinth the poet is describing, for in posing these questions the poet has been appealing to the reader's intellect; and the more the reader acknowledges the intellectual validity of the questions, the more deeply he identifies himself as an intellectual and implicates himself in the cycle of rationalization and recrimination that the labyrinth comprises.

Are there answers to these questions? None, King implies, that can be provided by human intellection, even as there are no strategies the intellect can devise on its own for coping with the experience of death. The intellect is part of the problem, and, unaided, it cannot provide a solution to what King calls "this home-bred tyranny." Instead, King can only abjure his intellectual pretensions and appeal to God for the insight which the human mind lacks. With a nod to Ezekiel (11:19), King calls upon God in his redemptive power to soften man's heart and "imprint" upon his "breast of flint" the marks of true contrition, for it is only through the genuine conversion of the heart that the mists clouding the mind will be dispersed. For King, as for his contemporaries, there was no inherent dichotomy between the mind and the emotions, the affections of the mind following directly from the disposition of the heart and soul. Thus, God is beseeched to provide not merely emotional reassurance but intellectual clarity, or "thy Grace's Clew," with which King, like some latter-day, Christianized Theseus, may aspire to thread his way through "this Labyrinth of Sinne/ My wild Affects and Actions wander in."

The skepticism with which King regards the powers of the human intellect very much affects the attitude he brings to the intellectual activity of writing poetry. If the intellect is impaired by its own frail mortality, then the verse that the intellect produces will be similarly inept, incapable of dealing satisfactorily with the experiences and paradoxes of the human condition. Indeed, in depicting the phenomenon of death, for example, as a text, as a book with its own lessons to impart, King explicitly calls attention to the deficiencies of his own text, his verse. Thus, in his early "Elegy Upon Prince Henrye's Death," King not only laments the passing of the young prince, but wonders how his own verse can ever do justice to the occasion or presume to vie in eloquence with the succinctly "Killing rhetorick" of death, which manages to embody "Woe's superlative" in only two words: "Henry's dead." Again and again, King's poetry runs a poor second either to the experience to which it responds or to the emotion it is intended to express. "And think not," he hastens to assure his deceased friend in "The Departure: An Elegy," that "I only mourne in Poetry and Ink." Rather, the "melancholy Plummets" of his pen "sink/ So lowe, they dive where th'hid Affections sitt." So impatient does King ultimately profess to become with the inadequacy of his verse that in his last datable poem, "An Elegy Upon my Best Friend, L. K. C." (Lady Katherine Cholmondeley; 1657), King announces his "long Farewell" from his poetry, "That Art, where with our Crosses we beguile/ And make them in Harmonious numbers smile"—a valediction in which King strives for that elusive fusion of art and life by burying his verse with his friend.

It is not to impugn King's sincerity to suggest that his insistence upon the deficiencies of his poetry owes a good deal to convention. As an apt student of poetry and poetic tradition, King would have been quite aware of the innumerable writers of and before his time who displayed their eloquence by lamenting their lack of eloquence, who emblazoned the depth of their passion or sense of loss by artfully expressing their inability to express their passion or loss. With King, however, the convention acquires something of the force of a personal signature. Loath to divorce his poetic craft for his life, he was even less willing to excise his verse from the principles and beliefs that gave his life its purpose. Convinced of the contingency and vulnerability of human existence, King could not consider his poetic exercises as anything but reflections of his own limitations. King would not have minded very much the gentle irony that the very powers he denigrated in his verse helped to ensure the continued survival and appeal of that verse.

BIBLIOGRAPHY

Berman, Ronald. *Henry King and the Seventeenth Century*. London: Chatto & Windus, 1964. King is presented in this study as embodying some of the paradoxes of the seventeenth century. It includes a biography and an in-depth look at King's world, his political and social philosophies, as well as an analysis of his poetry. Examples are used extensively and notes and bibliography follow the text.

Crum, Margaret, ed. *The Poems of Henry King*. Oxford, England: Clarendon Press, 1965. The introduction to this collection provides a biography, a short discus-

sion of the poems, and notes on the original texts. The poems themselves are followed by notes and appendices.

Keeble, N. H. Review of *The Sermons of Henry King (1592-1669), Bishop of Chichester*, edited by Mary Hobbs. *Notes and Queries* 40, no. 4 (December, 1993): 550. Keeble provides some biographical and historical information in an assessment of Hobbs's collection of King's sermons.

Tuve, Rosamund. *Elizabethan and Metaphysical Imagery*. Chicago: University of Chicago Press, 1947. This is a study of the imagery employed by the Elizabethan and metaphysical poets of the English Renaissance. The analysis stresses the intellectual, sensual, and charming aspects of the imagery. King and other poets as recent as William Butler Yeats are covered in the discussion.

Wallace, John M., ed. *The Golden and the Brazen World: Papers in Literature and History, 1650-1800*. Berkeley: University of California Press, 1985. This collection contains an essay by Cleanth Brooks on King's "The Exequy" and "The Legacy" titled "Need Clio Quarrel with Her Sister Muses? The Claims of Literature and History" (pp. 1-15). The essayist takes a biographical approach and gives a close reading of "The Exequy." He discusses seventeenth century theological beliefs, burial customs, and King's life and literary career in order to illuminate the poem on the light of its historical roots.

Thomas Moisan;
bibliography updated by the editors

GALWAY KINNELL

Born: Providence, Rhode Island; February 1, 1927

PRINCIPAL POETRY
What a Kingdom It Was, 1960
Flower Herding on Mount Monadnock, 1964
Poems of Night, 1968
Body Rags, 1968

First Poems, 1946-1954, 1970
The Book of Nightmares, 1971
*The Avenue Bearing the Initial of Christ into the
    New World: Poems, 1946-1964*, 1974
Mortal Acts, Mortal Words, 1980
Selected Poems, 1982
The Fundamental Project of Technology, 1983
The Past, 1985
When One Has Lived a Long Time Alone, 1990
Three Books, 1993
Imperfect Thirst, 1994
A New Selected Poems, 2000

Galway Kinnell

OTHER LITERARY FORMS

Although known primarily as a poet, Galway Kinnell in 1966 published the fable-like novel *Black Light* (revised 1980), set in Iran, which chronicles how a carpet maker's act of heinous murder propels him into a dark journey toward spiritual awakening. In *Walking Down the Stairs: Selections from Interviews* (1978), Kinnell offers his opinions about other poets and his own work, gleaned from interviews he gave between 1969 and 1976. *How the Alligator Missed Breakfast* (1982) is a children's book. Kinnell has also published numerous translations, including those of works by René Hardy, François Villon, Yves Bonnefoy, Yvan Goll, and Rainer Maria Rilke. Numerous magazines and literary journals have published articles by Kinnell, several of which have been reprinted as book chapters.

ACHIEVEMENTS

Galway Kinnell's poetry has garnered an ever-increasing and appreciative audience among both critics and the public. In 1971 he received the Shelley Prize from the Poetry Society of America, followed in 1975 by the Medal of Merit from the National Institute of Arts and Letters. For *Selected Poems*, Kinnell was awarded both the Pulitzer Prize and the American Book Award in 1983. He has been a Fulbright professor; president of the International Association of Poets, Playwrights, Editors, Essayists, and Novelists (PEN); a MacArthur fellow; the state poet of Vermont; and the Samuel F. B. Morse Professor of Fine Arts at New York University. *A New Selected Poems* won the National Book Award.

BIOGRAPHY

Born the fourth of four children to immigrant parents (his mother was from Ireland, his father from Scotland), Galway Kinnell spent most of his youth in Pawtucket, Rhode Island, where his father, James Scott Kinnell, earned his living as a carpenter and woodworking teacher. Kinnell left home his senior year of high school to attend Wilbraham Academy in Massachusetts on scholarship. From there he entered Princeton University, where for two of his undergraduate years he was a member of the U.S. Navy, training as an officer, and where he also met W. S. Merwin and Charles Bell. Bell became Kinnell's mentor. In 1949, following his graduation from Princeton summa cum laude, Kinnell received his M.A. from the University of Rochester. Between 1951 and 1964, Kinnell spent two years at the University of Grenoble in France as an instructor of American literature, two years in Iran as a lecturer and journalist, periods of teaching in Chicago and New York City, and periods of retreat to an abandoned farm he purchased in 1961 in northern Vermont. Kinnell's commitment to social justice during the period was evidenced both in his poetry and his membership in the Congress of Racial Equality. Later he would be an active participant in Poets Against the Vietnam War.

Marriage to Ines Delgado de Torres in 1965, and the subsequent arrival of a daughter, Maud, in 1966, and a son, Finn Fergus, in 1968, temporarily stinted Kinnell's wanderlust; in 1969, following two years in Spain and then short-term teaching engagements in California, Colorado, and Iowa, the Kinnells set up housekeeping in New York City for eight years. During this time the Kinnells hosted frequent gatherings, at both their New York apartment and the Vermont farm, at which friends such as James Wright, Saul Galin, Betty Kray, Mary Kaplan, and Etheridge Knight were known to converse, argue, and read their work aloud. In 1978, having been offered new teaching engagements, the Kinnells began globetrotting once again, this time from Nice, France, to Sydney, Australia, to Hawaii. In 1982 they resettled in New York City. In the years following, *Selected Poems* was awarded the Pulitzer Prize and was cowinner of the National Book Award, Kinnell and his wife were divorced, and Kinnell became the Samuel F. B. Morse Professor of Fine Arts at New York University, his first tenured position. He served as that institution's Erich Maria Remarque Professor of Creative Writing and as a chancellor of the Academy of American Poets.

ANALYSIS

Galway Kinnell's earliest poems demonstrate his ability to express himself in traditional poetic forms governed by rhyme and meter. "A Walk in the Country," "The Feast," and "First Song," among others, have each been critically acclaimed for their tenderness and delicacy. Citing constrictions on creative expression, however, Kinnell came to reject rhyme and meter—a position in agreement with Ezra Pound, T. S. Eliot, William Carlos Williams, and Walt Whitman, all of whose influences can be traced in Kinnell's poetry—and espoused free verse as the exclusive suitable medium for modern American poetry. Even in his "pre-enlightened" days, however, when the influence of William Butler Yeats was most evident, there was evidence of his preoccupation with secular sanctification of the material world and with humankind's hope for regeneration after death, though he rejected the possibility of bodily resurrection;

these themes would continue to mark his later work, though the form of that work would change considerably.

"FIRST SONG"

The last stanza of "First Song" carries suggestions of Kinnell's more dramatic, mature voice found in his monumental achievement "The Bear":

It was now fine music the frogs and the boys
Did in the towering Illinois twilight make
And into dark in spite of a shoulder's ache
A boy's hunched body loved out of a stalk
The first song of his happiness, and the song woke
His heart to the darkness and into the sadness of joy.

Boy and frogs playing together become, in their primitive (or perhaps primeval) communication, as one. The boy's "frogness" can be seen in his "hunched body," emphasized by the mention of "a shoulder's ache" and the "towering Illinois twilight." Clearly not as visceral or brutal in vocabulary and imagery as the later narrative, this poem nevertheless suggests that it is the animal nature of human beings that accesses the unconscious (here referred to as "the darkness") and brings wholeness to experience ("the sadness of joy").

Here, too, is an inkling that the boy's song flows from a place of suffering, just as the song that "blows across" the "sore, lolled tongue" of the dreaming poet of the "The Bear" flows from his wounded lurching across the tundra. "The Bear," oozing gustatory imagery, takes a darker, lonelier route than "First Song," but the two poems arrive at a similar life- and art-affirming destination.

Many of Kinnell's most celebrated poems keenly observe the animal kingdom. Besides the odoriferous he-bear splashing a trail of blood, there is a hen killed by weasels ("The Hen Flower"), a porcupine gutted while falling, wounded, from a tree branch ("The Porcupine"), a sow with fourteen suckling piglets ("St. Francis and the Sow"), and a mutating bird ("The Gray Heron"). The graphic descriptions of all these creatures are intended as heuristic paradigms to expand the reader's understanding of what it means to be an individuated human being.

MYSTICAL ELEMENTS

Documenting humanity's moments of wholeness is essential to Kinnell's mode. His universe, absent a Father God on whom to heap blame or credit for what has happened, what is happening, and what will happen, is lit instead by death's ever-burning candle. While Kinnell displays a rudimentary knowledge of Christian myth and ritual—using concepts such as "grace" and "agape" in some poems and making reference to Christ to provide a framework for a series of images, as he does in "To Christ Our Lord"—the hope and comfort he offers are based not in Christian orthodoxy but in a spirituality born of New Age pantheism. Christianity serves merely as fodder for irony.

Kinnell's evident belief in a vast, mystical union of all things existing, tangible and intangible, stretches from the "dark afternoons" that precede "a bright evening" in his early poem "Westport," to the fire blossoming out of wood that is "not *things dying* but just the *dying*," in "Flower of Five Blossoms" (*When One Has Lived a Long Time Alone*). It is from an acceptance of life as a brief journey that ends in nothingness—the loss of human identity and consciousness beyond the last breath, then a return into the creative essence of which all things earthly are derived—that Kinnell seems to draw the courage to live and die.

In "These Are Things I Tell To No One," from *Mortal Acts, Mortal Words*, Kinnell describes his "God" (his own quotation marks) as a "music of grace" that plays "from the other side of happiness." This music triggers worship of a "backward spreading brightness." In his 1969 essay *The Poetics of the Physical World*, he attributes to "something radiant in our lives" the human ability to "invent the realm of eternity." Yet he celebrates "another kind of glory," one that is connected to people's inability to enter the paradise they have invented.

That we last only for a time, that everyone around us lasts only for a time, that we know this, radiates a thrilling, tragic light on all our loves, all our relationships, even on those moments when the world, through its poetry, becomes almost capable of spurning time and death.

POETIC PHILOSOPHY

Besides reducing twentieth century divinity to human proportions, Kinnell's formula for earthbound transcendence formulates a modern reply to the argument, voiced as early as 1820 by Thomas Love Peacock, that

poetry has no intellectual place in a society committed to scientific progress. Through his form and content, Kinnell seems to say that postmodern poetry—the kind that employs frank language to describe common, everyday occurrences and objects in order to point to the sacredness of every part of creation—is necessary precisely *because* contemporary society is committed to scientific progress. Kinnell's poetics are grounded in a philosophy that affirms Percy Bysshe Shelley's *A Defense of Poetry* (wr. 1821, pb. 1840), which was written in response to Peacock's *The Four Ages of Poetry* (1820). Shelley pointed out that scientific discoveries could very well lead to a worsening of social inequities, absent humanitarian considerations.

Kinnell nurtures his readers' admiration for and identification with nature's workings through the use of metaphor. Through an intermingling of images—those that represent humans' inner struggle to transcend the suffering that comes with being mortal with those, both gentle and grisly, that represent outward processes drawn from nature, the city landscape, or his ordinary domestic routine—Kinnell formulates the argument that human transcendence comes in fleeting moments of surrender to primitive instincts arising from the unconscious.

"THE AVENUE BEARING THE INITIAL OF CHRIST INTO THE NEW WORLD" AND "VAPOR TRAIL REFLECTED IN THE FROG POND"

Aesthetic considerations rank high for Kinnell; his poems overflow with provocative imagery. He often communicates with his readers through the medium of song—not using the notes of the musical scale but arranging his words in indefinite verbal melodies, and even sometimes deliberately organizing his poems in accord with musical structures. Thus he appeals to his reader's inner rhythms without resorting to what he considers to be the inadequate patterns of formal meter and rhyme.

"The Avenue Bearing the Initial of Christ into the New World" and "Vapor Trail Reflected in the Frog Pond" typify yet another of Kinnell's approaches, an approach heavily Whitmanesque, designed to facilitate awakenings. Both address a social issue by painting a graphic picture of a spoiled environment. In terms of music, both reverberate with auditory descriptions.

The former is a long poem, organized in fourteen sections, incorporating onomatopoeia, one of Kinnell's preferred techniques. The three brief sections of "Vapor Trail Reflected in the Frog Pond," like musical suites all organized around a central theme, describe the reflection left by a bomber flying over a frog pond and move on to ruminate on the American involvement in the Vietnam War. The first suite introduces the scene: The speaker tells what he sees at the frog pond. The second suite branches away to record the speaker's mental journey, suggested by impressions of sounds from the racially torn South and a battlefield. The final suite, a wrenching tour de force, focuses on the anguish war brings, the violence it does to spirit as well as to flesh. Nevertheless, the poem suggests an ultimate triumph of nature in the cycle of life and death. "They gaze up at the drifting sun that gives us our lives," says Kinnell, "seed dazzled over the footbattered blaze of the earth."

Such images of light and fire—"the drifting sun," "seed dazzled," "blaze of the earth"—are characteristic of Kinnell. Secular glory shines throughout his poetry in variations on these two symbols of a mystic earthly presence awaiting recognition. In his poems things flash, sparkle, glisten, glitter, glimmer, glow, smolder, or burn.

"That Silent Evening"

In "That Silent Evening," the speaker tells how he and a lover once talked in bed in flickering firelight. Their talk is "low, silent," like the snowfall outside, and the firewood is giving up its ghosts "without a cackle," suggestive of intimacy rather than conversation. The speaker knows that he will remember the closeness of that fragment of time. Tracks the two have made in the snow become a metaphor for their relationship's journey, the weaving together and apart marking stretches of alienation interrupted by moments of completeness and bliss.

Branches "*scritch, scritch, scritch*," a chickadee "*dee, dee, dees*"—small sounds that suggest noumenal communications from the creative mystic fire that underlies everything. All the happenings of the world are reduced to a scratch in a field of snow. These auditory and visual images of impermanence are reminders of the ultimate insignificance of individual actions and the fu-

tility of ignoring the "end" built into the "beginning" of everything. The speaker muses that words come close to easing the worry over the inevitable loss of relationship ahead, by death if not by fracture, for whichever of the two lovers comes in need of reassurance. Yet it is in the anticipated remembering of the unspoken, loving oneness, that time past, present, and future overlaps. "The light/ that lives inside the eclipse doubles and shines/ through the darkness the sparkling that heavens the earth." Once again, Kinnell's "backward spreading brightness" penetrates the modern gloom to provide transcendence.

Kinnell has been criticized for "pseudo-shamanism," repetition of devices, overuse of certain tag words, and sentimentality. Yet few modern writers command such widespread respect among their peers, and almost none can match his skill in creating bold and beautiful endings. His mastery of the graphic, emotion-laden image and his ability to marshal language to create subtle yet powerful music ensure his place among modern American poets.

Other major works

LONG FICTION: *Black Light*, 1966, revised 1980.

SHORT FICTION: "The Permanence of Love," 1968.

NONFICTION: *The Poetics of the Physical World*, 1969; *Walking Down the Stairs: Selections from Interviews*, 1978; *Thoughts Occasioned by the Most Insignificant of Human Events*, 1982.

TRANSLATIONS: *Bitter Victory*, 1956 (René Hardy); *The Poems of François Villon*, 1965, rev. 1977; *On the Motion and Immobility of Douve*, 1968 (Yves Bonnefoy); *Lackawanna Elegy*, 1970 (Yvan Goll); *The Essential Rilke*, 1999.

CHILDREN'S LITERATURE: *How the Alligator Missed Breakfast*, 1982.

EDITED TEXT: *The Essential Whitman*, 1987.

Bibliography

Bly, Robert. "Galway Kinnell: The Hero and The Old Farmer." In *American Poetry: Wildness and Domesticity*. New York: Harper & Row, 1990. This is a revised version of the essay that originally appeared in Howard Nelson's *On the Poetry of Galway Kinnell: The Wages of Dying* (1987). The changes from its earlier form clarify meaning, and Bly's introductory chapters in the book set the stage for his thoughtful analysis of Kinnell's poetic voice.

Calhoun, Richard J. *Galway Kinnell*. New York: Twayne, 1992. Like other volumes in this series, a sturdy, safe introduction presenting biographical information and covering the major stages and works in Kinnell's career. Places him in the tradition of Theodore Roethke and Robert Lowell. Primary and secondary bibliographies.

Goldensohn, Lorrie. "Approaching Home Ground: Galway Kinnell's *Mortal Acts, Mortal Words*." *The Massachusetts Review* 25 (Summer, 1984): 303-321. After unraveling several of Kinnell's captured moments, Goldensohn lays them beside his professed philosophy and finds serious conflicts. Especially problematical, she points out, are the deficiencies in Kinnell's treatment of women. Goldensohn's feminist perspective provokes new questions and provides new insights.

Kleinbard, David. "Galway Kinnell's Poetry of Transformation." *The Centennial Review* 30 (Winter, 1986): 41-56. While Kleinbard focuses exclusively on Kinnell's *The Book of Nightmares*, exploring its relationship with Whitman's "Song of Myself" and Rainer Maria Rilke's *Duineser Elegien* (1923, *Duino Elegies*, 1930), his explication of language and image provides a paradigm to follow in reaching under Kinnell's surface rhythms for the unifying context of meaning.

Maceira, Karen. "Galway Kinnell: A Voice to Lead Us." *Hollins Critic* 32, no. 4 (October, 1995): 1-15. Maceira takes the occasion of *Imperfect Thirst* to present a shrewd and sympathetic assessment of Kinnell's growth as an artist.

Nelson, Howard, ed. *On the Poetry of Galway Kinnell: The Wages of Dying*. Ann Arbor: University of Michigan Press, 1987. This indispensable book is a collection of excerpts from previously published book reviews and articles together with essays—overviews, appraisals, analyses of specific poems, and a particularly insightful reminiscence—written specifically for the project. Writers include Charles Molesworth, Louise Bogan, Harold Bloom, Donald Davie, Joseph Bruchac, and Tess Gallagher. A chro-

nology and an extensive bibliography provide interesting and useful information.

Taylor, Granville. "From Irony to Lyricism: Galway Kinnell's True Voice." *Christianity and Literature* 37 (Summer, 1988): 45-54. Taylor explores Kinnell's emphasis on immanence over transcendence and the evolution of his form of grace. For readers interested in reconciling Kinnell's rejection of traditional Christian myths with orthodoxy, Taylor offers a solution.

Tuten, Nancy Lewis, ed. *Critical Essays on Galway Kinnell*. New York: G. K. Hall, 1996. Morris Dickstein, Mary Kinzie, Jay Parini, and Richard Tillinghast are some of the powerhouse commentators whose responses to Kinnell's work are gathered here. A judicious, balanced selection.

Zimmerman, Lee. *Intricate and Simple Things: The Poetry of Galway Kinnell*. Chicago: University of Illinois Press, 1987. Zimmerman's study is divided into five chapters and an epilogue, each of which focuses on one of Kinnell's collections, ending with *The Past*. Especially helpful are the author's discussions of the oppositions that form the heart of Kinnell's work, the literary context in which the work has evolved, and the effect on his message of the gradually increasing distance of the poet from his subject. An index facilitates use of this book for researching specific topics.

Virginia Starrett,
updated by Philip K. Jason

THOMAS KINSELLA

Born: Dublin, Ireland; May 4, 1928

PRINCIPAL POETRY
The Starlit Eye, 1952
Three Legendary Sonnets, 1952
The Death of a Queen, 1956
Poems, 1956
Another September, 1958, revised 1962
Moralities, 1960

Poems and Translations, 1961
Downstream, 1962
Six Irish Poets, 1962
Wormwood, 1966
Nightwalker and Other Poems, 1968
Poems, 1968 (with Douglas Livingstone and Anne Sexton)
Tear, 1969
Butcher's Dozen, 1972
A Selected Life, 1972
Finistere, 1972
Notes from the Land of the Dead and Other Poems, 1972
New Poems, 1973
Selected Poems, 1956-1968, 1973
Vertical Man, 1973
The Good Fight: A Poem for the Tenth Anniversary of the Death of John F. Kennedy, 1973
One, 1974
A Technical Supplement, 1976
Song of the Night and Other Poems, 1978
The Messenger, 1978

Fifteen Dead, 1979
One and Other Poems, 1979
Peppercanister Poems, 1972-1978, 1979
Poems, 1956-1973, 1979
One Fond Embrace, 1981, 1988
Songs of the Psyche, 1985
Her Vertical Smile, 1985
St. Catherine's Clock, 1987
Blood and Family, 1988
Poems from Centre City, 1990
Madonna and Other Poems, 1991
Open Court, 1991
From Centre City, 1994
The Collected Poems, 1956-1994, 1996
The Pen Shop, 1997
The Familiar, 1999
Godhead, 1999
Littlebody, 2000
Citizen of the World, 2000

Thomas Kinsella

OTHER LITERARY FORMS

In addition to his own poetry, Thomas Kinsella has published a large body of verse translated from the Irish. This work, which has been going on throughout his career, is most notably embodied in his celebrated version of the eighth century Irish epic *Táin bó Cuailnge* (*The Táin*, 1969) and in *An Duanaire, 1600-1900: Poems of the Dispossessed* (1981; with Sean O Tuama). ("An duanaire," literally translated, means "the poemery.") An appreciation of the significance which Kinsella attaches to the Irish-language tradition of Irish poetry, and the magnitude of his commitment to it, is crucial to an overall sense of his achievement. His introduction to *The New Oxford Book of Irish Verse* (1986), which he edited, provides convenient access to Kinsella's thinking on the subject of the Irish-language poetic tradition. The attitude expressed in that introduction recapitulates earlier statements contained in the poet's small but influential body of cultural criticism.

ACHIEVEMENTS

Thomas Kinsella is one of the most important Irish poets to emerge since the end of World War II. By means of a restlessly experimental formal and aesthetic sense, broadly conceived themes, and relentless self-scrutiny and self-exposure, his work has raised him above all his Irish contemporaries and placed him in the forefront of his generation of poets writing in English.

In the context of contemporary Irish poetry, his work has an unwonted syntactical density, complexity of imagery, and dramatic intensity. Since modern Irish poetry in English is noted more for lyric grace than for tough-minded plumbing of existential depths, Kinsella's poetry gains in importance because of its originality. Its essential inimitableness, in turn, commands respect by virtue of the tenacity of vision it embodies.

In recognition of his uniqueness and commitment, Kinsella has received widespread critical acclaim and has won the Guinness Poetry Award in 1958 for *Another September* and the Irish Arts Council Triennial Book Award in 1961 for *Poems and Translations*. He is a four-time winner of the Denis Devlin Memorial Award, in 1964-1966, 1967-1969, 1988, and 1994. He has also held two Guggenheim Fellowships.

BIOGRAPHY

Thomas Kinsella was born in Dublin on May 4, 1928. His family background is typical of the vast majority of native Dubliners—Catholic in religious affiliation, left-tending Nationalist in politics and lower-middle class in social standing: the kind of background detailed with such loving despair by one of Kinsella's favorite authors, James Joyce, in the stories of *Dubliners* (1914). Thomas Kinsella's father worked at the Guinness brewery and was active in labor union matters.

Educated at local day schools, Kinsella received a scholarship to attend University College, Dublin, to read for a science degree. Before graduation, however, he left to become a member of the Irish civil service, in which he had a successful career as a bureaucrat, rising to the rank of assistant principal officer in the Department of Finance.

Kinsella left the civil service in 1965 to become artist in residence at Southern Illinois University. In 1970, he was appointed to a professorship of English at Temple University, a position he retained until 1990. He eventually would teach for one semester a year at Temple, spending the rest of the year in Dublin running the Peppercanister Press.

Founded in 1972, Peppercanister is the poet's private press. It was established, in the poet's own words "with the purpose of issuing occasional special items." As well as being a notable addition to the illustrious private and small tradition of Irish publishing, Peppercanister has allowed Thomas Kinsella to produce long poems on single themes and to carry out fascinating exercises in the area of the poetic sequence.

In 1976 Kinsella founded Temple University's School of Irish Tradition in Dublin, enabling him to continue dividing his time between the United States and Ireland. Since his retirement from teaching in 1990, he has continued his direction of Peppercannister Press, as well as the Dolmen and Cuala Presses, both in Dublin.

ANALYSIS

From the outset of his career, Thomas Kinsella has shown an unremitting preoccupation with large themes. Love, death, time, and various ancillary imponderables are persistently at the forefront of Kinsella's poetic activity. Such concerns beset all poets, no doubt, as well as all thinking beings. More often than not, Kinsella grapples with these overwhelming subjects without the alleviating disguise of metaphor, and he confronts them without the consolations of philosophy. Their reality consists of the profundity of the poet's human—and hence, frequently baffled and outraged—experience of them.

Even in Kinsella's early love lyrics, it is impossible for the poet merely to celebrate the emotion. He cannot view his subject without being aware of its problematical character—its temporariness and changeability. Thus, to identify Kinsella's themes, while initially informative, may ultimately be misleading. It seems more illuminating to consider his preoccupations, which a reader may label time or death, as zones of the poet's psychic experience, and to recognize that a Kinsella poem is, typically, an anatomy of psychic experience, a rhetorical reexperiencing, rather than a particularly conclusive recounting. Such a view would seem to be borne out by the forms which his poems typically assume. Their fractured look and inconsistent verse patterns (unavoidably but not imitatively reproducing the prosody of T. S. Eliot and Ezra Pound) suggest an idea still developing. As Kinsella writes in "Worker in Mirror, at His

Bench": "No, it has no practical application./ I am simply trying to understand something/ —states of peace nursed out of wreckage./ The peace of fullness, not emptiness."

An immediate implication of this approach to poetry is that it owes little or nothing to the poet's Irish heritage. His concerns are common to all humanity, and while the conspicuous modernism of his technique has, in point of historical fact, some Irish avatars (the unjustly neglected Denis Devlin comes to mind), these are of less significance for a sense of Kinsella's achievement and development than the manner in which he has availed himself of the whole canon of Anglo-American poetry. In fact, an interesting case could be made for Kinsella's poetry being an adventitious, promiscuous coalescence of the preoccupations of poets since the dawn of Romanticism. Such a case might well produce the judgment that one of the bases for Kinsella's general importance to the history of poetry in the postwar period is that his verse is a sustained attempt to inaugurate a post-Romantic poetic that would neither merely debunk its predecessor's fatal charms (as perhaps T. S. Eliot desired to do) nor provide them with a new repertoire of gestures and disguises (which seems to have been Ezra Pound's project). The effect of this judgment would be to place Kinsella in the company of another great Irish anti-Romantic of twentieth century literature, Samuel Beckett.

A more far-reaching implication of Kinsella's technique is that it provides direct access to the metaphysical core of those preoccupations. Often the access is brutally direct. Throughout, Kinsella repeats the refrain articulated in the opening section of "Nightwalker": "I only know things seem and are not good." This line strikes a number of characteristic Kinsella notes. Its unrelieved, declarative immediacy is a feature which becomes increasingly pronounced as his verse matures. There is a sense of the unfitness of things, of evil, of times being out of joint. The speaker is strikingly committed to his subjective view. The line contains a representative Kinsella ambiguity, depending on whether the reader pauses heavily after "seem": Is "are not good" entailed by, or opposed to, "seem"? Readers familiar with Kinsella will hear the line announce a telltale air of threat and of brooding introspection. There is also, perhaps, a faint suggestion of meditative quest in "Night-

walker," which occurs in other important Kinsella poems from the 1960's (such as "Baggot Street Deserta," "A Country Walk," and *Downstream*). Such an undertaking, however, is hardly conceived in hope and does not seem to be a quest for which the persona freely and gladly volunteers. Rather, it seems a condition into which he has been haplessly born.

It is not difficult to understand Kinsella's confession that his vision of human existence is that of "an ordeal." In fact, given the prevalence in his verse of ignorance, darkness, death, and the unnervingly unpredictable tidal movements of the unconscious—all frequently presented by means of apocalyptic imagery—there is a strong indication that the poet is doing little more than indulging his idea of "ordeal," despite the prosodic virtuosity and furious verbal tension which make the indulgence seem an authentic act of soul-baring. Such an evaluation, however, would be incomplete. Also evident is the poet's desire to believe in what he has called "the eliciting of order from experience." Kinsella's verse is a continuing experiment in the viability of the desire to retain such a belief and a commitment to negotiate the leap of artistic faith which alone is capable of overcoming the abyss of unjustifiable unknowing that is the mortal lot. The possibility of achieving that act of composed and graceful suspension is what keeps Kinsella's poetry alive and within the realm of the human enterprise.

Although Kinsella's oeuvre exemplifies, to a dauntingly impressive degree, persistence and commitment in the face of the virtually unspeakable abyss, it has gone through a number of adjustments and modifications. Taken as a whole, therefore, Kinsella's output may be considered an enlarged version of some of its most outstanding moments, a sophisticated system of themes and variations. In the words of the preface to *Wormwood*, "It is certain that maturity and peace are to be sought through ordeal after ordeal, and it seems that the search continues until we fail."

One of the most important adjustments to have occurred in the development of Kinsella's poetic career is his emergence from largely private, personal experience, primarily of love. His early poems, particularly those collected in *Another September* and *Downstream*, seem too often to conceive of experience as the struggle of the will against the force of immutable abstractions. While these poems respect the necessarily tense and tentative character of experience, they seem also to regard mere experience as a pretext for thought. These poems share with Kinsella's later work the desire to achieve distinctiveness through allegories of possibility. Yet their generally tight, conventional forms have the effect of limiting their range of possibilities. In addition, the typical persona of these poems seems himself an abstraction, a man with only a nominal context and without a culture.

DOWNSTREAM

By *Downstream*, such isolation was being questioned. The concluding line of this collection's title poem—"Searching the darkness for a landing place"— may be taken (although somewhat glibly) as a statement emblematic of much of Kinsella's early work. Yet the collection also contains poems which, while painfully acknowledging the darkness, consider it as an archaeological redoubt. One of the effects of this adjustment is that the poet's personal past begins to offer redemptive possibilities. In addition, and with more obvious if not necessarily more far-reaching effects, a generalized past, in the form of Irish history, becomes an area of exploration. It is not the case that Kinsella never examined the past prior to *Downstream* ("King John's Castle" in *Another September* is proof to the contrary). Now, however, to the powerful sense of the past's otherness which "King John's Castle" conveys is added a sense of personal identification.

The poem in *Downstream* which demonstrates this development in Kinsella's range (a development that occurred around the time that the poet was preparing *The Táin*, his translation of an eighth century Irish epic and a major work of cultural archaeology) is "A Country Walk." Here, the persona, typically tense and restless, finds himself alone, explicitly undomesticated, with nothing between him and the legacy of the past discernible in the landscape through which he walks. The poem does not merely testify to the influential gap between present and past (a crucial preoccupation in all modern Irish writing) but also enters into the past with a brisk openness and nonjudgmental tolerance. "A Country Walk" reads like a journey of discovery, all the more so since what is discovered is not subjected to facile glorification. The fact that the past is so securely embedded in the landscape of the poem suggests that history is in the

nature of things and that there is as much point in attempting to deny its enduring presence as there is in trying to divert the river which is, throughout the course of the poem, never out of the poet's sight. The poem ends, appropriately, on a note of continuity: "The inert stirred. Heart and tongue were loosed:/ 'The waters hurtle through the flooded night. . . .'"

If anything, the present is circumvented in "A Country Walk." To ensure that the reader is aware of this, Kinsella daringly uses echoes of Yeats's "Easter 1916" to show how antiheroic is contemporary Ireland and to emphasize that the country is still, to paraphrase a line from Yeats's "September 1913," fumbling in the greasy till. This moment in "A Country Walk" prefaces the understandable admission "I turned away." The interlude, however, draws attention to a noteworthy feature of Kinsella's verse: its satire. From the outset, Kinsella's work was capable of excoriation. The addition of local, often contemporary, Irish subject matter has created the opportunity for some scalding satirical excursions.

NIGHTWALKER AND OTHER POEMS

Perhaps the most notorious of these sallies is to be found in the long title poem of *Nightwalker and Other Poems*, a poem which, in many ways, is an illuminating counterpart to "A Country Walk." Here, the setting is urban, contemporary Dublin, and the speaker, lacking the briskness of his opposite number in "A Country Walk," refers to himself as "a vagabond/ Tethered." The demoralizing spectacle of modern life is the poem's subject. Nothing is spared. In particular, Kinsella's years in the civil service are the basis for a damning portrait of national ideals stultified and betrayed. This portrait goes so far as to include figures from Irish public and political life who, although distorted by the poet's satirical fury, remain eminently recognizable and still occupy the highest positions in the land. Each of the poem's numerous scenarios is exposed as hollow social charades, and in direct contrast to the sense of release felt at the end of "A Country Walk," this poem concludes on a note of anticlimax: The speaker fails to find anything of redemptive value in current conditions.

While Kinsella has by no means forsaken the satirical mode (as *Butcher's Dozen*, Peppercanister's first publication, makes vividly clear), his career has developed more fruitfully through exploring the pretexts and presuppositions of his need that poetry be a salvage operation, acknowledging existence's many disasters and the intimacy of their wreckage and through acknowledgment saving face. Thus, in *Notes from the Land of the Dead and Other Poems* and *New Poems* the past is personal and the poems seem like diagnoses of memory and origins. Just as the setting for many of these poems is the poet's childhood home, so the poems reveal what has to be internalized for the sake of comprehending one's native land. In these poems, the speaker is the absorbed witness of others' agony, not only the agony of the deathbed but also the equally unrelenting travail described in "Tear": "sad dullness and tedious pain/ and lives bitter with hard bondage."

A MEDITATIVE VOICE

The poems in *Notes from the Land of the Dead and Other Poems* are also noteworthy for their degree of interaction with one another. Earlier, in *Wormwood*, Kinsella produced a strict yet supple poetic sequence. Now, the idea of sequence reemerges and takes more fluid form, a technique which can be seen embryonically in the interrelated sections of "Nightwalker" and which finds mature embodiment in many of the Peppercanister poems. This greater access to range and flexibility has enabled the poet to be less dependent on the singular effects of the dramatic lyric, where, as noted, there seemed to be a considerable degree of pressure to will experience to denote purpose. As a result of an increasing commitment to formal and metrical variety, Kinsella's voice has become more authentically meditative, its brooding habit engendering a measure of containment rather than disenchantment. This voice is present not only in such important Peppercanister collections as *One*, *A Technical Supplement*, and *Song of the Night and Other Poems* but also in some of the superb individual poems these books contain, notably, *Finistere* (*One*) and "Tao and Unfitness at Inistiogue on the River Nore" (*Song of the Night and Other Poems*).

OCCASIONAL POEMS OF PEPPERCANISTER PRESS

It is not clear, however, that Kinsella established Peppercanister with the expectation that such wonderful poems would result. On the contrary, the press came into being because of the need to publish an uncharacteristic

Kinsella production, a poem written for a particular occasion. The poem in question, *Butcher's Dozen*, was written in response to the killing in the city of Derry, Northern Ireland, of thirteen civil rights demonstrators by British troops. This event took place on the afternoon of Sunday, January 30, 1972, a day which will live in infamy in the minds of Irish people. The poem's immediate occasion is the horrifying event, but its subtitle clarifies the line of attack taken by Kinsella. The subtitle, "A Lesson for the Octave of Widgery," names the lord chief justice of the United Kingdom, Lord Widgery, chairman of the essentially whitewashing court of inquiry set up to examine the event. Thus, *Butcher's Dozen* is a critique not only of the troops' action but also of the mind-set such actions denote. The poem's incisive and abrasive couplets enact an alternative language and disposition to that of the Lord Chief Justice's report. While, from an aesthetic standpoint, *Butcher's Dozen* is hardly Kinsella's greatest poem, its significance as a cultural document is indisputable and is reinforced by the explanatory background notes which Kinsella wrote to accompany it.

The other occasional poems contained in the Peppercanister series also have to do with significant deaths. In order of appearance, the poems are *A Selected Life*, *Vertical Man*, *The Good Fight: A Poem for the Tenth Anniversary of the Death of John F. Kennedy*, and *The Messenger*. It has become standard practice to regard *A Selected Life* and *Vertical Man* together, two independent but intimately related treatments of the one event, the untimely death of the poet's friend, Seán Ó Riada. Again, the issue of cultural significance arises. Ó Riada, as well as being an accomplished composer of classical music (*Vertical Man* is the title of one of his compositions for orchestra), was also an extraordinary influence on Irish folk musicians. His conception of the rich tradition and important heritage of Irish folk music was the direct inspiration of the internationally acclaimed group The Chieftains. More relevant to the development of Kinsella's career, Ó Riada's scholarly, pleasure-giving rehabilitation of a dormant legacy is an important counterpart to the poet's explorations in Irish-language poetry. As the penultimate stanza of *Vertical Man* has it: "From palatal darkness a voice/ rose flickering, and checked/ in glottal silence. The song/ articulated and pierced."

THE GOOD FIGHT

In the light of the public demeanor assumed in *Butcher's Dozen* and the greater degree of interplay between textural openness and formal control contained in both Ó Riada poems, Kinsella undertook his most ambitious public poem, *The Good Fight*. Not only is the poem's subject matter ambitious, in particular given how rare it is for Irish poets to seek subjects outside the ambit of their own culture and tradition (a rarity which younger Irish poets such as Derek Mahon would work to dismantle), but also, formally speaking, *The Good Fight* is one of Kinsella's more daring experiments.

As in the case of earlier Peppercanister poems on public themes, *The Good Fight* has an author's note attached, which begins with the remark, "With the death of Kennedy many things died, foolish expectations and assumptions, as it now seems." In a sense, the poem is a collage of contemporary desires, a view borne out by the numerous allusions to and quotations from Kennedy speeches and other sources from the period. Yet such a view is contradicted by two other features of the poem. The most obvious of these are the various quotations from Plato's *Politeia* (*Republic*, 1701) and *Nomoi* (*Laws*, 1804), which are used to counterpoint the poem's development. This classical reference has the effect of measuring Kennedy's fate against some nominal yet conventionally uncontroversial standard of age-old wisdom. This feature in turn is seen in terms of the pervasive sense of unfulfilled aftermath which pervades the poem. It seems remarkable that this achievement is so little known.

THE MESSENGER

The significant death in *The Messenger* is not that of a well-known figure but of the poet's father. This immensely moving document testifies to Kinsella's growth as an artist. The poem's subject, death, has been a constant presence in his work since "A Lady of Quality," in *Poems*, and has been treated variously in such accomplished and representative poems as "Dick King" and "Cover Her Face." *The Messenger*, however, dwells more on celebrating the life that preceded its occasion than on the death of a man desiring to possess his culture: "The eggseed Goodness/ that is also called/ Decency." The poet's redemptive power and his cultural as well as personal responsibility to discharge it are seen to consummate effect in this powerful, moving work.

BLOOD AND FAMILY AND POEMS FROM CENTRE CITY

Blood and Family, Kinsella's first publication from a major publisher since the 1979 *Peppercanister Poems, 1972-1978*, is a reprint of more recent Peppercanister publications. This volume is the next place non-Irish readers will have to go for new Kinsella material. The volume contains *The Messenger, Songs of the Psyche, Her Vertical Smile, Out of Ireland*, and *St. Catherine's Clock*. The decision to open the volume with a reprint of *The Messenger* is a good one, given that it sets the cultural tone and prosodic idiom for the remainder of the poems. At the same time, it may be said that this volume consolidates rather than enlarges Kinsella's reputation, not merely because of the familiarity of some of its contents but because of the tension which its title invokes. The sense of belonging to two disjunctive collectives, family and nation, is here articulated thematically but also in terms of form and metrics. The result is an emphatic, diverse restatement of themes of brokenness and incompleteness which have informed the poet's vision from virtually its inception. While these themes are addressed and expressed with Kinsella's typical vehement, tight-lipped energy, the impression remains one of ground being reworked as worked anew, of a poet revisiting old preoccupations in search of unfamiliar nuances.

In the case of *Poems from Centre City*, however, there is evidence of a slightly different Kinsella. The poems in this Peppercanister pamphlet address the state of contemporary Dublin in a much more direct way than hitherto, lacking the range and ambition of, for example, "Nightwalker," and presenting themselves more intimately, as more the products of occasions, than is customary with this poet. Metrically simple and verbally direct, they attempt to come to terms with the decay—physical, moral, and institutional—of Kinsella's native place. Decay as a subject is no stranger to Kinsella's imagination. Yet, despite the comparatively fresh perspective on the poet's concerns that *Poems from Centre City* provides, it should not be assumed that the collection is intended to be thought of as a polemic. The inclusion of a poem on W. H. Auden, one of Kinsella's most permanent influences, may be understood as a caution against the reader's comprehending *Poems from Centre City* as a narrowly activist set of statements on, for example, an environmental theme.

At the same time, the diagnostic—or at least exploratory—thrust of much of Kinsella's work is once again in evidence in this small sampling of his work. The formal range is restricted; the subject matter is largely drawn from the immediacy and adventitiousness of an attentive citizen's experience. A number of the poems are suggested by memory, though all succeed in avoiding either moralizing or sentimentality. In terms of accessibility and immediate effectiveness, *Poems from Centre City* are among the most appealing of Kinsella's late works.

In terms of intensity and commitment, as well as the fascinating odyssey of his development, Thomas Kinsella is clearly a poet worthy of the utmost respect. As to his honesty and artistic integrity, it seems appropriate to allow a verse from the preamble to *The Messenger* to speak for those qualities: "The hand conceives an impossible Possible/ and exhausts in mid-reach./ What could be more natural?"

THE PEN SHOP

The 1990's found Kinsella publishing a number of poetry collections, often slight in size but heavy in themes and recollections. *The Pen Shop*, a small volume consisting of two sections titled "To the Coffee Shop," and "To the Pen Shop," focuses on the renewal of a poetic career late in the poet's life. Readers find Kinsella strolling through the streets of Dublin, visiting favorite haunts—the General Post Office, Grafton Street, the Guinness brewery, Trinity College—and seeing the specter of his father in every turn. He meanders to Nassau Street for "some of their best black refills" from the pen shop, and then finds himself at Bewley's, the city's famed tea and coffee shop. Rather than partake in tea or coffee, he instead consumes pills from a tin, needing the black draft of medicinal inspiration to enter his system "direct" with its taste of death, "foreign and clay sharp"; for only in this way may he be jolted into imaginative life and become the grand instrument of his muse's spectral writing: "The long body sliding in/ under my feet." Only then may he no longer be, like the other old men in Bewleys', "Speechless." Indeed, only then may he, like the first voices, "rising out of Europe,"

become "clear in calibre and professional,/ self chosen,/ rising beyond Jerusalem."

THE FAMILIAR AND GODHEAD

In 1999, Kinsella issued two short books simultaneously. *The Familiar* consists of the longer title poem and three short poems, all erotically charged and intimate, a style familiar to Kinsella readers. However, here the familiarity is of the flesh, with some mythical overtones. In the title poem, there are "demons over the door" and he has a "Muse on [his] mattress." When he goes to relieve himself during a night of lovemaking, he sees "three graces above the tank." The love scene ends with Kinsella invoking, in the volume's three short poems, a saint in "St. John's," a bride in "Wedding Night," and "Iris," the messenger of the gods.

Godhead consists of two short poems and a longer title poem. It has little in common thematically with *The Familiar*, since the two short poems are American seascapes ("High Tide: Amagansett" and "San Clemente, California: A Gloss") and the title poem is an evocation of the Holy Trinity of Father, Son, and Spirit. Yet both collections share a continuity in their terse, grainy, and stark poetic styles. His poems display a characteristic Irish style in their mythical and religious approach, yet at the same time are startlingly concrete and even irreverent. To speak of the crucifixion as "The Head hanging on one side,/ signifying abandonment" is gruesomely effective, while to end with the line "Dust of our lastborn" seems anticlimactic but haunting.

OTHER MAJOR WORKS

NONFICTION: *Davis, Mangan, Ferguson? Tradition and the Irish Writer*, 1970 (with W. B. Yeats); *The Dual Tradition: An Essay on Poetry and Politics in Ireland*, 1995.

TRANSLATIONS: *The Breastplate of Saint Patrick*, 1954 (revised as *Faeth Fiadha: The Breastplate of Saint Patrick*, 1957); *Longes mac n-Usnig, Being the Exile and Death of the Sons of Usnech*, 1954; *Thirty-three Triads, Translated from the XII Century Irish*, 1955; *The Táin*, 1969 (of *Táin bó Cuailnge*); *An Duanaire, 1600-1900: Poems of the Dispossessed*, 1981 (with Sean O Tuama).

EDITED TEXT: *The New Oxford Book of Irish Verse*, 1986.

BIBLIOGRAPHY

Abbate Badin, Donatella. *Thomas Kinsella*. New York: Twayne, 1996. An introductory biography and critical interpretation of selected works by Kinsella. Includes bibliographical references and index.

Harmon, Maurice. *The Poetry of Thomas Kinsella*. Atlantic Highlands, N.J.: Humanities Press, 1974. The author provides an overview of many of Kinsella's achievements, as well as helpful background information. Kinsella's preoccupation with the Irish language is also dealt with, and close readings of the major poems are offered. In addition, the poet's prosodical originality is analyzed. A valuable introductory guide.

John, Brian. "Irelands of the Mind: The Poetry of Thomas Kinsella and Seamus Heaney." *Canadian Journal of Irish Studies* 15 (December, 1989): 68-92. An analysis of the cultural implications of the two most important Irish poets of their generation. Kinsella's severe lyricism is contrasted with Heaney's more sensual verse. The two poets' senses of place, time, and history are also examined. The visions of Ireland produced are important evidence of the contemporary debate about Irish national identity.

_____. *Reading the Ground: The Poetry of Thomas Kinsella*. Washington, D.C.: Catholic University of America Press, 1996. A comprehensive study of Kinsella's poetry. John explores the poet's development within both the Irish and the English contexts and defines the nature of his poetic achievement.

Johnston, Dillon. "Kinsella and Clarke." In *Irish Poetry After Joyce*. Notre Dame, Ind.: University of Notre Dame Press, 1985. Kinsella's debt to his most important Irish poetic mentor is discussed. The origins and thrust of Kinsella's satirical tendencies are identified and analyzed. The poet's standing in the tradition of modern Irish poetry is also evaluated. An essential contribution to recent Irish literary history.

McGuinness, Arthur E. "Fragments of Identity: Thomas Kinsella's Modernist Imperative." *Colby Library Quarterly* 23 (December, 1987): 186-205. The poet's debt to, in particular, T. S. Eliot's theory and practice of poetry is considered. Kinsella's prosody is located in the context of modernism. His emotional timbre is evaluated in the light of the same context. The essay valuably addresses Kinsella's international poetic influences.

O'Hara, Daniel. "An Interview with Thomas Kinsella." *Contemporary Poetry* 4, no. 1 (1981): 1-18. The most comprehensive of the small number of Kinsella interviews. The poet speaks freely about his various artistic concerns, concentrating in his poetic practice. The intellectual atmosphere is bracing. Kinsella's interiority and the question of its formal consequences receive much attention.

_____. "Love's Architecture: The Poetic Irony of Thomas Kinsella." *Boundary* 2, no. 9 (Winter, 1981): 123-135. An elaborate theoretical assessment of Kinsella's achievement. The essay's approach is indebted to the criticism of Harold Bloom. The chief focus is on the metaphysical dimension of Kinsella's lyrics. A rigorous, intense account of Kinsella's art.

Skloot, Floyd. "The Evolving Poetry of Thomas Kinsella." *New England Review* 18, no. 4 (Fall, 1997): 174-187. Skloot reviews *The Collected Poems, 1956-1994* and in the process examines Kinsella's evolving style and themes. Offers a good retrospective look at Kinsella's body of work.

George O'Brien,
updated by Sarah Hilbert

RUDYARD KIPLING

Born: Bombay, India; December 30, 1865
Died: Hampstead, London, England; January 18, 1936

PRINCIPAL POETRY

Schoolboy Lyrics, 1881
Echoes, 1884 (with Alice Kipling)
Departmental Ditties and Other Verses, 1886
Barrack-Room Ballads and Other Verses, 1892
The Seven Seas, 1896
An Almanac of Twelve Sports, 1898
Recessional and Other Poems, 1899
The Five Nations, 1903

Collected Verse, 1907

A History of England, 1911 (with C. R. L. Fletcher)

Songs from Books, 1912

Sea Warfare, 1916

Twenty Poems, 1918

The Years Between, 1919

Rudyard Kipling's Verse: 1885-1918, 1919

Q. Horatii Flacci Carminum Librer Quintus, 1920 (with Charles L. Graves, A. D. Godley, A. B. Ramsay, and R. A. Knox)

Songs for Youth, 1924

Sea and Sussex from Rudyard Kipling's Verse, 1926

Songs of the Sea, 1927

Rudyard Kipling's Verse: 1885-1926, 1927

Poems, 1886-1929, 1929

Selected Poems, 1931

Rudyard Kipling's Verse: 1885-1932, 1933

Rudyard Kipling's Verse, 1940

OTHER LITERARY FORMS

Rudyard Kipling is best known for his short stories. His *Just So Stories* (1902), *The Jungle Book* (1894), and *The Second Jungle Book* (1895), are favorites with children and are among the most widely read collections of stories in the world. His novel *Kim* (1901) also ranks among the world's most popular books. Kipling's fiction, however, presents a critic with most of the problems that his verse presents, making it difficult to discuss one without the other. The fiction is often thought to be barbaric in content and representative of a discredited imperialistic point of view; too often, critics discuss Kipling's political views (which are often misrepresented) rather than his literary merits. Kipling's contempt for intellectualism makes him unfashionable in most critical circles, and those who admit to having admired him seem to be ashamed of their affection. Not all critics, however, have been ambiguous in their admiration of Kipling's work; especially since the 1960's, critics have made the short stories objects of serious study. In any case, Kipling's fiction has remained immensely popular from the late Victorian era to the present. It has been made into no fewer than thirteen motion pictures, including *Captains Courageous* (1937) and *The Jungle Book* (1942, 1967, and 1998). Kipling's fiction has the vigor and passion that appeal to the popular imagina-

tion, and a subtlety and brilliant prose style that are worthy of careful study.

ACHIEVEMENTS

Henry James called Rudyard Kipling a genius; T. S. Eliot called him a writer of verse who sometimes ascended to poetry. His *Departmental Ditties and Other Verses* brought him extravagant praise and fame. Some scholars assert that he was the world's best-known author from the 1890's to his death. Yet even his admirers have been uncertain of his achievement, particularly in poetry. Kipling often sang his poems while he composed them; they are often ballads or hymns, and all feature clear rhythms that urge a reader to read them aloud. Their surface themes are usually easy to understand; the language is clear and accessible to even casual readers.

Perhaps the accessibility of Kipling's verse is the source of the confusion; twentieth century critics have all too often regarded poetry that is popular among the

Rudyard Kipling, Nobel laureate in literature for 1907.
(© The Nobel Foundation)

great unwashed as automatically bad; obscurity has been the hallmark of much of the best of twentieth century poetry. Kipling's verse is informed by the Victorian masters, such as Alfred, Lord Tennyson, and Algernon Charles Swinburne. It is out of step with the modernist school, which may be why many readers think of Kipling as Victorian, even though he actively wrote and published into the 1930's; his autobiography appeared in 1937, the year after his death. His harsh views of ordinary people; his angry polemics, political conservatism, and lack of faith in so-called utopian societies; and the Cassandra-like prophecies of war which fill much of his verse, repel many aesthetes and political liberals. Kipling has been portrayed as a philistine. The truth is that he did not understand much of the social change of his lifetime, but he understood people, and in his verse he preserves the thoughts, emotions, hopes, and despairs of people usually ignored by poets. If one approaches his verse with an open mind, one will likely find brilliant prosody, excellent phrasing, surprising metaphors, and a poetic ethos that transcends literary and political fashion.

Kipling won the Nobel Prize for Literature in 1907. The award was, in part, a recognition of Kipling's worldwide appeal to readers; he touched more hearts and minds than anyone else of his generation. His work added phrases to the English language; few today realize that they paraphrase Kipling when they assert that "the female is deadlier than the male," or that "East is East and West is West."

BIOGRAPHY

Joseph Rudyard Kipling was born in Bombay, India, on December 30, 1865. His parents were John Lockwood Kipling and Alice (née Macdonald) Kipling. His father was then a sculptor and designer and was principal and professor of architectural sculpture of the School of Art at Bombay, and he later became curator of the museum at Lahore. His mother came from a family of accomplished women. John Lockwood Kipling set many of the high standards for literary skill that Rudyard endeavored to match in both fiction and poetry. Both parents encouraged their son's literary efforts and took pride in his achievements.

Except for a brief visit to England, Rudyard Kipling spent his first five years in India. In 1871 he was taken

with his sister Alice to England and left with Captain and Mrs. Holloway of Lorne Lodge in Southsea. After several unhappy years in the ungentle care of Mrs. Holloway, he left Lorne Lodge in 1877. In 1878, he was sent to United Services College in Devon. In 1882, he traveled to Lahore, where his father had found him a job as a reporter for the *Civil and Military Gazette*. He had seen little of his parents since 1871. Somewhat to his annoyance, he discovered that his parents had gathered the verses from his letters to them and had them published as *Schoolboy Lyrics* in 1881. In 1887, he joined the staff of the *Pioneer* of Allahabad, which he left in 1889. His experiences in England figure in many of his stories; his experiences as a journalist in India are reflected not only in his fiction but also in much of his best verse.

In 1888, Émile Édouard Moreau began The Indian Library, primarily to help Kipling and to capitalize on the young writer's talents. The first six volumes of the series consisted of Kipling's work. In 1889 Kipling traveled to Singapore, Hong Kong, Japan, through the United States, and to England. His *Departmental Ditties and Other Verses* was printed in England in 1890, and the response to his poetry moved him from the status of a promising young writer to the forefront not only of English letters but also of world literature. His writing from 1890 onward brought him wealth and lasting popularity. The initial praise of his work was extraordinary— in 1892, Henry James wrote to his brother William, "Kipling strikes me as personally the most complete man of genius (as distinct from fine intelligence) that I have ever known"—but by the 1900's he would suffer extraordinary abuse at the hands of the critics. Kipling married Caroline Starr Balestier in 1892 and moved to Brattleboro, Vermont, where her relatives lived. While living in the United States he had two daughters. Although he liked his home in Vermont, Kipling left the United States when his enmity with his brother-in-law became public and created a scandal. After some traveling, he returned to visit his mother-in-law; during a stay in New York he and his family fell ill; his wife, younger daughter Elsie, and baby son recovered quickly, but he nearly died and his elder daughter Josephine did die.

He settled at Rottingdean in England in 1897. His wife took charge of much of his family and social affairs, and A. P. Watt, a literary agent, handled his literary and business affairs. His life in Rottingdean was productive but isolated; as the years passed, he saw less and less of his literary friends. In 1907, to the chagrin of his detractors, he won the Nobel Prize in Literature. His poetry at the time warned England of impending war and of England's unpreparedness. When war began in 1914, his son, with his father's help, enlisted in the army. In late 1915, John Kipling was killed in a British attack during the Battle of Loos. From the end of World War I to his death, Kipling worked to perfect his literary art and vigorously expressed his opinions on politics and society. At the end of his life he wrote his autobiography and helped prepare the Sussex edition of his works. He died January 18, 1936, while embarking on a vacation. His ashes were buried in Westminster Abbey's Poets' Corner.

ANALYSIS

Rudyard Kipling's poetry is such a part of the culture of English-speaking people that one is hard put to approach his work without preconceived notions of its quality and content. In his own day, Kipling's poetry outraged many critics and provided handy epithets for politicians of many political leanings. Even today, scholars can be excited by his so-called racial and imperialistic topics. Myths thus abound. Kipling's verse is called racist; in fact, Kipling's verse repeatedly emphasizes that no one can rightfully be regarded superior to another on the basis of race or origin. "The White Man's Burden," he wrote, was to "Fill full the mouth of Famine/ And bid the sickness cease." Although imperialistic, the poem emphasizes not race but the obligations of Europeans and Americans to the oppressed peoples of the world.

"THE LAST OF THE LIGHT BRIGADE"

Kipling is said to glorify warfare by devoting much of his poetry to descriptions of the lives of soldiers; in fact, he shows war to be ugly and stupid. In "The Last of the Light Brigade," he portrays veterans of the Crimean War as destitute: "We leave to the streets and the workhouse the charge of the Light Brigade!" In the poem, Kipling calls attention to the differences between Tennyson's poetic description of the ill-fated charge and the degradation that characterized the soldiers' lives. Another myth is that Kipling's poetry is coarse and crude. The subject matter is, indeed, sometimes crude, but not the prosody. Even T. S. Eliot, who admired Kipling's

work, asserted that Kipling wrote good verse that occasionally ascended to poetry but that in general Kipling did not write poetry.

CRITICISM, FOUNDED AND UNFOUNDED

Some of the sources of misconceptions about Kipling's poetic achievement seem obvious: Casual or careless readings might glean only the surface remarks of subtle poems; Kipling's political poetry was and remains unpalatable to many people who condemn it on no other grounds than political distastefulness; his aggressive dislike of academics and admiration for men of action alienate many of those who would be likeliest to write about his poetry. Some of the negative myths are Kipling's fault. If one writes on the politics of the moment, one invites political interpretations of one's work.

Nevertheless, too much of the criticism of Kipling's poetry is clearly biased. Many rationales for denigrating the poetry seem contrived, as if covering reasons that would not bear exposure. After all, portraits of the hard lives of working people, as well as soldiers, dominate novels from Émile Zola to the present; such novels are often praised for their realism. One of the most highly regarded Anglo-American poets of the twentieth century, Ezra Pound, was a fascist who made propagandistic radio broadcasts from Italy during World War II. His avowed racism is well known and is as unpalatable to well-informed and compassionate people as anything to be found in the work of Kipling. Indeed, Kipling deplored Nazi Germany and dictatorships in general. Yet Pound was fashionable; Kipling was not.

Kipling's unfashionableness has its origins in two important aspects of his poetry: His versification was clear and usually unadorned, and his subjects were usually plain, working-class people. He began his career in the Victorian era, and his lyrical and narrative poetry has more in common with the styles of Tennyson, Robert Browning, and Swinburne than it has with the styles that have been predominant in a more modern age. One of the important aspects of modernism in poetry was the emphasis on metaphor; metaphors were used to make such works as Eliot's *The Waste Land* (1922) hauntingly remote from casual reading. Critics came to expect good poetry to demand close and sometimes prolonged reading in order for one to understand even the most basic meanings of the verse.

"LOOT"

Kipling's approach to his poetry was neither better nor worse than that of his later contemporaries; it was merely different, because he aimed for an audience other than the literary elite. Poetry had been a genre for popular reading; Kipling kept it such. His best poetry will reward close reading by perceptive readers; it will also reward the unskilled or casual reader with a basic surface meaning. For example, "Loot" provides a basic discussion of techniques for looting; the persona—the poem's speaker—says, "always work in pairs—/ It 'alves the gain, but safer you will find." A quick reading elicits the picture of a lowly soldier providing a description of an ugly but realistic aspect of war (and provides ammunition against Kipling for anyone who is determined to misread the poem as somehow glorifying looting). A close reading of the poem, however, reveals a careful use of language; Kipling uses his knowledge of soldiers and their ballads to give his persona an authentic voice. One will also discover a picture of the mindless violence and degradation of war at the level of the common foot soldier. Kipling's style was out of step with the literary movement of his day; it was judged by the wrong standards and often still is.

VICTORIANS AND COMMON FOLK

Poetry has traditionally been regarded as the elite of literary genres. The term *poet* was reserved in the sixteenth, seventeenth, and eighteenth centuries for those who had excelled in literature; it was a term of honor to which writers aspired. Poetry has been thought of as appropriate to high aspirations and great ideas; it has been considered "elevating." The Victorians added the notion that poetry was morally uplifting and that a poet was obliged to discuss high topics in grand language; thus, biblical phrasing and high-sounding archaisms such as "thee" and "thou" lingered in nineteenth century poetry. No matter how much they were involved with the literary revolutions of their time, Kipling's contemporaries were children of the Victorians. Many of the most admired poems of the first three decades of the twentieth century focused on the Arthurian legends or revived Latin poetic traditions.

Kipling's poetry, in contrast, focuses on common people, the active people whose raw manner of dealing with the world most interested him. Soldiers, as the frequent vanguard of the British Empire and the products of the laboring classes, were often subjects of Kipling's poetry; laborers themselves were also often the subject of his verse. Kipling gave these people voices; his keen insight made his language strikingly acute. It is coarse, harsh, and elemental. In addition, the poetry by which he is best known is in the ballad form. The ballad is a lyrical folk song that grows and changes with use and custom; it is heard in bars, at country fairs, and in the barracks of soldiers. Kipling's use of the ballad explains in part Eliot's judgment that Kipling is a verse-writer instead of a poet; the form is believed by some scholars to be beneath poetry.

Thus, elitism has had much to do with negative responses to Kipling; critics seem to believe that Kipling has degraded verse. Even though he was a conservative with some Victorian notions of poetry, Kipling was ahead of his time. Egalitarianism became one of the significant movements in the twentieth century; literacy burgeoned, as did access to literature. Kipling wrote for the broad literate mass of people; he gave voices to people who were generally left out of poetry, and he did not romanticize them. A soldier's achievement is to survive one more day; a laborer's achievement is to feed himself one more day. Their contempt for those who are not physically active fits well with Kipling's own disgust with aesthetes who are out of touch with much that is thought and done by those who provide the foundations for civilization.

"THE WAY THROUGH THE WOODS" AND "CITIES AND THRONES AND POWERS"

Kipling's verse is highly crafted poetry. It uses metaphors and prosody in unusual ways, but this is a strength, not a weakness. Kipling's mastery of metaphor is apparent, for example, in "The Way Through the Woods," which describes an eroded road that was closed some seventy years before. On its surface, the poem offers a wistful description of the encroachment by the wilderness on a road no longer used. It is more than that, however; there is an eeriness in its description of "coppice and heath," "ring-dove broods," and "trout-ringed pools," which all utterly hide a road that makes its presence felt only in echoes of the past. The lost road and the woods that have covered it are metaphors for the passage of time and the transitoriness of human works. The theme of the fragility of human achievements is an important one in poetry; in "The Way Through the Woods," Kipling makes the theme mystical and haunting.

The near futility of human endeavors when confronting time is a common motif of Kipling's work. Although "The Way Through the Woods" is remote in tone and metaphor, Kipling is perfectly willing to be blunt—and still metaphorical. In "Cities and Thrones and Powers" he uses flowers as metaphors:

> Cities and Thrones and Powers
> Stand in Time's eye,
> Almost as long as flowers,
> Which daily die:

The poem continues and turns tragedy into triumph:

> But, as new buds put forth
> To glad new men,
> Out of the spent and unconsidered Earth
> The Cities rise again.

Few readers would have trouble understanding the basic metaphor: Flowers die but leave seeds that grow into new flowers, and cities do the same. Even Kipling's eccentric phrase "Almost as long as flowers" is within easy reach of the unsophisticated reader: In the vastness of time, cities exist only briefly. The surface meanings of the central metaphor do not preclude subtlety. The transitoriness of "Cities and Thrones and Powers" is a melancholy topic, one that other poets have used to show the vanity of human achievements. Percy Bysshe Shelley's "Ozymandias" is the archetypal expression of the theme; a pedestal alone in the desert bears an almost meaningless inscription: "My name is Ozymandias, king of kings:/ Look on my works, ye Mighty, and despair!" Shelley adds: "Nothing beside remains." A city and civilization are reduced to desert. Kipling takes the same sad theme, attaches it to flowers, making the frail plants bear the weight of civilization, and in flowers he reveals that seeming transitoriness is in fact a cycle of renewal. "Time," he says, "Ordains . . . That in our very death,/ And burial sure,/ Shadow to shadow, well persuaded, saith,/ See how our works endure!" In the deaths of human works are the seeds of new works: One civilization begets another.

Kipling's interest in the passing and survival of civilizations also extended to current events. In "The Dykes" of 1902, he ponders the dangers to Britain posed by the militancy of Europe. "These are the dykes our fathers made: we have never known a breach," he says. The people of Britain have built protections against their enemies, but through neglect the "dykes" might be broken. "An evil ember bedded in ash—a spark blown west by the wind . . ./ We are surrendered to night and the sea—the gale and the tide behind!" Kipling the prophet uses metaphor to warn of war. "The Dykes" is dynamic and threatening; history has shown its warning to be apt.

"GUNGA DIN"

Kipling's narrative poetry is probably his best known. It includes "Gunga Din" and "The Ballad of East and West," both of which discuss British imperialism and cultural differences and are thus unfashionable. "Gunga Din" is as well known a poem as exists in English. In it Gunga Din, a water bearer for British soldiers in India, faithfully serves his masters and saves the life of the poem's narrator—giving up his own life in the process. Kipling uses the rhythm of the ballad form to create strikingly memorable phrases, including the last lines:

> You Lazarushian-leather Gunga Din!
> Though I've belted you and flayed you,
> By the livin' Gawd that made you,
> You're a better man than I am, Gunga Din!

The language is raw and the verse melodic; the combination is powerful. Gunga Din's life is shown to be miserable, and his masters are shown as beastly, but Gunga Din is revealed as having a noble quality that Kipling valued; Gunga Din cares enough for his fellow men to die for them. Thus, the last line summarizes the central theme of the poem; Gunga Din is the better man.

"THE BALLAD OF EAST AND WEST"

In a similar vein, "The Ballad of East and West" shows that all men can understand one another in the fundamental test of courage:

> Oh, East is East and West is West, and never the twain
>   shall meet,
> Till Earth and Sky stand presently at God's great
>   Judgment Seat;
> But there is neither East nor West, Border, nor Breed,
>   nor Birth,
> When two strong men stand face to face, though they
>   come from the ends of the earth!

Kipling admired men of action and physical courage. He asserted that men can communicate on fundamental levels that transcend the veneer of culture. In "The Ballad of East and West" two strong men are brought face to face, their differences seemingly beyond hope of peaceful resolution. They discover that they are alike and not as different as others would believe. Beginning as enemies, they part as friends.

"THE ABSENT-MINDED BEGGAR"

Kipling dealt with large metaphysical ideas, with the cycles of civilizations and the threats to Western civilization, yet for all his great themes, Kipling was at home with subjects no more lofty than the ordinary person's hope for a better future. In "The Absent-Minded Beggar," for example, Kipling reminds his readers of the hard lot of the dependents of the soldiers who fought in the Boer War. "When you've finished killing Kruger with your mouth,/ Will you kindly drop a shilling in my little tamborine/ For a gentleman in khaki order South?" The poem was written to help raise money for the needs of the families of the soldiers. The tone is sympathetic but honest. The British soldier has "left a lot of little things behind him!" The "little things" include his children—not necessarily legitimate—wives, lovers, girl-friends, and debts. The families will "live on half o' nothing . . . 'Cause the man that earns the wage is ordered out." The soldier is "an absent-minded beggar, but he heard his country call." Kipling's language demonstrates his understanding of his subject. The poem reveals the fundamental Kipling—not imperialist, not prophet, not poet playing with great poetic conceits—but a poet who understands people and cares about them. Few writers can be honestly said to have cared more about their subjects than Kipling.

Long after the politics of his day are forgotten and his polemics have become of interest only to literary historians, Kipling's essential efforts will still have meaning. Readers who approach Kipling's verse with a love for poetry can still declare as did scholar David Masson to his students at Edinburgh in 1890, while holding a copy of "Danny Deever," "Here's Literature! Here's Literature at last!"

OTHER MAJOR WORKS

LONG FICTION: *The Light That Failed*, 1890; *The Naulahka: A Story of East and West*, 1892 (with Wolcott Balestier); *Captains Courageous: A Story of the Grand Banks*, 1897; *Kim*, 1901.

SHORT FICTION: *Quartette*, 1885 (with John Lockwood Kipling, Alice Macdonald Kipling, and Alice Kipling); *Plain Tales from the Hills*, 1888; *Soldiers Three: A Collection of Stories*, 1888; *The Story of the Gadsbys*, 1888; *In Black and White*, 1888; *Under the Deodars*, 1888; *The Phantom 'Rickshaw and Other Tales*, 1888; *Wee Willie Winkie and Other Child Stories*, 1888; *The Courting of Dinah Shadd and Other Stories*, 1890; *The City of Dreadful Night and Other Places*, 1890; *Mine Own People*, 1891; *Life's Handicap*, 1891; *Many Inventions*, 1893; *The Jungle Book*, 1894; *The Second Jungle Book*, 1895; *Soldier Tales*, 1896; *The Day's Work*, 1898; *Stalky and Co.*, 1899; *Just So Stories*, 1902; *Traffics and Discoveries*, 1904; *Puck of Pook's Hill*, 1906; *Actions and Reactions*, 1909; *Rewards and Fairies*, 1910; *A Diversity of Creatures*, 1917; *Land and Sea Tales for Scouts and Guides*, 1923; *Debits and Credits*, 1926; *Thy Servant a Dog*, 1930; *Limits and Renewals*, 1932; *Collected Dog Stories*, 1934.

NONFICTION: *American Notes*, 1891; *Beast and Man in India*, 1891; *Letters of Marque*, 1891; *The Smith Administration*, 1891; *A Fleet in Being: Notes of Two Trips with the Channel Squadron*, 1898; *From Sea to Sea*, 1899; *Letters to the Family*, 1908; *The New Army in Training*, 1914; *France at War*, 1915; *The Fringes of the Fleet*, 1915; *Sea Warfare*, 1916; *Letters of Travel, 1892-1913*, 1920; *The Irish Guards in the Great War*, 1923; *A Book of Words*, 1928; *Souvenirs of France*, 1933; *Something of Myself: For My Friends Known and Unknown*, 1937; *Uncollected Prose*, 1938 (2 volumes); *Rudyard Kipling to Rider Haggard: The Record of a Friendship*, 1965 (Morton N. Cohen, editor).

MISCELLANEOUS: *The Sussex Edition of the Complete Works in Prose and Verse of Rudyard Kipling*, 1937-1939 (35 vols.).

BIBLIOGRAPHY

Carrington, Charles E. *Rudyard Kipling: His Life and Work*. 3d ed. London: Macmillan, 1978. This detailed study of Rudyard Kipling as a man of letters begins and ends by ranking Kipling with Daniel Defoe and Charles Dickens, as a popular writer whose appeal has never waned. Still the standard biography, it contains a chronology, a genealogical chart, a bibliography of printed and unprinted sources, notes, useful appendices, and an index.

Gilbert, Elliot L., ed. *Kipling and the Critics.* New York: New York University Press, 1965. A selection of classic essays about Kipling with a brief but detailed survey of the history of Kipling's criticism. The formidable array of critics includes T. S. Eliot, Bonamy Dobree, and Lionel Trilling. The essays by Eliot and Dobree in particular were responsible for revivals of interest in Kipling.

Harrison, James. *Rudyard Kipling.* Boston: Twayne, 1982. In this useful volume, Harrison divides Kipling's life into three periods; within each, he groups the stories thematically to show Kipling's preoccupations. Harrison sees more poetry in Kipling's prose than in his verse. The poems' didacticism regarding views many consider outdated and distasteful, he argues, will prevent them from regaining critical regard. The text contains notes and references, a bibliography, and an index.

Lycett, Andrew. *Rudyard Kipling.* London: Weidenfeld and Nicolson, 1999. Lycett's exhaustive biography provides invaluable insight into the life and work of Kipling. Includes bibliographical references and index.

Ricketts, Harry. *Rudyard Kipling: A Life.* New York: Carroll & Graf, 2000. Ricketts brings a fresh and sympathetic eye to Kipling's career. Ricketts brings vibrantly to life the diverse worlds of imperialist India and Victorian London that both inspired and betrayed Kipling's genius.

Tompkins, J. M. S. *The Art of Rudyard Kipling.* 2d ed. Lincoln: University of Nebraska Press, 1965. One of the best and most comprehensive critical assessments of Kipling's work. Focuses on the timeless human and moral themes in Kipling's fiction and verses and on his craftsmanship. Supplemented by an index and a list of the tales, essays and verses discussed in this study, along with their dates of publication and the sources in which they appear.

Wilson, Angus. *The Strange Ride of Rudyard Kipling: His Life and Works.* New York: Viking Press, 1977.

In this indispensable source, Wilson combines criticism and biography. He argues that while Kipling and his work may have suffered from his fear of self-knowledge, few writers have gone outside the usual range in so many different directions with such skill. References and an index supplement the text.

Kirk H. Beetz;
bibliography updated by the editors

LINCOLN KIRSTEIN

Born: Rochester, New York; May 4, 1907
Died: New York, New York; January 5, 1996

PRINCIPAL POETRY
Low Ceiling, 1935
Rhymes of a Pfc, 1964, revised and enlarged, 1967, 1980
The Poems of Lincoln Kirstein, 1987

OTHER LITERARY FORMS

Lincoln Kirstein published one autobiographical novel, *Flesh Is Heir: An Historical Romance* (1932), numerous books on the history of the ballet and ballet appreciation; and articles on his life and friendships. He cofounded and served as coeditor of *Hound and Horn* magazine, a literary periodical, while an undergraduate student at Harvard University in the late 1920's.

ACHIEVEMENTS

As a poet, Lincoln Kirstein is best known for *Rhymes of a Pfc,* which poet W. H. Auden described as the most honest appraisal of life during World War II. Kirstein received the Presidential Medal of Freedom in 1984 and the National Medal of Arts in 1985 for his career accomplishments as the founder of the American School of Ballet and the New York City Ballet, among other dance organizations.

BIOGRAPHY

Lincoln Kirstein was born in Rochester, New York, to Louis E. and Rose Stein Kirstein. His family later moved to Massachusetts. Kirstein's father was the head of the Boston Public Library. Kirstein's mother was a daughter of the Stein family, owners of the Stein-Bloch department stores in Rochester. Kirstein attended Phillips Exeter and graduated from the Berkshire School. Upon gaining admission to Harvard, he deferred for a year, starting in 1926, to work a year in the Connick stained-glass factory in Boston. A sequence of short poems in *Low Ceiling* records his experiences.

As a student at Harvard, Kirstein encountered such teachers as Alfred North Whitehead, whose lectures on metaphysics Kirstein attended. He was not a very dedicated student, but he had a way of absorbing culture and information just by being in conversation with people more learned than he or who had different experiences and backgrounds. He said reading Charles H. Grandgent, who translated Dante for the general reader, was the most important of his academic and literary experiences.

Kirstein formed two arts societies before he graduated from Harvard in 1930. The first was for the literary magazine *Hound and Horn*, which he coedited with Varian Fry, starting in 1927, with its title taken from the poetry of Ezra Pound, and in 1928, he started the Harvard Society for Contemporary Art. *Hound and Horn* featured writing by many important literary figures, including Ezra Pound, Yvor Winters, and Seán O'Faoláin. It was admired by T. S. Eliot and favorably reviewed in the United States and the United Kingdom.

In 1931, Kirstein moved to Manhattan, and in January, 1934, after persuading choreographer George Balanchine to come to America, Kirstein started the School of American Ballet. In 1941, Kirstein married Fidela Cadmus. For the rest of his life, he was among the most prominent figures in the New York performing arts world. Among his civic duties, Kirstien was the chairman of the Pierpont Morgan Library's Council of Fellows in the late 1950's and was an avid antique collector, especially of William Shakespeare memorabilia. His correspondence with book and antique dealer George Heywood Hill reveals Kirstein's sense of humor, his political support of the Civil Rights movement, and his passions and frustrations with the ballet. He died in New York in January, 1996.

ANALYSIS

In a prefatory statement to his 1987 collection of poetry, *The Poems of Lincoln Kirstein*, Lincoln Kirstein says he wanted to be an artist, but he felt he lacked the requisite talent to succeed. Of his poetry writing he said, "I liked to write verse; this was always play with no pretension. . . . Failing as dramatist and screenwriter, light verse served instead, with its game enhanced by rhythm, rhyme, and meter." Later, in his memoir *Mosaic: Memoirs* (1994), he elaborated, "I never had any focused aim to become a 'poet.' I liked to write light verse and later, in the army I produced bunch of rhymes, the result of a pastime filling gaps in duty" as a driver and translator for the army.

Kirstein favored the long line in his poetry, simple rhetorical devices and standard features such as iambics and couplets for his rhymes. He wrote to tell stories about a particular slice of life, describing the scene with visual and emotional accuracy from several points of view—his own as poet-speaker, that of his peers, and those from the world at large.

Kirstein named his models in verse writing as Thomas Hardy, Gerard Manley Hopkins, Rudyard Kipling, W. H. Auden, Marianne Moore, Ezra Pound, and T. S. Eliot. In *Rhymes of a Pfc*, he is particularly indebted to Kipling, whom he saw as the most competent and poetically versatile spokesman of World War I. Kirstein employs irony in some of his poetry, but typically he relies on a Romantic interest, almost Wordsworthian emphasis, on the uniqueness of individuals and the beauty of nature. *Rhymes of a Pfc* enabled Kirstein to manage the diversity of people and situations in wartime. Kirstein's poetry presents marked and striking skill in literary portraiture. The poems have specificity and particularity, proving Kirstein was an experienced observer of human nature.

LOW CEILING

The poems in *Low Ceiling*, Kirstein's first collection, dedicated to his friend Muriel Draper, also provide an opportunity to reflect on the different roles people play in their normal lives. The poems about his father's early career as a salesman resonate with compassion for the man who travels to a new town every day and has no real permanence or opportunity to reflect on his present or future opportunities. "Best Man's Song" is the story of a man looking on a pair of lovers with the eyes of experience. He sees the young "actor" without his makeup and stage identity able to attract a woman to marry him, and the speaker seems both worried and wistful, as though the actor has done something he is not ready to do.

The book also houses several longer poems, including "Lieder for Hitler," dedicated to British poet Stephen Spender; "Chamber of Horrors"; and "Change of Heart." The first is a sequence of five poems which concludes, "The spirit of Evil is loose in the land" and describes in the sequence how Chancellor Adolf Hitler seemed to have taken Europe by surprise in his rise to power. "Chamber of Honors" is presented as a mock trial of murderers detailing their premeditated acts of violence to each other. The last poem of the book, "Change of Heart," describes an "Actor" or a man's quest for place and fame in the world of "Muchness in Richness" and how, in the end, he is alone and discarded by those who would praise him once as he "adored delusion" and deluded himself that those around him really cared about him.

These early poems show Kirstein's awareness of the evocative power of words. He uses words to offer pictures of daily life with its successes, failures, and ordinariness. The speaker of many of these poems can be summed up in the character Kirstein creates for "Ghost Pasture," "a bright somnambulist. . . Outlawed, a guest disinherited, Rootless, a wanderer . . . bidden here . . . to dream."

RHYMES OF A PFC

Rhymes of a Pfc was first published in 1964 as a collection of sixty-five poems. The second edition of 1967 featured eighty-five poems, and the third separately published edition contained ninety-five poems in 1980. The third printing is the version included in the 1987 *Poems of Lincoln Kirstein*, with its explanatory notes identifying terms, places, people, and literary styles he used. It is evident Kipling influenced these poems in form and style as well as in content choices. From Kipling, Kirstein learned what to write about in a war, while from Hardy and Auden he learned how to provide depth in the narrative mode. For example, Kipling's "Paget M.P." provides a model for the individual character studies Kirstein produces, while

"Arithmetic of the Frontier" allows Kipling the opportunity to address the ironies of war and the wisdom it brings.

The collection is dedicated to poet Marianne Moore, and, as the title indicates, the poems rhyme. They range in subject matter from narratives of experience to descriptions of locations and treatments of ideas. In *Visions of War: World War II in Literature and Popular Culture* (1992), David K. Vaughan writes: "Lincoln Kirstein was an exceptional poet as well as a lyrical historian of an era."

The book's first three poems in the section labeled "World War I" describe how that war shaped Kirstein's life. He mentions the soldiers he saw on parade and records some childhood memories of ingenuity and suffering. The opening is consistent with the type of calculated craftsmanship that caused Vaughan to speculate that the revisions were consistent with Kirstein's aim to make *Rhymes of a Pfc* "a complete poetic statement about the war."

The second part of the book, "Stateside," with its fourteen poems, charts the solders' progress through basic training to overseas tours of duty. Poems in this section describe the discipline of the drill sergeant and the men's reactions to army life. The third and fourth parts of the book contain fifty-two poems. In these sections, he creates accomplished character sketches and a narrative of the daily experiences of the soldiers. Kirstein's focus is on the hardships of war on the soldiers. He attempts to balance his interpretation of England as a literary and historical subject against what he sees in such poems as "Tudoresque," in which at the poem's midpoint he asks, "What England meant to me/ Apart from bards on Widener's shelves and Jim Agee's brandied voice?" Here he is attempting to balance what he read in the Harvard library and heard from his friend the critic James Agee with "Britain: its earth" and the war-ravaged people he encounters.

When he is posted to France, the subject of the third part of the book, Kirstein writes of the stress of battle on his unit in such poems as "AWOL," in which a "Texan combat engineer" gets drunk, commandeers a jeep, and tries to escape, as the poet writes "from this man's army he resigns." In "Air Strike," Kirstein's interest in vivid adjectival lines is evident. This is characteristic of his later ballads and is first seen here in such lines as, "This was the morning to recall: steep azure, stunning, diamond-bright,/ An empty cloudless bell-clear shell, stupendous scale for such a sight."

The fourteen poems in the "Germany" section continue the theme of conflict and conflicting perspectives, as may be seen in "Das Schloss" (the castle) in which the poet-soldier comes upon a seventeenth century castle full of the "dynastic display of German legend." The soldiers have come to occupy the castle and have to explain to the countess that she must step aside for them as her son plays classical music in another room. For Vaughan, "Siegfriedslage" is the central poem not just of this section of the book but also of the whole collection, as it address how art can mediate the difficulties of war. The poem is based on Kirstein's chance encounter with his hero, W. H. Auden, the "Morden" of the poem, in Germany. In the poets' conversation, Kirstein is able to define and assert the role of art in the modern world. "Scraps" is an experimental poem in the collection, composed of scraps of headlines, postcards, and other forms of writing about the war.

"Peace" is the sixth section of the book, with its eight retrospective poems. As the war ends there is talk of monuments and celebrations; yet such enthusiasm is tempered by "Dear John" narrating a soldier's wife's decision to divorce her husband for a man she met on the swing shift. "Truce" focuses on soldiers' return to "normal" as they become wise men telling stories to the "next crop's youth" about the odds they faced and how they overcame them. The seventh and final section, "Postscript," features four poems on the themes of lost innocence and alienation.

THE POEMS OF LINCOLN KIRSTEIN

The Poems of Lincoln Kirstein was published in 1987 and has two sections. The first is "Poems of Patriot," thirty ballads written between 1955 and 1985. The second half of the book is composed of *Rhymes of a Pfc*. Auden's review of *Rhymes of a Pfc* from 1964 is appended. Auden especially admired Kirstein's ability to reproduce the voices of the American soldiers in what seemed to him an authentic way. Paul Fussell commented that Kirstein might well be considered the "greatest poet of the Second World War" given his accomplishments in *Rhymes of a Pfc*.

Here again, Kirstein uses the ballad form as a vehicle to show sensitivity to the varieties of people one encounters in daily life. The "urban section" opens the story of "Sunny Jim," a waiter at a Greek-owned delicatessen in New York, and moves through to the story of a boy who wants to be ballet dancer in "Look, Ma! I'm Dancing." The "Suburban" section commences with the story of a divorcing couple dealing with custody of their child in "Bar & Grille." Again, like Kipling, Kirstein draws portraits of ordinary people, such as Tom and Fred, who need to tell Tom's parents that Fred has acquired immunodeficiency syndrome (AIDS). The third section, "Between the Wars" features narratives of life for soldiers after World War II, a poem on the United Nations, and two other poems on racial tensions—"Stars, Bar & Stripe" and "Domes," a five-part ballad on how religion divides the peoples of the world.

The ballads are unified by their form and to some degree their tone more than their content. They present honest appraisals of human shortcomings, the role of pride and the lack of shame among people in their dealings with one another. The poems do not employ figurative language; they adhere to the conventions of poetic narrative, while any use of irony is circumstantial. In his poems, Kirstein is a nonjudgmental observer of human nature who lets the narrator or the lively characters he creates speak both as themselves and for themselves as he records the vagaries and varieties of lived life. There is an energy to all his poems which comes from his keen eye and his ability to use words precisely and evocatively.

OTHER MAJOR WORKS

LONG FICTION: *Flesh Is Heir: An Historical Romance*, 1932.

NONFICTION: *Dance: A Short History of Classic Theatrical Dancing*, 1936; *Movement and Metaphor: Four Centuries of Ballet*, 1970; *Ballet, Bias, and Belief: Three Pamphlets Collected and Other Dance Writings of Lincoln Kirstein*, 1983; *Quarry: A Collection in Lieu of Memoirs*, 1986; *By, with, to, and From: A Lincoln Kirstein Reader*, 1991 (Nicholas Jenkins, editor); *Mosaic: Memoirs*, 1994; *Tchelitchev*, 1994.

CHILDREN'S LITERATURE: *Puss in Boots*, 1992.

BIBLIOGRAPHY

Hamovitch, Mimi. *The Hound and Horn Letters*. Athens: University of Georgia Press, 1982. Collects the correspondence of the authors associated with Kirstein's Harvard literary periodical. Includes a preface by Kirstein, reprinted in *Mosaic* on the evolution of the magazine.

Vaughan, David K. "Snapshots in the Book of War: Lincoln Kirstein's *Rhymes of a Pfc*." In *Visions of War: World War II in Literature and Popular Culture*, edited by M. Paul Holsinger and Mary Ann Schofield. Bowling Green, Ohio: Bowling Green University Popular Press, 1992. Discusses Vaughan's view of the three voices in Kirstein's poetry and overviews the themes of the *Rhymes of a Pfc* in a biographical context.

Weber, Nicholas Fox. *Patron Saints: Five Rebels Who Opened America to a New Art, 1928-1943*. New York: Knopf, 1992. Art critic Weber looks at the lives of five artists, including Kirstein and his circle.

Beverly Schneller

CAROLYN KIZER

Born: Spokane, Washington; December 10, 1925

PRINCIPAL POETRY

The Ungrateful Garden, 1961
Knock upon Silence, 1965
Midnight Was My Cry: New and Selected Poems, 1971
Mermaids in the Basement: Poems for Women, 1984
Yin: New Poems, 1984
The Nearness of You, 1986
Harping On: Poems, 1985-1995, 1996
Pro Femina, 2000
Cool, Calm, and Collected: Poems, 1960-2000, 2001

OTHER LITERARY FORMS

Carolyn Kizer is the author of numerous critical reviews and articles on poetry and other literature. Many of these are collected in *Proses: On Poems and Poets* (1993) and *Picking and Choosing: Essays on Prose* (1995). She is a prolific translator of poetry from other languages, including Chinese, Japanese, Urdu, Macedonian, Yiddish, French, and French African. An account of an academic year spent in Pakistan, "Pakistan Journal," is included in her book of poetry translations *Carrying Over: Poems for the Chinese, Urdu, Macedonian, Yiddish, and French African* (1988). With Donald Finkel, she prepared *A Splintered Mirror: Chinese Poetry from the Democracy Movement* (1991). Kizer has written several short stories, one of which, "A Slight Mechanical Failure," appeared in *The Quarterly Review of Literature* in 1978. Kizer coedited, with Elaine Dallman and Barbara Gelpi, *Woman Poet, Vol 1: The West* (1980). She has also edited *One Hundred Great Poems by Women* (1995) and *The Essential Clare* (1992).

ACHIEVEMENTS

When the 1985 Pulitzer Prize for Poetry was awarded to Carolyn Kizer for *Yin*, her admirers considered that appropriate recognition was being given, if belatedly. Many others were undoubtedly asking, "Carolyn who?" because her work has not received a great amount of critical attention and consequently her name is not well known. During an interview following her winning of the Pulitzer Prize, Kizer offered two explanations for her relative neglect by critics: "For one thing, I think my poems are very clear, so my work lacks the interesting ambiguities that appeal to the critical mind. And I write in so many genres—free verse, formal verse, just about anything—that I can't be pigeonholed." Possibly another reason for critical neglect is that Kizer is a poet of relatively slender output, one who chooses to be known more for the excellence of her work than for the number of her poems. Nevertheless, in the wake of the Pulitzer Prize and with the increasing interest in gender studies on college and university campuses, Kizer is attaining greater recognition as a feminist writer and critic. Some of her writings about women, particularly *Pro Femina*, are and have for some time been well known to students of women's poetry.

Although she may not have achieved the name recognition of a Sylvia Plath or an Adrienne Rich, Carolyn Kizer's career as a poet has not been lacking in awards and honors. In the same year that she won the Pulitzer

Prize, she was awarded a five-thousand-dollar prize by the American Academy and Institute of Arts and Letters. Among her other honors are the Masefield Prize from the Poetry Society of America in 1983, the Governors Award from the State of Washington and an award from the San Francisco Arts Commission, both for *Mermaids in the Basement*, and the Theodore Roethke Memorial Foundation Poetry Award in 1988 for *The Nearness of You*. She is a recipient of the Frost Medal for Lifetime Achievement in Poetry from the Poetry Society of America.

BIOGRAPHY

Carolyn Kizer was born December 10, 1925, in Spokane, Washington, the only child of exceptional parents, Mabel Ashley Kizer and Benjamin Hamilton Kizer. Her mother had earned a Ph.D. in biology from Stanford University in 1904, taught at Mills College and San Francisco State while helping three younger brothers through college, administered the first federally sponsored drug clinic in New York, and worked as an organizer for the Industrial Workers of the World. She was in her mid-forties by the time she met and married Benjamin, a well-established Spokane lawyer and regional planner. Kizer's recollections of her childhood convey ambivalent feelings toward her distinguished but difficult parents. Her father's emotionally remote, authoritarian personality intimidated and disturbed her, yet she feels profound respect for his integrity, self-discipline, and achievements. Her brilliant mother's abandonment of a career for a near-neurotic obsession with her daughter, especially with her daughter's "creativity," also dismayed Kizer. She confesses that her mother's demands and expectations hampered her, and that she could only come into her own as a serious poet after her mother's death. Yet she also pays tribute to her mother as beloved muse: "I wrote the poems for her. I still do."

After receiving a B.A. degree from Sarah Lawrence College in 1945, Kizer began graduate studies at Columbia University, where she became a fellow of the Chinese government in comparative literature; she traveled to Taiwan, where she lived for one year. Upon her return she studied poetry with Theodore Roethke at the University of Washington and settled in Seattle. From 1948 to 1954 she was married to Charles Stimson

Bullitt, with whom she has three children: Ashley, Scott, and Jill. In 1959 she founded the Seattle-based poetry journal *Poetry Northwest*, which she edited until 1965. In 1964-1965 she was a specialist in literature for the United States Department of State in Pakistan. From 1966 to 1970 she was the first director of literature programs for the newly created National Endowment for the Arts, a position in which she aided struggling writers and promoted poetry readings in inner city schools.

In addition to writing, editing, and translating, she has, since 1970, lectured and given readings of her poetry at numerous colleges and universities throughout the United States and Europe. She has been poet in residence and visiting professor of poetry at the University of North Carolina at Chapel Hill, Ohio University, University of Iowa, University of Maryland, Stanford University, Princeton University, Washington University, Barnard College, and Columbia University. In 1975 she married John Marshall Woodbridge, an architect and planner.

The breadth of Kizer's interests in other times, other places, other cultures, other languages and literatures,

Carolyn Kizer (© Robert Turney)

has made her one of the United States' least provincial poets. Frequently her poems are grounded in the largest contexts of myth, history, and philosophy, so that they are not all as "clear" and easily accessible as she has avowed. An international perspective is evident in many ways in her work, in her love of Asian forms as well as in her translations. Her worldview is well summarized by her comment on *Carrying Over*, a book of poems translated from Chinese, Urdu, Macedonian, Yiddish, and French African: She refers to the book as "a kind of paradigm of our world as I wish it were, of the United Nations as I pray it might become: all of us, with sharply individual voices, but together—an orchestra!"

ANALYSIS

Although Carolyn Kizer has asserted that her poems are "very clear" and lacking in "interesting ambiguities that appeal to the critical mind," a number of them show considerable complexity of style, tone, and subject. Her poems based on Greek myth are an example of one kind of complexity, a complexity that has irritated at least some readers, who wish that she would express herself directly, without using myth. To this complaint Kizer would undoubtedly respond first by pointing to a large number of her poems in which she does express herself quite directly and second by observing that not everything can or should be so expressed. As Robert Frost said in a talk titled "Education by Poetry," "Poetry provides the one permissible way of saying one thing and meaning another. People say, 'why don't you say what you mean?' We never do that . . . being all of us too much poets. We like to talk in parables and in hints and in indirections." With characteristic insight, Kizer observes that people need to use metaphor, to speak of one thing in terms of another, because "the metaphor, like love,/ Springs from the very separateness of things." Additionally, she has spoken of the need to transform grim or painful experience by imposing a form on it through imagination and language.

THE UNGRATEFUL GARDEN

Not all her poems that use myth are difficult and obscure. The title poem in *The Ungrateful Garden* uses the familiar myth of King Midas and his golden touch to underscore the ironies of human attitudes toward nature. Having made nature unnatural, Midas is maddened by

the results. Furious to find his eyes blinded by golden flowers, his ears assaulted by "the heavy clang of leaf on leaf," his fingers pricked by golden thorns, his feet cut by golden stubble in his garden, he concludes: "Nature is evil."

At other times, Kizer uses Greek myth to write poems of metaphysical wit, such as "The Copulating Gods." The deities are amused by the way mortals have misunderstood the frank carnality of the gods. Unable to comprehend the gods' sensual pleasure, humans have invented histories for them and made them into a confused religion of "spiritual lust." "The headboard of our bed became their altar," declares a lascivious goddess as she returns to dalliance with her lover:

> Tracing again the bones of your famous face,
> I know we are not their history but our myth.
> Heaven prevents time, and our astral raptures
> Float buoyant in the universe. Come, kiss!
> Come, swoon again, we who invented dying
> And the whole alchemy of resurrection.
> They will concoct a scripture explaining this.

In another poem inspired by Greek myth, "The Dying Goddess," Venus is no longer the revered love goddess. The poem is a witty comment on a degenerate society in which love has been replaced. Some men are looking for mothers, others are taking to drink; still others join "odd cults . . . involving midgets,/ Partial castration, dismemberment of children," but none are worshipers of Venus. In the end, her image disappearing even from her own mirror, "she turns her face from the smokeless brazier." Kizer's attitude toward the modern world frequently conveys a feeling of decline or loss. In "The Old Gods," a lament for the lost splendor of the classical world, Zeus and his pantheon have fallen on hard times, replaced by Christianity ("that God-kissed girl, and her God-given Son") and other "windy deities" of disgusting meekness. The speaker in the poem is ambivalent: "You old Gods, I never cared about you./ I don't feel for the Greeks; I loathe the Romans." Still, the speaker's resentment at what has replaced the old gods rouses him to fight on their side, even knowing it is the losing side in this "battle of the Gods."

In other poems, Kizer uses Greek myth to develop feminist themes. In "Hera, Hung from the Sky," Hera is punished for having the audacity to dream of sexual equality, to imagine "that woman was great as man." Zeus punishes his wife by hanging her by her heels from the sky: having "lost the war of the air," she is left "half-strangled" in her hair, dangling, "drowned in fire." "Semele Recycled" is a quasi-comic, surreal account of what happened after Semele, a mortal, was burned to ashes when her lover Zeus appeared to her in all his blazing glory. The scattered parts of her body are horribly degraded but are magically reassembled at the god's command. God and mortal, their bodies meeting "like a thunderclap/ in mid-day," startling the cattle and bystanders, make love on a compost heap. Besides being a comment on the male god's absolute command over life, death, and rebirth, the poem is interested in the relationship between the "sacred" and "profane" aspects of love. Yeats's perception that "fair and foul are near of kin,/ And fair needs foul" is relevant here, as is Crazy Jane's statement that "Love has pitched his mansion in/ The place of excrement;/ For nothing can be sole or whole/ That has not been rent." Presumably, Kizer's Semele agrees.

In "Persephone Pauses," the goddess Persephone's bondage to Hades and the Underworld is a metaphor for woman's bondage to a sensual desire she is powerless to resist. Persephone's "dolor" and "dower" are the "sweet Hell" of female sexuality. The equivocal tone of the poem is perfectly conveyed when Persephone, realizing that her bondage means that only half her life is "spent in light," nevertheless descends with an almost cheery "Summertime, goodnight!"

"PRO FEMINA"

"Pro Femina," which first appeared in *Knock upon Silence*, is Kizer's fullest and most celebrated treatment of feminist themes. It does not use myth, but its form was inspired by classical literature. A three-part witty verse satire about "the fate of women," it turns the tables on Juvenal's Tenth Satire, which attacked women's vices, particularly vanity. Kizer's cunning strategy is to begin by conceding, "We *are* hyenas. Yes, we admit it./ While men have politely debated free will, we have howled for it,/ Howl still. . . ." The poem's catalog of injustices and outrages that women are expected to suffer in a male-dominated culture explains why women are "hyenas." Kizer's honesty compels her to acknowledge

in some cases women's complicity in their own suffering—for example, the "cabbageheads" "who, vague-eyed and acquiescent, worshiped God as a man." Far worse are the women who sold out, became "scabs to their stricken sisterhood,/ Impugning our sex to stay in good with the men." Kizer's sardonic comment: How the men "must have swaggered/ When women themselves endorsed their own inferiority!"

With canny eye for telling detail, Kizer loads the poem with examples of the ways women are dehumanized and trivialized, as in the culturally mandated feminine concern with "surfaces," with dress and appearance: "So primp, preen, prink, pluck and prize your flesh,/ All posturings! All ravishment! All sensibility!/ Meanwhile, have you used your mind today?" Some women, writers, try to escape marginalization by "aping the ways of the men," smoking cigars, swearing, drinking straight shots, all in hope of receiving the ultimate compliment: "*she writes like a man!*" Others are driven to opposite extremes, going "mad in a mist of chiffon," or become practical feminists such as the poet Sara Teasdale, who wore chiffon over red flannel underwear. Kizer reserves special scorn for the "Quarterly priestesses/ Who flog men for fun, and kick women to maim competition," but she believes that women writers are "emerging from all that, more or less," and perhaps better times for women are at hand.

Finally, having told the reader what she cannot stand, Kizer tells what she wants: free women of steady vision, discipline, and courage. These women, if unmarried, will keep their heads and their pride; if married, they will believe their creative work more important than doing dishes; if mothers, they will neither devour nor be devoured by their children. These women's husbands or lovers prefer and know how to cherish free women. This view in "Pro Femina" accords well with a statement Kizer made in an interview. Defining feminism as "equality with men in every way," she explains what that means to her:

> I don't want women to have to be superwomen. I want them to be able to be talented and good at what they do, and not have to be the perfect wife, the perfect mother, the perfect job-holder, and crochet besides. . . .

I want them able to make money commensurate with their efforts. I want them to have flextime so they can take time off for their children in emergencies. . . . I want them not to get fired if they get pregnant, and to have husbands who help out, not because they have to but because they want to.

Clearly, Kizer is not angry, radical, or separatist in her views, despite the harshly satiric tone of "Pro Femina." "I'm not particularly angry at men," she said. "I don't think anybody likes relinquishing power. If we lived in a matriarchy I wouldn't like to give it up either. The division of power is one of the things that make marriage a very complex relationship—trying to keep things in some kind of reasonable balance. . . . Constant attention has to be paid. . . ."

"Fanny"

To the three sections of "Pro Femina" just discussed, Kizer added a fourth section, "Fanny," when "Pro Femina" was reprinted in *Mermaids in the Basement*. ("Fanny" also appeared as a separate poem in *Yin*.) "Fanny," a long poem written in Roman hexameter, purports to be the diary of Frances, the fifty-year-old wife of Robert Louis Stevenson, written in Samoa in 1890 during the last year of his life. It is a singular account of hardship and harvest, triumph and terror. While her famous husband writes, Fanny builds a pig house, bakes bread in the rain, and, Earth Mother that she is, furiously plants—corn, potatoes, eggplant, pineapple, artichoke, cantaloupe, mangoes, strawberries, pumpkin. Samoa, however, is no Eden. The strawberries and potatoes rot, rats eat and horses trample the corn, the cantaloupe are stolen, and in the leaking and listing house, mildew spreads. Fanny, undaunted, goes on planting while her husband mocks her, calling her a peasant "because I delve in the earth." She broods a bit on this hurtful remark, but the rigors of everyday life leave her little time for such self-indulgence. Living with influenza epidemics, volcanoes, hurricanes, war, headhunters, and—what may be even worse—a vexing mother-in-law, an irritating clergyman, and someone who regularly reads and censors her diary, Fanny survives it all. Her husband dies, but Fanny triumphs: By removing her husband from London's unhealthy climate and nourishing him, she had "kept him alive for eight more years." She feels

well satisfied. Yet the reader sees the self-sacrifice and loneliness of a brave woman, which is all the more poignant because it is unconscious.

Possibly Kizer added "Fanny" to "Pro Femina" in order to provide a model of feminine virtue, or possibly she intended it as a negative example of woman as victim. Kizer's own attitude toward her remarkable character creation is not clear. What is clear is that she has written an extraordinary poem; its Keatsian richness of language, its beguiling portrait of Fanny, and its careful control of tone and distance have caused many reviewers to rank it among her best poems.

Poetry in translation

What impresses even a causal reader of Kizer's works is her mastery of a variety of subjects, styles, forms, and voices. She seems able to write a villanelle such as "On a Line from Sophocles" and free verse with equal ease. Her technical skill is widely acknowledged and at times dazzlingly displayed, as in some of her Chinese "imitations" and in her translations. A case in point is "Seven Sides and Seven Syllables" in *Carrying Over*. As is generally well recognized, poetry translation is itself an act of creation. In translating from French African, her difficult task was to preserve Edouard Maunick's seven-syllable lines while remaining faithful to the original poem's imagery and syntax. Printing the original text and her translation on facing pages, she invites qualified readers to judge the results for themselves.

Personal poems

Kizer has written political, comical, satirical, and lyrical poems. Some are public poems, while others seem more private. Among her personal poems, those about her parents and her children are particularly strong. One of the finest of these is "The Great Blue Heron," dedicated to her mother. A child playing sees a heron standing on the beach, "shadow without a shadow." Chilled by the sight of the spectral bird, the child runs to fetch her mother. They return just in time to see him "drifting/ Over the highest pines/ On vast, unmoving wings." The child suddenly realizes that her mother "knew what he was": The bird is death. Fifteen years later, her mother has died, everything has changed, except one thing: "Now there is only you/ Heavy upon my eye." No summary can convey the power of the poem and its image of the great heron, which becomes for the reader, as for the speaker in the poem, an objective correlative of death.

Another moving personal poem is "Antique Father," in which a speaker unsuccessfully implores a dying father to communicate, to utter some final word, perhaps some "grave secret." The spare, broken lines upon a mostly empty page perfectly reinforce the poem's meaning: the terror as they "gaze into the pit/ eternity," the breathless expectancy and urgency of this ultimate moment, the father's "terrible silence."

Kizer has written two poems for her daughter Ashley, one of which, "The Blessing," celebrates a complex grandmother-mother-daughter relationship. The daughter is self-controlled because the mother is not: "Holding me together at your expense/ has made you burn cool," mother tells daughter. Yet she realizes that she played the same role for her own mother—hence her references to "Daughter-my-mother" and "Mother-my-daughter." Ultimately, images of grandmother, mother, and daughter merge in this warmly autobiographical poem, in which the only certainty is that since there always will be "a hard time" for mother, a loving daughter is indeed a blessing.

LOVE POEMS

Kizer's love poems are as wonderfully various as she is. The witty "Food of Love" takes for its epigraph an observation by Samuel Butler II, "Eating is touch carried to the bitter end," and goes on from there:

> I'm going to murder you with love;
> I'm going to suffocate you with embraces;
> I'm going to hug you, bone by bone,
> Till you're dead all over.
> Then I will dine on your delectable marrow.

Moving to carefully controlled but extravagant metaphors of the Sahara and the Mediterranean Sea, the poem develops its theme of the inexhaustible renewal of love. "You will become my personal Sahara," but "I will be that green" of water and vegetation that transform a dusty desert into a "field in bloom." Then, "I will devour you, my natural food," once again.

"What the Bones Know" is indebted to William Butler Yeats for more than his philosophy of frank sensuality referred to in the poem: "I think that Yeats was right,/ That lust and love are one." The spare imagery (those

bones), the rhymes, the rhythms, the conversational tone, all pay homage. The repeated rhymes of death/ breath and the variations she plays on them are particularly effective in this concise meditation on sex and death. Kizer's great mentor and friend, Roethke, was also influenced by Yeats. (Can there be many contemporary poets who are not?) A reader catches echoes of Roethke in such images as "frozen brow" and the "shaking sides of lust."

A poem about love in quite a different mode is "The Patient Lovers." Its use of puns, its wordplay, and the extended conceit of love as illness are reminiscent of the Metaphysical poets; John Donne comes immediately to mind. Yet Kizer places her own individual stamp upon whatever she writes. Her own self-assured voice is the one the reader hears. An elegiac poem, "Winter Song," explores the dark winter of the soul when love has failed. Images of tedium and exhaustion convey the truth of prose-like assertion: *"Thinking of you, I am suddenly old."* The temptations of sentimentality (which must always be great in a poem on this subject) are resisted. The poem compellingly tells an unromantic truth: "We are separated, finally, not by death but life:/ We can cling to the dead, but the living break away." Some way to live with this melancholy fact is what the poem struggles to find.

HARPING ON AND COOL, CALM, AND COLLECTED

In her work of the 1990's and beyond, Kizer shows no loss of power and perhaps some gain. *Harping On* is a monument both to her experience and to her vitality. Some of this sharpness of wit is found in her cutting lines on Battista Franco's "Valley of the Fallen." While Kizer's voice is unmistakable, it is capable of many intonations, from a high poetic earnestness to a more low-down, sassy growl. Kizer's charm, in this collection and elsewhere, is in her constant ability to surprise, to satisfy, and to escape easy categorization. Another virtue is an accessibility that is never simplistic. At the end of her "A Song for Muriel," Kizer gently mocks and understates this gift: "It's all right here / Very clear." Only Kizer, in a career collection whose new poems slant toward the misgivings and hesitations of old age, could give her readers a title as zippy and unexpected as *Cool, Calm, and Collected.*

Surveying the achievements of Carolyn Kizer, one feels impelled to make lists of contraries: She is a poet of passion and control, of intellect and earthiness, of tradition and innovation, of classicism and modernity, of the mythic and the mundane, of the colloquial and the formal, to name a few of the possibilities. Yet what is important in her writing cannot by conveyed by schizophrenic-sounding lists. What is notable is the wise and knowing sense of an authentic self that informs her writing, a self that knows what is genuine and what is not. In an era of increasing fragmentation, incoherence, and tawdriness, it is good to have writers such as Carolyn Kizer to remind the reader of what wholeness, lucidity, and authenticity are all about.

OTHER MAJOR WORKS

NONFICTION: *Proses: On Poems and Poets*, 1993; *Picking and Choosing: Essays on Prose*, 1995.

TRANSLATIONS: *Carrying Over: Poems for the Chinese, Urdu, Macedonian, Yiddish, and French African*, 1988; *A Splintered Mirror: Chinese Poetry from the Democracy Movement*, 1991 (with Donald Finkel).

EDITED TEXTS: *Woman Poet, Vol. 1: The West*, 1980 (with Elaine Dallman and Barbara Gelpi); *The Essential Clare*, 1992; *One Hundred Great Poems by Women*, 1995.

BIBLIOGRAPHY

Finch, Annie, Johanna Keller, and Candace McClelland, eds. *Caroline Kizer: Perspectives on Life and Her Work.* Fort Lee, N.J.: CavanKerry Press, 2001. A significant collection of appreciations, both in poetry and in prose, plus interviews and a bibliography of Kizer's work. Maxine Kumin's short introduction leads to the work of such critics as Alfred Corn, Ruth Salvaggio (on Kizer's feminism), Robert Phillips (focus on mythology), Henry Taylor (perhaps the best overview of her career), and Judith Johnson.

Fulton, Alice. "Main Things." *Poetry* 151 (January, 1988): 372-377. A perceptive essay-review of *Mermaids in the Basement* and *The Nearness of You*, written with feminist concerns foremost in mind. Fulton scrutinizes some of Kizer's language choices and finds evidence of bias against women. She believes that Kizer's attitude toward women is ambivalent at times, but that overall the poet's strengths greatly outweigh her few weak moments. Along the way, Fulton offers many excellent insights into the poems.

Hampl, Patricia. "Women Who Say What They Mean." *The New York Times Book Review* 89 (November 25, 1984): 36. This essay-review of *Mermaids in the Basement* and *Yin* praises Kizer for having the courage of her early feminism but finds "Pro Femina" a less satisfying poem than others that are more lyrical and personal, such as "Thrall" and "Where I've Been All My Life." In some of her poems Kizer's humor seems forced and her tone uneven, but in her prose memoir "A Muse," humor and tone are perfectly managed.

Kizer, Carolyn. "Intensity and Effect: An Interview with Carolyn Kizer." Interview by Michelle Boisseau. *New Letters* 64, no. 3 (1998): 80-92. This interview had its first life on National Public Radio and is included in Finch, below. It provides an entertaining glance at Kizer's career as well as insights into the persona projected by the title of *Harping On.* Kizer addresses her years as literary-programs director at the National Endowment for the Arts and her fondness for Chinese poetry.

O'Connell, Nicolas. *At the Field's End: Interviews with Twenty Pacific Northwest Writers.* Seattle: Madrona, 1987. Kizer discusses the influence of her teacher and mentor Theodore Roethke in her development as a poet and credits him with making her a serious writer. She explains the importance of revision in writing, why reading poetry aloud is of supreme importance to her, why she believes that Asian influence on Western writers is good, and what being a feminist means.

Rigsbee, David, ed. *An Answering Music: On the Poetry of Carolyn Kizer.* Boston: Ford-Brown, 1991. Includes poems by Kizer, an interview, a detailed publishing history, and a group of enthusiastic responses to her work by such writers as Judith Johnson, John Montague, Laura Jensen, and Fred Chappell.

Karen A. Kildahl,
updated by Philip K. Jason

ETHERIDGE KNIGHT

Born: Corinth, Mississippi; April 19, 1931
Died: Indianapolis, Indiana; March 10, 1991

PRINCIPAL POETRY

"For Malcolm, a Year After," 1967 (a contribution
    to *For Malcolm: Poems on the Life and Death of
    Malcolm X*, 1967)
Poems from Prison, 1968
Black Voices from Prison, 1970
A Poem for Brother/Man, 1972
Belly Song and Other Poems, 1973
Born of a Woman: New and Selected Poems, 1980
The Essential Etheridge Knight, 1986

OTHER LITERARY FORMS

Etheridge Knight almost exclusively wrote poetry. A
few articles by him appeared in African American magazines such as *Black Digest* (with a format similar to
Reader's Digest), *Emerge* (similar to *Time* magazine),
and *Essence*, the foremost black women's periodical
publication.

ACHIEVEMENTS

Etheridge Knight opened the eyes of a nation to the
views and experiences of prisoners, a previously ignored
population. The initial acclaim lavished on *Poems from
Prison*, published in 1968, and the praise of honored
authors such as Gwendolyn Brooks and Robert Bly,
opened the door to a 1972 grant from the National Endowment for the Arts. His third collection, *Belly Song
and Other Poems*, earned 1973 Pulitzer Prize and National Book Award nominations. He received a Guggenheim Fellowship in 1974 and won the Shelley Memorial Award in 1984. His last book, *The Essential
Etheridge Knight*, earned the Before Columbus Foundation's 1987 American Book Award.

BIOGRAPHY

Etheridge Knight, one of Bushie and Belzora
(Cozart) Knight's seven children, came into the world
on April 19, 1931, near Corinth, Mississippi. During this
time the United States was gripped by one of history's

most sensational racial battles, the Scottsboro Boys trial.
Nine black males, ages twelve to nineteen, were taken
off a train near Scottsboro, Alabama, and charged with
the rape of two Huntsville, Alabama, white women,
Ruby Bates, eighteen, and Victoria Price, twenty-one.
The incident seeded a cloud of white fear and rage that
shadowed black men throughout the South for more
than thirty years.

Angered by the racial segregation and disgusted by
the backbreaking work of sharecropping, Knight dropped
out of school after the eighth grade and left home. He
wandered for about five years, then enlisted in the army
in 1947.

Knight was a medic, stationed in Guam, Hawaii, and
the battlefront in the Korean War until 1951, when he
was wounded by a piece of shrapnel. In 1957, the now
drug-addicted soldier was discharged. Drugs dominated
his life. In 1960, Knight was sentenced to prison for a
robbery in Indianapolis, Indiana, motivated by his need
to buy drugs. Doing time at Indiana State Prison in
Michigan City, Indiana, led Knight to self-discovery and
an increased desire to be more than an outcast in America. Those yearnings prompted him to write.

Poems from Prison, his first collection, was published
by Broadside Press in 1968, with an introduction by
Pulitzer Prize-winning poet Gwendolyn Brooks. She
mentored Knight, who eventually gained support from
members of the Black Arts movement, which gave artistic voice to African Americans' struggles for social rights
and political freedom. One of those members, poet Dudley Randall, was the founder and editor of Broadside
Press. Another, poet Sonia Sanchez, married Knight. By
year's end, Knight had gained a career, a wife, and three
stepchildren: Morani, Mongou, and Anita Sanchez. His
fame peaked between 1969 and 1975, when the movement waned. An anthology of prison writings, *Voce
Negre dal Carcere* (1968), first published in Laterza, Italy, broadened the popularity of Knight's work. Two
years later, Pathfinders Press released *Black Voices from
Prison* in the United States. Doors opened. The poet was
writer in residence at the University of Pittsburgh (1968-
1969), the University of Hartford (1969-1970), and Lincoln University (1972) in Jefferson City, Missouri. He
received a 1972 National Endowment for the Arts grant
and a 1974 Guggenheim Fellowship.

Etheridge Knight (University of Pittsburgh Press)

Knight's career was going well, but his personal life was in a downward slide. Drugs kept him in and out of Veterans Administration hospitals. The marriage to Sanchez crumbled into a 1972 divorce. On June 11, 1973, Knight married Mary Ann McAnally. The couple had two children: Mary Tandiwe and Etheridge Bambata. That same year, Broadside published the first collection of his poems written outside prison, *Belly Song and Other Poems*. In 1978, he married Charlene Blackburn. The relationship is celebrated in *Born of a Woman*, and with her he had a son, Issac Bushie Knight.

Knight continued to write. *The Essential Etheridge Knight*, was released in 1986, but Knight never regained prominence. He died of lung cancer in 1991 in Indianapolis, Indiana.

ANALYSIS

As black writers and artists in the late 1960's reached for words to politicize their expressions, Etheridge Knight's voice proved perfect. Like the works of LeRoi Jones (Amiri Baraka), Don L. Lee (Haki R. Madhubuti), Dudley Randall, and Sonia Sanchez, Knight's poems celebrate black heritage and criticize injustices. What readers will find in Knight's poetry is an attempt to un-

derstand belonging and racial isolation in U.S. society. As Cassie Premo wrote in *The Oxford Companion to African American Literature*, even dead, Knight "continues to testify to the power of freedom, and human capacity to envision it even when in prison."

He talked about life behind bars, unveiling a humanity in prisoners that most Americans, black or white, never knew existed. At the same time, his poetry revealed links between the ways black people survived on both sides of the wall.

Poems such as "Hard Rock Returns to Prison from the Hospital for the Criminal Insane" epitomized the standard for what in the early 1960's was still called Negro literature. A New York City poet then named LeRoi Jones (now Amiri Baraka of Newark, New Jersey) wrote in a 1962 essay, "The Myth of a Negro Literature":

Negro Literature, to be a legitimate product of the Negro experience in America, must get at that experience in exactly the terms America has proposed for it in its most ruthless identity.

As Patricia Liggins Hill wrote in "The Function of the New Black Aesthetic in Etheridge Knight's Prison Poetry," Knight's prison poems interweave temporal and spatial elements that "allow him to merge his personal consciousness with the consciousness of Black people."

The poet himself once said:

. . . a major part of discovering an aesthetic is coming to grips with oneself. The "true" artist is supposed to examine his own experience of this process as a reflection of his self, his ego.

Like many of the writers and painters during the Black Arts movement that surfaced in major urban centers between 1965 and 1975, Knight believed that a black artist's main duty was to expose the lies of the white-dominated society. In *Contemporary Authors*, he is quoted as saying that the traditional idea of the aesthetic drawn from Western European history demands that the artist speak only of the beautiful: "His task is to edify the listener, to make him see beauty of the world." That aesthetic definition was a problem because African Americans were identified in the traditional European mind as not beautiful. In fact, the broader society, then as now, saw everything in African American life as ugly. Black artists hoped to erase that mindset. They saw art as a force through which they could move people of all races toward understanding and respect. In *Contemporary Authors*, Knight is quoted as saying that the African American writer has to

> perceive and conceptualize the collective aspirations, the collective vision of black people, and through his art form give back to the people the truth that he has gotten from them. He must sing to them of their own deeds, and misdeeds.

Knight began to write poetry in prison, but he did not come to the task cold. Scholar Shirley Lumpkin states that Knight was "an accomplished reciter" before he entered prison. She explains that "reciters" in the African American tradition made "toasts," which were long, memorized, narrative poems, often in rhymed couplets, in which "sexual exploits, drug activities, and violent aggressive conflicts [involved] a cast of familiar folk." Like later rap and hiphop artists, reciters wove the stories in typically gritty, sometimes pornographic street language. Indiana State Prison toasts honed Knight's skill in the art form and opened his eyes to poetry's potential.

In *The Dictionary of Literary Biography*, Lumpking wrote:

> Since toast-telling brought him into genuine communion with others, he felt that poetry could simultaneously show him who he was and connect him with other people.

Poetry was what brought him into contact with Gwendolyn Brooks and Dudley Randall, who exposed Knight to the world.

In *Broadside Memories: Poets I Have Known* (1975), Randall states, "Knight sees himself as being one with Black people." As in the toasts, in rap and hiphop, rhyme becomes the glue in the black community. "Knight does not abjure rime like many contemporary poets," Randall wrote. "He says the average Black man in the streets defines poetry as something that

rimes, and Knight appeals to the folk by riming." Knight's view of the world and himself was forged in the anguish that comes from trying to make it as an outsider. His writings show that he saw African Americans as outcasts everywhere outside their culture, finding roots only in family connections.

"HARD ROCK RETURNS TO PRISON FROM THE HOSPITAL FOR THE CRIMINAL INSANE"

In "Hard Rock Returns to Prison from the Hospital for the Criminal Insane," Knight turns an uncontrollable prisoner into a new-day folk hero. Hard Rock is a Paul Bunyan without a pretty fate. The author understood that most African American lives, even mythic ones, do not have happy endings. The poem also shows that sometimes heroes are not what most people (meaning whites) see as nice or pretty. In the language of the incarcerated, Knight laid out the heroic stature:

> "Ol Hard Rock! Man, that's one crazy nigger."
> And then the jewel of a myth that Hard Rock once bit
> A screw on the thumb and poisoned him with syphilitic
>   spit.

To many, those details are as alienating as the description:

> Hard Rock was "known not to take no shit
> From nobody," and he had the scars to prove it:
> Split purple lips, lumped ears, welts above
> His yellow eyes, and one long scar that cut
> Across his temple and plowed through a thick
> Canopy of kinky hair.

The prisoner, Knight recognized, is an archetype of all black Americans, only nominally "free" but really imprisoned. In prison, the prisoner stays in a hole, a tiny cell devoid of light. The guards' intimidation cannot break the man's spirit, so the prison doctors give him a lobotomy. They take his ability to think. Knight saw that scenario as identical to the experience of the descendants of Africans in America. In Mississippi and other places, he had seen black people who tried to stand tall against the onslaught of racial oppression either killed or, like the fictional Hard Rock, tamed:

> A screw who knew Hard Rock
> From before shook him down and barked in his face
> And Hard Rock did *nothing*. Just grinned and looked silly.
> His eyes empty like knot holes in a fence.

The poem captures the disappointment and defeat Knight saw in black men on both sides of the walls:

We turned away our eyes to the ground. Crushed.
He had been our Destroyer, the doer of things
We dreamed of doing but could not bring ourselves to do.

"THE IDEA OF ANCESTRY"

Knight reflects on those connections in both "A Poem for Myself (Or Blues for a Mississippi Black Boy)" and "The Idea of Ancestry," in his *Poems from Prison*. In the first part of "The Idea of Ancestry," he wrote:

Taped to the wall of my cell are 47 pictures: 47 black
faces: my father, mother, grandmothers (1 dead), grand
    fathers (both dead), brothers,
sisters, uncles, aunts, cousins (1st & 2nd), nieces, and
    nephews. They stare
across the space at me sprawling on my bunk. I know
their dark eyes, they know mine. I know their style,
they know mine. I am all of them, they are all of me;
they are farmers, I am a thief, I am me, they are thee.

After exploring the variety of their individualism, he concludes differences cannot break family ties:

I have the same name as 1 grandfather, 3 cousins, 3
    nephews,
and 1 uncle. The uncle disappeared when he was 15,
    just took
off and caught a freight (they say). He's discussed each
    year
when the family has a reunion, he causes uneasiness in
the clan, he is an empty space. My father's mother, who
    is 93
and who keeps the Family Bible with everybody's birth
    dates
(and death dates) in it, always mentions him. There is
no place in her Bible for "whereabouts unknown."

Works written after prison extended Knight's reflections on connections. When considered to its fullest extent, what binds people is love. Knight's reflection on ancestry in "The Idea of Ancestry" reveals an understanding of a family, the accidental space where one shares traits and foibles with loved ones. Accidental refers to things outside a person's control. Patricia Liggins Hill acknowledged in a 1980 essay, "The Violent Space," that

"the form of the poem as well as the idea of ancestry in the poem also represents the problem of ancestral lineage for the Black race as a whole." The power to direct family lines was stripped from African Americans for generations. The practice of selling slaves without regard for emotional ties also made it hard to keep track of the existing linkages.

"A POEM FOR MYSELF"

Born of a Woman, *Poems from Prison*, *Black Voices from Prison* and *Belly Song and Other Poems* have pieces that openly grapple with questions of belonging. Those themes and styles resonate with legendary black poets such as Langston Hughes and Sterling Brown. This is particularly clear in the blues poem "A Poem for Myself (Or Blues for a Mississippi Black Boy)":

I was born in Mississippi;
I walked barefooted thru the mud.
Born black in Mississippi,
Walked barefooted thru the mud.
But when I reached the age of twelve
I left that place for good.

The narrative stanza sounds no different from the lines of a traditional Mississippi blues ballad. Many black poets, particularly during the Harlem Renaissance in the early twentieth century, used the style and meter of the music. Sung ballads usually have three iambic pentameter lines with the second line repeated. Knight slightly varies the meter, echoing the first line in the third and the second line in the fourth to create a more accessible feel and slightly disguise the poem's basic blues flavor.

In a review of *Born of a Woman*, Hill described Knight as a blues singer, "whose life has been 'full of trouble' and thus whose songs resound a variety of blues moods, feelings, and experiences and later take on the specific form of a blues musical composition." In *Obsidian: Black Literature in Review*, Craig Werner states that Knight "merges musical rhythms with traditional metrical devices, reflecting the assertion of an Afro-American cultural identity within a Euro-American context." If the blues form bodes defiance of established norms, it becomes as rebellious as the use of rhyme. It becomes yet another way to identify with the masses, which is clearly more of Knight's interest than meeting Western European standards. Lumpkin states that some critics find

Knight's language objectionable and "unpoetic." They judged his use of verse forms to be poor. In 1980, she wrote, "Some believe that he 'maintains an outmoded, strident black power rhetoric from the 1960's.'" She concludes: "Those with reservations and those who admire his work all agree . . . upon his vital language and the range of his subject matter. They all agree that he brings a needed freshness to poetry, particularly in his extraordinary ability to move an audience."

Knight died without ever finding the answers to the ties that bind people to something larger than themselves. However, as Premo wrote, "Knight's poetry expresses our freedom of consciousness and attests to our capacity for connections with others."

BIBLIOGRAPHY

Andrews, William L., Frances Smith Fuller, and Trudier Harris, eds. *The Oxford Companion to African American Literature.* New York: Oxford University Press, 1997. In this reference work, Cassie Premo briefly profiles the author, assessing his poetry's contribution to American writing. She concludes that his poetry expresses "our freedom of consciousness and attests to our capacity for connection to others."

Ford, Karen. "These Old Writing Paper Blues: The Blues Stanza and Literary Poetry." *College Literature* 24, no. 3 (October, 1997): 84-103. Ford weighs Knight's use of written and oral form in "For Malcolm, a Year After." She says that the "reciprocal, mutually informing and accommodating relationship" between them "dramatizes playful adaptation and rich potential."

Hill, Patricia Liggins. "The Violent Space: The Function of the New Black Aesthetic in Etheridge Knight's Prison Poetry." *Black American Literature Forum* 14, no. 3 (1980). The scholar analyzes how Knight's perspective, as seen in "Hard Rock Returns to Prison from the Hospital for the Criminal Insane" and other prison poems, fits within the aesthetic that often treats writing as a political act.

Randall, Dudley. *Broadside Memories: Poets I Have Known.* Detroit: Broadside Press, 1975. The poet is one of several authors Randall discusses. The publisher saw Knight's work as closer to the pulse of the

African American masses than that of most members of the Black Arts movement in the late 1960's.

Vendler, Helen Hennessy, ed. *Part of Nature, Part of Us: Modern American Poets.* Cambridge, Mass.: Harvard University Press, 1980. Shirley Lumpkin writes about "Hard Rock Returns to Prison from the Hospital for the Criminal Insane," tying the themes in the work that appears in *Poems from Prison* and *Born of a Woman* to his writings about Malcolm X and family. She highlights the work's sense of community and observes, "What renders the picture of 'Hard Rock' even more powerful is the first person plural's persona's voice, which uses black, prison, and standard vocabulary to explain what Hardrock's destruction means to the 'we' speaking in the poem."

Vincent F. A. Golphin

KENNETH KOCH

Born: Cincinnati, Ohio; February 27, 1925
Died: New York, New York; July 6, 2002

PRINCIPAL POETRY
Poems, 1953
Ko: Or, A Season on Earth, 1959
Permanently, 1960
Thank You and Other Poems, 1962
When the Sun Tries to Go On, 1969
Sleeping with Women, 1969
The Pleasures of Peace and Other Poems, 1969
The Art of Love, 1975
The Duplications, 1977
The Burning Mystery of Anna in 1951, 1979
From the Air, 1979
Days and Nights, 1982
Selected Poems, 1950-1982, 1985
On the Edge, 1986
Selected Poems, 1991
On the Great Atlantic Rainway: Selected Poems, 1950-1988, 1994
One Train: Poems, 1994
Straits: Poems, 1998
New Addresses: Poems, 2000

OTHER LITERARY FORMS

In addition to poetry, Kenneth Koch has published one novel, *The Red Robins* (1975), and books of dramatic pieces, including *Bertha and Other Plays* (1966) and *A Change of Hearts: Plays, Films, and Other Dramatic Works, 1951-1971* (1973). Both Koch's novel and his works for the stage are imaginative and improvisatory in their consistent portrayal of the comic drama of life.

The plays achieve their comic repercussions primarily through the juxtaposition of incongruous situations, and by means of rapid, often unpredictable changes of language, character, and scene. The plays echo and imitate older dramatic forms such as the Elizabethan chronical and the court masque, frequently appropriating the earlier dramatic conventions for comic purposes. *E. Kology* (1973), for example, a five-act play in rhymed verse, is as much masque as play. In it, the main character, E. Kology, persuades various polluters of air and water to abandon their destructive habits. An additional masque element is provided by a troupe of young men and women who assist E. Kology, performing a series of celebratory dances as part of the play's action. An even more masquelike play is *The Moon Balloon*, performed in New York's Central Park on New Year's Eve, 1969. *The Moon Balloon* is an entertainment in rhymed verse that makes use of spectacle, celebration, and metamorphosis.

History forms the basis for humor and metamorphosis in Koch's two historical plays, *Bertha* (1959), a historical pageant, and *George Washington Crossing the Delaware* (1962), a chronicle play. Bertha is a Norwegian queen who saves her people from the barbarian menace. She performs this feat regularly, whenever she becomes bored with routine rule. The humor of the play resides in the use of formal Elizabethan language to describe Bertha's idiosyncratic behavior, and in strangely concatenated literary allusions such as the linked references to *Antony and Cleopatra* (c. 1606-1607) and *Alice's Adventures in Wonderland* (1865), Bertha being related to both the tragic queen of Egypt and the mad queen of Wonderland.

George Washington Crossing the Delaware, perhaps Koch's best play, is part myth, part chronicle, part comedy. Its comic incongruities, its colloquial deflation of a more stately heroic language, and its juxtaposition of low comedy and high seriousness serve to make it a surprising and inventive theatrical entertainment.

ACHIEVEMENTS

Kenneth Koch's achievements are notable and varied. He has received numerous fellowships, including several from Fulbright (in 1950-1951, 1978, and 1982), a Guggenheim (1960-1961), and an Ingram Merrill Foundation Fellowship (1969). His literary awards are impressive: a National Institute of Arts and Letters award (1976), an Award of Merit for Poetry from the American Academy and Institute of Arts and Letters (1986), the Shelley Memorial Award (1994), the Bollingen Prize (1995), the Rebekah Johnson Bobbitt National Prize for Poetry for *One Train: Poems* (1996), a Chevalier de l'ordre des arts et des lettres, France (1999), and a National Book Award for *New Addresses* (2000). In 1995, he became an elected member of the American Academy of Arts and Letters.

BIOGRAPHY

Kenneth Koch was born in Cincinnati, Ohio, on February 27, 1925. Although he wrote his first poem when he was five, he did not begin writing seriously until he was seventeen, when he read the novels of John

Kenneth Koch (© Frank Lima)

Dos Passos and was thereby stimulated to imitate their particular style of stream of consciousness. Koch served as a rifleman in the U.S. Army during World War II. After the war, he earned a B.A. degree from Harvard University in 1948, and a doctorate from Columbia in 1959. At Harvard, Koch was a friend of John Ashbery and Frank O'Hara, poets who held similar views about the nature of poetry. Later, when they had settled in New York, Ashbery, O'Hara, and Koch came to be thought of as principal poets of the New York school.

Koch spent three important years in Europe, mostly in Italy and France. During that time, he was influenced by the humorous, surrealistic verse of Jacques Prévert. In a brief autobiographical account that appeared in *The New American Poetry* (1960, Donald Allen, editor), Koch noted that French poetry "had a huge effect" on his own work. Moreover, he acknowledged that he tried to get into his own writing "the same incomprehensible excitement" that he found in French poetry.

During the late 1960's and early 1970's Koch began teaching poetry writing at P.S. 61, a grammar school in New York City, and at a neighborhood museum in Brooklyn. A few years later he taught similar classes at a New York nursing home. Out of these experiences came a series of books about the teaching of poetry to children and the aged. The first of these, *Wishes, Lies, and Dreams: Teaching Young Children to Write Poetry* (1970), is perhaps the best known. A companion volume, *Rose Where Did You Get That Red?*, followed in 1973. Both are noteworthy for their inventive approach to teaching poetry, especially for the imaginative ways they keep reading and writing poetry together. An additional value of the books and of two later volumes (*I Never Told Anybody: Teaching Poetry in a Nursing Home*, 1977, and *Sleeping on the Wing: An Anthology of Modern Poetry with Essays on Reading and Writing*, 1981), is that all reveal something about Koch's poetic temperament and inclinations. The qualities that Koch encourages in his students' writing animate his own poems. Open forms, loose meter, memory and feeling, joy and humor, colloquial language, imaginative freedom—these reflect Koch's view that "there is no insurmountable barrier between ordinary speech and poetry."

Koch has taught at Brooklyn College (now of the City University of New York), Rutgers University, and The New School for Social Research. In 1971 he began his long tenure at Columbia University as a professor of English and comparative literature. Exhibitions of Koch's collaborative work have been held at the Ipswich Museum, England, in 1993; at the Tibor De Nagy Gallery, New York City, in 1994; and at Guild Hall, East Hampton, New York, in 2000. He lives in New York City.

ANALYSIS

At his best, Kenneth Koch is a good comic poet and a fine parodist. A poet of limited tonal range yet of a wide and resourceful imagination, Koch's random structures, open forms, and loose meters give his poetry freedom and surprise that occasionally astonish and often delight. Just as often, however, the formlessness of Koch's poems results in slackness and self-indulgence. The tension that one expects in good poetry, deriving largely from exigencies of form, is mission in Koch's poems.

In *The King of the Cats* (1965), F. W. Dupee compared Koch to Marianne Moore. Dupee notes that while both Koch and Moore make poetry out of "poetry-resistant stuff," Koch lacks Moore's patient scrutiny and careful, sustained observation. Preferring to participate imaginatively rather than to observe carefully, Koch often seems more interested in where he can go with an observation, with what his imagination can make of it, than in what it is in itself. At his best, Koch's imaginative facility translates into poetic felicity; at his worst, Koch's freedom of imagination obscures the clarity and lucidity of the poems, frequently testing the reader's patience.

Perhaps the most trenchant and perceptive criticism of Koch's work has been that of Richard Howard in his book on contemporary poetry, *Alone with America: Essays on the Art of Poetry in the United States Since 1950* (1969). Howard suggests that the central poetic problem for Koch is to sustain the interest of the instant, to hold onto the momentary imaginative phrase or the surprising conjunction of dichotomous ideas, experiences, and details. Koch frequently hurries beyond moments of imaginative vitality and verbal splendor; rather than sustaining or developing them, he abandons them. At his best, however, such abandonments lead to other moments that are equally splendid, culminating in convincingly coherent poems.

Some of Koch's most distinctive and successful poems are parodies. His parody of Robert Frost, "Mending Sump," in which he alludes to and satirizes the style and situation of both "Mending Wall" and "The Death of the Hired Man," is one of his most famous. A modestly successful parody, "Mending Sump" does not compare with Koch's brilliant and witty parody of William Carlos Williams's brief conversational poem, "This Is Just to Say." Koch entitles his parody "Variations on a Theme by William Carlos Williams." In four brief stanzas, Koch parodies the occasion, structure, rhythm, and tone of a poet whose work has powerfully influenced his own.

Although in his nonparodistic poetry Koch may not often attempt to imitate Williams, he does try to accomplish what Williams achieved in his best work: the astonishment of the moment; the astonishment of something seen, heard, felt, or understood; the magic and the beauty of the commonplace. Koch, too, can astonish—but not by acts of attention like those of Williams nor by his power of feeling. Koch astonishes by his outrageous dislocations of sense and logic, his exuberant and risk-taking amalgamation of utterly disparate experiences. His achievement, finally, consists of small surprises, delights of image and allusion, phrase and idea; his poems rarely possess the power to move or instruct, but they do entertain.

Among Kenneth Koch's long poems are *Ko: Or, A Season on Earth*, a mock-heroic epic in ottava rima about a Japanese baseball player, a poem with a variety of story lines; *The Duplications*, a comic epic about sex that employs trappings of Greek mythology and that in its second part becomes a self-reflexive poem concerned with the poetic vocation; and *When the Sun Tries to Go On*, a poem that goes on for one hundred twenty-four-line stanzas, in large part because Koch wanted to see how long he could go on with what was originally a seventy-two-line poem. All three poems are characterized by Koch's infectious humor, his far-fetched analogies, and his digressive impulse.

More interesting and more consistently successful are Koch's shorter poems, ranging in length from a dozen lines to a dozen pages. In the poems included in Koch's best collections, *The Art of Love* and *The Pleasures of Peace and Other Poems*, one encounters Koch at his most graceful and disarming. In the best poems from these volumes (and there are many engaging ones), Koch exhibits his characteristic playfulness, deliberate formlessness, and almost surrealistic allusiveness. The poems are humorous yet serious in both their invitations and their admonitions.

THE PLEASURES OF PEACE

Koch's major poetic preoccupations find abundant exemplifications in his volume *The Pleasures of Peace and Other Poems*. The title poem is divided loosely into fourteen sections, each section describing different kinds of pleasures: of writing, of peace, of pain, of pleasure itself, of fantasy, of reality, of memory, of autonomy, of poetry, and of living. The poem is both a catalog and a celebration of the rich pleasures of simply being alive. Its self-reflexiveness coexists with its Whitmanesque embrace of the range, diversity, and variability of life's pleasures. Another stylistic hallmark evident in this poem is a playful use of literary allusion. In addition to evoking Walt Whitman, Koch alludes directly to William Butler Yeats ("The Lake Isle of Innisfree"), Andrew Marvell ("To His Coy Mistress"), Robert Herrick, Percy Bysshe Shelley, and William Wordsworth. The allusions are surprising: Koch's lines modify and alter the words of the earlier poets as they situate them in the context of a radically different poem.

These observations about "The Pleasures of Peace" fail to account for what is perhaps its most distinctive identifying quality: a wild, surrealistic concatenation of details (pink mint chewing gum with "the whole rude gallery of war"; Dutch-speaking cowboys; the pleasures of agoraphobia with the pleasures of blasphemy; the pleasures of breasts, bread, and poodles; the pleasures of stars and of plaster). Moreover, amid the litany of the poem's pleasures occur several notes of desperation—for the horrors of war and suffering. Koch seems to find it necessary to remind his readers of the peaceful pleasures of life largely because the horrors of war and the futility of modern life allow them to be forgotten.

Although Sigmund Freud is an obvious influence on Koch's "The Interpretation of Dreams," a zany poem that imitates the syntax of dream in its associative structure, in its dislocations and disruptions of continuity, and in its oddly mismatched characters, Whitman is the dominant voice and force behind most of the other poems in the volume. Whitman's influence is discernible in "Hearing," a rambling play on sounds in which Koch makes music out of the disparate noises of waterfalls and trumpets, throbbing hearts and falling leaves, rain and thunder, bluebirds singing and dresses ripping. The poem, concluding with the words "the song is finished," owes something also to the other American poets it invokes: Ezra Pound, William Carlos Williams, and Wallace Stevens.

It is Whitman, however, who stands behind Koch's "Poem of the Forty-Eight States," especially the Whitman of "On Journeys Through the States"; and it is Whitman who hovers over the incantatory litany of Koch's "Sleeping with Women," especially the Whitman of "The Sleepers" and "Beautiful Women." Perhaps the most successful of Koch's Whitmanesque poems is "Faces," which, while less uniform in tone than "Sleeping with Women," with its hypnotic, anaphoric incantation, and while not as close to Whitman's own tone, nevertheless carries something of Whitman's power of suggestion in its implication that the variety of faces called up in the poem (Popeye and Agamemnon, Herbert Hoover and the poor of the Depression) reflect the life of the speaker of the poem. By implication, Koch seems to suggest that each reader could create a similar yet highly individual and personal collage of faces that, taken together, reflect the range and variety of his experience and that, in a concentrated yet variegated image, sum up his or her life.

THE ART OF LOVE

Koch's other important volume, *The Art of Love*, while retaining something of the humorous tone of *The Pleasures of Peace and Other Poems* as well as something of its imaginative wit, reaches more deeply in feeling and ranges more widely in thought. Many of the poems are cast in an admonitory mode; others are ironic, while still others include both irony and admonition. "The Art of Poetry" alternates between ironic posture and serious gesture in its descriptions of poetic attitudes, ideals, and practices. The speaker advises poets to stay young even while growing and developing, something

that Koch has consistently tried to do. He suggests that a poet should imitate other poets, try on other styles, and try out other voices in an effort to form, paradoxically, his own style. After addressing the problems of beginning a poem, sustaining and ending it (and also revising it), the speaker reminds the poet to absorb himself totally in poetry, for only such a total immersion will enable the poet to see poetry as "the mediation of life." Such is Koch's poetic credo.

This poetic creed notwithstanding, perhaps the most unusual and the most useful advice in "The Art of Poetry" is given in a set of questions and answers that further reveal the direction and impulse of Koch's own poetry: Is the poem astonishing? Is it wise? Is it original? Does it employ cheap effects, tricks, or gimmicks? Does it engage heart and mind? Would the poet envy another's having written it? If the answer is "yes" to all but the fourth question, the poem qualifies, if not for greatness, at least for honesty and integrity, qualities and standards certainly deserving of respect and admiration. In his "The Art of Poetry" Koch seems to have achieved them.

Although not overtly about the art of poetry, "Some General Instructions" can be taken as describing Koch's poems even as it gives more explicit advice about living. One statement in particular suggests the connection between poetry and life: "Things have a way of working out/ Which is nonsensical, and one should try to see/ How the process works." This implies that nonsense ultimately makes sense, that beneath the apparent confusion lies order, purpose, and meaning. The statement provides a helpful gloss on the best of Koch's poems, which often go by way of nonsense to make a final and useful kind of sense.

"Some General Instructions" alternates between aphorism and meditative commentary. Like any set of aphorisms, it bristles with contradictions. Even so, it shines with joy and radiates humor. Koch seems to enjoy juxtaposing serious moral and ethical advice with comic yet practical admonition. He advises, for example, that his readers be glad, that they savor life, love, pleasure, and virtue, and that they not eat too many bananas.

Although a similar tone mixing playful humor with thoughtful advice permeates Koch's lovely and beautiful "On Beauty," a rather different note is struck by two other poems in the volume. In "The Circus," a nostalgic reminiscence about the time he wrote an earlier poem with the same title, Koch wonders about the value of the earlier poem, and then, by extension, about the value of any of his poems, about the value of his poetic vocation. Moving out of a concern with poetry, "The Circus" becomes more somber, turning into a meditation on time, death, and loss, especially the loss of friends. In "The Art of Love," a how-to manual of eroticism, the speaker describes a set of outrageous sadomasochistic procedures. The practical nature of the advice ranges from how to meet and greet a girl, to how to get her to do the things described in the poem. "The Art of Love" ends with a catalog of questions about love, some serious, some humorous. Ludicrous answers are provided to each question. Full of high spirits, erotic fantasies, hyperbole, and insult, the poem needs to be taken ironically if it is not to be considered an offense against decency. Even then, its specificity of reference and particularity of detail make it seem less an ironic poem about the art of love than a degrading if witty description of perverse fantasies.

ON THE EDGE

Koch's 1986 volume *On the Edge* consists of two long poems, the title poem and "Impressions of Africa." The former is a strongly autobiographical work; the latter, as its title suggests, presents images and impressions gathered while the poet was in Africa. Although both present difficulties, with their fragmentations and free associations that attempt to represent experience and memory in Koch's unique way, the structure is not entirely haphazard. More than the usual Koch work, "Impressions of Africa" gives the reader a sense of how a place objectively appears, in lines that sometimes remind one of diary entries transformed into verse. "On the Edge" is harder to grasp. In the poem, events involving Koch and his friends circle an apparently fictional character named Dan. Moments of clarity are scattered among thoughts that interrupt themselves, such as "Our modern—fragmentary—Dan stands up—it's about time—reason." Koch's charm and sense of humor appear throughout, but the landscape of the work frequently exists so deep within the poet's consciousness that it seems indecipherable.

Koch's talent is perhaps best manifested in *The Pleasures of Peace and Other Poems* and *The Art of Love*.

While the poems do not range widely in style, theme, and technique, they do offer a distinctive set of pleasures for the accepting and patient reader, the pleasures of engaging an unusual and unpredictable poetic imagination as it reveals itself in a colloquially inflected idiom which is, by turns, earnest and ironic. The deliberate dislocations of logical organization, the profusion of incongruities in image and idea, the exaggeration and far-fetched analogies are all part of Koch's effort to avoid the predictable, the stodgy, and the dull. They are all part of his effort to create a poetry full of fun and surprise, which, even though it only infrequently ends in wisdom, nevertheless very often sustains the delight with which it begins.

STRAITS

In *Straits*, persons searching and journeying appear in the volume's title poem, a dazzling array of sentences of failure, success, discovery, and change, with everything happening at once. The "straits" of this collection represent a possibility, and they grant access to ecstasy, unity, freedom, and completeness. Running through *Straits* is Koch's preoccupation with time and making time run, not after him but in circles. Thus the seventeen quatrains of "Ballade," each titled for a year of the poet's life, undo chronology, beginning with the seventy-first and ending with the thirtieth, and ranging in age from five to seventy-three, in no particular order. Themes of aging, seasonal change, and "the loss of the sacred in everyday life" are amply evident (on being seventy-three, Koch comments, "I have lots of years and decades in me/ And they divide me like Sunday ads./ It's the Big Sale of the Week, when I can speak in song").

The volume spans a wide range of form and content, of experiences culled from Koch's life ("Currency") and those that are formed merely in an exuberant imagination. The sequence "The Seasons," dedicated to the eighteenth century poet James Thomson, maker of *The Seasons* (1730), is perhaps Koch's best contribution in this volume. Here linear time is supplanted by Koch's cyclic interpretations, the rhythms of day and night and of "The seasons' lazy susan." It calls forth New York urban pastoralism—hot-dog stands, the World Series, opera, and snowplows—and finds renewal even in autumn: "harbinger of rebirth/ Of school and love and work."

NEW ADDRESSES

In Koch's *New Addresses*, he presents fifty free-verse poems, each an ode to a different subject ("To Psychoanalysis," "To My Father's Business," "To 'Yes'"), making the "addresses" in his title quite literal. It is perhaps his most autobiographical collection, a volume that recalls, for the first time in his poetry, a pivotal moment in his life: his military service during World War II. Putting such an experience into verse proved a challenge he could not resist: "I'd never really been able to write [about the war] because it's like being psychotic to be in a war. You're walking around with a gun . . . and they shoot you!" However, the poet found that treating the war as a character, like any other person, "enabled me to get some of the feelings back, like the crazy idea that I couldn't be killed because I had to write." His encounter with a faulty explosive in "To Carelessness" is unnerving with its understated lesson in the dumb luck of staying alive in battle. "To World War Two," a much longer poem, captures the combatant's sense of his sheer insignificance: "If you could use me/ You'd use me, and then forget. How else/ Did I think you'd behave?/ I'm glad you ended. I'm glad I didn't die."

Other bits of Koch's life are also revealed throughout the addresses (for example, childhood is probed in "To Piano Lessons"; later periods in Koch's life in "To My Fifties"), where readers find the speaker accusing, praising, or querying abstract concepts, emotions, his character, and his past. Some are overtly emotional ("To My Father's Business" or "To Jewishness") while some favor his characteristic playfulness ("To Testosterone" or "To Some Abstract Paintings").

OTHER MAJOR WORKS

LONG FICTION: *The Red Robins*, 1975.

PLAYS: *Bertha*, pr. 1959; *George Washington Crossing the Delaware*, pr. 1962; *Bertha and Other Plays*, pb. 1966; *The Moon Balloon*, pr. 1969; *A Change of Hearts: Plays, Films, and Other Dramatic Works, 1951-1971*, pb. 1973; *E. Kology*, pb. 1973; *The New Diana*, pr. 1984; *The Gold Standard: A Book of Plays*, pb. 1996.

NONFICTION: *Wishes, Lies, and Dreams: Teaching Young Children to Write Poetry*, 1970; *Rose Where Did You Get That Red?*, 1973; *I Never Told Anybody:*

Teaching Poetry in a Nursing Home, 1977; *Sleeping on the Wing: An Anthology of Modern Poetry with Essays on Reading and Writing*, 1981 (with Kate Farrell); *The Art of Poetry: Poems, Parodies, Interviews, Essays, and Other Work*, 1996; *Making Your Own Days: The Pleasures of Reading and Writing Poetry*, 1998.

BIBLIOGRAPHY

Ashbery, John, and Kenneth Koch. *John Ashbery and Kenneth Koch: A Conversation*. Tucson, Ariz.: Interview Press, [1966?]. Insights into Koch's poetry emerge from this twenty-page interchange between the two poets.

Auslander, Philip. *The New York School Poets as Playwrights: O'Hara, Ashbery, Koch, Schuyler, and the Visual Arts*. New York: P. Lang, 1989. Auslander discusses the plays written by these poets who attended the New York School of Art. Their life in New York affects their artistic endeavors, regardless of their form: poetry, experimental drama, short story, or visual art. This survey is useful as it gives an idea of Koch's competency in varied artistic media.

Carruth, Hayden. "Kenneth Koch." In *Contemporary Poets*, edited by James Vinson and D. L. Kirkpatrick. 4th ed. New York: St. Martin's Press, 1985. Carruth, an outstanding poet in his own right, outlines Koch's background and work. Carruth first covers Koch's apprenticeship with the New York school of poets in the 1950's, and then discusses Koch's current poetry, which is simpler and more effective than his earlier work. A good introduction for all students.

Howard, Richard. *Alone with America: Essays on the Art of Poetry in the United States Since 1950*. New York: Atheneum, 1969. In his chapter on Koch, Howard discusses his emphasis on the individual moment and (paradoxically) its movement. Howard also notes Koch's ability to be funny, calling him a master parodist, and mentions devices that Koch uses in his "improvisational plays."

Koch, Kenneth. Interview by Anselm Berrigan. *Publishers Weekly* 247, no. 13 (March, 2000): 72. An interview with Koch and a discussion of *New Addresses: Poems*.

_____. "An Interview with Kenneth Koch." Interview by John Tranter. *Scripsi* 4 (November, 1986): 177-185. In this rare interview, Koch discusses the evolution of his work from his rebellious New York school of poetry days to his 1980's poetic style. He also talks about his work in the theater, which is experimental and plentiful. For all students.

Lang, Nancy. "Comic Fantasy in Two Postmodern Verse Novels: *Slinger* and *Ko*." In *The Poetic Fantastic: Studies in an Evolving Genre*, edited by Patrick D. Murphy and Vernon Ross Hyles. Westport, Conn.: Greenwood Press, 1989. This interesting article compares the use of fantasy for fun in Koch's *Ko: Or, A Season on Earth* and Edward Dorn's *Slinger*.

Merrin, Jeredith. "The Poetry Man." *The Southern Review* 35, no. 2 (Spring, 1999): 403-409. Merrin discusses Koch's poetry and nonfiction writing.

Moss, Howard. *The Poet's Story*. New York: Macmillan, 1973. Moss collects the short stories of twenty writers who are much better known for their poetry. In this collection, Moss includes Koch's short story "A Slight Mechanical Failure." Interesting, for it demonstrates Koch's versatility as a writer.

Robert DiYanni,
updated by Sarah Hilbert

YUSEF KOMUNYAKAA

Born: Bogalusa, Louisiana; April 29, 1947

PRINCIPAL POETRY

Dedications and Other Dark Horses, 1977
Lost in the Bonewheel Factory, 1979
Copacetic, 1984
I Apologize for the Eyes in My Head, 1986
Toys in the Field, 1987
Dien Cai Dau, 1988
February in Sydney, 1989
Magic City, 1992
Neon Vernacular: New and Selected Poems, 1993
Thieves of Paradise, 1998

Talking Dirty to the Gods, 2000
Pleasure Dome: New and Collected Poems, 2001

OTHER LITERARY FORMS

Despite his impressive poetic output—more than a book of poems every other year since 1977 and publication in all the major poetry journals—Yusef Komunyakaa has not been content to stay within these traditional confines. He has made a number of sound and video recordings of his readings of his work. One of the more interesting of these is *Love Notes from the Madhouse* (1997), a live reading performed with a jazz ensemble led by John Tchicai. He has written two libretti, "Slip Knot," with T. J. Anderson, about an eighteenth century slave, and "Testimony" (1999), about jazz great Charlie Parker. In *Thirteen Kinds of Desire* (2000), vocalist Pamela Knowles sings lyrics by Komunyakaa. Of his fight against traditional poetic boundaries, he notes: "I am always pushing against the walls [categories] create. I will always do this. . . . Theater and song won't be the last of me."

Blue Notes: Essays, Interviews, and Commentaries (2000), edited by Radiclani Clytus, is an eclectic mix of seven interviews with the poet from 1990 to 2000, as well as twelve short impressionistic essays by him and five new poems with commentary by the author. With Sascha Feinstein, he edited *The Jazz Poetry Anthology* (volume 1, 1991; volume 2, 1996). Together with Martha Collins, Komunyakaa translated the work of Vietnamese poet Nguyen Quang Thieu. His own poetry has been translated into Vietnamese as well as Russian, Korean, Czech, French, and Italian.

ACHIEVEMENTS

Many readers, critics, and fellow poets have long recognized Yusef Komunyakaa as a major poet of his generation. His poems about the Vietnam War place him among the finest writers who have explored this difficult terrain. His use of jazz and blues rhythms places him in the tradition of poet Langston Hughes and the best Southern writers. Of his many awards and honors, perhaps the most impressive is the 1994 Pulitzer Prize for Poetry for *Neon Vernacular*, which also won the Kingsley Tufts Award and the William Faulkner Prize. *Thieves of Paradise* was a finalist for the National Book Critics

Pulitzer Prize-winning poet Yusef Komunyakaa in 1996. (AP/Wide World Photos)

Circle Award. Komunyakaa has also won the Thomas Forcade Award and the Hanes Poetry Prize. In 1999, he was elected a chancellor of the Academy of American Poets.

He has been awarded creative writing fellowships from the National Endowment for the Arts, the Fine Arts Center in Provincetown, Massachusetts, and the Louisiana Arts Council. He has served as a judge for numerous poetry competitions and has been on the advisory board for the *Encyclopedia of American Poetry* (1998, 2001). His work has appeared in all the major poetry journals, as well as national magazines such as *The Atlantic Monthly* and *The New Republic*. One indication of Komunyakaa's appeal is the number of diverse anthologies that include his work. He appears repeatedly in the annual *The Best American Poetry*, collections of verse about Vietnam, and numerous periodicals.

BIOGRAPHY

The oldest of five children, Yusef Komunyakaa had a strained relationship with his father, which he chronicled vividly years later in a fourteen-sonnet sequence titled "Songs for My Father," which appears in *Neon Vernacular*. The Bogalusa of Komunyakaa's childhood was a rural community in southern Louisiana that held few opportunities economically or culturally, especially for a young black man. The main industry was the single paper mill, one that turned "workers into pulp," according to one poem. There was a racially charged atmosphere. The public library admitted only whites; the Ku Klux Klan was still active. In "Fog Galleon," Komunyakaa writes of these difficulties:

> I press against the taxicab
> Window. I'm black here, interfaced
> With a dead phosphorescence;
> The whole town smells
> Like the world's oldest anger.

Daydreaming and reading were ways of escaping and coping with a slow life. Daydreaming, which Komunyakaa now sees as an important creative act of his youth, is evident in his early identification with his grandfather's West Indian heritage. He took the name Komunyakaa from his grandfather, who, according to family legend, came to America as a stowaway from Trinidad. In the poem "Mismatched Shoes," Komunyakaa writes of this identification:

> The island swelled in his throat
> & calypso leapt into the air,
>
> . . . .
> I picked up those mismatched shoes
> & slipped into his skin. Komunyakaa.
> His blues, African fruit on my tongue.

The Bible and a set of supermarket encyclopedias were his first books. He has noted the influence of the Bible's "hypnotic cadence," sensitizing him to the importance of music and metaphor. James Baldwin's *Nobody Knows My Name* (1961), discovered in a church library when Komunyakaa was sixteen, inspired him to become a writer. Jazz and blues radio programs from New Orleans, heard on the family radio, formed a third important influence. Komunyakaa speaks fondly of those early days of listening to jazz and acknowledges its importance in his work.

After graduation from high school in 1965, Komunyakaa traveled briefly and in 1969 enlisted in the army. He was sent to Vietnam. He served as a reporter on the front lines and later as editor of *The Southern Cross*, a military newspaper. The experience of being flown in by helicopter to observe and then report on the war effort laid the groundwork for the powerful fusion of passion and detached observation that is a hallmark of his war poems, written years later. He was awarded the Bronze Star for his service in Vietnam.

Upon being discharged, Komunyakaa enrolled at the University of Colorado, where he majored in English and sociology, earning a bachelor's degree in 1975. A creative writing course there inspired him to pursue a master's degree in creative writing at Colorado State University, which he earned in 1978. He received his master of fine arts degree from the University of California, Irvine, in 1980. During this period he published limited editions of his first two short books of poems, *Dedications and Other Darkhorses* and *Lost in the Bonewheel Factory*.

Komunyakaa taught poetry briefly in public school before joining the creative writing faculty at the University of New Orleans, where he met Mandy Sayer, whom he married in 1985. That year he became an associate professor at Indiana University at Bloomington, where in 1989 he was named Lilly Professor of Poetry. He later became a professor in the Council of Humanities and Creative Writing Program at Princeton University.

ANALYSIS

Because Yusef Komunyakaa's poetry is so rich in imagery, allusion, metaphor, musical rhythms, and ironic twists, it possesses a freshness and a bittersweet bite whether the subject is the raw beauty of nature or the passions and follies of human nature. He has said that poetry does not work for him without "surprises." His poetry surprises both in its technique—the juxtaposition of disparate images and sudden shifts in perspective—and in its subjects. Generally his poems have a sensual quality even though the subject matter varies greatly: childhood memories, family feuds, race, war, sex, nature, jazz. Scholar Radiclani Clytus commented

early in Komunyakaa's career that the poet's interpretation of popular mythology and legend gave readers "alternative access to cultural lore. Epic human imperfections, ancient psychological profiles, and the haunting resonance of the South are now explained by those who slow drag to Little Willie John and rendezvous at MOMA." Komunyakaa's comment that "a poem is both confrontation and celebration" aptly captures the essence of his own work.

COPACETIC

Two early books, the first ones published by a major university press, introduce many of Komunyakaa's subjects and techniques and were the first to win him critical acclaim. *Copacetic* focuses primarily on memories of childhood and the persuasive influence of music. The narrator speaks of "a heavy love for jazz," and in fact musical motifs run throughout Komunyakaa's poetry. He has compared poetry to jazz and blues in its emphasis on feeling and tone, its sense of surprise and discovery, and its diversity within a general structure. Poems such as "Copacetic Mingus," "Elegy for Thelonious," and "Untitled Blues" convey the power of this kind of music, in which "Art & life bleed into each other." Depending on the poem, music can serve as escape, therapy, or analogy. Often it is combined with richly sensual images, as in "Woman, I Got the Blues."

I APOLOGIZE FOR THE EYES IN MY HEAD AND DIEN CAI DAU

I Apologize for the Eyes in My Head continues this motif while adding new subjects and themes. The ugly side of race relations in the United States is suggested in several poems. Komunyakaa also begins to explore the pain of the Vietnam War. "For the Walking Dead" is a moving account of "boyish soldiers on their way to the front" who seek respite with Veronica in a local bar.

The past wounds and present scars of the Vietnam War are the subjects of *Dien Cai Dau*, whose title means "crazy" in Vietnamese. The powerful yet exquisitely sensitive—and sensual—way in which Komunyakaa conveys the pain, loss, and psychic confusion of his experience in Vietnam found a receptive audience. Most present a moment or a reflection in a richly nuanced but undogmatic way. In "We Never Know" he juxtaposes a delicate image of dancing with a woman with the reality of an enemy in the field, whom he kills and whose body he then approaches. The moral ambiguity of the moment is highlighted by the tenderness with which the soldier regards the body:

> When I got to him,
> a blue halo
> of flies had already claimed him.
> I pulled the crumbled photograph
> from his fingers.
> There's no other way
> to say this: I fell in love.
> The morning cleared again,
> except for a distant mortar
> & somewhere choppers taking off.
> I slid the wallet into his pocket
> & turned him over, so he wouldn't be
> kissing the ground.

Poems such as "Tu Du Street" and "Thanks" are even more complex in their multiple, often conflicting, images. The former presents the bizarre reality of racial prejudice even in Vietnam, "where only machine gun fire bring us together." The women with whom the soldiers seek solace provide one common denominator:

> There's more than a nation
> inside us, as black & white
> soldiers touch the same lovers
> minutes apart, tasting
> each other's breath,
> without knowing these rooms
> run into each other like tunnels
> leading to the underworld.

In "Thanks" the narrator gives thanks to an unspecified being for the myriad coincidences that saved him one day in the jungle as he "played some deadly/ game for blind gods." The poet provides no resolution or closure, just a series of powerful, haunting images:

> Again, thanks for the dud
> hand grenade tossed at my feet
> outside Chu Lai. I'm still
> falling through its silence.

THIEVES OF PARADISE

Komunyakaa won an Academy of Arts and Letters award given to writers with "progressive and experimental tendencies." This book is an example of this art-

ist's ability to experiment with form and ease the reader into accepting poetry that is unfamiliar. Much of the subject matter is familiar—the grim reality of war and its psychological aftermath, the body's hungers and betrayals, the allure of memory and imagination—but the presentation is fresh and intriguing. "Palimpsest" is a seemingly random, kaleidoscopic series of four-quatrain poems that move from "slavecatchers" to tanks in Beijing's Tiananmen Square to the backwoods to jazz musician Count Basie. By confronting uncomfortable truths, the poet writes, "I am going to teach Mr. Pain/ to sway, to bop."

Several, such as "Nude Interrogation," "Phantasmagoria," and "Frontispiece," are prose poems that force one to rethink the nature of the form, while Komunyakaa's images work on the emotions. "The Glass Ark" is a five-page dialogue between two paleontologists.

This collection includes the libretto "Testimony," about Charlie Parker, written in twenty-eight fourteen-line stanzas. It captures the reckless allure of the man and the time:

> Yardbird
> could blow a woman's strut
> across the room. . . . pushed moans through brass. . . . High
> heels clicking like a high hat.
> Black-beaded flapper. Blue satin
> Yardbird, he'd blow pain & glitter.

TALKING DIRTY TO THE GODS

This volume stands apart from earlier works in its adherence to a strict, traditional form. Each of its 132 poems consists of sixteen lines, in four unrhymed quatrains. Much of the appeal of this collection stems from the freedom and friction Komunyakaa creates by presenting his unusual images and bizarre juxtapositions in a tightly controlled format. The gods he discusses are taken from the ancient and the modern worlds, the exotic and the commonplace. Whether discussing the maggot ("Little/ Master of earth"), Bellerophon, or Joseph Stalin, he is able to humanize his subject enough to win at least some sympathy from the reader.

NEON VERNACULAR

Neon Vernacular won considerable critical acclaim as well as the Pulitzer Prize. In addition to culling the best from earlier books, it adds gems of its own, including the unrhymed sonnet sequence "Songs for My Father," a powerful fourteen-poem sequence that chronicles the poet's complicated relationship with his dad. In "At the Screen Door," in which a former soldier murders because he cannot separate the past from the present, Komunyakaa returns to the psychological aftermath of Vietnam.

PLEASURE DOME

The publication of *Pleasure Dome* led to laudatory reviews not only for its poetic achievement but also for its high purpose: "Nearly every page of these collected poems will pull you from your expectations, tell you something you did not know, and leave you better off than you were," said the reviewer for *Library Journal*, while *Booklist* praised Komunyakaa's "fluent creative energy, and his passion for living the examined life." *Pleasure Dome* is an extraordinarily rich collection of more than 350 poems. All earlier books except *Talking Dirty to the Gods* are represented. There is also a section titled "New Poems" and another, "Early Uncollected." Among the new poems is "Tenebrae," a moving meditation on Richard Johnson, the black Indiana University music professor who committed suicide. The lines "You try to beat loneliness/ out of a drum" are woven throughout the poem with a cumulative, haunting effect.

OTHER MAJOR WORKS

NONFICTION: *Blue Notes: Essays, Interviews, and Commentaries*, 2000 (Radiclani Clytus, editor).

TRANSLATION: *The Insomnia of Fire*, 1995 (with Martha Collins, of poetry by Nguyen Quang Thieu).

EDITED TEXTS: *The Jazz Poetry Anthology*, 1991 (with Sascha Feinstein); *The Second Set: The Jazz Poetry Anthology, Volume 2*, 1996 (with Feinstein).

BIBLIOGRAPHY

Conley, Susan. "About Yusef Komunyakaa: A Profile." *Ploughshares* 23, no. 1 (Spring, 1997): 202-207. Conley gives a concise overview of the poet's career, his central themes and motifs, his views on race relations in America, and his usual method of writing poetry.

Dawidoff, Sally. "Talking Poetry with Yusef Komunyakaa." http://www.africana.com/DailyArticles/index_20010114.htm. 2000. This interview begins by discussing Komunyakaa's *Talking Dirty to the Gods*, then branches out into a variety of related subjects: political poetry, folklore and mythology, the jazz influence, and ways in which the poet can engage his or her audience.

Gordon, Fran. "Yusef Komunyakaa: Blue Note in a Lyrical Landscape." *Poets & Writers* 28, no. 6 (November/December, 2000): 26-33. Gordon terms Komunyakaa "one of America's most receptive minds" and "one of its most original voices." This interview provides a glimpse into the poet's thoughts on his background and early reading, his interest in nature and mythology, and his use of imagery and music in his poetry.

Gotera, Vincente. "Depending on the Light: Yusef Komunyakaa's *Dien Cai Dau*." In *America Rediscovered: Critical Essays on Literature and Film of the Vietnam War*, edited by Owen Gilman. New York: Garland, 1990. Komunyakaa differs from other war poets in his "devotion to highly textured language"; he refuses "to present Vietnam to the reader as exotica," but rather "underline[s] the existential reality" of his experience. That same year Gotera published an interview with the poet in *Callaloo*; he includes Komunyakaa's poetry in his 1994 *Radical Visions: Poetry by Vietnam Veterans*, published by the University of Georgia Press.

Ringnalda, Don. *Fighting and Writing the Vietnam War*. Jackson: University Press of Mississippi, 1994. As he does in "Rejecting 'Sweet Geometry'" (*Journal of American Culture* 16, no. 3, Fall, 1993), Ringnalda suggests that much of the poetry about Vietnam is too safe in both form and content. Because Komunyakaa realizes that the old paradigms are shattered, he "gains the freedom to explore subterranean, prerational landscapes. This results in a poetry of rich, disturbing associations."

Weber, Bruce. "A Poet's Values: It's the Words Over the Man." *The New York Times Biographical Service* 25 (May, 1994): 666-667. Written three weeks after Komunyakaa won the Pulitzer Prize, this brief account adds several new and interesting anecdotes about the poet's early years and his views on his craft.

Danny Robinson

KARL KRAUS

Born: Gitschin, Bohemia (now Jičin, Czech Republic;
    April 28, 1874
Died: Vienna, Austria; June 12, 1936

PRINCIPAL POETRY

Worte in Versen, 1916-1930 (9 volumes)
Poems, 1930

OTHER LITERARY FORMS

Karl Kraus, widely regarded as one of the greatest mid-twentieth century satirists, is not known primarily as a poet. His powerful cultural criticism took several forms, and poetry was but one of them. Kraus was most effective as a writer of prose, producing thousands of essays and aphorisms. He is also important as a dramatist, his greatest work in that form being his pacifist play *Die letzten Tage der Menschheit* (1922; *The Last Days of Mankind*, 1974), written during World War I. Most of Kraus's writings first appeared in his own journal, *Die Fackel*.

ACHIEVEMENTS

The vitriolic Karl Kraus, a man who hauled the powerful and the pitiful alike before a tribunal of total satire, was a legend in his lifetime, both adored and vilified by his contemporaries. Following a decade of desuetude, his work was rediscovered and reissued in Germany and Austria after World War II. Numerous editions, studies, and translations have focused critical attention on this satirist, whose dictum (*Spruch*) or contradiction (*Widerspruch*), "I have to wait until my writings are obsolete; then they may acquire timeliness," seems to be coming true. As literary critic and historian of German literature Erich Heller has put it, "Karl Kraus did not write 'in a language,' but through him the beauty, profundity, and accumulated moral experience of the German language assumed personal shape and became the crucial witness in the case this inspired prosecutor brought against his time."

Kraus's timeliness and, at long last, his relative exportability derive at least in part from certain parallels between his age and the late twentieth century, which

has need of his vibrant pacifism, his principled defense of the spirit against dehumanizing tendencies, and his "linguistic-moral imperative," as literary critic and expert of German literature J. P. Stern puts it, which equates purity of language with purity of thought, a return to the sources of spiritual strength, and steadfastness of moral purpose. Kraus lived a life that oscillated between love and hate. "Hatred must make a person productive," he once wrote; "otherwise one might as well love."

The thirty-seven volumes of *Die Fackel* represent a gigantic effort to fashion the imperishable profile of an age from such highly perishable materials as newspaper reports. The journal was an enormous pillory, a running autobiography, a uniquely personal history of Austria-Hungary (an empire which Kraus regarded as a "proving ground for the end of the world"), and a world stage on which Kraus dramatized himself and his satiric mission. His markedly apocalyptic stance as a "late" warner derives from his epoch's *Zeitgeist*: transitoriness, disintegration, and inner insecurity.

Kraus's unremitting satirical warfare against the press (and in particular the influential *Neue freie Presse* of Vienna) was motivated by his view of journalism as a vast switchboard that concentrated and activated the forces of corruption, dissolution, and decay. Recognizing a disturbing identity of *Zeit* and *Zeitung*, the age and the newspapers it spawned, with *Worte* (words) usurping and destroying *Werte* (values), he had apocalyptic visions of the world being obliterated by the black magic of printer's ink. Decades before Hermann Hesse coined the phrase *das feuilletonistische Zeitalter* (the pamphleteering period) in his utopian novel *Das Glasperlenspiel* (1943; *The Glass Bead Game*, 1949), Kraus recognized his age as "the age of the *feuilleton*," in which newspaper reports took precedence over events, form eclipsed substance, and the style, the atmosphere, the "package" were all-important. Excoriating the press, that "goiter of the world," for its pollution of language and its poisoning of the human spirit, Kraus anticipated the judgments of contemporary critics of the media, and his diagnosis still has relevance.

BIOGRAPHY

Karl Kraus was the son of a prosperous manufacturer of paper bags, and the family fortune supported him to a large extent for most of his life. In 1877, the family moved to Vienna, and Kraus spent the rest of his life in that city, with which he—like Sigmund Freud—had a love-hate relationship. After attending the University of Vienna without taking a degree, Kraus attempted a career on the stage. His failure as an actor irrevocably steered him to journalism and literature, though his talent for mimicry and parody as well as his penchant for verbal play found ample expression in his later public readings as well as in his writings. In 1892, Kraus began to contribute book reviews, drama criticism, and other prose to various newspapers and periodicals. In his twenties, however, his satirical impulse became too strong for any kind of accommodation, and Kraus rejected the prospect of becoming a sort of "culture clown" absorbed by a deceptively slack and effete environment and accorded, as he put it, "the accursed popularity which a grinning Vienna bestows."

Because work within the establishment seemed to be hedged in with multifarious taboos and considerations of a commercial and personal nature, Kraus rejected a job offer from the *Neue freie Presse* and founded his own journal, *Die Fackel*, the first issue of which appeared on April 1, 1899, and which from the beginning had an incomparably satiric *genius loci*. After 1911, the irregularly issued periodical contained Kraus's writings exclusively: "I no longer have contributors," he wrote. "I used to be envious of them. They repel those readers whom I want to lose myself." Kraus's periodical did continue to have numerous "contributors," albeit unwitting and unwilling ones: the people who were copiously quoted in its pages and allowed to hang themselves with the nooses of their own statements, attitudes, and actions.

Kraus's first major works were a literary satire titled *Die demolirte Literatur* (1897; the demolished literature), a witty diatribe about the razing of a Vienna café frequented by the literati, and an anti-Zionist pamphlet, *Eine Krone für Zion* (1898; a crown for Zion). (Kraus left the Jewish fold as early as 1898 and was secretly baptized as a Roman Catholic in 1911, but he broke with the Church eleven years later and thereafter remained unaffiliated with any religious group. He has been called everything from "an arch-Jew" and "an Old Testament prophet who pours cataracts of wrath

Karl Kraus

over his own people" to "a shining example of Jewish self-hatred.") If Kraus's early writings were directed largely against standard aspects of corruption, the second period of his creativity may be dated from the appearance of his essay *Sittlichkeit und Kriminalität* (1902, reissued in book form in 1908; morality and criminal justice), in which Kraus concerned himself, on the basis of contemporary court cases, with the glaring contrast between private and public morality and with the hypocrisy inherent in the administration of justice in Austria. In turning a powerful spotlight on a male-dominated society with its double standard, shameless encroachments on privacy, and sensation-mongering press, Kraus dealt with many subjects and attitudes that are germane to present-day problems: education, women's rights, sexual mores, child abuse. The gloomy, bitter wit of such essays gave way to lighter humor in Kraus's next collection, *Die chinesische Mauer* (1910; the Great Wall of China).

The outbreak of the war in 1914 marked a turning point in Kraus's life and creativity, and the outraged convictions of the pacifist and moralist inspired him to produce his most powerful and most characteristic work. Following several months of silence, Kraus delivered a sardonic public lecture on November 19, 1914. "In dieser grossen Zeit . . ." (in these great times . . .) may be regarded as the germ of his extensive wartime output. Kraus set himself up as the lonely, bold, uncompromising chronicler of what he termed "the last days of mankind" and "the Day of Judgment" for the benefit of a posterity that might no longer inhabit the planet Earth. Kraus's mammoth and all-but-unperformable play *The Last Days of Mankind*, written between July, 1915, and July, 1917, first appeared in several special issues of *Die Fackel* and then in book form. Its 209 scenes, with prologue and epilogue, take place "in a hundred scenes and hells" and feature people who, in Kraus's view, had all the stature, substance, and veracity of characters in an operetta yet were bent upon enacting the tragedy of humankind. The play is a sort of *phonomontage* in that the hundreds of real as well as fictitious persons reveal and judge themselves through their authentic speech patterns, with the satirist attempting to make language the moral index of a dying way of life as he uses actual speeches, newspaper editorials, war communiqués, and other documents.

The story of Kraus's postwar writings and polemics is basically the history of his disillusionment as his "homeland's loyal hater." The best that Kraus could say about the Austrian republic, a small country that was still bedeviled by "the parasites remaining from the imperial age and the blackheads of the revolution," was that it had replaced the monarchy and had rid Kraus of "that burdensome companion, the other K. K." (The reference is to the abbreviation of *kaiserlich-königlich*, "royal-imperial," the designation of many Austro-Hungarian institutions.) In the 1920's, Kraus engaged in extended polemics with the publicist Maximilian Harden (once an admired model), the critic Alfred Kerr, and the poet Franz Werfel (one of several apostles turned apostates). He castigated the unholy alliance between a police chief, Johannes Schober, and a crooked press czar, Imre Békessy, and Kraus succeeded with his spirited campaign to "kick the crook out of Vienna." The literary harvest of the Schober-Békessy affair was another documentary drama, *Die Unüberwindlichen* (pb. 1928, pr. 1929; the unconquerables). Another of the plays

written in the 1920's was *Wolkenkuckucksheim* (pb. 1923; cloudcuckooland), a verse play based on Aristophanes and presenting a sort of Last Days of Birdkind but with a Shakespearean solo by the lark at the end promising conciliation and peace.

Beginning in 1925, Kraus used "Theater der Dichtung" (theater of poetry, or literary theater) as a designation for many of his public readings of his own works and those of others, spellbinding one-man shows in which he presented poetry, prose, and entire plays to large audiences. (By the end of his life, he had made seven hundred such presentations in various cities.) These readings must be regarded as an integral part of his creativity and perhaps even as the apogee of his effectiveness. Kraus may be credited with the revival of interest in the nineteenth century Viennese playwright and actor Johann Nestroy, whom he presented in his full stature as a powerful social satirist and linguistic genius. William Shakespeare was also a living force in Kraus's life, and between 1916 and 1936 the satirist recited his adaptations of thirteen Shakespearean plays, also publishing two collections of plays and the sonnets in his translation. Kraus's special relationship with Jacques Offenbach dated back to his boyhood; he adapted and performed, with a piano accompanist, many of Offenbach's operettas. He appreciated these in programmatic contrast to the Viennese operetta of his time, which he regarded as inane, meretricious, and unwholesome.

"Mir fällt zu Hitler nichts ein" ("I can't think of anything to say about Hitler") is the striking first sentence of Kraus's prose work *Die dritte Walpurgisnacht* (wr. 1933, pb. 1952; the third Walpurgis Night). The title refers to both parts of Johann Wolfgang von Goethe's *Faust* as well as to the Third Reich. It was written in 1933 but not published in its entirety during Kraus's lifetime. That sentence, which lies at the heart of the misunderstandings and conflicts that marked and marred Kraus's last years, may have been indicative of resignation (though he *could* think of many things to say about Hitler and did indeed say them), but it was also a hyperbolic, heuristic device for depicting the Witches' Sabbath of the time. The satirist sadly realized the incommensurability of the human spirit with the unspeakably brutal and mindless power across the German border. Once again, language was in mortal danger, and the perpetrators of the new horrors obviously were not characters from an operetta.

In voicing genuine concern over Germany's pressure on his homeland, Kraus for once found himself in Austria's corner. Paradoxically, this led him to side with the clerico-fascist regime of Chancellor Engelbert Dollfuss, whose assassination in 1934 came as a severe shock to Kraus. Many of the satirist's erstwhile adherents expected him to join them in their struggle against Hitlerism, but they were disappointed at what they regarded as the equivocation of the essentially apolitical satirist. *Die Fackel* appeared at even more irregular intervals than before, and Kraus was content to reduce his readership to those who not only heard "the trumpets of the day" but also cared about Shakespeare, Nestroy, Offenbach, and German style, including Kraus's unique "comma problems." Preparing to "live in the safe sentence structure," Kraus strove pathetically and futilely to pit the word against the sword. His death of heart failure at the end of a long period of physical and spiritual exhaustion mercifully saved him from witnessing the Nazi takeover of Austria (to the cheers of most of its population), the destruction of his belongings, the deaths of close friends in concentration camps, and untold other horrors.

Analysis

Karl Kraus's poetry was not fully appreciated in his lifetime, being decried as derivative and excessively cerebral. In recent decades, however, Kraus's poetry has come to be regarded as an integral and important part of his oeuvre, and critics such as Werner Kraft, Leopold Liegler, and Caroline Kohn have written perceptively about this aspect of Kraus's creativity. When one realizes that much of Kraus's prose is lyrical or poetic, it is easy to see his poetry as only a special coinage from the same mint.

Kraus began to write poetry relatively late in life; his first poems did not appear in *Die Fackel* until 1912 and 1913, but then nine volumes of poetry and rhymed epigrams were published between 1916 and 1930 under the modest collective title *Worte in Versen*. In his verse, Kraus admittedly was an epigone rather than an innovator, indebted to the Goethean and Shakespearean tradi-

tions. He was "unoriginal" in that he usually needed some occasion to trigger his art. The poems are seldom "Romantic" in the sense of being products of rapture or intoxication; rather, they spring from the inspirations of language and logic.

Some of Kraus's poems are versified glosses and polemics, lyric versions of prose texts, or satiric ideas given purified and aesthetically appealing forms; others represent autobiographical excursions. Their abstraction and concision often presuppose familiarity with Kraus's other works, his life, and his personality; in this sense, the poems add up to a lyrical *roman à clef.* "I do not write poetry and then work with dross," Kraus once wrote; "I turn the dross into poetry and organize rallies in support of poetry." To a certain extent, Kraus's poetry is *Gedankenlyrik* in Friedrich Schiller's sense—poetry with a cargo of thought, reflecting a tradition coming to an end and an effort to preserve that tradition. The satirical poems are really *Gebrauchslyrik*, pithy poetry with a purpose. Yet Kraus's poetry also represents a kind of satirist's holiday in that the poet, so widely regarded as a hater, is here free to reveal himself fully and unabashedly in his love of humankind, the human spirit, nature, and animals. In this sense, it represents the "yea" of a great nay-sayer. Poetry to Kraus was like a freer, purer world, one harking back to the German classical tradition, in which the poet, freed from the goads of the satiric occasion and the burden of an ever-wakeful moral conscience, was able to reflect at leisure on love, nature, dreams, and wonderment.

Ursprung in poetry

The word *Ursprung* (origin or source) figures prominently in Kraus's thought and poetry. In his orphic epigram "Zwei Läufer" ("Two Runners"), Kraus depicts two antithetical forces alive in the human spirit, one that he loves and one that he hates. The world is perceived as a circuitous route back to the *Ursprung*. Intellectuality may be the wrong road, but it does lead back to immediacy; satire is a roundabout way to poetry; and poetry, to Kraus, is a philosophical or linguistic detour on the way to a lost paradise. Kraus saw himself as being midway between *Ursprung* and *Untergang*, the origin or source of all things and the end of the world (or of the human spirit) as conjured up by his satiric vision, and he viewed language as the only means of going back to the origin—

the origin that was forever the goal. This *Ursprung* represents a kind of naïve realism, a secular idea of Creation that is diametrically opposed to the tendency of speculative philosophy to make *homo cogitans*, cerebral man, the center of reality. In contrast to this, Kraus posits the unity of feeling and form from which all art, morality, and truth spring. This world of purity constitutes a timeless counterpoise to the world against which Kraus the satirist struggled, and such an inviolate nature stands in mute yet eloquent contrast to a contemporary world and society which Kraus, in a sardonic pun fully comprehensible only through an awareness of the subtleties of synonymous German prefixes, perceived not as a *Gegenwart* (present time) but as a *Widerwart* (repulsive age).

WORTE IN VERSEN

In his poetry, Kraus was guided by his conviction that the quality of a poem depended on the moral stature and ethical mission of the poet ("A poem is good until one knows by whom it is"). In his view, a satirist is only a deeply hurt lyricist, the artist wounded by the ugliness of the world. In *Worte in Versen*, rhyme and meaning are inseparably fused. Kraus's conception of rhyme is similar to that of the German Romantic critic Friedrich Schlegel, who described rhyme as the surprising reunion of friendly ideas after a long separation. Kraus's poem "Der Reim" ("The Rhyme"), for example, underscores this concept through the use of macaronic form: "Rhyme is the landing shore/ for two thoughts *en rapport*."

"NOCTURNAL HOUR" AND "THE DAY"

Two of Kraus's best-known poems make reference to his nocturnal working habits. "Nächtliche Stunde" ("Nocturnal Hour"), set to music by Eugen Auerbach in 1929, is a profound and poignant expression of Kraus's situation, written with great visionary power and economy of syntax and symbolism. It is structurally notable for the recurring unrhymed first and last lines of each of its three stanzas and the reiteration of the theme of transitoriness in the opening line of each. There is an increasing sense of inwardness and depth until the final synthesis of night, winter, life, spring, and death. Kraus himself pointed out that three times the unrhymed last line belongs to "the bird's voice which accompanies the experience of work through the stages of night, winter,

and life." Presumably, what the poet considers, weighs, and grades as he works is the possibility of changing this "language-forsaken" world through his efforts; a hero of creative work in Thomas Mann's sense, he continues to do his duty even as death approaches.

The beautiful poem "Der Tag" ("The Day"), set to music by Kraus's long-time piano accompanist, Franz Mittler, shares many of the motifs of "Nocturnal Hour." As the day breaks through the window, daring to disturb the claustrophobic intensity of the satirist's nocturnal labors, the bleary-eyed writer expresses surprise at the fact that the impure, desecrated day has the audacity to dawn after an apocalyptic night of struggle with the affairs of an ungodly, corrupt world—matters which the *Zeitgeist* keeps presenting in violation of an ideal, undefiled realm of pure humanity. The satirist has borne witness to the possibility of such humanity and has in mute, joyless toil erected an edifice of words in its support. The memento mori provided by a hearse outside, carrying some poor soul to his or her final resting place, gives the satirist an awareness of earthly evanescence and fills him with boundless sympathy with human suffering. His self-effacing, fanatical work in the service of the word, his ceaseless defense of language, and his search for eternal truths as a bulwark against the encroachments of the age have distinctly religious overtones: His prayer is for the poor soul outside as well as for himself but especially for a humankind gone astray and bound for perdition. It is properly understood, however, only in a larger context. Franz Kafka once described his obsessive writing as a form of prayer, and this was also Kraus's conception of his own work. One of his aphorisms is pertinent here: "When I take up my pen, nothing can happen to me. Fate, remember that!"

Ernst Krenek, who came under Kraus's spell at an early age, has included settings of both "Nocturnal Hour" and "The Day" in his song cycle *Durch die Nacht* (through the night), composed in 1930 and 1931, which also contains five other Kraus poems. "Schnellzug" ("Fast Train"), written in 1920 and set to music by Auerbach, has the evanescence and perceived meaninglessness of life as its theme and the dichotomy between inside and outside as its focus. The poet's staleness on a dirty, crowded train is contrasted with the fresh yet unspecific landscape outside, which tends to blur and blunt his perceptions. Though he is forced to stay aboard with the aimless multitude of his traveling companions, his disgust at his situation is a kind of rebellion. Being locked into his life of dedication and self-abnegation, he is fated to yearn for integration into the vanishing scenery.

TRIBUTE POEMS

A number of Kraus's poems are tributes to friends and other people he admired. Cases in point are "An einen alten Lehrer" (to an old teacher), a celebration of Heinrich Sedlmayer, his German and Latin teacher; "Die Schauspielerin" ("The Actress") and "Annie Kalmar," both in memory of the first of several women of uncommon physical and spiritual beauty in Kraus's life, a talented actress who died in 1901 at a tragically early age; "Peter Altenberg," a poetic obituary of one of the few contemporary writers whom Kraus befriended; and "An meinen Drucker" ("To My Printer"), a birthday tribute to Kraus's faithful printer, Georg Jahoda.

SATIRICAL POEMS

A number of satirical poems and songs form part of Kraus's plays. "Gebet" ("Prayer") is spoken by the Grumbler, the Kraus figure in *The Last Days of Mankind*, as is "Mit der Uhr in der Hand" ("With Stopwatch in Hand"), based on a 1916 news item about a submarine sinking a fully loaded troop transport in the Mediterranean in forty-three seconds. Also from that play is the trenchantly funny, self-exculpatory ditty sung by Emperor Franz Joseph in his sleep. "Die Psychoanalen" ("The Psychoanals"), from *Traumstück* (pb. 1923, pr. 1925; dream play), is a long chorus of the killers of dreams and blackeners of beauty, the exhibitors of inhibitions and purveyors of neuroses, people to whom even Goethe's poems are nothing but unsuccessful repressions. "Das Schoberlied" ("Schober's Song"), from *Die Unüberwindlichen*, is a mordant self-portrait of Vienna's police chief (and Austria's sometime chancellor), and "Das Lied von der Presse" ("The Song of the Press"), from the literary satire *Literatur: Oder, Man wird doch da sehen* (1921; literature: or, we'll see about that), sums up Kraus's feelings about the press. Among Kraus's autobiographical poems are "Bunte Begbenheiten" ("Colorful Goings-On"), about the Salzburg Festival and its commercialization and vulgarization—for which Kraus blamed its prime movers, Hugo von

Hofmannsthal and Max Reinhardt, as well as the Catholic Church—and "Nach dreissig Jahren" ("After Thirty Years"), which finds the satirist looking back on three decades of *Die Fackel* and taking stock of his achievements.

"SIDI" POEMS

Kraus evidently needed an idealized private sphere of wholeness, purity, and love to provide a counterpoint (and counterpoise) to the cacophony of corruption that he perceived all around him. Such a sphere was provided for him from 1913 to the end of his life by a Czech aristocrat, Baroness Sidonie Nádhérny von Borutin. Her family estate at Janovice, near Prague, became Kraus's *buen retiro*, a Garden of Eden six and a half hours from Vienna. A modern mythology about a Tristan and Isolde living through the last days of humankind is multifariously expressed in Kraus's letters to "Sidi" (long believed lost but rediscovered in 1969 and published five years later), in many of Kraus's poems addressed to her or inspired by shared experiences, and in the dedication of several volumes to the woman who, as Kraus once put it, had a true appreciation of only two books, "the railroad time-table and *Worte in Versen*."

Kraus proposed marriage to Sidonie on several occasions, but he was rejected and remained unmarried. Their relationship, however, survived Sidonie's engagement and marriage to other men. Among the approximately fifty "Sidi poems" are "Fernes Licht mit nahem Schein" ("Distant Light with Glow So Near") and "Wiese im Park" ("Lawn in the Park"), a poem with tragic undertones written on a sad Sunday in November, 1915. The poet wants to relieve the darkness of the times by recapturing the timeless past, in particular his childhood. His firm footing and reposeful communion with nature vanish, however, the spell is broken, and the present bleakly reasserts itself in the form of a "dead day."

USE OF SHAKESPEARE

Finally, mention must be made of Kraus's translations from Shakespeare. Kraus, who knew little or no English (or any foreign language, for that matter), used existing German translations of Shakespeare as a basis for versions (*Nachdichtungen*, free re-creations in the spirit of the original rather than accurate translations) which, he felt, would capture Shakespeare's spirit more fully and would add his works to the treasure house of German letters more enduringly than other translations had done. In this effort, he was guided by his superior poetic sense and his unerring linguistic instinct. Commenting on Kraus's edition of the *Sonnets*, Albert Bloch (Kraus's first translator into English) remarked that if Kraus had known English, his versions would not have been so beautiful. "Perhaps the result is not always immediately identifiable as Shakespeare," the reviewer admits; "certainly it is always undeniably Karl Kraus."

OTHER MAJOR WORKS

PLAYS: *Literatur: Oder, Man wird doch da sehn*, pr., pb. 1921; *Die letzen Tage der Menschheit*, pb. 1922, pr. 1930 (*The Last Days of Mankind*, 1974); *Traumstück*, pb. 1923, pr. 1925 (verse play); *Wolken-kuckucksheim*, pb. 1923 (verse play); *Traumtheater*, pb. 1924, pr. 1925; *Die Unüberwindlichen*, pb. 1928, pr. 1929; *Dramen*, pb. 1967.

NONFICTION: *Die demolirte Literatur*, 1897; *Eine Krone für Zion*, 1898; *Sittlichkeit und Kriminalität*, 1902 (serial), 1908 (book); *Sprüche und Widersprüche*, 1909; *Heine und die Folgen*, 1910; *Die chinesische Mauer*, 1910; *Nestroy und die Nachwelt*, 1912; *Pro domo et mundo*, 1912; *Nachts*, 1918; *Weltgericht*, 1919 (2 volumes); *Untergang der Weltdurch schwarze Magie*, 1922; *Epigramme*, 1927; *Literatur und Lüge*, 1929; *Zeitstrophen*, 1931; *Die dritte Walpurgisnacht*, wr. 1933, pb. 1952; *Die Sprache*, 1937; *Widerschein der Fackel*, 1956; *Half-Truths and One-and-a-Half Truths: Selected Aphorisms*, 1976.

MISCELLANEOUS: *In These Great Times: A Karl Kraus Reader*, 1976; *No Compromise: Selected Writings of Karl Kraus*, 1977.

BIBLIOGRAPHY

Iggers, Wilma A. *Karl Kraus: A Viennese Critic of the Twentieth Century*. The Hague: Martinus Nijhoff, 1967. A biographical study of Kraus and his life in Vienna. Includes a bibliography and index.

Theobald, John. *The Paper Ghetto: Karl Kraus and Anti-Semitism*. New York: P. Lang, 1996. A study of Kraus's relationship with his Jewish heritage. Includes bibliographical references and index.

Zohn, Harry. *Karl Kraus*. New York: Twayne Publishers, 1971. An introductory biography and critical study of selected works by Krause. Includes bibliographical references.

_____. *Karl Kraus and the Critics*. Columbia, S.C.: Camden House, 1997. A history of the critical response to Kraus's work. Includes bibliographical references and index.

Harry Zohn;
bibliography updated by the editors

MAXINE KUMIN

Born: Philadelphia, Pennsylvania; June 6, 1925

PRINCIPAL POETRY

Halfway, 1961
The Privilege, 1965
The Nightmare Factory, 1970
Up Country, 1972
House, Bridge, Fountain, Gate, 1975
The Retrieval System, 1978
Our Ground Time Here Will Be Brief, 1982
Closing the Ring: Selected Poems, 1984
The Long Approach, 1985
Nurture, 1989
Looking for Luck, 1992
Connecting the Dots, 1996
Selected Poems, 1960-1990, 1997
The Long Marriage, 2001

OTHER LITERARY FORMS

Maxine Kumin's novels include *Through Dooms of Love* (1965), *The Passions of Uxport* (1968), *The Abduction* (1971), and *The Designated Heir* (1974). She has published a collection of short stories, *Why Can't We Live Together like Civilized Human Beings?* (1982), and collections of essays, including *To Make a Prairie: Essays on Poets, Poetry, and Country Living* (1979) and *In Deep: Country Essays* (1987). In 1999 Kumin published *Quit Monks or Die!*, a murder mystery involving animal experimentation. More contemplative works were *Always Beginning: Essays on a Life in Poetry* (2000), which was notable for its depictions of modern country life as well as the author's ruminations on poetic craft, and, in the same year, *Inside the Halo and Beyond: The Anatomy of a Recovery* (2000), recounting Kumin's difficult recuperation from a horse-riding accident that left her, at the age of seventy-three, with two broken vertebrae in her neck. Kumin has also published numerous volumes of children's literature, several coauthored with Anne Sexton.

ACHIEVEMENTS

Most recognized for her rural poems, Maxine Kumin received a Pulitzer Prize in 1973 for her fourth volume of poetry, *Up Country*. She is applauded for her positive tone, her affirmation of life; for this life-affirming quality, her work is often contrasted to that of Anne Sexton and Sylvia Plath, in whose work critics find the negation of life. Among other awards, she has received a National Endowment for the Arts grant (1966), a National Council on the Humanities Fellowship (1967),

the Eunice Tietjens Memorial Prize from *Poetry* (1972), the American Academy and Institute of Arts and Letters Award for excellence in literature (1980), and an Academy of American Poets Fellowship (1986). She was U.S. poet laureate in 1981-1982. Awards garnered in the 1990's include the Poets' Prize in 1994 and the Aiken Taylor Poetry Prize in 1995, both for *Looking for Luck*, and the Harvard Graduate School of Arts and Sciences Centennial Award in 1996. She also served as the poet laureate of the State of New Hampshire from 1989 to 1994. She has published regularly, throughout her career, in the most prestigious magazines in the country, including *Poetry*, *The New Yorker*, and *The Atlantic*.

BIOGRAPHY

Born of Jewish parents in Germantown, Pennsylvania, in 1925 and educated as a child at a Catholic convent school, Maxine Kumin describes herself as an agnostic who believes passionately in poetry. Kumin's father, Peter Winokur, was a successful pawnbroker. As a teenager, Kumin trained to become an Olympic swimmer, but she abandoned this dream upon entrance to Radcliffe College, which lacked suitable training facilities. She received a bachelor's degree in 1946 and a master's in 1948, both from Radcliffe, but did not begin writing seriously until her late twenties, when, as a suburban housewife with small children, she turned to poetry for self-gratification. She met the poet Anne Sexton at a writing workshop at the Boston Center for Adult Education, and the two women developed a close personal and professional relationship, each installing an extra telephone line in her home so they could talk at length.

Kumin began her teaching career in 1958 at Tufts University in Massachusetts and has taught as visiting lecturer at Radcliffe, Columbia University, Amherst College, Princeton University, and Bucknell University, among others. She has been on the staffs of the Bread Loaf Writers' Conference (on numerous occasions) and the Sewanee Writers' Conference, and she served as poetry consultant to the Library of Congress from 1981 to 1982. In 1983, she traveled with the United States Information Agency on its Arts America Tour. Her academic appointments include stints at many colleges and uni-

Maxine Kumin

versities, and in 1995 she served as chancellor of the American Academy of Poets. She and her husband and three children have made their home on a horse farm in New Hampshire, where she prefers to spend much of her time.

ANALYSIS

The poetry of Maxine Kumin is concerned with loss (particularly loss through death or separation) and surviving such loss. Equally at home with natural and domestic images, Kumin organizes most of her poems into groups of pastoral or tribal poems. These groupings allow her to explore relationships found in nature and also relationships within extended human families. These pastoral and tribal poems connect through Kumin's recurring emphasis on the seasonal patterns of nature and the regenerative cycles of familial generations.

Kumin prefers to write in traditional forms (as opposed to free verse) and often employs exacting syllable counts, set rhyme and stanza patterns, and alliteration. She develops many of her poems with catalogs or extends them through simile, though in her later work simile appears less frequently. Her work has also changed through moving from a very personal, private voice to one that is more public.

HALFWAY

Images of the body abound in Kumin's poetry: skin, bone, knees, ribs, and thighs. Swimming recurs as a metaphor with associated water imagery, especially in her first volume, *Halfway*. This first book also shows a concern for the instructor-student relationship and sometimes, as in the opening poem, "Junior Life Saving," explores this relationship within the context of water.

The poem expresses concern with loss by drowning and the desire to prevent such loss. It begins with physical details, describing the young students, an "isosceles of knees," as they sit crosslegged and pick at their peeling sunburns. The lake assumes human powers; as the children enter the water to role-play the drowning victim and the rescuer, the lake seems to be smiling, "turned sudden to a foe." The speaker of the poem, who is aware of danger, gives instructions: "Class, I say, this is/ the front head release." Important is what the instructor, almost in a parental role, does not or cannot say: "Class, I say (and want/ to say, children,

my dears,/ I too know how to be afraid)." Instead, the instructor remains firm and practical: "I tell you what I know:/ go down to save."

The swimmer in "400-Meter Free Style" is again practical. Utilizing "thrift," he employs no movement that is not needed. This poem emphasizes images of the body, including references to the functionally clean movement of feet, muscle, wrist, heel, mouth, lungs, and heart. Furthermore, the typography of the poem suggests the movement of a swimmer's laps.

Both "High Dive: A Variant" and "The Lesson" suggest that mastery through practice can empower. The key word in "High Dive" (a sestina) is, in fact, "masterful": "Practice has made this come out right" so that "at peak" the male diver is "a schooled swan, arched and masterful." Although "The Lesson" (set in a natural body of water rather than a pool) approaches the theme more subtly, it announces itself flatly: "Eleven. Your hour of danger." The speaker-instructor continues to address the students, showing them how to do the sidestroke. Her directives are intertwined with observations of natural life in the water:

> it is the top leg goes forward
> forming the blade of the scissors,
> wherefore the cattails unseaming
> go rattletatat in the marshes,
> seeding the smallest of moments,
> all of us braver by inches.

The instructions seem themselves to cut through the poem and the water as if this concrete knowledge somehow lessens the danger of the lake. With the proper instruction, the swimmers learn to move through the water as if to do so were natural: "Up out and together we glide."

Kumin again explores the instructor-student relationship in "The Young Instructor in a Winter Landscape." The setting for this poem is a university campus rather than a body of water, but the poem begins with a reference to physical movements, reflecting on the fact that many college campuses are built on hills, so that teachers and students going to and from classes must exert themselves physically. The poem speaks of physical work and mental work as complementary: "Hills are warm work in icy weather:/ something the mind/ can chew on." It ends with a reference to the similarity between the instructor and his students and alludes to the passage of time in which they will replace him: "on that all-climbing hill of Sisyphus/ he sees it has begun to snow/ and all the faces facing him are his."

"Poem for My Son" and "The Journey: For Jane at Thirteen" are precursors of many poems in subsequent volumes on the separation of mothers and children. Separation in "Poem for My Son" is emotionally difficult; the mother remembers the oxygen tent that saved her son just after his birth and cannot force herself now to "unfasten from the boy." She knows that he will "wash away/ to war or love or luck,/ prodigious king, a stranger." It is a separation that she cannot make of her own will, yet by the end of the poem, she yields to the pull of life. "My pulse knit in your wrist/ expands. Go now and spend it."

Relinquishment of the daughter in "The Journey: For Jane at Thirteen" is not only difficult but also perilous: "It is a dangerous time./ The water rocks away under the timber." Luckily, the daughter carries with her, in her purse, magical objects that will protect her, "pale lipstick, half a dozen lotions," and she bears history and mythology texts and wears pennies in her shoes. Ultimately, though, her own self-confidence is most powerful: "You lean down your confident head./ We exchange kisses; I call your name/ and wave you off as the bridge goes under."

The last poem in the volume, "For Anne at Passover," is the first of many poems dedicated to Kumin's friend Anne Sexton. The speaker of this poem, again an instructor, ironically addresses Socrates (rather than Sexton) when she states that "one student says you sinned the sin of pride./ Another consecrates your suicide." This poem alludes to ironies within the women's backgrounds—Sexton's Catholicism and Kumin's Judaism—yet it ends on a note of faith in love and the return of spring:

> we pray and eat tonight in greening weather.
> Time swells the buds. A sharper rain begins;
> we are all babes who suck at love together.

UP COUNTRY

Kumin's poems celebrating love and spring (or summer) are among her most eloquent. Her rhythms soften.

For example, in the conclusion of "We Are," from her fourth volume, *Up Country*, she uses enjambment rather than her usual end-stopped lines, allowing her sentences to flow over line and stanza breaks:

> Even knowing
> that none of us can catch up with himself
>
> we are making a run
> for it. Love, we are making a run.

Images of survival are lush and ripe; in "Five Small Deaths in May," for example, the speaker makes plans to bury a much-loved dog "under the milkweed bloom/ where in July the monarchs come/ as spotted as he, as rampant, as enduring." In "Watering Trough," water suggests richness and plenty. A footed Victorian bathtub has been set outside as a trough for farm animals, and the speaker invites "all longnecked browsers" to partake of its "green water for sipping/ that muzzles may enter thoughtful/ and rise dripping."

Kumin uses the image of water similarly in "Morning Swim," one of her most successful poems. Here water serves as nourishment:

> My bones drank water; water fell
> through all my doors. I was the well
> that fed the lake that met my sea
> in which I sang *Abide with Me*.

The speaker of the poem attains this state of immersion "in chilly solitude," and the act of swimming is not actually physical but a movement within the speaker's imagination: "Into my empty head there come/ a cotton beach, a dock wherefrom/ I set out, oily and nude."

The amenities of solitude appear again in Kumin's series of hermit poems. Like Kumin's love poems, several poems in this series are quite sensuous. The sequence opens with "The Hermit Wakes to Bird Sounds": "He startles awake. His eyes are full of white light./ In a minute the sun will ooze into the sky." Kumin's description of night in "The Hermit Has a Visitor" is similar but more richly fertile than her reference to "night fog thick as terry cloth" in "Morning Swim": "Night is a honeycomb./ Night is the fur on a blue plum." For Kumin, blue is a color of ripeness. In "The Hermit Picks Berries," she describes the ripening of blueberries by noting their transformation in color, from "wax white" to "the green of small bruises" to "the red of bad welts": "Now they are true blue."

Kumin is even more sensual in "August 9th," but here she extols the deeper colors of black and purple. The poem revolves around the picking of dewberries, each berry "a black bulge fattening/ under its leaf blanket." The speaker experiences these berries in a purely physical manner, without spiritual overtones, because God is not present:

> in fact I am
> alone in the pasture,
> bending among deerflies
> and the droppings of porcupines.
> I am stripped to the waist.
> The sun licks my back.

But, ironically, the speaker, who seems very close to the hermit persona, uses plurals throughout the poem. It ends in exuberant command: "pinch!/ pull!/ purple your fingers!"

THE RETRIEVAL SYSTEM

Although Kumin's sixth volume, *The Retrieval System*, is quite different from *Up Country* in subject matter and tone, one of its poems, "Extrapolations from Henry Manley's Pie Plant" recaptures some of the earlier volume's lushness. The poem opens with a description of Henry's rhubarb: "The stalks are thick as cudgels, red/ as valentines."

In contrast to *Up Country*, *The Retrieval System* is structured thematically. In this book, Kumin confronts middle age and the loss of parents, children, and her friend Anne Sexton. In "Extrapolations from Henry Manley's Pie Plant" (one of a series of poems centered on Kumin's country neighbor), she reflects on the choices she has made: "I look at my middling self and recognize/ this life is but one of a number of possible lives." She considers some of these possible lives, then describes the one she has chosen: "Instead, mornings I commence with the sun,/ tend my animals, root in the garden/ and pass time with Henry." She does not regret this choice, because it has enabled her to live where the "goldfinches explode/ from the meadow."

In "Henry Manley, Living Alone, Keeps Time," the last and most successful poem of the series, Kumin considers the effects of aging: "Sundowning,/ the doctor calls it, the way/ he loses words when the light fades." Henry often cannot remember the names of those he loves, yet the poet recognizes that he "goes on loving them out of place." She is saddened by the separation of the body and the soul and notes his awareness of how loose his connection to life is becoming. At any moment his soul could slip out of his body, lightly and without warning, like the helium-filled balloon that floated from his grasp when he was a child.

Kumin titles a section of *The Retrieval System* "Body and Soul," and in one poem from this section, "Body and Soul: A Meditation," ponders the soul's physical location. In this poem, she is humorously regretful:

> Body, Old Paint, Old Partner,
> I ought to have paid closer
> attention when Miss Bloomberg
> shepherded the entire fifth grade
> into the Walk-Through Woman.

Though she remembers walking through the various chambers of the heart, she does not remember seeing the woman's soul, "that miner's canary flitting/ around the open spaces." She envisions the body's interior as a pinball machine in which the "little ball-bearing soul" rolls about, reversing direction as it clicks against various bones.

Kumin explores more serious regrets in this volume, confronting losses very specific and real. She refers to them explicitly in "Address to the Angels." These losses include the suicide of Anne Sexton, her father's fatal heart attack, and her daughter's move to Europe. She thinks that if she could go back in time she could prevent these bad occurrences: "I am wanting part of my life back/ so I can do it over./ So I can do it better."

In "How It Is" she wishes again that she could go back in time, this time so she could prevent Sexton's suicide; she thinks of the last day of Sexton's life, "how I would unwind it, paste/ it together in a different collage,/ back from the death car idling in the garage."

Several poems in this volume, which is dedicated to Kumin's daughters, concern the separation of parents and adult children, and particularly the separation of mothers and daughters. "Changing the Children" suggests the painfulness of adolescence and the distance it creates between parents and children. This distance is temporary, but by the time it closes, the relationship has changed: "Eventually we get them back./ Now they are grown up./ They are much like ourselves."

In "Seeing the Bones," Kumin mourns her separation from her world-traveling daughter: "now you're off to Africa/ or Everest, daughter of the file drawer,/ citizen of no return." Again Kumin wishes to return to an earlier time: "Working backward I reconstruct/ you. Send me your baby teeth, some new/ nail parings." Yet in "The Envelope," Kumin, although fearful of her own death, looks forward—to the near-immortality that her daughters will give her: "we, borne onward by our daughters, ride/ in the Envelope of Almost-Infinity."

Sometimes Kumin questions the possibility of surviving all these losses. In "July, Against Hunger," near the end of the book, she exclaims: "There are limits, my God, to what I can heft/ in this heat!"

NURTURE

Assuming a voice more political than personal in her tenth volume, *Nurture*, Kumin frets about the condition of the environment and the actual physical survival of animals. In "Thoughts on Saving the Manatee," she questions the possibility of the manatee's survival, for "experts agree that no matter/ how tenderly tamed by philanthropy/ [their] survival is chancy." The poem ends with a possible solution and a call to action reminiscent of Jonathan Swift's "A Modest Proposal":

> Let's revert to the Catch of the Day
> and serve up the last few as steak marinara.
> Let's stop pretending we need them
> more than they need us.

In this volume, and especially in the animal poems, Kumin displays a recurring concern for mothers and children. In "Thoughts on Saving the Manatee," she notes that the manatee in her area are "mostly cows and their calves." Quite a different scenario is presented in "Catchment," in which the speaker watches a female leopard pounce on a newborn antelope. Here the speaker faces a dilemma and wonders which animal she should root for—the helpless baby antelope or "the big cat, in whose camouflaged lair/ three helpless youngsters wait/ so starved for meat."

In the title poem, "Nurture," Kumin states her motherly interest directly: "I suffer, the critic proclaims,/ from an overabundance of maternal genes." Touched by a televised report of the surrogate parenting of a baby kangaroo, she is willing to open her heart and home to such an orphan—or to a human orphan, however wild: "it is safe to assume,/ given my fireside inked with paw prints,/ there would have been room." Considering the language she and the orphaned creature would share, Kumin constructs a list of forms of communication, alternating human and animal forms:

> Think of the language we two, same and not-same,
> might have constructed from sign,
> scratch, grimace, grunt, vowel:
>
> Laughter our first noun, and our long verb, howl.

Kumin again reflects on the language shared by animals and humans in "Sleeping with Animals." Keeping watch through the night over a mare ready to give birth, she finds herself and the mare in communion through "a wordless yet perfect/ language of touch and tremor." What they are saying to each other has to do with origins, "the wet cave we all/ once burst from gasping, naked or furred,/ into our separate species." As she meditates on the wonder of birth, Kumin considers her time with the mare well spent: "Together we wait for this still-clenched burden."

"Surprises," a "tribal poem," suggests a connection between Kumin and orphaned animals. Here, the poet, who is celebrating the success of her California peppers after fifteen years of failure, remembers how, when her mother's thriving roses finally caused the dilapidated trellis to collapse under their weight, "she mourned the dirtied blossoms more, I thought,// than if they'd been her children." While her mother "pulled on/ goatskin gloves to deal with her arrangements/ in chamberpots, pitchers, and a silver urn," Kumin was left to watch, "orphan at the bakeshop window."

Kumin moves forward to present time in "We Stood There Singing," which tells of a drive in Switzerland with her daughter and infant grandson. Kumin connects the grandson to the "wild child" in "Nurture" by using the verb "howled," again emphasizing the similarity between humans and animals. Kumin's grandson reappears in "A

Game of Monopoly in Chavannes." Thinking of him, she contemplates the passing of her own generation: "Our sole inheritor, he has taken us over// with his oceanic wants, his several passports." This grandson will someday replace her, will learn how to make his way through life, how to invest himself. Yet Kumin is not yet ready to leave. Mourning the deaths of her uncles in "Grappling in the Central Blue" makes her determined to hold on to life:

> Let us eat of the inland oyster.
> Let its fragrance intoxicate us
> into almost believing
> that staying on is possible
> again this year in
> benevolent blue October.

Some of Kumin's most beautiful poems, such as "Magellan Street, 1974," are about her daughter. Although she is again ruminating on the separation of mother and daughter, she is not sad but hopeful. She stands in her daughter's kitchen, bright with potted herbs, and is able to envision how the younger woman's life "will open, will burst from/ the maze in its walled-in garden/ and streak toward the horizon."

CONNECTING THE DOTS

Connecting the Dots appeared in 1996 and clearly reflects its times: "After the Cleansing of Bosnia" continues Kumin's poetic ruminations on her daughter, connecting her work in the trouble spots of the world—Haiti, Bangkok, and Bosnia—with the cruelty, and yet the beauty, of nature. Even in the midst of cruelty, "the hostile soldiers throw/ back/ bewildered babies that have dropped/ from the arms of exhausted women." Yet the knowledge that the cruelty of humans is part of the general cruelty of nature is revealed as a "false comfort" in the dream that concludes the poem, in which Kumin and her daughter see a barn owl eat a mouse.

The title poem of the collection, "Connecting the Dots," reflects on the passage of time and the role reversals it brings, as children begin to regard their parents with the same care for their well-being, and the same belief that they cannot be trusted to care for themselves, with which the parent formerly regarded the child:

> We're assayed kindly
> to see if we're
> still competent

> to keep house, mind
> the calendar
> connect the dots.

The children "still love us/ who overtake us" and yet they sound "the way/ we did, or like/ to think we did." The passage of time in the larger sense—the transition from one generation to the next—is echoed on a smaller scale by the seasonal cycle that marks the return of the children to check on their parents for "a week at Christmas/ ten days in August," while the parents "mind the calendar" in the time-honored country pursuits of "stack-/ ing wood for winter/ turning compost." The children live by the urban calendar of summer vacations in the country and Christmas holidays, while the parents abide by the routines of nature, the decomposition of mulch for the garden and the burning of dead wood to heat the chilly winter.

THE LONG MARRIAGE

In *Inside the Halo and Beyond*, Kumin wrote, in prose, of her recovery from a serious horse-riding accident that left her paralyzed with little hope of recovery. She managed to regain almost 95 percent of her movement, but the accident reverberates in the poems of *The Long Marriage*:

> The fact is, no conjecture can resolve
> why I survived this broken neck
> known in the trade as the hangman's fracture,
> this punctured lung, eleven broken ribs,
> a bruised liver, and more.

The image of hangman's fracture recurs in one of the most moving poems in the collection, "Oblivion," listing the "old details" seared into the memories of those who have found the bodies of suicides—"the tongue/ a blue plum forced between his lips/ when he hanged himself in her closet"—as well as the sense of inexplicable survival.

> for us it is never over
> who raced to the scene, cut the noose,
> pulled the bathtub plug on pink water,
> broke windows, turned off the gas,
> rode in the ambulance, only minutes later
> to take the body blow of bad news.
> We are trapped in the plot, every one.
> Left behind, there is no oblivion.

The near-rhymes of over/water/later and noose/gas/ news coupled with the perfect rhythm of the lines echo the sense of disjunction felt by the discoverer—can this really be happening? They are capped by the brutal descent into the reality of the situation in the alliterative "body blow of bad news." The final two lines slip back into the expected correlation of meter and rhyme, only to emphasize the finality of survival: "trapped in the plot" written by a dead loved one.

On the whole, however, Kumin's poetry is endlessly positive, celebrating the sensuousness of physical existence, the naturalness of movement and time. Had she published fewer volumes, choosing poems more selectively, her poetic achievement would have been more honed, her weaknesses less apparent. Yet solitary and social, personal and public, her poetry is a testament of affirmation within the context of painful losses.

OTHER MAJOR WORKS

LONG FICTION: *Through Dooms of Love*, 1965; *The Passions of Uxport*, 1968; *The Abduction*, 1971; *The Designated Heir*, 1974; *Quit Monks or Die!*, 1999.

SHORT FICTION: *Why Can't We Live Together Like Civilized Human Beings?*, 1982.

NONFICTION: *To Make a Prairie: Essays on Poets, Poetry, and Country Living*, 1979; *In Deep: Country Essays*, 1987; *Always Beginning: Essays on a Life in Poetry*, 2000; *Inside the Halo and Beyond: The Anatomy of a Recovery*, 2000.

CHILDREN'S LITERATURE: *Sebastian and the Dragon*, 1960; *Spring Things*, 1961; *Summer Story*, 1961; *Follow the Fall*, 1961; *A Winter Friend*, 1961; *Mittens in May*, 1962; *No One Writes a Letter to the Snail*, 1962; *Archibald the Traveling Poodle*, 1963; *Eggs of Things*, 1963 (with Anne Sexton); *More Eggs of Things*, 1964 (with Sexton); *Speedy Digs Downside Up*, 1964; *The Beach Before Breakfast*, 1964; *Paul Bunyan*, 1966; *Faraway Farm*, 1967; *The Wonderful Babies of 1809 and Other Years*, 1968; *When Grandmother Was Young*, 1969; *When Mother Was Young*, 1970; *When Great-Grandmother Was Young*, 1971; *Joey and the Birthday Present*, 1971 (with Sexton); *The Wizard's Tears*, 1975 (with Sexton); *What Color is Caesar?*, 1978; *The Microscope*, 1984.

MISCELLANEOUS: *Women, Animals, and Vegetables: Collected Essays and Stories*, 1994.

BIBLIOGRAPHY

Gioia, Dana. Review of *Our Ground Time Here Will Be Brief. Hudson Review* 35 (Winter, 1982/1983): 652-653. Although short, this review (in contrast to typical, merely descriptive reviews) is valuable for its critical assessment of Kumin's poetic achievement as reflected in a volume containing work from six previous volumes of poetry. Gioia suggests reasons for Kumin's popularity but argues that her poetic facility with language is limited.

Grosholz, Emily, ed. *Telling the Barn Swallow: Poets on the Poetry of Maxine Kumin*. Hanover, N.H.: University Press of New England, 1997. Essays form varied points of view dealing with Kumin's works. Includes bibliographical references.

Sexton, Anne, and Maxine Kumin. "A Nurturing Relationship: A Conversation with Anne Sexton and Maxine Kumin, April 15, 1974." Interview by Elaine Showalter and Carol Smith. *Women's Studies* 4 (1976): 115-136. In this rather lengthy, informal interview, Kumin and Sexton discuss their friendship and how each of them has influenced the other's work. Although both poets insist that they do not try to influence the other's voice, they do look at each other's work with an eye toward improvement. Of particular interest is Sexton's revelation that she suggested Kumin write a collection of country poems and that it be titled *Up Country*.

Nettie Farris, updated by Leslie Ellen Jones

STANLEY KUNITZ

Born: Worcester, Massachusetts; July 29, 1905

PRINCIPAL POETRY

Intellectual Things, 1930
Passport to the War: A Selection of Poems, 1944
Selected Poems, 1928-1958, 1958

The Testing-Tree: Poems, 1971

The Terrible Threshold: Selected Poems, 1940-1970, 1974

The Coat Without a Seam: Sixty Poems, 1930-1972, 1974

The Lincoln Relics, 1978

The Poems of Stanley Kunitz, 1928-1978, 1979

The Wellfleet Whale and Companion Poems, 1983

Next-to-Last Things: New Poems and Essays, 1985

Passing Through: The Later Poems, New and Selected, 1995

The Collected Poems, 2000

OTHER LITERARY FORMS

Stanley Kunitz has published numerous essays, interviews, and reviews on poetry and art. These are collected in *A Kind of Order, a Kind of Folly: Essays and Conversations* (1975) and in *Next-to-Last Things: New Poems and Essays* (1985). In addition, he has made extensive translations of modern Russian poetry, most notably in *Poems of Akhmatova* (1973, with Max Hayward) and *Story Under Full Sail* by Andrei Voznesensky (1974), as well as editing and cotranslating Ivan Drach's *Orchard Lamps* (1978) from the Ukrainian.

ACHIEVEMENTS

In more than seven decades of writing poetry, Stanley Kunitz has produced a corpus of work that is notable for its cohesiveness, its courageous explorations of the modern psyche, and its ever-broadening sympathies that adumbrate (with some fierce reservations and caveats) the unity of human experience. In language that always sustains a high degree of passionate dignity, never falling prey to the hortatory or didactic, Kunitz has boldly knocked again and again upon the doors of his obsessions with family, love, memory, and identity to demand that they surrender their secret meanings.

From the start of his career, Kunitz has paid consummate attention to mat-

ters of form, as bespeaking, to use his borrowed phrase, "a conservation of energy." Indeed, Kunitz has on numerous occasions spoken of form as a constant in art, as opposed to techniques and materials, which vary according to time and cultural necessity. Nevertheless, Kunitz's later poems have surprised his readers with their fresh embodiments: journal poems, prose poems, and free verse. At the same time, the poems retain the characteristically impassioned, sometimes bardic, voice of the earlier work, a voice that constitutes an unbroken thread running through all his poetry.

In many ways, Kunitz's work declares allegiance to the "flinty, maverick side" of American literature, the side inhabited by Henry David Thoreau and Walt Whitman, and holds to humanistic values, independent judgment, self-discipline, and a distrust of power in all its modern manifestations, particularly in the hands of the state. At the same time, the poems bear witness to the individual's spiritual yearnings in an age of decreasing sanctity at all levels. While not explicitly a religious poet ("I'm an American freethinker, a damn stubborn

Stanley Kunitz (AP/Wide World Photos)

one . . ."), Kunitz wrote poems that, nevertheless, remind readers of the tragic consequences that befall humans at the loss of that dimension. His achievement has been "to roam the wreckage" of his own humanity in a way that is both highly personal and representative and to ennoble that pursuit with the transformative powers of his art, an achievement that won for him the 1987 Bollingen Prize for Poetry. He received a National Book Award for Poetry in 1995. In 1998, he received the Frost Medal from the Poetry Society of America. In 2000, Congress named Kunitz the poet laureate of the United States

BIOGRAPHY

The son of immigrants, Stanley Jasspon Kunitz was born July 29, 1905, in Worcester, Massachusetts. Kunitz's father, Solomon, descended from Russian Sephardic Jews, committed suicide shortly before Stanley was born—an event that was to haunt the poet and that stands behind some of his most important and best-known poems. His mother, Yetta Helen, of Lithuanian descent, opened a dry goods store to support herself, her son, and two older daughters and to repay accumulated debts. Reared principally by his sisters and a succession of nurses, Kunitz grew up with his father's book collection, into which, as he put it, he would "passionately burrow." Though his mother shortly remarried, his stepfather, of whom he was fond, died before Kunitz reached his teens.

Educated in Worcester public schools, Kunitz edited the high school magazine, played tennis, and was graduated valedictorian of his class. Winning a scholarship to Harvard, Kunitz majored in English and began to write poetry, subsequently winning the Lloyd McKim Garrison Medal for poetry in 1926. He was graduated summa cum laude in the same year, and he took his M.A. degree from Harvard the following year. He worked briefly as a Sunday feature writer for the Worcester *Telegram*, where he had worked summers during college. He also completed a novel, which he later "heroically destroyed."

In 1927, Kunitz joined the H. W. Wilson Company as an editor. With Wilson's encouragement, he became editor of the *Wilson Bulletin*, a library publication (known now as the *Wilson Library Bulletin*). While at Wilson, he edited a series of reference books, including *Authors Today and Yesterday: A Companion Volume to "Living Authors"* (1933; with Howard Haycraft and Wilbur C. Hadden), *British Authors of the Nineteenth Century* (1936; with Haycraft), *American Authors, 1600-1900: A Biographical Dictionary of American Literature* (1938), and *Twentieth Century Authors: A Biographical Dictionary of Modern Literature* (1942; with Haycraft).

In 1930, Kunitz married Helen Pearse (they were divorced in 1937) and published his first collection of poems, *Intellectual Things*. The book was enthusiastically received by reviewers. Writing in *Saturday Review of Literature*, William Rose Benét observed, "Mr. Kunitz has gained the front rank of contemporary verse in a single stride." In 1939, Kunitz married a former actress, Eleanor Evans (from whom he was divorced in 1958), a union that produced his only child, Gretchen.

Kunitz's tenure with the H. W. Wilson Company was interrupted by World War II, during which he served as a noncommissioned officer in charge of information and education in the Air Transport Command. His second collection, *Passport to the War: A Selection of Poems*, appeared in 1944. A reviewer of that volume for *The New York Times Book Review* noted, "Kunitz has now (it seems) every instrument necessary to the poetic analysis of modern experience." Kunitz was awarded a Guggenheim Fellowship in 1945 and began a second career as an itinerant teacher, first at Bennington College, at the behest of his friend, the poet Theodore Roethke, then at a succession of colleges and universities, including the State University of New York at Potsdam, the New School for Social Research, Queens College, Brandeis University, the University of Washington, Yale University, Princeton University, and Rutgers University's Camden Campus.

In 1958, Kunitz married the artist Elise Asher, published *Selected Poems, 1928-1958*, which was awarded the Pulitzer Prize for Poetry in 1959, and received grants from the National Institute of Arts and Letters and the Ford Foundation.

During the 1960's, though based in New York City and Provincetown, Massachusetts, Kunitz was a Danforth Visiting Lecturer at colleges and universities throughout the United States. He also lectured in the Soviet Union, Poland, Senegal, and Ghana. In 1964, he edited a volume of the poems of John Keats and two years later translated selections from Russian poet Andrei Voznesensky's *Antiworlds and the Fifth Ace*. He continued to edit for the Wilson Company (with Vineta Colby, *European Authors: 1000-1900: A Biographical Dictionary of European Literature*, 1967) and coedited a memorial volume of essays on the poet Randall Jarrell. In 1968, along with artist Robert Motherwell and novelist Norman Mailer, he helped found The Fine Arts Work Center in Provincetown, a resident community of young artists and writers, and in 1969 he assumed the general editorship of the Yale Series of Younger Poets.

The Testing-Tree, a volume of poems and translations, appeared in 1971, prompting Robert Lowell to assert in *The New York Times Book Review*, "once again, Kunitz tops the crowd, the old iron brought to the white heat of simplicity." In 1974, Kunitz was awarded one of the nation's top official literary honors when he was appointed consultant in poetry to the Library of Congress. In addition to *The Testing-Tree* and the collected volume *The Poems of Stanley Kunitz, 1928-1978*, a book of essays and conversations titled *A Kind of Order, a Kind of Folly*, as well as three volumes of translations, appeared during the 1970's.

Kunitz published a thematic volume of old and new poems, *The Wellfleet Whale and Companion Poems*, in a limited edition in 1983, with the new poems later incorporated in *Next-to-Last Things: New Poems and Essays*, published in 1985. In recognition of his lifetime achievement, Kunitz was chosen as the first New York State poet, for the term 1987-1989.

In 1996, President Bill Clinton presented Kunitz with a National Medal of Arts. Kunitz's next volume of poems, *Passing Through: Later Poems, New and Selected*, received the National Book Award for Poetry in 1995. In 1998, he received the Frost Medal from the Poetry Society of America. Two years later, in 2000, Congress named Kunitz the poet laureate of the United States, a post that carries a one-year term and provides its incumbent with an office in the Library of Congress and a stipend of $35,000 for the year.

ANALYSIS

Stanley Kunitz has constantly sought to achieve higher and higher ground, both in his thoughtful aesthetic and in his themes. Kunitz's first poems were composed after the initial wave of modernism, led, in poetry, by T. S. Eliot and Ezra Pound, had crested. They resemble, to some extent, the earlier, tightly organized, ironic poems of Eliot, though the influence of the seventeenth century Metaphysical poets, particularly George Herbert (again an indirect influence of Eliot, who was largely responsible for the resurgence of interest in the Metaphysicals), is probably more preponderant. Moreover, by the 1920's, the work of Sigmund Freud had successfully invaded American arts and provided the introspective poet with a powerful tool for the analysis of self and culture.

INTELLECTUAL THINGS

The poems of *Intellectual Things* sketch many of the themes that will later be subject to elaboration and enrichment: the figure of the regenerative wound that is both the fresh scar of loss and the font of the power to transform experience into art, man's willful capriciousness (the "blood's unreason") and the inevitable cargo of guilt, and the search for the father, which is ultimately the search for identity, authority, and tradition, topics that pervade his later poems as crucially as they pervaded his early verse.

Eloquent and formally rigorous, the poems in this first collection show a poet already mature in his medium, writing of his "daily self that bled" to "Earth's absolute arithmetic/ of being." Characterized by paradox and a wish for transcendence (though that wish is frequently denied or diverted to another object), the early poems often poise upon niceties of intellection—though they are also fully felt—and suggest transport by language rather than the transcendence to which they aspire. From the first, Kunitz's poems have typically employed the language and images of paradox. In "Change," the opening poem to his first collection, man is "neither here nor there/ Because the mind moves everywhere;/ And he is neither now nor then/ Because tomorrow comes again/ Foreshadowed. . . ." In more characteristically personal poems, such as "Postscript," the poet observes, in what will develop into one of his ongoing themes, the self's phoenixlike destruction and subsequent regeneration: "I lost by winning, and I shall not win/ Again, except by loss." The losses Kunitz traces in *Intellectual Things* are those of past life (or of a past one that was denied), symbolized by the loss of his father, and the loss of love. In "For the Word Is Flesh" the poet admonishes his dead father: "O ruined father dead, long sweetly rotten/ Under the dial, the time-dissolving urn,/ Beware a second perishing. . . ." The second death is the doleful fate of being erased from the memories of the living. In a memorable passage that presages a later, more famous poem ("Father and Son"), Kunitz writes, "Let sons learn from their lipless fathers how/ Man enters Hell without a golden bough"—that is to say, uninstructed.

Some of the finest effects attained in *Intellectual Things* can be attributed to a high degree of control over phrasing, combined with the use of rhyme as a tool of force reminiscent of Alexander Pope, as in "Lovers Relentlessly": "Lovers relentlessly contend to be/ Superior in their identity.// The compass of the ego is designed/ To circumscribe intact a lesser mind. . . ." Kunitz uses rhyme also as a vehicle of wit, as in the shorter, three-beat lines of "Benediction": "God banish from your house/ The fly, the roach/ the mouse// That riots in the walls/ Until the plaster falls. . . ."

PASSPORT TO THE WAR

Passport to the War retains much of the density and bardic resonance of *Intellectual Things*, but the range of subject matter is broader: The self must now take its transformations into account against the background of recent history, for which regeneration is entirely problematic: "One generation past, two days by plane away,/ My house is dispossessed, my friends dispersed,/ My teeth and pride knocked in, my people game/ For the hunters of manskins in the warrens of Europe." To the question "How shall we uncreate that lawless energy?" the poet can only defer to the determinisms of time: "I think of Pavlov and his dogs/ And the motto carved on the broad lintel of his brain:/ "Sequence, consequence, and again consequence." If the shadow of history casts the representative self in a darker hue, the poet, like Matthew Arnold before him, clings to what is most central to the life of the individual: "Lie down with me, dear girl, before/ My butcher-boys begin to rave./ 'No hope for persons any more,'/ They cry, 'on either side of the grave.'/ Tell them I say the heart forgives/ The World." The strange weapons of intimacy and charity would seem ill-suited as protection in a bru-

tal world, but the sacramental element, the desire to raise the supposed commonplace, remains one of the bolts of a civilization unravaged by history. If history is the inevitable backdrop of our mortality, so do a representative mortal's most private strivings and sufferings themselves constitute a part of its fabric: "What the deep heart means,/ Its message of the big, round, childish hand,/ Its wonder, its simple lonely cry,/ The bloodied envelope addressed to you,/ Is history, that wide and mortal pang."

The visionary "Father and Son," perhaps Kunitz's best-known poem, establishes, in surrealistic images full of longing and regret, the poet's existential fate in the context of history. "Whirling between two wars," he follows "with skimming feet,/ The secret master of my blood . . . whose indomitable love/ Kept me in chains." Addressing his father "At the water's edge, where the smothering ferns lifted/ Their arms . . . ," the poet asks for his father's instruction: "For I would be a child to those who mourn/ And brother to the foundlings of the field . . . / O teach me how to work and keep me kind." Yet the summons brings only a shocking specter of discontinuity: "Among the turtles and the lilies he turned to me/ The white ignorant hollow of his face." One senses that what the poet asks is already, in some way, self-provided, though minus the love so deeply rooted in biology that it has the status of a cultural given. As war and upheaval expose these roots, one senses the poet's implication that, in a metaphorical sense, all are orphans.

"Open the Gates," another well-known visionary lyric, delivered in a grave voice that eerily suggests posthumous utterance, finds the poet "Within the city of the burning cloud," standing "at the monumental door/ Carved with the curious legend of my youth." Striking the door with "the great bone of my death," the poet stands "on the terrible threshold," where he sees "the end and the beginning in each other's arms." The seamless and incestuous image suggests the allegorical figures of Sin and Death in John Milton's *Paradise Lost* (1667), and the allusion holds to the extent that both figures are determinants of human fate. At the same time, the emphasis is less on moral conditioning than on the endlessly reforming fate of the human, as felt from the inside, in contrast with the wholeness of a life, glimpsed, so to speak, from a vantage somehow apart from it. Our lives, as William Shakespeare said, are "rounded with a sleep," and it is a matter of indifference whether one attempts an artificial distinction between the two sleeps, except that one's only knowledge takes place as human and forever from the vantage of one looking outward (even when looking inward). As for the question of inside versus outside, no other consciousness has yet much to contribute to the subject.

SELECTED POEMS, 1928-1958

In 1958, after another long hiatus, Kunitz published his *Selected Poems, 1928-1958*, more than a third of which are new poems. The new poems take up the modern subject of otherness, as in "The Science of the Night," in which the speaker contemplates his sleeping beloved "Down the imploring roads I cannot take/ Into the arms of ghosts I never knew." Even if he could track her to her birth, he admits, "You would escape me." He concludes, "As through a glass that magnifies my loss/ I see the lines of your spectrum shifting red,/ The universe expanding, thinning out,/ Our worlds flying, oh flying, fast apart." Always a time-bewitched poet, Kunitz brings to this and other new poems in the volume an added sense of urgency, for they are imbued with a love and desire that is unintentionally but nevertheless increasingly rearranged by the shifting weight of years.

THE TESTING-TREE

With amiable, if slow, regularity, Kunitz's fourth volume, *The Testing-Tree*, marks a departure from the rhetorical shimmer and elevated diction displayed in the previous collections. Written in a less knotty, more transparent syntax and style, the poems confront the upheavals of the 1960's, the guilt of failed marriage and inadequate parenthood, the ravages of time past ("the deep litter of the years"), and the inexplicable urge to carry on in the face of public and private failures: "In a murderous time/ the heart breaks and breaks/ and lives by breaking." The consolations of this volume, though sparse, strike the reader as all the more authentic for their scrupulous lack of facade, which, however, in no way implies a lessening of charity on the part of the poet.

One of the most notable poems in *The Testing-Tree* is "King of the River," a poem of the skewed hopes and unclear motives that disfigure and sometimes break a life but which are finally overtaken, with individual life itself transcended and transfigured by the relentless biological urge to perpetuate the species. The poem, whose central symbol is the chinook salmon swimming upstream to spawn, seeks to rebut the materialist's claim that "there is no life, only living things." By addressing the fish throughout as "you," the poet clearly implicates the reader in an allegory of life: "If the water were clear enough,/ if the water were still,/ but the water is not clear . . . If the knowledge were given you,/ but it is not given,/ for the membrane is clouded/ with self-deceptions." The psychological phrase helps swing the pointed finger around to the reader. "If the power were granted you/ to break out of your cells,/ but the imagination fails . . . If the heart were pure enough, but it is not pure . . . ," continues the litany of denial that underpins the allegory. The salmon ("Finned Ego") thrashes to a place of which it has no knowledge, for "the doors of the senses close/ on the child within." The blind, headlong rush to "the orgiastic pool" brings about dreadful change ("A dry fire eats you./ Fat drips from your bones") into something "beyond the merely human," where, despite the "fire on your tongue," promising that "The only music is time/ the only dance is love,/ you would admit/ that nothing compels you/ any more . . . but nostalgia and desire,/ the two-way ladder/ between heaven and hell." At the "brute absolute hour" when the salmon spawns only to die, when "The great clock of your life/ is slowing down,/ and the small clocks run wild," he ("you") stares into the face of his "creature self" and finds "he is not broken but endures," but at a price: He is "forever inheriting his salt kingdom,/ from which he is banished/ forever." The "forever" that rounds the conclusion, like a little sleep, suggests that the victory of life's mission to perpetuate itself is ironically accomplished at the loss of the human's vaunted objectivity and understanding.

In "Robin Redbreast," Kunitz reveals a similar, but distinct, necessity. In "the room where I lived/ with an empty page" (a room identified in "River Road" from the same volume as one the poet inhabited after his second divorce), the poet hears the squawking of blue jays tormenting a robin, "the dingiest bird/ you ever saw." Going out to pick up the bird "after they knocked him down," in order to "toss him back into his element," he notices the bullet hole that "had tunneled out his wits." The hole, cut so clean it becomes a window, reveals "the cold flash of the blue/ unappeasable sky." The sky's indifference to the poet's sympathy for the bird ("Poor thing! Poor foolish life!") or to his own condition (he lives "in a house marked 'For Sale'") provides the chilling backdrop for a revelation of the necessity for human charity toward all living things. The poem knowingly alludes to a passage in "Father and Son": "For I would be . . . brother to the foundlings of the field/ And friend of innocence and all bright eyes." As with that earlier poem, "Robin Redbreast" finds no consolation in received wisdom, either from a father's love or the heavens. What charity there is exists (as do humans) in what scientists dryly refer to as "terminal structure."

Memory is more directly the subject of "The Magic Curtain," a cultural tour of America during the 1920's. A paean to his nurse, Frieda, the poem affectionately recounts his happy childhood adventures with this blue-eyed, Bavarian maid, while his mother, "her mind already on her shop," unrolled "gingham by the yard,/ stitching dresses for the Boston trade." Frieda, identified as his "first love," in secret complicity with the knowing child, bestows "the kinds of kisses mother would not dream" and serves as his guide to the melodramatic, romantic world of the motion pictures where, during reels of *The Perils of Pauline* (1914), Keystone Kops, and Charlie Chaplin, "School faded out at every morning reel." The films also offer a hint of the glamorous world beyond for Frieda, who takes her cue in a cinematic cliché and runs off "with somebody's husband, daddy to a brood." Although the poet's mother never forgives her this abandonment, the older poet, returning to her in the sanctuary of memory, eagerly does, for each has in a different way unknowingly conspired in fulfilling the dreams of the other.

The uneasy subject and situation of parents (and parent figures) weighs heavily, if somewhat obliquely, in the poems of *The Testing-Tree*. In fact, the volume opens with "Journal for My Daughter," a poem in which the poet, in nine free-verse sections, confronts his own hesitations and guilt in the upbringing of his only child. He imagines himself through her eyes as beckoning "down corridors,/ secret, elusive, saturnine." Now that, he hopes, the smoke of these misgivings has cleared, he

declares, "I propose/ that we gather our affections." Looking back over his role in her life, he recounts his absence ("his name was absence") but claims, "I think I'd rather sleep forever/ than wake up cold/ in a country without women." He recounts too, drunken nights of bonhomie with his friend, the poet Theodore Roethke, "slapping each other on the back,/ sweaty with genius," while she "crawled under the sofa." While he confesses that he is now "haggard with his thousand years," he declares his solidarity with her 1960's protests: "His heart is at home/ in your own generation," and to prove it he equates her misspelled slogan *"Don't tred on me"* with the *"Noli me tangere!"* he used "to cry in Latin once." Though it seems implausible that one would cry out in Latin anyplace outside the Vatican or a course in Tudor poets, the point is well made. Recalling "the summer I went away," he carries her outside "in a blitz of fireflies" to observe her first eclipse. To this image he adds Samuel Taylor Coleridge's carrying his crying son outside and catching the reflection of stars in each of his suspended tears. The heavens and the natural world are captured, comfortably diminished, and naturalized as a way of sanctioning human folly and love. The reverse of this coin is that it is an illusion, a pint-sized reflection of a placid cosmos that will momentarily evaporate.

The book's title poem, composed in four sections of unrhymed tercets, concerns a ritualistic childhood game of stone-throwing ("for keeps") at a specific oak tree able to confer magic gifts: one hit for love, two for poetry, three for eternal life. In the summers of his youth, searching for "perfect stones," he is master "over that stretch of road . . . the world's fastest human." Leaving the road that begins at school at one end and that at the other tries "to loop me home," he enters a field "riddled with rabbit-life/ where the bees sank sugar-wells/ in the trunks of the maples." There, in the shadow of the "inexhaustible oak,/ tyrant and target," he calls to his father, *"wherever you are/ I have only three throws/ bless my good right arm."* In the final section, he recalls a recurring dream of his mother "wearing an owl's face/ and making barking noises." As "her minatory finger points," he steps through a cardboard door and wonders if he should be blamed for the dirt sifting into a well where a gentle-eyed "albino walrus huffs." Suddenly the scene shifts, and the highway up which a Model A chugs becomes the road "where tanks maneuver,/ revolving their turrets." He concludes, "It is necessary to go/ through dark and deeper dark/ and not to turn." With the clear implication that the poet is mindful of his approaching mortal hour, with or without his father's blessing, he cries, "Where is my testing-tree?/ Give me back my stones!"

The Testing-Tree differs from the first three volumes in being composed of nearly a quarter translations, all from postrevolutionary Russian poetry. It was during the 1960's that Kunitz met and befriended two of the Soviet Union's best-known poets, Yevgeny Yevtushenko and Andrei Voznesensky, and, in collaboration with Max Hayward, translated a selection of poems by a third, Anna Akhmatova. Clearly, the poems enabled Kunitz, with the aid of this fortuitous ventriloquism, to take aim at the brutality and inhumanity of the modern political bureaucracy, whether Soviet or American. In Yevtushenko's "Hand-Rolled Cigarettes," for example, the common man's practice of rolling cigarettes in papers torn from *Pravda* and *Izvestia*, the two chief organs of state propaganda, gives rise to a dandy send-up of the bureaucrat's contempt for the common man: "Returning late, the tired fisherman/ enjoys his ladled kvass's tang,/ and sifts tobacco at his ease/ onto some bureaucrat's harangue."

THE POEMS OF STANLEY KUNITZ, 1928-1978

The Poems of Stanley Kunitz, 1928-1978, like *Selected Poems, 1928-1958*, contains a section of new poems, titled "The Layers." Here, the poet returns to the garden of his obsessions—father, family, time, the wounds of guilt, and memory—in poems of reconciliation and commemoration. In the opening poem, "The Knot," the poet imagines that the knot "scored in the lintel of my door" keeps "bleeding through/ into the world we share." Like a repressed thought, the knot wants more than anything to grow out again, to become a limb: "I hear it come/ with a rush of resin/ out of the trauma/ of its lopping-off." Characteristically, the poet associates the wound with a door, a threshold. It is as though something in nature has had to be tamed in order to effect the domestic tranquillity so delicately limned here, but its desire to return to its true nature is such that it "racks itself with shoots/ that crackle overhead." Identifying a part of his own nature with that of the knot, the poet

completes the metaphor: "I shake my wings/ and fly into its boughs."

Kunitz returns to the theme of the lost father in "What of the Night?" and "Quinnapoxet." In the former, the poet wakes in the middle of the night "like a country doctor," having imagined, "with racing heart," the doorbell ringing. It is a messenger (Death) whose "gentle, insistent ring" finds the poet "not ready yet" and realizing "nobody stands on the stoop." Suddenly the poem switches focus from the grown son to the father: "When the messenger comes again/ I shall pretend/ in a childish voice/ my father is not home." His father has, in actuality, never been home, but in a deeper, metaphorical sense, he has never left home. In this light, just as the grown man must receive the messenger at the end of his life, so the son must protect the father in memory from the "second death," the oblivion of forgetting. The poet's task of remembering is obligatory, as his question earlier in the poem recognizes: "How could I afford/ to disobey that call?" "Quinnapoxet" takes place on a mysterious fishing trip where, on a dusty road similar to the one described in "Father and Son," the poet describes a hallucinatory vision of his mother and father "commingling with the dust/ they raised." His mother admonishes him for not writing, and the poet's response is simple: "I had nothing to say to her." Yet for his father who walks behind, "his face averted . . . deep in his other life," the poet, too awestruck to attempt speech, touches his forehead with his thumb, "in deaf-mute country/ the sign for father."

One of the most original of the new poems in this volume is "A Blessing of Women," a prose poem inspired by an exhibit of early American women painters and artisans mounted by the Whitney Museum. In the form of a litany, the poem briefly describes, in dignified understatement, the works and lives of five of the representative women: an embroiderer, a quilter, and three painters, "a rainbow-cloud of witnesses in a rising hubbub." He blesses them and greets them "as they pass from their long obscurity, through the gate that separates us from our history."

"Our history" is again the subject of "The Lincoln Relics," a meditation on Lincoln's passage from the "raw-boned, warty" mortal "into his legend and his fame." Written not long after the Watergate trauma during

Kunitz's tenure at the Library of Congress, the poem alludes to that episode by invoking the ancient struggle between idealism and materialism, no less fierce in Lincoln's day than in ours: "I saw the piranhas darting/ between the roseveined columns,/ avid to strip the flesh/ from the Republic's bones." The source of Lincoln's, the sacrificial redeemer's, strength is identified as his "secret wound"—that is to say, "trusting the better angels of our nature." It is this trust, evoked by the humble but talismanic relics—a pocketknife, a handkerchief, a button—found on his person after the assassination, that makes "a noble, dissolving music/ out of homely fife and drum."

The title poem of the new section, "The Layers," looks forward to the possibilities of new art. The poet has "walked through many lives" and from the present vantage sees "milestones dwindling/ toward the horizon/ and the slow fires trailing/ from the abandoned campsites." To the question, "How shall the heart be reconciled/ to its feast of losses?" the answer comes "In my darkest night" from a "nimbus-cloud voice" that thunders, "Live in the layers,/ not on the litter." Though the poet admits, "I lack the art/ to decipher it," he concludes, "I am not done with my changes."

NEXT-TO-LAST THINGS

Kunitz's work *Next-to-Last Things: New Poems and Essays* makes at least three important additions to his poetic canon. A dream poem, "The abduction," begins with the image of the beloved stumbling out of a wood, her blouse torn, her skirt bloodstained; she addresses the poet with the mysterious question, "Do you believe?" Through the years, he says, "from bits/ from broken clues/ we pieced enough together/ to make the story real." Led into the presence of "a royal stag,/ flaming in his chestnut coat," she was "borne/ aloft in triumph through the green,/ stretched on his rack of budding horn." In the next verse paragraph, the poet discloses that the episode was "a long time ago,/ almost another age" and muses on his sleeping wife (recalling, with the same image, the theme of otherness in "The Science of the Night"): "You lie in elegant repose,/ a hint of transport hovering on your lips." His attention shifts "to the harsh green flares," to which she is indifferent, that "swivel through the room/ controlled by unseen hands." The night world outside is "childhood country,/

bleached faces peering in/ with coals for eyes." His meditation leads him to realize that "the shapes of things/ are shifting in the wind," and concludes, "What do we know/ beyond the rapture and the dread?" echoing William Butler Yeats's famous question, "How can we know the dancer from the dance?" As a poem of transformation, "The Abduction" does not lend itself easily to interpretation—partly by design—for, at a very basic level, the preternatural images of transformation are rooted in undisclosed biographical events. As a poet of knowledge, however, Kunitz is poignant in his recognition that when people sleep, when they are most themselves, they are also most withdrawn and indifferent to their surroundings, even, or especially, from those they love. Yet by acknowledging, even honoring, the terms of this indifference, one most surely understands the unselfish nature of love.

"Days of Foreboding" begins with the announcement, "Great events are about to happen." The poet has seen migratory birds "in unprecedented numbers" picking the coastal margin clean. Turning to himself, he observes, "My bones are a family in their tent/ huddled over a small fire/ waiting for the uncertain signal/ to resume the long march." He too is migratory, warmed by the small fire of his heart. Presumably, the "uncertain signal" is in some way keyed to the signal by which the migratory birds decide to move on—that is, it is keyed to nature. Moreover, while the signal is uncertain in terms of time and origin, it is nevertheless inevitable. The ultimate phrase, "the long march," sings with historical resonance and the promise of an irreversible transformation at the end. In this poem and in others, Kunitz accepts the awful fact of mortality, not by making an abstraction of it but by naturalizing both it and the patch of history that is the bolt of time and circumstance given for its completion. Avoiding the need for consolation, it is a brave and existential view.

Certainly the centerpiece of *Next-to-Last Things* is the five-part meditative elegy, "The Wellfleet Whale," composed, like "The Testing-Tree," in tercets. Kunitz has noted that much of contemporary meditative poetry suffers from "the poverty of what it is meditating on," but this poem, occasioned by the beaching of a finback whale near the poet's home on Cape Cod, is rich in its suggestion that life's secret origins can be, if not revealed, then somehow embodied by the evocativeness of language, which is itself, as the poet notes elsewhere, "anciently deep in mysteries." The poem begins by ascribing to the whale, both Leviathan and deliverer of Jonah, Christ's precursor, the gift of language: "You have your language too,/ an eerie medley of clicks/ and hoots and trills. . . ." That language, to which humans are denied access (just as historical man, exiled from Eden, can no longer hear the music of the spheres), becomes only "sounds that all melt/ . . . with endless variations,/ as if to compensate/ for the vast loneliness of the sea." In the second section of the poem, the whale's arrival in the harbor is greeted with cheers "at the sign of your greatness." Unlike man, the whale in its element seems "like something poured,/ not driven," his presence asking "not sympathy, or love,/ or understanding,/ but awe and wonder," responses appropriate to deity. Yet by dawn, the whale is stranded on the rocks, and the curious gather in: "school-girls in yellow halters/ and a housewife bedecked/ with curlers, and whole families in beach/ buggies. . . ." As the great body is slowly crushed by its own weight, the Curator of Mammals arrives to draw the requisite vial of blood, someone carves his initials on the blistered flanks, and sea gulls peck at the skin. The poet asks, "What drew us, like a magnet, to your dying?" and answers, "You made a bond between us." This unlikely company, "boozing in the bonfire night," stands watch during the night as the whale enters its final agony and swings its head around to open "a blood-shot, glistening eye/ in which we swam with terror and recognition." The terror is that of witnessing "an exiled god" and the recognition that the creature, bringing with it "the myth/ of another country, dimly remembered" is "like us,/ disgraced and mortal," like all beings, and "delivered to the mercy of time." Despite the desecrations visited upon the creature, it remains an emissary from that other "country," the country of myth and inspired origin that stands at the beginning of human memory—and thus of identity—and so supervenes upon the noble disenchantment of the poem.

PASSING THROUGH

This collection of poems, published when Kunitz was ninety, is a slim volume that adds nine new poems to the body of Kunitz's work. Some of the poems in this collection are drawn from *The Testing-Tree*, *Next-to-Last Things*, and "The Layers." The title of the collection comes from a poem, "Passing Through," that Kunitz wrote on his seventy-ninth birthday and published in *Next-to-Last Things*. In this poem, he looks back upon his childhood and amplifies his quest for identity. Saying that his family never observed anniversaries, he matter-of-factly states, "my birthday went up in smoke/ in a fire at City Hall that gutted/ the Department of Vital Statistics." He goes on to say that only because a census report noted that "a five-year-old White Male/ [was] sharing my mother's address/ at the Green Street tenement in Worcester" did he have any identity at all. However, he concludes that "Maybe I enjoy not-being as much/ as being who I am," and continues whimsically, saying that—at seventy-nine, mind you— "I'm passing through a phase."

Similar in its quest for identity is "The Sea, That Has No Ending," which begins with the questions "Who are we? Why are we here,/ huddled on this desolate shore,/ so curiously chopped and joined?" The eternal sea, the forever sea, the sea that has always been and will always be, "The sea that has no ending,/ is lapping at our feet." Kunitz recounts, "How we long for the cleansing waters/ to rise and cover us forever!" Here he juxtaposes immortality and mortality, human time and eternity, reiterating forcefully his persistent concerns with time and space.

In his selection of poems for this volume, which in 1995 brought Kunitz the National Book Award in Poetry, the author included a range of works that detail ancient and modern events, broadly global and intensely personal occurrences, and events both real and mythical. On one hand, he celebrates the flight of Apollo 11 (the first to transport men to the Moon); on the other, he tells of the struggles of Roman gladiators.

"Around Pastor Bonhoeffer," his homage to Dietrich Bonhoeffer, who stood four-square against Adolf Hitler and his reign of terror in Nazi Germany, is stylistically among his most successful poems. Short, clipped lines capture the tension of the situation:

> *Kyrie eleison:* Night
> like no other night, plotted
> and palmed,
> omega of terror,
> packed like a bullet
> in the triggered chamber.

THE COLLECTED POEMS

Coincident with his being appointed the poet laureate of the United States in 2000, when he was ninety-five years old, this is the first complete collection of Kunitz's poems since the publication in 1979 of *The Poems of Stanley Kunitz, 1928-1978* by W. W. Norton. This volume, drawing on all the earlier volumes, provides readers with the full range of Kunitz's remarkably varied work. Reading through the entire volume, which is arranged chronologically, one becomes fully aware of the themes that most affected the poet and his work: innocence and love, including the loss of each; parental relationships, particularly the father-son relationship of which he was deprived by his father's suicide shortly before his birth; a tragic element connected with personal disappointments; an overwhelming optimism, articulated well in "The Long Boat," where Kunitz writes, "He loved the earth so much/ he wanted to stay forever." Kunitz is always aware of the tenuous relationship of time in human terms to eternity, which is a global concept. The poet urged young writers always to be explorers. In his ninth decade of life, Kunitz continued to be an explorer, seeking out new experiences and writing about them in new and uniquely wonderful ways.

The tension that is everywhere apparent between noble disenchantment and hard-won acceptance demonstrates the ruling dialectic in Kunitz's poems. At the very least, it reveals the long trail of a poetic career (poetic careers have been built on much less); at its most resplendent, this dialectic embodies, through its variously charted interests, experiences, and investigations, a reason for the mind's commitment to the things of this world. Standing simultaneously in their singular and typical natures, they suggest the duality that is both a curse and triumph and lead to an appreciation and understanding, as individuals rebound endlessly between the two, of the transformations that must be endured to ensure survival.

OTHER MAJOR WORKS

NONFICTION: *A Kind of Order, a Kind of Folly: Essays and Conversations*, 1975; *Interviews and Encounters with Stanley Kunitz*, 1993 (Stanley Moss, editor).

TRANSLATIONS: *Antiworlds and the Fifth Ace*, 1967 (with others; of Andrei Voznesensky's poetry); *Stolen Apples*, 1971 (with others; of Yevgeny Yevtushenko's poetry); *Poems of Akhmatova*, 1973 (with Max Hayward); *Story Under Full Sail*, 1974 (of Voznesensky's poetry); *Orchard Lamps*, 1978 (of Ivan Drach's poetry).

EDITED TEXTS: *Living Authors: A Book of Biographies*, 1931; *Authors Today and Yesterday: A Companion Volume to "Living Authors,"* 1933 (with Howard Haycraft and Wilbur C. Hadden); *The Junior Book of Authors*, 1934, 2d ed. 1951 (with Haycraft); *British Authors of the Nineteenth Century*, 1936 (with Haycraft); *American Authors, 1600-1900: A Biographical Dictionary of American Literature*, 1938 (with Haycraft); *Twentieth Century Authors: A Biographical Dictionary of Modern Literature*, 1942, 7th ed. 1973 (with Haycraft); *British Authors Before 1800: A Biographical Dictionary*, 1952 (with Haycraft); *Twentieth Century Authors: A Biographical Dictionary of Modern Literature, First Supplement*, 1955, 7th ed. 1990 (with Vineta Colby); *European Authors, 1000-1900: A Biographical Dictionary of European Literature*, 1967 (with Colby); *Contemporary Poetry in America*, 1973; *The Essential Blake*, 1987.

MISCELLANEOUS: *Next-to-Last Things: New Poems and Essays*, 1985.

BIBLIOGRAPHY

Barber, David. "A Visionary Poet at Ninety." *The Atlantic Monthly* 277, no. 6 (June, 1996): 113-120. This article includes a biographical survey and a brief review of some of the poet's earlier works before turning to a heartfelt appreciation of *Passing Through: The Later Poems, New and Selected*. Barber names Kunitz a "visionary" and sees his poetry as "transfiguring."

Campbell, Robert. "God, Man, and Whale: Stanley Kunitz's Collected Poems Show His Work Is All of a Piece." *The New York Times Book Review* 150 (October 1, 2000): 16. This review of Kunitz's poems, collected and published in his ninety-fifth year, offers comments about the broad spectrum of this poet's writing over seven decades. One of the most insightful brief overviews of Kunitz in print.

Henault, Marie. *Stanley Kunitz*. Boston: Twayne, 1980. A good introduction to Kunitz for the beginning reader. Presents biographical detail and criticism of his poetry, discussing his themes, form and techniques, and the "interior logics" of his poems. A sympathetic study lamenting the fact that Kunitz has not received the wide critical recognition he deserves.

Lowell, Robert. "On Stanley Kunitz's 'Father and Son.'" In *The Contemporary Poet as Artist and Critic*, edited by Anthony Ostroff. Boston: Little, Brown, 1964. Analyzes "Father and Son" and takes issue with a number of images in this poem, such as an orange being "nailed." Despite his unfavorable response, Lowell acknowledges that Kunitz has "never published an unfinished and unfelt poem."

Orr, Gregory. *Stanley Kunitz: An Introduction to the Poetry*. New York: Columbia University Press, 1985. A full-length criticism of Kunitz, noting that love and art are the two ways in which this poet seeks his identity. Discusses the key image, which Orr maintains is the single most important element in Kunitz's work. The chapter on *The Testing-Tree* is particularly recommended.

Plummer, William. "New Beginnings: At Ninety-five, Fledgling Poet Laureat Stanley Kunitz Finds Fresh Wood." *People Weekly* 54 (October 30, 2000): 159-160. Written for a popular audience, this overview of Kunitz's life and work emphasizes that the poet has continued to grow. An excellent, humane assessment of a life of creative endeavor.

Vinson, James, ed. *Contemporary Poets*. 3d ed. New York: Macmillan, 1980. The entry on Kunitz, by Michael True, examines his poetry as it retraces the "myth of the lost father." Cites his devotion to craft and the high standards he strove to maintain throughout his work. Notes Kunitz's earlier works as being more intellectual and his later ones as being more oriented toward feelings.

Weisberg, Robert. "Stanley Kunitz: The Stubborn Middle Way." *Modern Poetry Studies* 6 (Spring, 1975): 49-57. In this sympathetic article, Weisberg laments that Kunitz's "impressive" canon has aroused little critical interest. In discussing *Selected Poems, 1928-1958*, however, he criticizes Kunitz for being a "re-incarnation of John Donne" but praises "The Words of the Preacher" for the energy that his other metaphysical lyrics lack. Includes an analysis of *The Testing-Tree*.

David Rigsbee,
updated by R. Baird Shuman

REINER KUNZE

Born: Oelsnitz, Germany; August 16, 1933

PRINCIPAL POETRY

Vögel über dem Tau, 1959
Aber die Nachtigall jubelt, 1962
Widmungen, 1963
Sensible Wege, 1969
Zimmerlautstärke, 1972 (*With the Volume Turned Down*, 1973)
Brief mit blauem Siegel, 1973
Auf eigene Hoffnung, 1981
Eines jeden einziges Leben, 1986
Nicht alle Grenzen bleiben, 1989
Am Krankenbett des Tierbildhauers, 1991
Ein Tag auf dieser Erde, 1998

OTHER LITERARY FORMS

Although Reiner Kunze is known primarily as a lyric poet, he has also published two noteworthy volumes of prose and has distinguished himself as a prolific translator of modern Czech poetry. Kunze's first prose publication, *Der Löwe Leopold* (1970), was a collection of children's tales. Originally published in West Germany, the work subsequently appeared in a number of translations and was awarded the prestigious West German Youth Book Prize of 1971. It has never been published in the German Democratic Republic (GDR). Kunze's second prose volume, *Die wunderbaren Jahre* (1976; *The Wonderful Years*, 1977), has also appeared only in the West and consists of a series of short, critical vignettes describing various aspects of everyday life in the GDR. Kunze also worked closely with the producers of the film version of *The Wonderful Years* (1980).

Reiner Kunze (Courtesy of Reiner Kunze)

Achievements

Along with Günter Kunert, Volker Braun, Wolf Biermann, Sarah Kirsch, and Karl Mickel, to name only a few, Reiner Kunze belongs to the first generation of distinctively East German poets. These writers, who came of age in the late 1950's and early 1960's, took as their models poets from the preceding generation such as Peter Huchel and particularly Bertolt Brecht. Largely ignoring the prescribed canons of Socialist literary dogma, these poets lent an authentic voice to the experiences of their generation in the young German Democratic Republic.

Kunze in particular helped to bring honor and credibility to East German literature, as attested by the numerous literary prizes he has won, including the aforementioned West German Youth Book Prize and the Literature Prize of the Bavarian Academy of Fine Arts. In the year 1977 alone, Kunze was awarded the Andreas Gryphius Prize, the Georg Trakl Prize, and perhaps the most prestigious of German literary prizes, the Georg Büchner Prize. In 1984 he won the Eichendorff Literature Prize; in 1997, the Weilheimer Literature Prize; in

1998, the European Prize for Poetry, Serbia; and in 1999 the Friedrich Hölderlin Literary Award. Because his poetic diction relies heavily on untranslatable wordplay, he is not as well known outside the German-speaking countries as he deserves to be, but few who find their way to him fail to be captivated by his sensitivity, quiet dignity, and courageous humanism.

Biography

Although Reiner Kunze was ultimately forbidden to publish in the GDR and even became a nonperson in the eyes of the cultural bureaucracy, it is also true that if he had not attained maturity and received his education there, he might never have taken up writing. Born to working-class parents in the region of Thuringia, Kunze was originally destined to become a shoemaker, and he was somewhat surprised to find himself in 1951 with a completed secondary school diploma, facing a choice between art studies at the Academy of Art in Dresden or studies in journalism in Leipzig. As the son of a father who had been trained as a plumber but spent most of his life as a miner and a mother who supplemented the family income by crocheting piecework in her home, Kunze was an unlikely candidate for a learned profession. In keeping with the policies of the new regime, however, Kunze's talents received active encouragement precisely because of his working-class background, and therefore, in spite of his father's strong reservations, he studied journalism, philosophy, and literature in Leipzig from 1951 to 1955. Kunze was young, idealistic, more than a little naïve, and extremely grateful to the new government that had granted him such unexpected opportunity. It is not surprising, then, that his earliest poetic works, written during this period, contain a great deal of uncritical praise of the state and of the Socialist Unity Party, which Kunze had joined in 1949. To a certain degree, he was simply repeating the clichés and formulas taught him by his teachers but he also believed what he wrote. Although he later distanced himself from these early poems, which are now nearly inaccessible and justifiably forgotten, Kunze was sincere and cannot be charged with having consciously prostituted his art. At that time, he must have appeared to the authorities as everything they could wish for in the new generation of writers.

By 1959, however, Kunze's inability to reconcile Socialist theory with concrete experience led to severe political attacks upon him. Disappointed and disillusioned, he was forced to suspend his doctoral studies and teaching activities in the journalism faculty at Leipzig. Today, Kunze regards the year 1959 as the absolute low point, the "zero hour" in his life. Ironically, the year 1959 also saw the publication of his first major collection of poems, *Vögel über dem Tau* (birds above the dew).

Following a period of work as a manual laborer in the heavy equipment industry and as a truck driver in Leipzig, Kunze lived in 1961 and 1962 in Czechoslovakia while recovering from a serious heart ailment and waiting for permission to marry a Czech citizen, Dr. Elisabeth Littnerová, an oral surgeon who had begun a voluminous correspondence with the poet after hearing one of the poems from *Vögel über dem Tau* read on the radio in 1959. It was during this period that Kunze established his close ties with contemporary Czech poets. By the time he returned to the GDR in 1962 and settled in Greiz as a freelance writer, he had published his second volume of poetry in the GDR, *Aber die Nachtigall jubelt* (but the nightingale rejoices), as well as the first of numerous volumes of translations of modern Czech poetry. It is difficult for a lyric poet to earn a living from his work, but Kunze's wife was able to establish a successful medical practice in Greiz, and in the years from 1962 to 1968, Kunze kept busy primarily with his translations and as a contributor to Czech literary journals. The year 1963 saw the first publication of Kunze's work in the West, *Widmungen* (dedications), a collection of poems mostly from the period of his residency in Czechoslovakia but also containing several earlier poems which he did not wish to disclaim. Kunze's poetry of this period did not fit the cookbook conception of Socialist Realism demanded by some cultural policymakers, but neither did most of the new poetry being produced by young writers in what must be seen as a lyric renaissance and one of the numerous "thaws" in the cultural history of the GDR, and Kunze was neither singled out nor repressed by the regime.

It was not until 1968 that a period of tension with the authorities began—tension which gradually came to dominate Kunze's life and work until his expulsion from the GDR in April, 1977. The proximate cause was the invasion of Czechoslovakia by Warsaw Pact troops in August, 1968, a development which triggered Kunze's immediate resignation from the SED, the East German Communist Party. This, in turn, resulted in an almost total blacklisting of the poet. Except for a volume of poetry selected from earlier collections that was published in 1973 under the title *Brief mit blauem Siegel* (letter with a blue seal), no work of Kunze's has since appeared in the GDR. *Sensible Wege* (sensitive paths) and *With the Volume Turned Down* both appeared only in the West, and Kunze was fined in each instance under an East German law which prohibits authors from publishing material anywhere without first securing the permission of the Central Office for Copyrights.

As the East German repression of Kunze's works increased, so did the attention the poet received in the Western media. He was awarded numerous Western literary prizes, but was often prevented from traveling to receive them. Some Western commentators were clearly more interested in Kunze as a political martyr than as a poet, and their attempts to stylize him into the "Solzhenitsyn of the GDR" served only to increase his difficulties. Matters came to a head following the publication of *The Wonderful Years*, when Kunze was first removed from the East German Writers' Union in October, 1976, an action tantamount to a total prohibition against practicing the profession of writing in any form, and then "invited" to leave the GDR, an invitation the poet could scarcely afford to decline in view of the campaign of vilification and intimidation launched against him and his family.

Kunze settled near Passau in Bavaria, saddened at having to leave the country he once said he "would choose over and over again" but happy to be able to write in relative peace. In spite of the fears of those who saw in Kunze only the beleaguered and eventually exiled political dissident and to the disappointment of those who wished to embrace him only as a Cold War propaganda tool, he has not allowed himself to voice a position of such bitter political opposition that he can no longer speak in the idiom of the poet. The first volume of poetry that Kunze produced after coming to the West, *Auf eigene Hoffnung* (of my own hope), indicated that he was able to give poetic expression to the full range of human experience, both political and private, with which he was confronted in the West.

Analysis

Although initially in complete agreement with the ideals of humanistic Democratic Socialism, Reiner Kunze is by nature a shy, sensitive, reflective man whose poetic interests have always tended toward the private sphere, and it is ironic that he first became known to a wider audience primarily as a political dissident, as a sensational case in the often sordid history of East German cultural politics. As is the case with any writer living in a system where literary questions are by definition also political issues, it is impossible to avoid the political dimension when discussing Kunze's work. His achievement as a poet, however, rests on the modest virtues of directness, honesty, and basic humanity, not on any polemical stance.

Kunze has always been a "popular" poet, both before and after his exile from the GDR to West Germany. His poetic images are concrete, drawn almost exclusively from everyday life, and easily accessible without being merely simpleminded or naïve. From Heinrich Heine, Kunze learned satire and wit, from Federico García Lorca a bold metaphoric vision, and from Bertolt Brecht the knack of accommodating apparent opposites through dialectical thought; his chief claim to originality lies in his expansion of the possibilities of a lyric poetry of extreme brevity and concentration. His strength is the sudden, insightful aperçu, and some of his best work falls formally between epigram and graffiti. Kunze's playful, almost childlike view of the world, and of language in particular, allows him to exploit wordplay and create metaphors in ways that are both refreshingly original and genuinely insightful. He is capable of puckish good humor and wit, even when he has good reason for bitterness and despair. On the whole, his is a poetry of hope, however precarious. Kunze has said that he intends his poetry to reduce the distance and isolation between human beings, to make himself and his readers aware of their common humanity; at his best, he succeeds.

A fundamental characteristic of poetry can perhaps best be described as a tension between reason and emotion, between the demands of society and the needs of the private individual, between civilization and nature. In short, it is the clash of the Enlightenment with Romanticism. At different stages in his career, Kunze has resolved this tension now in one direction, now in the other, but his ultimate achievement lies in the dialectic reconciliation of opposites and the avoidance of false choices.

In Kunze's earliest poetry, contained in *Vögel über dem Tau, Aber die Nachtigall jubelt,* and, to a lesser extent, *Widmungen,* the Romantic elements clearly predominate. The first two volumes fulfill the promise of their titles, offering a great deal of nature imagery, with particular emphasis on birds and roses. The strophic forms as well as the rhymes of Kunze's early verse are simple, regular, and heavily indebted to folk poetry. Most of the poems of *Aber die Nachtigall jubelt* were intended to be set to music for use in East German puppet films for children, and Kunze has often said that he regards music as the queen of all the arts. The poet's preference for the realm of feeling is clearly apparent in the following lines from *Vögel über dem Tau:* "Love/ is a wild rose in us/ inaccessible to reason/ and not subjugated to it." Often the realm of nature and spontaneous feeling is defended against the demands or intrusions of a sterile, rational world of order and constraint, as in "The Song of the Strict Commander," whose troops are encouraged to break their close-order marching to pursue a pretty girl. Poetry itself is defended as a kind of refuge from an outside world that is often inimical to the spirit. Art and life become polarized, and there is no question which is to be preferred by the sensitive individual. In poems such as "Horizons" and "In the Thaya" from *Widmungen,* the rose is regarded as being almost subversive of the prevailing order. The latter poem contains the lines: "do you see how a rose is blooming in his hands?/ Don't you see it? A rose!/ But we're not in favor of roses/ We are for order./ Whoever is for the rose/ is against order." To a great extent, Kunze was simply reacting against the excessive demands of the state for personal and poetic regimentation, as clearly suggested by these lines from *Aber die Nachtigall jubelt:* "Art—it flees commands./ Reason alone does not control it./ It wants the artist's soul." The predominance of Romantic characteristics in these early poems also reflects Kunze's poetic naïveté and the fact that his earliest literary models were drawn from that era.

Some of Kunze's early poetry is flawed by excessive pathos and sentimentality, and at times he threatens to withdraw completely into a private realm of bird and flower metaphors. He was able to overcome that tendency by anchoring his poems in concrete, everyday experience. As he has matured, he has continued to portray landscapes, for example, but they have become clearly identifiable geographical locations with specific historical and social coordinates. Similarly, Kunze has withdrawn from metaphysical speculation about universal truths, seeking rather to illuminate problems in their specific manifestation from his own experience. In this way, Kunze's poetry has become more clearly autobiographical and direct, and his understanding of its function has undergone an evolutionary change. Whereas the realm of feeling and poetry once offered an inward, private escape from or alternative to the sterile world of reason and society, Kunze now sees art and life less as irreconcilable opposites than as necessary complements. The realm of poetry is to be furiously defended not because it offers an escape from life but precisely because it offers a means of coming to terms with it.

DEFENSE OF POETRY

Kunze attributes his maturation as a poet primarily to his contact with modern Czech poetry and today regards *Widmungen* as his first significant work. In that volume and in the subsequent collections *Sensible Wege* and *With the Volume Turned Down*, it is clear that he has turned away from Romantic models, with the exception of the sharp wit and barbed irony of Heine. His defense of poetry becomes more sharply focused, and the threats to it are more clearly identified and engaged; a 1972 article by Manfred Jäger, one of the earliest studies of Kunze's poetry, is titled "Eine offensive Verteidigung der Poesie" (an aggressive defense of poetry). Kunze's chief weapon in the defense of poetry is a dialectical, epigrammatic style indebted particularly to the late poetry of Brecht. In his poems of this period, Kunze frequently adopts a satirical tone, and his diction, deflated of its pathos, could even be called reductionist. An entire poem may turn on a single metaphor or a bit of wordplay;

grammatical markers fall away; and what is omitted is often more important than what is said. Sometimes, the polemical or didactic point of the poem lies in its title. All these features are evident in a poem titled "Gebildete Nation" (cultured nation): "Peter Huchel left the/ German Democratic Republic/ (report from France)/ He left/ The newspapers reported/ no loss." Kunze expresses dismay that a country which puts considerable emphasis on "storming the heights of culture" cannot feel or officially acknowledge the loss of a poetic talent of the magnitude of Peter Huchel. "Hymnus auf eine Frau beim verhör" (hymn to a woman being interrogated) illustrates Kunze's technique of setting the barb with a dialectical twist at the end: "Painful was/ the moment of/ undressing/ Then/ exposed to their glances she/ learned everything/ about them."

To be sure, the themes of Kunze's early lyrics do not altogether disappear, but they recede somewhat into the background; when they do appear, they share many of the stylistic features of the more overtly political poems. "Auf dich im blauen Mantel" (to you in a blue coat) is dedicated to the poet's wife: "Once more I read from the beginning/ the line of houses look for/ you the blue comma that/ makes sense of it." The fact that the poem itself desperately needs a comma between "houses" and "look" in order to make sense increases the poignancy of its thematic point. Kunze's ability to transform mundane experiences—such as the sight of his wife coming down the street—into a fresh poetic metaphor is one of his chief strengths. In *Widmungen* and subsequent collections, Kunze became a master of the short form, of the clever and penetrating but sometimes also moving aperçu. The previous romantic excesses gave way to a more balanced mixture of thought and feeling, and he emerged from an inward-turning lyricism to a poetry which engaged the world.

STRIVING TO COMMUNICATE

Indeed, the need for communication grew to occupy a central position in Kunze's life and art. One section of *Sensible Wege* is subtitled "Hunger nach der Welt" (hunger for the world), and the volume concludes with a cycle of twenty-one poems on the theme of the mail, a tenuous connection with the outside world for an increasingly critical East German poet whose standing with the authorities stood in inverse proportion to his growing reputation in both East and West. In one of these poems, Kunze refers to letters as "white lice in the pelt of the fatherland" awaiting the "comb" of the postal service.

Kunze fought all attempts at censorship and regimentation with the one weapon at his disposal, his poetry, which he could still publish in the West. The numerous literary prizes Kunze won in the West in the early 1970's afforded him a visibility which undoubtedly helped to protect him from cruder forms of repression, and, together with another "thaw" in cultural policies, probably accounted for the surprising publication of *Brief mit blauem Siegel* in the East in 1973. Nevertheless, Kunze was increasingly caught up in a process of escalating politicization that threatened to destroy all balance between political and private concerns and overwhelm his ability to respond creatively to them. Particularly with the publication of *The Wonderful Years*, Kunze came to be regarded by many in both East and West as a purely political phenomenon. He was embraced in the Federal Republic by anti-GDR forces who hoped to use him only as a propaganda weapon, and he was vilified in the East as an "enemy of the state"; it appeared for a time that Kunze was not going to be allowed to be "merely" a poet, to continue to give poetic expression to the full range of human experience.

AUF EIGENE HOFFNUNG

Although some observers assumed, perhaps understandably, that Kunze was indeed primarily a political dissident who would probably fall silent after his exile to the West, the move was instead very beneficial to him as a poet. Freed from the bitterness of repression and the glare of sensational publicity, Kunze was gradually able to produce the poems contained in *Auf eigene Hoffnung*, published some nine years after *With the Volume Turned Down*.

If Kunze began his career retreating from the world into romantic excesses and was then prevented from maintaining a balance between private and public life by forces largely outside his control, then the poems of *Auf eigene Hoffnung* appear to represent an achievement of equilibrium. The first section of the book contains poems written between 1973 and 1975, before his expulsion from the GDR; his weariness and concern over the politicization of his work is apparent. The section is sub-

titled "Des Fahnenhissens bin ich müde, Freund" ("I am tired of showing my colors, friend") a line from a poem based upon a wordplay made possible by the dual meaning of the German word *Fahne* ("flag" and "galley proof"). Ewald Osers, the British translator of *With the Volume Turned Down*, had written Kunze that he had just gotten the galley proofs (*Fahnen*) back from the printer and they were ready to be corrected, or "flown," depending on how one chose to understand the word. Kunze concludes his poem with the thought that the only *Fahne* to which he would care to swear an oath is one with a love poem on it. The same weariness with political themes is expressed in a poem titled "Tagebuchblatt 1980" (diary page 1980), obviously written during the West German election campaign: "The climbing roses are blossoming, as though the landscape were bleeding/ . . . / Even the landscape, they will claim, may/ no longer simply exist, it too/ must be for or against." Nature's pure colors thus become stylized into campaign propaganda for the Social Democrats, just as Kunze had recently been used for political causes that were not his own.

It may be understood, however, that Kunze is not mourning here his own lost innocence, the time when landscapes and roses were a form of inward, private escape; rather, he desires the right (and the peace of mind) to produce landscape and love poetry. When he does so in this volume, the poems display the tautness of language and boldness of metaphoric vision characteristic of his best work. In "Your Head on My Breast," for example, the entire poem is contructed around a single metaphor or wordplay based on the German word "Schlüsselbein" (which means collarbone, but since a *Schlüssel* is a key, the literal meaning is *key* bone). The abundance of landscape poems results in part, no doubt, from the poet's new freedom to travel. The latest volume even includes Kunze's impressions of America, gathered in 1980 when he held a guest professorship in the German department at the University of Texas. Kunze's eye is open to natural beauty, but he also locates his landscapes within their concrete social context. The placing of natural settings within their human context is perfectly symbolized in the metaphor that Kunze chooses for the heading of the section of poems on America: "Amerika, der Autobaum" (America, the auto-tree).

Although Kunze by no means seeks to avoid political themes, he is concerned that they are sometimes unsuitable for poetic expression. He is very much aware of the apology in Brecht's well-known poem "An die Nachgeborenen" (to posterity), which acknowledges that even righteous indignation distorts the features, and, as Kunze's poem "Credo on a Good Morning" suggests, he would rather avoid certain painful areas: "When you are writing a poem, that is, going/ barefoot in your heart,/ avoid the places where/ something shattered in you/ The moss/ is no match for the fragments/ It exists, the/ poem without a wound." As suggested, however, this credo does not prevent Kunze from adopting a critical stance with respect to political aspects of West German society. One poem shows how neo-Nazi attitudes are revealed in everyday life, as when a young Bavarian watching an international soccer match in a neighborhood bar comments upon a Dutch player who has just scored a goal: "Den ham's beim vagasn vagessn" (they forgot to gas that one). The man is obviously too young to remember the Nazi era, but the thoughtless remark reveals an appalling lack of sensitivity to Germany's past. Frequently, as in this poem, Kunze need only quote the target of his criticism directly in order to achieve a striking effect; the authorities in the GDR often made things easy for the poet in precisely this way.

THEMES BEYOND THE POLITICAL

Kunze has stated that he does not, in fact, choose his themes at all; rather, they choose him. In addition to its communicative intent, writing has for him also a personal, therapeutic function as a means of coming to terms with matters he can deal with in no other way. He vigorously rejects the thesis that he needs opposition in order to write and insists that he was never cut out for the role of political martyr. Kunze is relieved that the themes now choosing him—that is, the concerns impinging on his consciousness—are no longer almost all from the political sphere. Although he does not write prolifically, he has not fallen silent as many in the West feared he would, and the relative quiet that has grown around him has been productive, as expressed in the lines from a poem in *Auf eigene Hoffnung:* "Stillness gathers around me/ the soil for the poem/ In the spring we will/ have verses and birds."

EIN TAG AUF DIESER ERDE

Kunze has in fact not fallen silent and produced his first poetry collection in seven years in 1998. His collection titled *Ein Tag auf dieser Erde* (a day on this earth) seems to indicate a diary approach to poetry. However, the scope and purpose of the work is discernibly larger than a series of journal entries. While the passing of time sets immediate and inexplicable barriers to confine the human condition, no such limits restrict Kunze's poetic imagination, which here elaborates on the tangible, not always comfortable, intimacy of the cosmic order. An elegant sparseness accommodates Kunze's method, and wide-spanning acumen guides him in his task. There are six sections, and the brevity and subdued diction of the verse throughout allow for subtle gradations to take hold. Section One hints at timeless, local precedents for universal myths. Inevitable realities in human aging are beautifully, seamlessly linked to nature in the poem "November." Section Two expands to a tour of civilized history, with stops in a range of locales including Kyoto, for the cherry festival, and Namibia. The following two sections attend to events in recent German history and to the less-than-assuring ambivalence of ideal aspiration (two short poems in "Der himmel"). The penultimate section "Komm mit dem cello" touches on the unqualified consolations of art.

The book ends with a coda that gives the collection its title, a meditation on mortality in fifteen sections. Fish, bird, and river are the vibrant signs of transcendent life here, and there is a one-sided confrontation with God. Yet it is by a series of transformative, interwoven contrasts and reversals that the sequence becomes amazing, and so does the book as a whole, despite its emblematic familiarity. Without resorting to the readily available or conventional rhetoric of hope, *Ein Tag auf dieser Erde* builds to a quiet resolution, a calm right on the brink of a complete and devastating silence.

OTHER MAJOR WORKS

NONFICTION: *Die wunderbaren Jahre,* 1976 (*The Wonderful Years,* 1977); *Das weisse Gedicht: Essays,* 1989; *Am Sonnenhang: Tagebuch eines Jahres,* 1993.

CHILDREN'S LITERATURE: *Der Löwe Leopold,* 1970.

BIBLIOGRAPHY

Glenn, Jerry. Review of *Wo Freiheit ist . . . : Gespräche 1977-1993*, by Reiner Kunze. *World Literature Today* 69, no. 2 (Spring, 1995): 355. A review of a German collection of interviews with Kunze. Glenn's review provides an interpretation in English of the biographical material contained in the interviews.

Graves, Peter. "A Naked Individualist." Review of *Ein Tag Auf Dieser Erde*. *The Times Literary Supplement* (March 26, 1999): 26. Graves provides some biographical insights in his review of Kunze's work.

_____. "Reiner Kunze: Some Comments and a Conversation." *German Life and Letters* 41, no. 3 (1988): 312-322. A critical study of selected works by Kunze and an interview with the poet.

Hamburger, Michael. *After the Second Flood: Essays on Post-War German Literature*. New York: St. Martin's Press, 1986. A critical and historical study of several German poets including Reiner Kunze.

Dennis McCormick,
updated by Sarah Hilbert

L

JEAN DE LA FONTAINE

Born: Château-Thierry, France; July 8, 1621
Died: Paris, France; April 13, 1695

PRINCIPAL POETRY

Adonis, 1658

Le Songe de Vaux, 1659

Contes et nouvelles en vers, 1665 (*Tales and Short Stories in Verse*, 1735)

Deuxième partie des "Contes et nouvelles en vers," 1666 (*Part Two of "Tales and Short Stories in Verse,"* 1735)

Fables choisies, mises en vers, 1668-1694 (*Fables Written in Verse*, 1735)

Troisième partie des "Contes et nouvelles en vers," 1671 (*Part Three of "Tales and Short Stories in Verse,"* 1735)

Nouveaux Contes, 1674 (*New Tales*, 1735)

Poèmes et poésies diverses, 1697

OTHER LITERARY FORMS

The verse fable has attracted numerous writers over the centuries extending as far back as Aesop. Jean de La Fontaine's success in the genre, however, surpassed them all. Though his verse novel *Les Amours de Psyché et Cupidon* (1669; *The Loves of Cupid and Psyche*, 1744) may be considered a major work and he wrote plays, librettos, translations, and letters, La Fontaine's name has become, for young and old, inseparably linked with the fable, a genre that he brought to its ultimate fruition.

ACHIEVEMENTS

Jean de la Fontaine is unquestionably one of France's most beloved poets. He is a "classical" writer in the true meaning of the word. For centuries, French schoolchildren have learned his fables by heart. He is so important in France that he has often been compared with Dante and William Shakespeare as a national literary monu-ment. The poet's universal fame derives primarily from his *Fables Written in Verse*; La Fontaine developed this literary genre to perfection, and there have been no great fabulists after him (with the possible exception of the Russian writer Ivan Krylov). The *Fables* of La Fontaine culminated a long tradition in Western literature that began in antiquity with Aesop and Phaedrus. His works have been printed and reprinted in magnificent editions. They have been translated into many languages and have been illustrated by great artists down through the centuries: the *Fables* by Alphonse Oudry, Gustave Doré, and Marc Chagall; *Tales and Short Stories in Verse* illustrated by Charles-Dominique Joseph Eisen, Jean-Honoré Fragonard, and others.

La Fontaine unites the two major contrasting aesthetics found in the literature of seventeenth century France: artistic exuberance and classical restraint. Of the two, the former is best represented in poetry by the libertine poets, the so-called free spirits, such as Théophile de Viau and Marc-Antoine Saint-Amant. Temperamentally and in his general approach to life, La Fontaine belonged to this group of poets. His early works reveal a strain of playful sensuality and outspoken humor that are more representative of a hedonistic school of thought than one would normally expect from a renowned classical poet. Unlike other poets of his day, however, he was able to temper this natural tendency. One of La Fontaine's cardinal rules was that poetry should first of all give pleasure. He understood that pleasure is not an end in itself, that it must be deep and rich rather than facile or superficial. Wishing to please his readers, he hoped and believed that they would like what he himself liked.

Accordingly, he accepted the tenets of a classical doctrine that was very influential during this period. The influence of classical restraint is apparent in his mature works, especially the *Fables*. In matters of style (he strove for simplicity, clarity, brevity), choice of language (a restrained vocabulary), versification, and the insertion of old materials among new, La Fontaine showed himself to be a genuine classical author. Moreover, the meter of classical French poetry, with the ubiquitous Alexandrine, was at times threatened with monotony and stiffness. Through his writings, La Fontaine managed to infuse new life in French versification. He achieved a melodic depth unsurpassed by his contemporaries and proved to be a superb craftsman. The quick movement of his verse, with those sudden short lines and that frequent suddenness of feminine rhyme which can create surprise, fun, or intimacy, has been emulated by generations of French poets. Above all, he had the gift of being sincere, personal, and completely natural in his finest poetry, at a time when it was not at all fashionable to be so.

Biography

Jean de La Fontaine was born in the province of Champagne at Château-Thierry in 1621. In spite of his name, he was not of noble birth. His father held a government post as an administrator of forest and water resources. It was in the lush, green countryside of Château-Thierry that the poet spent his first twenty years. He loved the surrounding neighborhood with its familiar woods, waters, and meadows. He admired the natural world during a century when it went mostly unappreciated; indeed, to most of his contemporaries the term "nature" meant primarily human nature. Thus, his early upbringing set him apart from the other great classical writers of France's Golden Age, and the influence of nature and of country people is apparent in many of his tales and fables.

It is well documented that as a boy, La Fontaine was dreamy and absent-minded. He was also cheerful and lively, possessing an amiable disposition which remained with him throughout his life. In 1641, at the age of twenty, La Fontaine decided to study for the priesthood at the Oratoire in Paris, but he abandoned this pursuit after eighteen months and turned to the study of law. In 1647, his father transferred his official post to La Fontaine and married him off to a girl from an affluent family. The match proved to be a disaster, and the couple formally separated after eleven years of marriage. During this period, La Fontaine lived the life of a dilettante. He showed a disinclination for steady work and was content to spend much of his time in idleness; he was a voracious reader. He eventually sold his father's post and took up permanent residence in Paris.

La Fontaine began writing comparatively late in life, in his middle thirties. Throughout his career as a man of letters, he relied upon generous patrons for his support

and well-being. His first patron was also his most important—the wealthy finance minister Nicolas Fouquet. La Fontaine became a pensioner of Fouquet in 1656 and wrote for him such early major works as *Adonis* and *Le Songe de Vaux* (the dream of Vaux). Unfortunately for La Fontaine, Fouquet soon fell into disgrace. His opulent lifestyle aroused the envy and anger of the young King Louis XIV. Fouquet was accused of appropriating state funds and spent the rest of his life in prison. During Fouquet's ordeal, La Fontaine exhibited that particular virtue which would always be characteristic of him as pensioner—a deep sense of loyalty. He did not abandon Fouquet as did so many others, and he even wrote poems, including the "Elégie aux nymphes de Vaux," begging the king to be lenient. For this display of allegiance, he incurred the king's lasting enmity. He thus never received a pension from the government, as did many other writers and artists, and his election to the prestigious Académie Française was delayed on the king's order.

After Fouquet's downfall, La Fontaine was aided for a short time by the powerful Bouillon family and later

Jean de La Fontaine (Library of Congress)

by a royal patron, the dowager duchess of Orléans. He was by then forty years old, well into middle age for the times, and he was not a popular or well-known author. He realized that writing idyllic works such as *Adonis* would no longer be financially rewarding for him. Accordingly, he turned to more popular genres, such as tales and fables. He published his first tales in 1665. They were written in the tradition of Giovanni Boccaccio and Ludovico Ariosto, among others, and they became an immediate success. A second collection appeared a year later, in 1666; a third collection was published in 1671; and the final collection appeared in 1674. At that time, La Fontaine also began to publish those works on which his fame rests—the *Fables*. The first collection appeared in 1668, when he was forty-seven years old; the second, ten years later; and the last collection, in 1694, one year before his death.

The success of the *Fables* placed La Fontaine at the forefront of French writers. In 1669, he published *The Loves of Cupid and Psyche*, taken from the tale of Cupid and Psyche in Lucius Apuleius's *The Golden Ass* (second century). La Fontaine continued writing many occasional verses of small importance for various patrons. In 1684, despite earlier opposition by the king, he was finally elected to the Académie Française. In 1692, a serious illness occasioned a spiritual renewal, which, in turn, caused him to disavow publicly his earlier tales. In that same year, some of La Fontaine's fables were translated into English for the first time, by Sir Roger L'Estrange. In 1695, while attending a play, La Fontaine was struck ill and taken to the house of friends, the Haberts, where he died several days later. He is buried in the cemetery of the Saints-Innocents in Paris.

ANALYSIS

Jean de la Fontaine's poetic output mirrors the two major styles of seventeenth century French literature—that is to say, it lies between artistic exuberance, on one hand, and classical restraint, on the other. This has not always been apparent, however, since the fame of his *Fables* was such as to put his other poetic works in partial eclipse for a long period. Later scholarship has attempted to redress this imbalance. Such works as *Adonis*, *Le Songe de Vaux*, and *The Loves of Cupid and Psyche* reflect the grandiose splendor and fantasy char-

acteristic of the Baroque style of the period. Conversely, the brevity, clarity, and logic of the *Fables* are more typical of the classical style associated with the authors of France's "grand siècle."

ADONIS

La Fontaine presented his first major poetic endeavor, *Adonis*, to his new patron, Fouquet, in June, 1658. It was a fine example of calligraphy by Nicolas Jarvey, with the title page illustrated by François Chauveau. The poem was a long pastoral work whose subject was borrowed from Ovid. It relates the legend of the goddess Venus's love for a youth, Adonis, and of his untimely death. La Fontaine's work is only half the length of Shakespeare's better-known version, *Venus and Adonis*. Furthermore, La Fontaine's Adonis is not a cold and reluctant character, as is Shakespeare's. Instead, La Fontaine chose to emphasize the theme of youth cut off in the flower of strength and beauty. For La Fontaine, Adonis symbolizes the agony of helpless strength, a paradoxical antithesis characteristic of the Baroque. The poet's vivid and enjoyable descriptions of nature create a self-contained poetic world. It is not the real world, yet La Fontaine, a true lover of nature, has managed to make the setting of his poem so directly appealing to the senses and simple instincts of his readers that the illusion is all but complete.

On the other hand, his amorous poetry is too artificial and conventional. He composed his idyll in the Alexandrines typical of French poetry lines of twelve syllables, with four stresses to the line and rhyming in couplets. The stately Alexandrine was not well adapted to the subject matter of the poem. Even in the most tender passages, there is some monotony of cadence. A shorter verse line with its rapid movement would have smoothed the transitions between episodes in the narrative. Nevertheless, this first major poetic undertaking taught La Fontaine much about the writing of Alexandrines. For a long period unfairly neglected, *Adonis* deserves the recognition it has received during the past few decades. The poem contains verse worthy of La Fontaine at his best, and one can discern in it many of the traits which find fuller expression in his subsequent writings: skillful assimilation of source material, a refined musical style, close observation of human or animal life in a mythological setting, and, above all, an ability to infuse humor without compromising the decorous mood of the poem.

LE SONGE DE VAUX

Fouquet was pleased with *Adonis* and asked La Fontaine to undertake a new work in praise of Vaux, the magnificent white stone palace which the finance minister was engaged in creating for himself with the help of the best architects, garden designers, and artists in France. La Fontaine accommodated his patron with *Le Songe de Vaux*, a work which, as a result of the disgrace of Fouquet, was never completed. Nine fragments have survived, written in a mixture of verse and prose. The poem fits marvelously into the parklike landscape of Vaux in which La Fontaine places it. It is enveloped in a world of fantasy. Artificial as it may be, there is enough imagination to give a touch of fairyland to the scene. Wishing to give posterity a picture of Vaux as it would appear in all the beauty of its maturity, the poet used his imagination in describing Fouquet's magnificent estate. He proposed to describe—in lyrical, allegorical, and mythological terms—what the Vaux gardens, newly planted and only shrub-high, would be like in years to come.

The plot of *Le Songe de Vaux* revolves around the discovery of some imagined buried treasure on the palace grounds. A mysterious inscription on a jewel case leads to a kind of beauty contest in which the four nymphs representing architecture, painting, gardening, and poetry contest the honor of being responsible for the chief beauties of Vaux. The poem evokes an ideal world from which all ugliness is banished. In his *Young La Fontaine*, Philip Wadsworth has shown how La Fontaine had the rare gift, unique in seventeenth century France, of communicating in poetry the sensations aroused by colors and forms. This is particularly apparent in *Le Songe de Vaux*, a work permeated with poetic feeling for beauty, peace, and sensual pleasure akin to one of Charles Le Brun's paintings, which it celebrates. The verse, more smooth and melodious than in *Adonis*, seems to have developed effortlessly. The limpid simplicity of the shorter, octosyllabic lines assures a more flowing rhythm. The precious imagery and the choice of vocabulary help sustain the quiet enjoyment of varying moods.

THE LOVES OF CUPID AND PSYCHE

La Fontaine continued the practice of interweaving prose and poetry with *The Loves of Cupid and Psyche*, based on the classical tale of a jealous Venus who sends Cupid to make the beautiful maiden Psyche fall in love with an ugly creature, only to have Cupid fall in love with Psyche instead. This long novel-poem is set within the framework of a conversation in the park of Versailles among four friends—Polyphile, Acante, Ariste, and Gélaste. The gardens of Versailles and the surrounding area provide an atmosphere of fantasy similar in tone and style to the one depicted in *Le Songe de Vaux*. Indeed, La Fontaine transposed materials from the latter into this work. Once again, it is interesting to note the changes wrought by the poet on his source material—changes which enabled him to achieve effects unmatched by writers such as Vergil, Tasso, and Ariosto who had treated this myth before him. His Psyche is a much more complex character than any of her prototypes. She is sensual, tender, and open-minded, vain at times but always charming. Rather than portray her in bleak, isolated settings, as did his predecessors, La Fontaine shows her in beautiful surroundings. The joining of sensuous love and bucolic descriptions of nature bathe this work in an aura of voluptuous, Epicurean delight. *The Loves of Cupid and Psyche* is important as a transitional work in La Fontaine's oeuvre; it draws the curtain on the period of youthful ardor, of love and beauty, of preciosity and gallantry associated with the works of the Vaux period.

TALES AND SHORT STORIES IN VERSE

Second only to the *Fables* in their popularity, the *Tales and Short Stories in Verse* were first published in 1665. Three more collections of similar material appeared in 1666, 1671, and 1674. These tales belong to the Western literary tradition of stock ribald stories told and retold during the Middle Ages and the Renaissance by Boccaccio, Geoffrey Chaucer, Marguerite de Navarre, and many others. The predominant theme of these tales is illicit love: the frolicsome comedy of marital infidelity, the sexual prowess of men or lack of it, the frailty of women, the lustful desires of priests and nuns, and so forth. A total of thirty-five tales appeared over the years, of which "Joconde" and "Le Cocu battu et content" ("The Cudgelled and Contented Cuckold") are perhaps the most popular. In the later tales, the subjects include not only the illicit affairs of typically crafty women, paramours, and cuckolds but also the daily tribulations of ordinary people: a poor shoemaker, a cynical judge, a peasant and his master, among others. Like the fables, these tales first circulated in manuscript, soon winning favorable response from La Fontaine's friends. Licentious tales became extremely popular during the early reign of young Louis XIV; La Fontaine was aware of this trend and sought to cater to the salacious taste of the public. Nevertheless, the tales caused him enormous difficulties. Each collection was more licentious than its predecessors until the final published tales were ordered suppressed by the police. In his old age, La Fontaine publicly repudiated these tales, expressing regret at ever having written them; it should be noted, however, that this recantation was made during a period when strict moral severity prevailed at the court of Versailles.

NARRATIVE TECHNIQUE AND POETIC EXPRESSION

The fact that La Fontaine did not invent his plots—he borrowed freely from his precursors—enabled him to focus all his talents on details of narrative technique and poetic expression. It is in these two areas that he made his greatest contribution as a writer of tales. La Fontaine always had a flair for the dramatic, and in his tales he shows himself to be a master storyteller. His skill at creating action without impeding the progress of the plot (effected primarily by means of alteration in the rhythm of the poetry), his penchant for producing situations that shock or surprise, his ability to vary and freshen the treatment of old, banal themes—in brief, his talent for adroit handling of the strictly narrative aspects of the art—is his major appeal. Whatever plots he chose, his own special genius gave them new life.

In his tales, La Fontaine adopted a free-flowing conversational style. In fact, he seems to have gone to great lengths to ensure that the graceful, chatty style of these stories would appear as natural as possible to the reader. Toward that end, he employed an irregular and loose sort of verse, known as *vers libre* (not to be confused with modern free verse), consisting of lines in two or more meters without a fixed rhyme scheme. La Fontaine's two favorite verse forms were the eight-syllable line of the old French fabliaux and the ten-syllable line. These two verse lines, along with the lack of any clear-cut rhyme scheme, gave the tales a colloquial tone that one would normally expect to find only in prose. Such verse had

greater flexibility than anything previously written in French. It allowed the poet to tell his stories in a familiar, relaxed style, addressing himself directly to the reader. Curiously enough, he frequently felt a need to justify his use of this form, declaring that it was the most suitable and that it had given him as much trouble as the writing of regular verse or prose. In truth, it must be said that La Fontaine employed *vers libre* with great restraint. He introduced other rhythmic patterns as well, but only on rare occasions. His poetic expertise was to be found elsewhere: in the subtle interplay of rhymes, in evocative combinations of sounds, in complex rhythmic gradations and contrasts, in the joining of heterogeneous stanza forms, in the interplay of thought patterns with metrical patterns—all the stylistic characteristics that became associated with his masterpiece, the *Fables*.

FABLES

In the *Fables*, as in his tales, La Fontaine was reviving a genre which had been popular throughout the Middle Ages and the Renaissance. The *Fables* is a work of maturity, nourished by wide reading and a long apprenticeship in poetic technique. They were published in three cycles spanning twenty-five years. The first cycle, containing 125 fables, appeared in 1668. Ten years later, La Fontaine added nearly one hundred more, and the 1694 edition—the last edition published during his lifetime—included two dozen new fables. Thus, he wrote nearly 250 fables in all. The early fables owe a great deal to classical sources, in particular Aesop and Phaedrus; the later ones find their inspiration in Oriental stories.

These fables are the work of a man who had an intimate acquaintance with nature and an instinctive understanding of animals and country things. La Fontaine's *Fables* has always appealed to three distinct audiences: to children, because of the vividness and freshness of the stories; to literary students, because of their accomplished artistry; and to people of the world, because of their penetrating psychological observation of human behavior. Of these three disparate audiences, La Fontaine sought in particular the third category of readers, for he himself often said that his fables would be fully appreciated only by those who had had a long experience of life and people.

A comparison of La Fontaine's fables to others in the genre reveals the importance of his achievement. Traditional materials are handled with shades of feelings not to be found in earlier fables. In particular, his approach to the depiction of animals in the *Fables* is at variance with that of practically all the previous writers of fables who had found favor with the public. Like all fabulists, La Fontaine treats animals in anthropomorphic terms: They are used to depict certain human foibles. Moving beyond his predecessors artistically, La Fontaine's portrayals of the human as well as the animal aspects of his characters have not been surpassed by his followers and imitators. Strange, clumsy little creatures wander about, fiercely acting their parts to what is, at times, a merciless finish. These animals show the desires, appetites, and fears that are humankind's brutish inheritance. The dominant ones among them are forceful, secretive, cunning, and sharp-witted, and their ends are as elemental as their means are ingenious. Their victims are like those in the human world: muddleheaded, cringing before their masters, into whose maws they are ever ready to drop. The weak countenances of these victims remain plaintive, frightened, and pitiful—revealing the essential cruelty of existence.

What the *Fables* reveals, above all, is La Fontaine's conception of power (the first edition was dedicated to the future king of France). Animal hierarchies provided him with an opportunity to examine certain types of formal relations among control, resistance, and violence so that he could uncover, by implication, the same relationships in human society. In fact, the *Fables* constitute a survey of the struggle for power among men. La Fontaine views the political world as an arena in which the strong seek to defend and extend their powers and privileges. He posits a view of man that sees conflict as the only mode of action and insists that no moral considerations should be taken into account, the political aims justifying any means.

The prevalence of such motifs clearly indicates a substratum of belief which La Fontaine could not have derived from his learned sources alone. Themes such as these illustrate the extent to which he appropriated the idiom of the fable for his own wholly different ends. To study La Fontaine's fables is to investigate power *in extremis*. In the *Fables*, power must be exercised rather than merely possessed. It must be seized and maintained even at the cost of a progressive enslavement to its in-

stinctive violence. The traditional concept of power as a societal mechanism which lays down the law for everyone alike no longer applies. Animals, men, and institutions are treated and studied mainly as objects of domination. There is no reason to doubt that La Fontaine's contemporaries understood perfectly the "message" of this important work—one that has become obfuscated down through the centuries by the rote memorizations of schoolchildren and the musty compilations of scholars. One can also understand better why Jean-Jacques Rousseau denounced the use of such texts to shape young sensibilities.

Each generation takes a different approach to La Fontaine's individual vision. Certain past generations saw him as a detached observer of the human comedy, while others have seen him as a dissatisfied man with a gift for caricature, as a poet of the picturesque in nature and in rural life, as a dilettante with dregs of smug morality, or merely as a pleasant storyteller. No subsequent writer of fables has sustained such an intense emotional vision of man and of the forces that dominate and shape the world in which he lives as did La Fontaine. Above all, his fables repay study because of their poetic beauty and simplicity; they are a deeply felt artistic manifestation of the human condition, derived mostly from the bitter truth of experience.

OTHER MAJOR WORKS

LONG FICTION: *Les Amours de Psyché et Cupidon*, 1669 (*The Loves of Cupid and Psyche*, 1744).

PLAYS: *L'Eunuque*, pb. 1654; *Clymène*, pb. 1671; *Daphné*, pb. 1682 (libretto); *Galatée*, pb. 1682 (libretto); *L'Astrée*, pb. 1692 (libretto).

NONFICTION: *Relation d'un voyage en Limousin*, 1663; *Discours à Mme de La Sablière*, 1679; *Épître à Huet*, 1687.

MISCELLANEOUS: *Œuvres complètes*, 1933 (2 volumes); *Œuvres diverses*, 1942; *Œuvres, sources, et postérité d'Ésope à l'Oulipo*, 1995.

BIBLIOGRAPHY

Birberick, Anne L. *Reading Undercover: Audience and Authority in Jean de La Fontaine*. London: Associated University Presses, 1998. In her readings of La Fontaine's major poetic works, Biberick proposes the possibility of a "circular writing" resulting from the multiplicity of author/audience relationships in the poet's works, which allows La Fontaine room to criticize court patronage and tyranny, while nonetheless winning the necessary approbation of the Sun King.

_____. *Refiguring La Fontaine: Tercentenary Essays.* Charlottesville, Va.: Bookwood Press, 1996. In addition to Biberick's introductory summary of La Fontaine's critical reception since his death, this volume contains nine essays (three in French, six in English) that explore La Fontaine's adaptations of and challenges to literary structure, questions of discourse in the *Fables*, and new treatments of other, more neglected works by the poet. Of particular interest to an audience obliged to rely on translations from French is the last essay by David Lee Rubin, which examines three English translations of one fable in order to discuss how each translator's different approach informs, or distorts, the image of La Fontaine and his poetry.

Calder, Andrew. *The Fables of La Fontaine: Wisdom Brought Down to Earth.* Geneva: Droz, 2001. Arguing that it is essential to consider La Fontaine's *Fables* from a perspective both of utility and pleasure in some sixteen, self-contained chapters that look to the fables as lessons in life, Calder's book is also of interest in that it explores La Fontaine's philosophical similarities with schools of thought in antiquity and with his Renaissance predecessors, such as Erasmus, François Rabelais, and Michel Eyquem de Montaigne.

Collinet, Jean-Pierre. "La Fontaine et ses illustrateurs." In *Œuvres complètes.* Paris: Gallimard, 1991. Included in the Pléiade edition of La Fontaine's work, the most authoritative and extensively annotated French edition, this essay is a critical history of famous French illustrations of La Fontaine's poems, especially the *Fables*, from La Fontaine's lifetime through the famous illustrations by Gustave Doré in the nineteenth century.

Sweetser, Marie-Odile. *La Fontaine.* Boston: Twayne, 1987. In this very approachable critical biography of La Fontaine, Sweetser organizes her chapters by the chronological appearance of each of the poet's ma-

jor works. Her volume is also useful in that it makes available to a non-francophone readership a concise, well-documented synthesis of Continental scholarship concerning La Fontaine.

Raymond LePage;
bibliography updated by Joe Johnson

JULES LAFORGUE

Born: Montevideo, Uruguay; August 16, 1860
Died: Paris, France; August 20, 1887

PRINCIPAL POETRY

Les Complaintes, 1885
L'Imitation de Notre-Dame la lune, 1886
Des fleurs de bonne volonté, 1888
Les Derniers Vers de Jules Laforgue, 1890
Poésies complètes, 1894, 1970
Œuvres complètes de Jules Laforgue, 1902-1903 (4 volumes), 1922-1930 (6 volumes)
Poems, 1975

OTHER LITERARY FORMS

In Jules Laforgue's short but prolific writing career, he produced more than two hundred poems and many works in other literary forms, only some of which have been rescued from the papers left at his death. His surviving verse dramas include "Tessa," written in 1877, existing in a manuscript only recently discovered; *Pierrot fumiste*, composed in 1882, first published in 1892; and *Le Concile féerique*, published in 1886, compiled from five poems originally written for *Des fleurs de bonne volonté* (poems that Laforgue composed between 1883 and 1886 and that first appeared in 1888). These three cabaret farces command the attention of scholars eager to explore Laforgue's developing themes and ironic dialogue; they are not major contributions to theatrical literature.

Masterpieces of an original genre are Laforgue's six fanciful prose tales, *Moralités légendaires* (1887; *Six Moral Tales from Jules Laforgue*, 1928), retelling myths in details both mundane and psychologically plausible. Among these, "Hamlet" and "Persée et Andromède" ("Perseus and Andromeda: Or, The Happiest One of the Triangle") have provoked considerable admiring commentary. The actor and mime Jean-Louis Barrault performed a memorable adaptation of "Hamlet" in 1939. Several works of fiction have apparently been lost, but there survive a short autobiographical novel, *Stéphane Vassiliew*, written in 1881, first published in 1946, and a short autobiographical story, "Amours de la quinzième année," written about 1879, first published in 1887.

Laforgue's selected letters, especially those to his sister, created the legend of the poet as a self-conscious, sensitive, starving aesthete, but his letters to various other friends reveal his humor, his broad interests in philosophy, art, and music, and his acute observations of society. A fuller portrait of Laforgue's intellectual range emerges from his critical essays on Impressionist aesthetics, on the Symbolist poets Charles Baudelaire and Tristan Corbière, and on life in the German imperial court. Laforgue's translations of Walt Whitman's verse were published in 1886.

Among his other essays and drafts published posthumously are some provocative comments on the cultural definitions constricting the roles of women, including "La Femme—la légende féminine," among many others. Simone de Beauvoir, in *Le Deuxième Sexe* (1949; *The Second Sex*, 1953), and Léon Guichard, in his critical study of Laforgue, have evaluated these comments on feminine roles.

ACHIEVEMENTS

Jules Laforgue's poetry published in 1885 and 1886 earned for him praise from contemporary critics and established him as one of the leading innovators of poetic form at the time. The literary circle within which he moved made his classification as a Symbolist poet inevitable. His sudden death in 1887 gave his career a tragic plot, especially for literary historians eager to contribute to the mythology of doomed poets.

Laforgue's most significant contributions to the development of modern poetry are his rhymed free verse, his verbal playfulness, his juxtaposition of melancholy and gaiety in his ironic tone, and his psychologically complex monologues and dialogues, which give voice to the unconscious and to dream states, as well as to masks consciously assumed.

Although Laforgue has often been dismissed as a minor poet, his philosophical sophistication may deserve as much praise as his technical innovations. In his poetry, Laforgue explored the conflicts between the conscious and the unconscious, exposed the illusions of rational pessimism, and exploited the literary consequences of an idealist philosophy against those of determinism (as practiced by the Naturalists), but he set all these metaphysical confrontations in the real, familiar world of trivial remarks and superficial gestures.

BIOGRAPHY

Born in Uruguay, Jules Laforgue was sent at the age of six to a boarding school in Tarbes, France, where he remained until he was fifteen. Laforgue felt isolated and persecuted at school; he left an account of his childhood and adolescence in the autobiographical novel *Stéphane Vassiliew* (1946). His family returned from Uruguay in his sixteenth year, and the eleven children and two parents crowded into an apartment in Paris. That spring, his mother died after a twelfth pregnancy; she was thirty-seven. In "Avertissement," Laforgue wrote that he hardly knew his mother, but his awareness of her situation may be glimpsed in "Complainte du fœtus de poète," in which an unsympathetic and egotistic voice describes his birth, blithely unconcerned with any feelings but his own.

Laforgue attended the Lycée Fontanes (now Condorcet) but twice failed his oral examination for the *baccalauréat*. A paralyzing fear of failure afflicts many of Laforgue's poetic alter egos. After failing his examinations, Laforgue continued to study independently, reading omnivorously and attending lectures on the philosophy of art by the determinist Hippolyte Taine, whose assertions that art is completely determined by milieu, race, and historical moment Laforgue rejected.

In 1880, the twenty-year-old Laforgue met several influential men whose friendship helped launch his career. Gustave Kahn became a good friend, confidant, and literary editor. Kahn introduced Laforgue to the regular Tuesday readings by Stéphane Mallarmé and also to Charles Henry, an intellectual equally brilliant on scientific and literary topics. That same year, Laforgue also met the literary critic Paul Bourget, who generously criticized his writing and who arranged a job for Laforgue assisting the art critic Charles Ephrussi. He introduced Laforgue to the paintings of the Impressionists, and evidence from Laforgue's poems and essays indicates that the Impressionist aesthetic reflected his conviction that art aims at fusing a sensual and intellectual apprehension of life.

Late in 1881, Laforgue's father, who was dying from tuberculosis, moved the rest of the family to Tarbes, leaving Laforgue behind. Although he took a cheap room to remain in Paris, Laforgue was employed by Ephrussi, was writing poems, and was enjoying his literary life; ironically, a self-pitying letter written to his sister during this period, exaggerating his timidity and his loneliness and appealing for sympathy, later contributed to the legend of the starving poet.

That year, with the recommendations of Bourget and Ephrussi, Laforgue was appointed the French reader to the German Empress Augusta, a job which paid well, gave him leisure to write, introduced him to rich food and luxurious apartments, and required his residence in Germany. From November, 1881, through September, 1886, Laforgue lived with the peripatetic German imperial court for ten months of the year; he spent his long vacations of 1883, 1884, and 1885 in Paris, and his constant correspondence kept him in touch with contemporary literary developments in France.

Although he complained of his boredom in the German court, Laforgue worked steadily on his poems, and, during the court's residence in Berlin, he enjoyed the company of musicians and artists (especially his friends the brothers Théophile and Eugène Ysaÿe, a pianist and a violinist) and amused himself at the aquarium, circuses, music halls, museums, the opera, the ballet, and orchestral concerts. His experience of Berlin's cultural life influenced the imagery of his poems, in which one finds clowns, harlequins, underwater creatures, sublime music, and playfully improper cabaret patter.

On New Year's Day, 1886, Laforgue, who identified his anguished self-consciousness with Hamlet's character, visited the castle of Elsinore; he later reworked his experience of Hamlet's haunt into his *Des fleurs de bonne volonté* and his prose fantasy about the indecisive Dane. Back in Berlin, late in January, Laforgue met an English woman, Leah Lee, who had chosen to live independently from her family and who was supporting herself by teaching English. As he fell in love with her, he was reaching his decision to leave the German court position. He spent three weeks in Paris in late June and early July, then returned to the German court, and, by August, in the resort at Schlagenbad, he was writing his first poems in free verse.

Laforgue returned to Berlin with the German court on September 1, 1886, Lee accepted his marriage proposal on September 6, and he left the employ of the Empress Augusta that month. By October, Laforgue was living in Paris, waiting for his own wedding, reworking and finishing his poems in free verse, completing his *Moralités légendaires*, and discussing the movement newly named "Symbolist" with Édouard Dujardin and Teodor de Wyzewa (editors of *La Revue indépendante*) and his old friends Kahn (later editor of *La Vogue*) and Félix Fénéon (who edited and reshaped Laforgue's new poems in free verse). Laforgue's moral tales and his new poems were published in various issues of *La Vogue* and *La Revue indépendante*, so that by the autumn of 1886, Laforgue's star had burst onto the Parisian literary scene, with the publication of his tales, his free verse, *L'Imitation de Notre-Dame la lune*, and *Le Concile féerique*. Laforgue was being hailed as a leader in the avant-garde.

On the last day of that wonderful year, Laforgue and Leah married, in London (at St. Barnabas, where T. S. Eliot and Valerie Fletcher were married in 1957). Laforgue returned to Paris with a bad cough, which, as it developed, was a symptom of tuberculosis. For eight months, he was too ill to write much poetry, and he died on August 20, 1887.

ANALYSIS

Although the legend of his short, tragic life shaped the initial critical response to his work, Jules Laforgue is now recognized as one of the first modernist poets. Laforgue is notable for his technical innovations, for his ironic voices and psychologically complex persons, for his verbal and syntactic playfulness, and for his fusion of sublimely serious philosophical questions with the plainly vulgar language and concerns of ordinary life.

Laforgue developed the poetic form known as *vers libre*, or free verse, in which he used lines of varying length, subtle rhyming patterns, and diverse rhythms to correspond, flexibly, to shifts in mood and subject. Although Arthur Rimbaud also has been credited with inventing free verse (with his "Marine" and "Mouvement," poems written earlier than *Les Derniers Vers de Jules Laforgue*), Laforgue's innovative verse forms were published in periodicals before Rimbaud's examples, and his *Les Derniers Vers de Jules Laforgue* more directly influenced the free verse of modernist poets.

Most English and American readers know Laforgue through his influence on T. S. Eliot, Ezra Pound, Hart Crane, and Wallace Stevens. In 1908, Eliot read about Laforgue in *The Symbolist Movement in Literature*, by Arthur Symons; in 1909, Eliot read Laforgue's poems and letters selected in *Œuvres complètes*. Eliot's poems influenced by Laforgue's irony, dialogues, and verse forms include the 1909 "Nocturne," "Humouresque," and "Spleen," and the more famous "The Love Song of J. Alfred Prufrock," "Conversation Galante," "Portrait of a Lady," and "La Figlia che Piange," as well as sections of *The Waste Land* (1922). Pound and Crane both published translations of Laforgue's work, and Pound praised Laforgue's intellect dancing playfully among words. Laforguian irony and wordplay may be found in Pound's "Hugh Selwyn Mauberley" and in Crane's "Chaplinesque," among other poems. Stevens transformed Laforgue's Impressionist images and his verse forms extensively, but the French poet's diffused influence may be traced in such works of Stevens as "The Comedian as the Letter C," "Sea Surface Full of Clouds," "Peter Quince at the Clavier," and "Notes Toward a Supreme Fiction."

Laforgue anticipated the psychological narratives of both James Joyce and Marcel Proust in the interior monologue he developed in such poems as "Complainte de Lord Pierrot" and "Dimanches." He split his monologues and dialogues into multiple voices that are wittily self-aware and self-mocking. Although the contrapuntal dialogue of his "Complainte du soir des comices agricoles" was inspired by Gustave Flaubert (in a notorious scene in *Madame Bovary*, 1856; the overblown romantic language of a seduction is undercut by the vulgar realism of an animal auction at a country fair), Laforgue neither relied on simple antithesis nor assumed a superior moral stance; rather, his ironic conversations and monologues offer multiple perspectives which remain irreconcilable.

Pound and Joyce delighted in Laforgue's demolition and recombination of language. The amusing colloquialisms and revolutionary neologisms that appear in Laforgue's verse violated poetic etiquette but revealed the psychology of his speakers. They wittily or ignorantly combine two words from different realms to disclose an unexpected association. Examples include "sangsuelles," "éternullité," "voluptés," "spleenuosité," and "crucifige" (these neologisms are derived, respectively, from blood + sensual, eternal + nullity, violation or violence + voluptuous, spleen + sinuosity, and crucify + to clot). Laforgue often fused common words, but he also correctly employed arcane, archaic, and slang words in lines of impeccably sublime diction. The shock of contrast, with the implied assertion of the validity and significance of these verbal intrusions, radically changes the poet's relationship to language.

In his images and subjects, Laforgue, like the Impressionists and the Symbolists in painting and literature, claimed for his art both a psychological and a physical definition of reality and envisioned correlations between the sublime and the ordinary, between the spiritual and the objective worlds. Eliot, in his celebrated definition of the "objective correlative," drew on Laforgue's example.

Laforgue's literary legacy also includes his black humor. In poems such as "Excuse macabre," "Guitare," and "Complainte des blackboulés" ("Lament of the Blackballs"), his ironic but not pompous stance treated the grim themes of death, frustration, self-doubt, boredom, melancholy, alienation, nihilism, and the failure of passion with a racy wit, slipping often into gaiety. In this, Samuel Beckett is one of Laforgue's heirs.

The bathetic, self-centered misery of the gloomy poems Laforgue wrote from 1880 to 1882, for *Le Sanglot de la terre* (first pb. in *Œuvres complètes de Jules Laforgue*, 1902-1903), has provoked speculation about a period of depression he suffered, but these metrically conventional and sentimental verses, laboriously exploring correlations between an adolescent's passionate psyche and the world's turbulence, have a literary antecedent in the splenetic poems of Baudelaire, and they also betray the influence of the moral and metaphysical idealism of Schopenhauer. Recognizing the inadequacy of these early poems, Laforgue chose not to publish them.

From 1882 through 1884, Laforgue worked on a group of comic poems based on popular street ballads. In them, he experimented with unconventional metric forms, broken syntax, and introduced slang, puns, and vulgar words into poems that also played with liturgical images. In a letter, he described these poems as "psychology in the form of dream," and they contain free associations of words and sudden juxtapositions of sublime and tawdry images. These poems were written after Laforgue had immersed himself in the philosophy of Eduard von Hartmann, whose emphasis on the unconscious profoundly shaped the poet's definition of identity. The conflicting voices and shifting tones within Laforgue's poetry reflect his belief in the multiple selves that coexist in any personality. Consequently, his narrative verse seems to leap between dream states and waking, among past, present, and future experiences, and from unquestioning sympathy to biting mockery, while continuing to portray one persona. Publishing delays kept these poems from appearing until 1885, but, when *Les Complaintes* finally appeared, the volume was enthusiastically reviewed.

LES COMPLAINTES

Les Complaintes consists of two preliminary poems and fifty laments titled "Complainte de . . ."—with the titles playing upon the subjective-objective ambiguity of the genitive. The ambiguous titles reflect the multiple voices speaking within these dramatic poems and also the poems' themes. For example, "Complainte de Lord Pierrot" is a divided interior monologue spoken by Pierrot, and his lament also defines his identity; "Complainte du soir des comices agricoles" is set during the night of the country fair and may also be heard as the lament of that night; "Complainte des pianos qu'on entend dans les quartiers aisés" is both a lament of a man walking in well-to-do neighborhoods, who hears and is aroused by the sounds of girls' piano practice, and an imaginary dialogue between the man and the pianos

concerning the girls' inarticulate, romantic illusions, and their sexuality.

In "Complainte de Lord Pierrot," the individual is divided in time and in space, with Pierrot singing a self-mocking version of the ballad "Au clair de la lune," then commenting in rhymed couplets on his sexual timidity and inexperience, then in irregularly rhymed ten-syllable lines imagining himself under the influence of Venus, dressed as a swan, boldly coupling with Leda, then abruptly shifting to a mocking couplet, "—Tout cela vous honore,/ Lord Pierrot, mais encore?" ("All that pays you tribute,/ Lord Pierrot, but what next?"), which becomes a two-line refrain as it is repeated later in the poem. Similarly, in "Complainte des pianos qu'on entend dans les quartiers aisés," the lonely speaker meditates on desirable young girls who provoke his sexual longing, but a two-line refrain, echoing a popular song, seems to tease and mock him: "Tu t'en vas et tu nous quittes,/ Tu nous quitt's et tu t'en vas!" ("You depart and you leave us/ You leave us and you depart!"). As readers familiar with "The Love Song of J. Alfred Prufrock" will recognize, Eliot adopted Laforgue's device, the ironic couplet refrain, in his lines rhyming "come and go" with "Michelangelo."

Just as Pierrot's various moods are expressed in different verse forms, so the sexual longing, the self-doubting mockery, the erotic curiosity, and the contemptuous cynicism of a lonely man are represented in the shifting forms of "Complainte des pianos qu'on entend dans les quartiers aisés," in which the syllabic length of the lines changes with each stanza. The basic group of four verse forms, recurring five times in the same order, comprises a quatrain of irregular Alexandrines rhymed *abab*, followed by a rhymed couplet of seven-syllable lines, followed by a rhymed couplet of four-syllable lines, and concluded by a quatrain of seven-syllable lines rhymed *abab*, the first two lines being some version of the refrain, "Tu t'en vas et tu nous laisses,/ Tu nous laiss's et tu t'en vas." Although these shifts create the impression, on a first reading, of the free-flowing and disparate lines of thought within the lonely man's mind, the larger formal pattern is quite elaborate. The poem seems a patchwork of quatrains and couplets, in which the significant pattern of the whole shifts as one focuses on different combinations of the parts. Are the girls singing to the man? Is he imagining their mockery? The deliberate ambiguity reflects the psychological complexity of Laforgue's portrait and also the inevitability of change: from innocence to experience, from the sublimity of imaginary voyeurism to the vulgar reality of physical sexuality, from spiritual eroticism to the ordinary, routine materialism of life—embodied in the ludicrous exclamations on the month, the underclothes, and the routine meal of the final line: "Ô mois, ô linges, ô repas!"

L'IMITATION DE NOTRE-DAME LA LUNE

The twenty-two poems for *L'Imitation de Notre-Dame la lune* were written at lightning speed, in six weeks of 1885, and dedicated to Laforgue's friend Kahn and to Salammbô, Flaubert's fictional pagan priestess. These litanies in praise of the moon ridicule the excessive zeal and overstated piety that characterize both Salammbô's behavior and most public professions of idolatrous worship. Utilizing the literary conventions associating the moon and the cultural archetype "woman," Laforgue mocks the lunatic lover who throws himself at the feet of the woman ("aux pieds de la femme," in the poem "Guitare"), and his obsessive myth defining woman as mysterious, cruel, changeable, and purely sensual is exposed in the allusions to Delilah, Eve, the Sphinx, and La Joconde (the Mona Lisa).

The eminent lunologist in *L'Imitation de Notre-Dame la lune* is Pierrot, whose ancestor is Pagliacco, of the *commedia dell'arte*, but who, in the French tradition, became fused with Harlequin. The Pierrot figure in Laforgue's poetry has contradictory characteristics: He is both a disappointed lover, melancholy and vulnerable, and a deceiving lover, frivolous and cynical. In either mode, Pierrot avoids the entangling responsibilities of love. This clown, in whiteface, with his long skinny neck, dilated eyes, reddened mouth, and black skullcap, both longs for a woman and fears passion. He closely resembles Eliot's Prufrock.

DES FLEURS DE BONNE VOLONTÉ

Des fleurs de bonne volonté is, in part, a response to Baudelaire's *Les Fleurs du mal* (1857; *Flowers of Evil*, 1909). Written in 1886, these fifty-six poems reflect Laforgue's fascination with Hamlet's indecisiveness. Throughout these poems, he sprinkled epigraphs from Hamlet's and Ophelia's verbal duels, and his persona

agonizes over his own inability to marry. Like Hamlet, this character cannot allow himself to trust a woman. Unlike Baudelaire, who treats the infidelity of woman as a cosmic truth, Laforgue focuses on the psychology of the lover whose fear of betrayal paralyzes him. Like Jaques in *As You Like It* (1599-1600), this character's cynicism makes him miserable. His assertion in "Célibat, célibat, tout n'est que célibat" that human history is the history of one unmarried man at first seems ridiculous, a product of his obsession, but one may read the dramatic situation of these poems, the prolonged hesitation before risking a commitment, as an extended metaphor for human history.

Twelve different poems in this collection bear the title "Dimanches" (Sundays), and each portrays a profoundly melancholic state of mind; images of rain, gray skies, and the haunting refrain of a piano recur throughout. As Laforgue dissects ennui in these Impressionistic poems, it is self-generated and circles from dissatisfaction to longing for release, to fearing change, to resigning oneself to the misery of inaction.

"Dimanches" is representative. It consists of four stanzas, with the second and the fourth in parentheses. The first, invoking autumn, associates the fall of leaves with death and love's suffering; the second, replying parenthetically, pleads that the speaker can believe in himself only in moments when he is lost; the third raises the possibility of marriage; and the fourth replies with a hypothesis—what if he could believe in himself and then marry?—followed by a renunciation expressed in a self-wounding comparison: "C'est Galatée aveuglant Pygmalion!" (it is Galatea blinding Pygmalion!). Laforgue's use of myth here suggests that the artist, by dedicating himself to the abstract ideal of incorruptible beauty, comes to be transfixed by his own artifice; similarly, the woman, imprisoned in the statuesque role of perfect physical beauty, becomes a seductress as she embraces the one who created that role. The circular dialogue this speaker conducts with himself imprisons him in his own unhappiness.

When Laforgue decided to marry, he decided not to publish *Des fleurs de bonne volonté*, but he did rework several of the poems into his new poems in free verse. Laforgue's final poems develop his earlier themes with greater technical and psychological sophistication.

LES DERNIERS VERS DE JULES LAFORGUE

The twelve free-verse poems of *Les Derniers Vers de Jules Laforgue* cohere as twelve movements of one long symphony might; their interrelated themes and recapitulated forms reward close reading extended to the structure of the whole. Laforgue's extraordinary technical and thematic control reveals itself in the illusion of free-flowing lines, which, although irregular in length and grouped in no conventional stanzas, are linked by careful alliteration, internal harmonies, and end rhymes. The lines are grouped thematically, developing a mood, or symbol, or idea, in verse paragraphs, thus creating a verbal image of the memories, free associations, recurrent dreams, and self-conscious observations that compose an individual's interior universe.

Laforgue again treats the theme of an overly sensitive man, agonizing about the extent and the limits of his self-knowledge, who seeks release in a loving companion, but, associating sexuality with death, despairs of love. The personal tragedy, finally, is given broad cultural significance by Laforgue's allusions to historical events, to literary antecedents, to musical revolutions, to paintings, and to powerful myths. These poems, like Impressionist paintings, take into account the sensibility of the viewer and appeal to the imagination through associated sensual memories. Unlike Stéphane Mallarmé, Laforgue does not invoke the poet as sole symbol for humankind; moreover, the ivory tower of abstract thought and artifice does not confine Laforgue's persona, whose feelings and sensual impressions reflect factory smoke as well as fog, spittle as well as the sun's blinding white disk, the pettiness of objects consumed daily as well as the tragic grandeur of human mortality glimpsed in a sunset or in the coming of winter.

"L'Hiver qui vient," the first poem of the collection, illustrates the broader references and more radical techniques. Laforgue breaks poetic convention with his first line: "Blocus sentimental! Messageries du Levant!" (emotional blockade! Levantine carrier ships!). The line nullifies syntax by exclamation and alludes by echo to the glory and grim cost of the Napoleonic War's Continental System (known as the "blocus continental") and the eastern packet ships running the blockade. Neither national history nor seasonal change is the subject; rather, both are employed as correlatives of the persona's mood, a complex mixture of self-indulgent pity, rage against frustration, and ironic mockery. Facing the coming of winter yet again, the persona recalls associated feelings, images, and events: a child's loneliness at the *lycée*, the ennui of rainy Sundays, the end of a love affair, the suffering of soldiers far from home, the end of a fox hunt, each day's death of the sun, and the misery of urban life. From the music of Richard Wagner, Laforgue had learned to interweave distinctive themes representing complex passions. The weeping and sighing of autumnal rain and wind, the miserable coughing of a consumptive, the sad tones of hunting horns (imitated in "Ton ton, ton taine, ton ton!") resound in the poem, evoking compassion for the cornered creature, nostalgia for a lost social order, and the longing for an unattainable happiness. Laforgue's aim in these musical, free-verse poems may be understood in his last line of "L'Hiver qui vient": "J'essaierai en choeur d'en donner la note" (I will try, in this choir, to give it its note).

Perceiving the human situation as essentially hopeless and feeling the tragic disparity between glorious aspirations and sordid or merely ordinary lives, Laforgue nevertheless rejects the Romantic poet's uncontrolled sentimentalism, undercutting self-pity by vulgar language, tawdry details, and the wry commentary of a rhymed couplet. His characteristic fusion of sensitivity and ironic distance, his representation of divided psychological states, his masterful exploitation of free verse to evoke shifting moods and associated ideas, his consciously comic treatment of serious subjects, and his playful re-creation of language mark Laforgue as one of the first modernist poets.

OTHER MAJOR WORKS

LONG FICTION: *Stéphane Vassiliew*, 1946.

SHORT FICTION: *Moralités légendaires*, 1887 (*Six Moral Tales from Jules Laforgue*, 1928).

PLAYS: *Le Concile féerique*, pb. 1886; *Pierrot fumiste*, pb. 1892.

NONFICTION: *Lettres à un ami, 1880-86*, 1941.

BIBLIOGRAPHY

Arkell, David. *Looking for Laforgue: An Informal Biography*. New York: Persea Books, 1979. A biographical study of Laforgue with a bibliography and index.

Collie, Michael. *Jules Laforgue*. London: Athlone Press, 1977. A short introductory biography. Includes a bibliography and index.

Dale, Peter, trans. Introduction to *Poems of Jules Laforgue*. London: Anvil Press Poetry, 2001. Dale's twenty-page introduction provides a solid overview of the poet, his body of work, and the history of the texts. This bilingual English-French edition also offers notes on the text, a brief bibliography, and indexes of both French and English titles.

Franklin, Ursula. *Exiles and Ironists: Essays on the Kinship of Heine and Laforgue*. New York: P. Lang, 1988. Critical analysis considering the influence of Heinrich Heine on Laforgue's work. Includes a bibliography.

Holmes, Anne. *Jules LaForgue and Poetic Innovation*. New York: Oxford University Press, 1993. A critical analysis focusing on Laforgue's innovations in technique. Includes bibliographical references and an index.

Howe, Elisabeth A. *Stages of Self: The Dramatic Monologues of Laforgue, Valéry, and Mallarmé*. Athens: Ohio University Press, 1990. A study of the representations of the self in three nineteenth century French poets. Includes bibliographic references and an index.

Laforgue, Jules. *Poems of Jules Laforgue*. Translated by Peter Dale. London: Anvil Press Poetry, 1986. Peter Dale's introduction offers some biographical and historical insights into Laforgue's life and work.

Ramsey, Warren. *Jules Laforgue and the Ironic Inheritance*. New York: Oxford University Press, 1953. An in-depth critical assessment dealing with Laforgue's writing techique. Includes thorough bibliographic references.

_____, ed. *Jules Laforgue: Essays on a Poet's Life and Work*. Carbondale: Southern Illinois University Press, 1969. A collection of critical and biographical essays with bibliographic references.

Watson, Lawrence J. *Jules Laforgue: Poet of His Age*. Rev. ed. Mahwah, N.J.: Ramapo College of New Jersey, 1980. A short introduction to Laforgue and his work.

Judith L. Johnston;
bibliography updated by the editors

ALPHONSE DE LAMARTINE

Born: Mâcon, France; October 21, 1790
Died: Paris, France; February 28, 1869

PRINCIPAL POETRY

Méditations poétiques, 1820 (*The Poetical Meditations*, 1839)

La Mort de Socrate, 1823 (*The Death of Socrates*, 1829)

Nouvelles méditations poétiques, 1823

Chant du sacre, 1825

Le Dernier Chant du pèleringe d'Harold, 1825 (*The Last Canto of Childe Harold's Pilgrimage*, 1827)

Harmonies poétiques et religieuses, 1830

Œuvres complètes, 1834

Jocelyn, 1836 (English translation, 1837)

La Chute d'un ange, 1838

Recueillements poétiques, 1839

Œuvres poétiques complètes, 1963

OTHER LITERARY FORMS

Alphonse de Lamartine's attempts at drama are poor, often embarrassing, imitations of the works of Jean Racine, Pierre Corneille, and Voltaire, as well as William Shakespeare. Lamartine was somewhat more successful in the realm of prose fiction. He wrote two semi-autobiographical novels, *Graziella* (1849; English translation, 1871) and *Raphaël* (1849; English translation, 1849); the former was the more popular, while the latter is the better of the two. *Raphaël*, which is based on the poet's love affair with Julie Charles, has been criticized as a novel that was outmoded even in its time, as well as being excessively sentimental. Certainly, *Raphaël* bears the imprint of Jean-Jacques Rousseau's *La Nouvelle Héloïse* (1761; *Julia, or the New Eloisa*, 1773) but it is nevertheless an impressive treatment of Lamartine's favorite themes: religion, love, politics, and nature.

In the course of a long political career, Lamartine delivered some exceptionally eloquent and often politically perspicacious speeches before the French Chamber of Deputies. On the eve of the February Revolution of 1848, he published in eight volumes a fearless glorification of the French Revolution, *Histoire des Girondins*

(1847; *History of the Girondists*, 1847-1848). While not a historian's history, it offers such a colorful and sweeping vision of a period that in many ways it is really a historical novel in the guise of nonfiction. Among many other works, Lamartine also wrote popular histories of the 1848 Revolution in France, the Restoration, Turkey, and Russia.

ACHIEVEMENTS

The critic Henri Peyre has observed that among the great French Romantics, Alphonse de Lamartine demonstrated "the keenest political insight." His work in politics was as important as the politics in his works, but his formal, aesthetic accomplishments in poetry were strong, too. He made his first and his most lasting mark in poetry with *The Poetical Meditations*. This collection, which enjoyed tremendous success with the readers of its day, has been hailed as the first masterpiece of the Romantic movement in French poetry. Lamartine, seen by his contemporaries as an innovator, is often condemned by modern critics for his neoclassical diction, for his rhetorical flourishes, and for his sentimentalism. If one takes Lamartine's poetry on its own terms, however, and particularly if one appreciates its musical prosody, it will be clear why a handful of his poems have a permanent place in anthologies of French literature.

Alphonse de Lamartine (Hulton Archive)

BIOGRAPHY

Alphonse de Lamartine's life can be schematized as a pattern that shifts among four points: political commitments, a sentimental intermixture of women and natural scenery, a personalized and heretical form of Catholicism, and a semiautobiographical approach to poetry. Each, either through circumstance or through the poet's whims, was allowed periodically to reach an ascendancy over the others and to dominate his time and energy. To give emphasis to one over the other is to understand none of them; all must be considered in due course. If one is to understand Lamartine's heavily autobiographical poetry, one must consider his politics, his religion, and his love of women and nature.

Given his family and the events of his early years, it is no surprise that the adult Lamartine was to demonstrate an active interest in politics—although the leftward direction of that interest could hardly have been

predicted. On October 21, 1790, in the opening years of the French Revolution, Lamartine was born into a gentry family that was staunchly Royalist. His father was imprisoned for a long while during the Terror but was not executed. Lamartine's mother, a deeply religious woman who combined the ideas of Rousseau with Catholicism, gave Lamartine his early religious training and had a deep influence on him. At the Jesuit college at Belley, Lamartine again was exposed to liberal Catholic attitudes as well as to a broad range of world literature. It is a tribute to Lamartine's capacity for development that throughout his life he carried this liberalism in religion, as well as in politics, to points just short of radicalism, so much so that by old age he had evolved far beyond the paradigms of his youth.

An early and deep interest in nature and in love was to initiate Lamartine's metamorphosis. In 1811 and 1812, he visited Italy, which, as in the case of Johann

Wolfgang von Goethe several decades before, proved a great impetus to Lamartine's development as a poet. An affair with an Italian cigar maker of loose morals named Antoniella (the probable model for Graziella) had the effect of loosening those of the poet. The scenery, particularly that of the Bay of Naples, left a strong impression on several of his lyrics.

The real turning point, however, came during the autumn of 1816. While convalescing at a fashionable bath in Savoy, Lamartine met Julie Charles, who had all the requisite qualities for attracting the affections of a romantic poet: She was beautiful, consumptive, and married. They carried on an affair amid splendid alpine scenery, which helped to set the tone of pantheism in Lamartine's religious development. In spite of periodic separations, an amorous but perhaps unconsummated relationship continued until Julie finally died of tuberculosis in December, 1817. This affair left a permanent mark on Lamartine. Other affairs and even his marriage in 1820 to Marianne Birch, a wealthy Englishwoman, had no effect on his feelings for Julie and did not disperse the aura of melancholy that her death had imposed on him. Indeed, two further sorrows resulted from his marriage: the deaths of a son and a daughter.

Lamartine's career in the Chamber of Deputies, the elective legislative body of France during the first half of the nineteenth century and in the governments of the 1848 Revolution and the Second Republic is important historically and biographically. A consideration of this career is crucial to an understanding of Lamartine's political poetry. Charles-Maurice de Talleyrand-Périgord said of Lamartine that he had the acumen to penetrate to the heart of his country. He foresaw the dangers of military dictatorships—one of which was soon to materialize under Napoleon III. Lamartine also read an important message in the unsuccessful workers' riots in Lyons and in Paris (1831-1832). He foresaw the necessity for the political education of the working class, who he believed would initiate all future revolutions. (The events of 1848 and 1878 proved him, in great part, correct.)

Above all, Lamartine demonstrated an ability to adapt to a changing political climate—so much so that he was often a bit ahead of his time. Lamartine discovered to his sorrow that flexibility, no matter how logical, can be a fatal flaw in politics. What through twentieth century hindsight seems a sincere, if gradual, move from bourgeois liberalism to a moderately leftist stance seemed to his contemporaries to be inconsistency. Lamartine's sorrow was to have been a statesman in a time of political conservatives and opportunists, the worst and most formidable among whom was Napoleon III. Lamartine could easily have set himself up as a dictator, thereby gaining the support of the Right, but he decided instead to share his power as the head of the 1848 Provisional Government with the leader of the Left, A. A. Ledru-Rollin; this decision lost him the support of the wealthy ruling class.

Lamartine ran unsuccessfully for public office in 1848. Much of the remainder of his life was spent writing popular histories, biographies, and similar works to produce needed income. Lamartine's wife died in 1863; in 1867, the government of Napoleon III, acknowledging the relative poverty of the former statesman, granted Lamartine a substantial sum. Lamartine died in Paris on February 28, 1869.

ANALYSIS

Alphonse de Lamartine's poetry developed, as did everything in his life, by degrees, with no marked departures from the past. Rarely have life and art been so closely intertwined. All his passions became the stuff of his art, to be woven into complex patterns of alliteration and assonance. Perhaps he created only a handful of enduring works, but few poets can claim to have done more.

Lamartine's ability to accept and assimilate change as a Christian, a politician, and a poet demonstrates, more than any of his other qualities, his Romantic *Weltanschauung*. He did not merely accept nineteenth century historicism; he lived it. Change is the dominant theme of his poetry.

THE POETICAL MEDITATIONS

It is no surprise, then, that Lamartine's first collection of poems had a profound effect on the evolution of French poetry. Indeed, *The Poetical Meditations* demonstrates the same gradual development that characterized Lamartine the statesman. The work at the time seemed a radical departure from the neoclassical sensibility that continued to dominate French poetry under the Directorate, the Empire, and the early Restoration—indeed, it seemed so radical a departure that it was refused by the publisher to whom Lamartine first submitted it in 1817. What was acceptable in the prose of Vicomte François-René de Chateaubriand was, until 1820, not palatable in the more formalized realm of poetry. Lamartine took the first, appropriately cautious, step.

"THE LAKE"

The most famous and enduring work of this collection is "Le Lac" ("The Lake"); this lyric is also Lamartine's most frequently anthologized poem. The essential theme of the poem, mutability in the light of the permanence of nature, is introduced in the first stanza. Here, the natural world is treated metaphorically—"eternal night," "time's sea"—to suggest the uncertainty of human fate in the eternal flux. In short, the first stanza maintains a tradition that is at least as old as the first century Greek critic Longinus. Beginning with the second stanza, however, a new, albeit tentative, tone is struck. Natural objects, ceasing to be metaphors, have an existence all their own and are conveyed to the reader with a directness that had not been heard in French poetry for a long time. Although nature in Lamartine certainly lacks the concrete immediacy which it had already found in the poetry of William Wordsworth or Johann Wolfgang von Goethe, the lake, addressed as it is by the persona, is a natural object and not an imaginary shepherdess or an actual patron of the poet; thus, a new directness is gained. Stanzas 2 and 3 picture a time when the persona sat by an alpine lake with his beloved—a figure not individualized in the poem but based on Julie Charles.

The fourth stanza deals with a third Wordsworthian "spot in time": The persona recalls a night when Julie and he were rowing on the lake. This complex layering of three events is characteristic of Lamartine's obsession with time. Stanza 5 introduces the motif of a nature sympathetically resonant with human relations. The persona's beloved begins to speak, causing the shore to be spellbound and drawing the attention of the waves. The beloved's reply in stanzas 6 through 9 is still in the eighteenth century tradition; personified time is now addressed far more conventionally than in the persona's earlier address to the lake. Stanza 9 is a twofold culmination of the beloved's address. First, it gives clear expression to the *carpe diem* theme to which it has all been

leading: "So let us love, so let us love! let us hasten, let us enjoy the fleeting hour" ("Aimons donc, aimons donc! de l'heure fugitive,/ Hâtonsnous, jouissons!"). Second, the stanza returns to the opening image of the lyric, time as an expanse of water without a harbor: "Man has no harbor, time has no shore:/ It flows and we pass on."

In stanza 10, "jealous time" is addressed by the persona, who asks how time can take away the same "moments of intoxication" that it gives. In the last four stanzas, the persona addresses the "lake! mute rocks, grottos! dark forest!" asking them to keep alive the memory of the young couple's night on the lake. With measured rhythms, the poet appeals to all the different sounds of nature, "everything that is heard, seen, or breathed,/ Let all say: 'They loved!'" This musical voice of nature is a poetic credo that Lamartine repeats often in his poetry; the limpid rhythm and assonance that embody this natural music account for the great popularity of the poem.

"THE VALLEY"

A quick glance at another poem in the collection, "Le Vallon" ("The Valley"), indicates the unity of *The Poetical Meditations*. The theme and many of the motifs of "The Lake" are also found in "The Valley." Here, the persona again laments the brevity of life's pleasures, but the added motif of the anonymity of death sounds a new note. The waves and murmuring of the lake are replaced by those of two hidden streams, which meet to form one. The streams flow from their respective sources only to lose their individual identities by merging with each other. These natural images become metaphors for the persona's lost youth: "The source of my days like the streams has flowed away,/ It has passed without a sound, without a name, and without any hope of return."

In "The Valley," the poet employs one of his favorite metaphors: the capacity of sounds in nature to lull the senses and to heal hurts. These effects he sought, often with great success, in his lyrics: The persona says that, "Like an infant rocked by a simple chant,/ My soul is assuaged by the murmur of the waters" ("Comme un enfant bercé par un chant monotone,/ Mon âme s'assoupit au murmure des eaux"). The music of these lines, with their *n* and the *m* sounds, creates precisely the soothing effect that they describe. The water of the brooks and other images taken from nature are used to symbolize the transience of human life; paradoxically, for the poet, nature has the ability to console man because, although subject to change in its parts, it is permanent in its totality: "While everything changes for you, nature is the same." Behind nature is the quintessential permanence of God. For Lamartine, there is no consolation in change as manifested in natural phenomena such as water except in the thought that it is a part of some greater mystical whole.

"TRISTESSE"

It is both the strength and the weakness of *Nouvelles méditations poétiques* that Lamartine continues to explore the themes of *The Poetical Meditations*. "Tristesse" (sorrow) is a poem that draws upon Lamartine's experiences in Naples with Antoniella. As he often does in this volume, the poet draws upon images found in the earlier collection. For example, the "laughing slopes" of "The Lake" appear again in "Tristesse." The lake is now a bay, but it is still an expanse of water that provides a place for lovers to listen "to the gentle noise of the waves or the murmuring wind" ("Au doux bruit de la vague ou du vent qui murmure"); indeed, any hasty glance at Lamartine's poetry will demonstrate the poet's predilection for the word *murmure*—whether it is the murmur of the waves, wind, or foliage. The persona of "Tristesse," as the title implies, suffers in a state of melancholy and nostalgia for a happy past that is lost, never to return. Life and death are joined, a final paradox in which the poet wishes "to die in the place where he has tasted life." There are, however, some new elements in "Tristesse": There is a growing specificity both in the poet's description of the locus of Vergil's tomb and as he conveys his youthful passion with images of "enflamed Vesuvius once again arising from the bosom of the waves."

HARMONIES POÉTIQUES ET RELIGIEUSES

Harmonies poétiques et religieuses reflects the concerns of Lamartine the political figure. Indeed, even the religious aspects of this work can best be understood in a political context, for the separation of church and state was a crucial issue in the politics of nineteenth century France. This relationship between politics and religion must be kept in mind if the reader of *Harmonies poétiques et religieuses* is to comprehend Lamartine's

merging of Christianity with the secular historicism of eighteenth and nineteenth century France.

"LES REVOLUTIONS"

"Les Revolutions" (the revolutions) was first published in a review and later incorporated into *Harmonies poétiques et religieuses*. Inspired by the workers' uprisings in Paris and Lyon, which helped to provoke the turn left in Lamartine's politics, it demonstrates the concept of historical relativism that was to culminate in the works of G. F. W. Hegel, Charles Darwin, and Karl Marx. Lamartine shared a growing awareness that, in the evolution of social structures, whether religious or political, there are no absolute values. In this eloquent lyric, the poet expresses a genuine contempt for the backward-looking conservatism of the majority of his European contemporaries. He contrasts them metaphorically with the nomadic peoples of Arabia, who physically (if certainly not religiously or socially) packed up their belongings and passed on to new horizons. By contrast, the European conservatives are, as Lamartine tells them, "men petrified in [their] timid pride." Lamartine's preoccupation with change, previously applied to nature and to human relationships, is here applied to politics and religion; these human institutions are subject to the mutability that is part of a divine plan: "all things/ Change, fall, perish, flee, die, decompose" ("et toute chose/ Change, tombe, périt, fuit, meurt, se décompose") and all creation is subject to "divine evolutions."

Lamartine goes on, in a second section of "Les Revolutions," to say that the history of humankind is a course of changes, of rises and falls of empires: "All the course [of history] is marked out only/ By the debris of nations." The poet catalogs a variety of both religious and political forms that have been invented and discarded along the roadway of human history: "Thrones, altars, temples, porches, cultures, kingdoms, republics/ Are the powder covering the roadway." In this portion of the poem, Lamartine presents one of his comprehensive, universal visions of the history of Western civilization since ancient Egypt.

The final section of "Les Revolutions" gives perfect expression to Lamartine's conception of an evolutionary progression of human ethics and social structures—each valid only for a single day: "'Advance!' Humanity does not live by a single idea!/ Each night it extinguishes the candle that has guided it,/ it lights another from the eternal torch." Even religion evolves—even the sacred revelation of the Bible. Each generation reads its structures into the seemingly fixed text: "Page by page your epochs spell out the Gospel:/ Therein you have read but a single word, and you shall read a thousand;/ Therein your more venturesome children will read even more still!" God's revelation to man, for Lamartine, is not something fixed in time but is, rather, a dynamic, winged phenomenon: "In thunder and lightning your Word soars" ("Dans la foudre et l'éclair votre Verbe aussi vole"). Although many modern theologians share, in general outline at least, this notion of revelation, in Lamartine's day it represented a clearly heretical conception of the relationship between man and God.

JOCELYN

According to Henri Peyre, such a conception, which offers a new basis for Christianity, is also embodied in Lamartine's *Jocelyn*. The Church of Rome took such exception to the heretical nature of this work that it immediately placed it on the Index. *Jocelyn* is an epic work that was to be a part of an even larger, projected work, "The Epic of the Ages," never completed. A rather melodramatic narrative poem about a priest hiding in the Savoy Alps during the Terror, *Jocelyn* was nevertheless important in Lamartine's development, for in it he broke decisively with neoclassical norms of poetic diction, coloring his verse with real human speech.

LA CHUTE D'UN ANGE

Another work that was to form a part of "The Epic of the Ages," *La Chute d'un ange*, is little read today, but it contains an often anthologized passage, "Choeur des cèdres du Liban" (chorus of the Cedars of Lebanon), in which the poet reiterates his theme of the passage of time.

The ageless cedars are symbols for the continuity of nature and the transience of man: They have stood since before the Flood; they provided the wood for the Ark; they have witnessed the passage of sacred and profane history in the Levantine. Holy men, philosophers, and poets come to do homage to these trees; Lamartine himself saw them on his voyage to the Orient. They are emblems of the creation, the making, the *poesis* that is nature herself—"the great vital chorus" ("le grand choeur

végétal"). Nature is the inspiration for poetry: "And under our prophetic shadows/ They compose their most beautiful hymns out of the murmurs of our branches" ("Et sous nos ombres prophétiques/ Formeront leur plus beaux cantiques/ Des murmure de nos rameaux"). As Geoffrey Brereton has observed, this murmur of the cedars in the wind is an apt image for Lamartine's poetry, underlaid as it is with an all-important rhythm. The poet himself says that the trees roar "in glorious harmonies,/ Without articulated works, without precise language" ("en grandes harmonies/ Sans mots articulés, sans langues définies"). The emphasis on music over meaning that is found in Lamartine's most enduring lyrics foreshadows the verbal magic of Paul Verlaine and Stéphane Mallarmé.

OTHER MAJOR WORKS

LONG FICTION: *Graziella*, 1849 (English translation, 1871); *Raphaël*, 1849 (English translation, 1849); *Geneviève*, 1850 (English translation, 1850); *La Tailleur de pierres de Saint-Point*, 1851 (*The Stonesman of Saint-Point*, 1851).

PLAYS: *Toussaint Louverture*, pr., pb. 1850; *Saül*, pb. 1861; *Medée*, pb. 1873; *Zoraide*, pb. 1873.

NONFICTION: *Sur la politique rationelle*, 1831 (*The Polity of Reason*, 1848); *Voyage en Orient*, 1835 (*Travels in the East*, 1835); *Histoire des Girondins*, 1847 (*History of the Girondists*, 1847-1848); *Histoire de la révolution de 1848*, 1849 (*History of the French Revolution of 1848*, 1849); *Histoire de la Restauration*, 1851-1852 (*The History of the Restoration of Monarchy in France*, 1851-1853); *Histoire de la Turquie*, 1855; *Histoire des constituants*, 1855 (*History of the Constituent Assembly*, 1858); *Vie des grands hommes*, 1855-1856 (*Biographies and Portraits of Some Celebrated People*, 1866).

MISCELLANEOUS: *Œuvres complètes*, 1860-1866 (41 volumes).

BIBLIOGRAPHY

Araujo, Norman. *In Search of Eden: Lamartine's Symbols of Despair and Deliverance*. Brookline, Mass.: Classical Folia Editions, 1976. A critical interpretation of Lamartine's work with bibliographic references.

Barbin, Judith. "Liszt and Lamartine: *Poetic and Religious Harmonies.*" *The Comparatist Journal of the Southern Comparative Literature Association* 16 (1992): 115-122. A thoughtful essay that compares religious elements and musicality in Lamartine's poems in his 1829 book with selected works by the great Polish Romantic composer Franz Liszt.

Birkett, Mary Ellen. *Lamartine and the Poetics of Landscape.* Lexington, Ky.: French Forum, 1982. An excellent study that explores relationships between the representation of natural beauty in Romantic landscape painting and Lamartine's poetry. Like Barbin's study, this book examines the intimate connections between literature and the other arts that were so important during the Romantic period in France.

Bishop, Lloyd. "'Le Lac' as Exemplar of the Greater Romantic Lyric." *Romance Quarterly* 34, no. 4 (November, 1987): 403-413. This close reading of Lamartine's most famous poem explains how the poet's solitary meditation on the beauty of a lake reminds him of his deceased lover, with whom he often walked around the same lake. Argues that nature and death are important themes in Romantic lyric poetry.

Domvile, Margaret St. Lawrence Lady. *Life of Lamartine.* London: K. Paul, Trench, 1888. Written twenty years after his death this in-depth biography offers a nearly contemporaneous view of his life.

Fortescue, William. *Alphonse de Lamartine: A Political Biography.* New York: St. Martin's Press, 1983. Despite its title, this biography does not simply treat Lamartine's unsuccessful run for the French presidency and his opposition to the overthrow of the French Republic by Emperor Napoleon III in 1851. It also examines Lamartine's gradual evolution from a conservative Royalist to a fervent defender of democratic freedoms.

Lombard, Charles. *Lamartine.* New York: Twayne, 1973. Remains a clear introduction in English to Lamartine's lyric and epic poetry. Contains an annotated bibliography of important critical studies on the poetry.

Pirazzini, Agide. *The Influence of Italy on the Literary Career of Alphonse de Lamartine.* New York: AMS Press, 1966. This brief book provides a strong overview of Lamartine's social and political influences.

Porter, Laurence M. *The Renaissance of the Lyric in French Romanticism: Elegy, "Poëme," and Ode.* Lexington, Ky.: French Forum, 1978. A critical and historical study of nineteenth century French poetry including works by Lamartine. Includes an index and a bibliography.

Unger, Gérard. *Lamartine: Poète et homme d'état.* Paris: Flammarion, 1998. An in-depth biography of Lamartine's life as a politician and as a poet. Published in French.

Whitehouse, Henry R. *The Life of Lamartine.* Freeport, N.Y.: Books for Libraries Press, 1969. A reprint of a thorough biography originally published in 1918.

Rodney Farnsworth;
bibliography updated by Edmund J. Campion

CHARLES LAMB

Born: London, England; February 10, 1775
Died: Edmonton, England; December 27, 1834

PRINCIPAL POETRY

Blank Verse, 1798 (with Charles Lloyd)
Poetry for Children, 1809 (with Mary Lamb)
The Works of Charles Lamb, 1818
Album Verses, 1830
Satan in Search of a Wife, 1831
The Poetical Works of Charles Lamb, 1836

OTHER LITERARY FORMS

Charles Lamb began his literary career writing poetry and continued to write verse his entire life. He tried his hand at other genres, however, and is remembered primarily for his familiar essays. These essays, originally published in the *London Magazine*, were collected in *Essays of Elia* (1823) with another collection appearing ten years later, *Last Essays of Elia* (1833). In addition to his poetry and essays, Lamb wrote fiction, drama, children's literature, and criticism. He wrote one novel, *A Tale of Rosamund Gray and Old Blind Margaret*

(1798). In 1802, he published his first play, *John Woodvil: A Tragedy*, which was followed shortly by another attempt at drama: *Mr. H.: Or, Beware a Bad Name, a Farce in Two Acts* (1806). In addition to several prologues and epilogues, he published two other dramas: *The Pawnbroker's Daughter: A Farce* (1825) and *The Wife's Trial* (1827). In addition, he wrote (largely in collaboration with his sister Mary) several children's books: *The King and Queen of Hearts* (1805), *Tales from Shakespeare* (1807), *Adventures of Ulysses* (1808), *Mrs. Leicester's School* (1809), and *Prince Dorus* (1811). Lamb's criticism appeared in various periodicals but was never systematically collected and published during his lifetime. He did publish copious critical notes to accompany his voluminous extracts from Elizabethan plays, *Specimens of English Dramatic Poets, Who Lived About the Time of Shakespeare, with Notes* (1808).

ACHIEVEMENTS

Much of Charles Lamb's literary career was spent in search of an appropriate genre for his particular genius.

Charles Lamb (Hulton Archive)

He wrote poetry, drama, fiction, and criticism, but of these he truly distinguished himself only in criticism. When he happened upon the persona of Elia and the familiar essay, however, these early efforts contributed to his success. As if he had been in training for years preparing to create the *Essays of Elia*, Lamb applied what he had learned from each of the earlier literary forms in which he had worked. Incorporating his knowledge of the importance of rhythm, dramatic context, characterization, dialogue, tone, and point of view, he placed it into the *Essays of Elia* collections and created masterpieces.

Today's literary critics value the essays of Lamb because they embody and reflect in prose the Romantic predisposition found in the great poetry of the day. These familiar essays have a biographical impulse, organic form, symbolic representation, syntactic flexibility, and occasional subject matter. The popularity of Lamb's essays, however, does not depend upon their historical or theoretical relevance. The *Essays of Elia* collections were as celebrated in Lamb's day as they are in modern times and for the same reason: The character of Elia that Lamb creates is one of the most endearing personae in English literature. Elia's whimsical reminiscences may border upon the trivial, but that is insignificant, because the character of the speaker preempts the content of his speech. The personality of Elia becomes the focal point of the essay. His sentimentality, tempered by irony, elevates these pieces to the status of art, conferring upon them their timeless appeal.

Just as the character of Elia is essential to the success of the essays, Lamb's personality overwhelmed his accomplishments in his own day. No discussion of Lamb's achievements would be complete without mention of his many friends, who provided the essential ingredient for his famous nights at home and his fascinating correspondence. A list of his friends is a roster of the major figures of English Romanticism: Samuel Taylor Coleridge, Robert Southey, William Wordsworth, William Godwin, William Hazlitt, Thomas De Quincey, George Dyer, and Benjamin Robert Haydon. His midweek parties from 1801 through 1827 assembled writers, artists, actors, and critics for both frivolous and serious discussion. Port, mutton, cards, and tobacco made the following workday the longest of the week for Lamb. What the success of his weekly gatherings suggests, his correspondence corroborates: Lamb was an honest critic, a sensitive friend, and a sympathetic confidant. When he mentioned his many friends, he assumed his usual tone of self-deprecation, claiming that they were "for the most part, persons of an uncertain fortune." When talking of Lamb, his friends were less diffident. Henry Crabb Robinson epitomizes the opinion of Lamb's friends when he characterized Lamb as "of all the men of genius I ever knew, the one the most intensely and universally to be loved."

BIOGRAPHY

Charles Lamb was born in London to poor parents. His father was a servant and clerk to Samuel Salt, Esquire, of the Inner Temple, and his mother was Salt's housekeeper. Like his older brother John, Lamb went to Christ's Hospital School when he was seven, sponsored by Salt. There he met Coleridge, who was to become his friend for life. Because of a stutter, Lamb did not follow Coleridge to Cambridge on scholarship. Instead, at the age of fourteen, with his education complete, he went to work. His first two apprenticeships came to nothing. In 1792, however, he took a position as an accountant in the East India House, where he remained until his retirement in 1825. Lamb often complained about his position at the East India House, claiming that the work was boring and unimaginative. In fact, the routine about which he complained was a setting and stabilizing influence that his temperament needed and his art exploited. Lamb received an adequate income for a modicum of work, and, though not rich, he was comfortable by the standards of his day. Two other events in his life, however, diminished the happiness offered by this financial security.

Among celebrated bachelors, Lamb is one of the most famous. His unmarried status, however, was not of his own choosing. Sometime around 1792, he fell in love with Ann Simmons, a Hertfordshire neighbor of his maternal grandmother, Mrs. Field. Mrs. Field is said to have discouraged the relationship by pointing out that there was insanity in the Lamb family, and Ann married a London pawnbroker and silversmith named Barton. Lamb's poetry, letters, and essays testify to the sorrow he felt over his loss. Thirty years later in "Dream Children," Elia would fantasize about the woman he never married and the children he never fathered, who instead "call Bartram father." Mrs. Field's warning may have been a self-fulfilling prophecy. At the end of 1795, in despair over "another Person," Lamb committed himself to Hoxton Asylum for six weeks. In a letter to Coleridge dated May 27, 1796, he explains his condition: "I am got somewhat rational now, & *don't bite any one*. But *mad I was*—& many a vagary my imagination played with me."

The second unhappy event that crucially influenced Lamb's life was also related to madness. On September 22, 1796, his sister Mary went mad and fatally stabbed their mother with a kitchen knife. She was tried in the courts, found insane, and remanded to Lamb's custody for life, at his request. Because of his devotion to Mary, his life was altered permanently. Lamb and Mary had always been close, but now they became inseparable, except, that is, when Mary felt her madness coming on. Then the two could be seen walking hand in hand—crying and carrying Mary's straitjacket—to Hoxton Asylum where she would stay until she was well again. To make up for the family that neither of them had, they both cultivated a great number of friends. Stories abound concerning Lamb's remarkable personality, his charming wit, quick sallies, pointed puns, and clever ripostes. It was this engaging personality that Lamb managed to translate into his depiction of Elia. Elia first appeared in the *London Magazine* in August, 1820, with the essay "Recollections of the South-Sea House." Elia is however, a mask, but a mask sharing many of Lamb's traits and experiences.

In 1825, Lamb sent his last Elia essay to the *London Magazine*, and in that year he retired from the East India House. His retirement, eagerly awaited, proved disappointing. He missed the routine, the motivation, the camaraderie of the office. Worse was the frequent illness of Mary that left him alone more and more often. Lamb was not a man able to cope with loneliness, and his drinking increased. With the death of Coleridge in July of 1834, Lamb seemed to lose interest in life. On Saturday, December 27, 1834, he died in his home at the age of fifty-nine. He is buried in Edmonton churchyard, outside London.

ANALYSIS

Charles Lamb's attitude toward poetry evolved as he matured. As a young man, he considered himself an aspiring poet. He experimented with rhythms, modeled his diction after Sir Philip Sidney and his sentiment after William Lisle Bowles, discussed theory with Samuel Taylor Coleridge, and took pleasure in criticizing his own and others' work. In his early verse, there is little of the humor, irony, or modesty that typify his later writing. Lamb is not only serious but also self-consciously so, dealing with weighty topics in an elevated style. His early poems are heavy with melancholy and despair, even before Mary killed their mother. The poems are also personal and confessional and suggest an adolescent indulgence in emotion. Writing to Coleridge in 1796, Lamb explained, "I love my sonnets because they are the reflected images of my own feelings at different times."

Following Mary's disaster, Lamb's reality became as tragic as he had previously imagined. He wrote to Coleridge, "Mention nothing of poetry. I have destroyed every vestige of past vanities of that kind." This was the first of several renunciations of poetry made by Lamb throughout his life, but—like similar renunciations of liquor and tobacco—it was temporary. In a few months, he was sending Coleridge new verses, but the subject matter was altered. Lamb turned to poetry for solace and consolation, composing religious verse. His interest in poetry had revived, but the sensational occurrences that influenced the rest of his life encouraged him to become one of the least sensational of poets. From this new perspective, he counseled Coleridge to "cultivate simplicity," anticipating William Wordsworth's preface to *Lyrical Ballads* (1798). In his next letter to Coleridge, he praised Bowles and Philip Massinger and said he favored "an uncomplaining melancholy, a delicious regret for the past." Lamb's early sentimentality had been displaced by real tragedy, and his poetry changed accordingly.

With the healing passage of time, Lamb's literary interests shifted. In the years 1800 and 1805, he wrote several poems, but for the most part these middle years of his literary career were spent as a journalist. Around 1820, Lamb again began to write poetry, but of a completely different sort. The last period of his poetic pro-duction had been spent writing album verse and other occasional poems. As he matured, Lamb outgrew his earlier confessional mode and turned to people and events around him for subjects. He used his imagination to a greater degree, coloring reality, creating fictions, and distancing himself from his subject. His poetry changed with him, and it came to reflect a fictitious personality similar to the Elia of the essays. Like the Elia essays, Lamb's later poetry contains many autobiographical elements, but they are cloaked and decorous. In place of self-indulgent confessions is a distance and control not found in the early verse.

Lamb wrote and published most of his serious verse—that which today is most often anthologized—in the period between 1795 and 1800. His best and worst poems are among these efforts, which are autobiographical and despondent. They mourn the loss of love, of bygone days, and of happier times. They vary greatly in form, as Lamb experimented with different meters and structures. He was most successful in tight and traditional verse forms and least successful in blank verse. In fact, his blank verse is bad, a surprising situation since his strength in more structured forms is in the control and variation of meter and rhythm.

SONNETS

A favorite form of Lamb's throughout his life was the sonnet, which he began writing early in his career. Appropriately enough, two of his earliest and best poems are English sonnets, published in Coleridge's *Poems on Various Subjects* (1796). This first significant publication by Lamb shows the influence of the Elizabethans on his poetry. His syntax, imagery, and diction suggest the practice of two centuries earlier. One of these sonnets, "Was it some sweet device of Faery," mourns a lost love "Anna" and is clearly a response to the loss of Ann Simmons. The poem's sophisticated rhythm, with frequent enjambment and medial stops, transcends its commonplace subject. Here, as often in Lamb's poetry, the handling of rhythm turns what might be a mediocre effort into an admirable poem. His use of rhetorical questions in this sonnet is skillful, too. Unlike the stilted tone that such questions often provide, in this sonnet the questions actually help to create a sense of sincerity.

Another sonnet from the same volume, "O, I could laugh to hear the midnight wind," also treats the subject of lost love. The poem is nicely unified by the images of wind and wave, and it reflects the Romantic idea of the unity of man and cosmos. It also presents another Romantic concept, the value of the imagination and the powerful influence of memory. This poem is a reminder that much of Wordsworthian theory was not unique to Wordsworth. The ideas that the poem considers may be Romantic, but the style is that of an earlier day. The diction is antique, the imagery tightly unified, and the sonnet form itself conventionally developed. Lamb's prosody is pleasant but not novel.

In 1797, Coleridge's book of poetry went into a second edition, but with an amended title, ". . . to which are now added Poems by Charles Lamb." Lamb had already contributed four poems to the earlier edition, but now there appeared fourteen of his poems. The additional ones are, on the whole, inferior to the initial four; seven are sonnets written about the same time as those that Coleridge had already published. Of interest is one addressed to Mary and written before her tragedy, "If from my lips some angry accents fell." The closing lines give a sense of the personal nature of these verses:

> Thou to me didst ever shew
> Kindest affection; and would oft times lend
> An ear to the desponding love-sick lay,
> Weeping with sorrows with me, who repay
> But ill the mighty debt of love I owe,
> Mary, to thee, my sister and my friend.

The other poem of note in this volume was published in a supplement at the end of the edition. Lamb was signaling its inferiority, and his judgment was correct. "A Vision of Repentance" is an experiment in Spenserian stanza. It opens with a vision, "I saw a famous fountain, in my dream." The fountain turns out to be the waters of redemption that have attracted "Psyche" as well as the speaker. A dialogue between the two ensues, and Psyche reports that she has forsaken Jesus and given "to a treacherous WORLD my heart." After some further conversation, the speaker leaves Psyche with the wish "Christ restore thee soon." The poem is one of several by Lamb that deal with Christianity. Like his other religious verse, it is flawed: didactic, prolix, and unrhythmical.

BLANK VERSE

Lamb's failure with the Spenserian stanza is paralleled by his experiments in blank verse. In 1798, he and Charles Lloyd published a volume titled *Blank Verse*. Lacking the direction given by a tight form or a controlling convention, Lamb's blank verse is verbose, clumsy, and unsure. His autobiographical subject matter and confessional intent are uncomfortably couched in an elevated style reminiscent of John Milton. The two are not compatible. The volume, however, does contain one work by Lamb worthy of his talent.

"THE OLD FAMILIAR FACES"

"The Old Familiar Faces," though not in blank verse, is Lamb's best-known poem. The subject is typical of this period in Lamb's career; it is a lamenting revelation of intense personal grief and loss. Its power, however, lies not in its subject matter, but in the skillful way in which Lamb manipulates the prosody. The poem evokes man's essential isolation and loneliness in the dolorous tolling repetition of the phrase "All, all are gone, the old familiar faces."

The form of the poem creates the effect. Rather than blank verse or the thumping rhymed verse of which he was too fond, Lamb chose a three-line stanza that replaced rhyme with the repetition of the title line. In this way, he gained form without the convoluted syntax of the padded line that rhyme often demanded. The rhythm of the line is that used by Coleridge in "Christabel," and it is agreeable to think that it was Lamb who suggested this meter to his friend.

The poem is justly often anthologized; its rhythm is perfectly suited to the subject. Ian Jack in the *Oxford History of English Literature* (1963) suggests that the success of the meter conflicts with the other poems in the volume. He concludes, "It is hard to say how far the effect of the poem is due to metrical sophistication, and how far to a felicitous awkwardness."

"HESTER"

By 1800, the self-indulgent moroseness of Lamb's early verse was beginning to be displaced by a greater sense of reserve and control. These years saw less poetic activity by Lamb, but the poems he wrote are, on the whole, more able. An excellent example of the newfound discipline displayed by Lamb occurs in "Hester." The poem again deals with the subjects of loss, death, and despair, but he handles them with a new and previously uncharacteristic restraint. The tight rhyme scheme and the concluding hypermetrical iambic dimeter line provide Lamb with a form he uses well: a short line, a varied rhythm, and a regular stanza:

> A springy motion in her gait,
> A rising step, did indicate
> Of pride and joy no common rate
>   That flush'd her spirit

"Hester" is not one of the immortal poems in the English language, but it is a solid achievement worthy of a young poet. Ian Jack has compared it favorably with the lyrical ballads of Wordsworth.

"A FAREWELL TO TOBACCO"

Another poem from this period breaks the morbidity of Lamb's previous verse and prefigures the wit and urbanity found in *Essays of Elia*. Lamb wrote "A Farewell to Tobacco" in what he called "a stammering verse" because he used tobacco to retard his own stammering. Once again he turned to the short line, in this case an irregular eight-syllable trochaic line with rhyming couplets, and it well served his comic intent. Gone is the gross subjectivity; instead, the poem humorously indicts tobacco, while admitting that the habit is unbreakable. Good-natured wordplay and clever burlesque make the poem one of Lamb's most enjoyable. The comic tone established in "A Farewell to Tobacco" appears again in 1812 when Lamb composed one of his few political poems. "The Triumph of the Whale" gently ridicules the prince regent by comparing George with a leviathan. He satirizes the regent's girth, appetite, retinue, and failed constancy. The poem exists mainly, however, for the pun on which it ends: "the PRINCE of WHALES."

"WRITTEN AT CAMBRIDGE"

The last noteworthy poem of this period is a sonnet that illustrates Lamb's mature, relaxed, and personal style. "Written at Cambridge" is an autobiographical whimsy that details how the poet feels as he walks around the university. A note of disappointment begins the poem because the speaker regrets that he had been unable to attend such an institution. This sense of loss disappears, however, with the speaker's slightly foolish but nevertheless touching portrait of his imaginative usurpation of Cantabrigian wisdom while strolling its grounds. This poem is worthy of "gentle Charles."

THE POETICAL WORKS OF CHARLES LAMB

Of the original poems published in the posthumous collection *The Poetical Works of Charles Lamb*, almost half are from his last period, 1820 to 1834. Most of these are "album verse," a popular form in the 1820's. These occasional verses—written at the request of and about the album's owner—are humorous and light, built around epigrams, puns, and acrostics. Most of this album verse, while representative of the genre, is hardly memorable, with two exceptions. "On the Arrival in England of Lord Byron's Remains" is a good example of Lamb's mature tone, and it reveals his opinion of George Gordon, Lord Byron: "lordly Juan, damned to lasting fame,/ Went out a pickle, and came back the same." A more serious work which arrives at unpleasant conclusions is "In My Own Album," a poignant comparison of life to an album. The poem returns to the theme of self-reproach that colored so much of Lamb's early verse, but there exists a distance and a universality that was not at work before. Rhymed tercets provide Lamb the form in which he worked best, and his iambic hexameters are smooth and graceful. The music of his verse complements his rhythm and meter.

"ON AN INFANT DYING AS SOON AS BORN"

Two of Lamb's best poems, both products of this late period, nicely exemplify his mature serious and comic styles. Both were written after Lamb had won recognition as an essayist, when he no longer felt he had to prove himself as a poet. Freed from the necessity of competing with Edmund Spenser, John Donne, and Milton (not to mention Coleridge, Robert Burns, and Robert Southey), Lamb discovered his own rhythm and voice. These, his finest verses, are the products of his natural strengths, and not those borrowed from another time or another artist. Relaxed and self-assured, Lamb mastered the short line and the comic effect of rhyme. He cultivated forms that worked for him and his voice. "On an Infant Dying as Soon as Born" deals with loss and death in a poignant and moving way. The maudlin, pathetic tone is gone. In its place is an elegant lament for the state of all men, an elegy that transcends the single occasion, a threnody whose language and figures are worthy of Andrew Marvell or Henry Vaughan. The dead child, addressed as "Riddle of destiny," presents to the speaker an insoluble problem, the suffering of innocent men. The speaker concludes that "the economy of Heaven is dark" and that even the "wisest clerks" are unable to explain why an infant dies while

> shrivel'd crones
> Stiffen with age to stocks and stones;
> And crabbed use the conscience sears
> In sinners of an hundred years.

The poem closes with a traditional, but guarded, optimism.

SATAN IN SEARCH OF A WIFE

Lamb's longest and last poem published during his life, *Satan in Search of a Wife* (1831), consists of two books of thirty verses each. It is usually said that Lamb never valued this poem because he wrote his publisher not to mention that the "damn'd 'Devil's Wedding'" was written by the author of the *Essays of Elia*. Nevertheless, he thought highly enough of the poem to have it published. The ballad is Lamb at his best: light, jocular, ironic, punning, occasional, and personal. It begins with an echo of George Gordon, Lord Byron's *The Vision of Judgment* (1822) in reverse. Instead of St. Peter grown bored, the devil is out of sorts:

> The Devil was sick and queasy of late,
>   And his sleep and his appetite fail'd him;
> His ears they hung down and his tail it was clapp'd
> Between his poor hoofs, like a dog that's been rapp'd—
>   None knew what the devil ail'd him.

The tale continues, telling of the Devil's love for a tailor's daughter, his successful wooing of her, and the joyful wedding. Lamb's autobiographical propensity shows up even here, for lurking behind all the fun are serious complaints about bachelorhood, about women as lovers, women as mothers, and even women who murder, with the speaker concluding that "a living Fiend/ Was better than a dead Parent." The poem is, however, anything but maudlin. It is an energetic and fancy-filled romp which spoofs the devil, marriage, foreigners, and the Christian idea of Hell. It is vintage Lamb: genteel, a bit cynical, but kind and sincere. The essays of Lamb will continue

to earn him fame, but poems such as *Satan in Search of a Wife* have been too long neglected.

OTHER MAJOR WORKS

LONG FICTION: *A Tale of Rosamund Gray and Old Blind Margaret*, 1798.

PLAYS: *John Woodvil: A Tragedy*, pb. 1802; *Mr. H.: Or, Beware a Bad Name, a Farce in Two Acts*, pb. 1806; *The Pawnbroker's Daughter: A Farce*, pb. 1825; *The Wife's Trial*, pb. 1827.

NONFICTION: *Specimens of English Dramatic Poets, Who Lived About the Time of Shakespeare, with Notes*, 1808; *Essays of Elia*, 1823; *Last Essays of Elia*, 1833.

CHILDREN'S LITERATURE: *The King and Queen of Hearts*, 1805; *Tales from Shakespeare*, 1807 (with Mary Lamb); *Adventures of Ulysses*, 1808; *Mrs. Leicester's School*, 1809 (with Mary Lamb); *Prince Dorus*, 1811.

MISCELLANEOUS: *The Works of Charles and Mary Lamb*, 1903-1905 (7 volumes), 1912 (6 volumes); *The Letters of Charles Lamb*, 1935 (3 volumes).

BIBLIOGRAPHY

Barnett, George Leonard. *Charles Lamb*. Boston: Twayne, 1976. This volume is an excellent introduction to Lamb. Barnett supplies a biography interwoven with an analysis of Lamb's major works. Supplemented by a chronology of Lamb's life and work, an index, and a bibliography. Suitable for all students.

Cornwall, Barry. *Charles Lamb: A Memoir*. Boston: Roberts Brothers, 1866. Serious students of Lamb will find this old book essential, as it was written only thirty-two years after Lamb's death by a contemporary who knew him well. Lamb was astonishingly well loved, and his work held in high esteem by his contemporaries. It is interesting to see that the reputation of his work remains good today.

Hine, Reginald Leslie. *Charles Lamb and His Hertfordshire*. London: J. M. Dent & Sons, 1949. Lamb was born in London, in town, but his heart was in his adopted home in the country, in Herfordshire. This book sheds valuable light on Lamb's personality, which was shaped by his attachment to country life.

Contains paintings and drawings of Lamb and Herfordshire, a bibliography, and an index.

Howe, Will David. *Charles Lamb and His Friends*. Indianapolis: Bobbs-Merrill, 1944. Lamb was a lovable man and had many friends who wrote about him. Howe has stitched together many of these reminiscences and allowed the modern reader to see how Lamb's friends viewed him, and how he saw himself. Contains an index and a bibliography.

Lucas, Edward V. *The Life of Charles Lamb*. 5th ed. 2 vols. London: Methuen, 1921. This book remains the standard biography on Lamb. It is built on information gathered from Lamb's writings. Lucas provides a great deal of facts about Lamb's life but little critical analysis of his work. Valuable for all students.

Riehl, Joseph E. *That Dangerous Figure: Charles Lamb and the Critics*. Columbia, S.C.: Camden House, 1998. An examination of criticism by Lamb's contemporaries of his works whith extensive bibliographic references.

John F. Schell;
bibliography updated by the editors

WALTER SAVAGE LANDOR

Born: Warwick, England; January 30, 1775
Died: Florence, Italy; September 17, 1864

PRINCIPAL POETRY

The Poems of Walter Savage Landor, 1795
Gebir: A Poem, in Seven Books, 1798
Poems from the Arabic and Persian, 1800
Poetry by the Author of Gebir, 1800
Gebirus, Poema, 1803
Count Julian, 1812 (verse drama)
Idyllia Nova Quinque Heroum atque Heroidum, 1815
Idyllia Heroica Decem Librum Phaleuciorum Unum, 1820
Andrea of Hungary, 1839 (verse drama)

Giovanna of Naples, 1839 (verse drama)
Fra Rupert: The Last Part of a Trilogy, 1840 (verse drama)
The Siege of Ancona, 1846 (verse drama)
The Hellenics Enlarged and Completed, 1847
Poemata et Inscriptiones, 1847
Italics of Walter Savage Landor, 1848
The Last Fruit off an Old Tree, 1853
Heroic Idyls, with Additional Poems, 1863
The Poetical Works of Walter Savage Landor, 1937 (Stephen Wheeler, editor).

OTHER LITERARY FORMS

Walter Savage Landor's reputation rests primarily on his poetry, but he was a skilled writer of prose as well. His political writings are notable for their anger and his criticism for its insight into the mechanics of writing. All his prose is witty; it is frequently satirical. As with his poetry, Landor's prose works are carefully phrased and sometimes more perfect in their parts than their wholes. Ranked as one of the most important practitioners of nonfiction prose in the nineteenth century, he is viewed by critics as one of the outstanding prose stylists of the English language.

ACHIEVEMENTS

Walter Savage Landor's poetry has never had a wide readership. Much of its appeal is in its near-perfect phrasing and versification; such an appeal of skill almost inevitably attracts admirers among other poets, the fellow practitioners of a demanding art. Landor remains admired for the variety of poetic forms that he mastered and for the clarity of his phrasing; he is often faulted for the detached tone of his work—for the lack of emotional response to his subjects. His poetry often seems crystalline and fragile, as if unable to withstand the burden of a large audience. Fine prosody and marvelously apt phrasing when combined with the distant tone of much of his verse makes ranking him among poets a difficult task. Compounding the difficulty are his poetry's classical characteristics, which seem in conflict with the Romantic and Victorian eras during which he wrote. His poetry lacks the emotional vigor of Percy Bysshe Shelley's work but compares well with the beauty of John Keats's odes and is superior to George Gordon, Lord Byron's verse in ingenuity. He cannot match William Wordsworth in importance to the history of poetry, although many poets have valued his contributions to the understanding of prosody. Taken by itself, apart from its era and influence, Landor's poetry is equal in melodic beauty and economy of phrasing to much of the best in English poetry. As a poet, Landor might fairly be ranked behind Wordsworth and Robert Browning in overall achievement and behind Keats in imagery; he is second to none in phrasing and prosody.

BIOGRAPHY

Walter Savage Landor was a man given to fierce passions; he could burst out in either anger or generosity almost without warning. He was egotistical and given to romantic notions about life; this combination caused him much unhappiness and yet underlies much of his best writing. He was born on January 30, 1775, in Warwick. In 1780, he began his schooling at Knowle; in 1783, he was sent to study at Rugby. After eight years of annoying his teachers and antagonizing others with his satirical sense of humor, he was sent home. Landor, however, remembered Rugby fondly; while there, he developed his taste for poetry and demonstrated a precocious skill in composing verse. Reverend William Langley, of Ashbourne, Derbyshire, became Landor's tutor in 1792. The next year, Landor entered Trinity College, Oxford. While at Oxford he punctuated a political dispute by shooting at a neighbor's shutters; suspended from college for two terms, he left Oxford in 1794, never to return. He moved to London and had his poetry published under a grand title for a mere twenty-year-old, *The Poems of Walter Savage Landor* (1795). The volume brought him a small but loyal following among other writers and readers who had a taste for fine literature.

When his father died, Landor inherited a large fortune. This he spent on a large estate in Wales and on outfitting his own regiment to fight in Spain against the French. After the French left Spain, Landor's regiment disappeared, and he hastened home. In Wales, he tried to improve the lives of the peasants and to introduce enlightened methods of managing an estate. No one seemed to appreciate his efforts, and after losing much money, he abandoned the effort.

Walter Savage Landor (Hulton Archive)

In 1811, in one of his grand gestures, he married an attractive woman who was beneath him in both wealth and social station. Far from being grateful, his bride, Julia Thuillier, repeatedly cuckolded Landor and made his life unpleasant. She did not appreciate her husband's generous nature, his intellect, or his interests. Although she is often portrayed as a nasty and cruel woman, she and Landor seem to have had enough truces to produce a daughter and three sons. In 1814, Landor toured the Continent, where he was eventually joined by his wife. From 1816 to 1818, he stayed in Como, Italy, and in 1818 his first son was born. His daughter followed in 1820, while he was in Pisa. From 1821 to 1828, he lived in Florence, where his second and third sons were born in 1822 and 1825. By 1835, his family life was unbearable; his wife dedicated herself to embarrassing him publicly and committing adultery privately. Landor had doted on his children and spoiled them; nevertheless, when he left his wife and returned to England, they chose to remain with her, although in the 1840's his two eldest sons and his daughter visited him for months at a time. During the years of unhappy marriage, Landor continued to write, building a loyal following of admiring friends, including Ralph Waldo Emerson and John Forster.

Landor's trenchant wit and attacks on the misdeeds of public officials frequently involved him in trouble. In 1857, old but still fiery, he published attacks on a Mrs. Yescombe, whom he saw as a villainess because of an injustice visited on a young woman. Convicted of libel in 1858, he left England in 1859 to seek refuge from litigation in Fiesole, where he had maintained his family since 1835. Rejected by his family, he wandered to nearby Florence, where Robert Browning offered him a home. He died on September 17, 1864. He had wanted to be buried near Bath in England but was interred instead at Florence. He had wanted an epitaph that mentioned his closest friends but instead received one that mentions his wife and children.

ANALYSIS

The poems of Walter Savage Landor are like fragile crystals, the clarity of which disguises their masterfully crafted form. The meaning of Landor's verse often seems transparent; he believed in clarity as a poetic virtue. The seeming ease with which his verse can be understood belies the strenuous efforts Landor made to pare down his phrases and to present his ideas with near-perfect economy. Much of his success in economical phrasing comes from his mastery of a host of meters and poetic subgenres, chief among which were the verse drama, the dramatic scene, the heroic poem, and the Hellenic poem. Landor had a restless mind, requiring activity; he had a voracious appetite for ideas. Writing poetry provided him with relief from such intellectual demands. Poetry was thus more of a hobby than a career; Landor wrote verse for recreation, and the complexity of his prosody and the pureness of his language originate in part from this recreational aspect of his versifying. His poetry represented an effort to find peace of mind, to discharge some of his extraordinary intellectual energy. The literature of ancient Greece and Rome had a long history of amateur scholarly study and had inspired and informed the neoclassical period in England that was just ending when Landor was born, and he found ready materials for such agreeable study in a host of commentaries on form and style. The Greeks supplied him with ideas about life and human relationships; the Latin poets supplied him with high standards for poetic composition and style. He sometimes wrote in Latin, perhaps to capture the elegance and sense of sweet phrasing that typifies much of the best of the poetry of the classical Romans.

Landor's use of classical materials has long created problems for literary historians. His life spans the Romantic era and ends when the Victorian era was well under way. Although some Romantic poets—notably Percy Bysshe Shelley—used classical myths as subjects, they rarely employed classical forms. A classicist can be identified by his use of the standards of the ancient poets: an emphasis on phrasing, good sense, and logical order. A classicist restrains his emotions in favor of clarity of expression and tends to use classical works as models for his own. The Romantics, on the other hand, reacted to the preceding neoclassical age by emphasizing mysticism, nature, and traditional English poetic forms such as blank verse and the sonnet.

In his tastes and models, Landor was every inch a classicist and had more in common with Alexander Pope and Samuel Johnson than with Wordsworth or Shelley, but in his subjects he turned to nature as an ideal, somewhat as Wordsworth did and even more as did the Renaissance poet Sir Philip Sidney, and he wrote blank verse with a facility that had been alien to many of his neoclassical forebears. He had in common with his contemporaries a vast enthusiasm for poetry, but, whereas his contemporaries lived for their art, Landor's art was his servant. Emotional outbursts were reined in; uncontrolled poetic fervor was not for Landor. His spirit was as restless as Lord Byron's, but where Byron turned his restlessness into a poetic ideal, Landor used poetry to subdue his own restlessness. Thus, the determined and hard self-control evident in Landor's verse sets him apart from the poets of his time. Some critics call him a Romantic, though seemingly more for the age in which he lived than for the qualities of his work. He actually was the son of the neoclassical age; he followed a poetic path that was a logical extension of what the neoclassicists had achieved, while Wordsworth and the Romantics followed a poetic path that was a logical reaction against the neoclassicists. Landor was a classicist in a Romantic age.

VERSE DRAMAS

As a good student of the classical authors, Landor believed in poetic simplicity. His verse dramas reveal at once the strengths and weaknesses of the simplicity that gives his poetry its crystalline character. Although not the best of his dramatic efforts, perhaps the best known of his dramas is the tragedy of *Count Julian* (1812). The play resembles a child's perception of tragedy—all loud voices and grim visages. The characters exclaim instead of converse; each word seems meant for the ages. The welter of "Ohs!" and other short exclamations are sometimes more risible than dramatic. Even so, the subject of *Count Julian* has much potential for good drama. A Spanish warrior who has driven the Moors from Spain avenges the rape of his daughter by his king by leading the Moors back into his country, with disastrous consequences. The play's blank verse is austere, remote from the characters and their emotions. Landor had hoped that *Count Julian* might be performed, but its poetry is more important than its drama; it is now regarded strictly as a closet drama. *Andrea of Hungary* (1839) and its sequels *Giovanna of Naples* (1839) and *Fra Rupert: The Last Part of a Trilogy* (1840) are dramatically and poetically more successful. Blank verse and character blend well in these plays; the scenes between Andrea and Giovanna in the first of them are relaxed, revealing two interesting personalities. Landor cared little for plot, which he called "trick"; thus, the sequence of events in his trilogy of plays is predictable and has few twists. Andrea is murdered, probably at the instigation of the ambitious Fra Rupert; Giovanna remains a paragon of virtue through three marriages and is eventually murdered; Fra Rupert commits suicide, and his villainy is revealed. Landor uses the plot as a vehicle for some of his notions about power and politics and his blend of apt phrase, characterization, and good verse is often moving.

Landor's dramatic scenes also feature blank verse, though they are only short conversations. In "Essex and Bacon," for example, Landor shows the Earl of Essex meeting with Francis Bacon after the earl's condemnation to death for treason. Landor's interest in ambition and the abuse of power provides the scene's depth. Essex sees himself as greater than Bacon because he took a glorious chance by opposing Queen Elizabeth, and he cannot understand how his friend can call him "lower than bergess or than churl." Essex declares, "To servile souls how abject seem the fallen!/ Benchers and message-bearers stride o'er Essex." He dismisses Bacon with contempt. When alone, Bacon is allowed the last word, which, in summary, says that ambition is often mistakenly thought to be great by those who allow it to run their lives, when, in fact, it is arrogance. The dramatic scenes generally reflect Landor's concern with the abuse of power; "Ippolito di Este" perhaps makes Landor's feelings clearest. This short drama introduces the audience to the brothers Ferrante, Giulio, and the Cardinal Ippolito di Este. Ferrante has the misfortune to have his eyes admired by a woman whom his brother the cardinal desires; the cardinal has Ferrante's eyes removed. The dramatic scene is truly horrible, even if Ferrant is too saintly to be palatable.

GEBIR

Of Landor's heroic poems, his first (and his first important poem, written when he was perhaps twenty years of age), *Gebir*, is probably the best known. Gebir is king of Gades (Cádiz); he conquers Egypt and the heart of Queen Charoba then is assassinated. The poem takes him through heroic adventures, including a trip to the underworld. *Gebir* reveals Landor's extensive scholarship, based as it is on Arabian history. The verse is spare, already featuring Landor's emphasis on succinct phrasing; its scenes are dramatic and resemble the tragedies in structure. Unfortunately, the language of the poem is too remote for successful characterization; Gebir, who is a strong, dynamic young man, talks like an ancient Greek god. His love, Charoba, is more accessible to readers, although she, too, often merely declaims. *Gebir* displays much fine poetry; it may not always succeed, but it is good enough by itself to establish Landor's claim to poetic importance. Admired by contemporary critics and poets, including Robert Southey, the poem established Landor as a significant poet.

HELLENIC POEMS

Landor's so-called Hellenics are poems that are informed by ancient Greek myths and history. They encompass blank verse, lyrics, sonnets, and conversations. The best of these, such as "Coresos and Callirhöe," "The Altar of Modesty," "Acon and Rhodope," "Pan," and "The Marriage of Helena and Menelaos," are exquisite gems of the poet's art. Each is representative of Landor's classical principles; the poems are simple in form, their clarity of language being the result of much revision, and they reflect intelligent observation. They focus on characters and generally deliver homilies on love and life. In "Pan and Pitys," for instance, Pitys is loud in her derogation of Boreas, her suitor. Boreas hears her, and he drops a large rock on her. The exchanges between Pan and Pitys are loud and boisterous; her foolishness and insensitivity are also loud; perhaps she should have spoken more kindly of her suitor. In "Acon and Rhodope," a man loses sight of what is important in his life and loses all he cares for. The verse is thick with colors and odors that represent a mixture of life and death; apple trees have "freckled leaves" and oleanders have "light-hair'd progeny." The effect of the Hellenic poems is one of another world that is somehow part of the common one. The characters have thoughts, emotions, and problems, much like those that are common to humanity, but their world is richer, more intense than common experience. Such intensity is well evoked in "The Marriage of Helena and Menelaos," in which the sixteen-year-old Helena faces her husband-to-be and the prospect of adulthood for the first time. The gibes of siblings, the fears of appearing foolish, the sense of losing youth too soon, condense into a poignant, short series of events. "The Marriage of Helena and Menelaos" is a product of the mature Landor; it is alive with ideas, focused on a dramatic moment, and deceptively simple on its surface.

THE SIEGE OF ANCONA

Although Landor strove to use elevated language and to create clear, often austere, verse, his poetry contains much variety and life. Works such as "Homer, Laertes, Agatha" and "Penelope and Pheido" not only feature Landor's classicism but feature high poetry and are lively as well. Landor brings humanity to his poetry; he focuses on the difficulties people have when faced with problems larger than themselves. Like that of other poets who lived long lives, Landor's verse changed over the years; it began by being brash and noisy, as in *Gebir* and *Count Julian*; grew to reflect his thoughts on politics and power, as in *Fra Rupert*; and attained a blend of erudition and humanity that bring sensitivity to "The Marriage of Helena and Menelaos," written when Landor was eighty-nine.

Among his most sensitive and interesting works is the verse drama *The Siege of Ancona*. Typical of Landor's

work, it is known to only a few critics and admirers of poetry. Its verse is clear and its tone is heroic, without the declamatory faults of *Count Julian*; its psychology is subtle and its values those of a classicist who was nevertheless a part of the Romantic period. The Consul of Ancona asserts that "the air/ Is life alike to all, the sun is warmth,/ The earth, its fruits and flocks, are nutriment,/ Children and wives are comforts; all partake/ (Or may partake) in these" (III, ii, lines 48-52). Like Wordsworth, Landor found a universal metaphor in nature; unlike Wordsworth, he made his natural world Arcadian in the manner of English Renaissance poets. He labored at the classical ideal of spare verse and detached tone; he yielded to the Romantic desire to express his innermost spirit. At its best, his poetry is clear and crystalline, maintaining a warmth and sensitive empathy for the common joys, miseries, and confusions that people face in their daily lives.

OTHER MAJOR WORKS

LONG FICTION: *Imaginary Conversations of Literary Men and Statesmen*, 1824-1829 (5 volumes); *The Pentameron and Pentalogia*, 1837.

SHORT FICTION: *Dry Sticks Fagoted*, 1858.

NONFICTION: *Citation and Examination of William Shakespeare*, 1834.

MISCELLANEOUS: *The Complete Works of Walter Savage Landor*, 1927-1936 (16 volumes; Thomas E. Welby and Stephen Wheeler, editors); *Walter Savage Landor: Selected Poetry and Prose*, 1981 (Keith Hanley, editor).

BIBLIOGRAPHY

Dilworth, Ernest. *Walter Savage Landor.* New York: Twayne, 1974. An excellent critical introduction for those unfamiliar with Landor's work. The author points out the poet's aims and achievements as well as his shortcomings in style and substance. Frequent quotations support the text and a chronology, notes, references, and an excellent select bibliography are included.

Elwin, Malcolm. *Landor, a Replevin.* London: Macdonald, 1958. This is a rewriting of a book originally published in 1941 specifically for publication in England. The author's goal is to save the poet's reputation and work from misrepresentation and neglect. Written in a very personable style, he quotes both Landor's and others' letters extensively. Supplemented by a scholarly bibliography and a chronology.

Field, Jean. *Landor.* Studley, Warwickshire, England: Brewin Books, 2000. A biography of Landor with a selection of his works. Includes bibliographical references and index.

Hanley, Keith. Introduction to *Walter Savage Landor: Selected Poetry and Prose.* Manchester, England: Carcanet Press, 1981. Discusses Landor's role as a neoclassicist, the art of imitation, the classical structure of feeling, and his poetic style.

Pinsky, Robert. *Landor's Poetry.* Chicago: University of Chicago Press, 1968. This analysis of about twenty poems explores, among other things, Landor's repeated use of subjects and gives a fair picture of his poetic artistry. The author defends Landor and makes a case for the intellectual content of the poems. He shows some of the lesser verse to have real artistry behind it. Special attention is paid to an analysis of Landor's use of rhythms. Omitted in the discussion are Landor's tributes to other writers.

Super, Robert H. *Walter Savage Landor: A Biography.* New York: New York University Press, 1954. This lengthy, definitive biography replete with accurate detail includes material and documents hitherto ignored or undiscovered. The author corrects previous carelessness, errors in chronology, and other distortions. This fine example of biographical scholarship includes an index and an extensive system of notes and references displaying the meticulous accuracy seen throughout.

Kirk H. Beetz;
bibliography updated by the editors

WILLIAM LANGLAND

Born: Cleobury Mortimer(?), Shropshire, England; c. 1332
Died: London(?), England; c. 1400

PRINCIPAL POETRY

The Vision of William, Concerning Piers the Plowman, 1362 (A Text), c. 1377 (B Text), c. 1393 (C Text)
Richard the Redeless, c. 1395 (attributed)

OTHER LITERARY FORMS

William Langland is remembered only for his poetry.

ACHIEVEMENTS

Apparently, in its own day, *The Vision of William, Concerning Piers the Plowman* was a very popular work. More than fifty manuscripts of the poem in its various versions still exist. The poem's four printings before 1561 are evidence of its continued popularity. The audience of *Piers Plowman* was not, as it was for most poems of the alliterative revival, a small group of provincial nobles; rather, as J. A. Burrow (*Anglia,* LXXV, 1957) has shown, the poem would have been read by a broadly based national public of parish priests or local clergy whose tastes favored purely didactic literature. In addition, Burrow connects the poem with a growing lay public of the rising bourgeoisie, whose tastes were still conservative and generally religious. The didactic content of the poem, then, was its chief appeal in its own time.

By the sixteenth century, however, with the rise of Protestantism, William Langland's poem became acclaimed for its aspects of social satire. This strain in the poem had been underlined even in the fourteenth century, when John Ball, in a letter to the peasants of Essex during the revolt of 1381, mentioned Piers the Plowman. Possibly because of this mention, the very orthodox Catholic Langland came, ironically, to be associated with Lollardy, and to be looked upon as a bitter critic of the Roman Church and a precursor of Protestantism.

By the late sixteenth century, Langland's western Midland dialect had become too difficult for any but the most ardent reader, and so no new edition of *Piers Plowman* appeared until 1813. Though nineteenth century readers deplored Langland's allegory, they could still, like the readers before them, admire *Piers Plowman* as social satire, and, in addition, they could appreciate and admire the stark realism in such scenes as the confession of the seven deadly sins in Passus V (B Text). Their chief interest in Langland was historical: They viewed the poem as a firsthand commentary on the fourteenth century.

BIOGRAPHY

Virtually nothing is known of the poet who wrote *Piers Plowman*. At one time, in fact, there was some debate about whether a single author or perhaps as many as five were responsible for the three separate versions of the poem. That controversy has since ended, and scholarship has established a single author for all three versions.

That author's name was almost certainly William Langland. Two fifteenth century manuscript notes attribute the poem to Langland, and there is a line in the B Text which seems to be intended as a cryptogram of the poet's name: "I haue lyued in londe', quod [I], 'my name is longe wille." One manuscript declares that Langland was the son of a certain Stacey (Eustace) de Rokayle, who later held land under the Lord Despenser at Shipton-under-Wychwood in Oxfordshire; in all likelihood, Langland's father was a franklin. It has been conjectured that Langland was illegitimate, but the difference in surname is no real reason to assume this, such differences being common in the fourteenth century. Langland was not born in Oxfordshire but rather in Shropshire, at Cleobury Mortimer, some eight miles from the Malvern Hills which serve as the setting for the first two visions in *Piers Plowman*. Because the B Text is dated with some accuracy c. 1377 and because the poet in the B Text declares himself to be forty-five years old, the date of Langland's birth has been set at about 1332.

Whatever else is "known" about the author's life is conjectured from passages in the poem which describe the narrator's life and is based on the assumption that the narrator, "Will," and the poet Langland are one and the same. In the C Text, the poet speaks of having gone to school, and most likely he was educated at the priory of Great Malvern in Worcestershire. He would have gone through the usual training for the priesthood, but, according to evidence in the poem, the deaths of his father and friends left him without a benefactor and forced him to abandon his studies before taking holy orders. He would have been unable to advance in the Church, hav-

ing left school with only minor orders, partly because of his incomplete education and because, as the poet writes, he was married—a right permitted only to clerks in orders below subdeacon.

Because of these apparent facts, E. Talbot Donaldson assumes that Langland was an acolyte, one of the poor, unbeneficed clergy who had no official way of making a living within the Church hierarchy. Certainly he was poor, but he seems to have claimed exemption from manual labor by virtue of his being a tonsured clerk. W. W. Skeat conjectures that Langland may have earned some money as a scribe, copying out legal documents, since the poem displays a close knowledge of the form of such documents. Perhaps he was able to pick up odd clerical jobs here and there in the city of London, where, according to an apparently autobiographical account in the C Text, he went to live at Cornhill with his wife, Kitte, and daughter, Callote. According to this passage, Langland seems to have earned money by going about singing the office of the dead or other prayers for the living and making regular monthly rounds to the homes of his wealthy patrons.

Langland describes himself, though perhaps with some ironic hyperbole, as a singular character, apparently very tall and lean (his nickname is "Long Will"), wandering about dressed as a beggar, showing little respect for the wealthy who liked to parade their own importance, and spending time scribbling verses. Some considered him mad. Certainly it is true that he spent a good deal of time writing and rewriting *Piers Plowman*. He seems to have labored some thirty years, refining the poem and perhaps was still revising it at his death; the last two passus of the C version show little change from those of the B Text, suggesting that Langland may have died before he finished the last revision. To be sure, the date of Langland's death is even less certain than that of his birth; it is unlikely that the poet survived his century. If, as has often been disputed, Langland was the author of the poem *Richard the Redeless*, he was still alive in 1395.

ANALYSIS

PIERS PLOWMAN

Modern criticism has begun to concentrate, for the first time, on the artistry of *Piers Plowman*. Elizabeth

Salter (*Piers Plowman*, 1962) has pointed out how, with the return of so many modern poets to the free accentual verse similar to Langland's, readers are now more able to respond to the verse of *Piers Plowman*. Further, with the contemporary conviction that everyday themes and language are valid subjects for poetry, readers have become more sympathetic to some of Langland's finest passages, which treat everyday experiences in the vocabulary of the common man.

Yet it seems, ultimately, that the first readers of *Piers Plowman* were most correct: The poem's basic intent is didactic, and, for Langland, all artistry was secondary to the message he was trying to convey. Perhaps his greatest achievement is the theme itself, which is at once as simple and as complex as any in literature. Beginning as the Dreamer's simple question in Passus II (B Text), "How may I save my soul?," the theme turns into a multilayered search for individual salvation, for the perfection of contemporary society, for a mystical union with God, and for a way to put mystical vision to practical use in perfecting society. These searches are set against varied landscapes ranging from the contemporary world to the inner world of the soul, across biblical history, through Hell to Armageddon. For contemporary critics concerned largely with structure in literature, Langland's most remarkable feat is his ability, in spite of real or apparent digressions and inconsistencies, to put a poem of the encyclopedic range and depth of *Piers Plowman* together into a structured whole.

Piers Plowman is a difficult poem. One is not likely to find a more complex poem, nor one which poses quite so many problems. An entrance to the poem might best be achieved by an examination of those problems—problems of text, of form, of structure, and of interpretation—one at a time.

First, the poem exists in three totally different versions. The earliest version, known as the A Text, must have been written, or at least begun, about 1362, since it alludes to such things as the plague of 1361 and a certain great wind storm known to have occurred in January, 1362. This first version is a poem of some 2,500 lines, consisting of a prologue and eleven books or "passus." In the second, or B Text, William Langland revised his poem and added nine new passus, expanding *Piers Plowman* to more than 7,200 lines. This version must

have been written about 1377, since the fable of the cat and mice in the prologue seems to allude to events which occurred in the parliament of 1376-1377.

Langland thoroughly revised the poem one more time, increasing its length by another hundred or so lines, and this final version is known as the C Text. It contains no prologue but twenty-three passus. W. W. Skeat dated the C Text about 1393, believing that it reflected the differences which began in 1392 between the citizens of London and the king. An earlier date may be more accurate, however, since Thomas Usk seems to refer to the C version of *Piers Plowman* in his *Testament of Love* (1387), and Usk died in 1388. In the C version the poet often attempts to clarify ambiguities, and at times eliminates some of the social criticisms. He also eliminates some of the more dramatic scenes in B, such as Piers's tearing of Truth's pardon in Passus VII. Although the C Text may represent the author's ultimate intent, and although accurate critical texts of the C Text have made it more universally available, the vast majority of scholars and readers have preferred the B version, and so all references to the poem in this analysis are to George Kane and E. Talbot Donaldson's edition of the B Text.

PIERS PLOWMAN AND THE ALLITERATIVE REVIVAL

Having established the B version as the poem, however, one is not at all sure what sort of poem it is. *Piers Plowman* falls simultaneously into several categories, none of which defines it completely. It is, first, a poem of the alliterative revival. Poetry in English had originally been alliterative and followed strict metrical rules. When English verse began to appear once more in the west and north in the mid-fourteenth century, poets attempted to follow this native tradition. The Middle English alliterative line, however, was much freer than it had been in Old English: Lines had no fixed syllabic content, the number of stressed syllables was not always four, as in classic alliterative verse, but might be three, five, or six, and the alliterated sound was not always governed by the third stressed syllable, as in classic alliterative verse. The alliterative poets did, however, tend to rely on a special poetic diction and to decorate their poetry with elaborate rhetorical figures recommended by the poetic manuals of the time, such as that of Geoffrey of Vinsauf.

Langland, however, differed markedly from other alliterative poets. Possibly because his audience was not the aristocracy, he had no interest in elaborate rhetoric or poetic diction but rather used simple vocabulary and employed only those figures of speech which involved repetition, since his goal was to get his message across clearly. Langland did, however, continue and even furthered the trend toward a freer alliterative line, employing various rhythmic patterns as they suited the tone of his poem, sometimes alliterating a different sound in the second half-line than he had in the first, sometimes not alliterating at all, and often tossing in Latin quotations as nonalliterating half-lines. The overall tendency of Langland's verse, despite the Latin, is toward a naturalness of vocabulary and rhythm.

PIERS PLOWMAN AS SERMON LITERATURE

Piers Plowman also has a great deal in common with sermon literature. G. R. Owst saw Langland as drawing primarily from the pulpits of England his message of social reform, justice for the poor, condemnation for those who pervert the great institution of the Church, and a recommendation of love and work as opposed to revolution. Elizabeth Salter sees Langland's emphasis on teaching rather than fine writing and his use of metaphors and imagery in a purely functional manner to illustrate his material as consistent with sermon literature; however, *Piers Plowman*, in scope and complexity, goes far beyond even the most elaborate sermons, so again the label "sermon in verse" is inadequate.

PIERS PLOWMAN AS A DREAM VISION

The poem also takes the form of a dream vision. For the Middle Ages, influenced as they were by the biblical stories of Joseph and Daniel and by Macrobius's famous commentary of Cicero's "Somnium Scipionis" ("Dream of Scipio"), dreams were profoundly important, and could often take on oracular significance. Thus, beginning with Guillaume de Lorris Jean de Meung's thirteenth century *Le Roman de la rose* (*The Romance of the Rose*, 1370), there arose a genre of poetry containing a dreamer-narrator who relates his vision, which may be full of signs which the reader must interpret. Once again, however, *Piers Plowman* transcends the bounds of the form, for Langland writes not of one vision but of many. There are, in fact, ten separate visions in the poem, two of which are represented as dreams within dreams. More-

over, in contrast with the more typical medieval love visions, Langland seriously presents the visions as divine revelations. Perhaps Morton Bloomfield is more accurate, then, in describing *Piers Plowman* as an *apocalypse*: a literary work in the form of a vision revealing a divine message and deeply criticizing contemporary society.

A knowledge of its genre may help to explain some of the confusion in the structure of the poem. Anyone reading *Piers Plowman* for the first time must be struck by the bewildering plunges into and out of scenes, the unannounced and unexpected comings and goings of a multitude of new characters, the apparently unrelated sequence of events which seem to follow no cause-and-effect relationships. It could be argued that a dream vision would follow the logic of dream—of association and symbol rather than induction and deduction; this may be a partial answer. One could also say that the poem is not intended to be a narrative, which would follow a cause-and-effect pattern. It has, rather (like a sermon), a thematic unity. The Dreamer asks in the beginning, "What must I do to save my soul?," and the theme which unites the poem is the answer to that question. Essentially, the unifying motif is the quest for the answer, a quest which becomes a pilgrimage of the individual to God. Significantly, Langland calls the divisions of his poem *passus*, or "steps"—each new incident is another step toward the goal of the quest.

THE VISIO SECTION

Structurally, *Piers Plowman* is divided into two sections, the "Visio" and the "Vita." The *Visio* section depicts the world as it is, introduces the main themes, and prepares the way for the search which follows in the *Vita*. The narrator, Will (a persona for William Langland, but also a personification of the human will), falls asleep and relates his dream of a "fair field full of folk"—the people of Middle Earth as they work out their lives between heaven (a Tower of Truth) and hell (a dark dungeon). The Holy Church appears to Will as a lady and discourses on the fall of Lucifer and on love as the way to Truth. When the Dreamer asks how he may recognize falsehood, he is shown a series of scenes involving Lady Meed and her proposed marriage, first to Falsehood, then to Conscience. Lady Meed is the representation of *cupiditas*, the opposite of love: She is the love of earthly reward, and when she is driven out by Conscience and Reason, it represents the possibility of man's controlling his desire for worldly wealth by following the dictates of reason and conscience. In Will's second dream, Reason gives a sermon inspiring the people to repent, and there follows Langland's noted portrayal of the confession of the seven deadly sins. The people then begin a pilgrimage in search of Truth; here Piers the Plowman makes his first appearance, offering to guide them to Truth. First, however, Piers must plow his half-acre. The implied moral is that the needs of the body must be taken care of but that the will should desire no more than what is of material necessity.

The pilgrimage to Truth never takes place. Truth sends Piers a pardon, saying that those who do well will be saved. When a priest tells Piers that this is no pardon at all, Piers tears up the paper in anger. The point of this scene seems to be lost in obscurity. Robert Worth Frank considers the scene an attack on papal indulgences: The true "pardon" is God's command to do well. The priest, on the other hand, supports the idea of papal indulgences, which Piers angrily rejects by tearing the parchment, symbolically tearing up paper pardons from Rome. In a later interpretation, scholar Denise N. Baker denied that Piers's pardon is a pardon at all. The scene, according to Baker, reflects the Nominalist-Augustinian controversy of the fourteenth century, which concerned man's ability to do good works. The Augustinian position was that man was unable to do good works without God's grace, and Piers's tearing up of the pardon is Langland's emblem of man's dependence on God's gift of grace. Whichever interpretation is correct, Piers decides to leave plowing and begin a life of prayer and penance in order to search for Do-Well.

THE VITA SECTION

The *Vita* section of the poem is divided into three parts: the lives of Do-Well, Do-Better, and Do-Best. With the abandonment of the people's search for Truth, it is apparent that society cannot be reformed corporately but only on an individual basis. Will goes on an individual quest for the three degrees of doing well, for three grades of Christian perfection. The life of Do-Well is confusing: In the third dream, Will confronts his own faculties (Thought, Intelligence, Imagination),

as well as guides such as Study, Clergy, and Scripture. In the meantime, Will has a dream-within-a-dream wherein he follows Fortune for forty-five years. After he wakes, Will falls asleep again, and in a fifth vision, led by Patience and Conscience, he meets Haukyn, the Active Man, whose coat (his soul) is terribly stained with sin.

The sixth vision, the life of Do-Better, begins with Will's discourse with Anima, who rebukes Will for vainly seeking knowledge and extols the virtue of charity. Will falls into another, deeper, vision, in which he sees Piers Plowman as guardian of the Tree of Charity; sees Abraham, Moses, and the Good Samaritan as the personifications of Faith, Hope, and Charity; and learns about the Holy Trinity. In the eighth vision, the climax of the life of Do-Better and of the poem, the Dreamer witnesses the passion of Christ, sees Christ jousting in the arms of Piers Plowman, witnesses the Harrowing of Hell, a debate between the four daughters of God, and the Resurrection.

The two final dreams present the life of Do-Best. Piers Plowman is now Christ's vicar on earth. The Holy Spirit descends, bestowing gifts on the Christian body, enabling Piers to plow the field of the world. Conscience, seeing the Antichrist preparing to attack, directs all Christians to build a fortress, the Church of Unity, but the Christians are unprepared for battle. In the final vision, the Antichrist attacks. Conscience makes the mistake of letting a Friar into Unity, whose easy confessions corrupt the Church, and the people lose all fear. Conscience then vows to become a pilgrim and search for Piers Plowman to help in the fight, and the quest begins anew as the Dreamer awakes.

The poem is unified by the repetition of various themes. Salter gives the example of the recurring themes of the nature and function of sin, which is introduced in the section on Lady Meed, expanded upon in the confession of the seven deadly sins, restated in the picture of Haukyn's coat, and returned to again as the sins assist the Antichrist in the final attack on Unity. Even so, the nature and function of love in the universe, as it pertains to personal salvation and the reform of society, is the chief theme of the poem; and that theme is inextricably linked with the chief unifying motif of the poem, Piers the Plowman in his many incarnations.

ALLEGORICAL INTERPRETATIONS OF PIERS PLOWMAN

Deciding precisely what Piers signifies is part of the last and largest problem of the poem, that of interpretation. It is obvious that Langland's chief vehicle of expression in *Piers Plowman* is allegory, but it is unclear precisely how to read the allegory. Scholar Robert Worth Frank calls the kind of allegory which is typical of Langland "personification-allegory," which, he says, generally involves a single translation of the character's *name* (such as "Study," "Reason," "Scripture") into the abstract quality which it denotes. In this sense, the characters are "literal." It is a mistake to read more into the allegory than the form allows. In practice, however, this does not seem to work. "Sloth," for example, is simply sloth—one need inquire no further—but the more important characters, such as Do-Well, Do-Better, and Do-Best, are obviously much more complicated and seem to have multiple meanings.

An alternative approach to the allegory is that of D. W. Robertson and Bernard Huppé, who, in applying medieval exegetical criticism to literary texts, see a four-fold interpretation of the allegory. In discussing the complex symbol of the Tree of Charity, for example, they say that it allegorically represents the just; anagogically, Christ on the cross; and tropologically, the individual Christian. The difficulty with this approach is its rigidity: Some things are simply meant to be taken literally, while others may have multitudes of meanings far beyond these four.

A more beneficial approach to the meaning of these symbols is Salter's, which emphasizes a more open and flexible reading; here the reader is receptive to various sorts of significations, not necessarily in any exact order or category. The two most puzzling and multifaceted allegorical symbols are the three lives and Piers himself.

Do-Well, Do-Better, and Do-Best have been most often identified with the active, the contemplative, and the mixed lives. This may make more sense to modern readers if they realize, as T. P. Dunning notes, that the active life in the Middle Ages denotes not manual labor but rather the active practice of virtue, the works of prayer and devotion to which Piers devotes himself at the end of the *Visio*. This is the active life conceived of as the first stage of the spiritual life, and in the *Vita* it involves, first, the Dreamer's search through his own faculties, the emergence from intellectual error and then, with the repentance of Haukyn, the rejection of moral disorder. Do-Better would then represent the contemplative life, in which the Dreamer actually experiences a kind of union with God in a firsthand vision of Christ's passion. Do-Best, however, represents the mixed life, in which the individual must return to life in the world and, with the assistance of the Holy Spirit, work for the reform of society: Charity is not limited to love of the individual for God but includes love for others as well.

At the same time, the three lives may suggest the mystical theme of the soul seeking God, where Do-Well represents the purgative state and Do-Better the stage at which the mystic, like the Dreamer, achieves his illumination in a direct vision of God. For the mystic, however, there is no final unity in this world; he, like Conscience in the end, must continue the search and work toward another partial union. Do-Best reveals the practical results of illumination, which are in the service of others.

The three lives, then, suggest at least these things, and more, but Piers's meaning is more obscure. He appears in the poem only occasionally, but his presence dominates the action at crucial points. In the *Visio*, after the confession of the sins, Piers steps in, announcing that he is a friend and servant of Truth, and offering to lead all on a pilgrimage to him. First, however, he must plow his half-acre, and he organizes all the people to help with the work, thus establishing an ordered society in this world. At the end of the *Visio*, he receives the pardon from Truth for himself and his followers, which he tears up, pledging to leave his plow and search for Do-Well.

In the Do-Well section, Piers is mentioned by Clergy (Passus XIII) as one who preaches the primacy of love as opposed to learning. In Do-Better (Passus XV), Anima identifies Piers with Christ by means of a cryptic Latin comment about "Peter, that is Christ." In Passus XVI, Piers is warder of the Tree of Charity, which he explains to the Dreamer. The tree's fruit, identified as the patriarchs and prophets, is stolen by the devil, whom Piers chases, armed with a stave symbolizing Christ. Piers is then shown teaching Jesus the art of healing. At the climax, Christ fights for the souls of men, the fruit of Piers the Plowman, clad in Piers's arms.

In Do-Best, Piers returns to the poem. First the Dreamer sees a confused image in which Christ himself seems to be Piers, stained with blood and bearing a cross. The Holy Spirit then makes Piers the Plowman his vicar on earth, and Piers founds the Church, dispensing grace in the form of the eucharist, behaves like God in his charity to all, and then disappears.

THE FIGURE OF PIERS PLOWMAN

All this presents a confused figure who seems at times to be the symbol of moral integrity, at times Christ himself, and at the end perhaps the ideal pope whom conscience searches for to restore the corrupt and divided Church of the fourteenth century. The eminent literary historian Nevill Coghill thought that Piers personified Do-Well, Do-Better, and Do-Best successively. Later, Barbara Raw showed that Piers's career in the poem depicts the restoration of the divine image in man, somewhat distorted with the Fall but still present and restored at Christ's incarnation. According to Augustine and Aquinas, the restoration of this image took place in three stages, which may parallel Do-Well, Do-Better, and Do-Best. In Do-Better, Piers becomes the image of Christ because Christ has taken human form, Piers's arms. In Do-Best, Piers embodies the restored image of God in man: He has become like God. Salter sees Piers similarly: When Piers describes the way to Truth in Passus V, he declares that people will find Truth's dwelling in their own hearts. Piers represents this divine element in man, the Truth of God as it exists in man, and as the poem reaches its climax, it is revealed that God *is* to be found in man, as the man Piers becomes godlike. This, then, is Langland's ultimate message, which in spite of all the problems with *Piers Plowman* can still be stated with some certainty: Human beings bear the stamp of the image of God and can, through Christ, achieve Do-Best with Piers the Plowman.

BIBLIOGRAPHY

Alford, John A., ed. *A Companion to "Piers Plowman."* Berkeley: University of California Press, 1988. Contains nine essays on such subjects as the historical and theological context of Langland's *Piers Plowman*, literary and intellectual influences on the poet, and the text and language of the poem. Also includes an excellent introduction to the poem and its shape. Most essays provide good general overviews of the various scholarly opinions on the subjects covered and each essay includes abundant bibliographical details.

Brewer, Charlotte. *Editing "Piers Plowman": The Evolution of the Text.* New York: Cambridge University Press, 1996. An account of the more than fifty editions of the poem which have appeared since 1550. Brewer examines the lives and motivations of the various editors and the relationships between each successive edition.

Hewett-Smith, Kathleen M., ed. *William Langland's "Piers Plowman": A Book of Essays.* New York: Routledge, 2001. A collection of new critical essays examining the relevance of *Piers Plowman* to contemporary literary theory and to fourteenth century culture and ideology. Includes bibliographical references and index.

Krochalis, Jean, and Edward Peters, eds. *The World of "Piers Plowman."* Philadelphia: University of Pennsylvania Press, 1975. An interesting examination of the historical, intellectual, and social context in which Langland wrote. The editors provide a multitude of Middle English primary sources, from sermons to statutes to royal proclamations, as illustrations of Langland's world. Each general section, and many of the individual works, are prefaced with informative introductory passages. Not all spellings are modernized, and, despite marginal glosses, some texts may be difficult for the beginner. Still, this work offers valuable insight into the currents of thought in Langland's day.

Langland, William. *Piers Plowman: An Alliterative Verse Translation.* Edited and translated by E. Talbot Donaldson. New York: W. W. Norton, 1990. Donaldson's translation of *Piers Plowman* into modern English retains the alliterative qualities of Langland's verse while making it easily accessible to the reader with little or no knowledge of Middle English. Contains helpful glosses and margin notes and a useful list of suggestions for further reading.

_____. *The Vision of Piers Plowman: A Complete Edition of the B-Text.* Edited by A. V. C. Schmidt. London: J. M. Dent & Sons, 1978. Although this is primarily an untranslated edition of one version of

Langland's great work, the concise but thorough and accessible introduction and the excellent, copious commentary make this a valuable tool for the student of Langland. Commentary is divided into two sections: textual/lexical and literary/historical. Marginal glosses of words and phrases within the text are generous and will be enormously helpful to the student interested in a close examination of the text.

Martin, Priscilla. *Piers Plowman: The Field and the Tower.* London: Macmillan, 1979. The author focuses on irony and allegory in *Piers Plowman* and on the difficulties and paradoxes that result for both Langland and the reader as a result of the use of these literary devices. A good examination of Christian allegory is included.

Jay Ruud;
bibliography updated by the editors

SIDNEY LANIER

Born: Macon, Georgia; February 3, 1842
Died: Lynn, North Carolina; September 7, 1881

PRINCIPAL POETRY
Poems, 1877
Poems of Sidney Lanier, 1884 (Mary Day Lanier, editor)

OTHER LITERARY FORMS

Although Sidney Lanier is remembered primarily as a poet, he wrote in a surprising variety of genres. His *The Science of English Verse* (1880) is a handbook of prosody which is still valuable as a discussion of poetic theory and technique despite its overemphasis on the importance of sound. It was originally meant to be a textbook for Lanier's students at The Johns Hopkins University, and in fact his lecture notes were collected and published posthumously as *The English Novel* (1883) and *Shakspere and His Forerunners* (1902). Lanier's first book, however, was an autobiographical novel titled *Tiger-Lilies* (1867), which drew upon his Civil War experiences and his reading of the German Romantics.

His second published volume was *Florida: Its Scenery, Climate, and History* (1875), a travel book commissioned by the Atlantic Coast Line Railway and the standard guide to Florida for many years. Lanier was especially successful at revising classics, such as *The Boy's King Arthur* (1880) for juvenile audiences—a literary endeavor which appealed to his strong romantic sensibility while providing a welcome source of income. Finally, Lanier produced a remarkable number of essays, including "Retrospects and Prospects" (1871) and the four "Sketches of India" (1876), which were originally published in magazines. Lanier's writings are most readily available in *The Centennial Edition of the Works of Sidney Lanier* (1945).

ACHIEVEMENTS

Sidney Lanier was the first distinctively Southern poet to achieve a truly national recognition and acceptance. This is an honor usually accorded to Edgar Allan Poe (1809-1849), but unlike Poe, who was born in Boston, spent several of his formative years in Britain, and did much of his literary work in the Northeast, Lanier was a Georgian by birth who spent his entire life in the South. Nevertheless, by virtue of such works as "The Centennial Meditation of Columbia" and "Psalm of the West," Lanier came to be regarded as a spokesman for the American, rather than only the Southern, experience; yet, by one of those paradoxes of literary history, at the same time that he achieved this national status, Lanier won for Southern writers a degree of respect and credibility which was unprecedented in American literature and which is still evident today.

Lanier was one of the earliest American poets to use dialect in his verse, most notably the "Georgia cracker" speech utilized in "Thar's More in the Man than Thar Is in the Land." In this regard, Lanier was an early practitioner of "local-color" writing, that literary movement which flourished at the end of the nineteenth century. Imbued with a strong social conscience, Lanier was noted for his poetic treatment of current economic difficulties. In poems such as "The Symphony," he pleaded that love and music be used as antidotes for the miseries generated by "Trade" (read "industry and commercialism"), and in "Corn" and "Thar's More in the Man than Thar Is in the Land" he offered a practical solution to the economic problems of the postwar South: the cultivation of corn and grain instead of cotton. Lanier was also a tireless poetic experimenter. He is to be recognized for his ambitious attempts at metrical innovation (see "The Revenge of Hamish," an experiment in the use of loga-oedic dactyls), as well as his attempts to achieve heightened musical effects in his verse (see, for example, "Song of the Chattahoochee"). He also is remembered for his *The Science of English Verse* (1880), a textbook which is still interesting and perceptive, despite Lanier's unfortunate attempt to formulate a "science" of prosody which is analogous to musical notation.

Lanier is frequently cited as an example of a writer who could have achieved a great deal had he lived longer. There is no question that at the time of his death at age thirty-nine, his career was just getting under way. As Charles Anderson observes, Lanier wrote 164 poems; of these, 104 were written in two periods of intense creativity (1865-1868; 1874-1878), with the latter period producing his best work—58 major poems. At the time of his death Lanier had made plans for at least three more volumes of poetry, as is clear from the so-called "Poem Outlines" (see the *Centennial Edition*).

BIOGRAPHY

Sidney Clopton Lanier was born on February 3, 1842, in Macon, Georgia, a small city which was at the time the thriving center of the cotton industry. Both his parents were of good, long-established Virginia families who had settled comfortably into the urban, middle-class lifestyle of antebellum Macon. His father, Robert Sampson Lanier, was a graduate of Virginia's Randolph-Macon College and a practicing attorney; his mother, Mary Jane Anderson Lanier, was a devout Scottish Presbyterian who fostered in her children a deep appreciation for the writings of Sir Walter Scott. Sidney was the eldest child, with a sister Gertrude (born 1846) and a brother Clifford (born 1844), who occasionally collaborated with Sidney and who earned a minor literary reputation with the publication of his novel *Thorn-Fruit* (1867).

Lanier was a happy, bookish child noted for his good behavior and piety as well as for his love of literature, including works by Edward Bulwer-Lytton, John Keats, and the perennially popular Scott. He also demonstrated

exceptional musical ability at a very early age and eventually became expert at playing the violin, guitar, organ, and flute. In certain respects, Lanier's musical talent was unfortunate: The distinctive musicality of his verse too often overpowers the meaning, and his desire to become a professional musician often diverted his time and energies away from his career as a poet. At any rate, music was an integral part of his formal education. Evidently, Macon had no public-supported schools during Lanier's youth, so he was educated at private academies run by local clergymen. It is unclear how solid an education he received in this fashion, but at a time when only one out of thirteen adult white Southerners could read or write, it was certainly adequate to gain him admittance into a relatively new Presbyterian college, Oglethorpe University. Lanier matriculated at the age of fifteen: He was a good student, being especially adept at mathematics, and was named covaledictorian of his class. He returned to Oglethorpe in the fall after his graduation to serve as a tutor, a position secured for him by Professor James Woodrow. Woodrow (the uncle of Woodrow Wilson) possessed a degree of open-mindedness and cosmopolitanism which was unusual for Oglethorpe and something of a revelation for Lanier.

Before Lanier could explore the new worlds opened to him by Woodrow, however, the Civil War broke out. Lanier joined the Confederate Army in June, 1861, serving first as a private with the Macon Volunteers and later in the Mounted Signal Service. In 1864, while on signal duty on a blockade-runner, Lanier was captured and sent to a prison camp at Point Lookout, Maryland. Although Lanier was able to solace himself by playing his flute (which he had smuggled into prison inside his sleeve) and translating German poetry, the months spent at Point Lookout in 1864 and 1865 activated the latent tuberculosis which eventually killed him.

In 1867, Lanier married Mary Day, whom he had met while on furlough in 1863. It was not love at first sight: Lanier, a ladies' man of sorts, did not seem to notice Day until after his current sweetheart, one Gussie Lamar, jilted him. Day, an invalid, reportedly was advised by her physician that a marriage would improve her health (apparently it did: She outlived her husband by half a century, dying in 1931 at the age of eighty-seven). Despite the inauspicious circumstances surrounding the wedding, the marriage was a good one, and Lanier spent much of their fourteen years together attempting simultaneously to support his growing family (four sons), to satisfy his creative urges, and to find relief from his tuberculosis. From 1868 to 1873, he read law and clerked in his father's law office, an occupation for which he was temperamentally ill-suited, and which was all the more intolerable because of his worsening health and the frustration of having no time to write. He spent the winter and spring of 1872 to 1873 in Texas, and the trip, which had been undertaken because of his health, proved beneficial in another way. The Germans who played such a prominent role in San Antonio's cultural life encouraged him to pursue a career in music.

In 1873, with financial assistance from his brother Clifford, Lanier began his career as first flautist with the Peabody Orchestra of Baltimore. An extraordinarily talented player, Lanier was able to maintain his position with the orchestra intermittently for the next seven years. When his musical engagements were completed in the spring of 1874, he went to Sunnyside, Georgia, to spend a few months, and there he was deeply impressed with the region's cornfields. This led to the composition of "Corn," and his career as a poet began in earnest. "Corn," published in *Lippincott's Magazine* in 1875 after a devastating rejection by the *Atlantic Monthly*, was so successful that it resulted in commissioned work (including the guidebook *Florida*) and the opportunity to meet the writer-diplomat Bayard Taylor and Gibson Peacock, the editor of the Philadelphia *Evening Bulletin*, both of whom helped to further Lanier's career. In the first half of 1876, Lanier worked on two long poems: "The Centennial Meditation of Columbia," an assignment for the Philadelphia Centennial Exhibition, secured through the influence of Taylor, and "Psalm of the West," commissioned by the editor of *Lippincott's Magazine*. They are not among his best works ("The Centennial Meditation of Columbia" in particular was roundly criticized for its obscurity), but they did gain Lanier national attention.

In the summer of 1876, the exhausted Lanier moved with his family to a farm in West Chester, Pennsylvania, where he wrote a series of pot-boiling essays. That fall his health broke completely, and the generous Peacock financed a three-month vacation for Lanier in Tampa.

While in Florida, Lanier felt sufficiently well to write eleven poems, including "The Stirrup-Cup," but, homesick for Georgia, he left Tampa in April, 1877. Unsuccessful in his bid for a position in the U.S. Treasury, Lanier attempted to support his wife and children by borrowing from his brother and selling the family silver. He was fortunate enough, however, to be able to resume his position with the Peabody Orchestra. A few months later, in March, 1878, he began an intensive study of English literature at the Peabody Library in Baltimore in the hope that it would lead to a teaching position at The Johns Hopkins University. For once his hope was realized, and in the fall of 1879, he began to teach poetry and the English novel at the new Baltimore university.

The last few years of his life (from approximately 1877 to 1881) were remarkably full and productive. In addition to his research and teaching, Lanier was writing his best-known poems (including "Song of the Chattahoochee" in November, 1877, and "The Marshes of Glynn" in 1878), *The Science of English Verse*, and the series of books for children known as The Boy's Library of Legend and Chivalry. He also had published in 1877 his first and only book of verse, *Poems*, a slim volume (ninety-four pages; ten poems) issued by *Lippincott's Magazine*. The attempt to compress a lifetime's work into a few months was, however, ultimately self-defeating: Lanier's final bout with tuberculosis began late in 1880, and he died in the mountains of North Carolina in September, 1881.

ANALYSIS

Although literary historians are correct in maintaining that Sidney Lanier had only minimal influence on other writers, that influence is most apparent in the post-Civil War interest in the recording of regional dialects. Perhaps taking his cue either from James Russell Lowell's satirical, *The Biglow Papers* (1848, 1867) or Augustus Longstreet's humorous *Georgia Scenes* (1835), Lanier wrote several propagandistic poems in Southern dialect, in which humor was incidental rather than integral.

"THAR'S MORE IN THE MAN THAN THAR IS IN THE LAND"

Works written in dialect, yet serious in intent, were an innovation in American literature, and one of the first such works was Lanier's "Thar's More in the Man than Thar Is in the Land." Written sometime between 1869 and 1871, the poem was originally published in the Macon *Telegraph and Messenger* on February 7, 1871, and thereafter in newspapers throughout the South and Midwest. Lanier reworked a local story into a serious statement of what he personally felt was the soundest strategy for the survival of the postwar South: Resist the temptation to emigrate, and diversify crops.

The poem itself (despite the challenges of the dialect) is unusually straightforward for a work by Lanier, not only because of the paucity of imagery, but more important, because of Lanier's uncharacteristic avoidance of sentimentality. Written in ten sestets, it recounts how a man named Jones (appropriately enough a resident of Jones County, Georgia) was a failure as a farmer. Jones sold his farm to a man named Brown for $1.50 an acre and moved to Texas where ostensibly "cotton would sprout/ By the time you could plant it in the land." The redoubtable Brown "rolled up his breeches and bared his arm" and within five years had become a prosperous farmer, "so fat that he wouldn't weigh." One day while Brown was sitting down to "the bulliest dinner you ever see," Jones showed up, having literally walked back to Georgia to try to find work. Brown fed him and provided the moral of the poem: "'whether men's land was rich or poor/ Thar was more in the *man* than thar was in the *land*.'"

In a region of the United States still suffering from a deep depression fully five years after the war, Lanier's little parable must have been a breath of hope and encouragement. The poem, however, is far more than a paean to the advantages of working hard and staying in Georgia. It is the emphatic statement of an economic reality: Instead of continuing to raise "yallerish cotton" like Jones, one must grow corn and wheat. Thanks to crop diversification, Brown avoided the economic stranglehold which the Northern markets had on King Cotton (and, consequently, on the entire South), while enjoying the self-reliance that comes with raising a crop which one could literally consume. Whether or not the Southern audience noticed the poem's horticultural/economic message, they certainly admired "Thar's More in the Man than Thar Is in the Land," and its

immense popularity was due in part to its qualities as a poem. By virtue of its sing-songy rhythm, the familiar dialect, the predictable rhyme (generally *aabbbc*; the *c* invariably was the word "land"), and the surprisingly subtle humor (such as the broken rhyme "hum-/ Ble in stanza nine"), it was ideally suited to essentially rural, semiliterate readers who were accustomed to a rich oral tradition and who frequently found themselves in situations comparable to that of the unfortunate Jones.

"CORN"

Even the most cursory glance at his letters, poems, and essays reveals that Lanier sincerely regarded poetry as a noble calling, and he resisted the temptation to write broadly popular, potentially remunerative verse. He preferred producing poems that appealed to the finer aspects of individual, regional, or national character, or which expressed his personal views on economic or political matters. There was no affectation inherent in these twin didactic conceptions of poetry, and they were at least partly responsible for the cool reception which his poems often received in his lifetime. Still, Lanier's poems occasionally did manage to achieve some popularity, and only a few years after the regional success of "Thar's More in the Man than Thar Is in the Land," Lanier received his first national attention with "Corn."

"Corn" is a reiteration of the ideas presented in "Thar's More in the Man than Thar Is in the Land," but the two poems are handled in strikingly different ways. Lanier apparently began the composition of "Corn" in July, 1874, while he was staying in the hamlet of Sunnyside, Georgia. Evidently he was especially impressed by the extensive corn fields and the terrain. Unlike "Thar's More in the Man than Thar Is in the Land," this poem was definitely not intended for a semiliterate, rural Southern audience. In format, it is a sterling example of a Cowleyan ode. Unlike the technically rigid "Thar's More in the Man than Thar Is in the Land," "Corn" is irregular in stanza length, line length, and rhythm. It is so heavily enjambed that at first one may not even be conscious of the extraordinary degree to which Lanier relies on rhyme to give his poem coherence. The rhyming couplets and tercets, the eye rhyme ("hardihood"/"food"), and the leonine rhyme

("Thou lustrous stalk, that ne'er mayst walk nor talk") are testimonies to Lanier's fascination with sound—a fascination which, unfortunately, was largely responsible for the charges of obscurity, sentimentality, and even banality which have been leveled against Lanier's poetry throughout the last century.

One need not look beyond the first stanza of "Corn" to understand what these critics have in mind. The persona passes through some woods before he encounters the field of corn, but the little forest, as is typical of Lanier, has been personified and emotionalized to such an embarrassing degree that the first stanza sounds like a sentimentalized psychosexual dream. The leaves which brush the persona's cheek "caress/ Like women's hands"; the "little noises" sound "anon like beatings of a heart/ Anon like talk 'twixt lips not far apart"; and the persona clearly has abandoned himself to the pleasures of the sensuous forest.

The persona proceeds through the concupiscent forest until finally, in stanza three, he encounters the corn itself, which Lanier had intended to be the controlling image of the poem. In one of his more fortunate metaphors, Lanier likens the field of corn to an army, and although at times that metaphor is strained (one stalk functions as the "corn-captain"), what makes it especially appropriate is that there are in fact three "battles" going on in this poem: The corn stalks are competing for soil with the sassafras and brambles, the antebellum "King Cotton" economy is clashing with the new diversified crop system, and Lanier is positing life as a battle with The Poet as its hero and the corn-captain as his symbol. It is apparent, then, that Lanier is attempting to make the battle metaphor operate on at least three levels; although it is an interesting concept and Lanier makes a noble effort to realize it, in the final analysis it simply does not work. Instead of being mutually enriching, the various images result in a confusing clutter. This fundamental technical problem and a host of others are readily apparent to even the most sympathetic reader of "Corn."

In stanza four, the "fieldward-faring eyes" of the persona do not simply look at the corn, but harvest it in his heart. It is characteristic of Lanier that he favors the use of rather grotesque metaphors. What tends to make the metaphor a bit less dubious, however, is that Lanier is

not as interested in the physical corn as he is in the abstract qualities which he believes the corn embodies. Much as people can learn industriousness from bees and contentment from cows, Lanier felt that the cornstalk could teach readers about virtuous living.

One may reasonably question how a technically and thematically weak poem such as "Corn" could possibly attract a national audience. Part of the answer lies in the very matter of technique: At the time he was writing, Lanier was sufficiently innovative to generate interest. The second part of the answer is more a matter of sociology than of poetics. During the Reconstruction period, and in particular during the 1870's when Centennial enthusiasm was running high, there was an impulse toward reconciliation in the United States—an impulse which frequently took the form of Northern readers responding enthusiastically to any piece of writing from, or about, the South. Even though Lanier initially had some difficulty finding Northern periodicals which would publish his work, the fact is that these journals were far more receptive to Southern writers after the Civil War than they were at any time before it. Lanier's career actually came during an ideal time, for he was clearly, insistently a Southern writer, and nowhere is his Southern influence more apparent, perhaps, than in his two best-known poems, "Song of the Chattahoochee" and "The Marshes of Glynn."

"SONG OF THE CHATTAHOOCHEE"

"Song of the Chattahoochee" was written in Baltimore at the end of November, 1877, and its first verifiable publication (December, 1883) was in the *Independent*, a New York-based weekly paper with a wide circulation. It became so popular that for decades it was a staple of elementary school reading books, the only poem by Lanier with which many people were even vaguely familiar. That distinction is a dubious one, for in fact, "Song of the Chattahoochee" is not one of Lanier's better efforts, and yet the very qualities which tend to weaken it were those responsible for its popularity. In typical Lanierian fashion, its most striking feature is its sound. Ostensibly the Chattahoochee River itself is speaking the poem (an earlier version reprinted by F. V. N. Painter in his *Poets of the South*, 1903, is in the third person), and this provides a golden opportunity for Lanier to utilize diction which conveys the sound of moving water. Words featuring liquid consonants and alliteration are so common that at times the poem reads like a tongue-twister: "The willful waterweeds held me thrall,/ The laving laurel turned my tide." This effect is compounded by Lanier's heavy reliance on repetition, not only of individual words but also of phrases: Each of the five stanzas begins and ends with some variation of the opening couplet, "Out of the hills of Habersham, Down the valleys of Hall." Clearly Lanier is seeking to depict moving water onomatopoeically, and to a certain extent he succeeds, but in such a short poem (fifty lines) one simply does not need the phrases "the hills of Habersham" and "the valleys of Hall" repeated ten times each. The effect of soothing musicality which Lanier was trying to create becomes monotonous. It is so overwhelming that the reader may very well fail to detect either the structure of the poem or the theme.

"Song of the Chattahoochee" begins with the river explaining how it rises in Habersham County (in northeastern Georgia) and travels through Hall County on its way to "the plain." In stanza two, the speaker/river provides a catalog of the various small plants which attempt to delay it; stanza three is a catalog of the trees which seek to distract the river; stanza four reveals the rocks and minerals which try either to retard the flowing of the river or to dazzle it with their beauty. Then in stanza five, readers learn why the river resists these sensuous distractions: Compelled by a strong sense of Duty (with a capital *d*), it must both make itself useful through "toil" and allow itself to "be mixed with the main." It is possible to infer that the personified river represents a human being whose life is purposefully active and who willingly acknowledges the "rightness" of death (here conveyed as the merging of one's identity with the vastness of the ocean—an idea explored more fully in "The Marshes of Glynn"); but if this analogy were central to Lanier's purpose, he certainly did not handle it well, and as a result the depiction of the river as "dutiful" seems to be nothing more than a romantic imposition on the part of Lanier.

Despite its didactic impulse, Lanier's poem retained its popularity in elementary schools for many years and, consequently, among several generations of Americans. Brief and strikingly musical, it is ideally suited to introducing poetry to youngsters. "Song of the Chatta-

hoochee" also had the dubious but undeniable advantage of posthumous publication: To be frank, Lanier's career was never stronger than in the years immediately following his early death. Even so, he did enjoy some nationwide popularity in his lifetime, most notably with "The Marshes of Glynn."

"THE MARSHES OF GLYNN"

It is unclear when Lanier began the composition of "The Marshes of Glynn," although it is possible that it had been evolving over at least a three-year period before Lanier actually wrote it in the summer of 1878. The Glynn of the title is Glynn County, Georgia, noted for its salt marshes near the coastal village of Brunswick, a favorite haunt of the Lanier family for many years. Like "Corn," "The Marshes of Glynn" had its origins in Lanier's personal response to a specific element of the Georgia landscape, but it is notably more private and esoteric than that early effort. Both as an artist and as a man, Lanier had changed significantly during the four years following the composition of "Corn." For one thing, he had discovered Walt Whitman. Although Lanier (despite the distinctive sensuality of his imagery) was singularly reticent about sexual matters, he nevertheless was deeply impressed with Whitman's work, even going so far as somehow to amass the requisite five dollars and order a copy of *Leaves of Grass* (1855) from the Good Gray Poet himself. In a letter to Bayard Taylor in February, 1878, Lanier described that book as a source of "real refreshment" to him, and likened its effect, significantly, to "rude salt spray in your face." It is probably no coincidence that Lanier made that comparison only a few months before the composition of "The Marshes of Glynn," for the poem can justifiably be termed Whitmanesque in its remarkable range and sweep.

Lanier also had changed as a result of his discovery of Ralph Waldo Emerson. During his stay in Tampa in the winter of 1877, Lanier apparently read Emerson in earnest, an undertaking at least partly attributable to the precarious state of his health. By the late 1870's, Lanier was finally beginning to admit to himself that the tuberculosis with which he had struggled for a decade would probably kill him within a very few years, as indeed it did. This admission of imminent death, coupled with his lack of orthodox religious faith, apparently generated his interest in Emerson and fostered significant changes in the themes and techniques of his poems. These changes are especially evident in "The Marshes of Glynn," which shows Lanier in far better control of his material than was the case in "Corn."

The two poems begin in a similar fashion with an extensive catalog of the elements one encounters while walking through a forest, but in "The Marshes of Glynn" Lanier has carefully pruned the embarrassingly over-written sensual passages which are so striking in the opening of "Corn." True, he mentions "Virginal shy lights/ Wrought of the leaves to allure to the whispers of vows," but this is as purple a passage as one finds in the opening of "The Marshes of Glynn." Then with remark-able skill, the orientation is shifted from the association of the forest with love to that of religious faith, and from this point on, the rather long ode is devoted to spiritual matters. Unlike the irrelevant opening of "Corn," that of "The Marshes of Glynn" almost immediately presents Lanier's two concerns: the traditional belief that Nature is the great refresher of men's souls, and the contempo-rary Emersonian view that one may find the true God in the natural world. The intimate relationship between na-ture (specifically the forest) and the persona (transpar-ently Lanier himself) is first overtly presented in line 20, and it is at this point that the reader realizes that the pre-vious nineteen lines were actually an exceptionally elab-orate apostrophe to the forest. The persona's love for the beauties and mysteries of the wood is palpable, and that love is conveyed through Lanier's characteristic compound adjectives ("myriad-cloven"), alliteration ("beautiful-braided"), and assonance ("oaks"/"woven").

It is made abundantly clear, however, that the forest experience represents merely a phase in the persona's life which has now passed, a phase which was associ-ated with "the riotous noon-day sun." It is impossible to determine whether this represents a point in the per-sona's maturation (most likely his young manhood) or an earlier moment in his shifting orientation (when his concerns were more material or "earthly" than spiritual), or a combination of the two; but perhaps this is a moot point. What matters is that one phase of his existence (represented by the forest) is over, and that a new one (represented initially by the marshy beach) has begun. In keeping with the previous association of the forest with

noon, the new locale is associated with the setting sun, whose "slant yellow beam" seems "Like a lane into heaven." That this sunset is to be associated with an overwhelming spiritual experience (most likely death) is clear from the persona's observation that "now, unafraid, I am fain to face/ The vast sweet visage of space"—a space which a few lines later is depicted, significantly, as the "terminal" sea. Although the persona finds himself "drawn" to "the edge of the wood . . ./ Where the gray beach glimmering runs," he willingly submits and soon finds himself "Free/ By a world of marsh that borders a world of sea."

There is nothing even remotely frightening about the beach: It is gray (reportedly Lanier's favorite color), and it forms the transitional zone between something the persona has voluntarily rejected and something which he deeply desires. The Emersonian element of the poem is most evident as the persona reacts to the new freedom of the beach. At this point, the persona conveys his reac-tion to his spiritual freedom through two similes. First, "As the marsh hen secretly builds on the watery sod,/ Behold I will build me a nest on the greatness of God," and he also will fly as she does; second, "By so many roots as the marsh-grass sends in the sod/ I will heartily lay me a-hold on the greatness of God." The two meta-phors are perfect in their appropriateness and simplicity, and they usher in the third movement of the poem: the shift from sunset to night, and from marshy beach to ocean. Much as the persona's identity was blurred with that of the beach as he likened himself to the bird and grass, the identity of the beach is blended with that of the ocean as the tide rises, until finally "the sea and the marsh are one" and "it is night." The poem has pro-gressed so steadily to this climax that the final stanza sounds almost like a postscript.

It is unfortunate that Lanier did not live long enough to complete the series of projected "Hymns of the Marshes" of which "The Marshes of Glynn" was to be only a small part. Experimental in subject, scope, and technique (note the logaoedic dactyls and the long, loose Whitmanesque lines), "The Marshes of Glynn" is one of Lanier's best poems, revealing an intellectual maturity and a technical expertise which, had they been allowed to flower, might well have placed him among the fore-most American poets of the nineteenth century.

OTHER MAJOR WORKS

LONG FICTION: *Tiger-Lilies*, 1867.

NONFICTION: "Retrospects and Prospects," 1871; *Florida: Its Scenery, Climate, and History*, 1875; "Sketches of India," 1876; *The Science of English Verse*, 1880; *The English Novel*, 1883; *Shakspere and His Forerunners*, 1902.

CHILDREN'S LITERATURE: *The Boy's King Arthur*, 1880; *The Boy's Mabinogion*, 1881.

MISCELLANEOUS: *The Centennial Edition of the Works of Sidney Lanier*, 1945 (10 volumes).

BIBLIOGRAPHY

De Bellis, Jack Angelo. *Sidney Lanier*. New York: Twayne, 1972. De Bellis examines Lanier's growth by analyzing his growing awareness of the ways to make poetry express the morality of feeling. "The Symphony" is treated as a poem in which Lanier discovered how to symbolize the conflict between feeling and thought, and how to inject great feeling into the poem via the musicality of his verse. "The Marshes of Glynn" and "Sunrise" are shown to be rhythm experiments. Supplemented by indexes.

Gabin, Jane S. *A Living Minstrelsy: The Poetry and Music of Sidney Lanier*. Macon, Ga.: Mercer University Press, 1985. This study maintains that Lanier is unique in American literature because he is the only poet who is both active and accomplished in music. Gabin believes his poetry developed as a direct result of his pursuit of musical interests and that his achievements and innovations came as a direct result of his exposure to innovation in musical composition. Includes a bibliography and an index.

Mims, Edwin. *Sidney Lanier*. 1905. Reprint. Port Washington, N.Y.: Kennikat Press, 1968. Mims's study relies heavily on Lanier's letters and stresses his modernity. He suggests that the advances the poet made in "The Marshes of Glynn" and *The Science of English Verse* were negated by his weak health and short life. Supplemented by an introduction and illustrations.

Parks, Edd Winfield. *Sidney Lanier: The Man, the Poet, the Critic*. Athens: University of Georgia Press, 1968. Originally delivered as a Lamar Lecture at Wesleyan College. "The Man" provides a biographical sketch that adheres to authenticated facts. "The Poet" suggests obstacles that prevented Lanier from becoming a major poet, although his later poems are seen to override these weaknesses. "The Critic" reveals his inconsistencies as a critic by discussing his moralistic view of fiction.

Starke, Aubrey Harrison. *Sidney Lanier: A Biographical and Critical Study*. New York: Russel & Russel, 1964. Starke interprets all Lanier's work in the factual context of his life. He maintains that Lanier was sensitive to the development of the "New South" and was therefore a forerunner of the Fugitive-Agrarian writers, who responded to the ways materialistic society had replaced a traditional way of life. Starke says that in his poems, Lanier finds refuge by responding to music and nature. Supplemented by full notes, a documentation, and a bibliography.

White, Donna R. *A Century of Welsh Myth in Children's Literature*. Westport, Conn.: Greenwood Press, 1998. A chronological study of the adaptations in children's books of the Welsh legends collectively known as the *Mabinogi*. Includes a discussion of Lanier's *The Boy's Mabinogion*.

Alice Hall Petry;
bibliography updated by the editors

PHILIP LARKIN

Born: Coventry, England; August 9, 1922
Died: Hull, England; December 2, 1985

PRINCIPAL POETRY

The North Ship, 1945, 1966
The Less Deceived, 1955
The Whitsun Weddings, 1964
High Windows, 1974
Collected Poems, 1988

OTHER LITERARY FORMS

Although Philip Larkin is thought of today primarily as a poet, his first literary successes were novels: *Jill* (1946, 1964) and *A Girl in Winter* (1947). The two were widely acclaimed for their accomplished style, accurate dialogue, and subtle characterization. *Jill* was valued highly for its intimate look at wartime Oxford. The protagonist in each is an outsider who encounters great difficulty in attempting to fit into society, and the two novels explore themes of loneliness and alienation to which Larkin returns time and again in his later poetry. Larkin wrote comparatively little about literature and granted few interviews. His literary essays were collected into *Required Writings: Miscellaneous Pieces, 1955-1982* (1984). He also wrote extensively on jazz, chiefly in his reviews for the *Daily Telegraph*, and a number of those pieces appear in the volume *All What Jazz: A Record Diary, 1961-1968* (1970). His opinions of jazz works are frequently instructive for the reader who wishes to understand his views on poetry, particularly his comments on what he saw as the "modernist" jazz of Charlie Parker, which, like all modernism, concentrates on technique while violating the truth of human existence. True to his precepts, Larkin eschewed, throughout his career, technical fireworks in favor of a poetic that reflects the language of the people. He edited *New Poems*, 1958, with Louis MacNeice and Bonamy Dobrée, and he was chosen to compile *The Oxford Book of Twentieth-Century English Verse* (1973).

Philip Larkin

ACHIEVEMENTS

Few poets succeeded as Philip Larkin did in winning a large audience and critical respect for such a small body of poetry, and indeed his success may be attributable in part to the rate at which he wrote poems. Because he brought out, according to his own estimate, only three to five poems a year, he could give each one the meticulous attention required to build extremely tight, masterful verse. As a result, each of his slim volumes contains numerous poems that immediately catch the reader's attention for their precise yet colloquial diction.

His chief contribution to British poetry may well be his sustained determination to work in conventional forms and colloquial, even vulgar and coarse, language. In this attempt, as in his ironic self-deprecation and his gloomy outlook, he resembles Robert Frost. Also like Frost, he worked consciously against the modernist poetics of Wallace Stevens, T. S. Eliot, Ezra Pound, and their heirs, the poetics of disjunction and image. Most of

Larkin's poetry demonstrates a distrust of symbolic and metaphorical language, and a reliance instead on discursive verse. His insistence on plain language reflects a belief in the importance of tradition, a faith in the people who remain in touch with the land, and a suspicion of modern society, urban development, and technological advancement. Larkin stands as the chief example among his contemporaries of the line of counter-modernist poetry running not from William Butler Yeats and the Symbolists but from Thomas Hardy and Rudyard Kipling, for both of whom he had great admiration.

Larkin's popularity also results, in part, from his speaking not only as one of the people but for them as well. For all its bleakness and irony, or perhaps because of it, his poetry represents the attitudes of a segment of the British population that found itself with greatly diminished expectations following World War II; institutions were losing their traditional value and function, and the problems of empire (the crowning achievements of those institutions) were rushing home to roost. His poetry represents a search for meaning within the bewildering complexity of the twentieth century.

BIOGRAPHY

The Englishness of Philip Larkin's poetry is decidedly provincial; his England does not revolve around London, and in fact, there is a marked suspicion of the capital and the cosmopolitan urbanity it represents. From his diction to the frequency with which his speakers are seated in cars or trains traveling through the countryside, his poems reflect the provincialism of his life. Larkin was born August 9, 1922, in Coventry, where his father served as city treasurer throughout his childhood. He described his childhood as a bore and not worth mentioning, suggesting that no biography of him need begin before he turned twenty-one. Although he was not a particularly good student at the King Henry VII School in Coventry, he matriculated at St. John's College, Oxford, in 1940, hoping to get in a year of school before he was called into the military. As it eventually turned out, he failed his Army physical and stayed in college, graduating with first-class honors in 1943. His time at Oxford had a profound effect upon the youthful Larkin; in the introduction to *Jill*, he suggests that the war radically diminished the students' grand view of themselves, and this sense of reduced importance stuck with him in his poetry. Perhaps even more crucial to his development, though, were his friendships with budding writers Bruce Montgomery (Edmund Crispin) and Kingsley Amis. The Amis-Larkin friendship seems to have influenced both men, and their early writings share many attitudes and themes.

While at the university, Larkin published poems in the undergraduate magazines and in the anthology *Poetry in Wartime* (1942). (He had had one poem published in the *Listener* in 1940.) Fortune Press took notice and asked him to submit a collection; he did, and *The North Ship* was published in 1945. The poetry in that collection is heavily influenced by Yeats's work, to which he was introduced by the poet Vernon Watkins, who read and lectured at the English Club at Oxford and with whom Larkin subsequently developed a friendship.

After graduation, Larkin took a post as librarian in Wellington, Shropshire. He claimed that while there he began to read Thomas Hardy's poetry seriously, which allowed him to throw off the Yeatsian influence. He subsequently worked as a librarian in Leicester, in Belfast, and, after 1955, as head librarian at the University of Hull. His attitudes toward his work vacillated, and that ambivalence is displayed in his poems, particularly in "Toads" and "Toads Revisited." Nevertheless, he remained at his position as librarian and eschewed the life of poet-celebrity. He died in Hull on December 2, 1985.

ANALYSIS

If Rudyard Kipling's is the poetry of empire, then Philip Larkin's is the poetry of the aftermath of empire. Having lived through the divestiture of England's various colonial holdings, the economic impact of empire-building having finally come home, together with the ultimate travesty of imperial pretensions and the nightmare of Nazi and Soviet colonization in Europe, Larkin was wary of the expansiveness, the acquisitiveness, and the grandeur implicit in the imperial mentality. Many features of his poetry can be traced to that wariness: from the skepticism and irony, to the colloquial diction, to the formal precision of his poems.

Indeed, of all the writers who shared those ideals and techniques and who came to be known in the 1950's as the Movement, Larkin most faithfully retained his original attitude and style. Those writers—Kingsley Amis, Donald Davie, John Wain, Elizabeth Jennings, Thom Gunn, among others—diverse though they were, shared attitudes that were essentially empirical, antimodernist, skeptical, and ironic. Most of those views can be understood as outgrowths of an elemental alienation from society and its traditional institutions. Amis's Jim Dixon is the outstanding fictional embodiment of these attitudes; although he desperately wants and needs to be accepted into university society and the traditional power structure it represents, his contempt for the institution and those in it, bred of his alienation, carries him into situations that border on both hilarity and disaster. *Lucky Jim* (1954) is *the* Movement novel.

Isolation and alienation figure prominently in both of Larkin's novels, as well; yet it is in his poems that they receive their fullest development. The speakers of his poems—and in the great majority of cases the speaker is the poet himself—seem alienated from their surroundings, cut off from both people and institutions. While that alienation normally shows itself as distance, as irony and wry humor, it can sometimes appear as smugness, complacence, even sneering judgment. Larkin turns his sense of isolation, of being an outsider or fringe observer, into a position of centrality, in which the world from which he is alienated seems to be moving tangentially to his own sphere. In his best poems, that distance works two ways, allowing the poet to observe the world in perspective, as if viewing it through the wrong end of a pair of binoculars, so that weighty matters seem less momentous, while at the same time reminding the poet that he, too, is a figure of little consequence. When his poems fail, the poet risks very little of his own ego as he sits back in safety, judging others across the frosty distance.

Larkin gains his perspective in large measure through his belief that nothing lies beyond this world, that this existence, however muddled it may be, is probably the only one. His skepticism is thoroughgoing and merciless; he rarely softens his tone. In some writers such belief might provoke terror or a compulsion to reform the world. In Larkin, it gives rise to irony. He examines the feeble inhabitants of this tiny planet surrounded by the void and asks if it can all be so important.

The resulting sense of human insignificance, including his own, leads him to several of the characteristic features of his work. He rejects "poetic" devices in favor of simpler, more mundane vehicles. His diction, for example, is nearly always colloquial, often coarse, vulgar, or profane. His distrust of a specialized diction or syntax for poetry reflects his distrust of institutions generally. Similarly, he shies away from the intense poetic moment—image, symbol, metaphor—in favor of a discursive, argumentative verse. While he will occasionally resolve a poem through use of an image or a metaphor, particularly in *High Windows*, he more commonly talks his way through the poem, relying on intellect rather than emotion or intuition.

This rejection of the stuff of poetry leads him to a problem: If overtly poetic language and poetic devices are eschewed, what can the poet use to identify his poems *as* poems? For Larkin the answer lies in the external form of the poems: scansion, rhyme schemes, stanzaic patterns. The tension and the power of a Larkin poem often result from the interplay of common, unexceptional language with rigorously formal precision. "The Building," from *High Windows*, is an example of such

tension. The poet meditates upon the function of the hospital in modern society and the way in which it takes over some of the duties traditionally performed by the Church, all in very ordinary language. The poem, however, is stretched taut over not one but two sophisticated units: a seven-line stanza and an eight-line rhyme scheme (*abcbdad*). Rhyme pattern and stanzaic pattern come together at the end of the eighth stanza, but the poem does not end there; rather, the poet employs another rhyme unit, a stanza plus a line, as a means of resolving the poem. Even here Larkin's shrewd distrust of the intellectual viability of poetic forms displays itself: Ending neatly on the fifty-sixth line would be too neat, too pat, and would violate the poem's ambivalence toward the place. Similarly, although his rhyme schemes are often very regular, the same cannot be said for the rhymes themselves: speech/touch, faint/went, home/welcome. If Larkin recognizes his need for traditional forms in his poems, he recognizes also the necessity of altering those forms into viable elements of *his* poetry.

Finally, there is in Larkin a sense of an ending, of oblivion. For all his distrust of the "new apocalypse crowd," many of his poems suggest something similar, although with a characteristic difference. Where the "crowd" may prophesy the end of the world and everything in it, he, working out of his alienation, more commonly seems to be watching the string run out, as if he were a spectator at the edge of oblivion.

THE NORTH SHIP

Larkin's first volume of poetry, *The North Ship*, went virtually unnoticed at the time of its original publication and would be unnoticed still were it made to stand on its own merits. It has few. The poems are almost uniformly derivative Yeatsian juvenilia, laden with William Butler Yeats's imagery but shorn of its power or meaning; this is the verse of a young man who wants to become a poet by sounding like a known poet. No one has been more critical, moreover, of the volume than the poet himself, characterizing it as an anomaly, a mistake that happened when he did not know his own voice and thought, under the tutelage of Vernon Watkins, that he was someone else. That he allowed the republication of the work in 1966, with an introduction that is more than anything else a disclaimer, suggests a desire to distance the "real" poet from the confused adolescent.

Despite his objections, the book can be seen as representative of certain tendencies in his later verse, and it is enlightening to discern how many features of his mature work show themselves even when buried under someone else's style. A major difference between Larkin's poems and Yeats's lies in the use of objects: While the younger poet borrows Yeats's dancers, horses, candles, and moons, they remain dancers, horses, candles, and moons. They lack transcendent, symbolic value; objects remain mere objects.

There is also in these early poems a vagueness in the description of the phenomenal world. Perhaps that generality, that vagueness, could be explained as the result of the Yeatsian influence, but it is also a tendency of Larkin's later work. One often has the impression that a scene, particularly a human scene, is typical rather than specific.

One of the things clearly missing from this first work is a suspicion of the Yeatsian symbols, attitudes, and gestures, almost none of which the mature Larkin can abide. His assertion that it was his intense reading of Hardy's poetry that rescued him from the pernicious influence of Yeats may have validity; more probably, time heals youthful excess, and during the period when he was outgrowing the poetry of *The North Ship*, he began a salutary reading of Hardy.

THE LESS DECEIVED

A striking development in Larkin's second book of poems, *The Less Deceived*, is his insistence on the mundane, the unexceptional, the commonplace. In "Born Yesterday," a poem on the occasion of Sally Amis's birth, for example, he counters the usual wishes for beauty or brilliance with the attractive (for him) possibility of being utterly unextraordinary, of fitting in wholly by having nothing stand out. This wish he offers, he says, in case the others do not come true, but one almost has the sense that he wishes also that the others will not come true, that being average is much preferable to being exceptional.

He makes a similar case for the ordinary in the wickedly funny "I Remember, I Remember," which attacks the Romantic notions of the writer's childhood as exemplified in D. H. Lawrence's *Sons and Lovers* (1913). In other places he has described his childhood as boring, not worthy of comment, and in this poem he pursues that idea

vigorously. In the first two stanzas, he comes to the realization that he does not recognize the Coventry station into which the train has pulled, although he used it often as a child. When his traveling companion asks if Coventry is where he "has his roots," the poet responds in his mind with a catalog of all the things that never happened to him that supposedly happen to writers in their youth, "the splendid family/ I never ran to," "The bracken where I never sat trembling." Through the course of that list, he recognizes that the place looks so foreign now because it never gave him anything distinctive, that there is nothing that he carries with him that he can attribute to it. Then, in a remarkable about-face, he realizes that the location has very little to do with how his childhood was spent or misspent, that life is largely independent of place, that the alienation which he senses is something he carries with him, not a product of Coventry.

The poem at first seems to be an honest appraisal of his youth in contradistinction to all those romanticized accounts in biographies and novels, but the reader is forced finally to conclude that the poet protests too much. There is no childhood in which *nothing* happens, and in insisting so strongly on the vacuum in which he grew up, Larkin develops something like the inverse of nostalgia. He turns his present disillusionment and alienation back against the past and views it from his ironic perspective. Larkin is often the victim of his own ironies, and in this poem his victim is memory.

His irony, in this poem as in so many, is used defensively; he wards off criticism by beating everyone to the punch. Irony is in some respects safer than laying oneself open for inspection. In many of his finest poems, however, he drops his guard and allows himself to think seriously about serious subjects. The foremost example in *The Less Deceived* is "Church Going." The title turns out to be marvelously ambiguous, appearing at first blush to be a mere reference to attending church, but then becoming, as the poem progresses, an elliptical, punning reference to churches going out of fashion.

The first two stanzas are curtly dismissive in a manner often encountered in Larkin, as he describes his stop from a bicycle trip at a church that is apparently Ulster Protestant. Neither he (since he stops for a reason he cannot name and acts guilty as he looks around) nor the church (since it is not at all out of the ordinary) seems worthy of attention. He leaves, thinking the church "not worth stopping for." In the third stanza, however, the poem shifts gears in a way typical of Larkin's finest work: the dismissive attitude toward mundane existence, the wry observations give way to serious contemplation. "Church Going," in fact, contains two such shifts.

In stanzas three through seven Larkin reflects on the fate of churches when people stop going altogether—whether they will become places which people will avoid or seek out because of superstition, or become museums, or be turned to some profane use—and wonders, as well, who will be the last person to come to the church and what his reasons will be. Larkin has a sense, conveyed in a number of poems, that he and his generation of skeptics will be the end of religion in England, and in this poem he wonders about the results of that doubting. The final stanza contains yet another shift, this one rather more subtle. As if the "serious house on serious earth" were forcing the poet to be more serious, he shifts away from his musings about its fate, which are after all only another kind of dismissal, and recognizes instead the importance of the place. He suggests, finally, that the shallowness and disbelief of modern man cannot eradicate the impulse to think seriously and seek wisdom that the Church, however outmoded its rituals, represents.

THE WHITSUN WEDDINGS

The two finest poems in Larkin's succeeding volume display similar movements of thought. In the title poem, "The Whitsun Weddings," the movement takes on further embellishment; not only does the poem move from dismissiveness to contemplation, but also the language of the poem moves from specificity toward generality in a way that mirrors the theme. The poem also contains one of Larkin's favorite devices: the use of a train ride (occasionally a car ride) to depict the movement of thought.

The poem opens with the concern for specificity of someone who, like the speaker, is late; when the train leaves the station at "one-twenty," it is "three-quarters-empty." He catches glimpses of scenery along the way, none of it very interesting, much of it squalid and polluted. Not until the third stanza (suggesting the incompleteness of his detailed observation) does he notice the wedding parties at each station. Even then, it is with the dismissive attitude of someone who, as a professional

bachelor and alienated outsider, rather scorns the tackiness of the families gathered on the platforms to see the couples off, as well as that of the unreflective couples with whom he shares the coach. His ironical, detailed description takes up most of the next five stanzas.

Toward the end of stanza seven, however, he undergoes a change, has a moment of vision in which the postal districts of London appear as "squares of wheat." That image leads him, in the final stanza, to see the couples as symbols of fertility, so that finally the slowing train inspires in him an image of arrows beyond the scope of his vision, "somewhere becoming rain." That he loosens the reins of his vision, so that he can describe not merely what he sees but also what he can only envision, is a major development in his attitude from the beginning of the poem. It demonstrates a breaking down, however slight or momentary, of his alienation from the common run of existence and of his resistance to recognizing his own relationship with these others. The poem may ultimately be judged a failure because of the brevity of that breaking down, but the image it spawns of fertility and life just beginning is magnificent.

"Dockery and Son" displays a similar movement and is a stronger poem because the poet is forced to lower his defenses much earlier and reveal himself more fully during the course of his meditation. An offhand comment by the Dean that a fellow student now has a son at school sets the speaker's mind in motion. His first musings on the train home are again mundane, dismissive, of the "you-never-know-do-you" sort, and so boring that he falls asleep. On reconsideration, though, the poet experiences the shock of being brought up hard against the reality of having missed, irrevocably, what is for most men a major part of life—familial relations. Even this reflection remains thin and unsatisfactory, and he moves on to explore the nature of unquestioned and unquestioning belief and its source, deciding that it results not from wisdom or truth but from habit and style grown sclerotic. Yet those beliefs are what a man's life turns on, producing a son for Dockery and nothing for the poet.

At this point, very late in the poem, Larkin develops one of his marvelous reversals on the word "nothing." For most, it connotes an absence, a negation, a nonentity, but for Larkin "nothing" is a positive entity, a thing or force to be reckoned with, "Nothing with all a son's harsh patronage." The line suggests that the poet has had to wrestle with this "nothing" he has created even as a father, such as Dockery, has had to wrestle with the problems brought on by having a son. The similarity, however, does not stop there; the poet goes on to recognize the common fate that awaits not only Dockery and himself but everyone as well. Most commentators read the final phrase, "the only end of age," as meaning death, and certainly that meaning is there. Nevertheless, to understand it as *merely* meaning death is to lose some of the force it holds for the speaker. Rather, it must be read back through the stanza and the poem as a whole, so that the emphasis on nothingness informs that certain knowledge of death. That the poet not only knows he will die, but also that he has already tasted the nothingness he knows, as an unbeliever, that death entails, makes the experience of that knowledge the more poignant. As is so often true in Larkin's work, that poignancy, which could border on self-pity, is tempered by the understanding that he at least comprehends, and there lies behind the poem's ending an unstated irony aimed at those such as Dockery who engage life so fully as to obscure that reality.

Again, that constant strain of alienation insinuates its way into poem after poem. Throughout *The Whitsun Weddings* the poet feels himself cut off from his fellow humans, often struggling to retrieve a spirit of community with them, sometimes simply wondering why it is so. The volume, while it represents little change from its predecessor, renders a picture of a man in middle age who feels life passing him by, and who sees more and more clearly the inevitable. Settings are close, small; lives are petty, insignificant; society is filled with graffiti and pollution. In "The Importance of Elsewhere," he finds comfort in being a foreigner in Ireland, since at least he can explain his estrangement from his fellow inhabitants there. In England, ostensibly at home, he has no such excuse.

HIGH WINDOWS

A number of the poems in *High Windows* display that estrangement, often in unsettlingly smug tones. "Afternoons," in the previous book, shows Larkin at his judgmental worst, picking out nasty little details of petty lives and common tastes. In this volume, "The Old Fools," a poem that is often praised for its unexpected

ending, displays a similar attitude. After railing against the infirmity and senility of the elderly throughout the poem, the tag line of "Well, we shall find out" rings false, sounding too much like an attempt to dodge inevitable criticism.

"Going, Going" presents some of the same problems, yet it implicates the poet in his critique in a way that "The Old Fools" does not. What is going is England itself, and that entity, it turns out, is place, not people. People have ruined the landscape and the architecture, reducing everything to rubbish. The poem redeems itself through its linguistic implication of its creator. The piece remains polemical throughout, avoiding the impulse to resolve through metaphor, as if the misanthropic, gloomy sensibility demands a crabbed style distrustful of the richness of figurative language and, perhaps, mirroring the destruction of English literature: if "carved choirs," echoing as they do William Shakespeare's "bare ruined choirs where late the sweet birds sang," are ruined and replaced with "concrete and tyres," then this poem's language is the replacement for Shakespeare's. Everywhere the poet turns, he finds traditional institutions, including poetry, degraded into mundane modern forms.

A much finer expression of that discovery is to be found in "The Building," which brings together numerous themes and ideas from throughout Larkin's canon. Like "Dockery and Son," it is a meditation on the foretaste of death; like "Going, Going," a consideration of the degradation of institutions in the modern world; like "Church Going," a questioning of what man shall do without churches.

The first two stanzas examine the ways the building in which the speaker sits resembles so many other modern buildings—high-rise hotels, airport lounges—although there is something disturbingly unlike them, as well. Not until the end of the second stanza does he reveal that it is a hospital. What unites people here is the common knowledge of their own mortality; even if they are not to die immediately, they are forced by the place to confront the fact that they will die eventually. The inescapability of that knowledge tames and calms the people in the building, as once the knowledge of death and its aftermath quieted them in church.

The recognition of this similarity grows slowly but steadily throughout the poem. The words keep insinuating a connection: "confess," "congregations," a "locked church" outside. The reaction people have in the hospital also suggests a function similar to that of the Church; outside they can hide behind ignorance or refusal to face facts, while inside the hospital those illusions are stripped away and reality is brought into the clear, sharp light, the unambiguous clarity of hospital corridors. This growing realization culminates in a final understanding that unless the modern hospital is more powerful than the traditional cathedral (and Larkin, suspicious of all institutions, does not think it is), then nothing can stop the ineluctable fate that awaits humanity, although (and now the similarities are overwhelming) every night people bring offerings, in the form of flowers, as they would to church.

A remarkable poem such as "The Building" can overcome a score of "Afternoons," and what is more remarkable about it is the way Larkin overcomes his initial alienation to speak not only at, but also to and even for, his fellow humans and their very real suffering. His finest poems end, like this one, in benedictions that border on the "Shantih" of T. S. Eliot's *The Waste Land* (1922), giving the reader the sense that a troubling journey has reached a satisfying end.

COLLECTED POEMS

The publication of his *Collected Poems* (1988) brought to light scores of poems previously uncollected, long out of print, or unavailable to the general reading public. These poems will not significantly alter Larkin's reputation, other than to expand the base on which it rests. For fans of his work, however, the additions prove quite valuable, showing as they do the movement from juvenilia to maturity. The early work displays even more clearly than, say, *The North Ship* the various influences on the young poet: Yeats and W. H. Auden. A work such as "New Year Poem" demonstrates a remarkable prescience, dated as it is the day before (and written an ocean away from) Auden's famous "New Year Letter" of 1941; both poems look at the future and consider the social and spiritual needs in a time of crisis.

Larkin, ever parsimonious, wrote very few poems during the last decade of his life: *Collected Poems* reveals a mere seventeen. Many of those concern themselves with his standard topics—the ravages of age, the sense of not being in step with the rest of society, the approach of death. In "The Mower," for example, he ruminates on having run over a hedgehog in the tall grass, killing it. From this experience, he takes away a feeling of responsibility for the death, a sense of the loss of this fellow creature, and the reflection that, given our limited time, we should be kind to one another. This slight poem (eleven lines) sums up much of Larkin's thought in his later years: Death is a complete cessation of experience, not a transmutation but a blankness, an end, while life itself is a vale of unhappiness, and people therefore owe it to themselves and one another to make the way as pleasant as possible.

In "Aubade," perhaps the most substantial of the late poems, Larkin writes of the approach of death, now another day closer because it is a new morning. He declares that we have never been able to accept death, yet are also unable to defeat it. Once religion offered the consolation of afterlife; for Larkin, that promise is no longer valid. What people fear most, he asserts, is the absence of sensation, of affect, that is death, as well as the absolute certainty of its coming. His "morning poem" is really a poem of the dark night of the soul. The fifth, and final, ten-line stanza brings the light of day and the unmindful routine of the workaday world, the routine that acts as a balm by taking our minds off our ultimate problem. Indeed, the poem's closing image presents those representatives of the mundane, postal carriers, going among houses like doctors, their daily rounds offering temporary solace.

These two poems present Larkin's typically ironic approach to the literary tradition. "The Mower" is a highly unconventional garden song. While its title recalls Marvell's poems "The Garden" and "The Mower, Against Gardens," it shares none of their pastoral innocence or coyness. It finds death, not life, in the world of nature. Similarly, he subverts the traditional use of the aubade form to discuss not the coming day but also a coming night. In both cases he undermines traditionally upbeat forms. Yet these poems also point to the playfulness of which Larkin was capable even in his bleakest moments, finding amusement in poems of abject despair. That may prove to be his great gift, the ability to face darkness fully, to take it in, and still to laugh, to be ironic even about last things.

OTHER MAJOR WORKS

LONG FICTION: *Jill*, 1946, 1964; *A Girl in Winter*, 1947.

EDITED TEXT: *New Poems*, 1958 (with Louis MacNeice and Bonamy Dobrée); *The Oxford Book of Twentieth-Century English Verse*, 1973.

MISCELLANEOUS: *All What Jazz: A Record Diary, 1961-1968*, 1970; *Required Writings: Miscellaneous Pieces, 1955-1982*, 1984.

BIBLIOGRAPHY

Booth, James, ed. *New Larkins for Old: Critical Essays*. New York: St. Martin's Press, 2000. A collection of essays by established commentators on Larkin's work and by younger critics. Individual essays examine Larkin's novels and poetry in the light of psychoanalytical, postmodern, and postcolonial theories.

Brownjohn, Alan. *Philip Larkin*. Harlow, England: Longman, 1975. This little book (thirty-four pages with select bibliography), the first to deal with all four major volumes, is written with a poet's sensitivity to Larkin's verse. It includes a brief biographical section, followed by chronological discussion of the poems and concluding with an examination of the novels. A handy starting point for the student.

Day, Roger. *Philip Larkin*. Philadelphia: Open University Press, 1987. As one in the series of Open University Guides to Literature, this volume takes teaching as its primary focus. The focused questions and resulting commentary point students toward the important features of the poems and toward confidence in reading the poetry on their own, offering them suggestions for further reading and a select bibliography.

Hartley, Jean. *Philip Larkin, the Marvell Press, and Me*. Manchester, England: Carcanet, 1989. This memoir by the cofounder of the Marvell Press gives interesting insight into its most famous author. While the book deals with Hartley more than Larkin, it shows the exciting period of creative activity leading to and resulting from the publication of a truly important work, *The Less Deceived*, and it chronicles the lifelong friendship that resulted.

Hassan, Salem K. *Philip Larkin and His Contemporaries: An Air of Authenticity*. Basingstoke, England: Macmillan, 1988. Well researched, this volume places Larkin within the context of his Movement colleagues of the 1950's: John Wain, Thom Gunn, Kingsley Amis, and D. J. Enright. The first part discusses Larkin's poetry book by book. Part 2 devotes a chapter to careers of his four contemporaries, discussing their work in terms of his. The text also includes a select bibliography of primary and secondary sources, notes, and an index.

Motion, Andrew. *Philip Larkin: A Writer's Life*. New York: Farrar, Straus, Giroux, 1993. This short work provides an introduction to the man and his work. The book offers thematic and literary-historical overviews, although only one chapter on the poems themselves.

Rossen, Janice. *Philip Larkin: His Life's Work*. New York: Simon & Schuster, 1989. This intelligent and highly readable overview traces Larkin's development through the first two books, then looks at his lyric impulse, his firmly rooted Englishness, his sexual ambivalence, his use of vulgarity, and his struggle with mortality. The study ties in the poetry with the novels, jazz criticism, and literary criticism to develop a total view of the context of the poetry.

Thomas C. Foster;
bibliography updated by the editors

D. H. LAWRENCE

Born: Eastwood, Nottinghamshire, England; September 11, 1885
Died: Vence, France; March 2, 1930

PRINCIPAL POETRY

Love Poems and Others, 1913
Amores, 1916
Look! We Have Come Through!, 1917
New Poems, 1918
Bay, 1919
Tortoises, 1921
Birds, Beasts, and Flowers, 1923

OTHER LITERARY FORMS

D. H. Lawrence's productions reflect his artistic range. Accompanying his considerable body of poetry, the eleven novels published during his lifetime include *Sons and Lovers* (1913), *The Rainbow* (1915), *Women in Love* (1920), *The Plumed Serpent* (1926), and *Lady Chatterley's Lover* (1928). He wrote almost continuously for literary periodicals in addition to publishing five volumes of plays, nine volumes of essays, and several short-story collections including *The Prussian Officer and Other Stories* (1914), *England, My England* (1922), and *The Woman Who Rode Away and Other Stories* (1928). His final works, including *Apocalypse* and *Etruscan Places*, appeared between 1930 and 1933, and more poetry, essays, and drafts of fiction have since been collected in *Phoenix: The Posthumous Papers of D. H. Lawrence* (1936) and *Phoenix II: Uncollected, Unpublished, and Other Prose Works* (1968). Several of Lawrence's works, as well as Harry Moore's biography, *The Priest of Love*, have been adapted for the screen. The *Phoenix Edition of D. H. Lawrence* was published in 1957; Viking has printed *The Complete Short Stories of D. H. Lawrence* (1961) and *The Complete Plays of D. H. Lawrence* (1965).

ACHIEVEMENTS

D. H. Lawrence's work has consistently appealed to the adventurous and the perceptive. Ford Madox Ford, editor of the progressive *English Review*, printed Lawrence's earliest poems and short stories there in 1911, recognizing beneath their conventional surfaces potent psychological and emotional undercurrents previously unexplored in British letters. Before Freud's theories were widely known, Lawrence's *Sons and Lovers* daringly probed the dangerous multilayered mother-son-lover triangle he had experienced in his own life. After his elopement, itself a scandal, Lawrence produced *The Rainbow*, seized by Scotland Yard in 1915 and publicly condemned for obscenity. Lawrence's subsequent self-exile from England and his growing artistic notoriety came to a climax in the censorship trials of *Lady Chatterley's Lover*. Behind the alleged pornography, however, critics soon grasped Lawrence's genuine ability to convey what T. S. Eliot called "fitful and profound insights" into human behavior. Lawrence's admirers also included Edward Garnett, John Middleton Murry, Richard Aldington, Amy Lowell, and Rainer Maria Rilke, although Virginia Woolf perhaps illustrated her generation's ambivalence toward Lawrence most pungently: "Mr. Lawrence has moments of greatness, but he has hours of something quite different." Lawrence's own critical studies, particularly his pseudonymous *Movements in European History* (1921), and *Studies in Classic American Literature* (1923), reveal a

D. H. Lawrence (Library of Congress)

singular blend of historical perspective and instinctive understanding appreciated only after his death. Once the laudatory memories and abusive denunciations had died out, Lawrence's artistic reputation grew steadily, attributed generally to the craftsmanship of his short fiction and the uncompromisingly honest investigations of sexuality in his novels. As readers young in spirit increasingly observe, however, Lawrence's greatest gift, his affirmation of life, shines most brightly in his poetry.

BIOGRAPHY

David Herbert Richards Lawrence was born in Eastwood, Nottinghamshire, England, on September 11, 1885. His mother, Lydia Beardsall, had come from a fiercely religious middle-class family reduced in circumstances since the depression of 1837. Lydia, "a superior soul," as her third son called her, had been a schoolteacher, sensitive and musical, six years younger than her husband, to whom she was distantly related by marriage. His family had also lost money and position, and Arthur Lawrence, the proud possessor of a fine physique and a musical soul, had gone down into the mines as a child to work. Lydia's disillusion with her marriage, her husband's alcoholic degeneration, and the continual marital strife that haunted her son's childhood provided much of the conflict at the heart of Lawrence's work.

Out of hatred for her husband and a desperate resolve that her children should not sink to his level, Lydia used them as weapons against him. Much later, Lawrence regretted and in part redressed the unfavorable portrait of his father in his autobiographical "colliery novel," *Sons and Lovers*, which exhibits his mother's domination and his own fragile opposition through his love for Jessie Chambers, the "Miriam" whom he loved and left in literature as well as life.

Obedient to his mother's demands, Lawrence took a teaching position at Croydon, near London, in 1908. He was devastated by the ugly realities of urban life, disgusted by his savage pupils, and frustrated by the young women in his life. His mother's lingering death from cancer in late 1910, not long after he had laid an early copy of his first novel, *The White Peacock*, in her hands, sent him into a "heavy, bitter year," from which he emerged physically shaken by near-fatal pneumonia, unable to progress with his writing, and bent on leaving England. In the spring of 1912 he became smitten with "the woman of a lifetime," his former language professor's wife, the Baroness Frieda von Richthofen. Upon their elopement that May, they left behind them Frieda's children and Lawrence's England forever, except for a few brief and mostly unhappy intervals.

Lawrence then had to live by his pen, and he increased his output dramatically, pouring out not only fiction and poetry but also criticism and travel essays. After a painful stay in Cornwall during World War I, shunned because of Frieda's German connections and his own antiwar sentiments, Lawrence, shocked by British repression of *The Rainbow*, began the worldwide wandering which lasted the remainder of his life.

Lawrence almost realized his ambition of writing a major novel on each continent. After visiting Ceylon and Australia, he settled for a time with Frieda and a few friends near Taos, New Mexico, devoting himself to the idealization of primitivism as a vehicle for modern man's regeneration. Working on his novel *The Plumed Serpent* in Mexico in late 1924, he was struck simultaneously with harsh psychic and physical blows; he realized that his artistic position was untenable and went down "as if shot" with a combination of typhoid and the long-standing illness diagnosed then for the first time as tuberculosis.

Slowly recuperating on his ranch, Lawrence regained his creative equilibrium in a play, *David*, and a lovely fragmentary novel, "The Flying Fish," written, he said, "so near the borderline of death" that its spell could not be recaptured "in the cold light of day." There he proclaimed the belief in "regenerate man" to which he dedicated the rest of his short life. He returned in thought at least to England with *Lady Chatterly's Lover*, written on a sunny hill in Italy, a "novel of tenderness" that awakened violent protests and lawsuits, driving him even further into his metaphysical contemplation of human destiny. Very ill, holding to life through the strange bond of creativity alone, Lawrence worked out his conclusions on personal immortality in his *Last Poems*, until on March 2, 1930, in a sanatorium on the French Riviera aptly called "Ad Astra," "once dipped in dark oblivion/ the soul ha[d] peace, inward and lovely peace."

ANALYSIS

D. H. Lawrence had written poetry all of his creative life, but he did not set his poetic theory down until 1923. His poetry, as with nearly everything that he wrote, is uneven; and he knew it, distinguishing between his early self-conscious verse and the "real poems" that his "demon" shook out of him, poems he called "a biography of an emotional and inner life." In a preface to another man's poetry, Lawrence defined the process by which he himself transmuted "inner life," the core of his work, into art: "a bursting of bubbles of reality, and the pang of extinction that is also liberation into the roving, uncaring chaos which is all we shall ever know of God." Lawrence's poetry is thus best seen in the context of his life and through the painful paradox of his creativity, rooted in his most profound basic concept, the theory of human regeneration that he conveyed so often in the image of Paradise Regained.

As Richard Hoggart has observed, Lawrence's inner life spoke with both "the voice of a down-to-earth, tight, bright, witty Midlander" and "the voice of a seer with a majestic vision of God and life and earth." The Midlands voice first announced the major themes that Lawrence never abandoned: class, religion, and love. Lawrence very early felt the strictures of a working-man's life and the humiliation of poverty as keenly as he felt the happiness he shared at the Chambers' farm, among birds, beasts, and flowers threatened by encroaching industrialism. His "Rhyming Poems" also reflect his youthful love, quivering between the extremes of idealistic "spirituality" pressed upon him by his mother and Jessie Chambers, so fatally alike, and a powerful sexual drive crying out for satisfaction. At sixteen he abandoned his mother's harsh Congregationalism, though the "hymns of a man's life" never lost their appeal for him, and from 1906 to 1908 he was affected deeply by his experience of Arthur Schopenhauer's "Metaphysics of Sexual Love," which places sex at the center of the phenomenal universe, and Friedrich Wilhelm Nietzsche's works, probably including *The Birth of Tragedy*, which sees Greek tragedy as the result of creative tension between Apollonian rationalism and Dionysian ecstasy. Lawrence's prophetic voice had begun to whisper.

While his mother's slow death gradually disengaged him from her domination, Lawrence tried to weave his early concerns of class, love, and religion into an organic whole. Once he recovered from his own severe illness late in 1911, he looked toward new physical and creative horizons, and after his elopement with Frieda he at last was able to complete *Sons and Lovers* in a new affirmation of life. There were, however, characteristic growing pains. Frieda's aristocratic connections in Germany afforded him the social position that he, like his mother, had always envied while decrying its values, and he delighted in using his wife's baronial stationery at the same time that he was undergoing inevitable agonies at her cavalier disregard for sexual fidelity. The first book of Lawrence's "Unrhyming Poems," *Look! We Have Come Through!*, records the resolution of his complicated marital relationship in a form completely liberated from Georgian poetic convention. During World War I, Lawrence tried to locate man's vital meaning in a balance of power between love and friendship, replacing the God he had lost with the human values promised by his *The Rainbow* and the fourpart sexual harmony of *Women in Love*.

After the debacle of *The Rainbow*, Lawrence's social message became more strident. From 1917 to 1925, rapt in his dream of human regeneration—now fixed upon the figure of a patriarchal political leader—Lawrence went to the ends of the civilized earth. The fiction that he produced during that period urges progressively more primitivistic reorganizations of society, culminating in a faintly ridiculous neo-Aztec pantheon imposed upon Mexico in *The Plumed Serpent*, a novel embedding Lawrence's highest hopes in stubbornly incantatory verse and sometimes turgid prose.

At the midpoint of his career, a substantial conflict was brewing between Lawrence's urge for social reform and his prophetic sense of responsibility. The religious voice was clear in the poems of *Birds, Beasts, and Flowers*, where, as Vivian de Sola Pinto has observed, "the common experience is transformed and invested with mythical grandeur." Such a stirring transmutation proved incompatible with the "down-to-earth Midlands voice" calling for political answers to social questions. By 1923, possibly with memories of Nietzsche and Schopenhauer, Lawrence had defined his "simple trinity" as "the emotions, the mind, and then the children of this venerable pair, ideas." Lawrence also insisted that God's traditional position relative to human beings had changed, so that Christ could no longer serve as the pathway to the Father; the Holy Ghost would have to lead human beings to a "new living relation," nothing less than the spiritual regeneration that Lawrence hoped to bring to humankind from the wreckage of modern Western civilization.

When Lawrence collapsed upon completing *The Plumed Serpent*, he was forced to abandon his old dream of social rebirth through politically enforced primitivism. In the poetic "The Flying Fish" he announced that the Indian's "primeval day" and the white man's mechanism "nullified each other." Now, as de Sola Pinto remarked, Lawrence's "ecstasy controlled by the rational imagination" produced memorable poetry in *Birds, Beasts, and Flowers*, foreshadowing the affirmation of life eternal that Lawrence finally was to achieve.

Lawrence's irritation with Western materialism erupted once more late in his life in the angry little poems that he called his *Pansies* and *Nettles*, glimpses of man's stupidity, conceit, and boorishness encapsulated in stinging doggerel. Hardly his finest poetic achievement, these poems nevertheless represent more than a sick man's impatience with human frailty. They also demonstrate a quality of Lawrence's insight that he called "quickness," "the breath of the moment, and one eternal moment easily contradicting the next eternal moment."

By 1928, already gravely ill, Lawrence had turned almost completely to examining "the pang of extinction that is also liberation," the paradox, as he saw it, of physical death. His prophetic voice far outstripped the satiric note as he painted and wrote in the familiar archetypes of the Garden of Eden, regained, he felt now, through the apocalypse of death. His three original themes had coalesced into a great hymn of man's essential renewal, the "religion of wonder" that he had glimpsed in the Etruscans: "The whole universe lived; and the business of man was himself to live amid it all." Lawrence paid a heavy price for restoring man to Paradise, the unification of his Midlands voice and his prophetic voice in the acceptance of death as life's necessary other half. At last he was able to create a convincing myth as he had cre-

ated all his work, from the ideas born of his own mind and emotions. Lawrence's *Last Poems*, like Rainer Maria Rilke's terrible and beautiful angels, burst the bubbles of reality, and Lawrence closed his poems, like his life, upon the noble vision of resurrection.

"RHYMING POEMS"

Lawrence's "biography of an emotional and inner life" begins with his "Rhyming Poems," written between 1904 and 1912. Those he called "imaginative or fictional" he reworked twenty years later, mostly in his Midlands voice, "to say the real say," because "sometimes the hand of commonplace youth had been laid on the mouth of the demon." The subjective poems of his early years, "with the demon fuming in them smokily," were unchangeable.

One of the lessons that Lawrence had to learn as a young poet was when to leave his "demon" alone. "Discord in Childhood," a pain-filled record of the elder Lawrences' marital combat, had originally been a long poem, and, he said, a better one. Frightened by his own creativity, Lawrence burned the first poem as a young man, although he later worked the scene into *Sons and Lovers*. Characteristically, even the preserved version connects violent human emotion with nature and its forces: "Outside the house an ash-tree hung its terrible whips," while within, "a male thong" drowned "a slender lash whistling she-delirious rage" in a "silence of blood."

A similar sensuous absorption in brutal natural forces appears in the "Miriam" poems, darkening the mood of "Renascence," which celebrates "The warm, dumb wisdom" that Lawrence learned from his "Eve." The woman was to provide his pathway to creativity, the means to his apprehension of nature, and the viewpoint of sensitivity, but for now Lawrence only received "Strange throbs" through her, as when "the sow was grabbing her litter/ With snarling red jaws"; and, as in "Virgin Youth," "We cry in the wilderness."

Later, when he lived in Croydon, Lawrence saw violent urban deformation of nature, and it nearly shattered him; in "Transformations," beauty spills continuously into decay before him as men, "feet of the rainbow," are "twisted in grief like crumpling beech-leaves," and Lawrence is left to wonder at humanity's destiny: "What are you, oh multiform?"

He began to sense an answer looming in the growing recognition of his prophetic mission. In the poem "Prophet," he proposed "the shrouded mother of a new idea . . . as she seeks her procreant groom," using familiar biblical symbolism to stress the religious aspect of his utterance. Before the "shrouded mother," "men hide their faces," the fear bred of artificial social pressures forcing them to deny the powerful enriching role of sexuality in their lives. At last, in "Dreams Old and Nascent," Lawrence called for violent social action: "to escape the foul dream of having and getting and owning." For the first time, he attempted to define his affirmation of the vital impulse: "What is life, but the swelling and shaping the dream in the flesh?"

LOOK! WE HAVE COME THROUGH!

Lawrence shaped the dream of his own "crisis of manhood, when he marrie[d] and [came] into himself" in the cycle *Look! We Have Come Through!*, attempting in these highly personal poems a crucial connection between the lives of the flesh and the spirit. Greeting physical love in intimate Imagist lyrics like "Gloire de Dijon," he passed through "the strait gate of passion" in "Paradise Re-entered," in which his typically fierce human love must be "Burned clean by remorseless hate." His religious sense, too, had already departed materially from orthodox Christianity. In the same poem, he abandoned both God and Satan "on Eternity's level/ Field," and announced, "Back beyond good and evil/ Return we," with a distinctly Nietzschean echo suggesting his burgeoning preoccupation with spiritual evolution.

From the same nontraditional quarter came the promise that Lawrence incorporated into "Song of a Man Who Has Come Through," one of the closing poems of this cycle. Lawrence willingly yielded himself up to "the wind that blows through me," "a fine wind . . . blowing the new direction of Time." The wind of his prophetic aspect, to prove at times tempestuous, was the vehicle that Lawrence hoped to use "to come at the wonder" he sensed in the act of being, and with it he fashioned the personal experiences recorded in this set of poems into *The Rainbow* and *Women in Love*.

BIRDS, BEASTS, AND FLOWERS

The major poetic work of Lawrence's middle years was *Birds, Beasts, and Flowers*, which R. P. Blackmur

called "a religious apprehension" and de Sola Pinto has described as an "exploration of what may be called the divine otherness of non-human life." The social criticism that Lawrence vented in this volume is chiefly directed at America, "lurking among the undergrowth/ of Many-stemmed machines." Lawrence plainly confirmed his simultaneous fascination with and repulsion for "Modern, unissued, uncanny America" in "The Evening Land": "And I, who am half in love with you,/ What am I in love with?" Although Lawrence distrusted the American reliance on the machine, he saw "Dark, aboriginal eyes" in the American "idealistic skull," a "New throb," which, like his dramatic character David, he finally concluded was "the false dawn that precedes the real." The aspect of humanity that had always most repelled him, inflexible will, was even less acceptable to him in America than it had been in Europe, as he noted in "Turkey-Cock," "A raw American will, that has never been tempered by life." In several pieces of fiction, including "The Woman Who Rode Away" and *The Plumed Serpent*, he attempted to subdue that will by sheer force of primitive emotion and even compulsive self-sacrifice. Reversing that position in "Eagle in New Mexico," Lawrence candidly acknowledged the necessity of opposition to bloodthirsty will, negating his own proposal of primitivism as a remedy for modern civilization: "Even the sun in heaven can be curbed . . ./ By the life in the hearts of men." Finally, Lawrence unleashed considerable venom at "The American Eagle," which he had come to consider the symbol of civilization's disaster, "The new Proud Republic/ Based on the mystery of pride." Contradicting the very concept of political dominance by an "aristocracy of the spirit" that he had advocated for so long, Lawrence denounced the "bird of men that are masters,/ Or are you the goose that lays the . . . addled golden egg?"

None of the rancor of Lawrence's American-directed diatribes is present in the finest poetry of *Birds, Beasts, and Flowers* in which de Sola Pinto finds "an affirmation of the grandeur and mystery of the life of nature." Working from a mundane incident, a visit by a poisonous Sicilian snake to his water trough on "a hot, hot day," "Snake" illustrates Lawrence the poet at his most capable, commanding a deceptively simple style, ordinary speech, and a consummate adaptation of rhythm to meaning. The resulting interior monologue evokes a passionate mythopoeic response. The snake "had come like a guest in quiet," and Lawrence described himself as "afraid," but "honoured still more/ That he should seek my hospitality." In one of Lawrence's flashes of intuitive perception, the snake "looked around like a god" before retreating through a cranny in the wall. Lawrence's "voices . . . of accursed human education" impelled him to toss a log at the creature, a petty act that he shortly regretted profoundly: "And so, I missed my chance with one of the lords of life." "Snake" realizes a striking balance between mind and emotion, penetrating the mystery of civilized man's destruction of nature and eclipsing the conventional Christian symbolism of Evil Incarnate. In the snake's deathly potential, too, is the premonition that "the lords of life are the masters of death," an insight not developed fully until Lawrence had returned to Europe.

Still closer than "Snake" to expressing man's most archetypal need, the yearning after life renewed, Lawrence's "Almond Blossom" opens "a heart of delicate super-faith/ [in] . . . The rusty swords of almond-trees." Much of Lawrence's poetry has been assailed for supposed incoherence of utterance and Whitmanesque repetitiousness, but in "Almond Blossom," de Sola Pinto notes, Lawrence is "thinking in images." Lawrence's old Christian path to God, "The Gethsemane blood," bursts now into "tenderness of bud," a splendid annunciation of "A naked tree of blossom, like a bridegroom bathing in dew." The "new living relation" of man with God which Lawrence was proclaiming in his philosophical essays now assumed fulfillment in an emboldened image that merged social consciousness, love, and religion: "Think, to stand there in full-unfolded nudity, smiling,/ With all the snow-wind, and the sunglare, and the dog-star baying epithalamion."

PANSIES AND NETTLES

There is a marked shift in tone from *Birds, Beasts, and Flowers* to the following volumes of poems, *Pansies* and *Nettles*. In *Pansies*, Lawrence was immediately accused of obscenity for using "the *old* words [Lawrence's italics], that belong to the body below the navel." Those who knew him intimately, like Frieda, often referred to him as a puritan in sexual matters, and a purpose far different from obscenity motivated both his

Pansies and *Nettles*; he had a stern, almost Calvinistic urge to destroy what he considered genuine pornography, "the impudent and dirty mind[s]" that had condemned *Lady Chatterley's Lover*. Lawrence had never been a patient man, and his introduction to *Pansies* is one of his most savage jeremiads: "In the name of piety and purity, what a mass of disgusting insanity is spoken and written." Such social "insanity" was his greatest enemy, and he fought the mob "in order to keep sane and to keep society sane." His chief weapon was a hard-edged Swiftian wit that did not shrink from the scatological to make a point. In *Pansies*, Lawrence assailed most of the sacred cows of his time: censorship, "heavy breathing of the dead men"; "our bald-headed consciousness"; "narrow-gutted superiority"; the "Oxford cuckoos"; "ego-perverted love"; even "elderly discontented women."

His short series of *Nettles* must have stung his detractors even more viciously. In "13,000 People," a poem on the public reaction to the brief exhibition of his paintings abruptly terminated by British police, he flailed the "lunatics looking . . . where a fig-leaf might have been, but was not." He even figuratively neutered his "little Critics": "brought up by their Aunties/ who . . . had them fixed to save them from undesirable associations."

Despite his ferocity when assaulting social "insanity," the unhealthy forces of repression and censorship, Lawrence was still approaching a positive solution for modern man's woes in both *Pansies* and *Nettles*. In the little poem "God" in *Pansies*, he declared: "Where sanity is/ there God is," linking his own beliefs to the Supreme Being. He also dedicated several of the longer *Pansies* (*pensées*, or even heartsease, he had suggested in the introduction) to the Risen Lord, the new subjective path to God by which man could serve as his own Savior: "A sun will rise in me,/ I shall slowly resurrect." In "More Pansies," a still later group, Lawrence came even nearer the mystery of man's being, identifying the Holy Ghost as "the deepest part of our own consciousness/ wherein . . . we know our dependence on the creative beyond." Finally, as Lawrence struggled both in his poems and in his philosophic essays with the immensity of his apocalyptic vision, his satiric voice became only an overtone of the religious message he was attempting to enunciate. That message sprang from his "strange joy/ in a great [new] . . . adventure."

LAST POEMS AND APOCALYPSE

None of the poetry that Lawrence wrote during his life became him more than the *Last Poems*, which he wrote while leaving it. In his final prose work, *Apocalypse*, he was still clinging to the physical life he had celebrated so long and so rapturously, but in the *Last Poems* Lawrence was setting out gladly into a new country whose borders he had glimpsed in *Etruscan Places*, his vivid sense of place even capturing the paradoxical "delight of the underworld" in ancient tombs, "deep and sincere honour rendered to the dead and to the mysteries."

In "Bavarian Gentians," Lawrence powerfully enlarged the mythic role of nature's archetypes of resurrection as he descended into the "new adventure": "Reach me a gentian, bring me a torch!" Previously concentrating on Eve as man's mediatrix with Paradise Regained, Lawrence now saw woman as symbolic Persephone, "a voice . . . pierced with the passions of dense gloom." The image of biblical mystical marriage could satisfy him no longer, and Lawrence now looked toward the mythic "splendour of torches of darkness, shedding darkness on the lost bride and her groom."

With the relatively minor exceptions of poems dealing with the symbols of his *Apocalypse* and a few more prickly observations on man's social vicissitudes, *Last Poems* represents the birth pangs of Lawrence's incomplete poetic masterpiece, "The Ship of Death." He had seen a little model ship in an Etruscan tomb and it had carried his imagination toward the possibility of one long poetic testament, where, as Richard Aldington suggests, "suffering and the agony of departure are turned into music and reconciliation." The extant fragments of Lawrence's radiant vision center on a new concept in his stormy artistry, the peace of a soul fulfilled at last in its greatest adventure: "the long and painful death/ that lies between the old self and the new." Lawrence's long struggles with the nightmares of man's collective insanity were finally over, and he had "come through" his early preoccupations with the stresses of class and love and even religion, finding again within himself the possibility of a new dimension of human perception. At last

body and mind, life and death had become one for him, "filling the heart with peace."

Lawrence's poetic development from conventional Georgian verse to mythopoeic vision spanned only the first thirty years of the twentieth century, yet his ultimate vision approaches the universal. In his "moments of greatness," far from a willfully obscene *Weltbild*, he opens a breathtaking vista of the potential of the human condition in its entirety, not only body, not merely soul, but a creativity as vital as the Greek tragedy that Nietzsche had earlier proclaimed as the result of Apollonian-Dionysian tension. Lawrence's occasional Midlands lapses from literary propriety seem a small enough price to pay for the validity and vitality of his finest poetry, described best in the tenderly honest words of his fellow poet Rainer Maria Rilke: "act[s] of reverence toward life."

OTHER MAJOR WORKS

LONG FICTION: *The White Peacock*, 1911; *The Trespasser*, 1912; *Sons and Lovers*, 1913; *The Rainbow*, 1915; *Women in Love*, 1920; *The Lost Girl*, 1920; *Mr. Noon*, wr. 1920-1922, pb. 1984; *Aaron's Rod*, 1922; *The Ladybird, The Fox, The Captain's Doll*, 1923; *Kangaroo*, 1923; *The Boy in the Bush*, 1924 (with M. L. Skinner); *The Plumed Serpent*, 1926; *Lady Chatterley's Lover*, 1928; *The Escaped Cock*, 1929 (best known as *The Man Who Died*); *The Virgin and the Gipsy*, 1930.

SHORT FICTION: *The Prussian Officer and Other Stories*, 1914; *England, My England*, 1922; *St. Mawr: Together with "The Princess,"* 1925; *The Woman Who Rode Away and Other Stories*, 1928; *Love Among the Haystacks*, 1930; *The Lovely Lady and Other Stories*, 1933; *The Tales*, 1933; *A Modern Lover*, 1934; *The Complete Short Stories of D. H. Lawrence*, 1961;

PLAYS: *The Widowing of Mrs. Holroyd*, pb. 1914; *Touch and Go*, pb. 1920; *David*, pb. 1926; *The Plays*, pb. 1933; *A Collier's Friday Night*, pb. 1934; *The Complete Plays of D. H. Lawrence*, pb. 1965.

NONFICTION: *Study of Thomas Hardy*, 1914; *Twilight in Italy*, 1916; *Movements in European History*, 1921; *Psychoanalysis and the Unconscious*, 1921; *Sea and Sardinia*, 1921; *Fantasia of the Unconscious*, 1922; *Studies in Classic American Literature*, 1923;

Reflections on the Death of a Porcupine and Other Essays, 1925; *Mornings in Mexico*, 1927; *Pornography and Obscenity*, 1929; *Assorted Articles*, 1930; *À Propos of "Lady Chatterley's Lover,"* 1930; *Apocalypse*, 1931; *Etruscan Places*, 1932; *The Letters of D. H. Lawrence*, 1932 (Aldous Huxley, editor); *Phoenix: The Posthumous Papers of D. H. Lawrence*, 1936 (Edward McDonald, editor); *The Collected Letters of D. H. Lawrence*, 1962 (2 volumes; Harry T. Moore, editor); *Phoenix II: Uncollected, Unpublished, and Other Prose Works*, 1968 (Harry T. Moore and Warren Roberts, editors); *The Letters of D. H. Lawrence*, 1979-1993; *Selected Critical Writings*, 1998.

BIBLIOGRAPHY

Balbert, Peter, and Phillip L. Marcus, eds. *D. H. Lawrence: A Centenary Consideration*. Ithaca, N.Y.: Cornell University Press, 1985. Balbert and Marcus gather a collection of essays of leading scholars on concerns that Lawrence's writings continue to raise. Includes a chronology and directions for further reading.

Burgess, Anthony. *Flame into Being: The Life and Work of D. H. Lawrence*. London: Heinemann, 1985. Although primarily a novelist, Burgess has also written studies of other writers. Because he begins from a writer's point of view, his approaches are extraordinarily accessible and readable. This is the best single work on Lawrence, full of incisive insights. Contains no index, and the bibliography is limited to the memoirs.

Kermode, Frank. *D. H. Lawrence*. New York: Viking Press, 1973. In this study, a major literary critic presents an introduction that far surpasses most volumes of this type. Kermode surveys Lawrence's life and provides introductions to all the major works that are both informative and illuminating. A good first reference. Includes a complete index and a good introductory bibliography.

Kinkead-Weekes, Mark. *D. H. Lawrence, Triumph to Exile, 1912-1922*. New York: Cambridge University Press, 1996. A comprehensive telling of Lawrence's life, covering the period between his flight from England and his departure for Naples.

Meyers, Jeffrey. *D. H. Lawrence: A Biography*. New York: Alfred A. Knopf, 1990. This excellent "popular" biography covers all aspects of Lawrence's life and times and opens up new areas of investigation, especially as far as Lawrence's personal relationships are concerned. Augmented by a full index and a detailed bibliography.

Moore, Harry T. *The Priest of Love*. Rev. ed. New York: Farrar, Straus & Giroux, 1974. Although rather scholarly in some respects—the literary discussions are sometimes sophisticated—Moore's work is a solid biography that is particularly effective in examining Lawrence's working-class background. It offers a substantial index and a bibliography, but it is especially useful for the supplementary material in the appendices, illustrations, and maps.

Sagar, Keith. *A D. H. Lawrence Handbook*. New York: Barnes & Noble Books, 1982. Although not the standard literary handbook, this study is an unusually useful reference book. In addition to the customary bibliography and directions for further readings, it offers materials on mining regions and practices, social background, chronology in relation to world events, films and sound recordings, dialects, and maps.

Squires, Michael, and Keith Cushman. *The Challenge of D. H. Lawrence*. Madison: University of Wisconsin Press, 1990. Gathered in this volume are fifteen essays by leading scholars who were asked to provide fresh responses to recurrent topics in Lawrence's criticism. The essays cover most of the major issues in his life and work, and are regularly thought-provoking.

Worthen, John. *D. H. Lawrence, the Early Years, 1885-1912*. New York: Cambridge University Press, 1991. Describes Lawrence's upbringing in a small colliery town in Nottinghamshire and his years as a teacher before the blossoming of his literary career with *Sons and Lovers*. Drawing on a wide range of documentary and oral sources, many of them previously unpublished. It reveals a complex portrait of an extraordinary man.

Mitzi M. Brunsdale;
bibliography updated by the editors

LAYAMON

Born: Probably northern Worcestershire, England;
fl. c. 1200
Died: Unknown

PRINCIPAL POETRY
Brut, c. 1205

OTHER LITERARY FORMS

Layamon is known only as the author of the partially translated poetic chronicle known as Layamon's *Brut*.

ACHIEVEMENTS

Layamon's *Brut*, which J. S. P. Tatlock describes as "the nearest thing we have to a traditional racial Epic," is the first major literary work in Middle English, and the first version in English of the stories of King Arthur and of King Lear. Assessing Layamon's achievement is difficult because his *Brut* is a much expanded translation of Wace's *Roman de Brut* (c. 1155), itself an Anglo-Norman translation and expansion of Geoffrey of Monmouth's *Historia regum Britanniae* (c. 1136; *History of the Kings of Britain*). Consequently, it is necessary first to briefly describe these earlier versions and the influence they are known to have exerted.

Geoffrey of Monmouth, writing in Latin in about 1136, constructed a pseudohistory of the British (as opposed to the Anglo-Saxon) kings of England, beginning with the legendary Brutus (a grandson of Aeneas), continuing through the celebrated reign of King Arthur, and ending with the last British kings in the seventh century. The primary effect of Geoffrey's *History of the Kings of Britain* was to stimulate international interest in the legends of Arthur, which previously had been well known only to the Welsh and Breton peoples. Geoffrey's *History of the Kings of Britain* and the *Prophecies of Merlin* which make up its seventh book were translated in places as far away as Iceland. Centuries later, in Elizabethan times, Geoffrey's *History of the Kings of Britain* would be rediscovered by the Tudor kings, who wished to stress their ancient Welsh claims to the throne. As part of this new interest, the *History of the Kings of Britain* would provide subject matter for Edmund Spenser and

William Shakespeare. Spenser devotes a canto of *The Faerie Queene* (1590, 1596, Book II, Canto X) to a "Chronicle of British Kings," based on Geoffrey and derivative histories, such as Raphael Holinshed's *Chronicles* (1577). For his tragedy of *King Lear* (c. 1605-1606), Shakespeare consulted both Holinshed's and Spenser's versions. There he found the basic plot outline, including the opening love test, Lear's progressive humiliation by Goneril and Regan, and his eventual redemption (restoration in Geoffrey's *History of the Kings of Britain*) by Cordelia and the duke of France. To these elements Shakespeare added the parallel subplots of Gloucester, Kent, and the Fool, and he rearranged the ending in a masterful fashion typical of his treatment of source materials.

The influence of Geoffrey's *History of the Kings of Britain* on medieval Arthurian literature was primarily by way of the Anglo-Norman translation by Wace. Wace's courtly version in octosyllabic couplets motivated and stylistically influenced his immediate successors, Chrétien de Troyes, Marie de France, and Thomas of Britain. More substantial use of his subject matter was made by fourteenth century prose romancers, in the Vulgate *Merlin* and the *Morte Arthur*. The latter work was a major source for Thomas Malory's *Le Morte d'Arthur* (c. 1469), and thus one can trace a circuitous route from the first to the last of the great Middle English Arthurians. Malory also made use of the alliterative *Morte Arthure*, perhaps the Arthurian work closest in spirit and substance to Layamon's *Brut*. Even this product of the alliterative revival, however, is thought to be based not on Layamon but on Wace, or perhaps on the fourteenth century translation of Wace by Robert Mannyng of Brunne. Among medieval works, only Robert of Gloucester's chronicle (in its later recension, c. 1340) can confidently be said to have made direct use of Layamon's *Brut*.

Even though his chronicle, which survives in only two manuscripts, represented something of a dead end in the development of Arthurian legend, Layamon was rediscovered in the nineteenth and twentieth centuries. Both Alfred, Lord Tennyson and Ezra Pound made demonstrable use of Layamon's poetic style. Linguists continue to study the *Brut*'s early, more highly inflected dialect, and stylistic critics remain fascinated by its poetic form, which lies somewhere between the formulaic, alliterative meter of Anglo-Saxon poetry and the developing meter of the Middle English rhymed romances. The major modern contribution to Layamon scholarship, however, is the edition by G. L. Brook and R. F. Leslie.

BIOGRAPHY

All the known details concerning Layamon's life are derived from the opening section of his *Brut*, the first five lines of which read as follows (in Madden's translation, which includes the significant manuscript variants):

> There was a priest on earth (or in the land,) who was named Layamon; he was son of Leovenath (Leuca),—may the Lord be gracious to him!—he dwelt at Ernley, at a noble church (with the good knight,) upon Severns bank (Severn),—good (pleasant) it there seemed to him—near Radestone, where he books read.

The author's name, which has been spelled in a number of ways, is Scandinavian in origin, and is cognate with modern English "Lawman." The recorded variant spellings of his father's name are less confusing when one realizes that the scribe often writes *u* for *v*; "Levca" can then be seen as a shortened form of "Leovenath." Tatlock hypothesizes, in light of the familiarity with Ireland that Layamon exhibits in his poem, that perhaps Leovenath went to Ireland with the Norman invading force, married a Scandinavian Irishwoman (there having been a sizable Viking population in Ireland at that time), and later returned to England with his son. In any case, the only residence Layamon himself mentions is a church at "Ernley" on the banks of the Severn near "Radestone." These details accord well with a village variously referred to as Lower Areley, Areley Kings, and Areley Regis, not far from Worcester and the Welsh border. The books that Layamon mentions as having read (line 5) have usually been taken to be service books that he used in his role as a priest. Despite attempts to find the man behind these few details, however, Layamon remains little more than a name, an occupation (priest and translator), and a place-name. Even the time in which he "flourished" is derived from the supposed date of composition of the *Brut*, which is itself undergoing a reevaluation.

ANALYSIS

In order to analyze Layamon's *Brut*, it is first necessary to continue the discussion of his sources. As mentioned above, Layamon's main source was Wace's *Roman de Brut*, which in the edition that Madden consulted consisted of 15,300 lines, as opposed to the 32,350 lines in his edition of Layamon's *Brut*. Granted that Madden's lines (now termed half-lines) are shorter than the lines in Wace, it is still apparent that Layamon considerably expanded his main source. It has been suggested that Layamon may have used an already expanded version of Wace, which had been conflated with an earlier chronicle (now lost) by Gaimar. As this suggestion cannot be verified, however, most critics have looked elsewhere for supplementary sources. One recent modification in this matter of primary sources is the discovery that some of the material previously considered original in Wace derives instead from an extant "variant version" of Geoffrey. Furthermore, additions occurring in a Welsh version of Geoffrey are paralleled in Layamon.

Layamon in his preface mentions two works in addition to Wace: "the English book that Saint Bede made," and another book "in Latin, that Saint Albin made, and the fair Austin." Bede's best-known work, and the work potentially of the most use to Layamon, is his *Historia Ecclesiastica Genta Anglorum* (c. 732; *Ecclesiastical History of the English Peoples*), written in Latin and later translated into Anglo-Saxon. Albinus (died 732) reportedly helped Bede to gather source materials, and so a number of critics have assumed that Layamon erroneously attributed the Old English translation to Bede, and Bede's Latin original to Albius (and to the great apostle to the English, "Austin" or Augustine of Canterbury, died 604). Layamon claims both to have "compressed" these three books (including Wace) into one and to have used the latter two books "as a model." This second statement is closer to the truth, for Layamon did not in fact make any incontestable use of Bede. He was probably acting in a tradition of vague citation to a previous authority; Geoffrey before him had claimed access to a certain "most ancient" source book. Nor can Layamon be shown conclusively to have drawn upon Geoffrey in the original Latin, upon classical authors, upon French Arthurians (besides Wace), or upon Welsh records. Evidence does suggest, however, that he was familiar with late Anglo-Saxon homiletic literature, and may even have read classical Anglo-Saxon verse in manuscript.

The best known of Layamon's additions are those that contribute new material to Arthurian legend. Wace had made the first recorded reference to the Round Table, to which Layamon adds an account of the quarrels over precedence which led to its institution (11360ff.) To Arthur's biography, Layamon adds an account of the elvish gifts at his birth (9608ff.), a premonitory dream of his final misfortunes in the battle with Molred (13982ff.), and an expanded version of Arthur's mysterious departure to Avalon (14277ff.) Arthur as a character seems less a romance hero than a stern and successful king, feared and respected by all the kings and great knights of Europe. (Perhaps it should be noted that the better-known exploits of some of Arthur's knights, such as the Lancelot affair and the quest for the Holy Grail, do not appear in Geoffrey, Wace, or Layamon.) As for Merlin, Layamon reports more of his prophecies than Wace had done, and adds an account of his stay in the wilderness (9878ff.) that can be compared with the Welsh tales of Merlin Silvestris. A long list of Layamon's minor Arthurian additions can be found in R. H. Fletcher, *The Arthurian Material in the Chronicles* (1906).

BRUT

C. Friedlander discusses additions from other parts of Layamon's *Brut* in her examination of five of its longer episodes: those of Leir, those of the *Brut*, heroes and thanes." As an illustration he cites an interesting Arthurian passage, in which Wace's knights ascend a tower and joke gaily about the relative merits of wartime and peace. Layamon, on the other hand, first characterizes the "ancient stonework" of the tower (12419), in a motif that recalls the older Anglo-Saxon elegies. The gay debate becomes a tense exchange or "flit" (12459) that recalls the "flytings" of Anglo-Saxon and Old Icelandic narrative verse. Another "Saxon echo" frequently alluded to is found in the description of Loch Ness (10848ff.), which is populated with the same sea-creatures ("nicors") mentioned in *Beowulf* (c. 1000).

Lewis also finds Layamon "fiercer but kinder" than Wace; Tatlock comments on a pervasive delight in crushing enemies, and sees therein echoes of Irish saga literature. Also suggestive of Irish influence is Layamon's

greater emphasis on the marvelous and on appearances from the world of "faery." Layamon's additions concerning Arthur's weapons and the elvish smith who forged them evoke equally Anglo-Saxon and Irish legends. Finally, Tatlock also mentions Layamon's technical familiarity with matters of seamanship, which, together with other details from medieval life, contributes to the personal stamp that Layamon puts on his material.

Layamon achieves a further degree of originality simply by virtue of the poetic form he employs. Geoffrey's *History of the Kings of Britain* is in prose, and Wace's *Roman de Brut* is in octosyllabic couplets; Layamon's *Brut* is written in a combination of alliterating and rhyming half-lines. The presence of alliteration suggests an inheritance from Anglo-Saxon verse, though not without some attendant changes. Metrically, Layamon's lines favor an iambic trochaic rhythm rather than the predominantly trochaic rhythm of Anglo-Saxon verse. This change leads to a greater proliferation of unstressed syllables at either end of the half-line. Furthermore, alliteration seems to be more an ornament than a strictly regulated requirement in Layamon's verse.

In these aspects of form, Layamon's *Brut* resembles a few other Early Middle English poems, including some late poetic entries in the Anglo-Saxon chronicle, the "Worcester fragments," "The Grave," and "The Proverbs of Alfred." Tatlock remarks how these poems also all lack the understatement, parenthesis, and periphrasis that characterized Anglo-Saxon verse. To account for these developments, scholars have hypothesized that a less strict, more popular form of alliterative verse may have existed alongside the more refined Anglo-Saxon compositions, such as *Beowulf*, which were committed to manuscript. It may be that the tradition degenerated (partially as a result of changes in the language itself), or, again, it may be that Layamon and the others, perhaps additionally influenced by the "rhythmic alliteration" of Anglo-Saxon prose, imperfectly revived the old forms. Such a revival (variously explained) did occur in the later Middle Ages, yielding, for example, the alliterative *Morte Arthure* mentioned above.

Another feature that Layamon's *Brut* shares with the earlier Anglo-Saxon poetry is the presence of repeated lines and half-lines called *formulas*. Examples have been collected by Tatlock and Herbert Pilch, who also lists formulas that the *Brut* shares with Anglo-Saxon verse and with roughly contemporary verse. Formulas are present in much of the world's traditional narrative poetry, the recurrent epithets in Homer perhaps being the best-known examples. Early in the twentieth century, the Homeric scholar Milman Parry, supplementing his research with fieldwork on contemporary Yugoslavian oral epic, developed what is known as oral-formulaic theory to account for this widespread appearance of formulas. According to Parry and his student Albert Lord, formulas are learned by apprentice poets as a means whereby they may improvise long oral narratives. This theory has since been applied to Old English and some Middle English verse, even though many of Parry's original statements have had to be modified considerably. For example, Layamon as a translator is not improvising but rather working in close conjunction with a written text (even if he probably worked more "in his head" than modern poets tend to do). Why, then, would he have a need for ready-made formulas? He may instead have been using formulas ornamentally, in imitation of the earlier models, or there may have been other factors at work which made formulas desirable. Layamon seems to have been constrained to avoid ending his sentence units with the first half-line (as had often been the case in the earlier poetry). Formulas, which are more frequent in his second half-lines, may have represented a useful way to "pad out" the whole line, acting somewhat like the "rhyme tags" in metrical romances. Layamon's use of formulas differs in other ways from Anglo-Saxon practice. Fixed epithets, such as "athelest kingen" for Arthur, are more common, as are formulas that recur in similar situations, such as "wind stod an willen," often used in sea voyage descriptions.

Rhyme was likewise employed ornamentally in the Early Middle English poems mentioned above, prompting some scholars to hypothesize that rhyme was developing independently in England, probably under influence from Latin hymns. Surely the example of Wace strengthened this tendency toward the couplet, which would become the norm in rhymed romances. There may also be an Irish influence at work in Layamon's unusual rhyming by consonant classes and on contrasting stresses. Here are some sample rhyme-pairs, modernized from the episode of Arthur's final dream (13971ff.):

bestride/ride; tiding/king; son/welcome; fair knight/fare tonight. The first rhyme is exact; the second example rhymes an unstressed with a stressed syllable as does the third; yet here the consonants *m* and *n* do not match, but are related instead by way of a shared phonological class ("nasals"). The last example ingeniously interweaves homonyms and rhymes.

One final stylistic element distinguishing Layamon from his Anglo-Saxon predecessors is his use of the extended simile. Arthur's pursuit of Colgrim, for example, is compared (for eight lines, 10629ff.) to a wolf hunting down a mountain goat. Most of Layamon's extended similes, in fact, occur in this part of the Arthurian section, leading scholars to suppose that a single source may be responsible for this stylistic feature. Here, as elsewhere, however, the question of sources should not be allowed to overshadow Layamon's unique achievement. The *Brut* can and should be read for its own merits, as a poem and not simply as "Arthurian matter" divorced from its particular form.

BIBLIOGRAPHY

Bryan, Elizabeth J. *Collaborative Meaning in Medieval Scribal Culture: The Otho Layamon.* Ann Arbor: University of Michigan Press, 1999. Before print technology, every book was unique. Two manuscripts of the "same" text could present that text very differently, depending on scribes, compilers, translators, annotators, and decorators. The author questions whether it is appropriate to read such books, including *Layamon*, as products of a single author and finds cultural attitudes that valued communal aspects of manuscript texts: for example, a view of the physical book as connecting all who held it. Bibliographical references, index.

Donahue, Dennis. *Lawman's "Brut," an Early Arthurian Poem: A Study of Middle English Formulaic Composition.* Lewiston, N.Y.: Edwin Mellen Press, 1991. Examines the formulas and themes in the *Brut*, arguing that Layamon made artistic use of formulas, themes, and imagery in revising his Anglo-Norman source and creating darker portraits of Vortiger, Uther, and, especially, King Arthur. *Notes and Queries* comments that "undergraduates will certainly find the initial chapter on the development of the Parry/Lord theory most useful; the material presented in the appendices and analysed in the second chapter remains as valuable as it was fifteen years ago; and above all, it draws attention to the complexity of Layamon's narrative technique."

Layamon. *Layamon's Arthur: The Arthurian Section of Layamon's "Brut."* Edited by W. R. J. Barron and S. C. Weinberg. Austin: University of Texas Press, 2001. A fully edited version of the original text is accompanied by a close parallel prose translation, a substantial introduction, textual notes, and an updated bibliography. Sources are reviewed, as well as the social context of the poem and the structure. Includes a discussion of the Arthur character as hero and the *Brut* as a national epic.

_____. *Layamon's "Brut."* Translated by Donald G. Bzdyl. Binghamton, N.Y.: Center for Medieval and Early Renaissance Studies, 1989. This prose translation of the *Brut* is accompanied by an excellent bibliography that includes many articles and related studies. The introduction gives a good survey and appreciation of Layamon and the poem.

_____. *Selections from Layamon's "Brut."* Edited by G. L. Brook. Oxford, England: Clarendon Press, 1963. The selections specifically include the events preceding Arthur's birth, his marriage, the accession and victories over the Scots, Saxons, and Irish, the origin of the Roman War and the Morte. Includes notes, an excellent glossary, an index of names, and a select, short bibliography. The short introduction and biographical note is by the noted scholar and author, C. S. Lewis.

Le Saux, Francoise H. M. *Layamon's "Brut": The Poem and Its Sources.* Cambridge, England: D. S. Brewer, 1989. This study characterizes Layamon as more than the simple parish priest, as he is so often seen. Le Saux looks at many possible sources and traditions that inform the poem. She sees Layamon as a mixture of Welsh and English cultures—the allies against the Norman invaders. Previous scholarship is reevaluated and the thematic and stylistic relationship to the sources is examined. An exhaustive bibliography is also appended.

Paul Acker;

bibliography updated by the editors

EDWARD LEAR

Born: Holloway, England; May 12, 1812
Died: San Remo, Italy; January 29, 1888

PRINCIPAL POETRY

A Book of Nonsense, 1846, enlarged 1861
Nonsense Songs, Stories, Botany and Alphabets, 1871
More Nonsense, Pictures, Rhymes, Botany, Etc., 1872
Laughable Lyrics: A Fourth Book of Nonsense Poems, Songs, Botany, Music, Etc., 1877
Nonsense Songs and Stories, 1894
Queery Leary Nonsense, 1911 (Lady Strachey, editor)
The Complete Nonsense of Edward Lear, 1947 (Holbrook Jackson, editor)
Teapots and Quails, and Other New Nonsenses, 1953 (Angus Davison and Philip Hofer, editors)

OTHER LITERARY FORMS

Edward Lear's verse collections include three prose stories and three prose recipes called "Nonsense Cookery." A few of his fanciful botanical drawings are accompanied by whimsical texts. Like his poems, these pieces show Lear at play with language, blithely disregarding common sense.

Two volumes of letters, most of them to Chichester Fortescue, were published in 1907 and 1911. Enlivened by riddles, cartoons, and bits of verse, they demonstrate Lear's fascination with the sound and meaning of words. He uses puns and creative phonetic spellings; he coins words and humorously distorts existing ones. A cold January day in Corfu is so "icicular" that it "elicits the ordibble murmurs of the cantankerous Corcyreans." He complains of the proliferation of tourists, especially "Germen, Gerwomen, and Gerchildren," around his property in San Remo. Although he often revealed his loneliness and depression, Lear characteristically found something to laugh about—if not in his situation, then in his response to it: He called himself "savage and black as 90,000 bears," and wished he were "an egg and was going to be hatched." In 1883 he wrote, "I sometimes wish that I myself were a bit of gleaming granite or pomegranite or a poodle or a pumkin"; at seventy-one and in ill health, Lear's imperishable delight in wordplay pulled him out of self-pity.

He kept journals of his painting excursions; these were later published with his own illustrations. Lacking the warmth and spontaneity of the letters, these topographical and travel books are valuable to readers who relish pictorial description and wish to know the conditions of travel in the nineteenth century.

ACHIEVEMENTS

Edward Lear thought of himself as a topographical landscape painter, and his ornithological drawings are still highly regarded. Students of nineteenth century painting also admire his watercolor drawings—pen or pencil sketches executed out-of-doors and later elaborated and colored. Nevertheless, Lear's reputation as an author eventually overshadowed his painting, and he become famous as the father of nonsense literature and today is best known for the verses and cartoons he created to entertain children. He popularized the form that came to be known as the limerick, and his innovative comic drawings have influenced many artists, notably James Thurber.

BIOGRAPHY

Edward Lear was the twentieth of twenty-one children born to Jeremiah and Ann (Skerrett) Lear. Financial difficulties led to the dispersal of the family; although the Lears were later reunited, from 1816 Edward was looked after by his oldest sister, Ann. She was devoted to him and encouraged his interest in reading and painting, but the near-sighted, homely, rather morbid child brooded over being rejected, as he saw it, by his mother. His diary alludes mysteriously to another early trauma, perhaps a homosexual assault. His inclination to isolate himself grew after the onset of epilepsy (he called it his "demon") when he was five years old. He always felt that he was not like other people.

At fifteen he was earning his own living as a draftsman. Within five years, his skill in drawing birds brought him to the attention of Lord Stanley (later the thirteenth earl of Derby), who invited him to Knowsley to make drawings of his private menagerie. There he made acquaintances who would become lifelong patrons and began to create comical verses and drawings to amuse his host's children.

In 1837, the earl sent him to Italy to recover his health and to study landscape painting. From that time England was no longer his permanent home. Lear traveled throughout the Mediterranean world and lived in several places, explaining his wandering by saying that his health required a temperate climate, that he needed to make sketches as "studies" for his oil paintings, and that he must support himself by making his work available to wealthy tourists. His restlessness also suggests that he was searching for, and perhaps trying to avoid, something: an all-consuming interest.

Amazingly industrious even by Victorian standards, Lear generally spent most of his day sketching or painting; in leisure hours he read widely and taught himself a half-dozen languages. Hard work seemed to help ward off depression and epileptic attacks but did not prevent his being lonely. For thirty years his only constant companion was his Albanian servant, Giorgio Kokali, to whom Lear showed extraordinary kindness and loyalty. While busily preparing one set of illustrations for a

Edward Lear (Hulton Archive)

travel book and another for a volume of natural history, he decided to publish the series of limericks he had begun at Knowsley. His painting gave him less satisfaction than his nonsense verse, which he wrote for the children of friends and for other youngsters he met in hotels and aboard ships. His verse became a vehicle for self-expression, while painting all too often meant drudgery and frustration. Upon receiving a legacy at the age of thirty-seven, he studied for a time at the Royal Academy, as if hoping to win recognition as a serious artist. Lear apparently had small regard for the watercolor drawings he produced by the hundreds: They were "potboilers" and "tyrants" that required much time yet brought little money. Although he sometimes sold large landscapes in oil and received modest sums for his books, he often worried about his finances and had to rely on the patronage of wealthy friends.

Lear tried to be independent, but he constantly suffered from loneliness. He maintained a voluminous correspondence with scores of friends, sometimes rising early to write as many as thirty-five letters before breakfast. Occasionally he expressed wonder that "this child," an odd, moody fellow, should have so many friends. He confided in a few—Chichester Fortescue, Franklin Lushington, and Emily Tennyson (his ideal woman)—but even to them he could not reveal his dark memories or speak of his "demon." More than once he considered marriage but could never bring himself to propose, despite evidence that Augusta Bethell would have accepted him. Terrified of rejection, this charming and lovable man told himself and his confidants that he was too crotchety, ugly, poor, and sickly to be a good husband. Another impediment of which he may have been conscious was his tendency to homosexuality. His response to Lushington, a kind but undemonstrative person, can only be called passionate; for several years he fretted over Lushington's inability to give and receive affection. Emotional and spiritual intimacy were what he most craved, however, and his relationship with Lushington eventually became mutually satisfying. Throughout his adult years, Lear seems to have been happiest in the company of children.

Haunted by a sense of failure and determined to put an end to his wandering, in 1871 he moved into a house he had built in San Remo. Yet he traveled to India after his sixtieth birthday, making hundreds of drawings, and talked of going a second time. His last years were darkened by loneliness, illness, and a series of disappointments. He finally lost the will to work when his eyesight failed and he was near collapse. None of his friends was with him when he died.

ANALYSIS

Edward Lear is known as the father of nonsense literature, and he has never been surpassed in that genre. Charles L. Dodgson (Lewis Carroll) had the opportunity to learn from Lear, and Lear may have learned from him; however, Carroll's nonsense verse is much different: funnier, more intellectual, and less musical. Lear was a true poet, keenly sensitive to the sounds and "colors" of words. His poems have lasted not only because they are amusing and melodious but also because they express the innocence, melancholy, and exuberance of Lear himself.

THE LIMERICK FORM

According to Lear himself, he adopted the form for his limericks—or "nonsense rhymes," as he called them—from "There was a sick man of Tobago," published in *Anecdotes and Adventures of Fifteen Gentlemen* (c. 1822). Most of them begin with this formula: "There was an Old Man [or Old Person, or Young Lady] of [place name]." The last line is nearly the same as the first, with Lear typically using an adjective (sometimes appropriate, sometimes whimsical) before the character's designation. Each limerick is accompanied by a cartoon of its main character in action—riding a goose, sitting in a tree, refusing to respond sensibly to a sensible question. More than three-quarters of the limericks concern old people; even some of those called "young" in the texts appear elderly in the drawing. Most of Lear's folk are eccentrics. One old man runs through town carrying squealing pigs; another will eat nothing but roots. Physical oddities such as very long legs or huge eyes are common. Several characters with noses even more prodigious than Lear's deal variously with that handicap: One hires an old woman to carry it, another allows birds to roost on it, while a third adamantly denies that his nose is long. Lear's intended audience, children of the Victorian age, were surely amused not just by his characters' oddness but also by the fact that these laughable people were supposed to be "grown-ups."

FORMULAS FOR HUMOR

Lear often found humor in incongruity and arbitrariness. An old man of Dunrose, "melancholy" because his nose has been "seized" by a parrot half as large as himself, is said to be "soothed" upon learning that the bird's name is Polly. A few characters suffer terrible ends— drowning, suicide, choking on food, death from despair, being baked in a cake. Yet even their situations are amusing; either the text indicates that these people somehow deserve their fate, or the poem or cartoon indicates that they are not distressed by it. For example, the "courageous" Young Lady of Norway, flattened by a door, asks, "What of that?"

Lear's avowed purpose was to write "nonsense pure and absolute" for the amusement of "little folks." Consciously or not, he also dramatized the conflict between the individual and society. Even children must have noticed how often the limericks' heroes and heroines were at odds with the people around them. In Brill, Melrose, Parma, Buda, Columbia, and Thermopylae, and other real-world settings specified by Lear, "they"—representatives of Respectable Society—stare, turn aside, express disapproval, offer unwanted advice, and punish. A man who "dance[s] a quadrille with a Raven" is "smashed" by his countrymen; so is the fellow who constantly plays his gong. A fat man is stoned by the children of Chester. The reader is not surprised that one old man has "purchased a steed, which he rode at full speed,/ And escaped from the people of Basing." Aldous Huxley called Lear a "profound social philosopher" for his portrayal of the consequences of nonconformity (*On the Margin*, 1928). Lear's touch, however, was always light; even the limericks containing violence or death are not sad or horrific.

The eccentrics are more likely to be friendly with animals than with other human beings. They live with birds, ride bears, play music for pigs, and try to teach fishes to walk—but they can also be attacked by insects, bulls, and dogs (Lear was terrified of dogs). Apparently, being truly alive is a lonely, risky affair. Accidents, physical and mental afflictions, and rejection by others, all in the nature of things, seem especially likely for the person who is different from his neighbors. Yet, unpre-

dictably, "they" are sometimes solicitous and considerate, inquiring about the comfort of some irascible characters, warning others of imminent danger. "They" treat a depressed man by feeding him salad and singing to him; "they" glue together a hapless fellow "split quite in two" by a fall from a horse.

Lear's society, then, is committed to maintaining order and the general well-being—if necessary, at the expense of people who behave in ways "they" do not approve and cannot understand. This is the world we know. Without the preachiness of much contemporary children's literature—or rather, literature written for the edification of children—the limericks convey that civil, mannerly behavior is expected. From Lear's perspective, as from the child's, adult judgments appear arbitrary. For some reason, or no reason, "they" are delighted with a girl named Opsibeena who rides a pig; "they" seem less likely to appreciate innovation than to encourage decorum, however meaningless: One man ingratiates himself with his neighbors by sitting in his cellar under an umbrella.

IMAGINARY SETTINGS

The nonsense songs are set in an imagined world in which animals and objects talk, sing, and dance with one another. Some of these characters are heroes; others are bored and lonely misfits. Like Lear, an early admirer of Lord Byron, they seek happiness in love, companionship, and travel. Odd friendships and courtships, mysterious events, and unexpected reversals abound. Lear has created a world in which anything wonderful may happen. The rules of decorum do not apply, do not exist. An owl marries a pussycat, and the Poker woos the Shovel. The title characters in "The Daddy Long-Legs and the Fly," unwelcome in polite society, sail away to "the great Gromboolian Plain," where they spend their days at "battlecock and shuttledoor." Disgusted with idleness, a Nutcracker and a Sugar-tongs ride off on stolen ponies, never to return—ignoring the protests of their household companions. Less adventurous, a perambulating table and chair ask some friendly animals to lead them safely home. Most successful in their quest are the Jumblies of the green heads and blue hands. Despite the warnings of "all their friends" (akin to the limericks' "they"), the Jumblies go to sea in a sieve, discover "the Lakes, and the Torrible Zone,/ and the hills of the Chankly Bore," and return home after twenty years to be lionized by their neighbors. Unlike most of Lear's songs, "The Jumblies" has no undercurrent of melancholy or dread.

MARRIAGE, FAMILY, AND FREUDIAN INTERPRETATIONS

A wanderer for most of his life, Lear often wished for (but doubted that he really wanted) a home with a wife and children. His "laughable lyrics," which sometimes poke fun at the conventional sex roles, courtship rituals, and marriage, reveal that he was ambivalent about committing himself to a woman. As George Orwell remarked in his essay "Nonsense Poetry," "It is easy to guess that there was something seriously wrong in [Lear's] sex life" (*Shooting an Elephant and Other Essays*, 1950). More recent critics, reading nonsense literature as a manifestation of the author's repressed emotions, have noted that it is the pussycat, not the owl, who proposes matrimony; judging by Lear's cartoon, the owl is somewhat afraid of his bride. Again, a duck (a cigar-smoking female) talks a rather effeminate kangaroo into letting her ride around the world on his tail. Deserted by the girl he loves, the sorrowful title character in "The Dong with a Luminous Nose" wanders in lonely frustration; at night his great red nose, illuminated by a lamp "All fenced about/ With a bandage stout," is visible for miles. In pre-Freudian times this poem was surely "laughable" in a simpler way than it is now.

"THE COURTSHIP OF THE YONGHY-BONGHY-BÒ"

The hero of "The Courtship of the Yonghy-Bonghy-Bò" proposes to a married woman; when she regretfully refuses him, he flees to "the sunset isles of Boshen" to live alone. Remaining in Coromandel, "where the early pumpkins blow," the lady "weeps, and daily moans." So romantic and comical an ending would have been impossible if the Bò had offered himself to a woman who was free to marry him. "The Courtship of the Yonghy-Bonghy-Bò," one of the songs for which Lear composed a piano accompaniment, uses the verbal music of repetition, assonance, and alliteration. Indeed, in this and other songs he achieves a lyricism reminiscent of the Romantic poets. Parodying the Romantic manner as he made verse out of personal concerns and fantasies, he

was looking for a way to deal with his emotions. He once burst into tears while singing the song, written while he struggled to make up his mind about marrying "Gussie" Bethell.

"THE PELICAN CHORUS"

To the Nutcrackers and Sugar-tongs, domesticity—perhaps the most sacred of Victorian ideals—is a "stupid existence." Home is sweet only to the timorous table and chair, the phobia-ridden Discobboloses, and the cautious Spikky Sparrows. Mr. and Mrs. Sparrow don human clothing, ostensibly to protect themselves from catching cold but actually, it seems, to "look like other people." Lear does portray some happy and admirable couples. In "The Pelican Chorus," King and Queen Pelican sing of their present joys and recall their daughter's courtship by the King of the Cranes. They are content, even though they realize that they will probably never see Daughter Dell again. A less skillful poet would have allowed the song to become maudlin or merely ridiculous, but Lear maintains a balance of melancholy, nostalgia, and humor. He reveals the singers' pride in their "lovely leathery throats and chins" and pleasure in the "flumpy sound" their feet make as they dance. (This kind of music is impossible for the crane who, it is whispered, "has got no webs between his toes.") They complacently visualize Dell's "waddling form so fair,/ With a wreath of shrimps in her short white hair." The old pelicans' confusion—or fusion—of past and present is at once amusing and poignant; each stanza ends with this refrain:

> Ploffskin, Pluffskin, Pelican jee,
> We think no Birds so happy as we!
> Plumpskin, Ploshkin, Pelican jill,
> We think so then, and we thought so still!

"MR. AND MRS. DISCOBBOLOS"

"Mr. and Mrs. Discobbolos," another poem about a family, ends with what must be described as an entertaining catastrophe. For twenty years this couple lives in peaceful isolation atop a wall—because they are afraid of falling off. Then, quite suddenly, the wife begins to fret because their "six fine boys" and "six sweet girls" are missing the pleasures and opportunities of social intercourse. Disgusted, perhaps driven mad, Mr. Discobbolos slides to the ground and dynamites home and family "into thousands of bits to the sky so blue." One feels that he has done the right thing, even though his action is surprising and mysterious. Possibly he cannot endure mixing once again with conventional society or thinking that any of his children may marry such a "runcible goose" as his wife. Perhaps the poet is once again exploding the myth of the happy home. The attempt to make sense out of exquisite nonsense is part of the pleasure of reading Lear.

"INCIDENTS IN THE LIFE OF MY UNCLE ARLY"

No doubt he exposed more of his hopes and fears than he intended. Some of the songs, especially those written late in his life, involve the emotions in a way that the limericks do not. Since the poet sympathizes with the pain and joy of these creatures of fantasy, so does the reader. Lear's last ballad, published posthumously, is clearly autobiographical. "Incidents in the Life of My Uncle Arly," is a formal imitation of "The Lady of Shalott" which tells of the wanderings and death of a poor and lonely man. At last "they" bury him with a railway ticket (representing Lear's freedom and rootlessness) and his sole companion, a "pea-green Cricket" (symbolic, perhaps, of the poet's inspiration to make music of his own experience). Lear, the "Adopty Duncle" of many children, states four times that the hero's shoes are "far too tight." Among the many afflictions of the poet's last years were swollen feet. Arly's tight shoes may represent any of the constraints on the poet's happiness. Thomas Byrom has pointed out that Lear, like UncLE ARly, was a homeless traveler for more than forty years before building a villa in Italy (*Nonsense and Wonder*, 1977). Sad without being pessimistic, the poem characterizes a man whose life was lonely but rich in experience.

"ECLOGUE"

Lear's "Eclogue" is the product of his capacity for making fun of his sorrows and his tendency to self-pity and grumbling. In this parody of a classical genre, the singing contest between shepherds, Lear and John Addington Symonds catalog their woes; the latter's wife, Catherine, finally judges whose miseries are greater. The "Eclogue" is laughable, but the reader of Lear's correspondence sees how truly it reflects his assessment of himself and his career; but *A Book of Nonsense* saw thirty editions in his lifetime.

"THE QUANGLE WANGLE'S HAT"

Lear's pleasure in his verse is expressed most clearly in "The Quangle Wangle's Hat." Wearing a beaver hat one hundred and two feet wide, the title character sits sadly in a Crumpetty Tree, wishing (like Lear in San Remo) that someone would come to visit. Then he is approached by a series of exotic animals, some of them (like the Quangle Wangle himself) familiar from Lear's other writings. When they ask for permission to live on his hat, the hero welcomes each one. Enjoying a simple yet profound comradeship, an assembly of Lear's creatures blissfully dances "by the light of the Mulberry moon"—"and all [are] as happy as happy could be." Here in microcosm is Lear's imagined world, singularly free of conflict. The real world is not like this, but Lear persuades readers to imagine that it might be. Friendship and sharing of oneself offer the best hope of contentment in the fantasy world, as in the real one. The Quangle Wangle is Edward Lear.

OTHER MAJOR WORKS

NONFICTION: *Illustrations of the Family of Psittacidae: Or, Parrots*, 1832; *Views in Rome and Its Environs*, 1841; *Illustrated Excursions in Italy*, 1846; *Journals of a Landscape Painter in Albania, Etc.*, 1851; *Journals of a Landscape Painter in Southern Calabria, Etc.*, 1852; *Views in the Seven Ionian Islands*, 1863; *Journal of a Landscape Painter in Corsica*, 1870; *Lear in Sicily*, 1938; *Indian Journal*, 1953 (Ray Murphy, editor); *Edward Lear in Southern Italy*, 1964.

BIBLIOGRAPHY

Byrom, Thomas. *Nonsense and Wonder: The Poems and Cartoons of Edward Lear*. New York: E. P. Dutton, 1977. A full-length, sympathetic study of Lear that discusses his poetry in depth. The author has been generous in providing extracts of Lear's long poems, as well as reproductions of Lear's sketches accompanying his limericks. Possibly the most comprehensive literary criticism available on Lear's poetry.

Chitty, Susan. *That Singular Person Called Lear*. London: Weidenfeld & Nicolson, 1988. A biography of Lear, recommended for its appreciation of Lear, as well as for the breadth of knowledge about him. Discusses Lear's life and early development, his poetry, and his paintings. Essential background reading for Lear scholars.

Colley, Ann C. *Edward Lear and the Critics*. Columbia, S.C.: Camden House, 1993. A history of the critical reception of Lear's work. Includes bibliographical references and index.

Hark, Ina Rae. *Edward Lear*. Boston: Twayne, 1982. A useful introduction to Lear examining his nonsense poetry and its parallels with his life. The critical commentary covers his limericks, nonsense poems, and longer poems.

Levi, Peter. *Edward Lear*. New York: Scribner, 1995. A comprehensive biography of Lear's life and works. Includes a bibliography and an index.

Noakes, Vivian. *Edward Lear: Selected Letters*. Oxford, England: Clarendon Press, 1988. A thoroughly researched volume, containing an important selection of letters by Lear. Recommended reading for insight into Lear's thinking and inspirations for his works. Included among the letters are drawings by Lear.

Vinson, James, ed. *Great Writers of the English Language: Poets*. New York: St. Martin's Press, 1979. The entry on Lear gives a brief overview of his life and lists his works. Notes the irony that although Lear's nonsense poems originated as a diversion from his professional career as an artist, they were to become the key to his fame and influence. Acknowledges the strength of Lear's visual and linguistic playfulness.

Mary De Jong;
bibliography updated by the editors

LI-YOUNG LEE

Born: Jakarta, Indonesia: August 19, 1957

PRINCIPAL POETRY

Rose, 1986
The City in Which I Love You, 1990
Book of My Nights, 2001

OTHER LITERARY FORMS

The Winged Seed: A Remembrance (1995) is a memoir of Li-Young Lee's family's life in Jakarta, Indonesia, their years in exile, and their adaptation to life in a small Pennsylvania town. He remembers how the family suffered when his father was placed in prison for his political views. Acting out of love and loyalty, his mother spent endless hours waiting in lines outside the prison gates trying to see her husband. In the mother's absence, the responsibility for the safety of the home and family rested on Lee's sister Fei's shoulders as she guarded the house from the threat of looters and corrupt government officials. Most important, Lee focuses on his love for his father, love and respect mingled with fear, as he was often beaten by his father. Lee struggles to piece together his own memories of his past as well as the stories told to him by his parents. Moving between confusing and often painful images of his past and the present safety of his life with his wife and children, Lee blends history and present narrative as he seeks to make sense of his life.

ACHIEVEMENTS

Li-Young Lee's poetry is filled with the memories and stories of his family's life in exile and his struggle to bridge the gap between his own experiences as an immigrant and his Chinese heritage. Lee received National Endowment for the Arts Fellowships in 1986 and 1995 and a Guggenheim Fellowship in 1987. *Rose* won the New York University 1986 Delmore Schwartz Memorial Poetry Award and *The City in Which I Love You* was the 1990 Lamont Poetry Selection of the Academy of American Poets. Lee received the American Book Award, from the Before Columbus Foundation, in 1995 for *The Winged Seed*.

BIOGRAPHY

Li-Young Lee was born in 1957 in Jakarta, Indonesia, of Chinese parents. His maternal grandfather had been the first president of the Republic of China, and his father had been the personal physician to Mao Zedong in China before leaving for Indonesia. In Jakarta the senior Lee taught English and philosophy at Gamaliel University, which he helped establish. As a result of anti-Chinese sentiment, Lee's father spent a year as a

Critical Survey of Poetry

Li-Young Lee

political prisoner in President Sukarno's jails. In 1959, as the Lee family was being shipped to a detention center where they would be forced to live on a remote island, they were rescued by a former student of Lee's, who helped the family escape. They were taken in by a member of the congregation of the Ling Liang Assembly.

Fleeing from Sukarno, the family spent five years traveling throughout Hong Kong, Macao, and Japan. Lee's father preached in Hong Kong, where he drew large crowds for his revival meetings. After the family arrived in the United States in 1964, Lee's father became a Presbyterian minister in a small town in western Pennsylvania.

Li-Young Lee attended high school in Pennsylvania and earned a B.A. from the University of Pittsburgh in 1979. As an undergraduate he was allowed to take a graduate workshop in poetry taught by Gerald Stern, who later wrote the foreword to Lee's first book of poetry, *Rose*. In 1978 Lee married Donna L. Lee, and he and his wife settled in Chicago with their two sons. He attended the University of Arizona, Tucson, from 1979 to 1980, and the State University of New York, Brockport, from 1980 to 1981. He has worked as an artist for a fashion accessories company and has taught at Northwestern University and the University of Iowa. As Li-Young Lee's father aged, he became blind and helpless, and Li-Young cared for his father until his death in 1989.

ANALYSIS

Li-Young Lee's poetry draws on his memories of the refugee experience and stories recounted by family members. He explores the question of individual identity in a world where people have been uprooted from their culture and have not found acceptance in their new land. Many immigrants remain silent about their past lives, and their silence adds to the confusion and loss of identity that characterize the immigrant experience. Lee faces the complex issues of displacement as he seeks to understand earlier generations of his family. Fragmented memories of traumatic events haunt his life.

Lee uses the free-verse style and writes in the present tense as he fuses present experience with images from the past. The clarity and simplicity of his poems allow the reader to see ordinary scenes in a different way. His poems usually focus on a situation or character that sets the stage for his musings on love, friendship, and the meaning of life.

In the foreword to *Rose*, Gerald Stern wrote that "understanding, even accepting, the father is the critical event, the critical 'myth' in Lee's poetry." His father's life is so entwined with his own that at times he seems to become his father. For example, at the end of the poem "Ash, Snow, or Moonlight" he asks "is this the first half of the century or the last?/ Is this my father's life or mine?" Lee's poems show his reverence for both of his parents, but it is his loving but fearful father that he seeks to understand.

History is always present, coloring the way he sees his life. The gaps in his history haunt him, causing him to seek answers to his questions about the violent events that took place in Indonesia when he was a small child. He remembers images and scenes of terror, but he does not fully understand what happened.

"THE GIFT"

As the narrator of "The Gift" removes a metal splinter from his wife's hand, he recalls the scene when he was a boy of seven and his father removed a splinter from his palm. To distract the boy, the father told a story in a low and reassuring voice. The poem ends with the boy kissing his father as he holds up the splinter. In describing this ordinary scene, Lee reflects on the complex relationship that exists between father and son.

Although the son does not remember the story, he can "hear his voice still, a well/ of dark water, a prayer." He recalls his father's tenderness as he laid his hands against his face, but he also remembers "the flames of discipline/ he raised above my head." The hands that cared for him were the same hands that beat him.

Lee addresses the reader directly as he says "Had you entered that afternoon/ you would have thought you saw a man,/ planting something in a boy's palm." The reader would have witnessed an ordinary scene between a man and his son, but "Had you followed that boy/ you would have arrived here,/ where I bend over my wife's right hand." In performing this simple act, the father taught the son something about love, and the son reflects on the ways in which his father has influenced his life.

"PERSIMMONS"

When he was in sixth grade, Lee was slapped by his teacher for confusing the word "persimmon" with the word "precision" and was made to stand in the corner. Other words that caused him trouble were "fight" and "fright." Making a connection between the words, he thinks that "Fight was what I did when I was frightened/ fright was what I felt when I was fighting." In these lines Lee shows the confusion and fear that were part of the experience of learning to survive in a new culture.

When the teacher brings a persimmon to class, Lee knows that it is not ripe and does not join his classmates in eating a piece of the fruit. He then describes the ripe persimmons that he gave to his father. Now, years later "in the muddy lighting/ of my parents' cellar, I rummage, looking/ for something I lost." He finds a picture that his father had painted of the persimmons and takes the picture to his father. Now blind, his father says that he painted the persimmons so many times that he could paint them from memory. Lee reflects on the precision in his father's wrist as he painted the persimmons and makes the connection between his childhood experience and his father's precision as an artist. At the end of the poem the son sees that "Some things never leave a per-

son:/ scent of the hair of one you love,/ the texture of persimmons." Although he faced difficulties in school as a child of another culture, his heritage has endowed him with specific values.

"FURIOUS VERSIONS"

"Furious Versions" is a seven-part account of his family's years of exile. The poem is filled with images of the family's hardships. As he tells his family history, he is urged on by his father's words, "Don't forget any of this." He feels responsible for recording the family's experiences because, as he says, "I'm the only one/ who's lived to tell it,/ and I confuse/ the details." As he strives to reconstruct the events, his own viewpoint is confused with that of his father, causing him to ask,

> Will I rise and go
> out into an American city?
> Or walk down to the wilderness sea?
> I might run with wife and children to the docks
> to bribe an officer for our lives
> and perilous passage.

He provides this image to show his confusion:

> And did I stand
> on the train from Chicago to Pittsburgh
> so my fevered son could sleep? Or did I
> open my eyes
> and see my father's closed face
> rocking above me?

Some images stick in his mind as he recalls

> and everywhere, fire,
> corridors of fire, brick and barbed wire.
> Soldiers sweep the streets
> for my father. My mother
> hides him, haggard,
> in the closet.

Later an officer threatens his father as "A pistol butt turns my father's spit to blood." The following lines show that by recounting the events, Lee hopes to keep the memory of his father alive: "The characters survive through the telling/ the teller survives/ by his telling; by his voice/ brinking silence does he survive." He ends the poem by speaking of his life with his own sons as he kneels "to live a while/ at the level of his son's eyes."

"VISIONS AND INTERPRETATIONS"

In the poem "Visions and Interpretations," Lee and his son visit the grave of Lee's father, and as they rest against a tree Lee falls asleep and dreams. He describes the dream to his son, but neither of them understands the meaning of the dream. Lee talks of "The old book I finished reading/ I've since read again and again./ And what was far grows near,/ and what is near grows more dear." He is thinking of his past, trying to make sense of his father's life and his own history, but "between [his] eyes is always/ the rain, the migrant rain." He continues to try to make sense of his father's life in order to understand his own, but the confusion that was a result of his being uprooted from one culture and thrown into another has made it difficult to see his life clearly.

"INTERROGATIONS"

Lee was only a very young child carried in his father's arms when the family fled from Indonesia, and while trying to understand what happened during that traumatic time, he has met a wall of silence when asking relatives about the past. "Interrogations" is structured around pieces of dialogue as the first speaker asks the questions and the second answers. The first speaker has questions about the night they fled the house, but the second speaker does not provide the answers. One asks, "Which house did we flee by night? Which house did we flee by day?" and the other answers, "Don't ask me." The first speaker persists: "We stood and watched one burn; from one we ran away." The second answers, "I'm neatly folding/ the nights and days, notes/ to be forgotten." The questioner continues to describe shattered scenes from his memory—"There were fires in the streets"—and asks, "Who came along?/ Who got left behind?" The answer comes, "Ask the sea." Although the second speaker refuses to answer questions and says "I'm through/ with memory," the last line shows that the memories are still vivid: "Can't you still smell the smoke on my body?"

OTHER MAJOR WORKS

NONFICTION: *The Winged Seed: A Remembrance*, 1995.

BIBLIOGRAPHY

Engles, Tim. "Lee's 'Persimmons.'" *Explicator* 54 (Spring, 1996): 191-192. Engles shows how the words "persimmons" and "precision" represent the experiences of the poet's search for values from his "fading heritage." Engles says that the speaker of the poem "Persimmons" reflects on the warmth of his parents' love and the importance of their culture.

Lee, Li-Young. "To Witness the Invisible: A Talk with Li-Young Lee." Interview by Tod Marshall. *The Kenyon Review*, Winter, 2000, 129-147. Tod Marshall spoke with Li-Young Lee in Memphis, Tennessee, during the fall of 1996. In this interview Lee discusses his interest in quest poetry and talks about his own search for identity, coming to the conclusion that poetry comes out of a need to hear the voice of the universe.

Slowick, Mary. "Beyond Lot's Wife: The Immigration Poems of Marilyn Chin, Garrett Hongo, Li-Young Lee, and David Mura." *MELUS* 25, no. 3 (Fall/Winter, 2000): 221-242. Slovik explains that many immigrants find it difficult to speak of their experiences because they have been expelled from their homelands and have had to survive in a different and often hostile new culture. This silence leads to cultural ambivalence and a loss of cultural identity; families of immigrants live in a void between cultures. She discusses the poets whose lives are affected by the immigrant experience. The meaning of Lee's life lies not only in his own lifetime but also in the earlier generations of his family. The subject of Slowick's article is the effect of complex interfamily relationships on the poetry of these immigrant poets.

Stern, Gerald. Foreword to *Rose*. Brockport, N.Y.: Boa Editions, 1986. Gerald Stern, a former professor of Lee's when he was an undergraduate at the University of Pittsburgh, compares Lee's poetry to the works of such poets as John Keats and T. S. Eliot. Stern says that Lee's work is characterized by plain speech and a search for wisdom and understanding. According to Stern, the central focus of Lee's poetry is his desire to know, understand, and accept a powerful, remote, and loving father.

Zhou, Xiaojing. "Inheritance and Invention in Li-Young Lee's Poetry." *MELUS*, Spring, 1996, 113-132. Xiaojing Zhou shows that Lee's search for his own identity leads him to examine the years he and his family lived in exile as well as the sense of alienation he experienced as an immigrant. Zhou says that Lee's memories of his father and his Chinese cultural heritage combine to make his poetry unique.

Judith Barton Williamson

LUIS DE LEÓN

Born: Belmonte, Spain; 1527
Died: Madrigal de las Altas, Spain; August 23, 1591

PRINCIPAL POETRY

Poesías originales, 1637
Poesías traducidas de autores clásicos y renacentistas, 1637
Poesías traducidas de autores sagrados, 1637
Poems from the Spanish of Fra. Luis Ponce de León, 1883
Lyrics of Luis de León, 1928
The Unknown Light: The Poems of Fray Luis de León, 1979

OTHER LITERARY FORMS

Luis de León is considered the greatest Spanish prose writer of the sixteenth century as well as one of Spain's greatest poets. His prose masterpiece, *Los nombres de Cristo* (1583; *The Names of Christ*, 1926), is a treatise on the various names given to Christ in Scripture. *La perfecta casada* (1583; *The Perfect Wife*, 1943) is a commentary on Proverbs 31, with observations on marriage customs pertaining to medieval and sixteenth century women. His translations include the Song of Solomon, *El cantar de los cantares* (1561; *The Song of Songs*, 1936) and the Book of Job, *El libro de Job* (wr. c. 1585, pb. 1779).

ACHIEVEMENTS

Luis de León's life and work have come to symbolize for generations of Spaniards and Latin Americans the struggle for truth within the intellectual tradition of the Spanish Golden Age (1492-1680), a tradition which valued faith above knowledge. During his career

of forty-seven years at the University of Salamanca, in all his writings in Latin and Castilian, this Augustinian friar (frequently referred to as Fray Luis) fought valiantly to reconcile the Humanist tradition of the Renaissance with faith in the medieval Scholastic tradition based upon the authority of Aristotle and the church fathers.

In theology and exegesis, the two principal disciplines of the medieval university, the new learning implied for Fray Luis an uncompromising literalist position regarding sacred and classical texts. His insistence on an untranslatable spirit made concrete in language, his virulent criticism of his peers' imperfect understanding of texts, and the occasional unorthodox position that was a consequence of his understanding of Hebrew and Greek resulted in five years of prison while the Inquisition investigated his work for signs of heresy. Legend, unfounded in fact, has it that after his exoneration, he resumed his university lectures in the usual manner with the words, "As we were saying yesterday. . . ." Fray Luis has grown to represent the quality of forgiveness of those who misunderstood his passionate dedication to the pursuit of knowledge.

Fray Luis's translations from Greek, Latin, and Italian into Spanish, which constitute two-thirds of his poetic production, attest eloquently his knowledge of the nature of language and the art of translation. His work within the Augustinian Order and his prose writings reveal his belief in the perfectibility of man and man's institutions as well as the strength of his faith. Most important, however, Fray Luis's original verse established the Salamancan school of Spanish poetry, which rejected the full aesthetic force of the language in favor of a simplicity of style and profundity of thought which would lay bare the poet's struggle to reconcile modern concerns with awesome traditions.

BIOGRAPHY

One of six children, Luis de León was born Luis de León y Varela, the son of Lope de León and Inés Varela, in 1527 in the town of Belmonte. His family on both sides was extremely successful and included a professor of theology, a royal treasurer, a lawyer at the royal court, the secretary to the Duke of Maqueda, and the general Cristóbal de Alarcón, who had won fame and wealth in the Italian campaigns of Charles V. Lope de León himself was a successful lawyer in Madrid and Valladolid and was able to give his sons an outstanding classical education. When Luis was fourteen years old, he began to follow his father's and uncles' footsteps in the Faculty of Law at the University of Salamanca.

Perhaps because of the international reputation of the Salamancan theologians, perhaps because of a strong religious vocation, at age seventeen Fray Luis professed in the Order of Saint Augustine and, instead of studying law, began to study in the Faculty of Sacred Letters. His first public speech before the order reveals his determination that no kind of intimidation would force him to swerve from the truth as he perceived it. In that speech, Fray Luis claimed that, having given his life to Christ rather than to personal ambition, neither hypocrisy nor deception could constrain him to obedience. Within six years, he had begun the career which he would continue until his death, that of professor of theology at Salamanca.

Fray Luis was faced with winning and then every four years defending his position in public debates until he won a *cátedra*, or lifetime appointment to a chair with a fixed salary. These appointments became the source of fierce rivalry and heated debates between Augustinian and Dominican friars, and Fray Luis used every legal means available to guarantee his post until he had won a chair. Even then, to improve his position, he continued to challenge other professors for better-paying chairs as death provided opportunities. In one such opposition, he brought to trial Fray Bartolomé de Medina, a Dominican, for irregularities in Medina's appointment. The Salamanca conference decided in Medina's favor because of the latter's popularity among his students and colleagues. Fray Luis took the case to the royal council of Philip II, which decided in Fray Luis's favor by virtue of his seniority. This process and similar cases soon incurred his colleagues' disfavor and mistrust.

Fray Luis remained undefeated at Salamanca until he opposed another lion, León de Castro. Fray Luis denounced the latter's *Comentarios sobre Isaias* (1570) to the Inquisition and succeeded in having it suppressed. The *Comentarios sobre Isaias* contained a thinly veiled assault on the dangers of the Humanists' approach to Scripture because of their reliance upon Greek and Hebrew. León de Castro preferred the traditional Scholastic method of syllogistic deduction to the literalist method of translation, claiming that the literalist approach, particularly in the work of Martínez de Cantalpiedra and Gaspar de Grajal, represented a threat to the authority of the Vulgate (vulgar Latin) Bible. On a personal level, León de Castro attacked Martínez and Grajal and, by association, Fray Luis, as heretics.

In March of 1572, the seeds of dissension bore fruit. An accusation against fathers Grajal and Martínez implicating Fray Luis was filed with the Inquisition in Valladolid, calling for an investigation into their orthodoxy. Father Diego González initiated the process, declaring that he had learned from León de Castro that, like Grajal and Martínez, Fray Luis taught that the rabbinical interpretation of Scripture was as valid as that of the saints; that the prophets' words are meaningful to Christian and Jews alike; that there was no promise of eternal life in the Old Testament; and that the Vatablo and Pagninus Bibles were superior to the Vulgate. All three men, Diego González claimed, were *conversos* (converted Jews) who desired to observe the faith and law of their Jewish ancestors.

It is well known that Fray Luis, like Teresa de Jesús and much of the Spanish nobility, had Jewish forebears, that Fray Luis's maternal grandmother and great aunt had renounced Christianity and had been put to death in an *auto-da-fé*. During the Counter-Reformation in Spain, as during the plague-ridden fourteenth century, Spanish popular concern with *limpieza de la sangre* (purity of blood) reached fanatical proportions. On March 30, 1572, Fray Luis was arrested in Valladolid, where he would remain until 1577.

While in prison, Fray Luis finished *The Names of Christ*. The record of the trial reveals that Fray Luis valiantly refused to confess or to acknowledge his accusers' interpretations of the texts in question. While his judges declared that they felt Fray Luis was a dissembler and a deceiver, they refused to submit him to torture because of his delicate health. He was declared innocent of the charges only after the principal Augustinian professor of theology at Salamanca, Fray Domingo Báñez, turned the trial around by giving a Catholic meaning to Fray Luis's more ambiguous theological proposals. Báñez afterward advised Fray Luis that regarding scriptural studies, one might think with the minority but must speak with the majority. He was released with the threat of excommunication should he discuss the trial with anyone or try to seek out his accusers.

Fray Luis returned to Salamanca in triumph, but not to his original chair; he was given a lectureship in theology instead. On another occasion, he was denounced again to the Inquisition for opposing the teachings of Saint Thomas Aquinas and Saint Augustine regarding the nature of grace and predestination. Fray Luis held that grace was not a free gift of God but determined in part by men's actions or merit. This time the Inquisition refused to try the case.

Fray Luis left Salamanca in 1585 to represent the interests of the University in Madrid, specifically to defend the Colegio del Arzobispo against charges of irregularities in the granting of degrees. He was never to return, in spite of the efforts of Salamanca to have him back. Instead, he remained in Madrid, finished his commentary on the Book of Job, and became a close friend of Madre Ana de Jesús, a follower of Saint Teresa de Jesús of Ávila in the establishment of Reformed Carmelite convents.

Fray Luis's friendship with Madre Ana de Jesús and his sympathy with the Carmelite reforms were to become the strongest concerns of the last years of his life. When an opportunity arose in Salamanca to act upon the very issue for which he had been imprisoned by the Inquisition—the opportunity to correct the Vulgate in the light of Hebrew and Greek texts—he turned it down. He stated that such an undertaking was interminable and impossible since what was requested was not a literal translation but a re-creation of the spirit of the original texts, with the inevitable result that each revision would be worse than the last. Instead, in 1588, he visited Philip II at El Escorial Palace to speak with the king's confessor about the establishment of cloistered monasteries for Augustinian friars. The request was granted.

Later, Fray Luis aided Madre Ana de Jesús's efforts, as did Saint John of the Cross, to establish autonomy for the Reformed Carmelite nuns from the ambitious rule of Jesús María Doria. Fray Luis and Teresa de Jesús's favorite, Father Gracián, wrote Pope Sixtus V and received permission to provide a separate council for the nuns. Doria reacted by appealing to Philip II, and the King, in turn, ordered Fray Luis to desist in his support for the nuns. Fray Luis reacted by calling a general council to act immediately upon the directive of Pope Sixtus V. Doria appealed to the king, who sent an order to the meeting forbidding any innovations until the opinion of the new Pope, Gregory XIV, could be assessed.

Reportedly, Fray Luis left the meeting saying that none of his Holiness's orders could be carried out in Spain. This comment was overheard and reported to Philip II, who retaliated by temporarily blocking Fray Luis's appointment to Provincial of his order. Pope Gregory XIV eventually revoked the brief of Sixtus V, and Fray Luis died soon after in Madrigal de las Altas, having finally been appointed Provincial.

ANALYSIS

The poetry of Luis de León presents the pursuit of knowledge as a form of spiritual exultation. For him, the intellectual's contemplation of creation constitutes a joy approaching mystic rapture. In almost all of his original poems, he holds Neoplatonic philosophy and medieval Christianty in a tenuously balanced, unstable harmony which creates tremendous aesthetic tension. During his early years, his poems circulated in random manuscript form until he collected them at the request of his friend Don Pedro Portoarrero as a defense against misinterpretation. He divided his work into three books: original poems; translations from Horace, Vergil, Pindar, and Pietro Bembo; and translations of Holy Scripture.

In 1631, a similarly spirited poet, Francisco de Quevedo y Villegas, published all of Fray Luis's poetry. Quevedo recognized Fray Luis's depth and clarity, qualities which contrasted strongly with the elaborate Baroque preciosity of the style that was to become known as *Gongorismo*. Quevedo likewise recognized that Fray Luis's translations were in keeping with the classical orientation which informed his theory of language in *The Names of Christ* and which had led him to conclusions often dangerously at variance with those of his colleagues. In *The Names of Christ*, Fray Luis asserts that language when used by true and sound minds will reflect reality accurately without distortion; the triple complexity of words—in thought, speech, and writing—

can obtain absolute truth. This absolute, shared by many minds, leads to a harmonious world. Within this essentially Neoplatonic framework, Fray Luis includes the tradition of the Cabala and attributes to words an unconscious depth of meaning, realized through secret references and arbitrary associations.

RELIGIOUS POETRY

In Fray Luis's religious poetry, there is an intimacy of feeling and an occasional self-doubt that appear nowhere else in his work. The poem "En la fiesta de todos los santos" ("On the Holiday of All Saints' Day") illustrates the characteristic antithetical organization of his verse. The greatness of the remote past contrasts so strongly with the inadequacies of the present that the devotion to the early Christian saints continues to increase with each generation. A sense of being abandoned imbues his poem "En la ascensión" ("On the Ascension"), in which the poet asks Christ where his sheep will turn now that he has left them.

In one of his songs dedicated to the Virgin, "A Nuestra Señora" ("To Our Lady"), Fray Luis, in the depths of his despair at the persecution he has suffered, calls upon the Virgin Mary and, protesting his innocence and declaring his unworthiness, beseeches her to intercede for him against the hatred of his enemies and against their deceptions. He asks her to free him from the prison in which their misunderstanding has cast him. In this poem, Fray Luis expresses self-doubt, saying that if indeed he has succumbed to evil unknowingly, the Virgin's virtue will shine more brightly in forgiving a darker sin.

"TO CHRIST CRUCIFIED"

The song "A Cristo crucificado" ("To Christ Crucified"), by virtue of the brutal realism of the imagery and the poet's legalist perspective, reveals Fray Luis's faith in the law. While (for Fray Luis) the Virgin is the summa of the Divine Essence, Christ's humanity and suffering make him humble in Fray Luis's eyes and, therefore, accessible. The poem elaborates the theme of Christ the advocate fulfilling the law by granting pardon to all who call on him. He cannot flee because his feet are nailed. His heart is revealed through hs gaping wounds, and two words from a thief are sufficient to steal it. He dictates his will and New Testament before dying and, from the Cross, can deny no one's wish. His head drops upon his chest, and Fray Luis calls upon witnesses to affirm the gesture as a sign that the poet's request for pardon has been granted. Finally, since no testament is legally valid until the testator is dead, Christ fulfills the law to the letter and dies. While concluding the poem with the lines that Heaven, Earth, and Sun mourn Christ's death, the poet, because of his intellectual and legalistic perspective on the Crucifixion, demands—rather than seeks—justice.

LIRAS TO SAINT JAMES

The same intensity found in "To Christ Crucified" characterizes Fray Luis's *liras* dedicated to Saint James the Apostle and Moor Slayer, "A Santiago" ("To Santiago"). The poet portrays Saint James as the disciple who, after bringing Spain to Christ and returning to the East to suffer martyrdom, reappears during the Wars of Reconquest (780-1492) to avenge Spanish blood spilled by the Infidels. The poem exalts the theocratic dynamics of Spain's imperial expansion: the Spaniard's thirst for vengeance against the Moor, the Isabeline politics of African expansion, and the taste for awesome power, wealth, and fame acquired by the valiant conqueror who wages war for Christ. In this poem, Fray Luis proves that his range includes the grandiloquence associated with his contemporary Fernando de Herrera, founder of the Sevillian school.

THE PERFECT WIFE

Fray Luis's book *The Perfect Wife* still enjoys popularity in the Spanish-speaking world. Through a commentary on the last chapter of Proverbs, Fray Luis acknowledges that love between man and wife is the strongest of all human bonds. It is forged by nature and enhanced by grace, being the only institution in existence before the Fall of Adam and Eve. It is reinforced by social custom and tied by intricate mutual obligations. Fray Luis writes that the role of wife is more difficult than that of the average man because, aside from the chastity which is universally assumed, she is duty bound to profit her husband by managing his household economically, rearing his children wisely, and bringing him comfort and joy. Fray Luis contrasts the ideal wife with vain women who are incapable of physical work because they spend their days with cosmetics and jewelry; who scold servants to prove their authority; or who destroy their neighbors' reputations with frivolous gossip.

Because of her role as wife and mother, Fray Luis insists, a virtuous woman is the most powerful agent in society, providing she speak wisely and gently. He writes that, since reason cannot deceive and love does not wish to deceive, a loving and reasonable woman can bring her husband to perfection.

PEACE THROUGH SERVICE

For Fray Luis, in *The Names of Christ* and *The Perfect Wife*, perfection consists simply of fulfilling well one's station in life. In his own life, as a friar and scholar, service to the Church was of paramount importance. The poem "A la vida religiosa" (on the religious life) reveals through a dream the nature of Fray Luis's vocation. In the pastoral setting he so often prefers, he is called to exchange the glory of Earth for the glory of Heaven by renouncing present contentment, comfort, and wealth. Rather than follow the career of his father and uncles, the rewards of which he believes are feigned, he chooses the monk's bare cell, plain frock, hair shirt, and flagellation in order to free himself of vice, the world, the Devil, and the flesh. Thus freed, Fray Luis believes he will have everything the secular man strives for simply by serving God.

The ascetic life for Fray Luis does not lead, as for Saint John of the Cross, to mystic union with God. Rather, it frees him to engage in intellectual pursuits unencumbered by personal concerns. Through acquired rather than infused knowledge, he hopes to envision, enjoy, and realize in a social context his ideal of peace. His most famous and successful poems present this theme of peace through knowledge. This peace is obtained by achieving the Neoplatonic ideal of harmony, first within the soul, next between the individual and nature, and, finally, between the individual and a well-ordered society. Thus, in his poem "Morada del cielo" ("Dwelling Place in Heaven"), Fray Luis harmonizes the Renaissance idea of utopia with the Christian concept of Heaven through the conventions of the pastoral tradition. The Good Shepherd leads his flock to fields where knowledge becomes aesthetic delight, obliterating the sorrow, pain, and injustice of an imperfect temporal world.

This vision of peace stands in marked contrast to Fray Luis's combative life, yet in spite of his fierce competitiveness, in spite of his tendency to win through litigation what he could not win through friendship and approval, there are in his poems moments of that wholeness he so desperately desired. In "Dwelling Place in Heaven," Fray Luis reveals the height of his spiritual ambition, to hear the divine, silent music of the spheres played by God himself, the music which will transport him from his prison of imperfection to the eternal companionship of those who live free from error.

Fray Luis reveals his empirical certainty that such a paradise exists in his three most famous poems, "Vida retirada" ("The Secluded Life"), "A Salinas" ("To Francisco Salinas"), and "Noche serena" ("Serene Night"). Whenever he perceives the concert of number and harmony of disparities as he does in these poems—whether it be in the pastoral vision of nature, in the aesthetic pleasure of polyphonic music, in observing the heavens within a mythic Copernican perspective, or in the language of Humanistic dialogue and Renaissance verse forms—Fray Luis reaffirms his ideal of perfection and his belief in the perfectibility of man and his institutions. Because of the intensity of his struggle to harmonize the new learning of the Renaissance with the medieval traditions of Post-Tridentine Spain (after the Council of Trent, 1545-1563) and because of the valor of his struggle for intellectual integrity against his contemporaries' lack of understanding and his own self-doubts, Fray Luis de León has a permanent place in the history of Spanish culture.

OTHER MAJOR WORKS

NONFICTION: *Los nombres de Cristo*, 1583 (*The Names of Christ*, 1926); *La perfecta casada*, 1583 (*The Perfect Wife*, 1943).

TRANSLATIONS: *El cantar de los cantares*, 1561 (*The Song of Songs*, 1936); *El libro de Job*, wr. c. 1585, pb. 1779.

BIBLIOGRAPHY

Bell, Aubrey. *Luis de León*. Oxford, England: Clarendon, 1925. A biographical study in the context of the Spanish Renaissance.

Durán, Manuel. *Luis de Léon*. New York: Twayne, 1971. An introductory biography and critical study of selected works by Fray Luis. Includes bibliographic references.

Fitzmaurice-Kelly, James. *Fray Luis de León: A Biographical Fragment.* Oxford, England: Oxford University Press, 1921. A brief biography issued by the Hispanic Society of America.

Hildner, David Jonathan. *Poetry and Truth in the Spanish Works of Fray Luis de León.* Rochester, N.Y.: Boydell & Brewer, 1992. A critical analysis of selected works by de León. Includes bibliographical references.

Thompson, Colin P. *The Strife of Tongues: Fray Luis de León and the Golden Age of Spain.* New York: Cambridge University Press, 1988. A critical study of Fray Luis's works with an introducton to the history of Spain in the sixteenth century.

Vossler, Karl. *Fray Luis de León.* Buenos Aires: Espasa-Calpa Argentina, 1946. A short biography of Fray Luis.

Kenneth A. Stackhouse;
bibliography updated by the editors

LEONIDAS OF TARENTUM

Born: Tarentum (now Taranto, Italy); fl. first half of third century B.C.E.
Died: Unknown

PRINCIPAL POETRY
Epigrams, third century B.C.E.

OTHER LITERARY FORMS
Leonidas of Tarentum is not known to have written anything but epigrams.

ACHIEVEMENTS
Although a poet of the second rank in a period of scant literary achievement, Leonidas of Tarentum is notable for his attention to classes of people who had been ignored before the Hellenistic era. He was greatly admired by later epigrammatists, as is shown by scores of imitations produced in subsequent generations. More than any other Hellenistic writer, Leonidas can be cred-

ited with the expansion of poetry's vision to include the poor, the farmers, hunters, fishermen, tradesmen, merchant seamen, prostitutes, weavers, and others whose lives, although in no way remarkable, bore the common stamp of humanity in their labors. Although he did not limit his scope to the working world, Leonidas made proletarian life his special preserve, much as Theocritus made singing shepherds his poetic domain. Judging by the number of his immediate imitators, in fact, it would appear that Leonidas had a greater influence in his own time than the more celebrated Theocritus. When Vergil revived the pastoral, Theocritus had inspired barely two imitators (Bion and Moschus), whereas Leonidas's followers, both before and after Vergil's time, were legion.

The great paradox of Leonidas's achievement is his remarkable affinity for elaborate language to describe simple people. His poetry is full of ornamental adjectives and novel compounds and is characterized by a vocabulary that appears nowhere else in ancient Greek. His style is commonly characterized as baroque, exuberant in its highly calculated arrangement of words and ideas. Leonidas is an excellent Hellenistic example of the phenomenon of a writer vastly popular and influential in his own time but virtually unread today. Modern estimations vary widely: Gilbert Highet has called him "the greatest Greek epigrammatist of the Alexandrian era," but C. R. Beye finds him "heavy-handed, pedantic, and [overly] detailed"; Marcello Gigante sees him as the high-minded prophet of a new egalitarian society, and A. S. F. Gow as "a competent versifier, [but] hardly ever more than that." Whatever his merits as a poet, Leonidas deserves a careful reading by anyone who wishes to understand the dynamics of the age that gave classical Humanism its definitive shape.

BIOGRAPHY
Leonidas of Tarentum's biography, like that of most Hellenistic poets, is strictly conjectural, and, in the absence of contemporary references to him, is completely dependent on the evidence of his epigrams, in which he says very little about his own life. Most authorities place him in the first or second generation of Hellenistic poets, either early in the third century B.C.E., with Asclepiades, Callimachus, and Theocritus, or nearer the middle of the century, closer to such poets as Dioscorides and

Antipater, whose epigrams echo his style. An epigram purporting to be his own epitaph (Epigram 715 in book 7 AP. or Leonidas 93 G.-P.) represents him as a wanderer who died far from his native Tarentum, itself a plausible claim, because his one hundred-odd surviving epigrams represent people and places scattered all over the Greek-speaking world, the eastern Mediterranean littoral loosely referred to as the *oikoumenē*.

Though a native of Italy, Leonidas (like the Sicilian Theocritus) was in every sense of the word a member of the Greek world. His city (the modern Taranto) was colonized at the end of the eighth century B.C.E. by Spartans, and from the middle of the fifth century B.C.E. it was the leading Greek city of southern Italy. By the end of the next century, however, Tarentum came under pressure from Italian tribes to the north and depended on various mercenary leaders for protection. The last of these was Rome's famous adversary Pyrrhus, who left Tarentum to the Romans in 275. From about that time until the Hannibalic wars at the end of the century, the city regained stability and prosperity under Roman rule. Leonidas's supposed departure from Tarentum has been linked to the period of insecurity early in the third century, though, like other literary and intellectual figures from the Greek west, he would have been naturally attracted to such Greek capitals as Athens and Alexandria. His epigrams do not, however, suggest residence in any particular place, but rather an itinerant existence and a life shared mainly with the rural poor. Would-be biographers have leapt to the conclusion that Leonidas was in fact a destitute wanderer by choice who wrote about people with whom he shared his meager existence. This speculation is strengthened by occasional suggestions in Leonidas's epigrams that he was an admirer of the Cynic philosopher Diogenes and shared Cynic beliefs concerning poverty, simplicity, and the frailty of human life. It is possible that he followed in the footsteps of the popular Cynic philosopher Crates, adopting poverty as a way of life and traveling about the *oikoumenē* spreading a gospel of voluntary poverty and independence and consoling the victims of hardship, perhaps by celebrating their simple lives in his epigrams. Crates himself is said to have written poetry as a vehicle of his teaching, and some students of Leonidas see him as playing a similar prophetic role in his poetry.

Such speculation is difficult to reconcile with the highly sophisticated style of Leonidas's actual poems, which are seldom as austere or simple as the people he liked to write about. There is also the cosmopolitan range of his subjects, which include the most celebrated artistic, literary, and intellectual events of his time and, indeed, of previous generations. Wherever he spent his time, Leonidas did not isolate himself from the tastes or the events and concerns of his age. The public for whom he wrote was urban and well educated, with a sophisticated nostalgia for the simple lives of peasants and rural tradespeople. Like Theocritus's shepherds, Leonidas's working folk are as much a product of imagination as of observation, and there is no need to speculate that he spent most of his life among them. In short, no solid facts can be drawn from the epigrams to illuminate the mystery of Leonidas's life.

ANALYSIS

It is not known in what form Leonidas of Tarentum published his epigrams. A large number were published after his death in the *Garland* of Meleager, an anthology of epigrams put together early in the first century B.C.E., but it is probable that Meleager himself depended on earlier collections. Meleager's *Garland* is lost, although large parts of it were included when Constantine Cephalas, a church official in the palace at Constantinople in the late ninth century C.E., made a larger anthology of Greek epigrams. Within a century, Cephalas's collection (itself also lost) became a source of a still much larger anthology of Greek epigrams from the Byzantine, Roman, and earlier Greek eras, now known as the *Greek Anthology* or the *Palatine Anthology*. Cephalas's collection was also the source of an independent selection of epigrams put together in 1301 by the Byzantine monk Maximus Planudes. Eight or nine epigrams by Leonidas are extant only in the *Planudean Anthology*. The *Palatine Anthology* is so called because of its rediscovery in the Count Palatine's library at Heidelberg in 1606; modern editions are based on that tenth century codex as supplemented by the later Planudean collection. The numbering system used for references is either that of the *Palatine Anthology* (AP.) or that of the standard edition, *The Greek Anthology: Hellenistic Epigrams* (1965), edited by A. S. F. Gow and D. L. Page (G.-P.).

EPIGRAMS: HISTORY OF THE FORM

Historically and etymologically, an epigram is an inscription on something, usually a tomb, a statue, or a dedicatory plaque. At an early stage, epigrams were sometimes set to verse, and in time it was customary to write them in elegiac couplets consisting of a dactylic hexameter followed by a shorter pentameter line. The conciseness required of an inscription on metal or stone was a special challenge to the first epigrammatists, and from these circumstances evolved a miniature literary form that became extremely popular in the Hellenistic age, whose reading public was tired of rambling heroic poetry and prized concise workmanship.

One effect of this development was that the epigram became, by Hellenistic times, more or less independent of its inscriptional origins, not being intended for actual writing on anything more substantial than a piece of paper; still, it sometimes retained vestiges of its origins by masquerading in the form of an inscribed dedication or epitaph.

New types were also invented: The epideictic or display epigram is a versified comment about a statue, poem, or any other object, such as a fig tree or a carved piece of incense. The love epigram is a short poem about love, often not even ostensibly inscriptional or memorial in character. The protreptic, hortatory, or admonitory epigram is likewise not formally associated with an object; it is simply a versified bit of wisdom—"what oft was said but ne'er so well expressed"—usually in Hellenistic times a commonplace of popular Stoic, Cynic, or Epicurean philosophy. The tone as well as the type could vary, from somber to declamatory, playful, or mocking.

GREEK ANTHOLOGY

Leonidas of Tarentum's epigrams are arguably all epideictic, although most of them take the form of an epitaph or a dedication. If any of them were actually inscribed, however, it was probably after the fact and beyond the intentions of the author. The *Greek Anthology* preserves them, scattered among epigrams by other authors, under three main categories: Book 7, devoted to epitaphs or sepulchral epigrams, includes the largest number; book 6, containing dedicatory epigrams, has nearly as many; fifteen are preserved as epideictic epigrams in book 9. These three books of the *Greek Anthology* account for nearly all Leonidas's epigrams, with a dozen others distributed elsewhere, chiefly in Planudes' collection. The assignment of categories in the *Greek Anthology* is often careless, however, and is useful only as the most general guide to the kind of poems that Leonidas wrote.

RURAL THEMES

Too much attention to Leonidas's special interest in peasants, artisans, and the poor can obscure the fact that these subjects account for scarcely more than one-third of his epigrams. He can be credited with the "discovery" of simple folk as a subject of epigram, and he made himself their poet laureate, so to speak, but he did not limit himself to that subject any more than Theocritus limited himself to the poetic shepherds that made him famous. As has already been noted, Leonidas's complex style seems made for purposes other than the depiction of simple folk.

A survey of Leonidas's poems reveals, more than anything else, a love of complexity and variety. His work is a miscellany of people, places, and events that would seem novel to his city readers: They enjoyed reading about subjects outside their usual cosmopolitan ambit in Tarentum, Syracuse, Athens, or Alexandria. Hence the prominence of rural artisans, seamen, and the countryside and the significant absence of urban scenes and subjects. Hellenistic life was concentrated as never before in the cities, but taste was for anything but the here and now. Hence, also, the love of paradoxes, novelties, and curiosity items in Leonidas. He had no special loyalty to the class of people he put in his epigrams, no political posture, no philosophical ideology with which to indoctrinate his readers. Everything was subordinated to writing an epigram that his audience might find interesting, clever, and unconventional.

TIMELESSNESS

For these reasons, Johannes Geffcken's attempts to read historical allusions into Leonidas and Gigante's discovery of revolutionary protosocialist sentiment in the epigrams has had a cool reception among students of Hellenistic poetry. Leonidas is anything but topical; his epigrams, although often ostensibly tied to specific events, such as a fisherman's death or the dedication to Bacchus of some casks of wine, are almost always timeless or look back to an event in the distant past.

A small number of epigrams may be exceptional in this regard, such as a pair of quatrains dedicating spoils taken from Tarentum's ancient enemies, the Lucanians (epigrams 129 and 131 in book 6 AP. and Leonidas 34 and 35 G.-P.), but Leonidas's language is not specific enough to permit a definite dating within his probable lifetime; the epigrams may well be epideictic and patriotic rather than specific to a certain battle. An epigram on the occasion of Antigonus Gonatas's defeat by Pyrrhus in 273 B.C.E. (Epigram 130 in book 6 AP. or Leonidas 95 G.-P.) is a much better candidate for specific contemporary dating, if the ascription to Leonidas is correct.

Of the poets and artists celebrated in some eleven epigrams, only one belongs to Leonidas's own century: Aratus, the author of a poem on astronomy, the *Phainomena*, written shortly after 277 B.C.E. In his tendency to avoid the contemporary, Leonidas is like other poets of the third century: They preferred to write about the timeless or the mythical, and they tended to find only the poets and artists of earlier generations to be fit subjects for their praise.

ESCAPISM

This affinity with things set apart from the poet and his audience was not entirely new to Greek poetry; Homer wrote about events that took place nearly five centuries before his own time, and the Greek tragedians used even older myths for their plots. Yet the comedies of Aristophanes were unabashedly topical at the end of the fifth century B.C.E., and in the fourth century, Menander's comedies were also set in contemporary times (although they were not as politically topical). A certain escapism distinguishes Hellenistic poetry from that of earlier periods. Although some of their classical predecessors had used remote settings and characters only as a background for the presentation of their own immediate concerns and controversies, the Hellenistic poets—Leonidas, Callimachus, Apollonius Rhodius, Theocritus—used similarly removed situations as a means of turning away from their own milieu, which held little interest for them, to worlds more to their liking.

POETRY AS CRAFT

As a corollary of this impulse, art was cultivated for art's sake rather than for the traditional purposes of education and inspiration. When it inspired, it inspired disengagement rather than the heroic commitment that was typical, say, of Sophoclean tragedy. Poetry came to be viewed more as a craft than as a vehicle for great ideas. The many epigrams that Leonidas and his contemporaries composed in praise of ancient poets and artists suggest something like a cult of the artist whose art transcends rather than reflects. At the same time, they felt inferior to the geniuses of the past, and, rather than try to compete with them in epic or tragic poetry, the better poets sought uncharted territory for themselves, new kinds of poetry in which they would not be in the shadow of the grand masters of the past. With something of a pioneering spirit, every poet of talent sought to bring his readers something new and distinctive. In this way, Hellenistic poetry was a means of escaping the past as well as the present.

SUBJECT MATTER

Leonidas's novel attention to common people attracted many imitators—and, one must assume, a large audience. Some of what he provided his readers is now found in "human interest" journalism: "Man Half-Eaten by Sea Monster Buried Today" (Epigram 506 in book 7 AP. or Leonidas 65 G.-P.), "Lion Takes Refuge with Herdsmen" (Epigram 221 in book 6 AP. or Leonidas 53 G.-P.), "Four Sisters Die in Childbirth" (Epigram 463 in book 7 AP. or Leonidas 69 G.-P.). Others are less sensational curiosities, such as a die carved on a gambler's tombstone (Epigram 422 in book 7 AP. or Leonidas 22 G.-P.) or a fisherman who dies a natural death after a lifetime in a perilous trade (Epigram 295 in book 7 AP. or Leonidas 20 G.-P.).

Most of his subjects are bland in themselves: Three sisters dedicate their spinning and weaving implements to Athena on retiring from their labors (Epigram 289 in book 6 AP. or Leonidas 42 G.-P.); a gardener prays to the nymphs to see that his garden is well watered (Epigram 320 in book 9 AP. or Leonidas 6 G.-P.). The tone of such imaginary epitaphs and dedications is predictably calm; rarely does Leonidas inject the emotion expressed in Epigram 466 in book 7 AP. or Leonidas 71 G.-P., where a father grieves for his son, dead at eighteen. More often, there is a humorous note of mockery, as in the imaginary epitaph of a lady who drank too much and has a cup on her tomb: Her only regret in death is that the cup is empty (Epigram 455 in book 7

AP. or Leonidas 68 G.-P.). There are other joke epigrams, such as epigrams 236 and 261 in book 1 AP. or Leonidas 83 and 84 G.-P., in which a statue of the tutelary god Priapus threatens to abuse troublemakers with his overgrown phallus.

Sometimes an epigram will be built around a paradox: a cult statue of Aphrodite bearing warlike gear (Epigram 320 in book 9 AP. or Leonidas 24 G.-P.); a figure of Eros carved in frankincense that will be burned, although not with the fires of love (Epigram 179 in book 9 AP. or Leonidas 28 G.-P.). For the most part, Leonidas avoids erotic topics, although they were a favorite preoccupation in nearly all Hellenistic art and literature. He shows a greater interest in the commonplaces of Cynic philosophy; his longest poem is a sepulchral elegy of sixteen lines made up of Cynic sentiments on the frailty of life (Epigram 472 in book 7 AP. or Leonidas 77 G.-P.). Leonidas is not always consistent in his Cynic views, however, especially on the subject of poverty. Sometimes he praises it in good Cynic fashion because it implies independence and self-sufficiency, but in a rare autobiographical moment he prays that Aphrodite will save him from his "hateful poverty" (Epigram 300 in book 6 AP. or Leonidas 36 G.-P.). Moreover, he is as ready to make fun of a ragged Cynic guru (Sochares in Epigrams 293 and 298 in book 6 AP. or Leonidas 54 to 55 G.-P.) as he is to mock a man who goes to his grave without ever drinking too much (Eubulus or "Wiseman," in Epigram 452 in book 7 AP. or Leonidas 67 G.-P.). Less a philosopher than a poet, Leonidas shifts his point of view to suit his subject.

CHALLENGES OF TRANSLATION

Without reading Leonidas's epigrams in the original Greek, one is not likely to understand why they were read, copied, and imitated, even by generations whose tastes were not today's, because so much of Leonidas's art is invested in his use of language itself. The literary qualities most admired by Hellenistic readers and authors were highly formal, with relatively little emphasis being placed on the substance of a piece of writing. What mattered was not so much what one said, but how well one said it.

In translation, most of Leonidas's poetry will seem intolerably bland—as it will even in Greek, so long as one reads for propositional content. To read Leonidas as

his admirers did, one must read through Hellenistic eyes focused on felicity of phrasing, effective manipulation of word order (which is much more flexible in Greek than in English), freshness of diction, and creative management of the reader's expectations to stimulate curiosity, evoke surprise, and elicit humor. In his subordination of content to form, Leonidas (like many of his contemporaries) can be called a poet's poet. Christopher Dawson has shown by close analysis of several epigrams how successfully Leonidas exploited his material for maximum effect and, in particular, how he arranged his epigrams for a climactic focus at the end. His creation of poems leading up to a play of wit at the end took the epigram a step closer to the modern form first fully realized by the Roman poet Martial.

BIBLIOGRAPHY

Clack, Jerry. *Asclepiades of Samos and Leonidas of Tarentum: The Poems*. Wauconda, Ill.: Bolchazy, 1999. A collection and translation of the complete extant works of these two Greek epigrammatists, who set the course for this particular genre of poetry. As the book points out, for Leonidas the poetic form of the epigram went beyond the purely personal feelings of the author and allowed for social commentary, often alluding to the suffering and miseries of the poor, the infirm, and the aged.

Fowler, Barbara Hughes. *The Hellenistic Aesthetic*. Madison: University of Wisconsin Press, 1989. A general survey of the artistic thought and movements of the period which produced Leonidas. Although slight in its treatment of the poet and his individual poems, it is valuable for placing him and his work into an overall context.

Gutzwiller, Katheryn. *Poetic Garlands: Hellenistic Epigrams in Context*. Berkeley: University of California Press, 1998. A full-length study of the later, more literary Greek epigrams written by professional poets such as Leonidas. Gutzwiller traces the themes in Leonidas's work, including death, eroticism, and morality, and comments particularly on his epigram for the sponge-fisher Tharsys, attacked and half-eaten by a shark and so buried on both land and sea.

White, Heather. *New Essays in Hellenistic Poetry*. Amsterdam, Netherlands: Gieben, 1985. A good study of Leonidas and his contemporaries. The essay on Leonidas's work is useful, although somewhat technical in its examinations of the poetic and linguistic devices of the works of Leonidas. This is the sort of resource best used in conjunction with other more general studies of the poet and his writing.

Daniel H. Garrison;
bibliography updated by Michael Witkoski

GIACOMO LEOPARDI

Born: Recanati, Italy; June 29, 1798
Died: Naples, Italy; June 14, 1837

PRINCIPAL POETRY

Versi, 1826
Canti, 1831, 1835 (includes expanded version of *Versi*; English translation, 1962)
I paralipomeni della batracomiomachia, 1842 (*The War of the Mice and the Crabs*, 1976)
The Poems of Leopardi, 1923, 1973
Poems, 1963
Selected Poems of Giacomo Leopardi, 1995

OTHER LITERARY FORMS

Giacomo Leopardi was a child prodigy who began exercising both his talents and his erudition at the age of eleven. While as a poet he is best known for the *Canti* (literally, "songs"), and to some extent for the political satire *The War of the Mice and the Crabs* and other lyrical poems not included in the *Canti*, he did leave a great number of shorter poetic pieces or fragments, including translations, together with a similar number of brief prose pieces which in the aggregate round out an active literary personality. His philosophical "Imitazione," on Antoine Vincent Arnaut's "La Feuille," is possibly of 1818, or of 1828, the year of his polemical poem on style, "Scherzo." Four or five years before, he had translated freely a fragment of Simonides, and followed it with another translation of the same author. As early as 1809, inspired by Homer's *Iliad* (c. 800 B.C.E.), Leo-

pardi produced his first poem, "La morte di Ettore," and in 1812 he wrote *Pompeo in Egitto*, a tragedy denouncing tyranny. A number of extant poetic fragments cannot be dated accurately. In 1819, Leopardi wrote the pastoral tragedy *Telesilla*. In addition, there were many prose works, such as the remarkably erudite *Storia dell'astronomia* (1813; *History of Astronomy*, 1882), ranging from the beginning of the science to the comet of 1811, and the long *Saggio sopra gli errori popolari degli antichi* (1815; *Essay on the Popular Superstitions of the Ancients*, 1882), which revealed, among other things, the budding philologist. This philological dedication was to produce a number of projects in translation, vulgarization, and editing throughout his life, albeit more frequently in his earlier than in his later years because of his failing eyesight and health. As examples, one might mention his translations from the poetry of Moschus in 1815; the *Discorso sopra la vita e le opere de M. Cornelio Frontone*, the essay *Il salterio Ebraico*, and various vulgarizations of Homer and Vergil, all of 1816; and the *Crestomazia* (1827, 1828) of Italian literature in two volumes, as well as editions of Cicero and Petrarch, and an *Enciclopedia delle cognizioni utili e delle cose che non si sanno* during the 1820's, many volumes of which he never completed. A fundamental work is his 4,526-page notebook titled *Zibaldone*, which he began in 1817 and which represents an encyclopedic medley of thoughts and analyses, observations and recollections—philosophical, philological, critical, and personal—that occupied his mind until the end of 1832. It was published in the period from 1898 to 1900. From this notebook, in large part, he compiled a collection of thoughts titled *Cento undici pensieri* which was also published posthumously, in 1845 (*Pensieri*, 1981). To be noted, too, is his essay *Discorso di un Italiano intorno alla poesia romantica* (*Discourse of an Italian Concerning Romantic Poetry*) of 1818. Next to the *Canti*, Leopardi's most important work remains the collection of twenty-four short masterpieces of satirical prose known as the *Operette morali* (*Essays and Dialogues*, 1882), published and augmented three times during his lifetime: 1827, 1834, and 1836. Finally, an indispensable companion to Leopardi studies is his published correspondence, *Epistolario* (its nucleus was published in 1849), not only for its wealth of biographical indications but also, often in the manner of the *Zibaldone*, for its innumerable intellectual premises.

ACHIEVEMENTS

Giacomo Leopardi left an indelible mark on Italian poetry, in which category he is considered second only to Dante, and while Leopardi's influence on European letters does not match that of a number of transalpine contemporaries (Lord Byron, Victor Hugo, and Ludwig Tieck, for example), he is surely a greater poet than most of them and closer to the modern psyche—indeed, one of *the* truly significant poets of the nineteenth century. Leopardi was not only a consummate philologist in the classical sense, with all the linguistic and historical erudition which that term implies, but also he was one of those rare poets who, like Dante and Johann Wolfgang von Goethe, have been deemed worthy of consideration as a philosopher. Lyrical expression and philosophical reflection maintain a harmonious balance in his poetry at all times. Some critics see Leopardi chiefly as a scholar of broad humanistic and historical dimensions; others, as one of the sacred voices inspiring the movement for Italian unification; still others, as a pessimistic philosopher, a precursor of twentieth century Existentialism. Even in *Essays and Dialogues*, however, Leopardi was above all a poet—which is perhaps the most appropriately encompassing term available for him.

BIOGRAPHY

Count Giacomo Talegardo Francesco di Sales Saverio Pietro Leopardi was born in Recanati, in the province of the Marches, of a wealthy and noble family with a long tradition of service to the Church. His father, Count Monaldo, prided himself on his intellectual accomplishments, among which he included reactionary and scholarly writings and the building of an extensive and erudite family library in which the young Leopardi spent most of his formative years. Monaldo's sense of infallibility did not help him manage his inherited fortune, a responsibility undertaken by his wife, Marquise Adelaide Antici, an austere, bigoted, and despotic woman, whose harshness toward the sensitive Giacomo contrasted with her husband's affectionate paternal disposition. The priest who tutored Giacomo until he was

thirteen declared at that time that there was nothing more he could teach the boy, who read and studied daily until very late. Theology, mathematics, history, rhetoric, Greek, Latin, Spanish, French, Hebrew, English, German, the philosophers, the Enlightenment, the Italian classics, the commentators, astronomy: Leopardi's interests encompassed an encyclopedic range of intellectual activities, as described in *Zibaldone*, a "mad and most desperate [regime of] study," which inevitably and irreparably damaged his naturally frail constitution. His eyesight, his bones (rachitis), his back (he became a humpback), and other ailments (such as a cerebrospinal disease) were to plague him painfully for more than half of his brief life.

At first, Leopardi's consuming ambition was the acquisition of fame, "a very great and perhaps immoderate desire," but as the years passed, he realized that he had sacrificed his youth in pursuit of his ambition. Youth, "dearer than fame and laurels, than the pure light of day," lost "without a pleasure, uselessly," became a recurrent theme in his poetry. Frequently, he sat depressed in the library, or, during an afternoon stroll around the countryside, waves of melancholy overcame him, "an obstinate, black, horrible, barbarous melancholy," which convinced him that life could produce only misery.

Pietro Giordani, an Italian writer and patriot, befriended Leopardi, and for a while his spirits lifted. The subdued tones of earlier poems such as "Le rimembranze," "Appressamento della morte," "Primo amore" ("First Love"), and "Memorie del primo amore" were replaced by the more energetic tones of patriotic songs such as "All'Italia" ("To Italy") and "Sopra il monumento di Dante che si preparava a Firenze" ("On the Monument to Dante"). He tried to leave his "native savage town" of Recanati, but his parents discovered and frustrated the attempt, in the wake of which they imposed a close surveillance of his actions, complete with censorship of his correspondence. This situation produced meditations of deep melancholia, out of which grew a philosophy of sorrow, which for him constituted the necessary condition of the universe, in which beauty, love, glory, and virtue emerge as illusions that deceive wickedly and promote universal unhappiness. Yet illusion provided the only refuge from devastation occasioned by reason and reality, and the need for it made repeated claims on his soul and his worldview. During this period, from around 1819 to around 1822, many fine idylls came to light, such as "Il sogno," "L'infinito" ("The Infinite"), "La vita solitaria" ("The Solitary Life"), "La sera del dì di festa" ("Sunday Evening"), "Alla luna" ("To the Moon"), as well as the philosophical canzones "Ad Angelo Mai" ("To Angelo Mai"), "Nelle nozze della sorella Paolina," "A un vincitore nel pallone," "Bruto Minore" ("The Younger Brutus"), "Alla primavera, o delle favole antiche" ("To Spring: Or, Concerning the Ancient Myths"), "Inno ai patriarchi" ("Hymn to the Patriarchs"), and "Ultimo canto di Saffo" ("Sappho's Last Song").

Finally, in 1822, Leopardi received permission to journey to Rome—an experience which he anticipated with great enthusiasm, only to find in a short time disappointment and disillusionment. The capital, once the classical city of Caesar and Brutus, now the pontifical abode of Pius VII, academically still unemancipated from the corruption and veneered pomp of the eighteenth century Arcadia, appeared like everything else: It partook of the vanity of all things.

In 1823, the Milanese editor Antonio Stella offered Leopardi, by then returned to Recanati, the job of publishing the complete works of Cicero, a venture which saw the poet leave "the sepulcher of the living" for the Lombard capital in 1825. Completed by this time were the philosophical poem "Alla sua donna" ("To His Lady") and his famous prose work, *Essays and Dialogues*, his acid reflections on an undependable world. In Milan, he also worked on a commentary on Petrarch's poetry and on a double anthology of Italian verse and prose. Another poem, also in the philosophical vein, "Al Conte Carlo Pepoli" ("To Count Carlo Pepoli"), appeared. His reputation spread beyond Italy, so that offers of chairs reached him from the universities of Bonn and Berlin, but fear of the intemperate northern winters prompted him to refuse.

After a lapse of several years, Leopardi returned to his creative writing: "A Silvia" ("To Sylvia"), "Il risorgimento" ("The Revival"), "Il passero solitario" ("The Solitary Thrush"), "Le ricordanze" ("Memories"), "La quiete dopo la tempesta" ("The Calm After the Storm"), and "Il sabato del villaggio" ("Saturday Evening in the Village") are poems of sorrow and illusion,

of simple joys and lost youth, of evil and the pain of living. One of his greatest poems, "Canto notturno di un pastore errante dell'Asia" ("Night Song of a Nomadic Shepherd in Asia"), is dated 1829. Financial difficulties, aggravated by his parents' characteristic insensitivity, dented his pride when, in 1830, he accepted a sum of money raised by charitable friends headed by the historian Pietro Colletta. "I have lost all; I am a trunk which feels and suffers." In 1832, Leopardi was forced to ask his family for a modest allowance, an improbably small sum which, together with the previous year's Florentine printing of the augmented *Canti* (the idylls had appeared in Bologna in 1826 as *Versi*, and the broader and final collection appeared again in Naples in 1835), provided some economic respite. Yet, life continued to disillusion him, especially in his experience of unrequited and disappointing love. First, there had been a distant cousin, Gertrude Cassi, a lovely young lady of twenty-six who had come to Recanati for a brief visit that had filled the somber family mansion with some cheer, but had left the shy youth disenchanted ("First Love," written in 1817); then came Countess Carniani-Malvezzi of Bologna, a poet herself, with whom he established a comfortable intellectual relationship until his own emotions, growing warmer, forced a reluctant break in 1826; finally, between 1830 and 1833, having fallen in love with the wife of a Florentine professor, Fanny Targioni-Tozzetti, Leopardi discovered that she had merely been flattered by the attentions of a great man and had given him insincere encouragement. She became his "ultimate deception," the wounding return to reality from his illusions, echoes of which are heard in "Il pensiero dominante" ("The Ascendant Thought"), "Aspasia," "Amore e morte," ("Love and Death"), and "Consalvo," as well as in his most bitter poem, "A stesso" ("To Himself").

Leopardi knew many of the important figures of his day, and many others yearned to know him. Still, his circle of friends remained limited. Toward the end of his life, he became close companions with a young Neapolitan exile, Antonio Ranieri, first in Florence and then, after Ranieri was pardoned by King Ferdinand II, in Naples. Leopardi's health, already strained, declined rapidly, despite the more salubrious climate of Torre del Greco in the neighborhood of Mt. Vesuvius; the loving attention of Ranieri and his sister Paolina, as well as the doctors, could do nothing for Leopardi. By this time, he had written "Sopra un basso rilievo antico sepolcrale" ("On the Ancient Sepulchral Bas-Relief"), "Sopra il ritratto di una bella donna" ("On the Portrait of a Beautiful Lady"), "Palinodia al marchese Gino Capponi," as well as his monumental poem, "La ginestra, o il fiori del deserto" ("The Broom: Or, The Flower of the Desert"), and on his deathbed, just before he died, he dictated to Ranieri the end of his last poem, "Il tramonto della luna" ("The Setting of the Moon"). Death, which he had so often invoked as a liberation from the anguish of having been born, overtook him on June 14, 1837. He was buried in the small church of San Vitale in Fuorigrotta. Giordani provided the epitaph, in the course of which one reads: "philologist admired outside of Italy, consummate writer of philosophy and poetry, to be compared with the Greeks. . . ."

ANALYSIS

Giacomo Leopardi's prominence as a poet stems from the lyrical greatness of the *Canti*, but as *Essays and Dialogues* demonstrates, there was in him a talent for biting sarcasm and sardonic humor which *The War of the Mice and the Crabs* brings forth in no uncertain terms. He thought about this work from 1830, when he conceived it in Florence, to the end of his life, in Naples, where he completed it. An ironic fantasy, ringing with sociopolitical overtones, it was published abroad (by Baudry, in Paris), posthumously, in 1842, thanks to the faithful guardianship of Ranieri. The work, whose full original title means "things left out of the [pseudo-Homeric] War of the Frogs [also Crabs] and the Mice," is in eight cantos of eight-line stanzas (Leopardi had translated the original *Batrachomyomachia* three times), and takes to task any optimism based on the notion of social progress, liberals who claim to have the solution for national problems, the antimaterialistic postures of early nineteenth century philosophers, and political absolutism. Mixing together many elements, including the grotesque (the hell of the mice), the lyrical (a nocturne), and the polemical (statements against nature), Leopardi alludes to many Italian and European political realities of the first third of his century, without leaving too much room to doubt the identities of some of his characters, such as Camminatorto (Prince Clem-

ens von Metternich), Senzacapo (Francis I of Austria), Mangiaprosciutti (the Bourbon Ferdinand I), Rubatocchi (Joachim Murat, the "Dandy King" of Naples and Napoléon's ally), and so on. To regard the poem strictly as a political allegory of contemporary events, however, does not do it justice, for beyond the satirical and grotesque presentation in all of its varied fantasy is a panoramic view of human society conceived in broad, historical terms.

CANTI

The poetry of the *Canti* is elegant in its classical simplicity, its unpretentious yet effective imagery, its meditative philosophical tone, and its profoundly human tenderness. It reveals an overabundant inner life characterized by endless searching and above all by intellectual sincerity, a sincerity which found no compromise with reality. In the long run, Leopardi explained nothing (the mystery of life, after all, defies explanation), but he said everything. The "beautiful and mortal thing passes and lasts not"; all is vanity to which man falls prey, and those things he thinks he can turn to and rely upon—such as love, beauty, and nature—deceive him cruelly, for he is a microcosm in a macrocosm, subject to the universal destiny of sorrow existing in a world of ultimate nothingness. Yet as often as he proclaims universal disillusionment, the poet continues to nourish illusions of love, of goodness, of beauty, of human fraternity. The paradox harbors one implied refuge: art, that shaper of benign illusions. This is why he was a poet.

The *Canti* as read today follow the arrangement of the poems, approved by the poet, in the posthumous Florentine edition of 1845, faithfully executed by Ranieri. The form is free, usually in blank verse in lines of varying length but with sparse rhyme and above all a sophisticated use of assonance. For Leopardi, the lyric represented the summit of literary expression. With a truly classical regard for the importance of the word, he aimed at Homeric clarity—eschewing complexity and the pathological somberness of many of his northern contemporaries—no matter how pessimistic the thought. Suppleness and the cleanly contoured line had to coexist in order to maintain the tone of serenity that made for a feeling of beauty and a sense of music. In addition, the free style of the canzones allowed a more relaxed incorporation of philosophical reflection than would have been possible in a more rigid versification. At no time, however, did the poet lapse into discursiveness or pedantry. Meditations, like emotions, were subject to the simplicity and directness of Leopardi's style.

PATRIOTIC CANZONES

The first poems in the *Canti*, the patriotic canzones "To Italy" and "On the Monument to Dante," do not fit the ideological profile of a man who stood, ultimately, like his contemporary Alessandro Manzoni, above the political fray. Indeed, in later years, liberals who expected more utterances in this vein from Leopardi were disappointed. His conversations with Pietro Giordani undoubtedly underlie the nationalistic, youthful fervor reflected in these early poems, though as the years went by, his philosophical nature could not yield to political pragmatism, and he adopted more and more a metaphysical view of life's vicissitudes.

Of the two patriotic canzones, "To Italy" has enjoyed somewhat greater acclaim. It contains seven strophes of twenty lines each. The poet portrays a prostrate and reviled Italy, once so glorious yet today subject to foreign masters; her sons die fighting on alien ground, unlike the handful of noble Greeks, victors over the Persians at Thermopylae, who died for their own land. The poet Simonides could sing of that deed to posterity and thereby commingle his own fame with that of the Hellenic heroes. Tainted by occasional tones of "high-sounding oratory," in the opinion of Gian Carlo D'Adamo, the poem betrays the idealistic background of Petrarch and Ugo Foscolo, yet more personally it also rings with sincere concern and reveals that at twenty years of age, Leopardi was already an accomplished poet.

IDYLLS

Unlike the classical, Theocritan idylls which resembled verbal vignettes, Leopardi's idylls bear an autobiographical imprint. He defined them as "experiments, situations, feelings, historical adventures of my soul." Five poems in hendecasyllabic blank verse, the "small" idylls "The Infinite," "Sunday Evening," "To the Moon," "Il sogno," and "The Solitary Life," constitute the first significant phase in Leopardi's poetic development.

"The Infinite" is a mere fifteen-line idyll, yet it is a work of extraordinary depth. The poet is near Recanati, atop a hill that has always been dear to him. A hedge blocks his view of the horizon, but he imagines the silence of boundless space beyond it. The factor of time intrudes through the sound of the wind in the leaves, reminding him of eternity, of history, and of the present. "And so," he concludes, "in this immensity my thought is drowned: and in this sea is foundering sweet to me." The meditation strikes the reader because of the absence of concrete details; its indeterminateness is made vital by the evocative power of the words, the pauses, the enjambments, the oxymoronic arrangement of "foundering" and "sweet"—indeed, a whole rhythm of inner contemplation that halts on the threshold of fear before nothingness and reverts to losing itself completely in the immensity of being. A miniature drama played out in the mind, the poem has been considered Leopardi's masterpiece.

"Sunday Evening" recounts in forty-six lines how the poet cannot, like his beloved, indulge in pleasant fantasies during the calm evening after the holiday; nature allows him only tears. He compares the experience to the artisan's song that vanishes in the night's silence; on a grander scale, to the fall of the Roman Empire; and finally, to the anxiously awaited holiday that deceived him as a youth and choked his heart. The private theme of deception following in the wake of expectation is treated more objectively in "Saturday Evening in the Village." The effectiveness of this "holiday" poem derives from the moonlit setting, the sad, sentimental recollection, the dimmed semblance of a loved one, and the harshness of nature which favors others in preference to the poet.

"The Solitary Life" anticipates "The Solitary Thrush" with its theme of yearned-for solitude. A whole day is traced in its four unequal stanzas comprising 107 lines, from the morning patter of raindrops and the hen's fluttering wings, through the poet's lazy meditation by a quiet lake at noontime, where he remembers—despite the moving song he hears sung by a working girl from a nearby house—a disillusionment in love, to his greeting of the moon, which, unlike a thief or an adulterer, he wholly welcomes, as it sees him "wander through the woods and by the verdant banks, mute and solitary, or sit upon the grass, content enough, if only heart and breath be left for me to sigh." The movement of thought here surrenders to the motionlessness of silence.

PHILOSOPHICAL CANZONES

The next group of poems in the *Canti* is distinguished by a loftier language, and by a shift in subject matter from private to public concerns. These philosophical canzones number seven in all: "To Angelo Mai," "Nelle nozze della sorella Paolina," "Hymn to the Patriarchs," "A un vincitore nel pallone," "The Younger Brutus," "To Spring," and "Sappho's Last Song." This group of the early 1820's is usually expanded to include two poems composed slightly later, "To His Lady" and "To Count Carlo Pepoli," which share similar motifs.

In "To Angelo Mai," written in twelve fifteen-line strophes, Leopardi takes his Italian contemporaries to task because of their neglect of their illustrious past. To his "dead century" he opposes the philological discoveries of the erudite philologist and head librarian of the Ambrosiana and Vatican library, Angelo Mai, who had resurrected many significant texts. Philology is transfigured here to serve as a metaphor for civic regeneration. Though the poet feels decimated by sorrow and by lack of faith in the future, he evokes those "heroes" who lived and wrote before nature lifted the veil of comforting illusions from reality, before too much knowledge of the truth diminished man's imagination, before the sole certainty of existence—sorrow—had been fully disclosed, and before common opinion's notion of the sciences had pushed poetry into the background. Dante, Petrarch, Christopher Columbus, Ludovico Ariosto, Torquato Tasso, and Conte Vittorio Alfieri—all (except Ariosto) experienced deep sorrow, to which Leopardi relates his own experience in a manner which adumbrates the dominant pessimism of his subsequent poetry.

"The Younger Brutus," in eight fifteen-line stanzas, recalls the Roman hero after the battle of Philippi ridiculing the concept of virtue. The gods, he opines, are not moved by the fate of humans, who accept death with resignation. The hero claims a limited victory over such a destiny through suicide, which the gods are incapable of understanding. Why the divine injunction against suicide? Animals are not ruled by it, only the sons of Prometheus. Beasts and birds are ignorant of the world's destiny, and the stars are indifferent (adumbrations of the coming song of the Asian shepherd). On the threshold of death, Brutus will not invoke the gods or the stars

or posterity; his greatness will not enjoy understanding among men, so let his name and memory be lost. The poem stresses the hero's isolation; virtue, bitterly denounced at the outset, is exalted at the end. Leopardi's "agonism," as it has been called, consists of an active, if finally resigned, acceptance of fate, together with an eloquent protest against the laws of nature.

"Sappho's Last Song" portrays, in four sixteen-line stanzas, a legendary rather than historical Sappho: in Leopardi's words, "the unhappiness of a delicate, tender, sensitive, noble, and warm soul located in an ugly and young body," and, like Brutus, near suicide. The serene night and setting moon disclose a natural spectacle which once had brought comfort, but now, because of an adverse destiny, brings only misery. Why? No one can understand the lot of humankind; all is suffering, all is externality—the music and poetry of the deformed find no appreciation. Sappho will die; with illusions and youth gone, she will descend into the infernal black night. The poem mixes with great lyrical fantasy some of Leopardi's favorite themes, particularly the ironic contrast between the beauty of the world and the bleakness of human infelicity.

"GREAT" IDYLLS OF 1828-1830

As distinguished from the "small" idylls of 1819 to 1821—a term which many critics hesitate to accept (there is certainly nothing "small" about "The Infinite")—the "great" idylls of 1828 to 1830, perhaps better identified simply as further *canti*, treat Leopardi's familiar themes with more complex meditation and richer inspiration. They number seven: "The Revival," "To Sylvia," "The Solitary Thrush," "Memories," "The Calm After the Storm," "Saturday Evening in the Village," and "Night Song of a Nomadic Shepherd in Asia." Most of them are canzones in free form; they marked Leopardi's return to writing poetry after a lapse of several years.

"To Sylvia" underscores the theme of lost youth and the insensitive deception of nature. In its sixty-three lines in six uneven, free-form stanzas, the poem recalls the daughter of a coachman in Recanati, whose "happy and elusive" eyes and "constant song" he remembers. His life then was bright with hopes in a lovely landscape of gardens outlined in the distance by mountains and sea, but all of those hopes died, as Sylvia died, the victim of nature's cruelty, of a "strange disease" that preempted even her first acquaintance with words of love and praise for her beauty: "And with your hand you pointed from afar at chilling death and at a naked tomb." The poet, living on, can only lament the shattered illusions of youth, yet he does so without bitterness, with exquisite melancholy and refined sorrow that find relief in the re-creating power of the word.

"The Solitary Thrush," its three stanzas comprising fifty-nine lines, is a melancholy elegy evoking a festive spring day in the village, stressing, along with the theme of lost youth, the notion of isolation. The reasoning poet compares himself to the instinct-guided thrush that sings alone all day long while the other birds frolic in the sky. As the poet walks away from the celebrants in the village, the thrush leaves behind the joys of love and youth. It is an ending, in a way, and the sunset symbolizes it; while the bird will not mourn its losses, the poet will "many times look back at them, but quite disconsolate." Leopardi always revered solitude as a balm for the spirit and the imagination, but at the same time he recognized that it precludes communion with other people, and he saw in his penchant for solitude a dangerous inability to cope with life.

Written in seven free-style stanzas comprising 173 hendecasyllables, "Memories" recalls a train of images that had left their imprint on Leopardi's mind during his earlier years in Recanati. Returning to Recanati, the poet remembers how the "bright stars of the Bear" used to kindle dreams at night, and how by daytime the mountains suggested happiness beyond them. At that time, he did not know the malevolent crassness of his townsmen, nor did he expect a life without love. The pealing of the bell on city hall used to comfort his midnight fears, even as the "old halls" and the "frescoed walls" stirred his imagination then—when life held some promise. There was, too, the fountain in whose waters he had "thought of ending . . . my dreams." He remembers all of this with tenderness and regret, all of these "dulcet illusions," now that he has seen life in all of its squalid reality. No one can ever forget the lovely illusions of youth, like those associated with young Nerina, who was stripped of life when it seemed most promising. She has remained for him the lamented image of all that has departed. The poem is characteristic of Leopardi's more mature style in its blend of the lyrical with the reflective.

To the double tone of the lyrical and the reflective, "The Calm After the Storm" adds a third, the descriptive. It contains fifty-four lines in three free-style stanzas. After the storm, the town's rhythm resumes: the song of birds and the "refrain" of the hen, the artisan's tune, the women hustling after rainwater, and the screeching cart on the highway. Life truly seems welcome, as when one has escaped death. This is "bounteous" nature's sole gift: the avoidance of sorrow; pleasure is "relief from pain." The human race is "blest only when death relieves you from all sorrow." The original idyll becomes—not untypically for Leopardi—an ironic meditation.

"Saturday Evening in the Village," in four very uneven stanzas comprising fifty-one lines, again presents a series of images, all of villagers eager to complete their chores before the next day's holiday: the young lady with a bouquet of roses and violets, the old lady spinning at the wheel and recalling her youth, the children playing in the square, the farmer returning from the fields, the carpenter working until dawn. Yet the festive expectation will yield only ennui and the sad thought of the continuing drudgery of tomorrow. Youth is like Saturday—one should not be so eager to leave it behind. Echoes of Vergil and Tasso give this poem an archaic flavor, as do the moralizing hints at the end. Leopardi's idea is clear: Happiness is a factor of the imagination which anticipates, and to which one should cling, for it inevitably surpasses realization. The charm of the poem, however, resides in the gentleness with which it treats a potentially sermonic subject matter.

Generally acclaimed as one of Leopardi's finest poems, "Night Song of a Nomadic Shepherd in Asia," consisting of six stanzas comprising 143 lines, drew its inspiration from an item in the September, 1826, issue of *Journal des savants* concerning the Kirkis, a North-Central Asian nomadic tribe, some of whom "spend the night seated on a rock and looking at the moon, and improvising rather sad words on equally sad airs." The idea, however, had occupied Leopardi's mind for some time before 1826. The shepherd watches the "eternal pilgrim," the moon, as it crosses the sky and in turn watches the land. He does the same from dawn until evening, but what is the sense of the eternal movement of the stars and man's brief sojourn on Earth? Such is life: an old man who finally reaches his goal and disappears. Birth is difficult to begin with; then the parents must comfort the child "for being born"—so why struggle to live out the misery? Maybe the moon knows the why of things. The shepherd asks, but the question remains unanswered. Happy is the flock that knows nothing of destiny, though perhaps the lot of animals is equally unenviable, since "the day of birth is black to anything that's born." A surrogate for the poet, the shepherd in his primitive state knows as little about existence as the poet in his advanced modern age. Man has always asked himself the ultimate question, long before he started organizing his thoughts in writing; he always sensed that life is but an arduous journey toward death. All whys remain unanswered, and the moon, like the one Brutus saw, shines cold. Here again, because of the themes of pain, solitude, destiny, and universal mystery, the term "idyll" seems less suited than the term "elegy." In either case, however, the poem's supple rhythms give it a haunting, dirge-like quality.

THE ASPASIA CYCLE

The Aspasia cycle comprises "The Ascendant Thought," "Love and Death," "Consalvo," "To Himself," and "Aspasia," the last being a fictional name given by Leopardi to a woman he loved—unhappily: Pericles' beautiful and cultured courtesan represents the poet's Fanny Targioni-Tozzetti. All of the poems in the cycle are in blank verse, and with the exception of "Consalvo" and "Aspasia," which are in hendecasyllables, the style is free.

"The Ascendant Thought," in fourteen stanzas comprising 147 lines, refers to the effects of love, to the way in which the poet's mind is dominated by the thought of love "like a tower gigantic and alone in a solitary field." To him it seems impossible that he has tolerated unhappiness without turning to love, which thwarts death and gives life meaning. Love allows one to withdraw from reality as in a dream. What more can the poet ask than to look into the eyes of his beloved? The Platonic ideal of Leopardi's earlier "To His Lady" here modulates into a moving passion, sustained from beginning to end not with dreamy tones, but with ener-

getic emphasis. Here, Leopardi willingly throws himself into the arms of illusion.

On the other hand, "Love and Death," a slightly shorter poem of four stanzas comprising 124 lines, opposes death to the pleasures of love. The first effect of love is a languorous desire for death: While one needs love to escape the aridity of life, one knows also its "furious desire." Often, a lover in the heat of passion invokes death, and young lovers who kill themselves do so under the indifferent eyes of the crowd (for whom the poet ironically wishes emotionally barren longevity). As Benedetto Croce suggested, Leopardi addresses here the ravaging power of the senses: love as a "sweet and tremendous, elementary force of nature."

"To Himself" is Leopardi's most despairing utterance on the delusion of love, all the more powerful for its compression into a mere seventeen lines. The poet's heart will rest forever after the latest deception of love: "Bitter and dull is life, nothing more ever; and the world is mire." The only certainty is death; for himself, he has scorn, as he has also for nature, "and the infinite vanity of all things." Leopardi's style is as tense as his message; it is full of aesthetic silences that conjure up a wasteland of emotions, yet vibrant with the energy of disillusionment.

"Aspasia," consisting of 112 lines in four stanzas, concerns the mythologizing of woman. The poet sees Aspasia as a mother of incomparable beauty, elegance, and maternal femininity, a "ray divine." When he discovers that his image of her is largely fantasy, he blames her unjustly; in turn, she is unaware of the noble feelings that feed his delusion. The enchantment broken, the poet thinks of Aspasia in his tedium, "for a life bereft of sweet illusions and of love is like a starless night," but he finds comfort in lying on the grass to smile at "mortal destiny." The poem confesses Leopardi's humiliation for having been a slave in the throes of love, then rises to smile at the vanity of all things.

THE SEPULCHRAL CANZONES

The sepulchral canzones are only two in number: "On the Ancient Sepulchral Bas-Relief" and "On the Portrait of a Beautiful Lady." Both are written in free style, in lines of uneven length.

In the 109 lines of "On the Ancient Sepulchral Bas-Relief," the poet hesitates to call the dead young lady fortunate or unfortunate; perhaps she is happy, but her destiny inspires pity, since she passed away in the flower of her beauty. How could nature bring this upon an innocent person? Yet if death, a "most beautiful young maiden," is good, why lament it? Nature engenders illusions and struggles, so why should death appear frightening? If nature were not indifferent to man, she would not "tear a friend from friendly arms . . . and killing the one, the other keep alive." Sadly, Leopardi meditates, questioning the finality of things human; humankind's lot leaves not even death as the ultimate comforter. Against this despair, the poem adumbrates the theme of human solidarity, "brother [for] brother, child [for] parent, beloved [for] lover," that informs his last great poem, "The Broom."

"THE BROOM"

"The Broom," the poem that concludes the *Canti*, is Leopardi's most profoundly philosophical canzone. Its seven uneven stanzas comprise 317 lines. The setting is the sloping wastes of Mt. Vesuvius, where solitary broom plants grow. Under the lava once flourished famous cities; now there is only the plant's consoling scent. If one believes in man's "magnificent progressive destinies," one might come here to take note of nature's destructive powers and of man's impotence before her. The poet's "proud and mindless age" only *thinks* it progresses; its intellectuals praise the supposed accomplishments of the age, but the poet, who will be forgotten because of the bitter truths he utters, knows better. A humble, sick, yet generous man has nothing to hide about himself, but the one who foolishly ignores the misery of the human condition keeps making glorious promises to those who can be wiped out by natural disasters. On the other hand, those who admit humankind's frailty are noble—he who realizes that nature is *the* enemy and urges self-defensive brotherhood and the renunciation of wars. Under the starry sky where the poet sits, one cannot reconcile such immensity with the self-centered importance that man, "a mere dot," gives himself: "Laughter or pity, I know not which prevails." Nature treats man as the apple which falls from the tree and crushes the ant colony. After nearly two thousand years, the husbandman tending the vineyards still watches the crater closely and with constant apprehension. Tourists visit the unearthed Pompeii while the volcano keeps smoking, and nature does not heed human affairs. The broom plant, too, will succumb to the lava, but, free of "overweening pride," it is "far wiser and so much less infirm than humans," who believe in their immortality.

As a compendium of the *Canti*, "The Broom" reveals most of the best in Leopardi, although it does not achieve the melodic magic of "To Sylvia" or "Night Song of a Nomadic Shepherd in Asia." In the course of the collection, Leopardi establishes for himself a position of marked individuality in the poetic traditions of love, beauty, death, and nature, often by virtue of his melancholy cosmic view, emotionally powered by a deep sense of wonder. Narrowing his vision to a few common and familiar objects which serve as his points of departure, he opens them up, as it were, drawing himself away into the "infinite spaces" where his thought likes to roam freely. From this vantage, serenity dominates, rather than a pathological concentration on the ego. Although Leopardi is always at the base of his poetry, he stands there as an example, not as a display, of the human condition.

In the background of this seminal poem lie some of Leopardi's basic philosophical beliefs. "Against a reborn Catholic spiritualism and the idealistic currents," explains D'Adamo, ". . . Leopardi places his unchanged faith in materialistic and sensationalistic doctrines . . . ; he regrets that this body of thought which, after originating in Renaissance philosophy and developing successively during seventeenth century rationalism, freed us from medieval superstition and error, should be abandoned by the intellectuals of his day . . . in favor of new spiritualistic positions"—which included Catholic liberalism. Also in the background was the accusation of misanthropy leveled at Leopardi for his antiprogressivism, as well as the cruel charge that his pessimism was merely a consequence of his unfortunate physical condition.

As a symbol of man's helplessness, the broom plant encourages the poet in his message of brotherhood, which, after all, dates back to the origins of human life on Earth, and which bespeaks an innate moral sense in man. Leopardi appeals to man's reason; he wanted to end the *Canti* in this vein. The lyrical and the philosophical remain intertwined in this poetic discourse, though, as the composition unfolds, the two modes develop separately from each other in a brilliant interplay of reason and emotion.

Other major works

PLAYS: *Pompeo in Egitto*, wr. 1812; *Telesilla*, wr. 1819.

NONFICTION: *Storia dell'astronomia*, 1813 (*History of Astronomy*, 1882); *Saggio sopra gli errori popolari degli antichi*, 1815 (*Essay on the Popular Superstitions of the Ancients*, 1882); *Discorso sopra la vita e le opere de M. Cornelio Frontone*, 1816; *Il salterio Ebraico*, 1816; *Discorso di un Italiano intorno alla poesia romantica*, 1818 (*Discourse of an Italian Concerning Romantic Poetry*, 1882); *Crestomazia*, 1827, 1828 (2 volumes); *Operette morali*, 1827, 1834, 1836 (*Essays and Dialogues*, 1882); *Cento undici pensieri*, 1845 (*Pensieri*, 1981); *Epistolario*, 1849; *Zibaldone*, 1898-1900; *The Letters of Giacomo Leopardi, 1817-1837*, 1998.

Bibliography

Carsaniga, Giovanni. *Giacomo Leopardi: The Unheeded Voice*. Edinburgh, Scotland: Edinburgh University Press, 1977. A critical introduction to Leopardi's works with bibliographic references and an index.

Leopardi, Giacomo. *The Letters of Giacomo Leopardi, 1817-1837*. Selected and translated by Prue Shaw. Leeds, England: Northern Universities Press, 1998. Leopardi's correspondence offers invaluable insight into his life and writing habits as well as his relationships with family and acquaintances.

Nisbet, Delia Fabbroni-Giannotti. *Heinrich Heine and Giacomo Leopardi: The Rhetoric of Midrash*. New York: P. Lang, 2000. Provides a critical analysis of similarities between the rhetorical strategies of Heine's *Ludwig Börne: Recolections of a Revolutionist* (1881) and Leopardi's "Il Cantico del Gallo Silvestre" and the Midrashic process. Heine and Leopardi refer to biblical and historical events in their narrative and relate them to a contemporary situation to present their interpretation of an existential experience.

Press, Lynne, and Pamela Williams. *Women and Feminine Images in Giacomo Leopardi, 1798-1837*. Studies in Italian Literature 7. Lewiston, N.Y.: Edwin Mellen Press, 2000. A study of female images and man-woman relationships in Leopardi's works. Includes bibliographical references and index.

Singh, Ghan Shyam. *Leopardi and the Theory of Poetry*. Lexington: University Press of Kentucky, 1964. A biographical study of Leopardi and his thoughts on poetry. Includes a bibliographic essay summarizing Leopardi's works.

Sonzoghi, Marco, ed. *At the Year's Turning: An Anthology of Irish Poets Responding to Leopardi*. Chester Springs, Pa.: Dufour Editions, 1998. In addition to reprinting select poems in both Italian and English on facing pages, this collections offers insights into Italian influences on Irish authors.

Whitfield, John H. *Giacomo Leopardi*. Oxford, England: Blackwell, 1954. An in-depth biography of Leopardi with bibliographic references and an index.

Jean-Pierre Barricelli;
bibliography updated by the editors

Mikhail Lermontov

Born: Moscow, Russia; October 15, 1814
Died: Pyatigorsk, Russia; July 27, 1841

Principal poetry

Pesnya pro tsarya Ivana Vasilyevicha, molodogo oprichnika i udalogo kuptsa Kalashnikova, 1837 (*A Song About Tsar Ivan Vasilyevitch, His Young Body-Guard, and the Valiant Merchant Kalashnikov*, 1911)
Stikhotvoreniya M. Lermontova, 1840
Demon, 1841 (*The Demon*, 1875)
The Demon and Other Poems, 1965
Mikhail Lermontov: Major Poetical Works, 1983

Other literary forms

In addition to his position as one of the foremost Russian poets of the nineteenth century, Mikhail Lermontov holds the distinction of producing what many consider to be the first major novel in Russia, *Geroy*

Mikhail Lermontov (Library of Congress)

nashego vremeni (1840; *A Hero of Our Time*, 1854). The state of Russian prose during the 1820's and 1830's was far from satisfactory. Although several writers had tried their hands at historical novels in the 1820's, writers in the 1830's were still wrestling with such basic matters as narrative structure and a suitable literary language for the larger forms of prose fiction. Lermontov himself had begun two novels in the 1830's—a historical novel, *Vadim* (wr. 1832-1834), and a novel of St. Petersburg life, *Knyaginya Ligovskaya* (wr. 1836-1837; *Princess Ligovskaya*, 1965)—but he never completed them. In *A Hero of Our Time*, he solved the problems of structure and point of view by turning to the current fashion for combining a series of discrete short stories in a single cycle and taking it a step further. *A Hero of Our Time* consists of five tales linked by the figure of the central protagonist, Grigory Pechorin. Lermontov uses the device of multiple narrators and points of view to bring his readers ever closer to this hero, first providing second-hand accounts of the man and then concluding with an intimate psychological portrait arising from Pechorin's

own diary records, all the while maintaining his own authorial objectivity. The figure of Pechorin himself, a willful yet jaded egoist, made a strong impact on the reading public, and the Pechorin type had many successors in Russian literature.

Lermontov also wrote several plays, beginning with *Ispantsy* (1830; the Spaniards) and *Menschen und Leidenschaften* (1830; people and passions), which were inspired by the *Sturm und Drang* period of Friedrich Schiller's career, and concluding with *Maskarad* (wr. 1834-1835, pb. 1842; *Masquerade*, 1973), a drama exposing the vanity of St. Petersburg society. Lermontov is most remembered, however, for his prose and poetry.

ACHIEVEMENTS

In poetry, Mikhail Lermontov stands out as a Romantic writer *par excellence*. Influenced in his youth by such writers as Schiller and Lord Byron, he transformed Russian verse into a medium of frank lyric confession. The reserved and often abstract figure of the poet found in earlier Russian poetry gave way to a pronounced and assertive lyric ego in Lermontov's work, and Lermontov's readers were struck by the emotional intensity of his verse. Striving to express his personal feelings as forcefully as possible, Lermontov developed a charged verse style unmistakably his own. Although he seldom invented startling new poetic images, he often combined familiar images in sequences that dazzled his readers, and he utilized repetition, antithesis, and parallelism to create pithy and impressive verse formulations. Lermontov's poetic vision and his unabashed approach to the expression of his emotions had a considerable effect on subsequent Russian writers, from Nikolay Nekrasov in the next generation to Aleksandr Blok and Boris Pasternak in the twentieth century.

Iconoclastic in his approach to genre as well, Lermontov completed a trend already apparent in Russian poetry of the 1820's—the dismantling of the strict system of genre distinctions created during the era of classicism in Russian literature. Lermontov drew on disparate elements from various genres—the elegy, ode, ballad, and romance—and forged from them new verse forms suitable for his own expressive needs. The poet also showed a willingness to experiment with diverse meters and rhythms, and he employed ternary meters, primarily dactyls and amphibrachs, to an extent not seen previously in Russian poetry. Lermontov's exploration of such meters would later be continued by writers such as Nekrasov.

Although Lermontov's career was exceptionally brief, his accomplishments were extensive. He is justly considered to be, along with Alexander Pushkin, one of the two most important Russian poets of the nineteenth century. He left a rich legacy for future generations of Russian poets. Having moved past the poetic practices of Pushkin and his contemporaries, Lermontov forged a new style for the expression of the poet's emotions, a style both rugged and pliant, charged and evocative. His bold assertiveness as a poet and his skilled handling of rhythm and meter found an echo in the work of several generations of later writers. These achievements have earned Lermontov the right to one of the foremost places in the pantheon of Russian poets.

BIOGRAPHY

Mikhail Yurievich Lermontov was born in Moscow on October 15, 1814. According to family tradition, the Lermontovs were descended from a Scottish mercenary named George Learmont, who entered the service of the Muscovite state in the seventeenth century. Mikhail's mother, Mariya Arsenieva, belonged to an old and aristocratic family, the Stolypins, and her relatives did not approve of her match with Lermontov's father. Mariya died in 1817, and the child was reared by his maternal grandmother, Elizaveta Arsenieva, on her estate, Tarkhany. Because Lermontov's father Yury did not get along with Elizaveta Arsenieva, he left his son at Tarkhany and seldom met with him again before dying in 1831.

Lermontov had a comfortable upbringing. His grandmother provided him with a series of private tutors, and he occupied himself with painting and music as well as his studies. He moved with his grandmother to Moscow in 1827, and in the following year he entered a private preparatory school connected with the University of Moscow. There, he became interested in poetry and began to write voluminous amounts of verse, inspired by such authors as Schiller, Byron, Pushkin, Vasily Zhukovsky, and others. The influence of Byron and Pushkin is evident in Lermontov's first attempts at

narrative poetry, "Cherkesy" ("The Circassians") and "Kavkazsky plennik" ("A Prisoner of the Caucasus"). It was also during this period that Lermontov began work on his most famous narrative poem, *The Demon*.

In the fall of 1830, Lermontov entered the University of Moscow, where he remained immersed in his own personal world, reading and writing poetry and drama, including *Stranny chelovek* (1831; *A Strange One*, 1965). At the same time, he began to make a name for himself in social circles and experienced his first serious infatuations. His romance with one woman, Varvara Lopukhina, left a lasting imprint on his soul. Lermontov's romantic experiences and his encounter with society as a whole were filtered through his absorption with the figure of Byron. Constantly comparing his life with Byron's, he would become excited by any perceived similarities.

In 1832, Lermontov withdrew from the University of Moscow and sought admission to the University of St. Petersburg. Because the university would not give him credit for work done in Moscow, Lermontov instead entered the School of Guard Ensigns and Cavalry Cadets. There, he took up the lifestyle of an average cadet and wrote little in the way of serious poetry. Most of his creative energies went into the composition of salacious verse for his comrades' amusement, although he did begin work on his first novel, *Vadim*, a historical piece depicting the activities of a demoniac hero during the time of the Pugachev rebellion in the 1700's. After receiving his commission in the Life Guard Hussar Regiment stationed outside St. Petersburg in Tsarskoe Selo, Lermontov continued to sustain an active social life and rather calculatingly tried to generate a reputation as a Don Juan. Lermontov's cynicism about the values and mores of St. Petersburg society found expression in his verse play *Masquerade*, which, because of censorship problems, was approved for publication only after his death. In addition to this dramatic piece, Lermontov began work on the novel *Princess Ligovskaya*, which depicts an encounter between a young aristocrat and a St. Petersburg clerk, but the book was never finished.

Lermontov's literary reputation received a dramatic assist in 1837, when he wrote a bold poem about Pushkin's untimely death as a result of a duel in January of that year. The duel—the culmination of Pushkin's long frustration with life in St. Petersburg and with the attentions paid to his wife by Baron Georges d'Anthès, a French exile and the adopted son of a Dutch diplomat—had taken place on January 27. Pushkin was mortally wounded and died on January 29. Lermontov immediately penned a sharp poem expressing his dismay at Pushkin's death and the sufferings he had endured that led him to the duel. When some of d'Anthès's supporters began to cast aspersions on Pushkin, Lermontov added sixteen more lines which gave vent to his indignation with the court aristocracy itself. The poem received wide circulation in manuscript form and created a sensation in St. Petersburg. When it came to the czar's attention, Lermontov was arrested and sent to serve in the Caucasus.

This exile did not last long, however, and after several months in the south, Lermontov was transferred to Novgorod and then back to St. Petersburg. There, the poet circulated in society as a figure of note, and he reacted to the situation with ironic amusement. He also entered into close relationships with other important literary figures of the day—Zhukovsky, Pyotr Vyazemsky, and Andrey Kraevsky, the editor of the new journal *Otechestvennye zapiski*, in which several of Lermontov's poems appeared. Although his production of lyric poetry declined at this time, he completed several noteworthy works, including the narrative poems "Tambovskaya kaznacheysha" ("The Tambov Treasurer's Wife") and "Mtsyri" ("The Novice"), which contains the confessions of a young monk who had briefly fled the monastery to find out "if the earth is beautiful" and "if we are born into this world/ For freedom or for prison." The first portions of his great novel *A Hero of Our Time* also began to appear in 1839.

Early in 1840, however, Lermontov again found himself in trouble with the authorities. Within the span of a few weeks, he succeeded in insulting the czar's daughters at a masquerade ball and took part in a duel with Erneste de Barante, the son of the French ambassador. Again Lermontov was arrested, and again he was sent to the Caucasus for military service. Once there, Lermontov managed to obtain assignment with a regiment actively engaged in fierce battles with rebel Caucasian tribes, and he soon distinguished himself in hand-to-hand combat with the rebels. Suitably impressed,

Lermontov's commanders recommended that he be given a gold saber in recognition of his valor, but he never received this commendation, perhaps because he continued to incur the disfavor of the authorities back in St. Petersburg.

Having been given permission to take a two-month leave in the capital early in 1841, Lermontov overstayed his leave and was ordered to depart for the Caucasus within forty-eight hours. He was in no hurry to rejoin his regiment, however, and his return journey became a leisurely affair, during which he wrote several of his finest lyrics. Reaching the town of Pyatigorsk in May, he spent several weeks taking the waters and indulging in pleasant diversions with a company of friends and other young people. Unfortunately, Lermontov chose to mock a certain Nikolay Martynov, an officer and former schoolmate at the Guards' School who had adopted the habit of wearing native dress in an attempt to impress the women in town. Martynov took umbrage at Lermontov's repeated needling, and he finally challenged him to a duel. The duel took place on July 27, 1841. Deadly serious, Martynov advanced to the barrier with determination and shot Lermontov, killing him instantly. Lermontov was subsequently buried at Tarkhany.

ANALYSIS

The hallmark of Mikhail Lermontov's mature verse—a fine balance between the intensity of the poet's emotion and the controlled language he uses to express it—took several years to achieve. In his early work, Lermontov did not check his desire to convey his feelings directly, and his verse seems raw and effusive, often hyberbolic and unformed. He wrote hundreds of poems as an adolescent, and he later recognized their immaturity, for he refused to publish them with his subsequent work. They would appear only after his death.

EARLY POETRY

A study of the early poetry reveals Lermontov's aggressive absorption of the work of other writers. Imagery, phrases, and individual lines are taken whole from the poetry of such authors as Zhukovsky, Pushkin, Alexander Polezhaev, and Ivan Kozlov among the Russians, and of Byron, Thomas Moore, Alphonse de Lamartine, and Victor Hugo among foreign writers. Lermontov's tendency to lift excerpts from one work and to insert them into another was a lifelong characteristic of his artistic method. He not only appropriated elements from other writers' works but also cannibalized his own poetry. The narrative poem "The Novice," for example, contains elements drawn from an earlier work, "Boyarin Orsha" (the Boyar Orsha), which in turn contains elements from an even earlier work, "Ispoved" (a confession). As the Russian Formalist critic Boris Eikhenbaum put it in his noted study of 1924, *Lermontov* (English translation, 1981): "His attitude was not directed toward the creation of new material, but to the fusion of ready-made elements." In his greatest works, however, Lermontov's art of fusion resulted in some very distinguished pieces.

BYRON'S INFLUENCE

Perhaps the most influential figure in Lermontov's formative years as a poet was Byron. Lermontov's early lyrics repeatedly feature heroes who possess a special sensitivity or gifted nature but who have been crushed by fate. Such characters may carry a dark secret or wound in their souls, but they bear their suffering proudly and without complaint. Typical are these lines from a poem of 1831, "Iz Andreya Shenie" ("From André Chénier"): "My terrible lot is worthy of your tears,/ I have done much evil, but I have borne more." Lermontov himself recognized his affinity with Byron, while seeking at the same time to assert his individuality; a poem of 1832 begins, "No, I am not Byron, I am another/ As yet unknown chosen one." This sense of his own uniqueness is characteristic of the young Lermontov, and his fascination with the traits of the Byronic hero is further evident as he compares himself to Byron: "Like him, I am a wanderer persecuted by the world/ But with a Russian soul." Other Romantic features in the poem include a comparison between the unfathomable depths of his soul and the depths of the ocean (recalling Byron's celebrated verses on the same theme), a statement about the separation of the poet from "the crowd," and a complaint about the difficulty of expressing one's inner feelings. Lermontov airs this last concept in a demonstrative final line. Asking "Who will tell the crowd my thoughts?" the poet exclaims: "I—or God—or no one!" Many of Lermontov's poems conclude with such dramatic flair. Also characteristic here is Lermontov's penchant for concise lines structured by parallel-

ism and antithesis. Comparing himself with Byron, he writes: "I began earlier, I will end earlier." This line seemed particularly prophetic to the Russian reading public when the poem first appeared in 1845, after Lermontov's early death. Curiously, Lermontov's apprehension of an early death remained with him throughout his career.

"THE SAIL"

One of Lermontov's early lyrics, the short poem "Parus" ("The Sail"), became well known after his death. Written in three stanzas of iambic tetrameter, the most popular meter in Russian poetry at the time, the poem is wholly constructed on a strict scheme of parallels and repetitions. The first two lines of each stanza provide a description of a sea setting, while the second two depict the psychological condition of a person, perhaps a sailor, metonymically evoked by the image of the sail moving across the open sea (the word for "sail" in Russian is masculine, and the Russian pronoun *on* can be translated as either "he" or "it"). Within this framework of parallels, Lermontov utilizes a series of antitheses or oppositions which perhaps reflect the contradictory flux of emotions in the subject's soul. The poet asks in the first stanza: "What is it seeking in a distant land?/ What has it abandoned in its native region?" In the second stanza, however, he provides only negative answers: "Alas,—it is not seeking happiness/ And it does not flee from happiness!" Nor do the final lines provide a concrete resolution: "Rebellious one, it seeks the storm,/ As if in storms there is peace!" Lermontov's evocation of a rebellious spirit seeking peace through turmoil was given a political interpretation by some contemporary Russian readers, but the poem's generalized nature makes other interpretations possible, too. It is likely that Lermontov simply wanted to suggest the fundamental contradictions and confusion inherent in restlessness itself.

THE DEMON

Images of rebellion and negation occupied a prominent place among Lermontov's lyrics in the 1830's, and at the end of the decade he completed his most impressive portrait of a Romantic "spirit of negation"—the title character of the long narrative poem *The Demon*. Like many of Lermontov's other narrative poems, *The Demon* is less a tale involving several characters in a concrete setting than a forum for the lyric expression of the protagonist's emotional impulses. In its earlier versions, the poem was set in Spain, and the female protagonist was a nun, but Lermontov later shifted the setting to the Caucasus, and the austere mountain ranges of this region proved to be an excellent backdrop for his portrayal of human frailty and superhuman passion. The central character of the poem is the Demon, a dark spirit who becomes captivated by the beauty of a Georgian maiden, Tamara. After her fiancé has been killed, the Demon tries to persuade her to give her love to him, telling her that her love can restore him to goodness and reconcile him with Heaven. Having delivered his impassioned speech, he destroys her with a fatal kiss. As her soul is carried to Heaven by an angel, the Demon seeks to claim his victim, but the angel spurns him, and the furious Demon is left alone with his frustrated dreams.

The Demon is an enigmatic character. Lermontov does not provide the reader with a clear psychological portrait of his hero. He is not the stern, philosophizing rebel of Byron's verse drama *Cain* (1821) and of similar Western European treatments of the metaphysical Romantic hero. Rather, he resembles the protagonists of a number of Lermontov's other works in that he is a willful spirit motivated more by boredom than by Promethean ambitions. The Demon recalls happier times "When he believed and loved/ . . . And knew neither malice nor doubt," but his turn to evil is essentially unmotivated, and his speeches to Tamara are not logially structured arguments but rather dazzling torrents of charged phrases and images. When he identifies himself to her, he states: "I am the scourge of my earthly slaves,/ I am the tsar of knowledge and freedom,/ . . . And you see,—I am at your feet!"

When the Demon claims that he is ready to renounce evil and reconcile himself with the good, the reader is not sure how to gauge the Demon's sincerity. His attitudes are susceptible to instantaneous change. When he hears Tamara sing, he begins to enter her room "ready to love/ With a soul open to the good. . . ," yet when an angel blocks his way, he flares up: "And again in his soul awoke/ The poison of ancient hatred." He tells Tamara that as soon as he saw her, he suddenly hated his immortality and power, but as he tries to convince her to love him, he offers her both of these gifts. Perhaps the best way to understand the Demon is to view him as a figure who has truly become bored with doing evil ("He sowed evil without enjoyment/ . . . And evil grew boring to him"), and therefore he allows himself to become caught up in his own rhetoric about renunciation of evil and reconciliation with the good. At the moment of his declarations, he may feel sincere, but at the core of his soul, he is cold and unfeeling. Tamara, on the other hand, is given little to say; she seems to serve merely as a pretext for Lermontov's hero to pour out his soul.

The interaction between the Demon and Tamara is played out against the forbidding landscape of the Caucasus. Lermontov's descriptions of the icy mountains that stand guard over small patches of inhabited land serve as an apt emblem of the cosmos itself. The universe of *The Demon* and of many other Lermontov works is an impersonal realm in which human activity plays but a small and insignificant role. Lermontov's readers, however, have been less moved by his descriptions of nature than by the glittering oratory of the Demon, and the work has left significant traces on the creative consciousness of later Russian artists. The painter Mikhail Vrubel painted a series of studies inspired by *The Demon*, and the composer Anton Rubinstein wrote an opera based on the work.

"THE DEATH OF A POET"

Lermontov's development beyond the narrow thematics of his early Romantic period is most apparent in his shorter lyric works, beginning with his famous poem on Pushkin's death, "Smert poeta" ("The Death of a Poet"). The poem can be divided into three parts. The first two parts were written immediately after Pushkin's death, while the third was composed several days later. Throughout the poem, Lermontov's talent for declamatory verse comes to the fore. The first section, written in lines of iambic tetrameter, is marked by frequent exclamations, rhetorical questions, and strong intonational breaks, as in the lines: "He rose up against the opinion of society/ Alone, as before . . . and was killed!/ Killed!" In an interesting form of homage to Pushkin, Lermontov draws on Pushkin's own poetry to depict the poet's death, echoing the images used by the earlier poet in his brilliant novel in verse, *Evgeny Onegin* (1825-1833; *Eugene Onegin*, 1881).

During the second part of the poem, which is written in iambic lines of varying lengths, Lermontov adopts an elegiac tone as he questions why Pushkin left the peaceful diversions of close friendships to enter into "this society, envious and suffocating/ To a free heart and fiery passions." In the final section, also written in iambic lines of varying lengths, Lermontov's elegiac tone gives way to a torrent of bitter invective. His charged epithets and complex syntax seem to boil over with the heat of his indignation. He begins with a harsh characterization of those who spoke ill of the dead poet—"You, arrogant offspring/ Of fathers renowned for notorious baseness"—and he continues with an attack on the court itself: "You, standing in a greedy crowd around the throne,/ The executioners of Freedom, Genius, and Glory." After reminding these villains of the inevitability of divine punishment, which cannot be bought off with gold, Lermontov concludes: "And you will not wash away with all your black blood/ The righteous blood of the poet!" "The Death of a Poet" heralded Lermontov's growing maturity as a poet. Although revealing his continued reliance on certain Romantic formulas, it indicated that he was beginning to find a workable poetic style for himself.

"MEDITATION"

Lermontov employed the declamatory style of "The Death of a Poet" with great success in his late period. A forceful poem of 1838, "Duma" ("Meditation"), for example, presents a concentrated indictment of the coldness and emptiness of Lermontov's entire generation. The poem begins, "I gaze on our generation with sadness!" and it contains such well-known lines as "We are disgracefully faint-hearted before danger/ And contemptible slaves before power." As Lidiya Ginzburg points out in her important study, *Tvorchesky put Lermontova* (1940), the lyric ego of Lermontov's early works had become a more generalized "we"; this shift perhaps reflected a greater objectivity on Lermontov's part as he soberly measured himself and the society in which he had come to maturity. Certainly the poet knew how to pinpoint the falsity and vanity of his peers. In a poem of 1840 that begins "How often, surrounded by a motley crowd . . . ," Lermontov contrasts his feelings of boredom at a masquerade ball with his warm recollections of childhood and spontaneous dreaming. Noting that he hears "the wild whisper of speeches learned by rote" and is touched "with carefree audacity" by urban

beauties' hands, "which long ago had ceased to tremble," the poet concludes by confessing an urge "to confuse their frivolity/ And to throw boldly into their faces an iron verse/ Steeped in bitterness and spite!"

MATURE WORKS

Lermontov's declamatory "iron verse," however, was only one style he utilized in his mature work. It is futile to look for sharp genre distinctions in his late verse, for he did not pay close attention to such distinctions, and one can find in individual poems a blending of features from various genres. Eikhenbaum identifies three categories of poetry in Lermontov's mature period: poems of an oratorical, meditational character; poems of melancholy reflection; and poems resembling lyric ballads with a weakened plot. Indeed, several of Lermontov's late poems resemble small verse novellas: "Uznik" ("The Prisoner"), "Sosed" ("The Neighbor"), "Kinzhal" ("The Dagger"), "Son" ("A Dream"), and "Svidanie" ("The Meeting"). In part, Lermontov's predilection for such brief verse "novellas" may have signified a dissatisfaction with the unrestrained confessional tenor of his early work and a desire to create works which displayed greater objectivity and universality. For the same reason, perhaps, Lermontov also favored short allegorical poems in which natural settings and objects convey human situations and feelings. One example of this type is "Utyos" ("The Cliff"), the first stanza of which depicts a cloud nestling for the night against the breast of a great cliff. In the morning, the cloud moves on, "gaily playing in the azure," but it has left behind a moist trace in a crack in the cliff. The poem concludes with a picture of the cliff: "Solitarily/ It stands, plunged deep in thought,/ And quietly it weeps in the wilderness." Again, one can contrast the restrained evocation of abandonment and isolation here with the unchecked egotism of Lermontov's early work. The "plot" of this poem is further enhanced by the fact that in Russian, the word for "cloud" is feminine while the word for "cliff" is masculine. Also noteworthy is the trochaic meter of the verse; Lermontov moved beyond the poetic models of his predecessors to develop new rhythmic patterns.

"IT'S BORING AND SAD . . ."

At times, Lermontov's new rhythms produced an impression of ruggedness that aroused commentary from his readers. One such work is the poem "I skuchno i grustno . . ." ("It's Boring and Sad . . ."). Written in alternating lines of five-foot and three-foot amphibrachs, the poem stands out for its colloquial, almost prosaic diction, as at the beginning of the second stanza, where the poet writes: "To love . . . but whom? . . . for a short time—it's not worth the effort,/ But to love forever is impossible." After examining his situation and judging it dull, the poet concludes: "And life, if you look around with cold attentiveness,/ Is such an empty and foolish joke. . . ." The mood of pessimism and disillusionment is familiar from Lermontov's early work, but the detachment and impassivity of the verse are new. The poet is no longer swept away with the importance of his emotions. He surveys his own flaws and the flaws of his generation with an analytical eye that retains no illusions about the glamorous posturings of the Romantic hero. This detachment is precisely what makes Lermontov's portrait of Pechorin, the protagonist of *A Hero of Our Time*, so gripping and accurate.

"I WALK OUT ALONE ONTO THE ROAD . . ."

Lermontov's innovative approach to rhythmic patterns was perhaps most influential in his reflective poem of 1841, "Vykhozhu odin ya na dorogu . . ." ("I Walk Out Alone onto the Road . . ."). This work, one of the last which Lermontov wrote, depicts the poet alone in the midst of nature on a quiet, starlit night. Within his soul, however, he is troubled. He wonders why he feels so pained, and he confesses that he no longer expects anything from life; he merely wants to fall into a deep sleep. Yet it is not the sleep of the grave that he seeks; rather, he would like to fall asleep in the world of nature, eternally caressed by a sweet song of love.

Of special interest in this poem is Lermontov's use of trochaic pentameter with a caesura after the third syllable of the line. This meter creates a special rhythmic effect in which the line seems to fall into two segments. The first segment is often anapestic, because the first syllable is frequently unstressed or weakly stressed, while the second part of the line seems to consist of three iambic feet. This structure creates an impression of an initial upsweep of movement, emphasizing the semantic charge of the poem's first word—"výkhozhú" ("I walk out")—followed by a more calm or stable interval over the rest of the line. Such a contrast or imbalance is itself emblematic of the poem's message, for

despite the initial suggestion of movement conveyed by the poet's statement about walking out onto the road, he does not in fact go anywhere, and the poem concludes with images of passivity or stasis. This remarkable harmony between the rhythmic pattern of the poem and its message has had a lasting impact on the artists who followed Lermontov. Not only was the poem set to music and introduced to the general public as a song, but it also initiated an entire cycle of poems in which a contrast between the dynamic theme of the road or travel and the static theme of life or meditation is rendered in lines of trochaic pentameter. Among Lermontov's successors who wrote poems of this type were Fyodor Tyutchev, Ivan Bunin, Aleksandr Blok, Andrey Bely, Sergei Esenin, Boris Poplavsky, and Boris Pasternak.

OTHER MAJOR WORKS

LONG FICTION: *Vadim*, wr. 1832-1834, 1935-1937 (in *Polnoe sobranic sochinenii v piati tomakh*); *Knyaginya Ligovskaya*, wr. 1836-1837, 1935-1937 (in *Polnoe sobranie sochinenii v piati tomakh*; *Princess Ligovskaya*, 1965); *Geroy nashego vremeni*, 1839 (serial), 1840 (book; *A Hero of Our Time*, 1854).

PLAYS: *Tsigany*, wr. 1830, pb. 1935; *Ispantsy*, wr. 1830, pb. 1935 (verse); *Menschen und Leidenschaften*, wr. 1830, pb. 1935; *Stranny chelovek*, wr. 1831, pb. 1935 (verse; *A Strange One*, 1965); *Maskarad*, wr. 1834-1835, pb. 1842 (*Masquerade*, 1973); *Dva brata*, wr. 1836, pb. 1880 (*Two Brothers*, 1933).

MISCELLANEOUS: *Sochtsnentsya M. Ya. Lermontova*, 1889-1891 (6 volumes); *Polnoe sobranie sochinenii v piati tomakh*, 1935-1937 (5 volumes; includes all of his prose and poetry); *Polnoe sobranie sochinenii v shesti tomakh*, 1954-1957 (6 volumes; includes all of his prose and poetry); *A Lermontov Reader*, 1965 (includes *Princess Ligovskaya*, *A Strange One*, and poetry); *Michael Lermontov: Biography and Translation*, 1967; *Selected Works*, 1976 (includes prose and poetry).

BIBLIOGRAPHY

Eikhenbaum, Boris. *Lermontov*. Translated by Ray Parrot and Harry Weber. Ann Arbor: Ardis, 1981. A translation of the Russian monograph by a leading Russian critic of the 1920's, this thorough study of Lermontov's poetry and prose remains the seminal work on him. Many poems are offered in both Russian and English.

Garrard, John. *Mikhail Lermontov*. Boston: G. K. Hall, 1982. Like other volumes in Twayne's World Authors series, Garrard's monograph presents Lermontov and his works meticulously in a concise, easy-to-understand fashion. It lays the foundation for more ambitious studies of Lermontov in any language.

Golstein, Vladimir. *Lermontov's Narratives of Heroism*. Evanston, Ill.: Northwestern University Press, 1998. This study tackles the topic of heroism, prevalent in Lermontov's works, and how he presents and solves it. The emphasis is on "The Demon," "The Song," and Pechorin of *A Hero of Our Time*. Citations of works are in Russian and English translation.

Kelly, Laurence. *Lermontov: Tragedy in the Caucasus*. New York: George Braziller, 1977. A colorfully illustrated biography of Lermontov covers his childhood in the "wild" East, his education, the rise and fall in the society, and his attitudes toward war as reflected in his works.

Lavrin, Janko. *Lermontov*. London: Bowes & Bowes, 1959. This brief and very readable monograph presents all important features of Lermontov's poetry and prose. Lavrin succeeds in touching upon the salient aspects of Lermontov's works, stressing the comparison with other Russian and foreign writers. An excellent introductory monograph.

Reid, Robert. *Lermontov's "A Hero of Our Time."* London: Bristol Classical Press, 1997. This analysis of the novel casts light on Lermontov's work as a whole. Bibliographical references.

Turner, C. J. G. *Pechorin: An Essay on Lermontov's "A Hero of Our Time."* Birmingham, England: University of Birmingham, 1978. A pithy discussion of various aspects of Lermontov's main character, of the relationship of the narrator and the reader, the narrator and the hero, the hero and himself, the hero and the author, and the hero and the reader.

Julian W. Connolly;
bibliography updated by Vasa D. Mihailovich

DENISE LEVERTOV

Born: Ilford, Essex, England; October 24, 1923
Died: Seattle, Washington; December 20, 1997

PRINCIPAL POETRY

The Double Image, 1946
Here and Now, 1957
Overland to the Islands, 1958
Five Poems, 1958
With Eyes at the Back of Our Heads, 1959
The Jacob's Ladder, 1961
O Taste and See: New Poems, 1964
City Psalm, 1964
Psalm Concerning the Castle, 1966
The Sorrow Dance, 1966
A Tree Telling of Orpheus, 1968
A Marigold from North Vietnam, 1968
Three Poems, 1968
The Cold Spring and Other Poems, 1969
Embroideries, 1969
Relearning the Alphabet, 1970
Summer Poems, 1969, 1970
A New Year's Garland for My Students: MIT, 1969-1970, 1970
To Stay Alive, 1971
Footprints, 1972
The Freeing of the Dust, 1975
Chekhov on the West Heath, 1977
Modulations for Solo Voice, 1977
Life in the Forest, 1978
Collected Earlier Poems, 1940-1960, 1979
Pig Dreams: Scenes from the Life of Sylvia, 1981
Wanderer's Daysong, 1981
Candles in Babylon, 1982
Poems, 1960-1967, 1983
Oblique Prayers: New Poems with Fourteen Translations from Jean Joubert, 1984
The Menaced World, 1984
Selected Poems, 1986
Breathing the Water, 1987
Poems, 1968-1972, 1987
A Door in the Hive, 1989
Evening Train, 1993

Sands of the Well, 1996
This Great Unknowing: Last Poems, 1999

OTHER LITERARY FORMS

The Poet in the World (1973) gathers prose articles, reviews, criticism, statements to the press, and tributes to fellow poets. *Light Up the Cave* (1981), Denise Levertov's second volume of prose pieces, includes three short stories; articles on the nature of poetry and politics; speeches and political commentary; and memoirs and notes on other writers—Hilda Morley, Michele Murray, Bert Meyers, Rainer Maria Rilke, and Anton Chekhov. Of particular interest are the pages on dream, memory, and poetry and the details of her arrest and imprisonment experience as a war protester.

Levertov also wrote a novella, *In the Night: A Story* (1968), and the libretto for an oratorio, *El Salvador: Requiem and Invocation* (1983). With Kenneth Rexroth and William Carlos Williams, she edited *Penguin Modern Poets Nine* (1967). She produced translations of other poets' works, including *In Praise of Krishna: Songs from the Bengali* (1967, with Edward C. Dimock, Jr.), *Selected Poems*, by Eugene Guillevic (1969), and *Black Iris*, by Jean Joubert (1988). Her final prose work, *Tesserae* (1995), consists of autobiographical fragments that composed a "mosaic" of the poet's life.

ACHIEVEMENTS

Denise Levertov's first book of poems, *The Double Image*, was published in England in 1946. It brought her to the attention of British and American critics and poets such as Kenneth Rexroth and Robert Creeley. Eleven years later, her first American book was published, followed by many volumes of poems and several translations of other poets' work. She taught at many institutions, including Vassar College, Drew University, City College of New York, University of California at Berkeley, Massachusetts Institute of Technology, Brandeis University, Tufts University, and Stanford University. As the poetry editor of *The Nation* in the 1960's, she influenced the critical reception of new poets. She was elected to the American Academy of Arts and Letters. Her many awards include a Guggenheim Foundation Fellowship in 1962, the Lenore Marshall Poetry Prize in 1975 for *The Freeing of the Dust*, and in 1983 both the Elmer Holmes Bobst Award and the Shelley Memorial Award. Levertov won the Frost Medal in 1990 and in 1995, she was awarded the Academy of American Poets Fellowship.

BIOGRAPHY

Born near London, England, in 1923, Denise Levertov was reared in a multicultural environment: Welsh and Russian, Jewish and Christian. On her mother's side, her lineage was Welsh. Beatrice Spooner-Jones, her mother, was a daughter of a physician and great-granddaughter of a tailor, teacher, and preacher, Angell Jones, made famous by Daniel Owen, "the Welsh Dickens," in the novel *Hunangofiant Rhys Lewis* (1885). Beatrice Spooner-Jones had a beautiful singing voice and a stock of stories to tell of Welsh life. She loved to travel, and in Constantinople, where she was a teacher in a Scottish mission, she met a young Russian Jew, Paul Peter Levertoff, who had converted to Christianity. They were married in London, where he was ordained to the Anglican priesthood. His great passion in life was rec-

Denise Levertov (L. Schwartzwald, courtesy of New Directions)

onciliation between Christians and Jews. A daughter, Olga, was born to the couple, and seven years later, a second daughter, Denise.

In some ways, Denise felt like an only child. She never attended a public or private school; her mother, her only teacher, read many classic works of fiction to her. She visited museums and libraries in London and studied ballet for many years; for a time she considered a career in dance. When World War II came, she entered nurse's training and worked in a number of London public hospitals caring for children, the aged, and the poor. She had been writing poems since childhood and published her first volume of poems in England shortly after the war.

Levertov met and married an American writer, Mitchell Goodman, who was studying abroad. They lived in Europe until 1948, returning to Europe from New York for a period in 1950-1951. Her son Nikolai was born in 1949. In 1956, she became an American citizen. For the next thirty years, she published more than a dozen volumes of poetry with the same publisher, New Directions. During the Vietnam era, she wrote and spoke passionately against the war; in 1972, with Muriel Rukeyser and Jane Hart, she traveled to Hanoi. In the years of nuclear bomb testing in the air, she participated in the movement toward a test-ban treaty and the elimination of nuclear weapons altogether. Later, she vigorously supported protests against American involvement in civil wars in El Salvador, Honduras, and Nicaragua. She lived in Mexico for a number of years: Indeed, her mother grew to love Mexico and remained with a family in Oaxaca for twenty years before her death in 1977. After spending much of the last decade of her life in the Pacific Northwest, Levertov died in Seattle, Washington, on December 20, 1997.

ANALYSIS

Many major lyric poets who live a full, long life produce a body of work that encompasses between six and nine hundred poems. Denise Levertov published about six hundred poems. Yet despite this large number of works, her poems revolve around a few preoccupations and questions that continuously engaged her attention: the meaning of life, the issues of justice that have arisen in the twentieth century, and more personal concerns that have to do with friendships, family relationships, and immediate thoughts and feelings. Since the lyric poem captures a moment of intense feeling and thought (it is the most compressed form of literature), chronological analysis of Levertov's work gives access to a record of the poet's unfolding life. Levertov seems to have been uniquely placed in her family and time to inherit two great streams of lyric power—the Welsh gift of song and speech and the profound religious thought of her priest father's Jewish-Christian search for truth.

With such a combination of parental influences, the themes that prevail in Levertov's poetry—the nature and form of poetry, and the moral obligations of the poet to society—are hardly surprising. She once said that the Hasidic or mystical beliefs in her father's Jewish heritage gave her an ease and familiarity with spiritual mysteries. For the purpose of analysis, one can study these three areas of her concern—poetry, morality, and mystery—but in her poems they often appear not separately but together, coloring the mosaic of her words. She combines the skills of a craftsman and those of an artist, the vision of moral integrity and spiritual insight.

EARLY INFLUENCES

A young poet must establish her voice and style. Levertov learned from modernistic poets such as Charles Olson and William Carlos Williams, who used concrete, everyday words and familiar settings and events to convey profound truths. She drew also from Welsh hymn-singing lines. Lines and line breaks are essential to the sound quality of her poetry. Some of her inspiration comes from dreams, images, and dream sounds. Naturally, the technical apparatus of poetry making absorbs her interest as a poet and teacher of poetry writing: How should journals be used? How should a poet revise drafts? How does one evaluate poetry and distinguish what is good from what is bad? Who are the great poets of the twentieth century?

As to the second preoccupation in Levertov's poetry, the integrity of moral vision, the twentieth century has provided abundant evidence of the human capacity for sin as well as visionary leadership in the fight against evil. The age-old oppression of Jews by Christians flared into monstrous proportions as millions of innocent women, children, and men were gassed in death camps in Europe. The shock of this discovery in 1945 as World War II came to a close must have been intense for the young poet-nurse whose father was both Jew and Christian. In later decades, she felt an imperative to protest the horror and injustice of war. The effort to end the Vietnam War brought women together before the women's movement had gathered full force. The sight of children mutilated and burned by napalm aroused the conscience of many "unpolitical" people. Levertov's actions and her words expressed the outrage of many citizens. She explored the relevance of poetry to politics and questioned the moral responsibility of the poet in a time of peril. What use should be made of the gift of speech?

Early in her career, Levertov expressed her vision of unity in the physical and spiritual worlds. "Taste and See," the title poem of her seventh volume, has a biblical sound. Insisting that one cannot know a divinity apart from what is given to the senses, she probes the meaning of physical experience—a life affirmation—and considers its relationship to religious values. Decades before the general public awakened to the need to respect the physical world, Levertov spoke of the mystery in the objects people taste, touch, and see: the moon, food, a glass of water. She found both happiness and wisdom in the realization of mystery. Increasingly, in her later poetry, the value of mystical and religious experience became her theme.

RELIGIOUS SIGNIFICANCE

Levertov links the imagination with truth in poetry; thus the poem has a religious significance. As "religion" literally means "binding anew," she finds connections to be the essence or truth of imagination. In the poem "A Straw Swan Under the Christmas Tree," she writes, "All trivial parts of/ world-about-us speak in their forms/ of themselves and their counterparts! . . . one speech conjuring the other." The human emotion of sympathy depends on understanding the connections in animate and also inanimate life. "May the taste of salt/ recall to us the great depths about us," she writes in "The Depths." The principle of interrelated form applies even in the extreme case of the Nazi leader, Karl Adolf Eichmann. In "During the Eichmann Trial," she says that if we look accurately into another face, or into a mirror, one sees

"the other," even Eichmann. This oneness is a mystery, and something Eichmann did not know: "We are members/ one of another."

One should not conclude, however, that the truth of imagination Levertov seeks is an intellectual truth. Unlike the poet Dante, who moves from love and care in the physical world to a spiritual and intellectual understanding of love, Levertov remains firmly based in the physical realm, however far along the mystical path she may travel. Perhaps in the modern age the presence of evil within and without is so strong that the poet dares not abandon her mooring in the physical "real" world that needs so much assistance. Humanity is "a criminal kind, the planet's nightmare" (as she quotes Robinson Jeffers in the poem "Kith and Kin"). The truth she continually explores remains the connection in the patterns of human and natural life. Courage is a necessity, and models of courage may be found in her lean, economical poetic voice.

DICTION AND IMAGERY

A "speaking-voice" quality in Levertov's poems results from the open form of uneven line lengths. In keeping with the tone of a human voice in natural and varied cadences, her diction neither startles nor challenges the reader with rare and exotic words in the manner of Marianne Moore or Edith Sitwell. She "tunes up" or increases the vibrancy of her poems by making them "tight," with no excess words or phrases. She often omits subjects and verbs, punctuating a fragment as though it were a sentence, and alternates or intersperses fragments with complete sentences. Another skill is accuracy in word choice, using the best word to evoke the scene, the object, the person, or the feeling she is describing. She can change the feeling of a line by inserting words from another collocation—sets of words often found together. For example, in a late poem, "Those Who Want Out," from *A Door in the Hive* (1989), she describes people who are designing permanent colonies in space—their optimism, their love of speed and machines that are "outside of nature." Then a closing line judges them with icy and stern tone in six one-syllable words with biblical power: "They do not love the earth." This use of sparse, plain Anglo-Saxon English for a "stopper" of great power is found frequently in William Shakespeare.

Along with devices of diction, poetic speech uses images to convey truth. Levertov's images are most frequently from the natural world—plants, animals, and landscapes—and of everyday household objects. "In the Unknown" takes the reader to the poet's home: "As if the white page/ were a clean tablecloth,/ as if the vacuumed floor were a primed canvas." In "To the Muse" she describes the body as the house one lives in and the place to find one's inner poetry. There are many rooms in this house, and when the Muse seems to have departed, she is hiding, like a lost gold ring. One has forgotten to make a place for her, and to bring her back, one needs to attend to the house, find some flowers to decorate it, and be alert to the Muse with all of one's senses. Images of caves, mirrors, water, cloud, shadow, and moon fill her poems to make her feelings and ideas accessible to the common reader.

ROLES OF THE POET

In harmony with her use of diction and form, Levertov expressed a modest view of the poet: a person who can articulate feeling through the medium of language. She refused the exalted aura of a supersensitive person whose feelings are beyond the reach of ordinary human beings. Glorification by "temperament" was never attractive to her and was as suspect as misplaced romantic adulation—not a twentieth century ideal. It was the process of writing, not the result, that fascinated her. She saw poems as structures of meaning and sound that convey feelings accurately. The poet must revise and polish until the poem is complete. Technical skill with diction, form, rhythm, syntax, and sound—above all, sound—raise a poem from mediocrity to perfection. As a teacher, she had much experience to share. From her essays and articles on the subject of poetry one can gain information about many technical aspects of her craft. Her poems are more readily understood when one is familiar with these principles.

VERSIFICATION

Like many young poets, Levertov experimented in her early writings with various rhyme schemes, tones, and forms. A 1946 poem, "Folding a Shirt," uses Dante's interlacing *terza rima* rhyme pattern for six stanzas: *aba bcb cdc ded efe fgf*. "Midnight Quatrains" rhymes the second and fourth end words of each stanza. There are dramatic poems in dialogue form and ballads.

Typically, however, Levertov's poems have no end rhyme or regular meter. (The lack of regular rhyme and stressed beats in most modern poetry has been attributed to the chaos and irregularity in the twentieth century—poetry reflects life.) Her rhythm is subtle, moving with the line break. Uneven lines are the rule, not the exception. The placement of words and indentations create rhythmic ebb and flow, abrupt interruptions, slow pauses, and dramatic suspense. The eye follows a varied typography that signals rhythm with blank space and black ink, like a design for reading aloud. The "melos" or song quality of such an open form comes from the rightness of the line length—the line's appropriate length in the poem's internal system of meanings.

As well as obtaining rhythm by a masterful use of line breaks, Levertov excels in the construction of sentences within the poem. Often a poem is built like an argument: a proposition followed by a rebuttal, in the way of a sonnet. The poem's syntax often matches the idea of the poem. In "The Prayer," the poet is praying to Apollo at Delphi for the flame of her poetry to be maintained. As if the poem were the flame, it keeps going until the poet breaks the sentence when she begins to wonder whether the god is mocking her. The sentence ends at the same time that her belief in the god falters. The second sentence, a reprise, says that the flame is flickering, and perhaps it is some other god at work. In a very sensual poem, "Eros at Temple Stream," she pictures lovers bathing near a river, soaping each other with long, slippery strokes—their hands as flames. The poem's syntax—one long sentence with no punctuation at its close—mirrors the meaning.

NARRATIVE AND DRAMATIC POEMS

In Levertov's narrative and dramatic poems, she set the stage quickly. A mini-play, "Scenario," opens bluntly: "The theater of war. Offstage/ a cast of thousands weeping." A poem about animal life at the dump begins, "At the dump bullfrogs/ converse as usual." Often these poems begin with brief noun phrases, as in "A Hunger": "Black beans, white sunlight." Levertov's impulse for story and drama resulted in a number of long poem sequences and poetic plays. "Staying Alive," with its prologue and four parts with entr'actes, vividly recalls events and feelings at the height of the Vietnam War protests and the People's Park struggle in Berkeley,

California, in 1969. In 1983, an oratorio, *El Salvador: Requiem and Invocation*, was performed at Harvard University; the text by Levertov was set to music by the composer Newell Hendricks. Using the structures of the Johann Sebastian Bach passions and George Frideric Handel and Franz Josef Haydn oratorios, Levertov wrote voices for a narrator, Archbishop Oscar Romero, a questioner, nuns, and a chorus. She studied the speeches of the murdered archbishop and quoted his words as well as passages from Mayan prayers. The work was given to help fundraising efforts of relief organizations active in Central America.

POLITICAL POEMS

That the poet should be also a political person came as an early and natural revelation to Levertov. Her first published poem, "Listening to Distant Guns" (1940), tells of hearing "a low pulsation in the East" that "betrays no whisper of the battle scream." She actually heard the guns of World War II from the south coast of England, to where she, along with many young people, had been evacuated from the city of London. She herself was safe, but the war was very near. She describes the dismal feelings of the English people in "Christmas 1944," when no celebration could hide the blackout curtains on the windows, the knowledge of "fear knocking on the door" of so many Europeans. She gives a welcome: "Come in, then poverty, and come in, death:/ This year too many lie cold, or die in cold." During her impressionable teens and early twenties, she was surrounded with war. Although two decades would pass before her active involvement in the American antiwar movement, she had already expressed her grief at the mass destruction war brings.

In "On the Edge of Darkness: What Is Political Poetry?" (originally a lecture delivered at Boston University in 1975), Levertov defends the idea that a lyric poem can be simultaneously intimate, passionate, and political. Indeed, there is a long history of poets speaking out their political ideas—generally, though not always, in defense of liberty and peace. Contemporary "political" poets usually participate actively in the struggles of which they write. Specific issues give rise to topical poetry on race, class, environment, and gender problems. These poems, like the songs associated with the struggles, change the feelings of the listeners and readers; they alter the awareness of a community. The standards of aesthetic value apply to this poetry as to all other; it should arouse the whole being of the listener: mind, senses, and spirit.

ANTIWAR POETRY

By 1966, Levertov was writing poems about the war in Vietnam. The most influential and famous of these is probably "Life at War." Speaking for her contemporaries, she tells of war's pervasive influence in her century—"We have breathed the grits of it in, all our lives"—and then begins a long lament over the damage war has done to people's imaginations. The modern imagination, she argues, is "filmed over with the gray filth of it," because humankind (and here she lists wonderful and praiseworthy achievements and powers of human beings) "whose language imagines *mercy* and *lovingkindness*," can schedule the burning of children's bodies. "Burned human flesh/ is smelling in Vietnam as I write." As a former nurse, Levertov can bring her sensual awareness into her passionate denunciation of modern war. The poem closes with a statement that humankind needs the "deep intelligence" that living at peace can give. The violence to human imagination from war comes from its insult to intelligence.

Other antiwar poems were composed in the form of dialogues such as questions and answers about Vietnamese people or a narrator questioning a bomber pilot. Levertov's poems also protest the false language of war communiqués. She pays tribute to the young men and women antiwar activists—those who die, those who live, those who go to jail. One poem honors her friend and fellow poet Muriel Rukeyser, who went to Vietnam with her in 1972. Both women were rearing sons at the time—teenagers who were in line for a future military draft.

MARRIAGE AND FAMILY LIFE

Family life, and in particular marriage, inspired many of Levertov's most memorable poems. In keeping with her insistence on the beauty of sensual experience, she celebrated the joy of marriage. The short poem "Bedtime" puts the contentment of fulfilled love in natural terms: "We are a meadow where the bees hum,/ mind and body are almost one." "Hymn to Eros" praises the "drowsy god" who quietly circles in "a snowfall hush." Two beautiful poems to her son, Nikolai, are spaced years apart—one before his birth, "Who He Was," and one, "The Son," as he becomes a man. The first tells of his conception, gestation, and birth, and the second of skills he has gained.

The death of love and the contemporary difficulties in male-female relationships also provide subjects for notable poems. The much-quoted "About Marriage" begins with a cry for freedom, "Don't lock me in wedlock, I want/ marriage, an/ encounter," and concludes, "I would be/ met/ and meet you/ so,/ in a green/ airy space, not/ locked in." As the women's movement and the antiwar movement seemed to merge, the desire for peace and independence became the message of many women writers and poets. "The Ache of Marriage" compares marriage to Jonah's life in the belly of a whale; the poet and her spouse are looking for joy, "some joy/ not to be known outside it." Marriage is not discarded as an ideal, but its confinement brings problems to women who feel an urge to work in a wider field. In "Hypocrite Women" Levertov tells women that they should not be ashamed of their "unwomanly" traits but should admit boldly the truth of their lives.

The nature of another woman-to-woman relationship is explored in the "Olga poems." Levertov's sister, older by seven years, was estranged from her family for many years. Her death brought a recollection and definition of the two lives that were linked in dream and memory but separated by behavior, circumstances, and distance. The gaze of her sister's eyes haunts the poet: "eyes with some vision/ of festive goodness in back of their hard, or veiled, or shining,/ unknowable gaze." Poems to her mother and father join poems to other poets as Levertov continually seeks and writes about the connections in her life. Rilke, Rukeyser, Boris Pasternak, Robert Duncan, and Pablo Neruda are some of the poets she addressed in poems.

Travel and dreamscapes

Reflecting the world consciousness typical of Americans in the second half of the twentieth century, Levertov traveled widely. Many of her poems describe the people and places she visited in Europe, Mexico, the United States, and Asia. Distant places remain alive in memory with sensual evocations—dreamscapes. The perfume of linden trees in blossom in an ancient European town is recalled in "The Past." Feelings of comfort-

able married happiness mingle with the beauty of the setting. The poem "In Tonga" describes the life of sacred bats hanging in their caves, squeaking in night flight. The poet muses about them, "If they could think/ it would not be of us." "Poem from Manhattan" builds a prayer and invocation to New York City through its power, energy, and hope—"city, act of joy"—to its desolation—"city, gesture of greed." Moral and spiritual awareness accompanies the poet's sensory connections to the world.

Mysticism

The mystical and religious tones of Levertov's poetry can be traced from their beginnings to their full flowering in the poems of the 1980's collected in two volumes, *Breathing the Water* and *A Door in the Hive*. The daughter of a clergyman who was steeped in mystical Jewish Hasidism, Levertov showed her familiarity with religious texts in early poems. "Notes of a Scale" gives four moments of wonder; its reference note directs the reader to Martin Buber's *Tales of the Hasidim: The Early Masters* (1975). The poem "Sparks" includes passages from the Old Testament book of Ecclesiastes. In this work, Levertov moves easily from the ancient Hebrew text to the circumstances of a modern life. Not only Jewish mysticism but also Christian tradition inspired her poetry. Later poems take as their themes the annunciation to Mary, Jesus's parable of the mustard seed, and the path of Calvary.

Levertov's religious poetry is deeply imbued as well with thoughts on the lives and works of religious saints and writers. Saint Thomas Didymus, Julian of Norwich, William Blake, William Everson, and W. H. Auden are evoked in various poems. One should remember, also, that she translated religious poetry of the Bengali Vaishnava faith. Collaborating with the scholar Edward C. Dimock, Jr., she published this fascinating poetry under the title *In Praise of Krishna: Songs from the Bengali*. The warm emotional and erotic content of these poems has a kinship to Levertov's sensual approach to religious mysticism.

Dream-based poems

Access to religious symbols often comes in dreams. The immensely influential biblical accounts of dream visions (those of Ezekiel, Daniel, and John of Patmos, among others) echo in texts from every century. Many of these dream visions were part of Levertov's own home educational fare. She wrote of two childhood dreams: One consisted of a violent transformation from a rustic scene of happiness to a scene of burning and devastation. The other recurring dream was of a large country house made of a warm pink stone; its name was Mazinger Hall. These two dreams, like the later ones she used in poems, carry emotional content of joy and sorrow, gain and loss, security and terror. Gradually, her dream material was transformed into poems that evoke similar feelings in her readers.

In Levertov's early dream-based poems, the process of transferring a dream to a poem involved describing the dream content. The poet explained that later, after analytical work on her dreams, she abandoned that objectivity and gave her images stronger and clearer emotional force to present the dream content more directly to the reader. A third stage in this process came with the realization that the dream needs a literary form that cannot be imposed but must be listened for. Several times she found that a dream worked only as a prose tale. The stories "Say the Word" and "A Dream" began as poems that she transformed to a rhythmic prose. The experience of using dream material for a work of art teaches the poet that the poem must be not only visually clear but also morally or emotionally significant for the reader. An expression that is too private does not make an effective poem.

Another kind of dream poem may result from an auditory message received in a dream state, or as a combined visual and auditory dream. Levertov experienced each type and made poems of them. In "The Flight," she retells a vision of the poet and mystic William Blake, who spoke the words, "The will is given us that we may know the delights of surrender." She waited several years before composing a poem about that experience, to avoid a too-literal transcription. Again, an auditory message was received in a dream about the Russian poet Boris Pasternak. The visual scene disappeared from memory, but the words remained. In both instances, as Levertov explains, the quality of the resulting poem came from the poet's willingness to recognize and absorb a hidden quality that lay beyond the superficial appearances. Some dream images may indicate the questions or problems present at that moment in the poet's

life. In that case, the truth of the life and the truth of the dream provide an interplay that makes a powerful poem.

HONEY OF THE HUMAN

The religious message that hums (a favorite Levertov verb) throughout her poetry is the oneness of all life: all human beings, animals, trees, and the great elements of earth, air, fire, and water. The vision of air and water blended comes in poems about bees, honey, and ocean currents that hold "my seafern arms." The cleansing properties of honey in the hive, she writes in "Second Didactic Poem," neutralize even the poison of disease organisms. That hive with its transforming power may be the same as human activity—"honey of the human." Transformation may also move in the opposite direction, from a joyful morning self-confidence to a rapid pace that diminishes the person ("Remembering"). These apparent divisions between good and evil in a person's emotional life can be harmonized from a point of view that is wide enough to encompass the other side, or opposite, in what is experienced.

Certain lines of Levertov's poetry shine as lighthouse beacons across the restless waters of human experience: for example, "We are one of another" ("A Vision"), the lovely love song "We are a meadow where the bees hum" ("Bedtime"), and "To speak of sorrow/ works upon it" ("To Speak"). Why do these lines hum in the mind years after they are first encountered? In them one finds three qualities that characterize Levertov's poetic work: music, morality, and mysticism. Her best poems are true lyrics—songs, in their flowing rhythms and enchanting sound patterns of vowel and consonant combinations. Moreover, she teaches the lessons modern Americans need to hear, about respect for natural life and for unprotected, helpless human beings, especially children and the elderly. Then there is the wonder she shares in the magic of common things—the "gleam of water in the bedside glass" ("Midnight Gladness") and the moonlight crossing her room ("The Well"). Levertov said, "There is no magic, only facts"; her magic is found in accurate and loving observation of everyday shapes, colors, and sounds.

LEGACY

Yet beyond her mastery of the poem's form and even beyond the thought content, Levertov's poetry can be appreciated for the qualities of the poet herself. During the 1960's, before the women's movement had strengthened the fragile position of women poets, when a cult of death followed the suicides of Anne Sexton and Sylvia Plath, Denise Levertov lamented their loss, not only because they were fine poets but also because their deaths would confirm a popular conception of the poet as abnormally sensitive, often on the edge of madness. For her, alcoholism and nervous breakdowns were not signs of poetic talent. Creativity, she wrote, belongs to responsible, mature adults who take citizenship seriously. In the late 1960's and 1970's, she put this antiromantic view to the service of the peace and women's liberation movements—marching, protesting, speaking against social injustices. She called attention to the political poets imprisoned in many countries. In the 1980's, she produced poetry of great beauty on the human and material sources of her spiritual inspiration.

Indeed, the last volume of poetry published during her life, *Sands of the Well* (1996), showed the beginning of a pronounced shift away from her poems of social engagement to a more all-encompassing focus on a spirituality that transcended simple Christianity. Her lasting legacy was to show that a poet in the United States can support herself economically. Generously and with humor, she shared with students the fruits of her years of practicing her craft. In all these ways, she modeled a high standard for both poetry and the poet.

OTHER MAJOR WORKS

LONG FICTION: *In the Night: A Story*, 1968.

PLAY: *El Salvador: Requiem and Invocation*, pr. 1983 (libretto; music by W. Newell Hendricks).

NONFICTION: *The Poet in the World*, 1973; *Light Up the Cave*, 1981; *New and Selected Essays*, 1992; *Tesserae*, 1995.

TRANSLATIONS: *In Praise of Krishna: Songs from the Bengali*, 1967 (with Edward C. Dimock, Jr.); *Selected Poems*, 1969 (of Eugene Guillevic); *Black Iris*, 1988 (of Jean Joubert).

EDITED TEXTS: *Penguin Modern Poets Nine*, 1967 (with Kenneth Rexroth and William Carlos Williams); *The Collected Poems of Beatrice Hawley*, 1989.

BIBLIOGRAPHY

Brooker, Jewel Spears. *Conversations with Denise Levertov*. Jackson: University Press of Mississippi, 1998. This chronologically arranged volume collects interviews with Levertov conducted by various interviewers from 1963 to 1995. The most common themes addressed are faith, politics, feminism, and poetry.

Felstiner, John. "Poetry and Political Experience: Denise Levertov." In *Coming to Light: American Women Poets in the Twentieth Century*, edited by Diane Wood Middlebrook and Marilyn Yalom. Ann Arbor: University of Michigan Press, 1985. In this brief but valuable study, Felstiner shows that Levertov awakens human sensitivity—male and female—by insisting on the sacramental quality of all physical presence. In poetry, she finds hope while facing the horrors of war in Central America, in Vietnam, and in American cities. Felstiner's words on the oratorio *El Salvador: Requiem and Invocation* are particularly worthwhile.

Lacey, Paul A. "Denise Levertov: A Poetry of Exploration." In *American Women Poets*, edited by Harold Bloom. New York: Chelsea, 1986. Lacey considers the influence of Hasidism in Levertov's poetry: She treats the miraculous in a matter-of-fact tone. Her weakness in the early poetry, Lacey says, stemmed from an inability to deal seriously with evil in the world. Later, however, she grew into the political consequences of what it means to be, as she says, "members one of another."

Marten, Harry. *Understanding Denise Levertov*. Columbia: South Carolina University Press, 1988. One of the most important studies of Levertov in book form, Marten's analysis covers four decades of poetry. Individual chapters give an overview, a history of the earliest poetry, an analysis of the volumes that established her reputation, a consideration of her public voice, and a discussion of spiritual dimension in her later development. The annotated bibliography of critical articles is particularly helpful.

Pope, Deborah. "Homespun and Crazy Feathers: The Split Self in the Poems of Denise Levertov." In *A Separate Vision*. Baton Rouge: Louisiana State University Press, 1984. In Levertov's poems, divisions of the self appear in images of passivity and sleeping on one hand and cold, dark violence on the other. Her central concern for the woman artist becomes an effort to harmonize oppositions. In her later poetry, Levertov celebrates the freedom and power of a new role, the "wise woman."

Rodgers, Audrey T. *Denise Levertov: The Poetry of Engagement*. Rutherford, N.J.: Fairleigh Dickinson University Press, 1993. This treatment of Levertov's work examines her political commitment to antiwar themes in particular, placing poems on this topic in relation to Levertov's earlier work and her life. The author had access to Levertov herself and to previously unpublished letters in the preparation of this study.

Wagner-Martin, Linda. *Denise Levertov*. New York: Twayne, 1967. Although written when Levertov was in mid-career, Wagner's biography, survey of poems, and bibliography provide an excellent introduction to the poet's life and work. Seven chapters discuss Levertov's family and education in England, her poetic themes and forms, and influences from modernist poets. Includes a chronology and notes.

Doris Earnshaw,
updated by Leslie Ellen Jones

PHILIP LEVINE

Born: Detroit, Michigan; January 10, 1928

PRINCIPAL POETRY

On the Edge, 1963
Not This Pig, 1968
Thistles, 1970
Five Detroits, 1970
Pili's Wall, 1971
Red Dust, 1971
They Feed They Lion, 1972
1933, 1974
On the Edge and Over, 1976
The Names of the Lost, 1976
Ashes: Poems New and Old, 1979
Seven Years from Somewhere, 1979
One for the Rose, 1981

Selected Poems, 1984
Sweet Will, 1985
A Walk with Tom Jefferson, 1988
What Work Is, 1991
New Selected Poems, 1991
The Simple Truth, 1994
The Look of Things, 1996
Unselected Poems, 1997
The Mercy, 1999

OTHER LITERARY FORMS

Philip Levine has published a collection of interviews, *Don't Ask* (1981), in the University of Michigan's Poets on Poetry series. A series of autobiographical essays make up *The Bread of Time* (1994). Levine selected and translated *Tarumba: The Selected Poems of Jaime Sabines*, with Ernesto Trejo (1979) and *Off the Map: Selected Poems of Gloria Fuertes*, with Ada Long (1984).

ACHIEVEMENTS

Philip Levine's most important achievements in the early part of his career are the collections *Not This Pig* and *They Feed They Lion*. In the best poems of these two books, Levine reflects the influence of the surrealist and political poets of Spain and South America and takes on the subject of the city with a remarkable vitality. Along with James Wright, Allen Ginsberg, Denise Levertov, and Robert Bly, Levine has managed to incorporate politics into his poetry, going far beyond the immediate protest reaction to the Vietnam War. He writes about the working poor without condescension and with an empathy that puts him clearly in the tradition of Walt Whitman and William Carlos Williams; these poems are often about survivors, people who have suffered in their lives but refuse to quit.

Levine has won a number of poetry awards, most significantly the Lenore Marshall Award for *The Names of the Lost*, the National Book Critics Circle Award for *Ashes* and *Seven Years from Somewhere*, the American Book Award for *Ashes*, the National Book Award for *What Work Is*, and the Pulitzer Prize for *The Simple Truth*. He has also been honored with a Harriet Monroe Memorial Prize, a Frank O'Hara Prize, and the Ruth Lilly Poetry Prize.

BIOGRAPHY

Philip Levine was born in Detroit of Russian-Jewish immigrant parents; his experiences of the Depression and World War II in that city play a central role in his poetry. In an interview Levine said that he spent most of his childhood fighting against people who attacked him because he was Jewish. His father died when he was young (apparently in 1933, according to the poem titled "1933"), and both his parents often appear in his many poems that explore the past. According to Levine, the workers he knew as a child and as a young man had a great effect on him, and various immigrant anarchists had a lasting effect on his politics. He married Frances Artley in 1954, and they have three sons, Mark, John, and Theodore.

Since Levine often writes from personal experience, it is possible to draw a picture of him and his relationships from his poems. There are many poems about his grandparents, parents, brother, sister, wife, and each of his three sons. Not all the "facts" in his work, however, may necessarily be true. The poems do reveal much about the writer, but the poet's tendency to fictionalize must be kept in mind.

After holding a number of jobs, including working in a foundry, Levine attended Wayne State University, where he studied under John Berryman, receiving a B.A. degree in 1950 and an M.A. in 1955. He refused to serve in the Korean War, and although this was clearly a political protest on his part, he was declared 4-F for psychological reasons. He received a master of fine arts in creative writing from the University of Iowa in 1957 and won a fellowship to attend Stanford University. He taught at California State University, Fresno, for many years beginning in 1958. He has given readings of his poetry throughout the United States, often revealing a comic side of his character that is not obvious in his poetry. Levine was actively opposed to the Vietnam War, and his first trip to live in Spain in the late 1960's was taken, in part, to escape from America. In Spain, the Levines lived near the Catalan city of Barcelona, the stronghold of the anarchists during the Spanish Civil War, a city that Levine has said reminds him of the Detroit of his childhood. He has had an interest in the Spanish Civil War (1936-1939) for many years, sympathizing with the losing Republicans but identifying with the anarchists

Philip Levine

rather than the communists or Socialists, and he made Spain and that war the subject of some of his most memorable poems. For two years, Levine served as chair of the Literature Panel of the National Endowment for the Arts, and in 2000 he was elected a chancellor of the Academy of American Poets. Levine spends part of each year in Fresno, and part in New York, where he has led writing workshops at New York University.

ANALYSIS

When Philip Levine issued a new version of his first book *On the Edge*, he added to the title the words "and over," declaring the direction of his dark and fierce poetry. His poems examine a world of evil, loneliness, and loss, where a poem titled "Hymn to God in My Sickness" can only be a cry of unbelief. Paradoxically, there is a strong faith in human nature running throughout Levine's work. His is a poetry of community that at times holds out some distant but powerful dream of a better society. Often this is dramatized in the lives of the anarchists of the Spanish Civil War, celebrating their nobility and courage. His work expresses admiration for those who suffer but do not give in, those who fight against prejudice and pain. Many of his poems employ a second-person voice, and although they often have specific addressees, they are also addressed to the reader as a brother or sister to say "Your life is mine."

Levine is one of the most overtly urban poets in America today. His hometown of Detroit—its factories and foundries, its dead-end jobs, its dirt and smoke, its dying lives—plays a central part in his imagination. It is the city he escaped from—or tried to—to Fresno, California, a place often depicted by him as lonely and sad, a silent place where "each has his life/ private and sealed." Then there is the third city—Barcelona, Spain, where Levine often seems most at home, where he feels a greater sense of community and history, even though he carries what he sees as the political burden of America with him.

ON THE EDGE

The second poem in Levine's first book, *On the Edge*, "Night Thoughts over a Sick Child," sets off a central image and theme of his work, presenting the speaker helpless before the boy's suffering, with no faith in the efficacy of prayer. He finds the situation intolerable and refuses to justify it in any way:

> If it were mine by one word
> I would not save any man,
> myself or the universe
> at such cost: reality.

There is nothing for him to do but to face "the frail dignity/ of surrender." The mixture of suffering and helplessness, anger and sadness, points toward many of Levine's later poems.

In this early volume Levine is writing rather formal poetry, metrical or syllabic, with rhymes or off-rhymes. In poems about World War II and the Algerian War, he shows his concern for the public causes of suffering. In "Gangrene" he draws an ugly picture of torture, "the circus of excrement," and ends with a self-righteous address to the reader as being secretively thrilled by these descriptions of torture even though he fakes boredom. In later volumes Levine achieves a more satisfactory tone of identification with suffering of this kind.

Probably the best poem in *On the Edge* is "For Fran," a picture of the poet's wife as gardener, an image that appears also in later poems. She is seen preparing the flower beds for winter, and she becomes for the poet the person who bears the promise of the future: "Out of whatever we have been/ We will make something for the dark." These final lines can be taken as a kind of motto for Levine's later poetry, his attempt to make something in the face of the dominant darkness.

NOT THIS PIG

Levine's second volume, *Not This Pig*, is the key work in his development as a poet. There are some poems that are like the tightly ordered style of *On the Edge*, but a number of them indicate a new direction—more open, riskier, and more original. The fact that he is moving away from syllabics and rhyme—as did most poets of his generation in the 1960's—is not the main source of this originality; but a more daring language is in evidence, opening his work to a wider and deeper range.

His poem "The Midget," drawing on his experiences in Spain, is a fine example of this new range. In a café where the anarchists planned the burning of the bishop of Zaragoza, the speaker sits on a December day—off-season, no tourists—amid the factory workers and other laborers. A midget in the bar begins to sing of how he came from southern Spain "to this terrible/ Barcelona," telling them all that he is "big in the heart, and big down/ here, big where it really counts." The midget confronts the speaker with talk of his sexual prowess and insists that he "feel this and you'll believe." The speaker tries to turn away from him, buy him off with a drink, but the midget insists, tugging at him and grabbing his hand. The midget ends up sitting in his lap, singing of "Americas/ of those who never left." The others in the bar turn away in disgust, and then the drunken speaker begins to sing to the midget. In the final section, the poem goes beyond anecdote, stepping off into an eerie, mysterious world where the midget and the speaker merge in their opposition. They are both singers, old world and new, both strangers and outcasts. They come together in the brotherhood of freaks, the pain of being human.

The title of this volume comes from a brilliant tour de force, "Animals Are Passing from Our Lives," a poem told from the point of view of a pig. At first the pig seems complacent, going off to market "suffering children, suffering flies,/ suffering the consumers." He has no intention, however, of giving in, playing the human fool as the boy who drives him along believes he will. He will not "turn like a beast/ cleverly to hook his teeth/ with my teeth. No. Not this pig." This can be taken as a kind of slogan for the entire book, Levine's "Don't tread on me." In a somewhat similar vein is the poem "Baby Villon," about a 116-pound fighter who was robbed in Bangkok because he was white, in London because he was black; he does not give in—not this pig—he fights back. Different as they are, the poet and Villon become one: "My imaginary brother, my cousin,/ Myself made otherwise by all his pain."

Levine identifies with these tough losers, even though he admits that their pains are greater than his, their toughness surpassing his. His attitude toward suffering can be summed up in his often-anthologized poem, "To a Child Trapped in a Barbershop." In mock seriousness he tells the six-year-old that his case is hopeless, advising him not to drink the Lucky Tiger because "that makes it a crime/ against property and the state." "We've all been here before," he informs the boy: we have all suffered the fears of the barbershop and the sharp instruments, but "we stopped crying." The boy should do the same; that is, welcome the world of experience, its difficulties, fears, and pains.

THEY FEED THEY LION

In his next full-length volume, *They Feed They Lion*, and in the chapbooks *Red Dust* and *Pili's Wall*, Levine pushes further the discoveries that were made in poems such as "The Midget." As he said in his statement in *Contemporary Poets of the English Language*, he was influenced by the surrealistic Spanish and South American poets Miguel Hernández, Rafael Alberti, Pablo Neruda, and César Vallejo. These poets, as well as showing the way to a greater freedom of language, were political poets, all of them affected deeply by the Spanish Civil War. Possibly, though, the greatest reason for the renewed vigor of Levine's work is the discovery of his hometown, Detroit, as a subject for his poetry. This city is at the heart of *They Feed They Lion*, and it provides the starting point for some of the finest of Levine's poems.

When Levine returns to the city in 1968 in the poem "Coming Home," he finds it an affront to nature, a riot-torn city with "the eyes boarded up," the auto factories' dirt and smoke dominate the hellish landscape: "We burn this city every day." In "The Angels of Detroit" sequence, however, the poet again and again expresses his sympathy for the workers, people such as Bernard:

> His brothers are factories and
> bowling teams, his mother is the
> power to blight, his father
> moves in all men like a threat,
> a closing of hands, an unkept
> promise to return.

Out of such beaten lives comes Levine's most remarkable poem, the title poem, "They Feed They Lion." As that title illustrates, the poem breaks away from conventional language and syntax. It is a chant celebrating the workers who come "out of burlap sacks, out of bearing butter . . . out of creosote, gasoline, drive shafts, wooden dollies." "They lion grow," the refrain proclaims, "From 'Bow Down' come 'Rise Up.'" It is a cry of and for the workers, in praise of their resiliency and courage.

In the poem "Salami" Levine draws on his Spanish experience to praise the sausage and the culture it comes from. The poet draws a picture of a Spanish man rebuilding an old church all by himself, caring for his retarded child, and praying each night with "the overwhelming incense/ of salami." Then the poem returns to the speaker—so different from the old man—waking from a nightmare, full of guilt, fear, and chaos. He discovers his son sleeping peacefully, feeling that each breath of the boy carries a prayer for him, "the true and earthly prayer/ of salami." The salami gathers the figures of the poem into a community and draws from Levine an expression of reverence. It is an "earthly prayer," a praise of life in all its harshness and the beauty that, at times, comes from it.

After Levine had established his distinctive voice, he continued in a series of volumes—five in seven years—to mine the ore he had discovered in *They Feed They Lion*. None of these later volumes have quite the excitement and explosiveness of the earlier ones, yet all of them contain excellent poems. During this period, Levine often moves back and forth between personal and political poems, although sometimes the personal and political merge.

Despite the difficulties of his life, despite encounters with prejudice and brutality, he often looks back with pleasure to the child who thought he could be happy.

Now he knows that the earth will "let the same children die day/ after day." There is nothing one can do except "howl your name into the wind/ and it will blow it into dust." Everything is ashes and the best wish a man can make is to become "a fine flake of dust that moves/ at evening like smoke at great height/ above the earth and sees it all."

In the meantime, the poet seems to say, one can travel, looking for landscapes of greater beauty and intensity than the bombed-out cities of America. In the poem "Seven Years from Somewhere," Levine speaks of an experience, apparently in Morocco, where he was lost and a group of laughing Berber shepherds came to help him, even though they did not share a common language. One of the shepherds took his hand in an effort to communicate with him. After traveling on to "Fez, Meknes, Tetuan, Ceuta, Spain, Paris, here," he awakens to a world where no one takes his hand, and he remembers the shepherd's gesture:

> as one holds a blue egg
> found in tall grasses
> and smile and say something
> that means nothing, that
> means you are, you
> are, and you are home.

Human touch represents the hope that resides at the heart of many of Levine's best poems, and these poems show the way toward his directly political poetry. The poet Robert Bly, in "Leaping Up into Political Poetry," the introduction to *Forty Poems Touching on Recent American History* (1970), argues that one has to be an inward poet to write about outward events successfully, that "the writing of political poetry is like the writing of personal poetry, a sudden drive by the poet inward." Levine fits this notion of political poetry better than almost any other modern American poet, often exploring his own life while at the same time exploring the lives of the Spanish anarchists of the Civil War. He admits that someone else "who has suffered/ and died for his sister the earth" might have more to say than he, yet he feels the necessity to speak for those who have no other spokesman.

In "For the Fallen" Levine visits the graves in Barcelona of the leading anarchists who were executed during the war. After describing the sight of the graves amid the noise of the city, he remembers himself as a schoolboy in Detroit going on with his own life at the same time that the heroes were killed. The boy and others trudging home from their dreary jobs knew, in some mysterious way, that there was an important relationship between them and the men in Barcelona. After all these years the feeling the poet has for these men can "shiver these two stiff/ and darkening hands."

SWEET WILL AND A WALK WITH TOM JEFFERSON

In his volumes *Sweet Will* (1985) and *A Walk with Tom Jefferson* (1988) Levine began a subtle but important shift in his poetry. Overall, the tough bitterness appears less often and a quieter, more meditative element begins to dominate the feeling of these longer poems. Reviewers have been about equally divided in either regretting this change or praising it.

The poems often still have a strong narrative quality as Levine draws on events of his past or creates other speakers to reflect on their pasts. The harsh world of Detroit's neighborhoods and factories has become even more central to his work, but the poems sometimes end on surprisingly quiet notes. This is still, however, the work of Philip Levine; the horizons of hope remain darkened by storm clouds.

Levine has sometimes taken to turning the speaking roles in his poems over to others to tell their stories. The speaker in "Voyages" spent his early life working on ships on the Great Lakes, but one day he impulsively jumps ship and makes his way to another life. He settles for a middle-class existence and in the final lines insists—too strenuously—that he does not miss what he left behind:

> Not once has the ocean wind changed
> and brought the taste of salt
> over the coastal hills and through
> the orchards to my back yard, Not once
> have I wakened cold and scared
> out of a dreamless sleep
> into the dreamless life and cried
> and cried for what I left behind.

The speaker in "Buying and Selling" spends his life traveling the country buying and selling automotive parts but once, at the age of twenty, he "wept in the Dexter-/ Davison branch of the public library/ over the death of

Keats in the Colvin/ biography." The successful buying day ends on a note of sadness, a sadness for his lost youth, like "the sadness of children/ themselves, who having been abandoned believe/ their parents will return before dark."

When the poems are spoken by the poet himself, a sad note of acceptance becomes the dominant tone. In the ironically titled "I Sing the Body Electric" Levine pictures himself crossing the continent to bring audiences poems about the wars of which they never heard. In "Picture Postcards from the Other World," however, he imagines a reader, like himself, a middle-aged man or woman who "lost whatever faiths he held goes on/ with only the faith that even more/ will be lost." He hopes to bring such a reader his gift of language, even if it comes down to saying "nothing and saying it perfectly."

In the 1980's, Levine's meditative narratives became lengthier, and in the title poem of *A Walk with Tom Jefferson* he moved on to his largest canvas. Tom Jefferson is an elderly black Detroit factory worker, but his famous namesake drifts like a ghost at the heart of this ambitious poem. The narrator walks with Tom through his bombed-out landscape of Detroit's inner city, blocks left to rot since the riot of 1967. Tom's family came from Alabama when he was a child to work in the automobile industry for five dollars a day, but Tom still often remembers the world of his childhood.

The narrator muses on the lives destroyed by this industrial system that could not match their "ordinary serviceable dreams" and views the landmarks of the city with hatred—the Renaissance Center that "Ford built/ to look down on our degradation" and the auto plant "where he broke first our backs/ and then the rest." Tom Jefferson, however, still plants his vegetable garden every year, a habit brought from Alabama, and the garden flowers amid the wreckage of the ghetto. Tom is a believer, and his refrain of "That's Biblical" helps him interpret the sufferings of his life. The American Dream of the other Jefferson, the poem suggests, ended in the ugliness of cities like Detroit, but this Jefferson continues to survive and believe.

WHAT WORK IS, THE SIMPLE TRUTH, AND THE MERCY

Levine's collections of the 1990's demonstrate his continued poetic vitality and increasing depth of vision.

Both *What Work Is* and *The Simple Truth* were winners of major literary awards, bringing Levine a level of recognition long deserved. *What Work Is* takes a great leap in energy and impact over most of his volumes of the 1980's. This brilliant collection solidifies and extends Levine's lifelong concern with the exploited cogs in the industrial machine—the blue-collar workers. Nowhere is Levine's voice more assured, more capable of telling particularity, more sympathetically engaged. In poems like "Coming Close," Levine's own subtle mastery of craft embraces and exemplifies the work ethic he applauds. The four-beat lines and roughly patterned consonance let the reader feel the machinery and its interaction with the worker—its penetration. The book's masterpiece, found in the center of the collection, is the long poem "Burned." In this extended story and exfoliating image of the disasters of life in a factory town, Levine gives the reader, once and for all, the dark side of the American Dream.

In both *The Simple Truth* and *The Mercy*, Levine allows memory to replay events that go back decades. Always a poet whose work snuggled up near sentimentality, he manages even in these late, somewhat nostalgic poems to avoid crossing the line, to keep the language of emotion in check while letting the emotion itself rise out of the material. Levine's memories of his mother and the questions that remain about the father he never knew feed some of his finest work, especially the title poem of *The Mercy*, a poem that considers the meaning of his mother's voyage on the ship that brought her to America. The anger of his youth now somewhat subdued and at the same time complicated by even greater depths of thought and feeling, Levine in his seventies has clearly achieved a major and permanent place in the literature of his era.

Philip Levine is a prolific and ambitious poet. He found his essential subject—the suffering world of the industrial city—rather early in his poetic career, but he has managed to keep it vivid and vital through the decades by the depth of his talent and the seriousness of his commitment.

OTHER MAJOR WORKS

NONFICTION: *Don't Ask*, 1981; *The Bread of Time*, 1994; *So Ask: Essays, Conversations, and Interviews*, 2002.

TRANSLATIONS: *Tarumba: The Selected Poems of Jaime Sabines*, 1979 (with Ernesto Trejo); *Off the Map: Selected Poems of Gloria Fuertes*, 1984 (with Ada Long).

BIBLIOGRAPHY

Brouwer, Joel. "The Stubbornness of Things." *Progressive* 68, no. 8 (August, 1999): 44. This observant and respectful review of *The Mercy* singles out key passages from representative poems to illustrate Levine's fascination with the past and his "obsessive desire to get it right."

Buckley, Christopher, ed. *On the Poetry of Philip Levine: Stranger to Nothing*. Ann Arbor: University of Michigan Press, 1991. This first comprehensive look at the poet's career offers important reviews chronologically arranged plus a series of essays that focus on different aspects of Levine's work.

Holden, Jonathan. *Style and Authenticity in Postmodern Poetry*. Columbia: University of Missouri Press, 1986. In the concluding section of this analysis of contemporary poetry, Holden singles out a poem by Levine, "Milkweed," for special praise. He feels that it combines the attention to the world with the ability to make value judgments, the characteristics of postmodern poetry according to Holden.

Jackson, Richard. "The Long Embrace, Philip Levine's Longer Poems." *The Kenyon Review* 11 (Fall, 1989): 160-169. This is a detailed analysis of three long poems of Levine: "Letters for the Dead" (1933, 1976), "A Poem with No Ending" (*Sweet Will*, 1985), and "A Walk with Tom Jefferson," the title poem of the 1988 volume. He singles out the most recent poem as the most successful in sustaining intensity throughout a long poem.

Knight, Jeff Parker. Review of *The Simple Truth*. *Prairie Schooner* 71, no. 2 (Summer, 1997): 179-182. Knight claims that Levine measures the tension between truth and reality in *The Simple Truth* and in his other poems. Attending also to matters of craft, Knight praises "the perspective gained from an attentive lifetime."

Levine, Philip. "A Conversation with Philip Levine." *TriQuarterly* 95 (Winter, 1995/1996): 67-82. In a conversation with Davidson College students, Levine comments on his style, the biographical sources for his subjects, and the situation of contemporary American poetry. A very rich ramble.

Mariani, Paul. "Keeping the Covenant." Review of *A Walk with Tom Jefferson*. *The Kenyon Review* 11 (Fall, 1989): 170-171. Mariani compares Levine to Walt Whitman and William Carlos Williams, among others, in this laudatory essay. He concludes that his poetry has kept its covenant with the dispossessed.

Mills, Ralph. *Cry of the Human*. Urbana: University of Illinois Press, 1975. This is the clearest analysis of Levine's early work. Mills singles out "They Feed, They Lion" and "Angel Butcher" as remarkable achievements and concludes his analysis by calling Levine one of the best poets writing in English today.

Smith, Dave. *Local Assays: On Contemporary American Poetry*. Urbana: University of Illinois Press, 1988. Despite the fact that Smith feels that the work is sometimes marred by polemics, he states that Levine is a master of depicting daily life. He praises the work for its honesty and accessibility and finds the theme of communion at the heart of Levine's poetry.

Stein, Kevin. "Why 'Nothing Is Past': Philip Levine's Conversation with History." In his *Private Poets, Worldly Acts: Public and Private History in Contemporary American Poetry*. Athens: Ohio University Press, 1996. Stein explores the way in which the past impinges on the present in Levine's work. Levine carries on a dialogue with the past to reach "an understanding of the self that transcends the self."

Tillinghast, Richard. "Poems That Get Their Hands Dirty." *The New York Times Book Review* (December 18, 1991): 7. Compares Levine's *What Work Is* to Turner Cassity's *Between the Chains* and Adrienne Rich's *An Atlas of the Difficult World*.

Vendler, Helen. "All Too Real." *The New York Review of Books* 28 (December 17, 1981): 32-36. This is an all-out attack on Levine's poetry, an exception to the usual praise heaped on it. Vendler criticizes the metrics, the anecdotal subjects, and what she calls the sentimentality of the poetry. She states that Levine has too limited a notion of the real.

Michael Paul Novak,
updated by Philip K. Jason

LARRY LEVIS

Born: Fresno, California; September 30, 1946
Died: Richmond, Virginia; May 8, 1996

PRINCIPAL POETRY

Wrecking Crew: Poems, 1972
The Afterlife: Poems, 1977
*The Leopard's Mouth Is Dry and Cold Inside: Prose-
    poems*, 1980 (with Marcia Southwick)
The Dollmaker's Ghost, 1981
Sensationalism: Poems, 1982
Winter Stars, 1985
The Widening Spell of the Leaves, 1991
Elegy, 1997
The Selected Levis, 2000

OTHER LITERARY FORMS

Although Larry Levis primarily wrote poetry, much of his nonfiction prose is collected in *The Gazer Within* (2001), a volume in the Poets on Poetry series from the University of Michigan Press. The collection includes the title essay "Some Notes on the Gazer Within," originally published in 1980. Levis and his wife Marcia Southwick each contributed half of the fourteen prose poems that comprise *The Leopard's Mouth Is Dry and Cold Inside*. Sound recordings of Levis include a reading given on the program *New Letters on the Air*, broadcast in October of 1977, and a recording made with poet Thylias Moss in February, 1991, at the Library of Congress. A work of fiction, *Black Freckles: Stories*, was published in 1992.

ACHIEVEMENTS

Recognized early in his career as an outstanding young poet, Levis received the International Poetry Forum United States Award for *Wrecking Crew* as well as a YM-YWHA Discovery Award, both in 1971. The success of his first volume of poetry led to increased recognition in the form of a National Endowment for the Arts fellowship in 1973. Within three years he won the Lamont Poetry Selection Award, given in 1976 for *The Afterlife*. A third major work, *The Dollmaker's Ghost*, won the Open Competition of the National Poetry Series

in 1981. Levis received two additional fellowships from the National Endowment for the Arts, a Guggenheim Fellowship, and a Senior Fulbright Fellowship to Yugoslavia.

BIOGRAPHY

Larry Patrick Levis was born in Fresno, California, to William Kent Levis and Carol (Mayo) Levis. The Levis family owned vineyards and orchards, property that was referred to locally as "the ranch" and that was described by Levis as "a place that seemed to exist . . . in some motionless and unchanging moment." Adapted to this rural environment and the routine of farming, the Levis family life emphasized work and religion. Levis recalled his parents as ascribing to Victorian morals and conservative politics, harboring suspicion of social change, fearing communism, and disapproving of labor unions.

Carol Levis was a strong Irish Catholic who raised her children to believe in the "real presences rather than abstractions" of mystery, spirit and the Holy Ghost. Her efforts to instill her traditional faith in Levis failed, leaving him feeling "guilty for something" but unsure of what. Levis responded creatively, mistakenly confessing to adultery during his First Confession at age seven. In later years Levis portrayed the Catholic Church as a "garrison so effective it doesn't need soldiers." When he was twelve Levis came to believe, following a confrontation with his father over a nude caricature that he had drawn, that he was not a good person and would have to live outside conventional society—an event he later cited as a perfect beginning for a poet. As a teenager, Levis worked in the fields with Spanish-speaking migrant employees who found his innocence entertaining and endearing. Levis cared deeply for the men, absorbing their humorous stories and sharing their camaraderie while respecting their toughness.

While still in high school, Levis decided to become a poet, influenced by his love for the works of T. S. Eliot and Robert Frost. He attended California State University, Fresno, where he benefited greatly from instruction by the poet Philip Levine, who later claimed that Levis was his most inspired student. Levine became a trusted friend and the two men critiqued each other's writing for many years.

Levis graduated from California State University with a bachelor of arts degree in 1968. He then became a teaching assistant at Syracuse University in New York the following year, returning as an instructor to "Fresno State" in 1970. He taught at California State University in Los Angeles from 1970 to 1972 as a lecturer in English, and subsequently at the University of Iowa in Iowa City as a visiting lecturer. Levis was employed as an assistant professor of English at the University of Missouri at Columbia for six years, from 1974 to 1980; there he coedited the *Missouri Review* (1977-1980). During those years he published the prizewinning volumes *Wrecking Crew* and *The Afterlife*. A third prizewinning volume, *The Dollmaker's Ghost*, was published in 1981.

Upon leaving Missouri, Levis moved to the University of Utah in Salt Lake City, remaining there as an associate and later full professor of English until 1992. He also became the director of the university's writing program. His appointment as professor of English at the Virginia Commonwealth University in Richmond continued from 1992 until his death in 1996. His death from a heart attack at the age of forty-nine shocked and grieved his friends and colleagues, many of whom felt

Larry Levis (Erin Seals, courtesy of University of Pittsburgh Press)

that a promising career had been cut short at great loss to American poetry. His old friend Philip Levine edited the posthumously published *Elegy*.

ANALYSIS

Throughout his career Larry Levis drew upon the landscape of his childhood, from the vineyards and orchards of central California to the Pacific Ocean to the west and the Sierra Nevada to the east. He contrasted that edenic setting with his painful recognition of the sterility of urban development. On the other hand, his poems revealed a warm regard for the worth of individuals, especially ones whose lives were socially and economically difficult. Levis wrote about the lives and work of a wide array of people—photographers, poets, painters, laborers—in addition to his own.

At all stages of his career, Levis returned often to personal experiences that he would then recast into new poems. Although his use of memories remained constant, his style changed dramatically over the years. The "deep image" style that Levis employed early in his career utilized terse imagery and short lines, but Levis recognized that poets like Robert Bly and Charles Simic had succeeded so well in that mode that change was inevitable. He believed that the jewel-like imagery that had been used in the 1970's to embody emotional experience would ultimately lead to language devoid of meaning. He supported the trend of writers in his generation away from the hardened image in favor or a more relaxed approach. Levis gradually expanded his poems into meditative forms utilizing sweeping sentences generously spaced on the page.

Levis reflected constantly upon the force of death. His subjects inevitably move toward an unsettling end. Contrary to their somewhat romantic associations, magicians, ghosts, and angels represent disenchantment in his work. For Levis, death is a process that gives meaning only to life, because following death there is literally nothing. Over the years, Levis became ever more convinced of his assertion that death is the only arbiter of life; his argument culminated in the appropriately titled volume *Elegy*, itself published posthumously.

WRECKING CREW

Wrecking Crew portrays the ills of America through a narrator who is at once cynical and detached. The volume's hard-hitting style depicts old people "High on painkillers" and yawning go-go girls. In "For the Country" the narrator states, "I am the nicest guy in the world,/ closing his switchblade and whistling." Levis described his method as attempting "to build a great deal of energy into a very small system" and to avoid being "diffuse or discursive." This anger inspires a surrealistic treatment of the ordinary.

Discouraged by the Vietnam War and related events, Levis was drawn to "irrational realities" and assumed the persona of a magician, a popular figure in rock music, for a series of poems. These describe the birth of the Magician (who suffers an exit wound), his ride to the hospital, his pursuit by "pals [who] frowned like a firing squad," and attendance at his own revival. In the succeeding section, "Magician's Edge and Exit," the weather worsens, a frayed tire skids, and the Magician is (magically) "suddenly air." Finally the Magician notes that "a shrug of stars and years drifts through me." Levis was more successful in this type of acrobatic passage that "let the flesh go" than in more overtly political lines such as "You are America./ You are nobody./ I made you up."

THE AFTERLIFE

The Afterlife, like other works by Levis, is imagistic in style, but it contains a new emphasis on private matters. Far from submitting to the confessional tendencies that critics imagined, Levis attempted to create a personal mythology whose truths readers would recognize in their own lives. For example, in "A Poem of Horses" he writes of "going further into the blank paper" and finding "the dark trousers of your father" and the "hairpins of your mother." As a result, "You hold them in your hands." As if in stream-of-consciousness mode, the next stanza portrays a poor gelding waiting in the rain beside a jail in Santiago. Finally the time is given, 1946 (the year of Levis's birth), and, undressed, "They moved closer. As you began." At the same time the horse is being blindfolded and led "up the cliff while the shadows/ Pulled on their gloves one by one and went out,/ And left them alone." Thus conception is far from joyful and "your" life is shadowed from the very beginning.

Levis includes another poetic series in *The Afterlife*, this one dealing with the birds known as linnets. Death is introduced at the beginning, as Levis's brother admits that he has shot a linnet; and the poem then cuts to a scene in which the brother is found guilty by a "high court of linnets." Yet the sentencing is most punitive for the poet himself, who is to be thereafter haunted by linnets: As the feathers of the dead bird fall around him, each becomes an individual bird. When the poet throws down a stillborn linnet, another begins to sing. There follow a number of "songs" initially filled with dying animals and progressing to familial alienation. Eventually the speaker is reduced to whittling a wooden linnet. Death, which began the poem, also closes it: "one day in a diner in Oakland/ you begin dying." Drafts of poems are discarded when "a car backfires and drives away," and the poet becomes "father of that silence."

THE WIDENING SPELL OF THE LEAVES

In this last collection published during Levis's lifetime, Levis fully indulges his mature, meditative style. "The Perfection of Solitude: A Sequence" moving freely through time and place to create a landscape on the page that is populated by friends, strangers, and artists as diverse as Pieter Bruegel the Elder and John Coltrane. Use of a persona is no longer necessary. The sequence begins in "Oaxaca, 1983," in an empty plaza that "sleeps & is abandoned." Levis signs in at the Hotel França, but his signature appears to dry and fade "as if no one is ever at home inside a name." "Our Sister of Perfect Solitude," part 4 of the sequence, questions the very meaning of names: "One of my pastimes then was savoring the casual emptiness of names, any name." In "Coney Island Baby" the poet describes "a girl in the loveliness of her name," only to discredit the loveliness as the girl must "perform [her] whole life in a silence." Finally in "Coda: Kind of Blue" Levis uses jazz images in a listing that culminates with Beauty, a girl he charges the reader not to change, "even one syllable of her name." He closes by reminding the reader that the "song began" in solitude and "All things you are, & briefly, as, in solitude, it ends."

Searching and loss characterize "The Widening Spell of the Leaves," the title poem of the collection. Set at the "Carpathian Frontier" in the former Czechoslavakia in

October, 1968, the poem begins "Once, in a foreign country, I was suddenly ill." The poet suffers from fever and stomach pains while driving through villages where "there wasn't much point in/ Asking anyone for help." As the poet continues driving his illness worsens, yet he cannot communicate with the people, their language having changed from Slavic to German. He continues through higher and higher mountain passes, where the peasants seem to have a stillness embroidered into them. "Even as they moved," he observes, "The peasants, the herds of goats,/ And cattle, the spiralling leaves" become part of a spell of stillness.

Eventually, the poet comes to the end of the road; it is "Mistakenly erased," and facing a wide field filled with yellow leaves, he is afraid of disappearing into the spell. He then recalls a childhood experience with Mr. Hirata, a neighbor and photographer he feared would likewise disappear; young Levis believed that crocodiles would come out of one of Hirata's photographs to devour the man. The child's naïve alarm foreshadowed the neighbor's actual exile to Manzanar, a World War II detention camp in the Sierra Nevada, where he died of pneumonia. His skepticism aroused, the child refused to accept official claims that the death was accidental. He suspected that disease was "An equation that drank up light & never ended." Suffering fever and pain, the mature poet sees the leaves around him returning "year after, & the year after that, & every/ Year following," as he envisions leaves "So clear not one in a thousand trembled" and a spell that continues "until the end of Time."

ELEGY

The best poems of this posthumously published collection demonstrate what a vibrant contribution to American poetry Levis had made. Among the strongest short poems are "Boy in the Video Arcade" and "Anastasia and Sandman." The boy views the "end of it," and his reaction of "Big Deal" flattens the notes of Death's trumpet. Anastasia and Sandman are horses Levis recalls from his childhood but whose presences in this poem serve as reminders that Joseph Stalin confiscated horses from Romania to feed the starving Poles. Levis satirizes the communists by addressing "Members of the Committee on the Ineffable" and "Members of the Committee on Solitude." He calls on

> Old contrivers, daydreamers . . .
> Exhausted chimneysweeps of the spaces
> Between words, where the Holy Ghost tastes just
> Like the dust it is made of

to join him in discarding academia. What could be more important than "the angel hissing in its mist" and the two horses who once stood "Under the missing & innumerable stars."

The greater portion of the book is made up of a series of elegies with titles such as "Elegy with a Petty Thief in the Rigging" and "Elegy with a Bridle in Its Hand." In the final poem, "Elegy in the Sound of a Skipping Rope," Levis laments the "real head of state grinning through its veil/ of skin" and asserts that "When the State withers away it resembles/ The poor sections of Wichita or Denver." He ends with a girl wearing her communion dress and skipping rope

> until I could hear only the endless,
> Annoying, unvarying flick of the rope each time
> It touched the street.

OTHER MAJOR WORKS

SHORT FICTION: *Black Freckles: Stories*, 1992.
NONFICTION: *The Gazer Within*, 2001.

BIBLIOGRAPHY

Gilbert, Sandra M. "Where the Boys Are." *Poetry* 178 (July, 2001): 216-237. The final section of this essay asserts that Levis's work is representative of poetry as written in the United States over the last three decades of the twentieth century.

Halliday, Mark. "Levis and All Loss." *Chicago Review* 45 (Winter, 1999): 89-98. A revealing critical study of *Elegy* in which Halliday regrets the looseness of some associations in the work but claims that Levis's expansive achievement is the result of that same universalizing approach.

Kelen, Leslie. "After the Obsession with some Beloved Figure: An Interview with Larry Levis." *Antioch Review* 48 (Summer, 1990): 284-299. A long interview in which Levis freely discusses his writing from its early stages through *Winter Stars*.

Margaret A. Dodson

Janet Lewis

Born: Chicago, Illinois; August 17, 1899
Died: Los Altos, California; December 1, 1998

Principal poetry

The Indians in the Woods, 1922
The Wheel in Midsummer, 1927
The Earth-Bound, 1924-1944, 1946
The Ancient Ones, 1979
The Birthday of the Infanta, 1979
Poems Old and New, 1918-1978, 1981
Late Offerings, 1988
The Dear Past and Other Poems, 1919-1994, 1994
The Selected Poems of Janet Lewis, 2000

Other literary forms

Janet Lewis is best known for her four historical novels, critical and popular successes published between 1932 and 1959. The first and least acclaimed, *The Invasion: A Narrative of Events Concerning the Johnston Family of St. Mary's* (1932), shared with her early poems an interest in Native American life and the American wilderness. Three others, of which *The Wife of Martin Guerre* (1941) and *The Trial of Sören Qvist* (1947) are probably the best known, deal in a lucid, documentary style with historic cases of circumstantial evidence. Lewis's fictional prose reflected her apprenticeship in Imagistic poetry—a narrative style that, in her own words, is "supposed to be transparent."

Lewis also published a novel with a contemporary setting, *Against a Darkening Sky* (1943), and a collection of contemporary short stories, *Good-Bye, Son, and Other Stories* (1946), as well as children's books. She adapted *The Wife of Martin Guerre* as an opera, produced in 1956 by the Juilliard School of Music and subsequently at other schools. She wrote two other opera librettos, *The Swans* (1986) and *The Legend* (1987).

Achievements

In a career that spanned eight decades, Janet Lewis won a number of honors for her literary work, including the Friends of American Writers award in 1932 for *The Invasion: A Narrative of Events Concerning the*

Johnston Family of St. Mary's, a Shelley Memorial Award for poetry in 1947, and a Gold Medal from the Commonwealth Club of California in 1948 for *The Trial of Sören Qvist*. She held a Guggenheim Fellowship in creative writing for research in Paris from 1950 to 1951, won a Horace Gregory Foundation award in 1977, a Silver Medal from the Commonwealth Club of California in 1982 for *Poems Old and New, 1918-1978*, a University of Chicago Alumni Association Award for Professional Achievement in 1982, a Discovery Award/PEN (West) in 1982, and finally, a Robert Kirsch Award for Body of Work from the *Los Angeles Times* in 1985.

Biography

Janet Lewis was born on August 17, 1899, in Chicago, Illinois, the daughter of Edwin Herbert Lewis, a poet, novelist, and English teacher. In the summer, the family lived in northern Michigan, where Lewis came to know the Ojibwa Indians, the subjects of her first book. She published her first poem in *Poetry* when she was twenty-one, a book when she was twenty-three. Earning an A.A. at the Lewis Institute in 1918 and a Ph.B. at the University of Chicago in 1920, Lewis worked for the American consulate in Paris, for *Redbook* magazine in Chicago, and finally, for the Lewis Institute in Chicago, where she taught until stricken with tuberculosis in 1922. She moved for her health to Santa Fe, New Mexico, and became a friend of Yvor Winters, another Chicago poet convalescing in the West. On June 22, 1926, when Lewis was still in frail health, they were married and in 1927 moved to Stanford University in California, where her husband pursued his doctorate and began teaching in 1928.

The direct effect of Winters, Janet Lewis's famous husband, on her career is not easy to assess. They remained devoted to each other until his death from cancer in 1968, and her poetic style evolved in a way harmonious with his published critical stance. Both strict Imagists in the 1920's, Winters and Lewis began, in the 1930's, to work in traditional verse forms and with paraphrasable morals—a position hostile to the high modernist mode of T. S. Eliot and Ezra Pound and closer to the writing of Thomas Hardy than to any other major modern poet.

Meanwhile, writing in the mornings when the family was "off to school," Lewis established a national reputation as a novelist and published in 1946 what was to be for more than thirty years her last volume of poetry. It won for her the Shelley Memorial Award for poetry in 1947. Writing her books and assuming the public role of housewife in Los Altos, California, near Stanford University, Lewis apparently settled into a peaceful uniformity of life suggested in her poem "No-Winter Country." A Guggenheim Fellowship in 1950-1951 to do research in Paris for her novel *The Ghost of Monsieur Scarron* (1959) was perhaps the most significant interruption in her routine until her husband's death.

In 1971, still living in Los Altos, Lewis began writing poetry again, and her style again differed from what had gone before. The new work, in a more expansive and intimate voice, reestablished her reputation as a poet. For some years before and after her husband's death, Lewis taught writing at Stanford University. In 1976, she visited American Indian ruins in northern Arizona, making the last part of the journey on horseback and by foot, and her experiences on this pilgrimage back toward the Indian themes of her earlier work resulted in some of her strongest new poems, a thin volume titled *The Ancient Ones*. In the 1980's, she continued to write, publishing *Late Offerings* in 1988. She served as a lecturer at St. John's College in Santa Fe, New Mexico, in 1984 and as a lecturer at a writer's workshops in Aspen, Colorado, in 1987. She died on December 1, 1998, in Los Altos, California.

ANALYSIS

Janet Lewis's poetic output was slight but distinguished. The ninety-four lyrics in her collected poems, many of them brief, show a remarkable stylistic evolution through her career of nearly seventy years and display three distinct stages: compact Imagism in the 1920's, formal lyricism in the 1930's and 1940's, and, after a twenty-five-year hiatus, a free incantatory style in the 1970's, 1980's, and into the 1990's. The first two stages paralleled the career of Yvor Winters, who began as a strict and respected Imagist and became in the 1930's the leader of a self-styled "reactionary" return to traditional rhyme and accentual meter. Opinion is divided as to whether Lewis's formalist turn was well ad-

vised—whether her middle poems moved toward sentimentality and dryness or whether she wrote rich and finely crafted work in the tradition of Thomas Hardy and earlier English verse. A reviewer of the volume for *Poetry* described Lewis's poetic gift as "slight—I mean, both delicate and minor." Her husband, poet-critic Yvor Winters, praised her as a "stylist of remarkable native gift" but regretted her penchant for "domestic sentiment, which sometimes goes all the way to sentimentality."

Whatever the merits of these limiting remarks, Lewis was important as a verse stylist and as a participant in—and transcender of—modern literary quarrels regarding the use of traditional forms. Her first book of poems, perhaps one of the best collections in the strict Imagist mode, was published in 1922 in a series which included William Carlos Williams and Marianne Moore. Two books later, in 1946, she had evolved into her openly philosophical verse in traditional forms, and for it she won the Shelley Memorial Award for poetry. Her newer poems, a group begun when she was seventy-two years old, expanded her reputation and answered the complaints of sentimentality and dry formalism sometimes lodged against her work of the 1930's and 1940's.

In the 1980's and 1990's, Lewis's collected poems appeared at a time when fashion had caught up with her lifelong interests. The American Indian, the Sun Belt, and the lives of women had become, in the words of a *Parnassus* reviewer, "radical chic." In her eighties, Lewis achieved long-postponed recognition for decades of lyrical vision and craftsmanship.

THE INDIANS IN THE WOODS

The lyrics in her 1922 volume, *The Indians in the Woods*, average less than twelve lines and, with haiku-like compression, suggest the closeness between the lives of the Ojibwa Indians and the processes of nature, particularly the cycle of the harsh northern seasons. The poems are rigorously Imagistic, expunged of nearly all general statement or transition—each a sequence of evoked sensations and elemental feelings. Central to the sequence is the god whose return is celebrated in the spring; even without this underpinning of myth, however, the poems function individually as icons of time's destructive passage, the promise of rebirth, and the muted joy of participation in natural process. The narrator is repeatedly identified as female, at times a wife, at times a grandmother, so that the poems are genuinely feministic, with a male god playing the role of mysterious natural Other. In most of the poems, the god could as well be a mortal lover, the seasons as well figurative as literal, and the forest as well suburban as primeval. The reversal of literary gender roles—particularly in 1922—is reason alone to reread these poems. If stripped of their bibliographic history, they might as readily be attributed to the 1970's as to the 1920's. Like William Carlos Williams's poems in *Spring and All* (1922), which they antedate and resemble, the lyrics are spare and evocative; short lines play occasional run-ons against the expected pause at line's end. What the Ojibwa poems lack in range, they make up for in polished intensity.

IMAGISM AND TRADITIONALISM

Actually, though Imagism stands at the beginning of Lewis's collected poems, it was not her first style. "The Freighters," her earliest published poem, uses traditional accent and meter and describes trees along a bank as singing "with moving branches/ Songs of eternity." This is the sort of generalization which Lewis, as an Imagist, excluded from the 1922 volume, but to which she would return in her post-Imagist work after 1930.

Between 1922 and 1927, the years of her convalescence, Lewis was evolving toward a softer, more traditional style without sacrificing the Imagistic virtues of sensation and compression. Some of her most memorable short poems are from this transitional period. Generally domestic in subject, the poems often use traditional lyric forms but have compact images in the foreground. Some, like the title poem to her second book, "The Wheel in Midsummer," are stylistically similar to the Ojibwa poems.

Among the best works from her convalescent period are "The Reader," "Girl Help," and "Remembered Morning," which chart the direction in which her art was to evolve. "The Reader" is a delicately descriptive poem about a reader lost in a book, as the sun, the fire, and the leaves clamor ineffectually to recall him to sensory reality—all this shown with Imagistic directness. Then a newborn "creature"—presumably a moth—is at the screen door, "heaving damp heavy wings." Lewis's readers are left with the nascent symbol, no explanation. Less cryptic but equally delicate is "Girl Help," a three-quatrain rhyming poem in which a servant is shown to

pause and smell lilacs scented with promise. "Remembered Morning" succeeds with perhaps an even less promising subject, the remembrance of a happy summer's day in childhood. Yet Lewis's spare, evocative description rescues the poem from its conventional versification and a line such as "O happy early stir!" Less successful experiments with traditional verse include "Love Poem," "The Candle Flame," "The Manger," and "The Tennis Players," which fall into the mannerisms of early twentieth century magazine verse.

After her marriage and move to California, Lewis's style changed decisively, probably encouraged by her husband, who had recently made a sharp theoretical turn against "experimental" modern poetry and was already developing the position he would expound in his controversial critical books. Lewis's poems between 1927 and 1944 were in a style that adapted traditional prosody and direct paraphrasable purpose to the needs of twentieth century life. Some are flawed, at least from the mainstream perspective, by archaisms, inversions, predictable rhymes, and hackneyed similes—dangers deliberately courted by a reformed Imagist who knew what she was doing. The best are effective as beautifully crafted antiques newly made, and that was clearly Lewis's intention.

Among the best is "Time and Music," a philosophical poem in octameter couplets which uses its very formality as an extension of its content: the suggestion that willed form is life; its absence, death. "Country Burial" works in a more emotional mode, describing vividly a funeral procession across a flowery field, then turning away from the numbing, discomforting vision of a heaven without the wetness and color of earth. In this, and in "Baby Goat"—a poem saved from preciousness by the visual exactness of Lewis's descriptions—she contrasts the world of changing, doomed colors with the mysterious colorless world of Heaven, or unchanging form. This theme was implicit even in the "The Freighters" and the Ojibwa poems, but the best of the middle poems gain intellectual and moral density by making it explicit.

THE 1930'S AND 1940'S

In the poems written between 1930 and 1944, Lewis had clearly accepted the aim expressed in her husband's criticism and adopted by a school of California poets: to fuse fully realized descriptive detail with expressed abstract meaning through exertion of the conscious will in traditional verse. "Lines with a Gift of Herbs," "The Hanger at Sunnydale," "In the Egyptian Museum," and "Helen Grown Old" are successes in this effort, all reflecting on the contrast between particulars which change and universals which inhere through this change—the scent in dry herbs, the steel hanger of a lost dirigible, the jewelry of a dead civilization, and the mystery of Helen of Troy's unmemorialized old age. Though the verse, again, is sometimes too dry, too mannered for some modern tastes, these poems do seem to work through the willed fusion of image and explicit moral called for by Winters's theory. Nevertheless, despite the critical success of these poems, Lewis ceased writing poetry altogether between 1944 and 1971.

POEMS OLD AND NEW, 1918-1978

Her collected volume, *Poems Old and New, 1918-1978*, was received with almost universal praise, critics differing only about which poems to single out. In this book, Lewis collected her best poems in a wide range of styles, including the 1918 poem which won for her entrance into the Poetry Club at the University of Chicago. The most recent works in the volume, written after 1971, are a synthesis and extension of the styles which preceded them—returning to the free verse and American Indian subjects of her Imagistic period but exploring the powers of a complex, discursive long line. Without the Imagistic restrictions against abstract statement and paraphrasable content, Lewis displayed more freely her feeling for nature, her lyricism, and her sense of history.

When she took up verse again, it was free verse without rhyme or with casual rhyme in the manner of Ezra Pound or William Butler Yeats, and her lines set up a biblical narrative cadence not as free as Walt Whitman's but clearly in the same tradition. This was a clear break from the formalism of the middle years, though it was not a return to Imagism, for abstract statement and reasoning mix freely with description. Also, Lewis returned to the domestic and American Indian subjects of her pre-California lyrics. Here the interplay between the transient and the eternal received its most serene and poignant treatment in poems such as "For the Father of Sandro Gullota," "The Anasazi Woman," "The Ancient Ones: Betátakin," "In a Convalescent Hospital," and

"Geometries." Though Lewis maintained a recognizable voice through all of her changes, in the later poems she seemed to draw the reader closer, sharing her empathy with a child dying of leukemia, with the mummy of an indigenous woman, with a ruins of pre-Navajo people moved by universals of water and beauty, with a once-vital woman dying alone, and with geometric shapes replicated eternally in nature. The later poems in her collected volume are not uniformly her best, but they are a triumphant summation, suggesting or incorporating the best of what came before.

THE DEAR PAST AND OTHER POEMS, 1919-1994

A collection that includes some early uncollected poems as well as those from late in Lewis's life, *The Dear Past and Other Poems, 1919-1994* holds graceful meditations on the grievous passages of time, elegizing friends and family in subtly cadenced lyrics. These poems were not easily available to readers; none were included in her *Poems Old and New, 1918-1978*. A retrospective style dominates the volume, and most of its themes are elegiac. At the end of a sonnet titled "Garden Note: Los Altos, November," Lewis strives to understand how, as time passes, her garden is "still the same,/ And not the same," but her language, often supple and luminous, also recalls the sentimental hyperbole of old-fashioned poesy: "Fair names my garden has, and fairer fruit: Persimmon, loquat, and the pomegranate, Loved presences, fair memories, and fair fame." The poems find her both wistful and stoic, as in the moving conclusion of "River," in which memory itself becomes one of the imperatives of desire: "Remember for me the scent of sweet-grass/ In Ojibway baskets,/ Of meadow turf, alive with insects./ Remember for me." Her multicultural pursuits are again evident here, from her lifelong interest in Asian and American Indian cultures, her memories of a childhood spent among the indigenous communities of upper Michigan and Canada, and her time in northern New Mexico when she investigated the remains of the Anasazi.

OTHER MAJOR WORKS

LONG FICTION: *The Invasion: A Narrative of Events Concerning the Johnston Family of St. Mary's*, 1932, 1964; *The Wife of Martin Guerre*, 1941 (translated as

La Femme de Martin Guerre, 1947); *Against a Dark-ening Sky*, 1943; *The Trial of Sören Qvist*, 1947; *The Ghost of Monsieur Scarron*, 1959.

SHORT FICTION: *Good-Bye, Son, and Other Stories*, 1946.

PLAYS (LIBRETTOS): *The Wife of Martin Guerre*, pr. 1956 (music by William Bergsma); *The Last of the Mohicans*, pr. 1976 (music by Alva Henderson; based on James Fenimore Cooper's novel); *The Birth-day of the Infanta*, pr. 1977 (with Malcolm Seagrave; music by Seagrave; based on Oscar Wilde's tale); *Mulberry Street*, pb. 1981; *The Ancient Ones*, pr. 1981 (music by Henderson; cantata based on Lewis's book of poetry); *The Swans*, pb. 1986 (music by Henderson); *The Legend*, pb. 1987 (music by Bain Murray; based on Lewis's novel *The Invasion*).

CHILDREN'S LITERATURE: *The Friendly Adventures of Ollie Ostrich*, 1923; *Keiko's Bubble*, 1961.

EDITED TEXT: *Collected Poems of Yvor Winters*, 1978.

BIBLIOGRAPHY

Crow, Charles L. *Janet Lewis*. Boise, Idaho: Boise State University Press, 1980. This excellent study of Lewis's life and work provides careful, insightful, and detailed attention to her novels. Supplemented by an index and a bibliography.

Lewis, Janet. Interview. *The Virginia Quarterly Review* 69, no. 3 (Summer, 1993): 532. The transcript of an interview with Lewis in 1990 which provides invalu-able biographical material and insight.

McMurtry, Larry. "The Return of Janet Lewis." *The New York Review of Books* 45, no. 10 (June 11, 1998): 21-25. McMurtry discusses several books by Lewis, including *The Wife of Martin Guerre*, *Good-Bye, Son*, *The Invasion*, *The Trial of Sören Qvist*, and *The Ghost of Monsieur Scarron*.

Steele, Trimpi. "The Poetry of Janet Lewis." *The South-ern Review* 18 (April, 1982): 251-258. Provides a fine and detailed examination of the poetry of Lewis in terms of themes, symbols, and influences. Steele's analysis is well conceived and readable and provides an excellent introduction to Lewis's poetry.

William H. Green,
updated by Sarah Hilbert

LI BO

Li Po

Born: Chinese Turkestan; 701
Died: Sichuan Province, China; 762

PRINCIPAL POETRY
"Ballad of Chang-an" (as "The River Merchant's Wife: A Letter," in *Cathay*, 1915; Ezra Pound, translator)
The Poetry and Career of Li Po, 1950 (Arthur Waley, editor)
Li Po and Tu Fu, 1973 (Arthur Cooper, editor)

OTHER LITERARY FORMS
Some of Li Bo's letters and other prose writings sur-vive, but Li's reputation rests entirely upon his poetry.

ACHIEVEMENTS
Li Bo and his younger contemporary Du Fu (Tu Fu) rank as the two greatest poets in the three thousand years of Chinese literary history. Each has the reputation, and the merit, of William Shakespeare in the English tradi-tion.

By the age of forty, Li was a popular poet, well-known for the audacity of his poetry and his personality, but he was not widely considered an outstanding poet in his own lifetime. Contemporaries who liked his work despite its unconventional extravagance were highly enthusiastic about it. His friend Zui Zongzhi praised it as "incompa-rable," and for several years Li held a special position as a favored writer in the court of the emperor. In the last few years of his life, however, Li's influence waned.

Interest in Li's work began to revive several decades after his death, and the acclaim he received from the leading poets and critics early in the next century estab-lished him in the position of high regard that he has held ever since. His works were read, and memorized, by ed-ucated people throughout East Asia. Many later poets reveal debts to his compelling language, his gift for vi-sualizing imagined scenes, and his intensely personal way of viewing the world. Li's ability to produce a unique twist in image, language, or perspective set his poems apart, even those on traditional topics.

In many ways, Li's playfulness, his individualism, and his visionary flamboyance make him the most accessible of all traditional Chinese poets for the modern Western reader. One measure of Li's effect on modern-day readers of English is the number of translations available. Some of the strongest of Ezra Pound's poems after Chinese originals in *Cathay* are those attributed to "Rihahu," which is the Japanese pronunciation of the Chinese "Li Bo." Shigeyoshi Obata's free renditions will appeal to some readers, though others will find the English old-fashioned and too ornate. Arthur Waley's brief book on Li's life and poetry at times reflects Waley's lack of affinity with his subject. The layers of meaning in the poems are sometimes overlooked and the slippery facts of Li's life get muddled, but Waley's skill in Chinese and in English gives the book value. Extensive notes to individual poems are only one of the strengths of Arthur Cooper's translations.

Among the many excellent translations are the lucid, striking renditions by the poet David Young, and the more scholarly—but highly readable—work of Eiling Eide and Stephen Owen. In addition, most anthologies of translated Chinese poetry include works by Li. *Sunflower Splendor* (1975) makes an excellent starting place; it contains a bibliography of anthologies for further reading. Li's daring and robust spirit, his vivid sense of the sublime and the supernatural, and his profound understanding of the creative power of the poetic mind have as much to say to the modern Westerner as they have said to Asian readers for more than a millennium.

BIOGRAPHY

Li Bo lived at the height of one of China's richest eras of cultural and political greatness. The Tang Empire stretched in some places beyond the borders of China today, and trade flourished, ranging to India, Japan, the Middle East, and even Greece. The poets of Li's generation rode the crests of twin waves of innovation and the consolidation of earlier achievements. Despite the political instability that marred the final period of Li's life, he lived for forty-four of his sixty-odd years under an emperor whose reign is rightly called a golden age.

It is difficult to pin down the facts of Li's life. So colorful a figure naturally has inspired a number of legends. The poet evidently encouraged such legend-making in his own lifetime, the more extravagant the better, such as the story that he was fathered by the spirit of the planet known in the West as Venus.

While the great majority of the people under the Tang Empire, especially the people in power, were Han-Chinese, Li himself was probably at least partly of Turkish or Iranian descent. Li claimed that an ancestor of his had been exiled from China and that his family had lived for about a century in various settlements along trade routes in and around what is now Afghanistan. A good bit of evidence suggests the family's non-Chinese cultural orientation: Li's ability to write poetry in "a foreign language," several family members' names (including those of Li's two sons), the affinity for Central Asian culture shown in the content and form of many of his poems, and such stereotypically "foreign" personality traits as Li's love of drinking. None of this evidence is conclusive, but it is the first of several indications that Li's life was shaped by his position as an outsider in the Empire. The Tang taste for the exotic and the Turkish connections of the imperial family meant that the "foreigners'" work would have had a special appeal (many poets of the era were influenced by Central Asian themes and music), but Han-Chinese ethnocentricity meant that the "foreigner" himself would always have been regarded as exactly that.

Li's family moved to Sichuan Province, in southwest China, when he was about five years old. They were probably traders. Family wealth would explain how Li managed to live without a job in the government, which was the occupation of most male poets and scholars in traditional China, but the low status of merchants would have made his family background another strike against Li in the eyes of the establishment. Even to have grown up in Sichuan would have given him a markedly regional air. Owen points out the impact the particular traditions of the area may have had on Li in defining himself as a nonconformist, a bold and impulsive person, and a writer not of mainstream aristocratic verse, but of a poetry that returns to the greatness of the past.

Stories of Li's youth suggest the intelligence and the interest in occult learning revealed in his poems. The biographies of most poets of Li's era routinely claim that their subjects were brilliant students in childhood and that they could compose verse at an early age; the reports on Li are the same, but there is no reason not to believe them, if taken with a grain of salt. Poems written when he was about fifteen show Li's great talent and his already distinctive violation of contemporary ideas of "proper" restraint in poetry. Li apparently also lived and studied as a mountain recluse for some time before leaving Sichuan.

In his early twenties, Li began a period of wandering in the great valley of the Yangzi River in central China. The role he adopted, that of a daring and noble-hearted knight errant who righted wrongs with his sword, again shows his energy and his taste for an unconventional lifestyle.

At the time of Li's first marriage, in the early 730's, he was living in what is now Hubei Province, in the north-central Yangtze Basin. He made exaggerated claims for the ancestry of his wife, whose family name was Xu, as he did for his own. It was to her that his daughter Pingyang and his elder son Boquin were born. His younger son's name was Poli. The poet probably had one other formal wife and two concubines, but the facts are unclear.

Li then moved north and east to Shandong Province, where he continued writing and enjoying the company of friends, and from where he traveled to the scenic regions of southeast China. He enjoyed poem exchanges, banquets in the entertainment district, and poeticizing excursions to sites famous for their natural beauty. The constant succession of occasions calling for a poem had good results; like that of so many Chinese poets, Li's work developed greatly in his middle years.

It was during this period that Li met the Daoist religious teacher who finally arranged for his long-awaited introduction to the imperial court in 742. In that year or the next, the poet was granted a position in the Hanlin Academy, a prestigious group of scholars, holy men, and poets who enjoyed imperial favor.

The outsider had penetrated the inner sanctum of Emperor Xuanzong himself. Perhaps Li never took the civil service exams that were the more usual route of upward mobility because he disdained orthodox learning and officialdom, as he claimed, or perhaps he never took them because he lacked the well-rounded education and influential connections that were necessary to obtain a post. Not all of the famous male writers of the Tang era managed to pass the test, but, except for Li,

they all tried. Nevertheless, for nearly three years, Li was an eccentric and admired figure in a brilliant court, carousing, composing poems and song lyrics for the emperor and the women of the imperial household, and dashing off imperial decrees on command.

Things changed. The boastful, impetuous Li was no courtier. In 744, evidently as the result of an intrigue, he lost the emperor's favor and was given "permission" to "return to the hills." This banishment began another period of wandering and visiting whomever might take interest in the company of this colorful and brilliant poet. Li and Du Fu met when Li was in his early forties and Du in his early thirties; Du's many admiring poems addressed to Li suggest the force of the older poet's personality.

A decade later, a rebellion forced the emperor to abdicate. Li, who was then in the Southeast, joined the court of a secretly disloyal prince. It is not clear whether Li was naïve, coerced, or a willing participant in the treason, but when the prince was defeated in 757, Li was imprisoned and condemned to death. The poet's reputation saved him: His sentence was reduced to banishment to the far southwest frontier lands. Li dawdled on the long journey, was finally granted annesty in 759, and returned to his life of travel and visiting. Late in 762, the official and calligrapher with whom he was staying published the first collection of Li's works. The preface records that the poet was at the time seriously ill; this illness was evidently his last. There are, however, legends of his death by drowning, in a drunken attempt to embrace the moon's reflection on a river, and of the spirits who came on dolphin-back to summon him to heaven.

ANALYSIS

Li Bo acquired—and liked—the nickname Exiled Immortal. Its implication of a rule breaker who transcends conventional limitations describes his poetry as well as his life. He could use the standard devices and postures of his rich literary heritage, but he usually did so in his own original manner. He wrote many kinds of poems, in many moods and wearing many masks, but behind them all is the unique quality of the poet himself.

Among the poems by Li that have the greatest immediate appeal for the modern Western reader are those which suggest that the poetic mind operates on the level of the universe itself. This theme often appears in Li's poems about famous mountains, those nodes—in the traditional Chinese worldview—of cosmic spiritual energy. For example, in the poem "Climbing Mount Emei," the speaker of the poem ascends the best known of Sichuan's "faerie mountains," entering a realm of weird beauty that calls into question normal evaluations of both perception and ambition. At the summit, he proclaims, his aesthetic and his supernatural abilities are released, as he finally grasps esoteric Daoist teachings and the secrets of making poetry and music. Li closes the poem with a characteristically grand movement up and out: He is loosed from earthly ties ("All at once I lose the world's dust"), meets a youthful sprite, and hand in hand they move across the sky to the sun. This is not the only place where the poet sets himself in moments of inspiration on a par with the great forces of nature.

"Climbing the Peak of Mount Taibo"

Still, Li acknowledges, the human mind cannot always achieve this sublime state. Sometimes the power dwelling within the mountains is elusive, or the response to it is uncertain. In "Climbing the Peak of Mount Taibo," the mountain is again a jumping-off point for heavenly realms, but here the poet adopts a persona that imagines a transcendent journey of the spirit—straddling the wind and raising a hand that could almost touch the moon—only to hesitate at the end and ask, "Once I've left Wugong county/ When could I come back again?" This undercutting of the traditional spirit-journey motif is prepared for by a typical bit of linguistic playfulness. There is a multiple pun in the poem's third line: "Then Taibo speaks to me." "Taibo" is, first, the mountain itself, a peak in modern Shensi Province that was thought to be especially magical because one of the fantastic Daoist "cave-heavens" was said to be located within its summit. "Taibo" is also both the evening star (the ascent is made at sunset) and the very planetary spirit said to have been Li's true father. Finally, "Taibo" is Li's pen name; for an instant, at least, the reader is invited to wonder if the poet is talking only to himself.

"Wandering About Mount Tai: Six Poems"

One of the best examples of the multiplicity of stances and personas Li could adopt when considering the relationship of the individual to the supra-human is a poem cycle titled "Wandering About Mount Tai: Six Poems." In this description of travel around the easternmost of China's cosmos-ordering "Five Sacred Peaks," the poet achieves a mythic fusion of various traditional paradises: the ancient utopias located far away, across the sea or sky; the cave-heavens that riddle sacred ground; and the spiritually charged natural world itself. He also manages an emotional fusion of the various responses of a single persona to manifestations of the divine, ranging from frustration and embarrassment, through ecstasy and awe, to a final confident accommodation with the world and its spiritual force.

In the first poem of the group, despite the speaker's appreciation of the mountain's beauty, the stone gate of a cave-heaven is closed to him and the gold and silver pavilions of the Faerie Isles can be imagined but remain distant. Moreover, the beautiful "Jade Women" who come in response to the poet's magic, spirit-summoning whistle tease him, laughing and giving him nothing more than a cup of "Liquid Sunrise," the immortals' wine. He can only bow to them, ashamed of his mundane nature. Here as elsewhere, though he sorrows, he never lapses into self-pity. The second and third poems underline the theme of human limitations: The speaker meets a strange man who has achieved immortality through Daoist training, but the figure vanishes and the antique writing of the text he leaves behind cannot be deciphered; then, the wanderer has a moment of vision, only to chance upon a youthful divinity who laughs at him for trying to achieve immortality so late, "when I've lost my grip, rosy cheeks faded." The exuberant fourth poem records a moment of hard-won spiritual achievement gained through Daoist study, fasting, and chanting. This otherworldly goal is replaced in the following poem by an awareness of the power in the natural landscape itself.

The resolution appears in the last poem of the sequence, as the poet's persona travels through sublime scenery alive with spirits. Although he is cut off from that sacred force of the Dao in which nature and spirits participate so freely, the poet presents himself as capable of actively making contact with the transcendent: *He* imagines a wedding dance of spirits; *he* reaches up to grope among the constellations. It is precisely the force of his own capacity for vision which wins that vision. Even though he acknowledges the evanescence of this magical night, he closes by stating that he will still be able to see the variegated clouds of dawn, clouds that are traditionally vehicles for immortals and that remind the reader of the Liquid Sunrise wine that was his gift from the divinities in the first poem of the group. The ability for imaginative action upon the world's phenomena remains even when the moment of inspiration passes—as do the poems that have been created with it.

"In the Mountains: Question and Answer"

The theme of the "spirit journey" noted above, and other symbols found in China's ancient shamanistic tradition, appear in many of Li's works. Not all of Li's "mystical" poems, however, are so grandiose. In the famous "In the Mountains: Question and Answer," he quietly (and slightly smugly) strikes the pose of the reclusive sage who lives in the mountains for reasons that only a fool would ask to have put into words; behind this persona is the perhaps even more smug poet who has just done exactly that:

> You ask me for the reason
> I roost among emerald hills.
> I smile and yet do not reply,
> heart at its natural ease.
> Peach-blossom petals on Paradise Creek
> flow on their mysterious way.
> There is another heaven and earth
> that's not the human world.

Alchemy: "Gazing at Yellow Crane Mountain"

Parallel to Li's interest in the strange chemistry of poetic creation was his interest in alchemy. In China, this arcane science developed as part of the Daoist search for elixirs that could give long life or even immortality. Li used terms found in a textual tradition running back to the ancient holy book, the *I Ching* (sixth to third century B.C.E.; *Book of Changes*). Such language was popular in the poetry of the era; whether Li actually conducted experiments, alchemy served him well as a source of metaphors.

For example, in the poem "Gazing at Yellow Crane Mountain," alchemical imagery describes the catalytic moment in which mutability and human limitations are accepted. The mountain's cosmic power is forcefully

described in the opening lines. The peak is "bold and virile, thrusting up in mid-air"; it "gives birth to clouds"; as an *axis mundi*, it links earth and sky. It is famous, moreover, for the hermit living there who—unlike the poet—achieved transformation into an immortal long ago and left his stone cell for the Faerie Isles. At this point, the poem pivots. An alchemical reaction is described: "The Golden Crucible gives birth to a haze of dust." The concluding passage focuses on images of sustenance amid aging and physical frailty. Finally, the poet presents himself as making peace with the gap between mortal flesh and transcendental power: "I'll knot my heart's pledge, to lodge under blue pines,/ Awakened forever, my wanderlust done with!"

Wine: "Drinking Alone in the Moonlight"

Natural wonders, such as mountains, and mysteries, such as alchemy, are only two of the sources of recurring metaphors by means of which Li examines the multifaceted relationship of the self with the great forces outside it. The most famous of his metaphors are those concerning wine. In reading Li's many deservedly famous poems on wine, it is important to remember the traditional Chinese view of intoxication as exhilaration and release. Li the gregarious man enjoyed drinking; Li the lover of life's pleasures found in that enjoyment a solace for their brevity; Li the eccentric and spontaneous poet could hardly *not* have had a reputation for enjoying it—that was a hallmark of the type; finally, Li the seeker after actualization of his original unrestricted nature used the drug—as others had before him—as an instrument of that search. Poems such as the four on "Drinking Alone in the Moonlight" are the first to come to mind when this poet's name is mentioned. In this witty sequence, nature, personalized through the imaginative inspiration of wine, recognizes Li's particularity. The loneliness of individuality is eased by communion with the universal order, made possible through alcohol.

Chinese tradition: "The Road to Shu Is Hard"

In stressing Li's individualism, it is important not to overlook his adept use of Chinese tradition. Well-known poems such as "The Road to Shu Is Hard" show the unique qualities of his work: the bold language of the opening line ("Ee-hoo-hee! Steep, whoo! High, phew!"); the irregular and musical outpouring of the wildly varied lines and stanzas; the powerful evocation of the natural scene and of the visions it inspires in the imagination; and the insistence on his own panting, persistent voice ("With dangers, yes! like these,/ ahh, man from afar,/ why oh why come, eh?"). At the same time, the poem's title is that of an old folk song which for centuries had been used by educated poets as a point of departure, stressing the difficulties of the rugged mountain road just as Li does. Moreover, Li weaves into the poem evocative legends of the early history of the region; allusions to historical events and to classical literature are characteristic of his work. It is his revitalizing variations, in form and content, on familiar themes that make this and other such poems so rich.

Li, like many Chinese poets, sought to restore to the verse of his own era the greatness of the past, or his idealized version of the past. Throughout his oeuvre, there are reflections of his intimate knowledge of earlier poets, though the effect is never that of a mere imitation. One of his many "Ancient Airs," translated by Joseph J. Lee in *Sunflower Splendor*, proclaims, "I desire to select and transmit the old,/ So that its splendor will last a thousand ages."

Poems in this mode frequently combine the spare language and unadorned technique of earlier times with a strong moral statement. Another ancient air (translated by Ezra Pound as "Lament of the Frontier Guard") takes the traditional stance against the waste of human life and the cost to society when men serve as soldiers in the frontier lands. Such poems, with their serious messages and generally simple presentation, stood in conscious opposition to the decorative poetry associated with courtly writers of the preceding era.

FEMALE PERSONAS

Another group of poems in which Li approaches a traditional subject in his own way includes those written with female personas. (Many men in traditional China wrote poems in which the speaker was a winsome chanteuse or a lonely wife.) In works such as "Poem Written on Behalf of My Wife" and "Song of Changgan" (in Pound's translation, "The River Merchant's Wife: A Letter"), the poet expresses longings common to all people through the figure of a woman addressing her husband. The vivid pictorial presentation of scenes from such women's lives reminds the reader of the skill of the man behind the mask.

TECHNICAL SKILL

It may be that the very force of Li's images contributed to the traditional slighting of his technical skill as a poet. His was an era when many poets were directing their talents to the relatively recent "regulated verse," in which certain patterns of word pitch were to be created, somewhat like the stressed and unstressed syllables in English meter. Li, however, usually preferred the freer form of old-style verse, though like a good writer of free verse in English, he still used the sounds of his language. He played with alliteration, assonance, and off rhyme. He varied line length to suit content or rhythmic need. He created striking patterns of word pitch, for example, in his powerful description of the thunderstorm in "In a Dream, I Wander Tianmu Mountain: A Chant of Farewell."

One trait of inferior Chinese poetry is a tendency to break down into a string of neat two-line units; as Stephen Owen points out, Li's exuberant outpourings avoid this trap, though his effects are sometimes too easy or too loose. Eiling Eide's discussion of Li's use of allusion and "revived" clichés to enrich his poems and to tighten the links between lines suggests how well crafted the poet's apparently spontaneous verse could be at its best.

CONTRIBUTIONS TO VERSE FORM

In looking to the past for form, as he looked there for his poetic lineage, Li found a fertile base for his own distinctive way of writing. He wrote in a variety of genres, from the old rhapsodic "rhyme-prose," or *fu*, to pseudofolk songs, *yuefu*. A high proportion of his poems have words such as "song," "ode," or "melody" in their titles, and many were actually written to be accompanied by music. Li could write skillful, regulated verse when he chose or when the occasion (a formal farewell, for example) called for it. In addition, it may be that he was one of the first of the educated elite to write poems, called *ci* (lyrics), that were written to tunes of irregular line length; if he really wrote certain of these poems attributed to him, Li made an important contribution to the development of a verse form that was to dominate the subsequent poetic era. In form, then, as in mood and theme, Li's verse is marked by the skilled diversity often associated with greatness.

In all this wealth of poems, there is much for those who read Li more than twelve hundred years after the poet's death. Even in translation, the power of his images and of his poetic personality comes through. Without knowledge of Li's literary, political, or philosophical background, one can still experience his intense, expansive way of knowing the world. Indeed, Li's skill is such that the reader is moved to put on the masks which the poet fashioned and walk into the landscapes he painted. For the duration of such moments, one shivers in the Gobi wind, eyes a tipsy, lisping exotic dancer, or rakes one's fingers through the Milky Way.

BIBLIOGRAPHY

Aiken, Conrad. *A Letter from Li Po and Other Poems.* New York: Oxford University Press, 1955. Li Bo's letter provides insight into his poems selected in this collection.

Bornstein, George, ed. *Ezra Pound Among the Poets.* Chicago: University of Chicago Press, 1985. A study of the influence of several poets on Pound, including Li Bo as well as Homer, Ovid, Dante, Walt Whitman, Robert Browning, William Butler Yeats, William Carlos Williams, and T. S. Eliot.

Cooper, Arthur. *Li Po and Tu Fu.* Harmondsworth, Middlesex, England: Penguin Books, 1973. Poems selected and translated with a solid and extensive introduction. Contains Chinese calligraphy by Shui Chien-Tung.

Hagett, James M. "Li Po (701-762) and Mount Emei." *Cahiers d'Extreme-Asie* 8 (1995): 101-118. Sheds insight into Li Bo's poetic creativity and nature.

Owen, Stephen. *The Great Age of Chinese Poetry: The High T'ang.* New Haven, Conn.: Yale University Press, 1981. Provides information on Li Bo in the political and cultural milieu of the Tang Dynasty.

Waley, Arthur. *The Poetry and Career of Li Po.* New York: Macmillan, 1950. One of the earliest translations of Li Bo available today.

Wong, Siu-Kit. *The Genius of Li Po.* Hong Kong: Center of Asian Studies, University of Hong Kong, 1974. A concise analysis of Li Bo's poetic talent and imagination.

Young, David, trans. *Five T'ang Poets: Wang Wei, Li Po, Tu Fu, Li Ho, Li Shang-yin.* [S.l.]: Oberlin College Press, 1990. Provides an opportunity to appreciate Li Bo along with other contemporary poets in the Tang Dynasty.

Yu, Sun, trans. *Li Po: A New Translation.* Hong Kong: Commercial Press, 1982. A substantial collection in English and Chinese. It provides a good comparison with other translations of Li Bo's poems by English natives.

Jeanne Larsen;
bibliography updated by Qingyun Wu

LI QINGZHAO

Li Ch'ing-chao
Born: Near Licheng, China; 1084
Died: Zhejiang Province(?), China; c. 1151

PRINCIPAL POETRY

Only a small fraction of Li Qingzhao's work—fewer than seventy poems—is still extant. The authenticity of some of these poems is questioned. A good source for her *ci* poems, which constitute the majority of her work, is edited by Chiao Wan-li, *Jiaoji Song Jinren ci* (1931; collated *ci* poems by writers of the Sung, Chin, and Yuan dynasties). One modern edition is *Li Qingzhao ji* (1962; the collected works of Li Qingzhao).

OTHER LITERARY FORMS

Li Qingzhao was a serious scholar of antiquities and objets d'art and compiled book annotations and catalogs of antiques with her husband Zhao Mingcheng. An essay appended to one of the catalogs, *Jinshilu houxi* (c. 1135; epilogue to a catalog of inscriptions on bronze and stone), is a major source of biographical information. She also wrote a brief critical essay on *ci* poetry. A number of other prose pieces were collected posthumously, but nearly all of them are now lost.

ACHIEVEMENTS

Li Qingzhao's gender has certainly affected critical response to her work and has given her the mixed blessing of being regarded as "China's greatest poetess," but the high quality of her work is beyond question. It is impossible to know to what extent the preservation and transmission of those of her texts which have survived were influenced by traditional ideas of what kinds of poems were appropriate for women to write. Clearly, she understood and used the voices and the literary gestures of China's rich heritage of female persona poetry. Equally clearly, she could and did write on themes—politics and mysticism among them—outside the range found in the extant work of most Chinese literary women before the modern era.

One strength of Li's work, then, is its emotional variety. There are love poems ranging from the melancholy to the erotic. There are poems of despair at old age or at the defeat of the Northern Song Dynasty. Some poems exhort those in power to moral rectitude; others suggest with transcendental imagery the glories of spiritual transport to a world beyond this one.

Equally important are Li's contributions to the *ci* verse form. Her critical comments on the work of other *ci* poets suggest the seriousness with which she approached her art, as well as her capacity for innovation. At a time when the *shi* form—which had dominated Chinese poetry for nearly a millennium—was in danger of stagnation, she helped develop the newer kind of poetry, broadening its scope in theme and language.

The word *ci* is often translated as "lyrics"; indeed, the form had its origins in the lyrics to popular songs. Consequently, although *ci* were often beautiful to hear, they tended to focus on such lightweight topics as the pleasures of drinking and the appreciation of female beauty. Li, like her father's famous friend Su Shih (Su Dongbo) before her, wrote on more complex subjects and moods; her work retains the emotional delicacy associated with the *ci* while giving it more serious applications. Moreover, the wide range of levels of diction in her poems—from the elegant to the conversational—opened up new potential for self-expression and broadened options for later poets. One contemporary critic commented on her use of colloquialisms: "The fantastically vulgar expressions of the back alleys and streets, whatever suited her mood, she would write down in her poetry" (translation by Gaiyou Xu). Even after the old melodies were lost, *ci* were composed to set patterns of line length, word pitch, and rhyme; Li's variations on these patterns were so euphonious that they sometimes became the preferred versions. Finally, Li's skillful use of alliteration and assonance in this extremely difficult form has served as a benchmark of musicality that has seldom been equaled.

Ultimately, though, it is the effect of the individual poems that has earned for Li widespread critical regard. Her poetry retains a strongly personal vision without lapsing into self-absorption or self-pity; her sensuous descriptions of scenes come alive for the reader as they subtly express complicated moods through actions and objects in the external world. The poet used allusion to the literary tradition, as well as the repetitive phrases (for example, "chill, chill, clear, clear") that are a traditional ornament of Chinese verse. Both qualities show that her innovations were grounded in a sensitive understanding of the work of those before her.

BIOGRAPHY

Li Qingzhao's early life was one of privilege and happiness, but that happiness did not last. Political infighting resulted in her father's temporary exile and her father-in-law's disgrace. Her beloved husband's official duties caused repeated separations, and he died in his late forties. The conquest of North China by the Tartars meant the loss of her extensive art collection and difficult years as a widowed refugee. Despite the nostalgic and sorrowful tone of many of her poems, however, her work suggests the personal strength that enabled her to survive in such difficult times.

Li was born to a family that placed a high value on literature and education. Her father, Li Kefei, was an important figure in the national government and was well-known for such prose writings as his essay on the famous gardens of the city of Luoyang. Her mother, whose family name was Wang, was a poet who had been educated at home by her grandfather, an outstanding scholar and former prime minister. Family friends of talent, influence, and learning filled the household. The lively, intelligent girl's abilities were encouraged by this literary atmosphere and by the approval of the adults around her, despite the strictures concerning education for women that were prevalent in her time. Li's reputation for poems in the respected *shi* form was established while she was still in her teens, and she developed her talents for painting and calligraphy as well.

By most accounts, Li was eighteen when she married a young student from another important family, Zhao Mingcheng. The two were well-matched. In two years, Zhao entered the civil service, and the couple developed their collection of books, antique bronzes, and other art objects. In 1134, Li wrote a charming retrospective description of how the couple had enjoyed each other's company as they compiled information on their acquisitions. The marriage has attracted much interest. There is the story of Zhao's prophetic childhood dream, signifying that he would marry a poet, and another in which he attempts unsuccessfully to outdo his wife's poem "Zui huayin" ("Tune: Tipsy in the Flower's Shade"). A portrait of Li at age thirty-one depicts a woman of beauty and refined sensibilities.

The factional politics that caused her father's exile early in this period of Li's life also sent her father-in-law into disfavor. He died shortly after, in 1107. The two men belonged to opposing political groups, which must have made Li's position as a daughter-in-law difficult. Perhaps it also gave her a clearer perspective on governmental folly; her political poems suggest that this was so.

Li's husband's career was affected by his father's fall, but the following years, while Zhao was out of office, were perhaps the zenith of their happiness. In the early 1120's, Zhao returned to government service; poems written while he was traveling on official business or in search of items for their art collection suggest Li's unhappiness during his absence, for upper-class women were not allowed to travel as men did.

Li was in her early forties when North China fell to the Tartars in 1127. She fled Shandong for the South, where her husband was serving as a magistrate. Much of their valuable collection of books, paintings, and antiques was left behind and burned. After a brief time of reunion, Zhao was posted to another city, fell ill with malaria, and died.

Civil disorder increased as the Tartars pressed southward and the Chinese emperor retreated before them. Most of Li's remaining artworks were lost as she, too, repeatedly made her way to safety. Two unsubstantiated stories suggest further pressures on the poet. She was accused of attempting a treasonous bribery, and she is said by some sources to have had a brief and unhappy marriage. The cruelty of Zhang Ruzhou, the minor government official she reportedly married and divorced, was no more shocking to biographers of later centuries than Li's defiance of social expectations by remarrying.

Li's last years were evidently spent in the household of her younger brother, Li Hang, in Zhejiang Province in southeastern, China, but little else is known, except that she did continue writing. Most estimates of the year of her death put it soon after 1150.

ANALYSIS

Li Qingzhao's work combines affective force with the aesthetic appeal of refined, well-crafted expression. The emotions behind her poems were powerful, but they are never simply self-indulgent. The exquisite sound effects of the originals are lost in English versions, yet the images, and the textures of joy or contemplation or loss that they generate, convey the poet's emotions to Western readers.

"TUNE: TIPSY IN THE FLOWER'S SHADE"

One of the best-known and most frequently translated of Li's poems, "Tune: Tipsy in the Flower's Shade," shows her ability to develop such a texture, revealing feeling through ambiguous language and the accretion of sensations of vision, smell, and touch. The first line of the poem offers several possible readings. The "Thin mists—thick clouds" at the line's beginning are appropriate to the autumn festival day on which the poem is set, for the festival is associated with the uprising of the cloudy *yin* principle that, according to traditional Chinese cosmology, controls the autumn and winter months. It is the second half of the line that offers multiple levels of meaning. Are the mists and clouds themselves "sad all day long," or, as is often the case in Chinese poetry, is the subject of "sadness" an unstated "I," or is the line best understood as "Thin mists and thick clouds: sorrow makes the day endless"?

The poem's subsequent images build a tone of suppressed sexuality and murky melancholy: The reader catches the dull metallic gleam of an ornamental burner through streamers of incense smoke and feels the chill that works its way past the translucent gauze of the bed-curtains. The poem is said to have been sent to Li's husband, and the subtle eroticism of the boudoir setting is underlined by "midnight" and "jade pillow." The bedroom trappings conjure up the traditional figure of the attractive woman alone and longing for her absent beloved. "Jade" is a common ornamental epithet; the pillow was probably not literally made of jade, but the word would have suggested for Li's audience the cool whiteness of the speaker's skin. This suits the tone established at the poem's start, inasmuch as the *yin* principle is further associated with women and with sexuality.

In the second stanza, the poet intensifies the mood of painfully stifled passion with mention of "dusk," "furtive fragrances," and the force of a wind that pushes the blinds aside. Moreover, she uses the standard imagery linked to the festival in her own way, increasing the complexity of the mood established in stanza 1. The fourth century poet Tao Qian, whom Li admired greatly, invariably came to mind on the day of mid-autumn festival. Li's allusion to the "eastern hedge" mentioned in one of his most famous poems immediately recalls other images associated with Tao's work: Wine, a sad nobility in the face of the seasons' change, and the yellow chrysanthemums that endure when all the other flowers have yielded to the cold. The chrysanthemums of the last line also had been linked poetically with feminine beauty long before Tao's time; Li uses all of this in her much-praised closing assertion that she is "more fragile than the yellow chrysanthemum."

"TO THE TUNE: SOUND UPON SOUND, ADAGIO"

A similar nexus of coldness, wine, dark, and the wasted beauty of the late-blooming flowers appears in the famous poem "To the Tune: Sound upon Sound, Adagio." *Ci* were not required to fit their content to the old melodies' titles, but they sometimes did. Just as Li made use of the intoxication, the flowers, and the shadiness (literally, *yin*) indicated by the previous poem's title, here she creates a musical tour de force through repeated words and sounds and careful attention to the effect of word pitch. This dazzling focus on language—syllables falling one by one, like the fine rain she pictures drizzling drop after drop upon the autumnal trees—prepares the reader for the poem's final twist. The poet denies the adequacy of words to relieve, or even to express, her grief. "How," she asks, "can the one word 'sorrow' finish off all this?"

MELANCHOLY THEMES

Some of Li's other poems, especially those written in the final period of her life, explore this theme of melancholy. In the poem "Qingping yue" ("Tune: Pure Serene Music"), images of whiteness and purity—snow, plum blossoms, clear tears—set the scene for her description of graying hair that, to overtranslate the Chinese idiom, "engenders flowery patterns." The reference to intoxication, despite the ambiguous intimation that it is as if the plum blossoms themselves were exhilarating, is a reminder of the remarkable number of references to wine in Li's work. A great many Chinese writers in the nonconformist mode—including Tao Qian and the eighth century poet Li Bo—expressed their liberation from conventionality through praise of the effects of alcohol; it may be that the particularly bold stance necessarily taken, in traditional China, by the woman who claimed the role of artist made such references to the untrammeled state of inebriation especially apt. Just as characteristic is the closure, a depiction of nature that describes by implication the speaker's condition: The cutting evening wind suggests the force of aging as it scatters the pale flowers of spring.

AMATORY POEMS

Li's husband's death naturally figures in many of her poems of depression. The title of one well-known example is "Wuling chun" ("Tune: Spring at Wu-ling"). In an atmosphere that blends emotional stasis with a sense of time's inevitable passing ("The wind subsides—a fragrance/ of petals freshly fallen;/ it's late in the day . . ."), the speaker—like bereft women in poems written for centuries—neglects her grooming and broods on her man's absence. The poem's famous final image refers ironically to a place in the region where Li lived out her widowhood: "I hear at Twin Creek spring it's still lovely." She, no longer part of a happy couple, says she would like to go pleasure-boating there, but she fears that "at Twin Creek my frail boat/ could not carry this load of grief."

Earlier poems on temporary separations from her husband range from loneliness to a teasing reminder of the pleasures of reunion. "Xiaochongshan" ("Tune: Manifold Little Hills"), for example, exploits the conventional association of spring with burgeoning sexuality. The grass is green, the swollen plum-blossom buds are ready to open, and "Azure clouds gather, grind out jade into dust" as the trees burst into jade-white bloom. The speaker's sensuous enjoyment of the springtime ends in a plea to her absent beloved to return so that they might more fully enjoy the season.

The attribution to Li of some other openly amatory poems is questionable. Some editors were doubtless quick to assign any free-floating, female-persona poem to the woman poet who stood foremost in their minds; others must have been shocked at the thought that a married woman of good family might have written on such a topic. Yet there are poems that are certainly hers and are certainly sexual. The analysis by William H. Nienhauser, Jr., in an article published in *T'oung Pao* in 1978, of Li's poem "Ru mengling" ("Tune: As in a Dream a Song") shows how Li used the technique of accreted implications to develop a fabric of delicately suggestive language, rhythm, images, and action. The poem has enjoyed long-lasting popularity; as Nienhauser observes, it is not pornography but a work of aesthetically pleasing subtlety, requiring considerable poetic skill.

POLITICAL POEMS

If Li's poems of joy and nostalgia reflect the events of her private life, there are others which show her concern for the disordered state of her nation. Some of these poems remain in the personal mode. This is true of her poem "Caisang ci" ("Tune: Song of Picking Mulberry") (another poem written to the same tune is among the frankly erotic poems attributed to Li). Here, the huge exotic leaves of banana trees exemplify the strange new landscape of South China, to which Li and others from the fallen heartland of the empire have fled before the Tartar onslaught. In the poet's mind, the leaves, opening and furling, evoke human hearts pulsing with emotion. Here, too, the closely woven repetitions of sounds and words suggests the brooding, monotonous dripping of "rain at the midnight watch." The sentiments of grief and restless obsession voiced by this northerner are those of a generation in exile.

More strongly in a public voice are the admonitory poems that Li, like most of China's greatest poets, wrote on political themes. They display, in their form and their language, Li's understanding of the literary decorum so important in her culture. These poems are not *ci* but the older, loftier *shi*. (Some are written according to the rules of versification called "tonal regulation"; others

are in the freer "old style.") Most of Li's contemporaries would have considered *ci* no more appropriate to her public subject matter than a limerick would be. Moreover, the poems' diction suits the exalted positions of those to whom many of them were sent.

The message of these verses is that of the Confucian moralist, calling for righteousness on the part of the ruler and abstention from greed on the part of government officials. The poet reminds her readers of the value of learning and the consolations of study. She warns the emperor of the defeated dynasty against the reckless enjoyment of immediate pleasures and criticizes the nation-weakening dangers of political infighting. Through references, often satirical ones, to a variety of historical figures, the poet reveals her own knowledge of the classics. She also uses these allusions to cast her admonitions into a safer form. Indirectly, she censures the failure of the dynasty to stand up to the invaders and the subsequent appeasement of the Tartars.

WOMEN POETS, TRANSCENDENTAL THEMES

Li was not the first woman to write on transcendental themes. In the eighth and ninth centuries, for example, Xue Tao, Li Ye, and Yu Xuangji all drew in their own ways on the rich stream of Daoist visionary imagery. Still, it was not usual for women to write such poems. Unconventional or not, Li is successful in her evocation of spiritual longing. She describes the lure of the contemplative life and reminds her readers of the value of the ascetic's pursuit of ritual purity and immortality. In "Tune: A Fisherman's Honor," the speaker sails through the sky to the paradise of the distant Faerie Isles in a spirit journey that has its origins in the shamanistic cults of centuries before. A *shi* poem, "Dream at Daybreak," relates a journey through dawn clouds to the marvelous realm of the immortals. The speaker awakens, however, asking ruefully, "Since human life can be like this,/ Why must I return to my old home?" Finally, she sits in meditation, covering her ears against the clamor of this world, thinking deeply on what she will not meet with again, and sighing. The poem expresses such yearnings with ethereal grace.

What remains of Li's work both tantalizes and satisfies. The various *ci* and *shi* poems just discussed, the few remaining essays, and at least one long rhyme-prose (*fu*) believed to be her work, provide a frustrating glimpse of the much larger corpus of her poetry and prose that was once in circulation. Nevertheless, what has survived is enough to stand on its own merits. The evocative, sometimes surprising imagery, lively and musical language, sensitive depiction of emotional nuance, and range of mood and tone ensure that Li's poetry will continue to be read a thousand years after her death.

OTHER MAJOR WORKS

Li wrote essays and annotations, most of which are now lost. One source for the originals of those still extant is Xie Wuliang's history of Chinese women's literature, *Zhongguo funu wenxue shi*, 1916. Sections of her two best-known essays have been translated by Hu Pin-ch'ing and Ling Chung.

BIBLIOGRAPHY

Ch'en, Tsu-mei. *Li Ch'ing-chao P'ing Chuan*. Nan-ching shih: Nan-ching ta hsüeh ch'u pan she, 1995. Although written in Chinese, it contains a table of contents and a brief introduction in English. Extensive study of Li's life and her creative career, with a useful glossary and bibliography.

Cryer, James, trans. *Plum Blossom: Poems of Li Ch'ing-chao*. Chapel Hill, N.C.: Carolina Wren Press, 1984. A slim collection of Li's nature poems with artwork by Nieh Dan.

Hu, P'in-ch'ing. *Li Ch'ing-chao*. New York: Twayne Publishers, 1966. A concise study of Li's life and works, with thoughtful interpretations and critical comments.

Jiaosheng Wang, trans. *The Complete Ci-Poems of Li Qingzhao*. Philadelphia: Department of Oriental Studies, University of Pennsylvania, 1989. A more recent translation and more accurate to the Chinese texts. Bilingual text.

Kearns, Ann. *Four Poems of Li Ch'ing-chao: Soprano and Piano*. Bryn Mawr, Pa.: Casia, 1995. This English-language song cycle, with program and biographical notes and song texts preceding the score, speaks to the musicality of Li's poetry.

Kraft, Leo. *Songs from the Chinese: For Soprano and Flute, with Percussion*. New York: Seesaw Music Corp., 1990. Another famous musical setting for Li's poems, translated for this work by Kenneth Rexroth.

Li Qingzhao. *Li Ch'ing-chao, Complete Poems*. Translated by Kenneth Rexroth and Ling Chung. New York: New Directions, 1979. An insightful translation with sensitivity to Li's poetic style and images. With helpful notes and commentary.

McHugh, Vincent, and S. H. Kwock Li. *The Lady and the Hermit: Thirty Chinese Poems*. Translated by Ch'ing-chao. San Francisco: Golden Mountain Press, 1962. A creative translation of poems by Li of the Sung and Wang Fan-chih of the Tang Dynasty.

Mayhew, Lenore, and William McNaughton, trans. *As Though Dreaming: The Tz'u of Pure Jade*. Tokyo: Mushinsha, 1977. An excellent translation of Li's famous *Shu yu tz'u* from the Chinese text.

Jeanne Larsen;
bibliography updated by Qingyun Wu

LYN LIFSHIN

Born: Burlington, Vermont; July 12, 1944

PRINCIPAL POETRY

Why Is the House Dissolving?, 1968
Leaves and Night Things, 1970
Moving by Touch, 1970
Black Apples, 1971, revised 1973
Lady Lyn, 1971
Tentacles, Leaves, 1972
Mercurochrome Sun: Poems, 1972
Forty Days, Apple Nights, 1972
Museum, 1973
The Old House on the Croton, 1973
Poems, 1974
Audley End: Poems, 1974
Blue Madonna, 1974
The Old House Poems, 1975
Blue Fingers, 1975
Shaker House Poems, 1975
Upstate Madonna, 1975
Paper Apples, 1975
North Poems, 1976
Some Madonna Poems, 1976

Women Early Plymouth, 1977
Leaning South, 1977
Glass, 1978
Lips on That Blue Rail, 1978
Offered by Owner, 1978
35 Sundays, 1979
Sunday Poems, 1979
Blue Dust, New Mexico, 1982
Madonna Who Shifts for Herself, 1983
Naked Charm, 1984
Kiss the Skin Off, 1985
Remember the Ladies, 1985
The Camping Madonna at Indian Lake, 1986
Raw Opals, 1987
Red Hair and the Jesuit, 1988
Skin Divers, 1989
Not Made of Glass: Poems, 1968-1988, 1989
The Doctor Poems, 1990
Reading Lips, 1991
The Innocents, 1991
Marilyn Monroe, 1994
Shooting Kodachromes in the Dark, 1994
Parade, 1994
Color and Light, 1995
Blue Tattoo: Poems of the Holocaust, 1995
Jesus Christ Live and in the Flesh, 1997
Restrooms, Anyone? Plus a Classic Lifshin Reader, 1997
Cold Comfort: Selected Poems, 1970-1996, 1997
Before It's Light: New Poems, 1999

OTHER LITERARY FORMS

Although Lyn Lifshin is best known for her poetry, she has edited several major anthologies of women's writing that have received wide acclaim; two significantly different editions of *Tangled Vines*, collections of mother and daughter poems; a collection of women's diaries and journals; and a collection of women's confidences. She also has published an autobiography and a how-to book for writers.

ACHIEVEMENTS

Lyn Lifshin, sometimes called the Queen of the Small Presses, is one of the most widely published American poets of the last half of the twentieth century, with her work appearing in virtually every small press magazine from the least significant to the most prestigious. She has compiled more than ninety collections of her poetry, and her poems have appeared in most anthologies of women's poetry during her long career. As a performance poet, she has become something of a celebrity on the poetry-reading circuit, cultivating at times the persona of a rock star. For Lifshin, image is essential, and thus the Lifshin image at poetry readings of a waif with incredibly long blond hair dressed in tight blouses and miniskirts has become legendary in the American postmodern poetry culture.

While Lifshin has won many awards for her poetry, such as the Hart Crane Award, a Bread Loaf scholarship, numerous Yaddo fellowships, Millay Colony fellowships, a Jack Kerouac award, and others, she has yet to win, despite being nominated numerous times, the prestigious Pulitzer Prize or Ploughshare award—the awards through which the academic poetry establishment grants status. Despite her neglect by establishment poets and critics, she has become one of the most important antiestablishment poets, and her work is championed by iconoclast Black Sparrow Press.

BIOGRAPHY

Lyn Diane Lifshin was born in Burlington, Vermont, to a middle-class Jewish family. She grew up in Middlebury, Connecticut, where her father, with whom she was never close, worked unhappily in a family dry-goods store. Lifshin's poetic imagination manifested itself early, when, at the age of three, she remarked to her mother on a motor trip, "It looks like the trees are dancing." Although her mother wanted Lifshin to be an actress, she instead chose English as her main interest, both for the study of literature and for the writing of poetry. In the third grade she brought a poem home to her mother, one she had copied from nineteenth century poet William Blake, and claimed she had written it. Her mother, along with her teacher, then made her write another poem to show that she really could write poetry.

One of Lifshin's favorite stories concerns Robert Frost. The aging poet lived in her family's town and frequently shopped at the dry-goods store. One day her father showed the poet one of his daughter's poems. Frost wrote a note on the poem, "Very good saith Robert Frost," and asked to see more.

Lifshin attended Syracuse University, where she earned her bachelor of arts degree, and the University of Vermont, where she earned a master of arts degree. She began her prolific publishing career in 1966. Her first accepted poem was for the fall, 1966, issue of *Folio*, and her first appearance was for the poetry periodical *Kauri* in 1966.

The turning point in her career came after she left the Ph.D. program in English at the State University of New York (SUNY) at Albany in the late 1960's. As the youngest student in the program and one of the only women, she was subjected, she claims, to sexual harassment and humiliating remarks about her long hair and hippie-like clothes. Her adviser believed that she did not have the religious background to teach seventeenth century English poetry. No doubt, the rejecting of a doctoral candidate who later was to become a writer of Lifshin's stature remains one of the major embarrassments of the institution's English Department and one of the most famous legends of mid-twentieth century graduate school lore.

Lifshin did not take her failure easily. Instead she began expressing her anger through her poetry. Her first book, *Why Is the House Dissolving?*, has been treated by Hugh Fox as a vituperative rejection of academic life and a turning to poetry as an alternative career. Soon after her rejection by the SUNY English Department, she began writing and publishing at an astonishing rate. *Wormwood Review* published her first poem and then she began publishing in such little magazines as *Folio* and *Cardinal Poetry Quarterly*.

Thereafter she became one of the few American poets who have tried to make their living exclusively from the writing of poetry. Little-magazine editors of the 1970's and 1980's all have their stories to tell about receiving the Lifshin treatment, being swamped with one batch after another of Lifshin poems until they finally find some poems they like. Most of her career she lived in New York, but in the late 1990's and early 2000's she lived and worked in the Washington, D.C., area. Virtually all her books have been published by small independent presses with limited distribution, but beginning in 1997 her work was taken up by the prestigious Black Sparrow Press, adding to her reputation.

ANALYSIS

Lyn Lifshin rarely writes haiku, but one of her earliest poems, "The Leaving," from the summer, 1967, issue of *Cardinal Poetry Quarterly* revealed the early poet.

> You belong to sand
> To sea. Drift with the wind with
> The moonspun tide, go.

This poem, utterly undistinguished except in the context of its time, would often be considered mere student work. The haiku keeps rigidly to the requirements of its form (five syllables in the first line, seven in the second, five in the third) and tries to develop the one central image that will elicit the haiku moment of illumination, but it also breaks with tradition in the enjambment of lines one and two and thus reveals a direction that Lifshin's poems often were to take: toward compactness, rejection of poetic tradition and conformity, and abrupt thwarting of conventional expectations.

Naturally for a collection of poetry the size of Lyn Lifshin's, the range of her subjects is enormous and the breadth of their treatment diverse. Nevertheless, despite the large variety of Lifshin's poetic styles, certain characteristics typify most of her work from the beginning. Like the early haiku, most of Lifshin's poems are short, usually less than thirty lines, and most employ a short poetic line. Because her poems are often short with few words, they read quickly, causing Lifshin to be labeled the Queen of the Quickies.

Lyn Lifshin has written with wonderful humor throughout her career as she examines American culture to its fullest as a woman and as an interested observer. Her poetry proves respectable and accessible to a wide range of audiences from the academic, which originally spurned her, to large circulation audiences in such outlets as *Rolling Stone*. Although many of her early books are difficult to obtain because of their limited small press publications, two large collections, *Cold Comfort* and *Before It's Light*, contain many of her most popular poems. The mainstream publication of these two volumes signifies that, at last, one of America's most prolific poets has become a mainstay of the contemporary poetry scene.

"Fat"

Her most memorable poems are the personal poems and the poems built around personas from popular culture. "Fat," for example, derives its inspiration from Lifshin's obsession with weight. Evidently as a child she always felt overweight. In this poem, she contemplates what she has lost since she overcame her weight problems:

> Some of it I've
> given away, I guess that
> comes from thinking
> nobody could
> want it.
> Fat. Something you
> take in and just
> can't use.
> It hangs around
> reminding you of what
> wasn't totally
> digested, a layer of heavy
> water, grease.

Fat is the unwanted guest that stays despite all efforts at removal. Does fat represent something beyond excess body weight here? Probably not. As in most Lifshin poems, the imagery speaks for itself. The implications about the nature of being overweight can be discussed, or even the issue of whether one ought to judge overweight people as deficient in some way. The poem does not, however, directly address these banalities. It simply reports one woman's memory of her hatred for her fat, her attempt to hide her fat, and her feeling that fat, rather than (as some suggest) protecting one from cold makes one "more vulnerable,/ fat people having more/ places to bruise/ or scar."

"Hair"

Lifshin obviously takes pride in her hair as essential to her image: "Dig the hair," says Mary Battiata of *The Washington Post*, "I mean she wants you to. She's written poems about it. Her fairy-tale hair." An early trademark poem is "Hair," reprinted in *Cold Comfort*. Here the speaker protests her family's and society's efforts to make her conform with short hair, with hair pinned up, with hair that does not call attention to itself. In two particular life moments, however, she attempts conformity and fails. First in her wedding she accedes to family and patriarchal wishes:

> After
>
> the wedding I
> pulled pins out of
> that stiff hive
> for a week, afraid
> to touch it

Then, as she attempts to conform to male expectations in her graduate program, she again examines her hair:

> . . . I
> know they suspected
> me of being a
> hippie, a witch
>
> the college that
> said I couldn't stay
> on white cold paper
> wrote first can't you look more
> professional and
>
> dignified, wear
> it up.

The poem thus takes up a common theme for Lifshin: Women's conformity to expectations usually result in a loss of womanhood.

"You Understand the Requirements"

Lifshin develops the theme further in "You Understand the Requirements," a poem about the same period in her life, during which she was rejected by the SUNY English Department's committee:

> We are
> sorry to have to
> regret to
> tell you
> sorry sorry
> regret sorry that you have
> failed
>
> your hair should have been
> piled up higher

How can one be a woman and pass the examination into a man's world unless she becomes like a man? Here the reader witnesses the incredulity of the speaker, reading her rejection letter, which tries to state an obvious truth:

"you understand the requirements"—the requirement, by elimination of those traits she does not possess, being first that "you" be a man, and one, moreover, who is Protestant or at least Christian, not Jewish: with "sympathy for . . . English Anglicanism." The poem, though in the form of a rejection letter, seems filtered through the speaker's perception as she reads, as the key words "sorry" and "regret" echo and interrupt the form letter's flow, ironically emphasizing the coldness and finality of the judgment.

BARBIE POEMS

Lifshin patents this theme in her later poems of the 1980's and 1990's with several series of poems based on characters from popular culture, such as the toy doll Barbie, the actress Marilyn Monroe, Jesus, former First Lady Jackie Kennedy Onassis, famed husband abuser Lorena Bobbitt, and Lifshin's Mad Woman character.

In "Barbie Watches TV Alone, Naked," the doll contemplates why she must always be clothed to please all who play with her. She longs to be more than a toy:

> She is
> sick of having
> a rod jammed up in
> side her, of being
> boxed in with a
> hair brush that
> usually goes where
> it shouldn't.

In "Barbie Hunts Thru Medical Books Looking for What Is Wrong with Her," society's image of the perfect woman feels

> . . . empty, full
> of holes—some
> thing just for
> someone else
> to collect
> or abuse

OTHER MAJOR WORKS

NONFICTION: *On the Outside*, 1995; *Hints for Writers*, 1995.

EDITED TEXTS: *Tangled Vines*, 1978; *Ariadne's Thread*, 1982; *Lips Unsealed*, 1990; *Tangled Vines*, 1992.

BIBLIOGRAPHY

Battiata, Mary. "Madonna Who Writes Ten Poems a Day." *Washington Post*, August 17, 1997, p. W21. A valuable article that surveys the reputation and place of Lifshin in the contemporary poetry culture. It contains numerous assessments from well-known poets and critics.

Fox, Hugh. *Lyn Lifshin: A Critical Study*. Troy, N.Y.: Whitston, 1985. Although out of date because it covers only the early poetry of Lifshin, this study is a sensitive, detailed reading of most of the pre-1985 poems.

Fulton, Len. "Lifshin's Earth." *Small Press Review*, October/November, 1997. This is a typical but objective review of *Cold Comfort*.

Lynch, Mary Ann. *Lyn Lifshin: Not Made of Glass*. Video. New York: Women Make Movies, 1988. Readings of Lifshin's poems interspersed with her own and others' observations about her life and work.

Raindog. "Lyn Lifshin: Queen of the Small Press." *Lummox Journal*, Dec 27, 2000. While this is a typical interview of Lifshin after the publication of *Cold Comfort*, it does contain detailed comments on individual poems.

Paul Varner

VACHEL LINDSAY

Born: Springfield, Illinois; November 10, 1879
Died: Springfield, Illinois; December 5, 1931

PRINCIPAL POETRY

The Tramp's Excuse and Other Poems, 1909
Rhymes to Be Traded for Bread, 1912
General William Booth Enters into Heaven and Other Poems, 1913
The Congo and Other Poems, 1914
The Chinese Nightingale and Other Poems, 1917
The Golden Whales of California and Other Rhymes in the American Language, 1920
The Daniel Jazz and Other Poems, 1920

Collected Poems of Vachel Lindsay, 1923, revised 1925

Going-to-the-Sun, 1923

Going-to-the-Stars, 1926

The Candle in the Cabin, 1926

Johnny Appleseed and Other Poems, 1928

Every Soul Is a Circus, 1929

Selected Poems of Vachel Lindsay, 1931 (Hazelton Spencer, editor)

Selected Poems of Vachel Lindsay, 1963 (Mark Harris, editor)

The Poetry of Vachel Lindsay, 1984-1986 (3 volumes; Dennis Camp, editor).

OTHER LITERARY FORMS

Adventures While Preaching the Gospel of Beauty (1914) and *A Handy Guide for Beggars* (1916) are autobiographical accounts of Vachel Lindsay's walking tours, narratives that simultaneously articulate the populist ideals of his life and identify the sources for much of his poetry, the themes and characters that preoccupied him in the years before his great success. These and other prose works and designs are collected in *Adventures: Rhymes and Designs* (1968; Robert Sayre, editor); *Letters of Vachel Lindsay* (1979; Marc Chénetier, editor) offers a fair sampling of Lindsay's correspondence with the literary community after his fame was established. Lindsay produced quantities of broadsides and pamphlets on topics ranging from workers' rights in the mines, to racial injustice, to his own peculiarly passionate brand of Christianity. These, frequently set in frames of hieroglyphs of his own design or scrawled sketches vaguely in the style of Art Nouveau, suggest both his wide-ranging ambition and his lack of focus, his mercurial temperament.

ACHIEVEMENTS

Vachel Lindsay's achievements have always been measured by the size, enthusiasm, and attention of his audiences. The great recitals of the "higher vaudeville" poems of the 1910's aroused such enthusiasm that good critics responded with varying assessments: John Masefield, after meeting him in Indianapolis in 1916 and hearing him read in England in 1920, said flatly that Lindsay was "the best American poet," whereas Ezra Pound, polite at first, finally dismissed Lindsay with the observation that one could write such stuff "as fast as one scribbles." Poets as various as William Butler Yeats, Robert Graves, Stephen Vincent Benét, and Theodore Roethke all saw Lindsay's work as Masefield did, whereas Amy Lowell, Conrad Aiken, and many others not so politely scorned him.

The difference of opinion, finally, has less to do with Lindsay's style than with the two basic ways of perceiving poetry: hearing and reading. Lindsay's accomplishment was that he could write good poetry that could be read aloud well. The language, themes, and implications of his verse were profoundly American; they canvassed American culture clearly, affectionately, and critically. He built his poetry on his "tramps" through the land as well as in the city, "tramps" which taught him to see, as Walt Whitman, Robert Frost, and Carl Sandburg did, the particulars of American life that defied sentimentality and generalization. When he invoked the gods, they were American heroes, the names that the folk he met knew and revered, both successes and failures: Abraham Lincoln, John Peter Altgeld, William Jennings Bryan, and John Chapman (Johnny Appleseed). Just as important, however, his poetry sang; it moved those who sounded it and those who heard it. His British audiences in 1920 heard the unfamiliar cadences of American speech in song and were astounded. His American audiences heard the rhythms and voices of their own culture, normally absent from the esoteric world of the "New Poetry." This balance of theme and song, of creed in distinctive rhythm, is Lindsay's most durable accomplishment. With it he achieves what Whitman seemed to predict for the twentieth century American poet. Masterpieces like "General William Booth Enters into Heaven," "Santa Fe Trail," "Chinese Nightingale," "Flower-Fed Buffaloes," and others will remain among the classics of twentieth century American poetry, for they perfectly express the sounds and concerns of a complex moment in American history.

BIOGRAPHY

Nicholas Vachel Lindsay was born and died in his father's house next to the Governor's Mansion in Springfield, Illinois. His father, Dr. Vachel Thomas Lindsay, was a general practitioner whose home and financial stability made possible his son's slow progress toward a self-sustaining career as a poet. His mother, Esther Catharine Frazee Lindsay, a college mathematics teacher and instructor of painting before she married Dr. Lindsay, had the spirit and endurance to continue hopefully to support their son as he ambivalently moved from college (leaving Hiram College in June of 1900 without a degree after three years), to the Art Institute in Chicago, and on to New York to try to market his skills as an artist. His father may have hoped that his son would join his practice and settle down, but both parents were trampers and travelers in their own way. They had courted each other in the art galleries of Europe in the summer of 1875, and had taken the family to Europe in the summer of 1906, immediately after Lindsay's first American walking tour. In the spring of 1906, Lindsay had walked from Florida back north through the Okefenokee swamp to Atlanta, lecturing (on the Pre-Raphaelites), singing his poems ("The Tree of the Laughing Bells") all the way to Grassy Springs, Kentucky, and the home of relatives. The immediate leap to Europe, the Louvre, and the tomb of Napoleon was in some ways shocking, but Lindsay was comfortable in both milieux, marking the range of his experience, the talents and interests of his parents, and the end of the era of art and design as his principal interests.

His next "tramp" (in 1912) led directly to publication. He had tried "poem-peddling" in New York in the spring of 1905 without success, but now set out to trade rhymes for bread as he walked from Illinois to California. He caught the Santa Fe Trail in Kansas and felt charged with poetic material and enthusiasm. That the trip was hard was undeniable; there was less room for self-delusion or self-indulgence than in any other episode of his life. When he "gave up" and took the train from Wagon Mound, New Mexico, to Los Angeles, he felt defeated; but here, after gloom and despair, came the inspiration for "General William Booth Enters into Heaven." Booth of the Salvation Army had died almost a month earlier, but as Lindsay walked the city at night, the poem flashed into being.

"General William Booth Enters into Heaven" was his making, and, because it was such a showpiece to read, perhaps his unmaking as well. Lindsay's career has been divided into sections of composition and recital,

with the transitional stage between the publication of *General William Booth Enters into Heaven and Other Poems* by Kennerley in 1913 and *The Chinese Nightingale and Other Poems* by Macmillan in 1917. After this period, regardless of his own interests and enthusiasms, he was seen as a reciter of his own verse, a performer, an actor. His livelihood depended on the income generated from such recitals, and the verse he wrote later (with several notable exceptions) does not match the standard of the poetry of the 1910's.

It is important to note that Lindsay saw his public readings as the best way to reach the largest audience of American readers of poetry. If they all wanted to hear "The Congo," he would read it, repeatedly, even though he knew it was not representative of his best work. "I have tried to fight off all jazz," he said. He knew that it was he (as much as his verse, or more) who charmed or conjured his audiences; *he* had to read his work to have it go. He termed his reciting style and material a "higher vaudeville" and knew that in reaching new audiences he would have to alienate older or more traditional ones. In his day, however, academe did not scorn him: Yale, Wellesley, Oxford, Cambridge, all invited him to read, and they sat spellbound. Robert Graves, who introduced him to the circle of Oxford dons and students with the notion of showing off an American curiosity, was astonished at Lindsay's success. It is hard to reconstruct the experience: It depended on the power of Lindsay's delivery, but he asserted that the energy was there in the lines. In his passionate, reverent attention to his audience, his desire for its conversion, he poured himself out. Thus, in his reciting tours, Lindsay saw himself as no less than the Christian-democratic poet, a man who could, by the power of his poetry and personality, revive the artistic and moral sensibility of the nation.

Lindsay seemed more showman than troubadour, a performer, not a poet, primarily because he was more interested in speaking to America than to literary critics. The poets who supplanted him in American poetry anthologies consciously and particularly addressed themselves to the scholar-reader, the literary elite, the would-be student of literature. There is more to the contrast than this: Lindsay may have felt that he could not impress that literary elite beyond the first shock of amazement and delight at his readings: He may have doubted his staying power, his ability to follow "General William Booth Enters into Heaven" and "The Chinese Nightingale" with more of the same. Although Dr. Paul Wakefield (his brother-in-law) finally got him to the Mayo Foundation in Rochester, Minnesota, in June, 1924, for a diagnosis of his nervous condition, Lindsay must have feared the worsening of his serious physical and nervous disorder all his adult life. The word "epilepsy" was not mentioned until Eleanor Ruggles's biography (1959), but the severe seizures were public knowledge.

Celibate and unmarried until his mid-forties, but in love with a series of remarkable women who rejected his proposals, Lindsay married Elizabeth Conner on May 19, 1925, without revealing the secret of his seizures until after the ceremony. Paranoia, "morbid fancies," as Ruggles painfully documents them, insulting and insane accusations of family and stranger alike: These multiplied in the late 1920's and gave Lindsay's career a kind of lurid richness that tempts readers to consider the pathological case and not the poet. Lindsay drank a bottle of Lysol at home, upstairs, early in the morning of December 5, 1931, killing himself quickly but painfully. In the past decade he had read triumphantly in England, married a young, bright, determined wife, and was known internationally for poems many could recite from memory, but fear of the increased frequency of epileptic attack, financial anxieties, anger with critics who wanted "more of the same," and despair that he was tied to the task of reading to audiences that would not read him—these concerns, and doubtless others, resulted in suicide.

ANALYSIS

Music and message, rhythm and truth, Vachel Lindsay's best poetry offers extraordinary examples of the absolute interdependence of sound and sense. Lindsay finds ways of presenting on the page effects as various as the thump, whistle, and wheeze of a calliope ("The Kallyope Yell"), the staggered, percussive rattle of native dancing ("The Congo"), the smooth, mournful music of prairie birds singing in counterpoint to highway traffic ("The Santa Fe Trail"), and the unexpected brevity of a tall tale's punch line ("The Daniel Jazz"). Masterful as these effects are in themselves, they also illustrate Lindsay's affection for the details and the per-

sonality of his midwestern world. The gaudy steam calliope which blasted the fairgrounds with its din, the communities of blacks moving north to Illinois with their brand-new tempos of jazz music, the individual note of a bird called the Rachel Jane, the black servant's power in the household ("The Daniel Jazz") are all hard facts in his verse, keeping the dreams and generalizations, the hopes and fears of his populist idealism, rooted in the actual.

When, for example, Lindsay plucks General Booth out of his British setting for a tribute in a dream vision, marching deadbeats cruise around the courthouse in downtown Springfield. Here Lindsay harnesses the melting-pot theory of American meliorism to serve an evangelical cause, and where better to link the two powerful processes of social equality and salvation than on the courthouse steps that Abraham Lincoln climbed? The courthouse still dominates countless midwestern town squares, a kind of secular temple: Lindsay recognized its power as a symbol. The paradoxical quality of the courthouse is carried on in the paradox of "Booth the Soldier," the tension derived from the "salvation" army, almost oxymoronic, however Pauline and familiar, from Protestant hymns. Again secular power and spiritual grace unite in a specific figure.

Lindsay revered the ideals of the courthouse and the Salvation Army, but the poem really celebrates the transformation of the "blear review." When all are made new, the "blind eyes" which are opened are not specifically identified as Booth's, because *all* gaze on "a new, sweet world." Lindsay's concern for a mass of people is evident in this poem; the variety of their disabilities, their instruments, their crimes, all fascinate him. Their energy is captured in the way the lines begin—trochees and spondees abound and alliteration provides speed and percussion. The principal accents are often just two, forcing the reading voice to pace on as it makes sense of the line.

"GENERAL WILLIAM BOOTH ENTERS INTO HEAVEN"

In "General William Booth Enters into Heaven," Lindsay's technical genius can be appreciated; his belief in the new life of grace is given authority by the rippling power of the verse. In the first stanza, the alliteration and repeated stress at the start and finish of the first line exemplify Booth's confidence; the fact that he was blind makes this parade all the more bravely led. The undercurrent of the parenthesis "(Are you washed in the blood of the Lamb?)" changes the meter with its anapestic feet, implying the smooth confidence of the saint's question, but also slowing or interrupting the raucous motion of the parade. The couplet rhymes are remarkably appropriate as an organizing frame for this disorderly procession, but "the blood of the Lamb" never has its rhyme completed. Even in the last line of the poem, when the question is stripped of parentheses and quotation marks, when it comes straight to the reader/hearer, it has no echo, for it is Lindsay's unanswered, unanswerable question.

In the second stanza ("Every slum had sent . . .") Lindsay continues to move the reader/hearer through contradictory feelings: delight with the visual splendor of the scene (banners blooming and "transcendent dyes" in "the golden air") and awe or apprehension at the human forms that are here collected ("Bull-necked convicts," "Loons with trumpets"). The diction suggests salvation ("bloomed with glory," "transcendent," "upward thro' the golden air") while the subjects are clearly fallen, and likely to remain so.

The poem almost halts, therefore, caught by this paradox of evangelistic passion in fallen men, in the opening accounts of the third stanza with its three slow beats: "Booth died blind. . . ." Lindsay picks up the rhythm with uncharacteristic iambs, such as "and still by faith he trod," thus metrically emphasizing the miracle—dying blind but walking on. Lindsay hides the actual moment of transition here, as he does when the "blear review" is "in an instant" made new. In the middle of the stanza, with no italicized directions for music, Lindsay seems to lose the moment of salvation, and emphasizes instead the continuation of the parade of the purified host as it accompanies Booth to heaven.

Lindsay balances the familiar with the mystical perfectly. The parade of deadbeats playing musical instruments as they circle the town square becomes Booth's contribution to his world of slum victims, a metaphoric representation of his collected good works, and a fantastic vision of the heavenly scene.

It is easy to see that the italicized passages of advice ("Sweet flute music") are meant to invite the reader/

hearer to change attitude, to prepare for a new meter, to modulate tone. Lindsay's stage directions are meant to aid readers, not to stage shows or revise the verse. Lindsay structured his verse with care, setting lines on the page in groups indented or flush, with headnotes or numerical demarcation, always trying to slow the reader's headlong rush through a poem.

"THE GOSPEL OF BEAUTY"

Much more sober and conventional but no less successful is the trio of poems united under the title "The Gospel of Beauty." Lindsay sang the sections of this poem on his walking tours, and it is not hard to imagine the farmers of the plains listening with some pleasure to this celebration of their past and future. Once again, Lindsay's characteristic concerns emerge from the lines, although there is little of the jazzy movement of the Booth poem in these thoughtful stanzas. "The Proud Farmer" (the title of the first segment) was Lindsay's mother's father, whose town, church, fields, and cemetery he knew well. The poet sees the heroic accomplishments of the rural life and the failure of the town to grow and prosper according to his grandfather's design: "They sleep with him beneath the ragged grass . . ./ The village withers, by his voice unstirred." The poet, "a sturdy grandchild," is empowered by the meditation, this time admiring the characteristic American pioneer hero, the man who worked by day, read by night, preached the word, and sired a family to spread to the ends of the earth. Frazee, like Booth, was a hero, capable of converting and saving, and Lindsay feels his inheritance and expresses it in the run-ons of the last stanza. The inversions ("furtive souls and tame") and archaisms ("he preached and plowed and wrought") are not meant to ape the formal diction of poetic recollection; they are gestures of respect to a man of an earlier age, whose language was formed by biblical study.

The second section, "The Illinois Village," reminds the reader of Lindsay's preoccupation with Springfield as a holy and aesthetically charged place. *The Golden Book of Springfield* (1920) and *The Village Magazine* (pb. 1910, 1920, 1925, which he published several times at his own expense) were documents of his vision of Springfield as a site for political and spiritual rebirth, a new American life to start in the fields of Illinois. The three parts of "The Gospel of Beauty" move from one man on the land, to a village with promise, to a visionary city of the ideal future. "The Illinois Village" is Springfield in its youth, with the "village church by night" the image of "Spirit-power." Commerce is de-emphasized in favor of artful decoration ("fountain-frieze" and painters and poets); the church is the moral and cultural center. Lindsay's image of the church in moonlight and veiled by trees at dusty noon again places the fact between mere observation and fantasy, like the courthouse in "General William Booth Enters into Heaven": "The trees that watch at dusty noon/ Breaking its sharpest lines, veil not/ The whiteness it reflects from God."

"On the Building of Springfield" closes the work, its prophetic tone sharply in contrast to the meditative observations of the first two sections. Lindsay's dream here is like that of any booster of an "All-American city"; he wishes his city to claim its place with Athens, Oxford, and Florence. But his terms and rhythms are unique and defy casual description. "The Proud Farmer" saw the house of God and the farm to be one; in "The Illinois Village," the church organizes a square of town land, wreathed by trees; now a city is laid out in aisles, not streets, "where Music grows and Beauty is unchained." The renaissance of Springfield is larger than a religious conversion or a chamber of commerce scheme; it demands aesthetic appreciation, a vision beyond the practical payoff. Lindsay sees the danger of boosterism and calls Springfield "Ninevah" and "Babylon" unless it heeds his call, the proud farmer's heritage. Nature returns to assert its power when "Maple, Elm and Oak" are capitalized to suggest both the trees and the streets (as they are named in Springfield and almost every other American town); the trees again are the images of germinating genius in a town which tends to ignore the power of its own symbols. "Attics" are places to store rummage, not "sacred tears," as Attics of Athens might have shed. The curious choice of the verb form in the repeated line ("A city is not builded in a day.") reminds the reader/hearer of the process of the action, not its completeness: The open end of the trochee suggests both the incompleteness of the building and the hope for more.

"The Chinese Nightingale"

Thus Lindsay continues to combine vision and fact, myth and reality, all set in a form whose sound and me-

ter supports and explains the message. This pattern is still evident, on a larger scale, in "The Chinese Nightingale," a poem with its roots in the great tradition of nightingale poetry (Ovid, Samuel Taylor Coleridge, John Keats, Thomas Hardy, William Butler Yeats) and in the fairy tale (Hans Christian Andersen's tale of the bird and the emperor). Typically, Lindsay starts with a metrical and literary joke: The "How, how," of Chang is the musical salutation in Chinese which the reader/hearer understands only in English. Lindsay's sister and brother-in-law in China provided accurate images and diction for this poem. The question in reply to "How?" reminds the reader/hearer of William Wordsworth's silly questions to the leech gatherer, but instead of a lament over lost greatness and present drudgery, the artful objects that surround Chang conjure up the beauty of a civilization gone, like Yeats's piece of lapis lazuli. The nightingale, the joss, and the lady all sing with appropriate imagery and rhythm, to create the tapestry of sound that makes up the poem. The introduction of the lady's song, for example, is effected with a couplet of lifting iambs, ending with a double-rhyme that has an unaccented final syllable, a feminine ending: ("aflower . . . bower"), while Chang is solid in iambs at the lines' ends (his "countenance carved of stone/ ironed and ironed, all alone"). The living figure petrifies as the icons come alive: Keats would have approved, and Yeats did. The repetitions in the lady's song are mesmerizing, with their alterations ("bright bronze breast" and "bronze-brown wing") suggesting her accuracy, an accuracy which deteriorates in Chang's responses to short-line generalizations and vision of his San Francisco world. The Chinese laundryman is, like Keats, called back to his sole self after the nightingale's voice is stilled, but his memory of the dialogue between lady and joss whispers, hinting at evocative details, the remains of inspiration.

The tones of the song are distinct: The nightingale is the medium, the muse, whose brief invitation and occasional punctuation of the tale are done with almost nonsensical repetition. The lady sings gently, with fewer explosive consonants and more iambs at line-starts, dotting her lines with more anapestic feet ("I had a silvery name") than the "great gray joss" whose tone is more belligerent and stylized:

Hear the howl of the silver seas,
Hear the thunder.
Hear the gongs of holy China
How the waves and tunes combine
in a rhythmic clashing wonder, . . .

A comparison of the speaking voices here with Yeats's later "Byzantium" poems will reveal how many of the images are shared, and how differently the poems sound. Lindsay's details are, literally, taken from the laundryman's shelf, as Yeats's stone in "Lapis Lazuli" was from his own desk, but the integrity of the speaking voices and the metrical effects are pure Lindsay.

HOPES UNREALIZED

Whether Lindsay impersonates a joss or a calliope, or celebrates heroes like Pocahontas, John Peter Altgeld, Bryan, or Lincoln, the theme is frequently one of measured loss, hopes unrealized, populist dreams evaporating, death before accomplishment. In this regard, "General William Booth Enters into Heaven" and "The Daniel Jazz" form a jolly retelling of a familiar tale. The "Kallyope" runs out of steam and will not, finally, convert the proud, but it *has* insisted on the equation of "the gutter dream" and "the golden dream." The senseless notes that it sounds at the poem's close are invitations to enjoy pure body rhythm, which cannot succeed on the page or with the ear. Lindsay was fascinated by the loss of the dream and the bittersweet recollections of the promise once imagined. From "The Last Song of Lucifer," which he worked on in college, to "The Flower-Fed Buffaloes," published in *Going-to-the-Stars* in 1926, Lindsay seems to understand and accept the cycle of creation and destruction, hope and despair. This last poem, fifteen short lines, perfectly embodies the cycle in its music and diction.

"THE FLOWER-FED BUFFALOES"

"The Flower-Fed Buffaloes" opens with the title's descriptive phrase, evoking the perfect pastoral, then quickly turns to the song of the locomotive in the third line. Like Henry David Thoreau, Lindsay did not see the railroad as an evil force; both poets allowed their trains to sing. Still, the flowers that sustained the buffalo "lie low" under the ties, just as the "perfumed grass" gives way to the wheat. Although flowers and grass have been replaced by railroad tracks and wheat farms, the spring "still is sweet"; Lindsay is not cheaply nostalgic or willing to falsify his experience. Nevertheless, something is gone, not just the buffalo, but the tribes that fed on the species. Lindsay surprises the reader/ hearer with the intrusion of the Blackfeet and the Pawnees "lying low, lying low."

The savagery of the past age is captured in the diction describing the buffaloes' behavior ("They gore . . . they bellow . . . they trundle . . .") and the reader suddenly glimpses the vigor and violence of that age. Perfect pastoral? Not at all, but assuredly gone. The sibilant *s*'s the aspirate *f*'s and *wh*'s, and the lingering *l*'s create a mood that the bellowing and goring only briefly interrupt, for the spring *is* sweet, and the wheels of the harvesting machines and the railroad cars sweep through the prairie contentedly. Lindsay's point is to note the transition and loss and savor the memory, but not to hope for restoration.

LEGACY

Lindsay was an optimist, aware of history as creator as well as destroyer. His poetry urges the reader/hearer to hear and read: to know how we sound, where we came from, and "what to make of a diminished thing," that is, our future. When Frost used that phrase in "Oven Bird," he preceded it with "the highway dust is over all"; Frost, too, had "tramped" the American countryside in isolation and even despair. Frost and Lindsay represent different views of American culture, Frost so subtle and indirect, Lindsay so brassy; Frost so New England, Lindsay so plain; Frost so academically ironic, Lindsay so insistently proletarian. Lindsay exercised his power by singing, Frost be reflecting, but the two believed in a moral life, in which the poet's power to distinguish between what appears to be and what is, was supremely important.

OTHER MAJOR WORKS

SHORT FICTION: *The Golden Book of Springfield*, 1920.

NONFICTION: *Adventures While Preaching the Gospel of Beauty*, 1914; *The Art of the Moving Picture*, 1915; *A Handy Guide for Beggars*, 1916; *The Litany of Washington Street*, 1929; *Letters of Vachel Lindsay*, 1979 (Marc Chénetier, editor).

MISCELLANEOUS: *Adventures: Rhymes and Designs*, 1968 (Robert Sayre, editor).

BIBLIOGRAPHY

Chénetier, Marc, ed. *Letters of Vachel Lindsay*. New York: Burt Franklin, 1979. Chénetier's fine introduction focuses on Lindsay's vision of himself as a prophet leading the masses to an understanding of America and American art. Lindsay emerges not as a character from a modern folktale but as a serious thinker and scholar. The foreword is by Lindsay's son, Nicholas.

Engler, Balz. *Poetry and Community*. Tübingen, Germany: Stauffenburg, 1990. Includes bibliographical references and index.

Flanagan, John T., ed. *Profile of Vachel Lindsay*. Columbus, Ohio: Charles E. Merrill, 1970. This collection of essays deals with Lindsay's life and work. The essays are grouped into three approaches: reactions of critics during Lindsay's lifetime, reactions immediately after his death, and specialized critical articles written during the 1950's and 1960's. The book contains a chronology of the poet's life.

Hallwas, John E., and Dennis J. Reader, eds. *The Vision of This Land: Studies of Vachel Lindsay, Edgar Lee Masters, and Carl Sandburg*. Macomb: Western Illinois University Essays in Literature, 1976. Comparative analysis of these poets and their midwestern sense of place. Bibliography.

Harris, Mark. *City of Discontent: An Interpretive Biography of Vachel Lindsay, Being Also the Story of Springfield, Illinois, U.S.A.* Urbana: University of Illinois Press, 1992. Originally published in 1952, a novelistic biography of the poet well worth its insights, if somewhat romanticized. Harris's sympathetic interpretation deserves attention.

Massa, Ann. *Vachel Lindsay: Fieldworker for the American Dream*. Bloomington: Indiana University Press, 1970. Attempts to take all Lindsay's writings—poetry, prose, short stories, and articles—and describe their basic underlying philosophy. Explores Lindsay's life and his career as a public performer in the context of American thought at the time. Contains illustrations, including drawings by Lindsay, and a brief bibliography.

Masters, Edgar Lee. *Vachel Lindsay: A Poet in America*. New York: Charles Scribner's Sons, 1935. Masters was himself a poet and a longtime friend of Lindsay, and he wrote this biography only a few years after Lindsay's death, at the request of Lindsay's widow. In spite of several factual errors, this is an important critical study.

Ruggles, Eleanor. *The West-Going Heart: A Life of Vachel Lindsay*. New York: W. W. Norton, 1959. This frankly admiring but quite accurate biography presents Lindsay as something of an American legend, a larger-than-life figure in the tradition of Johnny Appleseed. Excerpts from the poems are used to illustrate Lindsay's life and ideas, but are not critically analyzed. Sixteen photographs are included.

Weston, Mildred. *Vachel Lindsay: Poet in Exile*. Fairfield, Wash.: Ye Galleon Press, 1995. Poet Weston provides her insights into Lindsay and his work.

Yatron, Michael. *America's Literary Revolt*. Reprint. Freeport, N.Y.: Books for Libraries Press, 1969. In addition to Lindsay, includes analysis of Edgar Lee Masters and Carl Sandburg, with whom he is often associated. Bibliographical references.

John Chapman Ward;
bibliography updated by the editors

THOMAS LODGE

Born: London(?), England; 1558(?)
Died: London, England; September, 1625

PRINCIPAL POETRY

Scillaes Metamorphosis, 1589
Phillis, 1593
A Fig for Momus, 1595
The Complete Works of Thomas Lodge, 1883 (4 volumes; Sir Edmund Gosse, editor)

OTHER LITERARY FORMS

Thomas Lodge wrote widely in genres other than poetry. His first prose work was *A Reply to Gosson* (1580), an answer to Stephen Gosson's *School of Abuse* (1579). His prose romances include *The Delectable Historie of Forbonius and Prisceria* (1584), *Rosalynde: Or, Euphues*

Golden Legacy (1590), *Euphues Shadow* (1592), and *A Margarite of America* (1596). Other prose works encompass miscellaneous subject matter: a biography, *The Famous, True, and Historicall Life of Robert Second Duke of Normandy* (1591); an invective in dialogue form, *Catharos* (1591); and a historical narrative, *The Life and Death of William Long Beard* (1593). *An Alarum Against Usurers* (1584), an exposé of contemporary money lenders, has the strong moral message of *A Looking Glass for London and England* (pr. 1588-1589), the play that Lodge wrote with Robert Greene. In about 1586, *The Wounds of Civill War*, another play he had written, was produced. His pamphlets on philosophical and religious topics include *The Divel Conjured* (1596), *Prosopopeia* (1596), and *Wits Miserie and The Worlds Madnesse* (1596). His later works are translations (*The Flowers of Lodowicke of Granado*, 1601; *The Famous and Memorable Workes of Josephus*, 1602; *The Workes of Lucius Annaeus Seneca*, 1614; *A Learned Summary upon the Famous Poeme of William of Saluste, Lord of Bartas*, 1625) and medical works (*A Treatise of the Plague*, 1603; *The Poore Mans Talentt*, 1621).

ACHIEVEMENTS

Thomas Lodge's poetry displays a facility in versification that, by itself, would mark him as a poetic talent. His experiments with verse forms—quatrains and couplets in *Scillaes Metamorphosis*; sonnets of ten to thirty-two lines ranging from tetrameters to hexameters in the poems appended to *Scillaes Metamorphosis*; poems mixing long and short lines in the miscellanies; and iambic pentameter couplets in the satires—show him to be much concerned with the craft of poetry, even when his experiments are not successful. He shows the same eagerness in trying new types of poems and subject matter, and his works range from sonnets to verse epistles, complaints, satires, eclogues, lyrics, and Ovidian narrative. His debt to the Romans in his verse epistles, satires, and Ovidian narrative is one that later writers also incurred, and Lodge to a great extent introduced these literary forms into English. Not all of his works are equally successful, and his facility at versification and image-making sometimes produces trivial or precious poems; nevertheless, he did point the way to later poetic development in English literature.

BIOGRAPHY

Thomas Lodge's biography is sketchy. The existing evidence prompted early biographers to portray him as a dissolute rake—disinherited by his family and jailed for debts—but more recent writers have been kinder. While his mother was apparently worried about Lodge's stability, she also favored him in her will above her other sons. Furthermore, even though there are ample records of suits and countersuits involving Lodge and various creditors, some of his problems seem to have been caused by naïveté, such as neglecting to get receipts and then being sued for ostensibly unpaid debts.

Lodge was born probably in 1558, since on taking his bachelor's degree in 1577 he would most likely have been eighteen or nineteen. Moreover, in a lawsuit with his brother William in 1594, he lists his age as being about thirty-six. In *A Treatise on the Plague*, he talks about London as if it were his birthplace, and presumably it was. His father was a prosperous grocer who became city alderman and, in 1562, Lord Mayor of London. As a child, Thomas Lodge may have been a page in the household of Henry Stanley, fourth Earl of Derby: *A Fig for Momus* opens with a dedication to Stanley's son, William, and reminds him of the time his "noble father in mine infancie . . . incorporated me into your house." If this reference is to a lengthy period of time spent in Stanley's household, he surely would have met the famous people of his day and acquired the attributes—and education—of a gentleman.

Lodge's affluence, however, was not to continue. By the time his father had finished his term as Lord Mayor he declared bankruptcy, a victim of financial problems caused by England's war with France and the 1563 outbreak of the plague. When Thomas Lodge entered the Merchant Taylor's School in 1571, he was one of a group of students who were admitted as the sons of poor men, paying reduced tuition. In 1573, Lodge entered Trinity College, Oxford. After taking his degree, he entered the Inns of Court in 1578.

His relationship with his parents at this period is problematical. When his father died in 1584, Thomas Lodge was not mentioned in his will. By this time Lodge had written pamphlets—his *A Reply to Gosson*—and perhaps had converted to Catholicism. Trinity College, which had been founded during Mary's reign, still reflected strong Catholic influences, and Lincoln's Inn also had strong Catholic affinities, numbering among its members many recusants. In 1581, Lodge had been called before the Privy Council to answer charges, perhaps stemming from his religion. His literary activity and new religion might have displeased his father enough to cause him to disinherit his son; on the other hand, his mother's will, made in 1579, had already left him a large estate, which perhaps accounts for his father's reluctance to leave him any more. Yet even his mother's intentions are open to speculation. She stipulated that Lodge was not to receive his bequest until he was twenty-five, prompting some biographers to believe that she doubted her son's stability. She also included a proviso that Lodge would receive a yearly allowance only if he stayed at Lincoln's Inn and conducted himself "as a good student ought to do." If his behavior displeased her executors, they were to distribute his bequest among her other sons; Lady Anne seems to have felt the need to exercise special control over this particular son. Early biographers tended to see Lodge at this period as a profligate and debt-ridden young man. This view, however, is based partly on Gosson's attack on Lodge's character, which is hardly a credible source. Lodge's youthful degeneracy seems to have been exaggerated in early accounts of his life.

Sometime between 1585 and 1588, Lodge made a sea voyage, a venture he was to repeat in 1591 with Sir Thomas Cavendish. This latter voyage shows the perils to which the Elizabethan sense of adventure could lead: The expedition was plagued with bad weather, a mutinous crew, and widespread disease. Throughout his life, Lodge had published regularly, no matter what he did on a day-to-day basis; in 1597, however, he turned to the study of medicine and from then on produced only translations or works on medicine. He took his medical degree from the University of Avignon and probably practiced for a while in Belgium. He later returned to England and, in 1602, had his degree from Avignon registered at Oxford, a formality that would, perhaps, have attracted English clients. During the plague of 1603, Lodge worked tirelessly, even publishing a treatise on the disease with the intent of discrediting quack doctors who were profiting from people's fear and ignorance.

In 1604 Lodge married the widow of an Elizabethan spy who had formerly been a Catholic working for the Pope. Although this man eventually became an atheist, his wife remained loyal to her religion, receiving a pension from Gregory XIII. Lodge's marriage to her—along with his own earlier conversion—apparently brought him under suspicion by the government, and the Royal College of Physicians denied him permission to practice in London. By 1605, Lodge was again practicing in Belgium. Finally, with the help of the English ambassador to France, he was allowed to return to England and, in 1610, entered the Royal College of Physicians. The plague again swept through London in 1625 and Lodge was made plague-surgeon. He died in 1625, presumably a victim of that disease.

In many ways Lodge's life exemplifies the variety of experience that a Renaissance man might have. While born to wealth, he was often involved in litigation over debts, whether incurred through real want or only through carelessness. A writer of delicate sonnets, he was also an adventurer who undertook two sea voyages. Although he was not persecuted for his religion as actively as some, his fortunes still rose and fell as his beliefs changed. Finally, the rather heedless young man acquired over the years a moral depth that caused him to work assiduously as a doctor throughout the plague years while others were fleeing London.

ANALYSIS

Perhaps Thomas Lodge's most famous work is the prose romance *Rosalynde*, the source for William Shakespeare's *As You Like It* (1590-1600) and a lively piece of writing by itself. While the prose narrative of *Rosalynde* lies outside the bounds of this analysis, it does contain lyrical poems that, for their excellence, rival the best of Lodge's work. Their beauty was appreciated by Lodge's contemporaries, and many reappeared in *England's Helicon* (1600). Containing simple and even homely images and language, they explore the paradoxes of the Petrarchan lover without being excessive; as usual, Lodge is a master of metrics and many of these lyrics are presented as songs. "Rosalynds Madrigal" is an especially good example of Lodge's success as a lyricist. The poem alternates long and short lines in the first quatrain of each stanza; the stanzas close with four consecutive rhyming lines and a final line which may or may not rhyme with one of the lines in the first or second quatrain. Lodge's craftsmanship is evident in the way he can alternate long and short lines and use intermittently rhyming final stanza lines to achieve a musical effect. The homely images—love builds a "neast" in Rosalynd's eyes—also give the poem a certain lightness of tone. Many of the poems he wrote for the miscellanies show the same light touch and metrical skill:

> My bonnie Lasse thine eie,
> So slie,
> Hath made me sorrow so:
> Thy Crimsen cheekes my deere,
> So cleere,
> Hath so much wrought my woe.

PHILLIS

When Lodge's lyrics fail they do so because they lack lightness and are not really profound enough to carry their serious, heavy tone; often they simply catalog the complaints of the Petrarchan lover and use balanced euphuistic lines to achieve a stately emphasis. Such emphasis seems misplaced, however, since the situations Lodge describes are often derivative. The sonnets in *Phillis* vary in quality. Some of them have the light touch of *Rosalynde*, although even in these Lodge is not consistent. Sonnet XIII opens by comparing Cupid to a bee: "If I approach he forward skippes,/ And if I kisse he stingeth me." The images describing love become more conventional as he goes along—tears, fire—and the poem ends with a conventional statement of constancy: "But if thou do not loue, Ile trulye serue hir,/ In spight of thee, by firme faith deserue hir." Sonnet XXXVII, containing heavy hexameter lines, lacks even the intermittently light tone of Sonnet XIII.

The *Phillis* sequence closes with a long medieval complaint, "The Complaint of Elstred." While hardly an inspired poem, it does show Lodge's affinities with pre-Renaissance verse. "Truth's Complaint over England" is also medieval in feeling and recounts Truth's lament over the condition of Lodge's England. Lodge's concept of satire seems mixed in his early works. "Truth's Complaint over England" achieves its social criticism through moralizing sentiments reminiscent of medieval complaint; Lodge's *A Reply to Gosson*, however, seems to show an awareness of different satiric possibilities. Confusing the etymology of *satire* and *satyr*—as most Renaissance writers did—Lodge gives a history of drama in which he asserts that tragedy evolved from satyr plays. The widely accepted Renaissance belief was that these plays allowed the playwright to scourge his audiences for their vices by having a satyr denounce them. In this way English writers came to think of satire as a harsh, uncouth form: Juvenal as opposed to the more urbane Horace. Lodge himself follows *Scillaes Metamorphosis* by a poem titled "The Discontented Satyr," a paean to discontent, the best emotion one can feel in a corrupt age.

A FIG FOR MOMUS

By the time he wrote *A Fig for Momus*, Lodge seems to have adopted this harsher Juvenalian mode of satire. This series of poems opens with a satire of flatterers and hypocrites, and Lodge is at his best in the imaginary characters and situations he evokes. Meeting an innkeeper with "a silken night-cap on his hed," the narrator is told that the man has had "An ague this two months." The narrator comments sardonically that "I let him passe: and laught to heare his skuce:/ For I knew well, he had the poxe by Luce." Lodge's second satire—incorrectly labeled the third—urges parents to set good examples for their children. The piece owes a special debt to Juvenal's Satire XIV on the same subject, and, if much of it seems simply moral preaching, the sheer number of vices which he catalogs keeps the poem moving. Perhaps Lodge's fourth satire offers his most memorable and bitter character study: a miser, old and decrepit, but still concerned with amassing a greater fortune. The gruesomely realistic description of the man shows Lodge at his best. His fifth satire opens with a paraphrase of Juvenal's Satire X, although his debt to Horace is also apparent in his description of the contented life. If this satire is less bitter and harsh than his others, it is perhaps because of the influence of Horace. In addition to introducing Juvenal into English literature, Lodge made one other lasting contribution to English satire: He was the first to use the epigrammatic pentameter couplet.

If *A Fig for Momus* does not seem, as a whole, the bitter invective that the satiric elements might lead one to expect, it is because Lodge has interspersed other genres: eclogues and verse epistles. His eclogues offer little new to English literature—Alexander Barclay, Barnabe Googe, Edmund Spenser, and Michael Drayton had already worked in this form—and their general theme of human corruption is not developed in an interesting way. Furthermore, their poetry, compared to Spenser's masterpiece in this genre, is noticeably deficient. Lodge's verse epistles, however, were the first to appear in English and, although they are uneven, the best of them have a lightness and wit that are typical of Lodge. The epistle "To his Mistress A. L." opens with a buildup in the first two lines which the following ones humorously deflate: "In that same month wherein the spring begins,/ And on that day when Phoebe left the twinnes/ (Which was on Saturday, the Twelfth of March)/ Your servant brought a letter seal'd with starch." The letter turns out to be a request for information on how to lose weight and the epistle cites various learned authorities on the subject, concluding that it is better to be "fat, slicke, faire" than "leane, lancke, spare." The epistle titled "In praise of his Mistris dogge" opens wittily enough with a request that his mistress "for a night . . . grant me Pretties place," and then proceeds to a canine history, ending with a pun: "Thus for your dog, my doggerell rime hath runne."

SCILLAES METAMORPHOSIS

If Lodge introduced the verse epistle into English, he was also one of the first to write Ovidian narrative, a literary type that would later appear in Christopher Marlowe's *Hero and Leander* (1598), Shakespeare's *Venus and Adonis* (1593), Drayton's *Endimion and Phoebe* (1595), and John Marston's *The Metamorphosis of Pygmalion's Image and Certain Satires* (1598). Ovid had, of course, been known before Lodge: Arthur Golding's translation of the *Metamorphosis* (1567) was a standard Elizabethan treatment of the Roman poet. Yet Golding allegorizes Ovid to make his eroticism acceptable; Lodge is far from finding any allegory in his source.

Scillaes Metamorphosis is noteworthy for its elaborate images and conceits: Lodge has taken Ovid's 143 lines and expanded them to nearly eight hundred. To the original story of Glaucus's love for the disdainful Scilla, Lodge adds an opening frame story in which the narrator, also a rejected lover, walks along the shore "Weeping my wants, and wailing scant reliefe." Finally he meets

Glaucus, the sea god, and hears his story. As Glaucus recounts Scilla's disdain to a group of nymphs, Venus appears with Cupid. Cupid cures Glaucus's lovesickness with an arrow and then shoots Scilla, who immediately falls in love with Glaucus, who now rejects her. Knowing her case to be hopeless, Scilla finally curses all men, whereupon she is beset by the personifications *Furie, Rage, Wan-hope, Dispair,* and *Woe,* who transform her into a flinty isle.

If one could sum up Lodge's handling of Ovid in one word, it would be *embroidery.* Whenever he can stop for a lengthy and sensuous description, he does. Some of these are very successful, such as the description of Venus after she has found the wounded Adonis: It ends with Lodge's touching lines "How on his senseless corpes she lay a crying,/ As if the boy were then but new a dying." The story of Venus and Adonis itself shows Lodge's leisurely narrative pace, since it is interpolated in the main story of Glaucus. Glaucus's description of Scilla is also leisurely and sensuous. Ovid simply says that she was *sine vestibus* when Glaucus saw her; Lodge's Glaucus minutely recounts her physical beauty, dwelling on her hair, cheeks, nose, lips, neck, breasts, and arms.

The flaws in Lodge's poem—and it is by no means of uniform quality—have to do in part with this massing of description and detail. Lodge does not seem to have any awareness that his poem cannot sustain the same high pitch stanza after stanza: Glaucus's laments, for example, all begin to sound alike. Lodge has partially dealt with this problem in the frame story at the beginning of the poem, the very place where the reader is unlikely to need a rest from the high pitch of the poem. Nevertheless, Lodge does offer an interesting double perspective on Glaucus that the rest of the poem might have done well to develop. After the narrator spends four stanzas crying and groaning over an unrequited love, Glaucus appears and berates the narrator's love-sickness in stanzas that almost bristle with moral advice. After counseling the narrator, however, Glaucus falls into exactly the same error and even faints while describing his own hopeless love. This humorous contradiction between Glaucus's words and actions lends an ironic perspective to the story which the rest of the poem does not explore. Indeed, the personifications from medieval allegory who transform Scilla seem totally out of place in Lodge's poem, as if he had not really decided what the dominant tone of Ovidian narrative should be.

His verse form is also ill-chosen, although he does the best he can with it. Composed of stanzas consisting of a quatrain (*abab*) and a couplet (*cc*), the poem has difficulty moving forward: The couplets are always stopping the flow of action. In one sense this hardly matters, since Lodge is more concerned with leisurely description than with fast-paced narrative action. The poem, nevertheless, is a narrative, however leisurely, and the recurring couplets do present a problem. Lodge almost seems to feel that this is so and usually manages to begin a new clause as the couplet begins, avoiding at least the awkwardness of the self-contained couplet having to continue the lines before it.

Hardly any of Lodge's long poems are unqualified successes, although they all have striking passages and show much facility of versification. That he was an experimenter is evident in the number of new poetic forms he introduced into English; experimenters cannot always produce perfect products. Nevertheless, music and lightness of tone mark many of Lodge's best works and make him a considerable figure in the development of Renaissance poetry.

OTHER MAJOR WORKS

LONG FICTION: *The Delectable Historie of Forbonius and Prisceria*, 1584; *Rosalynde: Or, Euphues Golden Legacy*, 1590; *Euphues Shadow*, 1592; *A Margarite of America*, 1596.

PLAYS: *The Wounds of Civill War*, pr. c. 1586, pb. 1594; *A Looking Glass for London and England*, pr. c. 1588-1589, pb. 1594 (with Robert Greene)

NONFICTION: *A Reply to Gosson*, 1580; *An Alarum Against Usurers*, 1584; *The Famous, True, and Historicall Life of Robert Second Duke of Normandy*, 1591; *Catharos*, 1591; *The Life and Death of William Long Beard*, 1593; *The Divel Conjured*, 1596; *Prosopopeia*, 1596; *Wits Miserie and the Worlds Madnesse*, 1596; *A Treatise of the Plague*, 1603; *The Poore Mans Talentt*, 1621.

TRANSLATIONS: *The Flowers of Lodowicke of Granado*, 1601; *The Famous and Memorable Workes of Josephus*, 1602; *The Workes of Lucius Annaeus Seneca*, 1614; *A Learned Summary upon the Famous Poeme of William of Saluste, Lord of Bartas*, 1625.

BIBLIOGRAPHY

Alexander, Nigel, ed. *Elizabethan Narrative Verse*. Cambridge, Mass.: Harvard University Press, 1968. Besides collecting eleven of the most important verse narratives, Alexander prefaces them with a twenty-six-page introduction that establishes the Ovidian background of these poems and comments on them individually. Contains interpretative and documentary notes, as well as a useful bibliography.

Conlon, Raymond, "Lodge's Rosalind." *The Explicator* 50, no. 1 (Fall, 1991): 7. Lodge's pastoral romance "Rosalind" is examined. Two sacrificial scenes in which Adam Spencer plays the dual role of nourisher and liberator of Rosader are discussed as part of a pattern in which the functions of the servant have symbolic importance.

Donno, Elizabeth Story. "The Epyllion." In *English Poetry and Prose, 1540-1674*, edited by Christopher Ricks. New York: Peter Bedrick Books, 1986. A leading authority on Elizabethan narrative poetry. Donno illuminates the conventions and qualities which characterize the forms. Places Lodge clearly against his cultural background. The thorough index demonstrates Lodge's manifold activities, and the bibliography covers all major works.

Hulse, Clark. *Metamorphic Verse: The Elizabethan Minor Epic*. Princeton, N.J.: Princeton University Press, 1981. Hulse's book is the modern authoritative study of the minor epic genre. Covers the field thoroughly, although much of the material is technical and sophisticated. The bibliography and index are complete.

Lodge, Thomas. *Rosalind: Euphues' Golden Legacy Found After His Death in His Cell Silexedra (1590)*. Edited by Donald Beecher. Ottawa: Dovehouse Editions, 1997. Beecher provides an informative introduction. Bibliographical references, index.

Muir, Kenneth. *Introduction to Elizabethan Literature*. New York: Random House, 1967. Muir is a major literary historian with unrivaled knowledge of this period. As a result, his commentaries are unusually insightful and learned. He brings out clearly Lodge's diverse interests and accomplishments. The bibliography, though dated, is useful; the notes and index offer significant help.

Ostriker, Alicia, and Leslie Dunn. "The Lyric." In *English Poetry and Prose, 1540-1674*, edited by Christopher Ricks. New York: Peter Bedrick Books, 1986. Ostriker and Dunn divide the field here, the former taking verse written independently, the latter lyrics written for music—a division first made during the Elizabethan period. Lodge is covered in both categories. The index demonstrates more of his diversity, and the bibliography collects the primary sources.

Rae, Wesley D. *Thomas Lodge*. New York: Twayne, 1967. Reprint. Irving Publishers, 1996. This 128-page book covers all aspects of Lodge's diverse activities, bringing them together in a common light—which does not often happen. It approaches Lodge's work chronologically, showing how his life sheds light on the writings. Includes a chronology, notes and references, an index, and a dated select bibliography.

Sisson, Charles J., ed. *Thomas Lodge and Other Elizabethans*. 1933. Reprint. London: Frank Cass, 1966. This volume collects five biographical studies, of which Sisson's, on Lodge, comprises more than 150 pages. The discussion devotes chapters to Lodge's father, his brothers, and Lodge himself, through painstaking reference to contemporary documents. A geneological chart of the Lodge family is appended.

Stagg, Louis Charles. *The Figurative Language of the Tragedies of Shakespeare's Chief Sixteenth-Century Contemporaries: Christopher Marlowe, Thomas Kyd, George Peele, Thomas Lodge, Samuel Daniel, Countess of Pembroke/Robert Garnier, Thomas Preston, Thomas Sackville and Thomas Norton, Robert Wilmot/ Inner Temple, Robert Greene, George Gascoigne/ Francis Kinwelmersh/Christopher Yelverton, Thomas Hughes, and Anonymous Authors of Shakespeare Apocrypha: An Index*. New York: Garland, 1984. This tome of more than one thousand pages serves scholars interested in the language of the plays, poetry, and other works of these Elizabethan authors. A standard reference.

Tenney, Edward Andrews. *Thomas Lodge*. Ithaca, N.Y.: Cornell University Press, 1935. Another biography of Lodge, this one supplements and updates that by Sisson.

Walker, Alice. *Life of Thomas Lodge*. London: Sidgwick and Jackson, 1933. A classic, if brief (33-page), biography.

Carole Moses;
bibliography updated by the editors

JOHN LOGAN

Born: Red Oak, Iowa; January 23, 1923
Died: San Francisco, California; November 6, 1987

PRINCIPAL POETRY

Cycle for Mother Cabrini, 1955
Ghosts of the Heart, 1960
Spring of the Thief: Poems, 1963-1968, 1963
The Zig-Zag Walk: Poems, 1963-1968, 1969
The Anonymous Lover, 1973
Poem in Progress, 1975
Aaron Siskind: Photographs/John Logan: Poems, 1976
The Bridge of Change: Poems, 1974-1980, 1979
Only the Dreamer Can Change the Dream, 1981
John Logan: The Collected Poems, 1989

OTHER LITERARY FORMS

Because John Logan's reputation stems from his poetry, his fiction has, for the most part, been overlooked. Logan's most sustained attempt at fiction, *The House That Jack Built: Or, A Portrait of the Artist as a Sad Sensualist* (1984), celebrated the discovery and sheer joy of language. Concerned with the poet's young life, the book offers childhood experiences, relationships, and images which reveal the intellectual and emotional development of Logan's poetic sensibility. Eighteen of Logan's stories, including five previously unpublished, are gathered in *John Logan: The Collected Fiction* (1991). As a teacher and critic, Logan contributed essays, interviews, forewords, and reviews to numerous magazines and books, most of which were collected in *A Ballet for the Ear: Interviews, Essays, and Reviews* (1983), edited by A. Poulin, Jr. This volume demonstrates Logan's wide-ranging scholarship and his dedication to the life of the poet. He explored with enthusiasm and keen insight such contrasting figures as Herman Melville and E. E. Cummings, and he developed provocative explanations for his own writing, his personal poetics, and the work and poetics of many contemporary writers. The passion of Logan's literary life, however, is best understood after hearing the poet read; his performances were often described as "spellbinding." Logan read from his work on a recording from the Watershed Foundation titled *Only the Dreamer Can Change the Dream.*

ACHIEVEMENTS

Often and incorrectly described as a confessional poet (a misnomer in John Logan's vocabulary since good confessional poetry confesses the reader), John Logan was one of the few truly personal poets to come to prominence in the twentieth century. James Wright tells an anecdote which best summarizes Logan's influence:

> I once stopped a fistfight between two of the best living poets I know, and I did it by reading aloud to them a poem by John Logan. . . . He is a genius of love in my lifetime, and, to my mind, one of the three or four masters we have to give to the world.

James Dickey placed Logan's work alongside the poetry of Robert Lowell, and Robert Bly wrote that "John Logan (was) one of the five or six finest poets to emerge in the United States in the last decades." Logan's reputation as a teacher equaled his reputation as a poet, and some of his noteworthy students, including Marvin Bell, have written at length about Logan's "humanistic" workshops. Logan received the Miles Modern Poetry Prize from Wayne State University in 1967, a Rockefeller Foundation grant in 1969, the Morton Dauwen Zabel Award from the National Institute of Arts and Letters in 1973, a Guggenheim Fellowship in 1979, a grant from the National Endowment for the Arts in 1980, and in 1982, three awards: the Robert Hazel Ferguson Award from the Friends of Literature in Chicago, the Lenore

John Logan (© Michael Nicholson/Corbis)

Marshall Poetry Prize, and the William Carlos Williams Prize from Ecco Press. He served as poetry editor for both *The Nation* and *Critic*, and he was also the founder and editor of *Choice*, a magazine of poetry and photography.

BIOGRAPHY

The speaker in John Logan's poetry is a wanderer, due, in part, to Logan's belief that poets are constant, spiritual travelers, but also because Logan's life could not be identified with any one particular place. The outward search for home, a place of rest, combined with Logan's inward search, gives the poems their universal appeal.

Logan was graduated magna cum laude from Coe College in 1943 with a degree in biology. In 1945, he married; it was a union that produced nine children but that finally ended in divorce. He received his M.A. in English in 1949 from the State University of Iowa, and in the years following, he did occasional graduate work in philosophy at Georgetown University and the University of Notre Dame. Beginning in 1947 and proceeding chronologically, Logan taught at St. John's College in Maryland, Notre Dame, St. Mary's College in California, the University of Washington, San Francisco State College, and, from 1966 until 1985, the State University of New York at Buffalo. Logan served as resident writer for countless poetry workshops and colonies, and because of his popular and distinctive reading style, he maintained a busy schedule of public appearances.

Logan was reared as a Protestant but converted to Catholicism after his marriage. His early work reflects a clear and strong religious orientation that takes the Christian God very seriously. After the early books, however, religious allusions eventually disappear, and only in a few later poems did Logan return to religious themes. He died of a heart ailment and complications from gall bladder surgery in San Francisco, California, on November 6, 1987.

ANALYSIS

Despite winning critical acclaim and the respect of his peers, Logan never enjoyed a wide readership. The reasons are many, but most important is the fact that, like Walt Whitman, Logan was an intensely personal poet who demanded an ultimate commitment from his reader. Logan's poetry transcends the ordinary form of things and transforms those things into something more real, more useful, than conventional reality. Consequently, the reader of a Logan poem cannot in any way remain passive; instead, he must confront the shadow or inarticulate counterself that exists within. Logan's commitment to this type of self-searching was absolute, and while such intensity may alienate some readers, his insistent demands lend power, depth, and psychological complexity to the poems. At his best, Logan explored the inner self without moral judgment, conceit, sentimentalism, or self-pity. Instead, he uncovered what at first seems threatening and perhaps grotesque in order to reveal what is finally beautiful in all living things.

John Logan built a personal poetry from his own obsessions: grace, the search for more than anonymous love, the friend or lover as rescuer, the father-son relationship, death, and poetry as rebirth.

"POEM FOR MY BROTHER"

"Poem for My Brother," a characteristic Logan poem, dramatizes the desire for acceptance and reconciliation between brothers that have grown apart. The younger of the two feels intimidated—or at least awkward—around his more athletic elder sibling and wants desperately to identify with him. This sense of physical and emotional alienation pervades Logan's poetry, paralleling a similar alienation in his career as a writer.

In "Poem for My Brother," Logan explained the many differences between the poet and his elder brother, but always with a desire for identification. The contrasts between the two remain sharp (as illustrated by the brothers' colors, blue and brown), and this is what gives the poem its natural power. A capsulized history of the color blue included in the poem explains that many societies still do not have a word other than "dark" for this "last of the primary colors to be named." "It's associated with black. . . ." Blue, for Logan, represented the *other*, the society of *other lovers* to which Logan sought admission—a place where, had he gained access, he would not have stayed. Logan realized that the redemption and grace of being accepted and forgiven is only temporary since any person soon finds himself alone again as he began, arguing only with himself, and being accountable, in the final analysis, only to himself. The tension between desire for the *other* and the knowledge that the consequent redemption is only temporary fuels much of Logan's poetry.

GRACE THROUGH RESCUE

Grace, by Logan's assessment, is the escape from anxiety through supernatural means—the sacraments and divine redemption—or through natural means: art and love. Logan's need for forgiveness and its subsequent grace motivated his outward and inward search, and his poems often showed that such rare and precious gifts are not easily won. Indeed, implicit in Logan's poetry was the necessity for taking risks. Even in the early *Cycle for Mother Cabrini*, Logan charged his poems with a nervous energy that thrives on the anticipation of danger. At the same time, the volume overflows with classical allusions, establishing Logan as an extension of the poetic tradition that he revered. He carried on "The Lives of the Poet," the first poem in *Ghosts of the Heart*, both figuratively and literally; that is, the book begins a tradition of poems celebrating the lives of other poets, Arthur Rimbaud and Lord Byron, that continues with E. E. Cummings, John Keats, James Joyce, and Dylan Thomas, to name only a few, through several of the other books. These homages, tributes, and elegies not only reassert the presence of literary figures in the reader's consciousness, but they often reveal a great deal about Logan's feelings and position as a poet.

Spring of the Thief deals primarily with the need for spiritual and physical change through imagination or uncanny transformation: the dread of stagnation suddenly transformed by new realization. This theme, however, does not fully mature until *The Zig-Zag Walk*. Although rich with translations of Georg Trakl and Tibor Tollas, the tone of *The Zig-Zag Walk* is more informal and the poetry less academic. Here Logan freed himself to explore personal relationships without the encumbrance of a superimposed poetic structure. Love becomes the central meaning of life, and it is love that saves the poet from his own self-destruction: " . . . as you reached for me/ . . . it was my self you hauled/ back from my despair." These lines from "The Rescue" resonate with lines from several poems, including the "Medicine Bow," in which the poet, shaking and losing his energy, is shocked back into life when he brings a handful of snow to his mouth. Such rescues always occur when the poet was on the edge, and, by their somber moods and continuing recurrence, the reader understands the transience of both rescue and relief.

Not until *The Anonymous Lover* is there any realization that the poet is also responsible for himself, that he is capable of self-rescue (as dramatized in "Medicine Bow"), and that he, indeed, must find or build his own refuge. In *Poem in Progress* (first published as a chapbook and then reprinted in *The Bridge of Change*), Logan managed to transcend many of the limitations that his younger obsessions seem to embody. He took up with authority the wealth he has learned and constructs the world of his imagination (his fear of death and the desire for rebirth) around an in-depth study of the father-son relationship.

POEM IN PROGRESS

Throughout *Poem in Progress*, the poet appeared variously as friend, brother, son, father (teacher), and lover, recapitulating many of the roles already estab-

lished in Logan's poetry. (When Logan shifted his role, companions would change their position as well. In "Lines for Michael in the Picture" from *The Zig-Zag Walk:* " . . . that transforming island fire/ that seems to fade in your eyes in the picture./ It makes you brother, friend, son, father.") From the poet's shifting viewpoint, *Poem in Progress* explores a series of personal relationships which, to some degree, originate in erotic attraction creating homoerotic overtones and suggesting incestuous fantasies. Some critics have made much of the text's "atmosphere" and have dwelled unnecessarily on what appear to be unfulfilled homoerotic confrontations. The characters in any one situation are of no importance to the total effect of the poem since love is fulfillment, even redemption, and love is not preferential about partners: "love in Plato's 'Phaedrus' is not thus: the need of man/ for woman, or of man for man, woman for woman;/ instead, it is the love that will be felt as fulfill-/ ment." Love that relieves human anxiety cannot be limited by predetermined judgments and prejudices. It must be accepted when offered and appreciated, for, as Logan knows all too well, its effects will not last.

Here, as in most of Logan's work, the poet was on an endless journey or search for the means to achieve grace. Moments of love and acceptance offer only brief respite from the continuing frustration of grace that eludes. For example, the poet in "IV Rescue in Florida: The Friend," feeling insecure and childlike before a reading, takes strength from a stranger sitting in the audience. This unknown person will soon receive the poet's love, and so, for that moment, the poet is not isolated or *anonymous*. The stranger, again, performs a temporary rescue.

The word *anonymous* recurs several times in *Poem in Progress*, and working at the center of this one-word refrain is Pablo Neruda's idea that poetry is "an exchange between strangers," a token of thanks, perhaps, for what is given unknowingly. For example, the young lovers in section five give the poet a wooden figurine in thanks for what his poetry has given them. This gesture is unexpected, and the poet as traveler identifies with the figure of the old Colombian man, sack over his back, with "fifty-year-old-hands." Yet, more than merely identification, the gesture of the gift returns to the poet some of what he has given: " . . . the breath/ he as breathed into it—or it has blown inside him—/ is given back again." Once more, Logan dramatized the respite from the search, the rest in the middle of the journey.

Art, however, like love, offers only a temporary rest, and the friends, sons, brothers, students, and lovers who rescued Logan from time to time on his journey could not offer what the poet ultimately sought—a permanent state of grace. Like Edgar Allan Poe, Logan was frequently subject to spiritual vertigo; just as Poe feared chaos and entropy, feared falling into the maelstrom or being sucked into the whirlpool, so Logan feared the ultimate falling away of his gifts and powers. This fear is evident in Logan's images of his youthful sons and friends—godlike and indestructible—and the poet's own admissions, even guilt, over his slowly diminishing powers: "(. . . but my Greek is no longer sure)." What saves Logan's poetry at this level is that the narrator is not morose about his insecurities and fears. His offhand comments about his slipping abilities and his celebration of youth and confidence come as the natural components of Logan's total embrace. *Poem in Progress* portrays the lost, searching, sometimes fragile poet at odds with the various roles thrust upon him, but a poet nonetheless reveling in a sea of anonymous lovers provided by the Mardi Gras where the heat of the sculptor's kiln consumes the outer coverings of both the poet and his friends leaving them "stark naked there as for making love or art."

LATER WORKS

"Believe It," the last poem in *The Bridge of Change*, is all at once a celebration of life's diversity and absurdity, an acknowledgment of fear concerning the loss of power and ability, the reassertion of the poet as a lifelong and constant traveler, and, finally, the reaffirmation of life and giving—an invitation to all the anonymous lovers that they are free to come and partake of the poet's joys.

OTHER MAJOR WORKS

LONG FICTION: *The House That Jack Built: Or, A Portrait of the Artist as a Sad Sensualist*, 1984.

SHORT FICTION: *John Logan: The Collected Fiction*, 1991.

NONFICTION: *A Ballet for the Ear: Interviews, Essays, and Reviews*, 1983.

BIBLIOGRAPHY

Chaplin, William. "Identity and Spirit in the Recent Poetry of John Logan." *The American Poetry Review* 2 (May/June, 1973): 19-24. Chapman does not attempt to validate specific events and places in Logan's poetry; instead, he asserts that everything worth knowing is in the poems themselves. As a result, he examines the pattern of feelings that emerge from the poems to gain insights into Logan's life and aesthetics. An important analysis that questions the conventional view of Logan's poetry as being confessional.

Dickey, James. *Babel to Byzantium*. New York: Farrar, Straus and Giroux, 1968. A highly personal and enlightening reading of Logan's poetry by an equally impressive novelist and poet. Dickey convincingly argues that Logan is one of the finest American poets ever. He offers important insight into the religions and literary influences that shaped Logan's work.

Hilgers, Thomas, and Michael Molloy. "A Conversation with John Logan." *The Iowa Review* 10 (Spring/Summer, 1980): 221-229. An excellent overview of Logan's life and work as told by the poet himself. Logan discusses the European locales that served as inspirations for many of his works, the influence of Rainer Maria Rilke, and the history behind many of his poems and his prose work, *The House That Jack Built: Or, A Portrait of the Artist as a Sad Sensualist*.

Petrosky, Anthony. "In and Out of John Logan's Workshops." *Ironwood* 15 (Fall, 1987): 97-101. A fascinating and illuminating personal account of Logan as a teacher, a poet, and an acquaintance, based on Petrosky's friendship with him. These recollections are a vivid study of Logan's personality, aesthetics, interests, and tastes. The numerous anecdotes—from Bach concerts to poetry workshops and meetings with other poets—offer valuable insight into Logan and his poetry.

Waters, Michael. *Dissolve to Island: On the Poetry of John Logan*. Houston: Ford-Brown, 1984. This first book-length critical study of Logan's poetry includes essays by Tama Baldwin, Marvin Bell, and Peter Makuck and is supplemented by selected poems. This valuable resource also contains bibliographic and biographical information.

Joseph Coulson

H<small>ENRY</small> W<small>ADSWORTH</small> L<small>ONGFELLOW</small>

Born: Portland, Maine; February 27, 1807
Died: Cambridge, Massachusetts; March 24, 1882

P<small>RINCIPAL POETRY</small>

Voices of the Night, 1839
Ballads and Other Poems, 1841
Poems on Slavery, 1842
The Belfry of Bruges and Other Poems, 1845
Evangeline, 1847
The Seaside and the Fireside, 1850
The Golden Legend, 1851
The Song of Hiawatha, 1855
The Courtship of Miles Standish and Other Poems,
 1858
Tales of a Wayside Inn, 1863
Flower-de-Luce, 1867
The New England Tragedies, 1868
The Divine Tragedy, 1871
Three Books of Song, 1872
Christus: A Mystery, 1872
Aftermath, 1873
The Hanging of the Crane, 1874
The Masque of Pandora and Other Poems, 1875
Kéramos and Other Poems, 1878
Ultima Thule, 1880
In the Harbor, 1882
Michael Angelo, 1883
Longfellow's Boyhood Poems, 1925

O<small>THER LITERARY FORMS</small>

Besides his poetry, Henry Wadsworth Longfellow produced a variety of works, most of them connected with his scholarly duties as professor of modern languages and literature at Bowdoin College (1829-1835) and at Harvard College (1837-1854). He created his own grammars: *Elements of French Grammar* (1830) and *Manuel de Proverbes Dramatiques* (1830). He wrote a series of scholarly articles in linguistics and literature for *The North American Review*, most of them reprinted in his collection, *Drift-Wood* (1857), and several other prose works. *Outre-Mer: A Pilgrimage Beyond the Sea* (1833-1834) was an account of his first European tour;

Hyperion (1839) was an account of his second, highlighted by an autobiographical reshaping of his romance with Fanny Appleton, whom he married three years later. *Kavanagh: A Tale* (1849) was his only attempt at writing a novel. He edited four anthologies of poetry: *The Poets and Poetry of Europe* (1845) contained selections from four hundred poets from ten different countries; *The Waif: A Collection of Poems* (1845) and *The Estray: A Collection of Poems* (1847) gathered together antislavery verses; and the thirty-one volumes of *Poems of Places* (1876-1879), one of the largest anthologies of poetry ever assembled. As the leading American poet of his age, Longfellow carried on a voluminous correspondence, writing more than five thousand letters, many of which have been published as *The Letters of Henry Wadsworth Longfellow* (1966-1974) by Harvard University Press. George T. Little reissued twenty-seven poems written during Longfellow's college days in an edition titled *Longfellow's Boyhood Poems* (1925).

A<small>CHIEVEMENTS</small>

Henry Wadsworth Longfellow was the most popular English-language poet of the nineteenth century. In both England and the United States, volumes of his poetry outsold all other verse and most fiction for nearly fifty years. When he died, more than a million copies of his poetry had been sold. He was granted private audiences with Queen Victoria, honorary degrees from Oxford and Cambridge, and a memorial in the Poets' Corner of Westminster Abbey, a distinction hitherto reserved for only the greatest of England's own poets. In America, a national holiday was proclaimed to celebrate his seventy-fifth birthday. From the late nineteenth century to the mid-twentieth, nearly every school-age child in the United States and most of those in Britain were required to read some of his lines. Apparently, few poets of any age had shown themselves better able to articulate the values, beliefs, and aspirations of their readership. The body of Longfellow's work can be seen as an index to some of the newly industrialized world's deepest self-images. Contemporaries praised "the sentiments of tenderness" in *Hyperion*, admired the "unexaggerated truthfulness" of *Evangeline*, and the "accuracy" of *The Song of Hiawatha*. They extolled the way he "obeyed the highest humanity of the poet's calling" in *The*

Golden Legend and repeatedly singled out the universal appeal of his voice: "force of thought" for the old, "melody" for the young, "piety" for the serious, and a "slight touch of mysticism" for the imaginative.

Longfellow was decidedly the most popular of a concentrated group of American poets that helped shape one another's stylistic response to the demands of such an audience. The group included James Russell Lowell, John Greenleaf Whittier, and William Cullen Bryant, all of whom catered primarily to a mass readership. They have frequently been called "Fireside Poets," meaning that they wrote not by but rather for the family hearth. They specialized in polite, sentimental, and traditional homilies for readers trying desperately to reaffirm some of their oldest and most cherished values during a period of unsettling and apparently chaotic change. Longfellow specifically imagined that each of his lines would be read aloud after dinner around the family circle, with young and old profiting by his every

Henry Wadsworth Longfellow (Library of Congress)

word. For them, he tried to picture a world where an omniscient God was still in control, where the human soul was still immortal, where death remained only "a beginning, not an end," where noble and courageous acts could still affect the outcome of a crisis, where the first duty of all was to sustain their spirituality by concentrating on the good, the beautiful, and the true, and where the duty of poets was to help their readers in this concentration on the sublime.

Longfellow was lionized for supporting these pieties in the nineteenth century and has been largely ignored because of them during much of the twentieth. A literate, scholarly, and compassionate man, Longfellow's verses probably merit neither critical extreme. At his worst, he could write prosaic and long-winded verse which seemed to aim principally at giving his audience the sentimentality they came to demand of him. At his best, he could struggle with his own and his age's doubts forthrightly; he could write movingly of the passing of traditional agrarian society and Christian ideals. Stronger minds than Longfellow's were puzzled by the abrupt changes which industrialization, urbanization, and political revolution had brought to their world. If he remained unsure of the qualities which the new world needed, he articulated with precision those qualities from the old which had been lost. There was an elegiac suppleness in his affirmations which created a tone of frailty and a sense of transience that often contradicted the superficial optimism which his readers demanded of him.

BIOGRAPHY

Henry Wadsworth Longfellow, the second of eight children, was born into an old and distinguished New England family. Stephen Longfellow, his father, was a prominent lawyer who had served as a representative in Congress and who could count among his ancestors New England patriarchs such as Samuel Sewell. His mother, Zilpah, could trace the Wadsworth name back through a Revolutionary War general to seventeenth century Plymouth Puritans such as John Alden. Schooled at the Portland Academy and Bowdoin College, Longfellow finished his formal education in 1825, graduating in a class which included Nathaniel Hawthorne. From the beginning, he had been expected to carry on the traditions of his two family groups: "You must adopt a profession which will afford you subsistence as well as reputation," his father had counseled him just before graduation. During his collegiate years, Longfellow had shown so much aptitude for foreign languages that Bowdoin actually offered him a newly established professorship in modern languages. The trustees of the college, however, insisted that their new professor travel to Europe at his own expense to round out his language training.

Accepting the offer, Longfellow toured Europe from 1826 to 1829, dividing his time between France, Spain, Italy, and Germany. By August 11, 1829, he was back at Bowdoin, preparing lecture notes and writing his own grammars and study texts. For the next six years, his scholarly duties at the college and his academic writing in linguistics and literature occupied most of his professional life. He did, however, find time to renew an interest in creative writing. His only book during the stay at Bowdoin, *Outre-Mer: A Pilgrimage Beyond the Sea*, was a prose account of his European travels, modeled on Washington Irving's *The Sketch Book of Geoffrey Crayon, Gent.* (1819-1820). Settling more comfortably into academic life, Longfellow married Mary Storer Potter on September 14, 1831, and devoted himself to extending his reputation by publishing literary criticism. Three years later, Harvard College was impressed enough with the quality of his academic writing to offer him the Smith Professorship of French and Spanish Languages, again contingent on his willingness to travel to Europe for further study.

He and his wife, Mary, sailed in April, 1835, to visit England, Denmark, Sweden, and Holland. In October, tragedy overtook the couple; Mary lost the child she was carrying and, in November, died from complications from the miscarriage. It took a year of grieving, studying, and falling in love again—this time with Fanny Appleton, the daughter of a prominent Boston family whom he had met in Switzerland—for Longfellow to recuperate fully from the loss. By the fall of 1836, he had returned to Harvard to continue his scholarly writing. By 1842, he had also finished *Hyperion*, a highly autobiographical account of his unrequited love for Fanny, and three volumes of original poetry. By 1843, he had apparently achieved enough recognition for Fanny to consent to marriage. The stay at Harvard marked the beginning of the most productive period of Longfellow's career, and his home life, with six children, was apparently a happy one. His creative writing blossomed: He issued three more volumes of poetry. His scholarly endeavors continued to absorb him, and he added to his academic bibliography two major collections of verse. By 1854, his poetry had gained so much recognition that he could afford to resign his professorship and devote himself to writing full-time. In the next seven years, he produced his most popular works: *The Seaside and the Fireside*, *The Golden Legend*, *The Song of Hiawatha*, *The Courtship of Miles Standish and Other Poems*, and *Tales of a Wayside Inn*. The flowering of Longfellow's productivity was again interrupted by personal tragedy: the death of his second wife in 1861. While sealing some letters with hot wax, Fanny set herself on fire and burned to death in the family living room. Longfellow himself was badly burned trying to rescue her. He never completely recovered from the loss, although he tried to lose himself in an ambitious verse translation of Dante's *The Divine Comedy* (c. 1320), in some passionate and realistic poems about the horrors of the Civil War, and in a dramatic narrative of the life of Christ.

Throughout the next decade, Longfellow devoted most of his flagging energies to reissuing previously published poetry, writing sequels to previously successful poems, and experimenting with a few new forms which he did not intend for publication during his lifetime. Much of his mature thought and many of his penetrating personal reflections were invested in an uncompleted drama about the life of Michelangelo. His health began to fail before the work was completed and he died from peritonitis after a short illness, on March 24, 1882, less than a month after his seventy-fifth birthday had been celebrated all over America.

ANALYSIS

Henry Wadsworth Longfellow worked in two entirely different poetic forms: short lyrical sketches which tried to point out similarities between passing, subjective emotions and lasting, objective settings or locations and long historical narratives which aimed at celebrating inspirational events. Like other Fireside Poets, Longfellow tailored both kinds of verse to an audience which, he envisioned, would read them aloud in front of the family hearth. He once defined the persona for most of these public works as "no unwelcomed guest," who, he "hoped, would have [his] place reserved among the rest" at "your warm fireside." Appropriately, his subjects were often chosen so that young and old might be elevated by his treatment of traditional values. They stressed home, family, romantic love, dutiful children, quiet acceptance of suffering and death, and the appreciation of nature, God, and country. He wrote in traditional metrical patterns which would be easy for his readers to follow. He selected a solemn, sometimes archaic, diction which might add a devotional tone to the after-dinner recitations. He characteristically kept his symbols and images simple, so that even his youngest listeners might understand his homilies at first hearing. After the shocking death of his second wife, it became more difficult for Longfellow to confine himself to the expectations of such an audience and to such a rigid series of poetic restrictions. Yet the progress of his work showed a single-minded commitment to continue fulfilling the dictates of this public role, long after he himself had outgrown them. Increasingly, Longfellow's later lyrics and narratives showed a quiet subversion of the subjects and styles which his adoring audience expected of their laureate. The later poems proposed the same simple formulas in the same simple intonations as the earlier works had, but they seemed to waver, often undercutting themselves with a quiet pessimism which directly contradicted their superficial cheeriness.

"THE BELLS OF SAN BLAS"

In the last lyric he wrote, "The Bells of San Blas," Longfellow seemed to reevaluate his poetic career and to dismiss it as belonging to a "dreamer of dreams" to "whom what is and what seems" were frequently "the same." Like the bells of the decaying Catholic Church, he claimed that the voice of his public persona had tried "to bring us back once more" to the "vanished days of yore," when the world was still "filled with faith, with zeal." But like many a nineteenth century artist, Longfellow concluded that such sounds were probably "in vain": The past could not successfully be called back again. The struggle to affirm publicly traditional values while privately doubting their efficacy provided the cen-

tral tension in much of his poetry. Even the twenty-seven short poems he composed during his college days and published in a variety of little magazines and academic journals were prophetic of the difficulties that Longfellow would encounter whenever he attempted to bring together the spirituality of the past with the progress of the present. Like "The Bells of San Blas," they were tinged with a solemn, mournful sense of desperation, rueful that the traditions, values, and wisdom painfully accumulated over humankind's previous three thousand years of history no longer offered much guidance to the present. The young Longfellow examined the deaths of a variety of heroic Indians, stoic ship captains, and brave infantrymen who had given their lives for some noble cause. He concluded sadly that such nobility produced little lasting effect: Theirs had been moments of brightness darkened by an unappreciative and uncaring present. In *Voices of the Night* (1839), a slim collection of nine short poems, Longfellow amplified the melancholy and focused it through a spokesman who was both confused and troubled by "life's deep storm." While striving to balance his images of life's forms, which could bring both "sorrow and delight," and life's sounds, which could both "soothe or affright," the collection kept straying to the darker, more negative pole.

BALLADS AND OTHER POEMS

Each of the nine major collections of lyrics which followed these tentative beginnings sustained his sense of confusion and foreboding. In *Ballads and Other Poems*, Longfellow examined the traditional lifestyles of a Viking warrior, a New England sea captain, and a simple village blacksmith with the same effusive sentimentality he had employed on a similar grouping during his undergraduate years. He characterized these simple lives as an accumulation of "toiling and rejoicing and sorrowing," emphasizing heavily "the sorrowing," and dismissed them as incapable of providing workable models for surviving the modern world. The tone of the collection was established by the resignation inherent in "The Goblet of Life," whose brim, Longfellow concluded, tended too often to overflow "with bitter drops of woe." The best anyone could hope for, given such pessimism, was the "strength to bear a portion of the care" which "crushes one half of humanity with despair."

THE BELFRY OF BRUGES AND OTHER POEMS

This pessimism was repeated throughout *The Belfry of Bruges and Other Poems*, whose title piece forced a tenuous metaphorical comparison between the "sweet sonorous clangor" of a city's bell tower and the poet's own "airy chimes," anticipating the image he would execute with greater skill in "The Bells of San Blas" almost forty years later. In 1845, Longfellow could only claim that the sounds from "the belfry of his brain" were, like the city's bells themselves, "scattered downward, though in vain" to a world no longer moved by "the hollow sound of brass." He complained that producing such irrelevant music might only "overburden his brain" and fill him with a sense of weariness and pain. He ended the collection with a downtrodden portrait of a morose poet, despondent because his book was "completed and closed." Painfully, he sensed that "dim" would "grow its fantasies"; soon "forgotten" they would "lie, like coals in the ashes . . . darken and die." Such abjection, Longfellow suggested, could only partially be relieved with a night which grew "darker and darker" as the "black shadows fall" and with the troubled observation that shortly "sleep and oblivion will reign over all."

THE SEASIDE AND THE FIRESIDE

Longfellow was never exactly sure which names or shapes to give the fears which haunted his early lyrics. It is true that the undifferentiated anxiety seldom paraded itself in his more frequently read historical narratives, but the fears had much to do with his sense that traditional solutions were failing to answer modern questions. In *The Seaside and the Fireside*, he conjured up a slightly paranoid image of a fisherman's daughter staring dumbly "out into the night" from behind the window of her family's cottage, hoping to see "some form arise." The child remained incapable of discerning what "tales the roaring ocean and the night wind, bleak and wild" might have to tell. But at the poem's end, those projected fears could beat "at the heart" of the child's mother and "drive the color from her cheek." It was more than a child's fascination mingled with fear of night mysteries which colored much of Longfellow's lyricism; it was a vague but omnipresent fear that something was dreadfully wrong with the direction of modern civilization. Keener minds than Longfellow's remained similarly mystified, unable to articulate the questions which by the twentieth century would evolve into a systematic pattern of angst.

"BIRDS OF PASSAGE"

The "Birds of Passage" sequence, which he distributed throughout many of the later collections of lyrics, confronted these fears as directly as Longfellow could. The poems purported to reproduce the sounds of modern life, "murmurs of delight or woe" and the "murmurs of pleasures and pains and wrongs" which comprised his polarized judgment. Like his earlier efforts, however, these dwelt on the negative side, frequently echoing "the only sound we can discern," the "sound of lament." Even these, "all this toiling for human culture," he worried, might prove to be "unavailing." The sequence showed Longfellow at his best: His lines filled with sophisticated internal rhymes, with sometimes startling end rhymes ("Flanders" and "commanders," "unafraid" and "cannonade," "mountbanks" and "tan and planks"), with easy musical rhythms.

The "Birds of Passage" sequence is representative of Longfellow at the height of his powers, groping sometimes toward a Whitmanesque mysticism which might redeem his early fears and negativities. "All the houses where men have lived and died are haunted houses," he offered as the cornerstone of his belief-system in one poem in the sequence: "The spirit world around this world of sense floats like an atmosphere." In the lyrics which transcended his sense of despair, Longfellow began to avow his own personal, haphazard mixture of New England mysticism, Bostonian New Thought, spiritualism, numerology, astrology, and staid Unitarianism, hoping to offer some redemptive spirituality to a world which frequently defined itself as a "dark abyss." "To the dark problems, there is no other solution possible," he wrote to James Russell Lowell, "except the one word, Providence."

BALANCING OPPOSITES

The last collections of lyrics wavered between the knowledge of how darkly a people tended to live their lives and the hope of how brightly those lives could be lived. The poems tended to deal more directly with the paradoxical ambiguities that had provided many of the tensions in the "Birds of Passage" sequence. They turned on life and death, daylight and moonlight, the heart of man, "blithe as the air is, and as free" and the heart of man so burdened "by the cares of yesterday" that "each to-day" was "heavier still." A view of the world in which defeats frequently turned out to be victories in disguise and the lowest ebbs were often only "the turn of tides" bound together *The Masque of Pandora and Other Poems, Kéramos and Other Poems*, and *Ultima Thule*. These collections suggested a more peaceful and accepting stance toward the dynamic balance of opposites which, Longfellow believed, characterized all of life.

LATE LYRICS

In the later poems, the destructive forces men could unleash were being quieted by the vaguely meditative and heartfelt notion that "God is All." His last lyrics, though never completely shaking the sense of despair, transience, and futility which had dogged his poetic vision, showed a Longfellow who was coming to terms with evil and who was growing surer with hope. In the complex polarities of "Victor and Vanquished," Longfellow seemed to suggest that even the worst of life could lead to the best. The victim, harried into a corner and confronted with certain death, could still stand unmoved and unafraid, taunting the victor with the chivalric challenge, "Do with me what thou wilt." Such spirit, Longfellow insisted, could make even "the vanquished here," the "victor of the field." Whenever "a noble deed is wrought" or "spoken is a noble thought," Longfellow articulated his redemptive code of hope: "our hearts, in glad surprise to higher levels rise." In *Ultima Thule*, he was explaining the presence of evil with the time-honored formula that "noble souls" inevitably "rise from disaster and defeat, the stronger." The effort would make them more conscious of "the divine with them." For these traditional platitudes, Longfellow could, at his best, often find fresh and moving imagery.

The collections of late lyrics were probably his most enduring works. They chronicled a troubled soul, torn with the doubts of his age, groping to articulate a sense of mystery, awe, and spirituality which might bring hope to a culture too concerned with its own certitudes and material advances. It was not these lyrics, however, but rather his long historical narratives which had brought him acclaim from his contemporaries. Neither the profound doubts nor the genuine hopes which animated his lyrics could be found in these more saccharine celebrations of traditional values.

At their worst, *The Spanish Student* (1843), *Evangeline*, *The Song of Hiawatha*, *The Courtship of Miles Standish*, *The Divine Tragedy*, *The Golden Legend*, and *The New England Tragedies* were dull prosaic narratives which have done much to discourage modern readers from discovering the strengths of Longfellow's talents. *The Spanish Student* was an infelicitous three-act verse comedy intended for the stage. It found no one willing to venture the capital necessary for producing it. *Evangeline* was the work which first won a mass audience for Longfellow. It was a simple tale, first spun by the clergyman, H. L. Conolly, while he dined with Longfellow and Nathaniel Hawthorne. Longfellow seized the story line, picked a formal, though not always formally kept, dactylic hexameter metrical pattern for it, and composed a long tale of the French Arcadienne, Evangeline, as she wandered through the forests of eighteenth century New England looking for her kidnapped lover. It was a cliché-ridden effort whose descriptive powers ran to portrayals of Evangeline as "living at peace with God and the World," to summaries of her relationship with her betrothed as "their two hearts, tender and true," and to a plot which described her quest for him as searches "in want and cheerless discomfort, bleeding, barefooted, over the shards and thorns of existence." When at the poem's and her own life's end Evangeline finally located her long-lost fiancé, the best Longfellow could fashion for an ending was to have her "meekly bow" her head and "murmur, 'Father, I thank Thee'" just before she died. The popularity of the poem probably revealed more about the tastes of Longfellow's readers than about his own talents.

THE SONG OF HIAWATHA

The same audience responded even more enthusiastically to *The Song of Hiawatha*. With its two-footed lines vaguely resembling the alliterative verse of traditional northern European epics like the Finnish *Kalevala*, with its heavy borrowings from Henry Rowe Schoolcraft's two volumes on North American Indians, and with its upbeat ending, the appeal of *The Song of Hiawatha* was quick and widespread. The tale borrowed the grandiose proportions of the European epic, picturing a Hiawatha whose every stride measured "a Mile," whose canoe needed no paddles "for his thoughts as paddles served," whose father was "the west wind," and whose true love was Minnehaha, daughter of the god of arrow makers. The poem's rhythmic devices could sometimes be interesting. Especially when read aloud, the Indian material could lend a freshness to the overworked conventions of the epic, and Longfellow's battle scenes, pitting Hiawatha against a variety of mythic creatures, were frequently well-paced. All this technical virtuosity, however, could not hold together the disconnected elements of the plot or prepare the reader for the arbitrarily imposed ending in which Hiawatha vacates his native village so that his fellow Indians might be more inclined to listen to the redeeming gospel of Christianity brought to them by European missionaries.

THE COURTSHIP OF MILES STANDISH

The same muddle of values and formlessness of plot marred *The Courtship of Miles Standish*. The poem returned to the dactylic hexameters of *Evangeline* and to the romantic love angle shared between two recognizably human historical figures. Set in seventeenth century Puritan New England, *The Courtship of Miles Standish* wavered between sustaining a heroic view of the Plymouth Colony and a lighthearted glance at the foibles of its founders. Longfellow could never quite make up his mind whether to emphasize the "strong hearts and true" of the pilgrims or to satirize the quirky leader who could lock himself in his room and cheer himself with passages from Julius Caesar: "Better be first, he said, in a little Iberian village/ Than be second in Rome, and I think he was right when he said it."

THE DIVINE TRAGEDY

With *The Divine Tragedy*, an epic about the life of Christ, *The Golden Legend*, a retelling of the Faust story, and *The New England Tragedies*, an unfinished grouping about Christianity in the New World, Longfellow began to lose the mass audience he had so carefully cultivated. These works marked the same kind of transition to a tentative but serious spirituality which had characterized his later collections of lyrics. These poems, far more earnest than his early narratives, constituted reevaluations of two thousand years of Western religious thought through which Longfellow hoped to sift beliefs which might still have meaning to his contemporaries. He originally planned a chronicle of the triumph of religious progress in the ancient, medieval, and modern worlds. But his own lack of conviction in doctrinaire

Christianity and his own unshakable doubts led him to undercut the tales of triumph by dwelling on those moments in which the purity of the original doctrines were perverted by fallible man.

The Divine Tragedy set out to recapture the original message, but neither Longfellow's scattered theology nor his limited talents lent themselves to a subject of Miltonic proportions. His Christ blandly mouthed excerpts from the King James Bible; his apostles turned out to be featureless; his plot was a pastiche of New Testament incidents only vaguely related to one another; and his ending was an inconclusive recitation of the Apostles' Creed, with each of the twelve taking turns uttering the lines. "Poor sad humanity," St. John says, summarizing the effort, "turns back with bleeding feet by the weary road it came."

THE GOLDEN LEGEND

With Longfellow's growing need to explain the tragedies which had befallen him, the turning back took the form of *The Golden Legend* and *The New England Tragedies*. Both sought to examine the storehouse of Western religious traditions and decide which "messages" from the "world of the spirits" could still animate contemporary man. "Death is the chilliness that precedes the dawn," he would declare in *Michael Angelo*, "then, we awake in the broad sunshine of the other life."

In *The Golden Legend*, Longfellow used the character of Prince Henry to examine how that belief in the other life came to be abandoned. His reshaping of both medieval and modern Christianity questioned, not the validity of the original doctrines, but the applications through which their adherents distorted them. His Faust figure in *The Golden Legend* was tempted by a sophisticated and worldly Lucifer, often disguised as a village priest, who counseled his charge not toward sin but toward a more modern point of view. Prince Henry was led to accept the belief in progress, materialism, the priority of the senses, and the certainty of the here and now. Lucifer eased his conscience. His temptations ran not to rejecting formal Christianity, but to ignoring its underlying sense of the mystical.

THE NEW ENGLAND TRAGEDIES

In *The New England Tragedies*, this temptation was accepted with fewer questions. "O silent, sombre, and deserted streets," says a forlorn John Endicott, noting the emphasis on progress instead of spirituality: "To me, ye're peopled with a sad procession and echo only to the voice of sorrow." Where Prince Henry had placed too much faith in the powers of the intellect, the New Englanders had overemphasized the social mission of Calvinism. Both, Longfellow maintained, had lost sight of the underlying mystery and awe evident in the original testament espoused in *The Divine Tragedy*. Late in his last two narratives, Longfellow came to recommend the same kind of inchoate spirituality which had displayed redemptive powers in the most hopeful of his lyric poems. He was not enough of a theologian to formulate a systematic creed, nor enough of a zealot to recommend one path over another; and he was too much of a symbolist not to believe that all religious systems were only rough approximations of the same underlying unity. Nevertheless, a direct, experiential contact with the mysticism in man and the mysticism in nature could, Longfellow felt, explain much of the darkness of life.

OTHER MAJOR WORKS

LONG FICTION: *Kavanagh: A Tale*, 1849.

PLAY: *The Spanish Student*, pb. 1843.

NONFICTION: *Elements of French Grammar*, 1830 (translation); *Manuel de Proverbes Dramatiques*, 1830; *Outre-Mer: A Pilgrimage Beyond the Sea*, 1833-1834; *Hyperion*, 1839; *Drift-Wood*, 1857; *The Letters of Henry Wadsworth Longfellow*, 1966-1974 (5 volumes; Andrew Hilen, editor).

EDITED TEXTS: *The Poets and Poetry of Europe*, 1845; *The Waif: A Collection of Poems*, 1845; *The Estray: A Collection of Poems*, 1847; *Poems of Places*, 1876-1879.

TRANSLATION: *The Divine Comedy of Dante Alighieri*, 1867-1869.

BIBLIOGRAPHY

Buell, Lawrence. *New England Literary Culture*. Cambridge, England: Cambridge University Press, 1986. Buell notes Longfellow's strong interest in New England life, a fact that many critics have neglected. His *The New England Tragedies* are the most comprehensive portrayal of the region by any nineteenth century poet. Longfellow's interest in religious epics is also stressed: The poet regarded *Christus: A Mystery* as his crowning achievement. Longfellow's religious vision was Unitarian, and he was worried by the possibility that religion is only a human projection.

Gartner, Matthew. "Longfellow's Place: The Poet and Poetry of Craigie House." *The New England Quarterly* 73, no. 1 (March, 2000): 32-57. Gartner discusses the symbolic status of the private home in Longfellow's poetry and in mid-ninteeth century America. The private home was seen as a sacred space whose high priestess was the wife and mother and Longfellow used his own home to advance his prestige and authority.

Pearce, Roy Harvey. *The Continuity of American Poetry*. Middletown, Conn.: Wesleyan University Press, 1987. The earlier edition (1961) of this work is a standard critical survey of American poetry. Pearce adopts a dismissive tone toward Longfellow. He lived in a closed world, constantly intent on proving that life is not an empty dream. His work was a constant and misguided search for certainty. In spite of his wide acquaintance with world literature and history, Longfellow was narrowly provincial in outlook. Preoccupied with his own thoughts, he was unable to see objects as they really are.

Suchard, Allen. "The Nineteenth Century: Romanticism in American Poetry." In *American Poetry*. Amherst: University of Massachusetts Press, 1988. In spite of Longfellow's reputation as a celebrator of the American way of life, he, in fact, was possessed by a gloomy vision. Cosmic abandonment is constantly present in his work. In "Hymn to the Night," he welcomes night and death as a release from life. His dark side became more prominent after the death of his second wife. The brooding quality of his verse is its best feature. Longfellow's sonnets have been unduly neglected: He is one of the foremost American masters of this verse form.

Tucker, Edward L. "The Meeting of Hawthorne and Longfellow in 1838." *ANQ* 13, no. 4 (Fall, 2000): 18-21. Tucker discusses a number of meetings between Longfellow and Nathaniel Hawthorne and comments on the omissions regarding the meetings in Longfellow's edited journals.

Turco, Lewis P. *Visions and Revisions of American Poetry.* Fayetteville: University of Alabama Press, 1986. Turco views Longfellow as a derivative poet of minor importance. He imitated the English Romantics, and, in spite of the bulk of his output, almost none has endured. "Ropewalk" is his greatest poem, and his Civil War carol "Christmas Bells" also ranks as outstanding. The greatness of the poem to a large extent consists of the fact that it illustrates pessimism, while ostensibly supporting a sunny outlook.

Waggoner, Hyatt H. "Five New England Poets." In *American Poets: From the Puritans to the Present.* Baton Rouge: Louisiana State University Press, 1984. Longfellow was the saddest of all American poets. His dominant theme is that time is man's enemy. He was unwilling to face his own vision and made constant efforts to cheer himself up. In his most famous poem "Psalm of Life," his message is that life must be worth living, but we do not know why. Waggoner contends that Longfellow was unintelligent and that his poems are often incoherent.

Philip Woodard;
bibliography updated by the editors

AUDRE LORDE

Born: Harlem, New York; February 18, 1934
Died: Christiansted, St. Croix, Virgin Islands; November 17, 1992

PRINCIPAL POETRY

The First Cities, 1968
Cables to Rage, 1970
From a Land Where Other People Live, 1973
New York Head Shop and Museum, 1974
Between Our Selves, 1976
Coal, 1976
The Black Unicorn, 1978
Chosen Poems, Old and New, 1982 (revised as *Undersong: Chosen Poems, Old and New*, 1992)

A Comrade Is as Precious as a Rice Seedling, 1984
Our Dead Behind Us, 1986
Need: A Chorale for Black Woman Voices, 1990
The Marvelous Arithmetics of Distance: Poems, 1987-1992, 1993
The Collected Poems of Audre Lorde, 1997

OTHER LITERARY FORMS

The Cancer Journals (1980) is a personal account of Audre Lorde's struggles with breast cancer. *Zami: A New Spelling of My Name* (1982), which Lorde called a "biomythography," is a retrospective narrative of her emerging sexuality. *Sister Outsider: Essays and Speeches* (1984) and *A Burst of Light: Essays* (1988) are collections of essays and speeches on poetry, feminism, lesbianism, and racism.

ACHIEVEMENTS

Audre Lorde received a National Endowment for the Arts grant and was a poet in residence at Tougaloo College in Jackson, Mississippi, in 1968. She also won the Creative Artists Public Service grant (1972 and 1976) and the Broadside Poets Award (1975). In 1975 she was named Woman of the Year by Staten Island Community College. She received the Borough of Manhattan President's Award for literary excellence (1987), the American Book Award from the Before Columbus Foundation for *A Burst of Light* (1989), a Walt Whitman Citation of Merit, and two Lambda Literary Awards for Lesbian Poetry: in 1993 for *Undersong* and in 1994 for *The Marvelous Arithmetics of Distance*. She was named poet laureate of New York in 1991.

BIOGRAPHY

Audre Lorde's parents emigrated from Grenada to New York City in 1924. Lorde, the youngest of three girls, was born in 1934. She recounted many of her childhood memories in *Zami*, identifying particular incidents that had an influence or effect on her developing sexuality and her later work as a poet. She attended the University of Mexico (1954-1955) and received a B.A. from Hunter College (1959) and an M.L.S. from Columbia University (1961). In 1962, she was married to Edwin Rollins, with whom she had two children before they were divorced in 1970.

Prior to 1968, when she gained public recognition for her poetry, Lorde supported herself through a variety of jobs, including low-paying factory work. She also served as a librarian in several institutions. After her first publication, *The First Cities*, Lorde worked primarily within American colleges and free presses. She was an instructor at City College of New York (1968-1970), an instructor and then lecturer at Lehman College (1969-1971), and a professor of English at John Jay College of Criminal Justice (1972-1981). From 1981 to 1987 she was a professor of English at Hunter College at CUNY and became a Thomas Hunter Professor for one year (1987-1988). She also served as poetry editor of the magazine *Chrysalis* and was a contributing editor of the journal *Black Scholar.*

In the early 1980's she helped start Kitchen Table: Women of Color Press, a multicultural effort publishing Asian American and Latina as well as African American women writers. In the late 1980's Lorde became increasingly concerned over the plight of black women in South Africa under apartheid, creating Sisterhood in Support of Sisters in South Africa and remaining an active voice on behalf of these women throughout the remainder of her life. She also served on the board of the National Coalition of Black Lesbians and Gays. With the companion of her last years, the writer and black feminist scholar Gloria I. Joseph, she made a home on St. Croix, U.S. Virgin Islands. Shortly before her death in 1992 she completed her tenth book of poems, *The Marvelous Arithmetics of Distance.*

ANALYSIS

Audre Lorde called herself a "black lesbian feminist warrior poet." At the heart of her work as poet, essayist, teacher, and lecturer lies an intense and relentless exploration of personal identity. Beyond the stunning portrayals of her deepest insights and emotions, her work is filled with powerful evocations of universal survival. The substance of her poetry and essays always reaches beyond the individual self into deep concerns for all humanity. Progressively, her work reveals an increasing awareness of her West Indian heritage in relation to her place in American society and its values.

All Audre Lorde's poems, essays, and speeches are deeply personal renditions of a compassionate writer,

thinker, and human being. Indeed, she drew much of her material from individual and multifaceted experience; she rendered it in writing that sought to reveal the complexity of being a black feminist lesbian poet. She expressed the feelings of being marginalized in an American society that is predominantly white, male, heterosexual, and middle class. Her writings reflected the changing constitution and perspective of American life, but she never relented to an easy optimism, nor did she make uninformed dismissals of society's ills. Her personal experiences made her compassionate toward those who suffer under oppressive regimes all over the world. By drawing from the history and mythology of the West Indies, she was able to refer to the racism and sexism that exist in other cultures.

The title of one of her essays is especially appropriate to inform her work as a poet, "The Transformation of Silence into Language and Action." In a self-

Audre Lorde (Ingmar Schullz, courtesy of W. W. Norton)

characterization when she was a poet in residence at Tougaloo College, Lorde said, "I became convinced, anti-academic though I am, that all poets must teach what they know, in order to continue being." Her insistent drive to exist according to the terms of her individual desires and powers was the focal point of many of her speeches and essays. Lorde was also active on the lecture circuit, and she was invited to speak to women writers in the Soviet Union and in Berlin. She documented many of her insights into various cultures and places in essays and poems.

The various forms of her writing provided many pieces to the whole picture that made up Lorde's life and work. She was unsentimental in naming the people who have been a part of her life and in evaluating the events that make up her experiences. Her parents and her sisters are addressed with some frequency in her poems. A girlhood friend, Genevieve, appears in *Zami*, and Lorde eulogizes her death in a poem titled "Memorial II." Many women are treated in several different poems, sometimes in cycles—for example, Martha and Eudora. In these ways, Lorde documented the people and the course of her life as she charted the changes and the progress that occur; at each turn, she sought to understand more deeply the situation and to learn which detours to take next.

When she was in her forties, Lorde was diagnosed with breast cancer. *The Cancer Journals* and the essay "A Burst of Light: Living with Cancer" are important pieces of personal writing that recorded her uncertainties, fears, and doubts about her mortality. Writing mostly in the form of a diary, Lorde allowed the reader to enter into her most private thoughts and emotions, with the hope that others may be encouraged to fight cancer. From her determination to survive, Lorde converted her struggles with cancer into energy for battling on behalf of other humanitarian concerns.

She set out rigorously to combat racism, sexism, heterosexism, and homophobia in her work. At times she dealt with the issues separately, but more frequently she spoke of the whole gamut, since she perceived that each stems from human blindness about the differences among people. What was remarkable about Lorde's insight is the balance that she sought in presenting her views. Overtly political in intent and social in content,

the essays and speeches ask all individuals to understand more deeply the ways in which human lives are organized. She then beckoned people to take charge of their lives, to confront the tasks at hand, and to take responsibility for making changes.

Much of Lorde's mature work evolved from her identity as a black feminist lesbian poet. These terms are essential conjunctions that expressed her existence and her vision. In the essay "The Master's Tools Will Never Dismantle the Master's House," Lorde made no apologies or defenses for her choices. She wrote, "For women, the need and desire to nurture each other is not pathological but redemptive, and it is within that knowledge that our real power is rediscovered." For Lorde, the power to exist and be alive came from her love—in all senses of the word—for women.

In her most often cited essay, "The Uses of the Erotic: The Erotic as Power," Lorde dislodged some of the negative assumptions that have sprung up around the terms "erotic" and "power," and offered new perspectives on how an individual must use her power and ability to love. For Lorde, the erotic was "a resource within each of us that lies in a deeply female and spiritual plane, firmly rooted in the power of our unexpressed or unrecognized feeling." Through a redefinition of the terms, Lorde showed how societal oppression numbs a woman's ability to feel and act deeply. Often the two—emotion and action—are in conflict with the values of a "racist, patriarchal, and anti-erotic society." Before individual human beings can come together as one society, each person must be in touch with his or her own feelings and be willing to express and share with others. These are the necessary first steps to effecting real political change.

Lorde contended that the need to share is a fundamental one that all people feel. Unfortunately, the prevailing attitudes of American society preclude true expression of individualism: If people do not fit into the norms or expectations of the dominant system of values, they are deemed "not normal" or deviant. Lorde argued against the hypocrisy of American values: Where is freedom if any forms of expression considered "unfit" are excluded? How might one such as herself, who is on the margins of all that is "normal," empower herself to take effective action?

These are the kinds of difficult questions Lorde raised from the beginning of her work as a writer and poet. She made efforts to answer them anew in much of what she produced. She emphasized the necessity of listening to others and teaching what she herself has learned in the course of her work. Always receptive to the notion of difference that exists among all people, Lorde set out to consider the meaning of her own experiences first, before she attempted to convey to others what those experiences might mean in the larger context of existence. On the one hand, her work was intensely personal; it may even be considered self-absorbed at times. Yet on the other, she managed to transform her deeply private pains and joys into universal and timeless concerns.

THE FIRST CITIES AND CABLES TO RAGE

In her early collections of poetry, *The First Cities* and *Cables to Rage*, Lorde expressed a keen political disillusionment, noting the failure of American ideals of equality and justice for all. When Lorde used the pronoun "we" in her poetry, she spoke for all who have been dispossessed. In "Anniversary," for example, she wrote, "Our tears/ water an alien grass," expressing the separation between those who belong and those who do not. In poems such as "Sowing," the poet revealed the land's betrayal of its inhabitants by showing images of destruction juxtaposed to personal rage: "I have been to this place before/ where blood seething commanded/ my fingers fresh from the earth."

She also demonstrated a concern for the children of this earth in "Blood-birth": Casting about to understand what it is in her that is raging to be born, she wondered how an opening will come "to show the true face of me/ lying exposed and together/ my children your children their children/ bent on our conjugating business." The image of the warrior, the one who must be prepared to go about the business of existing in an unjust world, signifies the need to take care of those not yet aware of unfulfilled promises.

If the rage in her early poems appears "unladylike," Lorde was setting out to explode sexual typecasting. Certainly, there was nothing dainty about her sharp images and powerful assessments of social conditions. As she confronted harsh realities, the portrayals were necessarily clamorous. Yet the poet's rage did not lead to a blind rampage. In "Conversation in Crisis," the poet

hoped to speak to her friend "for a clear meeting/ of self upon self/ in sight of our hearth/ but without fire." The poet must speak honestly and not out of false assumptions and pretenses so that real communication can occur. The reader and listener must heed the words as well as the tone in order to receive the meaning of the words. Communication, then, is a kind of contractual relationship between people.

FROM A LAND WHERE OTHER PEOPLE LIVE AND BETWEEN OUR SELVES

In the collections *From a Land Where Other People Live* and *Between Our Selves*, Lorde used a compassionate tone to tell people about the devastation of white racism upon African Americans. She mixes historical fact with political reality, emphasizing the disjunction that sometimes occurs between the two. In "Equinox," Lorde observed her daughter's birth by remembering a series of events that also occurred that year: She had "marched into Washington/ to a death knell of dreaming/ which 250,000 others mistook for a hope," for few at that time understood the victimization of children that was occurring not only in the American South but also in the Vietnam War. After she heard that Malcolm X had been shot, she reread all of his writings: "the dark mangled children/ came streaming out of the atlas/ Hanoi Angola Guinea-Bissau . . . / merged into Bedford-Stuyvesant and Hazelhurst Mississippi."

From the multiplicity of world horrors, the poet returned to her hometown in New York, exhausted but profoundly moved by the confrontation of history and the facts of her own existence. In "The Day They Eulogized Mahalia," another event is present in the background as the great singer Mahalia Jackson is memorialized: Six black children died in a fire at a day care center on the South Side; "firemen found their bodies/ like huddled lumps of charcoal/ with silent mouths and eyes wide open." Even as she mourned the dead in her poems, the poet seems aware of both the power and the powerlessness of words to effect real changes. In the poem, "Power," Lorde writes,

> The difference between poetry and rhetoric
> is being ready to kill
> yourself
> instead of your children.

Once the event has occurred, one can write about it or one can try to prevent a similar event from occurring; in either case, it is not possible to undo the first event. Therefore, as a society, people must learn from their errors and their failures to care for other people. Lorde even warned herself that she must discern and employ this crucial difference between poetry and rhetoric; if she did not, "my power too will run corrupt as poisonous mold/ or lie limp and useless as an unconnected wire."

COAL, THE BLACK UNICORN AND OUR DEAD BEHIND US

For Lorde, the process of learning all over again how to transform thought into action began with the awareness of her personal reality. In the collections *Coal, The Black Unicorn* and *Our Dead Behind Us*, the poet addressed more specifically the individual human beings in her life, creating vignettes of her relationships with other people. In particular, she returned again and again to images of her mother, Linda Belmar Lorde, whose relatively light-colored skin is mentioned in many of the poems. In "Outside," she links her mother's lightness to the brutal faces of racism: "Nobody lynched my momma/ but what she'd never been/ had bleached her face of everything." When Lorde questioned, "Who shall I curse that I grew up/ believing in my mother's face," she echoed the anger that also appears in the poem "Sequelae." There she stated explicitly the rage that evolved from the mother's lies, white lies: "I battle the shapes of you/ wearing old ghosts of me/ hating you for being/ black and not woman/ hating you for being white." (*Zami* elaborates many of the specific events to which Lorde referred in her poems about her mother.)

The return to childhood allowed the poet to come to new terms with her mother. In several of her poems, she also returned to even deeper roots constituting her identity. In "Dahomey," she referred to the African goddess Seboulisa, "the Mother of us all" or the creator of the world. In embracing the mother goddess, the poet was able "to sharpen the knives of my tongue." Because the subjects of her poetry are painful ones, Lorde empowered her own speech by always calling attention to the dangers of remaining silent. In "A Song for Many Movements," she stated simply and precisely the project of her poetry: "Our labor has become/ more important/ than our silence."

UNDERSONG

Three decades of production and the work from Lorde's first five published collections form her 1993 collection titled *Undersong: Chosen Poems, Old and New*, a reworking of her 1982 work, *Chosen Poems, Old and New*. It is not a "selected poems" in the usual meaning of the term, because it contains no work from her centrally important *The Black Unicorn*, which she considered too complex and too much of a unit to be dismembered by excerpting, and holds little of *Our Dead Behind Us*. Thus a large chunk of her strongest work is missing—including most of the poems in which she conjured and confronted "the worlds of Africa."

As she stated in an introduction, her revisions of *Chosen Poems, Old and New* were undertaken to clarify but not to recast the work—necessitating that she "propel [herself] back into the original poem-creating process and the poet who wrote it." Lorde returned to her work of *Chosen Poems, Old and New* after Hurricane Hugo wrecked her home in the Virgin Islands and she found "a waterlogged but readable copy of [the book], one of the few salvageable books from [her] library." The drama of the incident seemed to take an allegorical cast and inspired her to treat the anchoring of her poems in truth with the same fierce honesty she had devoted to confronting her childhood, her blackness, and her sexual identity. She thus seemed determined to keep her poetry under spiritual review with the same intensity that she devoted to the infinite difficulties of being an African American woman and lesbian in late twentieth century America. The changes she made in this collection seem limited to the excising of a handful of early poems, substituting others previously unpublished, and reworking line breaks and punctuation to give more space and deliberate stress to each stanza and image.

The themes of the book largely circulate on two central axes: The notion of changeable selves—the broken journey toward self—is a recurrent motif, as is her consuming involvement with issues of survival. In examining changeable selves, she juxtaposes the longing for completion with the awareness of change as a paradoxical condition of identity. In "October," Lorde appeals to the goddess Seboulisa, elsewhere described as the "Mother of us all":

Carry my heart to some shore
my feet will not shatter
do not let me pass away
before I have a name
for this tree
under which I am lying
Do not let me die still
needing to be stranger.

As the final couplet hints, the counterpoint to the search for self is the search for connection, and to that end, dialogue is used as a structuring device, creating a sense of companionship won in the face of a proudly borne singularity.

Poems with images of destruction also abound: the dead friend Genevieve; the father who "died in silence"; the "lovers processed/ through the corridors of Bellevue Mattewan/ Brooklyn State the Women's House of D./ St. Vincent's and the Tombs"; "a black boy (Emmett Till) hacked into a murderous lesson"; the lost sisters and daughters of Africa and its diaspora, whose "bones whiten/ in secret." Lorde's dual themes of the unending search for identity and a struggle for survival heightens the impact of the word "nightmare," which cycles endlessly throughout Lorde's work. The word represents her expression for history as glimpsed in surreal previsions and "Afterimages" (the title of a poem linking her memories of Emmett Till's lynching to television pictures of a Mississippi flood). One looks in vain for a "positive" counterweight, before realizing that the nightmare, for Lorde, is not a token of negativity but rather symbolizes the denied and feared aspects of experience that must be recalled and accepted for change to occur.

THE MARVELOUS ARITHMETICS OF DISTANCE: POEMS, 1987-1992

In her final collection of poems, published posthumously, Lorde displays a personal, moving, bare, and striking set of work that strives for poignant reckonings with her family. "Legacy—Hers" is about her mother, "bred for endurance/ for battle." "Inheritance—His" is about her father. She also has farewells to her sister, whom she forgives ("both you and I/ are free to go"), and to her son, whom she challenges ("In what do you believe?") She has many bouquets for Gloria, her partner.

She also visits her characteristic theme of politics in this collection. For example, she writes cinematically

about the destruction wrought by U.S. foreign policy in a ferocious "Peace on Earth: Christmas, 1989":

the rockets red glare where
all these brown children
running scrambling around the globe
flames through the rubble
bombs bursting in air
Panama Nablus Gaza
tear gas clouding the Natal sun.
THIS IS A GIFT FROM THE PEOPLE OF THE UNITED
STATES OF AMERICA
quick cut
the crackling Yule log
in an iron grate.

In "Jesse Helms," which begins "I am a Black woman/ writing my way to the future," she takes on the bigotry of the senator from North Carolina with intentional crudeness:

Your turn now jessehelms
come on its time
to lick the handwriting
off the walls.

In this sparse and commanding book, perhaps the most arresting lines are those in which she wrestles with the nearness of her own death. In "Today is not the day," she writes:

I am dying
but I do not want to do it
looking the other way.
Audre Lorde never looked the other way.

OTHER MAJOR WORKS

NONFICTION: *Uses of the Erotic: The Erotic as Power*, 1978; *The Cancer Journals*, 1980; *Zami: A New Spelling of My Name*, 1982; *Sister Outsider: Essays and Speeches*, 1984; *I Am Your Sister: Black Women Organizing Across Sexualities*, 1986; *Apartheid U.S.A.*, 1986; *A Burst of Light: Essays*, 1988; *The Audre Lorde Compendium: Essays, Speeches, and Journals*, 1996.

BIBLIOGRAPHY

Avi-Ram, Amitai F. "*Apo Koinou* in Lorde and the Moderns: Defining the Differences." *Callaloo* 9

(Winter, 1986): 193-208. *Apo koinou* comes from a Greek phrase meaning "in common." This original and ambitious essay discusses the uses of eroticism and the importance of a political consciousness in Lorde's work. The author situates Lorde's work in the context of other modernist poets. The argument is sophisticated and learned; its stimulating premise derives from a familiarity with literary history and Western philosophical thought.

Brooks, Jerome. "In the Name of the Father: The Poetry of Audre Lorde." In *Black Women Writers (1950-1980): A Critical Evaluation*, edited by Mari Evans. Garden City, N.Y.: Doubleday, 1984. This brief chapter deals with a topic to which Lorde gives little direct attention in her own essays—the death of her father. It is a useful analysis of a focused topic that clarifies the meaning of some of the poems in which the figure of the father appears.

Dilworth, Thomas. "Lorde's 'Power.'" *The Explicator* 57, no. 1 (Fall, 1998): 54-57. Examines the complex imagery in Audre Lorde's poem "Power," found in her collection titled *The Black Unicorn*. He argues that the poem is more than an expressive, rhetorical piece—it is a work of art.

Hull, Gloria, T. "Living on the Line: Audre Lorde and *Our Dead Behind Us*." In *Changing Our Own Words: Essays on Criticism, Theory, and Writing by Black Women*, edited by Cheryl A. Wall. New Brunswick, N.J.: Rutgers University Press, 1989. This is a thoughtful essay on one of Lorde's collections of poetry. While it refers to some contemporary critical theory, it is an engaging and accessible study that traces the trajectory of Lorde's work. Hull also assesses various critical reviews of the collection.

Lorde, Audre. *The Cancer Journals*. San Francisco, Calif.: Aunt Lute Books, 1997. A new edition with posthumous tributes from other writers and poets added to Lorde's autobiographical exploration of her breast cancer and mastectomy.

_____. "Sadomasochism: Not About Condemnation." Interview by Susan Leigh Star. In *A Burst of Light*. Ithaca, N.Y.: Firebrand Books, 1988. Lorde talks energetically about her sexuality, setting the discussion in the context of her life's work. This in-

terview is the first in a series of private meditations centered on her bouts with cancer.

Lorde, Audre, and Adrienne Rich. "An Interview: Audre Lorde and Adrienne Rich." In *Sister Outsider: Essays and Speeches*. Trumansburg, N.Y.: Crossing Press, 1984. The two poets speak about a wide range of topics such as power, knowledge, and eroticism. Lorde also discusses her views on the uses of prose and poetry, focusing on the process of perception.

Martin, Joan. "The Unicorn Is Black: Audre Lorde in Retrospect." In *Black Women Writers (1950-1980): A Critical Evaluation*, edited by Mari Evans. Garden City, N.Y.: Doubleday, 1984. This is a useful compendium of Lorde's work up to 1984, focusing on the collection titled *The Black Unicorn*.

Olson, Lester C. "Liabilities of Language: Audre Lorde Reclaiming Difference." *Quarterly Journal of Speech* 84, no. 4 (November, 1998): 448-470. Distortions around the naming and the misnaming of human differences are the central foci of Audre Lorde's speech "Age, Race, Class, Sex: Women Redefining Difference," which she delivered at Amherst College in Massachusetts on April 3, 1980. Here she exemplifies her deep understanding of what she refers to in an earlier speech as "that language which has been made to work against us."

Cynthia Wong,
updated by Sarah Hilbert

RICHARD LOVELACE

Born: Woolwich, England, or Holland; 1618
Died: London, England; 1656 or 1657

PRINCIPAL POETRY
Lucasta: Epodes, Odes, Sonnets, Songs, &c. to Which Is Added Aramantha, a Pastorall, 1649
Lucasta: Posthume Poems of Richard Lovelace, Esq., 1659
The Poems of Richard Lovelace, 1925 (2 volumes; C. H. Wilkinson, editor)

OTHER LITERARY FORMS

Apart from the lyrics published in the two volumes of his poetry, Richard Lovelace wrote two plays, neither of which appears to be extant. The youthful *The Scholar* or *The Scholars*, a comedy, may have been produced at Gloucester Hall, Oxford, in 1636, and repeated later at Whitefriars, Salisbury Court, London. The prologue and epilogue appear in *Lucasta* (1649). A second play, a tragedy titled *The Soldier* (1640), was written during the second Scottish expedition in 1640 but was never produced, according to Anthony à Wood, because of the closing of the theaters. Lovelace also wrote commendatory verses for a number of volumes published by friends or associates, versions of which appear in the collected editions of his poems. In addition, he wrote some lines, engraved under the portrait of Vincent Voiture, prefixed to the translation of the *Letters* by John Davies in 1657.

ACHIEVEMENTS

Although chiefly remembered for a handful of exquisite lyrics celebrating what Douglas Bush called the Cavalier trinity of beauty, love, and honor, Richard Lovelace has gradually risen to critical attention. Written for the most part against the somber landscape of England during the Civil War and Interregnum, Lovelace's poetry asserts more complex concerns and more authentic attitudes than those usually attributed to that "mob of gentlemen who wrote with ease." Decidedly a literary amateur in the Renaissance tradition of the courtier, Lovelace's sensibilities were deepened and roughened by the calamities that befell him, his cause, and his king. "To Althea, from Prison," and "To Lucasta, Going to the Wars" are justly admired along with a few other frequently anthologized pieces, but the achievement is considerably larger than their slight number and scope might suggest. In his ode "The Grasshopper," for example, written to his friend Charles Cotton, Lovelace fashions from an emblematic examination of the fate of that "poor verdant fool" an affirmation of human friendship that transcends particular circumstance and achieves an authentic tragic tone. In the lines written "To my worthy friend Mr. Peter Lely, on that excellent picture of his Majesty and the Duke of York, drawn by him at Hampton Court," Lovelace evokes the "clouded maj-

esty" of King Charles the First, transforming a typical genre piece describing a painting into a somber elegiac on human dignity and courage in the face of adversity.

Like most of his fellow Cavalier poets, Lovelace was indebted to the poetry of Ben Jonson and John Donne. To Jonson he owed what graciousness and form he achieved, especially in the choice of classical models. To Donne he owed some degree of intellectual toughness and delight in what ingenious conceits he could master. To the limitations of both, in different ways, he was indebted for those infelicities of style that came with too much striving and too much care. Among his immediate contemporaries he was, no doubt, influenced by his relative, the translator Thomas Stanley, who may have helped him in more substantial matters than verse. Other poets with whom Lovelace shared stylistic affinities and thematic concerns were Robert Herrick, Sir John Suckling, and Andrew Marvell.

BIOGRAPHY

The broad outlines of Richard Lovelace's life are easy enough to sketch; but when it comes to filling in the details, much remains conjectural. Born in 1618 either at the family manor of Bethersden, Woolwich, Kent, or in Holland, Lovelace was the eldest son of Sir William Lovelace and his wife Anne (Barne). (The Woolwich church register does not commence until 1663.) His mother spent some time in Holland, where his father served under Sir Horace Vere and was later killed at the siege of Groll in 1627. Her references to her son Richard in her will make it seem likely that he was born while she was with her husband in the Low Countries.

Richard had four brothers, Thomas, Francis, William, and Dudley (the last of whom was responsible for seeing *Lucasta: Posthume Poems* through the press after his brother's death), and three sisters, Anne, Elizabeth, and Johanna. There are no records of Lovelace's childhood. In January, 1630, Lady Lovelace married Jonathan Brown or Browne of London, Doctor of Laws, and it may be presumed that the family's fortunes were enhanced as a result. The poet was educated at Charterhouse and entered Gloucester Hall, now Worcester College, Oxford, as a gentleman commoner in 1634.

By all accounts, the young scholar was handsome and amiable. In his second year, according to Anthony à Wood, a not very reliable authority in the case of Lovelace, he attracted the attention of an eminent lady of the queen, who prevailed upon the archbishop of Canterbury, then chancellor of the university, to have him awarded a master of arts, though he was only of two years' standing. The following year Lovelace was at Cambridge University, where he met several young men then in residence who were to contribute commendatory verses to *Lucasta* twelve years later; among them was Andrew Marvell.

Upon leaving the university, Lovelace joined the court, where he attracted the attention of George, Lord Goring, later earl of Norwich, and was sent by him as an ensign in the first expedition against the Scots in 1639, under the earl of Northumberland. During the second of these ineffectual campaigns, he was commissioned captain. Although he apparently wrote the tragedy titled *The Soldier* during the second campaign, the only direct reference to the Scottish campaigns is the drinking song "To General Goring, after the pacification of Berwick." Among those who rode northward with Lovelace was the poet Sir John Suckling, whose "Ballad upon a Wedding" is traditionally thought to address Lovelace, although there is little, if any, substantive evidence for the attribution.

Following the Scottish campaigns, Lovelace returned to Kent and took possession of the family estates. In late April, 1642, he helped deliver the Kentish Petition to the House of Commons, for which he was confined in prison for perhaps as long as two months. The petitioners could not have hoped for any response less severe, especially as a similar petition of the previous month on behalf of the bishops and the liturgy had been ordered burned by the common hangman. In June, Lovelace was released on bail from his confinement, provided he remain in close communication with the Speaker of the House. Although he was forbidden to take an active role in the struggle between the king and Parliament, he outfitted his brothers Francis and William with men and money to aid the royalist cause and arranged for his younger brother, Dudley, to study tactics and fortification in Holland.

Lovelace probably spent the greater part of the years 1643-1646 in Holland and France. His departure may have occasioned the lyric "To Lucasta, going beyond the seas." In Holland he presumably learned the language and acquired an appreciation of the world of art then flourishing with Rembrandt at the height of his powers. Lovelace was present at the siege of Dunkirk in 1646, where he was wounded. A year later he was back in London and was admitted with the Dutch-born portraitist Peter Lely to the Freedom of the Painters' Company. In 1648 he and his brother were taken as prisoners to Peterhouse in London, possibly as a precautionary measure because of their past activities and the turbulent state of affairs in Kent at the time. It was during this second confinement, apparently, that he prepared his lyrics for publication in 1649. He was discharged on April 10, 1649, some ten months after his incarceration. During the year Lovelace sold what remained of his family estates, including the family portraits, among which was one of himself by an unknown artist. These later came to Dulwich College.

Virtually nothing is known of Lovelace's activities in the years preceding his death, which occurred sometime before October, 1657, the date of the publication of Eldred Revett's *Poems*, which contained an elegy on Lovelace. Wood provides an account of Lovelace's last days and death. It has achieved popularity as suiting the legend of the man, but that Lovelace died a miserable death in utter poverty seems less than likely. Fifteen months prior to his death he wrote "The Triumphs of Philamore and Amoret" for the celebration of the marriage of his friend Charles Cotton. The poem, itself, may account for Wood's version of Lovelace's wretched end. Its references to Cotton's aid, however, "when in mine obscure cave/ (Shut up almost close prisoner in a grave)/ Your beams could reach me through this vault of night," would seem not to call for Wood's exaggerated description of the event. That Lovelace's fortune and fortunes were gravely reduced by the end seems clear. He would hardly have been alone in facing such hardships. There were friends to help, and it is unlikely that such abject poverty would not have been hinted at, had it occurred, in the various elegies occasioned by the publication in 1659 of *Lucasta: Posthume Poems*. The community of lettered friends was closely knit and evidence exists that discounts the implications of Wood's narrative. The poet Thomas Stanley, Lovelace's kinsman, had helped several needy and deserving poets and royalists, among them Sir Edward Sherburne, John Hall, and Robert Herrick. Cotton clearly assisted Lovelace in his time of need, and it is well known that Marvell tirelessly aided Milton in the early years of the Restoration. These are examples of the kind of support that surely would have been available to such an important gentleman and poet. Lovelace's place of burial, in Wood's account, was "at the west end of the Church of Saint Bride, alias Bridget, in London, near to the body of his kinsman William." The church was completely destroyed in the Great Fire of London in 1666 along with any records that could verify the place of burial.

ANALYSIS

Richard Lovelace's name has epitomized the supposed values of the world he inhabited, while its later link with Samuel Richardson's villain in *Clarissa* (1747-1748) has added guilt by association. The poet was, however, neither villain nor fop. Whatever glitter or romance touched his poems was incidental to a career dominated by darkness and despair, against which he strove with considerable stoicism. Indeed, although the themes of love, friendship, and retirement appear frequently in his poems (along with an informed and highly cultivated notion of the role of the arts of music, painting, and literature in relation to the good life), a pervasive sense of disillusionment and tragic isolation gives the best of them a keen edge. More than one critic has noted a claustrophobic sense of entrapment that is never far from the surface of his work. The traditional themes of what Earl Miner calls the "social mode of cavalier poetry" celebrate the good life, the ruins and remedies of time, the ordering process of art set against the disorder of the age, and the special values of love and friendship in the face of loss. Yet the Cavaliers were forced increasingly to survive in a winter world, like that characterized by Lovelace in "The Grasshopper," a poem which has received considerable critical attention in recent years.

"THE GRASSHOPPER"

In this poem, as in "The Snail," "The Ant," and "A Fly Caught in a Cobweb," Lovelace turns to the emblems of nature for lessons that bespeak the necessary fortitude of all life faced with the inevitable process of mutability. He shares his desire to fashion ethical and political statements of an allegorical kind by means of a

microscopic examination of the natural world with other poets of his time, particularly Andrew Marvell, although the Anacreontic strain was most fully exploited by the royalist writers Thomas Stanley, Robert Herrick, and Abraham Cowley. Of the various reasons for examining the tiny creatures of the natural world, foremost was the wish to draw comparisons with the world of affairs amounting to little more than thinly veiled subversive propaganda. Although Lovelace and his fellow royalists were fascinated by the delicate craftsmanship that art shared with nature, "The Grasshopper" emerges as both a political and an ethical warning, as well as a pattern for refined artistry. The dual impulses in the poem, indeed, threaten its unity. In the end, it is only by recourse to paradox that Lovelace holds the disparate elements together.

In their enterprise to reinforce the royalist position by examples drawn from the world of nature, Lovelace and his fellow poets could not claim a monopoly on the material. Rebellion employed its own arguments from nature in support of human rights. When all else failed, the royalists found that their best alternative was a return to the nature found on what country estates were left to them, where they accepted a life of enforced retirement with whatever solace they could find. For Lovelace this last refuge from the political realities was no longer available.

LOVE, HONOR, AND TRUTH

The best known of Lovelace's lyrics are those that celebrate love, honor, and truth, especially "To Lucasta, Going to the Wars" and "To Althea, from Prison," the latter set by John Wilson for John Playford's *Select Airs and Dialogues* (1659). It is one of a number of royalist dungeon pieces which may be indebted to Vincent Voiture's *Dans la prison*, although prison philosophy was certainly something of a Cavalier convention. For all of Lovelace's asseverations that "iron bars do not a prison make," a sense of lost conviction lingers about the poem like Althea's whispering to her loved one "at the grates." While the poet extravagantly claims his right to lie "tangled" in his mistress's hair and "fettered to her eye," a feeling of suffocating doom weighs heavily on the poem. In comparison, the joyous, almost Elizabethan "Gratiana, dancing and singing," creates a world of exuberance, excitement, and courtly fascination, defining an atmosphere that exists, like Izaak Walton's trout-filled streams, in a world forever vanished. The theme of mutability sparkles through the verse like the golden tresses of Amarantha, that flower of another poem, which when loosened and shaken out will "scatter day."

In truth, for Lovelace it is sorrow that scatters his days, along with the realization that "joys so ripe, so little keep." Though the popular lyric "The Scrutiny" flaunted that brand of cynicism and masculine arrogance learned from John Donne through Thomas Carew and Sir John Suckling, the richer imaginative strain is the note that sounds touching true worth irretrievably lost. The general slightness of Lovelace's lyrics is, in one sense, a measure of what has vanished; and the brief attention span that shows itself in many of the poems, such as "Gratiana, dancing and singing," which disintegrates after the brilliance of the opening four stanzas, may be as much the result of distracted or shattered sensibilities as it is of limited poetic skills. The lyrics frequently end in fragments of broken vision or imaginative exhaustion. There are debts, as well, to the courtier poet Thomas Wyatt, whose verse, like Lovelace's own, was often crabbed and tortured but could rise to take the measure of a tawdry world.

THE INFLUENCE OF MARINO

Perhaps because he was an amateur poet and a connoisseur of art, Lovelace saw very clearly the value of restoring the ruins of time. Like many of his contemporaries, particularly Stanley, an indefatigable translator, Lovelace went to continental as well as classical models for his verse, including that fantastic lyricist of the previous generation, Giambattista Marino. It may be assumed that the Petrarchan themes employed by Marino and his followers fascinated the royalist imagination, both by their sensuousness and by the brilliance of their metaphorical transformations. If poetry could change things, such linguistic strategies as the Marinisti presented in search of the marvelous might be enlisted by the Cavaliers in support of the royalist vision. After all, in the king they were accustomed to see poetically and politically the divinely linked agent of the miraculous. Beyond this, translation became for the poets of the time a means both to enrich their own meager gifts and to reinforce the realm of humane letters that was, they believed, the special preserve of the royalist writers.

From Marino, Lovelace borrowed the ideas and images for a number of his better poems. In "Elinda's Glove," working from Marino's *Il Guanto* (c. 1600's) "Gli occhi di foco e'l sen di ghiaccio armata," Lovelace developed the images of sexual passion and feminine cruelty into an emblem that combined its sexuality with a social statement, transforming the intensely private into the mode of social convention and sophisticated tolerance, with tinges of mockery. Lovelace's "Song: To Amarantha, that she would dishevel her hair" develops one of Marino's favorite themes, while the complimentary verses of "Gratiana, singing and dancing" paraphrase the sonnet of Giovanni Leone Sempronio, "La bella ballerina," and Lovelace's lyric "The Fair Beggar" employs a motif developed in the poem "Bellissima Mendica" by the Marinist Claudio Achillini.

While much of his poetry written to celebrate friends and fellow artists was mere compliment, Lovelace often struck a note of sincerity that swept aside cant and allied human dignity with the longer life of art. On occasion these poems may owe something to models drawn from Marino's *La Galeria* (1619), but mere ingenuity gives way to the demands of authentic history and personal tragedy. In this regard, his poems written to Lely deserve a place in any appraisal of his accomplishments as a poet. In "Painture" (1659) he displays a fairly comprehensive understanding of painting and its particular fate in England, where the indifference of the average Englishman to anything but family portraits had troubled painters from Hans Holbein on. With Lely, Lovelace shares a sense of the importance of painting and seeks, by that bond, to establish an alliance against philistinism: "Now, my best Lely, let's walk hand in hand,/ And smile at this un-understanding land," where men adore merely their "own dull counterfeits."

LEGACY

Like his "Fly Caught in a Cobweb," as a poet and courtier Lovelace may seem to be a "small type of great ones, that do hum/ Within this whole world's narrow room." His vision as a minor poet, however, may display more clearly the age that produced him than do the more majestic tones of genius that rise above the humble chorus of voices from the land. In his "Advice to my best brother, Colonel Francis Lovelace," he counsels that "to rear an edifice by art so high/ That envy should not reach it," one must inevitably "build low." The lessons of humanity lie close to the surface of his poetry, more visible than the treasures of his wit. In the analysis of his poetry, that shallow part has satisfied most inquirers. Many have failed even to look that closely.

In his own day Lovelace's poetry achieved little serious recognition. A few poems were known and recognized, but he did not enjoy a reputation such as Suckling did, for example. By the eighteenth century he seems to have been almost forgotten. Had it not been for Bishop Thomas Percy, who reprinted his two most famous lyrics in his *Relics of Ancient English Poetry* (1765), he might easily have completely faded from sight. From his friend and benefactor Cotton he received a suitable estimate in an elegy written for *Lucasta: Posthume Poems*:

> In fortune humble, constant in mischance,
> Expert in both, and both served to advance
> Thy name by various trials of thy spirit
> And give the testimony of thy merit;
> Valiant to envy of the bravest men
> And learned to an undisputed pen.

OTHER MAJOR WORKS

PLAYS: *The Scholar(s)*, pr. 1636(?); *The Soldier*, wr. 1640.

BIBLIOGRAPHY

Allen, Don Cameron. "Richard Lovelace: 'The Grass-Hopper.'" In *Seventeenth-Century English Poetry: Modern Essays in Criticism*, edited by William R. Keast. New York: Oxford University Press, 1962. Examines the rich tradition embodied in the image of the grasshopper, at once the spend-thrift, the poet-singer, and the king. Concludes that the indestructible kingdom created at the end of the poem is an inner one created by the poem.

Marcus, Leah S. *The Politics of Mirth: Jonson, Herrick, Milton, Marvell, and the Defense of Old Holiday Pastimes*. Chicago: University of Chicago Press, 1986. Marcus couples Lovelace and Marvell, contemporaries whose poetry concerned cultural survival, and finds *Lucasta* a treasury of Cavalier political beliefs that Marvell later modified in his own poetry. Marcus accords only one of Lovelace's poems, "The Grasshopper," an in-depth analysis, but

that discussion is followed by a treatment of Marvell's Mower poems, which rewrite Lovelace's original poem.

Miner, Earl. *The Cavalier Mode from Jonson to Cotton*. Princeton, N.J.: Princeton University Press, 1971. Uses the emblem tradition to explicate Lovelace's "The Grasshopper," a poem that summarizes Lovelace's attitude to the "Grasshopper King." Miner's lengthy analysis also places the poem within another "mode," that of friendship, for the poem is addressed to his "Noble Friend, Mr. Charles Cotton."

Semler, L. E. *The English Mannerist Poets and the Visual Arts*. Madison, N.J.: Fairleigh Dickinson University Press, 1998. Offers an introduction to the parallel history of the Mannerist poets and artists with specific attention to Richard Lovelace among others. Includes bibliographic references and an index.

Skelton, Robin. *Cavalier Poets*. London: Longmans, Green, 1960. Skelton's monograph contains a chapter on Lovelace, the model of the Renaissance man but a poet whose lack of spontaneity and tendency to moralize are shortcomings. For Skelton, Lovelace is primarily concerned with the ideal and the idyllic and is also prone to rely on the pastoral manner.

Wedgwood, C. V. *Poetry and Politics Under the Stuarts*. Cambridge, England: Cambridge University Press, 1961. Wedgwood traces the disintegration of the defeated Cavaliers through her reading of Lovelace's famous "To Althea, from Prison," a poem that prompted many imitations by other Cavalier poets.

Galbraith M. Crump;
bibliography updated by the editors

AMY LOWELL

Born: Brookline, Massachusetts; February 9, 1874
Died: Brookline, Massachusetts; May 12, 1925

PRINCIPAL POETRY

A Dome of Many-Coloured Glass, 1912
Sword Blades and Poppy Seed, 1914
Men, Women, and Ghosts, 1916

Can Grande's Castle, 1918

Pictures of the Floating World, 1919

Legends, 1921

A Critical Fable, 1922

What's O'Clock, 1925

East Wind, 1926

Ballads for Sale, 1927

Selected Poems of Amy Lowell, 1928 (John Livingston Lowes, editor)

The Complete Poetical Works of Amy Lowell, 1955 (Louis Untermeyer, editor)

A Shard of Silence: Selected Poems of Amy Lowell, 1957 (G. R. Ruihley, editor)

Amy Lowell (Library of Congress)

OTHER LITERARY FORMS

In addition to collections of poetry, Amy Lowell published translations, criticism, and a literary biography. Her output was prodigious, fourteen of her books being published within a thirteen-year span. In addition, she wrote numerous essays and reviews and kept up an active correspondence, much of it concerning literature. Lowell edited three anthologies of Imagist poetry: *Some Imagist Poets* (1915), *Some Imagist Poets*, Volume II (1916), and *Some Imagist Poets*, Volume III (1917). Her three critical works were *Six French Poets* (1915), essays drawn from her lectures on the post-symbolist poets; *Tendencies in Modern American Poetry* (1917), essays also drawn from lectures on contemporary poetry and six poets in particular, including two Imagists; and *Poetry and Poets* (1930), essays compiled from her lectures and published posthumously. Although she did other translations (of operettas and verse dramas), Lowell's only published translations, with the exception of those in the appendix to *Six French Poets*, were those in *Fir-Flower Tablets* (1921), a collection of ancient Chinese poetry done in collaboration with Florence Ayscough. Lowell's monumental two-volume biography, *John Keats*, appeared in 1925, shortly before her death. A sampling of Lowell's letters can be found in *Florence Ayscough and Amy Lowell: Correspondence of a Friendship* (1945).

ACHIEVEMENTS

During her lifetime, Amy Lowell was one of the best-known modern American poets. This reputation had as much to do with Lowell the person and literary spokesperson as with Lowell the poet, though her work was certainly esteemed. Today her place in literary history as a whole is still to be determined, but her importance in the limited field of early twentieth century American letters is undisputed.

In her day, as F. Cudworth Flint has said, both Lowell and poetry were "news." Between 1914 and 1925, she spoke out for Imagism, free verse, and the "New Poetry" more frequently, energetically, and combatively than any of its other promoters or practitioners. She took on all comers in Boston, New York, Chicago, and any other city where she was invited to speak. "Poetry Society" meetings were often the best show in town when Lowell was on the platform.

Lowell's art probably suffered as a result of her taking on the role of promoter as well as producer of the new poetry, but she unquestionably helped to open the way for younger poets among her contemporaries and for free expression and experimentation in poetic form and theme. T. S. Eliot's *The Waste Land* (1922), which

Lowell did not admire, might not have had such an immediate impact on the development of modern poetry had Lowell not helped to prepare for its reception.

Critical opinion on Lowell's own poetry is divided. Her detractors argue that she lacks passion and feeling; that she is concerned only with the surfaces of things; that she is imitative, an assimilator without any original creative force. Some even say that she never really understood the new poetry she so tirelessly advocated, that she was temperamentally grounded in the conservatism and sentimentality of the nineteenth century.

Her supporters, on the other hand, cite the enormous variety of her subject matter; the breadth of forms she employed and the extent to which she developed rhythmical variation in her polyphonic prose; the freshness and vitality of many of her lyrics, particularly her poetry dealing with love; her brilliant and vivid sensory perceptions; the intelligence that complemented emotion in her poetry; and the range of emotions that her verse expressed. Contemporary feminist critics, in particular, in their revisionist readings of Lowell, have found her worthy of greater prominence than literary criticism has generally accorded her.

What most critics would probably agree on is that Lowell wrote at least a handful of excellent poems worthy of inclusion in any anthology of American poetry. There would also be general agreement that she played a paramount role in the poetic renaissance of the early twentieth century.

BIOGRAPHY

Amy Lowell was born in the family home (named "Sevenels" after her birth because there were then seven Lowells) in Brookline, Massachusetts, just outside Boston. Both of her parents were from distinguished and wealthy Massachusetts families. Her father, Augustus Lowell, was a member of the wealthiest branch of the Lowells, the prominent family who had come to America in 1639 and later had become a major force in the intellectual and industrial history of Massachusetts. The mill town of Lowell, Massachusetts, was named for the family. Lowell's mother, Katherine Bigelow Lawrence, was the daughter of Abbot Lawrence. The Lawrences were also an old American family, and another Massachusetts mill town was named for them.

Although the Lowells also owned a town house for the winter months, most of Lowell's childhood was spent at Sevenels, and she continued to live there, with the exception of summers in New Hampshire and abroad, until her death. After her parents' deaths, her mother's in 1895 and her father's in 1899, Lowell settled into Sevenels and made it her own, remodeling and refurnishing it extensively. The gardens there were the source of much of Lowell's imagery.

Lowell had two brothers and two sisters. Both brothers distinguished themselves, each in a different area. The elder, Percival, after ten years in the Orient and the publication of two books on the Far East, went to Flagstaff, Arizona, where he founded the Lowell Observatory and made discoveries concerning Mars. The younger brother, Abbott Lawrence, became president of Harvard University in 1909.

Lowell's formal education was limited. She was a mischievous pupil who was easily bored and a challenge to her teachers. Although she received a private school education, she did not attend college. Her own comment on her formal education was that "it really did not amount to a hill of beans." Most of her real education came from her avid reading in her father's library and in the Boston Athenaeum, a building she later wrote about and saved from razing. Her future profession was foreshadowed when she discovered Leigh Hunt's *Imagination and Fancy* and read it through and through. She was particularly taken with John Keats, about whom she later wrote a biography. Hunt's ideas about poetry were those of an earlier time, however, and were responsible, in part, for Lowell's unsuccessful first volume of rather old-fashioned poetry.

Because of a glandular condition, the five-foot-tall Lowell became obese in her adolescence and remained so, eventually weighing about 250 pounds. In spite of such corpulence, she was a successful debutante, having some sixty dinners given for her. Suitors, however, were few. Those who did appear were interested chiefly in her family connections. Lowell rejected two proposals of marriage and then accepted a third, only to be rejected later by her fiancé.

Eventually reconciled to spinsterhood, though not without much suffering, including a nervous breakdown requiring several years of convalescence, Lowell finally turned to poetry as a focus for her life. It also seemed to serve as a substitute for the orthodox Christian faith of her childhood, which she had rejected. Lowell had always been fascinated by the theater and was a creditable performer. Many thought that had she not been heavy, she would have become a professional actress. Her interest in theater, and indeed in all of the arts, continued throughout her life. Perhaps not so coincidentally, then, it was an actress, the great Eleanor Duse, who inspired Lowell to become a poet. It was 1902, the third time that she had seen Duse perform. Lowell later said that watching her "loosed a bolt in my brain and I knew where my true function lay." Having little training in poetry, Lowell began a long period of study and writing, with Hunt as her primary tutor. It was eight years before she published her first poems and ten before her first book appeared. During those years, she gradually withdrew from her many civic activities in order to concentrate on poetry. She received much support and encouragement throughout this period from Carl Engel, a young composer who also introduced her to new music.

On March 12, 1912, she met the person who was later to become her companion, critic, supporter, and confidante for life, Ada Dwyer Russell, an actress whom Lowell eventually coaxed into retirement. Many of Lowell's poems were inspired by, or written for, Mrs. Russell.

On October 12, 1912, her first collection of poems, *A Dome of Many-Coloured Glass*, was published to uniformly bad reviews, including one by Louis Untermeyer, who was later to become her friend and eventually to edit her collected poems. The year 1912 was an important one in American poetry. Harriet Monroe launched her new magazine *Poetry* in that year, a journal to which Lowell contributed both money and poems. The early issues of *Poetry* alerted Lowell to a group of poets in England who called themselves Les Imagistes and who were led by Ezra Pound and T. E. Hulme. Recognizing her own poetic tendencies in what she read, Lowell sailed for England, in the summer of 1913, to meet with Pound and the other poets and learn more about Imagism. She returned enthusiastic about what she had learned and about her own future. Within a year, Pound was in the center of a new movement, Vorticism, though he had recently edited a small anthology called

Des Imagistes. Lowell traveled to England again in 1914, meeting, among others, D. H. Lawrence, who was to become a close friend and whose talent Lowell immediately recognized. During that summer, Lowell and Pound parted in disagreement over the editorial policy of the next edition of *Des Imagistes*, and Lowell, with many of the poets on her side, took over the editorship of the anthology. She also took over the leadership of the Imagist movement and of the battle in America for the new poetic forms. Pound later dubbed the American movement "Amygism."

Lowell had learned much in two years, and *Sword Blades and Poppy Seed* was published in 1914 to great success, although only about a fourth of the poems were actually written in free verse. Lowell herself, in a short preface to the volume, used the term "unrhymed cadence." Three of the poems were written in what she called "polyphonic prose," a technique that she explained in the preface to a later book, *Can Grande's Castle*.

In 1915, 1916, and 1917, Lowell published the three volumes called *Some Imagist Poets*, picking up where Pound's *Des Imagistes* had left off and presenting seven to ten poems by each poet. Also in 1915, she published the successful *Six French Poets*, a book that brought her numerous speaking and reading engagements. From 1915 to 1918, Lowell was indefatigable. She gave countless lectures and readings, often traveling long distances on behalf of her own verse and of the New Poetry. She also wrote essays and reviews and produced several books. Always she was a friend to good writing and good writers, crusading tirelessly for others as well as for herself.

Men, Women and Ghosts, her next collection of poems, followed her French study. Next came another critical work, *Tendencies in Modern American Poetry*, followed by another volume of verse, *Can Grande's Castle*, her virtuoso production in polyphonic prose.

In 1916, Lowell injured herself lifting a carriage out of a ditch, causing the hernia which would eventually necessitate four operations and contribute to her death.

Her next publications were *Pictures of the Floating World*, reflecting her long study of the Orient, *Legends*, and *Fir-Flower Tablets*, translations of Chinese poetry done in collaboration with Florence Ayscough. *A Criti-*

cal Fable followed, and then Lowell began work on the book that was to be the culmination of a lifetime devotion to a single poet, John Keats. *John Keats* appeared in 1925; Lowell, driving herself to accomplish the task, became physically weaker and weaker during the course of its writing.

On May 12, 1925, she saw the side of her face droop while looking in a mirror, and in that moment, according to Damon, she "recognized her death." She died less than two hours later.

On August 25, *What's O'Clock* was published, and the following spring it won the Pulitzer Prize in poetry.

ANALYSIS

In its entirety, Amy Lowell's work is, as F. Cudworth Flint has observed, a history of the poetry of her time. Born in the 1870's, she died just three years after the publication of *The Waste Land.*

Although her first published work owed much, in both theme and form, to the Romantics and the Victorians, by her second book Lowell was planted more firmly in the twentieth century and, more specifically, in what has come to be known as the Poetic Renaissance. She herself used this term in her critical work, *Tendencies in Modern American Poetry.* It was a time of experimentation in all of the arts, in America as well as abroad. Lowell took control in America of the movement to revolutionize and modernize poetic forms and, by the end of her life at fifty-one, she was largely responsible for the acceptance in America of the "New Poetry." Poetry was popular in Lowell's day, and Lowell made it even more so. Though both her poetry and her ideas about it often enraged her audience, they never failed to elicit responses, and Lowell was such a dynamic saleswoman that she usually had the final word. Not a highly original thinker or writer, Lowell was able, nevertheless, to absorb the best of what was going on around her and build on it.

Lowell's work, though often faulted for being focused on externalities and devoid of emotion, is psychologically revealing, both of her own emotional states and, in some poems, of the ideas of Sigmund Freud and modern psychology. Many of her poems reveal her own experiences and emotions, and much of her imagery derives from her own life. Lowell's childhood at Sevenels,

at least into adolescence, when she became very heavy, was largely a happy one, and one of her greatest joys was her father's garden, later to become hers. Her knowledge and love of flowers, gardens, and birds permeates her work. The imagery is not all joyful, however, for Lowell lived out her life at Sevenels and her life also had its great disappointments and pain. Her obesity was probably responsible for her failure to marry and have a family, and, in disillusionment, she embraced poetry, almost as a spouse. Disillusionment about her work also occurs in the poems. In all, there is a tremendous amount of psychological as well as intellectual energy in her poems, partly a result of Lowell's driving need to achieve and compensate for what she had lost or never had. There is also peace in many of the poems, inspired by the security and contentment she found during the last eleven years of her life with Mrs. Russell. Many of the poems centering on love and devotion were inspired by Mrs. Russell.

Lowell's poetic subjects were wide-ranging. She wrote narratives on subjects as disparate as the frustration of a violinist's wife and the attempted rape of the moon by a fox. She wrote lyrics on such traditional subjects as love, disillusionment, artistic inspiration, and gardens, but she also wrote poems on buildings, cities, and wars. She wrote quasi epics that encompassed different centuries and countries, and dialect tales set in rural New England.

Glenn Richard Ruihley finds these diverse subjects unified by Lowell's transcendentalism, her search for the "Numinous or Divine" residing in all people and things. It was, according to Ruihley, the possibility of transcendence that she recognized that night while watching Duse act.

Her technical virtuosity was as great as her thematic range. Her use of metaphors and symbols was extensive. According to Ruihley, the only way to understand much of Lowell's work is through a study of "her chosen symbols." Though an outspoken advocate of poetic experimentation, she wrote in traditional forms as well as in free verse and polyphonic prose, often ranging through several forms in a single poem. Her virtuosity was unquestioned, but, like most virtuosity, it was exhausting as well as dazzling. She exhausted not through sheer variety of poetic forms but through a prolixity, particularly in much of her polyphonic prose, that left the reader drugged with sheer sensation and unable to absorb more.

Though she professed to be an Imagist, at least in her early work, and was the movement's leader in America, Lowell was never contained or restrained enough in her work to be truly Imagistic in the sense that the movement is usually defined. She was too expansive. In many of her poems, however, sometimes only in individual groups of lines, she did achieve what is usually thought of as Imagistic expression.

"ON LOOKING AT A COPY OF ALICE MEYNELL'S POEMS"

One of the recurring themes in Lowell's poetry is her disillusionment, selfdoubt, and even despair. A representative poem in this vein is "On Looking at a Copy of Alice Meynell's Poems: Given Me Years Ago by a Friend" (*Ballads for Sale*). When Lowell learned of Meynell's death in November, 1922, she turned again to the volume of Meynell's poems given to her twenty-five years earlier by Frances Dabney. In that year, 1897, Lowell had had her marriage engagement broken off by her young Bostonian suitor. Hoping to alleviate her grief, Dabney had given her the poems. In rereading the poems on Meynell's death, Lowell found little to admire, but the poems did renew her feelings of despair and bitterness.

Written in a rhyming, metered, and regular stanzaic form, the poem records Lowell's present and past reflections on Meynell's book. She evaluates it both as a gift and as a work of art. As she reads again the "whispered greeting" inscribed by Dabney, the memories surface, "dim as pictures on a winking wall," but vivid enough in the illumination of the moment to revive her emotions. Dabney's gift, intended "to ease the smart," was instead a painful "mirror," reflecting Lowell's own tragic lack of fulfillment, yet Lowell remembers how she once "loved to quote" these lines.

From her present perspective, Lowell wonders at both her own and Dabney's judgment. She distances herself from her memories as she contemplates the changes brought by time. Both Dabney and Meynell are dead, and the verses that once seemed so brilliant now seem merely "well-made." Lowell has "lived the almanac" since that time and still has "so much to do."

Though Meynell's and Lowell's old griefs seem insignificant now and Lowell refuses to linger any longer with them, she is still sympathetic to the pain, a sympathy tempered, however, by her awareness of old age and death and the ultimate futility of fame and happiness. These feelings are briefly captured in the magnificent and poignant third-from-the-last stanza: "So cried her heart, a feverish thing./ But clay is still, and clay is cold,/ And I was young, and I am old,/ And in December what birds sing!" Lowell cannot allow herself to remain in this mood, and in the final two stanzas, she returns the book to its shelf where "dust" will again cover the pain. For Ruihley, "Lowell's incompleteness" and "longing for wider satisfactions" are shared in some measure by everyone, albeit for varying reasons and in varying degrees. Her poem, then, transcends her own experience in its applicability and appeal.

RELATIONSHIPS BETWEEN PEOPLE AND THINGS

A second theme running throughout Lowell's work, and one that is suggested rather than directly stated, is the relationship between human beings and material forms. Lowell's pictorialism is brilliant and abundant, but rather than representing only surface effects as it was often unfairly accused of doing, it has its origin in sympathetic feeling and reveals a passionate heart. A beautiful example of this theme (and the poem which was most often requested at Lowell's frequent readings) is "Lilacs" (*What's O'Clock*).

"Lilacs" expresses clearly the relationship between things or places and people, a relationship indivisible and full of emotion. The poem expansively chronicles the spatial and temporal domain of the lilac. It is a list that finally incorporates the poet herself until she and New England and history and time and the lilac are one. Throughout the poem, the lilac is an active participant in its settings, playing many roles—conversing, watching, settling, staggering, tapping, running, standing, persuading, flaunting, charging, and calling. Having originated in the East, the lilac beckons to those who sail in from China, but it has become most fully itself in the soil of New England. The flower is both in its settings and of its settings, and finally it becomes its settings as it mingles with places and lives and takes on a significance far beyond that of any of its individual manifestations:

You are the great flood of our souls
Bursting above the leaf-shapes of our hearts,
You are the smell of all Summers,
The love of wives and children,
The recollection of the gardens of little children,
You are State Houses and Charters. . . .

In the last stanza, Lowell identifies herself directly with the lilac as it embodies her own soil, New England ("Lilac in me because I am New England"). Her litany of reasons for such a union, underscored by repetitive structures, serves to emphasize the force and passion of her feelings.

Another example of the emotional import of material forms in Lowell's work is the popular "Meeting-House Hill." The scene portrayed is a simple one. The poet, from the eminence of "a squalid hill-top," observes a quiet scene: "the curve of a blue bay beyond a railroad track" and "a white church above thin trees in a city square." The scene itself is unremarkable except as it affects the poet, who suggests that she must be "mad, or very tired." The bay seems to sing to her and the church "amazes . . . as though it were the Parthenon." The imagination and emotion of the poet give movement to the scene until it is transformed into the final arresting image, which occupies ten of the poem's twenty-five lines. The spire of the church becomes the mast of a ship just returned from Canton. As the ship enters the bay carrying "green and blue porcelain," the poet sees a "Chinese coolie leaning over the rail/ Gazing at the white spire." It is a vivid scene and the reader moves within the imagination of the poet so that the reader too feels the emotion of the moment and sees the transformation.

The "coolie" is both of the spire (the mast of his ship) and gazing at it, both passive object of contemplation and active contemplator, so that the two worlds of reality and imagination merge fully. This is far from a mere portrayal of the surfaces of things. Objects, landscapes, flowers, and birds are emblems in Lowell's work and are always portrayed with feeling.

LOVE AND DEVOTION

A third dominant theme in Lowell's poetry is that of love and devotion. It is "love in its combined physical and spiritual totality," as Jean Gould points out, that is celebrated in Lowell's work. Poems on this theme take many forms and honor many subjects, but the greatest are those inspired by Eleanor Duse and Mrs. Russell. Among those written for Russell are several of Lowell's most popular and enduring lyrics: "Madonna of the Evening Flowers," "Venus Transiens," "A Sprig of Rosemary," and "A Decade," all from *Pictures of the Floating World*; "In Excelsis" (*What's O'Clock*); and "The Taxi" (*Sword Blades and Poppy Seed*).

The scene in "Madonna of the Evening Flowers" is again simple. Lowell, tired from her day's work, calls for Russell. She is answered only by the wind and the sun shining on the remnants of her companion's recent activity—her books and her sewing implements. Though Lowell impatiently continues the search for her friend, the scene above has foreshadowed for the reader the simple domestic setting in which Russell will eventually be found. When finally spotted, Russell is "Standing under a spire of pale blue larkspur,/ With a basket of roses on [her] arm." The rest of the poem records Russell's practical responses to Lowell and Lowell's concomitant reflections. Lowell's attitude is worshipful, in contrast with the secular nature of Russell's concerns, and the natural and human scene merges with the divine as Lowell hears the imagined "*Te Deums* of the Canterbury Bells."

"In Excelsis" again strikes a worshipful note and one full of rapture. In it, Lowell sees Russell as both the creator of the natural world and the embodiment of it. It is Russell whose movements control the processes of nature and Russell who is herself the "air—earth—heaven" of Lowell's universe. As in "Madonna of the Evening Flowers," the poet's impulse is to kneel before such glory, but she restrains herself from excesses: "Heaven" is not a "boon deserving thanks." She will accept the life that Russell brings to her; her poems will be her thanks, "rubies" set in "stone."

"The Taxi" has a different tone. Probably written during one of Lowell's separations from Russell, the poem speaks of the pain of separation. The images are vivid and startling, hauntingly modern in their metaphors. In the loved one's absence, the world turns hostile to the poet. The streets "wedge" Russell away from Lowell, and the city lights "prick" Lowell's eyes. The night has "sharp edges" that "wound."

Other love poems are more tranquil, projecting neither the rapturous adoration of "Madonna of the Evening

Flowers" and "In Excelsis" nor the fearful tension of "The Taxi." The poet is often at peace in her love, admiring the beauty of her friend as if she were Botticelli's Venus ("Venus Transiens"), reflecting on the restfulness of her hands and voice ("A Sprig of Rosemary"), and savoring the simple nourishment of her presence ("A Decade").

Lowell's importance as a force in American literary history is undisputed. Her crusading efforts on behalf of modern poetry and poets had a formative influence on the development of American poetry in the twentieth century. The place of her own poetry is not as solidly determined. An untiring experimenter in verse forms, she was not a great poet, but she did write a few enduring poems which, it seems likely, will find a permanent place in the literary canon of her time.

OTHER MAJOR WORKS

NONFICTION: *Six French Poets*, 1915; *Tendencies in Modern American Poetry*, 1917; *John Keats*, 1925; *Poetry and Poets*, 1930; *Florence Ayscough and Amy Lowell: Correspondence of a Friendship*, 1945.

TRANSLATION: *Fir-Flower Tablets*, 1921 (with Florence Ayscough).

EDITED TEXTS: *Some Imagist Poets*, Volumes I-III, 1915-1917.

BIBLIOGRAPHY

Benvenuto, Richard. *Amy Lowell*. Boston: Twayne, 1985. Aims to give a fair and detailed reading of Lowell's poetry in order to suggest the strengths and limitations of her art, as well as to acquaint the reader with poems that, in Benvenuto's opinion, should not be neglected any longer. Besides being an erratic and uneven writer, Lowell was, Benvenuto argues, one of the most important literary figures of her time. Includes an annotated bibliography.

Flint, F. Cudworth. *Amy Lowell*. Minneapolis: University of Minnesota Press, 1969. This forty-eight-page pamphlet devoted to Lowell's life and work contains useful information about Lowell's participation in the Imagist movement. Addresses the question of how Lowell was able to achieve what Flint calls a "para-literary" eminence so quickly. Contains a bibliography.

Galvin, Mary E. *Queer Poetics: Five Modernist Women Writers*. Westport, Conn.: Greenwood Press, 1999. In an exploration of the relation between poetics and queer theory, Galvin presents a theoretical framework that can illuminate the way we read the specific poetic innovations of the writers in this study by placing them in a different social and epistemological context—that of "queer" existence.

Gould, Jean. *Amy: The World of Amy Lowell and the Imagist Movement*. New York: Dodd, Mead, 1975. This lengthy volume views Lowell's work in its historical context. Gould asserts that Lowell was one of the outstanding influences in the literary art of her time and focuses his discussion on her role in creating the Imagist movement. In her campaign for modern freedom of expression in poetry, Gould portrays Lowell as a vociferous advocate of revolutionary rhythms and free verse. Includes a bibliography.

Gregory, Horace. *Amy Lowell: Portrait of the Poet in Her Time*. Edinburgh, N.Y.: Thomas Nelson, 1958. Purports not to be a conventional biography but a portrait of the poet. The interpretative historical essay attempts to place Lowell among other poets of her day. Gregory sees Lowell as an archetypal "romantic" and discusses her role as advancer of the New Poetry.

Hughes, Glenn. "Amy Lowell: 'The Success.'" In *Imagism and the Imagists: A Study in Modern Poetry*. Stanford, Calif.: Stanford University Press, 1931. In this dated but excellent study of Lowell's life and work, Hughes, interested in the new effects of Lowell's work, discusses the polyphonic aspects of her poetry. Examines both her contribution to American poetry and her influence on it. Passages from individual poems are analyzed.

Ruihley, Glenn R. *The Thorn of a Rose: Amy Lowell Reconsidered*. Hamden, Conn.: Archon Books, 1975. One of the most useful critical studies on Lowell, this book assesses Lowell's rightful place in American literature. In attempting to redress the balance of critical opinion in her favor, the author argues that it is necessary to understand the inner character of Lowell's life and work—for example, the philosophical framework of her poetry. Focuses on the art of Lowell's middle and late periods. Contains a bibliography.

Elaine Gardiner;
bibliography updated by the editors

JAMES RUSSELL LOWELL

Born: Cambridge, Massachusetts; February 22, 1819
Died: Cambridge, Massachusetts; August 12, 1891

PRINCIPAL POETRY
A Year's Life, 1841
Poems, 1844
Poems: Second Series, 1848
A Fable for Critics, 1848
The Biglow Papers, 1848
The Vision of Sir Launfal, 1848
Ode Recited at the Harvard Commemoration,
    July 21, 1865, 1865
The Biglow Papers: Second Series, 1867
Under the Willows and Other Poems, 1869
The Cathedral, 1870
Three Memorial Poems, 1877
Heartsease and Rue, 1888
Last Poems of James Russell Lowell, 1895
The Complete Poetical Works of James Russell
    Lowell, 1896
The Uncollected Poetry of James Russell Lowell,
    1950

OTHER LITERARY FORMS
    Besides thirteen volumes of poetry, James Russell Lowell published during his lifetime ten collections of essays, most of which had already been printed in periodicals. The ten collections centered themselves on literary criticism, arising from his scholarly duties as professor of modern languages and literature at Harvard University (1855-1886), and political theory, arising from his contact with the Republican Party and his role as American ambassador to Spain (1877-1880) and England (1880-1887). The criticism—*Conversations on Some of the Old Poets* (1845), *Among My Books* (1870), *My Study Windows* (1871), *Among My Books: Second Series* (1876), *The English Poets: Lessing, Rousseau* (1888), *Latest Literary Essays and Addresses* (1891), and *The Old English Dramatists* (1892)—shows a fluid, informal style grounded on few theoretical principles. The early works tend toward a vaguely Romantic approach, emphasizing the authors whom Lowell found

inspirational. The later volumes are more conservative, based on more formal aesthetic principles. The same movement can be detected in Lowell's political theory. In *Fireside Travels* (1864) Lowell collected informal, chatty essays on Italy, Maine, and Cambridge. His *Democracy and Other Addresses* (1887) and *Political Essays* (1888) display a much more systematic approach to cultural commentary.
    Since most of the thirteen volumes of poetry and ten volumes of prose were first printed in magazines and newspapers, Lowell's primary audience was found among periodical readers and editors. He helped to shape many of the major American magazines of the nineteenth century. He was a contributing editor to short-lived literary magazines such as *The Pioneer* and *The Dial*, to abolitionist magazines such as the *Pennsylvania Freeman* and the *National Anti-Slavery Standard*, and to major publications such as *The Atlantic Monthly* and the *North American Review*. Much of the work that he did for these publications was reprinted in *Early Prose Writings of James Russell Lowell* (1902) and *The Anti-Slavery Papers of James Russell Lowell* (1902). Lowell saved some of his best prose for his personal friends, and the two-volume edition of his *Letters of James Russell Lowell* (1894; Charles Eliot Norton, editor) deserves to be more widely read.

ACHIEVEMENTS
    For James Russell Lowell, writing poetry was but one of several careers that he managed to sustain successfully and simultaneously. His first volume of poetry was composed during 1840 and 1841 while he was also trying to open his own law practice. His second was written while he was helping to launch a new magazine, *Pioneer: A Literary and Critical Journal*. After the magazine failed in 1843, Lowell threw himself into writing propaganda for the antislavery movement, accepting the post of editorial writer for Philadelphia's *The Freeman* and *Anti-Slavery Standard* simultaneously. From 1845 to 1848 he was also supplementing his meager income by writing literary criticism for *Graham's Magazine*. Despite the demands and prestige of the three assignments, he also found time to write three of his longest and best poems–*A Fable for Critics*, *The Biglow Papers*, and *The Vision of Sir Launfal*—all by 1848.

Lowell sustained such division of energy and interest throughout his career. In the 1850's, he mixed the publication of scholarly criticism, teaching at Harvard, and editing the newly founded *Atlantic Monthly* with his poetry. For good measure, he also started a novel. In the 1860's, he tried to edit the *North American Review*, keep his post at Harvard, issue collections of his prose works, and still write poetry. In the 1870's, he added a political career to his publishing, academic, and creative endeavors, campaigning to reform the Republican Party and accepting appointments as the nation's ambassador to Spain in 1877 and to Great Britain in 1880. He broadened the base of his readership and reputation by publishing a great deal of political commentary as well. In addition to being a poet, he was, said one of his admirers, "our acknowledged, foremost man of letters." Diplomat, journalist, critic, academic, and poet, Lowell's life was divided among a variety of interests, none of which seemed capable of holding his attention for very long.

This multiplicity of interests proved to be both the greatest strength and the greatest weakness of his literary career. It injected into the corpus of his poetry a fresh stream of ideas, moving them from stilted and derivative lyrics to bitter abolitionist verse, biting satire, political commentary, cultural meditation, and warmhearted regional description. The division of his energies, however, also robbed his poetry of the singularity of voice and consistency of tone that frequently mark poets of the first rank. Technically facile and frequently erudite, Lowell's poetry too often seemed to flow or ebb with the vagaries of his employment or the shifts in popular taste. His contemporaries thought that his poetry—which eventually filled 650 double-columned pages in the memorial edition of his work—was among the best their era had produced. He was generally acknowledged to be one of the two or three major American poets of the century. Twentieth century readers have not been so receptive, branding his ideas as commonplace, his style as derivative, and his voice as inconsistent. Lowell's poetry lacked the intensity to merit the praise it was given in the nineteenth century, but it deserves a more careful reading than it has been given by most twentieth century readers. With his range of tone, the fluidity of his cadences, the breadth of his intellect, the wit of his satire, and the accuracy of his depictions of nineteenth century American thought, Lowell's poetry remains much more than a historical curiosity.

BIOGRAPHY

James Russell Lowell was born into an important New England family that had been playing a prominent role in Massachusetts history ever since a wealthy merchant from Bristol, Percival Lowell, had helped to found the town of Newbury. Lowell's grandfather was a lawyer, a leading member of the Continental Congress. The poet's uncle, Francis Cabot Lowell, was one of the leading industrialists of the age, having given the family name to a factory town on the banks of the Merrimac River. His cousin was founder of Boston's Lowell Institute, and descendants of these Lowells, the poets Amy and Robert, kept the family name before readers well into the twentieth century. To be born into such a family meant that Lowell was outfitted for success from birth. His parents had him reading before he was four, translating French before he was ten, studying Latin and Greek in the small classical school run by William Wells, and gaining admission to Harvard by the time he was fifteen.

James Russell Lowell (Hulton Archive)

The youngest of six children, Lowell never quite outgrew the advantages his family so willingly bestowed on him. As it turned out, he lived and died in the same familial mansion, Elmwood, in which he was born. His father helped to subsidize his first three volumes of poetry. In 1854, his cousin helped to launch his academic career by paying him to deliver a series of lectures at the Lowell Institute. The lectures turned out well enough to convince a close family friend, Henry Wadsworth Longfellow, to campaign to have him appointed to a professorship at Harvard the following year. Another cousin, James Elliot Cabot, as well as Longfellow and Ralph Waldo Emerson, recommended him for the editorship of the newly established *Atlantic Monthly* in 1867. The Lowell name and fortune, together with the conservative political commentary that he wrote for the *Atlantic Monthly* and the *North American Review*, proved to be influential enough to launch him eventually on a diplomatic career. By 1877, his support of President Hayes had netted him an appointment as the American ambassador to Spain. By 1880, he had moved up to become the country's ambassador to England.

From the start, Lowell abetted these advantages with his own hard work, his serious commitment to the craft of writing, and his enviable record for accomplishing nearly everything he set out to do. The Lowell name may have opened for him many a door, but his own steady performance guaranteed that he would be offered positions of increasing importance and influence. Yet the same hard work and the responsiveness to the traditions and duties of his family kept him from finding the real James Russell Lowell. From the time when his Harvard classmates elected him to write and read their class poem during the 1839 commencement to the posthumous publication of *Last Poems of James Russell Lowell* in 1895, Lowell could be counted on to write what was expected of him rather than what he expected of himself. To gain the approval of his fellow graduates, Lowell could satirize the militancy and zeal of the abolitionist movement. To gain the approval, five years later, of his fiancé—Maria White was a protégé of social reformer Margaret Fuller and a militant abolitionist—he could turn his talents to editing the same abolitionist journals he had poked fun at in his commencement poem. When she died in 1853, Lowell lost either his interest in or sense of duty toward the abolitionist movement. Yet another family commitment, a contract to deliver thirteen lectures on the English poets for his cousin's Lowell Institute, moved him from his bent toward satire, his involvement in reform, and his formal lyric poetry to a career as a literary critic.

Lowell spent nearly fifty years as an apologist for institutional America, articulating clearly and sometimes passionately the principal social, aesthetic, and political beliefs of the educated upper class of America's Atlantic seaboard. It was a community of readers for whom his family, his friends, his training, and his temperament had made him a perfect spokesman. Beneath the public success, however, Lowell privately grew more despondent about spending his life as a publicist for the country's most influential periodicals, prestigious universities, and reputable literary circles. "I feel that my life has been mainly wasted," he complained only a few years before his death: "that I have thrown away more than most men ever had." His confession that he was "never quite pleased with what I do," that he had "spent most of my life" pursuing "the muse, without ever catching up to her," hinted at an underlying frustration. Lowell invested so much of his energy in meeting the obligations of his station that he never quite settled on who he wanted to be or what he wanted to write. Retired from his diplomatic appointments, Lowell spent the last two years of his life at Elmwood, living with his daughter and grandchildren, rearranging and rewriting his volumes for a "collected" edition of his works, and lamenting occasionally that his poetry seemed "to me, just like all the verses I read in the papers." He died at home on August 12, 1891.

ANALYSIS

Much of James Russell Lowell's poetry does not deserve as harsh a judgment as he himself accorded it. Partially, Lowell's sense of failure came from his inability to settle on what kind of verse he was most suited to write. He could pose as a lyric poet who was facile in dressing up contemporary ideas in traditional verse forms with appropriately suitable diction in the manner of the Fireside School. He could pose as a writer of light verse who could supply the periodical audience with historical romances such as *The Vision of Sir Launfal* or warmhearted, local-color sketches of New England eccentrics. He could pose as a satiric poet who could capture the foibles of the political and academic establishments. He could pose as a philosophical poet in the manner of William Wordsworth or Samuel Taylor Coleridge. Yet none of his four most frequently employed poetic stances seemed to be the genuine voice of James Russell Lowell. His regret that he had never "really caught up" to his muse was a complaint that many of his severest critics would echo. "In Mr. Lowell's prose works," a reviewer pointed out in 1848, "we have before observed a certain disjointedness." With his new *A Fable for Critics*, the "looseness," the "rambling plot," the "want of artistic finish," the "lack of polish" characteristic of his criticism had spilled over into his approach to poetry, the critic continued. In 1952, one of Lowell's ablest biographers branded his work as lacking the kind of "coherent personality" that could make his words endure.

Unable to find a voice of his own, too distracted by the various employment opportunities that came his way to spend much time rewriting or repressing the worst of his poetry, and betrayed by his own prodigious talents, which enabled him to dash off verses quickly and fluently, Lowell had produced by the end of his life much undistinguished poetry. In each of his four characteristic modes, however, individual poems can be found that display a high degree of craftsmanship, a quick wit, a sharp eye for detail, an easy, natural cadence, and a steady and thoughtful mind.

Six of Lowell's thirteen collections of verse were anchored by traditional odes, sonnets, and lyrics dressed up in a style that one of Lowell's contemporaries praised as a "masterful" blend of all "the chords of a lyre," sounding in "loud, but harmonious concert." In *A Year's Life*, the 1844 and the 1848 editions of *Poems*, *Under the Willows and Other Poems*, *Heartsease and Rue*, and *Last Poems of James Russell Lowell*, Lowell struggled with the poetic conventions of his day. Frequently, he lost. Imitating alternately the voices of John Keats, Wordsworth, Longfellow, and Alfred, Lord Tennyson, Lowell created a series of random reflections that stitched together pat phrases, formulaic ideas, long Latinate constructions, and overly generalized descriptions. These were the least successful of his four stylistic poses. They reworked well-worn subject matter: his love for Maria

White in the earlier volumes and his awe of the New England countryside in the later ones. Frequently, they were derived not from his actual life experiences but from secondary reactions to some other art form: a review of "The Mona Lisa" or "On Hearing a Sonata of Beethoven Played in the Next Room" or his sonnet sequences to Keats or Wordsworth. Many of these poems managed to sound "poetic" without displaying much originality or passion. They could offhandedly summarize Keats's poetry as "serene and pure, like gushing joy of light." They could describe Lowell's fiancé as a "maiden whose birth could command the morning-stars their ancient music make." They could explain the duty of the poet: "his nobleness should be God like high" so that "his least deed is perfect as a star."

On occasion, however, he could infuse even these traditional forms with a freshness of diction, a naturalness of rhythm, a precision of image, and an economy of language showing that when he found the time to write, he could write very well indeed. In *Under the Willows and Other Poems* and *Heartsease and Rue*, Lowell's facility at turning a phrase could frequently redeem his conventional material by unconventional animation. His skies could be "sweet as a psalm." A scorned lover, "walking alone where we walked together," could discover "in the grey autumnal weather" that "the leaves fade, inconstant as you." His philosophy of life could be compressed into the pithy "not failure, but low aim, is the crime."

When Lowell aimed his poetry lower, however, he frequently achieved greater success. His conventional lyrics, which were aimed at a cultivated audience who demanded conventional ideas in a conventional style, frequently deadened Lowell's enthusiasms. When he wrote down to a less educated readership with the aim of persuading, delighting, or entertaining, he often gave his natural wit full rein and created a series of lighthearted poems having the suppleness, spontaneity, and mischievousness of Mark Twain's prose or Ogden Nash's verse. His first three volumes contained few of these newspaper or magazine pieces, but *Under the Willows and Other Poems* and *Heartsease and Rue* were in the main collections of periodical pieces first printed in the *Atlantic Monthly*, the *Century Illustrated Monthly Magazine*, *The Nation*, and the *New York Ledger*.

"THE UNHAPPY LOT OF MR. KNOTT"

"The Unhappy Lot of Mr. Knott," which first appeared in *Graham's Magazine* in 1851, typified this happier Lowell with its sharp-edged portrait of the more shallow aspirations of New England's middle classes. His description of Knott's daughter's wedding, complete with its digressive and gratuitous advertisement, was characteristic of the stylistic pyrotechnics he sustained throughout the thousand-line cultural portrait:

> Accordingly, this artless maid
> Her father's ordinance obeyed,
> And, all in whitest crape arrayed,
> (Miss Pulsifer the dresses made
> And wishes here the fact displayed
> That she still carries on the trade,
> The third door south from Bagg's Arcade.)

His control of rhyme, rhythm, and narrative showed a technical virtuosity that he seldom duplicated in his more serious poetry.

"FITZ ADAMS' STORY"

Lowell's "Fitz Adams' Story," published in the *Atlantic Monthly* in 1867, displayed several additional devices in his arsenal of skills. Primary was Lowell's command of regional dialect. Ezra Weeks, the proprietor of the country inn where Fitz Adams was staying, could summarize his approach to cooking game birds this way:

> Wal, them's real nice uns, an'll eat A 1,
> Ef I can stop their bein' overdone;
> Nothin' riles me (I pledge my fastin' word)
> Like cookin' out the natur' of a bird . . .
> Jes scare 'em with the coals,—thet's my idee.

Lowell also exhibited a keen eye for detail and an even keener mind for universalizing the details he found. Above Weeks's mantel was this portrait of his parents:

> Mister and Mistress W. in their youth,—
> New England youth, that seems a sort of pill . . .
> Bitter to swallow, and which leaves a trace
> Of Calvinistic colic on the face.

Its breezy, iambic pentameter rhythm, accented with rhyming couplets, showed a playfulness and an experimental approach to metrics that kept the poem's cadences fresh for almost all of its 632 lines. In "The Flying Dutchman" and "The Voyage to Vinland," Lowell discovered that he could make the same informal approach to purely historical subjects. In his light verse, he seemed to find the freedom to overcome the deadening conventions that marred his more serious poetry. Yet his own sense of self-worth and his traditional attitudes toward what poetry should be prevented him from writing much verse in this, his happiest of styles. He had frequently proven that he was good at the pose, but he never quite let himself believe that the pose was good enough for him.

A FABLE FOR CRITICS

On occasion, Lowell could turn the warmhearted humor of his lighter verses into cool, even bitter, invective. Some of his satiric poetry managed to be as biting as some of Jonathan Swift's best prose and as angry as Alexander Pope's least charitable couplets. The most famous of his satires, and the most often anthologized, was his *A Fable for Critics*, which first appeared in 1848. It was a long, loosely structured narrative that gave Lowell the opportunity to demean most of the major and many of the minor writers in America. To a gathering of the gods on Olympus is summoned a critic who "bolts every book that comes out of the press/ Without the least question of larger or less." He was asked to review the careers of his fellow writers and find among them, "a rose." After ripping apart Bronson Alcott, Orestes Brownson, Theodore Parker, William Cullen Bryant, John Greenleaf Whittier, Richard Henry Dana, Edgar Allan Poe, and James Fenimore Cooper, the critic concluded that the best American has to offer Greece was but a thistle. If Lowell's critical summaries of rival authors tended toward brutality, he managed to leaven the tone of the whole by using the same playfulness he would later use in "Fitz Adams' Story." He filled *A Fable for Critics* with puns, condemning, for example, prophets who "got their name of augurs, because they were bores." He tightroped his way around the downright silly with an array of surprising rhymes. In one breathless sequence, he strung twelve feminine rhymes together: rely on, scion, ply on, try on, eye one, zion, buy one, fie on, lion, spy on, wry on, and die on.

What *A Fable for Critics* did for American letters, the two series of *The Biglow Papers* did for American politics. Prompted by Lowell's conservative reaction against the imperialism of the Mexican-American War, the first series of satires appeared in 1848 along with *A Fable for Critics*. The papers consisted of a series of letters, essays, poems, and commentaries supposedly written by a variety of New England eccentrics. They indicted recruiters (with "twenty rooster tails stuck onto their hats and eenamost enuf brass a bobbin' up and down"), soldiering ("Ninepence a day for killin' folks comes kind o' low for murder"), American conformity ("for one might imagine America to have been colonized by a tribe of those nondescript African animals the Aye-Ayes, so difficult a word is 'No' to us all"), jingoistic politicians in general, General Winfield Scott and Senator John Calhoun in particular, and hawkish newspaper editors ("the name 'editor' is [derived] not so much from *edo*, to publish, as from *edo*, to eat. . . . They blow up the flames of political discord to boil their own pots"). Lowell's satires could be telling displays of a lifetime accumulation of stored anger: at writers who did not take themselves as seriously as he did, at politicians more swayed by popularity than by principle, at the general thickheadedness of the American public, and especially, perhaps, at his own failures to confront these concerns in his own serious writing.

SERIOUS VERSE

On the few occasions when Lowell allowed himself to tackle serious thought with what he took to be serious verse, he produced a group of uneven reflections, sometimes brilliant, sometimes banal. In *Under the Willows and Other Poems*, *The Cathedral*, "The Ode for the 100th Anniversary of the Fight at Concord Bridge," "The Ode for the Fourth of July, 1876," "Agassiz," and *Ode Recited at the Harvard Commemoration, July 21, 1865*, Lowell tried to compress a lifetime of thought. Together, these poems show his growing conservatism, a rigidity of mind and form that bears little resemblance to the inventiveness of his lighter verse. In *Under the Willows and Other Poems*, he moodily reflects on the glories of nature without garnering much glory for his subject or for his treatment of it. Its nearly four hundred lines do little more than recommend being gentle on and with New England's best June days.

THE CATHEDRAL

In *The Cathedral*, probably his best philosophical poem, he centers on a visit to Chartres and explores with precision, depth, and compassion some of the material only briefly touched on in "Under the Willows." Man's relationship with nature, so fuzzily treated in the early poem, is amplified in *The Cathedral* as a mixture of the objective and the subjective. Whether inspecting willows on a hot June day or building a monument, "graceful, grotesque, with ever new surprise," man seeks always, Lowell claims, some sort of synthesis between his interior consciousness and his exterior environment. For him, the cathedral becomes "Imagination's very self in stone."

The visit to Chartres (as did similar visits by many nineteenth century authors) occasioned a regret-filled commentary on the lack of the spiritual and the mystical in contemporary life. Whether in communing with nature or constructing edifices to religious aspirations, "this is no age to get Cathedrals built." Instead, modern man seems more likely to demean the efforts of the past, asking questions such as: "Did Faith build this wonder? Or did Fear, that makes a fetish and misnames it God?" In blotting "out life with questions marks," in unduly relying on "secular conclusions," in its own hyperconsciousness of "earth's comedy," modern civilization has failed to realize, he claims, that "each age must worship its own thought of God." His own age has been unable to find a satisfactory image of this transcendental impulse and thus remains a world of "incompleteness" where "sorrow" is "swift, consolation a laggard." The sense of faith and purposefulness, displayed so extravagantly at Chartres, suggests answers of a sort desperately needed by modern man. Lowell tries to end the rumination optimistically: "Faith and wonder and the primal earth," he asserts, "are born into the world with every child." As much as Emerson or Walt Whitman, Lowell believed that the godly was still available to contemporary man; he was simply less sure than his forebears how it should be attained.

Lowell vaguely recognized that his culture seemed to lack the sense of idealism that had driven previous civilizations. His was an era content with pat answers from the past and blind optimism regarding the future. This awareness filled his satiric poetry with hard-edged bitterness, but in his philosophical poetry Lowell never quite found the right voice to articulate his concerns, nor the courage to betray the commitments of his public voice.

OTHER MAJOR WORKS

NONFICTION: *Conversations on Some of the Old Poets*, 1845; *Fireside Travels*, 1864; *Among My Books*, 1870; *My Study Windows*, 1871; *Among My Books: Second Series*, 1876; *Democracy and Other Addresses*, 1887; *Political Essays*, 1888; *The English Poets: Lessing, Rousseau*, 1888; *Latest Literary Essays and Addresses*, 1891; *The Old English Dramatists*, 1892; *Letters of James Russell Lowell*, 1894 (Charles Eliot Norton, editor); *Early Prose Writings of James Russell Lowell*, 1902; *The Anti-Slavery Papers of James Russell Lowell*, 1902.

MISCELLANEOUS: *The Complete Writings of James Russell Lowell*, 1904 (16 volumes).

BIBLIOGRAPHY

Beatty, Richmond Croom. *James Russell Lowell*. Knoxville: University of Tennessee Press, 1942. Reprint. Hamden, Conn.: Archon Books, 1969. Beatty's study is based on a thorough examination of Lowell's manuscripts and heavily criticizes the poet's political judgments at times. Includes bibliographical references.

Broaddus, Dorothy C. *Genteel Rhetoric: Writing High Culture in Nineteenth-Century Boston*. Columbia: University of South Carolina Press, 1999. An analysis of the use of rhetoric by several authors, including James Russell Lowell. Broaddus delves into the creation of high culture, character, and war. Includes bibliographical references and index.

Duberman, Martin B. *James Russell Lowell*. Boston: Houghton Mifflin, 1966. This well-researched biography is based mainly on manuscript materials and refers to the poetry and criticism of Lowell throughout. It provides a historian's evaluation of Lowell's political writings and activities. Supplemented by thorough notes, bibliographies, and an index.

Hudson, William Henry. *Lowell and His Poetry*. 1914. Reprint. New York: AMS Press, 1972. This volume of the Poetry and Life series is a reprint of a 1914 edition originally published in London. Hudson focuses on the poetry, not the life. In the course of his discussion, he quotes the full text of nine poems, which are listed in the beginning of the book. This brief study includes "The Changeling," "The First Snowfall," "After the Burial," and *Ode Recited at the Harvard Commemoration, July 21, 1865*.

McGlinchee, Claire. *James Russell Lowell*. United States Authors 120. New York: Twayne, 1967. The first chapter looks at Lowell in the context of nineteenth century American literature, and the second and third chapters offer a chronological account of Lowell's life through 1860. The following six chapters are devoted to his early poems, his criticism, details on his careers as professor, diplomat, and editor, his political verse (*The Biglow Papers*), and his later poetry (*The Cathedral* and the odes). Contains notes, an annotated bibliography, and an index.

Wagenknecht, Edward. *James Russell Lowell: Portrait of a Many-Sided Man*. New York: Oxford University Press, 1971. This book supplements Martin B. Duberman's more definitive biography by providing a less formal character portrait. Wagenknecht's facts are, however, authentic. (Duberman checked his manuscript.) Discussions of the poetic influences on Lowell and his approach to poetry make up two chapters, "Storing the Well" and "The Creative Life." Complemented by notes, a selective bibliography, and an index.

Philip Woodard;
bibliography updated by the editors

ROBERT LOWELL

Born: Boston, Massachusetts; March 1, 1917
Died: New York, New York; September 12, 1977

PRINCIPAL POETRY

Land of Unlikeness, 1944
Lord Weary's Castle, 1946
Poems, 1938-1949, 1950
The Mills of the Kavanaughs, 1951
Life Studies, 1959
Imitations, 1961
For the Union Dead, 1964
Near the Ocean, 1967
Notebook, 1967-1968, 1969

Notebook, 1970
The Dolphin, 1973
History, 1973
For Lizzie and Harriet, 1973
Selected Poems, 1976, revised 1977
Day by Day, 1977

OTHER LITERARY FORMS

Besides his free translations or rewritings of poems by writers from Homer to Boris Pasternak, which constitute *Imitations* and the similar translations of Roman poems in *Near the Ocean*, Robert Lowell translated Jean Baptiste Racine's play *Phaedra* (published in 1961, premiered at Wesleyan University in 1965) and Aeschylus's play *Oresteia*, which was published posthumously in 1979. *The Old Glory*, a trilogy of plays (*Endecott and the Red Cross, My Kinsman, Major Molineux*, and *Benito Cereno*) based on stories by Nathaniel Hawthorne and Herman Melville, was originally published in 1965; the latter two plays were premiered at the American Place Theater in 1964, winning for Lowell an Obie Award. A revised edition, with an expanded version of *Endecott and the Red Cross*, was issued in 1968, and *Endecott and the Red Cross* had its first performance at the American Place Theater in the same year. *Prometheus Bound*, Lowell's only other dramatic work, was presented at Yale in 1967 and published in 1969. Lowell also published a number of reviews and appreciations of writers; his *Collected Prose* was published in 1987.

ACHIEVEMENTS

Robert Lowell's poetry gives uniquely full expression to the painful experience of living in modern America; he speaks personally of his own experience as son, husband, lover, father, and mentally troubled individual human being, and publicly of American policy and society as a morally and spiritually troubled inheritor of Western cultural and Christian spiritual values. All the diverse kinds of poetry that Lowell wrote over a career in which he repeatedly transformed his art—religious, confessional, public—share a high degree of formal interest, whether written in traditional metrical forms or in free verse. Indeed, it was Lowell's ceaseless formal invention that enabled him to articulate, in so many different voices, the experience of modernity.

The poet was honored for his work on several occasions in his lifetime. He was twice awarded the Pulitzer Prize—in 1947 for *Lord Weary's Castle* and in 1974 for *The Dolphin*. He served as U.S. poet laureate from 1947 to 1948, and won the National Book Award for Poetry in 1960 for *Life Studies*.

BIOGRAPHY

Robert Traill Spence Lowell, Jr., the only child of Commander Robert Traill Spence Lowell, a naval officer, and Charlotte Winslow Lowell, was joined by birth to a number of figures variously prominent in the early history of Massachusetts Bay and in the cultural life of Boston. On his mother's side he was descended from Edward Winslow, who came to America on the Mayflower in 1620. His Lowell ancestors included a Harvard president, A. Lawrence Lowell, and the astronomer, Percival Lowell, as well as the poets James Russell Lowell and Amy Lowell. His ancestors' prominent roles

Robert Lowell (© Phil MacMullan, *Newsweek*, courtesy of Farrar, Straus and Giroux)

in the early history of Massachusetts and its culture made him feel implicated in the shames of that history—such as the massacre of the native Indians—and the failings of the Puritan culture that became the ground out of which a money-centered American industrial society grew. His sense of his family's direct involvement in the shaping of American history and culture was conducive to the conflation of the personal and the public that is one of the distinguishing features of his poetry.

The poet had a childhood of outward gentility and inner turmoil. He had his schooling at Brimmer School in Boston and St. Mark's Boarding School in Southborough, Massachusetts. His parents had limited means relative to their inherited social position, and his ineffectual father and domineering mother filled the home with their contention. Richard Eberhart, then at the beginning of his poetic career, was one of Lowell's English teachers at St. Mark's, and at Eberhart's encouragement he began to write poetry, some of which was published in the school magazine. In 1935 Lowell entered Harvard, intent on preparing himself for a career as a poet. He was disheartened by the approach to poetry of his Harvard professors, however, and frustrated in his search for a mentor. He was at a nadir of confidence, thrashing about for direction and desperate for encouragement, when an invitation to visit Ford Madox Ford, whom he had met at a cocktail party at the Tennessee home of Allen Tate, brought him to Tate's poetry and to Tate himself, who was to be a formative influence. Lowell was then torn between traditional metrical forms and free verse, and Tate brought him down, for the time being, on the side of the former. What Tate advocated was not bland mechanics but rather an intense struggle to apprehend and concentrate experience within the confines of form, depersonalizing and universalizing experience and revitalizing traditional forms.

His intimacy with Tate led to Lowell's immersion in the world and values of the traditionalist Southern agrarian poets who constituted the Fugitive group. After spending the summer of 1937 at the Tates' home, Lowell transferred from Harvard to Kenyon College to study with John Crowe Ransom, who had just been hired at Kenyon, which he would turn into a center of the New

Criticism. At Kenyon, Lowell met Randall Jarrell, with whom he began a personal and literary friendship that ended only with Jarrell's suicide in 1965. While apprenticing himself as a poet, Lowell studied Classics, graduating summa cum laude in 1940.

Also in that year, he married the young Catholic novelist Jean Stafford and converted to Roman Catholicism. He did a year's graduate work in English at Louisiana State University, studying under Cleanth Brooks and Robert Penn Warren, and then worked as an editorial assistant at Sheed and Ward, a Catholic publishing house in New York City. Then he and his wife spent a year with the Tates, a year in which Lowell and Allen Tate both did a great deal of writing under each other's inspiration. For Lowell, the year's output became the poems of his first book, *Land of Unlikeness* (1944), about half of which were subsequently revised and included in *Lord Weary's Castle* (1946), the book that launched his poetic career, winning him the Pulitzer Prize. Also during this period Lowell, having earlier tried to enlist, refused to serve in the army in protest against Allied bombing of civilian populations and served time in prison for this failure to comply with the Selective Service Act. In 1948, Lowell's marriage to Jean Stafford ended in divorce, and the following year he married the essayist and fiction-writer Elizabeth Hardwick.

The late 1940's saw the reemergence of Lowell's respect for William Carlos Williams's free verse. Lowell admired the unpoetical language of Williams's "American idiom," and developed a close friendship with the older poet, who succeeded Tate as his mentor. The impact of Williams's work and ideas is reflected in the free verse form of the poems in the last of the four sections of *Life Studies* (1959). From 1950 to 1953, Lowell and his wife were in Europe. Returning to the United States in 1953, he taught at the University of Iowa, where one of his students was W. D. Snodgrass; the younger poet, along with the older Williams, helped Lowell to develop the "confessional" mode pioneered in *Life Studies* and in Snodgrass's *Heart's Needle* (1959). Lowell's mother died in February, 1954, in Italy; "Sailing Home from Rapallo" (*Life Studies*) tells of his trip bringing her coffin, on which "Lowell" had been misspelled "LOVELL," back for her burial in the Winslow-Stark graveyard in Dunbarton, New Hampshire. From 1954 to the end of the decade, Lowell and his wife lived on Marlborough Street in Back Bay, Boston, while he taught at Boston University. His students included Sylvia Plath and Anne Sexton. His daughter Harriet was born in 1957. In 1960, *Life Studies* won Lowell the National Book Award for poetry, while Snodgrass's *Heart's Needle* took the Pulitzer Prize.

In 1960, Lowell moved with his wife and daughter to New York City. *Life Studies* was followed in 1961 by a volume of *Imitations*, translations of European poets intended to represent what the poets might have written had they been alive in contemporary America, and arranged not chronologically but in an expressive sequence of Lowell's own. From 1963 to 1977 he taught at Harvard. During the 1960's Lowell became active in the movement against American involvement in Vietnam. In June, 1965, in an open letter to President Lyndon Johnson, published in *The New York Times*, he refused an invitation to participate in the White House Festival of the Arts in protest against American foreign policy. He participated in the Pentagon March protesting American bombing and troop activities in Vietnam in October, 1967, and was active in Eugene McCarthy's campaign for the Democratic nomination for the presidency in 1967-1968, becoming a warm personal friend of McCarthy. His political experiences are recorded in *Notebook, 1967-1968* and the subsequent revisions of that book.

At the beginning of the 1970's, Lowell moved to England. He was a visiting fellow at All Soul's College, Oxford, in 1970, and taught at Essex University from 1970 to 1972. His book *The Dolphin* records the breakdown of his marriage of more than twenty years to Elizabeth Hardwick and his developing relationship with the English novelist Caroline Blackwood. While the emotional realities—entangled passion, fear, and joy in the relationship with Caroline, a period of mental breakdown, the pull of his old life and wife and their daughter Harriet—are vividly represented in the poetry, the events, except for the birth of Lowell's son by Caroline, are not always clear. In 1972 he was divorced from Elizabeth Hardwick and married to Caroline Blackwood.

By the late 1970's, Lowell was commuting back and forth between Ireland, where he and Caroline had a house, and America, where he was teaching a term each year at Harvard. His experience at that time, including the trouble into which his third marriage was falling and the experience of having a son late in life, is rendered in the poems of *Day by Day*, the title of which reflects its closeness to the recordings and reflections of journal writing. In the spring of the last year of his life, he took a trip to Russia. In September, 1977, he died of a heart attack in a taxicab in New York City, shortly after he had returned from Ireland.

ANALYSIS

American and European history and historical figures—military, political, and religious—and other writers and their works were very much present in Robert Lowell's consciousness. This influence is reflected in all of his poetry, although the learning is worn more lightly after *The Mills of the Kavanaughs*. As evident in his poetry as his historical sense and awareness of literary tradition is the intensity of his mental and emotional life, expressed indirectly through the vehicles of historical and fictional personas in his early poetry, and in undisguised, if more or less fictionalized, autobiography, beginning with *Life Studies*. Lowell's is a poetry in the Symbolist tradition; its symbols, whether used to convey religious significance (as in his first two books) or to express psychological realities (as in his subsequent works) are remarkable for their irreducible ambiguity. Ambiguity is indeed an essential feature of Lowell's mature vision. Symbolic resonance is accompanied in his work by a wealth of named particulars of the represented world; Norman Mailer has aptly described Lowell's language as "particular, with a wicked sense of names, details, places." His craftsmanship in prosody is remarkable in his early metrical verse, with its complex stanzaic forms and tension between the syntactical and the metrical structures. It is equally remarkable, albeit less flamboyant, in his later poetry, whether metrical or free verse. A gristly texture, partly the product of heavy alliteration, is characteristic of the sound of Lowell's verse. Also contributing to this characteristic choppiness is a syntax in which the subject-verb-adjunct sequence is frequently deferred or interrupted, especially by strings of adjectives, or broken off, leaving fragments interspersing the sentences.

Lowell's poetic career is remarkable for the number of times and the extent to which he transformed his art and for the frequency with which he revised his poems in public, publishing successive versions of a poem or different treatments of a single subject in successive volumes or incorporating passages from earlier pieces in new ones.

LORD WEARY'S CASTLE

Lowell's voice in *Lord Weary's Castle* is that of a Catholic convert raging against the spiritual depravity of the Protestant and secular culture of New England, of which his own family was so much a part, and that of a conscientious objector decrying the waging of war. A note reveals that the book's title comes from an old ballad that tells of "Lambkin," a good mason who "built Lord Weary's castle" but was never paid for his work; in Lowell's poems, the mason Lambkin becomes a figure for Christ and Lord Weary for the people who wrong God in their lives. The verse of this early collection is in strict metrical forms, which are strained by features in tension with the metrical pattern, such as terminal caesura followed by violent enjambment. Prominently heavy alliteration also helps to weave its characteristically rough texture.

Of the poems in this book, "The Quaker Graveyard in Nantucket," an elegy for Lowell's cousin Warren Winslow, whose ship had disappeared at sea in the war, has been the most frequently anthologized and extensively discussed. The poem is in seven parts, all in rhymed iambic pentameter verse, varied, except in parts II and V, by occasional trimeter lines.

Part I is a dramatic account, with much vivid and grotesque physical detail, of the recovery and sea burial of the drowned sailor's body, derived not from actual experience (Lowell's cousin's body was apparently never found), but, as Hugh Staples has shown, from Henry David Thoreau's *Cape Cod* (1865). It presents the sea as implacable in its power and the loss of life as irrevocable.

Parts II to IV elaborate on the power of the sea and view the newly dead sailor as joining dead generations of Quaker whalers who foolishly dared the sea's and the whale's might; Lowell takes his imagery from Herman Melville's *Moby Dick* (1851) and associates the fatal presumption of the Quaker sailors with Ahab's obsessive and fatal quest of the white whale. The whale in whose pursuit the earlier generations of sailors lost their lives is multivalent in its symbolic associations—at once the wrathful, inscrutable Jehovah of the Old Testament and the merciful Christ of the New.

In Part III, "only bones abide/ There . . . where their boats were tossed/ Sky-high, where mariners had fabled news/ of IS, the whited monster" alludes, Staples suggests, both to such a biblical passage as Exodus 3:14— ("And God said unto Moses, I AM THAT I AM: and he said, Thus shalt thou say unto the children of Israel, I AM hath sent me to you"—and to Christ under the epithet "*I*esus *S*alvator." Lowell's dead cousin, who joins the whalers in their "graveyard," is implicated in their guilt, together with the war-waging society of which he was a member.

Part IV closes with the question, "Who will dance/ The mast-lashed master of Leviathans/ Up from this field of Quakers in their unstoned graves?"—ambiguously alluding at once to Ahab and to the Christ whom the whalers are seen as having crucified again in their slaughter of the whale, as the contemporary soldier/sailors do in their killing in war.

Part V presents a horrific scene of whale-butchering as a sort of vision of apocalypse; drawing on the exegetical tradition that sees Jonah as a prefiguration of Christ, Lowell concludes this section with a prayer to the hacked, ripped whale, in the richness of its symbolic associations, "Hide,/ Our steel, Jonas Messias, in Thy side." The scene then switches abruptly from the violence of the sea to the pastoral serenity of the Catholic shrine of Our Lady of Walsingham in England, destroyed in the Reformation but recently restored. Yet, while the first of Part VI's two stanzas presents an attractive landscape, the Virgin Mother in the second stanza offers no accessible comfort: "There's no comeliness/ At all or charm in that expressionless/ Face . . ./ This face, . . ./ Expressionless, expresses God."

The final part returns the reader to the death-dealing sea, closing with a vision of Creation in which, even as "the Lord God formed man from the sea's slime," "blue-lung'd combers lumbered to the kill." After this formulation of the implacability and inscrutability of God's will, the poem closes with the line, "The Lord survives the rainbow of His will," offering, despite its recollection of the covenant at the end of the flood, no reassurance to the individual human creature who sins and dies, but only an assertion of an ultimate abiding that may or may not prove gracious to him.

The inscrutability and violence of God's ways in "The Quaker Graveyard in Nantucket" as well as the crassness and violence of the ways of men are typical of *Lord Weary's Castle*. This poem is also representative as a family elegy, a subgenre that was to become one of Lowell's most characteristic and successful. "At the Indian Killer's Grave" is another poem in which the poet confronts his dead ancestors, again censoriously. The cenotaph of his ancestors John and Mary Winslow is mentioned as one of the monuments in the graveyard behind King's Chapel, where the poet's persona meditates amid "baroque/ And prodigal embellishments," that are in vain against the grime and noise of the impinging city (a subway "Blacker than these black stones" lies beneath the graveyard, and its train "grinds . . ./ And screeches"). Unmentioned by name, but part of the public history to which the poem makes reference, is another ancestor, Josiah Winslow, who was noted as an Indian fighter and served as Governor of Plymouth during the war against the Indian leader King Philip (the English name for Metacomet, or Metacom). The conquered Indian was beheaded and his head set on a pole in Plymouth. In Lowell's poem, King Philip's head "Grins on a platter" and delivers a jeremiad to his and his people's buried killers, the poet's ancestors, evoking "nature and the land/ That fed the hunter's gashed and green perfection" in implicit contrast to the urban scene that has been sketched earlier in the poem, mocking the Puritans' notions of election as of no avail to save them. In the last of the poem's five rather long verse-paragraphs, the persona of the poet "ponder[s] on the railing" of the graveyard, wondering who the remote ancestor was "Who sowed so ill for his descent." The poem closes with paradise-garden imagery to answer the image at the beginning of the poem of the cemetery as fallen garden, and, in accord with Lowell's Catholic belief of the time, with an image of Mary conceiving Christ by the divine "Bridegroom," presumably suggesting divine mercy for both victims and victors.

THE MILLS OF THE KAVANAUGHS

Lowell's next significant collection, *The Mills of the Kavanaughs*, marks a sharp departure from the style and the outlook of *Lord Weary's Castle*. The long title poem and the other six poems of this volume are all at least partially dramatic monologue, and they deal mostly with situations of extremity—incest, madness, death—in the personal lives of their characters. They seem to follow from "Between the Porch and the Altar," a multipart poem of adulterous love in *Lord Weary's Castle*, with a third-person narrative section and a section of dramatic monologue by a woman, "Katherine's Dream." The Catholicism of the earlier book is gone, however; neither Christ nor Mary comes to offer the people of these poems a way to transcend the ills of their worlds. While *Lord Weary's Castle* is densely interlarded with biblical allusions, *The Mills of the Kavanaughs* draws heavily on classical literature. The allusions here are significantly different in their operation from those in the earlier book: While the apparatus of Catholic symbols was imposed on events by the poet in his interpretation of them, the myth of Persephone is very much a part of Anne Kavanaugh's consciousness and, as Richard Fein has pointed out, enters into her own efforts to interpret her situation, and the *Aeneid* (c. 29-19 B.C.E.) is similarly familiar to the old man in "Falling Asleep over the Aeneid," who assimilates his personal life to his literary experience. Randall Jarrell remarked that the title poem is an unremitting succession of nightmares and nightmarish visions all at the same high level of intensity, and several reviewers of the book objected to its monotonous violence. With hindsight, subsequent critics have seen the characters of the poems here as vehicles for Lowell to convey experiences of his own, including that of madness, that he would speak of straightforwardly in the first person in *Life Studies*. Certainly one acquainted with the poet's life will recognize autobiographical elements in "The Mills of the Kavanaughs"—the morally problematic heritage and the declining vitality and fortunes of an eminent family (the Kavanaugh family emblem, "Cut down we flourish," is that of the Winslows), Lowell's father's failed military career, and his own mental illness. Anne Kavanaugh seems to combine elements of Lowell's mother and of his wives. One of the remarkable features of the poem, indeed, is the extent to which it sympathetically conveys a woman's experience of a man who fails her; in this it is heralded by "Katherine's Dream" and anticipates " 'To Speak of Woe That Is in Marriage'" in *Life Studies*, the poems given to painfully moving quotations of Elizabeth Hardwick's letters in *The Dolphin*, and many other later poems.

LIFE STUDIES

After an eight-year silence, Lowell published *Life Studies*. The book is in four parts: The first consists of four poems close in form and mode (two are dramatic monologues) to Lowell's previous work, although the poem that opens the book, "Beyond the Alps," definitely announces a change of stance from the Catholicism of *Lord Weary's Castle*; the second is an autobiographical prose piece on the poet's childhood; the third consists of four poems on writers who influenced Lowell (Ford Madox Ford, George Santayana, Delmore Schwartz, and Hart Crane); and the fourth, which gives the book its title, "Life Studies," contains the poems that drew the epithet "confessional."

"Beyond the Alps" is actually a sequence of three sonnets, each with a different complex rhyme scheme. The speaker is on the train going from Rome to Paris in 1950, the year the Pope proclaimed the dogma of Mary's bodily assumption. At the end of the octet of the first sonnet, the speaker says, "Much against my will/ I left the City of God where it belongs"; in the sestet he characterizes the figure who has ruled there in his time, Benito Mussolini, as "one of us/ only, pure prose." The central sonnet treats the proclamation of Mary's Assumption as dogma, undercutting it by a description of the Pope listening to the crowds in St. Peter's Square that implies he too is "pure prose": "His electric razor purred,/ his pet canary chirped on his left hand." In the final sonnet, the "mountain-climbing train had come to earth," and the speaker somewhat ruefully owns that "There were no tickets for that altitude/ once held by Hellas."

In the third and fourth parts of this volume Lowell turns from the accentual syllabic metrics of his previous poetry to free verse rhythms much closer to those of conversation and, especially after the first part, from the relative impersonality and obliqueness of the earlier poetry to the confessional mode that *Life Studies* helped to pioneer. If the artifice is no longer obtrusive and the verse relatively transparent in Part IV, however, the poetry is no less artful in its construction: Rhyme and halfrhyme, used occasionally rather than systematically,

help to make the lines perceptible as units and to bind together stanzas; and alliteration continues to give the language a gristly texture. In imagery as well as in sound, these poems—sequences as well as individual poems—are unified.

The poems in the first section of Part IV, arranged in order of the chronology of their events in the poet's life, focus successively on Lowell's grandfather (the first three), his father (the next three), his mother (a further three), and an adult mental breakdown of his own (the final two). The last two in the first section take place in the world of Lowell's adult married life, and there is a continuity between their imagery of place and that of the poems in the second section, which focus on the writer's present, even if that present is preoccupied with memories (in "Memories of West Street and Lepke"). In "Man and Wife" and "'To Speak of Woe That Is in Marriage'" in the second section, Lowell's marriage, in the background in "Waking in the Blue" and "Home After Three Months Away" at the end of the first section, comes into the foreground. The particulars of decor, attire, and gesture with which these poems are richly furnished serve not to invoke an anagogic level of meaning, but at once to create a sense of actual experience in all its centrifugal detail and to convey character and psychological fate.

"Skunk Hour," the poem that closes the book, while highly particular in its dramatized situation, nevertheless has, more than any of the rest of these confessional pieces, a degree of independence from temporal succession, which, besides its power, has probably been a factor in the frequency with which it has been chosen to represent Lowell in anthologies. The eight six-line stanzas of "Skunk Hour" carry the speaker from detached, amusingly sharp observations of the foibles and failings of fellow residents of his New England summer resort town and the "illness" of its season to direct, mordantly sharp confession of his own neurotic behavior and his mind's and spirit's illness, and finally to the richly ambiguous image of vitality and survival in the face of the town's enervation, the season's fading, and the speaker's despair that concludes *Life Studies*. The first four stanzas are devoted to social observation—of "Nautilus Island's hermit/ heiress" who is "in her dotage" and "buys up all/ the eyesores facing her shore,/ and lets them fall"; of the disappearance of the "summer millionaire,/ who seemed to leap from an L. L. Bean/ catalogue," and the sale of his yacht; of the "fairy/ decorator [who] brightens his shop for fall," but finds "no money in his work" and would "rather marry." Significantly, where the first person pronoun appears, it is in the plural ("our summer millionaire," "our fairy decorator"); the poet speaks as a townsman, one of a community (albeit a derelict one). By the fifth stanza, however, he has ceased to be one of the people; now, apart from them, he tells the reader that he "climbed the hill's skull," where "I watched for love-cars." In a scene of anguished isolation suggestive of St. John of the Cross's "dark night of the soul," he declares, "My mind's not right." By the end of the sixth stanza, his voice has come to echo that of Milton's Satan: "I myself am hell;/ nobody's here." From this nadir, his attention swings to be arrested, in the final two stanzas, by "a mother skunk with her column of kittens" that "march[es] . . . up Main Street," "swills the garbage pail . . ./ and will not scare." If her crassness is appalling, her vitality is indeed a "rich air" against the town's stale atmosphere and the speaker's self-constructed cell. The significance of the image is as intractable in its ambiguity as its subject is stubborn in her determination to feed on the sour cream in the garbage.

FOR THE UNION DEAD

In *For the Union Dead*, Lowell's poetry continues to speak in the personal voice that emerged in *Life Studies*. Poems such as "Eye and Tooth" and "Myopia: A Night" are of the eye turned inward, focused on the "I," its tormenting memories and self-hatred. Others, notably "The Old Flame," "The Scream," "The Public Garden," and "Returning," revisit scenes of the poet's past as child or lover; interestingly, both "The Old Flame" and "The Public Garden" incorporate passages from poems in *The Mills of the Kavanaughs*, where the experiences in question were ascribed to dramatic characters rather than to the poet's self. A difference from the *Life Studies* poems is that these are separate lyrics and do not fit together into sequences. The theme of the cultural heritage of New England, treated in *Lord Weary's Castle*, is again treated here in a poem that speaks of Nathaniel Hawthorne and one that addresses Jonathan Edwards in intimate tones and with great sympathy.

(A similar intimacy and sympathy inform the poem addressed to Caligula, by whose name Lowell had been called by his classmates at St. Mark's.) There is, besides, a new element in this book: The poet deals with contemporary society and politics, not, as he had in *Lord Weary's Castle*, in Christian terms, as features of a world for which apocalypse was imminent, but with the same keen, painful observation and moral concern he had, since *Life Studies*, been bringing to bear on his personal life; he deals with them, indeed, as part and parcel of his personal experience.

The title poem, "For the Union Dead," revisits the old Boston Aquarium that the poet had gone to as a child, even as "The Public Garden" revisits that old "stamping ground" of Lowell and his wife. The difference is that while in the latter "[t]he city and its cruising cars surround" a private failure to "catch fire," in "For the Union Dead" the Aquarium is presented not as part of a personal landscape only, but, closed, its fish replaced by "giant finned cars," as emblematic of the course of Boston's, New England's, and America's culture. The other complex emblem in the poem is the monument to Colonel Shaw, friend and in-law to the poet's Lowell ancestors, who led the first regiment of free blacks in an attack on a fort defending Charleston Harbor, in which he and about half of his black soldiers were killed. The poem is in a sense another of Lowell's family elegies, but it opens beyond family history to national history. As the Aquarium's fish have been replaced by finned cars, the monument to the Civil War hero is now "propped by a plank splint" as support against the "earthquake" produced by excavation for a parking garage, and it has come to "stick like a fishbone/ in the city's throat." In a city of giant cars and parking garages, the martyred leader, "lean/ as a compass-needle," who "seems to wince at pleasure," is "out of bounds"; such firm sense of direction and such asceticism are no longer virtues the populace is comfortable contemplating or moved to emulate.

The poem is not, however, a sentimental one of pure nostalgia for an earlier period of the society's life or of the poet's, for the heroism of war before the World Wars or for the lost Aquarium and the child's pleasure in it. The fish that lived in the Aquarium tanks are described as "cowed, compliant," and the child's eagerness was "to burst the bubbles/ drifting from their noses." Colonel Shaw is said to have enjoyed "man's lovely,/ peculiar power to choose life and die"—hardly an unequivocal good, albeit preferable to the power to choose "a Mosler Safe, the 'Rock of Ages'/ that survived the blast" at Hiroshima to safeguard one's material wealth. Nor is the contemporary landscape presented as wholly desert; the steamshovels that excavate for the parking garages are "yellow dinosaur steamshovels . . . grunting/ as they cropped up tons of mush and grass," creatures not without appeal. Indeed, the attractiveness of martyrdom, as Lowell presents it, may not be that far removed from the appeal of fish behind glass or steamshovels behind barbed wire: "I often sigh still," says the poem's speaker, "for the dark downward and vegetating kingdom/ of the fish and reptile." There is, finally, an irreducible ambiguity in the poem's treatment of past and present, Aquarium and garage, Union soldier and contemporary Bostonian.

NEAR THE OCEAN

The title sequence of *Near the Ocean* consists of five numbered poems. The first two of these ("Waking Early Sunday Morning" and "Fourth of July in Maine") and the last ("Near the Ocean") are composed in rhymed couplets of iambic tetrameter lines, arranged in eight-line stanzas. This is the stanza form of Andrew Marvell's "The Garden" and *Upon Appleton House* (1681), a formal resemblance that may be taken to link Lowell's efforts to mediate between the private and the public realms of experience with the similar achievement of his seventeenth century predecessor. Of the remaining poems in the sequence, the third ("The Opposite House") is in nine-line stanzas of unrhymed short-line free verse; the fourth ("Central Park") is in iambic tetrameter couplets grouped in verse paragraphs. One cannot help being struck at the relative traditional formality of this verse after the free verse of *Life Studies* and *For the Union Dead*. Also very striking in the stanzaic verse is the fact that every one of the long stanzas is closed, giving each a tendency toward autonomy and setting the poem trembling with centrifugal forces. The blockiness and relative independence of these individual stanzas that yet for the most part do not stand quite free anticipates the fourteen-line blank verse units that will constitute *Notebook*.

Another striking feature of *Near the Ocean*—speaking, now, of the whole book—is that it consists partly of original poems, partly of translations (of Horace, Juvenal, and Dante). Lowell said in an interview that his translation enabled him to bring into English something that he would not dare write in English himself although he wished he could; thus, even where the translations are close, they are, to an important extent, expressions of Lowell's sensibility. If the translations are, thus, more of Lowell himself than one might at first take them to be, the original poems turn out to engage his poetic predecessors as significantly as do the translations. "Waking Early Sunday Morning" has its meaning in relation to Wallace Stevens's "Sunday Morning"; "Central Park" similarly evokes and responds to the "Sunday in the Park" section of William Carlos Williams's *Paterson* (1946-1958). The title poem of the sequence can be interpreted as a sort of Lowellian "Dover Beach."

While the poet of "Sunday Morning" was content that Earth should turn out to "Seem all of paradise that we shall know," the poet of "Waking Early Sunday Morning" finds no "heavenly fellowship/ Of men that perish and of summer morn" (Stevens) to supersede the failed fellowship of "the Faithful at Church," where the Bible is "chopped and crucified/ in hymns we hear but do not read." Lowell finds instead that "Only man thinning out his kind/ sounds through the Sabbath noon," and instead of the vision of earth as a paradisal garden with deer, whistling quail, ripening berries, and flocks of pigeons that closes Stevens's poem, Lowell sees the planet as a joyless "ghost/ orbiting forever lost," its people "fall[ing]/ in small war on the heels of small/ war." The world of Lowell's poem is a more complicated one than that of Stevens's in that it has a political aspect; the state with its monstrous militarism and the vulgarity of its leader, which is seen as "this Sunday morning, free to chaff/ his own thoughts with his bear-cuffed staff,/ swimming nude, unbuttoned, sick/ of his ghost-written rhetoric," is part of what the speaker here must assimilate. Furthermore the spiritual yearning of the speaker in Lowell's poem is more complex than Stevens'. The poem opens with his cry, "O to break loose," but not simply "to break loose"; rather "to break loose like the chinook/ salmon" that overcomes the current to reach its river birthplace "alive enough to spawn and die." The release longed for is the release of suicide. This is not all, though. Further on, the speaker voices an exclamation: "O that the spirit could remain/ tinged but untarnished by its strain!" This cry is preceded by a passage describing a glass of water fuzzed with condensation that looks silvery in the light of the sky; when it is seen from a shifted perspective, with brown wood behind it, the wood comes "to darken it, but not to stain." Salmon and glass of water, like key images in other Lowell poems, are profoundly ambiguous; there is no claim for objectivity in the anatomy of his world by a speaker who looks upon it through the dark glass of his own psychology—which is itself part of the world that the poem presents.

NOTEBOOK, 1967-1968

In his next book, *Notebook, 1967-1968*, Lowell again effects a striking formal transformation. The fourteen-line pieces in blank verse that Lowell used to register his various preoccupations—his marriage, wife and daughter, love affairs; his dreams; the Vietnam War, the Pentagon March, Eugene McCarthy's campaign for the Democratic presidential nomination, other political events by which he was affected or in which he was involved; other writers, both his friends among contemporaries and the predecessors who contributed to the literary tradition that he inherited; figures of history—were, he said in his "Afterthought" to *Notebook, 1967-1968*, "written as one poem." The organization of the pieces is partially according to Lowell's order of composition/experience, partially according to subject, setting, or season. Individual poems do, however, resist being subsumed in the whole book, either the original or the expanded edition of *Notebook*, in part because they are sonnet-like in more than number of lines and meter. In particular, Lowell's tendency to epigrammatic conclusions helps endowindividual poems with an autonomy stronger than the centripetal force exerted by a loosely seasonal organization.

Despite the frequency of the memorable concluding line or couplet, however, and despite the fact that these poems often embrace what Lowell called "the themes and gigantism of the sonnet," they do not have the sort of logical structure characteristic of the traditional sonnet. Their movement is typically associative, sometimes obscurely so; their phrases frequently do not join into complete sentences. The first poem in the section called "October and November" in *Notebook, 1967-1968*, "Che Guevara," can be taken as representative in its technique and in the spheres of reference—contemporary public affairs, the poet's personal life, the historical past—that it telescopes. Beginning with the notation, "Week of Che Guevara," it sketches Che's assassination and conveys Lowell's attitude toward it (as an instance at once of violence begetting violence and of a spirit having a certain grandeur being done in by meaner ones) in a series of participles and absolute constructions taking the first five lines. The scene then switches, by the mere transition of an "as" (which disappears in subsequent revision) indicating temporal simultaneity, to the poet's autumn in Manhattan, presented first through features indicating the season and evoking a mood—still-green leaves "burn to frittered reds," an oak tree "swells with goiters"—then through ones adumbrating the socioeconomic realities of the city—its "high white stone buildings over-/ shadow the poor"—then sliding through progressive subordination to the personal—"where our clasped, illicit hands/ pulse." Abruptly the final couplet first returns readers to the public event with which the poem began; then, taking up an association of the mentioned oak tree, the final couplet throws it into historical perspective, in a resonant, memorable conclusion: "Rest for the outlaw . . . kings once hid in oaks,/ with prices on their heads, and watched for game."

Both the heterogeneity of material treated as readers move from poem to poem, section to section, and the quick shifts within individual poems that are characteristic of their style (Lowell at one point makes explicit reference to this stylistic trait, saying, in the second poem of the "Harvard" section, "My mind can't hold the focus for a minute./ A sentence? A paragraph? . . ./ Flash-visions . . ."), create the impression of a mind besieged by an unremitting succession of disparate experiences that cannot be checked in their passing. When, in the second poem of *Notebook, 1967-1968*, the poet, killing a fly that has been "wham[ming] back and forth across" his daughter's bed, says "another instant's added/ to the horrifying mortmain of/ ephemera," he strikes a keynote for the whole book.

The succession of experiences do not, of course, all come from external events, but also from Lowell's reading and memory. The order in which subjects appear from poem to poem reflects his mental associations and the tensions in his thought as much as the flux of events in his life. In two poems on the Pentagon March, Lowell expresses his ambivalence toward pacificism and military valor. In the first, he compares the marchers he is among to "green Union Army recruits/ for the first Bull Run" and characterizes the soldiers who face them by a series of images, "the Martian, the ape, the hero,/ his new-fangled rifle, his green new steel helmet," conveying a profound ambivalence, confounding the two groups even as he distinguishes them and simultaneously both exalting and deflating each of them. The second poem on the March, which closes with Lowell helped staggering to his feet to "flee" the soldiers, is followed by an elegy on his ancestor Charles Russell Lowell, a "Union martyr," a cavalry officer who, struck and dying, "had himself strapped to the saddle . . . bound to death." It all seems to add up to the coexistence in Lowell's mind of pacifist convictions and an admiration for military heroism, which, Richard Fein has remarked, could not be more tellingly displayed.

"Obit," the poem that Lowell uses to end his book, looks toward the ending of the flux of experience in death, toward "the eternal return of earth's fairer children" (that has been adumbrated in the seasonal basis of the book's structure and in its attention to the poet's growing daughter), and back toward the onset and passage of moments of consciousness, as lovers' "unconquered flux, insensate oneness, their painful 'it was. . . .'" The question that constitutes the final couplet is not the typical rhetorical question. "After loving you so much, can I forget/ you for eternity, and have no other choice?" asks Lowell, while the accumulated context of this poem and of the whole book that precedes it indicate that his intellect would answer yes, his inclination, no.

HISTORY

Lowell did not stay satisfied with either the pieces or the whole of *Notebook, 1967-1968*. First, he revised poems and added to sections to produce the expanded *Notebook*; then, he separated the poems dealing with his marital life into *For Lizzie and Harriet* and rearranged the rest into a sequence following the chronology of history, filling in gaps with new poems and sometimes turning what began as autobiographical poems into po-

ems associating the same attitudes or experiences with historical or mythological figures; this revised sequence constitutes the volume Lowell titled *History*.

While the arrangement of *History*, as contrasted with that of *Notebook*, might at first seem superficial, the book has a thematic focus for which the ordering of poems in accord with the dates of their subject is appropriate. Stephen Yenser has pointed to the section called "The Powerful" in *Notebook*, an expanded version of that called "Power" in *Notebook, 1967-1968*, as the germ of *History*'s structure and theme. The poem that originally ended the chronological sequence of poems on historical figures in this section becomes, slightly revised, the conclusion of the whole book. It is a summational poem that articulates the relationship among the book's principal subjects—the mythical and legendary heroes and villains, the historical political and military leaders, the writers, and Lowell himself as writer and as a citizen and public man. Originally titled "New Year's 1968," it is, significantly, retitled "End of a Year." In a book dominated by the elegiac mode, it is an elegy of elegies. From an opening couplet that declares, "These conquered kings pass furiously away/ gods die in flesh and spirit and live in print," it moves to qualify that continued "life" in print as one of misquotation, then to look at the poet's writing of a run-out year "in bad, straightforward, nonscanning sentences," the year's "hero" the poet himself, of unsound mind (*demens*), his story, given in the imagery of the stories of "conquered kings," one of running his ship on the rocks. From the image of the foundering ship, the text slides to the scene present to the poet, where slush-ice in the Hudson "is rose-heather in the New York sunset"; then, dispensing with the requirements of complete clauses, the poem concludes abruptly and hauntingly with a juxtaposition of images of the landscape before the poet and the carbon that inks copies of his typescript (earlier in the poem compared to a Rosetta Stone): "bright sky, bright sky, carbon scarred with ciphers."

THE DOLPHIN

The thread of personal life that was drawn out of the weave of *Notebook* to constitute *For Lizzie and Harriet* is continued in *The Dolphin*, a slim volume which continues the use of the fourteen-line blank verse form. A feature that significantly differentiates *The Dolphin* from those others is the use of a central symbol, accreting in complexity and ambiguity over the course of the book. The dolphin, with variants (mermaid, "baby killer whale") and in its various attractive and fearsome aspects (graceful, playful swimmer; powerful predator), is associated with Caroline, and the contradictory connotations of Lowell's symbol reflect his ambivalence toward her. In the course of the book, Caroline is progressively mythicized and becomes a gigantic, ambiguous, and disturbing character set forth in the image of the dolphin, while Elizabeth, the wife Lowell is waveringly leaving, becomes an ever clearer, ever more human voice, presented principally through quotation from her letters.

"Fishnet" and "Dolphin," respectively the opening and closing poems of the book and serving as its frame, have become the best-known pieces of this collection. "Fishnet" begins with one of the series of nominals detached from any predication common in Lowell's poems of the *Notebook* form: "Any clear thing that blinds us with surprise,/ your wandering silences and bright trouvailles,/ dolphin let loose to catch the flashing fish." Already in its initial appearance, the dolphin symbol is ambiguous, associated with the appealing image of the "bright trouvailles," but presented as catching "the flashing fish" rather than as a flashing fish itself. In other poems the reader will find dolphin-Caroline presented both as a fish that the poet angles for and as a creature that may devour him. After its opening catalog of images, this first poem turns to reflect on the fates of poets; they "die adolescents, their beat embalms them." After several years of writing in the same verse form, Lowell was conscious that it was risky to continue with it any longer. (In a 1971 interview, he said of the form, "I mustn't tempt it.") The conclusion of the poem is affirmative in some of its diction, but ambivalent in its imagery. The poet presents his activity as a writer as "knotting, undoing a fishnet of tarred rope," the "undoing" presumably being a reference to his habitual revising and recasting of his previous work. In the closing couplet the product of this work is presented as surviving, but hardly in the manner in which, say, Elizabethan sonneteers spoke of their poetry as surviving: "the net will hang on the wall when the fish are eaten,/ nailed like illegible bronze on the futureless future." It seems that

Lowell foresees a time when his poetry will have ceased not only to be part of a life being lived, but even to be intelligible.

The final poem addresses "My Dolphin" as a guide, guiding "by surprise," "surprise" being conspicuous as the last word of the first line in each of the "frame" poems. The language in which the dolphin's activity is described is again ambivalent: She "made for my body/ caught in its hangman's-knot of sinking lines," the fishnet of the opening poem turned against its maker, become at once noose and weight. Focusing on his own making, the poet indicates that in his use of his life in his art, both in what he has altered and in what he has told as it was, he has done injury to others and to himself, and he calls the book that is ending "an eelnet made by man for the eel fighting," the ambiguity of "for" pointed up by the inversion of normal word order in the participial phrase. Ambiguity of reference is particularly insistent in the final line, "my eyes have seen what my hand did," which points at once to the poet's registering of his life in his poems and to his awareness of what his writings have done with and to his life. Such ambiguity is appropriate to the complexities of experience and of language.

DAY BY DAY

In his last book of poems, *Day by Day*, Lowell left the fourteen-line blank verse form in which he had been working for nearly a decade to write poems in a free verse more transparent and less marked with features such as sound repetition than that of *Life Studies* or *For the Union Dead*. The syntax has the looseness of the poems of *Notebook* and its progeny, without the tightness of their metrical form to resist its centrifugal pressures. Although lacking a single central symbol such as that of *The Dolphin*, this book has a central and insistent theme: age, the fear of aging and pain, the prospect of death. This theme is introduced in the first poem, "Ulysses and Circe"; in Lowell's interpretation of Ulysses' story, the old veteran of the Trojan wars, leaving a troubled affair with the young Circe, returns to Ithaca to find his wife "well-furnished with her entourage" and himself superfluous. Humiliated, cuckolded, his infuriated mind is set on the murder of Penelope's lovers. The situation of the aged lover and husband, here presented through the retelling of a much-retold tale, is presented through autobiographical poetry in the rest of the book.

The bulk of the book, its third part, bearing the title of the book, stays exceedingly close to a journal's day-by-day record of events and emotions. This final part is itself divided into three sections. The first covers a summer in England with Caroline, her daughters, and Lowell's son whom she bore. There is a measure of detachment and a certain urbanity in the reflections on the fate of England's great houses in poems such as "Domesday Book" and "*Milgate*." These poems of summer's fullness are all haunted, however, by intimations of coming emptiness; every subject becomes an occasion for meditation on infirmity and mortality. Most poignant, perhaps, is the edge given to the poet's sense of his age and apprehension of his death by his observation of his young son; a poem named for him, "Sheridan," finds its way to that ancient image of death, the scythe, presented, as is usual in Lowell's poetry, as a particular in the represented scene: "High-hung/ the period scythe silvers in the sun,/ a cutting edge, a bounding line,/ between the child's world and the earth." The second section of "Day by Day" covers a stay in Boston without Caroline, framed by poems of Caroline's departure and her return. This interlude is one for reencounter with figures and events of the past: A poem, "To Mother," ends "It has taken me the time since you died/ to discover you are as human as I am . . ./ if I am"; there is an imaginary dialogue with his father; his grandfather looms in two poems. A terrible memory from his St. Mark's days is told—being taunted to tears by his classmates and possibly having deserved it, having made a habit of harping on the defects of other boys to their friends; Lowell comes to a harsh self-judgment that "even now/ my callous unconscious drives me/ to torture my closest friend."

The third and final section, the most wrenching, records living with Caroline, ill from an old spinal injury, and a mental breakdown and then recovery. Lowell envisions himself and Caroline bound together as "seesaw inseparables," always "one up, the other down," represents her as experiencing "my sickness only as desertion." In sickness, his fear of sickness and expectance of death evoke nostalgia for his lost Catholic faith: "The Queen of Heaven, I miss her,/ we were divorced." Voices and memories crowd upon Lowell in this section, which begins, in "Turtle," with an invocation to memory. In that poem, a memory of hunting snapping turtles turns into a nightmare of death. In "Unwanted," words from an article on John Berryman, remembered words from a family psychiatrist with an ambiguous relation to his mother, and remembered words of his mother converge on his consciousness to bring home the recognition of his having been an unwanted child and of the impact of that on his psychological development—"to give my simple autobiography a plot," as the poet says wryly.

The last three poems bring the book to a gentle conclusion. "The Downlook" turns back with nostalgia to the previous year in Lowell's and Caroline's love, evoked in pastoral imagery as a time when "nothing dared impede/ the flow of the body's thousand rivulets of welcome"; such turning back in memory is a conclusion in "days of the downlook." The penultimate poem is a "Thanks for Recovery"; the last is an "Epilogue" that is an apologia, in which the poet regrets that "Those blessed structures, plot and rhyme," have been no help to him in this book, complains that his writings seem to him snapshots, neither fully true to life nor truly imaginary, but concludes by accepting and justifying his work as a response to the fact of mortality, giving "each figure in the photograph,/ his living name."

OTHER MAJOR WORKS

PLAYS: *The Old Glory*, pb. 1965 (includes *Endecott and the Red Cross*, *My Kinsman*, *Major Molineux*, and *Benito Cereno*); *Prometheus Bound*, pr. 1967, pb. 1969.

NONFICTION: *Collected Prose*, 1987.

TRANSLATIONS: *Phaedra*, 1961 (of Jean Baptiste Racine); *The Oresteia of Aeschylus*, 1979.

BIBLIOGRAPHY

Axelrod, Steven Gould, ed. *The Critical Response to Robert Lowell*. Westport, Conn.: Greenwood Press, 1999. A collection of critical essays covering the full spectrum of debate and response to Lowell's work. Prefaced with a survey of Lowell's life and his involvement in politics and literary movements, and concluding with a bibliography and chronology.

Cosgrave, Patrick. *The Public Poetry of Robert Lowell*. New York: Taplinger, 1970. While Lowell is usually seen as a "Confessional" poet, many of his greatest poems were on public issues. Cosgrave brings out that dimension in his poetry and locates it in the traditions of public poetry and modernism. Unfortunately, the book was published in 1970 and does not discuss Lowell's *Notebook*, a central text of Lowell's politics.

Hamilton, Ian. *Robert Lowell: A Biography.* New York: Random House, 1982. This book is occasionally sensational, but it is the best biography available. It traces Lowell's fascinating life in great detail and provides the contexts and occasions for many of his poems, which help readers understand them better.

Mariani, Paul L. *Lost Puritan: A Life of Robert Lowell.* New York: W. W. Norton, 1994. Mariani, a biographer specializing in the lives of poets and a poet himself, provides insights into Lowell's poetry with anecdotes from his crisis-filled life. Includes extensive bibliography.

Perloff, Marjorie G. *The Poetic Art of Robert Lowell.* Ithaca, N.Y.: Cornell University Press, 1973. One of the best books available on the specifics of Lowell's art. Perloff investigates with acuteness the images and syntax of many of Lowell's poems. She is especially helpful on the Winslow elegies and the sound patterns of the poems.

Rudman, Mark. *Robert Lowell: An Introduction to the Poetry.* New York: Columbia University Press, 1983. A brief overview of Lowell's poems useful for beginning readers of Lowell. It is a disappointing book, however, for anyone who knows Lowell well.

Wallingford, Katherine. *Robert Lowell's Language of the Self.* Chapel Hill: University of North Carolina Press, 1988. Wallingford uses psychoanalytic criticism to investigate the poems. She finds that Lowell knew Sigmund Freud and applied many of his analytic methods in his poems. Lowell's poetry invites this type of criticism, and this is the fullest use of it available.

Williamson, Alan. *Pity the Monsters: The Political Vision of Robert Lowell.* New Haven, Conn.: Yale University Press, 1974. Williamson discusses the violence as well as the political vision of Lowell. He is one of few critics to fully discuss *Near the Ocean* and *Notebook* (later published as *History*).

Eleanor von Auw Berry;
bibliography updated by the editors

LUCAN

Marcus Annaeus Lucanus

Born: Corduba, Roman province of Spain; November 3, 39 C.E.
Died: Rome, Italy; April 15, 65 C.E.

PRINCIPAL POETRY
Bellum civile, 60-65 C.E. (*Pharsalia*, 1614)

OTHER LITERARY FORMS

Thirteen of Lucan's lost works were known to Vacca, one of his major biographers, living in the sixth century. Vacca implied that these works were still extant; and several of them were confirmed by Suetonius, another biographer. Vacca is clear that the thirteen are minor works compared with the epic on the civil war, *Pharsalia*, but feels that some, at least, are valuable. The items on Vacca's list include the *Iliacon* from the Trojan cycle; the *Laudes Neronis*; the *Orpheus; De incendio urbis*, a description of the great fire which nearly destroyed Rome; *Saturnalia*, on the gaities of December; ten books of miscellaneous *Silvae*; the unfinished tragedy of *Medea*; a series of letters called *Epistulae ex Campania* (which, if they had survived, would surely have proved to be a fascinating addition to our specimens of ancient letter writing); as well as speeches for and against Octavius Sagitta. The latter suggest that (in 58 C.E.) Lucan, perhaps acting on the detective instinct, seized upon one of the most exciting murder trials of the day as material for two clever rhetorical showpieces.

ACHIEVEMENTS

Lucan's poetry covered a great variety of genres, although only his incomplete epic, the *Pharsalia*, is extant. Based on the titles, the subjects of a number of lost works range from tragedy to satire to occasional verse. The bulk of Lucan's poetry, including the ten books of the *Pharsalia*, was probably produced in about five years, beginning in 60 C.E. In the light of this information, his production can only be described as prodigious. The output is all the more remarkable when one considers that Lucan composed much of his poetry while he was involved in a political career. Most poets of antiquity who were also politicians postponed their poetic endeavors until they had withdrawn or retired from state business.

Lucan, then, enjoyed neither the leisure time of the retired senator nor the professional poet's singleness of purpose. Vergil was able to spend eleven years of his mature creative life working almost exclusively on the *Aeneid*, and the *Thebais* occupied Statius for twelve years, but Lucan, still in his early twenties, worked on the *Pharsalia* for no more than five years and possibly less than three. While he worked, he held an augurate and a quaestorship and joined a conspiracy to kill the emperor Nero.

BIOGRAPHY

Marcus Annaeus Lucanus was born in Corduba, Spain, on November 3, 39 C.E. The determining factors in his career were his descent from two prominent Spanish families and his rhetorical education. His father, Marcus Annaeus Mela, was the brother of Lucius Annaeus Seneca (the philosopher, poet, and statesman) and the son of Seneca the Elder. Lucan's mother was the daughter of Acilius Lucanus, a Corduban speaker of note. Thus, by birthright Lucan belonged to one of Spain's most distinguished families, whose talents had been widely recognized and who had obtained considerable wealth. Lucan was brought to Rome at an early age, where he enjoyed all the wealth and prestige that the Annaei could provide, particularly after 49 C.E., when Seneca was recalled from exile to become the tutor to Nero, the heir apparent to the throne. After formal training at the school of a grammarian, Lucan became the pupil of the Stoic philosopher Annaeus Cornutus, whose name suggests that he may have been a freedman of Lucan's own family.

Considering Seneca's position in Roman public affairs, which grew even stronger between 49 C.E. and 60 C.E., it is not surprising that Lucan was quickly drawn into the very heart of Roman social and political life. While this introduction to court life proved to be an incentive to Lucan, it ultimately caused his ruin. Lucan probably spent considerable time with Nero himself. After all, Lucan and Nero were only two years apart in age and both had a keen interest in literature. When

Lucan left Rome for Athens to pursue his education, Nero recalled him to join his entourage, the *cohors amicorum*. Soon, honors were being conferred upon Lucan, such as the quaestorship before the regular age of twenty-five and an augural priesthood. In 60 C.E., then twenty-one years old, he achieved his first public literary triumph with his *Laudes Neronis* at the festival of the Neronia, a newly established celebration in honor of the emperor.

At that time, Nero and his young admirer were on the best of terms; Lucan's position, however, became less secure as Nero's dislike for his tutor Seneca increased. Lucan, perhaps foolishly, entered a competition against Nero and so incurred the enmity of the emperor, who was clever, conceited, and egotistical. Suetonius, a biographer of Lucan, implies that the break between Lucan and Nero arose partly from Lucan's imagining that Nero's attitude toward his works was deliberately insulting and partly from Lucan's unbecoming mockery of the emperor's verses. Vacca attributes the quarrel to Nero's jealousy of Lucan's genius. In any case, Lucan was forbidden to engage in further poetic production or the pleading of law cases. The only avenue left open to the poet was covert satire, and he was prompted by Nero's persecution to join the Pisonian conspiracy. When the intrigue was discovered, Lucan was condemned to death. To avoid execution, after a sumptuous feast he had his veins opened. His last moments were spent reciting a piece of his own about a soldier similarly bleeding to death. When the emperor cut short Lucan's career, his epic was incomplete and published only in part.

ANALYSIS

Lucan was an audacious author. In touch with an imperial court, he dared to write his long poem *Pharsalia* glorifying the opposition to the founder of imperial power in Rome. Lucan must have been sufficiently aware of the arbitrary tyranny of Nero to recognize that in writing such an epic he played a game involving the highest of stakes. Conscious of his genius, independent in spirit, and impetuous in his youth, he was perhaps fascinated by a hazard with double danger. It was dangerous enough to challenge Nero in literary competition, but it was even more perilous to celebrate the defenders of the ancient Republican system. Theirs had been a lost cause, yet

Lucan makes idols of Pompey and Cato and so implicitly challenges Caesarism. There were several justifications for this anti-Caesarism. Corduba, the Spanish seat of his family, acknowledged a traditional allegiance to Pompey, and Lucan's own youthful imagination dreamed up rosy visions of a Republican past. His readings of Livy, the great propagandist for the Republic, confirmed his attitude. Nero's unfairness in trying to silence him drove him to detest the Caesarean dynasty.

Lucan's independent spirit affected not only the subject of his epic but also its composition. He broke away from epic tradition by resolutely rejecting mythology. Lucan's originality lay not so much in the choice of a Roman historical theme—there had been many epics, renowned and unrenowned, on national history—but in the treatment of his theme without the conventional introduction of the gods. The way in which Lucan introduced mythology as an appendix to geography only served to measure his contempt for it. When he described a region which had a legend, he told the legend with the proviso that it was not true. For Lucan, the strongest motive for relating a legend was that it was an incredible explanation of facts for which no credible explanation was forthcoming. Aware of the intrinsic greatness of the figures in a colossal struggle, Lucan relied for his effects more on history than on romance. In his theme, therefore, he broke away from Vergilian precedent and for legendary glamour substituted interest in a human conflict of a comparatively recent time.

PHARSALIA

Pharsalia is the only work by Lucan extant, and only ten books survive. This epic treats the war between Caesar and Pompey that erupted in 49 B.C.E. The title *Pharsalia* is borrowed from book 9, verse 985 of the poem. It consists of more than eight thousand hexameters but still does not complete the poet's design; the tenth book, about 150 lines shorter than the next shortest, ends abruptly, leaving Caesar at war in Egypt.

Modern critics have tended to condemn Lucan as tasteless and uninspired, and his *Pharsalia* is frequently (as has been said about John Milton's *Paradise Lost* of 1667) more talked about than read. In the Middle Ages, however, few classical authors were more widely read or praised than Lucan. In eighteenth century England, the *Pharsalia* not only was popular but also was considered to be the work of a poet even greater than Vergil. Lucan must be given credit for picturesque and striking language, but above all for his attempt to reinfuse a somewhat wilted Roman literature with the spirit of life. As Vergil had correctly seen, historical themes were not well suited to epic treatment. Nevertheless, Lucan was right in perceiving that Roman literature could not go on forever dealing with mythological fantasy, with ancient never-never lands and legendary history. If literature was to have any real meaning, it had to bring itself back to reality.

Lucan's attempt to make philosophy and science serve as the divine and mythological machinery had once served, however, is less than successful. The philosophical portions of the poem seem pompous, forced, and insincere, and require entirely too much argument. The scientific and pseudoscientific episodes are too long and detailed and clog the narrative. Lucan also failed to notice that if he was to write about real men and real history, he must write about them in "real" language and not in the high-flown, artificial style of the rhetorical schools.

The conflict between character and circumstance, each always victorious on its own ground, is the subject which gives interest and dignity to the *Pharsalia*. The poem opens with a delay of the action as Lucan describes the emperor Nero as a god and addresses him as sufficient inspiration for a poet. Lucan anticipates Nero's apotheosis and acknowledges that civil war was not a heavy price to pay for the blessings of Nero's reign. This opening probably owes something to Seneca, and certainly the poet is not at first so violently opposed to Caesar as he later becomes. Lucan is able to recognize that the war was a result of Pompey's inability to endure an equal and Caesar's inability to endure a master. It is a solitary gleam of insight. Referring to Pompey's lack of recent battle experience, Lucan unduly stresses his advanced age. In his fifty-seventh year, he was only four years older than his opponent, and, as Lucan more than once reminds his readers, had become Caesar's son-in-law by marrying Julia, whose death made the breach between them more probable. The poet, although sincerely embracing Pompey's cause, perceives him as a man overconfident because of previous battles and too trusting in the power of his name. The contrasting figure of Caesar is drawn forcefully although not sympathetically. He is a character who relies much on the sword and who enjoys creating havoc.

The strict narrative begins with Caesar's passage across the Alps, bringing his big plans to the small river Rubicon. (The adjectival antithesis is Lucan's.) Caesar is confronted with the majestic image of his native country protesting against further advance. The Rubicon is crossed; Arminium is taken; Caesar is met by his supporters. A summons for troops from Gaul presents an opportunity for digressions on Gallic tribes, tides, and Druids; then, a description of panic in Rome at Caesar's approach leads to the introduction of omens and expiatory rites. The book ends gloomily amid presages of disaster. Lucan, while he removes from his historical epic the conventional gods of epic poetry, puts in their place the supernatural, represented here by the symbolic figure of Roma, by portents, and by the prophecy of both an astrologer and a clairvoyant matron who has a vision of Pompey already lying dead.

Philosophy hesitantly opens book 2. The philosophical foundation of the *Pharsalia* is popular Stoicism, and the Stoics were perpetually confronted with the problem of reconciling belief in fate with divination. Why, asks Lucan, is man allowed to know future unhappiness through omens? He ends his philosophical discussion with a prayer that there might be hope amid fear and that the human mind be unaware of the coming doom. Mourning falls on Rome, and men pray for a foreign attack in preference to civil war. The passage is rhetorical in its earlier portion and argumentative at its close. The chief incidents of the book are: first, the remarriage of Cato to his former wife Marcia; second, the resistance to Caesar offered by Domitius, pointedly introduced because he was an ancestor of Nero; and, finally, the retreat of Pompey to Brundisium and overseas. Padding consists of digressions on the civil wars between Marius and Sulla and on the rivers of Italy. The introduction of Cato here is significant for book 9, where he plays a commanding part. For Lucan, Cato is the incarnation of virtue, never before guilty of shedding his country's blood, but now drawn by force into the struggle. Full of admiration for Cato's ascetic ordering of his life, the poet proudly

describes his Stoic ability to combine self-sufficing virtue with altruistic claims.

Book 3, mainly concerned with Caesar's activities on his return to Rome and his siege of Massilia, is ruined by a wearisome list of Pompey's eastern allies and the account of an interminable series of ingeniously horrible deaths which befall the soldiers. Among the compensating passages, however, are descriptions of Pompey's farewell to Italy and the eerie forest near Massilia. The former opens the book with a note of poetry and pathos, and the latter, describing the grave of the Druids, is a somber study touched with the spirit of Celtic romance. The reader is placed in a haunted wood at twilight, a place polluted by inhuman rites, shunned by birds, beasts, and forest deities. The leaves of the trees quiver, although there is no wind, and the whole forest is awesome with decay and nameless terrors.

Three episodes constitute most of the action of book 4: Caesar's Spanish operations; the failure of one of three Caesarean rafts to escape the Pompeian blockade in Illyria; and the arrival of a Caesarean general, Curio, in Africa, where he is defeated by Iuba and meets his death. The thirst suffered by the Pompeians in Spain prompts one of Lucan's denunciations of luxury, while the advice of the Caesarean commander to his men trapped on the raft to commit "mutual" suicide rather than surrender is argued in the strained style of a course in rhetoric. When the crew carries out their mutual slaughter, characteristic realism is employed to describe the crawling, bleeding, writhing agony of the lacerated men. This mass suicide closes with a reflection that consoled many of Nero's subjects as well as Lucan: Death is a ready way to elude tyranny. It is the Stoic speaking, recognizing the theoretical obligation of suicide and admitting that it was in certain circumstances defensible.

Book 5 opens with the assembly of the Senate friendly to Pompey and closes with his decision to send his wife Cornelia to Lesbos for safety. Nevertheless, Caesar is the dominant figure, especially when he cows the mutineers and crosses the Adriatic in a small boat on a stormy night to bring Antony. Caesar's willpower is dramatized in his defiant braving of the storm despite a fisherman's warning. He is content to have Fortune as his sole attendant in crossing the sea, but the storm is irresistibly tempting for Lucan. He exhausts his use of contending winds and then turns to hyperbole; mountains, having struggled in vain, crumble into the sea, as the waves roll portentously. Still full of hyperbole, but much more human, is the concluding episode, in which Pompey, deeply affected, can scarcely bring himself to tell his wife that for her safety they must part.

Overloaded with digressions, details of Caesar's scheme to enclose his enemy at Dyrrachum, and hyperbolical praise of the repulse of Pompey, book 6 is not on the whole successful. The action concentrates on one outstanding Caesarean who offers the resistance of an African elephant, tearing out and stamping on his own eyeball along with the arrow which pierced it. This and much more is neither poetry nor common sense. The rest mainly concerns the temporary setback of Caesar, who retreats to Thessaly and is followed there by Pompey. The mention of Thessaly offers the opportunity for digressions on geography and magic. There is a catalog of Thessalian spells for love, weather, rivers, mountains, and laws of the universe. The witches of Thessaly are more convincing in the work of Apuleius; yet Lucan does achieve a gruesome effect through Sextus Pompey's morbid longing to learn the future, not from oracles but from necromancy. He makes his way to the sorceress Erichtho and holds a midnight séance with her. Agreeing to his request, she selects a dead warrior, who is brought back to life by loathsome ingredients in order to foretell the future. The revelation is that the shades of the dead await both Sextus's father and his house. With that ominous response, Sextus returns to his father's camp before daybreak.

Although book 7 is not free from extravagance, it is the greatest book of the poem. It describes the feelings of both rivals before Pharsalus, as well as their fortunes in the battle. Pompey's men shout for battle and criticize their leader's caution. In a historically inaccurate scene, Cicero, who was not actually present, is introduced as urging Pompey to give battle. Pompey consents under protest. His men have their way, but many presage death in their pale coloring. The harangues to each side by the respective commanders are vigorous, full of bravado, and very readable. Despite Pompey's claim that his is the better cause, tyranny—in Lucan's view—is triumphant at Pharsalus. Lucan contrasts the fugitive Pompey,

looking back upon lost greatness, with Caesar, whose adversary from this point on is not Pompey but freedom and who, to discerning eyes, might be an object of pity: It was worse to win. The picture of the conqueror is not flattering. According to Lucan, Caesar encouraged his men to plunder, was the leader of the guilty side, callously surveyed the dead, withheld rotting corpses from cremation, and was hunted, Orestes-like, by avenging Furies.

The main interest of book 8 lies in Pompey's flight to Egypt and his murder as he is about to land. It is broken by reflections and apostrophes on both Egypt and Pompey. A prey to nervous fears, the defeated warrior escapes in a small boat to Lesbos, where he tries to console his grief-stricken wife. He sets sail with her in anxiety great enough to make unnatural his conversation with the pilot about astronomy. He holds a council of his supporters on his destination, suggesting they land in Parthia. His advisers consider this action dishonorable and persuade him to try Egypt, whose king, Ptolemy, owes his throne indirectly to Pompey. Thus does Pompey sail to meet death. Overmastering fate arranges that Pompey is enticed into a small boat where, in view of his wife and son, he is stabbed by a traitor. Pompey's head is cut off and carried to the boy-king Ptolemy. Having noted the majesty of Pompey's looks as preserved in death, Lucan yields to his obstructive passion for realism and spoils the pathos of the scene. Instead of Vergil's dignity in the face of sorrow, or beauty of simile, there are repulsive details of the still-gasping mouth and the drooping neck laid crosswise to be hacked through; there are sinews and veins to be cut; there are bones to break. Such realism is rendered unnecessary by the moving description of Pompey that follows. The headless body is retrieved from the sea by one of Pompey's Roman attendants and, after an incomplete cremation, is hastily buried. The book ends with imprecations and wild rhetoric on Egypt.

Pompey's apotheosis begins book 9. The lamentations of Cornelia, the threats of vengeance by Pompey's son, and Cato's dignified praise of the dead leader are preliminaries to the central theme of the book: the heroism of Cato. He marches with his men to Africa and gives many demonstrations of his endurance and courage. Cato's inspiring bravery is, however, almost smothered by a mass of irrelevant details about the origin of serpents in Africa and by catalogs of various species of serpents and various sorts of deaths from snakebite.

Book 10, on Caesar in Egypt, would fit better into an epic on mighty Julius than into the *Pharsalia*, yet it has energy in spite of a digression on Alexander the Great. The principal events are Caesar's visit to Alexander's tomb, his affair with Cleopatra, her magnificent banquet after a reconciliation with Ptolemy, and the plot to kill Caesar. The tenth book is incomplete, and there are many indications of an unfinished scheme. There is, for example, a reference to the postponement of a fated penalty, which implies that the poem was designed to continue up to Caesar's assassination in 44 B.C.E.

LEGACY

When it is remembered that the aim in academic rhetoric was to appear clever and striking at all costs, the central characteristic of Lucan's epic is at once grasped. The dominant note is one of display. The object is not to be natural but above all to be piquant and impressive. The parade of erudition which leads to catalogs and digressions employs Lucan's rhetorical training. The realistic detail is calculated to cause a shudder; the subtlety of argument makes a debating speech cogent; the hyperbole arrests attention; points, epigrams, and antitheses produce memorable phrases.

Realism in Lucan is morbid and grotesque. Too often it is paired with the desire to terrify the audience by dwelling on the horrible. Hence he enjoys describing tortures, the agonies of the wounded, the repulsive ghoulishness of a witch, and the revolting aspects of cremation. When realism is strained to the breaking point, it becomes unreal.

Despite such overemphasis on gory realism and hyperbole, Lucan's rhetoric is often brilliant, expressing his thought in brief, pointed form, often assisted by antithesis. These economical lines and phrases epigrammatically summarize a character, a situation, or—in the older meaning of *sententia*—a general truth.

Lucan's mannerisms and willful faults can blind his audience to his merits. It is true that he is rhetorical and sensational, yet when all his inaccuracies, distortions, and digressions have been held against him, his great passages prove that in spite of artificiality he can be fiery and irresistible.

BIBLIOGRAPHY

Ahl, Frederick. "Form Empowered: Lucan's *Pharsalia*." In *Roman Epic*, edited by A. J. Boyle. London: Routledge, 1993. Argues that Lucan's epic on the Roman Civil War was itself an internal struggle in which he sought to impose his own meaning on history, thus displacing that of Julius Caesar and his successor Augustus. "It is a political act as well as a political poem" in which Lucan "is matching himself against Caesar on two counts: one literary, one historical."

Bartsch, Shadi. *Ideology in Cold Blood: A Reading of Lucan's "Civil War."* Cambridge, Mass.: Harvard University Press, 1997. Bartsch approaches Lucan's epic as a paradoxical work, a combination of poetry and history where the historical "facts" are less important than the underlying "meanings" which Lucan imposes on them. Acknowledging that "Civil War" is a hard poem to read, Bartsch helps make sense of it through patient and sometimes inspired analysis.

Braud, S. H. Introduction to *Lucan, "Civil War."* Oxford: University Press, 1992. Braud's solid, meticulous translation is put into literary and historical context through his introduction, which reviews both the subject matter and style of the work and its altering reputation over the centuries.

Henderson, John. *Fighting for Rome: Poets and Caesars, History and Civil War*. Cambridge, England: Cambridge University Press, 1998. In a fashion similar to Ahl and Bartsch, Henderson looks at Lucan's *Civil War* as an attempt to rewrite history in terms of explaining its meaning if not changing its course. An interesting approach to what Lucan was attempting to do with his poetry and how successful he was in the task.

Johnson, W. R. *Momentary Monsters: Lucan and His Heroes*. Ithaca, N.Y.: Cornell University Press, 1987. Johnson points out that there are actually three "heroes" in Lucan's Civil War—Caesar, Cato, and Pompey—but that each of these is deeply, and perhaps fatally, flawed. These defects in their characters and perceptions cause them to become, as the title indicates, "momentary monsters" at crucial periods during the action of the poem. The question, which Lucan never resolves, is whether these flaws are prompted by events or are themselves the cause of those events.

Joyce, Jane Wilson. Introduction to *Lucan, "Pharsalia."* Ithaca, N.Y.: Cornell University Press, 1993. Wilson prefaces her lively and intelligent translation of Lucan with an introduction that places the poem in historical and literary context. While accepting much of the traditional scholarship that addresses the "poetry vs. history" puzzle the poem raises, she goes further to point out the underlying qualities which link the poem to other epics of the ancient world.

Masters, Jamie. *Poetry and Civil War in Lucan's "Bellum Civile."* Cambridge, England: Cambridge University Press, 1992. Lucan's poem not only is about civil war, Masters explains, but also manages to mimic the conflict in its structure, style, and characters. The tensions of the poem thus help re-create the struggle of the civil war itself, making form and contents merge.

Shelley P. Haley;
bibliography updated by Michael Witkoski

LUCRETIUS

Titus Lucretius Carus
Born: Probably Rome; c. 98 B.C.E.
Died: Probably Rome; October 15, 55 B.C.E.

PRINCIPAL POETRY

De rerum natura, c. 60 B.C.E. (*On the Nature of Things*, 1682)

OTHER LITERARY FORMS

Lucretius is remembered only for *On the Nature of Things*.

ACHIEVEMENTS

Lucretius wrote a single poem, not intended for public performance. The poem, *On the Nature of Things*, consists of the exposition of a philosophical system in exalted and ornate language and of an exhortation to follow that system and attain happiness.

BIOGRAPHY

Little is known about the life of Titus Lucretius Carus. Apart from the date of his birth, his literary activity, a curious statement concerning the publication of his poem, a possibly spurious anecdote of his intermittent insanity and possible suicide, and the date of his death, little else has survived. Modern scholars have argued against Lucretius's insanity by appealing to the intellectual stability and range, the subtlety, complexity, and orderliness of *On the Nature of Things*. The poem, while it does not solve the problem of Lucretius's insanity, does give some valuable insights into the history and personality of its author. *On the Nature of Things* shows that Lucretius was a scholar, and his knowledge of works such as the *Odyssey* (c. 800 B.C.E.) glows throughout his poem. He uses the story of Iphigenia to make the central point of his poem, which is the elimination of dangerous superstition. Lucretius was familiar with ancient science, Thucydides, Epicurus, and Empedocles, as well as early Roman authors. There are echoes of Ennius, the one Roman poet whom Lucretius praises by name, as a kindred rationalist in religion.

Lucretius's poem reveals his extensive knowledge, which in turn indicates his aristocratic, moneyed, cultured background. Like many other Roman youths in the same financial circumstances, he probably journeyed to Athens and so was introduced to science. Although the poem holds clues concerning Lucretius's library, as well as his literary habits, education, and social status, these assumptions can never be taken at face value.

In keeping with the allegation of insanity, Lucretius is said to have died by his own hand. According to another legend, followed by Alfred, Lord Tennyson, in his *Lucretius* (1868), Lucretius's wife killed him with a love potion. This notion has nothing to support it, and there is no evidence that Lucretius even had a wife.

ANALYSIS

Any discussion of the *On the Nature of Things* inevitably involves an explanation of the philosophical system which is its topic. The system is Epicurean, and Lucretius is, in fact, the chief authority of that system. Epicurus followed the atomistic theory, proposed by Leucippus. The philosopher Democritus worked out the theory, and through Epicurus it reached Lucretius. Like

Epicurus, Lucretius cared for physical speculations only insofar as they might help man to live a happy life. Democritus made it his main goal to seek causes; he would prefer, he said, to discover a true cause than to possess the kingdom of Persia. Epicurus and Lucretius were satisfied if they were convinced that something was the result of a number of possible causes, so long as these would not interfere with the happy life.

Epicurus held that both this and innumerable other universes, which he supposed to exist, are the result of chance conglomerations of atoms. These atoms are of all shapes but are very minute and fall eternally through space. As they fall, they swerve in an erratic way, making their motions unpredictable. Nothing is immaterial, although some things such as the soul are the result of the combinations of comparatively few and very fine, mobile atoms. As all things are, therefore, accidental compounds, all things are capable of dissolution. The two exceptions to this are the atoms themselves, which are too small to be broken into anything smaller, and the void, which, being nothing, cannot be injured. Man, therefore, has nothing to fear from death, which is mere dissolution followed by complete absence of consciousness. Man's one good is pleasure, yet this is not to be found in overindulgence of physical desires, which results in a surplus of pain, not of pleasure. The right course is to satisfy the physical needs in the simplest ways (hunger for example, by a reasonable amount of plain food) and to concentrate on gratifying and pleasing the mind. There is no need to disturb the mind with ambition, desire, or fear of death. The good Epicurean will live a quiet life and withhold himself from public employment and from all that would mar his tranquillity. He should devote much time to philosophic reflection and study. Such is the Epicurean system, which Lucretius set forth with much eloquence.

ON THE NATURE OF THINGS

On the Nature of Things is divided into six books. After a hauntingly beautiful address to Venus, Lucretius gives as his aim the release of men from fear by means of a philosophy which delivers humankind from the impieties of superstition. After laying down the fundamental principle that nothing can come from nothing or pass into nothing, book 1 then proceeds to state the atomic theory of matter as understood by the Epicureans.

Lucretius (Hulton Archive)

After an introduction in praise of philosophy, book 2 continues the subject and states the doctrine of "swerve." Book 3, which begins with praise of Epicurus, explains the nature of the soul. There are two parts of man: the *animus* or *mens*, which is situated in the chest, and with which man thinks and feels, and the *anima* or soul, which is dispersed throughout the body. Both the *animus* and the *anima* are composed of several sorts of minute atoms and both are mortal, passing out of the body and dispersing at death. Death, therefore, is not to be dreaded. The legendary tortures of the other world are nothing more than allegories of the woes which beset the foolish in this life.

The fact that book 4 has no introduction is one of many indications that the work never received final revision. It explains the Epicurean theory of perception and from this it passes to a discussion of sexual passion, explained as the effect of external stimuli acting on a system already suffering from an internal disturbance. Recognition of the purely physical nature of sexual passion and of the nonsupernatural causes of such conditions as barrenness will guard against the miseries of extravagant lovers and of the superstitious. Book 5, again having for its prologue an eloquent praise of Epicurus, is one of the most interesting of the poem. It gives the Epicurean theory of the history of the universe and of man. The universe is neither perfect, everlasting, nor divinely governed, and it will have an end as surely as it had a beginning. All of its phenomena, such as sunrise and sunset, have perfectly natural explanations. Book 6, clearly the least finished of all, progresses, after another tribute to Epicurus, to a somewhat miscellaneous series of discussions—first of celestial and meteoric phenomena, then of the curiosities on the surface of the earth (Mount Etna, the flooding of the Nile, and so on). Finally, the book moves on to the causes of disease, which are said to be largely the result of unwholesome or even unfamiliar air that is driven from one part of the surface of the earth to another. The poem concludes with Lucretius's rendering in verse of Thucydides' account of the plague at Athens.

STYLE AND LANGUAGE

Stylistically, Lucretius, the most Roman in character (honest, fearless, austere, orderly) of the Roman poets except perhaps for Ennius, is as an artist the most Greek. He has many traits associated with Hellenism. His science is Hellenistic and his didactic poems, full of learned lore, were much the fashion from Alexandrian times forward.

The excellence of the *On the Nature of Things* is principally of two sorts: first, in the command of the language, and second, in the eloquence of the passages of moral reflection and the descriptions of nature. Lucretius lived at a time when the Latin speech with which he was most familiar was the idiom of the Ciceronian Age. It was a clean and straight medium, more refined than the earlier language of Cato the Elder, but still natural and direct, retaining many expressions drawn from the law, the market, and the political arena.

It was during the Ciceronian Age that the literary force known as Alexandrianism made itself strongly felt in Roman poetry. Lucretius, however, was not attracted to Alexandrianism. At any rate, he did not imitate its wearying niceties of phrase and its emphasis on form. His deep although latent patriotism may have made him averse to a style so clearly foreign. Perhaps his own energetic nature craved a more energetic mode of expres-

sion. Because he was a devoted pupil of Epicurus, Lucretius may have believed that an intense preoccupation with the minutiae of style was unworthy of a poet who sought to free men from the haunting terror of death. Whatever the reason, Lucretius turned, rather, to the past, and there found a congenial model. He followed in the footsteps of Ennius; consequently, archaism is the most notable mark of Lucretius's style and diction.

By virtue of its dignity and energy, the older Latin speech seemed to be an appropriate medium through which Lucretius could proclaim Epicurus. Lucretius did not, however, imitate without discretion and taste, nor did he attempt to recapture the style and diction of a century before. For the most part, Lucretius avoided the extreme characteristics of Ennius's language: its uncouthness and grotesqueness. Lucretius's position in the history of Latin poetic style and diction is intermediate and transitional. Adopting the best that the past offered, he impressed upon Latin style his own energy and directness and passed it on to his younger colleague Vergil, who developed its qualities of gravity and flexibility still further.

Lucretius borrows many words and phrases directly from Ennius, but his archaism is not confined to such borrowings. In his fondness for the past, and in his desire to integrate his own poem with the traditions of older Roman literature, Lucretius often employs old words, old spellings of familiar words, and old idioms. The first of these categories strikes the attention of even the most casual reader (in Latin, of course, and not in translation). The reader is also at first surprised by a variety of old verbal forms.

Despite his conscious archaism, Lucretius was in no way a thoroughgoing and consistent antiquarian. He made no attempt to resurrect in its entirety the speech of Ennius and other early Latin poets and to write solely in their dying idiom. Had he done so, he probably would have ceased to be a poet and would have become simply a technician of words, devoid of energy and authenticity.

Another striking element of Lucretius's style is the fluidity and variety of his language. Like any other great poet, Lucretius used the literary sources at his disposal, but from them he developed a style that was uniquely his own; in so doing, he unified the several elements from which his style was drawn. One goal that Lucretius strove for was clarity. He hated obscure and pretentious language because it was objectionable in itself, but still more because of its exploitation by philosophers. Clarity of language may have been Lucretius's first aim, but it was, perhaps, also his greatest problem.

Epicurus had behind him a long tradition of philosophical writing in Greek. Lucretius was a pioneer in Latin in this field. His public was relatively unfamiliar with philosophical concepts and presumably with Greek philosophical terms. Lucretius found Latin equivalents for these terms but took care to insert them in contexts which help to clarify their meaning. Paradoxically, Lucretius had to be clearer than his master had been, and yet, as a poet who wished to write true poetry according to well-understood traditions, he was denied the full freedom of prosaic explanation and endured the tyrannies imposed by the hexameter. He did the best he could by employing different forms of words, adopting contracted forms, and borrowing or creating linguistic oddities. These practices account for the fluid nature of *On the Nature of Things.*

One of the conditions imposed by the need for clarity was a greater acceptance of repetition than was considered elegant by most contemporary poets, together with a comparative neglect of the conventional virtue of variety. Lucretius was disinclined to seek variations, although he did not exclude them, because he was not willing to sacrifice precision and clarity. What repetition Lucretius does use is sometimes rhetorical; he will repeat unusual or idiosyncratic words or phrases, thus attracting added attention to them. The repetition is deliberate and is used more as an artistic than as a didactic tool. Its object is to enliven expression, emphasize a point, or express the poet's feelings, which may be, in Lucretius's case, feelings of didactic earnestness.

Lucretius wrote his didactic poem in the epic medium, following the example of Empedocles, but he adapted the form to his own purposes. The ornamental epic simile (characteristic of Homer, Vergil, and John Milton) held little attraction for Lucretius. His similes, picturesque though they may sometimes be, are predominantly functional. The most famous Lucretian simile of all, about physicians administering wormwood to children (book 1, lines 936ff.), looks more like a conventional simile than most of his. It is, in fact, a severely practical personal statement of his own position as a philosopher-poet, and its language is strictly linked with the reality it is designed to illustrate. When Lucretius's similes are longer than usual, there is no extension of the simile as a picture in its own right, but as an additional illustration or further analogy. In fact, the longer similes often contain a series of analogies designed for the fullest possible clarification.

The functional character of the similes is closely connected with the Epicurean insistence on the validity of sense evidence. The normal function of these similes is to explain or illustrate, by an appeal to familiar experience, concepts or theories about invisible things (such as the atoms) or things remote in space (such as the movement of heavenly bodies) or in time (such as the infancy of the earth and the life of primitive man). The comparison is most commonly with man (his body or his actions), with living creatures familiar to man (such as dogs and cattle), or with the events of his life (such as a shipwreck) and things visible in his daily experience (such as smoke, flowing water, or sunrise). Since the similes are not conventional embellishments, they are not usually heralded by conventional introductory phrases, such as *ac veluti* (and just as), which mark a simile off from its context and direct special attention to it. They slip in simply and naturally, remaining closely integrated with the context, but are dismissed as soon as their task is done. They prove to be illustrations, comparisons, or analogies rather than similes in the conventional sense. Yet they are, in fact, another example of Lucretius's individualistic and serious-minded use of an element from the epic medium which he had adopted.

IMAGERY

Lucretius excels in another important feature of the poetic tradition: imagery. It has been said of Lucretius that he had that acute sensory awareness essential to all great poets. He was physically aware of textures, colors, and patterns of every kind. Imagery is an integral part of Lucretius's method, not at all in the conventional and superficial way in which it was to appear in the imperial poets.

Probably no poet of the Latin language, not even Vergil himself, exhibits so vast a range of imagery, so universal a vision of the world and its poetic possibilities as does Lucretius. The feel of a pebble in a shoe; the touch of the feet of an insect or of a strand of cobweb brushing across the face; the acrid smell of a just-extinguished wick; the taste of bitter medicine; the various parts of the human body—eyes, nose, hands, ears, internal organs, nerve fibers, and even teeth and their agonizing ache; the dead body tumescent and full of worms; a pig's-bladder balloon exploding; the hiss of a hot iron dashed into water; sparks flying from stone struck against stone or steel; the crash of a falling tree; clothes that grow damp when laid out near a body of water and then grow dry again when hung in the sun; the rumbling of carts over the paving stones of a Roman street; the wobbling of a vase when the water within it is disturbed; sheep on a mountainside; armies clashing on the plain; the foot of a bronze statue worn smooth and shiny where passersby have touched it; the light of the sun shining through varicolored awnings stretched over a theater; the springtime gaiety of birds and animals and even of fish; the curious snakelike majesty of the elephant and his trunk; and the sloppy contentment of pigs in the mud: These are only some of the many aspects of life that Lucretius uses for poetic and argumentative purposes. Although he is not often thought of in this respect, he was, in fact, one of the most brilliant word painters of life in the ancient world. His poem offers a wide panorama of the Mediterranean in the first century B.C.E. Lucretius saw that ideas are to be found only in things and that nothing proves a point quite so neatly as an appropriate series of pictures from life.

Consistently, Lucretius's images, down to the smallest detail, are functional, and their function is to clarify and enforce the argument of the poem. The *raison d'être* of Lucretius's poetry is that it sweetens the seemingly bitter but life-giving dose of Epicureanism. The *raison d'être* of the images is the rigorous logical work they are set to do in their contexts. This is one of the things which gives such intensity to the poetry of Lucretius, and it is a quality often lost in translation.

Lucretius expounds a materialist philosophy which explains the whole of the world and of experience in terms of the movements of invisible material particles. So, repeatedly, he must infer the behavior of these particles from the behavior of visible phenomena—rivers, wind and sea, fire, light, and all the rest. The philosophical subject matter of this poem is not an impediment to the poetry, but rather the stimulus for the impassioned observation and contemplation of the material world which contributes so much to the poetic intensity of the work.

GREEK MYTHS AND ALLEGORY

Another aspect of Lucretius's art is the use of Greek mythology for the purpose of allegory. Normally, Lucretius brushes aside myth as totally misleading, particularly the stock representations of Hell or the personalities of the Olympian gods. He does use the names of the gods as appropriate paraphrases, provided that nothing further is intended. Quite different is the opening of the first book, with its extended address to Venus and Mars, a fully developed allegory. There can be no doubt that Lucretius enjoys this sort of symbolism for its own sake. That is confirmed in his elaborate version of the sacrifice of Iphigenia in book 1, which is related with great force and pathos to demonstrate the moral of the evils of superstition.

The story of the Trojan War in book 1 is purely decorative. It is related in true epic style, simply as an example of an event which could not have happened had not the universe contained space as well as matter. The story of Phaëthon in book 5 is given as an illustration of the domination of the four elements over the others. Lucretius, however, dismisses it immediately as hopelessly naïve and unscientific. Yet the poet takes delight in relating both myths, and they serve the purpose of adding a personal interest to passages in which the human content is small.

In his imagery, sublime or lowly, Lucretius appears as a man who observes natural phenomena with a keen eye and expresses their essential significance in simple but effective language. If Lucretius is still worth reading, it is not only because of the brilliance of his descriptions or the power of his poetry, but also because he has something to say.

BIBLIOGRAPHY

Brown, Robert. *Lucretius on Love and Sex.* New York: E. J. Brill, 1987. An examination of the distinction Lucretius made between sexual pleasure and passion. Brown states that Lucretius's writings are "a body of sober sexual doctrine which sets off the elaborate central treatment of romantic passion and provides a basis for assessing the error and destructiveness of this emotion." In other words, the rational enjoyment of sex can and should be separated from the irrational effects of both lust and love.

Donohue, Harold. *The Song of the Swan: Lucretius and the Influence of Callimachus*. New York: University Press of America, 1993. Traces the connections and relationships of several of the key themes and techniques of classical poetry from Greek to Latin literature.

Fowler, Don, and Peta Fowler. Introduction to *Lucretius on the Nature of the Universe*. Oxford: Clarendon Press, 1997. Places Lucretius's philosophical and scientific poem within the contexts of Latin literature, Epicurean philosophy, and classical science. A good overview of the work and its contents which grounds it for the modern reader in terms of a vigorous modern translation.

Gale, Monica. *Myth and Poetry in Lucretius*. Cambridge, England: Cambridge University Press, 1994. *On the Nature of Things* is, essentially, a scientific and agnostic (if not atheistic) explanation of the universe and the transitory role of human beings in that universe. However, it is also a poem which makes extensive use of classical mythology and literary traditions. Gale examines these seeming contradictions and shows how they are resolved through Lucretius's artistry. This work helps to explain how Lucretius is both a part of the continuum of classical thought and a startlingly original individual in his own right.

_____. *Virgil on the Nature of Things: The "Georgics," Lucretius, and the Didactic Tradition*. Cambridge, England: Cambridge University Press, 2000. Gale points out that Lucretius's work is similar to Vergil's *Georgics* in that it explains, as scientifically as then possible, the workings of the natural world. Such understanding is not an end in itself (although that is worthwhile) but a means to live a more rational and ordered life. Good for helping the modern reader understand how a handbook on agriculture and a scientific treatise could be written in disciplined Latin verse.

Godwin, John. Introduction to *Lucretius: "De Rerum Natura" VI*. Warminster, England: Aris and Phillips, 1991. Although this translation is of only one book of what is, in fact, a long and intricate poem, Godwin's introduction provides a helpful overview of the entire work, including its techniques and meanings.

Sedley, David. *Lucretius and the Transformation of Greek Wisdom*. Cambridge, England: Cambridge University Press, 1998. A long-held view is that the Romans imported, with little or no change, entire segments of Greek culture, including scientific and artistic achievements. Sedley examines this concept and shows that it oversimplifies what actually happened, and that Lucretius in particular played a key role in making the Greek inheritance more fundamentally Roman.

Shelley P. Haley;
bibliography updated by Michael Witkoski

JOHN LYDGATE

Born: Lydgate, Suffolk, England; 1370(?)
Died: Bury St. Edmunds, England; 1451(?)

PRINCIPAL POETRY

Translation of Aesop, wr. c. 1400, pb. 1885
Complaint of the Black Knight, wr. c. 1400, pb. 1508
The Temple of Glass, wr. c. 1403, pb. 1477
The Life of Our Lady, wr. c. 1409, pb. 1484
The Hystorye, Sege, and Dystruccyon of Troye, wr. c.1420, pb. 1513 (better known as *Troy Book*)
The Siege of Thebes, wr. c. 1422, pb. 1496
The Pilgrimage of the Life of Man, wr. c. 1426, pb. 1899-1904
Guy of Warwick, wr. c. 1426, pb. 1873
Ballade at the Reverence of Our Lady, Qwene of Mercy, wr. c. 1430
The Dance of Death, wr. c. 1430, pb. 1554
Fall of Princes, wr. 1431-1439, pb. 1494

The Lives of Saints Edmund and Fremund, wr. c. 1433, pb. 1881

The Life of Saint Albon and the Life of Saint Amphabel, wr. c. 1439, pb. 1534

Queen Margaret's Entry into London, wr. c. 1445, pb. 1912

The Testament of J. Lydgate, wr. c. 1449, pb. 1515

The Secrets of Old Philosophers, wr. c. 1451, pb. 1511

OTHER LITERARY FORMS

John Lydgate wrote only one significant piece of prose, *The Serpent of Division*. Scholars are uncertain as to its exact date of composition, but Walter Schirmer, in his *John Lydgate: A Study in the Culture of the Fifteenth Century* (1961), suggests the year 1422. Drawing on Lucan's *Pharsalia* (c. 80 C.E.) and Vincent of Beauvais's *Speculum Historiale*, Lydgate here presents the first comprehensive account of the rise and fall of Julius Caesar ever written in English. As in other writings, Lydgate uses this story as an *exemplum*, a story used to teach morality. Here Lydgate's lesson had to do with civil war.

Certain of Lydgate's poems are very intimately connected with later English dramatic forms, especially the *masque*. His "mummings" were meant to accompany short pantomimes or the presentation of *tableaux vivantes*. For example, in 1424 *Mumming at Bishopswood* was presented at an outdoor gathering of London's civic officials. A narrator presented the verses while, at the same time, a dancer portrayed the Goddess of Spring with various gestures and dance steps. The lesson of the poem is conveyed through allegory, where immaterial entities are personified. Here Spring represents civil concord, and Lydgate argues that just as the joy, freshness, and prosperity of Spring replace the heaviness and trouble of winter, so too the various estates, the nobles, the clergy, and the commoners, should throw off their discord and work together in their God-given roles. Success in these "mummings" probably helped prepare Lydgate for his part in the preparation of the public celebrations for the coronation of Henry VI in 1429, and for the triumphant entry into London of the same king with his new queen, Margaret, in 1445.

John Lydgate (Hulton Archive)

ACHIEVEMENTS

John Lydgate was one of the most prolific writers in English, with 145,000 lines of verse to his credit. To match this, one would have to write eight lines a day, every day, for about fifty years. Furthermore, almost every known medieval poetic genre is represented in the Lydgate canon.

For hundreds of years the English literary public regarded Lydgate's achievement as equal to that of Geoffrey Chaucer or John Gower. Indeed, the three writers were generally grouped together into a conventional triad of outstanding English poets. George Ashby's praise in 1470 is typical:

> Maisters Gower, Chaucer & Lydgate,
> Primier poetes of this nacion,
> Embelysshing oure Englisshe tendure algate
> Firste finders to oure consolacion.

Furthermore, Lydgate was the glass through which his contemporaries understood and appreciated Chaucer, whom they considered a rhetorician, not a realist, the writer who finally formed English into a suitable vehicle for poetry, philosophy, and learning. In the end, perhaps Lydgate's greatest achievement was to consolidate this new status for his native tongue. Wholehearted monk, sometime administrator, and laureate versifier for kings and princes, Lydgate wrote poetry representative of his times and proper for someone of his position: sometimes prolix, often dull, but everywhere sincere, decorous, well-crafted, and worthy of remembrance.

BIOGRAPHY

John Lydgate was born into turbulent times. His life spanned seventy years of the Hundred Years' War with France, and, when he died, the Wars of the Roses were about to begin. In 1381, he witnessed the Peasants' Revolt; in 1399, he saw Richard II deposed. The earlier years of his life were those of the Great Western Schism, with popes in both Avignon and Rome. At the same time the anticlerical Lollards were stirring up trouble for the Church in England. Even nature seemed to conspire against the peace, for, beginning in 1349, the plague struck regularly, killing large portions of the English population.

Born of peasant stock, Lydgate was reared in the quiet village of Lydgate, far from the civil turmoil which raged elsewhere. He must have had a fairly normal childhood, for he later wrote: "Loth to lerne [I] loved no besyness,/ Save pley/ or merth . . . Folowyng alle appetytes longyng to childhede" (*Testament*, 11). His serious side prevailed, however, and perhaps as early as 1385 he joined the Benedictine monastery at Bury St. Edmunds, about sixty-five miles northeast of London. Bury St. Edmunds was one of the richest of England's monasteries, with eighty monks, twenty-one chaplains, and 111 servants. Here Lydgate received much of his formal education, although it is likely that he also spent a few years at Oxford, where he may have begun his literary career by writing his *Translation of Aesop*, the first book of fables written in Middle English. If Oxford was a good place to begin writing, however, the magnificent library of Bury St. Edmunds was just the place to nourish such a career, for it is thought to have contained about two thousand volumes, at the time making it one of the finest in England.

By the time he was ordained a priest in 1397, Lydgate probably had begun building a modest literary rep-

utation. Indeed, John Bale, a sixteenth century biographer, suggests that Lydgate had already started a school of rhetoric for the sons of noblemen. Although some scholars are dubious about this, it is certain that Lydgate at this time began to make friends among the aristocracy, many of whom were later to become his literary patrons.

As a matter of fact, Lydgate soon came to the attention of Prince Hal, later Henry V, who in 1409 charged him with writing a life of the Blessed Virgin Mary. Thus Lydgate wrote his first saint's legend, *The Life of Our Lady*. This was to be the start of a long and fruitful relationship between Lydgate and the Lancastrian dynasty, a dynasty which both the poet and his brother monks saw as a strong bulwark of Catholic orthodoxy against the Lollards.

Henry V was more interested in battle, conquest, and deeds of chivalry than in piety, however, and by October, 1412, he conceived a different sort of project for Lydgate's talent: a retelling of the popular story of Troy. It took Lydgate eight years, relying mostly on Guido delle Colonne's *Historia Troiana* (c. 1285), to construct this long epic of thirty thousand lines. His taste for versifying history, however, was hardly sated by this massive work, for very soon after completing *Troy Book*, Lydgate set out on another long poem: *The Siege of Thebes*. He found the frame for this tale in Chaucer's works; he presents the work as a continuation of *The Canterbury Tales* (1387-1400). Thus the pilgrim "Daun John" Lydgate himself tells the Thebes story—at length. In the prologue Lydgate shows his sense of humor, ironically contrasting his own appearance, "so pale, al devoyde of blode," to that of Chaucer's strong, lusty monk.

Lydgate's admiration for his master, Chaucer, knew no bounds; for Lydgate, Chaucer was the "lodesterre" of English letters. Although he probably never met the older poet, Lydgate was a very close acquaintance of Chaucer's son, Thomas, who was a wealthy country gentleman in Oxfordshire. A glimpse of the closeness of this relationship is seen in Lydgate's *Ballad to Thomas Chaucer* (1417).

In 1423, Lydgate moved closer to the circles of power at Windsor; he was given charge of the priory at Hatfield in Essex, a post which he retained, at least nominally, until 1434, when he was granted a *dimissio*, or formal written permission to return to Bury St. Edmunds "to seek the fruit of a better life." In fact, Lydgate probably resided at Hatfield only until 1426. It seems that in that year Lydgate was sent to Paris to take up a senior post on the staff of John of Lancaster, Duke of Bedford. Here, among other things, he wrote *Guy of Warwick*, an adaptation of an old epic poem glorifying a mythical English hero who saves England from the Danes by overcoming their champion, Colbrand.

While in France Lydgate met Thomas de Montacute, the fourth Earl of Salisbury, who was the second husband of Alice Chaucer, the granddaughter of the poet. Montacute had a great interest in letters and commissioned Lydgate's translation of Guilliam de Deguileville's popular *Pèlerinage de la vie humaine* (1330-1331), a long allegorical romance concerning the "pilgrimage" of man through this earthly existence.

It can be assumed that in Paris Lydgate mixed with people of the highest tastes and education, both English and French, for these years were productive ones for him, during which he wrote many of his satires and religious poems. He was inspired, for example, by one of the most popular themes of fifteenth century art, the *danse macabre*. Both in painting and in verse, this motif portrays the skeletons of men and women of all social classes dancing together as equals—in death. Lydgate's *Dance of Death* is a fairly close translation of verses which he discovered written on the colonnade surrounding the cemetery of the Église des Innocents in Paris.

In 1429, Lydgate returned to London for the coronation of the seven-year-old Henry VI. By this time, he was the premier poet of England, and thus he was commissioned to write an official *Roundel for the Coronation*, setting forth Henry's hereditary claim to the throne. Lydgate also had a hand in the planning of the official public celebrations for the event. He did the same in 1432 when Henry triumphantly returned to London from his coronation in Paris as king of France.

Fall of Princes, Lydgate's most important work, was commissioned in May, 1431, by Henry V's brother, Humphrey, duke of Gloucester, then warden of England. In some thirty-six thousand lines the poet chronicles the continual movement of the Wheel of Fortune, raising up and then casting down men and women of power and wealth. It took him eight years to complete, while he increasingly felt his powers being drained by age.

In 1433, the king spent four months at Bury St. Edmunds and in commemoration of the event Lydgate was asked to write a life of the monastery's patron, St. Edmund, for presentation to the monarch. Later, in 1439, Lydgate wrote his final piece of hagiography, *The Life of Saint Alban and the Life of Saint Amphabel*.

Lydgate received a lifelong pension from the king in 1439, but he was not left in peace at Bury St. Edmunds to enjoy it. In 1445, he was again given responsibilities for the planning of a public celebration, this time for the arrival in London of Henry VI's new queen, Margaret, daughter of King René of Anjou. For this occasion he wrote *Queen Margaret's Entry into London*, a work that no longer exists in its entirety.

In 1448, the poet, suspecting that his life was almost over, began his versified *Testament*, perhaps his most intensely personal poem. In it he denounces, somewhat conventionally, the levity of his youth, but he later proclaims in very moving terms his personal devotion to the name of Jesus. The tone and range of subject matter in Lydgate's *Testament* are much different from those of the more famous *Testament* written less than a decade later by François Villon.

Lydgate must have passed his last few years with some sadness over his country's fortunes. The Hundred Years' War was winding down, but not in England's favor. Further, the internal political turmoil which would eventually lead to the Wars of the Roses was growing in England. Lydgate's final work, which he left unfinished, is another attempt to offer wise counsel to the country's leaders. *The Secrets of Old Philosophers* is a translation of the *Secreta Secretorum*, supposedly written by Aristotle for his pupil Alexander. Benedict Burgh, who completed the work, relates that just after Lydgate wrote verse 1,491, "deth al consumyth," the pen dropped from his hand, and the much-honored poet passed into history.

ANALYSIS

Once the uncrowned poet laureate of England, Lydgate was appreciated by kings, princes, and nobility. In more modern times, he is often disparaged by literary scholars. Critics have charged that his poetry is dull, long-winded, and poorly wrought. Not all of these charges will stand scrutiny, however, and one could argue that Lydgate's fall is due primarily to a shifting of tastes in poetry rather than to poor craftsmanship on his part.

It is true that Lydgate's poetry consistently frustrates the modern reader, who expects poetry to be compressed and concise; Lydgate's poems are generally voluminous. Instead of irony or ambiguity, Lydgate usually assumes a rather prosaic straightforwardness. On the other hand, instead of ordinary words in their natural order, Lydgate uses obscure terms in complicated syntax. Far from writing "art for art's sake," Lydgate consistently insists on teaching sound doctrine and morality. Finally, in place of a uniquely personal vision and style, Lydgate always writes as a conventional public poet.

If one reads Lydgate through "medieval spectacles," however, these characteristics seem not only normal but praiseworthy as well. Lydgate saw himself as a rhetorician and thus felt it necessary to be both "sweet and useful" in his writing. Poetical art, to the medieval mind, was the application of rhetorical know-how to traditional themes and stories. Thus, he was first a craftsman, not a prophet or seer. He would not have considered his personal emotions or insights worthy of remembrance.

It is ironic, therefore, that Lydgate the careful craftsman has developed the reputation of being a poor versifier. If one assumes that his lines were supposed to be strictly iambic pentameter, this opinion may be justified. Fortunately, beginning with C. S. Lewis in 1939, certain scholars have suggested that Lydgate's line was based on a slightly different model, one which blends the French tradition of decasyllabic verse with the native tradition of balanced half-lines, thus allowing a variable number of stresses and syllables. In the light of these scholarly studies, Lydgate's verse seems consistently good.

Some critics, such as Schirmer (in *John Lydgate*) and Alain Renoir (in *The Poetry of John Lydgate*, 1967), argue that Lydgate is important as a poet of transition, since they find the seeds of Renaissance humanism in some of his work. While it would be foolish to discount their insights completely, however, the more traditional reading, expressed by Derek Pearsall in his *John Lydgate* (1970), still seems more satisfactory: "Looking for signs of humanism in Lydgate is an unrewarding task, because the whole direction of his mind is medieval." Lydgate will best be understood, therefore, if read as a medieval poet *par excellence*.

COMPLAINT OF THE BLACK KNIGHT

Much of what can be said about John Lydgate's art in the *Complaint of the Black Knight* can be applied very readily to the bulk of his writings, so it is a fitting piece with which to begin. The poem, written about 1400, is a conventional love complaint, a very popular genre of the age, of ninety-seven Chaucerian stanzas (stanzas of seven pentameter lines rhyming *ababbcc*). It begins with the poet, sick at heart, journeying out into the May morning to find some succor for his pain. He encounters birds singing, beautiful trees and flowers, a clear river, and a fountain which provides him water to refresh his spirits. All of a sudden, the poet discovers an arbor in which a handsome knight, dressed in black, sits moaning as if sick. After hiding, the poet discreetly listens to the lover's complaint.

The centerpiece of this poem is the highly artificial soliloquy which follows. Here the knight first confesses that he is tortured with overwhelming love; second, protests that his lady, because of false rumors about his conduct, disdains him; third, remonstrates with the God of Love, who, he claims, is unfair to honest lovers and rewards only the false; and fourth, offers his life to his lady: "My hert I send, and my spirit also,/ What so-ever she list with hem to do." Moved to tears by this complaint, the poet prays to the rising Venus, asking that she will have pity on this true lover. He then prays that all lovers will be true and that they will enjoy one another's embraces. Finally, he sends his poem off to his princess, hoping that this "little book" will speak eloquently of his pain in love.

The whole poem, in Derek Pearsall's words, is "a tissue of borrowings," not only from Geoffrey Chaucer's *Book of the Duchess* (c. 1370), Lydgate's main source, but also from many of the poems of the French allegorical school. Borrowing, however, is normal procedure for medieval poets, for, as Robert Payne has shown in his *The Key of Remembrance* (1963), they considered their primary task to be not poetic invention but rather the reordering and the embellishment of traditional truths or literary works. Lydgate here is true to his times, and he works as a craftsman, not a seer. His main talent, then, lies squarely within the confines of rhetoric.

The landscape in the *Complaint of the Black Knight*, for example, is not constructed from personal observation or experience, but is taken directly from conventional descriptions of nature which Lydgate found in "old books." He tries to construct a *locus amoenus*, an idealized natural site fit for idealized lovers, both successful and frustrated. Thus, he uses all the details, the May morning, the flowers, the birds, the clear stream, that the sources stipulated. Moreover, Lydgate borrows not only descriptions of nature but also many other traditional themes, images, and literary postures, making the poem entirely conventional.

After selecting his genre, his themes, and his sources, Lydgate, working methodically, amplifying, contracting, or rearranging parts according to his own tastes, next fashions a fitting structure for them. Finally, he adds the embellishment, the literary "colors," such as alliteration, antithesis, chiasmus, echoing, exclamation, parallelism, or repetition. Thus, in lines 232 to 233 the Knight describes his woes with an elaborate chiasmus, reminiscent of Chaucer's *Troilus and Criseyde* (1382), I, 420: "Now hote as fire, now colde as asshes dede,/ Now hote for colde, now colde for hete ageyn." In lines 400 to 403, Lydgate adapts an exclamation from *Troilus and Criseyde*, V, 1828-1832:

> Lo her the fyne of loveres servise!
> Lo how that Love can his servantis quyte!
> Lo how he can his feythful men dispise,
> To sle the trwe men, and fals to respite!

Lydgate regularly protests that he has no literary "colors," but this too is a conventional literary pose. On the contrary, one finds "colors" used carefully and continuously throughout the Lydgate corpus.

In fact, Lydgate is so much interested in the surface decoration of his poetry that he sometimes seems to neglect its deeper significance. The elaborate descriptions of nature in the literature of courtly love, for example, were meant to have a purpose beyond that of mere ornamentation; they were supposed to carry an allegorical meaning. In Chaucer's *Romaunt of the Rose* (c. 1370), from which Lydgate borrowed some of his landscape, the fountain of Narcissus represents the Lady's eyes, the garden represents the life at court, and the rose-plot is the mind of the lady wherein personified fears and hopes do battle. C. S. Lewis discusses these allegorical meanings at length in *The Allegory of Love* (1936), but he could not do the

same for Lydgate's version of the garden, for here the long description of the garden is not integrated with the rest of the poem. Once the Knight begins his soliloquy, Lydgate seemingly forgets the garden, whose description is thus solely a piece of rhetorical virtuosity. Indeed, that which is of most value in the poem is the part which is most intrinsically rhetorical: the formal complaint of the Knight. In Lewis's words, "The slow building up and decoration, niche by niche, of a rhetorical structure, brings out what is best in the poet."

In this context Lydgate's famous predilection for florid Latinate diction makes sense. The poet himself coined the term *aureate* to describe both a highly wrought style and an elevated diction. In *Fall of Princes* he describes his task in the following way: "Writying of old, with letters aureat,/ Labour of poetis doth hihli magnefie." The medium here fits the message, for Lydgate cannot resist twisting normal English word order. Moreover, the influence of Lydgate's style upon his successors was great indeed, for the use of "aureat lettres" came to dominate fifteenth century verse. It was not until the nineteenth century, when William Wordsworth began to attack "poetic diction," that "aureate" came to have pejorative connotations.

BALLADE AT THE REVERENCE OF OUR LADY, QWENE OF MERCY

Lydgate, however, felt that, just as the host of the Holy Communion was encased in a highly decorated monstrance for public adoration, so too religious matter should be placed in a suitably ornate poetic vehicle. His invocations to Mary in the *Ballade at the Reverence of Our Lady, Qwene of Mercy*, are often cited as prime examples of this suitably ornate diction. After invoking the "aureat licour of Clyo" to enliven his dull wit, Lydgate compares Mary to the stars, precious jewels, various birds, a red rose, and to many other things in a riot of exotic images expressed in extravagant terminology. Lines 36 through 39 are a good example:

> O closid gardeyn al void of weedes wicke,
> Cristallyn welle of clennesse cler consigned,
> Fructifying olyve of foilys faire and thicke,
> And redolent cedyr most derworthly ydyned.

These images certainly were not original with Lydgate; they are doubtless echoes of the *Song of Songs*, but Lydgate has presented them in fittingly sonorous language, filled with alliteration. Ian Robinson, in *Chaucer's Prosody: A Study of the Middle English Verse Tradition* (1971), summarizes the matter well when he remarks: "Material enters the Lydgate factory mud and leaves it terracotta."

RELIGIOUS VERSE

Not surprisingly, a great body of Lydgate's verse is explicitly religious, and nowhere is he more representative of his times than when he writes his saints' lives. Christian saints were the heroes of the medieval Catholic Church, and there was a great thirst on all levels of society for knowledge about them. Very early in the Christian era short narratives about the deaths of martyrs, *passiones*, or about the lives of confessors, *vitae*, began to be composed. These were meant to be read during the liturgy or the Divine Office. In the High Middle Ages, vernacular legends began to be written for the common folk, and, especially with the advent of the friars, these were used for public preaching. The legends, however, were viewed primarily as a literature of edification rather than as objective history or biography. Thus, "successful" structures, incidents, and even historical details were exchanged freely among the various legends. Generally speaking, then, medieval legend can be considered a type of popular formulaic literature.

THE LIVES OF SAINTS EDMUND AND FREMUND

In honor of the visit, in 1433, of Henry VI to Bury St. Edmunds, Abbott William Curteys commissioned Lydgate, who had written a number of *vitae* earlier, to write *The Lives of Saints Edmund and Fremund* for presentation to the King. Lydgate's response was an "epic legend," in which the life of Edmund, the former king of East Anglia (died 870), is retold in a suitably long (3,693 lines) narrative.

The work is divided into three sections. Books I and II recount the life, death, and burial of Edmund; Book III treats the life of Fremund, the king's nephew and avenger; and, finally, an appendix records several of Edmund's posthumous miracles. Most of the work is in Chaucerian stanzas.

Lydgate, using the Latin *Vita et Passio cum Miraculis Sancti Edmundi*, Bodlian Ms. 240, as his primary source, incorporates many of the standard characteristics of the *passio*. Thus, Edmund's birth is miraculously foretold by a strange widow when Alkmund, his Saxon father, is on a pilgrimage in Rome. In his youth, Edmund is pious and mature well beyond his years, so much so that his distant relative, Offa, chooses him as his successor to the East Anglian throne. After Offa dies, Edmund governs wisely and moderately, but despite his ability as a warrior, he comes to realize that bloodshed is hateful in the sight of God and repudiates warfare. Therefore, to protect his people from the marauding Danes, he offers his own life in return for their safety. When brought before the violent Hyngwar, leader of the Danes, Edmund refuses apostasy in the standard interrogation. Hyngwar loses self-control, as is typical of "evil judges," at Edmund's aggressive retorts and orders the King's execution. After undergoing a sustained round of tortures with superhuman endurance, Edmund is finally beheaded, but not before he sings out a long panegyric to God in which he asks to die as God's "true knight." The head of the slain king, although hidden, is miraculously protected by a wolf until it is found by Edmund's subjects. Other miracles follow before Fremund is introduced in Book III.

In this legend Lydgate uses his sources freely, carefully choosing incidents that serve his own purposes. The posthumous miracles, for example, are chosen to illustrate his theme that tyrants and other prideful people are eventually punished by God. His arrangement of those miracles indicates concern for symmetry, balance, and artistic control. In short, Lydgate's contribution to the history of the Edmund legend is that of a masterful rhetorician who fitted the legend into an elegant structure, added rhetorical flourishes such as prologues, prayers, and epilogues, and finished the surface with the appropriate sonorous diction.

FALL OF PRINCES

The literary cousin to the saint is the fallen prince, for one can fashion an *exemplum* from each. If medieval audiences could be edified by the courage of the former, they could be taught detachment and humility from the life of the latter: for example, from the lives of Priam and Saul, Alexander and Caesar, Arthur and King John of France.

The theme of the world's transitoriness was another medieval commonplace, but Giovanni Boccaccio's *De Casibus Illustrium Virorum* (1358) treated the theme in a systematic and comprehensive way for the first time. In this work, all of the kings just mentioned, and many more besides, pass before the Italian poet and complain of their downfalls. Boccaccio's work became extremely popular and was translated into French in 1409 by Laurent de Premierfait. In 1431, Duke Humphrey of Gloucester commissioned Lydgate to translate it into English, and this free translation was titled *Fall of Princes*. The task took Lydgate eight years.

Working from the French translation, Lydgate expands Boccaccio's work even more, filling in abbreviated stories, adding missing ones, inserting exhortations, and writing envoys for the end of each chapter. The result is a massive medieval history book (36,365 lines), a mirror for princes, an encyclopedia of world biography. Lydgate follows his medieval penchant for inclusion rather than concision, and thus the sheer bulk of the work is both a positive attribute—it contributes to an impression of weight and solemnity—and a fault—Boccaccio's fine structure seems completely lost.

Fall of Princes may be called a book of tragedies, for the medieval definition of tragedy was much simpler than Aristotle's: "For tragedie, as poetes spesephie,/ Gynneth with ioie, eendith with adversite:/ From hih estate [Men] caste in low degre." Lydgate follows both Boccaccio and Laurent in deprecating the blind goddess Fortune, a personification blamed as the fickle distributor of both tragedy and good luck. In the prologue to Book I, Lydgate describes her as "transitory of condicioun," "hasty & sodeyne," since "Whan men most truste, than is she most chaungable." One often encounters medieval representations of the "Wheel of Fortune," where one sees the blindfolded goddess spinning a wheel to which various men are attached. Those on the top, the rulers, enjoy the favors of good fortune, whereas those on the bottom, paupers or prisoners, are in misery. Figures on either side, however, the rising courtier or the falling prince, emphasize that the wheel is never static, and that both kingdoms and rulers pass away.

There were several common reactions to these lessons in mutability. First of all, they inspired sorrow over time's passing. Thus the *Ubi sunt?* (Where are they?) theme is found in much of medieval poetry, from the Anglo-Saxon *Wanderer* to the "Ballade des dames du temps jadis" ("Ballad of the Ladies of Bygone Times")

of Villon. Poets using this theme complain that everything beautiful, noble, or great in this world eventually passes away. Lydgate repeats this theme often and at length in *Fall of Princes*. In the Envoy to Book II, Lydgate ponders the fate of Rome. "Where be thyn Emperours, most sovereign of renown?" he asks. "Where is now Cesar"; where "Tullius?" His answer is not as poetic as Villon's "But where are the snows of bygone years?" for he states directly that "Off alle echon the odious ravyne of time/ Hath be processe the brought to ruyne."

If, on one hand, time brings everything to an end and princes are brought low by Fortune's variability, on the other hand, a good Christian ought to see God's Providence working through Fortune, punishing pride or arrogance. Thus, by pondering tragedy, men of power can learn meekness, detachment, and humility, and place the highest value on spiritual things. "Ley doun thi pride," cries Lydgate; "Cri God merci, thi trespacis repentyng!" For the Romans, of course, it is too late, but it is not too late for Lydgate's contemporaries.

One wonders how many medieval princes read completely through all nine books of Lydgate's *exempla*. Even the Knight from Chaucer's *The Canterbury Tales*, for example, could stand only so many of the similar tragedies told by Chaucer's Monk: "good sire, namoore of this!" he cries, for "litel hevyness/ Is right ynough to muche folke" (Prologue to the *Nun's Priest's Tale*). Even Lydgate himself grew tired of his forced march through the ruins of history, for he complains about his fatigue in the Prologue to Book VIII. Moreover, Lydgate expanded on his sources less and less with each succeeding book.

All this has led Pearsall to speculate that perhaps the best way to read *Fall of Princes* would be to read only extracts of the best passages, which "are too good to miss." The structure of the work is basically inorganic and encyclopedic, since Lydgate, again being true to the aesthetics of his age, seems to have expanded on his sources to include in his work all "useful knowledge" rather than critically selecting and editing his material to allow an organic structure to emerge. Moreover, Pearsall remarks that probably Lydgate's contemporaries more often read the poem in extracts than as a whole, since parts of the work often appear detached from the rest in surviving manuscripts. Practicality supports this view, for there is much repetition and dull elaboration in the poem which most people would rather avoid; but, on the other hand, more detailed work needs be done on the poem's structure before it can be said that here Lydgate completely lacked structural control.

VERSIFICTION: "BALANCED PENTAMETER"

The versifying in *Fall of Princes*, as in most of Lydgate's work, has traditionally given critics problems. Although most of his lines can be scanned as rather regular iambic pentameter, a large number cannot, and these have in the past led certain writers to call Lydgate a bungling versifier. Recent critics have been fairer to the poet, however, and for good reason. First, medieval scribes were notoriously free in "correcting" their copy, adding or deleting words or changing spelling according to regional pronunciations. Especially with regard to the final *-e*, the sounding of which had probably ceased by the fifteenth century, scribal practices varied widely. Second, for all the current philological sophistication, medievalists are still not sure how Lydgate's contemporaries would have pronounced their native tongue. In short, all scansion of Lydgate's poetry is tentative at best.

The best approach to Lydgate's line seems to be that of Ian Robinson. He claims that Lydgate wrote a "balanced pentameter" line, a line which was meant to work both in half-lines and as a full line of five metrical feet. The English metrical line was in transition at the time, and this means that there were two sometimes conflicting traditions competing in the art not only of Lydgate but also of Chaucer. The first was the rather recently adopted French decasyllabic line, later to evolve into the English iambic pentameter of William Shakespeare. The oldest English tradition of verse, however, revived in the thirteenth and fourteenth centuries, constructed lines based on stress and alliteration rather than on syllable count. Thus the opening lines of *The Vision of William, Concerning Piers the Plowman*, a poem of the fourteenth century Alliterative Revival, run as follows: In a sómer séson // whan sóft was the sónne/ I shópe me in shróudes // as I a shépe wére." Although one generally finds four stressed syllables per line (the first three of which were usually alliterated), the total number of syllables per line, stressed and unstressed, varied widely.

That is why it makes no difference, metrically speaking, whether the final unstressed syllables italicized above were pronounced or not. In either case these lines are good alliterative verse since both read smoothly in rhythmic half-lines.

So too with Lydgate. If his verse is read with a strong medial caesura, letting the stresses, whether two or three per half-line, fall where they are most natural, the lines hardly ever seem awkward. On the contrary, they are generally easy to scan. Some lines, especially the "broken-backed" variety—lines with only four stressed syllables—seem to fit the English side of the tradition a bit more, whereas others, being to the modern sensibility more "regular," favor the French side. Line 4,465 from Book II, for example, "Off slaúhtre, móordre // & outráious róbbyng," even offers a hint of alliteration in the stressed syllables. On the other hand, lines such as "Thĭ bíldyng gán // off fáls dĭscéncĭoún" can be seen as favoring the French side of the tradition, although it still breaks easily into two smooth half-lines.

OTHER MAJOR WORKS

NONFICTION: *The Serpent of Division*, wr. 1422(?), pb. 1559.

BIBLIOGRAPHY

Dane, Joseph A., and Irene Basey Beesemyer. "The Denigration of John Lydgate: Implications of Printing History." *English Studies* 81, no. 2 (April, 2000): 117-126. Dane considers the traditional evaluations of John Lydgate in English literary history against a background of his publication history. Originally thought to be the style of the works, it was instead, the content of the works that led to a decline in Lydgate's popularity.

Ebin, Lois A. *John Lydgate*. Boston: Twayne, 1985. This concise yet thorough book-length study serves as a useful introduction to the Lydgate canon and contains chapters on his courtly poems, moral and didactic poems, and religious poems. Includes a chronology of Lydgate's life, complete notes, including a list of secondary sources, references, and an index.

Edwards, A. S. G. "Lydgate Scholarship: Progress and Prospects." In *Fifteenth Century Studies*, edited by

Robert F. Yeager. Hamden, Conn.: Archon Books, 1984. Edwards's bibliographic essay examines twenty-five years of scholarship devoted to the works of John Lydgate. While this study includes brief, insightful accounts of book-length studies and editorial work concerning Lydgate, its primary value is found in its extended bibliographic notes.

_____. "Lydgate Scholarship: Some Directions for Future Research." In *Manuscripts and Readers in Fifteenth Century England: The Literary Implications of Manuscript Studies*, edited by Derek Pearsall. Cambridge, England: Cambridge University Press, 1983. Discusses Lydgate's work in terms of audience and provenance. Devotes its attention to textual criticism of illuminated manuscripts and the identification of scribes in regard to Lydgate. Contains good notes and serves as a guide for the gaps in the study of Lydgate's works.

Lawton, David. "Dullness and the Fifteenth Century." *English Literary History* 54 (Winter, 1987): 761-799. The primary purpose of this lengthy article is to expose the treatment of humility in Lydgate's works. It is important because it provides a good comparison of Lydgate's works in this regard with those of George Ashby and Thomas Hoccleve. Illuminates the sources of these works as being partly from Geoffrey Chaucer and John Gower. Contains specific notes and references.

Lawton, Lesley. "The Illustration of Late Medieval Secular Texts with Special Reference to Lydgate's *Troy Book*." In *Manuscripts and Readers in Fifteenth Century England: The Literary Implications of Manuscript Studies*, edited by Derek Pearsall. Cambridge, England: Cambridge University Press, 1983. As the title implies, this work is devoted to the role of illustrations in medieval texts, especially Lydgate's *Troy Book*. Here, the relationships of the illustrations to the text are examined as they relate to the work's structure and its audience. Provides an interesting account of this often neglected idea and is supplemented with notes.

Pearsall, Derek Albert. *John Lydgate (1371-1449)*. Victoria, B.C.: University of Victoria, 1997. A bibliography of works by and about Lydgate with a brief biographical sketch.

Gregory M. Sadlek;
bibliography updated by the editors

M

GEORGE MACBETH

Born: Shotts, Scotland; January 19, 1932
Died: Tuam, County Galway, Ireland; February 17, 1992

PRINCIPAL POETRY

The Broken Places, 1963
A Doomsday Book, 1965
The Colour of Blood, 1967, 1969
The Night of Stones, 1968
A War Quartet, 1969
The Burning Cone, 1970
Collected Poems: 1958-1970, 1971
The Orlando Poems, 1971
Shrapnel and a Poet's Year, 1973
In the Hours Waiting for the Blood to Come, 1975
Buying a Heart, 1978
Poems of Love and Death, 1980
Published Collections, 1982
Poems from Oby, 1982
The Long Darkness, 1983
The Cleaver Gardens, 1986
Anatomy of a Divorce, 1988
Collected Poems: 1958-1982, 1989
Trespassing: Poems from Ireland, 1991
Patient, 1992

OTHER LITERARY FORMS

In addition to his numerous volumes of poetry, George MacBeth published poetry pamphlets, chapbooks, and limited-edition books. Many of these, initially published in small editions, became parts of larger books and have thus been incorporated into the mainstream of MacBeth's work. MacBeth also published children's books, novels, plays, and an autobiography, and he edited several volumes of poetry.

The sheer volume of MacBeth's production reveals his almost obsessive dedication to writing and the breadth of his interests. Among his publications other than poetry, the autobiography *My Scotland* (1973) probably holds the greatest interest for the reader of his poetry because of what it reveals about MacBeth's background and development. MacBeth himself described the book as a nonlogical, non-narrative, massive jigsaw of autobiographical bits, a collection of about two hundred short prose pieces about being Scottish.

ACHIEVEMENTS

A co-recipient of Sir Geoffrey Faber Award in 1964, George MacBeth was one of the most prolific poets of twentieth century Britain. Volume alone, however, did not account for his significance as a poet; rather, he earned his stature for the diversity of his writing. He was, in the best sense of the word, an "experimental" poet: absolutely fearless in his willingness to attempt new forms and take on unusual subjects, yet simultaneously fascinated by traditional meter and rhyme, as well as by material that has fueled the imagination of poets for centuries. *Poems of Love and Death* contains poems ranging from the dangerously romantic "The Truth," with its didactic final stanza which includes the lines "Happiness is a state of mind,/ And grief is something frail and small," to the satiric "The Flame of Love, by Laura Stargleam," which mocks the dime novel plotline that it exploits. MacBeth is as likely to write about a missile commander as about evening primroses, and the reader familiar with his writing is not at all surprised to find these disparate topics dealt with in a single book, in this case *Buying a Heart*. In fact, it is the sense of discovery and the vitality of MacBeth's imagination that continues to attract many readers.

BIOGRAPHY

Born in Scotland near Glasgow, George Mann MacBeth lived the greater part of his life in England. This circumstance had a substantial impact on his poetry, leading him to view himself as something of an exile. Although he felt comfortable in England, he did not regard himself as English and remarked on the sensation of detachment, of living and working in a foreign country. The Scotland he left as a child remained in his mind as a lost world, a kind of Eden which could never be regained, and his sense of loss helped make him, in his own evaluation, "a very retrospective, backward-looking poet." Perhaps more significantly, his detachment, or rootlessness, enabled him to embrace a larger part of the world than is available to most writers.

Another significant element of MacBeth's life was his long-term association with the British Broadcasting Corporation, where he worked as a producer of poetry programs. This position bought him into contact with the leading poets in England and around the world and exposed him to everything that was happening in poetry. MacBeth himself acknowledged that his close work with a broad variety of poets over the years influenced his writing, particularly in the areas of technique and structure. Always careful not to become too involved in purely "English" writing, he consciously tried to keep in touch with poetic developments in the world at large, and his accomplishments as a poet can be measured most accurately if they are considered in the context of that endeavor.

By the late 1980's MacBeth had moved to Ireland, continuing to work there as a freelance broadcaster, a

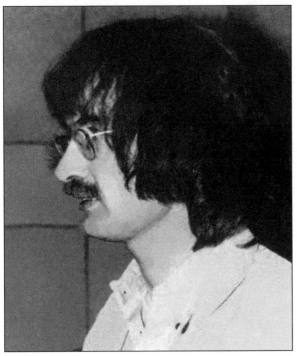

George MacBeth

teacher, and a writer, and traveling frequently to give readings of his poetry abroad. His life was tragically cut short when, in 1992, he died of motor neuron disease, in Tuam, County Galway.

ANALYSIS

George MacBeth once remarked that he considered the word "experimental," often used to describe his work, to be a term of praise. While he acknowledged the possibility of failing in some of his excursions into new forms and new subjects, he obviously felt the risk to be justified. His strongest impulse as a writer was to test the bounds of poetry and, wherever possible, extend them.

This daring push toward the limits of his craft is nowhere better revealed than in the fourth section of his *Collected Poems: 1958-1970*, where MacBeth employs his no-holds-barred approach and enjoys doing it. Indeed, the sense of pleasure that MacBeth manages to communicate, his pure delight in the shape of language on the page, is essential to the reader because it helps to carry him through poems which at first glance may repel rather than attract.

"TWO EXPERIMENTS" AND "LDMN ANALYSIS OF THOMAS NASHE'S 'SONG'"

Two such forbidding poems which challenge the analytical mind in satiric fashion are "Two Experiments" and "LDMN Analysis of Thomas Nashe's 'Song.'" The first of these poems, divided into two sections, presents a "Vowel Analysis of 'Babylonian Poem' from the German of Friederike Mayröcker" and a "Numerical Analysis of 'Brazilian Poem' from the German of Friederike Mayröcker." If the ponderous and unlikely subtitles are not enough to warn the reader not to be too serious, the actual text should be sufficiently illuminating. The first section is a listing of vowels, ostensibly from the Mayröcker poem, presented in the following fashion: "U EE-EI A I AE-IIE-EIE UE EOE U EI; E." Thus runs the first line, and the second section begins in the following way: "(. .2 2 6 2 3 5: 2 3 3-6 3 8: 3." Clearly, these representations are meaningless, but they do make a point, not a very positive point, about the analytical approach to poetry: that critical analyses of poetry may make no more sense than these vowel and number analyses. A similar statement is made in "LDMN Analysis of Thomas Nashe's 'Song,'" which offers an arrangement of *L*'s, *D*'s, *M*'s, and *N*'s, presumably as they might be extracted from the Nashe poem.

As might be expected, the response to such experimentation has not been universally positive, and a number of readers have questioned whether such strategies can properly be called poetry. Ironically, this may be the very question that MacBeth wants the reader to ask, the ultimate critic's question: "What is poetry?" MacBeth himself is as sincere as any reader in his search for an answer, for he offers no dogmatic views of his own; he merely tosses out experiments in an effort to determine where the boundaries lie.

"THE SKI MURDERS" AND "FIN DU GLOBE"

Other poems that are somewhat less eccentric but nevertheless experimental are "The Ski Murders" and "Fin du Globe." The first is an "encyclopaedia-poem" consisting of twenty-six individual entries, one for each letter of the alphabet. The entries themselves are written in a prose style that might have been taken from a spy novel, and the reader is invited to construct his own story by piecing the vignettes together in whatever fashion he wishes. The second poem is presented as a game containing fifty-two "postcards" and four "*fin du globe*" cards. The players (the readers) are instructed to deal out the cards as in an ordinary deck and to read, in turn, the brief postcard message printed on each. When a *fin du globe* card is turned up, the game is over. Again, the question arises—Is this poetry?—and once again MacBeth is challenging the reader while exploring the limits of his craft and trying to extend his artistic territory. Even the most skeptical reader can, if he allows himself, find pleasure in these and similar experiments, for they are clever and entertaining, and one can sense the pleasure that MacBeth himself must have experienced in giving free rein to his imagination.

"A POET'S LIFE"

Among MacBeth's most successful comic poems is "A Poet's Life," which first appeared in *In the Hours Waiting for the Blood to Come* and has since developed into a kind of serial poem published in various installments. In its original form, the poem consists of twelve episodes focusing on various aspects of the poet's life. The point of view is third person, to permit MacBeth as much distance as possible from his subject, himself. The result is a poem, which avoids the gloomy seriousness of typical introspection and yet focuses on some serious themes, showing the poet to be as human as anyone else. The first section of the poem is representative of MacBeth's technique; it shows the poet at home, trying to write and jotting down the following lines: "today I got up at eight, felt cold, shaved,/ washed, had breakfast, and dressed." The banality here reflects a larger tedium in the poet's life, for nothing much happens to him, except in his imagination. It is not surprising, then, when his efforts to write lead nowhere and he turns to the television for an episode of the *Avengers*, a purely escapist adventure show.

Viewed almost as a specimen or as a caged animal might be viewed, the poet is an amusing creature, sipping his "peppermint cream" and sucking distractedly on his pencil; and yet he is also pitiable. There is, in fact, something of the fool about the poet, something reminiscent of Charlie Chaplin's little tramp, for although he evokes laughter or a bemused smile there is something fundamentally sad about him. The poignancy comes from the realization that the poet, no matter how hard he tries to blend into the common crowd, must always remain isolated. It is the nature of his craft; writing poetry sets him apart. Consequently, when he goes to the supermarket, dressed in "green wranglers" to make himself inconspicuous, he still stands out among the old women, the babies, and the old men. He is "looking/ at life for his poems, is helping/ his wife, is a normal considerate man," and yet his role as poet inevitably removes him from the other shoppers and from the world at large.

Technically, "A Poet's Life" is rather simple and straightforward, but several significant devices work subtly to make the poem successful. The objective point of view enables MacBeth to combine the comic and the pathetic without becoming maudlin or self-pitying; this slightly detached tone is complemented by MacBeth's freewheeling, modernized version of the *Don Juan* stanza. It is typical of MacBeth to turn to traditional forms for inspiration, to borrow them and make them new.

"HOW TO EAT AN ORANGE"

Not a poet to break the rules without first understanding what the rules are, MacBeth is fascinated by traditional forms as well as by those that are new and experimental. It is a measure of his poetic temperament that he is able to take a traditional form and incorporate it into his general experimentation. The reader often encounters regular rhyme and meter in MacBeth's work and occasionally recognizes something like a sonnet or sestina. Invariably, though, the standard form is modified to conform to MacBeth's urge to experiment. "How to Eat an Orange" is as nearly a sonnet as it can possibly be without actually being one. It has fourteen lines and a Shakespearean rhyme scheme, including the final couplet; but it lacks the iambic pentameter. In fact, it has no regular meter at all, although the iambic does surface from time to time like a theme played in the background. Form, then, is not an end in itself but a means to an end, and MacBeth employs whatever forms he finds useful, including the traditional, in communicating his ideas.

"WHAT METRE IS"

MacBeth's attitude toward form is captured most provocatively in a poem titled "What Metre Is." A tour de force of technique, this poem stands as the poet's manifesto. The controlling idea is that the poem itself will provide examples of various poetic devices while they are being discussed. For example, when alliteration is mentioned, it appears in the context of the following passage: "leaping/ long lean and allusive/ through low lines." The uses of prose are considered in this fashion: "Prose is another possibility. There could be three/ sentences in the stanza. This would be an example of/ that." Other aspects of metrics discussed and illustrated in the poem are syllabics, free verse, word and interval counting, internal rhyming, rhythm, assonance, and finally, typography, "its mos/ t irrit/ ating (perhaps) manif/ estation." Irritating and mechanical it may be, representing the voice of the typewriter and the "abdic/ ation of insp/ iration," but still the poet feels compelled to say "I li/ ke it." He likes it because it is "the logica/ l exp/ ression o/ f itsel/ f." Having gone through his paces, the way a musician might play the scale or some well-known traditional piece just to prove he can, MacBeth turns finally to the experimental, which, despite its flaws, holds some irresistible attraction for him. He can manage traditional metrics, and he illustrates this ability in the poem, but he can also handle the riskier, less traditional devices. This poem, then, embodies on a small scale the range of poetic techniques one is likely to encounter in MacBeth's poetry: the traditional, often with modifications, and the experimental, always with MacBeth's own particular daring.

CHILDHOOD, WAR, AND VIOLENCE

If MacBeth takes chances with the form of his poems, he also takes considerable risks with the content. Many of his poems are violent or sexually explicit, and some readers have found his subject matter objectionable. Perhaps the chief characteristic of the content of his poetry is a fascination with fear and violence, which MacBeth feels can be traced to his childhood. As a boy during World War II, MacBeth lost his father and experienced the bombing of his house. He collected shrapnel in the streets after air raids, spent night after night in the shelters, and grew up surrounded by physical violence and the threat of death. This kind of environment affected him strongly, and MacBeth felt that it led ultimately to a kind of obsession with violence that finds an outlet through his poetry.

The connection between his childhood experience of the war and such poems as "The Sirens," "The War," and "The Passing Ones" is obvious because these poems are explicitly about that experience, about "those bombed houses where/ I echoed in/ The empty rooms." Other poems, such as "Driving West," with its apocalyptic vision of a nuclear war, are less concerned with the actual experiences of World War II than with the nightmare vision it instilled. MacBeth's childhood fear of bombs has been translated into an adult's vision of the end of the world: "There was nothing left,/ Only a world of scrap. Dark metal bruised,/ Flung soup of blood, anchors and driven screws." This is the inheritance of Hiroshima and Nagasaki, a vision of the potential that man has to destroy himself and the entire planet.

"THE BURNING POEM"

The same influences are operating, though less obviously, in "The Burning Poem," which ends with the following passage: "Burning, burning,/ and nothing left to burn:/ only the ashes/ in a little urn." Here the violence has been freed of its war context with only a passing reference to suggest the connection: "rice paper, cartridge-paper,/ it was all the same." The merging of art, as represented by the rice paper, and war, represented by the cartridge paper, suggests the relationship between MacBeth's experiences of the war and his poetry. He is, in effect, "Spilling petrol/ on the bare pages." There is a sense in which many of MacBeth's poems are burning with the effects of remembered violence.

"A Confession"

Inevitably, the violence loses its war context entirely and becomes associated with other things, just as it must have been absorbed into MacBeth's life. In "A Confession," for example, the topic is abortion, and the woman who has chosen to abort her child remembers the procedure as "the hard cold inrush of its killer,/ Saw-teeth, threshing fins, cascading water,/ And the soul spat like a bubble out of its head." The act was not clinical or antiseptic but personal and highly violent. The woman, in the course of her dramatic monologue, reveals an obsessive guilt and an inability to deal with what she has done. She wonders, finally, what her punishment might be "For crucifying someone in my womb." In this case MacBeth is somewhat removed from the poem because he uses the persona of the woman, but in "In the Hours Waiting for the Blood to Come" and "Two Days After" he approaches the topic of a lost or aborted child in a much more personal way, considering the impact of the death on the people involved in the relationship. In "Two Days After" the couple make love but the act has less to do with love than with guilt and a kind of spent violence.

Often, MacBeth's images seem designed specifically to shock the reader, to jolt him out of complacency. It is important, however, to realize that MacBeth employs violent and sexually explicit passages for more than merely sensational purposes. He wants to consider the darker side of human nature; violence and fear are alive in the world, and acknowledging their existence is a first step toward coming to terms with them.

"The Red Herring"

It would be a mistake to regard MacBeth as merely a poet of sex and violence, for he has more dimensions than those. MacBeth himself seems bothered by the attention that has been given to the more sensational aspects of his poetry to the exclusion of other elements, and has remarked that he does not find his poetry any more violent than anyone else's. In terms of his total body of work, he is right, but the shocking and explicit poems inevitably call more attention to themselves than those that are more subdued in tone and subject matter, especially the very fine children's poems and MacBeth's engaging forays into the fantastic or surreal.

"The Red Herring" is a good illustration of MacBeth's poetry for children. The elements of the poem are a dried red herring, a bare wall, a ladder, and a man with a hammer, a nail, and a long piece of string. After the man has tied the red herring to the string suspended from the nail in the top of the wall and gone away, the poet addresses the question of why he would bother to make up such a simple story: "I did it just to annoy people./ Serious people. And perhaps also/ to amuse children. Small children." Undoubtedly, a child could take pleasure in this poem, but it is not entirely limited to the child in its appeal. The adult who is able to put off his seriousness for a moment or two will find himself smiling at the poem because of its saucy tone and at himself because he was probably gullible enough to enter the poem with a serious mind, even though the title itself warned him that things were not what they seemed. The playfulness here is characteristic of MacBeth's sense of humor, and, as usual, it is designed to make a serious point as well as to please.

"Scissor-Man"

Related to the children's poems are MacBeth's trips into the fantastic, as reflected in "Scissor-Man." The speaker, a pair of scissors used to cut bacon rind, contemplates his position in life, grousing about being kept under the draining board rather than in the sink unit. Further, he worries about what might be going on between the nutcrackers and the carrot grater and vows that if he should "catch him rubbing/ those tin nipples of hers/ in the breadbin" he will "have his/ washer off." Clearly, this is not meant to be children's poetry, but it is, perhaps, a kind of children's poetry for adults, for it engages the imagination in the same way that nursery rhymes and fairy tales do. In this case, MacBeth's humor seems designed to be an end in itself, an escape into the purely fanciful.

If one were to compile a list of adjectives to describe MacBeth's poetry, he would include at least the following: experimental, traditional, humorous, serious, violent, compassionate. The fact that these adjectives seem to cancel one another is significant, for MacBeth is possessed of a vital desire to encompass everything. In all his diversity, MacBeth is an original and important contemporary poet, a risk-taker who is continually trying to extend the boundaries of his art.

OTHER MAJOR WORKS

LONG FICTION: *The Transformation*, 1975; *The Samurai*, 1975; *The Survivor*, 1977; *The Seven Witches*, 1978; *The Born Losers*, 1981; *The Katana*, 1981; *A Kind of Treason*, 1982; *Anna's Book*, 1983; *The Lion of Pescara*, 1984; *Dizzy's Woman*, 1986; *Another Love Story*, 1991; *The Testament of Spencer*, 1992.

PLAYS: *The Doomsday Show*, pr. 1964; *The Scene-Machine*, pr., pb. 1971 (music by Anthony Gilbert).

NONFICTION: *My Scotland*, 1973.

EDITED TEXTS: *The Penguin Book of Sick Verse*, 1963; *Penguin Modern Poets VI*, 1964 (with J. Clemo and E. Lucie-Smith); *The Penguin Book of Animal Verse*, 1965; *Poetry 1900-1965*, 1967; *The Penguin Book of Victorian Verse*, 1968; *The Falling Splendour*, 1970; *Poetry for Today*, 1983; *The Book of Cats*, 1992 (with Martin Booth).

CHILDREN'S LITERATURE: *Noah's Journey*, 1966; *Jonah and the Lord*, 1969; *The Rectory Mice*, 1982; *The Book of Daniel*, 1986.

BIBLIOGRAPHY

Booth, Martin. *Travelling Through the Senses: A Study of the Poetry of George MacBeth*. Isle of Skye, Scotland: Aquila, 1983. A brief assessment of MacBeth's poetic work.

Dooley, Tim. Review of *Collected Poems, 1958-1982*. *The Times Literary Supplement*, January 26, 1990, p. 101. According to Dooley, the poems in the volume under review reveal a healthy development: "Formal scrupulousness replaces formal daring and self-examination replaces self-regard." Dooley praises the "new tenderness" that has accompanied Mac-Beth's increasing attention to form.

Ries, Lawrence R. "George MacBeth." In *Poets of Great Britain and Ireland Since 1960: Part 2, M-Z*, edited by Vincent B. Sherry, Jr. Vol. 40 of *Dictionary of Literary Biography*. Detroit: Gale Research, 1985. A judicious appreciation that calls attention to MacBeth's black humor and dexterity as a "trickster." Some biographical facts are given, but the piece is primarily a survey of the achievements (and disappointments) of MacBeth's poetry through *Poems from Oby*. The references cited at the end reveal that MacBeth's work gets reviews but very little extended critical attention.

Rosenthal, Macha Louis. *The New Poets: American and British Poetry Since World War II*. New York: Oxford University Press, 1967. Rosenthal discusses Macbeth in the context of all English language poets in the last half of the twentieth century. Macbeth is one of the most prolific and experimental poets writing today. He defines his times as well as being a product of them. Contains a bibliography.

Schmidt, Michael, and Grevel Lindop. *British Poetry Since 1930: A Critical Survey*. Oxford, England: Carcanet Press, 1972. A useful overview that places MacBeth's poetry in context. MacBeth gives shape to the alienation of modern life by being one of the most fecund and experimental of modern poets. Useful for all students who seek a broad view of modern poetry and an understanding of where Macbeth fits in.

Thwaite, Anthony. *Twentieth-Century English Poetry: An Introduction*. New York: Barnes & Noble, 1978. Discusses MacBeth as a member of "The Group," with only a very brief characterization of his poetry itself but providing an overview of the twentieth century British poetry that can serve as a context for a student of MacBeth. Contains a bibliography and an index.

Neal Bowers;
bibliography updated by the editors

MICHAEL MCCLURE

Born: Marysville, Kansas; October 20, 1932

PRINCIPAL POETRY
Passage, 1956
Peyote Poem, 1958
For Artaud, 1959
Hymns to St. Geryon and Other Poems, 1959
The New Book/A Book of Torture, 1961
Dark Brown, 1961
Ghost Tantras, 1964
Two for Bruce Conner, 1964

Thirteen Mad Sonnets, 1964

Poisoned Wheat, 1965

Dream Table, 1965

Unto Caesar, 1965

Mandalas, 1965

Love Lion Book, 1966

Hail Thee Who Play, 1968, revised 1974

The Sermons of Jean Harlow and the Curses of Billy the Kid, 1968

The Surge, 1969

Hymns to St. Geryon/Dark Brown, 1969

Little Odes and The Raptors, 1969

Star, 1970

The Book of Joanna, 1973

Solstice Blossom, 1973

Fleas 189-195, 1974

An Organism, 1974

Rare Angel (writ with raven's blood), 1974

September Blackberries, 1974

A Fist Full (1956-1957), 1974

Jaguar Skies, 1975

Man of Moderation, 1975

Antechamber and Other Poems, 1978

Fragments of Perseus, 1983

Selected Poems, 1986

Rebel Lions, 1991

Simple Eyes and Other Poems, 1994

Three Poems: Dolphin Skull, Rare Angel, and Dark Brown, 1995

Huge Dreams, 1999

Rain Mirror: New Poems, 1999

Touching the Edge: Dharma Devotions from the Hummingbird Sangha, 1999

The Masked Choir: A Masque in the Shape of an Enquiry into the Treena and Sheena Myth, 2000

OTHER LITERARY FORMS

Michael McClure is the author of more than twenty plays. A production in New York of *The Beard* (pr., pb. 1965) won Obie Awards for best play and best director. In 1978, McClure's *Josephine, the Mouse Singer* was produced at the WPA Theatre in New York and won the Obie Award for Best Play of the Year.

McClure's autobiographical novel *The Mad Cub* (1970) set many of the central themes, moods, and goals for his writing. *Meat Science Essays* (1963) provides scientific and ecological background for McClure's other writings. *Scratching the Beat Surface* (1982) and *Lighting the Corners* (1993) offer theories of art, memoirs of the Beat generation, and interviews.

McClure's work as an editor is revealed in *Ark II, Moby I* (1957) and *Journal for the Protection of All Beings* (1961). Performances by McClure have been recorded on video in *Love Lion* (1991) and in the audio recording *Howls, Raps, and Roars* (1993). He may also be seen in the film *The Source* (2000).

ACHIEVEMENTS

Michael McClure has been committed to full and open exploration of consciousness, perception, sexual fulfillment, and artistic action. To this end, McClure pursued an interdisciplinary approach to his work. He argues against environmental destruction and seeks to protect and enhance the planet. In all, he stands as a positive and unifying force in art, science, literature, and ecology. Often published through small presses dedicated to artistry in the making of books, his work re-

Michael McClure (© Larry Keenan, Jr., courtesy of New Directions)

flects a combination of spontaneous creativity and enduring, specialized publication.

McClure has been the recipient of grants from the National Endowment for the Arts, the Guggenheim Foundation, and the Rockefeller Foundation, and has won the Alfred Jarry Award (1973), several Obie Awards for his theater work, and a Pushcart Prize (1991). In 1993, the National Poetry Association honored McClure for distinguished lifetime achievement in poetry.

BIOGRAPHY

Michael Thomas McClure was born to Thomas and Marian Dixie Johnston McClure in Marysville, Kansas, and he soon gained a sense of the immensity of the plains. Following the divorce of his parents, he lived in Seattle, Washington, with his maternal grandfather, whose interests included medicine, ornithology, and horticulture. In Seattle, the rich forests and stunning beaches excited McClure's young imagination. At age twelve, McClure returned to Kansas, where he lived with his mother and her new husband.

In high school, McClure and his friend Bruce Conner developed an interest in abstract expressionist painters, including Clyfford Still, Mark Rothko, and Jackson Pollock. As a writer, McClure pursued traditional forms and patterns, composing a collection of villanelles as his project for a creative writing course at Wichita University. At the University of Arizona he studied anthropology and painting, but after meeting Joanna Kinnison, McClure fell in love, married, and traveled with her to San Francisco. Though disappointed not to find Mark Rothko and Clyfford Still teaching in San Francisco, McClure took delight in the Bay Area's natural splendor. Upon meeting the poet Robert Duncan, McClure reaffirmed his focus on poetry, exploring the tension between Duncan's advice to experiment and McClure's own need to work with traditional forms.

In 1956, McClure's first publication of his poems appeared in *Poetry*: two villanelles dedicated to Theodore Roethke. In the same year, McClure coedited *Ark II, Moby I*, in which he brought together San Francisco writers with Black Mountain writers, including Charles Olson and Robert Creeley. The maturation of McClure's poetics followed, in large part, from an extended correspondence with Olson. In 1956, *Passage*, McClure's first book of poetry, was published.

A production of McClure's play *The Beard* was offered at the Actor's Workshop in San Francisco in 1965; the play's sexual frankness resulted in the arrest of several of the actors and producers. With support from the American Civil Liberties Union, *The Beard* survived efforts to stifle its production.

With these varied accomplishments behind him, McClure settled into a diverse and prolific artistic career. He is an avant-garde figure whose participation in and commentaries about spontaneity, music, art, and the environment are central to understanding his artistic generation. In addition to sustaining academic positions or fellowships at institutions such as the California College of Arts and Crafts (Oakland), State University of New York, and Yale University's Pierson College, he has edited literary and ecology journals, has lectured widely, and has continued to publish.

ANALYSIS

Michael McClure's first published poems were two villanelles dedicated to Theodore Roethke published in the January, 1956, issue of *Poetry*. The works reveal McClure grounded in the requirements of the villanelle, but in "Premonition," he expresses his need to soar and fly. "Beginning in the heart," writes McClure, "I work towards light." He insists, "My eyes are spiralled up"; he adds, "Feet burn to walk the mackerel sky at night," and "Ears are aching for the Great Bird's bite." Nevertheless, the poem concludes with the idea that McClure's earthly "skin and wingless skull . . . grow tight." He longs for ascent, but his longing is not yet fulfilled.

The second villanelle reinforces and intensifies the sense of confinement and limitation. McClure is mindful of "Elysium" but finds that it "is dwindled." His body is likened to a "corpse," his hands are his "defeat," and his eyes are "dumb." The "ouzel" (a thrush) and the "undine" (a water spirit) represent the loftiness that McClure longs for, but the poem declares that they are "past and future sense, not circumstance." In these poems McClure reveals the heavy thought and meticulous craftsmanship of Roethke, but McClure outlines the aim at transcendence that marks all of his subsequent writings.

The historic second issue of *Evergreen Review* includes poems also found in *Passage* and *Hymns to St. Geryon and Other Poems*. "Night Words: The Ravishing" expresses calm and satisfaction as McClure declares, "How beautiful things are in a beautiful room." He enjoys "ambrosial insomnia," finds that the "room is softened," and repeatedly states pleasure about the fact that the features of the room are "without proportion."

"THE RUG"

In "The Rug," McClure draws a contrast between experience and the poem as a record of the experience. Describing intimacy, McClure writes, "I put my hands// to you—like cool jazz coming." Yet even in the act of describing the intimacy, words are insufficient, and McClure insists, "THIS IS NOT IT." The poem may be colorful and elegant but ultimately "is failure, no trick, no end/ but speech for those who'll listen." Nevertheless, the insufficiency of language does not prevent experience from rising to special excitement.

"THE ROBE"

In "The Robe," McClure returns to the subject of intimacy, telling his lover that they "float about each other—// bare feet not touching the floor." McClure writes, "Aloof as miracles. Hearing/ jazz in the air. We are passing—// our shapes like nasturtiums." Although "HEROIC ACTS/ won't free" the lovers, they do find blissful sleep. The poems in this issue of *Evergreen Review* present McClure alongside Jack Kerouac, Allen Ginsberg, Lawrence Ferlinghetti, and other major writers of the so-called San Francisco scene, marking McClure as a major contributor to the San Francisco poetry renaissance.

"HYMN TO ST. GERYON, I"

Donald Allen's *The New American Poetry* presents poems from *Hymns to St. Geryon and Other Poems* and *For Artaud* and places McClure in the context of a broad national awakening in poetry marked by multiple and interacting schools of poetry. The poems in *The New American Poetry* fully demonstrate McClure's attempt to liberate himself and the form of poetry through experimentation in language and sensory experience. The lines are not aligned but are freely distributed on the page. Rhyme and metrics have no place in the record of the action of the mind and body.

"Hymn to St. Geryon, I" is a statement of poetic philosophy and method. At the outset, McClure cites abstract expressionist Clyfford Still, who commits himself to "an unqualified act" and states, "Demands for communication are presumptuous and irrelevant." McClure insists, "But the thing I say!! Is to see." He wants to turn "THE GESTURE" into "fists" so that he can "hit with the thing" and "make a robe of it/ TO WEAR" and thereby "clothe" him and his readers "in the action." McClure asserts, "I am the body, the animal, the poem/ is a gesture of mine."

"PEYOTE POEM, PART I"

In "Peyote Poem, Part I," McClure explores hallucinogenic experience, aware that he and his belly "are two individuals/ joined together/ in life." His mind rides high "on a mesa of time and space," yet his body exerts its authority with "STOMACHE." The effect of the peyote is intense, but McClure is calm in his intensity, saying, "I smile to myself. I know/ all that there is to know. I see all there/ is to feel." In sum, peyote provides a transcendent experience.

"FOR ARTAUD"

Like "Peyote Poem," "For Artaud" describes the effects of hallucinogens, including heroin and peyote. McClure writes, "I am free and open from the blackness." He asks, "Let me feel great pain and strength of suffering." In the spirit of French writer Antonin Artaud, McClure seeks heightened awareness through derangement of his ordinary sensory impressions.

SELECTED POEMS

In 1986, McClure published *Selected Poems*, which gathered material from nine of his previous books. From *The New Book/A Book of Torture* McClure selects "Ode to Jackson Pollock," a tribute to the abstract expressionist who rendered "the lovely shape of chaos," found "the secret/ spread in clouds of color," and pressed experience through himself "onto the canvas." From *Little Odes and The Raptors* appears "Hummingbird Ode," in which McClure addresses a dead hummingbird. McClure speaks to this "spike of desire" that met its end by smashing into a plate-glass window. McClure asks the hummingbird, "WHAT'S/ ON YOUR SIDE OF THE VEIL??/ DO YOU DIP YOUR BEAK/ in the vast black lily/ of space?"

From *Star* McClure selected "The Surge," an exclamatory poem that McClure, in a prefatory note, describes as "the failure of an attempt to write a beautiful poem."

McClure insists that there is "a more total view!" asserting, "The Surge of Life may not be seen by male or female/ for both are halves." He asks, "Is all life a vast chromosome stretched in Time?" From *September Blackberries*, McClure includes "Gray Fox at Solstice," a poem in honor of the fox that savors "the beat of starlight/ on his brow, and ocean/ on his eardrums." At home in his "garden," the fox "dance-runs through/ the Indian paintbrush." A similar appreciation of wildlife occurs in "To a Golden Lion Marmoset," which is selected from *Jaguar Skies*. The animal is an endangered species, and McClure declares, "Your life is all I find/ to prove ours are worthwhile."

A selection from the long poem "Rare Angel" (1974) concludes *Selected Poems*. This poem "tracks vertically on the page" and seeks "luck—swinging out in every direction." Testing the limits of perception, consciousness, and reality, McClure writes, "We swirl out what we are and watch for its return."

McClure notes that he does not include any sampling of *Ghost Tantras* in *Selected Poems* because "beast language" does not coordinate with his other verse. *Ghost Tantras* is dominated by phrases such as "GOOOOOOR! GOOOOOOOOOO!" mixed with a few intelligible phrases, creating poetry based on sound rather than meaning, aiming at "the Human Spirit & all Mammals."

LATER POEMS

McClure's later poetry looks to both the past and present. *Huge Dreams* regathers the work of the early Beat period, and *Three Poems* presents anew *Rare Angel* and *Dark Brown*, McClure's long and boldly erotic "ROMANTIC CRY." New in *Three Poems* is "Dolphin Skull," a long poem revealing subconscious and conscious artistic production. McClure writes, "Never say: Hold, let this moment never cease," then reverses himself, declaring, "HOLD, LET THIS MOMENT never cease. Drag it out/ of context look at the roots of it in quarks/ and primal hydrogen. It's the sound/ of Shelley's laugh in my ears." Both *Rain Mirror* and *Touching the Edge* are intended as vertical poems that scroll down. In *Rain Mirror*, the first series of poems is titled "Haiku Edge," and McClure writes, "HEY, IT'S ALL CON/ SCIOUSNESS—thumps/of assault/ rifles/ and/ the/ stars," pitting "con" against "consciousness" and violence against nature's serenity. The haikus often focus on such dualities. The second series of poems is "Crisis

Blossoms," a sequence of "graftings." The poet explores memories and contemplates death: "BYE/ BYE/ SWEET/ OLD/ STORY/ HELLO/ FUTURE/ MAYBE/ UH/ WITH/ GHOST SMILE." *Touching the Edge* is a set of dharma devotions divided into three sequences: "RICE ROARING," "OVAL MUDRA," and "WET PLANK." McClure asks to be "cheerful/ and modest" as he reflects on the diversity around him, noticing not only fruit, flowers, and wildlife, but also chain saws, airplanes, and asphalt. He is calmly aware of both destruction and creation, and ultimately concludes that these forces are one and the same.

OTHER MAJOR WORKS

LONG FICTION: *The Mad Cub*, 1970.

PLAYS: *The Beard*, pr., pb. 1965; *The Growl*, pr. 1971; *Minnie Mouse and the Tap-Dancing Buddha*, pr. 1978; *Josephine, the Mouse Singer*, pr. 1978, pb. 1980.

NONFICTION: *Meat Science Essays*, 1963; *Scratching the Beat Surface*, 1982; *Lighting the Corners*, 1993.

EDITED TEXTS: *Ark II, Moby I*, 1957 (with James Harmon); *Journal for the Protection of All Beings*, 1961.

BIBLIOGRAPHY

Jacob, John, ed. "Symposium on Michael McClure." *Margins* 18 (1975). This special issue is entirely devoted to analysis and discussion of McClure.

Phillips, Rod. "Let Us Throw Out the Word Man: Michael McClure's Mammalian Poetics." In *"Forest Beatniks" and "Urban Thoreaus": Gary Snyder, Jack Kerouac, Lew Welch, and Michael McClure*. New York: Peter Lang, 2000. Philips emphasizes McClure's fascination with nature and his combination of poetry with biology and ecology.

Stephenson, Gregory. "From the Substrate: Notes on the Work of Michael McClure." In *The Daybreak Boys: Essays on the Literature of the Beat Generation*. Carbondale: Southern Illinois University Press, 1990. Stephenson provides a clear and thorough survey of McClure's writings, appreciating McClure's effort to heal humankind, to reconcile body and spirit, and to develop harmonious coexistence with the environment.

Thurley, Geoffrey. "The Development of the New Language: Michael McClure, Philip Whalen, and Gregory Corso." In *The Beats: Essays in Criticism*, edited by Lee Bartlett. Jefferson, N.C.: McFarland, 1981. Thurley examines McClure as a poet experimenting with hallucinogens, especially in "Peyote Poem," but expresses reservations about the validity of McClure's triumphs in perception while under the influence of narcotic substances.

Watson, Steven. "Michael McClure." In *The Birth of the Beat Generation*. New York: Pantheon, 1995. Watson provides a sketch of McClure's youth, education, and career, with recognition for McClure's interdisciplinary role among the Beats and his dedication to science and the environment.

William T. Lawlor

Hugh MacDiarmid

Christopher Murray Grieve
Born: Langholm, Scotland; August 11, 1892
Died: Edinburgh, Scotland; September 9, 1978

Principal poetry
A Moment in Eternity, 1922
Sangschaw, 1925
Penny Wheep, 1926
A Drunk Man Looks at the Thistle, 1926
The Lucky Bag, 1927
To Circumjack Cencrastus: Or, The Curly Snake, 1930
First Hymn to Lenin and Other Poems, 1931
Scots Unbound and Other Poems, 1932
Selected Poems, 1934
Stony Limits and Other Poems, 1934
Second Hymn to Lenin and Other Poems, 1935
A Kist of Whistles, 1947
In Memoriam James Joyce: From a Vision of World Language, 1955
The Battle Continues, 1957
Three Hymns to Lenin, 1957
Collected Poems of Hugh MacDiarmid, 1962

A Lap of Honour, 1967
Complete Poems, 1920-1976, 1978 (2 volumes)

Other literary forms

Hugh MacDiarmid wrote prolifically through most of his life. His more than seventy books include social criticism, political polemics, autobiography, and literary criticism. He edited earlier Scottish poets such as William Dunbar and Robert Burns and several poetry anthologies, and he founded and edited a number of Scottish periodicals.

Achievements

Only slowly has Hugh MacDiarmid come to be recognized as a major twentieth century poet. He spent most of his life laboring in one way or another for Scotland and won his earliest acclaim there. He was a founder, in 1927, of the Scottish Center of PEN, the international writers' organization, and of the National Party of Scotland the following year, although his always radical political views led him into the Communist Party in the 1930's.

Despite his extreme social and political views, his friends were legion. He once observed that few other people could boast of friendships with William Butler Yeats, T. S. Eliot, *and* Dylan Thomas, and the circle of his admirers extended worldwide. After many years of promoting, usually undiplomatically, Scotland and Scottish culture, he was awarded a Civil List pension in 1950, and although his criticism of Scottish education continued unabated, Edinburgh University awarded him an honorary Doctor of Laws degree in 1957.

Not until the 1960's, however, did MacDiarmid's poetry begin to appear in British and modern poetry anthologies. Despite a general awakening to his greatness since that time, reliable commentary of his work remains largely in the hands of Scottish critics. It is safe to say that the study of his poetry to date represents a tiny portion of what will emerge in the years and decades to come. As an innovator in modern literature, MacDiarmid deserves to be ranked with Eliot, James Joyce, and Samuel Beckett.

Biography

Born Christopher Murray Grieve on August 11, 1892, in Langholm, Scotland, near the English border,

Hugh MacDiarmid adopted his pen name in the early 1920's. His father's side of the family worked mostly in tweed mills, while his mother's people were farmers; throughout his life, MacDiarmid championed the working class. His father, who was a rural postman, died while MacDiarmid was still a teenager. Educated at Langholm Academy and Broughton Junior Student Center, Edinburgh, the young man worked thereafter as a journalist and became active in politics. In World War I, he served in the Royal Army Medical Corps in Salonika, Italy, and France.

In 1918, MacDiarmid was married, and he settled after the war in Montrose, Angus, where he continued as a reporter, local politician and contributor to the Scottish Renaissance and Nationalist movements. Although MacDiarmid adopted his pen name in the early 1920's, he continued to write prose under his given name for years afterward. He lived in England most of the time between the years 1929 and 1932, working at temporary jobs, perfecting his antipathy to the English, and suffering the breakup of his marriage.

After being remarried in 1932, MacDiarmid returned to Scotland, worked briefly in Edinburgh, and from 1933 to 1941 lived in Whalsay in the Shetland Islands, where he developed the geological interest which permeates his poems of this period. He performed factory and merchant tasks during World War II, after which he traveled considerably, including trips to Communist nations. As late as 1964, when he was seventy-two, he stood as Communist candidate for Parliament in the district of Kinross and West Perthshire, insisting as always that his Communist and Nationalist commitments in no way conflicted. The publication of *Collected Poems of Hugh MacDiarmid* in the United States in 1962, while omitting many good poems, brought him to the attention of a wider reading public, and in his final years, he was acknowledged as one of Scotland's greatest poets. He died at the age of eighty-six on September 9, 1978.

ANALYSIS

When MacDiarmid began writing poetry seriously after serving in World War I, the Scots literary tradition had reached one of its lowest points. In the century following the deaths of Robert Burns, Sir Walter Scott, and Lord Byron, Scottish poetry consisted largely of ener-

vated and sentimental effusions which imitated the surface mannerisms of Burns's lyrics. Under the circumstances, it is hardly surprising that MacDiarmid wrote his earliest poems in standard English. Although his style was reminiscent of English Romanticism, it had from the start more vigor and individuality than the work of most of his contemporaries.

A MOMENT IN ETERNITY

The best of these early poems, *A Moment in Eternity*, first appeared in MacDiarmid's *Annals of the Five Senses* (1923), which contained chiefly experimental prose. This poem establishes his essentially Romantic disposition, "searching the unsearchable" in quest of God and immortality. Although his style and technique were to change radically, these ambitions remained with him, and "eternity" remained to the end of his career one of the most frequent words in his poetic vocabulary. His rhythms in this early poem are supple, varied, but basically iambic; his diction, pleasant but rather conventional.

SANGSCHAW AND PENNY WHEEP

It was not long, however, before he began to write under his pseudonym in a vocabulary forged from various local Scottish dialects and words from literary Scots dating as far back as the late medieval period of Scottish literary glory, when Robert Henryson, William Dunbar, Gavin Douglas, and others overshadowed the best English poets. He charged this "synthetic Scots" with a surprising vitality in two early books of lyrics, *Sangschaw* and *Penny Wheep*. The poems were about God, eternity, the Scottish countryside, love, and other subjects. Because he broke with the stereotypes of recent Scottish poetry and because he challenged his traditionally literate countrymen with a diction reaching back to a time of Scottish literary ascendancy, MacDiarmid was basing his strategy on an appeal to the best in his readers.

A DRUNK MAN LOOKS AT THE THISTLE

Before the publication of the second of these works, he was already shaping another book. *A Drunk Man Looks at the Thistle*, also issued in 1926, proved a much more ambitious work: a sequence of lyrics and meditative poems making up one long, symbolically unified poem. Although MacDiarmid was to write many long poems, he would never find a structural principle more effective than the one he used here. While some critics have objected to the titles of the fifty-nine poems as interfering with the unity of the book, anyone reading through the sequence will have no trouble perceiving its integrity. The first title, "Sic Transit Gloria Scotia," signals the poet's concern with the cultural and literary decline of his native land and suggests his intention of arresting that decline personally. *A Drunk Man Looks at the Thistle* has come to be recognized as more than a regional achievement, though MacDiarmid took several risks which probably delayed recognition of the scope of his achievement.

In the first place, the title, while accurate, is an odd one for an ambitious literary work, as it seems to lack seriousness and in fact to cater to the common perception of the Scottish peasantry as whiskey-guzzling ne'er-do-wells. His employment of a Scots vocabulary also posed problems. The vocabulary threatened to repel English readers, who expected poets to clothe respectable verse in literary English. The numerous dialect words required heavy use of a specialized dictionary. Even if willing to wrestle with the words, however, such readers were likely to associate Scots with feeble imitations of Burns. MacDiarmid appeared unconventional and frivolous not only in choosing a drunkard as the poem's speaker but also in choosing the lowly thistle, rather than a more "worthy" flower such as a rose, as his central symbol. Who else had made anything of such a homely weed since the rhetorical question of Matthew 7:16: "Do men gather grapes of thorns, or figs of thistles?"

Nevertheless, MacDiarmid had reasons to hope for a harvest. His format permitted him a series of lyrical, comical, and satirical reflections in a variety of meters and stanzas, both rhymed and unrhymed, with the concomitant advantage of showing off his technical versatility. He could also expect that his more extravagant poetic flights, being merely the dreams of a drunken man, would not reflect on him. Apparent digressions were no problem, either, for everyone expects a drunken man to meander. Therefore, while his character indulged in a leisurely display of reactions to all that ailed him and Scotland, the poet could carefully guide his inebriated speaker along a purposeful path.

The drunkard begins by complaining of the difficulty of keeping up with his drinking partners, especially since the Scotch does not compare with the old-time variety, thereby establishing that everything Scottish now seems to be "destitute o'speerit," including the appalling poetry now produced by supposed devotees of Burns. An immediate dilemma presents itself: How can one be a good Scot yet shake off the Scottish lethargy and mediocrity? Interestingly, MacDiarmid's method involves the occasional incorporation of translations and adaptations from French, Belgian, German, and Russian poets, and two original lyrics addressed to Fyodor Dostoevski. MacDiarmid obviously considered the great Russian novelist a kindred spirit in the struggle to repossess imaginatively a stubbornly recalcitrant homeland. To be a good Scot meant, among other things, to accept competent assistance wherever available.

In a poem called "Poet's Pub," based on a poem by Aleksandr Blok, the drunkard resists the idea of going home to his wife, Jean, who is sure to nag him. Instead, he hopes to discover the truth said to be in wine, especially those truths ordinarily dark to him and to his cronies. He catches sight of a "silken leddy" in the pub, but she soon fades from sight, and eventually he stumbles outside to begin his homeward trek. The fourth poem of the sequence introduces the thistle and the image with which MacDiarmid customarily pairs it, the moonlight: "The munelicht's like a lookin'-glass,/ The thistle's like mysel," he observes, one of the resemblances being that he needs a shave.

In the poems that follow, the symbolic values of thistle and moonlight proliferate. A poem addressed to "The Unknown Goddess"—again adapted from Blok—presumably refers to the mysterious lady of the pub, who may represent his muse but is certainly the opposite of Jean. The drunkard's attention alternates between depressing reality ("Our Educational System," "The Barren Fig," "Tussle with the Philistines") and inspired visions ("Man and the Infinite," "Outward Bound," "The Spur of Love"). The drunken man is not sure of much: "And yet I feel this muckle thistle's staun'in'/ Atween me and the mune as pairt o' a Plan." He regards himself as his nation's "soul" and thus free to appropriate the humble thistle: In one of his flights he compares his homeward course to the wanderings of Ulysses; in another he sees himself "ootward boond" toward eternity. The thistle may serve to unite man and the infinite, or it may simply take off on its own and leave man nothing but the hole in which it was once rooted. Periodically his thoughts return to Jean, who "ud no' be long/ In finding whence this thistle sprang," for it is in her absence that the plant has grown for him.

The man's thoughts oscillate between Scotland—materialistic, Philistine, ill-educated, yet worth redemption—and himself as representative of the more general human condition—earthbound and mortal yet aspiring to eternity. The thistle has, despite its general ugliness, the capacity to flower, to put out at its tip a "rose" that permits MacDiarmid the traditional associations of that flower in a different context. In "The Form and Purpose of the Thistle," the speaker reflects on the "craft" that produced the odd, prickly stalk capable of breaking into flowers "like sudden lauchter," a craft of puzzling contrarieties. In "The Thistle's Characteristics," the poet ranges over man's illusions and presumptions. "For wha o's ha'e the thistle's poo'er/ To see we're worthless and believe 't?" Later he employs the Norse myth of Yggdrasill, the ash tree which binds together Earth, Heaven, and Hell; in this case, however, man is a "twig" on a giant thistle that, far from uniting creation, "braks his warlds abreid and rives/ His heavens to tatters on its horns." The Yggdrasill poem insists on man's suffering and ends by seeing humans as so many Christs, carrying their crosses "frae the seed," although as the drunkard slyly puts it, most feel it far less than he "thro' bein' mair wudden frae the stert!" Such satiric thrusts at his countrymen occur frequently in the work as a whole. However painful the life, the soul will soar in its "divine inebriety." Intoxication, then, is also a metaphor in this poem, standing for the poetic imagination that can rise above, and gain solace by reflecting on, humankind's common "Calvary."

The drunken man contemplates the oppressive English rule over an exhausted and often foolish Scotland, but even more often, his thoughts wind between Heaven and Earth, between the aspirations of the rose and the limitations of the rooted stalk. He longs for the mysterious lady, then is gripped by the recollection of practical Jean at home. Near the end of the work, he sees himself, God, the Devil, and Scotland all on a great cosmic wheel which sums up Scotland's and man's slow journeys through history. Pondering Scottish resistance to change and new ideas, he wonders if he must "assume/ The burden o' his people's doom" by dying heroically for his re-

calcitrant fellows. He falters over the decision, not exactly rejecting heroism but choosing to return to Jean's arms. The last lyric of the poem pays eloquent tribute to what he has left of his vision: silence. The conclusion is a joke, for he imagines what Jean will say to that: "And weel ye micht,/ . . . efter sic a nicht!"

The final lines of the poem are consistent with the whole work: Despite his insistence on the dignity of human imagination, the drunken man is always aware of the indignity of human circumstances and his inability to grasp the meaning of life. Only a drunk—that is, only a person intoxicated by life generally and the life of the mind particularly—would bother with such a spiritual quest.

TO CIRCUMJACK CENCRASTUS

MacDiarmid's next book of poetry, *To Circumjack Cencrastus*, is more of a miscellany, but one stanza of the poem aptly titled "MacDiarmid's Curses" holds a particular irony:

> Speakin o' Scotland in English words
> As it were Beethoven chirpt by birds;
> Or as if a Board school teacher
> Tried to teach Rimbaud and Nietzsche.

Although these lines do not precisely deny the possibility of a shift to "English words," they scarcely foretell the fact that within a few years MacDiarmid would virtually cease to write in his Scottish amalgam, even when "speakin' o' Scotland." By the middle 1930's, he would be creating a very different sort of poetry using standard English.

HYMNS TO LENIN

In the meantime, MacDiarmid continued to employ Scots for his first two "hymns to Lenin." Many intellectuals of the time shared his hope, but few his enduring faith, in the efficacy of Communism. It remains difficult to read objectively the "First Hymn to Lenin," in which the Soviet leader is hailed as a successor to Christ, or to appreciate it as poetry. MacDiarmid seems to have traded metaphysical doubts for political assurance, and the exchange does not enhance his poetry. He was always extreme in his enthusiasms, but from this point on, his polemical voice invaded his poetry more frequently. Within *First Hymn to Lenin and Other Poems*, however, is found "At My Father's Grave," with its eight lines of flexible blank verse meditating hauntingly on his father, as if from "across a valley."

Stony Limits and Other Poems

With *Stony Limits and Other Poems*, MacDiarmid moved into a new phase of his poetic career. He still included poems in Scots, notably a group called "Shetland Lyrics," but he was now working in a literary English that differed markedly from that of his very early poetry. The English poems were at this point more discursive, somewhat less concrete, and considerably more formal. The title poem, in nine ten-line stanzas, pays tribute to Charles Doughty, a poet, geologist, and travel writer who delighted in the lonely occupation of studying the soil and rock formations of remote regions, his most famous book being about the Arabian desert. Gregarious himself, MacDiarmid could respond enthusiastically to Doughty's serenity, his indifference to the crowd, and his capacity for appreciating realms of silence. When this book appeared, MacDiarmid had retreated to the Shetland Islands, where, without ceasing his political involvements, he had begun to study the geology of this northern outpost. He created a new difficulty for his reader, for "Stony Limits" is peppered with terms such as "xenoliths," "orthopinacoid," "striae," and "microline." The geological terminology signals his camaraderie with Doughty and also a growing love of precision quite distinct from the passion for suggestiveness which created the thistle and moonlight images in *A Drunk Man Looks at the Thistle*. This elegy is quiet, almost reverent, but without the defiant tone of his hymns to Lenin.

"On a Raised Beach"

He carries his scientific enthusiasm further in a longer poem in the same collection, "On a Raised Beach." The poem begins "All is lithogenesis—or lochia," a line hardly calculated to appeal immediately to the laity, but since the first term signifies rock formation and the second the discharge from the womb after childbirth, the line immediately juxtaposes the contrasting elements of the poem, stones and human life. Actually, the first twenty-four of the poem's more than four hundred lines teem with technical geological terms, most of which cannot be found in an ordinary desk dictionary. Anyone who braves this formidable initial barrier, however, discovers an arresting meditation on the human situation vis-à-vis that of the stones, which "are one with the stars."

MacDiarmid points out that specific terms can be given to scientific phenomena, but man finds more difficulty in expressing his convictions and preferences. The permanence of stone emphasizes the transience and impatience of man. Early in the poem, he compares man unfavorably to the one other creature stirring on the beach, a bird whose "inward gates" are, unlike man's, "always open." MacDiarmid argues that the gates of stones stand open even longer. The poet's admiration for these enduring veterans of a world older than man can easily imagine resembles Henry David Thoreau's for living nature, and a number of the lines have a Thoreauvian ring to them—for example, "Let men find the faith that builds mountains/ Before they seek the faith that moves them." As in Thoreau, nature teaches the perceptive person humility. Life is redundant, says MacDiarmid, but not stones. Human culture pales before the bleak but beautiful sentinels of time on a scale beyond man's ordinary comprehension.

As the stately free verse moves on, MacDiarmid alludes to various stones with human associations: the missile that David hurled at Goliath, pebbles with which Demosthenes filled his mouth, the rock that guarded Christ's tomb. Human culture is like Goliath, doomed to fall, and no orator can hope to rival the lithic earth in eloquence. Stones not only draw men back to their beginnings but also lead them on to their end. No stone can be rolled aside like the "Christophanic" one to release death, but death is not on that account to be feared, because dying is less difficult than living a worthwhile life.

Despite the weightiness of "On a Raised Beach," despite its rather sepulchral tone, the poem does not oppress but conveys a breath of caution, a salutary deflation of human arrogance. The poem might have benefited from a beach more specifically evoked, like Matthew Arnold's Dover Beach, but it nevertheless communicates effectively the "capacity for solitude" by which MacDiarmid strives to imitate the great stones.

Lucky Poet

The virtual disappearance of Scots lyrics after *Stony Limits and Other Poems* seems to be not a repudiation of the poet's earlier theory but an acknowledgment that after several hundred poems in that medium he needed to test the linguistic possibilities of English. Like Burns before him, MacDiarmid could sing best in Scots and create more comedy and humor than he ever seemed to have tried in literary English. Advocates of his poetry (many of whom are Scottish) have tended to prefer the Scots poems, but the best of his English poems have their own excellence, and it is of a sort appropriate to an older man. They are sober, thought-provoking, and reflective of the intensity of a poet deeply committed to his art and alert to the world about him. Like Yeats and Eliot, he changed his style in middle age to produce a kind of verse in sharp contrast to that which gained for him his initial audience.

Not until the publication of his autobiography, *Lucky Poet*, in 1943 did MacDiarmid formulate in detail his prescription for the poetry he had been attempting to practice for a decade. This book contains several previously unpublished poems, one of which, "The Kind of Poetry I Want," sets forth vigorously the theory that he had been developing. The diction and rhythms of this long poem are prosaic, and its topical allusions date it severely, but it rings with conviction. Probably no poem ever written realizes all of its specifications. According to MacDiarmid, the poet must be a polymath who can base his or her work on "difficult knowledge" in many fields, including the sciences, and must be technically accomplished and equipped with "ecstasy." Poetry must reflect closeness to and knowledge of nature. The poet must know the countryside and the technological order and must deploy linguistic and historical learning. Poetry must be factual and still illuminate values, argues MacDiarmid; it must integrate the knowledge of its various sources and—as a crowning touch—must reflect a poet uninterested in personal success. At one point, MacDiarmid concedes that such poetry must await social reorganization, presumably along communistic lines.

MacDiarmid was better equipped than most to pursue his poetic ideal. By mid-career, his poetry bristled with learned allusions to Russian, Hebrew, Turkish, Chinese, Greek, and Gaelic poetry, to name a few. Not all the poems in *Lucky Poet* are learned, but they are all provoking. Two of them excoriate the cities of Edinburgh and Glasgow for their bourgeois sins, and the good humor of his earlier social criticism has vanished. Clearly, he is less willing than ever to cater to merely conventional taste and expectations.

In Memoriam James Joyce

By the time of *In Memoriam James Joyce: From a Vision of World Language*, MacDiarmid was brewing a poetry in some ways like Joyce's prose, packed with recondite allusions, quotations in many languages, puns, technical vocabulary, and an often tortuous syntax. The tone was more likely to be oracular and insistent. How many of his poetic tenets he was then fulfilling is disputable, but he clearly was not integrating knowledge, and perhaps he was inadvertently demonstrating the impossibility of such integration in the second half of the twentieth century, with its myriad specialists. Reminiscent of his previous work is the poem "We Must Look at the Harebell." MacDiarmid is at his best when "looking" rather than persuading, and this poem has fresh observations not only of the harebell but also of the pinguicula or butterwort (a small herb), the asphodel, the parsley fern, and other flora to be found by a person willing to climb rocks and descend into bogs. The plants he observes are interesting, but even more interesting is his determination to reveal the prospects of nature.

A Lap of Honour

MacDiarmid appears to have written relatively little new poetry after the publication of *In Memoriam James Joyce*, but because *Collected Poems of Hugh MacDiarmid* omitted a number of his earlier poems, the volume *A Lap of Honour*, which appeared five years later, when the poet turned seventy-five, was an important addition. It contained some poems that had appeared only in periodicals and others from books difficult to obtain in 1967. One of the most important inclusions was "On a Raised Beach," only a short extract of which had appeared in the 1962 collection. There were several, by then welcome, Scots poems from an earlier day. Thus, this volume made accessible to many readers for the first time a sampling of MacDiarmid's work over the decades of his greatest vitality, the 1920's, 1930's, and 1940's.

Later poetry

The innovations of his later poetry have an importance beyond the success of individual poems. In an age when many poets knew little about science and even affected to despise it, MacDiarmid was trying to widen the range of the poet's expertise. While the scientific knowledge of even an amateur such as MacDiarmid is bound to seem inadequate to a well-trained scientist, he was often able to enhance his subjects with metaphors drawn from science. Thus, in "Stony Limits," he compared his projected poem in praise of Doughty to the process of crystallization in rocks and to the growth of lunar formations, and in "Crystals Like Blood," he could liken the memory to the extraction of mercury from cinnabar. Such metaphors doubtless have very little effect on a scientifically illiterate reader, but his fear was of a poetry that failed by appealing only to the badly educated. His aspiration to the precision of the exact sciences was probably unrealistic, but he was doing his part to integrate the "two cultures" at a time when many intellectuals were dividing into mutually antagonistic and uncomprehending camps. His efforts to apply the discoveries of modern linguistics to poetry were unsuccessful, but there is no telling what they may have suggested to younger poets. He carried allusion and quotation beyond what many readers would consider tolerable limits, but he did not shrink from challenging those who were able and willing to follow him. Like Eliot, MacDiarmid was trying to use tradition creatively, and like Ezra Pound, he often moved outside the Western tradition favored by Eliot. Few poets have worked so diligently for so long to widen the possibilities of poetry.

By a curious irony, MacDiarmid's poems in English, because of their high density of technical words and obscure quotations and allusions, present greater difficulties than his earlier ones in Scots. Lacking the humor and lyricism of the early poems, his English poems often repay the reader's careful attention with their insight into the natural world and their challenge to conventional ways of looking at the world and of expressing the results of such observations. Nevertheless, his early mission to rescue Scottish poetry by creating a composite dialect out of folk and literary sources and to speak to a materialistic generation of the possibilities of a richer culture and authentic spiritual life was doubtless his greatest accomplishment. Even without consulting the glossary of *Collected Poems of Hugh MacDiarmid*, the English-speaking reader can take pleasure in the energy and lyrical buoyancy of *A Drunk Man Looks at the Thistle*, and with very little trouble the full meaning is available to all. It has been suggested that this poem is the modern equivalent of the medieval dream vision. Undoubtedly, only a poet steeped in literary tradition could

have written it. Taking advantage of a form that allows a comprehensive and uninhibited vision, MacDiarmid fashions a poem that is highly original because it reflects a modern, skeptical sensibility, and is readily understandable because it is made from the materials of everyday life. While aiming at universality in his later poetry, he achieved it most fully in his odyssey of a drunken cottager beneath the Scottish "mune."

Other major works

NONFICTION: *Albyn: Or, Scotland and the Future*, 1927; *The Present Condition of Scottish Music*, 1927; *At the Sign of the Thistle: A Collection of Essays*, 1934; *Scottish Eccentrics*, 1936; *The Islands of Scotland*, 1939; *Lucky Poet*, 1943; *Burns Today and Tomorrow*, 1959; *David Hume: Scotland's Greatest Son*, 1961; *The Company I've Kept*, 1966; *Scotland, 1968: Selected Essays of Hugh MacDiarmid*, 1969 (Duncan Glen, editor).

EDITED TEXTS: *Northern Numbers, Being Representative Selections from Certain Living Scottish Poets*, 1920-1922 (3 volumes); *The Golden Treasury of Scottish Poetry*, 1940.

MISCELLANEOUS: *Annals of the Five Senses*, 1923.

Bibliography

Bold, Alan. *MacDiarmid: The Terrible Crystal*. London: Routledge & Kegan Paul, 1983. A full-length study of MacDiarmid's poetry. In addition to critical commentary of his works, Bold compares him to other writers, particularly those who influenced him, and discusses both the political and mystical elements in his works.

Buthlay, Kenneth. *Hugh MacDiarmid*. 1964. Rev. ed. Edinburgh, Scotland: Scottish Academic Press, 1982. A comprehensive and lively introduction to MacDiarmid, expanded and revised from the first edition in 1964. This study is an illuminating account of MacDiarmid's development as a poet, with critical examination of individual poems and technical devices.

Gish, Nancy K. *Hugh MacDiarmid: The Man and His Work*. London: Macmillan, 1984. A critical appraisal of MacDiarmid's work, with emphasis given to such poems as *A Drunk Man Looks at the Thistle*,

Stony Limits and Other Poems, as well as the later long poems. Includes a glossary for "On a Raised Beach." The author interviewed MacDiarmid for this work, which provides much important background information on the poet and his thinking.

Glen, Duncan, ed. *Hugh MacDiarmid: A Critical Survey*. Edinburgh, Scotland: Scottish Academic Press, 1972. A collection of essays, all but one previously printed, affirming the significance of MacDiarmid's poetry. This useful volume offers solid literary criticism of MacDiarmid's work from his early poetry to his later poems.

_____. *Hugh MacDiarmid and the Scottish Renaissance*. London: W. & R. Chambers, 1964. Considered the definitive introduction to MacDiarmid's life and work by a notable scholar of the poet. This thoroughly researched volume places MacDiarmid among Scottish writers who revived Scottish traditions.

_____. *Hugh Macdiarmid: Or, Out of Langholm and into the World*. Edinburgh, Scotland: Akros Publications, 1992. A short biographical study of MacDiarmid with bibliographic references.

Herbert, W. N. *To Circumjack MacDiarmid: The Poetry and Prose of Hugh MacDiarmid*. New York: Oxford University Press, 1992. A critical study of selected works by MacDiarmid. Includes bibliographical references and index.

McQuillan, Ruth. *Hugh MacDiarmid: The Patrimony, a Tale of the Generations of Men, and a Golden Lyric*. Edinburgh, Scotland: Akros Publications, 1992. A brief analysis (thirty-two pages) with bibliographical references.

Riach, Alan. *Hugh MacDiarmid's Epic Poetry*. Scotland: Edinburgh University Press, 1991. A well-known scholar of Scottish culture, and MacDiarmid in particular, offers interpretations of the poetry. Bibliographical references, index.

Scott, P. H., and A. C. Davis. *The Age of MacDiarmid: Essays on Hugh MacDiarmid and His Influence on Contemporary Scotland*. Edinburgh, Scotland: Mainstream Publishing, 1980. An important collection of essays from eminent scholars of MacDiarmid. The first group of essays is largely autobiographical in nature; the second group addresses themes such as MacDiarmid's nationalism, politics, and the language problem in his work.

Robert P. Ellis;
bibliography updated by the editors

CYNTHIA MACDONALD

Cynthia Lee
Born: New York, New York; February 2, 1928

PRINCIPAL POETRY
Amputations, 1972
Transplants, 1976
(W)holes, 1980
Alternate Means of Transport, 1985
Living Wills: New and Selected Poems, 1991
I Can't Remember: Poems, 1997

OTHER LITERARY FORMS

Although Cynthia Macdonald is known primarily as a poet, she also wrote the libretto for the opera *The Rehearsal*, with music by Thomas Benjamin, which was produced in 1980 at Northwestern University in Evanston, Illinois. That same year, her lyrics were set to music by Judy Collins for "This Is the Day," recorded on Elektra. Macdonald is also the author of reviews, essays, memoirs, and commentaries on her own poems and on the writing process, which have appeared in various books and periodicals.

ACHIEVEMENTS

Cynthia Macdonald has won critical acclaim both for her originality in tone and expression and for her mastery of technique. Early in her career, she was given grants by the MacDowell Colony, the National Endowment for the Arts, the Yaddo Foundation, and CAPS, as well as an award from the National Academy of Institute of Arts and Letters in 1977. She was named a Rockefeller Foundation Fellow in 1978.

In 1991, Macdonald's collection *Living Wills: New and Selected Poems* was chosen by *The New York Times Book Review* as one of the Notable Books of the Year.

The following year, the Folger Shakespeare Library awarded Macdonald its O. B. Hardison Poetry Prize.

Another of Macdonald's major achievements was her work with the University of Houston's creative writing program, which she was asked to develop in the late 1970's. Within less than two decades, it was being ranked as one of the best graduate programs of its kind in the United States.

BIOGRAPHY

Cynthia Macdonald was born on February 2, 1928, in New York City, to Leonard Lee, a department store buyer, and Dorothy Kiam Lee. Cynthia's younger sister died in childhood. When Cynthia was eight, the family moved to Southern California, where Leonard Lee became a film writer. Four years later the Lees were divorced. Dorothy took Cynthia back to New York and enrolled her in the prestigious Brearley School, where she remained for five years.

At twelve, Cynthia attended her first opera and was so impressed that eventually she resolved to become an operatic performer. However, her parents persuaded her to go to Bennington College instead of to a music school. After graduating in 1950, she returned to New York to prepare for her musical career. Even after her marriage in 1954 to E. C. Macdonald, a Shell Oil executive, she continued to appear with small opera companies and to sing in restaurants where the staff performed.

Her husband was moved so frequently that Cynthia Macdonald found it difficult to establish herself in her own career. However, while she was at home with her two children, Jennifer Tim, born in 1956, and Scott Thurston, born in 1959, she began writing poetry. By the time the family returned from three years in Japan, Macdonald had decided to give up music and to concentrate on her writing.

After receiving her M.A. in 1970 from Sarah Lawrence College, Macdonald began teaching there. When her husband was transferred to Houston, she did not accompany him. They were divorced in 1975. That same year, Cynthia Macdonald became a professor at the Johns Hopkins University, where she remained until 1979, when she accepted the University of Houston's offer of a position as codirector of its new creative writing program.

During the 1970's, Macdonald had published her first two collections of poems. From the beginning, critics found much to admire in her works. Although they found some stylistic flaws in the first collection, *Amputations*, they praised the poet for her verbal wit and her imaginative imagery. *Transplants* and *(W)holes* also received generally favorable reviews.

In Houston, Macdonald began preparing for still a third career. In 1986, having completed a four-year course at the Houston-Galveston Psychoanalytic Institute, she entered private practice, specializing in problems such as writer's block. Perhaps her training accounted for the more compassionate tone many noted in Macdonald's fourth volume, *Alternate Means of Transport*, in the newer poems in *Living Wills: New and Selected Poems*, and in *I Can't Remember: Poems*. While from the first she had been regarded as a poet with a unique talent, Cynthia Macdonald was eventually applauded as a truly impressive artist.

ANALYSIS

The early work of Cynthia Macdonald is sometimes described as too preoccupied with the grotesque and too flippant in tone. However, from the first, the poet was admired for her way with words. She has the narrative skill of a fine short story writer, initially capturing the attention of her readers with a startling image or statement, then maintaining the suspense up to an ending which, though usually less than happy, is always interesting and often memorable.

AMPUTATIONS

As the title suggests, the poems in Macdonald's first collection were almost uniformly grotesque. Most of them deal with literal amputations. Sometimes there is no explanation of the circumstances, as in "Inventory," where the persona lists his father's finger as one of the items that appears from time to time in his own ever-present suitcase.

Often, however, a first-person narrator explains in a matter-of-fact manner why the mutilation was not accidental, but necessary. Thus in "Departure," a mother treats her son's cutting off his feet as an inevitable stage in the process of becoming independent, while in "Objets d'Art," it seems perfectly logical to the speaker that she should respond to a stranger's calling her a "real ball cutter" by relieving as many men as possible of their testicles. These narrators not only treat the amputations as perfectly normal but also take pride in the care with which they treat their relics. Such narratives were undoubtedly symbolic, meant to point out the disjunctive nature of relationships, but most critics felt that their impact was diminished by the poet's sardonic tone.

However, the poems in *Amputations* did demonstrate that Macdonald was already well on her way to mastering her craft. In "Departure," for instance, she captures the reader's attention with a striking first line: "When he cut off his feet I knew he was leaving." As she proceeds, she roots surreal scenes in reality with homely details such as "striped sheets" and "Spaghetti sauce" and makes her descriptions vivid by using unexpected imagery, "corrugated toenails," for example. She drops hints of deeper meanings, as when the mother speaks of being left "alone/ With souvenirs and my spondees," thus raising issues of time, memory, and the isolation of the artist. The ending of the narrative, however, is as starkly simple as its beginning: "I love you. I have kept the feet in perfect condition."

Whether they focus on feminist issues, like "Objets d'Art"; on parent-child relationships, like "Departure"; on marital failure, like the autobiographical poem "A Family of Doll House Dolls"; or on an artist's frustrations, like "The Platform Builder," Macdonald's poems show human life as a desperate search for meaning. When he fails at committing suicide, the title character in "The Holy Man Walks Through Fire" becomes convinced that he must have been saved in order to lead his country, though to what he does not know. After a public relations firm has made him famous, he decides to prove his worth by walking through fire on live television. He ends up with third-degree burns, a failed prophet, only too aware that, as he puts it, "My country has not made it through the fire."

TRANSPLANTS

In her second collection, *Transplants*, Macdonald again uses grotesque images to symbolize the discontinuity of human existence. In this volume, published the year after Macdonald's divorce, marriage and family life are routinely shown as destroying women. The ten "Doctor Dimity Poems," for example, show family life at its most brutal. More subtly, "Instruction from Bly" demonstrates

that women cannot escape their commitments. Even though the poet-narrator has taken a year's leave from her family so that she can write, she is too concerned about her children and too uncertain about her husband's capacity for fidelity to focus on her poetry.

In her essays, Macdonald admits that there is an autobiographical basis for many of her poems. During her childhood, Macdonald came to identify with her mother, whom she saw as being made miserable by an uncaring husband. Her own reaction to her mother's death is the subject of two very moving poems in this collection, "Inheritance" and "The Late Mother." In both of them, the daughter takes on her mother's personality and her nurturing role. In "The Late Mother," as Macdonald holds her dying mother in her arms, she sees herself becoming "her mother and my own."

ALTERNATE MEANS OF TRANSPORT

The influence of Macdonald's intensive study of psychology and psychiatry is evident throughout *Alternate Means of Transport*. Instead of the grotesque images of the early poems, Macdonald now uses subtler, more complex symbolism, such as the red hats in one of her epigraphs, whose source is listed as *The Psychoanalytic Dictionary of Dream Symbols*. Her work is now both more varied and more profound. A sequence of seventeen poems, also titled "Alternate Means of Transport," though presented as a whimsical set of variations on the subject of hats, in fact deals with love, lust, hatred, death, disease, joy, art, and the quest for the meaning of life.

The anger that was often evident in Macdonald's early poems now has been replaced by a more balanced, thoughtful tone, the sardonic humor by an appealing playfulness. Even though in "Benefit Ball for Save the Children," the poet points out how ironic it is that the rich would stuff themselves to help starving children, the poem is a comment, not a diatribe. This new self-control, which makes her poetry all the more effective, can be seen even when she deals with issues about which she feels strongly, such as what marriage does to women. "Why Penelope Was Happy" makes its point through humor: Penelope is weeping tears of joy not just because her husband is safe but also because he is safely distant.

I CAN'T REMEMBER

In *I Can't Remember*, Macdonald continues to use a light touch to make her point about serious matters. In the feminist poem "Victoria's Secret," the persona moves through free association from the glamorous female body on the cover of a *Victoria's Secret* catalog to the free-spirited novelist Victoria Woolf, then to Queen Victoria, whose lust for her husband Albert proved how wrong the men of her era were about the sexual nature of women, and finally to the persona herself, as eager as that earlier Victoria to assume the role of "Venus couchant" in her lover's arms.

There are also frequent autobiographical references in this collection. In "The Weekend He Died," Macdonald deals with her feelings for her two fathers, "the birth father who killed himself," and her stepfather, who was both her "father by choice" and, in a play on words that is typical of the poet, is also described as a "Choice father," representing all that is best in fatherhood. However, the poem proceeds to a more general consideration of human helplessness. Her stepfather's accidental death reminds her that in reality it is not choice, but chance, that dominates human existence. Macdonald muses, "There is too much/ we cannot outwit."

In her essay "Heaven Is God's Throne; Earth, His Footstool," Macdonald explains how being reared as a nonobservant Jew in a society that was at least nominally Christian intensified her own sense of alienation. Macdonald's poems reflect a growing preoccupation with her Jewish heritage. Among the eleven poems in this collection that begin with chickens is one titled "Jewish Chicken Examines the Difference between Heaven and Hell," which pits Protestant theology against the reality of death in the Auschwitz concentration camp. Macdonald also refers to her Jewish background in "Miriam's Grandmother" and in "Singing Miriam's Lament." In "Maps and Globes," she comments that if her family had not left Europe in 1840, she might well have died in a concentration camp a hundred years later. Again, it was pure chance that determined her fate.

Though, like her characters, she would like to believe in a divine plan and a providential God, Macdonald cannot see that the evidence justifies such a faith. If there is a God, she asserts in "Casual Neglects," He must be as careless as some human parents. The compassion that is evident in Macdonald's later poetry is well illustrated in the lines with which this poem ends: "the empty sky of Paradise is pocked with small pink shells,/ those baby fingernails which couldn't quite keep holding on."

OTHER MAJOR WORKS

PLAY: *The Rehearsal*, pr. 1980 (libretto; music by Thomas Benjamin).

BIBLIOGRAPHY

Hosmer, Robert. "What We See and Feel and Are." Review of *Living Wills: New and Selected Poems. The Southern Review* 28 (Spring, 1992): 439-441. An incisive discussion of the difference in tone and focus between Macdonald's first three books and her later works. Beginning with *Alternate Means of Transport*, her poetry has a "new, spiritual dimension."

Macdonald, Cynthia. "Heaven Is God's Throne; Earth, His Footstool." *Prairie Schooner* 72 (Fall, 1988): 46-60. An autobiographical essay about the internal conflicts that resulted from the author's being reared in a household that was neither Christian nor Jewish. The poem "And Cause His Countenance to Shine upon You" illustrated the points made in the essay.

_____. "Mosaic Law: The Bits and Pieces from Which One Woman's Poems Are Made." In *Where We Stand: Women Poets on Literary Tradition*, edited by Sharon Bryan. New York: W. W. Norton, 1993. Discusses the unique problems women writers face in their search for a literary tradition. The poet has chosen to utilize "bits and pieces" from her reading and her studies in order to create "mosaics" that are hers alone.

_____. "The Role of the Stars in Psychoanalysis." *Yale Review* 79 (Summer, 1990): 579-603. In this memoir, much of which is written as a conversation between the poet and her analyst, Macdonald comments on how events in her childhood have affected her life and her works. Two of her poems, "Separations" and "The Murderer's Daughter: Inside and Outside," are discussed at length. Concludes with a segment from "Tracking Connections," presented as an example of "an all-purpose ending."

Rosenberg, Liz. "Poetry at a Gallop." Review of *Living Wills: New and Selected Poems. The New York Times Book Review*, June 30, 1991, p. 26. This collection is interesting as a record of the poet's development; over the years her works have become both more compassionate and more profound. A highly favorable review.

Scharf, Michael. Review of *I Can't Remember*. *Poetry* 173 (February, 1999): 318. A perceptive consideration of the poet's sixth volume. Points out how she utilizes explicit Freudian associations in order to reveal what often proves to be a comic view of life.

Widmann, R. L. "The Poetry of Cynthia MacDonald." In *Feminist Criticism: Essays on Theory, Poetry, and Prose*, edited by Cheryl L. Brown and Karen Olson. Metuchen, N.J.: Scarecrow Press, 1978. This essay, which originally appeared in the spring, 1974, issue of *Concerning Poetry*, remains a valuable study of Macdonald's first collection. Presents a detailed textual analysis of "Objets d'Art," "Inventory," and "Departure."

Rosemary M. Canfield Reisman

Wᴀʟᴛ MᴄDᴏɴᴀʟᴅ

Born: Lubbock, Texas; July 18, 1934

Pʀɪɴᴄɪᴘᴀʟ ᴘᴏᴇᴛʀʏ

Caliban in Blue and Other Poems, 1976
One Thing Leads to Another, 1978
Anything, Anything, 1980
Working Against Time, 1981
Burning the Fence, 1981
Witching on Hardscrabble, 1985
The Flying Dutchman, 1987
Rafting the Brazos, 1988
After the Noise of Saigon, 1988
Night Landings, 1989
The Digs in Escondido Canyon, 1991
All That Matters: The Texas Plains in Photographs and Poems, 1992
Where Skies Are Not Cloudy, 1993
Counting Survivors, 1995
Blessings the Body Gave, 1998
Whatever the Wind Delivers: Celebrating West Texas and the Near Southwest, 1999
All Occasions, 2000

Oᴛʜᴇʀ ʟɪᴛᴇʀᴀʀʏ ꜰᴏʀᴍꜱ

Walt McDonald's short stories have appeared widely in literary magazines, anthologies, and in the collection *A Band of Brothers: Stories from Vietnam* (1989). As a scholar and critic, he has published essays in many journals and reference works, and he coedited *A "Catch-22" Casebook* (1973) with Frederick Kiley and *Texas Stories and Poems* (1978) with James P. White.

McDonald has also published art books with archivist Janet M. Neugebauer including *All That Matters: The Texas Plains in Photographs and Poems* (1992) and *Whatever the Wind Delivers: Celebrating West Texas and the Near Southwest* (1999). These volumes present McDonald's poetry alongside historic photographs from the Southwest Collection, creating a strong aesthetic effect and an engaging interpretive social history.

Aᴄʜɪᴇᴠᴇᴍᴇɴᴛꜱ

In addition to his poetry collections, McDonald has published more than nineteen hundred poems in periodicals, and his works have appeared in more than sixty anthologies and textbooks. *The Flying Dutchman* won the Elliston Poetry Prize, *After the Noise of Saigon* won the Juniper Prize, and *Blessings the Body Gave* won the Ohio State University Press/*The Journal* Award in Poetry. In 1999, McDonald was named poet laureate of Lubbock, Texas (a lifetime honor), and, in 2000, Texas poet laureate for 2000-2001. He has received two creative writing fellowships from the National Endowment for the Arts and six awards from the Texas Institute of Letters, including the Lon Tinkle Memorial Award for excellence sustained throughout a career. Four of his books have won the Western Heritage Award from the National Cowboy Hall of Fame.

Bɪᴏɢʀᴀᴘʜʏ

Walt McDonald was born and reared in Lubbock, Texas, to Vera Graves McDonald and C. A. McDonald, a veteran of World War I who had worked as a cowboy in his youth and later as a commercial painter. After earning his B.A. from Texas Tech University in 1956, McDonald was accepted into U.S. Air Force pilot training. Since his class would not begin for another year, he stayed at Texas Tech and completed his M.A. in English. In 1959, he married Carol Ham.

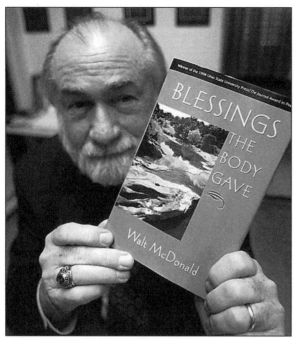

Walt McDonald at his office on the campus of Texas Tech in 1998. (AP/Wide World Photos)

After pilot training, McDonald taught English at the Air Force Academy. Later he attended the Writers' Workshop at the University of Iowa, where he studied fiction writing with R.V. Cassill and Vance Bourjaily. At this time he had no interest in poetry and did not take a single poetry-writing class. After completing his Ph.D. in 1966, he returned to his teaching assignment at the Air Force Academy.

In 1969, McDonald, now the father of three children, was sent to Vietnam, where he served as a ground officer at Tan Son Nhut and Cam Ron from late 1969 to early 1970. After a medical discharge from the Air Force, McDonald returned to Texas Tech in 1971, where he started the creative writing program and remained its director. He began serving as Paul Whitfield Horn Professor of English and poet-in-residence.

A significant aspect of McDonald's story for readers to remember is this: Although he customarily writes in the first person, he is not the speaker in his poems. As he told interviewer Darryl Tippens,

> Always I'm writing poems, not autobiography. In the sense that poems expose some of my interests, obses-

sions, the regions of the mind I keep prowling, sure. But almost *only* in that sense. . . . I'm not there, frank and undisguised, in a poem or a short story. Experience is valuable for what it is; then the writing takes over.

In other words, he is not the soldier or the pilot, the cowboy or the hardscrabble rancher, who speaks from the pages. Yet he does share a part of those characters' history and culture, and the common experience makes the poems rich and real.

ANALYSIS

Though early in his career Walt McDonald was considered a "Vietnam poet," he is best known as a Southwest regionalist. In an interview with Fred Alsberg, he suggested that his regions are not so much real places as "regions of the mind," "cluster[s] of images or obsessions that a writer draws on over and over, for poems." What he is describing is more accurately an intellectual complex than any particular place on the map. Thus as the term "region" applies to McDonald's work, "Texas" and "Vietnam" are rightly understood as regions, but so are "flying" and "family life."

CALIBAN IN BLUE AND OTHER POEMS

Informed by his years as a pilot, service in Vietnam, and literary study, the poems in McDonald's first book, *Caliban in Blue and Other Poems*, are carefully crafted, allusive, and detached. After reading the book, poet Donald Justice asked, "Where's Texas in your poems, Walt?"—a question that would prove to be a turning point. Though *Caliban in Blue and Other Poems* was an excellent book, its foremost critical importance may reside in what it lacked: Texas.

McDonald responded with four collections in five years in which Vietnam recedes, replaced by increased attention to family relationships and southwestern scenes and culture. The ironic detachment of *Caliban in Blue and Other Poems* erodes: The voice becomes more engaged, less critical, more forgiving of the human condition; literary allusions grow less frequent and less schoolish, more casually effective; the vignettes gain narrative continuity; the voice seems more aware of joy.

BURNING THE FENCE

Burning the Fence culminates this transition, in that it establishes the trajectory of craft and theme that Mc-

Donald's later work would follow. All his "regions" are here: family, the mountains, flying, Texas, and Vietnam. Most important, however, *Burning the Fence* highlights a sophisticated merging of the physical and spiritual. "Tornado Alley," a poem ostensibly about a family's yearly storm preparations, becomes in its final line— "We search the sky. There's time"—a comment on the fragile comfort humans take in putting off death. "First Solo" warns a new pilot, "Give everything you have to the runway./ You will have all night to dream," clearly a statement about how to live one's life as much as how to land one's plane. Finally, the collection's title poem features a quasi-personified fence doing its best to resist burning. As the flames "waver within cracks" and the posts "hold in their flames," the fence is "unwilling to stop being fence," just as humans resist their own material and temporal limitations.

HARDSCRABBLE COUNTRY

By the early 1980's, McDonald had mastered his method and charted his regions, the most frequented of which is the Texas hardscrabble country. Hundreds of his poems not only portray the region's countryside and culture but also exploit its metaphoric richness. By attending to everyday particulars, McDonald discovers its grandeur as well, portraying what critic Michael Hobbes has called the poet's "hardscrabble sublime." His apparently simple vignettes of common tasks consistently suggest truths about how to be human in a difficult world—Texas or elsewhere.

That often means acting on faith. In "Starting a Pasture," the narrator, against common sense and in spite of the real or imagined jeers of his neighbors, fences a new pasture in dry cotton country. The poem is at once a self-deprecating monologue and a testament to the stubbornness necessary to exist in a harsh environment. "Living on Buried Water" portrays similar determination, lightened by persistent faith. The arid conditions naturally trigger poems about finding wells—often by "Witching with sycamore." "Sometimes a twig drags down to water," the speaker tells us, "and we risk digging." "We haven't found it," he confesses, but ends with an affirmation: "we believe it's here."

In "Digging for Buried Water," the narrator has risked shoveling a well and has struck water, resulting in a near-religious ecstasy. At the signs of success, the dig-

gers begin scooping "like a rescue team in a cave-in/ delirious, convinced we hear tapping." "Rigging the Windmill" relates the story of a narrator whose labor has been successful, but its difficulty has suggested questions both practical and theological. He wonders "how many cows/ it will water, how many angels dance/ in whirlwind, how many times/ a pump goes around before breaking." "Wind and Hardscrabble" reflects further the tenuous life. Only the cattle, untroubled by human doubt, do not worry the brutal heat—so long as the wind keeps turning the windmill's blades. The final image is one of Canaan-like abundance:

> Parched, they wade still pastures
> shimmering in heat waves
> and muzzle deep in stock tanks
> filled and overflowing.

Cattle may not realize the fragility of life, but cattlemen do. "The Witness of Dry Plains" portrays an arid world in which "a hawk rises high in the heavens," sees a rabbit, and dives, "wings stiff and wide, totally silent." McDonald often refers to nature "red in tooth and claw," but that situation is, it would seem, part of the sublimity. The death of the rabbit and the salvation of the hawk are a single act—a part of that balance in which humans are not simply observers but participants: "All is as it will be, in a desert./ Even the trees are balanced."

It takes a determination to stay. According to "Living on Open Plains," the only source of water, the Ogallala water table, is dropping three feet every year, but the narrator has no intention of leaving. Looking out into the dark evening, he claims, "wherever others on the road a mile away/ are going, we are here." To live on hardscrabble, people must be willing to accept "whatever the wind delivers." In the poem by that title, the narrator and his wife accept the dust, "the earth we live on, the dust our fingers/ string new fences on, holding each other/ one more night with loving words."

FLYING

McDonald has returned to his "flying" region throughout his career, often with vignettes that find power simply in their clear telling of a story. In "Ejecting from Jets," Kirk, the pilot, has become inverted and ejected "downward like a dart." In a flatly stated but horrific final image, his head is found crushed in his helmet, and "under the burned fuselage,/ the bones of his hand/ squeezing the trigger like a gun." Strong as this poem is, McDonald often reaches for a greater metaphorical resonance. A similar situation occurs in "For Dawes, on Takeoff," but with a different effect:

> They found his head
> stuck to his helmet.
> In trees downrange, they found his arms
> flung out from the body as if asking why.

The image of Kirk is one of desperation, but the image of Dawes, though similarly horrific, suggests greater philosophical significance: In death Dawes asks the most important question, "Why?" "First Solo in Thunderstorms" works toward a more subtle thematic weight. The pilot, flying at night in hard weather, reflects that there is nothing to be done but fight the panic and believe that "storms like our lives/ have to end, that wings never/ level enough could hold me,/ that only a turbine was burning." Flying here clearly becomes a metaphor for human lives: frail, tenuous, demanding of faith in the face of doubt.

"After the Noise of Saigon"

Though after *Caliban in Blue and Other Poems* the theme of Vietnam temporarily disappeared from McDonald's poems, it eventually returned in a few poems in each volume. Many of these present a soldier's straightforward emotional observations: "The Children of Saigon" and "The Food Pickers of Saigon," for example, portray destitute Vietnamese eking out a living on the waste of American military bases. Poems such as "The Last Still Days in a Bunker" and "War Games" create realistic scenes of the danger shared by many soldiers. More often, however, the Vietnam experience is felt as a subtle but controlling presence, one of several psychic forces.

By using that region in this more understated manner, McDonald achieves powerful compression and is able, often with a single term or phrase, to trigger a complex psychological response. In "After the Noise of Saigon," the Vietnamese landscape never appears—the poem is ostensibly about hunting in the mountains. Yet the simple phrase "after the noise of Saigon" suggests a complex of meaning that informs the way readers understand the narrator's actions in pursuit of a wounded

cougar. As the speaker states, "These blue trees have nothing/ and all to do with what I'm here for/ after the noise of Saigon." Because of the suggestiveness of the lines—and because, too, no doubt, his poems gain a cumulative effect as the volumes progress—such minimalism turns rich in the reading. Readers grasp intuitively the implied metaphor, understanding on a visceral level how hunting allows the speaker to work through his Vietnam experience, to handle "the simple bitter sap that rises in me/ like bad blood I need to spill/ out here alone in the silence." The bitterness which in the poems in *Caliban in Blue and Other Poems* might have vented from a detached distance is here an emotional force that leads to a hard-won self-knowledge.

"For God in My Sorrows"

The potential pitfall of working and reworking his regions is monotony. Yet while McDonald's poems do use the language of his regions, or intellectual complexes, they are not merely about those regions. Texas and flying and Vietnam are less the subjects of McDonald's poems than they are languages in which to consider what it means to be human.

As critic Darryl Tippens has suggested, place for McDonald is "vehicle rather than tenor, and what he ultimately reveals through geography is timeless, universal, and spiritual." Other critics, too, have noted a tendency to deal more directly with religious questions in the later work. "For God in My Sorrows" is nothing short of an impassioned plea: The speaker is reaching beyond that which can be seen, not to the stars but to "whatever scattered them." He seems to find his answer:

> When I close my eyes, magically,
> it's here. This, this is what I need,
>   without lights or cities
> man-made and dying, somehow to know I'm known.

Though close study of McDonald's work reveals intricate and sophisticated religious thinking throughout his career, this poem is arresting in its directness: The poet is not simply alluding to a story from the Bible or making observations about life that imply a Judeo-Christian understanding of evil and good. He is directly asking the most basic and speculative of theological questions. Further, he is doing so not in a narrative, but in something very close to a purely lyrical meditation.

OTHER MAJOR WORKS

SHORT FICTION: *A Band of Brothers: Stories from Vietnam*, 1989.

EDITED TEXT: *A "Catch-22" Casebook*, 1973 (with Frederick Kiley); *Texas Stories and Poems*, 1978 (with James P. White).

MISCELLANEOUS: *All That Matters: The Texas Plains in Photographs and Poems*, 1992 (with Janet M. Neugebauer); *Whatever the Wind Delivers: Celebrating West Texas and the Near Southwest*, 1999 (with Neugebauer).

BIBLIOGRAPHY

Beidler, Philip D. "Poets After Our War." In *Rewriting America: Vietnam Authors and Their Generation*. Athens: University of Georgia Press, 1991. Emphasizes the increasingly subtle and contextualized—but nevertheless important—role that Vietnam plays in the poet's work.

Gotera, Vicente F. "Walter McDonald: After the (Machine) Noise of Saigon." In *Radical Vision: Poetry by Vietnam Veterans*. Athens: University of Georgia Press, 1994. Examines Vietnam poetry in relation to traditional American interpretive myths. Particularly insightful on the thematic place of technology in McDonald's work.

Hobbs, Michael. "Walter McDonald." In *Updating the Literary West*, edited by Thomas J. Lyon et al. Fort Worth: Texas Christian University Press, 1997. Useful article that introduces the concept of "hardscrabble sublime." Claims *Witching on Hardscrabble* (1985) is McDonald's best volume.

Tippens, Darryl, ed. *Christianity and Literature* 49, no. 2 (Winter, 2000). Special issue focusing on McDonald's work. Includes an interview by Tippens, four articles on McDonald's poetry, and a select bibliography.

William Jolliff

PHYLLIS McGINLEY

Born: Ontario, Oregon; March 21, 1905
Died: New York, New York: February 22, 1978

PRINCIPAL POETRY

On the Contrary, 1934
One More Manhattan, 1937
A Pocket Full of Wry, 1940
Husbands Are Difficult: Or, The Book of Oliver Ames, 1941
Stones from a Glass House: New Poems, 1946
A Short Walk from the Station, 1951
The Love Letters of Phyllis McGinley, 1954
Merry Christmas, Happy New Year, 1958
Times Three: Selected Verse from Three Decades, with Seventy New Poems, 1960
A Wreath of Christmas Legends, 1967

OTHER LITERARY FORMS

In addition to light verse, Phyllis McGinley wrote several books for children using a variety of different styles. These include Christmas stories, variations on traditional tales, fantasies, verse tales, and alphabet books. Some of her most popular works for children are *The Most Wonderful Doll in the World* (1950) and *The Year Without a Santa Claus* (1957).

McGinley also wrote several collections of essays. In both *The Province of the Heart* (1959) and *Sixpence in Her Shoe* (1964), she dealt primarily with the role of the housewife and with life in the suburbs. In *Saint-Watching* (1969), she portrayed the lives of several saints, emphasizing their warmth and humanity rather than their sanctity.

ACHIEVEMENTS

One of Phyllis McGinley's greatest achievements was to make poetry accessible to a wide audience. This was one of the main reasons she chose to write about everyday people and occurrences. As she commented in an interview that appeared in *Time* magazine in 1965: "At a time when poetry has become the property of the universities and not the common people, I have a vast number of people who have become my readers. I have kept the door open and perhaps led them to greater poetry."

In addition to her popular success, McGinley received many academic honors and awards. *The Love Letters of Phyllis McGinley* received the Edna St. Vincent Millay Memorial Award, and *Times Three* won the

Pulitzer Prize. She was elected a member of the National Institute for Arts and Letters and was selected to read her work at the White House. *Wonderful Time* was honored as one of the best books for children of 1966 by *The New York Times*. She received honorary doctorates from many institutions.

BIOGRAPHY

Although Phyllis McGinley was born in Ontario, Oregon, her family moved to a ranch near Iliff, Oregon, when she was only three months old. Both she and her brother felt isolated and friendless there because of the remote nature of her home. In spite of the fact that she entertained herself by developing a love for reading, she was much happier when the family moved to Ogden, Utah, after her father's death.

After her graduation from the University of Utah, McGinley taught school in Ogden. Since she had won numerous literary awards in college, she began submitting her poetry to various national magazines. She later moved to New Rochelle, New York, and began teaching English at a junior high school. At first, her poems were lyrical and serious. An editor at *The New Yorker*, however, encouraged her to begin writing light verse—which had the advantage of paying more than serious poetry did. After the principal of the school objected to her moonlighting as a writer, she gave up teaching and moved to New York City, first working at an advertising agency and then accepting a job as the poetry editor at *Town and Country* magazine.

In 1936, McGinley married Bill Hayden, and the couple moved to the New York suburb of Larchmont. Her first daughter, Julie, was born in 1939, followed by Patsy in 1941. McGinley enjoyed her role as a housewife and mother. She incorporated her experiences into her poetry, continuing to send her work to a wide range of magazines and publishing several volumes of verse. The triumphs and tragedies of daily living became the source of much of the humor in her work.

Because McGinley often championed the role of the suburban housewife, she was frequently viewed as a defender of domesticity against the attacks of such writers as Betty Friedan, who in *The Feminine Mystique* (1963) equated the role of a housewife with a type of mental illness. Although McGinley, as well as some of her critics,

pointed out that as a successful author, she was hardly a typical homebody. Her two books of essays, *The Province of the Heart* and *Sixpence in Her Shoe*, present witty and charming pictures of coping with daily life in the home.

After her husband died in 1972, McGinley moved to an apartment in New York City. She resided there until she died in 1978.

ANALYSIS

One of the best modern writers of light verse, Phyllis McGinley stands out for presenting the reader with clever and recognizable portraits of the twentieth century world. While a few of her poems are dated because they are so closely connected with a particular time period, most survive because they deal with everyday situations: visiting family, shopping, fighting with the machines in the household that never seem to work correctly, waiting in line, listening to the dentist. These poems are based on her own experiences and present a wry and witty view of urban and suburban life. However, McGinley also derives many of her poems from newspaper headlines. In fact, glancing through *Times Three* shows that many of her best poems were inspired by her responses to headlines that she found intriguing, humorous, or outrageous. In his introduction to this Pulitzer Prize-winning book, the poet W. H. Auden comments that she is "coolly realistic . . . she merely observes what is the case with deadly accuracy."

McGinley's work stands out not only for her unique perspective, but also for her technical virtuosity. She experiments successfully with many different poetic styles and rhyme forms, adapting the sonnet as easily as the nursery rhyme to her themes.

STONES FROM A GLASS HOUSE

Stones from a Glass House collects primarily poems that were published in various magazines during the years from 1940 through 1946. The first portion of the book, "The Time Is Now," contains sonnets describing suburban living, recording such incidents as upsets at a beauty parlor and the scene at a railroad station when the commuter train returns from New York. It both laments the problems and praises the joys of middle-class life. For example, in "The Chosen People," the speaker uses the style and rhythm of a nursery rhyme to complain about taxes: "I'm a middle-bracket person with a middle-bracket spouse/ And we live together gaily in a middle-bracket house." On the other hand, the speaker in "Confessions of a Reluctant Optimist" describes herself as unable to find anything to disparage about her life.

The second section, "It Seems Like Yesterday," focuses on war poems. While McGinley still employs the ironic language, rhythm, and style of light verse, most of these poems present serious subjects. In addition, many view war from the woman's point of view: the wife, the mother, the villager walking through the park who mourns the absence of the young men. The elegant sonnet "Dido of Tunisia" comments not only on war's destruction but also on its futility. "Hamburg" mourns for the destruction of that city, noting that "Gretchen for her children weeps no louder/ Than Rachel wept."

A SHORT WALK FROM THE STATION

McGinley opens *A Short Walk from the Station* volume with an essay, "Suburbia, of Thee I Sing," that challenges the "literary cliché" of the suburbs as a barren wasteland where conformity and hypocrisy flourish. Instead, she describes a suburb as an attractive and comfortable location, filled with ordinary people who have a mixture of virtues and vices. She emphasizes the role of such a place in raising children. Three of the sections in the book, "Landscape with Figures," "Sonnets from Westchester," and "Views from a Terrace," contain both new and old poems gathered to provide examples for the thesis McGinley sets forth in the introduction. This defense does not blunt her sharp observation of the world around her. In "Reactionary Essay on Applied Science," she parallels the major discoveries of the scientific world with those minor ones that make life simpler: "Deciding on reflection calm,/ Mankind is better off with trifles:/ With Band-Aid rather than the bomb,/ With safety match than safety rifles."

THE LOVE LETTERS OF PHYLLIS MCGINLEY

Linda Welshimer Wagner points out that McGinley's later poems are more technically complex than her earlier work. McGinley adopts more elements of free verse and begins to "move from accentual to syllabic verse," where the length of the lines depends not on accented words but the total number of syllables. This gives many of the poems in *The Love Letters of Phyllis McGinley* a greater freedom of movement and expression.

The selection of poems, as well, includes a wide range of subjects and styles. The volume begins with "Apologia," a rather wistful acknowledgment of the need for the middle-aged to accept and even celebrate the world as it is, being thankful "for the lily,/ Spot and all." Several other poems also deal with growing older and all that means for a mother. "Ballade of Lost Objects" begins with a catalog of items that disappear around the house, a technique McGinley often uses. However, the last line in the first stanza shifts the poem's tone abruptly as the speaker wonders *And where in the world did the children vanish?* Another poem developing this theme even further is "The Doll House." McGinley approaches a blank-verse style in this poem, which gives it a freer and more narrative tone. As in "Ballade of Lost Objects," an extensive catalog of details provides a backdrop for a mother's musings as the objects in the dollhouse remain unchanging:

> The fire
> Painted upon the hearth would not turn cold,
> Or the constant hour change, or the heart tire
> Of what it must pursue,
> Or the guest depart, or anything here be old.

TIMES THREE

In her early books, McGinley explores themes that she would use throughout her career. One of the clearest ways to identify these subjects is to review *Times Three: Selected Verse from Three Decades, with Seventy New Poems*. McGinley groups the poems she selected for inclusion both chronologically and thematically. Thus, the section titled "The Thirties" includes poems from *On the Contrary* and *One More Manhattan*. In addition, several poems from *A Pocket Full of Wry* and even *Husbands Are Difficult* are also represented here, since they were first published in popular magazines in the 1930's. She then organizes these poems into four distinct categories. The first, "Personal Remarks," includes humorous reflections on a wide range of subjects with universal appeal. For example, "Melancholy Reflections After a Lost Argument" cleverly captures the frustration most people experience when they come up with the perfect response just a bit too late. In "Lament of the Normal Child," the speaker longs for a complex or fixation, since that seems the only way to attract adult attention. "On the Town," as the title suggests, presents her portraits of urban life. "The House of Oliver Ames" contains a series of poems dealing with husbands and marriage.

The final section, "The Threadbare Times," includes more serious subjects. "Trinity Place" uses irony to convey the suffering of the unemployed during the Depression, contrasting the pigeons who "preen" in a churchyard with the unemployed men, sitting idle on the benches: "It is only the men who are hungry. The pigeons are fed." "Carol with Variations" was inspired by a newspaper headline, which appeared during Christmas week in 1936. It noted that the armies of the world currently contained more than 7.6 million men. She parodies several different carols to pair the original lyrics extolling peace with the realities of the decade:

> Sing hosanna, sing Noel.
> Sing the gunner and the shell.
> Sing the candle, sing the lamp,
> Sing the Concentration Camp.
> Sing the Season born anew
> Sing of exile for the Jew,

OTHER MAJOR WORKS

PLAY: *Small Wonder*, pr. 1948.

NONFICTION: *The Province of the Heart*, 1959; *Sixpence in Her Shoe*, 1964; *Saint-Watching*, 1969; *Confessions of a Reluctant Optimist*, 1973.

CHILDREN'S LITERATURE: *The Horse Who Lived Upstairs*, 1944; *The Plain Princess*, 1945; *All Around the Town*, 1948; *A Name for Kitty*, 1948; *The Most Wonderful Doll in the World*, 1950; *Blunderbus*, 1951; *The Horse Who Had His Picture in the Paper*, 1951; *The Make-Believe Twins*, 1953; *The Year Without a Santa Claus*, 1957; *Lucy McLockett*, 1959; *Sugar and Spice: The ABC of Being a Girl*, 1960; *Mince Pie and Mistletoe*, 1961; *Boys Are Awful*, 1962; *The B Book*, 1962; *A Girl and Her Room*, 1963; *How Mrs. Santa Claus Saved Christmas*, 1963; *Wonderful Time*, 1966.

BIBLIOGRAPHY

Allen, Everett S. *Famous American Humorous Poets*. New York: Dodd, Mead, 1968. The chapter on McGinley provides a good introduction to her work, including a biography, evaluation of McGinley's stature as a poet, and a discussion of her themes and style.

Hasley, Louis. "The Poetry of Phyllis McGinley." *Catholic World*, August, 1970, 211-215. Hasley analyzes the different verse patterns that McGinley used throughout her career. He demonstrates the range of McGinley's technical artistry by comparing her work to a set of standards for judging the various categories of light verse. He concludes that her work contains many characteristics of the Cavalier poets of seventeenth century.

Richart, Bette. "The Light Touch." *Commonweal* 9 (December, 1960): 277-279. Richart praises McGinley's use of poetic devices and her technical skill in the composition of her poetry. However, she believes that McGinley's choice of subject matter often weakens her poetry, making it trivial. She also finds McGinley's tone in some of these works is overly complacent. Richart contrasts such light poems with McGinley's more serious work on such topics as age and youth, such as "The Dollhouse," a work that she ranks as serious poetry.

Semansky, Chris. "Overview of 'Reactionary Essay on Applied Science.'" In *Poetry for Students*. Vol. 9. Detroit: Gale, 2000. Semansky discusses the dispassionate point of view that McGinley adopts in this poem, as well as her effective use of catalog and contrast. The entry also contains a biography and bibliography.

Sullivan, Kay. "From Suburbs to Saints: Phyllis McGinley." *Catholic World*, September, 1957, 420-425. This article is a source of rich biographical detail.

"The Telltale Hearth." *Time* 18 (June, 1965): 74-78. In this interview, McGinley provides many anecdotes about her life, as well as describing her views on poetry, feminism, and her role in modern literature.

Wagner, Linda Welshimer. *Phyllis McGinley*. New York: Twayne, 1971. Wagner identifies and analyzes the major themes in McGinley's work throughout her career, as well as noting the technical development of her poetic skills. Several poems are analyzed in depth. One chapter is devoted to a comparison of the characteristics of light verse and serious poetry. While the main focus of the book is McGinley's poetry, her essays and children's books are also discussed briefly. A helpful chronology and annotated bibliography are included.

Mary E. Mahony

THOMAS MCGRATH

Born: Near Sheldon, North Dakota; November 20,
1916
Died: Minneapolis, Minnesota; September 20, 1990

PRINCIPAL POETRY

Longshot O'Leary's Garland of Practical Poesie,
1949

Letter to an Imaginary Friend: Parts One and Two,
1970

The Movie at the End of the World: Collected Poems,
1973

Passages Toward the Dark, 1982

Echoes Inside the Labyrinth, 1983

*Letter to an Imaginary Friend: Parts Three and
Four*, 1985

Selected Poems: 1938-1988, 1988

Death Songs, 1991

OTHER LITERARY FORMS

"Conquering Horse," "Choruses for the City," and
"Paradise" (all undated) are three of more than a dozen
screenplays completed by Thomas McGrath. These are
primarily sociopolitical documentaries, written for such
noted directors as Mike Cimino. McGrath was the author of two novels—*The Gates of Ivory, the Gates of
Horn* (1957, revised 1987) and *This Coffin Has No Handles* (1988)—and completed a number of interviews and
brief biographical and nonfiction prose pieces, as well as
short literary essays. He helped to found or served as editor of *Crazy Horse, Masses and Mainstream*, and the
California Quarterly.

ACHIEVEMENTS

Well into his lifetime Thomas McGrath began to receive recognition in the upper Midwest. Some readers
have complained, however, of critical neglect on a wider
scale, which they attribute to literary and political biases.
(A few of McGrath's works were initially received more
positively outside the United States than within it.) His
incredible formal range may have precluded his neat assimilation into any particular literary camp. He produced traditional folk ballads, surrealist free verse, nar-

rative blank verse, and prose poems; he published a
collection of very short, haiku-like lyrics, as well as a
sprawling, two-volume, experimental autobiography in
verse, comparable to Walt Whitman's *Leaves of Grass*
(1855), William Wordsworth's *The Prelude* (1850), William Carlos Williams's *Paterson* (1963), and Hart Crane's
The Bridge (1930). He wrote social satire and political
invective as well as intimate, personal meditations.

Despite his somewhat ambiguous or incomplete
critical acceptance, however, McGrath was awarded—
primarily late in his career—a number of distinguished
prizes and honors: the Lenore Marshall Poetry Prize
(1989), the Shelley Memorial Award (1990), a Rhodes
Scholarship, an Amy Lowell Traveling Fellowship in
Poetry, two National Endowment for the Arts Fellowships, a Guggenheim Fellowship, and two Bush fellowships. Not long before his death, he was awarded a
Senior Fellowship by the Literature Program of the
National Endowment for the Arts and was presented the
Distinguished Achievement Award by the Society for
Western Literature.

BIOGRAPHY

Thomas McGrath was born and reared on a farm
near Sheldon, North Dakota, southwest of Fargo. His
parents were second-generation Irish homesteaders, and
the land they farmed was remote, desolate, and climati-
cally extreme. When roads were impassable and the
family's radios inoperable, Tom's father recited poems,
sang, and told stories to the family. From an early age,
Tom assisted the seasonal crews on their steam threshers
and witnessed the lingering Wobbly agitation of that
period. In 1939 he was graduated from the University of
North Dakota with a Rhodes Scholarship. His financial
lot throughout undergraduate school, however, had been
poor, reducing him at times to life on the streets. (According to one story, he even stole potatoes one night
from the garden of a university president.) Such hardships no doubt played their roles in his lifelong commitment to socialist reform and revolution. In 1940 he attended graduate school in English at Louisiana State
University, where he studied with Cleanth Brooks and
worked with Alan Swallow in the founding of Swallow
Press. Throughout graduate school his interest in the
plight of the working class flourished, and, upon gradua-

tion with his M.A., and after teaching briefly at a college in Maine, he worked as a labor organizer on the New York waterfront in 1942. He served in the United States Army during World War II and then finally took advantage of his Rhodes Scholarship by attending the University of Oxford.

Back in the United States, McGrath taught at Los Angeles State College from 1951 to 1953. During this time he was called before the House of Representatives Committee on Un-American Activities. His subsequent blacklisting resulted in employment problems for many years, and he was forced to take a variety of temporary odd jobs, including work in a wooden-toy factory. He spent time in Greece, Portugal, Great Britain, and South America, and for ten years he taught at state universities in North Dakota and Minnesota. In 1983 he retired to Minneapolis, Minnesota, where he died in September, 1990.

Thomas McGrath

ANALYSIS

Any glance at Thomas McGrath's oeuvre reveals him to be a poet of formal playfulness. Though his work through the years shows contemporary influences, he never slips into any predictable mode or style and never abandons the concerns he embraced so passionately as a young student in the Depression. His key concerns seem to be human suffering brought about by political and economic oppression, a desire for transformation, and the exile that results from efforts to bring about change. His astounding output—including the two-volume epic *Letter to an Imaginary Friend*—is far too much to examine in a brief overview.

"A LITTLE SONG ABOUT CHARITY"

In his earliest work, McGrath's key themes appear mainly in political terms. Indeed, his first several books, selections from which were gathered in *The Movie at the End of the World*, are unarguably Marxist and at times didactic. Each poem has aesthetic integrity, its political concerns being integral rather than extraneous or imposed. Nevertheless, those interests are, in many of these earlier works, particularly overt. An extreme example is "A Little Song About Charity," from *Longshot*

O'Leary's Garland of Practical Poesie. In this playful satire with its songlike refrain, the speaker mocks the so-called charity of bourgeois capitalists:

> The boss came around at Christmas—
> Oh smiling like a lamb—
> He made me a pair of gloves
> And then cut off my hands.

This boss comes around again to give the speaker shoes for his birthday, only to cut off the speaker's feet as well. By the end, the readers are told that if they care about their family and about the working class, they must carefully reserve their affections: "Don't waste it on the cockroach boss/ But keep your love at home."

"A Little Song About Charity" is one of the most message-oriented and two-dimensional of McGrath's earliest works. Certainly the whole of *Longshot O'Leary Garland of Practical Poesie* is "practical" or utilitarian, as its title suggests and as the Marxist view of art instructs. Yet a number of the early poems reveal as well the complexities with which McGrath struggled throughout his writing career.

"THE DIALECTICS OF LOVE"

"The Dialectics of Love" shows a merging of traditional poetic concerns, private dilemmas, and political ideology. The poem is made up of rhymed couplets, a pattern traditionally suited to poems of wit (such as those of Alexander Pope). Section 1 describes an unfaithful lover's corpse, the earth above him ironically pressing "closer . . . than any lover." The man who in life sought freedom from permanence now experiences the most terrible permanence. In section 2, the perspective widens to include "the human winter,/ And civil war in every sector." Typically for McGrath, personal concerns in and of themselves are not worthy material for poetry (his own marriage was very likely failing at about the time this poem was written). He resists the merely personal, and where it does appear, he connects it nearly always to larger, universal concerns. In "The Dialectics of Love," infidelity in an individual relationship becomes emblematic of an essential human conflict: the desire for security and permanence versus the contrasting desire for freedom. While section 1 derides the changeable lover, section 2 works its way to a realization of the world's inherent mutability. Therefore, "He must seem false who would be true." In other words, the one who is faithful, who is always the same, now seems to this speaker false to life itself.

Characteristically, McGrath next relates this "dialectic" between conflicting human needs to the Marxist dialectic, or class struggle. Section 3 sees "Over the public eye and lip/ The seal of personal ownership." The desire to own property is like the wish to keep a relationship constant, or the desire to resist time's havoc. Because such constancy is folly, "personal love/ Changes, if it is pure enough." In the last lines of the poem, the corpse seen earlier, lying in the permanence of death, is now viewed instead as subject to constant change, "the transience of the winding year." The idea in section 1 is thus neatly reversed in section 3: In death people are given over entirely to the changes that natural forces inflict.

"The Dialectics of Love," with its metaphysical wit and proper dose of ambiguity, demonstrates the influence of its literary period and of McGrath's graduate study. Its archaic inversions and poeticizing ("When right hand and left divided are/ And the split heart cannot love the more") further shows it to be an immature work. Typically, however, McGrath is more than competent with whatever style he chooses, and "The Dialectics of Love" is no exception.

ALIENATION

Other poems of *The Movie at the End of the World* reveal McGrath's themes somewhat more characteristically. The metaphysical permanence versus flux dialectic often transmutes into the more earthy conflict of community membership versus exile. The speaker of these poems is solitary, one who watches from a distance, excluded. The sometimes desperately poor young man who left his Irish family's farm for college must indeed have felt a rift: While his education separated him to some extent from his family, his rural roots separated him from the academic communities at the University of North Dakota and Louisiana State. In the first part of his personal epic, *Letter to an Imaginary Friend*, he describes this transition from farm life to college and his first encounter with a college dean: "a pithy, pursy bastard" who winds up saying "nothing but *money money*." The farm boy cannot accept his college scholarship, because the rules require that he live in a dormitory, and he lacks the necessary resources. As a burgeoning Communist in the 1940's and 1950's, McGrath no doubt felt himself alienated more profoundly than ever, and his blacklisting in 1953 both confirmed and enforced this exile.

McGrath was excluded, however, in more ways than one. For most of his career, he was something of a literary outlaw, a status described early in his "Ars Poetica: Or: Who Lives in the Ivory Tower?" Here the speaker suggests some possible roles for the poet: the craftsman and wordsmith, the political caller-to-arms, the documenter of street life and of the real conditions of the working class. Each such suggestion is knocked down, however, by the voices of housewives ("Get out of my technicolor dream with your tragic view and your verses"), editors ("take the red flags out of your poem—we mustn't offend the censor"), hobos on the street ("I respect your profession as much as my own, but it don't pay off when you're hungry"), and even representatives of academia ("Your feet are muddy, you son-of-a-bitch, get out of our ivory tower"). McGrath indeed did not fit neatly into any niche, literary or otherwise, and his exile is evident throughout his work.

TRANSFORMATION

This theme of separation typically connects with a companion concern for transformation, particularly in three early poems, "A Long Way Outside Yellowstone," "Love in a Bus," and "Such Simple Love." In each of these pieces the speaker comes upon or is accidentally privy to a couple's lovemaking—an awkward occasion that would doubtless reinforce an already lonely person's separateness. In each of these poems the speaker remarks approvingly of the couple's disregard for convention: In two of the poems the couples are in public places, and in one they are unusually rambunctious, causing the building the speaker also occupies to shake dramatically. In each poem as well the speaker notes that love, however fleeting and inglorious, is the only thing of permanence and worth in the human world, perhaps the only means of transcendence: "their hands touching deny you,/ Becoming, poor blinded beggars, pilgrims on the road to heaven." For McGrath, the only heaven possible is one that happens in material terms. He had perhaps seen too much of tangible human misery—life on the streets, the financial struggles of his family—to accept some dubious, remote, Platonic realm, mystical transcendence, or religious salvation. The material determinism of Marx reflected and reinforced the young poet's inclinations in this regard: The world evolves through material, rather than spiritual, struggle between the classes, and these clashes will necessarily result in some ultimate material change, a revolution and worker's utopia right here on earth.

Despite this ever-present desire for transformation, McGrath never appears naïve. Most of his pieces, even the earliest, engage the theme of incapacity or futility, the ambiguities attendant on any plan for worldly change. In "Such Simple Love," a caustically cynical poem, he says, "But love without direction is a cheap blanket/ And even if it did no one any harm,/ No one is warm." In "A Long Way Outside Yellowstone" there is a similar epigrammatic statement: "Poverty of all but spirit turns up love like aces/ That weren't in the deck at all." In other words, genuine love comes only when material luxuries are stripped away, or when one's material well-being is otherwise nonexistent. This is hardly an optimistic sentiment. In "The Heroes of Childhood," the speaker laments his loss of faith in human gods, including his Marxist heroes. Such poems as "A Letter for Marian" reflect an essential isolation and loss of comradeship, community, and love: "When the telephone

rings there's a war on each end./ The message arrives, but there's no one to sign for it."

"You Can Start the Poetry Now"

By the end of section 3 of *The Movie at the End of the World*, McGrath's central concerns and formal virtuosity are more than evident. The fourth and final section, titled "New Poems," continues the development of those concerns. It also heralds, however, a more immediate, spoken voice, a still bolder formal range, and the influence of literary trends of the late 1950's and the 1960's.

This section begins with the playful prose poem "You Can Start the Poetry Now: Or, News from Crazy Horse." The poem gives an account of an actual poetry reading, with the alternating voices of a poet who has stood up to perform and the admonitions of the audience he faces. The poet begins seemingly in mid-thought, with total disingenuousness: "—I guess all I'm trying to say is I saw Crazy Horse die for/ a split level swimming pool in a tree-house owned by/ a Pawnee-Warner Brothers psychiatrist." The audience interrupts to remind him gently that he can "start the poetry now." The poet, however, continues his previous thoughts, and the audience continually breaks in, increasingly loudly and angrily, to insist that he "START THE POETRY!! START THE POETRY NOW!!" Something of an antipoem, this piece seems to mock conventional notions of the poet's relationship to his public. Certainly this poem itself is formally unconventional.

Yet "You Can Start the Poetry Now" is immediately followed by an end-rhymed poem in six-line stanzas and iambics. McGrath is simply not a predictable poet, and even in many later poems he surprises the reader with dramatic shifts in form and voice. The "New Poems" section reveals the influence of William Carlos Williams ("Legend" appears to be written in variable feet), of Wallace Stevens (the metaphysics and imagism of "from: A Sound of One Hand"), and Whitman ("Return to Marsh Street" with its long cadenced lines). Contemporary influences are also apparent. Through the work of such writers as Robert Bly, many American poets of the 1960's discovered South American and Asian literature, and McGrath was no exception. Such lyrics as "For Alvaro" and "Old Friends" are haiku-like in their brevity and lack of abstraction, while "Hoot!" suggests the surreal imagist mode that many writers of the 1960's adopted and that McGrath was to explore further in later books. "Praises" is a tribute to the sensual and metaphorical lushness of vegetables, much along the lines of Pablo Neruda's celebrated odes to socks and salt. Numerous other poems from this section show McGrath's interest in South American writing.

While his later work is somewhat dark, this last section of *The Movie at the End of the World* is for the most part one of relative lightness. He even presents a friendly parody of Bly's poems, the titles of which often begin with a present participle. (McGrath's parody is called "Driving Towards Boston I Run Across One of Robert Bly's Old Poems.") The section ends with an amusing (though serious) rejection of capitalism and the military machine in "Gone Away Blues," as didactic as the much earlier "A Little Song About Charity" but more light-hearted. Some thirty years after his first poems about the plight of the working class, about exile and longing for revolution, McGrath here expresses, with seeming ease, the same concerns.

Lᴀᴛᴇʀ ᴘᴏᴇᴛʀʏ

Probably McGrath's most brilliant output came after *The Movie at the End of the World*. The poems of *Passage Toward the Dark*, for example, have an immediacy, a mature insight, and a dark richness that, arguably, the early and middle-period work simply does not show. Some of his later motifs are more ambitious as well. In the latter part of *Letter to an Imaginary Friend*, McGrath develops a new symbol for revolution: the Blue Star Kachina, a Hopi spirit of radical change, suggesting the transforming power of the imagination and of poetry itself, in all its shapes and modes. Certainly McGrath's poems, which *The Movie at the End of the World* aptly displays, are themselves very like the Kachina. For poetry as versatile and engaging as any in the twentieth century, a reader would do well to explore the work of Thomas McGrath.

Oᴛʜᴇʀ ᴍᴀᴊᴏʀ ᴡᴏʀᴋꜱ

ʟᴏɴɢ ꜰɪᴄᴛɪᴏɴ: *The Gates of Ivory, the Gates of Horn*, 1957, revised 1987; *This Coffin Has No Handles*, 1985 (serial), 1988 (book).

Bɪʙʟɪᴏɢʀᴀᴘʜʏ

Di Piero, W. S. "Politics in Poetry: The Case of Thomas McGrath." *New England Review* 17, no. 4 (Fall, 1995): 41. An analysis of the political aspects of McGrath's *Letter to an Imaginary Friend*.

Gibbons, Reginald, and Terrence Des Pres, eds. *Thomas McGrath: Life and the Poem*. Urbana: University of Illinois Press, 1992. Originally published as a special issue of *TriQuarterly* in 1987, contains some valuable biographical information on McGrath, including a firsthand account of his waterfront years as a labor organizer and agitator. It includes the reminiscences of former students as well.

McGrath, Thomas. "Surviving as a Writer: The Politics of Poetry/The Poetry of Politics." Interview by Jim Dochniak. *Sez: A Multi-Racial Journal of Poetry and People's Culture* 2/3 (1981): A-L, special section. This is a twelve-page transcript of an informal interview at the University of Minnesota. McGrath here touches on the childhood sources of his writing, his socialist politics, and his international travels. He distinguishes between tactical and strategic poetry and discusses his struggle to survive financially.

McKenzie, James. "Conversations with Thomas McGrath." *North Dakota Quarterly* 56 (Fall, 1988): 135-150. Compiled here are anecdotes and excerpts from McGrath discussions, interviews, and panel events at the University of North Dakota throughout the years. Topics include McGrath's association with the Beat poets and the autobiographical background to *Letter to an Imaginary Friend*. His former wife Alice McGrath joins in.

North Dakota Quarterly 50 (Fall, 1982). In this special issue, titled *Dream Champ: A Festschrift for Thomas McGrath*, an assortment of writers, students and friends reflect, sometimes whimsically, on McGrath and his work. Edited by Robert W. Lewis, it includes poems written in honor of McGrath and important essays on his filmscript career and his politics, as well as McGrath's "Statement to the House Committee on Un-American Activities."

Stern, Frederick, ed. *The Revolutionary Poet in the United States*. Columbia: University of Missouri Press, 1988. A two-hundred-page collection of critical essays, retrospectives, and scholarship on McGrath. This book includes work by Diane Wakoski, Hayden Carruth, Studs Terkel, and E. P. Thompson. The volume is a good collection of supplementary material as well, including a chronology of works, biographical sketch, and complete bibliography.

Cynthia Nichols;
bibliography updated by the editors

ANTONIO MACHADO

Born: Seville, Spain; July 26, 1875
Died: Collioure, France; February 22, 1939

PRINCIPAL POETRY

Soledades, 1902 (dated 1903)
Soledades, galerías, y otros poemas, 1907 (*Solitudes, Galleries, and Other Poems*, 1987)
Campos de Castilla, 1912 (*The Castilian Camp*, 1982)
Poesías completas, 1917
Nuevas canciones, 1924
De un cancionero apócrifo, 1926
Obras, 1940
Eighty Poems of Antonio Machado, 1959
Antonio Machado, 1973
Selected Poems of Antonio Machado, 1978
Selected Poems, 1982
Times Alone: Selected Poems of Antonio Machado, 1983
Roads Dreamed Clear Afternoons: An Anthology of the Poetry of Antonio Machado, 1994

OTHER LITERARY FORMS

Although the majority of Antonio Machado's sparse published work is poetry, he collaborated with his brother, Manuel, on a number of plays for the Madrid stage. These began in 1926 with adaptations of Spanish dramas of the Golden Age and culminated in 1929 with the very successful *La Lola se va a los puertos* (the *Lola* goes off to sea). The last of their plays to be staged in Madrid was *El hombre que murió en la guerra* (the man who died in the war), in 1941. Several series of prose commentaries on a variety of subjects, principally literary and philosophical, originally appeared in periodicals and were eventually collected and published in 1936 in the somewhat amorphous yet interesting *Juan de Mairena* (English translation, 1963).

ACHIEVEMENTS

Antonio Machado was one of the the two great lyric poets of Spain's *generación del 98* (Generation of '98), the other being Juan Ramón Jiménez. In 1927, Machado was elected to the Royal Spanish Academy.

BIOGRAPHY

Antonio Machado y Ruiz was born into an interesting family of relatively successful professionals. His paternal grandfather had been to the New World, studied medicine in Paris, practiced for a time in Seville, published a philosophical and scientific journal there, and became governor of the province. Machado's father studied but never practiced law, devoting himself to the study of Spanish folklore, especially flamenco song and poetry, and publishing four important collections. His mother was a vivacious woman who dedicated herself to her family and four sons, most particularly to Antonio, who was attached to her throughout life and whose death preceded hers by only a few days. Machado's memory of the home where he was born and for eight years led a peaceful existence in charming surroundings never left him.

When Machado's grandfather received a professorship in Madrid, the family accompanied him there. Life in the capital was turbulent and somewhat more hazardous than in Seville. Machado and two of his brothers were enrolled in the Free Institute, a private school founded by Francisco Giner de los Ríos, a friend of the Machado family, and dominated by the principles of *Krausismo*, named after an obscure German philosopher Karl Christian Friedrich Krause (1781-1832), whose system of philosophy, which attempted to combine pantheism and theism, was promoted in Spain by Julián Sanz del Río in an effort to establish a new, liberal educational system. Although he completed his secondary education in Catholic institutions, Machado was to remain faithful to the tenets of *Krausismo* and anticlerical to the end. At the conclusion of this first phase of his education, Machado's family was undergoing a reversal of fortune, and in 1892 and 1895, respectively, his father and grandfather died.

Antonio Machado

Although Machado became "the man of the family," he did not assume any responsibilities. Rather, he led a somewhat Bohemian life, as before, and began a literary career by writing satirical sketches for *La caricatura* under the pseudonym of "Cabellera" ("Long Hair")—his brother Manuel wrote as "Polilla" ("Moth")—meanwhile thinking of entering the theater. In 1899, Antonio and Manuel at last obtained paid positions as translators and editors for Garnier Brothers in Paris. What they accomplished at Garnier's is not clear, but they did frequent the literary circles of Paris and became acquainted with many of the celebrities of the day, such as Jean Moréas and Darío. At the same time that the Machados were exploring new interests, they were reading, discussing, and beginning to write poetry.

Little is known of Antonio's first efforts in France and Spain, but the small volume *Soledades* appeared in 1902 (although it was dated 1903) and soon began to enjoy some success in Madrid. Dissatisfied with the *Modernista* aestheticism of these early poems, however, Machado immediately started work on an expanded *Soledades*, in which the spiritual and the ethical would dominate and

from which a number of the earlier poems would be excluded. During this period of rapid growth and maturation, the great influence on the poet was that of Miguel de Unamuno y Jugo, who, in an open letter of 1904 in *Helios*, had urged Machado to abandon the principle of art for art's sake. In an article of 1905 on Unamuno's *La vida de Don Quijote y Sancho* (1905; *Life of Don Quijote and Sancho*, 1927), Machado admires his mentor's recreation of Miguel de Cervantes' hero, in which spirit and feeling transform ideas into poetry.

As a result of his contact with Unamuno, Machado abandoned his semi-Bohemian life and, during 1906 and 1907, prepared for a serious profession. Considering himself too old to attend a university, he studied French and Spanish language and literature at home and passed the arduous examinations to become a professor. He was appointed to a post at the Institute in Soria, in the heart of Old Castile, where he spent five years. Soria was not what it had been in ancient and medieval times, and the Institute ran pedagogically and politically in ways far removed from the principles of *Krausismo*. Patient and unassuming, Machado adjusted to the school's dull atmosphere, accepting old-fashioned patterns of unenthusiastic teaching and rote learning and ignoring local politics. His salvation lay in a few friendships with men of strong cultural interests and in the setting, steeped in the history and traditions of Spain.

Although an attractive man, Machado was timid and unaggressive with women, as was characteristic of the generally unromantic Generation of '98, who placed the blame on old Spanish customs regarding courtship. In late 1907, however, when he was past thirty, Machado met Leonor Izquierdo, the daughter of the family in whose boardinghouse he lived. The girl was only thirteen at the time, and Machado had to wait until she was fourteen to court her; they were married in 1909. A simple, provincial girl of limited education, augmented only by short stays in Madrid and Paris, Leonor nevertheless pleased her husband, and his love for her endured well beyond the grave. While they were in Paris in 1911, where Machado had been awarded a fellowship, she fell seriously ill with tuberculosis and died in 1912, some time after their return to Soria.

After his wife's death, Machado secured a transfer to Baeza in Jaén. His native Andalusia did not comfort him, however, and he sank into a depression that brought him close to suicide. His mother joined him for a time, which must have helped, and the success of *The Castilian Camp* made Machado aware of possessing a useful talent that he did not have the right to destroy. His faith in life was restored above all by a serious study of philosophy, including not only the work of modern philosophers, especially Henri Bergson, but also of the ancients and the languages to read them in the original. Unable to emulate Unamuno in his mastery of Greek, Machado nevertheless managed during several summers in Madrid to pass the necessary examinations to acquire his doctorate in 1918, at the age of forty-three.

In Baeza, Machado, older, heavier, careless of his appearance, resumed his old way of life. He was a seemingly aimless, somewhat lame, but indefatigable walker, usually alone. He sought the company of a few friends in a *tertulia*, at the Institute, or in the local pharmacy. Sometimes there would be an organized excursion to visit a point of interest; other times he would participate in the literary homages that are a part of Spanish culture, as when he read his "Desde mi rincón" (from my corner) in Aranjuez to honor José Martínez Ruiz (Azorín) and Castile. In 1915, Federico García Lorca, also an Andalusian, came to meet Machado at a cultural gathering in Baeza. Machado continued his work as a critic of Spanish society, concentrating on that of Baeza as most typical of the nation, except for Madrid. In his correspondence with Unamuno, he decried the state of religion in Baeza, dominated as it was by women. Both Machado and Unamuno were evolving from the Cain-Abel theme applied to Spain to a reaffirmation of Jesus's principle of Christian charity, yet Machado was not yet prepared to be an open activist.

Resigned but not satisfied in Baeza, and his inspiration grown thin, Machado obtained a post in Segovia in 1919. Segovia possessed everything that Soria had offered the poet and more, and Madrid was near. He would toil during the week in Segovia, pursuing other interests, especially in the theater, on his weekends in Madrid. Machado's scant poetic production during this time is varied in nature and high in quality. Outwardly he revealed little of his thoughts and feelings, but his mind was teeming with ideas and projects. One project that Machado eagerly worked to realize was the Segovian

activists' Popular University. To it he contributed, with all its political overtones, his philosophy of an active Christian brotherhood outside the hierarchy of the Church. Further, he delivered a lecture on Russian literature in which he declared the Revolution a failure because of a lack of philosophical tradition, but praised Russian literature for its universality, founded on Christian brotherhood.

In the mid-1920's, Machado began to feel discontented with his image as a somewhat eccentric widower and schoolteacher and as an isolated poet exploiting a few memories. Furthermore, the poets of the Generation of '98 were being displaced by those of the Generation of '27. It was time to do something new. During this period, Machado began to collaborate with his brother on a series of plays. His desire for rejuvenation also led him henceforth to use pseudonyms and to seek and find a new love. As Machado's passion was at first for an imaginary lady, it was long thought that his "Guiomar" did not exist, but he met Pilar Valderrama in 1926 and soon was in the grip of a schoolboy's infatuation for the mediocre poetess, who was also a married woman and a mother of three. It was an infatuation that, despite her coolness, he maintained for many years, deriving from it a metaphysical system for all consolation.

Except for the theater, Machado's significant production after 1925 consisted of two open-ended, interrelated works. In 1926, he published a brief, intensely concentrated book in prose and verse, *De un cancionero apócrifo* (apocryphal songbook), in which his first important persona, Abel Martín, expresses Machado's persistent belief that the poet is constantly torn between philosophy and poetry. All great poets must be backed by an implied metaphysics, so that, like Plato and perhaps Machado, poet and philosopher are one. The prose parts explain Machado's ideas, each of which is illustrated by a poem. The idea of love is expressed, for example, in "Canciones a Guiomar" ("Songs to Guiomar"). *Juan de Mairena*, published as a series in the *Diario de Madrid* and as a book in 1936, was entirely in prose, with increased emphasis by Mairena-Machado on political themes, for the Spanish Civil War was then in progress.

In 1927, Machado was elected to the Royal Spanish Academy, normally the greatest of honors for a man of

letters in Spain, but his increasingly revolutionary political ideas made him less sympathetic toward the conservative Academy, and he never completed his acceptance
speech. In 1931, under the Republic created after the ab-
dication of Alfonso XIII, Machado was appointed professor of Spanish literature at the Instituto Calderón de
la Barca in Madrid, but his hope for the future of Spain
could not keep him from putting all of his creative energy into *Juan de Mairena*, and he continued to be a dry,
dull professor.

In the tradition of civil wars, the Spanish Civil War
set the Machado brothers against each other, Manuel
producing propaganda for the Nationalists in Burgos,
Antonio performing the same service for the Republicans, first in Madrid, then in Valencia, and finally in
Barcelona. In January, 1939, as that city was about to
fall to the Nationalists, Antonio, his mother, and others
of the family fled to France. Both mother and son were
gravely ill, and Antonio died in Collioure of pneumonia
on February 22; his mother died three days later. After
the war, Machado's work continued to be honored, and
today the poet is widely recognized as one of the greatest of the Hispanic world.

ANALYSIS

The two great lyric poets of the *generación del 98*
(Generation of '98), Juan Ramón Jiménez and Antonio
Machado, were both Andalusians. The latter is equally
representative of Castile, however, in his preference
for intellectual, philosophical, and classical solutions to
existential problems. At first influenced by the *Modernismo* of Rubén Darío, who characterized him as profound, Machado soon abandoned that style as superficial in its constant striving for effect. For him, true
lyricism consisted of deep spirituality, of an animated
exchange between the soul and the world.

Machado's output was not large, and his themes
were few in number. His *Soledades* (solitudes) stressed
recollections of his youth and the dreams of a young
man in an Andalusian setting. In *The Castilian Camp*,
the landscape with which Machado communes is that of
the province which historically and culturally came to
epitomize Spain, and which after many years of residence he adopted as a second native region. In this collection as in *Nuevas canciones* (new songs), there are

also memories of Leonor Izquierdo, the young woman
whom Machado met, married, and soon lost to death in
Soria; wishes for the renaissance of Spain, shared with
the other intellectuals of the Generation of '98; and
meditations on the passage of time, life and death, and
the search for God. Discarding early in his career the
influences of Impressionism, French Symbolism, and
Hispano-American *Modernismo*, Machado forged a personal yet traditional style. His restrained, highly concentrated verse provided a valuable alternative to the aestheticism of his great contemporary, Jiménez.

SOLEDADES

The editions of Antonio Machado's *Soledades* dating from 1917 remained substantially unchanged and
represent the mature poet. Despite successive modifications and excisions, the collection continues to reflect
important influences of earlier poets. Gustavo Adolfo
Bécquer, a Sevillian post-Romantic who wrote intimate
lyrics in opposition to the realistic or bombastic poetry
of his day, persisted in Machado's literary affections.
Bécquer's idea of poetry as high perfection, impossible
to attain, is symbolized by a disdainful virgin or a fleeing doe (poem 42 in *Soledades*) or, as life became sad-
der and more disappointing, illusion turned to chimera
(poems 36 and 43). Like Bécquer, Machado became the
poet of reverie par excellence, creating brief, intimate
lyrics of traditional octosyllabic lines and subtle assonance.

Inevitably, he was somewhat influenced also by
Darío's work, especially the brilliant and erotic *Prosas
profanas* (1896; *Profane Hymns and Other Poems*, 1922).
Although Machado, like the others of his grave generation, eschewed the sensual, he fell under the spell of
Darío's "Era un aire suave" ("The Air Was Soft") when
he composed "Fantasía de una noche de abril" (fantasy of
an April night) in elegant *arte mayor*, musical twelve-
syllable lines of balanced hemistichs. Although Machado
relegated the poem to a minor section of *Soledades*, he
did not reject it. In the poem, the poet ardently seeks
love one night in Moorish Seville, but lacking confidence and considering himself an "anachronism," his
hopes disintegrate with the elaborate form of the poem.

Another strong though brief influence on Machado's
work was that of Paul Verlaine, particularly the Symbolist's use of nature, as in the garden with a fountain, to ex-

press the poet's feelings at a given moment, as well as the Edgar Allan Poe-like theme of fatality discovered through the French poet. Although by 1907 he had rejected most of his poems in the manner of Verlaine, Machado became a poet who, like Marcel Proust in his poetic novels, developed memory as a powerful instrument to reveal his inner self.

The poetic renovation accomplished by Machado's *Soledades*, a traditional title well suited to his purpose, progressively and rigorously excluded frank confession and the anecdotal as well as the stylistic excesses of Luis de Góngora y Argote. Here, Machado is preoccupied with time, and as he reworks a few symbols, such as the gallery, the road, the fountain, and the river, he seeks constantly to re-create the past and meditates on a possibly better future. Many lines in these simple poems strike deep and lasting chords in the reader responsive to the same existential problems.

THE CASTILIAN CAMP AND NUEVAS CANCIONES

Although somewhat late in joining Unamuno, Azorín, and Pío Baroja in their celebration of Castile, with *The Castilian Camp* Machado earned membership in the Generation of '98, the only poet to do so, for Jiménez chose not to write on the Spanish theme. Influenced above all by Unamuno and Azorín, considerable portions of *Nuevas canciones* exploited the theme further. Machado dealt with the problems and destiny of Castile and Spain, centered on Soria as typical of the region and nation. Along the same lines, another group of poems praised those who advanced the culture of Spain. A third group gave the history of Machado's love for his wife, the shock of her death, and the continuing sense of loss, all in the same setting of Soria.

In the long run, however, the outer view was not the one with which Machado felt most comfortable. Toward the end of *The Castilian Camp*, in a poem unique in tone, "Poema de un día" or "Meditaciones rurales" ("Poem for a Day" or "Rural Meditations"), he offhandedly details his extreme loneliness and expresses his intention to withdraw once more into philosophy. The form is a rather complex variation of Jorge Manrique's medieval elegy; in his solitude, the poet is intensely conscious of his surroundings—the changing winter weather outside, the constant ticking of the clock inside. The latter causes him to think about the meaning of time, and

the former leads him mentally to follow the raindrops to the fountain, then to the river, and finally to the sea, which symbolically evokes the anguish of the agnostic. Machado's only consolation lies in his books, particularly those of Unamuno, whose latest work, probably *Del sentimento trágico de la vida en los hombres y en los pueblos* (1913; *The Tragic Sense of Life*, 1921), he possesses. As for his old master, Henri Bergson, Machado ironically accepts the author's conclusion in *Essai sur les données immédiates de la conscience* (1888; *Time and Free Will*, 1910) that time and being according to his definitions made free will inescapable. After a walk amid the banalities of Baeza and its provincials to clear his head, the poet returns to his study, again ready to face solitude and his own efforts to cope with the human condition.

Despite the inclusion of many different kinds of poems, *The Castilian Camp* presents a relatively unified picture of Machado in his effort to reach out to the reality of Spain—its landscape, its problems, its important cultural figures—and to create a meaningful personal life. Moreover, there is a strong continuity from *Soledades* to *The Castilian Camp*, for many of the symbols of the former became realities in Soria, and the poet's obsession with time found a firm basis in the strong sense of history in the typical Castilian town. When his wife's death forced him back into himself, Soria became more vivid as he sought to re-create time and life in memory. It is interesting to note in passing that what the Andalusian Machado did for Castile, his contemporary, Robert Frost, did for his adopted New England.

PROVERBIOS Y CANCIONES

The third and most complex body of poems by Machado is that in which he strove hardest to reconcile his metaphysical and aesthetic concerns. First in *The Castilian Camp*, then in *Nuevas canciones*, one finds long series of "Proverbios y canciones" (proverbs and songs), poems of one stanza presenting a bit of philosophy in highly concentrated form. They culminated in the major poems with prose commentaries, somewhat in the tradition of Saint John of the Cross, of the two parts of the *De un cancionero apócrifo* in *Obras completas de Manuel y Antonio Machado* (1946). This collection clearly reflects the poet's need to renew his inspiration and his desire to find love again.

DE UN CANCIONERO APÓCRIFO

As his protagonists represent Machado in his dramas, so do a series of related personas in the *De un cancionero apócrifo*. Lacking systematic training in philosophy, the poet hesitated to express himself directly. Moreover, the use of spokesmen permitted him a degree of objectivity in dealing philosophically with the great themes of love, God, and death, which were either disturbing personally or shocking to a Catholic readership. Noteworthy, too, is the mask of ironic humor which the poet wears throughout to conceal his anguish.

It is clear that Machado thought of poetry as the expression of intimate, personal experience. When, in the second part of the prose discussions in the *De un cancionero apócrifo*, he attacks Spanish Baroque poetry of the seventeenth century as too conceptual and artificial and insufficiently intuitive, he is attacking also the poetry of his day and of all the vanguard to the present. More important, Machado, through another of his spokesmen, Jorge Meneses, satirizes the mechanistic, materialistic society of the contemporary world, which has rendered individual sentiment unnecessary and ineffectual for poetry. Meneses has invented a kind of protocomputer into which are fed the terms significant in the kind of poetry desired; the machine thus produces a poem for the masses. When, with the words "man" and "woman," the computer is programmed to create a love poem, however, the result merely proves that love and the heightened existence which it is supposed to provide are illusory. As before, then, Machado acknowledges defeat for lyric poetry and for himself as a poet, a defeat brought about by excessive intellectualization. However accurate his predictions for the future of lyric poetry, Machado's poetic work nevertheless lives on, as fresh and human as when he conceived it.

OTHER MAJOR WORKS

PLAYS: *Desdichas de la fortuna, o Julianillo Valcárcel*, pr. 1926 (with Manuel Machado); *Juan de Mañara*, pr. 1927 (with Manuel Machado); *Las adelfas*, pb. 1928 (with Manuel Machado); *La Lola se va a los puertos*, pr. 1929 (with Manuel Machado); *La prima Fernanda*, pr., pb. 1931 (with Manuel Machado); *La duquesa de Benamejí*, pb. 1932 (with Manuel Machado); *El hombre que murió en la guerra*, pr. 1941 (with Manuel Machado).

NONFICTION: *Juan de Mairena*, 1936 (English translation, 1963).

MISCELLANEOUS: *Obras completas de Manuel y Antonio Machado*, 1946 (includes *De un cancionero apócrifo*).

BIBLIOGRAPHY

Cobb, Carl W. *Antonio Machado*. New York: Twayne, 1971. An introductory biography and critical study of Machado by an expert in Spanish poets and the translation of Spanish poetry into English. Includes a bibliography of Machado's work.

Hutman, Norma Louise. *Machado: A Dialogue with Time, Nature as an Expression of Temporality in the Poetry of Antonio Machado*. Albuquerque: University of New Mexico Press, 1969. A critical analysis of selected poems by Machado. Includes a bibliography of Machado's poetry.

Krogh, Kevin. *The Landscape Poetry of Antonio Machado: A Dialogical Study of "ampos de Castilla."* Lewiston, N.Y.: Edwin Mellen Press, 2001. Krogh analyzes Machado's description of the countryside of Castile, Spain. Includes bibliographical references and indexes.

Ribbans, Geoffrey. *Antonio Machado (1875-1939): Poetry and Integrity*. London: Hispanic and Luso Brazilian Council, 1975. A transcription of a lecture dealing with Machado's life and poetry. Ribbans has written extensively on various figures in Spanish literature and has edited collections of Machado's poetry.

Round, Nicholas Grenville. *Poetry and Otherness in Hardy and Machado*. London: Queen Mary and Westfield College, 1993. A critical study comparing the poetic works of Thomas Hardy and Antonio Machado. Includes bibliographical references.

Walters, D. Gareth. *Estelas en el mar: Essays on the Poetry of Antonio Machado*. London: Grant and Cutler, 1992. This collection of essays from the Glasgow Colloquium focuses on technical aspects of specific poems. Studies such as "Questioning the Rules: Concepts of Deviance and Conformism in *Campos de Castilla*," by Robin Warner, reevaluate the works' meanings in their historical contexts. Other studies analyzing neo-mysticism, the nostalgic vision of *Canciones a Guiomar*, and the poetry of cultural memory offer fresh approaches to contemporary classics.

Whiston, James. *Antonio Machado's Writings and the Spanish Civil War*. Liverpool, England: Liverpool University Press, 1996. A study of the influence on Machado's writing of Spanish Civil War propaganda and the resulting schism between the poet and his brother.

Young, Howard Thomas. *The Victorious Expression: A Study of Four Contemporary Spanish Poets, Miguel de Unamuno, Antonio Machado, Juan Ramón Jiménez, Federico García Lorca*. Madison: University of Wisconsin Press, 1964. An introductory critical study of four Spanish poets. Includes bibliographical references.

Richard A. Mazzara;
bibliography updated by the editors

CLAUDE MCKAY

Born: Sunny Ville, Jamaica; September 15, 1889
Died: Chicago, Illinois; May 22, 1948

PRINCIPAL POETRY
Songs of Jamaica, 1912
Constab Ballads, 1912
Spring in New Hampshire and Other Poems, 1920
Harlem Shadows, 1922
Selected Poems of Claude McKay, 1953

OTHER LITERARY FORMS

Even though he is probably best known as a poet, Claude McKay's verse makes up a relatively small portion of his literary output. While his novels, *Home to Harlem* (1928), *Banjo* (1929), and *Banana Bottom* (1933), do not place him at the forefront of American novelists, they were remarkable at the time for their frankness and slice-of-life realism. *Home to Harlem* was the first best-selling novel of the Harlem Renaissance,

yet it was condemned by the majority of black critics, who felt that the black American art and literature emerging in the 1920's and 1930's should present an uplifting image of the African American. McKay, however, went on in his next two novels to express his admiration for the earthy ways of uneducated lower-class blacks, somewhat at the expense of black intellectuals. The remainder of McKay's published fiction appears in *Gingertown* (1932), a volume of short stories.

McKay also produced a substantial body of literary and social criticism, a revealing selection of which appears, along with a number of his letters and selections from his fiction and poetry, in *The Passion of Claude McKay: Selected Poetry and Prose, 1912-1948* (1973), edited by Wayne F. Cooper. An autobiography, *A Long Way from Home* (1937), and an important social history, *Harlem: Negro Metropolis* (1940), round out the list of his principal works.

ACHIEVEMENTS

Claude McKay received a medal from the Jamaican Institute of Arts and Sciences (1912), the National Association for the Advancement of Colored People's Harmon Foundation Award (1929) for *Harlem Shadows* and *Home to Harlem*, an award from the James Weldon Johnson Literary Guild (1937), and the Order of Jamaica. He was named that country's national poet in 1977.

McKay's contribution to American poetry cannot, however, be measured in awards and citations alone. His peculiar pilgrimage took him from Jamaica to Moscow, from Communism to Catholicism, from Harlem to Marseilles. He lived and worked among common laborers most of his life, and developed a respect for them worthy of Walt Whitman. He rejected the critical pronouncements of his black contemporaries and, as poet and critic Melvin Tolson points out, he "was unaffected by the New Poetry and Criticism." His singular blend of modern political and social radicalism with the timeworn cadences of the sonnet won for him, at best, mixed reviews from many critics, black and white.

In any attempt to calculate his poetic achievement, however, one must realize that, with the exception of his early Jamaican dialect verse (certainly an important contribution in its own right to the little-studied literature of the British West Indies) and some rather disappointing poetry composed late in his life, his poetic career spanned little more than a decade. At the publication in 1922 of *Harlem Shadows*, the furthest extent of his poetic development, he was only thirty-three. McKay should be read as a poet on the way up, who turned his attention almost exclusively to prose after his initial success in verse.

Surely there is no more ludicrous task than to criticize a writer on the basis of his potential, and so one should take McKay as one finds him, and indeed, in those terms, he does not fare badly. His was the first notable voice of anger in modern black American poetry. Writing when he did, he had to struggle against the enormous pressure, not of white censure, but of a racial responsibility that was his, whether he wanted it or not. He could not be merely a poet—he had to be a "black poet," had to speak, to some extent, for countless others; such a position is difficult for any poet. Through it all, however, he strove for individuality, and fought to keep

Claude McKay (Library of Congress)

from being bought by any interest, black or white, right- or left-wing.

Largely through the work of McKay, and of such Harlem Renaissance contemporaries as Countée Cullen and Langston Hughes, the task of being a black poet in America was made easier. *Harlem Shadows* marked a decisive beginning toward improving the predicament so concisely recorded by Cullen, who wondered aloud in the sonnet "Yet Do I Marvel" how a well-intentioned God could in his wisdom do "this curious thing:/ To make a poet black and bid him sing."

Bɪᴏɢʀᴀᴘʜʏ

Festus Claudius McKay was born in 1889 on a small farm in Clarendon Parish, Jamaica. His parents were well-respected members of the community and of the local Baptist church. He received his early education from his older brother, a schoolteacher near Montego Bay. In 1907, he was apprenticed to a wheelwright and cabinetmaker in Brown's Town; this apprenticeship was short-lived, but it was in Brown's Town that McKay entered into a far more fruitful apprenticeship of another sort. Walter Jekyll, an English aristocrat and student of Jamaican culture, came to know young Claude and undertook the boy's literary education. As McKay recalled years later in his autobiography, *A Long Way from Home*, Jekyll opened a whole new world to him:

> I read poetry: *Childe Harold, The Duncaid, Essay on Man, Paradise Lost*, the Elizabethan lyrics, *Leaves of Grass*, the lyrics of Shelley and Keats and of the late Victorian poets, and . . . we read together pieces out of Dante, Leopardi, and Goethe, Villon and Baudelaire.

It was Jekyll who first recognized and nurtured McKay's gift for writing poetry, and who encouraged him to put that gift to work in the service of his own Jamaican dialect. The result was the publication of *Songs of Jamaica* and *Constab Ballads*. The first is a celebration of peasant life, somewhat after the manner of Robert Burns; *Constab Ballads* is more like Rudyard Kipling, drawing as it does upon McKay's brief stint as a constable in Kingston, Jamaica.

Kingston gave McKay his first taste of city life, and his first real taste of racism. The contempt of the city's white and mulatto upper classes for rural and lower-class blacks was an unpleasant revelation. The most blatant racism that McKay witnessed in Kingston, however, was not Jamaican in origin—it was imported in the form of American tourists. He would come to know this brand of racism much more intimately in the next few years, for, after only eight months in the Kingston constabulary, he resigned his post and left for the United States. In 1912 he enrolled, first at Tuskegee Institute, then at Kansas State College, to study agronomy. His plan was to return to Jamaica to help modernize the island's agriculture. The plan might have succeeded but for a gift of several thousand dollars from an unidentified patron—most likely Walter Jekyll—that paid McKay's way to New York, where he invested his money in a restaurant and married Eulalie Imelda Edwards, an old Jamaican sweetheart. Neither marriage nor restaurant survived long, but McKay found a certain consolation in the bustle and energy of the city. One part of town in particular seemed to reach out to him: Harlem.

In the next five years or so he worked at a variety of jobs—bar boy, longshoreman, fireman, and finally porter, then waiter, on the Pennsylvania Railroad. This was yet another apprenticeship, one in which he further developed the sympathy for the working class that remained with him all his life. Since his youth he had leaned politically toward socialism, and his years among the proletariat solidified his beliefs. His race consciousness developed hand-in-hand with his class consciousness. During this period of apprenticeship and developing awareness, he wrote. In 1918, he began a long association with Max Eastman, editor of the Communist magazine, *The Liberator*. McKay began publishing poems and essays in this revolutionary journal, and eventually became an associate editor. In 1919, in response to that year's bloody postwar race riots, McKay published in *The Liberator* what would become his most famous poem, "If We Must Die." The defiant tone and the open outrage of the poem caught the attention of the black community, and practically overnight McKay was at the forefront of black American poets.

Then came another of the abrupt turns that were so much a part of McKay's life and work. Before his newly won reputation had a chance to flourish, he left for England where he stayed for more than a year, writing and editing for a Communist newspaper, *Workers' Dread-*

nought, and, in 1920, publishing his first book of poetry since the Jamaican volumes, *Spring in New Hampshire and Other Poems*. He returned to New York early in 1921 and spent the next two years with *The Liberator*, publishing a good bit of prose and verse and working on his principal book of poems, *Harlem Shadows*. Upon its publication in 1922, observes Wayne Cooper, McKay "was immediately acclaimed the best Negro poet since Paul Laurence Dunbar." Once again, however, he did not linger long over success. He was tired and in need of a change, especially after a chance meeting with his former wife reopened old wounds. Late in 1922, he traveled to Moscow for the Fourth Congress of the Third International. He quickly became a great favorite with Muscovites, and was allowed to address the Congress on the plight of American blacks and on the problem of racism within the Communist Party. As McKay described it, he was greeted "like a black ikon in the flesh." He was, it seemed, on the verge of a promising career as a political activist; but despite his successes in Russia, he still saw himself primarily as a writer. When he left Russia, he was "eager to resume what he considered the modern writer's proper function—namely, to record as best he could the truths of his own experience."

The 1920's were the decade of the Expatriate Artist, but though he spent most of his time in France until settling in Tangiers in 1931, McKay had very little to do with such writers as Ernest Hemingway and F. Scott Fitzgerald; his exile was too different from theirs. During his stay in Europe and North Africa, McKay published all his major fiction, along with a number of magazine articles. His first two novels, *Home to Harlem* and *Banjo*, were financially successful, in spite of the outraged reaction they drew from most black American critics. *Gingertown*, a collection of short stories, was not nearly so successful, and McKay's third novel, *Banana Bottom*, was a critical and financial disaster. Financially ruined, McKay was forced to end his expatriate existence.

With the help of some American friends, McKay returned to New York in 1934. He hoped to be of service to the black community, but upon his return, observes Wayne Cooper, "he found a wrecked economy, almost universal black poverty, and little sense of unity among those black writers and intellectuals he had hoped to work with in years ahead." As for his literary ambitions, the Harlem Renaissance was finished; black writers were no longer in vogue. Not only could he not find a publisher, he was unable to find any sort of a job, and wound up in Camp Greycourt, a government welfare camp outside New York City. Fortunately, Max Eastman was able to rescue him from the camp and help him to get a job with the Federal Writers' Project. In 1937 he was able to publish his autobiography, *A Long Way from Home*. Once again, he was publishing articles in magazines, but his views isolated him from the mainstream black leaders; he felt, again in Cooper's words, that "their single-minded opposition to racial segregation was detrimental to any effective black community organization and to the development of a positive group spirit among blacks." McKay's thought at this time also shows a drift away from Communism, and a growing disillusionment with the fate of the "Grand Experiment" at the hands of the Soviets.

A Long Way from Home was neither a critical nor a financial success. Neither was his next and last book, *Harlem: Negro Metropolis*, a historical study published in 1940. By then, in spite of the steady work provided him by the Federal Writers' Project, his literary reputation was declining steadily. Despite his final acceptance of American citizenship in 1940, he could still not bring himself to regard America as home. His exile from both the black leadership and the left-wing establishment was becoming more and more total; worse still, his health began to deteriorate rapidly. Once again, like Walter Jekyll and Max Eastman in earlier years, a friend offered a hand. Ellen Terry, a Catholic writer, rescued McKay from a Harlem rooming house, and McKay's life took one last unexpected turn. As a young man he had rejected the fundamentalist Christianity of his father, and during his varied career had had little use for religion. Through his friendship with Terry, and later with the progressive Chicago bishop, Bernard Scheil, McKay experienced a change of mind and heart. In the spring of 1944 he moved to Chicago, and by fall of that year he was baptized into the Roman Catholic church.

At last he seemed to have found a refuge, though his letters reveal a lingering bitterness over his lot. With his newfound faith, however, came a satisfying involvement in Chicago's Catholic Youth Organization and the op-

portunity to go on writing. His health continued to decline, and on May 22, 1948, McKay died of heart failure. He had recently finished preparing his *Selected Poems of Claude McKay* for publication. It is probably just as well that the volume appeared posthumously, as it took five years to find a publisher; at the time of his death, all of his works were out of print. After a requiem mass in Chicago, McKay was brought back to Harlem for a memorial service. He was buried in Queens, "a long way from home."

ANALYSIS

At the conclusion of his essay "The Renaissance Reexamined," which appears as the final chapter of Arna Bontemps's 1972 book, *The Harlem Renaissance Remembered*, Warrington Hudlin insists that any true appreciation of the Harlem Renaissance hinges on the realization that this celebrated literary phenomenon "opened the door" for the black writing of today. The Harlem Renaissance will always be remembered for this reason. It will be valued for its merits. It will come again to importance because of its idea." The poetry of Claude McKay must be read in much the same light. Though it is easy enough to find fault with much of his verse, he did help to "open the door" for those who would follow; as such, he deserves to be valued for his merits, judged by his strengths.

"INVOCATION"

Though progressive enough in thought, McKay never felt compelled to experiment much with the form of his poetry. In content he is a black man of the twentieth century; in form he is more an English lyricist of the nineteenth, with, here and there, Miltonic echoes. The effect is, at times, a little peculiar, as in "Invocation," a sonnet in which the poet beseeches his muse to

> Let fall the light upon my sable face
> That once gleamed upon the Ethiopian's art;
> Lift me to thee out of this alien place
> So I may be, thine exiled counterpart,
> The worthy singer of my world and race.

Archaic trappings aside, there is a kind of majesty here, not bad work for a young man in his twenties. The Miltonic ring is probably no accident; McKay, it must be remembered, received something of an English gentleman's education. As the work of a black man pursuing what had been to that time primarily a white man's vocation, McKay's "Invocation" bears comparison with John Milton's "Hail native Language." One of the young Milton's ambitions was to vindicate English as poetic language, deserving of the same respect as Homer's Greek, Vergil's Latin, or Dante's Italian. McKay found himself in the position of vindicating a black man's experience of a white culture as a worthy subject for poetry.

"The Tropics in New York"

Not all of McKay's verse concerns itself specifically with the theme of interracial tension. Among his poems are love lyrics, idyllic songs of country life, and harsher poems of the city, where "the old milk carts go rumbling by,/ Under the same old stars," where "Out of the tenements, cold as stone,/ Dark figures start for work." A recurring theme in McKay's work is the yearning for the lost world of childhood, which for him meant memories of Jamaica. This sense of loss is the occasion for one of his finest poems, "The Tropics in New York":

> Bananas ripe and green, and ginger-root,
> Cocoa in pods and alligator pears,
> And tangerines and mangoes and grape fruit,
> Fit for the highest prize at parish fairs.

The diction here is simple; one can almost hear Ernest Hemingway in the loving list of fruits. The speaker's memory stirs at the sight of a shop window. In the midst of the city his thoughts turn to images of "fruit-trees laden by low-singing rills,/ And dewy dawns, and mystical blue skies/ In benediction over nun-like hills." Here, in three straightforward quatrains, is the mechanism of nostalgia. From a physical reality placed by chance before him, the observer turns his eyes inward, visualizing a happy scene of which he is no longer a part. In the final stanza his eyes are still involved in the experience, only now they have grown dim, "and I could no more gaze;/ A wave of longing through my body swept." All of the narrator's senses tune themselves to grief as the quickening of smell and taste turns to a poignant hunger for "the old, familiar ways." Finally, the poem closes on a line as classically simple and tersely musical as anything in the poems of A. E. Housman: "I turned aside and bowed my head and wept."

Indeed, the poem is reminiscent of "Poem XL" in A. E. Housman's *A Shropshire Lad* (1896):

> Into my heart an air that kills
> From yon far country blows:
> What are those blue remembered hills,
> What spires, what farms are those?

It is a long way, to be sure, from Shropshire to Clarendon Parish, Jamaica, but the issue here is the long road back to lost experience, to that "land of lost content" that shines so plain, "The happy highways where I went/ And cannot come again." Any fair assessment of McKay's verse must affirm that he knew that land, those highways, all too well.

"We Wear the Mask"

That same fair assessment, however, must give a prominent place to those poems upon which McKay's reputation was made—his poems of protest. McKay, in the estimation of Arna Bontemps, was black poetry's "strongest voice since [Paul Laurence] Dunbar." Dunbar's "racial" verse is a good indication of the point to which black American poetry had progressed by World War I. His plantation-style dialect verse tries, with a certain ironic cheerfulness, to make the best of a bad situation. At their best, these poems exhibit a stinging wit. At their worst, they are about as dignified as a minstrel show. In his poems in literary English, Dunbar is more assertive of his racial pride, but with an emphasis on suffering and forbearance, as in "We Wear the Mask." This poem, which could be read in retrospect as an answer to those critics and poets who would later disown Dunbar for not being "black" enough, speaks of the great cost at which pain and anger are contained:

> We smile, but O great Christ, our cries
> To Thee from tortured souls arise.
> We sing, but oh, the clay is vile
> Beneath our feet, and long the mile;
> But let the world dream otherwise,
> We wear the mask.

The anguish is plain enough, yet the poem, couched in a prayer, seems to view this "wearing of the mask" as an ennobling act, as a virtuous sacrifice. McKay was not inclined to view things in quite that way.

"IF WE MUST DIE"

From the spring through the fall of 1919, numerous American cities were wracked by bloody race conflicts, the worst of which was a July riot in Chicago that left dozens dead and hundreds injured or homeless. While he was never the object of such violence, McKay and his fellow railroad waiters and porters walked to and from their trains with loaded revolvers in their pockets. Not unexpectedly, his reaction to the riots was far from mild; his concern was not with turning the other cheek, but with returning the offending slap. When the sonnet "If We Must Die" appeared in *The Liberator* it marked the emergence of a new rage in black American poetry:

> If we must die, let it not be like hogs,
> Hunted and penned in an inglorious spot,
> While round us bark the mad and hungry dogs,
> Making their mock at our accursed lot.

Again, the form is of another century, the language dated, even by late nineteenth century standards—"O kinsmen! We must meet the common foe! . . . What though before us lies the open grave?" The message, however, is ageless, avoiding as the poem does any direct reference to race.

On the heels of much-publicized violence against black neighborhoods, the implications were clear enough, but the universality of the poem became more obvious with time. A Jewish friend of McKay's wrote him in 1939, "proclaiming that . . . ["If We Must Die"] must have been written about the European Jews persecuted by Hitler." In a more celebrated instance, Winston Churchill read the poem before the House of Commons, as if, in the words of black poet and critic, Melvin Tolson, "it were the talismanic uniform of His Majesty's field marshal." The message reaches back to Thermopylae and Masada, and forward to Warsaw, Bastogne, and beyond. In its coverage of the bloodbath at the New York State Prison at Attica, *Time* (September 27, 1971) quoted the first four lines of McKay's sonnet as the "would-be heroic" effort of an anonymous, rebellious inmate. McKay might not have minded; he stated in his autobiography that "If We Must Die" was "the only poem I ever read to the members of my [railroad] crew." A poem that touches prisoners, railroad workers, and prime ministers alike must be termed a consid-erable success, despite any technical flaws it may exhibit.

Even so, one must not altogether avoid the question of just how successful McKay's poems are as poems. James Giles, in his 1976 study, *Claude McKay*, remarks on the disparity "between McKay's passionate resentment of racist oppression and his Victorianism in form and diction," finding in this conflict "a unique kind of tension in many of his poems, which weakens their ultimate success." Giles is probably correct to a point. In many cases McKay's art might have found fuller expression had he experimented more, let content more often shape form; he had shown abilities in this direction in his early Jamaican poems, and he was certainly open to experimentation in his later prose. The simple fact, however, is that he consistently chose to use traditional forms, and it would be unfair to say that it was a wholly unsuccessful strategy.

"THE LYNCHING"

Indeed, the very civility of his favorite form, the sonnet, sometimes adds an ironic tension that heightens, rather than diminishes, the effect of the poem. For example, one could imagine any number of grisly, graphic effects to be achieved in a *vers libre*, expressionistic poem about a lynching. In McKay's "The Lynching," though, one cannot help feeling the pull of an understated horror at seeing the act translated to quatrains and couplets: "and little lads, lynchers that were to be,/ Danced round the dreadful thing in fiendish glee." No further description of the "dreadful thing" is necessary. When McKay uses his poems to focus on real or imagined experience—a lynching, a cornered fight to the death, an unexpected remembrance of things past—his formal restraint probably works most often in his favor.

ANGRY SONNETS

In poems that set out to convey a self-conscious message, however, he tends to be less successful, not so much because the form does not fit the content as because poetry and causes are dangerous bedfellows. Some of McKay's other angry sonnets—"The White House," "To the White Fiends," "Baptism"—may leave readers disappointed because they preach too much. McKay's specifically sociological, political, and, later, religious views receive better expression elsewhere, in his prose. Perhaps that is why he did not devote so much of his time to poetry after the publication of *Harlem Shadows*. In any case, his position in black American poetry is secure. Perhaps he should be judged more by that which was new in his poems, and that which inspired other black writers to carry on the task, as later generations have judged the Harlem Renaissance—as a bold and determined beginning, a rolling up of the sleeves for the hard work ahead.

OTHER MAJOR WORKS

LONG FICTION: *Home to Harlem*, 1928; *Banjo*, 1929; *Banana Bottom*, 1933.

SHORT FICTION: *Gingertown*, 1932.

NONFICTION: *A Long Way from Home*, 1937 (autobiography); *Harlem: Negro Metropolis*, 1940.

MISCELLANEOUS: *The Passion of Claude McKay: Selected Poetry and Prose, 1912-1948*, 1973 (Wayne F. Cooper, editor; contains social and literary criticism, letters, prose, fiction, and poetry).

BIBLIOGRAPHY

Cooper, Wayne F. *Claude McKay: Rebel Sojourner in the Harlem Renaissance*. Baton Rouge: Louisiana State University Press, 1987. This first full-length biography of McKay is a fascinating and very readable book. Special attention is paid to McKay's early life in Jamaica and the complex influences of his family. Includes nine photographs and a useful index.

Gayle, Addison, Jr. *Claude McKay: The Black Poet at War*. Detroit: Broadside Press, 1972. This brief study looks closely at four poems—"Flame-Heart," *Harlem Shadows*, "To the White Fiends," and "If We Must Die"—as they demonstrate McKay's growing skill and militancy throughout his career. Gayle argues that McKay was an important revolutionary poet.

Giles, James R. *Claude McKay*. Boston: Twayne, 1976. This study examines McKay's work as it was influenced by his homeland of Jamaica, the Harlem Renaissance, the Communist Party, and the Roman Catholic church. Giles asserts that McKay's fiction represents his major achievement. The book includes a chronology and a briefly annotated bibliography.

Hathaway, Heather. *Caribbean Waves: Relocating Claude McKay and Paule Marshall*. Bloomington: Indiana University Press, 1999. A biographical and critical study of the lives and works of two writers and the way that their works have been shaped by their backgrounds as Caribbean immigrants.

James, Winston. *A Fierce Hatred of Injustice: Claude McKay's Jamaica and His Poetry of Rebellion*. New York: Verso, 2000. A critical study of McKay's early writing with a focus on the poet's use of Jamaican creole in two early collections, *Songs of Jamaica* and *Constab Ballads*, and in his previously uncollected poems for the Jamaican press. An anthology of the latter is provided together with McKay's comic sketch about Jamaican peasant life and his autobiographical essay.

LeSeur, Geta. "Claude McKay's Marxism." In *The Harlem Renaissance: Revaluations*, edited by Amritjit Singh, William S. Shiver, and Stanley Brodwin. New York: Garland, 1989. This article examines McKay's struggle to find in Marxism the solution to the "Negro question" and looks at his trip to Russia to assess Marxism in action firsthand in 1922 and 1923.

Richard A. Eichwald;
bibliography updated by the editors

ARCHIBALD MACLEISH

Born: Glencoe, Illinois; May 7, 1892
Died: Conway, Massachusetts; April 20, 1982

PRINCIPAL POETRY

Songs for a Summer's Day, 1915
Tower of Ivory, 1917
The Happy Marriage, 1924
The Pot of Earth, 1925
Streets in the Moon, 1926
The Hamlet of A. MacLeish, 1928
Einstein, 1929
New Found Land: Fourteen Poems, 1930
Conquistador, 1932
Poems, 1924-1933, 1933
Frescoes for Mr. Rockefeller's City, 1933

Public Speech, 1936
Land of the Free, 1938
America Was Promises, 1939
Brave New World, 1948
Actfive and Other Poems, 1948
Collected Poems, 1917-1952, 1952
New Poems, 1951-1952, 1952
Songs for Eve, 1954
The Collected Poems of Archibald MacLeish, 1962
The Wild Old Wicked Man and Other Poems, 1968
The Human Season: Selected Poems, 1926-1972,
    1972
New and Collected Poems, 1917-1976, 1976
On the Beaches of the Moon, 1978
Collected Poems, 1917-1982, 1985

OTHER LITERARY FORMS

In addition to some twenty volumes of poems,
Archibald MacLeish presented innumerable lectures, to
college students, librarians, and the general public. Some
of these are recorded in the volumes of prose essays he
published, many on the public role of the poet as guardian
of his own society. Several others concern social issues of
the 1930's through the 1960's. The essays analyzing poems and commenting on the responsibility of the poet,
such as *Poetry and Opinion: The "Pisan Cantos" of Ezra
Pound* (1950) and *Poetry and Experience* (1961), illuminate MacLeish's own work as well as distinguish him
from such contemporaries as Ezra Pound and T. S. Eliot.

The other major literary genre in which MacLeish
worked was verse drama. One of his earlier works,
Nobodaddy: A Play (1926), whose title is derived from
William Blake's name for the Old Testament God of
vengeance and restrictions, presents an interpretation of
the stories of Adam and Eve and Cain and Abel. A
closet play, it dramatizes the relationship between self-
conscious humanity and indifferent, alien nature. In 1934
he collaborated with Nicholas Nabokoff on a ballet,
Union Pacific, but much of his creative energy in the
1930's was devoted to writing hortatory verse plays for
radio, such as *The Fall of the City* (1937), *Air Raid*
(1938), and *The American Story: Ten Broadcasts* (1944).
These works approach propaganda in their enthusiasm
for the freedom of democracy and their attempts to warn
Americans against the dangers of fascism.

Archibald MacLeish (Library of Congress)

Of the later plays, *The Trojan Horse* (1952) presents
implicit criticism of the McCarthy era while *This Music
Crept By Me upon the Waters* (1953) dramatizes the individual's quest for happiness and the transitory, paradoxical nature of that happiness. *J. B.: A Play in Verse*
(1958), MacLeish's most popular and widely-read play,
is an adaptation of the story of Job to modern American
life; it ran successfully on Broadway for ten months.

ACHIEVEMENTS

Archibald MacLeish's reputation has remained
undeservedly small in view of his contributions to both
literature and public life. In addition to his achievements
as a writer, MacLeish was highly successful in government and academic posts. His name is known today for
a handful of lyrics that are widely anthologized, but he
also wrote screenplays and plays for the stage. Although
academic scholars have paid relatively little attention to
his work, he received many awards and honorary academic degrees, including—among many others—the
John Reed Memorial Prize (1929), the Shelley Memorial Award for Poetry (1931), three Pulitzer Prizes (in

1933 for *Conquistador*, in 1953 for *Collected Poems, 1917-1952*, and in 1959 for his drama *J. B.*), the Order of Commander from the French Legion of Honor (1946), the Bollingen Prize (1953), the National Book Award in poetry for *Collected Poems, 1917-1952* (1953), an Antoinette Perry ("Tony") Award in drama (1959), an Academy Award for Best Screenplay for *The Eleanor Roosevelt Story* (1966), an Academy of American Poets Fellowship (1966), the Presidential Medal of Freedom (1977), the National Medal for Literature (1978), and the Gold Medal for Poetry, awarded by the American Academy of Arts and Letters (1979).

MacLeish is probably most noteworthy for his refusal to "escape" into his art, for his effort to be a whole human being: husband, father, teacher, soldier, public servant, as well as poet. Unlike Eliot and Pound, who longed nostalgically for the lost order of past European culture, MacLeish committed himself to the New World—to both the present and the future. He sought, through experiments with traditional verse forms and metrics, to adapt the techniques of poetry and drama to the American idiom and contemporary life. He wrote not for posterity but for his contemporaries. As Hyatt Howe Waggoner points out in *The Heel of Elohim* (1950), MacLeish was the only poet of the early twentieth century who understood and wrote about the modern revolution in physics, the space-time continuum, and the four-dimensional universe. This pervasive awareness of profoundly shocking scientific discoveries may turn out to be one of MacLeish's major contributions to modern literature, but most significant is MacLeish's attempt to fulfill the ancient but neglected tradition of the poet as prophet—in Percy Bysshe Shelley's words, the poet as "unacknowledged legislator of mankind."

The present critical consensus is that MacLeish has written some magnificent lyric poems, that the longer works, such as *Conquistador*, are flawed, and that some of them, such as *The Hamlet of A. MacLeish*, tend to be derivative. Given the size of MacLeish's corpus, its variety, and the topical political content of some works, it is probable that decades must pass before he can be judiciously ranked as a writer. As a whole man, speaking to other men of his time, he must be admired. He not only reflected upon the timeless paradoxes of being human but also acted as a Socratic gadfly, pricking

the consciences of his fellow citizens of a threatened republic.

Biography

Archibald MacLeish was born in Glencoe, Illinois, on May 7, 1892. Some aspects of his early life seem to have influenced his mature concept of the poet. His father was a Scots immigrant, that circumstance perhaps explaining MacLeish's preoccupation with westward migration and his emphasis on America as a melting pot. More important, both his parents fostered a strong sense of moral responsibility in the young MacLeish. After attending the Hotchkiss School, MacLeish was graduated from Yale with a B.A. degree in 1915, showing his propensity for being a well-rounded man by distinguishing himself in sports, academics, and the writing of poetry. He went on to Harvard Law School, marrying Ada Hitchcock in 1916; but his education was interrupted by his enlisting in the army in 1917. MacLeish served in France, attaining the rank of captain. He returned to Harvard and received his law degree in 1919 and then taught for a year before joining a Boston law firm. After practicing law and trying to write poetry for three years, MacLeish quit his job and moved his wife and two children to Paris to devote his full efforts to poetry. During the five years of his expatriation, MacLeish associated with other American writers such as Pound, John Dos Passos, F. Scott Fitzgerald, and Ernest Hemingway, the latter becoming a close friend. MacLeish's poems of this period show the influence of the poetics of Pound and Eliot and also of the spare style of Hemingway. His poems of this period tend also to reflect the introspective influence of the decadent poets.

Unlike many other American expatriates of the 1920's, MacLeish never intended to abandon his homeland. Having achieved recognition as a poet, in 1928 he returned to the United States, to a farm at Conway, Massachusetts. From that point on, his writings express a strong patriotic commitment. In the next year MacLeish traveled on foot and mule through Mexico, tracing the path of Hernando Cortes and preparing to write his epic, *Conquistador*. In the meantime he published *New Found Land* which, as the title suggests, heralded a renewed affirmation of America. Thus MacLeish turned away from the preoccupation with European tradition and the past that characterized Eliot and Pound, and embraced the promise and the problems of his native land.

MacLeish became increasingly vocal about the problems of America in the Great Depression, acting out his belief that a poet must speak to his own time about real issues, rather than to an elite group of aesthetes. He joined the editorial board of the new *Fortune* magazine and wrote articles of distinction on contemporary social issues. During the 1930's, he spoke out for the preservation of democracy not only through his poems but also through exhortative verse radio plays and a poetic commentary on photographs illustrating rural poverty. The last work in particular led in 1939 to MacLeish's controversial appointment by President Roosevelt to the post of Librarian of Congress. In the early 1940's, MacLeish also served as director of the Office of Facts and Figures, assistant director of the Office of War Information, Assistant Secretary of State, and after the war, as head of the United States delegation to the founding of UNESCO. During the political debates of the 1930's and 1940's, he remained both anti-Marxist and anti-Fascist, a staunch supporter of American democracy, and a severe critic of the big capitalists who, he felt, were exploiting the land.

In 1949, MacLeish returned to private life and to teaching. He was Boylston Professor of Rhetoric and Oratory at Harvard until 1962. From 1963 to 1967, he was Simpson Lecturer at Amherst College. During this later phase of his career MacLeish turned in his plays and poems to the fundamental and universal issues of human life. After the death of Robert Frost in 1962, MacLeish succeeded him as the unofficial poet laureate of the United States, publishing, for example, a poem on the 1969 moon landing in *The New York Times*. This poem typifies MacLeish's concept of the role of the poet. While it describes a specific political and scientific feat, the poem concludes with an ironic twist that broadens the context of this historical event into a reflection on man's universal preoccupation with the mysteries of existence. The moon landing shows technology capturing man's oldest symbol for time, change, and imagination; once on the moon, however, man discovers its essence as a symbol of reflection: He sees an impossible sight, his own home, the earth, rising like the moon before his eyes. By following his seemingly impossible aspirations, man finds knowledge of himself and his illu-

sions. MacLeish died in Conway, Massachusetts, on April 20, 1982.

ANALYSIS

Public and private man, humanist, social critic, poet, Archibald MacLeish presents a rare wholeness of vision throughout his long career as a writer. This is not to say that his poetry remains static, that for over fifty years he wrote the same poem over and over again. Indeed, his focus and style shift at two major points, dividing his corpus roughly into three stages: the 1920's, the 1930's, and the postwar period. As Hyatt Howe Waggoner points out, MacLeish was the first among a very few twentieth century poets who have recognized, grasped, and used in their work the discoveries of post-Newtonian physics. He refused to polarize poetry and science because to do so would be escapism. It is the poet's role to express the mysteries of existence and experience. To oppose poetry to the contemporary understanding of nature and the universe, of origins and time and space, is to rob the poet of his subject and his mission. Throughout his works, MacLeish reiterates the value of the real, the concrete experience of the senses and feelings. Philosophically, he resembles the British empiricists of the eighteenth century, though without being reductive about experience. He distrusts abstractions, in the political arena no less than in the aesthetic. MacLeish is always in agreement with William Wordsworth's concept of the poet, "a man speaking to men." Unlike Eliot and Pound, he did not write for posterity nor for an elite group of preservers of western culture. He sought a metaphor for contemporary man, particularly American man. Like the eighteenth century English Augustans, he wrote social criticism with a public voice, with a sense of civic responsibility. Unlike neoclassicists of all periods, however, from Alexander Pope to Eliot, MacLeish refused the temptation to look back with nostalgia to a golden past. Rather, he sought to remind his readers of the true American dream. In *A Continuing Journey* (1968), he defines this dream as a reverence for the dignity of man, his self-determination, and his possibilities for unbounded knowledge.

If MacLeish were only a public poet, addressing only contemporary social issues, he would soon lose his audience. His genius inheres in his synthesis of the "public-private world in which we live." He is always a poet, a superb craftsman meditating on the exigencies of human experience. The main fact of human experience for MacLeish is man's finiteness, the inevitability of death. In fact, the three stages of his poetic development can be understood according to their attitude toward death. Early in his career, MacLeish lost his brother in World War I; he also suffered the death of a child. In the first period, there is an outcry against meaningless death. Man's transient existence in the vast universe of twentieth century physics offers a temptation to deep bitterness, but MacLeish refuses to yield to it. In later prose essays and poems, he criticizes the existentialists, who reduce man's lot to absurdity. The poetry of the second stage, written in the 1930's, turns away from the search for the relationship between man and the universe, focusing instead on death in its more political and historical context: death from war, oppression, and hunger. In the final period, MacLeish returns to death as a topic, but now as a concrete, highly personal event. He writes elegies for his friends, for other writers. He dwells on growing old, on his own inevitable death. These later poems invite comparison with the last poems of William Butler Yeats. They are affirmative, yet also ironic and sometimes tragic. In terms of the paradox presented in John Keats's "Ode on a Grecian Urn," these poems choose the death that results from living rather than the immortality of stasis.

NEW AND COLLECTED POEMS, 1917-1976

In *New and Collected Poems, 1917-1976*, MacLeish included the poems he published in the 1920's, together with three earlier poems published in 1917 in *Tower of Ivory*. The poetry of this early period reflects to some degree the influences MacLeish encountered during his five years in France. These poems had elicited critical comments that tended to denigrate them by stressing their derivative nature, though, in general, such evaluations are unfair. It is true that influences tend to be obvious, but the poems also embody MacLeish's personal synthesis of technique and vision. These works develop a core of personal symbols, using the techniques of the French symbolists as well as the Poundian juxtaposition of concrete images and the fusion of ancient myth and modern life used so successfully by Eliot in *The Waste Land* (1922). The early poems show an almost Meta-

physical wit in their use of paradox and irony, also revealing traces of William Shakespeare, William Blake, Keats, and Yeats, to name a few. Hemingway, his close friend during the expatriate period, seems, surprisingly, to have influenced MacLeish's style in a very lasting way. Throughout his career he tends to use short concrete words grouped into coordinate clauses, with relatively little subordination. He seems to want to state the "bare facts," not to embellish them. Yet the poems of the 1920's reveal highly successful experiments with music and sound. Critics agree that MacLeish was a technical master of the musical aspect of lyric poetry.

THE HAPPY MARRIAGE

The Happy Marriage is a sequence of sonnets about love, paradoxical in the manner of John Donne, using plain language yet with striking musical effects. The poems are not allusive; they dwell on real life as opposed to books, on great moments of sense perception as opposed to ideas and abstractions. Not "love" or the "lover," but particular, concrete visual and tactile moments of sensation compose man's reality. In *The Dialogues of Archibald MacLeish and Mark Van Doren* (1964), MacLeish states that Algernon Charles Swinburne was his initial source, and intense sensibility is evident in these poems, as in the earlier *Tower of Ivory*, though they are never decadent.

THE POT OF EARTH

The Pot of Earth is a long narrative poem using a ritual taken from Sir James G. Frazer's *The Golden Bough* (1890-1915) as an epigraph; it works through allusion as an ordering structural and thematic principle in the story of a contemporary girl's reproductive cycle. The fertility ritual, part of the cult of Adonis, describes women cultivating plants in pots of earth. The plants grow rapidly under the sunlight, but wither for lack of roots. After eight days the plants, along with images of the dead Adonis, are thrown into the sea or springs. This use of Frazer invites comparison with *The Waste Land*; the two works utilize the lore from Frazer in a parallel manner. The resulting poems, however, are very different in subject matter, mode, and tone. Whereas Eliot reflects on the sterility of Western culture after World War I, associating it with abortive fertility rites and degraded or impotent lovers, MacLeish expresses the age-old rhythms of the female life cycle, its inescapable connection with nature and death. While the species lives on, the individual, who rebels against her unwilled participation in the cycle, dies. *The Pot of Earth* itself is "pregnant" with the techniques and symbols that MacLeish developed in succeeding works. Images of the moon, sun, sea, and leafy trees shadowed against the moon or sun recur throughout MacLeish's works, sometimes as opaque images or details and sometimes as symbols fraught with almost allegorical significance. The themes born here are meditation on death, man's (here woman's) relationships to time, nature, and the revolving planets, and the flesh as intractable reality, somehow mysteriously connected with "self."

In this poem, sensuous, concrete images of nature work together with the narrative structure to communicate the tension between the individual heroine (or victim) of the poem and the inexorable rhythms of nature in which she participates by maturing, making love, conceiving, bearing a child, and dying as a result. The epigraph of the poem, from Hamlet's "mad" talk with Polonius about Ophelia, establishes the sun as a symbol of the male fertilizing principle. Hamlet's "let her not walk i' the sun" puns on the word "sun," meaning that his (the son's) love for her is threatening. In the same way, MacLeish uses the sun as both a death-bearing fertilizing principle and beckoning romantic love. The moon is a relatively clear symbol, in its influence on the tides, of the inevitable cyclical processes of nature: birth, maturity, death, and rebirth. The individual, however, is not reborn; the species is. The tragedy of the individual thus inheres in a conflict with nature's preservation of the species. MacLeish plays with point of view in the poem to bring out this conflict. Part I, "The Sowing of the Dead Corn," begins with an objective third-person description of nature's "death," winter, shifting to a limited third-person with insight into the young girl's fear of menstruation. This is carried further into a first-person interior monologue, jumping from the thirteen-year-old to the seventeen-year-old girl. The loss of virginity on Easter Sunday is told in the third person through juxtaposed natural images of sowing, together with brief explanatory statements.

Part II, "The Shallow Grass," begins with the marriage of the young woman, juxtaposing her behavior with the sensuously depicted newly plowed fields which function typically as an objective correlative for the body of the bride. The poem moves back and forth from nature, in the context of the Adonis ritual, to the particular woman, now pregnant, just beginning to try to separate her identity from her uncontrollable body. Part III, "Carrion Spring," reveals her as a "reaped meadow," dead. In Parts II and III, the poet turns to the reader and comments cryptically on the mystery of the process. In tone, *The Pot of Earth* is not optimistic; its insistence on the absolute presence of flesh and bone, on their mysterious inviolability, is present in *The Happy Marriage* and ties in with the conclusion to *Einstein*, another long poem of the 1920's.

EINSTEIN AND THE HAMLET OF A. MACLEISH

MacLeish's technique of structuring in *The Pot of Earth*—allusion to the Adonis ritual—is similar to his use of marginal glosses in both *Einstein* and *The Hamlet of A. MacLeish*. Both long poems rely on marginal glosses to provide order and context for their verses; the latter is similar in tone to *The Waste Land*, and similar in conception to the "Hamlet" of Jules Laforgue. The speaker is a poet beating his breast in the void, bewailing the inadequacies of words and knowledge. The ghost of Shakespeare's *Hamlet, Prince of Denmark* (c. 1600-1601) represents the mystery of meaning that man assumes to be at the center of experience. There is a sense of the moon as the boundary of the human corner of the vast indifferent universe. The poet-speaker bemoans the pain of mortal existence, without any illusion of a responsive chord in the universe. *The Hamlet of A. MacLeish* typifies his more personal poems in that it is both autobiographical and universal. He mentions the loss of his brother and child, while always remaining a representative figure, the poet-man facing the exigencies of life in a universe without meaning. Along with *Einstein*, this poem is among MacLeish's most pessimistic, and he rejected its self-pitying aspects during the following decade.

STREETS IN THE MOON

Streets in the Moon, like *Einstein*, grapples with the image-defeating concepts of modern physics such as the time-space continuum and the fourth dimension. Whereas *Einstein* suggests a laboratory notebook, being a factual description of man's felt disjunction with a vast, yet closed and indifferent universe, *Streets in the*

Moon is a series of more "poetic" lyrics. These poems on various topics, such as death, technological man, and poetics, range from the playful to the nostalgic. Their language tends to be plainer, more abstract and conversational than that of earlier poems. They are united, however, by their uses of the moon as a symbol and the Einsteinian universe as setting. Many of the poems are ironic in the disparity between their titles and their contents. The moon, always haunting MacLeish's poems, seems to be a Janus-faced symbol, with contradictory meanings. It is a traditional beacon of imagination, of the dream world of myth and symbol, but it is also a satellite in the indifferent universe, representing a time-space continuum that mutely destroys man's aspirations toward meaning. Even MacLeish's most famous lyric, taken from *Streets in the Moon*, "Ars Poetica," is permeated by the symbolic moon.

"ARS POETICA"

"Ars Poetica," a twenty-four-line poem with a Horatian title implying high seriousness, is perhaps the single poem for which MacLeish is best known and the one most often anthologized. It has been taken both too seriously and not seriously enough by some critics. The title suggests a disquisition on the true nature of poetry. Companion poems such as "Some Aspects of Immortality," "Man!," and "Hearts' and Flowers,'" however, reveal a technique of ironically deceptive titles. The titles do relate to the subject at hand, but not in the imposing or sentimental way the reader expects. For example, "Hearts' and Flowers'" sounds like a sentimental valentine, but it is a musical compilation of scientific descriptions of sea anemones. The further irony results from the erotic rhythms and connotations of the scientific words. Thus the reader comes full circle from romantic expectations, through surprise at the scientific terminology, and back to erotic and romantic response on an intuitive level.

"Ars Poetica" operates analogously. At first reading it appears to be, not a treatise on poetics, but a paradoxical, anti-intellectual riddle. It has been rejected by some readers (and with some justification) as the epitome of art for art's sake. In the 1920's, MacLeish's poetry was much more attuned to aestheticism than it was later. The first section of "Ars Poetica" states that a poem should be a concrete object, using four similes to suggest the desired qualities of muteness and palpability: a "globed

fruit," "old medallions," stone casement ledges, and the "flight of birds." In other words, a poem should be felt and experienced, not rationally analyzed. It should be a "real" and immediate experience, like the inviolate life of the flesh referred to in earlier poems. Certainly it is paradoxical to ask that a poem, a collection of words, be silent and wordless.

The second eight lines of "Ars Poetica" begin and end with the same two lines comparing the poem's motionlessness in time to the moon's climbing. The first uses a kind of philosophical synesthesia to communicate the time-space continuum that informs *Einstein* and *Streets in the Moon*. The moon, of course, does not climb; only from the perspective of an earthly observer, man, does it appear to do so. The earth turns (and man with it) and the moon circles the earth, but all he sees is an apparently static moon that yet moves higher and higher. Thus the poem seems to have deceptive qualities. The poem, like the moon rising behind the branches of a tree which serve as a standard to gauge its movement, passes through the memories and experiences of the mind.

Whether these mental events are the poet's or the reader's is not clear. Possibly MacLeish refers to the creative process, the relationship between the poet's personal experiences and the impersonal work he forges from them. Most often quoted are the final eight lines, which argue that a poem should not be read as a statement of some idea or external meaning. Rather, a poem is a created object, a whole self-contained experience. Here there is a suggestion of Eliot's objective correlative, which MacLeish had also frequently used in the poems of the 1920's. An image is offered for the reader to experience directly, to feel the emotion that the poet wants to express. Metonymy rather than metaphor is the appropriate figure of speech. The image or poem is an instance of the emotional complex rather than an analogue of it. The obvious trap in "Ars Poetica" is to extort "meaning" in the sense of a general theory of poetics from a poem that warns against interpreting poems as vehicles of meaning. Thus it sets the reader up to expect a theory of poetry, thwarts that expectation by its content, yet does fulfill the title's promise in a negative way.

NEW FOUND LAND

The final volume of MacLeish's initial stage, *New Found Land*, is a transitional work. Like his other collections, it offers a variety of lyrics on death, time and space, travel and migration, and it uses various experimental styles in combination with the recurrent symbols of sun, moon, sea, and leafy branches. Many of MacLeish's best-known lyrics are to be found here; but they are nostalgic, looking back to the Old World and the preoccupations of MacLeish's expatriate years. Only with "American Letter," at the end of the volume, is the promise of the collection's title fulfilled. "American Letter" shows the poet reluctantly turning from the sirens of Old World culture, the tempting foreign olive and palm trees. This poem is often described as an affirmation of America, but it is a difficult, painful affirmation. America is strange because it is neither a land nor a race. It is only a promise of a New World. MacLeish is in a sense a "reborn" American, avowing his kinship with the land and the mixed blood of America.

CONQUISTADOR

MacLeish's return to the United States in 1928 and his tramp through Mexico following the path of Cortes marked a rather dramatic change in the purpose and preoccupations of his poems. His research for *Fortune* magazine plunged the poet into awareness of social problems caused by the Great Depression. His poetry became oriented toward the New World, the present time, and the immediate future; he criticized society, but with an affirmative faith in the possibilities for freedom's triumph. The first poem of this period, *Conquistador*, builds on the narrative techniques used in his earlier works but with a new kind of subject matter. *Conquistador* is closer to a true American epic than most other attempts, such as William Carlos Williams's *Paterson* (1946-1958) or Hart Crane's *The Bridge* (1930). It explores the historical, cultural, and ideological origins of the New World, and what it finds is violence and the rape of the land, a theme shared by the subsequent volume, *Frescoes for Mr. Rockefeller's City*.

Conquistador makes no explicit value judgments; it merely presents the story of Cortes's discovery and violent capture of Mexico. The facts are presented, however, in the context of Dante's *Inferno*. The dedication is from the deepest pit of hell, from Ulysses' speech to his sailors as he leads them out of the world of men toward their death. Ulysses' sin is his driven, unprincipled search for new realms to explore and conquer; he is severely punished for venturing out of his appropriate realm, using deception to inspire his followers. A persistent motif of MacLeish's poetry is man's insistent drive to push westward, to explore, but mostly to discover the "land's end." This drive is neither praiseworthy nor evil in itself, but it has often led to trouble. In addition to the framing quotation from Dante, *Conquistador* uses a kind of modified terza rima, based not on rhyme but on other techniques of sound repetition, predominantly assonance and consonance. A further echo of the *Inferno* is the prologue, which is reminiscent of book VI of Vergil's *Aeneid* (c. 29-19 B.C.E.), the descent to the underworld, and the context for *The Divine Comedy* (c. 1320). The speaker of the poem descends to find the dead followers of Cortes to obtain the story of Bernál Díaz, one of the soldiers whose actual record of the journey MacLeish had read. It is Díaz's somewhat disjointed memories, difficult to recover, that form the substance of the poem. Because it is made up of somewhat harshly juxtaposed concrete images, *Conquistador* resembles Pound's *Cantos* (1925-1972), yet it is unified by a single plot, the conquest of Tenochtitlan, and a single narrative consciousness, that of Bernál Díaz.

Conquistador picks up one of MacLeish's earliest themes, applying it to the writing of history. In *The Happy Marriage* and even in "Baccalaureate," one of his very first poems, MacLeish contrasts book-learning and abstract ideas with felt concrete experience. In the preface to *Conquistador*, Díaz protests against the "official" historical accounts of the conquest of Mexico, especially the one written by a priest named Gómara. Such records falsify reality by labeling it with dates and neat words. For Díaz and the other soldiers, the conquest was a matter of blood and terror and guilt and finally death. It was a collection of acutely felt sense impressions and emotions. The style of the poem, written in fifteen books, embodies the confusion of Díaz's ghost as he summons his long-submerged memories. They are hazy and missing links, but acute when they surface. Clauses are repeatedly strung together with "and," as a child would speak.

Critics have read *Conquistador* as a poem more about the consciousness of the narrator than about the conquest of Tenochtitlan. MacLeish, however, seems to aim at objectivity by finding the most real, most accurate account available, the story of a participant in the action. The unglorious, unheroic attitude of the soldier lends realism to a story that might be idealized by a more distanced third-person narrative. MacLeish is essentially an empiricist; thus the sense impressions of one subject are the only accurate matter of knowledge. As always with a first-person point of view, the reader is left to evaluate the narrator and his reliability, to weigh the facts for himself. The ironic distance between author and narrator becomes greatest in the final book, in which Díaz describes the "beautiful victory," meaning the utter destruction of a highly developed culture which would never again live. Díaz calls it a "Christian siege," words which are oxymoronic in themselves. The ethnocentric attitudes of the Spaniards follow MacLeish's interesting attempt in book II to represent the alien yet beautiful culture of the Aztecs through the speech of Montezuma on death. It is almost impossible to make rational sense out of the words because they seek to transcend Greek-Judeo-Christian categories of thought.

Frescoes for Mr. Rockefeller's City

Frescoes for Mr. Rockefeller's City, published a year after *Conquistador*, weaves its implicit criticisms of the rape of the land and its natives into a more explicitly North American tapestry. These lyrical poems are a series of written paintings metaphorically intended to adorn New York City. Many of them attack the major capitalists, such as Andrew Mellon, J. P. Morgan, and Cornelius Vanderbilt, who built the railroads and controlled the stock market. MacLeish seems to blame them not only for massacring the Indians and alienating the earth with technology, but also, more immediately, for causing the Depression. In "Oil Painting of the Artist as Artist," MacLeish clearly criticizes the expatriate artists with whom he lived and learned during the 1920's. While his criticism of exploitative capitalists might suggest that MacLeish became a Communist during the 1930's, his poem "Background with Revolutionaries," a sarcastic critique of Lenin, actually earned him the venomous wrath of his Communist contemporaries. From 1928 on, MacLeish had a clear conception of Jeffersonian democracy as a standard for American government. He did not fall into the political extremes of Communism in the 1930's or of McCarthyism in the 1950's.

Public Speech and America Was Promises

Two other volumes of the 1930's, *Public Speech* and *America Was Promises*, while also criticizing the abusers of democracy, are both powerfully affirmative in their overall impressions. *Public Speech* sets forth brotherly love as the means for healing. *America Was Promises* juxtaposes the ideals of the Founding Fathers with the exploitations of capitalists, but it ends on the idea that America's promise is still intact for those who wish to seize it by preserving freedom.

The long final stage of MacLeish's career synthesized the poles of the two earlier, formative stages. In the 1920's he studied poetic techniques, both traditional and modern, dwelling in the realm of art for art's sake, expressing fine shades of sensibility and railing against the fact that man must live and die in a vast mathematical universe without inherent meaning. In the 1930's, on the other hand, MacLeish faced his homeland squarely, shouldering his heavy social responsibilities as a poet in a suffering and disillusioned republic. The 1940's were another transitional phase, in which MacLeish was still dwelling on public issues, but returning as well to earlier preoccupations, such as the Einsteinian universe and man's place in it.

Actfive and Other Poems

"Actfive" is a successful synthesis of many of MacLeish's earlier techniques and themes, a poem in which he asks what the nature of the world will be after the attempted genocide and atomic bombs of World War II. The context is Shakespeare's metaphor that "All the world's a stage." The poem is essentially an allegory, a technique that MacLeish uses often in the short, Blakean lyrics of his later period. God has departed, the King is unthroned, and man is murdered. "Actfive" seeks a hero, surveying the ineffectual types proposed in the modern era: the scientist, the magnate of industry, the revolutionary, the Nietzschean great man, the victim, the State, the narcissistic ego, and the masses. The poem is as negative as a realistic understanding of World War II requires, yet it ends on a note shared by *Einstein* and by William Faulkner's speech accepting the Nobel Prize. The "something inviolate" of *Einstein*, the mysterious, concrete life force inherent in flesh and bone will survive. Faulkner's belief that man will not merely endure but will prevail is anticipated in MacLeish's hope that man will dare to endure and love. The poems of *Actfive and Other Poems* are lyrics that look back to the "Metaphysical" wit of the 1920's and forward to the more Yeatsian poems of the later years. They are paradoxical and meditative, seeking a new reconciliation of private and public voice.

The lyrics of the 1950's through the 1970's are studded with gems. Nature is no longer the vast universe of contemporary physics, but the age-old habitat of man. MacLeish's style becomes markedly plain, the syntax often blunt. Many of the poems deal with death as a very concrete event, adopting the accepting attitude of Keats's "To Autumn." The majority of the lyrics use a technique new for MacLeish. They hinge, sometimes ironically, on a single correspondence between a natural image and a human idea or feeling. The correspondences range from emblems to metaphor to allegory. The natural images tend not to be static but rather brief processes or structures of experience, such as the sudden flight of birds from a tree. There may be a strong Japanese influence in MacLeish's new technique and simplicity. Related to the use of analogy is a strong thematic concern with the ordering of experience, as captured in Wallace Stevens's poem "Anecdote of a Jar." Thus, MacLeish becomes simultaneously more intellectual and more concrete. He becomes far more personal in his subject matter and voice, while at the same time appealing to a wider audience. Not everyone shares his concern over the abuses of capitalism, but most readers do share a concern about death's imminence. Many of the later poems are topical, but in a more personal way than the poems of the 1930's. They are elegies for MacLeish's friends and comments on the sickness of the McCarthy era. "National Security" presents the political sickness of the 1970's by dealing with Cambodia, Laos, and Vietnam as three names locked in a classified file. Two juxtaposed metaphors produce the bitter irony of the lyric: the names as classified files and the names as bodies whose blood oozes from the file drawer, through the Capital, and into the continent.

"OLD MAN'S JOURNEY"

The lyric "Old Man's Journey," published in 1968, is typical of the later poems. It is a sixteen-line poem, in rhyme scheme identical to a Shakespearean sonnet except for the extra couplet at the end. To accentuate the pattern, the poem is spaced as three quatrains followed by two couplets. Unlike traditional sonnets, the poem is not iambic pentameter. It is predominantly tetrameter, although the rhythms and lengths of the lines vary to suit the sense of the poem, as in free verse. Thus technically the poem typifies MacLeish's synthesis of constrictive, traditional poetic forms with contemporary innovations, especially in free verse. Using musical sound repetitions, thirteen of the poem's lines describe the salmon's relentless return upstream to its birthplace to die. Only the title, line four, and the appended couplet reveal the analogical nature of the natural description. The salmon is somewhat anthropomorphized with the goal of eternity and the idea of memory. Line four explains that return to the nostalgic past is a human compulsion, a fault.

As in most of his later lyrics, MacLeish does not expound upon the human significance of the poem. The emblem or analogy, the image drawn from nature, receives the emphasis, the reader being forced to draw his own conclusions. The poems speak by implication. The salmon becomes infected with restlessness at the memory of its birthplace, so it halts its journey and swims upstream to die. In human terms this suggests the way old people's minds often dwell on their earliest experiences, but it could also imply a return to a geographical place or to earlier values. The final couplet broadens the context of the poem through literary allusion even as the earlier long poems use marginal glosses and epigraphs from *The Golden Bough*, *Hamlet*, and the *Inferno*. Here, as in *Conquistador*, the reference is to Dante's version of Ulysses as a wanderer compelled to explore ever farther from home. "Old Man's Journey" thus implies that just as a salmon's nature drives it to return at last to the stream where it was spawned, so man's nature drives him to remembrance or literal return to his earliest experiences on the way to death.

Such lyrics as these, however, are best read for their concrete images of nature, allowing their human implications to unfold on an intuitive level. While MacLeish clearly rejected any hint of art for art's sake by 1930, his best poems live up to the injunctions of "Ars Poetica": that a poem is not an abstract exposition but rather a self-contained object.

OTHER MAJOR WORKS

PLAYS: *The Pot of Earth*, pb. 1925; *Nobodaddy: A Play*, pb. 1926; *Union Pacific: A Ballet*, pr. 1934 (libretto; with Nicolas Nabokoff); _Panic: A Play in Verse_, pr., pb. 1935; _The Fall of the City: A Verse Play for Radio_, pr., pb. 1937; _Air Raid: A Verse Play for Radio_, pr., pb. 1938; _The States Talking_, pb. 1941; _The American Story: Ten Broadcasts_, pb. 1944; _The Trojan Horse: A Play_, pb., pr. 1952 (broadcast); _This Music Crept By Me upon the Waters_, pr., pb. 1953; _J. B.: A Play in Verse_, pr., pb. 1958; _Three Short Plays: The Secret of Freedom, Air Raid, The Fall of the City_, pb. 1961; _Herakles: A Play in Verse_, pr. 1967; _Scratch_, pr. pb. 1971 (inspired by Stephen Vincent Benét's short story "The Devil and Daniel Webster"); _Six Plays_, pb. 1980.

NONFICTION: _Housing America_, 1932; _Jews in America_, 1936; _Background of War_, 1937; _The Irresponsibles: A Declaration_, 1940; _The American Cause_, 1941; _A Time to Speak: The Selected Prose of Archibald MacLeish_, 1941; _American Opinion and the War_, 1942; _A Time to Act: Selected Addresses_, 1943; _Poetry and Opinion: The "Pisan Cantos" of Ezra Pound_, 1950; _Freedom Is the Right to Choose: An Inquiry into the Battle for the American Future_, 1951; _Poetry and Experience_, 1961; _The Dialogues of Archibald MacLeish and Mark Van Doren_, 1964; _The Eleanor Roosevelt Story_, 1965; _A Continuing Journey_, 1968; _The Great American Frustration_, 1968; _Champion of a Cause: Essays and Addresses on Librarianship_, 1971; _Riders on the Earth: Essays and Reminiscences_, 1978; _Letters of Archibald MacLeish: 1907-1982_, 1983 (R. H. Winnick, editor).

BIBLIOGRAPHY

Cohn, Ruby. _Dialogues in American Drama_. Bloomington: Indiana University Press, 1971. Although this volume does not contain much analysis of MacLeish's earlier plays since the author believes they are merely unsuccessful adaptations of his poetry to dramatic form, Cohn's incisive reading of _J. B._ makes this volume worth consulting.

Donaldson, Scott. _Archibald MacLeish: An American Life_. Boston: Houghton Mifflin, 1992. Donaldson's biography of MacLeish discusses his education at Hotchkiss, Yale, and Harvard Law School; his expatriate life of writing in Paris; his editorship of _Fortune_; and his political career.

Drabeck, Bernard A., and Helen E. Ellis, eds. _Archibald MacLeish: Reflections_. Amherst: University of Massachusetts Press, 1986. This oral autobiography, drawn from recorded conversations the editors pursued with MacLeish from 1976 to 1981, is a valuable, unique compendium of MacLeish's commentary on his own poetry and prose and that of his peers. The preface by Richard Wilbur is especially helpful in placing MacLeish's achievements in centennial perspective.

Falk, Signi. _Archibald MacLeish_. New York: Twayne, 1966. The best extant source of exposition and biographical information on MacLeish, even though it is basically a handbook or primer on him rather than a full-fledged biocritical study. Falk methodically examines each work in MacLeish's oeuvre and offers a sound critical judgment of its merits.

Kirkpatrick, D. C., ed. _American Writers Since 1900_. New York: St. James Press, 1983. This standard reference tool contains a chronology of MacLeish's life and a comprehensive bibliography of his work. The short, evaluative article by Robert K. Johnson is a worthy overview of MacLeish's achievements in poetry and drama.

Leary, Lewis G., and John Archard. _Articles on American Literature, 1968-1975_. Durham, N.C.: Duke University Press, 1979.

Leary, Lewis G., Carolyn Bartholet, and Catharine Roth. _Articles on American Literature, 1950-1967_. Durham, N.C.: Duke University Press, 1970. These reference volumes contain comprehensive bibliographies of periodical articles related to MacLeish's criticism.

MacLeish, Archibald. _The Letters of Archibald MacLeish, 1907-1982_, edited by R. H. Winnick. Boston: Houghton Mifflin, 1983. Published posthumously, these letters represent the most important source of autobiographical information on MacLeish's life and the sources, influences, and personal memories of his most famous poems and plays. Contains a helpful index.

MacLeish, William H. _Uphill with Archie: A Son's Journey_. New York: Simon & Schuster, 2000. A beautifully written and deeply involving look at the life and the world of Archibald MacLeish by his youngest son. Partly an homage, partly an attempt to come to terms with the man, *Uphill with Archie* speaks to all sons and daughters who have never completely resolved their feelings about powerful parents.

Smith, Grover. *Archibald MacLeish*. Minneapolis: University of Minnesota Press, 1971. This pamphlet in the well-known University of Minnesota series offers a concentrated analysis of MacLeish's poetry with some attention to the poetic drama, *J. B.* The short biography and bibliography is a useful starting place for research.

Eve Walsh Stoddard;
bibliography updated by the editors

Louis MacNeice

Born: Belfast, Ireland; September 12, 1907
Died: London, England; September 3, 1963

PRINCIPAL POETRY
Blind Fireworks, 1929
Poems, 1935
Poems, 1937
The Earth Compels, 1938
Autumn Journal, 1939
Selected Poems, 1940
The Last Ditch, 1940
Poems, 1925-1940, 1940
Plant and Phantom, 1941
Springboard: Poems, 1941-1944, 1944
Holes in the Sky: Poems, 1944-1947, 1948
Collected Poems, 1925-1948, 1949
Ten Burnt Offerings, 1952
The Other Wing, 1954
Autumn Sequel: A Rhetorical Poem in XXVI Cantos, 1954
Visitations, 1957
Eighty-five Poems, 1959
Solstices, 1961
The Burning Perch, 1963
The Collected Poems of Louis MacNeice, 1966 (E. R. Dodds, editor)

OTHER LITERARY FORMS

Although he was a poet first and foremost, Louis MacNeice published a number of important works in other genres. His only novel, *Roundabout Way* (1932), not very successful, was published under the pseudonym Louis Malone. MacNeice's only other venture into fiction was a children's book, *The Penny That Rolled Away* (1954), published in England as *The Sixpence That Rolled Away*.

An area in which he was no more prolific, but much more successful, was translation. The combination of his education in classics with his gifts as a poet led him to do a successful translation of Aeschylus's *Agamemnon* (1936). E. R. Dodds, an eminent classics professor at Oxford and literary executor of MacNeice's estate, calls the translation "splendid" (*Time Was Away*, 1974, Terence Brown and Alec Reid, editors). W. B. Stanford agrees that in spite of the almost insurmountable difficulties of Aeschylus's text, MacNeice succeeded in producing an eminently actable version, genuinely poetic, and generally faithful to the original. MacNeice's translation of Johann Wolfgang von Goethe's *Faust* (1951) for radio presented very different problems—in particular, his not knowing German. The radio medium itself also produced problems in terms of what the audience could follow. MacNeice collaborated with E. L. Stahl on the project, and on the whole it was successful. According to Stahl, MacNeice succeeded in rendering the work's unusual combination of the dramatic with the lyric, producing excellent versions of the various lyrical passages.

MacNeice wrote several plays for the theater and nearly one hundred radio scripts for the BBC. Except for *The Agamemnon of Aeschylus*, his theatrical works are not notable, although *Station Bell* was performed by the Birmingham University Dramatic Society in 1937, and a similar play, *Out of the Picture*, was performed in 1937 by the Group Theatre in London, which had also done *Agamemnon*. The verse play was accounted a failure, while having its moments of very good poetry and wit. It was similar to the plays that W. H. Auden and Christopher Isherwood were producing for the Group Theatre in the 1930's: cartoon-like parodies in the service of leftist political views. MacNeice's play does, however, show a serious concern with love. Much later, in 1958,

MacNeice wrote *One for the Grave* (published in 1968), patterned on the medieval morality play. It exemplifies his growing interest in allegory, described in *Varieties of Parable* (1965). During World War II, MacNeice wrote documentary dramas for radio, contributing much that was original, though not of lasting literary value, to the genre. His later radio dramas, such as *Out of the Picture*, and his late poems tend toward allegory and quest motifs. *The Dark Tower and Other Radio Scripts by Louis MacNeice* (1947) is the most successful of these dramas in its equilibrium between realism and allegory.

MacNeice also wrote an unfinished prose autobiography, published posthumously as *The Strings Are False* (1965); several works of mixed poetry and prose, most notably *Letters from Iceland* (1937) with Auden; and several volumes of literary criticism. These works illuminate MacNeice's poetry, offering insight into the self-conscious relationship of one poet to his predecessors and his craft. *Modern Poetry: A Personal Essay* (1938) is significant as a manifesto of one of the new poets of the 1930's, who believed that poetry should speak directly to social and political issues. *The Poetry of W. B. Yeats* (1941), written before the major scholarly commentaries on William Butler Yeats, offers lucid insights into particular poems, as well as illuminating MacNeice's own goals as a poet. *Varieties of Parable*, a posthumous printing of MacNeice's Clark Lectures of 1963, elucidates his concern with writing poetry that operates on two levels simultaneously, the realistic and the symbolic, moral, or allegorical.

ACHIEVEMENTS

Louis MacNeice is most notable as an exemplar of Socrates' maxim that the unexamined life is not worth living. The major question surrounding his reputation is whether he ranks as a minor or a major poet, whether his poems show a progression of thought and technique or an essential similarity over the years. No one would deny that his craft, his mastery of prosody and verse forms, is of the highest order. Most critics agree that in his last three volumes of poems MacNeice took a new point of departure. Auden asserts in his memorial address for MacNeice (*Time Was Away*) that posterity will endorse his opinion that the later poems do advance, showing ever greater craftsmanship and intensity of

Louis MacNeice (Kim Kurnizki)

feeling. Auden claims that of all his contemporaries, MacNeice was least guilty of "clever forgeries," or dishonest poems. This honesty, combined with an ingrained temperamental skepticism, is at the root of both his major contributions to poetry and what some people see as his flaws. MacNeice is a philosophical poet, Auden says, without a specific body of beliefs, except for a fundamental sense of *humanitas* as a goal and standard of behavior. He is a harsh critic of general systems because he is always faithful to the complexity of reality.

MacNeice's achievements as a poet are paradoxical: He combines an appeal to large audiences with highly learned allusions, and he focuses on everyday events and political issues while also exploring ultimate metaphysical questions. Most interesting is his transition from the 1930's view that the poet is chiefly a *communicator*, almost a journalist, to the belief that poetry should operate on two levels, the real and the allegorical. It is these contradictory qualities, along with the literary-historical value of recording a thoughtful person's ethical responses to the trials of modern life, that will ensure MacNeice's poetry a lasting reputation.

Biography

Louis MacNeice was born on September 12, 1907, in Belfast, the son of a well-respected Church of Ireland rector. Because his early childhood experiences inform the imagery and ideas of almost all his work, the details of MacNeice's early life are important. His father, John Frederick MacNeice, and his mother, Elizabeth Margaret, were both natives of Connemara in the west of Ireland, a bastion of wild tales and imagination. Both parents communicated to their children their strong attachment to the Ireland of their youth as opposed to the stern, dour, Puritanical atmosphere of Ulster. MacNeice's father was extraordinary among Protestant Irishmen in his outspoken support for Home Rule and a united Irish republic. Thus the young poet started life with a feeling of displacement and a nostalgia for a culture and landscape he had never seen. Life in the rectory was, of course, pervaded by religion and a sense of duty and social responsibility. MacNeice had a sister, Elizabeth, five years his elder, and a brother, William, in between, who had Down's Syndrome and therefore did not figure heavily in the other children's play. The children were fairly isolated and developed many imaginative games. Louis showed a tendency toward gothic preoccupations in his fear of partially hidden statues in the church and in the graveyard that adjoined his garden. Of special significance is his mother's removal to a nursing home and subsequent death when Louis was seven. She had provided comfort and gaiety in the otherwise secluded and stern life of the Rectory. Louis, the youngest, had been particularly close to her and his poetry reflects the rupture in his world occasioned by her loss. Without their mother and intimidated by the misery of their father, the MacNeice children became particularly subject to the influences of servants. On the one hand, the cook, Annie, was a warm Catholic peasant who spoke of fairies and leprechauns. On the other hand, Miss MacCready, who was hired to take care of the children when their mother became ill, was the antithesis of both Mrs. MacNeice and Annie, a puritanical Calvinist, extremely dour and severe, lecturing constantly about hell and damnation.

In 1917, MacNeice's father remarried. Though she was very kind and devoted, the new Mrs. MacNeice had a Victorian, puritanical outlook on life which led to further restrictions on the children's behavior. Soon after the marriage, MacNeice was sent to Marlborough College, an English public school, further confusing his cultural identity. From this point on, England became his adopted home, but the English always regarded him as Irish. The Irish, of course, considered him an Anglo-Irishman, while he himself always felt his roots to be in the west of Ireland. Both at Marlborough and later at Merton College, Oxford, MacNeice was in his milieu. At Marlborough he was a friend of Anthony Blunt and John Betjeman, among others. He flourished in the atmosphere of aestheticism and learning. At Oxford he encountered Stephen Spender and the other poets with whom he came to be associated in the 1930's. MacNeice studied the classics and philosophy at Oxford and these interests are second only to the autobiographical in their influence on his poetry. He was graduated from Oxford with a double first in Honour Moderations and "Greats."

Having rebelled against his upbringing by drinking heavily and rejecting his faith at Oxford, MacNeice in a sense completed the break by marrying a Jewish girl, Mariette Ezra. Together they moved to Birmingham, where he was appointed lecturer in classics at the University. In Birmingham, MacNeice encountered the working class and taught their aspiring children at the University. He had always been protected from the lower classes of Belfast and in English schools had lived among the upper classes. The new contact with working people led to a healthy respect for the ordinary man and a broadening of MacNeice's social awareness. At the same time, he was becoming recognized as a member of the "poets of the thirties," with Auden, Isherwood, Spender, and C. Day Lewis, whose sense of social responsibility led them to espouse Marxism. MacNeice never became a Communist, but he did write about social issues and questioned the comfortable assumptions of traditional English liberalism. While at Birmingham, MacNeice became friendly with E. R. Dodds, who was later to become his literary executor. In 1934 he and his wife had a son, Dan, and in 1936, she left them both abruptly for an American graduate student at Oxford, Charles Katzman. This abandonment, parallel to the death of his mother, haunted MacNeice for many years and is reflected in his poetry. In the later 1930's, MacNeice traveled twice to Spain, reporting on the Spanish

Civil War, and twice to Iceland, the second time with Auden. In 1936 he became lecturer in Greek at Bedford College for women at the University of London. In 1939 and 1940, he lectured at colleges in the United States, returning to what he felt to be his civic responsibility to England following the outbreak of World War II.

From 1941, MacNeice worked for the British Broadcasting Corporation as a scriptwriter and producer, except for the year and a half in 1950-1951 that he served as Director of the British Institute in Athens, Greece. In 1942 he married a singer, Hedli Anderson; they had a daughter, Corinna, the following year. In the 1940's and 1950's MacNeice traveled extensively, to India, Greece, Wales, America, Africa, Asia, France, and Ireland. His premature death in 1963 was the sort of paradoxical experience he might have used in a poem on the irony of life. He was going far beyond the call of duty for the BBC by descending a chilly manhole to check the sound transmission for a feature he was producing. He suffered from exposure, contracted pneumonia, and died. Such a death appears to represent the antithesis of the poetic, yet for MacNeice, poetry spoke about the ordinary as well as the metaphysical and it was intended to speak to the ordinary man. His death resulted from the performance of his ordinary human responsibility, his job.

Analysis

Louis MacNeice was an extremely self-conscious poet. He wrote several books of literary criticism, gave lectures on the subject, and often reflected upon the role of the poet in his poems. In an early essay, written in 1936, he reveals his allegiance to the group of poets represented by W. H. Auden, who believed their chief responsibility to be social rather than purely artistic. MacNeice divided art into two types: parable and escape. William Butler Yeats and T. S. Eliot, while unquestionably great, represent the latter, the less valid route. MacNeice always retained his belief in "parable-art," that is, poems that appear naturalistic while also suggesting latent moral or metaphysical content—although he came to realize in later years that journalistic or overly realistic art has its defects while "escape-art" often addresses fundamental problems. MacNeice's lasting conception of the poet's task is remarkably close to William Wordsworth's in the preface to the *Lyrical Bal-*

lads (1800): The poet should be a spokesman for and to ordinary men. In order to communicate with a large audience, the poet must be representative, involved in current events, interested in the news, sports, and so on. He must always place the subject matter and the purpose of his art above a pure interest in form. In *Modern Poetry: A Personal Essay*, he echoes Wordsworth's dictum that the poet must keep his eye on the object. A glance at the titles of MacNeice's poems reveals the wide range of his subjects; geographical locations, artists, seasons, classical and mythical figures, types of people, technological objects, and types of songs are a few representatives of the plurality embraced by his poems. Furthermore, like Wordsworth, MacNeice studies external objects, places, and events closely, though his poems often end up really being about human consciousness and morality, through analogy or reflection on the experience.

Telling vs. showing

Thus, MacNeice's fundamental approach to poetry also resembles Wordsworth's. Many of his poems are a modernized, sometimes journalistic version of the loco-descriptive genre of the eighteenth century, arising from the description of a place, object, or event, followed usually by a philosophical, moral, or psychological reflection on that event. Although MacNeice attempts to use a plain, simple style, his training in the classics and English literature tends to produce a rich profusion of allusive reverberations. The relationship between the topical focus of the poem and the meditation it produces varies from association to analogy to multiple parallels. In technique, MacNeice differs from the Imagistic, symbolist thrust of T. S. Eliot, Ezra Pound, and the modern American poets influenced by them. The framework of MacNeice's poems is primarily expository; he tells rather than trying to show through objective correlatives.

Poet of ideas

As Terence Brown argues in *Louis MacNeice: Sceptical Vision* (1975), MacNeice is most notable as a poet of ideas. In his study of Yeats he emphasizes the importance of belief in giving substance to a poet's work. Many critics have mistakenly criticized MacNeice's poetry on this basis, finding it superficial and devoid of philosophical system. Brown argues cogently that MacNeice is deceptively philosophical because he remains a skeptic. Thus the few positive beliefs underlying his poetry appear negative. Many of his poems question epistemological and metaphysical assumptions; depending on one's interpretation, MacNeice's "final" position may seem positive or negative. Many of his poems represent what might loosely be called an Existentialist position. Although he never stops evaluating the validity of religion, MacNeice ceased to believe in God in his late teens, after being brought up in the home of a future Anglican bishop. The loss of God and Christianity left a huge gap in the metaphysical structure of MacNeice's thought, and he resisted replacing it with another absolute system such as Marxism. He retained a strong sense of moral and social duty, but he found no objective sanctions for value and order. In his poems he explores the conflicting and paradoxical facts of experience. For example, he believes that a new social order will benefit the masses, but he is honest enough to admit his fondness for the privileges of the elite: good education, clothes, food, art. He remains obsessed with the Heraclitean theory of flux, that we can never step into the same river twice. Yet when we face the absence of certainty, belief, and absolute value, we can celebrate plurality and assert ourselves against time and death. Brown distinguishes the modernity of MacNeice in "a sceptical faith, which believes that no transcendent reality, but rather non-being, gives being value."

STYLISTICS

The most striking technical features of MacNeice's poems evince his sometimes conflicting concerns with reaching a large audience of ordinary people and with reflecting philosophically on experience. In line with the former, he attempts to use colloquial, or at least plain, language, and often to base his rhythm and style on popular musical forms, from the folk ballad, nursery rhyme, and lullaby to modern jazz. His concern with contemporary issues, coupled with his classical training, makes irony and satire inevitable. Like the English Augustans (with whom he did not want to be identified), MacNeice cannot help contrasting reality with the ideals of past literature, politics, and belief systems. His satire of contemporary society tends to be of the urbane, gentle, Horatian type, only infrequently becoming harsh and bitter. Other stylistic features mark his concern with metaphysical issues. He uses analogy and paradox,

accreting many resonances through classical and biblical allusions, usually simultaneously. Many poems pose unresolved questions and problems, circling back on their beginnings at the end. The endings that repeat initial statements or questions would seem to offer closure, or at least a definite structure, to the poems, but paradoxically they do not. Rather, they emphasize the impossibility of answering or closing the issue.

Another stylistic feature that recurs throughout MacNeice's work is the list, similar to the epic catalogs of Homer. Rather than suggesting greatness or richness as they usually do in epics, MacNeice's catalogs represent the irreducible plurality of experience.

EVOLUTION VS. STASIS

In addition to the question of his belief system or lack thereof, critics have disagreed over whether MacNeice's work develops over time or remains essentially the same. The answer to this question is sometimes viewed as a determinant of MacNeice's rank as a poet. An argument can be made for both positions, but the answer must be a synthesis. While MacNeice's appreciation of the complexity of life, its latent suggestions, grows as his poetry develops, certain interrelated clusters of themes and recurring images inform his work from beginning to end.

For example, the places and events of his childhood shape his problematic identity and worldview, including his obsessions with dreams and with Ireland as a symbol of the more gothic, mysterious, and mystical sides of experience. Connected with his upbringing in the home of an Anglican rector is a preoccupation, mentioned above, with disbelief in God and religion, and faith in liberal humanism. The disappearance of God results in complex epistemological and moral questions which also pervade many poems. Another related thematic cluster is a concern with time, death, and Heraclitean flux. Closely related to this cluster is an increasing interest in cycles, in repetition versus renewal, reflected in many poems about spring and fall.

Although these themes, along with recurring images of train journeys, Ireland, stone, dazzling surfaces, and time represented as space, among others, continue to absorb MacNeice's attention, the types of poems and emphases evolve over time, particularly in response to changes in the political temper of the times. His juvenilia, written between 1925 and 1927, reflects the aesthetic focus of his student years, playing with sound and rhetorical devices, musing on sensation, death, God, and self-consciousness. MacNeice did not really emerge as a poet until the 1930's, when his teaching, marriage, and life among the workers of Birmingham opened his eyes to the world of social injustice and political reality. At that point he was influenced by Auden, Stephen Spender, and C. Day Lewis, and came to see the poet's role as more journalistic than purely aesthetic.

FROM POLITICAL TO PHILOSOPHICAL

The poems of the 1930's reflect his preoccupation with the disheartening political events in Spain and Germany and his belief that the existing social order was doomed. The poetry of this period is more leftist than at any other stage in MacNeice's career, but he never espouses the dogmas of Marxism. During World War II, his poetry becomes more humanistic, more positive in its treatment of man. MacNeice's faith in human nature was fanned by the courage and generosity he witnessed in his job as a fire watcher in London during the war.

After the war his poems become at first more philosophical, reflecting a revaluation of the role of art and a desire for belief of any kind, not necessarily in God. At this point the poems express an existential recognition of the void, and a disgust with the depersonalization of England after the war; they also play with looking at subjects from different perspectives. His last three volumes of poems, published in 1957, 1961, and posthumously in 1963, represent what most critics consider to be the apotheosis of MacNeice's career. The lyrics of his latest poems are austere and short, often using tetrameter rather than pentameter or hexameter lines. Many of these poems are "parable-poems" in the sense that MacNeice described in his Clark Lectures of 1963, published as *Varieties of Parable* (1965); that is, they use images to structure a poem that is in effect a miniature allegory. The poems appear to be topical or occasional, but they hold a double or deeper meaning.

"THE KINGDOM"

Because MacNeice was essentially a reflective, philosophical poet, his poetry records an ongoing dialectic between the shaping forces of his consciousness and the events and character of the external world. Thus certain techniques, goals, and preoccupations tend to recur, though they are different in response to historical and personal developments in MacNeice's life. Since he was a skeptic, he tends to ask questions rather than give answers, but the more positive values that he holds become clearer by the last years of his life. In particular, the idea of a kingdom of individuals, who lay claim to their freedom and create their lives, is implicit in many of the later poems, after being introduced in "The Kingdom," written around 1943. The members of this kingdom counteract flux and fear by their genuineness, their honest seeing and feeling, their incorruptibility. The Greek notion of *arête*, sometimes translated as virtue or excellence, but without the narrowly moral meaning usually attached to "virtue," comes to mind when one reads the descriptions of exemplary individuals in "The Kingdom." This kingdom is analogous to the Kingdom of Christ, the ideal Republic of Plato, and the Kingdom of Ends in Immanuel Kant's moral system. Yet it does not depend on absolutes and thus it is not an unattainable ideal but a mode of life that some people manage to realize in the ordinary course of life. Moreover, the members of this kingdom belong by virtue of their differentness, not because they share divine souls or absolute ideas of reason.

"BLASPHEMIES"

MacNeice sees himself in terms of stages of development in such poems as "Blasphemies," written in the late 1950's, where he describes his changing attitude toward God and belief. The poem is a third-person narrative about his own feelings toward religion since his childhood. In the first stanza he is seven years old, lying in bed pondering the nature of the unforgivable sin against the Holy Ghost. In the second stanza he is seventeen, striking the pose of a blasphemer, parodying prayers. The middle-aged writer of the autobiographical poem mocks his earlier stance, seeing the hollowness of rebellion against a nonexistent deity. The third stanza describes how, at thirty, the poet realized the futility of protest against an absence, and turned to a new religion of humanism and realism, facing facts. The mature MacNeice undercuts these simple new faiths by ending the stanza with a question about the nature of facts for a thirty-year-old. Stanza four finds the poet at forty attempting to appropriate the myths of Christianity for purely symbolic use, and realizing that their lack of absolute meaning makes them useless to him. At the age of forty he has reached a crisis of sorts, unable to speak for himself or for humankind. The final stanza sums up MacNeice's ultimate philosophical position: that there are no ultimate beliefs or postures. He finally throws off the entire issue of Christianity, finding divinity neither above nor within man.

The irreducible reality is that he is not Tom, Dick, or Harry, some archetypal representative of ordinary man. He is himself, merely fifty, a question. The final two lines of the poem, however, in typical MacNeice fashion, reintroduce the problem of metaphysics that he has just dismissed. He asserts that although he is a question, that question is as worthwhile as any other, which is not saying too much. He then, however, uses the word "quest" in apposition to the word "question," reintroducing the entire issue of a search for ultimate meaning. To complete the confusion, he ends with a completed repetition of the broken-off question which opens the poem: What is the sin against the Holy Ghost? The repeated but augmented line is an instance of the type of incremental repetition used in folk ballads such as "Lord Randall," and it suggests the kind of dark riddle often presented in such songs. The final question might be just idle intellectual curiosity or it might imply that ultimate questions of belief simply cannot be escaped by rationality.

"TO HEDLI"

MacNeice's dedicatory poem, "To Hedli," which prefaces the 1949 *Collected Poems, 1925-1948*, serves as a good introduction to his technique and themes. The poem is clearly occasional and autobiographical, using the first-person point of view that he often eschews in later poems. While employing fairly plain diction, the poem is a sestina, a highly restrictive verse form made up of six stanzas, each having six lines ending with the same six words throughout the poem. In addition, the final word of each stanza is repeated as the last word of the first line in the succeeding stanza. MacNeice takes a few liberties, adding a tercet, or half-stanza, at the end, and substituting the word "returning" for "turning" in stanza four. The poem is typically self-reflective, calling into question the poetic efforts represented in the collected poems, regretting the unanswered question present in the volume. The content of the poem thus radiates

out from a highly specific event, the collecting of Mac-Neice's poems from 1925-1948, and their dedication to the listener of the poem, his second wife Hedli. From this focus the poem reaches back to the poet's past practices and beliefs and outward to suggest a broad metaphysical stance. The poem is therefore typically occasional, personal, and philosophical. Although the poem does not make explicit reference to World War II, its recent horror is implicit in the anger of those who believed they knew all the answers and the "grim past" which has silenced so many poets.

Two recurrent themes that pervade this poem are the need for belief and the motif of repetitive cycles, with the question of renewal. The sestina form, so highly repetitive, mirrors the concern with cycles. Stanza one calls the poetic moments in the collection "April Answers." In MacNeice's works, spring and fall always signal, on one level, the cycles of time and life. In "Day of Renewal," he says he has measured all his experience in terms of returning autumns. The answers that come in April are the positive side of cycles; they herald renewal if not rebirth. The poems, or answers, implicitly compared to perennial plants, seem to have "withered" off from their bulbs or roots, their questions. The questions, or sources of the poems, are akin to the frozen barrenness of winter, perhaps representing despair. Stanza three picks up the metaphor implicit in the word "withered" by comparing the "Word" to a bulb underground. MacNeice is writing this poem during the period when he began attempting to deal with religious matters symbolically, so it is clear that "Word" has no literal Christian significance. It is rather the source of true poetry, informed by some body of belief. The cycles of renewal in MacNeice's past work are contrasted with a larger cycle in which this word is awaiting a new generation of poets who will produce "full leaf" and "bloom" of meaning and image.

The alternating stanzas, two and four, criticize more clearly what MacNeice sees as his own weaknesses as a poet. He has lived too much in the present, in a no-man's-land of belief, between unknown gods to come and the rejected gods of his ancestors. This position parallels, though without the defined system of belief, Yeats's prophecy in "A Second Coming." There is a milder sense than Yeats's of the crumbling of the old order in the outpouring of angry sound from those who knew the answers, perhaps enthusiasts for Communism. Stanza four explains MacNeice's past contentment with "dazzle," the poetic mirroring of intense moments in the flux of life, and with chance gifts washed up by the sea of life. These gifts were fragments from older castaways who could never return. This statement suggests that while nature repeats its cycles endlessly, men die. The final half stanza suggests that the poet is growing older and has nothing but half answers; his end is in sight. Stanza five begins with the word "But," clearly contrasting the poet's past contentment with his present goals. He refers to the autumn in which he is writing this dedicatory poem (November, 1948) and parallels the leaves' turning brown with the gilt's flaking off his poetic images. The poem ends with a definite desire for some fundamental answers to metaphysical questions. Unlike later poems, "To Hedli" at least implies that such answers may exist.

"An Eclogue for Christmas"

Among the earlier poems in the 1949 collection, "An Eclogue for Christmas" (December, 1933) marks an early point of departure, a turning toward serious poems of social commentary. In his fragmentary prose autobiography, *The Strings Are False* (1965), MacNeice describes his absorption in his home life during the early 1930's. His sister, in "Trees Were Green" (*Times Was Away*), comments on the special pleasure Christmas always represented for her brother. MacNeice explains that when he had finished writing this poem he was taken aback by the depth of his despair over Western culture's decay. Like many of the poems of this period, "An Eclogue for Christmas" combines colloquial language with a classical form, the eclogue, which is a dialogue between shepherds, often on love or poetry, or the contrast between city and country life. The two speakers of MacNeice's poem, *A.* and *B.*, represent the city and the country, the country in this case being the world of the landed gentry in England. There is no disagreement between the two speakers; they mirror each other's prophecies of doom in terms of the societies they represent. Neither city nor country escapes the horrors of the times. *B.*, the representative of country life, tells *A.* not to look for sanctuary in the country. Both places are equally bad. The poem describes a time like that in

Yeats's "A Second Coming," but in a more dominant way than "To Hedli." It seems that MacNeice could clearly see the coming of World War II. The poem satirizes contemporary upper-class British society as mechanistic, slick, and superficial. The rhythms of jazz pervade the hectic and chaotic life of the city, and people like *A.* become automatons. Rather than being individuals like those in MacNeice's later "The Kingdom," people are grotesque in their efforts to be unique.

The motif of cyclical return is what motivates the poem, the reflection on Christ's birth as represented by "old tinsel and frills." This is a hollow repetition, not a renewal or rebirth. The elaboration of technological "improvements" has alienated people from the genuine reality of life. The cyclicity of history is suggested in the metaphor of the Goths returning to silence the pneumatic drill. Yet MacNeice is such a skeptic that he is unable to make a wholesale condemnation of modern industrial society. He admits that a narcotic beauty can be perceived in the lights and bustle of the city, which he here calls an "organism" rather than a machine. *B.* attacks the country gentry in Marxist terms, as a breed whose time is about to end. He alludes to the destruction of the "manor wall" by the "State" with a capital "S," and also to private property as something which is turning to "poison and pus." Much of this part of the dialogue is carried on in questions, so it is difficult to assign a positive attitude to either speaker, let alone the author. *A.*, who seems closer to MacNeice, counters the Marxist-inspired questions of *B.* with questions about the results of violent revolution. *A.* is clearly the skeptic who sees the problems inherent in capitalist society but cannot accept the Marxist solution. *A.* interrupts *B.*, telling him not to "gloat" over his own demise, suggesting the irony of an upper-class Communism. The poem ends with self-mocking assertions on the part of both speakers; they have no choice but to cling to the few good, real things they have in life.

Like so many of MacNeice's poems, this one circles back to its opening occasion, the significance of Christmas. The ending holds out a somewhat flippant hope for renewal, but it is extremely "ephemeral," like the few positive ideas in the last part of the poem. Thus, "An Eclogue for Christmas" shows MacNeice facing an "evil time," the discord and injustices of modern industrial society, but unwilling and unable to accept the premises of a new regime founded on violence and the subordination of the individual to the state. This skepticism sets him apart from the group of poet-friends surrounding Auden.

Autumn Journal

Six years later, in the fall of 1938, MacNeice wrote *Autumn Journal*, a long poem in twenty-four cantos, commenting specifically on the depressing political events of the time: the Munich Pact and the Spanish Civil War. In a prefatory note he categorizes the poem as half lyric and half didactic, hoping that it presents some "criticism of life" with some standards beyond the "merely personal." The poem, however, is a journal (as the title states) and its record of events is tinged by fleeting personal response. It is a huge, complex version of his shorter poems in its intertwining threads of autobiography, travel, politics, philosophy, morality, and poetics. The personal-ethical response to political events is the strongest of these threads, coloring the entire poem. Because it takes its impetus from the private and public events of the days and months of late 1938, from late August until New Year's Eve, it does not have an overall architectonic structure; each individual canto rounds itself out as a separate unity which is enhanced by its relationship to the whole.

The poem as a whole is given closure by the parallels between the dying summer at the beginning, the dying year at the end, and the threatened death of European civilization from the impending world war throughout. The narrative is basically chronological, following the poet's first day of the fall term, through trips to Oxford and finally to Spain. The narrative technique resembles stream of consciousness, the thoughts and memories of the poet creating the subject matter. The poem is more fluently lyrical than many of MacNeice's poems, which have been criticized as being "flat." It uses an alternating rhyme scheme like that of ballad stanzas (*abcbdefe* . . .), but the effect resembles terza rima.

As in most of MacNeice's works, the meditations are rooted in specific observations of actual times, places, and events. Canto I begins with a catalog of concrete images of summer's end in Hampshire, ordinary people leading ordinary lives, insulated within their families. The poet-narrator is in a train, as in so many of his poems. The train ride comes to symbolize the journey of

life, the time line of each individual. In an ambiguous tone, MacNeice mentions his dog lying on the floor of the train, a symbol of lost order. This is picked up both more seriously and more ironically in Canto VII when the dog is lost while political treaties are dying and trees are being cut down on Primrose Hill in order to make an antiaircraft station. The loss of the dog is the close of the "old regime." In MacNeice's personal life, the "old regime" represents his marriage to Mariette, but in larger terms it is the demise of traditional Western capitalist society. At the end of this canto, the speaker tries to work up enthusiasm for a war which he cannot romanticize. He realizes exactly what it is, yet he also realizes that he may have to become uncritical like the enemy, like Hitler propagandizing on the radio.

Canto VIII builds, through satirical popular song rhythms, to a climax of fear about the outbreak of war. At the end of the canto the poet learns that the crisis is averted through the sacrifice of Czechoslovakia. He does not explain his response directly except to say that he has saved his own skin as an Englishman in a way that damns his conscience. The poet-narrator feels a terrible conflict between a natural desire to avert war and a sense of duty, which might in earlier times have been called honor, to face up to the threat of Hitler and defeat him. This conflict is implicit until Canto XII, in which he describes people, himself included, lacking the heart to become involved in ethics or "public calls." In his private debate with his conscience, MacNeice recalls the soldiers training across the road from his home when he was a child during World War I. Having described the beginning of classes in Canto IX, cynically and mockingly stating that *we* are safe (although the Czechs are lost), the poet is reading Plato in preparation for teaching his philosophy course. The ethical differences between Plato and Aristotle form an important context for the progress of MacNeice's feelings and thoughts in the poem. In Canto XII, he rejects Plato's ideal forms as a world of capital initials, preferring instead the Heraclitean world of flux, of sensation. He admits at the end of Canto XII that his desire is to be "human," in the fullest sense, to live in a civilized community where both mind and body are given their due. He undercuts this desire by satirizing the professors of humanities who become "spiritually bankrupt" snobs, yet conceding his own willingness to take the comforts that such a profession provides. Though the connection is not explicitly made here, the reader must keep in mind the overwhelming threat to civilization that forms the background of these reflections. *Autumn Journal* traces MacNeice's emotional and moral journey from reluctant self-interest to reluctant determination to do his share to protect humanity in the impending war.

Canto XIII is a mocking, slightly bitter rejection of the elitist education, particularly in philosophy, that MacNeice has received. The bitterness arises from the disjunction between the promise and world of thought and the real world he must inhabit. He must be happy to live in the world of appearances and plurality, life in the particular rather than the eternal and ideal realm. The poet's synthesis between skepticism and moral and civic responsibility is revealed in the next canto where he describes a trip to Oxford to help drive voters to the polls. While he cannot commit himself to political ideologies, he does mobilize himself to act for a "half-believed-in principle." Imperfect though it is, the parliamentary system is England's only hope for political progress. Here MacNeice comes to the important realization that to shun politics for private endeavor is to risk the conditions that support or allow that private endeavor. As he drives back to London at the end of Canto XIV, MacNeice has a new understanding of the need for all Englishmen to unite against the threat of Fascism. This new resolution allows the cheerful final image of the sun caressing the plurality of nature, wheelbarrows full of oranges and apples. This serenity is undercut in the following canto by a nightmarish effort to escape through drink the horrors that threaten, horrors associated in MacNeice's mind with his childhood fears and bad dreams.

In Canto XVII, at nine o'clock on a November morning, the poet savors a moment of almost Keatsian escape in a bath, allowing responsibility to die. Metaphorically he speaks of the ego merging into the bath, thus leading himself into a meditation on the need of man to merge, or at least interact, with those outside himself. Significantly, MacNeice affirms Aristotle's ethical notion that man's essence is to act, as opposed to Socrates' idea that man's crowning glory is to think. The canto ends with his refusal to "drug" himself with the sensations of the

moment. This climactic decision to act is followed by cantos satirizing industrialized England, implying, as William Blake does in *Songs of Innocence* (1789) and *Songs of Experience* (1794), that church and state conspire to allow social injustice. While MacNeice is not a Communist, he fairly consistently condemns *laissez-faire* economics as an instrument of evil. While Canto XVIII is very bitter about England's social and political failure to act, it ends with the affirmative statement that the seeds of energy and choice are still alive. Canto XX, trying to sound bitter, relaxes into a nostalgic longing for Christmas, a week away, a "coral island in time." This beautiful image is typical of MacNeice's conflation of space and time. Any poem about consciousness exists in the stream of time, but to be comprehensible the passing of time must be anchored to spatial reference points. MacNeice frequently concretizes this space/time relationship by metaphorically imaging time as a geographical space. Christmas here is an ideal moment, described through an allusion to the lotus eaters of the *Odyssey* (c. 800 B.C.E.). The remainder of the canto speaks respectfully of Christ but ends on a satirical note about people exploiting the season to beg for money. This carries additional overtones, however, because if one remembers the spirit of Christmas rather than the selfish pleasures it brings, nothing is more appropriate than to celebrate Christ's birthday by giving money to beggars.

Canto XXI returns to the notion of Canto XVII, that one must live a life beyond the self, in spite of the wish to quit. The poem, like the year, ends with MacNeice's train journey through France to Spain. Significantly, the poem skips Christmas, implying that neither the hollow religion of Christianity nor the personal pleasures of the holiday have a meaningful place in the ethical and political events at hand. MacNeice goes to face the New Year in Spain, a place where metaphorically all of Europe may soon stand in time. He goes to confront his duty as a man of action and a citizen of a free country. His New Year's resolutions, detailed in the penultimate canto, reveal his self-criticisms and determination to seek the roots of "will and conscience," to participate. The final canto is a sleep song, gentle in tone, allowing some peace after the hard-won resolutions of Canto XXIII. MacNeice addresses himself, his parents, his ex-wife, and all people, to dream of a "possible land" where the individual can pursue his natural abilities in freedom and understanding. He tells of his hope to awaken soon, but of his doubts to sleep forever.

VISITATIONS, SOLSTICES, AND THE BURNING PERCH

Most critics agree that MacNeice's final three books of poems, *Visitations*, *Solstices*, and the posthumous *The Burning Perch*, achieve new heights of technical precision and depth of meaning. The themes of flux and renewal become even more prominent than in the past. According to his own statements in literary criticism, MacNeice was attempting to write more "parable-poems." The use of the train journey and of Christmas Day in *Autumn Journal* exemplifies the multiple layers of meaning he could achieve in describing an actual event, object, or place. In these later poems there is more respect for the mysterious, the dark side of experience. The focus on life as a paradox is playfully yet darkly expounded in poems resembling folk ballad riddles, poems such as "A Hand of Snap-shots," "The Riddle," and parts of "Notes for a Biography." In particular, the poems of *The Burning Perch* give brief nightmare sketches of the gothic side of experience. Connected to the motifs of riddles and paradoxes is a new concern with perspective or various ways of knowing, as in Part I of "Jigsaws," "The Wiper," "The Grey Ones," and perhaps "Budgie."

"The Wiper," from *Solstices*, is a perfect example of the kind of "parable-poem" MacNeice sought to write in his later years. On the literal level it starts with a concrete description of the driver's and passengers' perspective of the road from inside the car on a dark, rainy night. The first stanza portrays the glimpses of the shiny asphalt when the windshield wipers clear the window, only to blur it when they move back the other way. The focus shifts to the nature of the road and then to an outside view of the wet cars on the road. The fourth stanza turns to the memory of the car's passengers, to the relationship between past and present, while the final stanza looks not very invitingly to the "black future," literally the dark night ahead on the road. Only through subtle double meanings does MacNeice suggest the allegorical or symbolic nature of the poem. The words "mystery" and "always" in stanza two and "black future" in stanza five are the only obvious indicators of a level of meaning beyond the literal.

The poem symbolizes life as a journey with the potential of being a quest, a potential limited by the restrictions of partial blindness. The riders in the car can see only brief snatches of a black road, a mysterious road with unknown dimensions. The darkness of night, the meaningless void of existence, is broken intermittently by the lights of other people insulated and partially blinded in their own "moving boxes." Significantly, while each driver is able to see very little through the dark and rain, his or her car gives off light that illuminates the way for other drivers, if only transiently. The dials in the cars measure speed and distance covered. In Aristotle's terms, these are indicators of efficient causes, but the final cause, the destination and the daylight, is not indicated. The final line of the poem is highly characteristic of MacNeice in its qualified, pessimistically positive assertion. In spite of ignorance and clouded perceptions, living in a world of night and rain, the drivers manage to stay on the road.

MacNeice is a poet of contradictions, a learned classicist who sought to write in a colloquial idiom and appeal to a broad audience, a man who sought belief but was unable to accede to the dishonesty of systematizing. His poems are above all honest. They study life in the fullness of its antinomies and paradoxes.

OTHER MAJOR WORKS

LONG FICTION: *Roundabout Way* (as Louis Malone), 1932.

PLAYS: *Out of the Picture*, pr., pb. 1937; *Station Bell*, pr. 1937.

RADIO PLAYS: *Christopher Columbus*, 1944; *The Dark Tower and Other Radio Scripts by Louis MacNeice*, 1947; *The Mad Islands and The Administrator*, 1964; *One for the Grave*, pr. 1966, pb. 1968; *Persons from Porlock and Other Plays for Radio*, 1969.

NONFICTION: *Letters from Iceland*, 1937 (with W. H. Auden); *I Crossed the Minch*, 1938; *Modern Poetry: A Personal Essay*, 1938; *Zoo*, 1938; *The Poetry of W. B. Yeats*, 1941; *Astrology*, 1964; *The Strings Are False*, 1965; *Varieties of Parable*, 1965.

CHILDREN'S LITERATURE: *The Penny That Rolled Away*, 1954.

TRANSLATIONS: *The Agamemnon of Aeschylus*, 1936; *Goethe's Faust, Parts I and II*, 1951 (with E. L. Stahl).

BIBLIOGRAPHY

Brown, Terence. *Louis MacNeice: Sceptical Vision.* New York: Barnes & Noble Books, 1975. This book is concerned with the themes in MacNeice's poetry. The author presents the argument that the poet's real contribution is as a proponent of creative skepticism. The result is a dependable, authoritative study. Contains a good bibliography and notes.

Brown, Terence, and Alec Reid, eds. *Time Was Away: The World of Louis MacNeice.* Dublin: Dolmen Press, 1974. These essays, a grab-bag collection including personal tributes, reminiscences, and evaluations of MacNeice's work, are of uneven quality. Several pieces are of interest—including one by MacNeice's sister which contains personal biographical information. Other selections look at MacNeice's Irishness, his poetry, and his reaction to his mother's death. Includes W. H. Auden's "Louis MacNeice: A Memorial Address" to introduce the collection.

Devine, Kathleen, and Alan J. Peacock, eds. *Louis MacNeice and His Influence.* New York: Oxford University Press, 1998. Essays by leading experts on MacNeice's work examine the range and depth of his achievement, including his influence on Michael Longley, Derek Mahon, Seamus Heaney, and Paul Muldoon. Includes bibliographical references and index.

Longley, Edna. *Louis MacNeice: A Study.* London: Faber & Faber, 1988. The first complete study after MacNeice's death. Explores the dramatic nature of MacNeice's poetry, stresses the importance of his Irish background, and credits William Butler Yeats's influence, hitherto downplayed. This piece of historical criticism moves chronologically, linking MacNeice's life and times. Special attention is given to his English, war, and postwar poems. Bibliography.

McDonald, Peter. *Louis MacNeice: The Poet in His Contexts.* 1991. Reprint. New York: Oxford University Press, 1996. An examination of MacNeice in the context of Northern Ireland and its poets. W. J.

Martz, reviewing for *Choice* magazine, notes the author's "need to see MacNeice as MacNeice . . . in his contexts rather than those that have hitherto been thought to be his." Bibliography, index.

McKinnon, William T. *Apollo's Blended Dream: A Study of the Poetry of Louis MacNeice.* New York: Oxford University Press, 1971. After a skeletal biography the author suggests that MacNeice has been underestimated and proposes to reevaluate his work in a new perspective. He characterizes him as a poet-philosopher and then goes into a detailed analysis of his linguistic techniques. Although rather dry in approach, this is a valid study with interesting perceptions of the poet.

Marsack, Robyn. *The Cave of Making: The Poetry of Louis MacNeice.* New York: Oxford University Press, 1982. This book looks at MacNeice as a poet of the 1930's and focuses on despair and disillusionment in his work. Contains commentary on the poet's craft and process based on papers, drafts, and notes made available to the author. Extensive notes and an excellent bibliography make this a helpful companion to reading MacNeice.

Moore, Donald B. *The Poetry of Louis MacNeice.* Leicester: Leicester University Press, 1972. This descriptive study traces the poet's development chronologically, starting with early influences and following him through the war years and to his death. Tracks thematic lines such as self, society, and philosophy through MacNeice's work. The final chapter gives a retrospective and general critical overview. Includes a select bibliography with citations of related works.

O'Neill, Michael, and Gareth Reeves. *Auden, MacNeice, Spender: The Thirties Poetry.* London: Macmillan Education, 1992. A close analysis of the major works of three giants of 1930's English poetry.

Stallworthy, Jon. *Louis MacNeice.* New York: W. W. Norton, 1995. Poet and Wilfred Owen biographer Stallworthy produces the first full-scale biography of MacNeice, tour de force "not likely to be superseded," according to the W. J. Martz, reviewer for *Choice* magazine: "The author in effect presents MacNeice as an example of the tragedy of an individualist in the twentieth century." Supported by pictures and copies of manuscript pages, each dated. Bibliography, notes, and index.

Eve Walsh Stoddard;
bibliography updated by the editors

SANDRA MCPHERSON

Born: San Jose, California; August 2, 1943

PRINCIPAL POETRY

Elegies for the Hot Season, 1970
Radiation, 1973
The Year of Our Birth, 1978
Sensing, 1980
Patron Happiness, 1983
Streamers, 1988
Designating Duet, 1989
The God of Indeterminacy, 1993
Edge Effect: Trails and Portrayals, 1996
The Spaces Between Birds: Mother/Daughter Poems, 1967-1995, 1996

OTHER LITERARY FORMS

Sandra McPherson has published a number of essays about contemporary poetry, among them "You Can Say That Again" (*Iowa Review*, Summer, 1972), "The Working Line" (*Field*, April, 1973), "Saying No: A Brief Compendium and Sometimes a Workbook with Blank Spaces" (*Iowa Review*, Summer, 1973), "Secrets: Beginning to Write Them Out" (*Field*, Spring, 1986), and "The Two-Tone Line, Blues Ideology, and the Scrap Quilt" (*Field*, Spring, 1991).

ACHIEVEMENTS

Since the mid-1960's, Sandra McPherson has been one of the United States' most important poets. Well received by critics and readers for poems noted for their empathy and unusual syntactical arrangements, McPherson has earned numerous high-profile literary grants and awards, including two Ingram Merrill grants (1972 and 1984), three National Endowment for the Arts grants, the Helen Bullis Prize from *Poetry North-*

west, the Bess Hokin Prize from *Poetry*, the Emily Dickinson Prize from the Poetry Society of America, and the Blumenthal-Leviton-Blonder Award from *Poetry*. Her first book, *Elegies for the Hot Season*, was a selection of the National Council on the Arts university press program. Her second book, *Radiation*, received the Pacific Northwest Booksellers Prize. *The Year of Our Birth* was nominated for a National Book Award, and *Streamers* was nominated for both the *Los Angeles Times* Book Award and the Bay Area Book Reviewers Association Award.

BIOGRAPHY

The unusual facts of Sandra McPherson's biography come to figure both directly and indirectly in many of her poems. Born in San Jose, California, she was given up for adoption at birth. Her adoptive parents lived in San Jose; McPherson grew up there and went to San Jose State University. Not only has McPherson's adoption helped to form her worldview, but her adult reunion with her birth parents in 1981 has also provided the poet with a heightened sense of both the random and orderly forces at work in the universe. Now that she is intimate with two sets of living parents, many of McPherson's poems, especially those in *Patron Happiness*, have come to focus on the similarities between her own ways of perceiving and those of her blood relatives. They also take up attendant questions concerning identity formation and the way a person's life inevitably progresses along unpredictable paths. (See "Earthstars, Birthparents' House," "Wings and Seeds," "Helen Todd: My Birthname," and "Last Week of Winter" in *Patron Happiness* and "The Pantheist to His Child" and "Big Flowers" in *Streamers*.)

After continuing her education at the University of Washington, where she studied with the celebrated poets David Wagoner and Elizabeth Bishop, McPherson worked for a short time as a technical writer for Honeywell, a defense contractor. Poems that reflect this experience are "Preparation" and "Resigning from a Job in the Defense Industry" in *Elegies for the Hot Season*. After marrying poet Henry Carlile in 1966, she gave birth the following year to a daughter, Phoebe. She has taught at the University of Iowa's writing workshop, Portland State University, the University of California at Berkeley, and the University of California at Davis, where she continues to teach. In 1999, McPherson founded the Swan Scythe Press.

ANALYSIS

In her poems, Sandra McPherson repeatedly takes up the issue of survival. She is especially concerned with the tenuous life of objects and beings at the mercy of forces outside their control. In "World of Different Sizes," from her first book, *Elegies for the Hot Season*, she admits a desire to help small objects or beings survive. Her subjects range from slugs and flowers to cats and dogs to human beings and the natural world at large. The lives of children and women as well as adult love relationships are also favorite topics. Usually written in the voice of a narrator who is empathic with whatever or whoever is threatened, her poems express a deep admiration for the idiosyncrasies of the world's fragile inhabitants. McPherson draws connections between the inability of a being to protect itself and special traits of that being. The poet believes that those traits are highly deserving of care and admiration, because they cannot be found in any other being and therefore will disappear when that being dies. For McPherson, the beauty of a thing is closely related to its degree of helplessness. As she intimates in "Worlds of Different Sizes," she believes that all things—no matter what their size—have an invisible and endangered spirit that is laboring for life.

McPherson's belief in the delicate and essential inward energy of plants and animals (and sometimes even inanimate objects) produces a poetry which continuously examines that aspect of a thing that gives it its distinctive identity. In her poem "The Plant," she recognizes a houseplant's distinctive life, suggesting that its blossoms emerge from a special place in the plant, a kind of botanical soul. As in many of McPherson's poems, however, this soul is finite and cannot always weather the menacing forces of its environment.

McPherson's work is not important merely because of her ability to prize those beings threatened by uncontrollable forces. Her genius lies in her talent for wedding this extraordinary empathic faculty with her own idiosyncratic syntactical mode. Her idiom is clearly her own—and it virtually resists mimicry. Few other poets

write like Sandra McPherson. Her poetic language does not soar like that of Dylan Thomas or Theodore Roethke in passionate lyric bursts. She is one of the most significant poets of her era because she renders her concern for the unique qualities of vulnerable beings in a poetic diction that is often contrapuntal, involuted, highly detailed, and, in her best poems, mysterious and surprising. The linguistic structure she creates is often as unusual as the subjects she is describing. The great aesthetic strength of McPherson's poetry is that in key ways her verse is like many of her subjects: exclusive, irreproducible, one-of-a-kind. Her poems can be difficult; they frequently require close reading in the way many of Marianne Moore's poems do. People, animals, and things are depicted not only with a care for detail but also with an eye for aspects of the subject that have heretofore gone undescribed.

McPherson's poems are often marked by a shimmering, highly refined voice, one that speaks out of an uncanny identification with the inner life of fellow creatures. While McPherson's growing canon will probably leave a lasting mark, her voice also seems somehow fearful of its own mortality, of its human fragility. Beginning with Wallace Stevens, most of the major poets of the twentieth century lament the fact of human mortality. Yet few poets use tone and imagery to render convincingly the nervous fear that not only is one capable of dying but indeed that one may die at any moment. One of McPherson's earlier poems, "Lions," uses lions as images of incompletely socialized, unpredictable, and dangerous human instincts. This simultaneous and self-conscious awareness of one's own power to kill and ability to die is echoed in McPherson's language and serves to amplify her assertion that all beings—especially those that survive for the pleasure of others—must be the focus of wonder and care.

ELEGIES FOR THE HOT SEASON

To examine McPherson's five books in order of their appearance is to witness in midcareer the evolution of a style of poetic language that simultaneously describes and mirrors the tenuous and idiosyncratic nature of its subjects. Her first book provides a small preview of the complex syntactical and imagistic poetics she has come to employ more and more. The title poem is the best in a remarkably sophisticated first volume. In the two-part

"Elegies for the Hot Season," snails and caterpillars are the foci of her empathy as well as metaphors for the finite lives of humans. In the first section, called "The Killing of the Snails," the narrator remembers how her father would circle the house on humid moonless nights during the summer, hunting for snails to destroy. She could hear him on the other side of the walls as he crunched them with his feet. The next day she would search for them. The signature characteristics by which one can recognize the poems of McPherson's fifth book are prefigured here in her attention to detail and imaginative phrasing. Like her later poetry, this first section does not end with an obvious thematic turn. There is surprise in the section's closure; the poet does not dwell on what might be a young girl's horrific fascination. Rather, she notes the perseverance and perhaps the retribution of the surviving snails.

The second section, "The Killing of the Caterpillars," does not, however, end the poem by focusing on the persevering traits of caterpillars. In this sequence the narrator has watched her neighbor torch nests of tent caterpillars in the branches of his cherry tree. The neighbor is a musical "conductor," but the music is the sound of immolation, the burning caterpillars. The exploding larvae begin their strange, hallucinatory fall through the branches. McPherson finds the exact metaphor to describe the scene and renders it here in exotic imagery and exquisite free verse sound. The fiery caterpillars have been part of a terrible and oddly beautiful show. After they burn out into black crisps, the narrator's fixation with burning appears in her attention to light, specifically that of her father's flashlight illuminating the dead caterpillars. The poem ends with a hopelessness that had been temporarily suppressed by the closing retribution of the first section. In many ways "Elegies for the Hot Season" establishes a paradigm for the kinds of poems that McPherson has written since it first appeared. With an imaginative care for specific visual details, the poem focuses on the fragile existence of small, nonhuman creatures and demonstrates a sympathy for their circumstance. Furthermore, "Elegies for the Hot Season" considers the deadly human power of the environment those creatures inhabit.

At least two other poems from *Elegies for the Hot Season* are representative of McPherson's range. "Re-

signing from a Job in the Defense Industry" is not an overcharged political manifesto; rather, it considers the manner in which people in the narrator's workplace would cope with their life of building weapons of mass destruction. Typically, McPherson's narrator found herself fascinated with names. Her coworkers attempted to minimize the nearly unimaginable gravity of their work by distracting themselves. Some decorated their holiday plants and trees. Others made art for the company talent show. Like the poet's artistic impulse, the creative process of the coworkers was a gesture against the mechanics of death. In "His Body," which expresses a woman's view of her lover's body, the narrator is fascinated by the unusual aspects of a being's physical self. In this case, these aspects correspond to the invisible characteristics that distinguish one human being from all others. While the language is syntactically straightforward, the poem manifests McPherson's penchant for clever observation. While "His Body" closes on a loving note, it also affirms the poet's belief that being alive dictates the condition of isolation.

RADIATION

McPherson continues her inquiry into identity in her second book, *Radiation*. Employing a quote from French poet Paul Valéry as an epigraph, she establishes a severe context for the poems that follow. Is it true that good people are fundamentally evil? That evil people have good hearts? Valéry understands that his hypothesis is unprovable, and McPherson, too, recognizes that the notion that each individual may actually be a character opposite, like a film negative, is probably too simple. Yet the epigraph provides her with a tool for understanding human nature: People may not be duplicitous character opposites, but they are certainly not entirely how they project themselves. Human beings are, rather, complex entities who can be both savage and caring. The kind may at times be cruel, and the cruel may at times be kind. In McPherson's view, such irony must be accepted if one is to appreciate one's dual position as destroyer and caregiver. One's survival and the survival of others may depend on one's recognizing one's own animality.

McPherson believes that human beings are animals in the best and worst sense of the word. People are born feral, and several poems in *Radiation* concern the instinctively self-directed nature of humankind. In "Peter

Rabbit" McPherson retells the children's story of Peter, the small rabbit that disobeys his mother and wanders far from home, barely escaping from Mr. McGregor's garden and losing his pretty blue jacket in the process. The poem is narrated by a bright child to whom the story is being read. The child knows that mothers, too, can be unkind, even Mother Rabbit. Though the child sympathizes with Peter, the child also knows that Peter is not always good, that he is a thief. At the same time, the child understands that being bad may be part of being alive. In the next lines the child recognizes an affinity with Peter—almost a complete identification. McPherson creates an endearing children's diction to dramatize the innate good-bad split in human beings. Such a language emphasizes the child's innocence, but innocence here does not mean moral purity. The child needs protection, despite the fact that the child can be "naughty" and knows it. The child is needy and desirous of all good things, including Peter's safe deliverance from Mr. McGregor. The child also knows how the story will end. Endlessly yearning for pleasures, the child wants to put off the inevitable displeasure of that cessation.

Like many of the poems in *Radiation*, "Peter Rabbit" is a more penetrating investigation of the issues McPherson began to explore in *Elegies for the Hot Season*. The poems of the second book take greater associative leaps, each image leading quickly to another. When she was writing these poems, she was clearly influenced by the work many of her peers were doing with "deep imagery," a style of writing characterized by leaping, often surreal images intended to stir buried emotions in the reader. Such images were usually referred to as archetypes, especially by proponents of Jungian poet Robert Bly's theories regarding poetry and the operations of the unconscious mind. This kind of archetypal imagery is effective in McPherson's "Cinderella," a poem that retells the old story by placing an aging Cinderella at a window out of which, at the end of the poem, she stares, full of longing. Soon, however, Cinderella finds a gold leaf, and she is again temporarily satisfied. The poem first leaves the reader with a sensation of deliverance. Just as Peter Rabbit escaped the foot of Mr. McGregor, and just as the child narrator hopes for a provider of infinite pleasures, Cinderella is once more saved from her life of drudgery—or so it may seem, for this Cinderella

is perhaps too much like the child in Peter Rabbit. She has not learned what all adults must learn: to find redemption in the self.

THE YEAR OF OUR BIRTH

In *The Year of Our Birth* themes involving the painful realities of children, women, parents, and the natural world are rendered in a complex style often marked by great associative leaps, deep imagery, ellipses, and uncommon syntax. The poems of *The Year of Our Birth* are among McPherson's most ambitious, difficult, and rewarding. One critic found her rhythms awkward, but he may have misunderstood McPherson's deliberately contrapuntal accents, which are intended to reflect the peculiarities of both the thing perceived and the process of perception.

Such a surprising syntactical arrangement begins "Children," a poem about the complex symbiotic relation between mother and daughter. The poet establishes a strange and affecting density in the first line by mixing the pronoun "you" into the sentence four times. The effect of this and other techniques is a certain indeterminacy. The reader is temporarily adrift, trying to establish meaning and order. McPherson intends to disrupt the conventional, linear style of expression, because she wants the poem's language to mirror the relationship between the mother and daughter—that is, a state out of equilibrium, always in dynamic flux, indeterminate.

McPherson uses similar diction as well as a more radical, leaping imagery in "A Coconut for Katerina," an extraordinary poem about a friend's miscarriage. The poem never explicitly states that its subject is a miscarriage. The reader's immediate dislocation is like Katerina's flustered consciousness. One must suspend typically linear thought in order to follow the poem's movement. As with many of the poems in *The Year of Our Birth*, reading "A Coconut for Katerina"—perhaps the poet's best poem—requires an intuitive approach. Filled with poetic surprises, the entire first stanza works against structural order, and the sentence of the second stanza is actually a fragment. The third sentence suggests that Katerina is holding up a coconut as if for display. Many of the poem's lines shift direction in meaning, until understanding is obscured by the shifts.

Such shifting, indeterminate writing can be disarming when first encountered, but, when a reader learns to release the desire for instantaneous conventional interpretation, the poem takes on a salient life. In this poem, the reader can eventually come to sense that Katerina is despondent over a miscarriage, despondent to the point of a near psychotic experience. Many of McPherson's poems require an unusual way of reading; not only must the reader float from strange image to image in the associative drift of a distressed consciousness, but that reader also must allow those images first to pique emotional responses and, second, to come to the surface of the reader's own consciousness. The reader experiences the situations and resulting feelings McPherson is uncovering. Reading in this way provides a free-floating sensation.

Immediately following the strange images of milk at the end of the first stanza, the reader finds rope imagery. The atransitional movement from milk to rope is an example of McPherson's rapid leaps. The poem is elliptical in that it provides few linking terms. McPherson eschews transitions and requires her readers to shift rapidly. The sudden introduction of the first-person narrator is another quick shift. Who is she or he? Later in the poem, the narrator is transformed into the first-person plural "we." Perhaps the narrator is a friend, then a group of friends. The narrator apparently empathizes intimately with Katerina, experiencing the anxiety she feels. Yet the narrator is simultaneously conscious of something more. Katerina—like the children, Peter Rabbit, the snails, the caterpillars, and all the other objects of McPherson's concern—is representative of the vulnerable being who must suffer random fates.

McPherson is of great literary importance because in taking such risks with language she is advancing one of the collective projects of twentieth century American poetry: to render thought processes and emotional life via poetic language. A poem such as "A Coconut for Katerina" is not simply decoded; rather, it is experienced, felt. The sequence of archetypal moments in the poem provides a surprisingly fast series of imaginative episodes that correspond to those of Katerina and her friends. The reader knows a central facet of their lives. To empathize with them is, in McPherson's view, a good thing. The poem ends with a series of sea and water images, which generate an awareness of future possibilities.

The poet's care for all things vulnerable is an explicit concern of many other poems in *The Year of Our Birth.* "In a Garden" offers a proposition in less dense language than either "Children" or "A Coconut for Katerina." In "Centerfold Reflected in a Jet Window," McPherson is frightened for all women, especially her daughter, who are too often exploited by certain kinds of men. The narrator is sitting in an airplane behind a man who is staring at a naked woman in a magazine. First she imagines the woman exposed and freezing outside the plane. Quickly the woman is transformed into the narrator's freezing daughter. Eventually the poem employs another surreal and deep image—that of a disappointed old woman who is riding inside the earth, alone, wanting love after giving it all her life.

PATRON HAPPINESS

McPherson's fourth major book, *Patron Happiness,* is also deeply concerned with women who aspire to succeed in a tragically unloving world. One of its most affecting poems is "The Steps," subtitled "Mother Once in the '40's." The poem is about a mature woman who faints every other year or so and who seems to desire some kind of lighter, otherworldly existence. A kind of mystic feminist fantasia, the poem asserts a woman's desire to transcend her mundane and empty existence after her children are grown. The poem intimates that her survival depends on her periodic dream states, in which she can know a less binding, more rapturous state of being. The trance becomes a method of adapting to a world that conspires against her fulfillment.

If the poems of McPherson's first three books primarily depict a world of vulnerable beings menaced by dark forces, *Patron Happiness* exhibits a romantic option by which those who are endangered may find some solace. Just as "A Coconut for Katerina" closes on a note of regenerative possibility, poems such as "The Steps," "Helen Todd: My Birthname," and "Urban Ode" seem to favor a life of speculative wonder. In these poems the imagination can serve as comfort or relief. For example, in "Helen Todd: My Birthname" McPherson imagines the identity she would have had if her birth parents had kept her. The poem is one of McPherson's most popular, because its subject is striking and its execution poignant. The poet's imagination allows her to know two lives in the one being. Astonished to learn her birth name, Helen

Todd, she converts this astonishment to an empowering realization that she may actually have doubled her life.

"Urban Ode," the last poem in the book, has a theme of openness to the enabling possibilities of the imagination. It begins in a diner from which an angry boy has been quietly ejected after flinging a chair that just misses the narrator. The boy's behavior leads the narrator to ponder his probable painful loneliness—a loneliness that she, too, has felt. Now, after hours of therapy and piano playing, however, she may be past the debilitating effect of that loneliness. The poem ends with images of children running around a bush. One of the children asks her friend Ava to come see a jay, but Ava says no because she has already seen a jay. She knows what it is, what it looks like. While Ava disregards something she has already seen, her friend has learned to see wonder in the bird—and, by extension, in all common things. Because McPherson is uncertain that such potential can exist in herself, the poem is not a sure affirmation of imaginative potential. McPherson herself wonders whether this state of surprise that can negate a paralyzing loneliness is truly possible for adults.

STREAMERS

Like *Patron Happiness*, McPherson's *Streamers* chronicles her development from great worry and doubt to a modest hope. With a naturalist's eye for details, the book often focuses on marine and plant life while carrying on her inquiries into the renascent methods of the vulnerable. The book also demonstrates McPherson's new interest in poems that are longer than her usual one- or two-page length. The best poem in the volume is the title piece, which draws a comparison between the lives of persevering women and the cyanea, a stinging jellyfish that can attain a diameter of seven feet. Written in forty-one irregular stanzas, the poem is set initially at the sea, where the narrator and a friend are propped on elbows, looking down from a dock at a large jellyfish. Unlike other women, this woman friend has not left for other parts of the world; she owns five houses but lives alone. The poem, about women finding independent means to happiness, shifts from the friend's reminiscences and observations to those of the narrator, with an intervening quotation from Sherlock Holmes about the great distracting vision of beautiful women. The key to the poem lies in the elasticity of the jelly-

fish, its "streamers," which never seem to harden. Unlike the friends who have left their husbands (and perhaps unlike men who too often survive by armoring themselves emotionally), the two women come to see that achieving vitality and an adaptable flexibility is the key to retaining their own identity as independent women while surviving. "Streamers" moves toward this conclusion in a long, undulant wave of comparisons. Unlike many of McPherson's earlier poems, its syntax is relatively natural, as close to conversational as she ever writes.

The volume ends with "Kindness," a poem of twenty-three regular four-line stanzas, comparing flowers to the tensionless hands of the narrator's lover. The narrator understands that she has come to love this man because he chooses "not to threaten" and she can therefore live a less anxious life. Like "Streamers," "Kindness" moves with an easy, uncomplicated pace. Like "Streamers"—and many of McPherson's other poems—it draws its surprising conclusions from intriguing likenesses. The lover is as gentle as a plantain, and both he and the narrator are like naturalists, in love with the things of the natural world as well as with each other. Where some people might callously destroy the undefended, mysterious beings of the world, this man kindly accepts their enigmatic or unknowable selves.

"Streamers" and "Kindness" are representative of McPherson's ongoing poetic and thematic growth. For more than twenty years, she has demonstrated an extraordinary talent for perceiving the unique attributes of common things and rendering her insights in a language that is as distinctive as the things themselves. Her evolution from *Elegies for the Hot Season*, published in 1970, to *Streamers*, published in 1988, is marked principally by an increased confidence in the redemptive powers of the imagination and the regenerative powers of sentient beings. As she becomes somewhat less anxious about the dangers of an unfeeling environment and a bit more comforted by the enduring possibilities of imagination, her poetry demonstrates a less apprehensive voice while retaining its diligence, complexity, and insight.

THE GOD OF INDETERMINACY, EDGE EFFECT, AND THE SPACES BETWEEN BIRDS

Those traits are responsive to an ever-widening range of subjects in her collections of the 1990's. *The God of*

Indeterminacy has as its center the broad world of folk art. McPherson at once admires the men and women who practice these traditional art forms, exploring the meanings of community and experience that they symbolize, and involves readers in a provocative measuring of the differences between folk art and the kind of art McPherson herself aspires to create. She pays particular attention to quilting and to blues music. In *Edge Effect*, McPherson turns her attention to natural history as well as to the creative efforts of marginalized individuals, including the mentally ill. There is a connection between these two books forged by McPherson's interest in traditional folk arts, and *Edge Effect* connects as well with another volume of the same year, *The Spaces Between Birds*, in which the poet fashions a work both lyrical and narrative about the raising of her autistic daughter, Phoebe. Some of Phoebe's poems interact with those of her mother. Through her career, McPherson has managed, in a voice that is all her own, to blend compassion with directness, celebration with unpleasant truths about the human experience.

BIBLIOGRAPHY

Boruch, Marianne. "No Perimeters." *American Poetry Review* 18 (March/April, 1989): 41-43. In this review of *Streamers*, Boruch applauds McPherson's sense of discovery and surprise. Boruch discusses "Fringecups" and "The Feather," analyzing McPherson's deliberate manner of coming to realizations. The review finishes with a declaration that, like those of William Carlos Williams, McPherson's poems are rare because they do not compromise.

Jackson, Richard. Review of *Patron Happiness*. *Prairie Schooner* 59 (Winter, 1985): 109-116. Jackson's review is a positive evaluation of *Patron Happiness*, which he sees as recording a romantic journey toward personal identity.

McPherson, Sandra. "Dialogue with Sandra McPherson." Interview by Cecilia Hagen. *Northwest Review* 20, nos. 2/3 (1982): 29-55. In this lengthy and wide-ranging interview, McPherson discusses her intuitive closeness to nature, her writing styles, contemporary poets, world and national history (including the Vietnam War), politics, feminism, liberalism, her travels, and her first three books of poems. Of partic-

ular interest are her comments about American literary politics, especially as applied to Western poets, and her references to Elizabeth Bishop.

Stitt, Peter. Review of *The Year of Our Birth*. *The Georgia Review* 33 (Summer, 1979): 463-470. The most critical of all pieces written about McPherson's work, this review of five books by different poets devotes only two adjectival paragraphs to *The Year of Our Birth*. Stitt dislikes the opening poem, and he finds the rhythms of others awkward. He does cite "Centerfold Reflected in a Jet Window" and "Senility" as good poems.

Young, David. "Overview." *The Longman Anthology of Contemporary American Poetry*. 2d ed. London: Longman, 1989. One of the best, most insightful pieces written about McPherson, Young's brief introduction presents a highly laudatory description of her work. He commends the intricacies of her poems as well as her imaginative and specific manner of observation. Young discusses "Gnawing the Breast," "Games," "The Museum of the Second Creation," "Resigning from a Job in the Defense Industry," and "A Coconut for Katerina."

*Kevin Clark,
updated by Philip K. Jason*

HAKI R. MADHUBUTI

Don L. Lee
Born: Little Rock, Arkansas; February 23, 1942

PRINCIPAL POETRY
Think Black, 1967, 1968, 1969
Black Pride, 1968
Don't Cry, Scream, 1969
We Walk the Way of the New World, 1970
Directionscore: Selected and New Poems, 1971
Book of Life, 1973
Earthquakes and Sunrise Missions: Poetry and Essays of Black Renewal, 1973-1983, 1984
Killing Memory, Seeking Ancestors, 1987

GroundWork: New and Selected Poems of Don L.
Lee/Haki R. Madhubuti from 1966-1996, 1996
Heartlove: Wedding and Love Poems, 1998

OTHER LITERARY FORMS

Although Haki R. Madhubuti began his writing career as a poet and continues to write poems, he soon asserted that poetry was not only an aesthetic process, but also a sociopolitical act. Two themes permeating his work, then, are also political goals: black unity and black power (through that unity). Because his efforts as a poet and writer demand total dedication to his political concerns—whether in his personal lifestyle or in his publishing ventures—Madhubuti has essentially chosen the role of poet-as-prophet. As he puts it, "*black* for the black poet is a way of life." It should come as no surprise, then, that less than half of his published writing has been poetry (despite its having been his initially favored genre), for Madhubuti does not intend to elevate his status in the black community by his writing so much as he seeks to transform the community through the writing act itself. To that end, he has become one of the foremost social essayists in the Black Nationalist movement, along with Imamu Amiri Baraka (LeRoi Jones), Maulana Ron Karenga, and Julius K. Nyerere.

Madhubuti has consistently used the social essay to espouse and develop the ideals, difficulties, and goals of what has come to be called "cultural nationalism." His book *From Plan to Planet, Life Studies: The Need for Afrikan Minds and Institutions* (1973) perhaps best expresses the emphasis on "social content" in Madhubuti's use of the essay and "Blackpoetry," which, as he says in the preface to *Don't Cry, Scream*, is to "tell what's *to be* & how to *be* it," as vehicles for black liberation. The book, a collection of thirty brief essays organized into four distinct sections, is unified by the underlying premise that black survival, meaning the survival of all peoples of African descent anywhere in the world, including Africa, is threatened both by the political power of European and American governments and by the racism—latent and manifest—in those two Aryan-derived cultures.

In the attempt to unify the diaspora of African culture, Madhubuti begins by examining the individual's situation in an oppressive culture and asserts the necessity to "*create* or *re-create* an Afrikan (or black) mind in a *predominantly* European-American setting." (*Afrikan* here and throughout Madhubuti's writing is so spelled in order to indicate a harder *c* sound indigenous to African languages before the "contamination" of sound and spelling—implying sociopolitical domination—by European colonialism: the change in "standard" spelling is seen as a "revolutionary" act.) This first section, appropriately untitled in recognition of the difficulty involved in establishing a cultural perspective with which to begin a plan of unity, might be called "To See with Afrikan Eyes." The second section, "Life Studies," moves from the concern for the black individual to the problems inherent in the local black community. Here Madhubuti shifts from the necessity of self-esteem, or "positive identity," to the necessity for a black value system, *Nguzo Saba*, that subordinates individual success to the best interests of the black community as a whole. The code of *Nguzo Saba* nurtures self-reliance through cooperative education, business, and industry (urban or rural). To this end, he asserts that widely diverse and geographically scattered communities can form a "psychological unity" that will result in a Black Nation. Madhubuti's synthesis here achieves less theoretical complexity but more pragmatic clarity than similar ideas from his sources: Nyerere's *ujamaa*, African-based socialism; and Karenga's *kawaida*, African tradition and reason.

From this plan for cultural unity despite geographical disparity, Madhubuti focuses on the responsibility of the artist in "The Black Arts." Black artists, in these recommendations, bear the role of "culture stabilizers" who affirm racial identity, maintain political purpose, and define cultural direction in accordance with the principles of the previous section. They are, by implication, prophets who create and fulfill the prophecy of a Black Nation. Through cooperative publishing, teaching, and distribution, the artists help create new wealth, thus new power, for blacks in America—but only insofar as the black community gains unity, not merely in any sense of individual achievement. In the fourth section, "Worldview," Madhubuti extends the prior concerns for individual, community, and artist to blacks throughout the world. Loosely based on Nyerere's concepts and drawing upon ideas in Frantz Fanon's *The Wretched of the Earth* (1965), as well as many other sources, he analyzes the rise of European colonialism from a cultural nationalist viewpoint and reasserts the necessity for the values defined in section two on a global as well as a national scale. While Nyerere bases his doctrine on a philosophy of issues that reaches toward love to nurture the culture, Madhubuti, revising those ideas, asserts that the "nationbuilding" of love within the community must focus on people—black people—not on issues. (*Love* is defined by him as "familyhood," "mutual involvement in one another," and "the brotherhood of man.")

The implicit contradiction throughout the essays, however, is that whites are not only perceived as the enemy of blacks in America, but as "the world's enemy." No such contradiction in "a brotherhood of man" exists as long as Madhubuti speaks of blacks. In fact, it is worth noting that, aside from his condemnation of European and American colonialism (in its various forms), he argues from a pro-black rather than an antiwhite position. His antagonism to negative positions is explicitly stated: "Our struggle should not be based upon the *hate* of anything." In addition to this central contradiction, there are a number of flaws, particularly in unidentified sources and poor documentation, that weaken the polemic of this volume. It remains, however, an important tool in understanding the poetry of Madhubuti; in fact, considered with *Enemies: The Clash of Races* (1978), the work may be said to overshadow the poetry itself, for Madhubuti has moved increasingly to this literary form as his primary means of expressing his sociopolitical (which is to say artistic) vision.

One further major literary concern for Madhubuti has been literary criticism, especially the definition of "new Blackpoetry" in the light of the concepts of *ujamaa* and *kawaida*. His collection of critical essays, *Dynamite Voices: Black Poets of the 1960's* (1971), is significant in two respects: It established a responsibility for the black critic to evaluate seriously the merits of the emerging "cultural nationalist school" of black poets, and it provided a model for doing so (if sometimes uneven and superficial in its judgments). Here, too, Madhubuti shows a tendency for his social criticism to overrun his literary evaluation, but the book will remain an important contribution to the development of aesthetic standards for black literature. (Some of Madhubuti's in-

sights have already been explored and expanded much more carefully and thoroughly than in his own book by Stephen Henderson and Addison Gayle, Jr.) In this context, it is also necessary to note that Madhubuti regularly contributes a column, "Worldview," and book reviews to his journal *Black Books Bulletin*. Other reviews, short essays, polemical statements, and introductions are widespread in anthologies and journals such as *The Negro Digest* (later *Black World*), *Third World*, and *The Black Scholar*. In addition to his writings, recordings of Madhubuti are also available that add a great deal to the printed poem on the page. Like the work of Dylan Thomas, much of the delight in hearing Madhubuti's poetry—based as it is on the improvisations and unpredictable qualities of jazz and urban black speech patterns—is lost when his voice is absent. More so than for a great many poets, his work becomes more powerful when heard.

ACHIEVEMENTS

Perhaps Haki R. Madhubuti's single most impressive accomplishment has been not his success with new forms of poetry, his articulation of new social criticism, his formulation of new aesthetic principles, or his success as a publisher and editor, but his ability to accomplish all of these goals, for which, he asserts, a black poet must struggle. Madhubuti *is* the black poet of his proposed "total dedication" to black liberation and "nationbuilding." In his embodiment of his principles and commitment, Madhubuti has reached into corners of the black community that have been heretofore untouched by black literature or liberation politics. Within four years of the publication of his first book, he had "sold more books of poetry (some 250,000 copies) than probably all of the black poets who came before him combined" (*The Black Collegian*, February/March, 1971). One would be hard-pressed to name *any* American poet who could boast such a large figure in such short time—twenty-five thousand copies, ten percent of Madhubuti's sales, might be considered a phenomenal success. Clearly, Madhubuti's popularity does not rest on library or classroom purchases; it is based on the very "market" he seeks to speak to: the black community. Having defined his audience as exclusively the blacks of America in his social criticism, he has found a quite remarkable response from that desired audience even though he is frequently blunt in his sarcastic ridicule of blacks who aspire to imitate whites. In taking the black community seriously as an audience, Madhubuti has discovered that the audience accepts him seriously. This interaction, then, seems to be the epitome of the "mutual involvement" between artists and community of which he writes in his social criticism.

Madhubuti's popular reception, however, has not diminished his success in a more narrowly defined black literary community. His influence on young black poets and writers of the 1970's is pervasive; one sees imitations of him and dedications to him in many black literary journals. His extensions of Baraka's theoretical positions in cultural nationalism have forced older black critics to reexamine and reevaluate their criteria for black aesthetic standards. His publishing and editing efforts have enabled many young black writers to reach print, as attested by his numerous introductions and reviews of their work. Most important, however, Madhubuti has succeeded continuously in educating (he would say *reeducating*) ever-increasing numbers of individuals within the black community to participate in that dialogue and to perpetuate it within the community. He has been, and remains, an essential leader in working toward black pride, unity, and power, or as he puts it, in giving "identity, purpose and direction" to black "nationbuilding."

BIOGRAPHY

Haki R. Madhubuti (who changed his name from Don L. Lee to his Swahili name in 1973), born in Little Rock, Arkansas, moved to Chicago with his parents Jimmy and Maxine Lee midway through his childhood. After graduating from high school, Madhubuti continued his education at Wilson Junior College, Roosevelt University, and the University of Illinois at Chicago Circle. His formal education has been tempered, however, by a wide range of jobs which have increased his rapport with varied classes and individuals within the black community. After serving in the United States Army from 1960 to 1963, Madhubuti returned to Chicago to begin an apprenticeship as curator of the DuSable Museum of African History, which he continued until 1967. Meanwhile, he worked as a stock department clerk for

Montgomery Ward (1963 to 1964), a post office clerk (1964 to 1965), and a junior executive for Spiegel's (1965 to 1966). By the end of 1967, Madhubuti's reputation as a poet and as a spokesman for the new black poetry of the 1960's had grown sufficiently to enable him to support himself through publishing and teaching alone.

In 1968-1969, Madhubuti was writer-in-residence at Cornell University. Similar positions followed at Northeastern Illinois State College (1969-1970) and the University of Illinois at Chicago Circle (1969-1971), where he combined poet-in-residencies with teaching black literature. From 1970 to 1975, Madhubuti taught at Howard University, except for a year at Morgan State College where he was writer-in-residence for 1972-1973. The extensive popular reception of his poetry and the increasing frequency of his social essays made him a favorite if controversial reader and lecturer with black college students across the country. His influence and popularity also enabled him to found, in Chicago, the Institute of Positive Education in 1971, which publishes *Black Books Bulletin* edited by Madhubuti and for which he served as director from 1971 to 1991. He is also the publisher and editor of Third World Press, one of the United States's largest and most successful independent African American book publishers, since 1971. In conjunction with his publishing roles, Madhubuti is also a professor of English and director emeritus of the Gwendolyn Brooks Center at Chicago State University. Madhubuti has also held important executive positions with a number of Pan-African organizations such as the Congress of African People. Madhubuti's publishing, editing, teaching, and writing continue to maintain his stature within the Black Nationalist movement.

ANALYSIS

Much of Haki R. Madhubuti's poetry was initially greeted by outright condemnation on the part of white critics whose standards of aesthetic judgment were antagonistic, to say the least, toward the nationalist assumptions inherent in much of the new black poetry of the 1960's. Jascha Kessler, for example, in a review in *Poetry* (February, 1973), said that in "Lee all is converted to rant/ . . ./ [he] is outside poetry somewhere, exhorting, hectoring, cursing, making a lot of noise/ . . .

you don't have to be black for that/ . . ./ it's hardly an excuse." Madhubuti's sociopolitical concerns, in short, were viewed as unfit for poetic rendering, and his urban, rap-style jazz rhythms and phrases in his poems were dismissed as simply disgruntled, militant ravings. Ironically, that sort of reception—and inability to move beyond the parameters of the New Criticism—supported exactly what the new black poets were claiming: White critical standards forced blacks to write as if they were white themselves and thereby denied them their own cultural heritage and suppressed their experience of oppression. Indeed, this is the dilemma in which the young Lee found himself; if he were to "succeed," he would need (even as a poet) to obliterate his own identity as a black man.

The writings of Amiri Baraka, probably more than any other poet's, as well as his independent studies in African culture (probably begun at the DuSable Museum), violently ruptured the assumption that accommodation to the dominant culture was the sole means by which blacks could survive in America. With the break from accommodationist thought, as Marlene Mosher suggests in *New Directions from Don L. Lee* (1975), Madhubuti began his struggle to create identity, unity, and power in a neo-African context that would preserve his heritage and experience while creating a possibility for the black community as a whole to free itself from the oppressive constraints of mainstream American culture. Madhubuti progressed from the accommodationist period through a reactive phase, then through a revolutionary program, to a prophetic vision. These four aspects of his poetry are distinct not only in the ideological content of his work, but also in the structure of the poems themselves. Once the prophetic vision had been embraced, it was necessary to begin a pragmatic clarification of that vision; the necessity to describe specifically the new Black Nation led, ironically, to an increasing devotion to prose, and thus Madhubuti's poetry seemed nearly to disappear—at least in publication— after his book of poems, *Book of Life*. That the vision of his poetry should result in the suspension of his poetry writing in favor of concrete description was, for those who laud his poetry, a great loss. It is not, however, incomprehensible, for Madhubuti, in urging the embodiment of his poetic vision and in describing *how* to build

that vision in realistic terms, is actually carrying out what he first proposed as the goal of his work: to construct an African mind and to create a Black Nation. One assumes, then, that his activities left little time for him to pursue his poetry. Fortunately, he began again to publish books of poems in 1984.

The period of accommodation in Madhubuti's work is available only through autobiographical references found in the early poems of the reactive phase. This early "pre-poetic" time is, appropriately, marked by a lack of articulation. Without his own voice, there are no poems, no prose, no statements of any kind. To speak as oneself for one's community was to react to that accommodation. Madhubuti's "confession" of that period, therefore, is marked by bitterness, hatred, and condemnation of almost everything he associated with white America, including himself. Several poems in his first book, *Think Black*, are testimonial as well as vengeful; it is clear in these poems that Madhubuti had been "liberating" himself for several years, and only then was testifying to that personal struggle through accommodation. He was to say later, in "Black Sketches" (*Don't Cry, Scream*), that he "became black" in 1963 and "everyone thought it unusual:/ even me."

THINK BLACK

Both the accommodationist period and the reactive phase are seen in *Think Black*, but the point of view is nearly always that of a reaction against accommodation. In "Understanding But Not Forgetting," Madhubuti speaks of his family life and his "early escape/ period, trying to be white." Among his images are those of an intellectual accommodationist who "still ain't hip," an uneducated grandmother "with wisdom that most philosophers would/ envy," misery-filled weekends with "no family/ but money," a twenty-two-year-old sister with "five children," a mother involved in prostitution but "providing for her family," and a cheating white newspaper distributor who kept "telling/ me what a good boy I was." Reexamining his childhood and adolescence in this poem, Madhubuti concludes: "About positive images as a child—NONE," and further that "About negative images as a child—all black." In his attempt to understand his social conditioning and view it in the larger context of American culture, he is forced to conclude that education, democracy, religion, and even the

"BLACK MIDDLE CLASS" (to which he has aspired) have failed him because of "the American System." It is, in fact, those very outcasts of the black community itself—the grandmother and the prostitute-mother, who "read Richard Wright and Chester Himes/ . . ./ [the] bad books," that offer examples of survival against overwhelming oppression.

BLACK PRIDE

Madhubuti had not, however, accomplished much more at that time than rejection of the value system which had created his anger and despair: The awareness of *how* to "think black" is vague. The last poem in the book, "Awareness," is a chant of only three words: "BLACK PEOPLE THINK." In the variations of syntactical arrangement of these words, however, one is left with the unmistakable impression that he will struggle to learn from those outcasts of mainstream society just what it does mean to "THINK BLACK." These lessons are the heart of his second book, *Black Pride*, which is still reactive but nevertheless substantial in its discovery of identity. While many of these poems remain confessional, there is an increase in the clarity of Madhubuti's sociopolitical development. In the brief lead poem, "The New Integrationist," he announces his intention to join "negroes/ with/ black/ people." The one-word lines of the poem force the reader to contemplate not only the irony in his use of "integration," but also the implications inherent in the labels "negro" and "black." It is an appropriate keynote for the fulfillment of that vague awareness with which his first book ended.

Perhaps the growth in self-identity that characterizes *Black Pride* begins, paradoxically, most clearly in "The Self-Hatred of Don L. Lee." The confessional stance of the poet first acknowledges a love of "my color" because it allowed him to move upward in the accommodationist period; it "opened sMall [sic]/ doors of/ tokenism." After "struggling" through a reading list of the forerunners of cultural nationalism, Madhubuti then describes a breakthrough from "my blindness" to "pitch-black/ . . ./ awareness." His "all/ black/ . . ./ inner/ self" is now his strength, the basis for his self-identity, and he rejects with "vehement/ hatred" his "light/ brown/ outer" self, that appearance which he had previously exploited by accepting the benefits of tokenism. While Madhubuti had escaped accommodation by this time, he

had not yet ceased to react to it; instead of having skin too dark, he had skin too light. He was, as black oral tradition puts it, "color-struck." He had, however, moved much deeper into the problem of establishing an identity based on dignity rather than denigration.

The growth of identity and black pride still remains, then, a function of what is not blackness instead of what is, or will become, Madhubuti's new Black Nation. In several poems such as "The Primitive," Madhubuti describes the loss of black values under American slavery and the subsequent efforts of blacks to imitate their oppressors who "raped our minds" with mainstream images from "Tv/ . . ./ Reader's Digest/ . . ./ tarzan & jungle jim," who offered "used cars & used homes/ reefers & napalm/ european history & promises" and who fostered "alien concepts/ of Whi-teness." His message here is blunt: "this weapon called/ civilization/ . . ./ [acts] to drive us mad/ (like them)." For all of his vindictive bitterness, however, Madhubuti addresses himself to the black community more than he does to white America—self-reliance for self-preservation emerges as the crucial issue. As he suggests in the final poem "No More Marching Now," nonviolent protest and civil rights legislation have been undermined by white values; thus, "public/ housing" has become a euphemism for "concentration camps." His charge is typically blunt: "you better wake up/ . . ./ before it's too late."

Although the first two volumes of Madhubuti's poems exist in the tension between accommodation and reaction, they do show growth in the use of language as well as in identity and pride. His work, at times, suffers from clichéd rhetoric and easy catchphrases common to exhortation, but it also possesses a genuine delight in the playfulness of language even while it struggles forward in the midst of serious sociopolitical polemic. In his division of "white," for example, where the one-syllable word is frequently cut into the two-syllable "whi-te" or the second syllable is dropped completely to the next line, Madhubuti demonstrates more than typographical scoring for the sound of his poem, for he displays the fragmentation between ideals and the implementation of those ideals in American culture. In contrast, "Black man" appears frequently as one word, "blackman," sometimes capitalized and sometimes not—to emphasize the gradual dissolution of the individual's ego, to suggest the necessity for unity in the community for which he strives. Capitalization, in a similar way, sometimes connotes pride in his use of "BLACK." At other times, he uses derogatory puns, such as when "U.S." becomes "u ass." His models are street language, urban speech patterns, jazz improvisation, the narrative form of the toast, and the general inventiveness of an oral tradition that belongs wholly to black culture.

DON'T CRY, SCREAM

These early poems continue to develop both thematically and technically in Madhubuti's next two books, *Don't Cry, Scream* and *We Walk the Way of the New World*, in which he began to outline his revolutionary program. Mosher suggests that these works are consciously much less antiwhite and much more problack in their sociopolitical commitment. Madhubuti's artistic commitment fused completely with his politics; as he says in the preface to *Don't Cry, Scream*, "there is *no* neutral blackart." Black poetry is seen as "culture building" rather than as a tool to criticize either white society or blacks who seek assimilation. In this programmatic work, the hate, bitterness, and invective of the earlier two books give way to music, humor, and a gentler insistence on change. The poems are more consciously crafted than previously, but they do not compromise their essentially urgent political fervor.

In perhaps the most widely anthologized poem by Madhubuti, "But He Was Cool or: he even stopped for green lights," he humorously undermines the stance of black radicals who are far more concerned with the appearance of being a revolutionary than with a real commitment to working for change in the black community. His satire here is more implicit than explicit, for the reader views the "supercool/ ultrablack" radical in "a double-natural" hairstyle and "dashikis [that] were tailor made." His imported beads are "triplehip," and he introduces himself "in swahili" while saying "good-by in yoruba." Madhubuti then becomes more explicit in his satire by dividing and modifying "intelligent" to read "ill tel li gent," but he quickly moves back to implication by a rapidly delivered "bop" hyperbole that describes the radical as "cool cool ultracool/ . . ./ cool so cool cold cool/ . . . him was air conditioned cool" and concludes that he was "so cool him nicknamed refrigerator." The dissonance of the last word with the "ice box cool" ear-

lier in the delivery clashes not only in sound, but also in economic and political connotation. This radical is so busy acting the role of a revolutionary that he has been seduced by the very goals of Western culture that Madhubuti is rejecting: money, power, and sex. By his superficial use of gestures, the "radical" has taken himself even farther away from an awareness of the real needs in the black community. In the aftermath of riots in "detroit, newark, [and] chicago," the would-be revolutionary must still be informed that "to be black/ is/ to be/ very-hot." Despite the humor, music, and wordplay in one of Madhubuti's most consciously and carefully "aesthetic" poems, the message is still primarily political. Although the poem does react to the shallowness of the radical, it is worth noting that the poem is no longer essentially reactive in its tone; by the very act of informing the radical of his ignorance in the closure of the poem, the implication is established that even this caricature has the possibility of redemption in Madhubuti's version of Black Nationalism.

Throughout *Don't Cry, Scream*, Madhubuti begins to embrace a wider range of sensibilities in the black community while continuing to denounce those who would betray the needs of black people. In "Black Sketches," he describes Republican Senator Ed Brooke from Massachusetts (then a self-proclaimed liberal advocate of civil rights) as "slashing/ his wrist/ because somebody/ called him/ black," and portrays the conservative (relative to Madhubuti) Roy Wilkins as the token figure on the television show, "the mod squad." He is relentless in his attack on black leaders who work within mainstream politics. In another poem, however, "Blackrunners/ blackmen or run into blackness," Madhubuti celebrates the Olympic medal winners Tommie Smith and John Carlos for their Black Power salutes in 1968 during the awards ceremony. One could hardly describe their gesture as revolutionary, but Madhubuti accepts and praises their symbolic act as a sign of solidarity with his own sense of revolutionary change. In other poems, he is equally open to the role of black women, intellectuals, and Vietnam veterans. By the final poem of the volume, he is even willing to concede that the "negroes" whom he has denounced in earlier work may also be receptive to his political message. In "A Message All Blackpeople Can Dig (& a few negroes too)," Madhubuti announces that "the realpeople" must "move together/ hands on weapons & families" in order to bring new meanings "to/ . . ./ the blackness,/ to US." While not exactly greeting antagonists with open arms (the parenthetical shift to the lower case in the title is quite intentional), his emphasis has changed from the coarse invective found in *Think Black* to a moral, political force that proceeds in "a righteous direction." Not even whites are specifically attacked here; the enemy is now perceived as "the whitimind," attitudes and actions from "unpeople" who perpetuate racism and oppression. The message, in short, is now much closer to black humanism than it ever has been before: "blackpeople/ are moving, moving to return this earth into the hands of/ human beings."

WE WALK THE WAY OF THE NEW WORLD

The seeds for a revolutionary humanism planted at the close of *Don't Cry, Scream* blossom in *We Walk the Way of the New World*. The flowers are armed to be sure, but in signaling this change, the author's introduction, "Louder but Softer," proclaims that the "cultural nihilism" of the 1960's must give way to the "New World of black consciousness" in which education and self-definition (in the context of the community) will create not noisy, pseudorevolutionaries but self-confident leaders who pursue "real" skills—"doctors, lawyers, teachers, historians, writers"—for ensuring the survival and development of African American culture. Madhubuti's scope and purpose in this book is no less committed than it has been before, but it is far more embracing, compassionate, and visionary. His concern is the establishment of "an ongoing process aimed at an ultimate definition of our being." The tone of urgency ("We're talking about our children, a survival of a people") remains constant and clear, but its directions have moved completely "from negative to positive." While the ideas are not new in *We Walk the Way of the New World*, they do form Madhubuti's most consciously articulated and poetically designed program: Of the three sections that shape the book, "Black Woman Poems," "African Poems," and "New World Poems," he says, "Each part is a part of the other: Blackwoman is African and Africa is Blackwoman and they both represent the *New World*." What is new in the fourth volume, then, is the degree of structural unity and, to a certain extent, a greater clarity in describing the specific meaning of *Nguzo Saba*, a black

value system: "design yr own neighborhoods/ . . . teach yr own children/ . . . but/ build yr own loop/ . . ./ feed yr own people/ . . ./ [and] protect yr own communities."

The unifying metaphor for the book is the pilgrimage into the New World. Arming the heroic, everyman figure "blackman" (unnamed because he is potentially any black man in the service of community rather than in pursuit of individual, egotistical goals) with a knowledge of the contrasts between black women who are positive role-models (with their love tied inextricably to black consciousness) and black women who aspire to imitate white middle-class, suburban women, Madhubuti then distinguishes the values of precolonial Africa from those which have become "contaminated" by Western industrialization. Here his emphasis is on rural communalism, loving family life, and conserving natural resources. By the final section, "blackman" has ceased to function as a depersonalized hero and is embodied in the individuality (having derived such from the community) of real black men, women, and children. This section largely recapitulates the themes and messages of earlier work, but it does so in an affirmative tone of self-asserted action within *kawaida*, African reason and tradition. In the long apocalyptic poem "For Black People," Madhubuti dramatically represents a movement of the entire race from a capitalistic state of self-defeating inactivity to a socialistic economy where mutual love and respect result in an ecologically sound, peacefully shared world of all races (although the "few whi-te communities/ . . . were closely watched"). The movement of the poem, symphonic in its structure, is, in fact, the culmination of Madhubuti's sociopolitical growth and artistic vision to this point.

BOOK OF LIFE

With *Book of Life*, Madhubuti introduces little new thought, but his ideas are expressed in a much more reserved political tone and poetic structure. His role is that of the visionary prophet, the wise sage offering advice to the young children who must inevitably carry on the struggle to build the New World which he has described. Indeed, the book's cover shows a photograph of his own son in the center of a star, and the volume is dedicated to him "and his sons, and their sons." Throughout the book, photographs of Madhubuti sitting or fishing with his son testify to his affirmation of the future. His introduction still affirms "black world unity" and looks to *kawaida* as the source of this new African frame of reference, but only six new poems speak explicitly to the political dimensions of his vision. The second section, captioned after the title of the book, is composed of ninety-two meditations that echo Laozi's *Dao De Jing* (c. third century B.C.E.). The language is simple but profound; the tone is quiet but urgent; the intended audience seems to be his son, but the community overhears him; the poetics are nearly devoid of device from any cultural context, but the force of the didacticism is sincere and genuine. Madhubuti, thinking of black poets who talk "about going to the Bahamas to write the next book," denounces those "poets [who] have become the traitors." It may well be that his sense of betrayal by black artists whom he had expected to assist him in his struggle for the New World and his own growing quietism combined to bring an end to his poetry—at least since the 1973 publication of this work. He seems to have followed his own proverb in *Book of Life*: "best teachers/ seldom teach/ they be and do."

Madhubuti demonstrated an astonishingly rapid growth in his poetry and thought—in only six years. With that sort of energy and commitment, it is not surprising that he should do what he has asked of others, shunning the success of the "traitors": to be and do whatever is necessary for the building of the New World. For Madhubuti, that necessity has meant a turning away from publishing poetry and a turning toward the education of the future generation. One might quite easily dismiss Madhubuti as a dreamer or a madman, but then one would need to recall such visionaries as William Blake, who was dismissed too much too soon.

EARTHQUAKES AND SUNRISE MISSIONS AND KILLING MEMORY, SEEKING ANCESTORS

In the 1980's the growth in Madhubuti's poetry is clearly evident. A sizable portion of his later poems teach through the impact of artful language, rather than sounding merely teacherly. In Madhubuti's two poetry collections of the 1980's, *Earthquakes and Sunrise Missions* and *Killing Memory, Seeking Ancestors*, represent some of his strongest writing as he trusts that his keen observation will yield a bold enough political statement.

For example, in "The Shape of Things to Come," written about the earthquake in Naples, Italy, he ob-serves: "quicker than one can pronounce free enterprise/ like well-oiled rumors or elastic lawyers smelling money/ plastic coffins appear and are sold/ at dusk behind the vatican on the white market./ in Italy in the christian month of eighty/ in the bottom of unimaginable catastrophe/ the profit motive endures as children replenish the earth/ in wretched abundance."

Poems from these volumes, such as "Abortion," "Winterman," "The Changing Seasons of Life," "White on Black Crime," and "Killing Memory" all reflect his increased technical control and subtle political commentary. Poems collected here also show that ideologically, Madhubuti no longer continues to fight all the old battles. Christianity gets a break now, as do some white individuals. He has not, however, wavered in his fundamental commitment to black liberation and in his belief that cultural awareness can ignite and help sustain progressive political struggle. The love in him and for his mission has not diminished. If anything it has grown.

HEARTLOVE

Ten years after the publication of his previous volume of poetry, Madhubuti produced *Heartlove: Wedding and Love Poems*, an elegant collection drawn solely from Madhubuti's poetry and prose and designed to capture and celebrate the essence of love in marriage, family meditations, caring, commitment, and friendships. Acting as a poetic script for the cast of a wedding—minister, bride and groom, the maid of honor, and the best man—Madhubuti counsels, "rise with the wisdom of grandmothers, rise understanding that creation is ongoing, immensely appealing and acceptable to fools and geniuses, and those of us in between."

Each poem offers words of encouragement and advice to new couples or words of tribute to the lives that have influenced Madhubuti's. From "Wedding Poems" to "Quality of Love" to "Extended Families," *Heartlove* addresses crucial questions about building partnerships and and the struggle to preserve community.

OTHER MAJOR WORKS

NONFICTION: *Dynamite Voices: Black Poets of the 1960's*, 1971; *From Plan to Planet, Life Studies: The Need for Afrikan Minds and Institutions*, 1973; *Enemies: The Clash of Races*, 1978; *Black Men: Obsolete, Single, Dangerous?*, 1990; *Claiming Earth:*

Race, Rage, Rape, Redemption—Blacks Seeking a Culture of Enlightened Empowerment, 1994.

EDITED TEXTS: *To Gwen with Love: An Anthology Dedicated to Gwendolyn Brooks*, 1971 (with Francis Ward and Patricia L. Brown); *Say That the River Turns: The Impact of Gwendolyn Brooks*, 1987; *Confusion by Any Other Name: Essays Exploring the Negative Impact of "The Blackman's Guide to Understanding the Blackwoman,"* 1990; *Why L.A. Happened: Implications of the '92 Los Angeles Rebellion*, 1993; *Black Books Bulletin: The Challenge of the Twenty-first Century*, 1995; *Million Man March, Day of Absence: A Commemorative Anthology—Speeches, Commentary, Photography, Poetry, Illustrations, Documents*, 1996 (with Maulana Karenga); *Releasing the Spirit: A Collection of Literary Works from "Gallery Thirty-seven,"* 1998 (with Gwendolyn Michell); *Describe the Moment: A Collection of Literary Works from "Gallery Thirty-seven,"* 2000 (with Mitchell).

MISCELLANEOUS: *Earthquakes and Sunrise Missions: Poetry and Essays of Black Renewal, 1973-1983*, 1984.

BIBLIOGRAPHY

Madhubuti, Haki R. "Hard Words and Clear Songs: The Writing of Black Poetry." In *Tapping Potential: English Language Arts for the Black Learner*. Edited by Charlotte K. Brooks et al. Urbana, Ill.: Black Caucus of the National Council of Teachers of English, 1985. In this article, Madhubuti outlines some of his poetic philosophy. He explains why he writes, as a poet, and as an African American. Helpful to understanding Madhubuti's outlook.

Mosher, Marlene. *New Directions from Don L. Lee.* Hicksville, N.Y.: Exposition Press, 1975. This volume is one of the only available book-length studies on Madhubuti, so it is extremely valuable to any student of his work. Mosher provides criticism and interpretation of Madhubuti's important writing up to the mid-1970's. Includes a bibliography and an index.

Thompson, Julius E. "The Public Response to Haki R. Madhubuti, 1968-1988." *The Literary Griot: International Journal of Black Expressive Cultural Studies* 4, nos. 1/2 (Spring/Summer, 1992): 16-37. A study of the critical treatment and public response to the works of Madhubuti.

Michael Loudon,
updated by Sarah Hilbert

FRANÇOIS MALHERBE

Born: Caen, France; 1555
Died: Paris, France; October 16, 1628

PRINCIPAL POETRY

Les Larmes de Saint Pierre, 1587
Consolation à Monsieur Du Périer sur la mort de sa fille, c. 1600
À la reine, sur sa bienvenue en France, 1600
Prière pour le roi Henri le Grand, 1605
Prière pour le roi allant en Limousin, 1607
Ballet de Madame, 1615
Poésies, 1626

OTHER LITERARY FORMS

Friendship with the Stoic Guillaume Du Vair brought François Malherbe in contact with the writings of Livy and Lucius Annaeus Seneca, some of which he began to translate as early as the turn of the seventeenth century. The first of these efforts was published in 1617, and most of the rest posthumously. These translations are of little if any interest to the modern reader. Of greater import are his numerous letters to many of the major literary figures of his time; some of these were anthologized as early as 1625, although most of them did not see print until 1645; of particular interest to students of the history of ideas are his letters to Nicolas Fabri de Peiresc, perhaps the most universally learned man of the era. His commentaries on contemporary poems and plays—marginalia published posthumously—are essential to an understanding of the poet's doctrine, but they must be taken with a grain of salt: Sallies of a very temperamental man, they are always excessive, and perhaps were intended more to draw attention to the ambitious

Malherbe than to detract from the work of his colleagues (although unpublished, these commentaries were widely circulated).

ACHIEVEMENTS

"At last, Malherbe came," said Nicolas Boileau in 1674, giving credit to him for having brought order and reason to poetry. "Everyone followed his rules [of prosody]," continued Boileau, although some twenty years later, in a letter to François de Maucroix, he was to admit that "in truth, nature had not made [Malherbe] a great poet; but he made up for that . . . with work, for no one worked harder than he over his poems." This composite has misled many generations of students and critics who insisted on overstating François Malherbe's influence and teachings while belittling or disregarding his genuine achievements as a poet. Thanks to the efforts of scholars such as René Fromilhague, David Lee Rubin, and Philip A. Wadsworth, that error has been largely rectified. It should further be stated that it is precisely in that area of poetics in which Malherbe's influence was most categorically posited—prosody—that close analysis shows it to be minimal. In matters of prosody, Malherbe had little or no effect on the poets of his century, not even on "pupils" such as François Maynard and Honorat de Racan. It would be dangerous, however, to limit one's vision to prosodic matters, for to do so would be to allow the mechanics of the genre to obscure its essence. In his pronouncements, Malherbe concentrated on (indeed, limited himself to) the former; in his own poetry, particularly in his "grandes odes," he most definitely strove for that "higher, hidden order" in which the latter resides.

Unlike the posturing and opportunistic theoretician, Malherbe the poet arranged syllables and words not because such intellectual games had intrinsic value, but because he saw that clarity and harmony were essential to the aura of grandeur and majesty with which he wished to imbue his official poetry. His labors over finding the one right word or expression were the butt of many jokes, but they yielded sensible, rational images, striking in their accuracy and psychological truth. These images are never mere ornaments, as they tend to be in Mannerist poetry, but integral parts of the symbolic and metaphoric structures from which the poems derive their profound unity. Through them, commonplaces are given life and raised to new evocative powers.

One has but to read one of Malherbe's odes aloud to realize that this "arranger of syllables," as he called himself, thoroughly understood what most of his contemporaries did not—that lyric poetry, by definition and by nature, is a musical art. His balanced phrases and carefully chosen words not only give strength to his lines but also are pleasing to the ear; their all-pervasive harmony makes the auditor forget about the labors detected by the punctilious critic. It then becomes evident that all of Malherbe's prosodic strictures were born of his concern for order and harmony.

In Malherbe's poetic world, intricate (hidden) structural patterns are made to reinforce poetic abstractions representing the material, historic reality. Few poets, if any, followed Malherbe's specific prosodic rules; many saw that such strictures were motivated by the profound conviction that craftsmanship was necessary if the poet were ever to imbue his work with any semblance of metaphoric coherence and with any degree of lyricism. These loftier considerations behind the specific rules and practices were understood by poets such as Tristan l'Hermite and Jean de La Fontaine, and in that broader understanding of poetry, they, and not the likes of Maynard and Racan, are perhaps to be considered the true "students" of Malherbe.

BIOGRAPHY

François Malherbe received his early education in his native Caen. When he was sixteen, he was sent by his father, newly converted to Protestantism, to study in Germany for two years. In 1577, Malherbe became the secretary of Henri d'Angoulême, illegitimate son of Henry II, and, glad to get away from his father's extreme Protestantism, which he loathed, followed his new master to Provence, where the young prince was to assume the role of governor. A devoted political servant, Malherbe was to remain with his master in the south of France for nearly ten years. There, he married the daughter of a local *président* and, except for a preliminary piece written for a colleague's poem, gave little indication of having literary aspirations. In 1586, Malherbe and his wife were back in Caen when his master was assassinated in Aix. The following year, Malherbe was in

Paris, where he presented his first major poem, *Les Larmes de Saint Pierre* (the tears of Saint Peter), to King Henry III; he was given a sizable financial reward, but not the pension or post he had sought. In 1594, he was elected alderman of Caen, but this duty did not keep him from spending more of the next ten years in his wife's native province—particularly in its dazzling capital, Aix—than in his native Normandy. He was in Aix in 1600 when the new Queen, Marie de Médicis, on her way to meet Henry IV, whom she had married by proxy, stopped in that city. A member of the welcoming party, Malherbe presented her with his first official ode, the 230-line "À la Reine: Pour sa bienvenue en France."

In 1605, Malherbe went to Paris and was presented to Henry IV, who requested a poem of him. The resulting "Prière pour le Roi allant en Limousin" so pleased the king that he granted the poet a pension and a job with his Master of the Horse, Bellegarde. It was to be the beginning of a lifelong association with the court: Malherbe became the official poet of the Crown until his death in 1628. Astute, careful, fawning, Malherbe survived the unsettled regency of Marie de Médicis, singing her praises as he had sung those of her husband and as he was to sing those of the ambitious Cardinal de Richelieu when he early perceived his rising star.

Fundamentally—and admittedly—lazy, Malherbe was a great lover of law and order. He was sincere in his vehement defense of Crown and Church and lavishly praised the martial inclinations of a king if aimed at quelling anarchy. His orthodoxy, in short, political or theological, was more a question of desire for peace than one of philosophic cogitation and decision. Antoine Adam is quite right when he suggests that in London, Amsterdam, or Zurich, Malherbe would have been a good Protestant. The bitterness so prevalent in his later poems, and so diametrically opposed to the quiet Stoicism he professed and demonstrated in earlier works, is undoubtedly due to the sorrows (such as the death of his son in a duel) and travails (such as the endless pains to which he had to go to collect his various pensions) which banished peace and contentment from the last years of his life. Marie de Médicis had appreciated the sallies of his wit and the pomp of his pen; her son, Louis XIII, did not share her sensitivity, and although Malherbe never lost his position at court, he readily

sensed and deeply resented his diminished presence. When he died in 1628, it was not simply because his health had been broken; his spirit too seemed to have given up.

ANALYSIS

François Malherbe's poetic production is far from extensive; it is, nevertheless, considerably varied and of uneven merit. Much of his success at court was due to the ballet libretti which he wrote; these are of interest to court historians, but their literary value is negligible at best. His epigrams today seem derivative and forced. Of primary interest are his great odes and other solemn occasional poems such as the "Prière pour le Roi allant en Limousin." Also of interest are his religious poems and, to a lesser degree, his erotic ones.

"RÉCIT D'UN BERGER"

Nearly everything that Malherbe wrote for public consumption was a political statement. That is the case even for seemingly innocuous poems such as the "Récit d'un berger" of the *Ballet de Madame* of 1615, a lavish court festivity celebrating the marriage of Elizabeth, sister of Louis XIII, to the future Philip IV of Spain. The "ballet" was really a revue of court notables in sumptuous costumes parading through equally sumptuous settings activated by what were then astonishing machines. Malherbe's "Récit d'un berger" allowed its speaker to praise the efforts of the young king and of the Queen Mother on behalf of peace, and to vaunt the advantages of what was a far from popular alliance of royal families. Malherbe's lines had been commissioned by the Queen Mother, and in addition to the usual flattery, they faithfully reflected her policy and desires. It is almost impossible to divorce Malherbe the poet from Malherbe the political animal. In 1617, with the rise to power of D'Albert de Luynes, Malherbe lost his privileged status at court; the need to write disappeared and he seriously thought of "abandoning the Muses." In fact, until 1623— by which date de Luynes had died and Richelieu was quickly rising in power, welcoming Malherbe back into the official fold—Malherbe concentrated his literary efforts on his letters and translations; the poet was silent.

Under the circumstances, it is no wonder that these poems are so hyperbolic in their flattery and allusions as to defy credibility—an ingredient no one expected anyway—and to verge on sycophancy. The most indecisive military encounter could, with such a pen, be transformed into a momentous and stupendous triumph. Today, the reader of such excesses may be tempted to smile, but it must be kept in mind that for an official court poet, as for the painters of the *portraits d'apparat*, the presentation of the royal apotheosis was a very serious matter.

Asked why he did not write any elegies, Malherbe is said to have answered, "Because I write odes," referring to the form he considered to be the ultimate endeavor in lyric poetry. He used the term only for long poems dealing with great matters of state, and he called "stances" those poems dealing with less lofty subjects—or, as in the case of his famous "Prière pour le Roi allant en Limousin," briefer treatments of lofty themes—a distinction his successors were not to maintain. It is these odes which are today considered the omphalos of Malherbe's official poetry.

For generations, the guardians of academic truths steadfastly maintained that Malherbe's odes were characterized by rigorous composition, striking articulation, and, above all, a strictly logical discourse from which all digressions were ruthlessly banished. Recently, however, Wadsworth, by closely analyzing the great odes, has shown that "a forceful argument . . . is not necessarily a logical one," and that these poems, using a certain fragmentary, accumulative process, do in fact violate the rules of deductive logic more often than not. For all that, Wadsworth does not suggest that Malherbe's official poems lack structure. Rather, he points to the age-old theory of the ode as an inspired creation, one "in which elevation of style mattered much more than obedience to rules of composition." He hints that beyond that apparent "beautiful disorder," there might be found a higher, hidden order. It is precisely this more subtle order which Rubin has analyzed. Looking closely at the six completed odes, he concludes that they contain both literal and figurative structural elements; that the literal ones include successions of facts "from whose less-than-rigorous presentation stems the surface disorder noted by Professor Wadsworth"; that the figurative ones, however, contain "the techniques by means of which Malherbe integrated the fragmentary literal elements into a [higher, hidden order]." It is at this level that the

poet established—through intricate, yet coherent, systems of figures—series of correlations yielding a not-too-obvious but profound metaphorical unity.

"ALLANT CHÂTIER LA REBELLION DES ROCHELOIS"

In his prosody, Malherbe avoided the unusual, achieving striking variety within the framework of conventional forms. Five of the six completed odes are in isometric (octo- and heptasyllabic) *dizains*, the variety deriving from the diverse rhyme schemes and syntactic breaks. Much the same can be said of the poet's manipulation of metaphors, which are relatively few and conventional. The allusions are set up early in the poem so that all comparisons may be derived therefrom. Thus, in the opening stanza of the ode to the King "Allant châtier la rebellion des Rochelois," the first line contains a reference to the (Herculean) labors of the King; the second line deifies Louis by references to Jupiter's thunderbolt and to the Lion of Judah; the third and fourth lines represent the rebellious enclaves as so many Hydra's heads, of which this godlike Hercules will now strike off the last.

It is noteworthy that in the last stanza of this ode, Malherbe explicitly demonstrates what he has only implied earlier, that the king and his bard enjoy a symbiotic relationship. He enters into his poetic tableau much as a medieval painter introduced himself into a lordly fresco. The king's glory is made eternal precisely because Malherbe's poetry, a verbal temple, will last forever, unlike the bronze or marble of monuments. In this temple, both the icon (Louis) and the high priest (Malherbe) are simultaneously of this world and transcend it, but for the king to be assured of eternity, he must rely on his poet's pen, which alone can make a god of him. Malherbe would be nothing without his monarch's generosity and would be mute were it not for Louis's deeds, which furnish him with suitable subject matter; but without these odes, Louis would also be unable to fulfill his destiny. As Rubin concludes, "thus the poet establishes himself as the king's greatest—that is, most powerful and efficacious—subject and, paradoxically, his most generous patron."

It would be difficult to ascribe with certainty any sort of deep religious feelings to Malherbe, in view of his private behavior and admissions to friends. Most critics agree that to him, religion was a matter of political orthodoxy and social compliance; he was a Catholic in much the same way that he was a royalist. Yet, it is impossible to read the best of his religious poems without admiration: A thorough professional, he took modes of expression—such as the paraphrase of Psalms, *stances spirituelles*, and consolations—and, avoiding the prevalent excessive ejaculations of facile penitence and humility (frequently spoiled by intrusions of Humanistic secularism and even pagan mythology), he produced poems of pure religious expression that were to serve as models for generations to come. There is no exaltation to be found here but, as in the occasional poetry, an aura of grandeur and solemnity.

"PRIÈRE POUR LE ROI ALLANT EN LIMOUSIN"

Malherbe's Catholicism, as expressed in these poems, is one strongly affected by his preoccupation with Seneca, but that Stoicism never interferes with the expression of a most orthodox dogma. It adds to a primordial aura of pomp and majesty one of resignation and melancholy. It should not be thought, however, that Malherbe advocated an ascetic or contemplative faith; rather, he saw the Monarchy and the Church as inextricably conjoined, the former being the temporal arm of the latter, and several of his works dealing with this relationship cannot be categorized as either exclusively spiritual or exclusively temporal. Such is obviously the case with the already mentioned "Prière pour le Roi allant en Limousin," but there are others—less self-evident, perhaps, yet revealing the close relationship that Malherbe espoused.

Such a poem is the paraphrase of Psalm 128, written for the Queen Mother in 1614. In that year, a league of princes had rebelled against the regency of Marie de Médicis, who bribed them into submission. It is this purchase of peace which Malherbe treats by having the young king praise God for saving him and his realm from evil and turmoil. The praise of God is intertwined with castigation of the perfidious rebels whose snares the youthful Louis escaped only because of the powers watching over him. It is here that a deliberate ambiguity is introduced. God is the watchful Father protecting His royal son. God has turned the tide, but it is the Queen Mother who has implemented His wish. Not only is the benevolent paternity shared by God and the queen, their roles and attributes so closely intertwined as to make

distinctions impossible, but also the king is depicted as that offspring of a noble race who, now that he is delivered from the hands of his foes, will bring happiness to his once-oppressed people. His role in establishing a peaceful realm on Earth is nothing short of messianic. This is not blasphemy: A monarch by divine right, Louis could be expected to do no less, at least in theory.

It can readily be seen that such a poem, although inspired by the Bible, is entirely Gallic in tone. The references are French, as are the expressions. Even the short biblical formulations yield to more sophisticated compound sentences, and the artistic expression is delicately enhanced by qualifiers rare or absent in the Psalms. By definition, a "paraphrase" suggests that the author has been struck by a thought he wishes now to comment on and amplify. In Malherbe's case, the impetus is not biblical—spiritual or historic—but official or personal. It is intended as an exposition of a rational and coherent concept or attitude. There is lyricism; even more, there is drama; above all, there is persuasive reason. Dramatic beginnings in these poems—such as those of the paraphrase of Psalm 145 or of the famous "Consolation à M. du Périer," the latter's striking exordium sustained by tightly knit and sustained images—are part and parcel of a unified structure for which the word "theatrical" would not be out of place. After such an initial exhortation, there are always reiterations of imperatives (as in the paraphrase of Psalm 145) and energetic rhythms to sustain the initial impact. Today, drama and theology may seem like ill-suited partners; such was not the case in a century in which the stage and the pulpit were the centers of attention and of admiration. When, in 1715, before the crowned heads of Europe and their representatives, Jean-Baptiste Massillon, of humblest origins, began the funeral oration of Louis the Great with "God alone is great, my brothers," he was electrifying his audience in much the same way that Malherbe had startled his readers a full century earlier.

Malherbe's production in the realm of spiritual poetry is even less voluminous than in the official, occasional arena. Quality cannot be assessed on the basis of volume, nor can influence. Racan, Pierre Corneille, Antoine Godeau especially—all the successful writers of spiritual verses—show the undeniable imprint of Malherbe's daring and forceful creation.

BIBLIOGRAPHY

Abraham, Claude. *Enfin Malherbe vint: The Influence of Malherbe on French Lyric Prosody, 1609-1674.* Lexington: University Press of Kentucky, 1971. Explains very clearly Malherbe's poetics as presented in his acerbic commentary on the poems of his contemporary Philippe Desportes and the extraordinary influence of Malherbe's theories on French poets and literary critics during the first three decades of the seventeenth century. This is still one of the best books in English on Malherbe. Contains an excellent bibliography of primary and secondary sources.

Campion, Edmund J. "Poetic Theory in Théophile de Viau's 'Élégie à une dame.'" *Concerning Poetry* 20 (1987): 1-9. Describes why Malherbe's contemporary Théophile de Viau rejected Malherbe's attempt to impose one standard on all poets. Unlike Malherbe, Théophile de Viau believed that a truly original poet must develop his or her unique style and voice.

Chesters, G. "Malherbe, Ponge, and Revolutionary Classicism." In *The Classical Tradition in French Literature.* London: Grant and Cutler, 1977. Describes well the arguments in Francis Ponge's 1965 book *Pour un Malherbe* in which this eminent twentieth-century French poet attempted rather successfully to rehabilitate Malherbe's poetry but not his poetics.

Gershuny, Walter, "Seventeenth-Century Commemorative Verse." *Cahiers du dix-septième* 3, no.1 (Spring, 1989): 279-289. Explains very clearly formal poems which the court poet Malherbe wrote to honor the French kings Henry IV and Louis XIII.

Rubin, David Lee. *Higher, Hidden Order: Design and Meanings in the Odes of Malherbe.* Chapel Hill: University of North Carolina Press, 1972. A book-length study on the rhetoric of praise and blame in the numerous odes that Malherbe wrote during the late sixteenth and early seventeenth centuries. Like Abraham, Rubin argues that Malherbe was a more successful and effective poet than traditional criticism indicates.

Claude Abraham;
bibliography updated by Edmund J. Campion

STÉPHANE MALLARMÉ

Born: Paris, France; March 18, 1842
Died: Valvins, France; September 9, 1898

PRINCIPAL POETRY

L'Après-midi d'un faune, 1876 (*The Afternoon of a Faun*, 1956)
Les Poésies de Stéphane Mallarmé, 1887
Un Coup de dés jamais n'abolira le hasard, 1914 (*Dice Thrown Never Will Annul Chance*, 1965)
Igitur, 1925 (English translation, 1974)
Poems by Mallarmé, 1936 (Roger Fry, translator)
Herodias, 1940 (Clark Mills, translator)
Selected Poems, 1957
Les Noces d'Hérodiade, 1959
Pour un "Tombeau d'Anatole," 1961 (*A Tomb for Anatole*, 1983)
Poésies, 1970 (*The Poems*, 1977)

OTHER LITERARY FORMS

Stéphane Mallarmé is known chiefly for his poetry. A selection from his numerous critical essays and reviews, including some important theoretical statements, was published in *Divagations* (1897). Following the example of Charles Baudelaire, Mallarmé translated Edgar Allan Poe. He also published an idiosyncratic introduction to English philology, *Petite Philologie à l'usage des classes et du monde: Les Mots anglais* (1878; little philology for classroom use and for society: English words). It should be noted that Mallarmé wrote a number of prose poems, treated by some critics as prose works. The best edition of Mallarmé's poetry and essays is the Pléiade *Œuvres complètes de Stéphane Mallarmé* (1945), prepared by Henri Mondor and G. Jean-Aubry, although it is not a complete collection.

ACHIEVEMENTS

Stéphane Mallarmé's work is both the culmination of French Romanticism and the harbinger of the more hermetic poetry of the twentieth century. His vision of poetry as a sacred art, created with considerable sacrifice by an elite, derives from the Romantic image of the poet as prophet, typical of Victor Hugo. Mallarmé's "pure poetry," without reference to history or to social reality and characterized by a dense and elliptical style, however, deliberately abandons the attempt of many Romantics to bring poetry closer to life and to make it a social force. Very early in his career, Mallarmé said that it was heresy to try to make poetry understandable to a large audience. He sought instead to give expression to a higher form of intellectual experience in a language that is suggestive and indirect. Mallarmé's disciples, notably Paul Valéry, used the term "Symbolism" to describe the new poetry. Mallarmé exerted a great personal influence on the theories developed in modernist artistic circles through his Tuesday receptions in his apartment on the rue de Rome in Paris.

BIOGRAPHY

Stéphane Mallarmé was born into a middle-class Parisian family of government administrators. His mother died when he was five. He was taken in by his maternal grandparents, who placed him in a series of boarding schools from the time he was ten. This forcible separation from a family environment was particularly painful because it deprived him of the company of his only sibling, his sister Maria, who was younger by two years. He

Stéphane Mallarmé, center, with Édouard Manet, right, and an unidentified woman.
(Library of Congress)

continued to write to her until her death at the age of thirteen. This disappearance of mother and sister, both idealized figures strongly linked in Mallarmé's mind to the religious life, seems to have caused Mallarmé to abandon conventional religious beliefs and to seek in his adolescent poetry a way of preserving the memory of these beloved presences. At the same time, Mallarmé's active sexual life seems to have left him disappointed and perhaps guilty about physical pleasure.

In 1860, Mallarmé took a position with the French administration, then went to London in 1862 with a young German woman, Maria Gerhard, whom he married in 1863. At the end of that year, he took his first position as a teacher of English. His entire professional career consisted of a series of appointments in secondary schools, first in the provinces and then, after 1871, in Paris. He retired in 1894. During the 1870's, Mallarmé published translations, textbooks, a women's fashion magazine, and his own poetry.

His period of great celebrity began around 1884, when Paul Verlaine and Joris-Karl Huysmans acclaimed him in their own works. During the last fifteen years of his life, Mallarmé exercised enormous influence on the younger poets, who hailed him as the prophetic exemplar of Symbolism. Mallarmé himself did not seek honor or public attention. He left the publication of manifestos to his followers and preferred to devote his time to research for his oeuvre, his great "work," which he never finished. His poetic works, considerable as they are, did not live up to his ambition, although his manuscripts give evidence of intense labor.

ANALYSIS

"Everything in the world exists to end up in a book," wrote Stéphane Mallarmé in 1895. It is this attitude toward reality and toward the importance of the book that makes Mallarmé the preeminent Symbolist poet. For him, reality exists only in the symbol, which, in poetry, is constructed out of language. This position, apparently influenced by Hegelian idealism, does not mean that poetry is necessarily about language—although a number of Mallarmé's poems are about language and poetry themselves—but rather that language provides the only systematic and rational framework, the only escape from randomness, in a world in which there is no sign of a personal God. Mallarmé's poetry is a kind of metaphysical poetry, in that it aspires to go beyond the physical reality of everyday life to uncover the mysterious world of a pure ideal that can exist nowhere except in the mind and in language.

Even though many of Mallarmé's poems seem at first to be completely obscure, in most cases careful reading will reveal that a kernel drawn from everyday life has been transformed into a spare, unsentimental, timeless formal variation (in the way that a composer makes a variation on a musical theme). The effect is neither an enshrinement of a particular moment, place, or picturesque character nor an appeal to emotional sympathy. It is still less a moral or political message. Instead, such poems invite the reader to experience the power of the mind and of language.

For Mallarmé, the most important experience is the experience of the poem itself, and if such a statement seems commonplace and even trite, it is because Mallarmé's influence has been so pervasive. For him, however, the experience of the poem was particularly concrete and precise, and he frequently wrote about acts and objects connected with writing and reading with a kind of religious awe. The word *livre* (book) and such kindred terms as *grimoire* (book of magic incantations) and *bouquin* (old book) have in his vocabulary an importance rarely found in other bodies of poetry except in religious texts, where "the book" is the sacred scripture explaining and justifying the world. Mallarmé attempted during his life to create a nonreligious scripture.

Most of his poems, however, are playful occasional pieces such as "Eventail de Madame Mallarmé" ("Madam Mallarmé's Fan"); brief poems written in honor of other artists, such as the "Hommage" to Richard Wagner and "Le Tombeau d'Edgar Poe" ("The Tomb of Edgar Poe"); erotic poetry based on elliptical sexual fantasy, such as *The Afternoon of a Faun* and "Victorieusement fui le suicide beau" ("The Beautiful Suicide Victoriously Escaped"); or the long series of poems lamenting the difficulty of escaping from the base material world and of

writing the higher kind of poetry. The last category includes the well-known "L'Azur," sometimes called the "Swan Sonnet," "Les Fenêtres" ("The Windows"), and "Le Pître châtié" ("The Clown's Punishment"). Only the three longer poems, *Herodias, Igitur* (read to friends in unfinished form and published posthumously), and *Dice Thrown Never Will Annul Chance* (published in the magazine *Cosmopolis* in May, 1897, but not published in book form until 1914) give some idea of the form of Mallarmé's more ambitious projects.

There is nevertheless a stylistic and thematic coherence in Mallarmé's work, which proceeds by a kind of condensation and subtraction. The extremely difficult but logical grammar absorbs the reader in the enigmatic possibilities of meaning, thus fixing attention on the poem's language. Objects and persons named in the poems are described as absent or "abolished."

"ALL THE SOUL INDRAWN . . ."

A good way to begin with Mallarmé's poetry is to look at his brief poem "Toute l'âme résumée . . ." ("All the Soul Indrawn . . ."), which is a witty response to a survey on free verse. Mallarmé compares making poetry to smoking a cigar. The successive rings of smoke are "abolished" by those that follow, and the ash keeps falling away from the "bright kiss of fire." Poetry is not what is left behind, Mallarmé implies; it is rather the process itself, momentary but renewed. Because the word *âme* can mean both "soul" and, with some etymological delving, "breath," and *résumée* means both "summed up" and "drawn in," Mallarmé has put into play a metaphor for the content of poetry which eludes the traditional distinction between form and content, vehicle and tenor. The breath is what permits the cigar to keep burning; it is also the proof that one is alive. Yet this thing, which is so essential to smoking and to life, is empty. Similarly, the burning tip of the cigar, the thing showing that the cigar is "alive," is the fire that can survive only by emptying itself of the ash. Like smoking, Mallarmé suggests, poetry should be regarded as pure activity, without product and without connection with any external reality. After making this comparison explicit in the third quatrain, which advises writers to exclude vile reality, Mallarmé concludes with a distich that pointedly inverts the usual literary and rhetorical values of his day: "A too precise meaning scratches out/ Your vague literature." The more definite and specific the reference a poem makes to reality, the less it can be considered precisely literary.

"MY OLD BOOKS CLOSED AT THE NAME OF PAPHOS"

Another celebrated poem centered on the powers of literature, considered this time from the point of view of the reader, is "Mes bouquins refermés sur le nom de Paphos" ("My Old Books Closed at the Name of Paphos"). The speaker of the poem tells of closing his book and looking out on a snowy landscape where he imagines a Mediterranean scene. There is a parallel between the foam of the sea splashing against a ruin in the first quatrain and the white snow presented as part of the reader's material reality in the second quatrain. The speaker makes clear, however, that he will not wail a funereal lament (*nénie*) if the snowy reality does not coincide with his imagined seascape. The tercets make clear why the speaker so calmly accepts the divorce of dream from reality. The absence of things, which one notices because literature draws one's attention to such lacunae, is presented as a superior value. Mallarmé's negative approach, his preference for hollowing out a dream world by "abolishing" elements of the everyday world, appears in the speaker's claim: "My hunger, which is satisfied here by no fruits/ Finds in their learned lack an equal savor." To be satisfied by "no fruits" is not the same as being unsatisfied. It is a state in which the learned vision imposes a preference for the dream.

The second tercet goes even further, recalling that absence is not merely in the speaker's present world but in the scene imagined as well. Apparently addressing a lover, he confesses: "I think longer, perhaps desperately,/ Of the other, with the seared breast of an ancient Amazon." The scene is not only absent but also organized around an absence, the missing breast of one of the legendary warrior-women who founded the city of Paphos. Even these two absences are not all one can find here. The adverb translated as "desperately" or "distractedly" to describe the speaker's preoccupation with the Amazon is *éperdument*, which contains the word *perdu* (lost). The speaker, as reader, is thus also in some way lost to the everyday world and to ordinary love.

"HER PURE FINGERNAILS ON HIGH OFFERING THEIR ONYX"

The procedure of creating a scene by "abolishing" is taken closer to Mallarmé's project of a great magical work in the sonnet "Ses purs ongles trés haut dédiant leur onyx" ("Her Pure Fingernails on High Offering Their Onyx"), known as the "Sonnet in yx" because of its unusual rhymes. This sonnet apparently describes a deserted parlor belonging to a magician, the "Master," who has gone to get tears in the underworld from the river Styx. The vessel the Master will use is a *ptyx*. This is a word that has a meaning in Greek but none in French. Mallarmé may have meant it to remain meaningless, for the *ptyx* is called "this unique object of which Nothingness is proud." Furthermore, the *ptyx* is designated in the poem only as an absence: "in the empty parlor: no ptyx,/ Abolished trinket of sonorous inanity."

Scholars have studied the problem of the *ptyx* at length with reference to its ancient meanings, ranging from "book" to "seashell." As one scholar has noted, however, the more meanings that are proposed for the word, the less it actually signifies. It has become an empty form that traps the reader into deep and repeated investigations of semantic, phonetic, and etymological networks in the sonnet in the hope of finding some meaning. This sonnet certainly follows the precepts of "All the Soul Indrawn . . ." in avoiding a "too precise sense." It also exemplifies the kind of dream to which Mallarmé wanted to lead his readers. Although psychoanalytic readings of Mallarmé have been among the most interesting, Mallarmé himself did not use the word *rêve* (dream) to designate a person's unconscious. For Mallarmé, "dream" suggested both the aspiration to a world of pure thought without material limitation (this is particularly clear in "The Windows") and the realm in which language unfolds in all of its ambiguity. The Master's absence from this parlor could be interpreted as the author's desire to absent himself from the scene within which the reader can experience the possibilities of language, including the possibility that the most important words exist anagrammatically within the evident ones.

HERODIAS

Of Mallarmé's longer poems, those that seem to be part of his "great work," only *Herodias* and *Dice Thrown Never Will Annul Chance* gave the public some idea of the synthesis of poetic research of which he often spoke. Those works and the posthumous publications are all extremely difficult to interpret, but they seem to have at their core a struggle between the magic of the poetic symbol and the Nothingness (*le Néant*) that, for Mallarmé, constituted the universe. Because he rejected the physically present world for an ideal one and yet did not believe in religious spirituality, the magic of the great work would be to create a place where the ideal could exist. The language of the great work would have to be a special one, not the "unrefined and immediate" but the "essential" word free from the "chance" of usage, as he wrote in a preface to a work by René Ghil.

Herodias, a verse drama with little of the apparatus of a theater script, unites the themes of incantation, abolition, cerebral eroticism, and the preservation of the memory of the beloved dead. In most editions of Mallarmé, *Herodias* is divided into an "overture," in which the nurse of Princess Herodias describes the imaginary setting; a "scene," consisting of a dialogue between Herodias and her nurse; and a "canticle," in which the voice of John the Baptist sings at the moment of his decapitation. In the overture, the palace is evoked as empty and abandoned, like the parlor of the "Sonnet in yx." The king is long absent, the basin deserted by its swan, the sun rising red for the last time.

Even if one could create such a setting on the stage, the words of the overture make it clear that the real stage for these words is in the mind. The nurse, for example, speaks of a voice that evokes the past and then asks, "Is it my voice ready for the incantation?" If the speaker responsible for the exposition is not sure whether she has spoken, this suggests that she has merely thought the words. Moreover, the words that her voice may be ready to pronounce are an evocation of the past. Future and past thus join to create a situation in which imminent doom, nostalgia, and uncertainty about time coexist in a paradoxical equilibrium. The abstract quality of this setting is further emphasized by such metaphors as "the bed with pages of velum." The princess's bed is thus characterized as entirely chaste, while the whole drama takes on the aura of something entirely within a book.

In "Scene," the nurse tries to persuade Herodias to satisfy her awakening sexuality, while the princess insists that she loves the "horror" of being virgin and that she cannot tolerate any touch. In place of touch, sight becomes the only sense through which Herodias can open herself to sexuality or even to consciousness. The scene is full of mirrors, described as cold and distant like "water frozen from boredom." All the mirrors serve to reflect the princess's image, excluding the menacing outside world. In the last lines, Herodias, at the departure of the nurse, announces that she is waiting for an unknown thing and that she has lied to her nurse about her voluntary solitude.

The connection between "Scene" and "Canticle," which follows it, is not cle ar, although the fragments edited by Gardner Davies in *Les Noces d'Hérodiade* permit some conjectures. Several critics have advanced the idea that John the Baptist has seen Heriodas, who then feels that only his death can restore her sense of intactness. The saint is what the fragment calls the "somber pretext" for the princess's full achievement of self-consciousness. His crime is to be different from a mirror, which offers a neutral image without judgement. According to "Canticle," there is a tension between the ideal and the physical in John as well, and this tension is released by the decapitation, in which the saint sees salvation. Mallarmé, however, avoids religious statement by concluding with the word *salut*, which can mean both "salvation" and "salute." The word describes both the movement of the head as it follows its trajectory up and then down and the hope expressed by baptism. In the unfinished version of this drama, Herodias seems to have captured the dying glance of John and to consider herself united to the prophet in a wedding that is both sexual and ideal. She addresses the head, saying "I reason for you, head, not about you."

Herodias's hope to snatch consciousness from death was apparently the long-term result of Mallarmé's adolescent poetic meditations on death. It is also a hope that appears in the fragmentary *A Tomb for Anatole* (edited by Jean-Pierre Richard), in which the poet tried to recreate the life of his dead son through imagination. In a passage similar to that in which Herodias declares that she will think for John, Mallarmé tells his dead son that the poet will *be* the son hereafter. The question of the apparent futility of such a project is addressed by two other long poems by Mallarmé, *Igitur* and *Dice Thrown Never Will Annul Chance*.

IGITUR

Igitur, a prose poem written between 1867 and 1870 and left unfinished at Mallarmé's death, was edited by the scholar Edmond Bonniot, the poet's son-in-law, who discovered the manuscript in 1900. The poem relates the adventures of Igitur, a prince haunted by a supreme "Idea" and by the destiny imposed by his race, which has somehow projected Igitur outside time. The next-to-last section is titled "A Roll of Dice" and takes place in the family tomb. There, Igitur confronts the problem of the relationship among personal action, necessity, and chance. Understanding that action is absurd except as a return to infinity, which is a form of the pure absolute, he throws the dice before laying himself on the ashes of his ancestors. This metaphysical hero, described by critics as a Hamlet stripped of psychology, confronts the problems of individual time-bound existence (versus a timeless ideal) and of the tradition of a nation or race. This can be considered as Mallarmé's own problem, for the poet is both haunted by the literary and scriptural tradition and faced with the apparent randomness of his own efforts. Mallarmé's flight from a psychological and emotional poetry toward an intellectual and apparently impersonal one corresponds to the desire to escape from chance into a pure rationality in which everything would be determined and necessary, although not foreseeable to the human mind.

DICE THROWN NEVER WILL ANNUL CHANCE

Dice Thrown Never Will Annul Chance follows from *Igitur* and seems to be the work that most closely approaches Mallarmé's ambition for "pure poetry." This work has had a wide influence on such twentieth century movements as Dada, Surrealism, and Lettrism, not because of its theme but because of its innovative typographical form. Mallarmé had the text set in type of various sizes and specified the exact location of each word on the double-page layouts. Some pages have as few as four words, while others have nearly a hundred. The poet can control more than the verbal aspect of the poem by dealing directly with the visual domain usually left to the printer. Mallarmé here manifests his obsessive concern for the concrete aspects of the book, for the obliteration of the distinction between form and content, and for the reduction of chance in the production of a literary work. The title of the poem runs in the largest type

through the poem in such a way that the last word, "Chance," appears only on the ninth double-page unit (out of a total of eleven). Interrupting the title sentence are qualifications expressed in subordinate clauses and in various forms of apposition in various smaller type sizes. The effect is one of suspense, like that which attends a throw of the dice. The last small line of the poem reveals an application of the metaphor of the dice: "Every thought makes a roll of the dice."

Even though Mallarmé eschewed appeals to a broad public, and despite the fact that, aside from a half-dozen shorter poems frequently taught in *lycées* and colleges, his work does not have a wide readership, he has had an enormous influence on twentieth century poets, artists, and critics.

OTHER MAJOR WORKS

NONFICTION: *Petite Philologie à l'usage des classes et du monde: Les Mots anglais*, 1878; *Les Dieux antiques*, 1880; *Divagations*, 1897; *Correspondance*, 1959-1984 (10 volumes); *Documents Mallarmé*, 1968-1971 (3 volumes).

TRANSLATION: Les Poésies de Stéphane Mallarmé, 1887.

MISCELLANEOUS: *Album de vers et de prose*, 1887; *Pages*, 1891; *Vers et prose*, 1893; *Œuvres complètes de Stéphane Mallarmé*, 1945; *Selected Prose Poems, Essays, and Letters*, 1956; *Mallarmé*, 1965; *Selected Poetry and Prose*, 1982.

BIBLIOGRAPHY

Cohn, Robert Greer. ed. *Mallarmé in the Twentieth Century*. London: Associated University Presses, 1998. A collection of essays by many of the most eminent figures in the study of Mallarmé, including Julia Kristeva, Mary Ann Caws, Albert Cook, Anna Balakian, and Robert Cohn. An important summary of the state of scholarship on the poet.

Lloyd, Rosemary. *Mallarmé: The Poet and His Circle*. Ithaca, N.Y.: Cornell University Press, 1999. A literary biography of the poet and his period. Mallarmé hosted gatherings attended by writers, artists, thinkers, and musicians in France, England, and Belgium. Through these gatherings and voluminous correspondence Mallarmé developed and recorded his friendships with Paul Valéry, André Gide, Berthe Morisot, and many others. Includes bibliographical references and index.

Millan, Gordan. *A Throw of the Dice: The Life of Stéphane Mallarmé.* New York: Farrar, Straus, Giroux, 1994. This biography of Mallarmé, who has a reputation for difficulty and obscurity, proves equally valuable to students and specialists. The narrative is aimed at the general reader while the ample footnotes provide material for the specialist. The text draws on previously unpublished correspondence and new documentation and includes bibliographical references and an index.

Pearson, Roger. *Unfolding Mallarmé: The Development of a Poetic Art.* New York: Oxford University Press, 1996. An account of the development of Mallarmé's poetry from his earliest verse to his final masterpiece. Close readings demonstrate the intricate linguistic and formal play to be found in many of his major poems.

Temple, Michael, ed. *Meetings with Mallarmé.* Exeter, England: University of Exeter Press, 1998. Critical interpretation of Mallarmé's major works. Includes bibliographical references and index.

John D. Lyons;
bibliography updated by the editors

OSIP MANDELSTAM

Born: Warsaw, Poland, Russian Empire (now in Poland); January 15, 1891

Died: Vtoraya Rechka, near Vladivostock, Russia, U.S.S.R. (now in Russia); probably December 27, 1938

PRINCIPAL POETRY

Kamen, 1913, enlarged 1916, 1923 (*Stone*, 1981)

Tristia, 1922, second edition 1923 (English translation, 1973)

Stikhotvoreniya, 1928 (*Poems*, 1973)

Complete Poetry of Osip Emilievich Mandelstam, 1973

Voronezhskiye tetradi, 1980

The Voronezh Notebooks: Poems, 1935-1937, 1996

OTHER LITERARY FORMS

Osip Mandelstam was writing essays on Russian and European literature as early as 1913. Many of the theoretical essays were collected, some in considerably revised or censored form, in *O poezii* (1928; *About Poetry*, 1977). These, as well as his otherwise uncollected essays and reviews, are available in their original and most complete versions in *Sobranie sochinenii* (1955, 1964-1971, 1981; *Collected Works*, 1967-1969). Mandelstam's prose was not republished in the Soviet Union, with the exception of his single most important essay, "Razgovor o Dante" ("Conversation About Dante"), written in 1933 but not published until 1967, when an edition of twenty-five thousand copies sold out immediately and was not reprinted. Mandelstam's prose has been seen both as a key to deciphering his poetry and as a complex body of nonpoetic discourse of great independent value. All of his prose has been translated into English.

ACHIEVEMENTS

Osip Mandelstam's poetry won immediate praise from fellow members of Russian literary circles, and he now holds an indisputable position as one of Russia's greatest poets. Like many of his contemporaries, however, Mandelstam experienced anything but a "successful" literary career. His work appeared often in pre-Revolutionary journals, but Mandelstam was not among the writers whom the Bolsheviks promoted after 1917. By 1923, the official ostracism of independent poets such as Mandelstam was apparent, though many continued writing and publishing whenever possible. Mandelstam did not write poetry between 1925 and 1930, turning instead to prose forms which were as inventive and as idiosyncratic as his verse. Attempts to discredit him intensified after 1928. He was arrested twice in the 1930's and is believed to have died while in transit to a Siberian labor camp.

Even during the "thaw" under Premier Nikita Khrushchev, Mandelstam's works were kept out of print, and it was not until 1973 that his "rehabilitation" was made credible by the publication of his poetry in the prestigious *Biblioteka poeta* (poet's library) series. That slim volume was reissued. During the Soviet era in Russia, scholarly writing about Mandelstam, although limited, appeared; his name was mentioned in many but by no means all studies of literature. Official publications, such as textbooks or encyclopedias, relegated him to minor status and often commented disparagingly on his "isolation" from his age. The deep respect commanded by his poetry in the Soviet Union was nevertheless measured by the evolution of scholarly interest in his work.

Mandelstam's reputation outside Russia was initially slow in developing because of the extreme difficulty in obtaining reliable texts of his works and because of the scarcity of information about the poet. As texts and translations became available, Mandelstam's reputation grew steadily. The single most important factor in making his work known in the West was the publication of two volumes of memoirs by his wife, Nadezhda Mandelstam. *Vospominania* (1970; *Hope Against Hope: A Memoir*, 1970) and *Vtoraya kniga* (1972; *Hope Abandoned*, 1974), issued in Russian by émigré publishers and translated into many Western languages, are the prime source of information concerning Mandelstam's life. Works of art in their own right, they also provide invaluable insights into his poetry.

BIOGRAPHY

Osip Emilievich Mandelstam was born in Warsaw, Poland, on January 15, 1891. His family moved almost immediately to St. Petersburg, where Mandelstam later received his education at the Tenischev School (as did Vladimir Nabokov only a few years later). Mandelstam's mother was a pianist; his father worked in a leather-tanning factory. Little is known about Mandelstam's childhood or young adulthood; he recorded cultural rather than personal impressions in his autobiographical sketch, *Shum vremeni* (1925; *The Noise of Time*, 1965).

Mandelstam took several trips abroad, including one to Heidelberg, where he studied Old French and the philosophy of Immanuel Kant at the University of Heidelberg from 1909 to 1910. He returned to St. Petersburg University's faculty of history and philology but seems never to have passed his examinations. Mandelstam had a highly intuitive approach to learning which foreshadowed the associative leaps which make his poetry so dif-

ficult to read. His schoolmate Viktor Zhirmunsky, later a prominent Formalist critic, said of Mandelstam that he had only to touch and smell the cover of a book to know its contents with a startling degree of accuracy.

Mandelstam had been writing in earnest at least as early as 1908, and he began publishing poems and essays in St. Petersburg on his return from Heidelberg. By 1913, his literary stance was defined by his alliance with the Acmeists, a group dedicated to replacing the murky longing of Russian Symbolism with a classical sense of clarity and with a dedication to the things of this world rather than to the concepts they might symbolize. Among the acquaintances made in the Acmeist Guild of Poets, Mandelstam formed a lifelong friendship with the poet Anna Akhmatova.

The ideological positions taken by poets were soon overwhelmed by the political upheavals of the decade. Mandelstam did not serve in World War I. He greeted the Revolution with an enthusiasm typical of most intellectuals; he grew increasingly disappointed as the nature of Bolshevik power became apparent. Mandelstam worked in several cultural departments of the young Soviet government, moving between Moscow and St. Petersburg (renamed Leningrad) in connection with these and other jobs. In May, 1919, he met and later married Nadezhda Yakovlevna Khazina. The civil war parted the Mandelstams at times, but they were virtually inseparable until Mandelstam's second arrest in 1938. Nadezhda Yakovlevna became far more than her husband's companion and source of strength. She recorded his poems after he had composed them mentally; she memorized the poems when it became clear that written texts were in jeopardy; and she ensured her husband's poetic legacy many years after his death with her two volumes of memoirs and her lifelong campaign to have his poems published.

An early indication of Mandelstam's difficulties came in 1925, when the journal *Rossiya* rejected *The Noise of Time*. Living in or near Leningrad after 1925, Mandelstam busied himself with popular journalistic articles, children's literature, translations, and, by the end of the decade, hack editorial work. Although he published volumes of poetry, prose, and literary criticism in 1928, an attempt to entrap him in a plagiarism scandal the same year demonstrated the general precariousness

Osip Mandelstam

of his status under the new regime. Nikolai Bukharin, who saved Mandelstam more than once, arranged a trip to Armenia and Georgia which proved crucial in ending his five years of poetic silence. Mandelstam wrote a purgative account of the plagiarism trial, *Chetvertaia proza* (written in 1930 but never published in the Soviet Union; it is available in English translation as *Fourth Prose*, 1966), as well as poetry and prose inspired by the Armenian land and people.

After the journey, Mandelstam and his wife lived in near poverty in Moscow. Though he gave several readings, Mandelstam saw his prose work *Puteshestviye v Armeniyu* (1933; *Journey to Armenia*, 1973) denounced soon after its publication in the periodical *Zvezda*. On May 13, 1934, Mandelstam was arrested, ostensibly for a poem about Stalin's cruelty; the act of reciting such a poem even to a few friends was characteristic of his defiance of the authorities and of the Soviet literary establishment, which he openly despised. Bukharin again intervened, and the terms of exile were softened considerably. First sent to Cherdyn, the Mandelstams were allowed to select Voronezh, a southern provincial

city, as the place where they would spend the next three years.

Mandelstam attempted suicide in Cherdyn and suffered intense periods of anxiety whenever Nadezhda Yakovlevna was away, even briefly. He could find little work in Voronezh. Despite periods of near insanity, Mandelstam wrote (and actively sought to publish) three notebooks of poems in Voronezh. In May, 1937, the couple returned to Moscow, where Mandelstam suffered at least one heart attack. Heart ailments had plagued him for years, and throughout his poetry, shortness of breath was always to be a metaphor for the difficulty of writing.

In the fall of 1937, a final respite from the hardships of Moscow was arranged. In the sanatorium in Samatikha, Mandelstam was again arrested in the early morning of May 2, 1938. In August, he was sentenced to five years' hard labor for counterrevolutionary activities. In September, he was sent to a transit camp near Vladivostock, from which he wrote to his wife for the last time. The actual circumstances of Mandelstam's death will probably never be known. The conditions of the camp almost certainly drove him, and not a few others, to the point of insanity. In 1940, his brother Aleksandr received an official statement that Mandelstam had died December 27, 1938, of heart failure.

Nadezhda Yakovlevna Mandelstam lived another forty-two years, sustained by her friendship with Anna Akhmatova and by her commitment to preserving her husband's poems for a generation that could read them. As Mandelstam's works began appearing in print, Nadezhda Mandelstam published her two invaluable volumes of memoirs, *Hope Against Hope* and *Hope Abandoned*. On December 31, 1980, she achieved her great wish, an achievement rare enough for Russians of her generation: She died in her own bed.

ANALYSIS

In Osip Mandelstam's first published essay, "O sobesednike" (1913; "On the Addressee"), he describes the ideal reader as one who opens a bottle found among sand dunes and reads a message mysteriously addressed to the reader. Mandelstam's poetry, like the message in the bottle, has had to wait to find its reader; it also demands that a reader be aggressive and resourceful. His poems are intensely dependent on one another and are frequently comprehensible only in terms of ciphered citations from the works of other poets. The reader who wishes to go beyond some critics' belief that Mandelstam's lexicon is arbitrary or irrational must read each poem in the context of the entire œuvre and with an eye to subtexts from Russian and European literature.

ACMEISM

Mandelstam's attempt to incorporate the poetry of the past into his works suited both the spirit and stated tenets of Acmeism, a movement he later defined as a "homesickness for world culture." Mandelstam always saw the Acmeist poets as the preservers of an increasingly endangered literary memory. "True" poetry could arise only from a celebration of its dependence on the old. Poetry plows up the fields of time, he wrote; his own poems bring forth rich layers of subsoil by their poetics of quotation. Apparently opaque lyric situations, when deciphered, yield transparent levels of meaning. Mandelstam especially loved the myths of Greece and Rome, though his quotations are most often from nineteenth and twentieth century Russian poets.

Using another metaphor, perhaps the most typical metaphor for the Acmeists, Mandelstam wrote in the early 1920's that Russian poetry has no Acropolis. "Our culture has been lost until now and cannot find its walls." Russia's words would build its cultural edifices, he predicted, and it is in the use of the word that one must seek the distinctive feature of Mandelstam's poetry.

"HAPPILY NEIGHING, THE HERDS GRAZE"

An example of Mandelstam's use of quotations will indicate how far interpretation of his poetry must stray from the apparent lyric situation. Referring to Mandelstam's first collection of poems, *Stone*, Kiril Taranovsky has noted that a line in the poem "S veselym rzhaniem pasutsia tabuny" ("Happily Neighing, the Herds Graze") quotes Alexander Pushkin's famous statement, "My sadness is luminous." Mandelstam's line is "In old age my sadness is luminous." Nineteen years later, Mandelstam wrote, in a poem memorializing Andrei Bely, "My sadness is lush." The epithet here comes from the *Slovo o polku Igoreve* (c. 1187; *The Lay of Igor's Host*), but the syntax still recalls Pushkin. Interpreting the stylized line "My sadness is lush" thus requires knowing

Pushkin and *The Lay of Igor's Host*, to say nothing of Mandelstam's first quotation of Pushkin in "Happily Neighing, the Herds Graze" or the often ornate works of Andrei Bely.

In "Happily Neighing, the Herds Graze," Pushkin's presence is also felt in the poem's seasonal setting, his beloved autumn. The month mentioned, August, suggests Augustus Caesar, and the ancient Roman context is as significant as the Pushkinian overtones. The poem thus has more to do with the ages of human culture than with grazing herds; the poem contrasts the "classical spring" of Pushkin's golden age of Russian literature with the decline of Rome. The dominant color in the poem is gold, specifically the dry gold of harvest. Russia in the year 1915 resembled Rome during its decline, as the Romanov dynasty faced its end, so that three historical periods come to bear on an interpretation of this apparently pastoral poem. The rise and decline of civilizations do not upset this poet, for whom the cyclical nature of the seasons suggests that historical change is itself cyclical. As Mandelstam wrote in 1918, "Everything has been before, everything will repeat anew. What is sweet to us is the moment of recognition." To achieve such moments, the reader must allow Mandelstam's metaphors to acquire meaning in more than one context. The contexts will border on one another in surprising ways, but it is his peculiar gift to his readers that when they read his poems, they see past poets and past ages of man from new vantage points.

STONE

Mandelstam's first volume of poetry, *Stone*, was published in 1913, with successive enlargements in 1916 and 1923. *Stone* contains short lyrics, many of only three or four quatrains. The title evokes the volume's dominant architectural motifs. Aside from the well-known triptych of cathedral poems in *Stone*, there are also poems of intimate interiors, designs in household utensils, and sea shells. The patterns of crafted objects or complex facades allow Mandelstam to write in *Stone* about the structures of language, about how poems may best be written. At times, his metapoetic statements emerge completely undisguised. A landscape is described by the technical language of poetics in "Est' ivolgi v lesakh" ("There Are Orioles in the Woods"), in which the birds' singing is measured by the length of vowel sounds, their lines ringing forth in tonic rhythms. The day "yawns like a caesura."

Mandelstam pursues the probable relationship between the oriole and the poet in "Ia ne slyxal rasskazov Ossiana" ("I Have Not Heard the Tales of Ossian"). Here, a raven echoing a harp replaces the oriole; the poem's persona intones, "And again the bard will compose another's song/ And, as his own, he will pronounce it." Mandelstam contrasts his own heritage with that of another land, as distinct as the singing of birds and men. Despite the differences between the battles of Russian soldiers and the feigned tales of Ossian, the poet's entire received heritage is "blessed," "the erring dreams of other singers" ("other" connotes "foreign" as well as "not oneself" in Russian). It is in making the dreams his own that the poet finds victory.

In "Est' tselomudrennye chary" ("There Are Chaste Charms"), Mandelstam concludes with an equally victorious quatrain. The poem has evoked household gods in terms derived from classical Rome and from eighteenth century poetry. After three quatrains of listening to ancient gods and their lyres, the poet declares that the gods "are your equals." With a careful hand, he adds, "one may rearrange them."

Among the poems which both assert and demonstrate Mandelstam's strength as an independent poet is "Notre Dame," the shortest and most clearly Acmeist of his three 1912 cathedral poems. The Acmeists consistently praised the Gothic optimism of medieval architecture and art, and they shared that period's devotion to art as high craft. In "Notre Dame," Mandelstam praises the church's "massive walls," its "elemental labyrinth." The cathedral becomes both that which the poet studies and that from which he is inspired to create something of his own. The outstretched body of Adam furnishes a metaphor for the opening description of the cathedral's vaulted ceiling. Adam's name, and his having been "joyful and first," had once provided an alternative name for Acmeism, Adamism, which never took hold. The name "Adam," nevertheless, invokes in "Notre Dame" the poetic principles of the movement, its clarity, its balance, its sense of the poem as something visibly constructed. "Notre Dame" is as close to a programmatic statement in verse as Mandelstam ever came; the poem does what a Gothic cathedral should do, "revealing its secret plan from the outside."

TRISTIA

Mandelstam's second volume, *Tristia*, appeared in 1922, with a second edition in 1923. Compared to the architectural poems of *Stone*, many drawing on the Roman tradition in classical culture, *Tristia* depends more on the myths of ancient Greece. It evokes the landscape of the Mediterranean or Crimean seas to frame tender, interiorized poems. The title is the same as that of a work by Ovid, written during his exile, and the connotations of *tristia*, both emotional and literary, resonate throughout the volume, though the title was not initially of Mandelstam's choosing. The title poem, "Tristia," addresses the difficulties of separation, the science of which the speaker says he has studied to the point of knowing it well. There are several kinds of separation involved, from women seeing men off to battle in stanza 1 to men and women facing their particular deaths in stanza 4. The poet feels the difficulty of moving from one kind of separation to another in stanza 3, where he complains, "How poor is the language of joy." Ovid's exile has been a continuous event since he wrote his *Tristia* (after 8 C.E.). There is joy in recognizing the repetition of historical and personal events; Mandelstam here performs his usual chronological sleight of hand in juxtaposing several ages in history, rising toward divinations of the future in the final stanza.

The moment of recognition or remembrance is sought after in vain in "Ia slovo pozabyl, chto ia khotel skazat'" ("I Have Forgotten the Word I Wanted to Say"). Like its companion poem "Kogda Psikheia-zhizn' spuskaetsia k teniam" ("When Psyche-Life Descends to the Shades"), the poem evokes the failure to remember poetic words as a descent into Hades. The close correspondence between these two psyche poems is characteristic of Mandelstam: The presentation of variants demonstrates his belief that the drafts of a poem are never lost. These poems also demonstrate the general Acmeist principle that there is no final or closed version of any work of literature.

PSYCHE POEMS

In the psyche poems, mythological figures are mentioned, such as Persephone or Antigone for their descent into the Underworld or for their devotion to the funeral ritual, respectively. The river mentioned in both poems is not Lethe, the river of forgetfulness, but Styx, the boundary of Hades. Forgetfulness plagues both poems, however; "I Have Forgotten the Word I Wanted to Say," a formula repeated in one poem, equates the fear of death's oblivion with the loss of poetry. The images of the dry riverbed, of birds which cannot be heard, of a blind swallow with clipped wings—all suggest an artist's sterility. It is the dead who revive an ability to remember (hence their avoidance of the river Lethe), to recognize meanings as significant as those of the divining women at the end of "Tristia." With the slowness so crucial to the entire volume, something develops in "I Have Forgotten the Word I Wanted to Say." In "When Psyche-Life Descends to the Shades," the soul is slow to hand over her payment for crossing the river. The "unincarnated thought" returns to the Underworld, but the black ice of its remembered sound burns on the poet's lips. For Mandelstam, lips (like breathing), suggest the act of composing poetry, so that these twin poems conclude with a kind of optimism, however fearful.

Several poems in *Tristia* treat the social causes of Mandelstam's fear of poetic failure, among them two of his most famous: "Sumerki svobody" ("The Twilight of Freedom") and "V Peterburge my soidomsia snova" ("In Petersburg We Shall Meet Again"). Both poems respond to the Revolution of 1917 ambiguously if not pessimistically. The sun both rises and sets in "The Twilight of Freedom," where the "twilight" of the title could mean "sunset" as well as "dawn." "In Petersburg We Shall Meet Again" also chooses an ambiguous source of light; the sun is buried and the "night sun" illuminates the final stanza.

Images from the psyche poems reappear with more pronounced political overtones. In "The Twilight of Freedom," there are immobilized swallows, bound into "fighting legions." The people appear as both powerful and restrained, expressing perfectly Mandelstam's perception of the Revolution as potentially empowering but finally overpowering. In "In Petersburg We Shall Meet Again," the "blessed, meaningless word" which the poet feared forgetting in the Psyche poems seems miraculously renewed. The poem displays terrifying sights and sounds, from ominous patrols to whizzing sirens, yet the speaker clings to his "word" as if oblivious of everything else. The poem closes with a crowd leaving a theater, where the end of the performance suggests the end of an entire culture. Yet, as in the exhortation to be brave in "The Twilight of Freedom," the poetic voice affirms its power to live beyond the threats of "Lethe's cold" or the "Soviet night." What endures in *Tristia*, though with difficulty, is what seemed immutable in *Stone:* faith in the word as the center of Russian culture.

POEMS

In 1928, Mandelstam published a volume of poems comprising revised versions of *Stone* and *Tristia*, as well as some twenty new poems. Several had appeared in the second edition of *Tristia*. These poems are even less optimistic than the ambiguous poems of *Tristia*; they are permeated by a fear of disorder which so threatened Mandelstam's voice that he ceased writing poems altogether from 1925 to 1930. The city arches its back threateningly in "In Petersburg We Shall Meet Again"; the back is broken in "Vek" ("The Age"). The age is dying in "Net, nikogda nichei ia ne byl sovremennik" ("No, I Was Never Anyone's Contemporary"), a poem whose first line discloses as well as any of his works Mandelstam's alienated state of mind. The source of light in these poems is not the sun, not even the occluded or nighttime sun, but stars which look down menacingly from the evening firmament. The air is steamy, foamy, dark, and watery, as impossible to breathe as the sky is to behold. Not being able to breathe, like not being able to speak, conveys Mandelstam's extraordinary difficulty in writing during this period.

"THE HORSESHOE FINDER" AND "SLATE ODE"

Two of Mandelstam's most startling and most difficult poems date from the early 1920's: "Nashedshii podkovu" ("The Horseshoe Finder") and "Grifel' naia oda" ("Slate Ode"). The poems test and affirm poetry's ability to endure despite the shifting values of the age. "The Horseshoe Finder" binds together long, irregular verse lines without rhyme (a new form for Mandelstam) by repeating and interweaving clusters of consonants. Rejecting the slow realizations of *Tristia*, the poem moves quickly from one metaphorical cluster to another. Finding the horseshoe, also a talismanic emblem for poetry in "Slate Ode," is like finding the bottled message in Mandelstam's essay "On the Addressee." The past can still be transmitted in "The Horseshoe Finder": "Human lips . . . preserve the form of the last spoken word," but these lips "have nothing more to say."

"LENINGRAD" AND POETRY AFTER 1930

Mandelstam resumed writing poetry in 1930, and, had the official literary establishment not been forcing him out of print, there could easily have emerged a third volume of verse from the poems written in Moscow and Voronezh. A clear task unites many of these poems, a task of self-definition. The fate of the poet has become a metaphor for the fate of the culture, so that intensely personal poems avoid all solipsism. The triangular relationship "world-self-text" emerges as a conflict to be resolved anew in each poem. Mandelstam returned to Leningrad, "familiar to the point of tears." In his poem "Leningrad," Mandelstam proclaims against all odds, echoing the famous Pushkin line, that he does not want to die. Death moves inevitably through the poem, though, as his address book leads only to "dead voices"; the poet lives on back stairs, awaiting guests who rattle a ball and chain.

Mandelstam was arrested for the often-quoted epigram about Stalin; describing "cockroach whiskers" and "fat fingers, like worms," the poem was perhaps his angriest of the period. The secret police could have arrested Mandelstam, however, for any number of works from the early 1930's. Hatred of the "songs" with which the Soviets had supplied the new age, disgust at the ethos of the Socialist Utopia, and fear that Russia's genuine cultural heritage would perish are frequent themes. Mandelstam wanted no part of the changes around him; he names himself as the "unrecognized brother, an outcast in the family of man" in a poem dedicated to Anna Akhmatova, his dear friend and fellow poet who also suffered ostracism.

In the South and in Moscow, Mandelstam was befriended by several biologists. They inspired him to read Jean-Baptiste Lamarck, Charles Darwin, and other authors who in turn provided Mandelstam with a new metaphor for expressing his dislike of the age's paeans to "progress." In "Lamarck," Mandelstam chooses to occupy the lowest step on the evolutionary ladder rather than join in the false advances urged by the government. These steps bring man down in the evolutionary chain, observes the poet, toward species which cannot hear, speak, or breathe—toward those which do not produce poetry. The age, in copious images of the silence of deafness, has grown dumb; self-definition nears self-denigration as the surrounding cultural edifices crumble and threaten to bring the new Soviet literature down with them.

Destruction, pain, death, terror—these are the themes which dominate the post-1930 poems to a degree which would separate them from the poems written before 1925 even if there were no other distinctions. As Mandelstam wrote poems inspired by the chaos around him, so also the poems formally demonstrated the pervasiveness of chaos. Disintegration became both subject matter and structuring principle: The late poems demonstrate an openness, fragmentation, and avoidance of conventional poetic diction, meter, and rhyme which would have been inconceivable in the beautifully formed poems of *Stone* or *Tristia*. The early predilection for exact rhyme is reshaped by an admixture of near rhymes of all sorts. The poems grow rich in internal paronomasia, where interweavings of sounds create controlling structures in lines which seem otherwise arbitrarily ordered. The rhythms grow freer during the 1930's as well. Mandelstam had used free verse in the 1920's, as in "The Horseshoe Finder," and returned to it for longer, more complex works such as "Polnoch' v Moskve" ("Midnight in Moscow"). Conventionally metered poems include aberrant lines of fewer or more metrical feet or with entirely different schemes; conversely, the free verse of "Midnight in Moscow" permits interpolated lines of perfect or near-perfect meter.

The spontaneity which the late poems explore represents the final version of Mandelstam's longstanding commitment to the openness of the poetic text. Including fragments of conversation and unconventional constructions in these poems, Mandelstam was converting the destructive chaos around him to his own ends. Hence the fluidity of "cross-references" in his poetry, particularly in the late verse, where there are not only "twin" or "triplet" poems, as Nadezhda Yakovlevna Mandelstam called them, but also entire cycles of variants, among them the poems on the death of Bely in 1934. Moving beyond the concrete referentiality of the early poems, the late Mandelstam dramatizes rather than describes the act of self-definition. The communicative act between poet and reader overrides the encoding act between poet and world, as the reader is drawn deeply into the process of decoding the poet's relationships with his world and his poems.

Mandelstam's confidence that a reader would someday seek to understand even his most labyrinthine poems shines through unexpectedly during the late period. There are love poems to his wife and others—among the most remarkable is "Masteritsa vinovatykh vzorov" ("Mistress of Guilty Glances")—as well as poems wherein renunciation yields extraordinary strength. Mandelstam's enduring gift, long after he had himself fallen victim to the society at odds with him, was to find strength in the deepest threats to his identity. Hence, the halfhearted desire to write an ode to Stalin, which might save his wife after his own death, gave rise instead to a host of deeply honest poems which were as hopeful as they were embattled. Though the simple longings of the late poems may be futile, the act of recording his desires into completely threatened poems represents Mandelstam's typical achievement in the late works.

OTHER MAJOR WORKS

NONFICTION: *O prirode slova*, 1922 (*About the Nature of the Word*, 1977); *Shum vremeni*, 1925 (autobiography; *The Noise of Time*, 1965); *Feodosiya*, 1925 (autobiography; *Theodosia*, 1965); *O poezii*, 1928 (*About Poetry*, 1977); *Chetvertaia proza*, wr. 1930 or 1931, 1966 (*Fourth Prose*, 1970); *Puteshestviye v Armeniyu*, 1933 (travel sketch; *Journey to Armenia*, 1973); *Razgovor o Dante*, 1967 (*Conversation About Dante*, 1965); *Selected Essays*, 1977; *Slovo i kul'tura: Stat'i*, 1987.

CHILDREN'S LITERATURE: *Dva tramvaya*, 1925; *Primus*, 1925; *Shary*, 1926; *Kukhnya*, 1926.

MISCELLANEOUS: *Sobranie sochinenii*, 1955, 1964-1971, 1981 (*Collected Works*, 1967-1969); *The Complete Critical Prose and Letters*, 1979.

BIBLIOGRAPHY

Baines, Jennifer. *Mandelstam: The Later Poetry*. New York: Cambridge University Press, 1976. Scholarly treatment of Mandelstam's poems written in Moscow and Voronezh in the 1930's, the study of which has been somewhat neglected because of their enigmatic nature.

Brown, Clarence. *Mandelstam*. New York: Cambridge University Press, 1973. The best authority on Mandelstam in the English-speaking world presents his seminal work, covering all aspects of Mandelstam's life and work. Brown's analyses of Mandelstam's poems are particularly valuable.

Broyde, Steven. *Osip Mandelstam and His Age: A Commentary on the Themes of War and Revolution in the Poetry, 1913-1923*. Cambridge: Harvard University Press, 1975. A detailed analysis of Mandelstam's poems inspired by, and centered on, war and revolution. There are many citations of poems, in Russian and in English.

Mandelstam, Nadezhda. *Hope Against Hope: A Memoir*. New York: Atheneum, 1970.

_____. *Hope Abandoned*. New York: Atheneum, 1974. The two-volume memoirs of Mandelstam's wife deal mostly with biographical details, but also with the genesis of many of Mandelstam's poems.

Omry, Ronen. *An Approach to Mandelstam*. Jerusalem: The Magnes Press, 1983. A descriptive, interpretative, and detailed commentary of two of Mandelstam's longer poems, "The State Ode" and "1. January 1924."

Pollack, Nancy. *Mandelstam the Reader*. Baltimore: The Johns Hopkins University Press, 1995. A study of Mandelstam's late verse and prose. The two genres receive approximately equal treatment, but the analyses of poems tend to be deeper.

Prsybylski, Ryszard. *An Essay on the Poetry of Osip Mandelstam: God's Grateful Guest*. Translated by Madeline G. Levine. Ann Arbor, Mich.: Ardis, 1987. This book-length "essay" offers the views of a noted Polish scholar. He treats Mandelstam's attraction to, and reflection of, Greek and Roman classicism, the musical quality of his poetry, his affinity to architecture and archeology, and other features of the poetry. The author places Mandelstam in the framework of world literature.

Zeeman, Peter. *The Later Poetry of Osip Mandelstam: Text and Context*. Amsterdam: Rodopi, 1988. Detailed interpretations and analyses of Mandelstam's poems written in the 1930's. Zeeman uses primarily contextualization and historical reconstruction in his discussion of the poems, some of which are among the most difficult of all Mandelstam's poems.

Stephanie Sandler;
bibliography updated by Vasa D. Mihailovich